A RELIGIOUS HISTORY OF THE AMERICAN PEOPLE

SYDNEY E. AHLSTROM

A RELIGIOUS HISTORY OF THE AMERICAN PEOPLE

NEW HAVEN AND LONDON: YALE UNIVERSITY PRESS

Library of Congress catalog card number: 72–151564
International standard book number: 0–300–01475–9 (cloth),
0–300–01762–6 (paper)

Designed by Sally Sullivan
and set in Linotype Baskerville type.
Printed in the United States of America by
Vail-Ballou Press, Inc., Binghamton, N.Y.

19 18 17 16 15 14 13 12

FOR

MY MOTHER

CONTENTS

PART VII: THE ORDEALS OF TRANSITION 731

PART VIII: THE AGE OF FALTERING CRUSADES 873

PART IX: TOWARD POST-PURITAN AMERICA 965

ILLUSTRATIONS

by Michael Graham

Page 15: The mission church San Luis Rey de Francia, near Oceanside, California, built under the supervision of Padre Antonio Peyri between 1811 and 1815. The mission had been founded in 1798 by Padre-Presidente Fermin de Lasuén.

Page 121: The second meetinghouse of the church in Plymouth, Massachusetts, built in 1683. A conjectural rendering based on early specifications and sketches.

Page 261: Independence Hall, Philadelphia, Pennsylvania, originally the Pennsylvania State House, designed by Andrew Hamilton and Edmund Wooley and constructed between 1732 and 1748. The wooden steeple depicted here was taken down in 1781 but restored along more elaborate lines in 1828.

Page 385: An evangelical camp meeting. A conjectural rendering based in part on a drawing (c.1820) by the French artist and naturalist J. G. Milbert and on George Caleb Bingham's painting *Stump Speaking* (1853–54).

Page 511: Temple B'nai Yeshurun, Cincinnati, Ohio, the first Neo-Moorish synagogue in America. Designed by James Keys Wilson and constructed in 1864–65, when Rabbi Isaac Mayer Wise was spiritual leader of the congregation.

Page 633: The old African Methodist Episcopal Zion Church in Tuskegee, Alabama, in which Booker T. Washington convened the first classes of the Tuskegee Normal and Industrial Institute on 4 July 1881.

Page 731: Trinity Church (Episcopal), Boston, Massachusetts, designed in 1872 by Henry Hobson Richardson and completed in 1877, though significant alterations and additions were made in later years.

Page 873: The Greek Orthodox Church of the Annunciation, Milwaukee, Wisconsin, designed by Frank Lloyd Wright and consecrated in 1961.

Page 965: Composition, after a photograph by Edward Weston, *North Wall,* Point Lobos, 1946.

PREFACE TO THE FOURTH PRINTING

It is about two years now since the manuscript of this book was committed to the printer. It has been a period, as Tacitus said of his own day in Rome, "fertile in vicissitudes, pregnant with sanguinary encounters, embroiled with intestine dissensions, and even in the intervals of peace, deformed with horrors." [1] The American people, to whose religious concerns my efforts are directed, have experienced even greater moral disquiet and more uneasiness of spirit than I could have recorded or anticipated when I wrote my concluding reflections. The nation's latest traumas have thus provided additional warrant for the foreboding tone of those reflections. With the national bicentenary now over the horizon, and with ideological reconstruction so urgently needed, it would seem that an account of the country's spiritual development continues to serve a significant purpose.

This book of history, of course, does not deal with every aspect of the national experience, yet it has been one of my primary purposes in these chapters so to entwine the moral and religious elements of American life in the larger context that it would be difficult or impossible for any reader to keep them in separate mental compartments. It may be appropriate, therefore, to reiterate the concern for the future that is expressed—and duly qualified—in the final sentence of this volume. Hope, in the fine phase of Samuel Willard, "oyles the wheels, warms the heart, and gives activity to compassion." Having that in mind, I would urge every reader to seek out and draw strength from "the profounder elements" of the American tradition.

With this printing the publisher has decided to issue a paperbound edition and to reduce the outer dimensions of the trade edition. The decision should have a favorable counterinflationary effect on the one hand, and bring muscular relief to both hands. In no sense, however, is this a revised edition, though the occasion has given me a better opportunity than heretofore to

1. Publius Cornelius Tacitus, *The History*, book I, par. 2 (The Oxford Translation, Revised. London, 1889).

correct various errors of fact and typography. At the same time, fortunately, I can also express my gratitude to very many extremely thoughtful reviewers and to the many others who have written letters. From both I have gained much encouragement and assistance; and I deeply regret that academic duties have delayed my personal responses. Though the inexorable effect of yielding to the suggestions and criticisms I have received would be greatly to enlarge an already ponderous tome, I value them exceedingly. It is often remarked that an author can learn much from his readers—even as to his own purposes and method. And I am glad to confess here that they have impressed upon me how strong a personal commitment I have to an historical emphasis on the living intentionality of human beings, as against mute social forces and structures. Whatever I may do in a later revised edition, this commitment, I feel, will not change.

S.E.A.

Yale University
New Haven, Connecticut
15 January 1974

PREFACE

Postmodern man proclaims himself to be also posthistoric—or at least he often exhibits himself as present-minded. Eschewing tradition, fearing the grip of the past, pessimistic about the future, he lives—or tries to live—within the narrow confines of today. The life of one-dimensional man is thus temporally flat; he avoids the mysteries of time and process; he does not take his own historicity seriously. Even when he is radically critical of society, he often ignores both the social circumstances of his protest and the historical sources of his critique.

Yet no work of history can be written from such a standpoint, regardless of its purpose or the sources of its inspiration. And this particular book was written in the firm conviction that the moral and spiritual development of the American people is one of the most intensely relevant subjects on the face of the earth. The United States—its nature and its actions—presents one of the world's most difficult challenges to the understanding, and a comprehensive account of its religious history holds promise of bringing light where light is sorely needed. Unlike Philip Schaff and many of my predecessors in this field, however, I do not believe that the necessary illumination can be provided by "church history" in its classic forms. Only a minority of Americans have ever believed that Christianity holds the central ruling position in history, or considered themselves to be part of what Schaff called the objective, organized, visible Kingdom of Christ on earth.[1] Christianity is by no means the only current in American religious history, although it has been the major one. Even this current consists of many quite discrete substreams, and from one or another of these separate confessional positions much of America's religious history has been interpreted in terms of heresy. So a broader stance, a wider conception of the "rule of charity,"

1. Schaff elaborates his profound conception of Christian church history in section 4 of the general introduction to his *History of the Apostolic Church* (first German ed., 1851; first English ed., 1853). His multivolume *History of the Christian Church* is surely one of the greatest works of history by an American. Yet Schaff's doctrinal stand severely limits the scope of his prodigious labors (see chap. 38, n. 3).

is essential, and this sympathy must be extended far beyond the explicitly Judaeo-Christian traditions. Not least it must include the propensity of Americans to view the state itself in a religious light. All of the country's varied religious movements, however, can be brought within a reasonably comprehensive and coherent account if four conditions are observed. Since these have been guidelines for me, they should be enumerated.

First, religious history as a field of study must be placed not only spatially but theoretically within the larger frame of world history. It enjoys no rights of sanctuary, no immunity from the demands for evidence and plausibility that are made on historians generally. The historian cannot claim divinely inspired sources of insight, nor can he place one body of holy scripture above another. "Orthodoxy" and "heresy" may not be used as dogmatic judgments, but only as historically conditioned designations. This prescription, it may be added, even disqualifies the kind of *theologia gloria* that has informed many supposedly secular accounts of this Redeemer Nation.

Second, the concept of religion must be extended to include "secular" movements and convictions, some of which opposed or sought to supplant the churches. Agnosticism does not preclude religiosity and moral seriousness. In 1970 the courts were taking this step by broadening the acceptable grounds for conscientious objection to war, and religious historians must similarly widen their scope.

Third, constant attention must be given to the radical diversity of American religious movements. This means that holistic interpretations of a single, unified "American tradition" must be cautiously employed. The national experience has, to be sure, put its mark on all of the country's disparate religious impulses, and white Anglo-Saxon Protestantism enjoyed a long hegemony. Yet one must constantly observe both the diverse denominational forces that flowed within this "mainstream" and the varying responses of groups outside the "quasi-establishment."

Fourth, the social context—including its demographic, economic, political, and psychological dimensions—must ever be borne in mind. Churches, sects, cults, and denominations exist as human communities, despite the unique sanctions and commitments that distinguish them from many other human groups and institutions. Their search for a transcendent reference above and beyond mundane considerations undoubtedly gives them a special character; indeed, it is this persistent search for absolute grounds for faith and action that makes them so fundamental—and so revealing. Yet the religious historian must remember that for this very reason his responsibility for rigorous analysis is intensified rather than reduced.

That I have fallen short of these exacting demands goes without saying. I exist in the middle of things and inherit the limitations of my situation. Not only the inadequacy of my knowledge, but also my hidden presuppositions and my unexamined major premises will in due course be exposed. I encourage my readers to call attention to these shortcomings with all possible speed and thoroughness.

In the meantime let me suggest the extent of my indebtedness, first of all to the innumerable band of historians who have worked in this field before me. Let no man say that he can in one lifetime write an American religious history "from the sources." If my obligations to the work of other scholars had been fully expressed in footnotes, this book would have been barnacled to the sinking point. In general, therefore, I have usually cited only those works which I directly quote at some length, though my annotation does increase slightly as I approach the contemporary period. For the same reason my bibliography has been limited largely to relatively recent works which themselves contain valuable bibliographical data on the subjects they treat. Works cited without publication data in the footnotes are listed in the bibliography. For similar reasons of space and efficiency the index is intended to take the place of innumerable footnote cross-references.

My most ardent thanks are, of course, conveyed to my wife, Nancy, who did not type a single word of the manuscript, but who bore with me. Her constant demands for clarity should benefit many readers. I must also make amends to my children, Alexander, Promise, Constance, and Sydney, who remember few times in their lives when one chapter or another was not denying them various imagined pleasures, but who have been, withal, remarkably considerate of the task that kept me so many hours in library and study.

Then how should I acknowledge my teachers and colleagues? The debt runs back to Carl G. Tideman in my Cokato, Minnesota, high school and Conrad Peterson in Gustavus Adolphus College. With deepening specificity it includes my professors and many fellow graduate students at Harvard and my colleagues at Yale. To mention names is impractical, despite the vividness of my remembered indebtedness. I hope they know—or knew—the depth of my gratitude. To Clarence C. Goen, Robert L. Ferm, Robert Stuart, Sanford Wylie, Vera Houghtlin, and several other research assistants, and to many exceedingly considerate typists—especially Helen Kent, Florence Sherman, Rose Stone, and Ascencion Day—I am grateful in ways beyond telling. In a special category are the Bollingen Foundation, which provided a generous grant, and the staff of the Yale University Press, who have transformed a huge pile of manuscript into a book. I would like to thank especially Cynthia Brodhead, whose careful editing of every page redounds to the benefit of every reader including myself, and Constance Sargent, who made the index. A word of special gratitude is owed to Michael Graham, whose illustrations grace the book.

For both the routine and the extraordinary solicitude shown by librarians and curators of special collections in dozens of institutions I feel a special sense of indebtedness. To the Yale University Library I am most of all beholden, and particularly to Raymond P. Morris and the Yale Divinity School library staff.

Then there are the dozens of scholarly readers of individual chapters, groups of chapters, or the entire manuscript, who have made me the beneficiary of their knowledge and wisdom. In a similar category are the many undergraduate, graduate, and divinity students at Yale University who in lecture courses and seminars have disputed and corrected my views and brought fresh insights to the subject through their research papers and discussion. That I have not and could not acknowledge the contributions made by these many concerned and talented people is sadly obvious, but I cherish the interest they manifested, thank them for the many ways in which they have saved me from error, and exonerate them absolutely from the flaws that still testify to my ignorance and perversity.

Yet my final thought is of another sort entirely. It springs from an intense awareness of the numberless communities of faith and moral conviction with which I have dealt inadequately or not at all. Faced with the inescapable limitations of space, and also of time, I think of Bishop Joseph Hall's Elizabethan lament: "This field is so spacious that it were easy for a man to lose himself in it; and if I should spend all my pilgrimage in this walk, my time would sooner end than my way." Remembering the many written pages that had to be abandoned or rudely abridged and countless cases where my interest had to be restrained, I can now only hope that these pages do succeed in presenting something of the vitality and diversity of the religious commitments that over the years have brought the American people to their present engagement with the future.

S. E. A.

Yale University
New Haven, Connecticut
16 December 1971

1

AMERICAN RELIGIOUS HISTORY IN THE POST-PROTESTANT ERA

History in its earliest and primal form celebrates the deeds of men and of gods, often of god-like men and man-like gods. And many of these very elements are wonderfully exhibited in what is possibly the oldest document of American history, the Icelandic *Saga of Eric the Red.*

> Eric was married to a woman named Thorhild, and had two sons; one named Thorstein and the other Leif. . . . Thorstein lived at home with his father in Greenland [while] Leif had sailed to Norway where he was at the court of King Olaf Tryggvason. . . . Upon one occasion the king came to speak with Leif, and asked him, "Is it thy purpose to sail to Greenland in the summer?" "It is my purpose," said Leif, "if it be your will." "I believe it will be well," answered the king, "and thither thou shalt go upon my errand to proclaim Christianity there." . . . Leif put to sea when his ship was ready for the voyage. For a long time he was tossed upon the ocean, and came upon lands of which he had previously had no knowledge. There were self-sown wheat fields and vines growing there. . . . Leif found men upon a wreck, and took them home with him [to Greenland], and procured quarters for them all during the winter. In this wise he showed his nobleness and goodness, since he introduced Christianity into the country, and saved the men from the wreck; and he was called Leif the Lucky ever after.[1]

1. Julius E. Olson, ed., "The Voyages of the Northmen," in *The Northmen, Columbus, and Cabot, 985–1503* (New York: Charles Scribner's Sons, 1906), pp. 23–26. Of the two major Icelandic narratives of Leif Ericson's discoveries, this one is regarded as the more reliable and older (ca. 1310–20). The passage quoted is, of course, a very minute portion of the evidence for Norse visits to the North American continent.

Already present in this medieval account are the major themes of the American saga: a religiously oriented sense of mission, an abundant land, a noble hero, and a favoring Providence. Even the vital ingredient of luck was there. And as soon as English settlers in the New World began sending reports back to the Old, the same themes recur. Overcoming strong contradictory evidence, the Reverend Alexander Whitaker's *Good Newes from Virginia* began the celebrationist tradition in 1613. Edward Johnson extended it to New England in 1654 with his *Wonder-Working Providence of Sions Saviour*. A half-century later Cotton Mather in his *Magnalia Christi Americana* provided copious documentation of "Christ's Great Deeds in America." Even Jonathan Edwards took up the refrain as he pondered the Great Awakening in 1740:

> 'Tis not unlikely that this work of God's Spirit, that is so extraordinary and wonderful, is the dawning, or at least a prelude, of that glorious work of God so often foretold in Scripture, which in the progress and issue of it shall renew the world of mankind. . . . And there are many things that make it probable that this work will begin in America.[2]

Following the lead of Johnson, Mather, and Edwards, American historians have continued without hesitation to see God Almighty and the Lord Jesus Christ as day-by-day participants in the country's struggles. "It is the object of the present work," wrote George Bancroft in the 1876 edition of his vast American history, "to explain how the change in the condition of our land has been brought about; and, as the fortunes of a nation are not under the control of blind destiny, to follow the steps by which a favoring Providence, calling our institutions into being, has conducted the country to its present happiness and glory." [3]

In the later twentieth century the mythic quality of the American saga has evaporated. The historian of the American religious experience who draws his work to a close as the nation's bicentennial observance draws near must speak in terms more somber than those which Bancroft used. The air seems less salubrious, the future more ominous. Institutionalized urban ghettoes and the "warfare state" make it impossible to see America's "present happiness and glory" as proof of a "favoring Providence." Indeed, if one forswear "blind destiny" as a guiding principle, the categories of divine judgment and wrath seem more appropriate. Yet the present day gives us no vantage point for making Olympian judgments. The historian of one age,

2. Jonathan Edwards, *Thoughts on the Revival in New England*, in *The Works of President Edwards*, 4 vols. (New York: Robert Carter & Brothers, 1879), 3:313.

3. George Bancroft, *History of the United States*, 1:3. In this revised edition Bancroft let these words of his introduction stand substantially as first written in 1834, when Andrew Jackson was in the White House.

as Leopold von Ranke insisted, stands no closer to God than those of other times—not even when the churches of God are his special subject matter, we might add. Each generation can only say that a different portion of the past is open for its examination, that its angle of vision is altered, and that new standards of explanation and relevance prevail. A new present requires a new past; and the historian's responsibility for creating a meaningful and usable past depends more on his interpretation of accepted historical knowledge than on his additions to the world's overflowing treasury of fact.

The latter chapters of this book describe the conditions under which this first chapter and all those that follow had to be written. There is no human escape from that enclosing circle. One experiences very vividly the truth of Max Lerner's retrospective comment on the ten years he spent in writing *America as a Civilization* (1957): "I found when I came to the end of the decade that a number of things I had written about America were no longer valid. The American civilization had been changing drastically right under my fingertips as I was writing about it." [4] The present-day historian's predicament is, if anything, more difficult than Lerner's, in that social and intellectual developments of the last decade have profoundly altered our interpretation of the entire course of American history. The terrible moral dilemmas that began to intensify during the sixties have had an especially rude impact on long-accepted views of the country's religious development.

In addition to this revolutionary situation, the sheer brevity of American history makes it particularly susceptible to revisionism. The United States offers the first major instance in the modern world of "the birth of a nation." Not only was it discovered and colonized in the clear light of recorded history, but it constituted itself as an independent republic as the Atlantic community entered its late modern phase. John Ruskin declared that he could not "even for a couple months, live in a country so miserable as to possess no castles." [5] As late as 1789 the "American" barely existed. Having almost no past of his own and lacking the confident selfhood of older nations, he lived for the future. In 1909 Israel Zangwill in his celebrated play *The Melting-Pot* still spoke in the present progressive tense: "[Here] all the races of Europe are melting and re-forming. . . . God is making the American." [6] The historian of America, even when he speaks in the present tense, is dealing with national parturition.

The religious history of the American people—like the political and so-

4. Thomas R. Ford, ed., *The Revolutionary Theme in Contemporary America* (Lexington, Ky.: University of Kentucky Press, 1965), p. 1.

5. John Ruskin, *Fors Clavigera,* Letter 10 (7 September 1871).

6. Israel Zangwill, *The Melting-Pot* (New York: Macmillan Co., 1909), p. 37. See also pp. 157, 193.

cial history of which it is the spiritual corollary—is, nevertheless, one of the grandest epics in the history of mankind. The stage is continental in size, and the cast is produced by the largest transoceanic migration and the most rapid transcontinental dispersion of people the world has ever seen. More difficult for the historian than the newness of America, therefore, is the unequaled complexity of its makeup. The compounding of the country's ethnic and confessional diversity has continued almost unabated since Spain founded Saint Augustine in 1565. In the radical antinomian tradition alone the accretions have been continuous, from Mistress Anne Hutchinson in the 1630s to Timothy Leary in the 1960s—both of whom, incidentally, confronted the upholders of public order in the neighborhood of Boston before carrying their message to more remote regions. As these instances suggest, moreover, many strong religious impulses have not been neatly housed in churches. The sheer multifariousness of the American religious heritage is the central problem of any historian who would undertake the general synoptic task.

A traveler in 1700 making his way from Boston to the Carolinas would encounter Congregationalists of varying intensity, Baptists of several varieties, Presbyterians, Quakers, and several other forms of Puritan radicalism; Dutch, German, and French Reformed; Swedish, Finnish, and German Lutherans; Mennonites and radical pietists, Anglicans, Roman Catholics; here and there a Jewish congregation, a few Rosicrucians; and, of course, a vast number of the unchurched—some of them powerfully alienated from any form of institutional religion. With the passing years the variety would increase, and in the year of the nation's officially recognized independence (1783) Ezra Stiles in his famous sermon "The United States Elevated to Glory and Honor" prophesied that in due course the country would "embosom all the religious sects and denominations in Christendom"—and allow freedom to them all.[7]

As the great tide of immigration poured in, Stiles's prophecy began to be fulfilled. In 1854 Philip Schaff, somewhat less ecstatically, observed that the United States offered "a motley sampler of all church history," [8] though the sample was then far from complete. But by the 1920s the Monophysite Church of Armenia—the oldest established church in Christendom—had put down American roots, as had each of the three main branches of the Syrian church—Jacobite, Nestorian, and Orthodox. Virtually every surviving heresy and schism in Christian history had its representatives in Amer-

7. Ezra Stiles, *The United States Elevated to Glory and Honor: A Sermon* (New Haven, 1783).

8. Philip Schaff, *America: A Sketch of Its Political, Social, and Religious Character*, p. 80.

ica. Small wonder that in the 1930s Dietrich Bonhoeffer would comment that "it has been granted to the Americans less than any other nation on earth to realize the visible unity of the Church of God." [9]

For many decades this plenitude of religious variation was little more than a cause of scorn, an occasion for bitter polemics, or a source of fascinated bewilderment. Among those with more scholarly interests, however, another response came to be manifested. It took the form of handbooks dealing with these diverse "religious bodies" according to one or another scheme of classification. Hannah Adams, a Unitarian school teacher, set high standards for this genre in 1784 with her *Alphabetical Compendium of the Various Sects,* which through several editions also pioneered in the field of world religions. She has been followed by a long line of authors who adopted the same method, from Samuel Goodrich later in the nineteenth century to Frank Mead and Frederick E. Mayer in the twentieth. Some of these efforts have been extremely useful, even profound; the genre should by no means be deprecated. But it is not history except in a very limited sense.

Another venerable solution was candidly adopted by Samuel D. McConnell in the 1880s, when he set out to write a history of American Christianity—and I single him out from among many only because his rationale was better stated:

> It has been frequently noticed that the Christianity of America possesses characteristics of its own. It is not only different in many regards from that which subsisted in Europe at the time of settlement of the colonies; but it is different from that which subsists in any other portion of Christendom now. Christianity here wears a garment of American weaving and American adornment. The religious history of the country is quite as striking as its political; it has had as many and as marked epochs; the influences which have shaped it have to be sought for in more numerous and more diverse sources; and those influences are more actively at work now than are those which produce political changes.
>
> With this fact in view I thought to trace the stream of religious life in the United States to its many various sources, to estimate the relative size and importance of the affluents which have colored it, and maybe to forecast its future course.

9. Dietrich Bonhoeffer, *No Rusty Swords: Letters, Lectures, and Notes, 1928–1936, from the Collected Works of Dietrich Bonhoeffer,* vol. 1, ed. Edwin H. Robinson (New York: Harper & Row, 1965), p. 94.

McConnell, one notes, had laudable objectives. He was proposing a genuinely cultural interpretation. He goes on, however, to announce a decision that many another historian has envied: "I found the project to be so difficult that I abandoned it. . . . The coherence of the facts in the religious history of our land cannot yet be seen. The facts themselves are abundant to embarrassment; but they cannot yet be strung upon any single thread which I have been able to discover." Noting that the unity of the church in America had lagged far behind the political development of the country, he insisted that "while this condition of things remains there cannot be written a history of the American Church." He then announced an anticlimactic decision: "I have undertaken therefore the more modest task to set out the history of the Protestant Episcopal Church in the United States." [10]

McConnell, of course, was not the first who chose to concentrate on a single denomination. Indeed, some of the greatest achievements in American religious historiography have been made in this realm, with Governor Bradford and Cotton Mather producing classics in the early colonial period. Even as McConnell went about his task, Philip Schaff was projecting the American Church History Series, in which some of our finest ecclesiastical history was published. But both of these alternatives (i.e. handbooks and denominational histories) are evasions of a responsibility that could not be escaped; and long before McConnell took the easy way out, more temerarious souls had forged a strong American tradition of synoptic interpretation.

In retrospect one can see that the decisive preparation for the emergence of general histories was provided by the colonial Great Awakening. Only through that convulsive outburst of piety did "American Evangelical Protestantism" become aware of itself as a national reality and alive to its culture-shaping power. The Revolution, moreover, as we have already heard Ezra Stiles testify, was to add another vital ingredient to the American's sense of religious solidarity. The Puritans had long thought of England as an Elect Nation, and Jonathan Edwards spoke of it with complete assurance as "the principal kingdom of the Reformation." By a remarkable process of transfer this notion was now attached to the raggle-taggle republic being created in America. Even in 1777, when the military issue was still unclear, Timothy Dwight would pen his incredibly confident lines:

> Columbia, Columbia, to glory arise,
> The queen of the world, and the child of the skies;

10. *History of the American Episcopal Church, 1600–1915,* pp. xvii–xix.

Thy genius commands thee; with rapture behold,
While ages on ages thy splendors unfold.[11]

The realistic view of man's sinfulness that tempered Dwight's optimism gradually disappeared in later forms of patriotic piety, and after the Loyalists had departed, only an occasional very eccentric American ever doubted that the Star-Spangled Banner waved over the Lord's Chosen Nation. In many minds the American was conceived as a new Adam in a new Eden, and the American nation as mankind's great second chance. Nothing better illustrates the continuity of this tradition than the patriotic hymns that were entered in the national book of psalms—from *America,* struck off in an inspired moment by an Andover seminarian for a Fourth of July observance in 1832, to *The Battle Hymn of the Republic,* written by Julia Ward Howe as if by the hand of God in 1861, to *America the Beautiful,* published in the *Congregationalist* in 1893. This mythic theme of America as a beacon on a hill and an exemplar for the world became a constituent element in historical interpretations of the nation's religious life.

Equally powerful as an integrating idea was the metaphor of the melting pot, the conception of the United States as a crucible in which the diverse base metals of the world would be marvelously transformed into pure Anglo-Saxon Protestant gold. A former French soldier who temporarily underwent that transformation described the process in his *Letters from an American Farmer,* published in 1782:

> Here individuals of all nations are melted into a new race of men. . . . The Americans were once scattered all over Europe; here they are incorporated into one of the finest systems of population which has ever appeared. . . . Here religion demands but little of him: a small voluntary salary to the minister and gratitude to God; can he refuse these? The American is a new man, who acts upon new principles; he must therefore entertain new ideas and form new opinions. . . . This is an American.[12]

Crèvecoeur would have been disappointed and surprised by the Second Awakening, which would soon transform the slumbering churches and make the "evangelical united front" a potent force in the land. But he would probably have been assuaged by the degree to which his melting pot metaphor became a working principle of Protestant historical interpretations during the entire course of the century which followed. Anti-Catholi-

11. See Kenneth Silverman, *Timothy Dwight,* pp. 40–41, 139–40.

12. J. Hector St. John de Crèvecoeur, *Letters from an American Farmer, and Sketches of Eighteenth-Century America,* ed. Albert E. Stone (New York: Signet Classics, 1963), p. 64.

cism and nativism would flame up recurrently; then as the great revivals followed one after the other, a quasi-establishment of evangelical Protestantism emerged. Not even the great antebellum sectional controversy interfered with its progress, because evangelicalism deepened its hold in both the North and the South. The Civil War, indeed, became a kind of double holy war. In 1893 the general secretary of the American branch of the Evangelical Alliance, Josiah Strong, looking beyond the shining seas, depicted the American nation as the new Rome whose destiny it was to "Anglo-Saxonize" the entire world.[13] During the Gilded Age this spiritual hegemony was threatened by factories, immigrants, and disconcerting modern ideas, but the united evangelical front closed ranks for the temperance crusade, the Little War of 1898, and the Great War of 1914–18. Protestant America, consequently, did not really face its first great moment of truth until it marched onto the moral and religious battlefields of the twenties, the tumultuous decade of prohibition, immigration, evolution, jazz, the KKK, short skirts, the movies, Al Smith, and the Crash. Here, indeed, was the antipodes of the Great Awakening. Yet a general awareness of the painful fact that evangelicalism was no longer a culture-shaping power was almost miraculously delayed for another thirty years. Only in the 1960s would it become apparent that the Great Puritan Epoch in American history had come to an end.

Perhaps inevitably it was during the last century of this epoch that the twin motifs of the elect nation and the melting pot gained their fullest historiographical expression. A new synthesis of American church history emerged—proud, nationalistic, and stridently Protestant. Most decisive in shaping its major lineaments was Robert Baird, an American Presbyterian missionary to Roman Catholics in Europe who published his famous *Religion in America* (1843) first in England, then in other languages and in several widely read American editions. This was not simply the first important panoramic history of American religion: it was a manifesto for a worldwide reformation of Christianity that took American Protestant voluntaryism as its model. To Baird the religion of America simply *was* revivalistic evangelicalism—though he did include a brief, condescending section on the unevangelical bodies. His basic value judgment is suggested by the mere two pages he allotted to the Roman Catholic church, which was in 1850 the largest denomination in the United States.[14]

The next historian-laureate of note was the Methodist Daniel Dorchester,

13. Josiah Strong, *The New Era; or, the Coming Kingdom* (New York, 1893), pp. 41–80, esp. p. 80.

14. See the critical abridgment of Baird's *Religion in America,* edited by Henry W. Bowden. Because of Baird's great zeal for facts, Schaff and many other historians relied heavily on him. Though not an influential interpreter of the American religious tradition, Schaff probably did more than

a prominent temperance leader and sometime national superintendent of Indian schools. He described himself as an admiring disciple of Baird, but he worked on a far vaster scale and with much greater attention to factual and statistical detail. His eight-hundred-page account *Christianity in the United States* (1887) is probably the finest work of its kind ever published. It is far more balanced and open-minded than Baird's book in its treatment of "unevangelical" movements, relatively generous in the amount of space allotted to Catholicism, and uncensorious on intra-Protestant doctrinal issues. Yet Baird's heavy evangelical and outspokenly nativist bias remains. Both in its distributions of praise and in its thematic structure Dorchester's book belongs in the "great tradition" of the American Protestant historiography.

At the century's end, Leonard Woolsey Bacon was chosen to provide the capstone volume for the American Church History Series. And his *History of American Christianity* (1897) deserves remembrance. It is a masterpiece of organization, with a steady kind of eloquence that sweeps the reader from triumph to triumph. Its judgments show the moderating force of theological liberalism; yet at bottom, Bacon presents still another version of the Protestant American's *theologia gloria,* in which patriotism and religion are inextricably entwined. "By a prodigy of divine providence," he begins, "the secret of the ages [that a new world lay beyond the Western Sea] had been kept from premature disclosure. . . . If the discovery of America had been achieved . . . even a single century earlier, the Christianity to be transplanted to the western world would have been that of the church of Europe in its lowest stage of decadence." He ends with his heart still strangely warmed by "those seventeen wonderful September days of 1893" when the World Parliament of Religions had met in Chicago as part of the four hundredth anniversary celebration of Columbus's discovery. With the memory of that truly ecumenical gathering in mind (representatives of other world religions had also attended), Bacon closes his work with thoughts of "great providential preparations as for some 'divine event' still hidden behind the curtain that is about to rise on the new century." Incapable of pessimism as he seems to have been, one suspects that his vision included the Melting Pot, perhaps in the shape of the Holy Grail, containing all of America's churches, Catholic and Protestant, amalgamated somehow, but in such a way that Protestants would have no problems in adjusting to the new reality.[15]

any other church historian to establish the "historical standpoint" in the American mind (see James H. Nichols, *Romanticism in American Theology: Nevin and Schaff at Mercersburg*).

15. *History of American Christianity,* pp. 2, 419. Bacon, who had Yale degrees in both theology and medicine, was a widely traveled Congregational minister.

The Protestant synthesis by no means culminated in the work of Bacon, however. That honor unquestionably belongs to William Warren Sweet (b. 1881), whose *Story of Religions in America* first appeared in 1930, and who from 1927 to 1946 was extremely influential as professor of the history of American Christianity at the University of Chicago. Deeply and permanently impressed by Frederick Jackson Turner, Sweet's thought was dominated by the shaping force of the frontier. Even more important in the long run was the way in which his accent on cultural factors in church history eclipsed the pious providentialism of his predecessors. Yet we should not overstate the case, for Sweet emphatically did not betray the great Protestant tradition of historiography. He translated it into the idiom of the "scientific history" and accented the role of the Baptists and Methodists; but the uncritical celebrationism of Baird remains an aspect of his many books.[16] The older forms of nativism disappear, yet Catholics, Eastern Orthodox, Jews, Negroes, immigrants, and the city are on the periphery of his scholarly interest. Anti-intellectualism and the idea of progress consistently undermine his treatment of Puritanism, systematic theology, doctrinal developments, and the rise of humanistic modernism.

Due in part to Sweet's example, an active new generation of American church historians arose. Among them were many who stemmed from the "Chicago School," as the mere mention of Brauer, W. E. Garrison, Handy, Hudson, Marty, Nichols, and above all, Sidney E. Mead makes apparent. Few of these Chicago men, furthermore, were subservient to Sweet, and some were explicitly critical. Yet the revival of interest in the American field was by no means limited to Chicago. Indeed the surge of scholarship became too vast to be considered here, except insofar as this book as a whole is a tribute to it.[17] Even in the new generation, however, the major concern continued to be the rise and development of the Protestant tradition. Until fairly recently, moreover, seminary professors have provided the great bulk of the published work; and these men have been understandably concerned with problems of diagnosis and prescription for the white Protestant churches. Very few of them have been fundamentally critical of the mainstream trend, or of its relation to American culture as a whole, or of that culture itself. Their tendency, with vital exceptions, has been to contribute to the "concensus tradition" in American historiography.[18]

16. In addition to general accounts, Sweet turned his American church-historical attention to the Civil War, revivalism, and his own Methodist denomination.

17. One or more works by each of the historians who are mentioned by name only in this chapter are included in the bibliography of this volume.

18. Perhaps the man whose work best incorporates this Protestant consensus into a

Certain powerful countervailing tendencies did appear, however; and some of these dissents from the received interpretation have been of great personal significance to me. One trend of this sort, showing some Marxist influence, is marked out by Vernon L. Parrington's famous *Main Currents of American Thought* (1927–1930) and by H. Richard Niebuhr's *Social Sources of Denominationalism* (1929). Another is the remarkable rediscovery of Puritanism pioneered by Samuel Eliot Morison, Kenneth B. Murdock, and William Haller. This tradition culminates in the massive works of Perry Miller—who, coincidentally or not, also had a link to Chicago that preceded his long identification with Harvard. In this context one must also include the powerful Neo-orthodox impulse, represented best, perhaps, by H. Richard Niebuhr's *Kingdom of God in America* (1937) with its thoroughgoing reconsideration of judgments rendered by the previous generation of liberals. The combined impact of these dissents brought a serious challenge to the optimistic progressivism that had heretofore dominated the historiographical mainstream.

To complete the picture one must add the name of the elder Arthur Meier Schlesinger, whose pivotal essays "The Significance of the City in American History" and "The Critical Period in American Religion," along with countless other works which he wrote, edited, or inspired, made him a major figure in America's rediscovery of the city as a vital factor in its religious history.[19] Nor is this tribute sufficient, for Schlesinger also played a major role in the revival of concern for the history of immigration and ethnic minorities. In this effort he by no means labored alone, in part because many immigrant groups inspired their own historians to impressive accomplishments. Due to the importance of religion to the cultural cohesion of these groups, many eminent works on specific religious traditions have been published. To mention individual achievements would be impossible, but Monsignor John Tracy Ellis and Oscar Handlin stand out—both for their own works and for the innumerable students they have guided and inspired.

Against this background of vigorous activity, Henry F. May in 1964 could describe a veritable thirty-year "renaissance" in the writing of American church history; and with this revived and renovated situation before them, later authors of general American religious histories have done their work. So valuable have the works of these scholars been to me that I must

---

full-scale interpretation of the American mind is Ralph Henry Gabriel in *The Course of American Democratic Thought.*

19. Among many other titles in my bibliography, those of A. I. Abell, T. L. Smith, Ira Brown, W. R. Cross, and H. F. May testify to Schlesinger's strong influence.

acknowledge my indebtedness: to Clifton E. Olmstead's *History of Religion in the United States* (1960) for the first major presentation of the whole story since that of Sweet; to the impressive two volumes of expertly interpreted documents of *American Christianity* (1960) edited by H. Shelton Smith, Robert T. Handy, and Lefferts A. Loetscher; to the survey accounts of Winthrop S. Hudson (*Religion in America,* 1965) and Edwin Scott Gaustad (*A Religious History of America,* 1966); and finally, to the editors and authors of *Religion in American Life* (4 vols., 1961), which provided the first comprehensive overview of the American religious experience since that given in the American Church History Series of the 1890s. Especially memorable in this composite work was the learned two-volume bibliography prepared by Nelson R. Burr.[20] It is this last-mentioned work more than any other which justifies the decision to limit the extent of my own bibliography.

As the foregoing survey very inadequately suggests, and as Burr's bibliography incontestably shows, anyone in the 1970s who would again venture a general history of American religion is the legatee of an awesome body of scholarship. It behooves him not only to profess his profound gratitude, but to say why he has deemed it worthwhile to devote a decade of his life to the task. Such an apologia does not come easily, but the simplest answer is that the "renaissance" described by Professor May calls for a new, synthetic effort on a fairly large scale. Closer to the heart of the matter is the conviction, declared early in this chapter, that events have so radically transformed the American situation that our whole view of what is relevant in the past must be revised. A new set of circumstances now stands in need of historical explanation. We are driven to an awareness of historiographical crisis by the mere mention of John XXIII and John Kennedy, of Martin Luther King, Malcolm X, and the Beatles, or if we think of the student movement, the environmental awakening, the alleged death of God, and the new mood in which American priorities at home and abroad are being reevaluated. Post-Protestant America requires an account of its spiritual past that seeks to clarify its spiritual present. And such an account should above all do justice to the fundamentally pluralistic situation which has been struggling to be born ever since this country was formally dedicated to the proposition that all men are created equal.

The basic paradigm for a renovation of American church history is the black religious experience, which has been virtually closed out of all syn-

20. James W. Smith and A. Leland Jamison, eds., *Religion in American Life.* Volume 4 consists of the two book-length parts of Burr's bibliography. Volume 3 has not yet been published.

optic histories written so far—closed out despite the obvious fact that any history of America that ignores the full consequences of slavery and non-emancipation is a fairy tale, and that the black churches have been the chief bearers of the Afro-American heritage from early nineteenth-century revivals to the present day. This paradigm of restoration must then be applied to the other traditions that the Protestant synthesis left to one side, such as the Catholic, Jewish, and Eastern Orthodox, as well as such large nonecclesiastical religious movements as New Thought, Theosophy, and Rosicrucianism. In the same spirit one is led to emphasize more strongly than has been usual two seemingly contradictory aspects of American church history: the degree to which denominational traditions even in the Protestant mainstream modify the behavior of individual churches, and the way in which the long development of modern religious ideas undermines these confessional commitments and thus prepares the ground for the emergence of radical theology in the 1960s.

Basic to the effective fulfillment of all these aims is the recognition of the degree to which American civilization is a New World extension of Christendom. Unique it certainly becomes, but its distinctiveness springs almost as much from the continuing impact of diverse and sometimes contradictory European influences as from the fact that it occupied a vast and rich wilderness. An account of its religious development thus requires a constant concern for men, movements, and ideas whose origins are very remote in both time and space. One must, of course, forswear the temptation to make American religious history a pretext for writing the history of Western civilization; yet it has seemed imperative, for example, to deal with such immensely significant developments as the rise of East European Jewish Orthodoxy or the shaping of the Greek Orthodox Christianity, even though the full impact of these religious impulses was not felt in the United States until early in the twentieth century. It is for such reasons that this history does not begin with the traditional American sequence running from the Reformation on the Continent through that in Great Britain and on to the planting of the American colonies, but opens instead with chapters on Western Catholicism, New Spain, and New France. In this way one can better understand the ways in which medieval Christianity was still very much alive even in the catechisms and sermons of Puritan New England.

I
EUROPEAN PROLOGUE

For the Lord had said vnto Abram, Get thee out of thy Countrey, and from thy kindred, and from thy fathers house, vnto the land that I will shew thee. And I will make of thee a great nation, and will blesse thee, and make thy name great, and thou shalt be a blessing. I will blesse them also that blesse thee, and curse them that curse thee, and in thee shall all the families of the earth be blessed. [Genesis 12:1–3]

Being the text used by the Reverend William Symonds, preacher at Saint Savior's, Southwark, in A Sermon Preached At White-Chappel, In The Presence of . . . the Aduenturers and Planters of Virginia, . . . Published For The Benefit And Vse Of The Colony, Planted, And to bee Planted there, and for the Aduancement of their Christian Purpose. (25 April 1609)

America became the Great Frontier of Western Christendom in 1492, and five centuries after Columbus opened the sea trails to this New World the people of the United States in overwhelming numbers still recognize Europe as the source not only of the languages they speak, but of much that animates their most dearly held convictions. Even those with ties to Africa or Asia or those most ancient of migrants from Asia who are called Indians spend most of their lives in contexts and institutions that were shaped by the Western tradition. The American who listens to news of Marxism in China on a Japanese transistor radio may well wonder if Europe is not the chief source of an emerging global civilization.

The imperial designs awakened in European capitals by the discovery of America and the process by which those designs became an actuality were closely related to the religious turmoil which featured European history during the age of discovery and colonization. It is the purpose of Part I to consider this background. It begins with a chapter on Roman Catholic Christendom before the Reformation, which is followed by accounts of New Spain and New France, the two Catholic empires that long encircled the English colonies. These are followed by a chapter on the Continental Reformation, followed by two others that deal with religious developments in Great Britain. It closes with a chapter that surveys the belated and sporadic—yet remarkably successful—enterprises by which England and, in passing, the Netherlands and Sweden, carried out their imperial intentions along the North Atlantic mainland during the seventeenth century. As a result of these efforts Protestantism, predominantly in its Puritan form, became a major factor in the spiritual shaping of a "great nation."

2

WESTERN CATHOLICISM

On Saint George's Eve, 22 April 1418, the forty-fifth and last general session of the Council of Constance was dissolved, and the departing prelates were granted full absolution by the new pope, Martin V. The most splendid assembly that Western Christendom had ever seen, after lasting three years and six months, came to an end without any tumult (though Europe's peace was broken elsewhere), without any rise in the prices of provisions (though the city was crowded with visitors), and without any extraordinary sickness (though a plague broke out soon after). This council, said one of its eminent participants, "was more difficult than any other general council that preceded it, more strange, surprising, and hazardous in its course, and lasted a longer time." [1]

The Great Schism of the papacy was no more: this was the leading fact. In November 1417 the considerably reconstituted College of Cardinals had elected as Christ's new vicar Oddo Colonna, one of their number who had come to Constance with Pope John XXIII. Rival claimants were safely out of the way: John was now a prisoner in Heidelberg Castle, Gregory XII had abdicated, and Benedict XIII was a shadow pope soon to be isolated till he died on Peñíscola, a miniature Gibraltar rising out of the sea near Tortosa, Spain.[2] Martin V began his return to Rome in May 1418, traveling

1. Cardinal Guillaume Fillastre's Diary, in John Hine Mundy et al., eds., *The Council of Constance: The Unification of the Church*, Records of Civilization no. 63 (New York: Columbia University Press, 1961), p. 446.

2. When Cardinal Angelo Giuseppe Roncalli was crowned pope in 1958 he became John XXIII, thus using a name which had lapsed since the John XXIII known to historians was deposed at Constance. Number XXIII was used again because the church recognizes Gregory XII as the true pope up to the time of Martin V's election at the Council of Constance. Gregory XII was in the line of popes who had stayed at Rome after Gregory XI had returned from Avignon in 1377. Benedict XIII, also deposed at Constance, belonged to the line that returned to Avignon, and along with his single predecessor he is designated an "antipope." At the Council of Pisa (1409), which sought to remedy the Great Schism, Alexander V was elected, and John XXIII became his successor in 1410; but these popes of the "Pisan

with great pomp as the only head of a united church; and although he was unable to enter the Eternal City until 1420, he was able eventually to swing all factions in the church to his support. In June the Emperor Sigismund quietly left Constance, knowing that his determination to reunite the Church had at least made possible the council's chief accomplishment.

One can hardly conclude, however, that the Council of Constance reformed the Roman church "in head and members," as many had hoped it would. It had convened with three ostensible purposes: to heal the disastrous schism, to deal with heresy, and to reform the church. Its spectacular achievement of the first two goals blunted the desire for reform; and the new pope, once his election was confirmed, was anxious for the council to adjourn before it meddled too much in the internal affairs of the papacy.

But Constance, as an event, does provide most remarkable testimony to the complex character of the church in late medieval times. There at the Christmas Mass in 1414 had stood Emperor Sigismund, wearing the stole and dalmatic of a deacon, taking part in the holy office as lector for the day—but symbolizing nevertheless the authority of the secular power which was to be so decisive in the council's result. In the same cathedral three days later preached Cardinal Pierre d'Ailly, chancellor of the University of Paris and indefatigable champion of reform. He upheld the supremacy of a general council with a persuasiveness that made his words the manifesto of the conciliar party, and personified a different principle of authority. Also in the cathedral on 6 July 1415, John Huss, the patriot reformer of Bohemia, whose spiritual descendants three centuries later would be evangelizing the Indians in Pennsylvania, was condemned as a heretic and led out of the city to be burned for the manner of his invoking still another principle of authority, that of the Bible. There, almost a year later, on 30 May 1416, having recanted his recantation, Jerome of Prague, philosopher, humanist, orator, and superb Latinist, met the same fate, praising Huss as the smoke filled his lungs and leading the cultured Poggio Bracciolini of Florence to lament that the world had lost its most remarkable humanist scholar. At Constance, the learned Poggio, symbol of the new love for antiquity, would set aside his nominal duties as a papal secretary to forage in nearby monastic libraries for lost manuscripts of his beloved Latin classics, and would rejoice to find what still remains our best manuscript of Quintilian. His quest symbolized the rising interest in classical antiquity as still another principle of authority. On 1 February 1415, Con-

line" are also regarded as antipopes. In the fifteenth century, of course, these determinations had not been agreed upon. Perhaps there is some significance to the fact that the modern Pope John XXIII was a church historian.

stance had witnessed a contrasting ceremony in which Pope John XXIII proclaimed the canonization of Saint Brigitta of Sweden—mystic, seer, reformer, pilgrim, doer of many charitable works—a fitting tribute to ancient ideals not otherwise much in evidence.

All these tendencies converged in the old imperial free city on the Bodensee, giving rise to the conflicts between secular and churchly power, the problems of religious authority, the clamor over corruption and abuse, the reassertion of medieval mystic piety, the flowing tide of Renaissance enthusiasm, and much more. The fifteenth is an exciting century: it is the quattrocento of Italian art and humanism; it marks the critical stage in the struggle between curialism and conciliarism; it unfolds many portents of the upheaval we call the Reformation. It is also an open-ended age that reveals the changing texture of European culture.

THE ETHOS OF THE AGE

These hundred years are frequently viewed as a one-way street from Constance to Wittenberg, or from Constance to Trent, depending on whether the viewer is Protestant or Catholic. Historians with humanistic inclinations have taken a less specifically religious route and charted the literary and artistic wonders of the Renaissance to their flowering in Medicean Florence and Rome. Those whose concern is primarily economic have mapped the fifteenth century as a time of expanding trade culminating in a "commercial revolution" and the discovery of new worlds. And there are other categories by which to describe the period.

Each of these modes of interpretation captures an essential aspect of fifteenth-century life and therefore can claim a measure of validity. But our understanding of church history can be enriched, perhaps, if we pause for a moment and regard the period as a self-contained epoch in which to observe the manifold interests, the depths and wonders, the spirit and zest of Western Christendom before the tumultuous events of the Reformation harden party lines between Roman Catholics and various reforming groups. Protestants sometimes forget that this culture produced other religious phenomena besides Tetzel and Pope Leo X—for example, Luther and Calvin, not to mention Loyola and many other Catholic reformers. The vast reservoir of popular piety, the widespread acceptance of mystical devotion, the intermingling of world and church—these are all factors that help to explicate the religious resurgence of an age which is also prologue to the whole American adventure.

Popular Piety

Historians, in their concentration upon leaders of thought and action, tend to neglect the common people whose belief and devotion necessarily undergird and nourish the Church's institutional life in every period. Johan Huizinga has reminded us of this danger in his sensitive discussion of the forms of life, thought, and art in the late Middle Ages. He puts his finger on an elemental factor in the fervor of the age.

> To the world when it was half a thousand years younger, the outlines of all things seemed more clearly marked than to us. The contrast between suffering and joy, between adversity and happiness, appeared more striking. . . . Calamities and indigence were more afflicting than at present; it was more difficult to guard against them, and to find solace. . . . Honours and riches were relished with greater avidity and contrasted more vividly with surrounding misery. We, at the present day, can hardly understand the keenness with which a fur coat, a good fire on the hearth, a soft bed, a glass of wine, were formerly enjoyed.[3]

Modern man has almost lost the sense of darkness; he can hardly imagine a dark village, a dark city street, a dark monastery. By the same token, alas, he has lost the full sense of light and of day. He has made silence almost unknown; hence he can hardly comprehend the greatest of late medieval sounds, the ringing of church bells. Modern man's mobility, moreover, has robbed him of that sense of place and station, of both isolation and rootedness, which were familiar facts in the Western nations until the last century or two. We can scarcely conceive a time when each district, even each town, spoke the vernacular language with a dialect or accent of its own. And because of these cultural changes we are hindered in understanding the piety of premodern ages. A considerable imaginative effort is required.

The first step in any such effort to reenter this late medieval atmosphere is an obliteration of the sharp distinction moderns make between the sacred and the secular.[4] Because we separate the churchly from the worldly more decisively than Geoffrey Chaucer or Martin Luther would or could, we

3. *The Waning of the Middle Ages,* trans. F. Hopman (London: E. Arnold & Co., 1927), pp. 1–2.

4. No distinction essential to a discussion of religion and the church offers greater obstacles to clarity than that suggested by the two sets of terms *sacred, religious, churchly,* etc., on the one hand, and *secular, profane, worldly,* etc., on the other. The 1960s, in particular, were deluged by a literature which has significantly altered the traditional value judgments. Theologians, both Christian and Jewish, have sought "nonreligious" categories and stressed the excellencies of "secularity." Historians have emphasized the profane contributions of the churches. Regardless of these trends, however, the objective function of the distinction remains, and without praise or blame intended, it is used as needed throughout this book (see Michael J. Taylor,

tend to consider Luther's *Table-Talk* as vulgar and Chaucer's *Canterbury Tales* as anticlerical. But the fact is that the tension between the Christian and the world, which was real enough to first-century Christians in their hostile and religiously heterogeneous world, had almost disappeared, and Christianity (in the West, at least) was not only politically established but so socially domesticated that the sense of an alien "world" over against the church was almost unknown. For one thing, the Church—with its institutions, its clergy, its confraternities and lay-brotherhoods—had become omnipresent. Its rites surrounded not only the great life events of birth, marriage, and death, but also the organizations of crafts and professions, the acts and offices of government, and international relations. Theology and science were also interpenetrated. In the fifteenth century, indeed, the Church was enjoying its last years as the relatively unchallenged custodian and interpreter of the cosmos.

What we call superstition was ever-present in all of its many forms. "The sky hung low," says Shirley Jackson Case in describing the thought-world of the early Church; and after the passage of a millennium it had not lifted noticeably. It may even have lowered. Demons, fairies, sprites, and the mysterious workings of unknown and largely unpredictable powers had a firm hold on the imagination. It follows that the interpenetration of the sacred and the secular became characteristic of this realm as well. Worship, theology, and biblical exegesis often incorporated fanciful and magical elements. Even the sneeze had theological overtones, which our "bless you" still commemorates. By a reverse process, folklore and mythology were sublimated or partially reshaped to Christian purposes. Thomas Malory's *Le Morte d'Arthur,* printed by William Caxton in England in 1485, provides an excellent example of this process, and latter-day scholarly battles over the origins of this masterpiece emphasize the way in which sacred tradition had been woven into five centuries' accumulation of historical fact, heroic legend, courtly romance, and chivalric aspiration. Here incontinent desire, ideal love, and the Holy Grail coexist, but the range and tone of the narrative as well as the unselfconscious blending of earthiness, chivalry, barbarity, adultery, and other-worldly piety have made the work an open door to the late medieval mind just as surely as Tennyson's eminently respectable *Idylls of the King* is to the Victorian.

If the piety of the common people lacked depth, it certainly did not lack outward expression. Measured in terms of church buildings, attendance at worship, endowment bequests, charitable deeds, religious pilgrimages, and

ed., *The Sacred and the Secular* [New York: Prentice-Hall, 1968] and William A. Clebsch, *From Sacred to Profane America*).

a thousand other modes of pious expression, there is no evidence that popular devotion flagged. Especially in northern Europe it flourished with great zeal and sincerity. As Gerhard Ritter has remarked, "Even the most passionate and most embittered German criticism of the church could still be called the anger of disillusioned love." [5]

Devotional Life

The spirit which characterized the piety of the common people came to classical expression in the devotional writings and sermons of the Rhineland mystics. The roots of this impulse go deep into the preceding centuries. Behind the Rhenish "Friends of God" stands the commanding figure of the Dominican mystic, Meister Eckhart (1260–1328?), in whose train come that distinguished group, Heinrich Suso (1295–1366), Johannes Tauler (1300–1361), and the author of the *Theologia Germanica* (ca. 1350). Each of these made a permanent contribution to the Church's devotional life which was to be studied and republished by Dominicans and Jesuits no less than by Martin Luther and John Wesley. Their widespread appeal, then and since, has probably stemmed as much from their practical piety as from their speculative theology. To read them is to be stirred into a personal search for the meaning of love, which Tauler called the "beginning, middle, and end of virtue," and which he taught could be found only by losing oneself in the love of God as a drop of water is lost in the ocean.

The *devotio moderna* of the Brethren of the Common Life and the Windesheim Congregation of monasteries in the Netherlands endeared itself even more strongly to later generations. *The Imitation of Christ* by Thomas a Kempis (1380–1471), a canon of Saint Augustine at Windesheim, has become the most treasured work to issue from this spiritual movement. It is an extended gloss on the dominical message, "He who follows me shall not walk in darkness." The exceedingly human tendency apparent at every stage of history, to convert the Christian life into a well-defined and legalistic regimen, was much in evidence in the world that Thomas contemplated. So were many grosser corruptions. But Thomas summoned professing Christians to a higher life of discipleship. Then as in all succeeding centuries great numbers responded; the dedicated Christian life which these men and movements exemplified, and the ageless way in which they sought to bring persons directly to a deeper understanding of the mercy and holiness of God and the nature of Christian discipline, are intrinsic aspects of the age.

5. Gerhard Ritter, "Why the Reformation in Germany," *Church History* 23 (June 1958): 103.

The Secularization of the Church

If the church was not an alien in the world, neither was the world a stranger to the church. The distinction between what we are pleased to call the sacred and the secular was further blurred by what, for lack of a better term, may be styled the secularization of the church. In saying this, however, one can transcend the harsh debates of G. G. Coulton, Cardinal F. A. Gasquet, and G. K. Chesterton concerning the religiosity of cultures such as Chaucer's "merrie England." The point is that with so large a portion of Europe's resources under the church's jurisdiction, and with so large a percentage of the population numbered among the "religious," secular interests and "worldly" ways of life and thought entered cloister and chapter house. Abbots and archbishops became rulers, priests became secretaries of state or administrators, monks became wandering men of letters (like Erasmus), other clerics became physicians and scientists (like Copernicus), papal secretaries were humanistic dilettantes (like Poggio), and a pope (Julius II) even served as a field general. Gentleladies like Chaucer's winsome pilgrim became nuns without ceasing to be gentleladies—which may remind us that pilgrimages, too, became something more than simple works of penance or piety. All of this could be established by quoting only the great reformers of the religious life: Saint Odo of Cluny, Saint Bernard of Clairvaux, or Thomas a Kempis—not to mention the writings of Erasmus or countless other less friendly observers.

Though an isolated, unchallenged, and basically agrarian culture, medieval Europe was the most completely realized "Christian society" the world has yet seen. Its fabric was even then rent by urbanism, capitalism, nationalism, and science—making "neomedievalism" impossible—but one can hardly deny its beauty, profundity, or overall achievement. As for its faults, none pointed to them more relentlessly than churchmen themselves: Pierre d'Ailly's reform sermon at Constance was on a theme to which many of Christendom's greatest and most dedicated men devoted themselves. They held Pope Martin V to his promise to call another general council in five years, but the proceedings at Pavia and Siena in 1423 came to an indecisive conclusion. When Martin died in 1431, they bound his successor, Eugenius IV, to convene another general council immediately. How the Council of Basel got out of hand, defied the papal decree of dismissal and elected a counterpope, only to see the official proceedings transferred to Italy, is a complex series of events which cannot be surveyed here. The outcome was that papal power and "curialism" triumphed, and that a general pacification was achieved in time for the jubilee celebrations of 1450.

Pacification was not reform, however; and although the main lines of the superficial settlement made by Pope Nicholas V (1447–55) were held intact until the Reformation, discontent and frustration continued to build up. Neither the popes nor the dominant leaders of the papal Curia during the next half-century were able to apprehend the explosive power that ecclesiastical malpractice was generating throughout the length and breadth of Europe. Even if Nicholas V, or Alexander VI (1492–1503), or Julius II (1503–13) had been aware of the depth of concern that was stirring men everywhere, it is doubtful that they could have channeled it into a genuine reformation without the kind of cataclysmic disruption that broke into the pleasant and cultured world of Leo X (1513–21).

Even the word "cataclysm" scarcely suggests the magnitude of the forces then at work. In many ways they were greater than either the reformers, the pope, or the emperor. The old order for the Western nations and for the sprawling Roman church was crumbling. This was true in all realms—social and political, intellectual and spiritual. The Reformation as a whole is an event of the magnitude of the Fall of Rome, and one does not pinpoint some single occurrence or circumstance as the "cause" of it except as a form of amusement. For the Holy Roman emperors as for their Roman predecessors, the whole material and spiritual world was subjected to such pressures that its institutional structures, no longer amenable to modification, gradually cracked and fell to pieces. And the forces active in this process would not only promote the formation of new ideologies and structures in Europe, but almost inevitably they would bring American history—and American church history—into actuality. It is important to see that the impulses which led Luther to the Wittenberg church door were integrally related to those which sent Spanish caravels out across the Western Sea.

SOME FACTORS OF CHANGE

The New Learning

One factor altering the situation was that complex of attitudes and enthusiasms which are associated with the Renaissance: the so-called rebirth of learning, the revival of antiquity, the passionate reassertion of individuality, and with these, the search for standards of beauty, truth, and relevance independent of the Church and its dogmas. Philosophy, theology, ethics, and art—not to mention political and economic theory—were taken out of the Church's domain and patronized by princes, merchants, and bankers; and they were now often practiced by laymen, as well as priests who regarded holy orders very casually. The vast scholastic enterprise was often jettisoned as a preoccupation of the "dark ages." For some, Latinity almost replaced theology as the "queen of the sciences." Castiglione's *Life of the Courtier* replaced the *Golden Legend* of the saints as a guide to personal behavior, and Machiavelli's *Prince* would in due course replace the medieval "mirrors for kings" as a guide for rulers.

Machiavelli also suggests another aspect of the intellectual trend of the century: the growing concern for reality as against ideality. Just as Machiavelli was to describe the way a successful prince *did* rule rather than the way he *ought* to rule, so an increasing number of men were becoming concerned with *how* events in the physical universe occur rather than *why* things are as they are. Observation and induction began to displace speculation and deduction. In artistic expression as well, realism came to the fore: compare, for example, a Madonna by Duccio to one by Raphael. In philosophy, nominalism as taught by William of Ockham began to prevail. At the University of Padua, where the most signal scientific advances were to be made, there was a more direct continuity with Aristotle and the scholastics than with the antiquarian effusions of the humanists; but the results were entirely new, and they fired new aspirations by inspiring a new confidence in the power of human reason. At this point at least, the scientific movement joined hands with the humanistic.

But by no means all of the ancient concerns of the Church were abandoned, for the new learning was also opening up the "strange world of the Bible." In France, the Low Countries, England, and Germany, many men turned with renewed vigor to the Scriptures—encouraged in theory at least by the nominalists, with their emphasis on the supreme will of God and the limitations of reason in matters of faith. At Oxford John Colet (1467–1519) was lecturing on Romans, and his enthusiasm seems to have aroused Erasmus to more serious religious concerns. In France the biblical studies of Jacques Lefevre d'Étaples (1450–1537) directed the humanistic group of Meaux into more evangelical interests, and ultimately influenced both Luther and Calvin. Erasmus's Greek text of the New Testament, published by Froben of Basel in 1516, was not only the first work of its kind (Ximénes's Complutensian Polyglot was prepared earlier though not published until 1517), but a major milestone in the textual study of the Bible. Together with a parallel emergence of Hebrew and Old Testament studies, it became the basis of most of the scientific exegesis of the entire Reformation period. This renascence of biblical study on the part of men who, for the most part, were inclined less to speculate than to investigate, is an important confluence of scientific and humanistic interests in the service of theological inquiry and religious concern.

Economic Factors

The chief economic reality that underlay the profound dislocations and anxieties of the pre-Reformation century are summed up in the statement that Europe, first in Italy and then farther north, was making a transition from an "economy of status" to an "economy of money." This "commercial revolution" was enjoyed by almost no one but the great merchants and bankers, and even they were constantly attacked by rulers and populace as scapegoats in a process which few understood. The dynamic instabilities of early capitalism appeared: men of lowly origin grew rich and powerful enough to put even kings and popes in their debt, the old guilds became moribund, knights and squires went begging, peasant debt reached intolerable proportions. The entire social and economic equilibrium of medieval society was upset. In an effort to stem the tide, governments passed laws and the church invoked traditional moral sanctions; but in the last analysis there were usually more who preferred the monetary advantage of trade, rent, and interest to the security of status. In their distress men reaffirmed the ideals they were abandoning, but the change went on.

The result was that the institutions of capitalism prospered. Above all, the cities grew into great centers of industry, trade, and banking: Florence, Milan, Venice, Antwerp, London, Augsburg, Basel, Cadiz, Lisbon, and many others. As trade increased, the possibilities for extending it were enlarged. Africa, India, and the Spice Islands beckoned, and it was Portugal under the leadership of Prince Henry which made the first bold response. After a few tentative thrusts down the west coast of Africa, Bartolomeu Dias in 1488 rounded the Cape of Good Hope, and ten years later Vasco da Gama made his way around to India and back. These early efforts encouraged explorers from other nations to brave uncharted seas in search of new routes to riches, a development which has obvious implications for the history of Christianity.

National Feeling

To mention Portugal is to draw attention to another factor in the late-medieval upheaval, the rise of national states and the emergence of national feeling. "Nationalism" is too strong a word to describe the phenomenon in this early period; but both of its chief psychic and organizational elements, patriotism and the nation-state, were clearly taking shape. In England geography cooperated with the trend of the times; and after the house of Tudor secured the throne in 1485, national feeling grew apace. In France, too, a self-conscious spirit was developing, and not even the diplomacy of Pope Nicholas V could resist the demands of Gallican churchmen for more liberties. In Germany and Italy the "national reality" was obscured by petty rivalries among tiny states and independent cities which existed in a heterogeneous pattern at once more parochial and more cosmopolitan than in other countries. Yet Luther would lay bare a German national consciousness not dissimilar to that called forth in Bohemia by John Huss a century earlier; and Machiavelli would join others in the vision of a peninsular unity transcending Italy's continual intercommunal strife.

Just as the interests of the new learning converged on the biblical text to usher in a new era in the study of the Scriptures, so the new forces of economic concern and national feeling combined to inaugurate a new period in Western imperialism. 1492 was particularly fateful. In this year Pope Alexander VI undertook to send out a venerable Benedictine monk to supervise the long-neglected diocese of Gardar in Greenland, an interesting commentary on the dissolution of what had once been a promising link to new and distant worlds.[6] As if to document the rapidly developing activities in warmer waters, the same pope two years later arranged between Spain and Portugal the famous Line of Demarcation defining their respective areas of exploitation and evangelism. More significant to Spain than a treaty (which would be often flouted) was the hard fact that in 1492 Queen Isabella, "the Last Crusader," finally achieved the definitive expulsion of the Moors from Iberian soil, thus ending the long Islamic occupation that had begun under the Ommiad caliphs in 711.

When Columbus on 12 October 1492 dropped anchor at San Salvador in the Bahama Islands, his feat symbolized as nothing else could the way in which the lure of trade and the emergence of a strong united nation would combine to kindle anew the missionary zeal of the Church. Francisco Garcia Cardinal Ximénes (1436–1517) was then archbishop of Toledo, primate of Spain, chancellor of Castile, and chief adviser to Isabella. Ascetic Franciscan, zealous reformer, and energetic promoter of learning, he would do much to make Columbus's discovery the beginning of a new era in Spanish and world church history. And from Spain would come many other heroes of the faith, for there the Catholic Reformation was earliest and most completely realized.

Interrupting or culminating these many forces of transition came that convulsive series of events which constitute the Reformation proper, the decisive rupture of Western Christendom, and the emergence of evangelical territorial churches in most of Northern Europe as well as large Protestant

6. Excavations made during 1963 on the northernmost peninsula of Newfoundland strengthened already existing evidence that the Vikings actually did reach and live in "Vinland," the lands west of Greenland of which their sagas frequently speak.

movements in several Roman Catholic countries. The significance of these events can hardly be exaggerated; far more than the so-called Renaissance they brought an end to the old order in Europe and inaugurated the modern age. Through several accidents of history the American colonies, out of which grew the United States, were molded by the Reformation with a directness and intensity unequaled in any other country. For this reason the history of these colonies must begin with the emergence and development of Protestantism on the Continent and in Great Britain (see chaps. 5 and 6, below). The general course of Roman Catholic history, however, though also profoundly altered by the Reformation, was not changed in so fundamental a manner. In Spain and Italy where Protestant inroads were slight, as in France and Germany where religious conflicts were long and severe, Roman Catholicism was in the long run powerfully challenged and aroused by the Reformation. Everywhere, however, its response was ordered and informed by ancient heritage and medieval tradition. The character and advancement of the great Roman Catholic empires in the New World, therefore, are best understood without prior preoccupation with the details of Protestant church history.

ROMAN CATHOLIC REFORM MOVEMENTS

Individual Efforts

In March 1517, a half-year before the Ninety-five Theses would be posted in Wittenberg, the Fifth Lateran Council—ecumenical in theory, Italian in fact—concluded five years of fitful sessions during which the perennial problem of reforming the Church terminated in the same impasse which had frustrated so many similar proceedings. Gilles of Vitterbo, general of Luther's own order of Augustinians and a participant in the revival of interest in their great patron saint's theology, had opened the meetings with a ringing summons to renewal. He voiced the universal complaints against the corruption of the clergy and the cupidity of the Curia. Yet a great Roman Catholic historian summarizes the result in negative terms:

> The times were not ripe for a profound transformation of manners in the Italy of the Renaissance. The corruptions of the Curia were not corrected. Pope Leo X, sunk in the utterly profane luxuries of his court and worship of the arts, remained inert in the face of the church's needs.[7]

7. L. Christiani, *L'Eglise à l'Époque du Concile de Trente,* ed. A. Fliche and V. Martin (Paris, 1948), p. 247. My translation.

To say that "the times were not ripe," however, or that early efforts toward ecclesiastical reform lacked papal leadership, is not to say that reformers were nonexistent. A deeply rooted concern for purifying the Church was manifest in several sectors of European Christendom; and the most important of these many impulses maintained their characteristic spirit despite the events of 1517 and after.

One prominent example is the fiery Dominican preacher, Girolamo Savonarola (1452–98), who became the virtual ruler of Florence in 1496–97 and almost succeeded in turning that center of Renaissance culture into a penitential city. (He is best remembered by Protestants for his great hymn, "Jesus, Refuge of the Weary.") In quite another and far less sensational way this reforming spirit was also revealed by the austere Dutchman, Florensz Dedal, who for the last twenty months of his life succeeded Leo X as Pope Adrian VI (d. 1523). Rising from humble origins to become tutor of Charles V, cardinal-bishop of Tortosa, and a papal legate in Spain, he had shown his moral rigor as a reformer, especially of the monastic life. His pontificate was too short to be influential, but he personified a religious type that would finally awaken the Roman church from its complacency and impotence.

In theological realms diverse movements of correction were also found. A long line of scholars, often in the nominalist tradition of William of Ockham, had been stressing the need for study of the Bible in its central literal sense, often supporting such claims by an emphasis upon the unknowableness of God and his will by any other means. These tendencies had doctrinal corollaries in men who were emphasizing again Saint Augustine's and Saint Bernard's concern for justification by faith. Perhaps most outstanding of these efforts were those fostered by Guillaume Briçonnet in France. As abbot of Saint Germain-des-Prés and later (1516 ff.) as bishop of Meaux he encouraged and then applied the pronouncedly evangelical biblical labors of Lefevre d'Étaples and his circle—a circle in which John Calvin himself for a time was numbered.

Even among the humanists a deep strain of piety often fused with outspoken enthusiasm for the new learning, leading them from an exclusive passion for classical scholarship to a concern for church reform. And of these men none was more accomplished and famous than Erasmus of Rotterdam (1466?–1536), whose work ranged from the blistering ridicule of church and clergy in his *Praise of Folly* (1509) to his epoch-making Greek edition of the New Testament. He also edited many works of the early church fathers and wrote a simple, earnest, and widely read *Handbook of the Christian Soldier*.

More directly important for the Catholic Reformation, however, were those movements which were more consciously rooted in medieval piety and motivated by a concern for reinvigorating ascetic ideals and practices. The reforming impulse of the order of Augustinian Hermits indicates the degree to which, in Germany especially, sensitive souls reacted against the prevailing laxity. The Franciscans also evolved a new and stricter branch, the Observants, in 1517, and yet another ultra observant branch, the Capuchins, in 1525. It is unquestionably true that in Europe as a whole the monastic orders were so deeply enmeshed in social and economic affairs that total root-and-branch reformation was impossible, but the instances cited were more than isolated examples. Everywhere during the fifteenth century, as during most preceding ages, important movements of monastic reform were set in motion.

Of the individual champions of spiritual renewal perhaps none was more profound or influential than Saint Theresa of Avila (1515–82) who, despite the dates of her lifespan, represents a long-developing Spanish tradition; and Saint John of the Cross (1542–91), who was virtually her spiritual son. Both were of aristocratic birth, both entered the ranks of the Carmelites, and both became fervent exponents of rigorous asceticism, mystical devotion, and the contemplative life. For years they labored together to found and foster the Reformed, or discalced, order of Carmelites, in which the monastic rule was observed with all possible austerity. Like so many others who were equally highborn and elitist in their strategy, they sought to reform the Church not by wide-sweeping legislation or popular appeals, but by the spiritual renewal of individuals, especially the clergy and religious orders. Their central concerns were the knowledge of "the dark night of the soul," the subjugation of self, and the attainment of "the spiritual and secret kingdom of God." Yet such efforts were not "sectarian" in spirit even when they were pronouncedly individualistic, nor were they at first "counterreformatory" in temper. This quest for mystical union with God through withdrawal from the world and stringent self-discipline sprang from within the ancient life of the Church. Nowhere more than in Spain was the ascetic ideal combined with ecclesiastical discipline to enforce a program that would elevate morals, educate priests, and coerce heretics. Given the long tradition of the crusade against the Moors, it was perhaps natural enough that the land of Ximénes and Isabella would produce a Loyola while Germany was producing a Luther.

New Monastic Orders

Such efforts at reform had several parallels in Rome itself, a fact which gave them an obvious special significance. Here the most influential line of development was represented by the Society of Divine Love, a confraternity of secular priests whose activities centered in the Church of Saints Sylvester and Dorothea. Officially recognized by Leo X in 1514—three years before Luther's Ninety-five Theses—it was led by Saint Cajetan of Thiene (1480–1547), an almost archetypical representative of sixteenth-century Catholic reformation. He sought systematically to arouse intense ardor for the sacraments, along with a program of rigorous asceticism, moral earnestness, and charitable sacrifice. Though never numbering more than sixty, the society was able to attract to its ranks many able and zealous men, who were often very influential members of the papal court. Both in Rome and as emulated elsewhere this type of movement became a powerful instrument for reform. Similar in some respects were the later efforts of Saint Philip Neri (1515–95). His oratory in Rome, with its authorized congregation (1575), directed its efforts to the devotional life, sacramental practice, and theological commitment of the laity. The oratory not only attained important influence in the Curia, but won acceptance as a model in other countries, notably in France.

Saint Cajetan, however, went further in harnessing this kind of zeal, and in 1524 he gained papal approval for an order of clerks regular, the Theatines, which he hoped would provide a disciplined and elite model for reforming the clergy and redirecting its concern for the whole parish ministry. Pietro Caraffa (1476–1559), formerly associated with the Society of Divine Love, became the first superior of the Theatines. He was a Neapolitan nobleman who began his active career as a reformer in 1504 after becoming bishop of Chieti. In later years while serving as a papal legate in several countries, his determination deepened, largely due to the influence of the Spanish reformers like Ximénes and Dedal. He became archbishop of Brindisi as well, but renounced these offices to enter the new order. Later as Pope Paul IV (1555–59) he would personify the Counter-Reformation in its most strenuous, authoritarian, and uncompromising form. In post-Reformation years still other prelates, like Bishop Gian Matteo Giberti of Verona (1495–1543) and Archbishop Carlo Borromeo of Milan (1538–84), both of them closely affiliated with Saint Cajetan, continued and broadened this type of reform, concerning themselves with all aspects of diocesan life, piety, and worship.

By far the most momentous aspect of these reforms was the new way in which the monastic life was conceived. Out of such efforts emerged a new kind of religious order, a creative contribution equal in importance to the mendicant idea embodied in the Dominican and Franciscan orders. Its newness lay in adapting the ascetic ideal to the needs of the time by organizing priests under a strict rule or into an order, but for the purpose of intensifying their priestly and pastoral labors "in the world." This objective often required the substitution of new disciplinary measures for the old cloistered life and corporate participation in the daily offices of worship. Inwardly the priests were dedicated to the renewal of Christian piety, charity, and instruction, and they submitted themselves obediently to such demands as this task would impose. Following the example and impetus afforded by the Oratory of Divine Love and the Theatines, several such orders were formed in Italy during the sixteenth century, but not all of them adopted Cajetan's rigorous demands that even the order as such remain poor and without endowments.

The order founded upon these general principles which played by far the most revolutionary role and whose activity marks most decisively the transition to Counter-Reformation objectives was the Society of Jesus, founded by Saint Ignatius of Loyola (1491–1556). His army career cut short by a crippling wound, Loyola resolved in August 1521 to live a life of self-denial in the service of Christ. In 1522 he placed his sword and dagger on the altar of Our Lady Montserrat, and exchanged his fine clothes for the sackcloth gown and pilgrim staff of a knight of God. He then walked on to Manresa, where for almost a year he practiced the most rigorous asceticism, deepening his devotional life and continuing his meditation on the life of Christ. Finally, in a vision received nearby on the river Cardona, he felt the climactic "enlightening of the understanding" that was to make him both a great spiritual teacher and the founder of a militia that would put itself in the service of Jesus. Hereafter he would be a soldier of the Virgin.

During this stay at Manresa, Loyola also wrought out a series of remarkable Christ-centered spiritual exercises by which to discipline himself and others whom he persuaded to adopt his rigorous program. As fully articulated over the years, the *Spiritual Exercises* provide in twenty-eight general divisions a specific and detailed routine for every hour of every day; they include intense contemplation of some biblical event, invocation of the presence of Christ, examination of the sinful self, and meditation on the glories of redemption. Loyola was so severe in his piety and so zealous in recruiting converts to his system of spiritual discipline, not only at Manresa, but on his pilgrimage to the Holy Land, and later at Barcelona, Alcala, and Salamanca, that he incurred the suspicion of the officers of the Inquisition and suffered considerable persecution.

In Paris in 1528 Loyola devoted himself to arduous study in order to overcome his educational deficiencies; but he remained alert for young men whom he could overpower with his enthusiasm for self-sacrificial labors on behalf of the Church. Among the able youths mastered by his indomitable energy were Peter Faber, Francis Xavier, Alfonso Salmeron, Jacob Lainez and Nicholas Bobadilla—all Spaniards or (like himself) Basques. On 15 August 1534 (the anniversary of the Assumption of the Virgin), in Saint Mary's Church at Montmartre, these men took upon themselves a most solemn vow to enter upon missionary work in Jerusalem, or, if this were impossible, to go without questioning wherever the pope might send them. They received formal recognition from Paul III as the Company or Society of Jesus on 27 September 1540, and from that time forward they increased rapidly in numbers and influence. The Jesuits, as they were called, soon moved into many diverse positions of influence, and after a very few years they were able to shape the policy of the entire church. With their avowed aim "the greater glory of God," they became the most effective agents for reclaiming many vast segments of Protestantism for the Roman Catholic church, for evangelizing large portions of the newly opened lands of the East and West, for founding and maintaining great educational institutions, and for strengthening the authority of the pope within the church. Their flexibility, adaptiveness, and perennial interest in innovation would be constantly evident in these undertakings. Just as the *Spiritual Exercises* were the soul of the constitution which Loyola provided for his order, so did the Society of Jesus institutionalize some of the deepest themes of the Catholic Reformation.

Culmination

From 1534 to 1549 the chair of Peter was occupied by Paul III, under whom reform decisively reached the papacy. He not only brought to the office a measure of discipline—although his successors were by no means agreed in their estimates of his austerity and zeal—but he granted formal recognition to the Jesuits and cooperated with the forces that had long sought a definitive council to deal with corruption and to formulate doctrine in answer to the charges of the Protestants. The Council of Trent is both the culmination and the documentation of the entire process of Roman Catholic Reformation. Like the Jesuits, who had so much to do with its outcome, it represents the double aspect which all Roman Catholic activity showed after 1541, when the failure of the Conference of Regensburg revealed the hopelessness of reconciliation with the Protestants. On the one hand, it was intensely loyal to the medieval heritage of the Church. On the other, it took calculating cognizance of the Protestant revolt, anathematizing its distinctive tenets and formulating Catholic dogma in an unprecedentedly thorough way.

The Council of Trent met in three main sessions from 1545 to 1563, one adjournment lasting nearly a decade while Pope Julius III provided a brief Indian summer for the Renaissance. Between its beginning and end there were frequent changes in personnel, and consequently, in opinion. On many issues opposing views clashed sharply, and mediating positions were adopted —making the council far less reactionary than most Protestants and many Roman Catholics have supposed. But its final results constitute an ecclesiastical landmark as important as the rupture between the Eastern and Western churches. In this sense Trent is the birthplace of modern Roman Catholicism and "post-Tridentine" becomes one of the most meaningful adjectives in church history. In its decrees the council defined the authority of Scripture and holy tradition, the nature of Original Sin, and the doctrines of the sacraments; it devoted a long section to justification by faith as a specific answer to Protestants, and closed by asserting that the authority of the pope was "to be preserved." Thus the door to rapprochement with Protestants was shut, and it would remain closed for almost exactly four centuries. Within Catholicism itself large areas of doctrine previously open to discussion were narrowed to more precisely defined limits. As interpreted by those charged with carrying out the work of Counter-Reformation, Trent's decrees became a standard of inflexible conservatism.

The council's importance will be appreciated more fully when, in a later chapter, the Reformation is considered. Before describing anti-Roman movements, however, it is worthwhile to follow out the colonial and missionary endeavors of the two Roman Catholic powers whose imperial designs became involved in American religious history. We must, of course, remember that after 1517 Europe was shaken to its roots by the Reformation. Yet it remains true that in the vast Roman Catholic empires pre-Reformation piety and Counter-Reformation zeal were dominant influences. For this reason the imperial ventures of Spain and France are recounted before we consider the religious background which had the heaviest early influence on the future United States.

3

THE CHURCH IN NEW SPAIN

American church history begins on Thursday, 11 October 1492, and the circumstances are set down tersely in the journal of Christopher Columbus, "Admiral of the Ocean Sea, Viceroy and Governor of whatever territory he might discover."

> The course was W.S.W. and there was more sea than there had been during the whole of the voyage. They saw sand-pipers, and a green reed near the ship. . . . Everyone breathed afresh and rejoiced at these signs. . . . After sunset the Admiral returned to his original west course, and they went along at the rate of 12 miles per hour. As the caravel *Pinta* was a better sailer, and went ahead of the Admiral, she found the land, and made the signals ordered by the Admiral. The land was first seen by a sailor named Rodrigo de Triana. But the Admiral, at ten o'clock, being on the castle of the poop, saw a light, though it was so uncertain that he could not affirm it was land. . . . At two hours after midnight the land was sighted at a distance of two leagues.[1]

On the following day Columbus landed, took possession of this island in the name of King Ferdinand and Queen Isabella, and named it San Salvador (Holy Savior). To the assembled natives he gave "red caps, and glass beads to put round their necks, and many other things of little value, which gave them great pleasure, and made them so much our friends that it was a marvel to see." He surmised that they would be "more easily freed and converted to our holy faith by love than by force." With an optimism that the Anglo-American experience of succeeding centuries would hardly jus-

1. Edward G. Bourne, ed., "The Voyages of Columbus and of John Cabot," in *The Northmen, Columbus, and Cabot, 985–1530* (New York: Charles Scribner's Sons, 1906), pp. 108–10.

tify, he also declared, "I believe that they would easily be made Christians, as it appeared to me that they had no religion."

After returning to Spain, Columbus made a final entry in his journal (15 March 1493) voicing the same confidence:

> I know respecting this voyage that God has miraculously shown his will, as may be seen from this journal, setting forth the numerous miracles that have been displayed in the voyage, and in me who was so long at the court of your Highnesses, working in opposition to and against the opinions of so many chief persons of your household, who were all against me, looking upon this enterprise as folly. But I hope, in our Lord, that it will be a great benefit to Christianity, for so it has ever appeared.[2]

Thus, in the very year that Granada's fall terminated "the Last Crusade," the vista for another vast campaign opened before the Catholic rulers of Spain.

SPAIN'S EARLY ACTIVITIES IN THE NEW WORLD

Exploration and Conquest

Unlike England, which in 1497 remunerated the intrepid John Cabot with "ten pounds for him that found the isle" and followed this generous act with nearly a century of exploratory and colonial neglect, Spain responded with vigor. At the insistence of Ferdinand and Isabella, Pope Alexander VI issued two bulls, *Inter Caetera I* and *II,* which granted to Spain all lands not under Christian rule and set a line at one hundred leagues (263 miles) west of the Azores and Cape Verde Islands, beyond which all future discoveries not held by a Christian ruler on 25 December 1492 would belong to Spain. This was in May 1493. In September Columbus set sail again, not with three ships and ninety reluctant men, but with an imposing armada of seventeen ships bearing over twelve hundred men (but no women), at least five priests, livestock, seeds, and building materials. On Hispaniola (Haiti), where the colony was planted, very little was to flourish besides discontent and disease, but Spain had made a serious colonizing effort which would be followed by countless others before the revolutions of the nineteenth century collapsed her American empire.

After his third voyage in 1500, Columbus and his two brothers were accused by the colonists of maladministration and sent home in chains. Although he managed to clear himself in time to make a fourth and last voy-

2. Ibid., pp. 257–58.

age in 1504, his authority over his discoveries was transferred permanently to the crown. By this time, other adventurers—many of them his former captains—had added three thousand miles of South American coastline to the gradually growing knowledge of the cartographers. Alonso de Ojeda and Juan de la Cosa, Vincente Yãnez Pinzón, Peralonso Niño, Diego de Lepe, and others had coasted and traded from the Isthmus to far down the Brazilian shore. In 1513 Vasco Núñez de Balboa pushed across Panama to discover the Pacific Ocean; and scarcely fifteen years later Lucas Vasquez de Ayllón and Esteban Gómez were bringing in sketchy reports of the North American coast to Nova Scotia.

Added to the thrilling feats of the navigators were the exploits of the *conquistadores.* By 1515 Puerto Rico and Cuba were conquered and San Juan and Havana founded. Cortes toppled the Aztec empire in 1521, establishing Spanish control of central Mexico and launching the earliest probes of the Pacific coast. Guzmán made savage forays into north-central Mexico. Pizarro began the sorties that were to culminate in his victories over the Incas and the founding in 1535 of Lima, City of the Kings and future capital of all South America.

Government of the Settlements

To consolidate these gains and regulate the new empire, a House of Trade (1503) and a governing council of the Indies (1524) were organized in Spain. Furthermore, all the conquered territories from Florida to Honduras, the patrimony of Isabella of Castile, were in 1527 put under the supervision of the *audiencia* of New Spain, with headquarters in Mexico City. After 1535 the chief administrative officer was the viceroy. A similar office was established for South America five years later. Beneath the viceroy were governors appointed in more settled areas, or captains-general in areas requiring military defense. Beneath these in the administrative hierarchy were the *alcaldes, mayores,* and *corregidores,* who represented royal authority in towns and metropolitan districts. At the lowest level were the various municipal offices which, though elective at first, soon became appointive. Colonial administration was held accountable to the crown: short terms, the requirement of detailed reports, and a constant flow of royal inspectors strove to maintain strict control. In this way the absolutism of the Spanish monarch reached out into the New World. But because of the enormous difficulties of supervision, the fruits of autocratic paternalism—graft, venality, and the decay of civic concern—were evident from first to last.

The Participation of the Church

Churchmen were important at every level of the social and political structure in New Spain. The spirit of Spanish Catholicism, forged in the long campaign against Jews and Moors, was transplanted with little attenuation of either its fierce orthodoxy or its ardent piety. Perhaps most decisive for the future was the fact that, by embarking on the course of empire a full century before her northern competitors, Spain transmitted to the New World a culture that had been little affected by the Renaissance, the Reformation, or the commercial revolution. "Thus a medieval civilization, revering intellectual and spiritual as well as political authority, acquired a new lease on life and became the heritage of modern Hispanic America." [3]

From the first, conquest and conversion were assumed to go together, and every ship that brought soldiers and settlers brought also its share of priests. The representatives of the church were backed by the same royal power that dispatched the captains and the viceroys. A series of papal concessions to the Spanish monarchs, known as the *Real Patronato,* had granted to the Spanish king ecclesiastical powers which were extraordinarily large even for the home country but which for lands across the sea made him virtually a vice-pope. He had authority to collect all tithes and to present the candidates for all churchly offices from the lowliest curate up to an archbishop; he had arrogated to himself the right to review the decrees of all councils and synods held in the Indies; and he demanded the privilege of approving papal decrees, bulls, and ordinations affecting Spanish interests before they were allowed to become official.

With this vast grant of authority it was, of course, Spain's responsibility to promote the church throughout her growing empire—a duty that she did not shirk. Especially after the Protestant Reformation gave increased emphasis to the missionary motive, evangelism was prosecuted with determination, though not always with charity. In Spain as nowhere else, church and state partook of the same spirit, sought the same goals, and to a large extent employed the same methods. The religious zeal of rulers like Isabella, Charles V, and Philip II (whose combined reigns covered more than a century), no less than the administrative ability of ecclesiastics like Ximénes and his successors, made certain that the Great Commission to baptize all nations was taken seriously. Especially notable were the procedures

3. Irving A. Leonard in his foreword to Mariano Picón-Salas, *A Cultural History of Spanish America, from Conquest to Independence,* p. x.

and policies established by the archdeacon of Seville, Juan de Fonseca, who served as virtual colonial minister during the entire reign of Ferdinand and Isabella and Father García de Loaísa (ca. 1479–1546), general of the Dominican Order and later cardinal-archbishop of Seville, who served as president of the Council of the Indies.

In 1523 Charles V granted to Vásquez de Ayllón the right to plant settlements on the North American coast "eight hundred leagues up" from San Domingo. The *cedula* by which this ill-fated colonial enterprise was authorized was explicit and typical in its exhibition of the emperor's religious interest:

> Our principal intent in the discovery of new lands is that the inhabitants and natives thereof who are without the light of the knowledge of faith may be brought to understand the truths of our holy Catholic faith, and that they may come to the knowledge thereof and become Christians and be saved, and this is the chief motive you are to bear and hold in this affair, and to this end it is proper that religious persons should accompany you . . . and I command that whatever you shall thus expend in transporting the said religious, as well as in maintaining them and giving them what is needful, . . . and for the vestments and other articles required for the divine worship, shall be paid entirely from the rents and profits which in any manner shall belong to us in the said land.[4]

In 1526 this colony of San Miguel was founded near where Jamestown would rise nearly a century later. The colony benefited from the ministrations of Antonio de Montesinos, the Dominican friar who had already become an outspoken champion of Indian rights, but the problems of survival precluded active evangelism. Ayllón himself died; and after a cold winter marked by mutiny, a slave revolt, and Indian attacks, the 150 men who remained of the initial 600 returned to Hispaniola. But a chapel had been built, and the Mass celebrated.

After a half-dozen failures the first permanent colony in what would become the United States was finally established at Saint Augustine in 1565 by Pedro Menéndez de Avilés in order to protect the sea route of treasure ships. Here all of the characteristics of the sixteenth-century church were evident. Intolerance was savagely manifested at the massacre of the French Huguenots who had settled at the mouth of the Saint Johns River to the north. (Spain at that time was exceedingly jealous of exclusive rights in her newly discovered domains, and would make no concessions to any other

4. Quoted in John G. Shea, *The Catholic Church in Colonial Days*, 1:104–107.

group, least of all to Protestants.)[5] As in Spain, church and state were closely identified; indeed, the entire life of the citadel-town revolved around the *plaza mayore* facing the harbor, the chapel on one side, and the governor's palace on the other. Later two hospitals and a convent were added, and missions to the Indians were begun. The first efforts by Jesuits under Menéndez proved abortive, but permanent labors were resumed in 1568 and expanded in 1595 with the arrival of eleven Franciscans. Among several ambitious Jesuit ventures was another unsuccessful attempt to found a mission colony in the Chesapeake area (1570–71). By 1634 some thirty-five Franciscans were maintaining forty-four missions and ministering to twenty-five or thirty thousand Indian converts. Catechisms were translated and some elementary schooling attempted.

Although church life in Florida was under the jurisdiction of the bishop of Santiago de Cuba, the whole system suffered from inadequate supervision. The British were expanding in the north; and when the War of the Spanish Succession broke out in 1701, the whole fragile structure of Spanish life in Florida began to crumble. The consecration of a resident bishop for Saint Augustine in 1709 did not halt the decay. When the third bishop, Ponce y Carasco, arrived in 1751, there were in the immediate vicinity of Saint Augustine only four Indian missions, with 136 souls; in other words, there was no Catholic presence in Florida outside of the Spanish population of the city. It was only out in the west, far from the British and French, where imperial wars were but rumors and where a more settled type of Indian civilization prevailed, that the characteristic institutions of the Church of New Spain were to reveal their genius—in sharp contrast with the Anglo-Saxon mode of expansion.

THE EXPANSION OF NEW SPAIN

Florida never became a vital part of Spain's empire. The dangers and difficulties were many; the attractions few. In the Caribbean Islands (notably Hispaniola and Cuba), in the viceroyalties of South America, and especially in "New Spain" (which extended from Panama City to Monterey), her empire flourished. From this last area came a series of northern thrusts which constitute one of the most colorful chapters in North American history. Drawing men into these unknown lands were the tales of wanderers like Cabeza de Vaca, that amazing survivor of the Narváez expedition to Tampa Bay (1528), who finally emerged from his wanderings on the Rio Fuerte in

5. This short-lived colony was founded at a time when Huguenot influence in French government was strong. Subsequently, New France was closed to Protestants (see chap. 4).

Mexico in 1536. In 1540, enticed by reports of the fabulous Seven Cities of Cibola, the viceroy commissioned Francisco Vásquez de Coronado to lead a major expedition; this resulted in the discovery of the Grand Canyon, Kansas, Oklahoma, the Texas panhandle, and some pueblo villages of the Zuñi in western New Mexico—a vast mission field, but no silver or gold. For sixty years interest in the northern country languished. It was left for Don Juan de Oñate to enter the northern lands in 1598, claim them for Spain, and found at San Juan de Caballeros the first colony in what is now New Mexico.

New Mexico

Oñate's initial company included over a hundred soldiers, four hundred settlers, seven Franciscan fathers and two lay brothers under Father Martinez, many slaves, eighty-three wagons, and seven thousand head of stock. It came to stay, and despite many difficulties it did stay. In 1609 Oñate was replaced as governor by Pedro de Peralta. He moved the capital to Santa Fe, which became the permanent center of Spanish dominion in New Mexico. *Encomiendas* were granted to soldiers and settlers; other towns were founded, and a new agricultural commonwealth began to flourish. As missionaries the friars made rapid if somewhat superficial headway, in 1630 reporting fifty priests at work in twenty-five missions embracing sixty thousand converts in ninety pueblos.

A fierce revolt by the Indians in 1680 resulted in a terrible massacre, and the remaining Spaniards were forced back to El Paso for over twenty years. But near the centenary of Oñate's entry, the territory was reconquered and the old Spanish pattern of life restored for another century and a quarter. The Indians, sullen but subdued, were the basic source of labor in the fields, the mills, and the mines. With the passing years their burden was increased by heavy debts to Spanish and *mestizo* merchants and lenders. Nor was this system of virtual vassalage obnoxious to the friars, who were generally content to work within the existing framework of colonial rule, though they were in almost constant conflict with the civil authorities over control of the Indians.

By 1744 the slowly growing non-Indian population had risen to about ten thousand, with two-thirds of the people living in the four principal cities, Santa Fe, Santa Cruz, Albuquerque, and El Paso. At that time the Franciscans were still administering about twenty-five missions and about 17,500 Indians. Yet the missionary work was seriously retarded by the failures of the friars to learn the Indian languages and by jurisdictional conflicts with the bishop of Durango. By 1800 the number of Indians in the missions had fallen to about ten thousand. The Apaches, moreover, remained a constant threat throughout the eighteenth century. Mercantilistic trade regulations also limited the area's economic growth. The great event of the year was the annual caravan down to Chihuahua when the agricultural produce of New Mexico could be exchanged for needed goods from abroad. There was naturally some illicit trading with the French in Louisiana, the British, and later the Americans; but these outside avenues of trade became important only after Mexico's independence and the opening of the Santa Fe Trail to Saint Louis, both of which occurred in 1821. Amid the anticlericalism and political disorder of the early decades of Mexican rule the state of the church deteriorated still further. When the province of New Mexico (including Colorado, Utah, Nevada, and most of Arizona) became part of the United States in 1848, it had a population of about sixty thousand, perhaps half of which was Spanish or *mestizo*. Twenty or more priests were serving the area, but the missions were in nearly total disorganization. Two years later the vicariate of New Mexico was erected to order the church's affairs in the region. Chosen to direct the task was a French-born priest then serving in Kentucky, Jean-Baptiste Lamy. When he resigned as archbishop in 1875, he reported fifty-six priests and 203 places of worship in his vast province.

Arizona

Except for the area south of the Gila Valley, much of modern Arizona—or Piméria Alta, as it was called—had a character and history of its own. Unlike New Mexico, it experienced little white occupation and few extended missionary efforts, remaining for the most part a forbidding, dangerous and half-explored challenge to a relatively small number of intrepid Jesuits and their Franciscan successors. Even in the south, missionary efforts were not begun until the 1680s—and with few enduring results. Yet much dedication was displayed by the Black Robes who did seek the conversion of the hostile tribes in this area, and one of their number has become almost the archetypical hero of the Spanish borderlands. Eusebio Kino (1644–1711), born in the Tyrol and educated at Ingolstadt, came to Mexico in 1681 and entered upon his life work in the north in 1687. Before his death twenty-four years later he had baptized four thousand Indians, covered thousands of miles in over forty expeditions, explored and mapped the area, introduced stock raising in five or six valleys, and assisted in the founding of several missions. These missions, however, remained precarious due to Indian hostility, the shortage of priests, and quarrels with civil authorities. And even the small gains made were decimated after 1783 when the decree of Charles III expelling the Jesuits was carried out.[6] Here as elsewhere the Franciscans strove to maintain the work, but aside from the beautiful new

6. See pp. 65–66, 338, 530, and 534 below.

church erected at San Xavier del Bac (1797), little remained of the Arizona mission in 1821, and still less when the United States acquired the territory.

Texas

Spanish concern for the Texas territory was aroused by the arrival of LaSalle and the French in the lower Mississippi Valley between 1682 and 1689, though a few missionaries had ventured east and north from El Paso during the preceding decades. Under Alonso de Léon, governor of Coahuila, a series of expeditions was sent out, and in 1690 he claimed the area for Spain. San Francisco de los Tejas (Texas) was founded as a Spanish mission in that year by the Franciscan Father Damian Massanet, but it was abandoned three years later. In 1718 renewed efforts produced more permanent results, of which the San Antonio, or Alamo, mission is the most famous. By 1722 there were ten missions, four *presidios,* and four centers of settlement in the Texas territory; and a governor resided at Los Adaes (now Robeline, Louisiana).

The overall Spanish influence in Texas was very weak, however, because of the unavailability of settlers and the intractability of the Comanches and Apaches. From 1762 to 1800 even the military occupants were withdrawn from Texas, for France had ceded to Spain the entire Louisiana territory. In 1810 the Spanish population of Texas probably did not exceed 3,000—and only 432 Indians were left in the six missions that remained. The United States purchased Louisiana in 1803, Mexico broke away from Spain in 1821, and Texas won independence from Mexico in 1836, at which time only two priests of Mexican origin remained, and they were a source of scandal. The religious history of old Texas contains a record of fifty missions and much heroism, but the end result in so vast and unsettled a region was barely discernible. Subsequent immigration, however, has again given Texas a considerable population of Spanish Catholic heritage.

California

In the Far West the early story is very similar to that in Texas. During the great period of Spain's expansion in the New World, California was largely ignored. In the 1540s Juan Rodríguez Cabrillo, Bartolomé Ferrelo, and others had pushed up the western coast, and in 1602 Juan Vizcaino bestowed names on many of the bays and islands he discovered along the coasts of California and Oregon. But not until 1702 did Father Eusebio Kino, as he pressed out from inland settlements, determine after extensive labors in Arizona that Lower California was a peninsula and not an island. Attention was focused on Texas; and while Father Salvatierra and other

Jesuits were advancing an important work in Lower California, the upper part of that region was forgotten or ignored.

All this was changed by the Russian advance down the coast from Alaska. In 1728 the Russian captain Vitus Bering had sailed through the straits that now bear his name, and in 1741 he reached Alaska, whereupon he claimed for Russia a slice of America as large as western Europe. As with Texas, the presence of an alien power spurred Spain to action. José de Gálvez, the vigorous visitor-general of Spain's new and energetic King Charles III, organized an expedition in 1769, putting Don Gasper de Portola in charge. Because of the expulsion of the Jesuits from the Spanish Empire, six Franciscans were assigned the spiritual tasks, with Father Junípero Serra (1713–84), a university-trained native of Majorca, as their leader. In July 1769 the mission of San Diego de Alcala was founded, and nearby, the *presidio*. The expedition then struggled northward over rugged terrain in search of Monterey, which they missed; but in November they became the first white men to view the Golden Gate and the magnificent bay that lies behind it. A year later they found Monterey and established the San Carlos (Borromeo) mission, and by 1772 three others. Then, after an heroic search for an overland route, Juan Batista de Anza, commander of Tubac (Arizona), with Father Francisco Garcés as guide, led out the company of soldiers and friars —thirty families in all—that were to constitute the first Spanish post on San Francisco Bay. While he was seeking a suitable site for a settlement in the bay area, far away in Philadelphia a group of American patriots were signing their names to a Declaration of Independence. A few years later, after Spain had joined France in an anti-British alliance, Father Serra would enjoin his brothers to pray for the success of the Revolution.

In the next decade Santa Barbara, San Jose, Los Angeles, and others were added to the thin line of missions around which was to be gathered the romantic history of old California. There were also four military *presidios* and three small towns along the coast, but even as late as 1800 a Spanish population of only twelve hundred lived there. In California the mission system prospered as nowhere else, chiefly because the Indians were not warlike, olive trees flourished, grain grew bountifully, and sheep and cattle multiplied so rapidly that whole herds had to be slaughtered for lack of an adequate market. Equally important was the fact that white settlers did not swarm in to disrupt the situation. In the later eighteenth century, Spanish settlers were not swarming anywhere, and in any event there were vast tracts awaiting potential claim seekers in the more accessible southern areas. The gold for which Coronado and others had searched so tirelessly was not discovered until after the American flag flew over the *cabildo* in

Monterey—a fact which Methodist Bishop Matthew Simpson would interpret as a sure sign of God's special role for the United States. The *presidios* were there, of course, and with them came the perennial conflicts between secular and ecclesiastical authority that were the ugliest feature of the church's work in New Spain. But in California the Franciscans had less interference than elsewhere, and the full scope of the mission idea could be expressed, not least because their work was led for fifteen years by a friar who to an unusual degree combined an intense ascetic piety with great administrative ability. By every external standard, indeed, Father Serra seems to have embodied the Spanish ideal of the missionary as saint.

Each of California's twenty-one missions was adjacent to a village where from one to three thousand Indians lived. Between 1769 and 1845 perhaps a hundred thousand of them were baptized through the labors of 146 Franciscans, of whom 45 were at work in 1805—their year of maximum strength. After they had been won from their wilderness ways, they were given the rudiments of Christian nurture, then fitted to the demands of a hundred Western tasks. In the Spanish sense of the terms, they were Christianized and civilized. They tilled the land, herded stock, tanned cowhides, built roads and bridges, and in order to raise a mission chapel, they quarried stone, hewed beams, and molded bricks. At the period of greatest prosperity there were in the twenty-one missions over 230,000 head of cattle, 268,000 sheep, 8,300 goats, 3,400 swine, 3,500 mules, and 34,000 horses, with the farms yielding 125,000 bushels of grain.

The missions were thus the most important institutions of Old California, undergirding both its social and economic life. Aside from them life was meager. Towns were small, soldiers had few duties, and Indians did the work. Government was at a minimum, the viceroy was far away, the king farther still. Life was slow, graceful, and easy.

LIFE IN THE BORDERLANDS

The Spanish domains which became parts of the United States were all borderlands. Advances into these areas were always chiefly defensive; and in every case except Arizona and New Mexico the initial threat was imperial—British, French, or Russian. This was a frontier civilization: vastly different from the peculiarly Anglo-American frontier about which Frederick Jackson Turner launched his bold thesis, yet a frontier nevertheless. To interpret the life of the area, this fact must always be kept in mind, for none of these border provinces attained the complex cultural development of the Spanish lands to the south. Although a score of Spanish-American universities conferred 150,000 degrees before 1821, formal educational institutions were virtually nonexistent in the borderlands. Books were exceedingly rare. The Far Southwest did not have its first printing press until after Mexican independence. The chief artistic achievements were architectural, for the Spanish mission occupies an honored place in the procession of great occidental architectural styles. Its unique loveliness is not owed merely to borrowings from the Moorish, baroque, or classical, or even the American Indian, but rather to a creative, harmonious, and profound response to the demands of the spirit, the land, and the times. Nowhere else have frontiers led to the creation of such timeless beauty.

The most important institutions peculiar to the borderlands were the *presidio* and the mission. The former was the military outpost, consisting usually of an unruly company of soldiers which the padres wanted to keep as far from the Indians as possible, and a commander whose efforts to aggrandize his power and profit often precipitated a clash with the clerics. The mission, on the other hand, represented the religious and educational —and thus the civilizing—forces on this remote frontier. In addition to these major institutions, there were many private ranches, or *encomiendas,* often originating with generous grants and almost invariably dependent on Indian labor. Finally, there were the widely scattered towns which grew up around military or governmental centers and became by a natural process the centers of trade and of whatever social life existed. There were, properly speaking, no cities in the borderlands except perhaps New Orleans, but it was Spanish only from 1763 to 1800.

The fundamental feature of the borderlands was the Spanish way of life itself, which not even the rude demands of the frontier could deprive of grace and color. An English gentleman who visited Saint Augustine just two years before Florida was purchased by the United States in 1819 caught something of its character:

> I had arrived at the season of general relaxation, on the eve of the Carnival, which is celebrated with much gayety in all Catholic countries. Masks, dominoes, harlequins, punchinellos, and a great variety of grotesque disguises, on horseback, in cars, gigs, and on foot, paraded the streets with guitars, violins, and other instruments; and in the evenings, the houses were open to receive masks, and balls were given in every direction. . . .
>
> Dancing formed one of their most common amusements. . . . These

> assemblies were always informal, and frequented by all classes, all meeting on a level; but were conducted with the utmost polite decorum, for which the Spanish character is so distinguished.[7]

The same impression is provided by the picture of California towns during the late 1830s painted by Richard Henry Dana in his *Two Years before the Mast* (1840). It is worth quoting at length.

> It was a fine Saturday afternoon that we came to anchor at Monterey; the sun was about an hour high, and everything looked pleasant. The Mexican flag was flying from the little square presidio, and the drums and trumpets of the soldiers, who were out on parade, sounded over the water, and gave great life to the scene. There is no working class (the Indians being practically serfs, and doing all the hard work) and every rich man looks like a grandee, and every poor scamp like a broken-down gentleman. I have seen a man, with a fine figure and courteous manners, dressed in broadcloth and velvet, with a noble horse completely covered with trappings, without a *real* in his pockets, and absolutely suffering for something to eat.
>
> The women wore gowns of various texture—silks, crape, calicoes, etc.—made after the European style. . . . They wore shoes of kid or satin, sashes or belts of bright colours, and almost always a necklace and earrings. . . . If their husbands do not dress them well enough, they will soon receive presents from others. . . . Next to love of dress, I was most struck with the fineness of the voices and the beauty of the intonation of both sexes.
>
> The houses here as everywhere else in California, are of one story, built of adobe. . . . Some of the more wealthy inhabitants have glass to their windows, and board floors; and in Monterey nearly all the houses are white-washed on the outside. . . . The Indians . . . do all the hard work, two or three being attached to the better houses, and the poorest persons are able to keep one at least; for they have only to feed them, and give them a small piece of coarse cloth and a belt for the men, and a coarse gown, without shoes or stockings, for the women. . . .
>
> Nothing but the character of the people prevents Monterey from becoming a large town. The soil is as rich as man could wish, climate as good as any in the world, water abundant and the situation extremely

7. G. R. Fairbanks, *The History and Antiquities of the City of Saint Augustine* (1858), quoted by Herbert Ingram Priestly, *The Coming of the White Man, 1492–1848*, History of American Life Series, vol. 1 (New York: Macmillan Co., 1929), pp. 80–81.

> beautiful. The harbour, too, is a good one. . . . There are a number of English and Americans . . . who have married Californians, become united to the Roman church, and acquired considerable property. Having more industry, frugality, and enterprise than the natives, they soon get nearly all the trade into their own hands.[8]

Are such descriptions within the proper realm of religious history? It would seem so. They form an authentic picture of a way of life nurtured by centuries of Roman Catholicism as it prevailed in the Latin civilizations of Europe. These modes of living are as important as the missions and the padres. They are as rooted in church history as Puritan severity; and as Dana's final paragraph suggests, the lineaments of each culture were to have a crucial bearing on the growth and conflict of empires in the New World. The prevalence of this "un-American" way of life helped perpetuate the colonial status of New Mexico and Arizona—and during the so-called Progressive Era even delayed their admission to statehood for a decade.

THE SPANISH HERITAGE

The nineteenth century brought rude shocks to the vast Spanish Empire. In the home country the impact of the French Revolution and Napoleon's invasion was in many respects annulled by the Congress of Vienna and the reestablished monarchy. But in the New World, where the United States now stood for another type of revolution, the old imperial order sustained heavy blows. Led by Miranda, Bolívar, San Martín and others, independence was won in country after country. In Mexico it came in 1821—just three hundred years after Cortez's victory over Montezuma. But the initial royalist conservatism under Augustín de Iturbide soon yielded to three decades of political chaos during which Texas won its independence. In 1819, meanwhile, Spain had sold Florida to the United States lest it be lost without remuneration. By 1854 all of New Spain that was ever to become part of the continental United States had been obtained through revolution, annexation, conquest, or purchase. We very naturally ask, therefore, what was the religious significance of these vast acquisitions?

In evaluating the American legacy from New Spain, one's first temptation is to accept Father O'Gorman's summation:

> In time the work of the Spanish Church in the territory of the United States extended from 1520 to 1840. . . . In space it extended from the

8. Richard Henry Dana, *Two Years before the Mast* (New York: Penguin Books, 1948), pp. 73–86.

> Atlantic to the Pacific. . . . It was a glorious work, and the recital of it impresses us by the vastness and success of the toil. Yet, as we look around us today, we can find nothing of it that remains. Names of saints in melodious Spanish stand out from maps in all that section where the Spanish monk trod, toiled, and died. A few thousand Christian Indians, descendants of those they converted and civilized, still survive in New Mexico and Arizona, and that is all.[9]

Yet this minimal statement will not do. The marks of Spanish Catholicism on American religious and cultural life were more deeply etched. Aside from the large Spanish-speaking ethnic minority in the United States, much of which has come from Puerto Rico and Cuba as well as from Mexico, considerable weight must be given to the place that old imperial Spain occupies in the consciousness of all Americans, though especially of Roman Catholics. Because the federal Union came to include most of the Spanish borderlands, many Americans can draw sustenance from the fact that the country's oldest heritage is not Puritan but Catholic. Other Americans are usefully reminded of Spain's larger cultural achievement, a work that Herbert Eugene Bolton has eloquently described:

> One of the marvels in the history of the modern world is the way in which that little Iberian nation, Spain, when most of her blood and treasure were absorbed in European wars, with a handful of men took possession of the Caribbean archipelago, and by rapid yet steady advance spread her culture, her religion, her law, and her language over more than half of the two American continents, where they still are dominant and still are secure.[10]

Within this larger memory, moreover, the Spanish mission has lived on as symbol and inspiration—through crumbling ruins in New Mexico, the haunting beauty of Santa Barbara, or at the Alamo, now a shrine overlaid with still other kinds of memory. The mission represents a concern for Christian conversion and a humane regard for primitive peoples despite the background of governmental corruption, ecclesiastical cynicism, and ruthless subjugation. The missions, of course, were instruments of imperial politics, and their immense economic involvement inevitably affected their inner life. They also encouraged a kind of serfdom which, early and late, led to violent uprisings. In the northern borderlands which became part of the United States the end effect was worse than elsewhere. Due to the small Spanish population and the attenuated cultural context, the Indian

9. Thomas O'Gorman, *History of the Roman Catholic Church in the United States*, ACHS, vol. 9 (New York, 1895), pp. 111–12.

10. Herbert E. Bolton, *The Mission as a Frontier Institution in the Spanish-American Colonies*, pp. 1–2.

was left in a state of disorientation, uprooted from his old ways, yet unwesternized. But from beginning to end the missions did bear witness to an ideal that was far removed from the savagery of the *conquistadores* and the exploitative social order that prevailed in succeeding centuries.

These developments north of the Rio Grande naturally invite attention to the work of missionaries in New Spain generally, and to the long record of holiness and zeal written by the Dominicans, Jesuits, Carmelites, Augustinians, Mercedarians, and, above all, Franciscans, who together accomplished one of the most epoch-making expansions in the history of the church. In 1521 Pope Leo X gave extravagant authority to the Franciscans in this new mission field; and after 1524—when their first company arrived—they swiftly won a reputation for piety, zeal, and effectiveness. By the time Don Juan Zumarraga became the first archbishop of Mexico in 1533, he reported that they alone had baptized one and a half million Indians. Other orders were soon engaged with equal vigor, and within a century Mexico south of the Rio Grande was at least superficially a Christian country. Certain characteristics of the indigenous culture and its religions made their work easier, as the utter failure to Christianize or subdue the Apaches and Comanches serves to indicate. A willingness to adapt to the religious tendencies of the Indians was equally important. But a passion for saving souls was the prime necessity—and this passion the spirituality of the Spanish church provided in abundant measure.

An excellent indication of the success as well as the methods of Spanish evangelism is the great shrine of Our Lady of Guadalupe, one of the richest and most lavishly decorated of Mexican churches, which was erected on "the very place sacred to the goddess Teotenantzin, 'mother of gods' who among all the figures in the Mexican pantheon, most closely resembles the Holy Virgin." [11] The Mary beheld in the miraculous portrait which is the central object of veneration for the throngs who visit the church is in every feature an Indian.

From the legal standpoint the Indian was from the first a subject of

11. Charles S. Braden, *Religious Aspects of the Conquest of Mexico*, pp. 302–07. Our Lady of Guadalupe is the name of a picture, transferred to a church, and thence to a town. The events connected with its origins are among the most remarkable in the church history of sixteenth-century New Spain. On 9 December 1531, just a century before the settlement of Boston, a fifty-five-year-old Indian, a Franciscan neophyte, beheld a vision of the Virgin, who bade him ask the bishop to build a church at that spot. On the next day, fulfilling the demand for a sign, she instructed him to pick roses in a certain place, though they were out of season. He did, and brought them to the bishop. As the Indian opened his tilma to exhibit the roses, however, he discovered upon it the now famous picture of the Virgin. The church was built and, upon becoming New Spain's most popular shrine, has been repeatedly enlarged. In 1754 Pope Benedict XIV decreed Our Lady of Guadalupe to be the national patron of Mexico and made 12 December a holy day of obligation.

the crown. For the Spanish ruling class in Mexico, the Indian was an underling, not a caste apart (given the shortage of Spanish women), but above all a source of labor, a peon; and in the long run he was to respond with resentment, revolution, and anticlericalism. The church, though inescapably part of this cloven society, unequivocally regarded the Indian as a child of God and sought to bring him within her embrace. The Dominican Antonio Montesinos (ca. 1486–ca. 1530) inaugurated a campaign to prevent the rise of Indian slavery, and Bishop Las Casas (1474–1566) was successful in gaining its formal prohibition. It was the friars, however, traveling on foot, living amid the Indians without wealth or display and learning their languages, who came to understand the Indian: "In contrast to the chronicles of the great military leaders or aristocratic observers of the Conquest," writes Mariano Picón-Salas, "the friar-historians, who were almost always at odds with these overlords, touched what might be called the inner life of the aborigines." [12] Because of facts such as these the achievements of the missionaries are a meaningful challenge to Anglo-Saxon Protestant solutions of similar problems. It is by no means an accident that Helen Hunt Jackson's *Ramona* (1884), which was part of a campaign to reform American Indian policy, portrayed Spanish California in idyllic tones.

On the other hand, Spain participated actively in Western Christendom's rape of Africa and soon instituted Negro slavery in its empire on a vast scale, though far less in Mexico than in the islands, and almost not at all in the northern borderlands. Spanish church leaders, moreover, did not extend their solicitude for American Indians to African blacks with equal zeal, and the antislavery efforts of the Jesuit Alphonso Sandoval and others came to naught. Both canon and civil law did provide a measure of protection to slaves, but enforcement was often lax. It thus becomes apparent that comparative judgments in the complex area of slavery and race relations cannot be made until scholarship on these matters gives detailed attention to the full historical and cultural experience of each New World country.

Effect on Other Nations

The final and most enduring consequence of Spanish exploration and settlement for American religious history was that it spurred France and England to increasingly vigorous imperial activity. Quite aside from its internal qualities, the mere existence of the Spanish empire became a vital stimulus to nations which were already profoundly affected by the Reformation. French Catholics, once their domestic religious wars were over,

12. Picón-Salas, *Cultural History of Spanish America*, p. 59.

saw an opportunity to regain in the New World what they had lost in the Old; while England saw on distant shores a new Canaan that must be made safe from the encroachments of popery.

The account of English exploits must follow a discussion of the Reformation, but the establishment of New France should be viewed in conjunction with Spain. Both empires were pervaded by the influence of Roman Catholicism, and after 1701 the Bourbon kings on both Spanish and French thrones frequently collaborated in their colonial enterprises. Moreover, both of these empires stood as massive challenges to the main thrust of Anglo-American advances in the New World. Especially in the seventeenth and eighteenth centuries this "Popish menace" would condition the attitudes and loyalties of the American colonists. The anti-Catholicism thus engendered would be strengthened and further stimulated by various domestic and international factors down at least to the Spanish-American War of 1898. Well into the twentieth century it was a vital component of Protestant patriotism and a spur to expansionist ambitions.

American religious history is strangely incomplete if Europe's competition for American empire is ignored. We proceed, therefore, to a survey of the empire which the French tardily launched, and in which pre-Reformation piety and counter-Reformation zeal were far more pervasively evident than in France itself.

4

THE CHURCH IN NEW FRANCE

During the fierce winter of 1604–05 the entire American empire of France consisted of one miserable colony which lay freezing and half-dead with scurvy on the little island of Saint Croix in Passamaquoddy Bay. Yet this winter of suffering was the prologue to a continuous process of French expansion which would end only with the fall of Montcalm on the Plains of Abraham a century and a half later. In sharp contrast, the Lions of Castile had already in the sixteenth century been borne to the heartlands of two continents, and a new Spanish colonial civilization had taken root. By 1604 Mexico City had a cathedral, a university, and two theological seminaries. Indians were kneeling at the shrine of Our Lady of Guadalupe. Saint Augustine was an established citadel-town, and New Mexico had been subdued.

Why, one may ask, was France so dilatory in pushing her colonial enterprises when for many reasons she might have been first? Cousin, it is claimed, sailed to Newfoundland in the 1480s; and fishing fleets from Saint-Malo and other Breton and Norman ports made repeated voyages to the Grand Banks during the fifteenth century. Cardinal Richelieu, moreover, was essentially right in declaring that "No realm is so well situated as France to be mistress of the seas, or so rich in all things needful." Why then were not these early expeditions followed by many more? The answer is not easily given.

It is true that under Francis I (1515–47) the potential prosperity of the French people began to be realized. But the very force of this fact brought France into the fierce dynastic struggles of the period, causing her to dissipate her energies on the battlefields of Italy and Spain. For a time the king himself was a hostage of his bitter rival the Emperor Charles V. An uneasy truce followed the Peace of Cambrai (1529), but soon another shadow fell across the realm. The Protestant Reformation shattered the unity of Roman Christendom—and with it the unity of France. In 1534, the year that Jacques Cartier first sailed into the Saint Lawrence Gulf, a brilliant young lawyer from Noyon was converted to evangelical views and forced to flee the land. And in 1536, the year Cartier returned from his second voyage, this lawyer—John Calvin—dedicated his *Institutes of the Christian Religion* to the French king in an immortal preface which assured that monarch he had nothing to fear from a revival of evangelical Christianity.

With the Concordat of Bologna (1516), Francis I had gained a drastic subordination of the church to the state. Yet he vacillated for a time in his attitude toward the reformers—for political reasons and because a strain of piety and humanistic concern ran strong in his own family. Then after 1533 he adopted a policy of vigorous suppression which was continued by his successors, but the strength of the Protestant party nevertheless continued to grow. Between 1562 and 1594 France was ravaged by the Wars of Religion. It had become a nation divided against itself.

At several points the balance of power was such that the Huguenot Admiral Coligny was able to send out small colonies to the New World. In 1564 one such group went to the Saint Johns River in "Florida," where it was viewed as a threat to the interests of Spain and annihilated by Menendez, the founder of Saint Augustine. Coligny himself was struck down in the massacre of Saint Bartholomew's Eve (1572); and another period of bloody fighting began. The assassination of Henry III in 1589 left Henry of Navarre, the Huguenot hero, as the only surviving heir to the throne. But because not even a victorious Protestant could hope to rule France peacefully, he renounced his "heresies" and was received into the Roman Catholic church. (As cynics have put it, he decided "Paris was worth a Mass.") He became Henry IV, founder of the Bourbon dynasty. Protestant liberties were secured by the Edict of Nantes promulgated at Henry's insistence in 1598. Thus peace came to the distracted kingdom, which then entered upon another era of prosperity and power.

The interest in overseas empire, however, was still small. Henry and Sully, his great minister of state, shared the immemorial view of Frenchmen that there is no place like France, and so did little more than yield grudging permission to adventurers of various types. First, they undertook a series of mere trading voyages. The De Monts colony, already mentioned, set forth in 1604. It, too, would have been only another dismal episode, had not one of its survivors been Samuel Champlain, the royal geographer and a man of extraordinary vision and determination. Champlain aroused renewed interest in the colonial venture, and in 1608—on the third of his eleven voyages to Canada—he founded Quebec. All but eight men perished in that first Canadian winter; but by the time of his death in 1635 Champlain could believe that a permanent foothold had been gained. Meanwhile other Frenchmen returned to the Bay of Fundy and began to make Port Royal a center of French influence.

French outposts in North America rested on an exceedingly tenuous footing, remaining little more than fur trading posts until Richelieu's rise to power in 1627. Richelieu was far more interested in aggrandizing royal prerogatives and advancing the French cause in European power struggles than he was in colonies, but he gave New France at least a semblance of support. He organized the Company of One Hundred Associates to control and sustain the colonists in Canada, and encouraged positive measures for settlement. These steps, however, were more impressive in theory than in substance.

COLONIAL POLICY AFTER 1663

After the death of Cardinal Mazarin, who had continued the policies of Richelieu, Louis XIV assumed personal responsibility for foreign policy, including the work of colonization. This was in 1661. Two years later Canada was made a royal domain. The old Company was upbraided for its pitiful performance and dissolved; supervision was transferred to the intendant (a new royal office), and a Sovereign Council composed of the governor, the bishop of Quebec (after 1674), and five councilors appointed by the king. In addition, the new minister of finance, Jean Baptiste Colbert, promoted a thoroughgoing mercantilist policy whereby the mother country was to enjoy a trade monopoly in its colonial empire. Under Colbert, France became a serious competitor of her European rivals in the race for empire.

The condition of Canada was nevertheless still deplorable, chiefly because of her widely scattered population. About twenty-five hundred traders, officials, and priests were clustered in small, isolated settlements which were totally defenseless against the ever menacing Iroquois. The new form of government also failed to inaugurate an era of peace and prosperity, for the governor was often arrayed against the royal intendant on one hand and the bishop on the other. Brushes with the British frequently led to bloody battles along the disputed border line. And after the passing of Colbert and Louis XIV, military and economic support from the homeland became sporadic and undependable. Yet in spite of these difficulties, New France continued its immense territorial expansion.

In a sense, the source of both the expansion and its difficulties was that dreamer, adventurer, and explorer, René Robert Cavalier, Sieur de la Salle (1643–87). It was he who first conceived the highly contagious idea of a greater New France. After a series of incredibly long and difficult expeditions, he convinced the royal court that the fleur-de-lis should fly over a fortified area extending from Quebec to the mouth of the Mississippi, and from the headwaters of the Ohio to the Rocky Mountain springs of the Missouri. This would make New France a vast inland empire covering the entire Great Lakes basin and the heart of the North American continent. La Salle's own colonizing venture at the mouth of the Mississippi ended in tragedy, but the grandiose idea had been sown.

The next years saw a series of ventures in expansion. Pierre le Moyne, Sieur d'Iberville, established Fort Maurepas on Biloxi Bay in 1699, while his brother, Jean Baptiste le Moyne, Sieur de Bienville, planted New Orleans in 1718. Fortresses were built at crucial points in the north: Louisbourg on Cape Breton (1720), Niagara on Lake Ontario (1720), Vincennes on the lower Wabash (1724), and several others, including Fort Duquesne (Pittsburgh) in 1753. In the west Pierre Gaultier de Varennes, Sieur de la Verendrye, prepared to defend the Saskatchewan and the Missouri valleys (1734, 1738).

The area thus fortified was both thinly populated and badly governed. John Law's infamous Company of the Indies had backed the founding of New Orleans in hope of speedy profits, but maladministration threatened the very existence of the settlement. In 1731 "Louisiana" was rescued from total pandemonium by being placed under royal control as Canada had been, with a governor and an intendant. But by this time the end of French domination was near.

In 1713 at the Treaty of Utrecht the Hudson's Bay area was signed away to England. Even more vitally, so was Nova Scotia. Around Port Royal the old French inhabitants were at first permitted to remain, but later (during King George's War) they were suspected of anti-British activities. In 1755 Colonel Charles Lawrence, governor of Nova Scotia, drove six thousand Acadians into exile. Their tragic fate entered the American consciousness belatedly with the publication of Longfellow's *Evangeline* in 1847. In 1762 the entire Louisiana territory was ceded to the Bourbons of Spain to keep it out of English hands, and so it remained almost until the Louisiana Purchase of 1803. By that time Canada, too, would be gone. It was ceded to

Great Britain in 1763, but General Wolf's capture of Quebec in 1759 was the decisive military event.[1]

France may have been late in entering the competition for empire in America; her efforts may have often miscarried; her colonial government may have been haphazard or unwieldy; even her greatest successes may have been impermanent. But taken as a whole, New France was an astonishing achievement, and its church-historical dimension both in the mother country and in the vast reaches of North America merits our concern.

THE ECCLESIASTICAL BACKGROUND IN SEVENTEETH-CENTURY FRANCE

Royal Absolutism and the Church

In France as in Spain, church and state were closely interwoven, and both institutions had been powerfully affected by the rise of national feeling. Though France had no *Real Patronato* granting her rulers nearly papal powers in governing the ecclesiastical establishment, both king and clergy

1. France's "race for empire" was a peripheral but inseparable part of a great European power struggle which dated at least to the Reformation era and included, later still, the devastating Thirty Years War (1618–48). Usually included among the "French and Indian Wars" on the North American continent are the following:

Date	*In Europe*	*In America*	*Major American Results*
1688–97	War of the League of Augsburg	King William's War	Treaty of Ryswick. Port Royal, though captured by English, returned to France.
1701–13	War of the Spanish Succession	Queen Anne's War	Treaty of Utrecht. Hudson's Bay area and Nova Scotia (Port Royal) ceded to England.
1740–48	War of the Austrian Succession	King George's War	Treaty of Aix-la-Chapelle. Louisbourg on Cape Breton Island though captured by English and colonials, returned to France.
1756–63	Seven Years War	The French and Indian War	Treaty of Paris. All of continental New France in Canada and east of Mississippi ceded to England. Spanish Florida to England; Louisiana territory, west of Mississippi, ceded to Spain.

In America all of these wars involved intermittent but often cruel and bloody border fighting, burnings of towns, massacres, and continuous feelings of suspicion and hostility. Each war also featured one or more military efforts on a larger scale. After the "World War of the American Revolution" England returned Florida to Spain, who sold it to the United States in 1819. Napoleon recovered the Louisiana territory from Spain in 1800, but sold it to the United States in 1803.

were exceedingly jealous of "ancient Gallican liberties." Philip IV had defied Rome by disputing papal claims to supremacy and cutting off papal revenues, and had forestalled excommunication by imprisoning Pope Boniface VIII in 1303. The "Pragmatic Sanction" of 1438 and the Concordat of Bologna (1516) had further reduced papal authority in France. The quondam Protestant Henry IV showed scant solicitude for papal desires; and as his Bourbon successors accelerated the trend toward royal absolutism, the papal voice in French affairs became increasingly weak. Louis XIV, with the concurrence of Bishop Bossuet, declared in 1682 that the temporal sovereignty of kings was independent of the pope, that a general council was above the pope, that the usages of the French church limited papal interference, and that the pope was not infallible. Louis also successfully appropriated the income from all vacant bishoprics.

One must not conclude, however, that Gallicanism loosened the ties between church and state within the nation; actually it strengthened them. Churchmen could and did serve as statesmen to advance the national interest—as did Cardinal Richelieu under Louis XIII, the Italian-born Cardinal Mazarin during the regency of Louis XIV, and Cardinal Fleury during the regency of Louis XV. Men like these, as much as the kings themselves, were architects of a foreign policy of which the chief goal was dynastic and territorial gain. During the religious wars that wracked the continent in the wake of the Reformation, they supported the Protestant cause (or even the Turks) against the pope and the Hapsburgs whenever this would advance the interests of France. And within France, king and clergy worked together, though only so long as the latter conceded that their traditional prerogatives were a dead letter and that a new absolutistic order prevailed.

New Movements in French Catholicism

During the century in which France's colonial aspirations awakened, there also occurred a remarkable resurgence of Catholic piety. Reform in the French Catholic church had been delayed by the Wars of Religion, but a revival beginning with the coming of peace reached its peak under Louis XIV. The Society of Jesus spread rapidly and widely, opposition by the Sorbonne notwithstanding. Capuchins, Recollects, reformed Cistercians, and Benedictines were joined by newer orders in stimulating the return to purified religion.

One of the most influential of these reformist impulses was the new order of secular priests constituting the French Oratory, founded by the pioneer of modern French mysticism, Pierre de Bérulle (1575–1629). Under his successor, Charles de Condren, the oratory's interest in revitalizing the clergy continued, but Condren also became a strong champion of the devotion to the Sacred Heart of Jesus, a form of piety which before long gained a most remarkable popular appeal due to the support of the Jesuits and the testimonies of Saint Margaret Mary Alacoque.[2]

Bérulle and Condren had a decisive influence on Jean-Jacques Olier (1608–57), who founded several seminaries and through them the Society of Saint Sulpice (named for his church located in a Paris slum, where he carried on a vigorous program of reform), and on Saint Vincent de Paul (1576–1660), who formed in 1625 the Congregation of the Priests of the Mission and in 1633 the Sisters (or Daughters) of Charity. Other reformers were Saint Francis de Sales, who left a treasure of writings on the life of the spirit; Saint Jean Eudes, who established the Congregation of the Good Shepherd (the Eudists) to care for fallen women and inaugurated the liturgical worship of the Sacred Hearts of Mary and Jesus; and Saint Jean de la Salle, whose work in founding schools earned him recognition as one of the fathers of modern pedagogy in France.

The Catholic Reformation in France was free from neither theological controversy nor political interference. A revival of Augustinianism, emphasizing divine predestination, personal religious experience through conscious conversion, and direct relationship of the believer with God, was promoted by Cornelius Jansen (1588–1638), bishop of Ypres. He was followed by Antoine Arnauld, author of *Frequent Communion;* Pasquier Quesnel, author of *Moral Reflections of the New Testament;* Blaise Pascal, famous for his *Pensées* and a fierce attack on the Jesuits in his *Provincial Letters;* and by a large group of "Jansenists" centered at the abbey of Port Royal, near Paris. Because the Jansenists were openly critical of the Jesuits' alleged Pelagian tendencies and utilitarian ethics, they incurred the bitter opposition of the Jesuits, who badgered both king and pope until they secured the condemnation of Jansenism in the bull *Unigenitus* (1713).

Of a different nature was the controversy over the Neoplatonic and "quietistic" mysticism of Madame Guyon and François Fénelon. They were opposed by Bishop Bossuet, who persuaded the pope to condemn their views and the king to proscribe their activities. Finally and most unfortunately for France, the Jesuits pressured Louis XIV into revoking the Edict of Nantes in 1685, marking the culmination of a long process by which Protestant privileges had been gradually withdrawn. Very soon large numbers of Huguenots, among them some of the country's wealthiest, most industrious

2. The devotion to the Sacred Heart, which experienced so strong a revival in seventeenth-century France, is an important clue to the intense and often sentimental ardor that pervaded the period. On the history and controversies related to this devotion, see Josef Stierli, ed., *Heart of the Saviour* (New York: Herder and Herder, 1957).

citizens, emigrated to Germany, Holland, England, and America, thus dealing a severe and permanent blow to the vitality of the French nation and strengthening the economic and political life of France's chief Protestant rivals. For her colonial empire, however, the revival of Catholic fervor in France itself had a direct and powerful significance. To a most remarkable degree the New World beyond the sea and its heathen population became the object of pious zeal.

FRENCH MISSIONS IN AMERICA

In New France the faith and institutions of the Roman church gained a centrality and importance that was equaled in no other empire, not even New Spain. The statement can be narrowed further: it was not simply transplanted French Catholicism, but preeminently the Society of Jesus, which shaped the spirit of New France. George Bancroft's assertion is not significantly overdrawn: "The history of missionary labors is connected with the origin of every celebrated town in the annals of French Canada; not a cape was turned nor a river entered but a Jesuit led the way." [3]

Early Labors in the East

Before the first Jesuit team, consisting of Pierre Biard and Ennemond Massé, arrived at Port Royal (Nova Scotia) in 1611, two secular priests had been there and had baptized more than a hundred Indians. In 1615 the Recollects, a semicontemplative reform branch of the Franciscan order, began their mission out of Quebec with four priests; and that summer Fathers Le Caron and Jamet set off up the Saint Lawrence River for the country of the Hurons. But after only slight success and many difficulties with the trading company, the Recollects themselves requested aid from the Society of Jesus, not least because this would provide more leverage at the centers of power. In 1625 the first five Jesuits arrived at Quebec, and for a time the Society was assigned the sole responsibility for French missions out of Quebec. They faced a disappointing prospect. There were only fifty-one winter residents in all of New France; and the first news they received was that the Recollect Father Viel had just been drowned or murdered while returning from his mission to the Hurons. Then Champlain died in 1635. But under the leadership of Paul LeJeune the Jesuits began to write a magnificent chapter in the history of Christian missions and the expansion of New France. By 1649 eight of them had won the martyr's crown.

The story of almost any one of these early missionaries would illustrate

3. George Bancroft, *History of the United States*, 2:300.

how fervent piety combined with a passionate desire to Christianize Canada's Indians could draw men and women out of the familiar institutional life of France and impel them to sacrificial labors in the wilderness. That of Jean de Brébeuf serves as well as any. Born in 1593 to a prosperous manorial family living near Saint Lô in Normandy, he entered the Society of Jesus in 1617. He was serving as a college administrator when his plea to join the first Jesuit mission to Quebec was accepted. For the rest of his life—except for a brief return to academic work during the British occupation—the conversion of the Hurons was virtually his sole earthly preoccupation. Living with this harassed and plague-ridden tribe, learning its ways, preparing a grammar and lexicon of its language, trying tirelessly (for a time as superior of the mission) to win converts and to allay suspicions that the missionaries were the source of tribal woe, baptizing the dying and the newborn, he personifies the concept of total commitment. At the same time his notebooks record a personal religious life of unabated self-discipline and ecstasy: "On the 9th of May, [1640] when I was in the village of Saint Joseph, I was, as it were, carried out of myself and to God by powerful acts of love, and I was transported to God, as if to embrace Him." This union, he goes on to say, was disturbed by the appearance of an old woman whom he supposed to be the devil in disguise. In a later entry (27 May) he speaks of his experience while at prayer before the Blessed Sacrament on the feast of the Pentecost: "I saw myself in a moment invested in a great fire which burned everything which was there around me, without consuming aught. While these flames lasted, I felt myself inwardly on fire with the love of God, more ardently than I had ever been."

Nine years later the flames would be real. Just as some signs of large scale conversions were being detected, the Hurons were set upon even more furiously than before by the western Iroquois. Amid the carnage Brébeuf was captured, and after brutal preparatory punishment he was scalded and burned to death on 16 March 1649 at a village then named for Saint Ignace on the Sturgeon River, near the easternmost bay of Lake Huron. "At his death," writes the most thorough historian of these exploits, "began the irreparable ruin of the Huron nation." [4] Soon the whole Huron tribe, on whom such great labors had been expended, was uprooted and driven west to Wisconsin by the Iroquois, who were backed by the Dutch and English in an effort to limit French expansion and control of the fur trade. Yet the Jesuits continued their efforts undaunted, following the Hurons westward.

4. Francis X. Talbot, *Saint among the Hurons: The Life of Jean de Brébeuf*, pp. 213, 214, 300, 310. Already at his burial Brébeuf was regarded as a martyr and saint. Pope Pius XI proclaimed his canonization along with seven other Jesuit martyrs in 1930.

After 1680 the Society of Jesus also worked strenuously among the Abenakis of Maine. Among these Indians the Capuchins had conducted a mission between 1632 and 1655, but even with Jesuit aid during the subsequent years, their efforts had resulted in only a few feeble villages of transplanted converts. The arrival of Father Sebastian Râle in 1694 led to a revival of the mission and they finally gained the whole tribe's lasting commitment to the Christian faith. Unfortunately, this story is so intertwined with Anglo-French hostilities, Indian intrigue, and frontier fighting that the Abenaki mission is very difficult to evaluate. Despite his effectiveness as a missionary, events conspired against Râle, beginning in 1704, when the Indian allies of the French perpetrated the famous massacre at Deerfield, Massachusetts. In 1713 the Treaty of Utrecht conveyed Hudson's Bay, Newfoundland, and Nova Scotia (Acadia) to England. Border disputes and intermittent raiding followed, and finally, in 1722, the English declared war. Two years later Râle was shot and scalped. During the last years of New France missionary activity declined, and the work in Maine languished. Yet the Abenaki remnant was true to its new faith, and after the American Revolution they were allowed to receive the ministrations of a Roman Catholic priest.

Though not alone in their efforts, the Jesuits were also particularly successful in arousing interest in France for their projects in the New World. They recruited supporters from other orders as well as among laymen. Of greatest importance was a Sulpician group including Jean Jacques Olier himself, which obtained a grant on the island of Montreal and convinced a pious military officer, Paul Chomedy, Sieur de Maisonneuve, to lead a colony to the place. In 1641 he sailed with a small company that included one Jesuit priest and Mademoiselle Jeanne Mance, who was to found Montreal's Hospital of Saint Joseph. In the following spring, Maisonneuve began his twenty-four year stay at that dangerous outpost. Further reinforcements arrived in 1653, including four Sulpician priests and Sister Marguerite Bourgeoys, who soon carried out her intention of founding the Congregation de Notre Dame and its school for girls. After a trip to France in 1659, the two women returned with further helpers for the work—six nuns and two Sulpician priests. In time, an enclave of Sulpician influence and piety developed here, never powerful, but testimony nonetheless to a deep measure of missionary concern.

In Quebec French piety flowered similarly among courageous women. Madame de la Peltrie, of Normandy's *haute noblesse,* was a leading spirit: fired by Jesuit appeals, she devoted herself and her fortune to the Indian women of Canada, first enlisting the help of the Ursulines, a teaching order closely related in its founding to the Jesuits, then coming herself to Quebec in 1639. Under their Mother Superior, Marie de l'Incarnation, the Ursulines began a school for Indian girls. At the same time, a hospital was begun under the patronage of the Duchess d'Aiguillon by a group of nuns who arrived on the same ship with the Ursulines.

Evangelism and Exploration

In eastern Canada, missionary efforts were rendered impractical not only by the hostility of the Indians but by determined English and Dutch resistance to France and to Catholicism. Jesuit attention consequently was shifted farther west and north, far beyond Iroquois and foreign influence, until Sault Sainte Marie and the western Great Lakes region became the final scene of their labor. In this new locale their concern began to shift from evangelism to exploration. Missionary interest remained, of course, but the charting of unknown territory and careful reporting on the land and its savage people took on increased importance. The missionaries lost their early optimism.

The exemplar of these later endeavors is Father Jacques Marquette (1637–75), whose exploits have become an enduring part of American folklore. Born in Laon, he entered the Society of Jesus at the age of seventeen, came to New France in 1666, and for four years labored on the upper Great Lakes. Devout and intrepid, he was in every sense a true counterpart of the early Jesuit martyrs. In 1673 he joined the trader and explorer Louis Joliet in a search for the Mississippi River, an expedition which took them more than twenty-five hundred miles by birchbark canoe. After paddling from the Mackinac Straits through Green Bay and up the Fox River, they went overland to the Wisconsin River and down it to the Mississippi, which they followed as far as the mouth of the Arkansas River. Convinced now that the great river emptied into the Gulf of Mexico rather than the Pacific Ocean, and fearing to go farther lest they fall into the hands of the Spanish, they returned by way of the Illinois River. Here Marquette conceived his final venture, the founding of a mission in the Illinois country. This was fulfilled in 1674 with the establishment of the mission of the Immaculate Conception of the Blessed Virgin at Kaskaskia (near present-day Utica, Illinois); but Marquette contracted dysentery on the trip and died the following spring on the eastern shore of Lake Michigan.

Decline of Jesuit Influence

Despite their energetic efforts, the Jesuits with the passing years gradually lost their missionary monopoly. The Sulpicians at Montreal were one small encroachment. Far more significant, indeed, one of the most important events in the church history of New France, was the appointment of a bishop for Quebec. François Xavier de Laval-Montmorency (1623–1708) was the Jesuits' own choice. Descended from one of the great families of France, he had early been caught up by the Catholic revival. Educated by the Jesuits at La Flèche and the Collège de Clermont in Paris, ordained priest in 1647 and appointed archdeacon of Evreux, he was leading a semi-cloistered life of contemplation when he was consecrated bishop of Petraea *in partibus infidelium* and sent as apostolic vicar to Quebec in 1659. Yet jurisdictional disputes continued. His education notwithstanding, Laval soon intruded on Jesuit prerogatives. The archbishop of Rouen, moreover, objected that this papal appointment violated Gallican rights.

Despite such resistance, Laval was installed in 1674 as bishop of the newly erected see of Quebec; and in this role he was a powerful alternate ecclesiastical force in New France until his resignation in 1688. Enormously jealous of episcopal authority, he made clear from the beginning to governors, intendants, and clergy that he would be bishop in very fact. Laval led the long, bitter fight against trading brandy to the Indians. He founded his own diocesan seminary and obtained for it the right of transferring and recalling the parish clergy of the diocese. In short, he laid foundations and established precedents that go far to explain the resolutely church-oriented culture which ultimately flourished in the region whose spiritual center was Quebec.

Another event fraught with great significance for Jesuit missions was the appointment of Louis de Buade, Comte de Frontenac (1620–98), as governor of New France in 1672, just as Louis XIV was becoming involved in another exhausting war. The "Iron Governor" was a capable leader, and he would demonstrate that fact even more clearly during his second term (1689–98) than during his first (1672–82). He distrusted the Jesuits because of their ultramontane sympathies and removed them on every possible occasion, replacing them with Recollects and Sulpicians wherever he could. La Salle, his great lieutenant, was in complete agreement with this view; indeed, three of the Recollects who accompanied La Salle are among the most memorable heroes of their order: the adventurous Father Louis Hennepin, explorer of the upper Mississippi and teller of tales; Gabriel Ribourde, murdered in Illinois by a band of Kickapoos; and Zenobe Membré, "the Franciscan Father Marquette," whose martyr death came in the wilds of Texas when Indians slaughtered the last remnant of La Salle's ill-fated expedition (1689).

La Salle himself never saw the consequences of his prodigious efforts, but the Cross was carried to the vast lands his enterprises opened. In addition to the overwhelming scope of the task, however, three major factors impeded missionary progress: a succession of governmental arrangements that kept civil affairs on the verge of anarchy, bitter jurisdictional conflicts between the bishop of Quebec and the missionary orders on the one hand and between the Jesuits and Capuchins or Recollects on the other, and finally, the unmistakeable waning of religious fervor both among the supporters of missions in France and in the missionaries themselves. Dedicated men did give their lives to the missionary cause: at his death in 1689, after indefatigable work throughout the inland area, Father Allouez was said to have baptized ten thousand Indians. Yet in 1750 Father Vivier reported only a handful of converts and great irreligion in the scattered French villages.

In the later years of New France the Jesuits finally suffered the penalty for their aggressive advances. They came to be hated as masters of intrigue in both Catholic and Protestant countries. When Louis XIV died (1715), the archbishop of Paris forbade them to preach or hear confession in his diocese. By 1750 they were in disrepute everywhere. Portugal expelled the order from all its lands in 1759, and France followed suit between 1761 and 1764, just when particularly evil times had befallen Canada. Spain did likewise in 1767. Harshly criticized by several earlier popes, the society was suppressed by Clement XIV in the bull *Dominus ac redemptor noster* (21 July 1773). In New France they were deported and their properties sold at public auction; and despite its recent cession to Spain, this was done in Louisiana as well.

THE LASTING EFFECTS OF NEW FRANCE

The century and a half during which France carried out its bold design for a North American empire was rarely free from conflict. The clash of two civilizations underlies the entire story of the rise and fall of New France. Every European struggle had its American counterpart in colonial retaliations and Indian wars. But from the earliest times, the blows struck by the English, whether from the mother country or the colonies, were the most decisive. There might be momentary reversals when European treaties would forfeit American conquests, but ineluctably New France yielded—at Port Royal, Newfoundland and Cape Breton, in the Hudson Bay area, and finally at Quebec and New Orleans.

This was more than mere "competition for empire," however. It was also a conflict of cultures beneath which lay two contrasting interpretations of the Christian faith. Precisely because fiercely contended religious issues underlay the constant warfare, the most enduring effect of New France on the British colonies was to intensify an already vehement hatred of "popery." The antipathy, moreover, long outlasted the political peace treaties. American Protestantism would sustain itself on memories of "the Old French Wars" until nineteenth-century immigration provided new grounds for nativist persecutions. The continued loyalty of French-Canadians to the Roman Catholic church, on the other hand, was strengthened by their determination to preserve their cultural integrity against the politically dominant British.

The third culture involved in the struggle for North America, the Indian, played a special role. Every power with an interest in America sought to use the Indians, both as protective buffers and as allies in offensive campaigns. The Dutch and later the British generally maintained an alliance with the Five Nations of the Iroquois, while the French remained friendly with the Abenakis, the Hurons, and the Algonquins. French missionary activity thus became more and more politically motivated, and Indian treachery was often charged to priestly intrigue. The way in which missionaries were regarded as a military necessity is shown by a letter of 1726 from the ecclesiastical director of the Company of the Indies in Louisiana to the French minister of the navy:

> Allow me, Sir, to detail in the present conjuncture my own remarks:
>
> 1) It is necessary to establish missionaries among the savages. We have dared to diminish our troops on the supposition they will be granted. They are, therefore, essential.
>
> 2) The first missionaries must be placed around *the savages who separate us from the English,* and since the latter try incessantly to gain them in order to stir them up against us, it is absolutely necessary that the missionaries sent to them be men of spirit, active, alert.
>
> 3) Among the religious bodies of the whole world *the Jesuits alone are such;* therefore, we need them.[5]

The Indian's strategic importance for the success or failure of individual white settlements as well as of large imperial designs ruled out benign and altruistic Indian policies on all sides. And with the passage of time not even the elimination of French competition for empire would alleviate the problem. In areas not yet open to settlement, as in the trans-Mississippi West during the days of the "mountain men," the American would prove to be

5. Claude L. Vogel, *The Capuchins in French Louisiana, 1722–1766* (New York: Joseph F. Wagner, 1928), p. 87.

quite as capable of "embracing" the Indian as anyone else. With the gradual westward movement of the American population, however, neither the French nor the Spanish "solution" to the problem was a live alternative. Perhaps the surest fact is that only one misfortune to befall the Indian was greater than his being caught up in the crosscurrents of imperialism; his greatest tragedy was to be overrun and enveloped by the "Atlantic Migration," the centuries-long movement of Europeans into the British dominions of North America.[6]

Apart from these legacies of intolerance and misfortune, there was a record of saintliness and heroism written by the French missionaries that challenges even the rhetoric of professional hagiographers, and in modern times it has come to be widely appreciated. Protestant Americans no longer consider Sebastian Râle as the type of the sinister Jesuit, but modify the image of the wilderness conspirator with that of the martyr dying at the foot of a cross in the village square of the tribe with the largest Christian population north of New Mexico. At the same time, the early record of holy exploits has provided Roman Catholics in America with an heroic colonial tradition.

The lasting impact of New France on American religious life has been slight. In that part of La Salle's imagined empire which became United States territory, very little that was French or Roman Catholic endured except, as in New Spain, a treasure of melodious but soon hopelessly mispronounced place-names. A few small communities remained along the Mississippi and its tributaries, but these were soon enveloped by America's westward expansion. Only in New Orleans and the Louisiana bayou country, where the transplanted Acadians settled, did anything like French culture leave a lasting deposit; and even here three decades of Spanish rule left traces of yet another culture. In this area, however, religious affairs were radically different from those in Quebec. Disorder and laxity were the rule; and not until 1785, under Spanish rule, did New Orleans receive a resident bishop. Only after the purchase of Louisiana by the United States was ecclesiastical anarchy gradually ended and a reunion of church and people attempted.

The reasons for the evanescent character of French Catholicism in the region between the Saint Lawrence River and New Orleans are readily apparent. The French were disinclined to emigrate, and as the wars of Louis XIV continued, his ministers discouraged what little migratory impulse there was. The one group that did leave in such large numbers as to affect

6. On the nature and extent of this continuing migration to the United States see chaps. 7, 31, 33, 45, 57, and 59, esp. pp. 749–50.

the vitality of the nation—the Huguenots—were not allowed to settle in New France. Those who came to America contributed their wealth and acumen to the British colonies instead.[7]

One might expect that a lasting contribution of the French in America would have resulted from their Indian missions. Yet even here the verdict must be negative. The priests mollified the Indians, interpreted them, and probably understood them. To some degree they may have influenced tribal attitudes and politics. They also baptized innumerable infants and dying adults—yet genuine conversions were extraordinarily rare. The North American Indians were very resistant to Christian conversion. It seems likely that, even against these odds, and despite growing population pressures on the frontiers, the Indian missions in the various British colonies were more successful, though they have been far less heralded by historians.

Yet New France did not die, even though Great Britain won the French and Indian Wars. The integrity of French Canada was respected in the Treaty of Paris of 1763, and even honored (to the exasperation of English colonials) by Parliament's Quebec Act of 1774, which extended Canada's boundaries south to the Ohio River and granted the Roman Catholic church a privileged position in a highly centralized colonial government. The French Canadians continued to be a powerful faction in Canada long after it became British, doing much to keep it loyal to the crown during the American Revolution. The province of Quebec would perpetuate the spirit of the *ancien régime* long after it had died in France. Successfully resisting assimilation, this proudly French province would in the later twentieth century become the catalyst of a much larger Canadian resistance to the Americanization of the country. French-Canadians would nevertheless move in growing numbers into the New England commonwealths that had once mounted campaigns against Quebec and Louisbourg. But this is rather a chapter in the history of American industrialism, immigration, and politics.

The church of New France, meanwhile, would become a confusing element in the average American's badly focused picture of Canadian history: on the one hand, dark complicity in colonial wars, Indian massacres, and a reactionary social order; on the other, a colorful saga of intrepid explorers and supremely dedicated missionaries.

7. In 1763 the population of lower Louisiana numbered about five thousand, plus half again as many slaves; the Saint Lawrence region, about sixty thousand. The population of the English colonies, by contrast, exceeded one and a quarter million at this time.

5

THE REFORMATION

The Spanish conquest of the New World had taken large strides before the great events of the Reformation shook the structures of Europe. This blow to the universality of the Roman church did provide Spain with a powerful external stimulus to missionary zeal, religious rigor, and intolerance; but the spirit and purpose of the Reformers had no other positive effect on her empire in America. When New France came into existence more than a century later, France itself had been racked by decades of controversy and religious war. But again, the work of the church in the colonial empire was inspired and conducted chiefly by those who were most determined to rejuvenate the ancient Catholic faith and to counteract Reformed influences. In both Spain and France imperial rivalries were heightened and intensified by a Counter-Reformation spirit. Except in this indirect way, however, the Reformation failed to put its mark on the colonial culture and institutions of either New Spain or New France.

On the other hand, the primarily British "intermediate empire" which in time forced its way between these two Roman Catholic giants was molded by the Reformation in ways that are almost beyond the possibility of exaggeration. Here, too, economic and imperial rivalry was a factor at once fierce and enthusiastic; but far more importantly, the spirit of the colonies that took shape along the Atlantic coast was with few exceptions informed and shaped by the spiritual resurgence which broke the unity of Roman Christendom in the sixteenth century. The Reformation, of course, was closely related to innumerable other secular developments that, taken together, constitute a decisive abrogation of the medieval tradition. The effects of this vast revolution are also visible in Britain's New World empire. But just as no true or adequate comprehension of the Reformation is possible without a vision of its setting in the late Middle Ages, so an understanding of American colonial foundations must rest on a comprehension of that evangelical unleashing which constitutes the heart of the Reformation.

The great Reformation events have roots that twine their way back into virtually every crevice of Europe's medieval experience. Interpreters of the Reformation have traditionally stressed certain historical factors. In the immediate ecclesiastical realm they point to the decay of papal prestige and the increase of corruption, which accelerated national feeling in both the secular and religious realms, aroused the advocates of conciliarism, and provoked widespread demands for reform. In the closely related area of popular piety, the growing dissatisfaction with worldly church leadership and overly institutionalized forms of religious expression, together with official unresponsiveness to the religious needs of individual Christians, spawned in virtually every part of Europe a steady succession of movements for spiritual, devotional, mystical, and evangelical renewal. The importance of underlying economic transformations is generally acknowledged, with particular stress given to the increase of commercial activity, the growth of towns and cities, important shifts in the bases of economic power, and the emergence of new social groups with increasingly secular sources of patronage.

Almost inseparable from economic transitions are political changes, both general and specific: above all, the steady rise of something that may with caution be termed the "national state," and within such states, the advent of rulers determined to overcome the splintering effects of feudal tradition, papal power, and the church's independence. The widening of certain intellectual horizons and the narrowing of others in the "Renaissance" is perhaps the most complex influence of all, for this phenomenon includes not only the rebirth of interest in the literature, art, and philosophy of antiquity, but also a renewal of interest in scholarship of all kinds and an advance in man's knowledge of both nature and mankind based on scientific observation, experimentation, and exploration. All of these modern forces tended to cast medieval formulations into disfavor.[1] Quite independent of these developments were others equally disturbing: the rising Turkish menace on the eastern frontier, and at least one circumstance for which not even the most zealous Marxist has been able to give an economic explanation—the appearance of Halley's comet in 1531 and other celestial

1. In his important psychoanalytic study *Young Man Luther* (New York: W. W. Norton & Co., 1962), Erik Erikson speaks of the "grim willingness" of both Luther and Freud "to do the dirty work of their respective ages: for each kept human conscience in focus in an era of material and scientific expansion" (p. 9). He also sees "Luther's emancipation from medieval dogma [as] one of the indispensable precursors both of modern philosophy and psychology."

visitations during the years 1554, 1556, and 1558. Religious life, theology, and the functioning of the church were profoundly affected. Specifically religious interests, in turn, conditioned the course of these secular developments.[2]

The interplay of so many convergent forces makes it impossible to designate any one person, event, or set of conditions as the *cause* of the Reformation. Nothing so demonstrates the pervasive spontaneity of the Reformation or shows to what a remarkable degree this vast uprising was the response of Europe's soul to Europe's condition as does the wide range of religious reform, redefinition, and revitalization which was manifested during its central decades. That the Reformation was in one fundamental sense a great time of Christian revival is best indicated by considering the several major forms of the impulse for renewal.

These many reform movements may with small injustice be grouped under the traditional headings: Lutheran, Anglican, Reformed, and Radical (as well as the Roman Catholic renewal already considered in chaps. 2, 3, and 4). A history of religion in America obviously cannot treat these separate movements in all the details of their entanglement with Europe's social, political, and diplomatic history. But because of their crucial importance for American Christianity, the dominant forms require brief exposition. This résumé, however, will give special emphasis to the character of the *Reformed* tradition (or as it is so often misnamed, the "Calvinistic" tradition). Because this phase of the Continental Reformation struck Great Britain with far greater transforming power than either the Lutheran or Radical movements, special attention must be given to its driving concerns and central ideas. In a later chapter we will consider the ferment which "Reformed" theology aroused in England, and how, quite independently of Continental Radicalism, it ultimately generated its own Anglo-American type of radical "Puritanism," which would in turn become one of the most vital elements in the foundations of American thought and culture.

THE LUTHERAN REFORMATION

When Martin Luther celebrated Mass in Rome during his visit there in 1510, he was appalled that the Italian priest at the adjacent altar had said his last amen before Luther had gone farther in the order of service than

2. On the terminological hornet's nest that the decade of the 1960s has built around the distinction between the secular and the religious or sacred, see p. 21, n. 4 above. I think the distinction is necessary, though the referent of the concepts keeps changing. The Reformation itself had a massive impact on this whole discussion, especially Luther, with his emphasis on the goodness of the Creation and all that is therein.

reading the gospel lesson. At San Sebastiano he saw seven masses completed in an hour; and he encountered priests who did not know how to hear confession. Only at the "German Church" on the Piazza Navona did he find liturgical practice passably reverent. Both provincialism and Germanic pride may have conditioned his judgment; yet in the years ahead Saints Cajetan of Thiene and Philip Neri would inveigh against the same liturgical abuses; and many an Italian traveler in Germany, both earlier and later, would remark on the greater religious earnestness of northern Catholicism. Catholic and Protestant historians have agreed that it was this earnestness that made the German situation critical, with Catholics lamenting that so promising a circumstance should have been disrupted, and Protestants seeing the "disruption" as a proper flowering of evangelical truth. There is widespread agreement that the prevalence of ecclesiastical abuse, clerical ignorance, and theological decadence made this vast reservoir of popular religious concern highly explosive. So long as reformist demands were merely legalistic or institutional, and so long as criticism was chiefly the game of Renaissance humanists, large-scale effects were unlikely. Only if these various types of unrest were aroused by a thorough and profound protest would the existing structure be broken. And this, as Gerhard Ritter has eloquently stated it, was precisely what came to pass with the publication of the Ninety-five Theses and the emergence of Martin Luther (1483–1546).

> He is the man of the people, an agitator in the grandest style, and the most popular speaker and writer that Germany has ever produced. . . . He shares the moral indignation of his contemporaries over the outward corruption of the church; he uses all the slogans of anticlerical and antipapal opposition of the preceding hundred years and still outdoes them—but at the same time he is the most brilliant and profound theological thinker, the most powerful and strong-willed prophet-figure of his people, and a religious genius whose experience of faith is of unprecedented inwardness and intimacy.[3]

In this light it is not difficult to explain why, when Luther was summoned before Charles V and the Imperial Diet in 1521, the populace of Worms greeted him in the streets as a liberating hero.

Yet that aspect of the Reformation to which Luther's name is attached was not radical. The old and often used phrase, "Evangelical principle, Catholic substance," very aptly describes both Luther's intention and the Lutheran church which gradually came into existence. Though his doc-

3. Gerhard Ritter, "Why the Reformation in Germany," p. 106.

trine of Christian freedom was fundamentally radical, the reformation he sought was conservative. Luther's thought had been profoundly affected by Saint Augustine, the hero if not the founder of his order; and "justification by faith," so often designated the "material principle" of Lutheranism, was preached to his satisfaction by saints and doctors of the Church in all centuries. *Sola gratia,* defended so doggedly by Augustine, recurs in Aquinas, and had been affirmed by the Council of Trent. There is considerable truth in the contention of some Roman Catholic scholars that efforts for the reunion of Christendom must be channeled toward a thoroughgoing reevaluation of Luther. There is also much truth in the Roman Catholic claim that if Luther had possessed a profound knowledge of Saint Thomas or even of the full tradition of medieval exegesis of Saint Paul, he would have been spared much anguish. But these points are at best academic, for the assault on Thomism had begun even before the Angelic Doctor's death, and it had continued unabated. In succeeding centuries the influence of Duns Scotus, William of Ockham, Pierre d'Ailly, and John Gerson was far more pervasive than that of Saint Thomas, and new nominalistic methods of biblical interpretation were widespread. The tradition in which Luther was schooled was the *Via Moderna,* stemming from Ockham and maturing in Gabriel Biel. And this tradition probably deserved the evangelical antischolastic strictures which Luther delivered against it, as well as the emphasis on justification by faith which he championed. Moreover, his cry of "grace alone" did run counter to the prevailing emphasis of the *Via Moderna* and, above all, to the practical working of the Church's sacramental system as the average lay Christian experienced it in 1500.

The "evangelical principle" in Luther's thinking is probably most forcefully expressed through his *theologia crucis* (theology of the Cross), in which he elucidated the righteousness of God and God's gift to man.

> All good things [he said in 1518] are hidden in the Cross and under the Cross. Therefore they must not be sought and cannot be understood except under the Cross. Thus I, poor little creature, do not find anything in the Scriptures but Jesus Christ and Him crucified. For Jesus Christ is every benefit which is attributed to the righteous men in the Scriptures, such as joy, hope, glory, strength, wisdom. But He is a crucified Christ. Therefore only such people can rejoice in Him as trust and love Him, while they despair of themselves and hate their own name.[4]

4. From a lecture on the Psalms, 1518. Quoted by Regin Prenter, "Luther on Word and Sacrament," in *More about Luther* (Decorah, Iowa: Luther College Press, 1958), pp. 65–66.

Luther was to repeat again and again that only the Word in preaching and sacrament was the vehicle of God's grace; but he always returned to his insistence that there must be a death of self and a new birth in Christ. His famous emphasis on Holy Scripture was also rooted in the *theologia crucis:* he insisted that the substance of the Bible was the central divine act—God's judgment and forgiveness in and through the incarnate, crucified, and risen Jesus Christ. This is "the Gospel" and this message shaped Luther's understanding of both Old and New Testaments, freeing him from literalism and the trammels of traditional interpretation. Probably never in the history of the Church has any one person shown such rich theological insight in biblical interpretation, or made the Scriptures speak to people with such power and relevance. Basic to this timeliness and ethical relevance were three other persistent themes.

One was the conception of Christian freedom expounded in his classic treatise *On Christian Liberty* (1520). It left no ground for legalism (or salvation by the law), but rooted man's faith, love, and hope in God's unbounded mercy, and defined the Christian life as a free response to God's self-giving love. Here one also perceives his opposition to a *theologia gloria* according to which the visible Church was a safe ark of salvation if only one climbed aboard and obeyed the captain's rules. A second theme was his understanding of man as "at once justified and sinner" (*simul justus et peccator*) which stood squarely across the tempting road to perfectionism and spiritual arrogance, at the same time that it turned man to acts of love in this world. Finally, Luther's thought was suffused by a deep emphasis on God the Creator. All the orders of Creation—that is, the institutional structures of the secular world: family, government, marketplace, etc.—were seen as divinely ordained means of serving one's neighbor in one's vocation. Every just human calling was an opportunity for "faith active in love." Man's proper response to God's love-engendering deed in Christ lay in the callings of this world, not in withdrawal from them or in ascetic denials of man's essential nature. If we remember the enormous degree to which the Church had, for a thousand years, been directing Europe's most talented and pious people into the clergy and the monastic establishment, the full force of this Reformation demand becomes more apparent.

That there is much "Catholic substance" in these insistences goes without saying; but the most explicit witness to Luther's basic conservatism, and the most momentous for the subsequent development of the Reformation churches, is his stand on the sacraments, especially the Eucharist. He made his position explicit at the Colloquy at Marburg in 1529—possibly a watershed in Reformation history—where Luther and Melanchthon met the reformers of Strasbourg and Zurich, Martin Butzer and Huldreich Zwingli. "Hoc est corpus meum: this is my body," Luther wrote on the table; and no amount of discussion could shake his insistence on Christ's Real Presence in the sacrament. Better the Roman Mass, he would declare, than to understand the Lord's Supper in memorial, symbolic, or spiritual terms. *Vos habetis alium Spiritum quam nos,* "You are of another spirit," was his famous summation; and because Luther also had grave doubts about advancing the evangelical cause by force of arms, the great alliance projected by Zwingli and Landgrave Philip of Hesse was unachieved. Zwingli seems to have been moved from a purely memorial to a more spiritual view of the sacrament by these and other discussions; and Calvin would later teach a noncorporeal presence which was still closer to the Lutheran position. Yet the cleavage remained a basic point at issue between the Lutheran and nearly all other phases of the Protestant Reformation.

Luther and his successors would face "the floodgates of Protestantism" in Germany as well; but these experiences with radicalism only strengthened Lutherans in their conservatism. Their protest was not against the time-honored government, vestments, and liturgy of the Church; it was a reform within traditional channels, which entirely justifies the term "magisterial reformation." In Sweden even the apostolic episcopal succession remained unbroken, and in Scandinavia generally the externals of worship and church government were continued. Luther all his life denied that there was any "Lutheran" church; and the Augsburg Confession of 1530, which became the great manifesto of his evangelical cause, was one of the most remarkably irenic documents of a polemical century.

The writings of Luther and the news of his deeds soon reached far beyond the borders of Saxony, arousing intellectual and spiritual ferment in Germany, England, the Netherlands, France, Switzerland, Austria, Bohemia, and Scandinavia. In countless places unquenchable evangelical movements of reform arose, and often extremist elements carried the movement far beyond Luther's intention or desire. In other areas traditional views and powers quickly asserted themselves. Within a decade or two of the Peace of Augsburg (1555), however, churches acknowledging the Augsburg Confession had been formed in most of the provinces of Northern Germany, along the Baltic, and in Scandinavia. By 1580, when the Formula of Concord was agreed upon by many of these churches, Lutheranism had achieved something like its "classic" positions on the main disputed issues, and had established itself for the most part in the areas where it would continue to prevail for centuries despite wars of religion and continuing controversy.

THE REFORMED TRADITION

Before the pope or the emperor or even Luther had fully realized the significance of the events in Wittenberg, an almost completely independent series of Reformation events took place in Switzerland. There, as elsewhere, discontent was rife. A scandalous incident of indulgence selling, parallel to Luther's encounter with Tetzel, had occurred, and in some respects conditions were particularly acute because the Confederation itself and especially the cities within it had attained an independence which the church's diocesan arrangements did not recognize. The bishops were not only corrupt symbols of an older feudal order; they were also foreigners. Other nationalistic motives included widespread resentment against the use of Swiss mercenaries. By 1523, the magistrates of Zurich, led by their great preacher-theologian Huldreich Zwingli (1484–1531), had instituted a full-fledged purge and reform of the church. On some points Zwingli voiced the central demands of Luther, as in his denunciation of works-piety and the proclamation of justification by faith. But he went much farther: the Mass was abolished, its liturgy denounced, and frequent celebration of Holy Communion discouraged. The traditional government of the church was disallowed; and very soon, as the Zurich example took effect in the other German cantons of Switzerland and then in many parts of Germany along the Rhine, this movement assumed a characteristic theological spirit and religious temper. As it advanced into the French cantons and into France itself, it merged with other reformist impulses of humanistic spirit, and gained some of its most influential apostles. William Farel, for example, left the evangelical group at Meaux and helped to prosecute the reform in French Switzerland. The movement began to take on the main features that mark it as a distinct phase of the Reformation. In fact, the Reformed tradition was an established reality by the time John Calvin (1509–64), another French humanist, was converted to evangelical views in 1534, the year after King Francis I embarked on a positive policy of repression. Calvin became a major prophet with the publication of the first edition of his mighty *Institutes of the Christian Religion* in 1536, and he continued to imbue the Reformed movement with confidence and theological rigor. Although in many ways he sought (though largely without avail) to make that movement less radical, basically he became a part of it. For this reason it is more accurate to speak of the tradition with which he is so inseparably associated as "Reformed" rather than as "Calvinistic." The power of his words and the influence of his work is incalculable. After Geneva became his permanent home in 1541, he stands out as the chief source of energy and inspiration during the "second phase" of the Reformed tradition's development. Especially important among the new areas won during this period were Scotland and the Netherlands.

Calvin very directly influenced John Knox (c.1513–72), the man who came almost to personify the Scottish Reformation. Knox was an admiring participant in Geneva's reformation during his exile, and upon his return in 1558 he brought his native land decisively into the Reformed tradition, laying the groundwork for a system of presbyterian government which would in later years have vast influence on American church order.

In the Netherlands, the early seeds of Reformation were sown by many Augustinian canons regular who perpetuated the devotional emphasis of Gerhard Groote and Thomas a Kempis, by Lutheran writings and converts, and by considerable Anabaptist activity. Gradually, however, Reformed ideas (with much help from Calvin) came to dominate the Protestant movement. In 1571, strongly influenced by the French Reformed, the Dutch adopted the Belgic Confession prepared ten years earlier by Guy de Bres. The conversion of William the Silent in 1571 was a vital turning point for these provinces, and by 1609 they had thrown off Spanish domination and become an independent Dutch republic.

In France, too, as we have seen (chap. 4), Reformed views made considerable headway. In 1559 a synod met in Paris and took its stand upon the Gallic Confession which, like its sister confession in the Netherlands, owed much to Calvin and the Reformed tradition. The movement's growth led to fierce wars of religion and an ambiguous sort of Huguenot "victory" under Henry of Navarre, though he abjured his Protestantism in order to occupy the throne in 1589. Henry soon flouted papal desires, however, by promulgating an edict of toleration in 1598 which remained in effect until revoked by Louis XIV in 1685. There were also significant Reformed advances in Bohemia, Hungary, Austria, Poland, in the German Rhineland and, as will be indicated later, in England.

The lineaments of the Reformed outlook on God, man, society, and history have become very familiar; but both familiarity and controversy have obscured the genius and power of the movement with which Calvin's name is inseparably associated. The best clues to the animating spirit of this movement are the confessions which its leaders formulated, defended, and died for: the Heidelberg Catechism in Germany, several Helvetic confessions, the Belgic, Gallic, and old Scottish confessions, and most detailed of all, the formularies issued by the Westminster Assembly in Great Britain (1643–45). The themes that run so consistently through these great confessions and the writings of their chief expositors deserve reiteration; for they are ideas which had an enormous impact on subsequent history. For the United States they were to become a powerful culture-forming influence.

First of all, one must underline a truism and designate the notion of God's awful and absolute sovereignty as a central precept. One historian argued that this emphasis on God's eternal decrees gave theological grounds for the Puritan's disinclination even to celebrate the Festival of the Incarnation, Christmas. This goes too far, but not in the wrong direction. The majesty, power, "otherness," utter transcendence, and unknowableness of God were themes upon which Reformed thinking and meditation constantly dwelled. Early and late this austere Hebraic legacy led men away from sentimentalism, triviality, and all efforts to cajole the Almighty.

If God is sovereign, man is not. The doctrine of human depravity also stood to the fore in Reformed preaching, and with it, in all of its sharp clarity, a doctrine of "double predestination," that God in his almighty wisdom had elected some men to eternal salvation and reprobated others. Within the Reformed churches organized dissent from this strict logic did appear—notably in the School of Saumur (France), among the Arminian "Remonstrants" of the Netherlands, and, as will appear later, in Great Britain and America. In their early stages, however, even these deviationists did not move far from the central tradition. For both the strict and moderate parties, however, the doctrine of assurance—how to know if one is among the Elect—became increasingly important. In this way the doctrine of predestination portended much, both in theory and in practice, for the future history of religious "enthusiasm." Men could not help speculating on the signs of election, nor could they help being tempted to conceive of the church as constituted by those who bore those signs. The experience of regeneration or of "God's effectual call" necessarily took on earthshaking significance. In many ways the various national or territorial "Reformed" churches were as "magisterial" as those of the Lutherans; but in their aroused concern for designating the Saints, or Elect of God, they share a vital trait with many of the "Radical" reformers soon to be discussed.

The third characteristic or theme also flows from the doctrines of divine sovereignty and human depravity, namely, the intense concern of Reformed theology for God's revealed Law. First and most obviously, this concern was applied to churchly matters. It was rarely if ever doubted that the Scriptures provide authoritative direction for the church with respect to doctrine, discipline, and worship. The visible Church, in other words, was literally "re-formed" or reconstituted according to biblical prescription, the *jus divinum*. All the rites, offices, and ceremonies that were not explicitly provided for in the Bible were prohibited, including "profane" hymnody and instrumental or polyphonic music and even great festivals like Christmas. The Sabbath, on the other hand, came to be observed with almost Judaic austerity and legalistic rigor. As in so many other cases, Calvin himself counseled moderation in the application of such reasoning; but he was by no means successful in preventing the rise of extreme legalism in the Reformed tradition.

God's Law also regulated personal behavior. Reformed theologians dissented vigorously from Lutherans and insisted that the Law was an explicit guide to human morality. They held (in the famous phrase) to the *tertius usus legis,* the third use of the Law: that it was a teacher. In this traditional formulation the first use of the Law was to proclaim God as the Creator of the universe; in this context the law in all its forms, but especially as enforced by governments, keeps the sinful proclivities of men in check. The second use was to judge man by laying bare the deficiencies of his faith and conduct, and to bring him to repentance and humility.

This emphasis on the Law led to a fourth feature of Reformed theology, one which Puritanism would make highly consequential in America. Reformed theologians—like most Christian thinkers of the time—felt that the Church and the world, Christ and culture, existed in a tension-filled relationship. Church and world were not at odds, but neither was to be dominated by the other. Yet within this consensus Reformed thinkers to a remarkable degree regarded the world as amenable to Christian control and discipline. Even though culture was understood to be fallen, perverted, and opposed to Christ, it could be shaped and regulated—or "converted," to use the term H. Richard Niebuhr has employed in his profound analysis *Christ and Culture* (1951). Reformed leaders were thus exceedingly optimistic in their plans for reorganizing society and institutions according to their understanding of God's law. Indeed, they were made strong in their purposes by the belief that they were but instruments in God's plan for reordering human society. When coupled with the insistence that monasticism had no legitimate place in the world, and that every Christian had a calling (*vocatio*) to service and work in the world rather than to withdraw from it, this doctrine provided a sure basis for that austere "this-worldly asceticism" which devoted Reformed communities have demonstrated the world over.

A final and inclusive way in which the Law assumed a distinctive place in the Reformed tradition was through its enlivening of an Old Testament world view. The most tangible evidence of this tendency is the frequency with which Reformed adherents named their children after Israel's heroes.

But of all the aspects of this Old Testament attitude, none would have more momentous consequences (for America especially) than the Puritan determination to make God's revealed Law and the historical example of Israel an explicit basis for ordering the affairs of men in this world, and their conviction that this could be done to God's glory by specific colonial commonwealths or even by an entire nation.

THE RADICAL REFORMATION

Christian radicalism, of course, is as old as the Church. The gospel is a radical message. Saint Paul was already dealing with "radical" tendencies in his letters to the Corinthians. And a long succession of often very strong heretical movements testify to the continuing tension between the world and the faith of the Christian Church. Radicalism is premodern even if we define it so as to include only those protests against compromise, acculturation, and institutionalization which become "sectarian" in form. During its first three centuries, the Church often heard demands that it be purged of all but the visible saints, that it eschew all that is formal and objective in worship, or that it establish itself as a perfectionist community withdrawn from the world. In the Middle Ages much of this potential radicalism was channeled into the monastic and mendicant orders and the lay brotherhoods associated with or similar to them. There were also signs of it among the Waldensians, the Lollards of England, and the Hussites. But in the age of the Reformation there was a mighty and immensely diversified resurgence of such radicalism. So mighty was the popular resurgence, in fact, that both rulers and spiritual leaders of the "magisterial reformation" (whether Lutheran or Reformed) feared that the "left wing" would take over. Luther rushed back to Wittenberg from his hiding place in the Wartburg to deal with the excesses of Carlstadt. And as other radical movements arose, Zwingli and Calvin showed similar fears about the Swiss Anabaptists. In Austria, the Lowlands, and around Strasbourg apprehension and controversy rose to a higher pitch. At times this radicalism in religion was accompanied by revolutionary violence, as in the Peasants' Revolt (1524) and in the seizure of the city of Münster (1534). Such actions provoked both secular repression and churchly anathemas.

In spite of persecution and polemics, however, several enduring radical movements emerged, at least three of which are perpetuated in America. One of these, the least organized, consisted of "spiritual reformers," the free spirits in every land, but especially in Spain, France, and Germany, who together constituted an almost subterranean mystical tradition. Rejecting the world and its demands, recoiling from the objectivity of formal worship, forsaking objective scriptural interpretation, living in the tradition of earlier mystics, they emphasized the primacy of spirit and the Christlike life. Kaspar Schwenkfeld (1489–1561) was one of these persecuted wanderers; and some of his followers, the "confessors of the Glory of Christ," were one day to seek refuge in Pennsylvania. Erasmus himself has been placed in this category, and there were many others, some of them highly sophisticated expositors of spiritual religion, others simpler advocates of inner peace and moral self-discipline.

More rationalistic in character were the antitrinitarians, best organized in the Socinian movements of Poland and Transylvania, but probably best remembered through the adventurous thought, and martyrdom in Calvin's Geneva, of Michel Servetus. The connection between these movements and the latter-day Unitarians of Boston would be largely sentimental, but the rationalistic tendency which they represent was to be of continuing significance during the intervening centuries.

The most widespread form of radicalism was the composite movement which included the true "Anabaptists"—those widely separated yet interrelated efforts to restore or revive the primitive Church according to the biblical pattern. Their profoundest wish was to gather a visible church of true Christians; yet their search for an adequate understanding of what form this "true Church" might take was almost as tortuous as efforts of later historians to penetrate the polemical histories of their enemies. Gradually, however, certain more or less distinct movements defined themselves despite strong centrifugal tendencies: the Swiss Brethren on whose development Conrad Grebel and Balthasar Hübmaier had much influence; the harried and wandering Hutterites whom Jacob Hutter molded into an enduring community that was at once church and *societas economica;* and the Mennonites, the largest body to survive, comprising the followers of Menno Simons of the Netherlands, whose preaching led to the foundation of many small congregations in his homeland, in northern Germany, Alsace, and elsewhere.

Unity was something that these Anabaptist groups never achieved, and it is doubtful that even the absence of persecution would have improved matters in this regard. They are nevertheless united by certain persistent convictions; above all, by the desire to reconstitute the Church as a community of earnest believers whose conversion had been sealed by adult baptism (they rebaptized, hence Anabaptist). Behind this lay their protest against state churches and their insistence that the Church as a whole had "fallen" when it entered into cooperation with rulers, identifying itself with whole peoples regardless of their personal dedication. Almost universally these Anabaptists were pacifists; personal uprightness and charitableness were the constant conditions of good standing in their churches. Their frequent refusal to deal with governments meant that invariably they experienced an enormous tension with the world of magistrates and economics. These traits drove them toward a communitarianism which was at times almost tantamount to a new noncelibate monasticism. They are best known in contemporary America as devout and sequestered communities, archaic, simple, and prosperous.

Many of the principles for which Anabaptists struggled and testified would be realized in America, above all the separation of church and state. This American tradition, however, probably owes far more to the simple fact of religious pluralism than to these harried underground churches. What the sixteenth-century radicals most relevantly manifested was the dynamic fertility of the European religious consciousness during Reformation times. They reveal with special clarity the kind of internal logic that seemed to press the reforming spirit into all social classes and out across the whole possible spectrum of theological and ecclesiastical solution.

In due season, virtually every aspect of the Continental Reformation which has here been touched upon, and many variations that have not even been mentioned, would find their place on American soil. In later chapters these events will be dealt with to such lengths as space will allow. For the present, however, it is imperative to consider more directly the way in which the Reformation was being carried out in Great Britain. From this realm would come the colonial impulses—imperial, commercial, and evangelistic—which would form the chief foundations—political, economic, and religious—of the American tradition.

6

THE REFORMATION IN GREAT BRITAIN AND THE AGE OF PURITANISM

With Richard III dead on Bosworth Field and the army of the house of York in flight, the victorious Henry Tudor, earl of Richmond, had England's royal crown set upon his head. This was 21 August 1485. All England hoped that the long turbulence of the War of the Roses was over, and Parliament authenticated the universal desire for peace, stability, and orderly government by validating the victor's claim to reign. In November he was officially crowned as Henry VII, and four months later, as if to concede the arrival of a new day, the archbishop of Canterbury died. Ecclesiastical affairs continued in their normal course for a while, but a turning point in the history of the English church had been passed. During the next half-century, England would become capable of a world-historical role that one could hardly have expected in 1485.

THE REFORMATION IN GREAT BRITAIN

The Reign of Henry VIII, 1509–47

When Henry VII died in 1509, his energetic and brilliant son inherited a remarkably consolidated nation. Of serious rivals for the crown there were none; the feuds of Lancaster and York were past, domestic peace was sure, prosperity beckoned. Of great moment for the future of the church, governmental authority had been centralized to a remarkable degree. What his father had begun, Henry VIII continued, aided by the incomparable

Thomas Cardinal Wolsey, lord chancellor, archbishop of York, and papal legate with authority over the whole English clergy. Wolsey's ability and zeal were equal to the authority given him by the king, and his pride matched his power. On the other hand, his diplomatic failures and military involvements on the Continent caused fiscal difficulties and aroused popular animosity which were ultimately his undoing. Yet his self-assertiveness had one far-reaching result: he taught his monarch how to manipulate the church. This lesson proved helpful in 1527 when Henry determined to seek a divorce from Catherine of Aragon, his brother's widow, whom he had married after receiving a papal dispensation. Even the cardinal was forced to bow to the royal will. Wolsey, failing to obtain papal sanction for the divorce after two years of negotiations, was stripped of power, accused of treason, and summoned for trial. He died while en route to London, but his enormous unpopularity was turned to the king's advantage.

Pope Clement VII at the time was a virtual prisoner of Charles V, Holy Roman emperor and nephew of Catherine; thus he had neither the inclination nor the ability to grant Henry's wish. The king decided to take matters into his own hands, and in a swift series of royal and parliamentary acts, England's ties with the papacy were cut, one by one. By 1531 the clergy had been cowed into accepting the king as "Singular Protector, only Supreme Lord, and, as far as the law of Christ allows, even Supreme Head" of the church in England. This was followed, without the qualifying reservation, by the famous Act of Supremacy in 1534. "Thus in the course of a few years Henry had carried through a major revolution . . . [in which] the Church of England had played little part. . . . It is, therefore, no exaggeration to say that the English Reformation, at any rate in its earlier stages, was 'a parliamentary transaction,' or an 'act of state.' "[1]

The same could be said for the king's next series of moves. By 1539 England's entire monastic establishment was liquidated, its vast lands transferred to lay owners, its inmates scattered, and its buildings left to moulder. This was done for money or favor, without reforming fervor or theological justification; yet so thoroughly had the institution decayed or outlived its usefulness that not even the monks and friars offered serious resistance or manifested much concern for their vows, though at least three abbots were hanged for resisting the crown's action. People and Parliament seemed, in general, to have accepted the deed without protest.

When Henry died in 1547, the English church presented the most anomalous state of affairs in the Christian world. An enormous revolution had

1. John R. H. Moorman, *A History of the Church in England*, pp. 168–69. He in turn quotes F. M. Powicke, *The Reformation in England*, pp. 1, 38.

been accomplished; nearly nine hundred years of undisputed papal authority had been overthrown and the entire edifice of medieval monasticism spoliated. Yet doctrine was for the most part unchanged, popular piety was relatively undisturbed, and parish life went on much as before. Despite earlier signs of opportunism and vacillation, the traditional faith and order of medieval Catholicism were perpetuated by the Six Articles of 1539 and the King's Book of 1543.

But England had not been insulated from the Continental Reformation. At Cambridge Luther's writings were already stirring Thomas Cranmer and the circle of future bishops who had counseled Henry on his marital problems in 1529. Henry VIII himself had won a papal title as Defender of the Faith for an anti-Lutheran polemic. In later years, however, the king contemplated a league with the Protestant princes of Germany, and with this end in mind he and his theological counselors came close to signing the Wittenberg Articles in 1538. The Ten Articles of 1536 also exhibit definite Reformation influences. Vernacular translations of the Bible, certain to be a potent force in the nation's religious life, were beginning to circulate: and although the version of Tyndale was suppressed, the Coverdale and Rogers versions were licensed and the "Great Bible," a somewhat more tradition-minded version of "Matthew's Bible," was published by royal order in 1539.[2] Cranmer, who had become archbishop of Canterbury in 1533, was advocating plans for liturgical reform, and he succeeded in translating a great litany into English before Henry's death. The king had also put his son under Protestant tutelage.

The Reign of Edward VI, 1547–53

The son of Henry VIII and Jane Seymour was a frail lad of nine years when he came to the throne. Having received a Protestant education, he was hailed by some as a new Josiah to purify the Temple of its idolatries. In view of his minority, however, the real responsibility of ruling devolved upon two successive regents, both of whom were chiefly motivated by political and economic considerations. The king's uncle, Edward Seymour, duke of Somerset, was protector from 1547 to 1549 and permitted moderate reforms; he was displaced by John Dudley, earl of Warwick and duke of Northumberland, who encouraged far more radical religious policies. Thus during the brief reign of Edward VI, the nation moved many long strides down the road to reformation—though often by legislative fiat no more popular or churchly than Henry's enactments.

Gradually, however, Protestant influence began to deepen and become

2. On English versions of the Bible see n. 9 below.

more pervasive. Lutheran refugees from the Augsburg Interim (1548) were welcomed, while brilliant and forceful Reformed theologians became professors in Oxford and Cambridge. Among the latter were Peter Martyr Vermigli, a former Capuchin, now a distinguished Reformed theologian, Martin Butzer, the reformer of Strasbourg, and John à Lasco, an influential Polish Protestant. Moreover, an energetic and capable group of "Henrician exiles" were back at work in the English church after instructive sojourns in Reformed centers during the previous king's final reactionary period. Under these several influences and with the hearty cooperation of the archbishop, the protectors, and Parliament, new and far more drastic reforming acts were passed. In 1549 and 1552 new prayer books were prepared and enforced by Acts of Uniformity. In 1553 the Forty-two Articles of Religion were issued; and they, like the latter prayer book, revealed a decided influence from the Reformed tradition. Although subscribing to the common Reformation doctrines, Cranmer tended toward Reformed formulations, most notably perhaps with regard to predestination and on the crucial Eucharistic issue which divided Lutherans and Reformed. He moved steadily in the direction of those views of the Eucharist advocated by Tyndale, Rogers, Hooper, and many other English reformers of the time.

Edward died three weeks after signing the Forty-two Articles, but by that time the form and spirit of the English church, as well as a whole range of externals, had been massively altered. While early Lutheran influences remained visible and important in the prayer book and English Bibles in general, Lutheran conservatism and Luther's distinctive theological emphases—especially on law and gospel—yielded to the more radical attitudes of the Reformed tradition, particularly to the evangelical reformulation expounded by Zwingli and Bullinger in Zurich, Oecolampadius in Basel, and other Rhineland reformers. To a surprising degree the theological groundwork for later English Puritanism, including its emphasis on the covenant, was laid during these years. In the same spirit, action was taken to forbid many traditional practices and ceremonies and to destroy "popish" vestments, ornamentation, and church furnishings. Indeed, John Hooper, bishop of Gloucester during these years, has been justifiably named the "father" of Puritanism. The transformation wrought under these auspices, however, was accompanied by surprisingly little overt resistance—evidence that the reforms were still lacking in depth or popular appropriation.

The Reign of Mary, 1553–58

Nothing indicates the superficiality of the Edwardian reforms so well as the astonishing enthusiasm with which the fervently Roman Catholic Mary

Tudor, half sister of Edward, was welcomed to the throne, and the ease with which she persuaded Parliament to repeal nearly all of the church legislation of the previous two regimes. The only surviving child of Catherine of Aragon by Henry VIII, she felt compelled to reverse insofar as possible the national apostasy which had begun with the illegal and unholy divorce of her parents. Had Mary sought only to return to the compromise which Henry VIII tried to achieve, she might have been successful; but nothing less than a complete purge of Protestants and a full return to Rome would suit her.

In 1554–55 the Protestant bishops Hugh Latimer, Nicholas Ridley, and John Hooper were burned at the stake. The next year Archbishop Cranmer suffered a similar fate, while Cardinal Reginald Pole (who as papal legate had absolved the nation and readmitted it to the Catholic fold) was consecrated as his successor on the very next day. Three hundred others, immortalized in John Foxe's *Book of Martyrs,* "made their sad way out to face the fires of Smithfield," led by the protomartyr John Rogers, editor of the pseudonymous "Matthew's Bible" of 1537.

Popular displeasure mounted. Yet even the reconciliation with Rome (1555) might possibly have been accepted had not Mary already sealed her doom by marrying Philip II of Spain (12 January 1554), and then by becoming deeply involved in Continental military ventures that brought defeat and humiliation to the nation. The almost simultaneous death of the harassed queen and her archbishop in November 1558 seemed like a decisive stroke of providence.

The Reign of Elizabeth, 1558–1603

The daughter of Henry and Anne Boleyn—untested but surely Protestant—succeeded to the throne. English Protestants who had been nursing their sorrow in exile on the Continent or in quiet seclusion at home waited hopefully to see what the new sovereign would do. Her decision, however, was gauged to give unqualified satisfaction to no one.

> Her father may be said to have seized the church. Her brother and sister before her had in contrary ways and with unhappy results tried to reform it. She perceived that she must govern it or be ruined. . . . What she chiefly wanted, after all, was to be queen of England and live. She had the common sense to know that her people would permit her to do this provided they also were permitted to live and go about their accustomed affairs with as little interference as might be. So, without troubling to be either logical or zealous, she made herself safe. . . .

The only religious test she unfailingly insisted upon was willingness to swear allegiance to herself as the church's governor.[3]

The queen's determination to ensure the institutional continuity of the Church of England was indicated by her provision for an apostolic episcopacy. She appointed Matthew Parker, who had been ordained to the priesthood before the break with Rome (1527), as archbishop of Canterbury in 1559.[4] The principles which underlay Elizabeth's policy of comprehension and accommodation were documented in two acts of Parliament passed the same year. The Act of Supremacy designated her as the "supreme governor" of England's church and provided an oath to be subscribed by the clergy. The Act of Uniformity reinstituted a significantly moderated version of the second Edwardian prayer book (1552). The publication of a full doctrinal statement was delayed until 1563, and not until after she had been excommunicated by the pope was subscription to it made compulsory for all the clergy (1571). The Thirty-nine Articles of Religion as then promulgated were based on the Forty-two Articles of 1553, and they have never been substantially revised.

The spirit and meaning of the Elizabethan Settlement is apparent when one examines the Book of Common Prayer and the Articles of Religion. Both are clearly aimed at maximum inclusiveness within the limits of uniformity and loyalty, yet both show the continuing appeal of the influences which had been operating at the time of their formulation during the closing years of Edward's reign. The Thirty-nine Articles naturally show more doctrinal precision than the prayer book, and they indicate the immense degree to which the Reformed tradition had made its mark on the leading English divines of the Edwardian and Elizabethan periods. They are moderate, to be sure; considerable evidence of Lutheran influence remains, and at important points they are purposely vague. But it is not accidental that precise Puritan theologians like Increase Mather would at a later day find them "substantially consonant" with the rigorous doctrines of the Westminster Confession. In Elizabeth's day, however, and far more explicitly since, they were understood as an historical document rather than as a church confession, as something not to be contradicted rather than as an exposition of the church's faith.

3. William Haller, *The Rise of Puritanism*, pp. 6–7.

4. The Roman Catholic historian Philip Hughes would refer to the English bishops as a "self-consecrated hierarchy of heretics" (*A Popular History of the Catholic Church* [New York: Macmillan Co., 1951], p. 251), and Pope Leo XIII declared Anglican orders null and void in 1896; but Queen Elizabeth was excommunicated in 1570 by Pope Pius V. Matthew Parker, her first archbishop of Canterbury, had been consecrated by four bishops, two of whom had been consecrated in the reign of Henry VIII under the old order.

The Book of Common Prayer, both under Elizabeth and throughout the subsequent history of the Anglican communion, has been infinitely more powerful in its influence. Quite appropriately it served as the virtual standard of doctrine in the decade preceding the promulgation of the Articles of Religion in 1571. It is by far the greatest and most lasting monument of the early Tudor phase of the English Reformation. It garners an immense wealth of the church's liturgical treasures from English medieval, Eastern, and Lutheran traditions and renders it in an English that only the strictest Puritans could resist. The rich stamp of Cranmer's ecumenical genius remains on every page. At the same time, his sacramental doctrine is retained, along with many of the sharply Reformed features of the 1552 version, with the result that in some ways it is far more Protestant than Henry VIII would have expected, more so than many of the contemporary Lutheran liturgies. Stately in language, scriptural in quality and in much of its substance, it endeared itself to generation after generation, becoming in time the quintessential expression of Anglicanism.

Undoubtedly the Reformed spirit of the Elizabethan Settlement would have been less marked if the Queen and her immediate advisers had prevailed. But in 1559 a vigorous and numerous reforming party was already in existence, whose demands not only could not be ignored, but whose loyalty was urgently needed on account of the European political situation. At the convocation of 1562–63 these "Puritans" very nearly gained control. But even when frustrated in their more extreme efforts, they were grateful to have a defender of the Protestant cause as queen, and they tempered their demands accordingly. With Continental Protestantism in confusion, Good Queen Bess was, after all, the very palladium of the Reformation's stand against the resurgent Roman host. She gave purpose, focus, and even glamor "to the fresh ideology of that age—Protestantism." [5] During the reigns of her Stuart successors her accession on 17 November was remembered as a "birthday of the gospel," and for Puritans and other opposition elements its anniversaries became a rally day.

THE AGE OF PURITANISM

The great "second phase" of the English Reformation, stretching from the accession of Elizabeth to the Restoration of Charles II (or perhaps to the Glorious Revolution), may be justly designated the "Puritan Century."

5. Sir John E. Neale, "England's Elizabeth" (Paper delivered on the Fourth Centenary of the Accession of Queen Elizabeth I, Folger Shakespeare Library, Washington, D.C., 17 November 1958), pp. 2–8.

From the standpoint of America, the reforming movement which sharpened the religious issues of the age is so important that its nature and aims will receive more extended discussion in a later chapter (chap. 8). For the present its place in England's church history can be only briefly suggested.

Characteristics of Puritanism

Puritanism in its very vital negative aspect has been defined by Professor G. M. Trevelyan as "the religion of those who wished either to 'purify' the usage of the Established Church from the taint of Papacy, or to worship separately by forms so 'purified.' "[6] Its affirmations are inevitably more important, however, though more easily ignored. Puritans, like devoted Christians in every age, were first of all determined to conform the Church Militant to their understanding of the fact that man's redemption is of God in Christ. With remarkable intensity they focused their reformatory zeal in Alan Simpson's excellent phrases, on what they deemed to be two kinds of wickedness, that of people who appeared to be "living without any benefit of religion" and those "who had embraced the wrong religion."[7] They sought not only to "purify" England's religion, but to revive it. The peculiar power and distinctive witness of the Puritans are explained by their adherence to Reformed theology in the midst of a situation where centuries of spiritual decline and decades of political and ecclesiastical upheaval had left both clergy and laity alike, in almost every sense of the term, unreformed, and where the established institutional and liturgical forms impeded their program for renewal of the church.

The negative as well as the positive convictions which they held had been brought to England first by fugitive tracts and books, then by living emissaries like Martin Butzer and Peter Martyr; these influences in turn were constantly reinformed by a stream of letters and other writings from the Continental reformers—most prominent of which were Heinrich Bullinger's *Decades* and, later, John Calvin's masterful *Institutes of the Christian Religion*. In this way those who came to be known as Puritans drew upon a firm tradition of English Protestantism that had been established during the reigns of Henry and Edward. The returning Marian exiles, most of whom had taken refuge in Reformed strongholds on the Continent, added their passionate testimony to the chorus.[8] To encourage still others there

6. George M. Trevelyan, *England under the Stuarts*, 16th ed. (London: Methuen and Co., 1933), pp. 60–71.

7. Alan Simpson, *Puritanism in Old and New England*, p. 7.

8. Miles Coverdale (1488–1568), famed as a translator of the Bible but also a strenuous Puritan, was back from his third exile. He fled first in the days before the Act of Supremacy, next during Henry's period of reaction, and finally under Mary. Between 1551 and 1553 he was bishop of Exeter.

was the example of Scotland, where John Knox—come straight from Geneva—had so successfully challenged the "monstrous regiment of women" and by 1560 made over the Kirk of Scotland along presbyterial lines.

The growing influence of the Bible served to increase popular dissatisfaction with England's religious situation. In fact, Holy Scripture was both the practical and the theoretical fountainhead of the movement. Among the clergy scriptural study completely renovated the role and method of theological inquiry, while among the people it created a vast hunger for evangelical preaching. Puritanism was a "movement of the Book" among an increasingly literate people, and an essential accompaniment of its expansion was the publishing of popular versions of the Bible. The earliest of these was the Geneva Version of 1560, with its highly provocative yet immensely instructive marginal notes.[9]

The Growth of Puritanism

The first solid impact of the Puritan movement was felt during the days when the Elizabethan Settlement was being hammered out. Its theological leader at that time was Thomas Cartwright, a professor at Cambridge for whom presbyterianism was the only lawful, scriptural church polity, and who saw in Geneva or Scotland the proper model of a Christian establish-

9. The first English effort to render the Scriptures in the vernacular was that of John Wycliffe (1380), a translation of the Latin Vulgate. William Tyndale's translation from Erasmus's Greek text was printed surreptitiously in Antwerp and distributed in England after 1526. The first complete Bible in English was done by Miles Coverdale in 1535 with considerable indebtedness to Tyndale and Luther; it included the intertestamentary "apocryphal" books. John Rogers issued in 1537 a translation based on the work of Tyndale and Coverdale which was printed under the pseudonym "Matthew," and hence called "Matthew's Bible." A recension of this by Richard Tavener appeared in 1539. The "Great Bible" of 1539 was the first Bible to be specifically prescribed for use in the churches of England. It, too, was virtually a reissue of Matthew's Bible, edited by Coverdale. The second and later editions bore a preface by Archbishop Cranmer commending its use. This is the version quoted in the Book of Common Prayer.

The Geneva Bible (1560) was the work of several Marian exiles, including Coverdale. Its numbered verses, lucid prose, improved scholarship, extensive prologues, and marginal notes gave it wide popularity. It was authorized for use in Scotland, and until superseded by the King James Version, it was the most widely distributed English Bible. The "Bishop's Bible," a revision of the Great Bible supervised by Archbishop Parker and carried out by him, his fellow bishops, and a few other scholars who later became bishops, appeared in 1568, but it was never widely accepted in either churches or households. The Douai-Rheims Bible (N. T., 1582; O. T., 1609–10) was translated by exiled Roman Catholics for use in England; as revised from time to time it has remained a standard Roman Catholic Bible in England.

The version which captured the hearts and minds of English speaking non-Catholics for three centuries is, of course, the one authorized by King James in 1604—his sole positive response to the many complaints brought by churchmen and theologians to the Hampton Court Conference of that year. The king himself paid close attention to the work, and the translation was accomplished by forty-seven men drawn from the best scholars of the day. It was first issued in 1611. See F. F. Bruce, *The English Bible, A History of Translations* (New York: Oxford University Press, 1961).

ment. Among all but the most zealous of these early reformers, however, there was little inclination to become "separatistic" or openly disloyal; most Puritans were willing to "tarry for the magistrate." They would even follow Calvin's counsel to accept the traditional episcopate when it did not hinder truth. Only later in Elizabeth's reign were there any sizable groups advocating "reformation without tarrying for anie"—in Robert Browne's famous phrase (1582).

During the reign of James I (1603–25), who as King James VI of Scotland had developed a jaundiced view of presbyterianism, royal opposition to Puritanism became increasingly overt. Among Puritans, therefore, the grounds for hope and the willingness to tarry became appreciably less. One indication of the declining optimism about national reformation was the gradual rise of increasingly congregational ways of thinking. This trend was evident even among the great theologians and preachers who had made Cambridge University, and especially Emmanuel College, a nursery of Puritanism. The sense of estrangement deepened as James's political behavior became more autocratic and as he showed increasing solicitude for religious spokesmen and leaders of the Arminian, less strictly Reformed, more ritualistic type. Even then, however, the majority resisted separatism. John Foxe and others had imbued them with the conviction that England was an "Elect Nation" destined to save the Reformation; and they still hoped for some circumstance by which church and state could be bound together in a single polity and a single confession of faith. Despite the unfavorable shift of ecclesiastical power, those who yearned for a more complete purification could sustain their hope so long as the see of Canterbury was occupied by men such as Parker, Grindal, Whitgift, Bancroft, and Abbot—these men were all Calvinists, and to a degree Puritans also.

In 1625, however, Charles I took the throne, and also took to himself a Roman Catholic queen; worse still, he showed marked favoritism to a new party in the church which was both "Armininian" and dogmatically "prelatical." Charles made the leader of that party, Bishop William Laud of London, one of his most trusted advisers, and in 1633 appointed him archbishop of Canterbury. Coupled with the king's high-handed dealings with Parliament and his weak foreign policy in the face of the growing power of Roman Catholic France, these policies began to dim Puritan hopes for England's future. As a consequnce the more dogmatic and especially the more congregationally inclined among them began in ever larger numbers to despair of root and branch reform. Singly or in groups some fled to Holland. Then, during the decade of the 1630s, the great Puritan migration to America took place.

When the "swarming of the Puritans" ceased, it was largely due to the fact that in 1640, after the failure of Charles and Laud's schemes for subjugating Scotland, the Long Parliament met with the antiprelatical party in the ascendancy. Episcopacy was abolished and plans for a Puritan reformation of the Church of England were carried forward with vigor. An assembly of divines was summoned to prepare a blueprint for the new establishment. To gain Scottish support the antiprelatic Solemn League and Covenant was pressed upon the English nation, and Scottish commissioners were added to the assembly. A strictly Reformed *Directory of Worship* was prepared and enacted by Parliament; a presbyterian form of church government was prescribed and partially enacted. Archbishop Laud having been executed, the assembly proceeded to formulate its famous confession, and then the larger and shorter catechisms which were adopted by the General Assembly of the Church of Scotland and, in slightly modified form, by Parliament, with the subscription of over two-thirds of England's beneficed clergy.

Taken together, these Westminster standards constitute one of the classic formulations of Reformed theology. That so many learned and contentious men in an age of so much theological hair-splitting could with so little coercion establish so resounding a consensus on so detailed a doctrinal statement is one of the marvels of the century. Nor were these formulations forgotten amid wars and violence; they remain normative in Scotland and their immense influence on the thought and practice of American Congregationalists, Presbyterians, and Baptists makes them by far the most important confessional witness in American colonial history. Insusceptible to easy or brief summary, they and the derivative confessions deserve close attention from any student of early American Protestantism. Westminster is the pinnacle confession of Reformed scholasticism of the strict predestinarian covenant school.

Westminster notwithstanding, more radical tendencies in religion soon emerged, especially in the Parliamentary army. After the execution of the king in 1649 and Oliver Cromwell's assumption of political authority, congregational "Independency" and other far more extreme groups flourished. Baptists grew in number, and left-wing sectarian movements proliferated. Toleration was soon seen as the only viable solution. To mark off their position in this turbulent scene, the Independent divines met at the Savoy Palace in 1658 to formulate the Savoy Declaration, affirming congregational principles of church order but otherwise following Westminster very closely. But by then the lord protector was dead; and in the chaos that followed, it was less than two years before Presbyterians cooperated with the episcopal party to restore Charles II and the traditional church order.

The Puritans in their time of triumph had proved unable to provide peace, order, and stability, or to gain popular support and sympathy.

The restored church was Laudian without apology or mercy; compromise and accommodation were forsworn. Successive acts of uniformity and restoration were enacted. For Puritans of all types, the Great Persecution began on Saint Bartholomew's Day 1662, when two thousand nonconforming clergymen were deprived of their livings. For Presbyterians, Congregationalists, Baptists, and Quakers—not to mention Roman Catholics and Unitarians—social inequality, imprisonment, and legal harassment became the order of the day.

Puritan nonconformity had become dissent, and the tradition continued to show considerable vitality in several ways quite apart from American developments. An immense spiritual treasure was conveyed to the whole Christian world through an entire library of devotional literature. John Bunyan's *Pilgrim's Progress,* the most widely read of Puritan classics, was produced during the Baptist author's twelve-year stint in Bedford jail. Other popular works included Richard Baxter's *Saint's Everlasting Rest* (1650), then Philip Doddridge's *Rise and Progress of Religion in the Soul* (1745) and the hymns of Isaac Watts. Even later, when Puritanism as an integrated theology, way of life, and intellectual movement had passed out of existence, Puritan morality would make a deep mark on both the established church and the wider ranges of English life. One historian has designated the decades before and after 1700 as a time of "moral revolution." [10] Puritanism's legacy figured strongly in the organized activities of that period and in eighteenth-century political thought.

The New Anglicanism

No less certainly forged on the anvil of the Puritan century, however, was "normative Anglicanism," which came properly into its own and took its distinctive and enduring shape during the period between 1660 and 1690. Between Henry's Act of Supremacy and the Restoration the religious travail of England had turned upon one many-faceted problem: What should Anglicanism be? What form should the church of the English nation be given? With the coming of the Stuarts to England's throne, the further question of Scotland's church was added. The Restoration settled the basic issue. Scotland was allowed to go its way with a Presbyterian church, though "Anglicanism" survived there as a form of recognized dissent. In England, however, episcopacy won the day, due to the determined efforts of a fairly small group of Cromwellian exiles led by Edward Hyde

10. Dudley Bahlman, *The Moral Revolution* (New Haven: Yale University Press, 1957).

(Lord Clarendon), who until 1667 at least did more than any other statesman to steer the course of England's restored monarchy and restored church. The Glorious Revolution of 1688–89 modified the harsher lineaments of this settlement, but the Anglicanism which emerged from these struggles became normative during the centuries which followed.

Several elements or tendencies vied for centrality in this "new" Anglicanism. One was the idea of continuity with England's Catholic past, the determination to retain traditional forms of the ministry and the ancient diocesan government of the church. Another was a preference for the liturgical forms enshrined in the Book of Common Prayer substantially according to its Elizabethan revision, though some six hundred minor changes were made. Both of these factors ensured a strong link between church and state. Since the Thirty-nine Articles were also retained, the Reformation heritage of the church with its strong biblical or evangelical emphasis was preserved. Most decisively, however, the idea of a comprehensive church as it had been affirmed by King Henry, Archbishop Laud, *and* the Westminster Assembly was abandoned. The existence of other Christian communions in the United Kingdom was recognized. Indeed, the expulsion of Nonconformists created "Dissenting churches" which after 1689 were given a measure of toleration. The idea of Christian "denominationalism" as it had been formulated by a few of the congregational "dissenting brethren" at Westminster was thus given a kind of official recognition.

In theology "Anglicanism," though still defiantly anti-Roman and much influenced by Puritan moral attitudes, became pronouncedly anti-Calvinistic, Arminian, and rationalistic. In this way certain not always entirely compatible elements of England's long Reformation experience were retrospectively appropriated as "Anglican," while others were extruded. Especially appreciated were Cranmer's liturgical reforms, the King James Version of the Bible, Richard Hooker's views on polity, law, reason, and tradition, the irenic rationalism of the Cambridge Platonists, and the preaching tradition and forms of piety associated with George Herbert, Lancelot Andrewes, Jeremy Taylor, and other kindred spirits. Within strict institutional limits "normative Anglicanism" was by nature broad, undogmatic, and, as time would shortly reveal, extremely open to the new currents of "reasonableness" associated with John Locke and the Enlightenment.

The reign of Charles II (1660–85) was religiously ambiguous, in that "Anglicanism" was firmly established and enforced despite the prevailing laxity in public morals. For Puritans and Roman Catholics it was a time of persecution, as the king's solicitude for the latter was harshly countered by Parliament. Charles II was received into the Roman Catholic church in his last hours, and his brother and successor, James II (1685–88), was avowedly a Catholic. He remained "governor" of the Church of England, and like his brother, he sought unsuccessfully to win toleration for both Dissenters and Roman Catholics. Unpopular in any event, he was forced in the brief Glorious Revolution to flee the realm and thus make way for Parliament's settlement of the crown on his Protestant daughter, Mary, and her Dutch Reformed consort, William of Orange. Nonjuring Anglicans who refused to swear a new oath of loyalty, including four hundred clergy, six bishops, and the archbishop of Canterbury, were deprived, and in due course they were replaced by men more agreeable to the "revolution." The Bill of Rights as well as a toleration act was passed in 1689. Non-Anglicans continued to suffer many humiliating disabilities and inequities, but England moved into a new and clearly postreformation phase of its history with Parliament greatly enhanced in its authority and as an officially Protestant country.

In retrospect, the impact of the Puritan century on English civilization is incalculable. R. H. Tawney's judgment on this point is not exaggerated:

> The growth, triumph and transformation of the Puritan spirit was the most fundamental movement of the seventeenth century. Puritanism, not the Tudor secession from Rome, was the true English Reformation, and it is from its struggle against the old order that an England which is unmistakably modern emerges. But, immense as were its accomplishments on the higher stage of public affairs, its achievements in that inner world, of which politics are but the squalid scaffolding, were mightier still. . . . The revolution which Puritanism wrought in Church and State was less than that which it worked in men's souls, and the watchwords which it thundered, amid the hum of Parliaments and the roar of battles, had been learned in the lonely nights, when Jacob wrestled with the angel of the Lord to wring a blessing before he fled.[11]

What is true for England applies equally to America. By the most remarkable happenstance, almost the entire spectrum into which Christian life and thought were refracted by the tumultuous English Reformation was recapitulated in the American colonies. Sometimes the circumstances were strangely reversed, with Quakers dominant in Pennsylvania, Roman Catholics in Maryland, and Congregationalists in New England—while Anglicans often found themselves an unprivileged minority. In the colonies, moreover, private and public life could respond to all of the vital forces

11. R. H. Tawney, *Religion and the Rise of Capitalism,* p. 165.

unleashed by the Reformation. In one colony or another each major reformatory tradition would gain full expression; and because of the principle of toleration, other non-English traditions would in due course make their contribution. Persecution and harassment of minority groups would also erupt in the New World, but ultimately all churches would flourish in a degree of freedom unknown elsewhere. Puritanism, above all, would leave a legacy in America no less significant than the impact of Luther upon the German nation.

7

EMPIRE, COMMERCE, AND RELIGION: A SURVEY OF EARLY COLONIZATION

Just how merry "merrie England" was in the late fourteenth century when Geoffrey Chaucer told his tales has been a subject of violent dispute. There is little doubt, however, that England's economy was stagnant, that her people were poor, and that immediate prospects for improvement were dimmed by the large role of agriculture, serfdom, and the manorial system in her national life. But by the time of Shakespeare, this state of affairs had changed no less drastically than the language itself. The two intervening centuries had witnessed steady but in the long run drastic social change. Continental demands for wool had disrupted the old methods of farming, so that herds of sheep now grazed where serfs had toiled. With the increase of available manpower, textile manufacturing had grown in importance; new markets were being sought and found. Towns grew, trade guilds were formed, and the rising merchant class gained increasing economic and political power. During the years 1575–1620 these several trends culminated in a minor industrial revolution.

As money circulated more freely, economic localism was less pronounced and dependence on foreign shipping declined. Merchants and rulers alike became convinced that a favorable balance of trade, and hence the inward flow of more money, was necessary for national prosperity. With the centralization of government under the Tudors came acceptance of the mercantile system, which in turn meant redoubled efforts in the search for advantageous markets and a growing desire for a colonial empire. The chief purpose of this chapter, however, is not to follow these internal developments but to survey the process by which England reached out across the Atlantic. First to be considered are the new land itself and the fate of its native Indians. Then will follow an account of colony-founding on the North American mainland and an examination of the way in which the economic, imperial, and religious aspects of this complex sequence were interrelated. In subsequent chapters each of these colonies or groups of colonies will be discussed separately with special attention to its religious significance.

THE NEW LAND AND THE FIRST AMERICANS

The land which England was now poised to occupy was vaster and richer than anyone then knew; but the English would discover only very slowly that its wealth was not like that which had dazzled Cortez and Pizarro. The material abundance, so decisive in shaping the character of future Americans, was not there for the taking; it would have to be produced by an industrious people—and their slaves. Between the dream and the achievement of a flourishing colonial empire, however, was the Indian.

The British knew, of course, that the terrain of the future United States was already inhabited. In fact, the conversion of heathen tribes would figure prominently among the stated objectives of imperial expansion in the New World, and long-lasting stereotypes of the Indians, as well as of the newly discovered Africans, were already taking shape. Yet nobody knew or could have guessed how diverse these indigenous people were, or how resistant to conversion and incorporation they would be. As for the Indians—who have so often been depicted standing on the shore in friendly expectation as a sailing ship hove into view—they even less could have imagined that the ships would not stop coming until the greatest folk migration since the Germanic invasions of Europe had brought over forty-five million rapidly multiplying people to America.

The Indians living north of present-day Mexico in 1600 probably numbered around a million. More conservative estimates run toward 750,000, which is not far from the size of the Indian population of the United States and Canada in 1970. Their presence in America was the result of a long process that had begun possibly thirty thousand years ago during the last glacial age and continued for perhaps twenty centuries. Asian peoples of widely differing physical types and speaking diverse tongues seem to have made their way across Bering Strait (and possibly by sea to points other than Alaska) and then slowly spread out over the two continents, moving in various directions for a variety of reasons, adapting to the land in such ways as the topography and other tribes allowed. (A three-mile move per week could bring a nomadic group from California to southern Argentina in seventy years—though no one has suggested that such a journey was ever undertaken.)

By the time European settlement began, Indian civilization had achieved a degree of stability, though intertribal conflict continued, and a war between the Iroquois and Hurons was in progress when the French arrived on the St. Lawrence. All of the habitable areas were occupied, albeit very thinly, by more or less Mongoloid peoples who had no more in common than the varied Caucasian peoples of Europe. The Indians north of Mexico were divided into more than two hundred linguistic groups which spoke mutually incomprehensible languages and many dialects, about half of which survive. Beneath these groupings were many civil or tribal organizations, some very small, others large and, as with the Iroquois, politically complex. Despite many enclaves and anomalies, the Indian population was also divided into widely variant cultural groups according to the distinctive means of existence prevailing in various physiographic regions of the country. All across the far north from the Aleutians to Greenland were the Eskimos, the most linguistically unified group and probably the latest to arrive. In almost all of the other areas the confusion of tribes and tongues was more pronounced: the vast Athabascan region west of Hudson's Bay, the great plains, the northeastern and southeastern woodland areas, the north Pacific, the northwest mountain-plateau area, California, and the far southwest. The major differences in ways of life among these regions (and many subregions) had much to do with geography and climate, and most present-day Americans know or can imagine something of the variety that prevailed.

Likely to be forgotten, however, are the vast changes in the Indian way of life that would reach all the way to the Pacific even before Americans began scouting the trans-Appalachian region. "The hunting economy of the red man," writes one sympathetic and experienced scholar, "was doomed from the moment that prancing Arab chargers were taken off the Spanish caravels; from the moment that the crude cannon and muskets of Champlain sounded out across the waters of the lake that bears his name. It was a doom slow in progress, but as inevitable as the procession of day and night." [1] Whether doom was that inexorable can be questioned, but there is no doubt that even by 1750 the horse had altered the lifeways of almost every tribe from the Mississippi to the mountains—while guns, traps, and the fur trade were extending their effects far out beyond the Great Lakes and into the upper Missouri. Spanish Christian culture, meanwhile, was

1. Gustavus E. E. Lindquist, *The Indian in American Life* (New York: Friendship Press, 1944), p. 7.

moving northward from Mexico and after 1769 into California. Defensive needs were already leading to intertribal cooperation and confederation.

With regard to the Indian's religion, the modern American imagination falters. The Christian has considerable difficulty understanding the piety of the Jew (and vice versa), but the spiritual life of the pre-Columbian Indian is removed at another order of magnitude. Beyond this fact is the sheer diversity of cultures. Ruth Benedict, for example, tells how one type of supernatural vision experienced in many North American tribes functions differently in each of them.[2] Anthropological and archaeological data on fertility rites, harvest festivals, war and sun dances, death and birth ceremonies, or chants and prayers for rain and the healing of disease are phenomenologically empty unless described in a precise cultural context. But with distinguished anthropologists disagreeing on the interpretation of individual tribes, generalizations about *all* of the tribes must be of the simplest sort. It is almost futile to speak of "Indian religion" in general. One can say perhaps that the American Indian, like other peoples, stood in awe and relative helplessness in the face of the mysteries of nature and life. His religion was a response to this circumstance and a means of conditioning the forces of nature. His beliefs were animistic—the world of multifarious forces and things was animated or controlled by a hierarchy of spirits whose acts and intentions could in some degree be interpreted or conditioned through shamans and by appropriate ceremonies and rituals. Genesis myths often told (in diverse ways) how the world in ages past had been transformed by a culture hero whose messianic return was expected. For these and other reasons most tribes tended to regard the earth and its powers with greater veneration and respect than the Europeans who would cut down the trees and plough up the prairies. It seems clear, too, that the Indian's way of life contrasted sharply with the Puritan view of work and individual advancement. Western acquisitive society with its notions of fee simple land tenure mystified and outraged him. Though he sought the new trading wares, he did not envy or imitate the ways of the newcomers, and with surprising tenacity he maintained his own culture despite deprivation and mistreatment. For this reason prophecies of cultural "doom" and predictions of assimilation have been only very slowly borne out. Indians of the Taos Reservation who in 1970 had 48,000 acres of land returned to them made their plea on religious grounds—this land was sacred to them, nature is their church, Blue Lake their *sanctum sanctorum*. Essential to our understanding, however, is the fact that the religion of each of the many tribes and nations upon which the white man intruded was a functional

2. Ruth Benedict, *Patterns of Culture*, pp. 35–40.

element of its culture. The sanctions and consolations of religion were and are intricately related to a whole way of life. The gun, the horse, and the trap, therefore, were as powerful instruments of religious change as the missionaries; and the subsequent encroachments of modern technology, individual wage earning, private property, and American politics would have an even heavier impact. From the earliest days, however, the most massive and irresistible instrument of change was the arrival, year after year, of more immigrants whose livelihoods in Europe had been disrupted by strange unbidden social forces not totally unlike those which may have led the Indians to leave the Asian continent long before. As these new Americans occupied the land and moved westward frontier after frontier, the United States became a theater of more direct contact between Indian and European peoples than was the case in New Spain.

As actors in this great continental drama Junípero Serra, Jacques Marquette, Johan Campanius, and John Eliot (to name four dedicated missionaries, Spanish, French, Swedish, and English Puritan) committed their lives to very similar evangelistic aims; they all sought to Christianize the Indian. Yet the differences between these mission enterprises were enormous, and they sprang from the large imperial situation. New Spain, with vast lands and few immigrants, would seek to integrate the Indian into a New World form of Western Catholic culture. New France during the brief and harried existence of its great forest empire would seek (with very modest success) to convert Indians to Christianity within the old tribal context. The Anglo-American empire, with equally vast lands, but with immigration accelerating at a rapid rate, would for more than two centuries treat the Indians as independent nations or wards of the government who had a right to a share of the land; most Christian missions were conducted within that assumption and on reservations. Yet as settlement moved westward countless battles and wars were fought, an American epic was written, and as Teddy Roosevelt would say, the West was "won." Yet the principle of the Indian's right to land, despite centuries of perfidy, would not be abandoned, as 55,340,000 acres in his possession in 1971 still attest. Yet most of the land (almost all of the good land) was cleared of its earlier inhabitants in the name of progress and the greatest good, and the Indian was pushed into various pockets and corners. During the late decades of the twentieth century, when the idea of inevitable progress seemed less convincing than in its nineteenth-century heyday, the Indian's inexorable absorption and disappearance is neither advocated nor predicted with the old confidence. When every aspect of America's racial dilemma was being reconsidered and when an environmental crisis had awakened a nationwide need for the Indian's respect for nature, the questions of cultural encounter and Indian policy were receiving renewed attention. But this by no means meant that a consensus on policy was any nearer than it had been a century before. Both white and red Americans were still about evenly divided between "romantic" and "realistic" views, with the more forceful Indian militants moving toward their more numerous Mexican-American brethren in demanding greater equality and participation in American society rather than a return to tribal life on reservations. To say this is, of course, to get far ahead of the story—but at least a glimpse of the tragedies that lay ahead is essential to a consideration of the beginning.

ENGLAND'S COLONIAL ENTERPRISE IN AMERICA

Early Efforts

During the first century after Columbus's momentous discoveries, England's response was anything but vigorous or concerted. Authorized by Henry VII, John Cabot sailed from Bristol in 1497 and returned with enough information on the northern regions of Newfoundland, Nova Scotia, or Labrador to stimulate interest and backing for a second expedition, which carried him down the North American coast possibly as far as the Chesapeake Bay. Cabot thus by the law of prior discovery established the basis for England's claim to the northern American landmass. English interest in western lands and waters then languished for a half-century, but sprang to life upon the accession of Queen Elizabeth, for whom the papal demarcation line was more a challenge than a hindrance. John Hawkins and Francis Drake made their famous inroads on Spain's American empire in the 1560s and 1570s, while in 1576–78 Martin Frobisher led three voyages to northern waters in search of gold and a northwest passage to the Orient. Between 1585 and 1587 John Davis made three more such excursions, while Humphrey Gilbert and his half-brother, Walter Raleigh, made abortive efforts to plant colonies in the New World, on the Newfoundland and North Carolina coasts respectively.

Only after 1588, when Spain's "Invincible Armada" was swept from the seas, did England begin to attain that maritime mastery which would make possible the entertainment of imperial dreams. Again there were a series of failures; but finally on 2 May 1607, three ships brought to the mouth of the James River a company of 105 colonists, with whom the history of continuous Anglo-American settlement begins. This first planting resulted from an effort by a group of London and Plymouth merchants to establish a trading outpost in the New World. Having organized a joint-stock company, they obtained in 1606 a charter which designated two tracts of land along the Virginia coast, each one hundred miles square, for colonization. As revised in 1609 and again in 1612, the charter allowed the Virginia Company all powers "fit and necessary" for the government of the colony; and in 1619 the company saw fit to establish popular government. Exasperated by the violent factionalism among the company's leaders and dismayed by their meager accomplishments, King James finally annulled the charter in 1624 and made Virginia a royal colony.

The cost of the experiment was high. The company lost over £200,000 in the enterprise, and finally collapsed in bankruptcy. By 1616 some 1,600 colonists had been sent from England; but only 350 were still alive. By 1618 the population had grown to about 1,000, yet in 1623, despite the immigration of 4,000 more, the population still numbered only 1,200. Ravaged by Indian massacres, pestilence, misgovernment, sloth, avarice, disorderliness, and neglect, the Jamestown settlement all but expired. But Virginia survived, and the colony's unbroken church history begins immediately after the first landing, with the celebration of Holy Communion by the Reverend Robert Hunt, pastor of the struggling outpost of English civilization.

The Settlement of New England

After Virginia, the next permanent English plantations were in New England. The first of these, organized by the "Pilgrim Fathers" whom America has taken so close to her heart, was intended to be within the grant of the Virginia Company. In an epoch-making royal decision, James I had promised freedom from molestation to this radical dissenting group.[3] But they landed, apparently by accident, far to the north, within the vast grant of the Council for New England, a loosely organized venture headed by Sir Ferdinando Gorges, the mayor of Plymouth, England. Dominated by men of strong "prelatical" and royalist inclinations, the council had already begun one permanent settlement in Newfoundland; but when its other efforts came to naught, it surrendered its charter (1635), leaving the Pilgrims at Plymouth without royal title to their lands. The Plymouth colony, however, was permitted to conduct its own affairs until it was incorporated in the reconstituted royal colony of Massachusetts by the charter of 1691.

The next decade saw only desultory colonial activity in New England. After its first agonizing winter, the Plymouth colony grew very slowly, num-

3. Concessions by the king were made, however, only after the "Pilgrims" themselves had made extremely sweeping concessions as to royal authority, even in ecclesiastical affairs.

bering scarcely three hundred by 1630. A dozen or so other tiny outposts also maintained a bare existence at various points along the coast. The decade's end, however, was marked by the arrival of a colonial enterprise of much grander dimensions. Its beginnings lay in a fishing post established in 1623 at Cape Ann on the Massachusetts coast by a group of Dorchester businessmen. In 1626 the colonists, led by Roger Conant, moved to Salem. Meanwhile John White, a Dorchester clergyman of moderate Puritan sympathies and great missionary zeal, persuaded various Puritans of means to form a new company. This enterprising group first obtained a grant from the Council for New England; but when it was contested, they applied directly to the king and achieved one of the most surprising coups in colonial history. In March 1629 Charles I chartered the Massachusetts Bay Company with a land grant that carved the heart out of the council's vast though substantially unsettled tract. It extended from three miles north of the Merrimac River to three miles south of the Charles River, and, with the prodigality born of imperial optimism and geographical ignorance, "from sea to sea."

As the prospect for Puritans darkened in Laud's England, the leaders of the company voted to transfer its charter and government to a group which was planning a large scale migration under John Winthrop. In 1630 nearly a thousand of these congregationally inclined Puritans set sail from Southampton in eleven ships. Bearing their charter with them, they crossed to Massachusetts Bay, founded a cluster of towns and established a virtually independent self-governing colony. As the prospect for church reform grew even dimmer in England and the plight of earnest Puritans proportionally more dire, New England attracted an increasingly large number of immigrants. By 1641, when the power of the king and his archbishop was finally broken, at least another twenty thousand had migrated, though not all of these were of one mind in theological matters, and a fair number had no more than a passing interest in church affairs. Yet the Bible Commonwealth which they founded and settled endured as such until its charter was revoked in 1684.

Although the Bay Colony held the dominant place in New England, neighboring colonies soon were founded. In 1632 Massachusetts men began exploring the Connecticut Valley where the Dutch and later Plymouth had set up outposts. Within four years practically the entire congregation from Newtown had migrated with their pastor, Thomas Hooker, to found a new colony. As others joined the trek, settlements grew at Windsor, Hartford, and Wethersfield; and by 1662, just before it was joined with New Haven, Connecticut included fifteen towns. Though often remembered for its more liberal franchise, this colony was a Bible Commonwealth pervaded by much the same spirit and ideals as its parent colony—a fact made very clear in the Fundamental Orders adopted in 1639, and even more clear by its subsequent history.

By this time Theophilus Eaton, a London merchant, and his pastor, John Davenport, had founded another independent jurisdiction at New Haven, with affiliated settlements at nearby points. These towns formalized their relations in 1643, when they adopted a frame of government. The New Haven colony enforced stricter principles of church membership and took the example of ancient Israel more seriously than any other of the Bible Commonwealths. It lacked a formal charter, however, and much to Davenport's chagrin, New Haven was annexed to Connecticut in 1662.

Down the coast from New Haven still another Puritan outpost was founded in 1635 on a grant which two ambitious Puritan noblemen, Lord Saye-and-Sele and Lord Brooke, had obtained from the Council for New England three years previously. John Winthrop, Jr., son of the Massachusetts governor, was the first head of this small settlement at the mouth of the Connecticut River; but he enlarged the field for his administrative talents by engineering in 1644 the sale of Saye-Brooke to the colony of Connecticut —of which he became governor in 1657. In 1662 he succeeded in obtaining from Charles II a royal charter for Connecticut, whose sole title up to this point had been possession of its land and an arrangement with the Bay colony. At this time it was incorporated with New Haven, which had incurred the royal wrath by harboring three of the regicides of 1649. The younger Winthrop thus brought Connecticut to approximately its present size.

The New England colonies mentioned so far, in addition to a fair number of tributary communities in Maine, New Hampshire, and Long Island, were all in substantial agreement on matters pertaining to Christian doctrine and the ordering of God's church. So much could not be said of Rhode Island, which was founded by nonconformists expelled from the Bay Colony. By far the most important of these exiles was Roger Williams, whose irreconcilable differences with the established colonies led him to found Providence on Narragansett Bay in 1636. In the next few years, various neighboring settlements were begun by other outcasts and bold spirits: Pocasset (Portsmouth) by Anne Hutchinson and her friends in 1638, Newport by William Coddington in 1639, and Shawomet (Warwick) by Samuel Gorton in 1643. (Portsmouth and Newport united in 1640.) For this entire group Roger Williams was able to obtain from Parliament in 1644 a land patent and permission to form a government. None was established until 1647, however, probably because of the hesitancy of these freedom-loving radicals to form a central government of even the loosest kind. The first charter had no legality after the Stuart Restoration, but John Clarke, the colony's patient emissary, was able to secure from Charles II in 1663 a royal charter confirming the land grant, approving the government, and guaranteeing religious liberty. From the beginning the colony had separated church and state and offered freedom of conscience to all, with the result that it became a sanctuary for Baptists, Quakers, and other independent spirits, including those who wished freedom from *any* kind of religious obligation. Rhode Island was thus unique in New England, though its history was hardly less informed by the Puritan spirit than was that of its imperious and more authoritarian neighbors.

The Middle and Southern Colonies

The decades of the twenties and thirties, so eventful in New England, were also a time for diverse kinds of colonizing activity further south. First to arrive were the Dutch, for whom Henry Hudson had explored in 1609 the great river which bears his name. By 1624, when the first permanent settlers arrived at Manhattan Island, Dutch traders had already set up posts at widely scattered points on Long Island Sound and on the Hudson and Connecticut rivers. When Spain finally recognized the long-declared Dutch independence in the Peace of Westphalia in 1648, a major cause for emigration was removed, and New Amsterdam was only very slowly peopled by a small multinational group of settlers. In 1655, when the shifting European situation made it propitious, Peter Stuyvesant (who governed New Netherland from 1647 to 1664) conquered and annexed the small Swedish settlement that had been planted on the lower Delaware River in 1638.

The Dutch West India Company was a trading concern, never interested in a thriving agricultural community overseas, and the government it provided was harsh, dictatorial, and generally unattractive. The patroon system of vast baronial estates on the Hudson never flourished because of widespread discontent with the company's land policies, arbitrary rule, and religious intolerance. When England took possession of the little colony in 1664, therefore, there was little internal resistance and much relief in the neighboring colonies. With the duke of York (later James II) as the sole proprietor of this vast, ill-defined tract, New York became a thriving and much more religiously tolerant colony. He and his governors ruled with a strong hand, but in 1683 the need for a more adequate taxation system led to the establishment of a representative colonial assembly. The chief legacy of the colony's founders was a self-conscious minority of Dutch people and the Dutch Reformed church, which maintained a continuous and lively existence, especially in New York and New Jersey. The Swedish colony in the meantime disappeared almost without a trace. Its small population of four hundred soon lost its identity, while the Swedish Lutheran church gradually and by a natural affinity merged with colonial Anglicanism.[4]

Immediately to the south of the Swedish settlement on the Delaware arose another almost contemporary colony. Maryland, though English, was in some respects even more alien to the emerging pattern of settlement than the Dutch and Swedish colonies. It was conceived by George Calvert, Lord Baltimore, secretary of state under James I, a former stockholder in the Virginia Company, and founder of an unsuccessful Newfoundland colony. After becoming a Roman Catholic, Calvert obtained in 1632 an extremely liberal proprietary grant from Charles I. By no means a simple charter for a trading company, this grant resembled a feudal fief that awarded the proprietor the independence and authority of a "Count Palatine." When carried into actuality by his son Cecilius, the colony purported to be chiefly a refuge for harassed Roman Catholics; but to achieve this end it became necessary (or at least highly expedient) to establish the principle of toleration. Maryland has the distinction of being the first colony to announce this principle, though in other respects an anachronistic semifeudal social order was planned. In the first two shiploads of colonists arriving on 3 March 1634, Roman Catholics were dominant, but from the first Protestants were a numerical majority.

The two decades between the ending of Charles I's personal rule (1640) and the Restoration of Charles II (1660) was a period of salutary neglect for the American colonies and a time of internal growth and consolidation. Political and commercial regulation was at a minimum, and only Maryland was seriously torn by civil strife—a Puritan revolution which overturned Roman Catholic rule between 1655 and 1658. A second rebellion in 1689 led two years later to the assertion of royal authority, which continued to be

4. The legal situation of "Delaware" (as we now call it) became uncertain after the Dutch collapse and remained so until the American Revolution. The duke of York "leased" it to William Penn in 1682; but his title to lands west of the Delaware River was very uncertain (as Penn, the duke, and most others continued to recognize). With these leases, however, Penn asserted effective rule over the "three counties" (a subdivision of the area instituted by Governor Andros of New York in 1680). The people in the "lower counties" remained restive, however, and finally gained the right to secede in the Pennsylvania charter of liberties of 1701. Their separation was authorized by the Privy Council in 1703 and exercised in 1704. Its governor was appointed by the proprietor of Pennsylvania, but otherwise the territory was a royal colony, though it was never closely regulated, nor were the laws of its assembly reviewed in England.

exercised even after the proprietary was returned in 1716 to the next Lord Baltimore, now become an Anglican. No new colonies were founded on the mainland during the Interregnum, though Cromwell's "Western Design" did involve activity in the Caribbean and resulted in the acquisition of Jamaica.

The return of the monarchy brought varied sorts of enterprises, including the formulation of more definite governmental and commercial policies. In New England, Connecticut was consolidated and chartered, Rhode Island was chartered, and the scattered settlements of New Hampshire organized as a royal colony. Several new colonies also were formed. New Netherland yielded to New York in 1664; then three and a half months later the duke of York made over a large part of his domain—Nova Caesaria, or New Jersey—to John Lord Berkeley and Sir George Carteret, who were already proprietors of an undeveloped Carolina grant. They regarded themselves as "true and absolute Lords" of this sparsely settled and disorganized tract, but their hopes for prosperity were lost in a welter of confused land grants and governmental concessions. In 1670 Berkeley finally sold his rights to two Quakers, and in 1684 the Carteret interests were sold to a group of twenty-four oddly assorted men, most of whom were Quakers. With complications thus compounded, the crisis deepened, until finally in 1702, at the recommendation of the Board of Trade, all of the proprietors were required to surrender their governmental authority, and New Jersey became a royal colony of the usual type. So ended thirty-eight years of conflict and litigation that nearly destroyed the colony.[5]

Carolina, too, originated in the immediate post-Restoration period, when in 1663 a vast tract of land south of Virginia was made over to a group of proprietors on terms similar to those for Maryland. With feudal visions even more grandiose than the Calverts', these men faced many hindrances, not least of which was their own inexperience. After several false starts, they inaugurated their enterprise in 1670 with a plantation at Charles Town, vaunting an absurd neofeudal constitution in which John Locke allegedly had a hand. Farther north around Albemarle Sound, meanwhile, other groups had settled. This "North Carolina" district received its own governor in 1712, though proprietary ineptitude and poor transportation long kept formal governance to a minimum.

The final seventeenth-century colony to be founded was the great proprietary province of Pennsylvania, whose early history is inseparable from the life and ideals of its founder, William Penn (1644–1718). Son of the

5. The governor of New York served as its governor until 1738. Reflecting the colony's dual origins, its assembly alternated its place of meeting between Perth Amboy (East Jersey) and Burlington (West Jersey).

great Admiral Penn, he was eminently a man of the world: sometime student at Christ Church (Oxford), Saumur, and Lincoln's Inn, friend of the duke of York, manager of his father's Irish estate, widely traveled and deeply involved in the affairs of his time. Yet he was also a man of the spirit: youthful convert to Quaker principles and their lifelong defender, friend of George Fox, John Locke, and Algernon Sidney, compassionate humanitarian, mystic, theologian, and profound political theorist. No man was better fitted to undertake a colonial venture whose express purpose was to provide a sanctuary for the persecuted people of Europe. Particularly disturbed by the disabilities imposed on his fellow Quakers, he began after 1679 to lose his confidence in England; and like John Winthrop a half-century before, he set his eyes and hopes on the New World. From his involvement in the miserable tangle of New Jersey, he also knew at least one way *not* to proceed. On 1 June 1681 his charter received the great seal. There were discordant notes in that charter—its extensive grant of authority to the proprietor and his heirs, for example, in addition to its insistence on obedience to royal authority and English trade laws—but it gave the great idealist an opportunity to carry out his "Holy Experiment." For his vast, rich, inland domain, Penn provided a full set of laws, "a code of Quaker principles applied to actual government." The Frame of Government called for a resident governor, a small elective council, and a large elective assembly with very limited powers. The franchise was restricted to men with land and property. Preferential treatment for Anglicans was nominally exacted by the charter, but freedom of worship and toleration were assured for all who believed in God.

When Penn arrived in 1682, the population had already reached four thousand, and a year later people were reported to be "coming in fast." As Penn's brochures and advertisements circulated throughout the British Isles and northern Europe, the tide of immigrants swelled. Germantown was founded in 1683. Welshmen and Englishmen came too; and after the Glorious Revolution the people demanded and ultimately obtained greater political rights.

The widely divergent backgrounds and outlooks of the people brought together in Pennsylvania created many tensions and problems. In 1705 Penn himself was discouraged: "I am a crucified man between Injustice and Ingratitude there [in America] and Extortion and Oppression here [in England]." Yet as Charles M. Andrews says,

> Two circumstances favored him: his charter was less proprietary than had been the earlier ones; and he himself was an idealist. On the other hand, two things were against him: first, aristocratic by instinct, he was

> certain to be influenced by the power he exercised; secondly, neither practical nor sagacious, he had to learn by bitter experience that ideals are difficult of application.[6]

Though troubles and dissensions naturally came, for the most part they were transcended. The colony grew strong and prospered despite its boundary disputes, governmental clashes, and personal dissensions. By 1709, when the British Parliament provided for the naturalization of foreign (i.e. American) Protestants, Pennsylvania flourished as a model state where people of diverse ethnic and religious backgrounds could live together under equitable laws in a single commonwealth. Despite the heavy predominance of Quakers in managing the affairs of the colony, and despite the large vestiges of proprietary privilege, its solutions to these manifold problems made it more nearly a paradigm of latter-day American democracy than any other colony.

The "Empire" in Retrospect

In 1714 Queen Anne died and the Stuart line of English monarchs passed into history. Her death marks the end of an era, making this a convenient point to cast a retrospective eye over the farflung empire created during the rule of her predecessors.

By one way of reckoning, England's seventeenth-century empire building on the North American coast would hardly be called a "burst of colonial activity." A score or so of feeble "plantings" plus two others gained by conquest constituted a few islets of Western civilization along a thousand-mile stretch of coastal plain. Such a result from a century's labor calls for moderate language. Yet compared with the colonial accomplishments of her two chief competitors (Spain and France), England's achievement assumes dramatic proportions. Pennsylvania, for example, had more European colonists in 1710—thirty years after its founding—than the whole vast expanse of New France from Quebec to New Orleans had attracted in a century. And France not only had begun her North American empire almost simultaneously with England, but had given to Quebec alone more royal subsidies than all the Anglo-American colonies had received together. At the same time, the white population of Mexico also outnumbered that of New France; but the population of New England alone, containing just over a third of those in the English colonies, outnumbered the entire white population of Spain's enormous holdings in the New World—and this despite Spain's head start of an entire century. In view of these facts, the energy

6. Charles M. Andrews, *The Colonial Period in American History*, 3: 303–04.

and vitality of the English nation arrest attention and require explanation. And in a religious history such as this one, religious factors in relation to commercial and imperial concerns must be especially probed.

RELIGION AND THE NEW AGE

The connection of the religious upheaval of the sixteenth century to England's imperial expansiveness is both undeniable and extremely difficult to describe. If even the economic effects of an objective event like the dissolution of the monasteries are nearly impossible to establish, the larger fact of the abandonment of the monastic *idea* involves long-term ramifications that overwhelm the imagination. Other problems are still more baffling. Difficulty has not stopped speculation, however, and some of the most challenging theories of historical action have been focused on these intriguing issues. Oldest and most continuously asked are questions of causation and explanation that almost any historical narrative (including this one) must confront and seek to answer.

A traditional but very superficial approach to the problem of relating religion to English colonization is the classification of colonies as "religious" or "nonreligious." In this manner, the Puritan commonwealths, Maryland, and Pennsylvania are often put in the first category, and the others in the latter. But such a procedure takes much too simple a view of the motives of both founders and settlers: in the first place, men simply do not act single-mindedly for patriotic, or commercial, or religious reasons, any more than they go to the beach single-mindedly to swim, or sun, or watch other people. Even if the founders had such a singleness of purpose, they would have been unable to exclude less purely motivated settlers from their colonies. The situation is complicated by the presence of settlements of intensely dedicated religious groups in colonies such as New Jersey or Carolina, whose proprietors were chiefly interested in profits. Another anomaly was the Puritan population of Roman Catholic Maryland, which had already become a majority when this colony's famous Act of Toleration was passed in 1649.

A much more useful mode of analysis is that which stresses the remarkable degree to which religious and missionary motives functioned in the thought of the entire age, even for Elizabethan sea dogs like William and John Hawkins. "Serve God dayly, love one another, preserve your victuals, beware of fire, and keep good companie"—thus Sir John admonished his crew when he led a slaving expedition to Guinea and thence to the West Indies in 1564–65. Later, when he quoted the Bible to excuse his failure to intercept the Spanish treasure fleet, the Virgin Queen replied, "This fool went out a soldier and is come home a divine."

The seventeenth century was an age of faith, a time when few Englishmen would take lightly any precept clearly set forth in Scripture, and when God's providence was seen behind every occurrence. Scoffers and skeptics were the exception. To forget this fact is to imperil our understanding of these undertakings. In the early colonial period the United States has its one historical contact with a civilization that was still recognizably medieval. It is thus as dangerous to attribute purely secular motives to anyone as it is to regard pious phraseology as proof of any exceptional degree of religious concern. We must also concede that no instruments are at hand for gauging the depth and seriousness of statements made or acts performed. When was a chaplain taken along merely as a talisman, and when did his presence show a genuine desire to maintain Christian worship? And who can get behind the rationalizations?

More important relationships of religion, commerce, and colonization may be seen in the immense stress placed by the clergy upon the New World as a challenge to Christian evangelism. Here we face a vital chapter in the development of the British Empire, for in England the clergy played a leading role in awakening kings, ministers, merchants, and people to their obligation to carry the gospel to all parts of the earth, and especially to the New World, a Western Canaan for the claiming and evangelizing of which the English were a chosen people. There was a strong anti-Roman Catholic animus to their pleading, as well as a fervent hope that the "errors of popery" would not be sown in areas still unclaimed; and in fact, a fierce tradition of anti-Catholicism, both visceral and dogmatic, is one of Puritanism's most active legacies to Anglo-American civilization. Yet John Donne, when dean of Saint Paul's, transcended such acrimony in his lofty summons to the stockholders of the Virginia Company in 1622:

> You shall haue made this Iland, which is but as the Suburbs of the old world, a Bridge, a Gallery to the new; to ioyne all to that world that shall never grow old, the Kingdome of Heauen. You shall add persons to this Kingdome, and to the Kingdome of heauen, and adde names to the Bookes of our Chronicles, and to the Booke of Life.[7]

Few could express the ultimate vision so well as Donne; yet hundreds of others stated the same case, putting before patriots, merchants, and church-

7. *A Sermon Vpon the VIII. Verse of the I. Chapter of the Acts of the Apostles* (1622), quoted in Louis B. Wright, *Religion and Empire: The Alliance between Piety and Commerce in English Expansion, 1558–1625*, p. 111. This valuable book has also been used and quoted in other parts of this chapter.

men the challenge of a divinely appointed destiny. In the process, they took it upon themselves to prove that colonial expansion would also cure England's other ills, whether moral, social, economic, or political. On no other set of issues were all of the preachers, Conformist and Puritan, so nearly in agreement. All this took place, moreover, when the pulpit had an importance in English life that it has enjoyed in no other period.

But not even in the widespread proclamation of missionary duty do we reach the principal nexus of religion and England's expansion. The most basic aspects of the relationship are far more subtle, far less explicitly rationalized. True it may be that England was spurred to large-scale Protestant colonial expansion in North America by the challenge of Spain and France. But why, we must ask, *why* did the English respond with such energy and power? What dynamic motive underlies the swarming of the English in the New World? What is the secret not only of England's expansion but of her expansiveness? Even partial answers to these exciting questions lead into some of the most heated controversies of recent historiography. The appearance of historical interpretations based on economic materialism in its Marxian form did most to intensify these debates. Later in the nineteenth century positivists contributed their deterministic emphasis on environmental factors. Romantics and idealists kept the controversy well heated. Concern with such issues may, to be sure, carry one beyond the traditional boundaries of church history, yet it is difficult to see how they can be avoided.

Most insistently these controversies have had to do with the relation of the great Reformation events and ideas to the growth of modern institutions, attitudes, and ideals. What effect, it is asked, did the Reformation—particularly the Protestant Reformation—have upon the rise of democracy, of individualism, and of capitalism? Each of these questions looms large in a discussion of England's energetic role in international affairs in the Elizabethan and subsequent periods. In answering, one must first insist upon the inadequacy of any simple "economic interpretation." It will never do to explain historical events, religious or otherwise, solely as functions of the social environment. Ralph Barton Perry's words are to the point:

> Men act when they decide; men act together when they agree. Having gone so far, there is no just ground for denying the potency, the unique social potency of those interrelations, reciprocities, and identities of emotion and expectation which constitute collective ideals. . . . If a factor such as an ideal makes any difference, then there may be situations in which it makes all the difference.[8]

8. Ralph Barton Perry, *Puritanism and Democracy*, pp. 22–23.

The ideas which shape ideals have a life of their own; and, almost like meteors from outer space, many great ideas come into the world on the wings of individuated human genius—by means of a Luther, a Newton, a Rousseau, or an Adam Smith. Believed, propagated, and subtly altered by many devotees, these ideas become operative forces in history, hindering or encouraging the course of events of which they become a part.

Reformation ideas or events, of course, did not cause the commercial revolution that transformed England, any more than the economic upheaval caused the Reformation. Yet the spirit of capitalism latent in so much of England's expansion was intensified by the way in which the Reformation accentuated certain motifs of the Judaeo-Christian tradition, motifs which for centuries had a dynamic effect on Western civilization. The Reformation, in the British Isles as elsewhere, was essentially a Christian revival in which the biblical understanding of man and history was forcefully proclaimed. This meant a renewal of concern for *this* life, *this* world, and all their impinging problems, moral and social. Other religions may be otherworldly; but the Jew, the Christian, and even the Moslem are all impressed by the prophetic demands of the Bible and its peculiar concern for the irreversible course of history, in which men participate in this world as morally responsible persons.

Beyond being simply Christian, the English Reformation was a vast and variegated evangelical revival which felt the impact of each major phase of the Continental Reformation. Most important of all was the influence of the Reformed tradition on English life; the total outlook involved in this rigorous and radical reconception of Christianity implied a whole new social order. In certain small areas and for a short time this "new social order" would be made explicit; in this fact lies the fascination (and possibly the wider importance) of New England's Bible Commonwealths. But the implicit order was equally important. This is the vital truth behind R. H. Tawney's previously quoted pronouncement that "the growth, triumph and transformation of the Puritan spirit was the most fundamental movement of the seventeenth century. Puritanism . . . was the true English Reformation, and it is from its struggle against the old order that the England which is unmistakably modern emerges."[9] In the social and political order, in other words, the expansion of Reformed and Puritan convictions had revolutionary implications; it was a threat to arbitrary and despotic governance. The English "revolution" of 1640–90 is unimaginable and inexplicable if the concomitant "Puritan reformation" is not borne in mind.[10]

9. R. H. Tawney, *Religion and the Rise of Capitalism,* p. 165.

10. Stuart E. Prall states that modern scholarship on the role of Puritanism in England's

Yet "struggle" and revolution should not be overemphasized. Richard Hakluyt, who had as great an influence on English expansion as any other single Englishman of the sixteenth century, provides an excellent case in point, for his lifelong effort to awaken England to her colonial destiny was not a "struggle against the old order" in the political or institutional sense. He had been converted to geography as a schoolboy, and he simply wanted to awaken Englishmen to their world mission. Throughout his life (1552–1616) he was a favorite of the Elizabethan court and the object of much preferment. The same could be said of many of those churchmen whom he influenced most, Samuel Purchas, for example, or George Abbot, who became archbishop of Canterbury. These men were unaware of accomplishing a revolution; yet what happened in their lifetimes was the transformation of character implicit in Reformed Christianity as a whole—not just its "Protestant ethic," or its repudiation of monasticism, or its emphasis on the "priesthood of all believers," or its advocacy of congregational or presbyterian polity. The essence of it was expressed in the archepiscopal pronouncements of every English primate under Elizabeth and James; there is more of it even in Archbishop Laud than he knew, and it reappears in more secularized form under Charles II, in the sermons of his appointee to the see of London, John Tillotson.

Elemental to this transforming power was the knowledge that God rules the world which he made, that the earth is the Lord's, that all the orders and stations thereof are good, and that man's highest worldly duty is to glorify God. Sloth and idleness dishonor the Creator. Typical abhorrence for such dishonor was shown by the Reverend Richard Eburne, when he pleaded with King James I for more royal support for the colonies. "Our so long continued rest and peace . . . our unspeakable idleness and dissolute life, have so corrupted and in manner effeminated our people generally . . . that they cannot endure the hearing, much lesse the doing of any laborious attempts, of any thing that shall be troublous or any whit dangerous unto them." [11] In other contexts the same insistence was echoed up and down the land and throughout the realm, decade after decade. Long after its overarching theology had crumbled, men spoke of the "gospel of work" in semireligious accents.

---

great upheaval of 1640–60, "has really done nothing to undermine the essential accuracy" of his title, though he also wishes to make clear that he is not dealing with the "Glorious Revolution" of 1688–89 (*The Puritan Revolution: A Documentary History*, p. x). Actually the latter revolution documented what the earlier one had wrought—and what Charles II and James II had tried to ignore. Taken together they constitute the "English Revolution."

11. *A Plain Path-Way to Plantations* (1624); quoted by Wright, *Religion and Empire*, p. 149.

Most influential was the new emphasis on serving the Lord in one's vocation—as a tradesman, as a merchant, as an artisan, or as a magistrate or "citizen." Formerly it was thought necessary to withdraw from the tainted world in order to develop the highest spirituality; monasticism was the surest way to perfection. Now it was the life of withdrawal which was regarded as tainted and opposed to God's will. In the Reformed tradition especially, an additional premium was put on austerity, frugality, and sober living. The effect of such zeal—such "this-worldly asceticism," to use Max Weber's famous phrase—on commercial life and attitudes is apparent.[12]

There were other more subtle influences. One of these was the inevitable concern aroused in human hearts by the transcendence of God, a major emphasis of Reformed theology. This was acted out in an abhorrence of all the ways by which the Church had previously sought to make God's nature and works near and almost palpable in painting, sculpture, architecture, and liturgical ceremony. To speak in the Reformed and Puritan manner of the transcendence of God is basically to witness to his power and to the inscrutability of his ways; and in no way were these doctrines more firmly underlined than by that much-discussed doctrine of election, of God's absolute predestinating decrees unto salvation or unto damnation. This was awesome doctrine; and in a sermon-dominated age when it was preached from every pulpit—by no one more firmly than by that arch-Conformist, Archbishop Whitgift—only very blithe or very hardened souls would regard lightly the burning question of assurance: "Am I of the chosen?" And again, rare would be the person who, taking the question seriously, would proclaim his unfavored status by profligacy, dishonesty, or laziness. Reformed theology unquestionably encouraged rectitude, probity, and industry; and it did so even among those who in no way entertained the "bourgeois heresy" that worldly success is a sure sign of election, or worse still, a means of earning redemption.[13]

Individual responsibility in religious matters was made even more explicit by the doctrine of the priesthood of all believers which the Reformers affirmed so emphatically. Most obviously, this doctrine led to the increased importance of the laity in Protestant church life. It also put a new emphasis upon personal confrontation with the great issues of the faith,

12. Max Weber, *The Protestant Ethic and the Spirit of Capitalism.* The vast ensuing literature is sampled and bibliography given in Robert W. Green, *Protestantism and Capitalism: The Weber Thesis and Its Critics.* My general inclination to Weber and kindred thinkers is apparent.

13. It may be doubted that any responsible Christian ever entertained this so-called "bourgeois heresy" in either of its forms—except perhaps as a desperate effort of self-justification.

thus giving still another whirl to the "inner gyroscope" which a contemporary sociologist has used to symbolize a classic but now disappearing type of personal moral responsibility. Indeed the rise of moralism was an inescapable consequence of the blows to sacramental and sacerdotal religion struck during the Puritan century. In this sense Puritanism won a resounding, long-term victory. By the time of Queen Anne "the active religious life of the whole of England, as of most of Scotland and Wales, had become Puritan." [14] In the Evangelical Revival of the eighteenth century and the Victorianism of the nineteenth, it would continue to be a dynamic factor in British life. By the affinity of its assumptions and claims, Reformed and Puritan theology also smoothed the way for the progress of social-compact notions of government, as well as for other scientific and philosophical departures from tradition.

Britain's transformation was wrought by many other forces besides religion. The New World itself, to which preachers and church leaders pointed with such eagerness, became a great frontier for all of Europe and a leaven to European life in a hundred ways. It would disrupt monetary systems as well as cosmologies. Yet in a religious age, one indeed given over to churchly contentions and rivalries that none could ignore, Christian concern was a shaping force of such strength as to be almost unfathomable to the modern mind.

14. Maurice Ashley, *England in the Seventeenth Century, 1603–1714* (London: Penguin Books, 1958), p. 238.

II
THE PROTESTANT EMPIRE FOUNDED

Government seems to me a part of religion itself, a thing sacred in its institution and end. For if it does not directly remove the cause, it crushes the effects of evil and is as such (though a lower yet) an emanation of the same divine power that is both author and object of pure religion. . . . But that is only to evil doers, government itself being otherwise as capable of kindness, goodness, and charity as a more private society. They weakly err that think there is no other use of government than correction which is the coarsest part of it. Daily experience tells us that the care and regulation of many other affairs, more soft and daily necessary, make up much of the greatest part of government and [this] must have followed the peopling of the world had Adam never fell and [it] will continue among men, on earth, under the highest attainments they may arrive at by the coming of the blessed Second Adam, the Lord from Heaven.

William Penn, Preface to the Frame of Government of Pennsylvania (1682)

For no country was the travail of Reformation more protracted than for Great Britain: nowhere was it more tumultuous, and nowhere were the consequences so revolutionary. It is no figment of Whiggish pride or British insularity that the Glorious Revolution (whether misnamed or not) marked the advent of modern democratic individualism and put the *ancien régime* on borrowed time. It was only in a series of almost accidental colonial commonwealths strung along the North American seaboard, however, that the distilled essence of this Puritan Revolution could manifest its full historical significance.

In the "howling wilderness" between Maine and Georgia, plans for medieval baronies were cancelled by physical circumstance. Old World commercial ventures fell into disarray. Yet of far greater importance to the gradual emergence of this strange piecemeal empire was the English government's willingness to encourage the founding of almost any kind of colony and to welcome into them almost any interested person or group, however radical or eccentric. Equally significant is the fact that nearly all who did come to America were disposed in one way or another to make the most of the liberties made available by England's revolution and America's "free air."

The most influential colony founders were those with clear, firmly held ideals and a determination to institutionalize the distinctive results of the British Reformation. Because people who shared these views were dominant in several colonies and numerous almost everywhere, the society which gradually emerged did embody many of these intentions. There were, of course, countercurrents: leaders with aristocratic ideals, and many settlers who opposed Puritan radicalism. Migrants from the European continent often had their own aspirations. Far more fateful were the importation of Africans and the steady extension of chattel slavery. Yet the coexistence of so much diversity—religious, ideological, and ethnic—tended to foster a libertarian consensus and advance the practice of religious freedom. The foundations of the American religious tradition, therefore, are best understood through the separate consideration of the various colonial commonwealths that took shape along the Atlantic coast during the seventeenth century.

8

THE RISE AND FLOWERING OF THE PURITAN SPIRIT

Under Henry VIII England had gained a national church without reformation, but the power of Protestantism proved irresistible. In due course it visited upon Great Britain the longest and most turbulent Reformation experience in Christendom. By the time of the Glorious Revolution in 1689, the country's settlement of religious and civil affairs had gone through at least a dozen major stages, two kings had been deprived of rule, and a civil war had been fought. By this time Britain had also become a major Atlantic power, and its rapidly growing empire was becoming a prosperous extension of English civilization. Great Britain, in short, had experienced an economic, political, imperial, and religious transformation. In comparison with the changes wrought in the mother country, moreover, the colonial civilization taking shape on the North American continent represented an even more drastic break with the old order in Europe. Because unrest at home had prevented regulation of the very emigration which it had stimulated, the American colonies were developing in unexpected and unprecedented ways. Among other things, they had become the most thoroughly Protestant, Reformed, and Puritan commonwealths in the world. Indeed, Puritanism provided the moral and religious background of fully 75 percent of the people who declared their independence in 1776.[1] In order to understand the new civilization that was arising in the wilderness, therefore, a sympathetic effort to comprehend the Puritan impulse is peculiarly important.

1. If one were to compute such a percentage on the basis of all the German, Swiss, French, Dutch, and Scottish people whose forebears bore the "stamp of Geneva" in some broader sense, 85 or 90 percent would not be an extravagant estimate.

The term Puritanism in its broadest sense refers to a widely ramified movement of religious renovation that gradually took shape in Great Britain under the leadership of men who were committed to the Continental Reformed tradition. The movement began to gain a special kind of self-consciousness under the reign of Queen Elizabeth (1558–1603). During the next century its votaries increased greatly in both numbers and variety, achieving political dominance in England for a time after the Civil War, and moral dominance for a still longer period after the Glorious Revolution. From the outset these reformers were determined to achieve a threefold program for purifying the visible church: through a purging of popish remnants and the establishment of "apostolic" principles of worship and church order, through the implantation and teaching of Reformed doctrine, and through a revival of discipline and evangelical piety in clergy and laity alike. The first of these objectives was the most disruptive, because convictions as to church polity naturally took such clear and objective institutional forms. Yet the movement as a whole embraced a wide range of ecclesiastical arrangements. Many Puritans—with Calvin's word to support them—were content to accomplish their reforms within an episcopal church under the crown's governance. A growing number of others began to conceive of "purification" in increasingly radical terms, and gradually institutional changes of a more drastic nature were proposed. Voltaire in the eighteenth century was commenting on the divisive effect of this ferment on the left when he observed that the English, alas, have a hundred religions but only one sauce.

The appearance of multitudinous sects does not alter the fact that some "Anglican" archbishops as well as some itinerant Ranters can properly be referred to as Puritans. The latter group simply carried their program for England's church to an individualistic extreme. This great diversity of expression has led some scholars to regard England's ferment as totally amorphous:

> Before the Revolution the term was almost invariably pejorative, and if one knows the circumstances surrounding its use, one may easily enough understand why the word is used and what is communicated by that use. But the conclusion arising from detailed knowledge of the prerevolutionary uses of the term is that "puritan" is the "x" of a cultural and social equation: it has no meaning beyond that given it by the particular manipulator of an algebra of abuse.[2]

2. Charles and Katherine George, *The Protestant Mind of the English Reformation: 1570–1640*, p. 6.

Such a statement, unfortunately, overlooks both the common origins and the shared objectives of Puritan reformers. A primary purpose of this chapter, therefore, is to consider England's great contribution to the family of Reformed traditions. If special concern is shown for the groups which came to dominate the Holy Commonwealths of Massachusetts and Connecticut, it is only because those particular groups provide especially vivid instances of a broad impulse which was of great consequence to the entire American colonial scene.

THE PURITAN SPIRIT

A Revival of Experiential Piety

In some ways the Puritan spirit is ageless. One senses a fundamental aspect of its temper in the prophetic demands of Amos:

> Seek good, and not evil,
>   that you may live;
> And so the Lord, the God of hosts, will be with you,
>   as you have said.
> Hate evil, and love good,
>   and establish justice in the gate;
> it may be that the Lord, the God of hosts,
>   will be gracious to the remnant of Joseph.
>
> . . . .
>
> Woe to those who are at ease in Zion,
>   and to those who feel secure on the mountain of Samaria. . . .
> Woe to those who lie upon beds of ivory,
>   and stretch themselves upon their couches,
> and eat lambs from the flock,
>   and calves from the midst of the stall;
> who sing idle songs to the sound of the harp,
>   and like David invent for themselves instruments of music;
> who drink wine in bowls,
>   and anoint themselves with finest oils,
>   but are not grieved over the ruin of Joseph!
>
> [Amos 5:14–15; 6:1–6]

In 1115 the same moral passion led Saint Bernard out into the wilderness of the Aube valley to reconstruct Benedictine life within the somber, unadorned walls of Clairvaux, and to begin there the Cistercian movement of monastic reform. Hugh Latimer also heard this ancient call in the early days of England's reformation. His grief over "the ruin of Joseph" spurred him to attack "unpreaching prelates" with sharply drawn contrasts between apostolic simplicity and episcopal magnificence; it nerved him to dramatize this theme even on that day in 1525 when the bishop of Ely entered Cambridge's Great Saint Mary's while Latimer was preaching, and it strengthened him as he was led to the fires by Queen Mary's executioners a quarter-century later. John Milton's *Lycidas* (1645) would express the same outrage. Gradually this demand for purity came to inform a popular movement.

No less was the Puritan spirit infused with what Perry Miller calls "the Augustinian strain of piety":

> I venture to call this piety Augustinian . . . simply because Augustine is the arch-exemplar of a religious frame of mind of which Puritanism is only one instance out of many in fifteen hundred years of religious history. . . . There survive hundreds of Puritan diaries and thousands of Puritan sermons, but we can read the inward meaning of them all in the *Confessions* [of Saint Augustine].
>
> Puritan theology was an effort to externalize and systematize this subjective mood. Piety was the inspiration for Puritan heroism and the impetus in the charge of Puritan Ironsides. . . . It was foolishness and fanaticism to their opponents, but to themselves it was life eternal. . . . It blazed most clearly and most fiercely in the person of Jonathan Edwards, but Emerson was illuminated, though from afar, by its rays, and it smoldered in the recesses of Hawthorne's intuitions.[3]

At times one can even find among professed Puritans the sort of mystical piety which transported Augustine from the window in Ostia into other realms of being and led him to discover that there was no peace outside of rest in God. Thomas Hooker in Connecticut shared this spirit: "The soul was made for an end, and good, and therefore for a better than itself, therefore to enjoy union with him, and communion with those blessed excellencies of his. . . ." The recurrence of these mystical flights reminds us that the Puritans were heirs not only of the Reformation but of the medieval tradition out of which it grew, and that they also communed with those Platonic ideas which so often offered the Renaissance humanist a way of rejecting scholastic theology.

Yet there was an element in Puritan inwardness more basic, more decisive, and far more fraught with historical consequences than Platonic mysti-

3. Perry Miller, *The New England Mind: The Seventeenth Century*, pp. 3–5.

cism: it was the inescapable example of Saint Paul on the road to Damascus. The Puritans were spiritual brethren with a practical mission. They called England, and later America, to a spiritual awakening; and nearly every one of those who uttered the call had had his own road to Damascus. For Henry Burton, who had his ears lopped off as Laud's prisoner but who returned to work with a Puritan following during Parliament's power, the great personal awakening came at Cambridge University. He describes the impact of sermons by Laurence Chaderton, master of Emmanuel College, and William Perkins, also of Emmanuel and the "angelical doctor" of the movement: "From my first entrance in the College, it pleased God to open mine eyes by their ministry, so as to put a difference between their sound teaching, and the University Sermons, which savoured more of humane wit, than of Gods word." Thomas Goodwin, perhaps the most influential of the Independent "dissenting brethren" at the Westminster Assembly, states in his autobiography that the change occurred "Monday the second of Octob. 1620 in the Afternoon," when he casually attended a Cambridge funeral service being conducted by Thomas Bainbridge. The experience was a watershed between a life in Adam's bondage, when "God was to me as a wayfaring Man," and one of assured implantation into Christ.

Yet assurance that the transition had truly been made was often the result of prolonged—even continual—self-analysis. In Perry Miller's words, the Puritans "liberated men from the treadmill of indulgences and penances, but cast them on the iron couch of introspection." Whether or not the Puritan made conversion experiences normative, he always regarded the Christian faith as a decisive, renovating commitment. Anglo-American Puritanism is in fact the fountainhead of a new conception of evangelical inwardness, a type of piety in which the unmerited and purely gracious work of divine mercy in the human soul becomes a cardinal fact of Christian existence. In due course this experiential tradition would inspire a rich body of hymnody and a devotional literature that stands in marked contrast to the older mystical tradition.[4]

Emphasis on Law and Discipline

Puritanism at its core, however, was something more than an austere exodus from the fleshpots of Egypt or a resurgence of experimental piety. It was a vigorous effort to bring God's discipline to this world, its people, and, preeminently, to God's Church. If the Puritan's Bible reading led him

4. Puritanism is thus a major source of the religious outlook which animated the great evangelical revivals of the eighteenth century and the rise of pietism on the Continent. See F. Ernest Stoeffler, *The Rise of Evangelical Pietism*.

to Amos and Saint Paul, it also led him to Moses. The Law was dear to his heart, and through the centuries he and his Reformed kindred have dwelt unremittingly on the value of the Law as teacher and moral guide for the Christian. Detesting those who were "at ease in Zion," determined to have a church whose holiness was visible, the Puritan turned to Holy Scriptures, where he found a witness to the Creator that inspired him to be a fruitful part of God's order as a citizen and in his vocation. He recognized that governments, constitutions, and laws were instituted to restrain man's sin and hence were truly of God. So long as conscience allowed, therefore, he was law-abiding and loyal. He also found much specific guidance in the Scriptures, very often in the Old Testament, for the ordering of personal life, the regulation of society, and the structuring of the Church.

With regard to personal life, the Puritan demanded of himself—and of others—a reformation of character, the rejection of idle recreations and vain display, and sober, obedient godliness. Meditation on God's Law revealed in Holy Writ brought him to contrite awareness of his sinful condition. If he were favored with an experience of the Holy Spirit's regenerating work, he would, as a "visible saint" nevertheless continue to live out his life in a "covenant of evangelical obedience." The Puritan preachers sought nothing less than a new kind of Englishman. Their aims, to use a modern expression, were countercultural; their straightforward, earnest, plain-style sermons were meant to accomplish "a revolution of the saints."

In the public realm the Puritan sought, in Governor John Winthrop's words, "a due form of government both civill and ecclesiastical." In civil affairs this demanded respect for England's legal tradition, system of government, and social traditions. Because of his concern for dutiful living, the Puritan was usually more orderly than disruptive so long as governments did not obstruct or harass those who sought to obey God's Law. When free to speculate or encouraged to innovate, however, the more thoroughgoing Puritans moved toward modern democratic ideas. The practical advocacy of Governor Winthrop, Thomas Hooker, Roger Williams, or William Penn is of a piece with the theoretical writings of Puritanism's greatest political philosopher, Algernon Sidney.

The Scriptures—even passages like the one from Amos quoted above—provided explicit directives regarding church order, and the Puritan was determined to follow these directives. Collision with established practice thus became almost inevitable, for liturgies, ceremonies, vestments, church furnishings, and ecclesiastical institutions were both public and visible, on the one hand, and regulated by canon or civil law, on the other. The Puritan's characteristic "precisianism" nearly always exhibited itself first in such matters. Often Puritan wrath was directed at seemingly trivial externals, such as the giving of a ring in marriage or the wearing of the surplice. At other times, however, such massive social realities as the bishop's office or a state-established church were called in question. Perhaps most characteristic and revealing was the creation of the "Puritan Sabbath" as a meticulously observed tribute to the glory of God and the authority of his Law. Matters of this sort, both little and large, offered almost infinite occasion for controversy, schism, and violence. Even separated congregations in exile would be disrupted by conflicts over such issues; and the New World, as we shall see, was by no means exempt.

Calvinistic Theology and the Covenant

However deeply the Puritan was convinced of his call from God, however inflamed with prophetic fire, however moved by a conversion experience, his response was very rarely one of unstructured enthusiasm. Even left-wing movements like the Quakers did not defend religion without doctrinal ordering, careful biblical exegesis, and theological responsibility. Mainstream Puritans shared a strong systematic propensity. Their leaders were usually university graduates and often academicians who were also bent on making the universities more fit instruments of reform. "Dumme Doggs" in the pulpit were anathema, a learned ministry and an informed, literate laity were prime necessities. Though looking back with thanksgiving to the great confessions of the Reformation era, the Puritans also entered into the making of new confessions with thoroughness and vigor. In Britain, as it happened, their thinking seemed to lead almost inexorably to the doctrinal views so carefully articulated in the Westminster standards and their derivative symbols. Doctrine, moreover, was almost always felt to stand in need of support from both philosophical reason and common experience. Puritanism, in short, is generally marked by careful thought; it is an intellectual tradition of great profundity.

One of the most characteristic tendencies of Puritan theology was to adapt Reformed dogma to the needs of public and personal religion by means of the idea of covenant. Federal theology, as it is called (*foedus,* covenant), has, of course, a long pre-Puritan history. Some of its roots are to be found in certain writings of Calvin, and they achieve special clarity and emphasis in the extremely influential writings of Heinrich Bullinger, Zwingli's successor in Zurich. Prominent in the Heidelberg Catechism (1563), covenant ideas were developed in more detail by a succession of theologians in the Rhineland and the Netherlands. In England they were elaborated by several great Puritan divines at Cambridge University: William Perkins (1558–

1602), John Preston (1587–1628), Richard Sibbes (1577–1635), and above all, William Ames (1576–1633). Ames had to give up his university appointments in 1610 because of his refusal to wear the surplice. Later he fled to Holland, serving as professor of theology at the University of Franeker from 1622 to 1632. His pupil, Johannes Cocceius (1603–1669), carried federal theology to its fullest and most systematic expression and became the leader of an extremely influential school of thought. Ames himself was the chief theological mentor of the New England Puritans. His *Medulla Theologiae* (Amsterdam, 1623; translated in 1642 as *The Marrow of Sacred Divinity*) was their prime theological text; his *De Conscientia* (*Cases of Conscience,* 1632, translated 1639) their chief guide to moral theology.

In Scotland, meanwhile, the particular adversities of the Reformed cause gave special strength to the covenanting idea by making individually sworn covenants the means of formalizing opposition to prelacy of all types, whether Roman or Anglican. Scottish Presbyterians became literally a people of the covenant. These various influences converged in the Westminster Assembly and made its historic declarations the most definitive covenantal confession in post-Reformation history. As followed or adapted by later groups and churches, the Westminster Confession would become by far the most influential doctrinal symbol in American Protestant history.[5]

The heart of covenant theology was the insistence that God's predestinating decrees were not part of a vast impersonal and mechanical scheme, but that, under the Gospel dispensation, God had established a covenant of grace with the seed of Abraham. This was to be appropriated in faith, and hence was irreducibly personal. Puritans disagreed as to how much was God's work, and how much preparation for grace the natural man could do; but they tended to agree that the effectual call of each elect saint of God would always come as an individuated personal encounter with God's promises. One would then make a covenant with God, as had Abraham of old (Gen. 17). Of course, the encounter was at the divine initiative, and therefore a gift of grace; by the Covenant of Redemption, indeed, God the Father had covenanted with his Son to accomplish man's salvation. But more was demanded of man than mere intellectual acknowledgment of

5. Adherence to the doctrines of the Westminster Assembly was attested at the Cambridge Synod of the New England Puritans in 1648. In 1680 the Massachusetts "Reforming Synod" and in 1708 the Connecticut Saybrook Synod adopted explicitly that version of Westminster formulated by the English Independents in 1658 and published as the Savoy Declaration. Westminster was also adapted by the English Baptists in 1677, and in 1707 this London Confession was adopted by the immensely influential Philadelphia Association of Baptists in America. The unaltered Westminster Confession (and Catechism) were made normative for the Church of Scotland in 1689, and in due course for American Presbyterians as well.

divine mercy. True faith involved inward, overt, and obedient preparation, appropriation, humility, dedication, gratitude—and a commitment to walk in God's way according to his Law. A specific conversion experience was at first rarely regarded as normative or necessary, though for many it was by this means that assurance of election was received. Gradually, as Puritan pastors and theologians examined themselves and counseled their more earnest and troubled parishioners, a consensus as to the morphology of true Christian experience began to be formulated. In due course—and with important consequences for America—these Nonconforming Puritans in the Church of England came increasingly to regard a specific experience of regeneration as an essential sign of election. In New England and elsewhere "conversion" would become a requirement for church membership. After Cromwell's ascendancy these notions would also become widespread in England.

THE PURITAN SPECTRUM

The proper manner of organizing particular churches, the relation of these congregations one with another, and the question as to whether established national churches were sanctioned by Scripture occasioned constant and inevitable controversy. Those who believed that a formal church covenant was required of local congregations, or even that a national covenant was the responsibility of a committed commonwealth, raised other problems, as did underlying doctrines of the ministry and the sacraments. As thoughtful men addressed these diverse issues and sought to develop self-consistent views, patterns gradually emerged which make it useful for the historian to describe a broad spectrum of Puritan reformism. At the right was the Prelatical party, which accepted the ancient structures of England's church and at least the basic notion of a Book of Common Prayer, but which doubted the values of strict conformity, stressed the need for a renewal of preaching and pastoral care, for greater ceremonial austerity, and for an increase of Christian discipline at all levels. Carrying these ideas somewhat further were the Presbyterians, who took the established church of Geneva or Scotland as their model. Like the Episcopalians, they accepted the notion that the church should be nationally organized, but prelacy was to be replaced by a system of ascending judicatories or church courts: local sessions, presbyteries, synods, and a general assembly, with the clergy and laity of the presbytery serving as a kind of elective, representative, and composite "bishop." It would still be the church of the entire nation, and infant baptism would prevail everywhere. Such advocacy was strong in Elizabeth's time; and later, under the Long Parliament, Presbyterians had their way for a time in England. Many Puritans of this general persuasion also emigrated to America, but only much later, when joined by thousands of Presbyterians of Scottish background, would their church principles be fully institutionalized.

Puritans of congregational tendency became more numerous as covenantal notions gained deeper hold and as Stuart intransigence made national reform seem unlikely. They conceived of the church as ideally a congregation of "visible saints" who had covenanted with God and with one another. A church so formed they regarded as utterly complete in itself: it could determine who were the saints, discipline and excommunicate its members, and ordain its duly called ministers, who would administer the ordinances (sacraments) only to those in the covenant. Congregationalists, however, were not of one mind as to how separate a particular church should be, nor were they agreed in their judgments of the "unreformed" Church of England. Some "Separatists" viewed the established church as no better than Romanism and hence not a church of Christ at all. With Robert Browne they would refuse to "tarry for the magistrate" and go their own way. Still others, the Baptists, would press the covenant logic even farther, abandon the idea of infant baptism, redefine this sacrament as simply the external seal of the Spirit's work, and insist upon complete separation of church and state. They would also diminish the significance of ordination and the Lord's Supper. Such Separatists, whether Baptist or not, often put themselves in a position where exile or persecution was their lot. Radical separatism, however, was rare in the period before the Civil War, though various kinds and degrees of "Independency" flourished during the Interregnum.

The great majority of congregational thinkers and covenant theologians remained within the establishment in the hope that they could reform it according to their views. With varying degrees of recalcitrance these non-separating Congregationalists discharged their religious obligations within the Church of England. They did not deny that it was a true church and they hoped for a national settlement on their terms, but in the meantime they carried Nonconformity as far as conscience demanded or as bishops allowed. The repressive measures of Charles I and Archbishop Laud finally convinced many of this persuasion that their hopes for reform were in vain, thus providing the impetus for the great Puritan migration to America. Even then they were conspicuously *not* separating from the Church of England, but simply providing an example for the world to see. After 1640, when Parliament made it possible for Puritans to reorganize the national church in England, the Presbyterians were dominant, and Congregational delegates were again forced into dissent. Under the Commonwealth, however, more radical tendencies flourished: Baptists became numerous, and to their left still other groups took shape. Most notable of these was the Society of Friends, among whom a Spirit-filled fellowship took the place of an ordained ministry and objective sacraments. Other groups were more radical still: some completely individualistic, some consumed with millennialist doctrines, some with social revolution in mind. Yet even in these extremes there remained a common interest in reform, revival, and personal faith that made at least some of the radicals recognizable spiritual companions of at least some bishops at the other extreme of the Puritan movement.

Nearly every component of this wide spectrum, and still other components as well, would enter into the religious life of colonial America. An "Anglicanism" deeply colored by Puritan convictions would shape the early religious life of Virginia—as long as possible, to the legal exclusion of other churches. In due course similar but less homogeneous Anglican establishments would be erected in Maryland, the Carolinas, New York, and Georgia. Quakers would be prominent among both founders and settlers of New Jersey and Pennsylvania, and would also find their way in significant numbers to Rhode Island and the Carolinas. In virtually all of the colonies Baptists would found churches—first in Rhode Island, most influentially in eastern Pennsylvania, but also in the South. Presbyterians were widely scattered, but in the Middle Colonies they were able to organize a farflung presbytery in 1706. This group also won many neighboring Congregationalists to their persuasion, and shared important aspects of their tradition with the Dutch, German, and French Reformed who gathered in the same colonies. Plymouth is remembered as the colony of more or less separatistic Congregationalists. Among the early founders of Rhode Island were extremist Puritans of various sorts, many of them exiles. Finally, in the Holy Commonwealths of Massachusetts, Connecticut, and New Haven, a "magisterial" nonseparating Congregationalism would be so fully institutionalized that the very term Puritan has often been reserved for them alone. Because they are in a sense archetypical, and because for almost two centuries it was their fortune to be spared both encroachment or molestation, logic if not chronology makes them the proper starting point for an account of religious developments in the American colonies.

9

THE HOLY COMMONWEALTHS OF NEW ENGLAND

All over the world New England is known as the place where Puritanism achieved its fullest, least inhibited flowering. And for well over two centuries after its founding, this region self-consciously understood its own vocation in these terms. These colonies, to be sure, were not the only ones to have some special sense of purpose. William Penn, Lord Baltimore, and Roger Williams also launched their plantations as holy experiments of one sort or another. But the four chief New England colonies were instilled with a peculiarly corporate spirit. In each of them, covenantal ideas, though no magic bar to schism or fragmentation, put a curb on purely individualistic endeavors, while an underlying conception of government by social compact gave further strength to the feeling of solidarity. The idea of a "national covenant" also bound together the people of each commonwealth, as well as the visible saints, in a common task. In the early years, this sense of a common calling was strengthened by the widely held conviction that the reformation being carried out in these commonwealths was actually a decisive phase in the final chapter of God's plan for his Church in this world. England in these latter times was conceived as truly an "Elect Nation," and the Puritans of New England were now corporately performing its ultimate task.

THE PLANTING OF PLYMOUTH

There is no better place to begin an account of New England church life than with Governor William Bradford's *History of Plimoth Plantation,* for none can match his description of the Pilgrims' arrival in Cape Cod Bay in November 1620.

Being thus arived in a good harbor and brought safe to land, they fell upon their knees & blessed ye God of heaven, who had brought them over ye vast & furious ocean, and delivered them from all ye periles & miseries thereof, againe to set their feete on ye firme and stable earth, their proper elemente. . . .

But hear I cannot but stay and make a pause, and stand half amased at this poore peoples presente condition; and so I thinke will the reader too, when he well considers ye same. . . . They had now no friends to wellcome them, no inns to entertaine or refresh their weatherbeaten bodys, no houses or much less townes to repaire too, to seeke for succoure. . . . And for ye season it was winter, and they that know ye winters of ye cuntrie know them to be sharp & violent, & subjects to cruell & feirce stormes, deangerous to travill to known places, much more to serch an unknown coast. Besids, what could they see but a hidious & desolate wildernes, full of wild beasts & willd men? and what multituds ther might be of them they knew not. Nether could they, as it were, goe up to ye tope of Pisgah, to vew from this wildernes a more godly cuntrie. . . . For sumer being done, all things stand upon them with a wetherbeaten face; and ye whole countrie, full of woods & thickets, represented a wild & savage heiw.[1]

A month of anxious searching for a harbor and town site followed, until finally on Christmas Day they asserted their freedom from "popish festivals" by beginning work on their common stores building. But before landing they had formed a "combination" as "ye first foundation of their governmente in this place; occasioned partly by ye discontented & mutinous speeches that some of the strangers amongst them had let fall." The famous Mayflower Compact reads as follows:

In ye name of God, Amen. We whose names are underwriten, the loyall subjects of our dread soveraigne Lord, King James, by ye grace of God, of Great Britaine, France & Ireland king, defender of ye faith, &c., having undertaken, for ye glorie of God, and advancemente of ye Christian faith, and honour of our king & countrie, a voyage to plant ye first colonie in ye Northerne parts of Virginia, doe by these presents solemnly & mutualy in ye presence of God, and one of another, covenant and combine our selves togeather into a civill body politick, for our better ordering & preservation, & furtherance of ye ends aforesaid; and by vertue hereof to enacte constitute, and frame such just & equall lawes, ordinances, acts, constitutions, & offices, from time to time, as

1. William Bradford, *Of Plimoth Plantation* (Boston, 1901), pp. 94–95.

> shall be thought most meete & convenient for ye generall good of ye Colonie, unto which we promise all due submission and obedience. In witness whereof we have hereunder subscribed our names at Cap-Codd ye 11. of November, in ye year of ye raigne of our soveraigne lord, King James, of England, France, & Ireland ye eighteenth, and of Scotland ye fiftie fourth. Ano. Dom. 1620.[2]

The social compact thus accomplished accords with Puritan political theory and stands in close relationship to an event sixteen years before, when some of these very persons in the manorhouse at Scrooby had, "as ye Lords free people, joyned them selves (by a covenant of the Lord) into a church estate." They had consciously separated from the Church of England, and were therefore "hunted & persecuted on every side." Their afflictions were made no easier by the epithet "schismatic" visited upon them by non-separating Puritans no less than by the strictest Conformists. Realizing the impossibility of their predicament, the Scrooby congregation had decided in 1607 to flee to the Netherlands. After many misadventures the congregation was gradually assembled in Leyden, "yet it was not longe before they saw the grime & grisly face of povertie coming upon them like an armed man, with whom they must bukle & incounter . . . and though they were sometimes foyled, yet by Gods assistance they prevailed and got ye victorie." Due to their "hard and continuall labor" they prospered. Under the able ministry of John Robinson and Elder William Brewster "they grew in knowledge & other gifts & graces of ye spirite of God . . . and many came unto them from diverse parts of England, so as they grew a great congregation." Influenced doubtless by the large-spirited Robinson, their temper moderated to a much more charitable form of Separatism than many had previously shown.

Yet a comfortable life in Holland was not their goal, and inquietude over this prospect eventually led them to contact the Virginia Company in London. In this they were favored by both the company's desperate need and the deeply sympathetic efforts of Edwin Sandys, but even these advantages did not preclude an enormously complex series of negotiations. After the most vexatious delays, the little Leyden group set sail from Delfshaven on 22 July 1620 in the *Speedwell.* Joined by others of their group in England, the whole company finally took passage on the *Mayflower,* which left Plymouth harbor on 16 September, an overcrowded and underprovisioned ship, bearing, in addition to its crew of forty-eight, one hundred and one passengers. Of the latter, fifty-six were adults, fourteen were servants and

2. Ibid., p. 110.

hired artisans (not Separatists), and thirty-one were children, of whom at least seven belonged neither to the passengers nor to any English Separatist, but were probably waifs and idlers. The figures include thirty-five from Leyden and sixty-six from London and Southampton who were recruited for the venture. On the voyage itself, though it took sixty-five days, only one passenger died, while two were born. But the first winter compensated horribly for that good fortune: by spring half of the company had died of scurvy, general debility, and other unascertainable causes.

The heroic beginnings and unostentatious life of the Plymouth colony have won for it a secure place in American hearts. From the viewpoint of church history, moreover, its symbolic significance is great, for it remains the classic instance in America of congregational Separatism. From humble or lower middle class backgrounds, the "Pilgrim Fathers" had few intellectual or academic pretensions or aspirations. Less than twenty university men came to the colony during its first three decades, and only three of them, all ministers, remained. For fifty years the colony lacked a public school and sent no one away to a university. Perhaps as a consequence of these facts, but also because the colony as a whole attracted few immigrants, its churches were frequently without ministers. Until 1629 there were none in the whole colony; indeed, it is something of an anomaly that for almost a decade these pious Pilgrims scarcely had a church even by their own definition. A Dutch visitor in 1627 saw them marching in solemn procession and by drumbeat to Sabbath meeting, where Elder Brewster, a layman, "taught twise every Saboth, and yt both powerfully and profitably, to ye great contemment of ye hearers, and their comfortable edification; yea, many were brought to God by his ministrie." But Brewster, on advice from his Amsterdam pastor, did not administer the sacraments; and until the Reverend Ralph Smith came from Salem, Plymouth had no regular minister. The company had sent the Reverend John Lyford, an Anglican of sorts, in 1624; but when he proved unworthy, Bradford ran him out of Plymouth.

Only a few men—notably Elder William Brewster, Deacon Samuel Fuller, Edward Winslow, and possibly the fabled Myles Standish—are remembered as significant champions of the colony's "way." As to literary achievements, Governor Bradford's simple yet eloquent history stands almost alone as its great religious epic. John Robinson, their most powerful advocate, remained in the Netherlands, where he died in 1625 before he could join his congregation. The American representatives of Separatism at Plymouth were not theologically minded, nor were they aggressive or self-conscious in their churchmanship. It is unlikely that they influenced the church views of the Bay Colony, and in later years they probably adopted the Massachusetts demand for a converted church membership. They sought and found freedom to create a "body politick" and a thoroughly congregational church way, and this is the chief significance of their courageous venture.

There are reasons for the failure of the Pilgrim Fathers to achieve greatness—which they never aspired to in the first place. For one thing, "the howling wildernesse" to which they came was something less than lush. Having landed outside of the Virginia grant, moreover, they were involved in financial and legal difficulties which were not resolved until the "Old Colony" became duly chartered in 1691 as part of Massachusetts. The government nevertheless was orderly. All freemen voted for the governor and seem to have elected John Carver even before they left England. When he died, Bradford took his place and through thirty annual terms of office came virtually to personify the mind of the colony. In 1636 the *Great Fundamentals,* a legal code, was enacted; and in 1643 a representative form of government was established for the ten towns then existing. Their delegates met annually in Plymouth with the governor and his assistants as a unicameral general court. Despite the absence of a religious test, the franchise became no broader than it was in the Bay Colony—limited in practice to propertied men of stable orthodox views.

For reasons not entirely clear, the colony grew only very slowly. It took two years to replenish the losses of the first year's decimation. After a decade there were only three hundred, and by 1643 there were about twenty-five hundred people widely scattered among ten towns. As the attraction of remoter lands increased, Bradford reported that Plymouth town itself became "thin and bare." In 1691 the colony's population was estimated at seventy-five hundred. By that time its mode of life, its problems, and its churches had lost most of their distinctiveness. The nature of this transformation, as well as of the colony's most besetting problem, is better highlighted in the history of Plymouth's large and overbearing neighbor to the north.

THE COLONY AT MASSACHUSETTS BAY

Preliminary Activities

To suggest that New England waters and harbors were seething with activity between 1620 and 1630 would be misleading, but it would be still more inaccurate to imagine a time of empty silence broken only by the prayers of the Pilgrims. Actually a great deal happened. Through the efforts of Ferdinando Gorges the Plymouth Company (a branch of the old Virginia Company) was reorganized in 1620 as the Council for New England. The group of aristocrats who accomplished this feat was then incorporated as a land company, with a grant to all the territory between 40°N and 48°N.

Though unauthorized within the council's grants, Thomas and Andrew Weston founded an unruly and short-lived colony at Wessagusset (Weymouth) in 1622. Captain Wollaston led a similar venture to Mount Wollaston (Quincy) about the same time. When it failed, Thomas Morton, a London lawyer of dubious virtue, regrouped the colony in accordance with his plans for traffic with the Indians in liquor and firearms; but by 1628 Myles Standish of Plymouth had driven him out. Gorges and the council also encouraged sporadic activity in Maine, where fishing and furs were the primary attractions. In 1623–24 Robert Gorges (son of Ferdinando), now invested with formal authority and the high-sounding title of governor general, had hopes of a vast proprietary principality at Wessagusset; but after a miserable winter he decamped, leaving several of his men behind. One of these, the Reverend William Blaxton, established himself in self-sufficient isolation on Beacon Hill. Other settlements or trading posts at Nantasket and several other points were set up, some of them by fishermen, including those from Plymouth. In 1623 there were at least forty authorized sailings to areas held by the Council for New England; and in 1625 at least fifty ships were fishing in New England waters. By that time there must have been several hundred permanent or semipermanent "settlers" at various points along the coast besides those at Plymouth.

Only one of these scattered efforts has any place in church history, except insofar as they all made the area better known. This single important exception begins with the colony at Cape Ann (Gloucester) founded by a company organized in the Wessex seaport of Dorchester by John White, the minister of Holy Trinity Church there. White was a man of Puritan sympathies who had a deep pastoral concern for the fishermen and crewmen in New England. Since there seemed to be promising commercial advantages as well, the Dorchester Company was organized. Fourteen men were sent out in 1623, and thirty-two more in the year following. When after three years they had turned no profit and provided little pastoral care to wandering mariners, the company called on Roger Conant, a merchant who had spent one year in the Plymouth colony and had recently visited Nantasket, to take over the company's New England affairs. By the time he accomplished his mission, however, the company had collapsed, having discovered that "no sure fishing place in the Land is fit for planting, nor any good place for planting found fit for fishing, at least neere the Shoare, And secondly, rarely any Fisher-men will worke at Land, neither are Husbandmen fit Fisher-men but with long use and experience." [3] Conant was left in America as a kind of caretaker "governor" to pick up the debris, a task which he accomplished well by moving the colony's twenty souls to Naumkeag (Salem), where a viable agricultural colony could be maintained. On observing the situation there, he wrote back to White that this new site "might prove a receptacle for such as upon account of religion would be willing to begin a foreign plantation," and received assurances in turn that appropriate measures would be taken.

In England meanwhile the efforts of White and some of his Dorchester associates converged with the interests of "some Gentlemen of London" and the colonial desires of an earnest group of Puritans in East Anglia. Ninety of these interested persons ultimately gained legal status and were chartered in 1628 as the New England Company, with a title (such as it was) to lands "from the Atlantic Ocean to the South Sea" between a point three miles north of the Merrimac River to a point three miles south of the Charles. Under these auspices and with John Endecott as "chief-in-command," a party of about forty sailed from Weymouth on the *Abigail* on 20 June 1628, reaching Naumkeag on 6 September. Here, with little solicitude for the "Old Planters" under Conant, Endecott ruled with a hard hand until 1629, when word was received that the New England Company had been reconstituted on a radically different basis as the Massachusetts Bay Company.

The Salem Settlement

When the imperious Endecott began to exercise his authority, the old settlers of Naumkeag rose up in resentment. A peace of sorts was worked out, and the settlement was renamed "Salem," meaning "peace." The colony began to prepare for winter, and since their preparations seem to have been adequate, perhaps we may infer that Edward Johnson's idyllic picture of the first winter applied to that which was soon upon them.

> They made shift to rub out the Wintern cold by the Fire-side, having fuell enough growing at their very doores, turning down many a drop of the Bottell, and burning Tobacco with all the ease they could, discoursing betweene one while and another, of the great progresse they would make after the Summers-Sun had changed the Earths white furr'd Gowne into a greene Mantell.[4]

3. Clifford K. Shipton, *Roger Conant, A Founder of Massachusetts* (Cambridge, Mass.: Harvard University Press, 1945), p. 55.

4. Ibid., p. 62.

If these men talked about their homeland, as undoubtedly they did, it was no doubt frequently about the declining state of affairs there and the likelihood that many would soon be seeking refuge in New England. With the summer of 1629, the situation of the settlement was drastically altered. The Massachusetts Bay Company gave instructions for the appointment of Endecott as governor, and the formation of a council of twelve. The Old Planters were placated by receiving two representatives on the council, a generous grant of fine land, and the right to grow tobacco, though sale of the latter to company settlers was forbidden "unless upon urgent occasion, for the benefit of health." Later instructions permitted it "to be taken privately by ancient men, and none others," a restriction which was more than a Puritan foible, for King James himself had written *A Counterblast on Tobacco* in 1604. As it turned out, something more substantial than tobacco was to become necessary, for during June and July four ships bearing nearly three hundred settlers arrived—the largest and best equipped expedition which had been sent to New England up to this point.

Since the new arrivals included three ministers of pronounced Puritan persuasion, John Higginson, Samuel Skelton, and Francis Bright, the governor set aside 20 June 1629 as a special day for investing them with authority. The morning was given over to prayer and teaching, the afternoon to the solemnities of election. The candidates spoke on the subject of the ministry, and were found to be thoroughly congregational in conviction. Ballots were cast by "every fit member."

> So Mr. Skelton was chosen pastor and Mr. Higginson to be teacher; and they accepting ye choyce, Mr. Higginson with 3. or 4. of ye gravest members of ye church, laid their hands on Mr. Skelton, using prayers therwith. This being done, there was imposission of hands [on] Mr. Higginson also.[5]

Another "day of Humiliation" was set for 6 August, when deacons and elders were to be elected. But before that time it was decided that the church in Salem must itself be more properly constituted, and thirty persons, including Roger Conant and probably some others of the Old Planters, were by some means selected for the task. What criteria they used is not known, but there is no evidence that accounts of saving experience were required. The now famous Salem church covenant was then prepared and signed:

5. Charles Gott to William Bradford, 30 July 1629, in Bradford. *Of Plimoth Plantation*, p. 317.

> We Covenant with the Lord and one with an other; and doe bynd our selves in the presence of God, to walke together in all his waies, according as he is pleased to reveale himself unto us in his blessed word of truth.[6]

Since a body with proper ecclesiastical powers now existed, not only to rule upon the admission of new members and to discipline themselves, but also to call a ministry, in due course Skelton and Higginson were again "ordained to their several offices." In this way the Massachusetts Bay Colony had a ministry ordained in New England even before Plymouth did, for it was late in 1629 before Ralph Smith, a Separatist minister who had come out on the ship with Higginson, having "exercised his gifts" among the Pilgrims, was duly called and ordained there.

Considerable controversy has arisen over both the "facts" and the significance of these events. Most agitated has been the argument over the "Deacon Fuller myth"—the theory that during the winter and spring Plymouth's good but rather eccentric physician, while attending the ailing settlers at Salem, persuaded the Massachusetts men that in Congregationalism as practiced at Plymouth was the true Scripture doctrine of the church. By this chance occurrence, it is claimed, the whole ecclesiastical drift of the Bay Colony was so altered that its leaders, lay and clerical, intoxicated by the "free aire" of the New World and torn from the old ways by the persuasions of Deacon Fuller, changed their minds about the Church of England and became Separatistic Congregationalists. Following this line of reasoning, even the learned Leonard Bacon found the "germ of New England" in the church founded at the house of William Brewster in Scrooby. Far more plausible, however, is the view that Higginson, already silenced and on the verge of arrest in England, insisted that a covenanted church be formed in Salem in order to validate his ministry there. This view conforms with the words he allegedly uttered as his ship left England: "We will not say, as the separatists were wont to say at their leaving of England, 'Farewel, Babylon' . . . but . . . 'farewel, the Church of God in England.' " Men who for years had been pondering and debating these matters of doctrine and polity, and who were ready to risk exile rather than violate their convictions, were not likely to be deflected from their course by hearsay accounts of a Separatist church in Plymouth. Deacon Fuller's visit probably did convince Endecott that the facts were "farr from ye commone reporte that hath been spread of you." In other words, Endecott perceived

6. Williston Walker, *The Creeds and Platforms of Congregationalism,* p. 116.

that his people could be in communion with the church at Plymouth. Considering the reputation that Separatists had in the eyes of many nonseparating Puritans, and that acknowledged fellowship with extremists could hardly please the Massachusetts stockholders in England, this was no small accomplishment on Deacon Fuller's part. It proved permanent, too, for in churchly matters moderately good relations between New Plymouth and the Bay Colony continued.[7]

Removal of the Massachusetts Bay Company to New England

What neither Governor Endecott nor Deacon Fuller could have known or even imagined had meanwhile been accomplished by the Bay Colony's leaders in England. Meeting on 28 July at Sempringham, the stockholders in East Anglia conceived the bold idea of transferring the entire company to New England, and of taking with them the charter with its surprisingly large grant of governmental authority. On 26 August twelve of these Puritans met in Cambridge and signed an agreement "to inhabite and continue in New England. Provided, always that . . . the whole government together with the Patent for the said plantacion, bee first by an order of Court legally transferred and established to remayne with us and others which shall inhabite upon the said plantacion." Two days later the proposal was presented to the General Court by the company, and on 29 August the way was officially cleared for the colony to displace the company.

With the election of John Winthrop (1588–1649) as governor in October, emigration plans were pressed vigorously. By spring a fleet of eleven ships had been assembled at Southampton, and vast amounts of stores had been purchased. England's largest colonial migration was under way. The first four ships with four hundred passengers set sail on 29 March 1630, with Governor Winthrop in the *Arbella*. Before the year was out six hundred more would follow; and by 1643, when the reins of government passed from Charles I to the Puritan-dominated Long Parliament, opening new opportunities for reform in England itself, more than twenty thousand people had made their way to Massachusetts. But before discussing this "swarming of the Puritans" in New England, it would be well to inquire into the convictions, hopes, and ideals of those who projected and guided this Holy Commonwealth.

They were, of course, Puritans in the broad sense in which that move-

7. Plymouth sent fraternal messengers to the Cambridge Synod in 1647, and its church institutions came gradually to resemble those in the Bay Colony, even to include the requirement that a candidate for membership give account of his experience of God's effectual call.

ment has been defined in foregoing pages. They shared its Reformed and reforming spirit and its convictions about the need for the magistrate and the church to cooperate in establishing a civil and ecclesiastical order. More specifically, they were a self-conscious, tightly knit group within the larger movement. They had gone beyond presbyterian conceptions of a national church to one that was categorically congregational. They no longer accepted the pure preaching of the gospel and correct administration of the sacraments as sufficient marks of a true church. And they believed that the church should consist only of "visible saints" and their children, with a knowledgeable profession of faith and consistent God-fearing behavior as the tests of visibility. In the darkening fourth decade of the seventeenth century, they had finally abandoned hope that such a church way could be established in England. They could "tarry for the magistrate" no longer, lest they be extinguished altogether. As a saving remnant they left England behind, to become a kind of Church of Christ in Exile, a "citty on a hill" for all the world to see, or even the final purification of church and state before the Last Days.

Yet they were not separating themselves from England's church any more than Higginson had when at Land's End he saw England slipping from view. This conviction was expressed in the *Humble Request* which Winthrop and the other leaders had written just before they departed.

> We . . . esteem it our honor to call the *Church of England* from whence we rise, our dear mother . . . ever acknowledging that such hope and part as we have obtained in the common salvation we have received in her bosom and sucked it from her breasts. We leave it not, therefore, as loathing that milk wherewith we were nourished there; but blessing God for the parentage and education, as members of the same body, shall always rejoice in her good.[8]

Congregationalism was not synonymous with Separatism, nor was the distinction a labyrinthine sophistry. Though convinced of grave defects in England's church, these Puritans did not consider it the Whore of Babylon or an engine of Antichrist. They sometimes emigrated as groups from English parishes, as did those from Chelmsford who were reunited with their former preacher, Thomas Hooker, in Newtown, Massachusetts; but they simply could not unchurch the relatives, friends and fellow-Christians they left behind. Their willingness to see implicitly—and hence authentically—

8. Quoted in a very important account of the matter by Perry Miller, *Orthodoxy in Massachusetts*, p. 139.

covenanted churches and truly "called" ministers in Old England was a realistic and charitable refusal to yield to fanaticism.

The one crucial characteristic of "classic" New England Puritan thought that is not revealed by the famous Salem events was the conviction that particular churches should be formed only by men and women who could give credible evidence that they had inwardly experienced God's effectual call. On this point they had not arrived at consensus by 1630, though years of private introspection and collective searching of hearts led in that direction. By 1635, however, with John Cotton probably leading the way, the leaders of the Bay Colony reached this significant corporate decision. They made a narration of the experience of regenerating grace a requirement of adult church membership. Seen in full perspective, this was a radical demand. For the first time in Christendom, a state church with vigorous conceptions of enforced uniformity in belief and practice was requiring an internal, experiential test of church membership. Many future problems of the New England churches stemmed from this decision. It would appear, moreover, that its influence beyond New England was proportionate to its revolutionary character.

Building the Bay Colony

Formation of the Holy Commonwealth began immediately, for the simple act of joining the enterprise was taken to mean involvement in and responsibility for its corporate tasks in the world. Even aboard the *Arbella* Governor Winthrop had drawn out some of these implications:

> It is of the nature and essence of every society to be knit together by some covenant, either expressed or implied. . . .
>
> For the work we have in hand, it is by mutual consent, through a special over-ruling providence and a more than ordinary approbation of the churches of Christ, to seek out a place of cohabitation and consortship, under a due form of government both civil and ecclesiastical. . . .
>
> Therefore we must not content ourselves with usual ordinary means. Whatsoever we did or ought to have done when we lived in England, the same must we do, and more also where we go. . . .
>
> Neither must we think that the Lord will bear with such failings at our hands as He doth from those among whom we have lived. . . .
>
> Thus stands the cause between God and us: we are entered into covenant with Him for this work; we have taken out a commission, the Lord hath given us leave to draw our own articles. . . .

We shall find that the God of Israel is among us. . . . For we must consider that we shall be as a city upon a hill, the eyes of all people are upon us.[9]

On 12 June the *Arbella* arrived at Salem and put ashore its weary, weakened passengers. As other ships arrived, Winthrop shifted the colony's center to the fine landlocked harbor at the mouth of the Charles River. Soon Boston, on its easily protected peninsula, became the seat of government. Before the year was out, eleven ships had come, and the colonists they brought had made the beginnings of a famous cluster of towns in the Bay area.

Prompt measures were taken to establish the civil government on the foundation provided in the royal charter they had brought with them. On 23 August 1630 Governor Winthrop, Deputy Governor Thomas Dudley, and seven "assistants" of the company began their governmental tasks. But on 29 October, at a meeting thrown open to "the whole body of settlers," they carried out a minor political revolution: it was decided "by the generall vote of the people, and ereccion of hands" that the freemen of the colony, not the stockholders of the company, "should have the power of chuseing Assistants . . . and the Assistants from amongst themselves to chuse a Governor and Deputy Governor, whoe with the Assistants should have the power of makeing lawes and chuseing officers to execute the same." At the next meeting of the General Court 116 newcomers were added to the original group of twelve "freemen"; this probably included most of the adult males. In 1632 the freemen were empowered to elect the governor and deputy governor directly.

The trading company thus became a commonwealth, though it was far from being a "democracy" in the modern sense. The governor and assistants were still to enact such laws as God's Word and passing exigencies might require; and only church members had the franchise. In 1634 the freemen asked and received still larger concessions, according to which the representatives of the several towns gained legislative powers. The Bay Colony governed itself by the resultant bicameral system without essential modification for over sixty years. To call it a "theocracy" is therefore absurd. Its franchise was wider than England's, and "of all the governments in the Western world at the time, that of early Massachusetts gave the clergy least authority."[10] The clergy's influence was large, to be sure; but it was both informal, depending on the Puritan's reluctance to ignore ministerial coun-

9. Perry Miller, ed., *The American Puritans*, p. 82.

10. Edmund S. Morgan, *The Puritan Dilemma, The Story of John Winthrop*, p. 96.

sel, and indirect, resting largely on the minister's important role in determining church membership.

Towns in the Bay Colony were laid out more or less after the pattern of an English manor. Population growth meant new towns; but in order to guard against the dispersion and isolation of families that an unlimited land supply made possible, each new town was incorporated with responsible proprietors in charge. At its center were the meetinghouse, the common pasture, and the village. In 1642 and 1647 laws requiring a common school were passed. Radiating from the center of town were the fields and farmlands. The church was not only the geographical and social focus of town life, but its spiritual center as well, formed at the earliest possible time by the covenanting of the town's visible saints. Thereupon the lay officers were elected and a minister called, who in due course would be ordained, in all probability for a lifetime ministry in the same town, possibly dividing his duties with a colleague (or "teacher") if the town were able to obtain full clerical "equipment." With a church formed, a meetinghouse would be erected for worship and civic assembly, a plain and usually small building, with a centered pulpit, no holy altar (only a serviceable table), and no "popish" tower until a much later day. On the Sabbath there were morning and afternoon services—each with its lengthy free prayers, discordantly sung psalms, and a very long sermon. The sermons, delivered in plain style on a wide range of subjects, offered solid biblical exposition, stated the doctrine explicitly, and gave particular attention to its practical "use." The congregation was concerned above all with the way of salvation and its moral implications.

Town meetings were at first both civil and ecclesiastical in their scope, electing hogreeves and selectmen, attending to the repair of roads, and arranging for the maintenance of minister and meetinghouse. In some instances they retained this dual character on into the nineteenth century. Since an increasingly large number of townsmen failed to meet the experiential demands of church membership, strictly ecclesiastical elections and discipline came to be reserved for the church itself, while more general matters of supporting public worship fell to the town or "parish." The General Court in turn made such support obligatory and in many ways sought to uphold the churches and protect them from their enemies. The civil government also enforced the "first table" of the Decalogue, punishing blasphemy, heresy, and vain swearing, and requiring that the Sabbath be kept. Urian Oakes (1631?–81), minister in Cambridge and sometime president of Harvard, stated the theory behind this close cooperation of church and state with admirable precision and typical Puritan confidence:

> According to the design of our founders and the frame of things laid by them the interest of righteousness in the commonwealth and holiness in the Churches are inseparable. . . . To divide what God hath conjoyned . . . is folly in its exaltation. I look upon this as a little model of the glorious kingdom of Christ on earth. Christ reigns among us in the commonwealth as well as in the Church and hath his glorious interest involved and wrapt up in the good of both societies respectively.[11]

The New England Way as exemplified in the Bay Colony rested on the conviction that the entire commonwealth was intended to be as faithfully "under God" as it could possibly be.

The general welfare thus required the maintenance of a learned ministry. *New England's First Fruits* (1643) stated that need in memorable words:

> After God had carried us safe to *New England,* and wee had builded our houses, provided necessaries for our liveli-hood, rear'd convenient places for Gods worship, and settled the Civill Government; One of the next things we longed for, and looked after was to advance *Learning* and perpetuate it to Posterity; dreading to leave an illiterate Ministry to the Churches, when our present Ministers shall lie in the Dust.[12]

To this end in 1636 the General Court voted "to give 400 [pounds] towards a schoale or colledge." A year later, they chose a plot in Newtown (later Cambridge), where Thomas Shepard was minister, and appointed as master Nathaniel Eaton, brother of Theophilus Eaton, the London merchant and cofounder of New Haven. The first classes were held in 1638, and in that year, too, John Harvard, a young minister and Cambridge graduate, died and left his property and library to the infant nursery of learning. Although Eaton proved unsatisfactory, the next president, Henry Dunster, brought many improvements. Before Dunster's conversion to Baptist views required his resignation in 1654, the college had received a new charter (1650—and still in effect at present), was granting degrees, and had self-consciously committed itself to liberal education in the old university tradition. In 1674 President Hoar could publish the names of two hundred Harvard graduates.

The first printing press in the American colonies was set up at Cambridge in 1639, and from it in 1640 issued the first book, *THE VVHOLE BOOKE OF PSALMES Faithfully TRANSLATED into ENGLISH Metre, Whereunto is prefixed a discourse declaring not only the lawfullnes, but*

11. Urian Oakes, *New England Pleaded With* (1673), p. 49.

12. Samuel Eliot Morison, *The Founding of Harvard College,* p. 432. Appendix D gives the document in its entirety.

also the necessity of the heavenly Ordinance of singing Scripture Psalmes in the Churches of God. It is not clear why a new metrical version and so large a printing venture was undertaken; but the desire to indicate the Bay Colony's ecclesiastical self-sufficiency was probably paramount. Whatever the reason, the accomplishment was impressive. It suggests the degree to which a miniature Puritan version of English civilization had taken shape in a corner of the vast American wilderness.

Of all the achievements of Puritanism, however, none was more important than that which the Puritan himself would have insisted to be a work of God: its capacity to shape a type of person. It could take a brilliant young Cambridge graduate like John Cotton, who might easily have been led by vanity and his own rhetorical gifts into the very kind of hireling ministry that Milton excoriated in *Lycidas,* and turn him down the hard path to exile. Or it could take a young country gentleman and graduate of Trinity College, Cambridge, like John Winthrop, and so utterly reshape his life's purpose that he would sacrifice all the security of England to lead the Bay Colony's venture. Only through biographical study of such men as these —clerical or lay—can the movement's central achievement be grasped. And it is no small feat that the colony itself would similarly shape a new generation of men and women—even a long posterity.

10

TENSIONS IN THE NEW ENGLAND WAY

The New England Zion was never an untroubled Christian utopia. Settlement brought unsettlement. Indian wars, political crises, and problems of diplomacy were added to the serious difficulties of economic depression which ensued after the victories of Cromwell brought an end to the great Puritan emigration from England. In due course, the Restoration created other issues. Intrinsic religious tensions also emerged, at least five of which raised major problems. The first involved the fundamental theological question as to the place of law and "legal obedience" under the gospel order, a matter with which the American churches were still wrestling in the later twentieth century and which in one form or another has aroused heated controversies during most of the intervening decades. The second and third had to do with ordering the church, with settling ecclesiological questions that stand very near to the center of the Puritan idea of reformation. The fourth was peculiarly American in that it involved the matter of how properly to regard the indigenous Indian population. The fifth was the comprehensive problem of sustaining the fervor of the Holy Commonwealths—more specifically, how to halt or roll back the seemingly inexorable process of routinization and declining fervor.

NATURE AND GRACE

Early and late one central question recurs in Christian history: What is man's role and what is God's in the work of redemption? And if the Reformation opened the question anew, it certainly did not close it. For the Puritans as for Augustine the issue was serious and inescapable. The builders of the Bay Colony had barely addressed the problems of physical survival before they encountered the question—and dealt with it in their characteristic way.

First of all, like all Reformed theologians, they allowed neither the doctrine of predestination nor that of human depravity to undermine their conception of man as a responsible moral being, living under God's law and obliged to glorify his Creator by obedience regardless of his state of grace. Their firmness did not make them "Arminians" or "Pelagians," since they did not attribute saving merit to such obedience. But their violent disagreements as to whether or not external amendment of life was a sign of election made the "Antinomian Controversy" the opening chapter in American intellectual history.

Closely related to this conflict was the question of preparation for grace which had agitated theologians since the earliest days of the Reformation. Could the natural man, or one who was merely in the "external covenant" by virtue of baptism, respond to God's promises? Could he (or must he) prepare his heart for the moment of the Spirit's regenerating work, for his "effectual call"? Most of the early Puritan leaders said yes. Such great founding fathers of the New England Way as Thomas Hooker of Hartford, Thomas Shepard of Cambridge, and Peter Bulkley of Concord, each in his own way, developed elaborate doctrines of preparation for grace until the process came to be regarded as an essential stage in the order of salvation. John Cotton of the Boston church, on the other hand, stressed the unconditional nature of election and understood regeneration as a more arbitrary work of grace; his powerful emphasis on the inner experience of regeneration, moreover, went far toward making a credible account of the Spirit's internal work a requirement of church membership in Massachusetts. Yet strongly felt disagreements on these issues doubtlessly contributed to the founding of New England's second Bible Commonwealth.

In 1634 Thomas Hooker and most of his congregation moved far westward, out of the Bay Colony's grant, to plant Hartford and a cluster of towns in the lower Connecticut Valley. Although desire for more land was a major cause of their exodus, Hooker also had a larger conception of the work of the Law in conversion and hence a broader conception of his ministry and a less restrictive conception of church membership. The need for greater freedom, a wider franchise, and more restricted exercise of the magistrate's authority seems also to have figured in the decision. In any event, Hooker and Cotton probably were too forceful and too much at odds for one small colony. Once established, the Connecticut colony did not categorically require freemen to be church members. Hooker, too, was less stringent in applying the experiential test of true sainthood. Yet the conception of church and state underlying the Fundamental Orders of Connecticut (1639) was in actual practice no more "liberal" than the constitution of the Bay Colony. Hooker, in fact, remained an honored exponent of the New England Way, opposed those who would alter its basic principles, and, in his great posthumously published treatise, *Survey of the Summe of Church-Discipline,* provided an officially approved defense of New England Congregationalism. In the long run his colony became the most impregnable bastion of those principles in the entire region.

The founding of Connecticut was not the only "event" to issue from the nature and grace problem, however, for in John Cotton's Boston congregation there appeared that remarkable woman, lay theologian, and prophetess, Anne Hutchinson. An admirer of Cotton from his days in Old England's Boston, she not only praised him for his insisting on inward signs of saving grace but criticized those who stressed sanctification as a sign and taught a mere Covenant of Works. The so-called Antinomian Crisis resulted—one of the most basic and revealing controversies of the early years. In 1637 even Hooker came back to moderate a ministerial synod which condemned eighty-two Hutchinsonesque propositions. Lest both the peace and reputation of the colony be shattered, the General Court then took very decisive action, exiling Mrs. Hutchinson's brother-in-law, the Reverend John Wheelwright (who thereafter founded a dissident congregation in Exeter, New Hampshire). The unfortunate prophetess rendered her already difficult case impossible by invoking special revelations that had purportedly come to her. She was banished by the General Court in November 1637 and in exile exerted a small influence in the development of Rhode Island. Cotton was slow to recognize error in his admiring parishioner, but ultimately he made an ambiguous peace with his ministerial brethren.

"Preparation" thenceforward became a recognized feature of the New England Way, occupying a large place in the works of its most influential early expositors. They by no means defended Arminianism, for they did not believe that God's sovereign will could be coerced by human effort; but they demanded a law-abiding response to God's gracious promise, recognized the role of God's Law in bringing sinners to humble contrition, and emphasized the need for godly obedience in all who chose to live in the commonwealth. It is hard to see how they could have done otherwise without relinquishing their conviction that their commonwealth as a whole was in a "national covenant" with God. A steady drift toward Arminianism was to become visible in the decades that followed, but only in the eighteenth century, under very different conditions, would an emphasis on man's cooperation in his redemption be frankly preached. In that day Jonathan

Edwards would oppose these liberal tendencies with a stricter predestinarianism than New England's great founding divines had been able to accept.

THE PROBLEM OF SEPARATISM

A second difficulty sprang from the psychology and practice of Separatism, which in various manifestations was a serious threat to the very existence of a holy commonwealth. The most thoroughgoing and troublesome exemplar of this tendency was Roger Williams (1603?–83) who reached the Bay Colony in 1631. Called to minister to the Boston church, he refused on the ground that it had not formally separated itself from the Church of England and would not expressly repent its past connection. He further antagonized the leadership of the colony by denying the right of the magistrate to enforce the "first table of the Law" (i.e. that part of the Decalogue having to do with man's direct responsibility to God), by objecting to the practice of having unregenerate persons take an oath (i.e. swear) in God's name, and by denouncing the charter as an unlawful expropriation of lands rightfully belonging to the Indians. Made unwelcome in the Bay Colony, he then spent a controversy-ridden two years in Plymouth. The General Court of Massachusetts finally moved against him in 1635 when, after returning as the newly elected minister of Salem, he threatened the order and uniformity of the colony by asking that church to separate from the other churches of Massachusetts. In October he was ordered to leave the colony. To escape deportation, he fled in January 1636, journeying through the wilderness first to Plymouth and then on again farther, where he founded Providence and began what in time would become the charter colony of Rhode Island. Since Anne Hutchinson, whose views also savored of Separatism, and many other extremists took refuge in Rhode Island, orthodox Puritans began to regard that colony as a veritable "sewer of New England."

Epithets, however, could not solve the problem. In Rhode Island it would receive a historic solution through the legal separation of church and state. The Quakers would work toward the same end in New Jersey and Pennsylvania. Yet the problem was undoubtedly intrinsic to the Puritan idea of a truly purified church of regenerate Christians. The state could always be suspected of bringing impure influences to bear on ecclesiastical affairs and of making unacceptable demands on "visible saints." Quite aside from the state, moreover, a given church's fellowship with other allegedly impure churches might at any time come to be regarded as intolerable in God's sight. Hence separatism would remain a latent source of turmoil in churches of the strict Puritan tradition. During the Great Awakening and in all subsequent periods of revived piety, even in the twentieth century, the old issue was repeatedly to provoke rancor and division.

QUESTIONS OF CONNECTIONALISM

A third besetting problem of New England's leaders was the indefinite state of theory with regard to the proper relation of one particular church to all the others. On this matter the position of New England's churches had never been precisely settled. When civil war erupted in England with the Presbyterian party predominant, radical movements of many sorts all increased their agitation, making questions of polity crucial. In Massachusetts the Williams and Hutchinson incidents had also created serious problems of interchurch authority; the latter difficulty, indeed, provoked the call of a ministerial "synod." Then in 1645 Robert Child and others raised a formidable threat by petitioning for "presbyterian" church order, vowing to appeal their case to Parliament if it were rejected. In September 1646, therefore, at the behest of certain ministers, the General Court called a synod, and, after reluctant compliance by the Boston and Salem churches, the Cambridge Synod began its historic sessions.

The sessions were attended by delegates from all of the twenty-nine Massachusetts churches except Concord as well as two delegates from New Hampshire and a few goodwill observers from Plymouth, New Haven, and Connecticut. The synod reconvened on 8 June 1647, after a long adjournment during which the Independent cause triumphed in England, and then, at a final session in August 1648, announced its result:

> A PLATFORM OF CHURCH DISCIPLINE GATHERED OUT OF THE WORD OF GOD AND AGREED UPON BY THE ELDERS AND MESSENGERS OF THE CHURCHES ASSEMBLED IN THE SYNOD AT CAMBRIDGE IN NEW ENGLAND. TO BE PRESENTED TO THE CHURCHES AND GENERALL COURT FOR THEIR CONSIDERATION AND ACCEPTANCE IN THE LORD.

This document became the seventeenth-century platform of the New England churches, marking them off as clearly Congregational at a time when British Puritanism was dividing between a strict Presbyterian party and a kind of "Independency" which would tolerate all sects and allow each particular group to revel in whatever "heresy" it might prefer.

Against the Presbyterians the Cambridge Platform defined the polity of Congregationalism in great detail, documenting the New England Way as history had already exhibited it yet making explicit "the communion of churches one with another" and giving to councils and synods strong advisory and admonitory powers but not legal coercive authority. Opposing the principle of toleration, it committed the churches to the doctrinal position of the Westminster Assembly. The delegates also declared that uniformity was to be maintained by the power of the magistrates, "the nursing fathers" of the church; heresy, disobedience, and schism were "to be restrayned, & punished by civil authority."

Almost simultaneously with the publication of the Result of the Cambridge Synod there also appeared a number of apologetical works answering various attacks on the New England Way. Among them were John Cotton's *The Way of the Congregational Churches Cleared, in Two Treatises,* Thomas Hooker's *Survey of the Summe of Church Discipline,* and John Norton's *Responsio,* as well as other works by John Davenport and Thomas Shepard. Taken together, these works constitute an illustrious definition of one of the major ecclesiastical traditions in modern Protestantism, and they set New England's Holy Commonwealths on their course. Many critical problems were left unresolved, but a crucial foundation had been laid. So supported, the Cambridge Platform long held a central place in the confessional history of American Congregationalism.

EVANGELISM AND THE INDIANS

It may seem odd to move from problems of church order to Indian relations, but the Indian has always been tragically odd in American history, and the Puritans had their share of difficulty. Their conviction that England was an elect nation tended to minimize other peoples, and it may be that the theology of the covenant had a similar effect. Yet the Bay Colony's charter did contain a clear pledge to "wynn and incite the Natives of the Country to the knowledge and obedience of the onlie true God and Savior of Mankinde, and the Christian fayth." Further incentive to evangelism was provided by theories that the Indians were descendants of the Lost Tribes whose conversion would betoken the prophesied return of Christ, an event which the early Puritans longed for—and expected. Nevertheless, the extension of settled areas into Connecticut and the failure of most of the colonies to respect Indian rights led to the Pequot War (1637) and, as a defensive measure, the New England Confederation (1643).

War notwithstanding, the latter year also saw the beginning of Thomas Mayhew's mission to the Indians on Martha's Vineyard, a work which ministers in his family sustained for a century with permanent results. The first Puritan to become famous in England for his knowledge of the American

Indian was Roger Williams. He had from the first shown extreme solicitude for their land rights, and in 1643 he published *A Key into the Language . . . of the Natives in that part of America, called New England.* He expressed his hope that God "in His holy season" would bring this race sprung "from Adam and Noah" away from their idols; but later, as Williams became more radical, his interest in evangelism waned. He is properly remembered for an understanding and respect for the Indian that was most unusual for his age—or later ages.

In the field of Indian missions the labors of John Eliot are most memorable. As a minister in Roxbury, near Boston, he began a lifetime's dedication to this work in 1646, and within thirty years he had inspired a mission that claimed the conversion of about four thousand Indians, who were gathered in twenty-four congregations, some of them with ordained Indian ministers. He published an Indian-language catechism for his converts in 1653, and in 1661–63 the Old and New Testaments, the first Bible printed in America. Eliot and his colleagues also publicized the American missionary challenge and contributed to the interest that led Parliament in 1649 to incorporate the Society for the Propagation of the Gospel in New England—an organization that was still able to support Jonathan Edwards in his work among the Indians over a century later.[1]

The years 1675–76 brought a tragic interruption to this promising work in the form of King Philip's War, in which the Wampanoags and Narragansets devastated the outlying white settlements, pressed back the frontier, and but for the coordinated offensive of the New England Confederation might have carried the day. In the end, southern New England was permanently cleared of Indian danger, but in the north the Abenaki tribe turned to France for aid. And in a very few years the terrible French and Indian Wars would begin, holding New England at bay and restricting its northward and westward expansion until the fall of Quebec in 1759. With massacre and treachery an actuality or an imminent possibility, missions were necessarily restricted, but they by no means came to a halt, despite suspicions of French intrigue and the near disappearance of an accessible Indian population. Yet a decline in Indian evangelism tended to accompany the same general decline of zeal in the Bible Commonwealths that led many to interpret King Philip's War as a divine punishment. Considering the total seventeenth-century predicament of the New England colonies, however, one may claim for them a degree of concern for and success in Indian

1. This "New England Company," as it came to be called, is not to be confused with the Society for the Propagation of the Gospel in Foreign Parts, founded by the Church of England a half-century later (see chap. 4, especially pp. 219–21).

missions which equals the far more heralded efforts of New Spain and New France. Unlike these great Catholic empires, moreover, New England and her American neighbors were already beginning to experience the surge of European migration which would continue for three centuries in ever increasing volume. In the face of this steady movement of peoples all "solutions" of the Indian problem would crumble.

DECLENSION AND THE QUESTION OF CHURCH MEMBERSHIP

The most troublesome spiritual problem for the Puritan commonwealths was the decline of "experimental" piety that was almost inevitable in communities organized at so high a pitch of fervency. Very significant for this trend was a series of disputes over the qualifications for church membership and the rights of children to baptism. On these issues the founders of New England's "church-way" had been from the first between two fires. Presbyterians applauded them for not yielding to the doctrine of believer's baptism but denounced them for seeming to render baptism almost nugatory by their radical demand for a personal religious experience as a prerequisite to communicant status in the church. Baptists, on the other hand, commended their demand for congregations of regenerate saints but lamented their continuation of infant baptism. The New England Puritans for the most part compromised by limiting infant baptism to the children of parents who had owned the covenant. Yet this situation was highly unstable and confusing. Some churches, more "presbyterian" or simply more lax than others, either did not "quibble too much" over evidences of a conversion experience or defined the family in broad terms. More radical individuals, like Roger Williams or Henry Dunster of Harvard College, became openly Baptist.

More distressing than theological uncertainty was a circumstance which normal biological processes laid bare. Among the second and later generations of Puritans (as well as among the immigrants who continued to arrive) there were many duly baptized members to whom the experience of saving grace never came. Though these unconverted persons were usually professing Christians and leading morally respectable lives, they were still only in "external covenant" and therefore could not present their children for baptism. This problem was already looming large in the controversies leading to the Cambridge Synod of 1648, but that body ignored its instructions and evaded the matter. The issue continued to be a cause for concern, however, in part because various social and psychological factors gave it political and economic overtones, but chiefly because it posed a critical ecclesiastical problem. The colonial establishment was being plagued by the very forces that had made the Church of England's parish system odious. Their people, including many baptized children of saints, were becoming a mere cross-section of English types, the pious and impious, the fervent and the stolid.[2] Of professing Christians there was no lack, but many were not qualifying for full membership even though it brought both access to the Lord's Table and the right to bring children to baptism. The churches, despite their wide responsibilities for the spiritual welfare of individual lives and the body politic, simply were not being nourished by a sufficient influx of "visible saints." Fears arose that the saving remnant would become too small to save. Baptists, in the meantime, kept alive the doctrinal conflict on the meaning of baptism, while many others raised theological objections to the prevailing restrictions on the sacraments.

The clamor increased during the 1650s. In 1657 a Connecticut-Massachusetts ministerial council met and approved certain "half-way" measures; but the Massachusetts General Court went further and summoned a formal Synod in 1662. According to its historic deliberations, baptism was declared to be sufficiently constitutive of church membership to allow its recipients to bring their children also within the baptismal covenant, although an experience of regeneration was still required of full communicant members. This so-called Half-Way Covenant gained wide acceptance throughout New England, making its way even into the strict New Haven jurisdiction after that colony was merged with Connecticut in 1662. This is not to say that the Half-Way Covenant met no opposition, however. Just as some churches had practiced "half-way" measures long before 1662, many resisted it after. In Connecticut several churches were split in a dispute over its adoption, including those at Hartford, Windsor, and Stratford. The Reverend Abraham Pierson of Branford led a majority of his congregation to New Jersey, where they perpetuated the old New Haven constitution in New Ark. Here, ironically, they were gradually absorbed into the Presbyterianism of the Middle Colonies, though not without injecting some New England leaven

2. As with the *Mayflower*'s company in 1620, the great migration to New England and to other parts of America was very much a mixed multitude. Early and late the ministers lamented that most of the population was chiefly interested in making money and getting ahead. In enlarging on this point the scholarship of Darrett Rutman and others (see bibliography) has done much to improve our understanding of New England society. It is important to remember, however, that what made New England a distinctive social order and what accounts for its spiritual influence was the winnowed Puritan minority and its leaders, including not only the clergy, but such lay persons as Theophilus Eaton, Governor Winthrop, and Anne Hutchinson. Demands for increased rigor and discipline—as among the Baptists—were often lay movements even late in the century, though the trend for a time was in the other direction. Yet a great revival lay in the not too distant future.

into the Scottish tradition. John Davenport, the venerable pastor of the First Church in New Haven who bitterly opposed both the half-way measures and New Haven's absorption by Connecticut, was called by a majority of the First Church in Boston to oppose the innovation there, whereupon the minority withdrew to form the Third, or "Old South," Church of that city.

Widespread adoption of the Half-Way Covenant solved some important doctrinal uncertainties, but it could hardly be expected to relieve New England's religious ills. "Declension" continued uninterruptedly, the lamentations of the clergy intensified, and their sermonic jeremiads came to constitute a major literary genre. To the generalized woes of declining piety were added the very material facts of royal Restoration, which brought England's reassertion of governmental authority and the regulation of trade. On top of these developments came other tragedies: an increase of shipwrecks and pestilence, enormous losses of life and property in King Philip's War, and the devastating Boston fires of 1676 and 1679. In desperation the General Court finally called for a synod to make "full inquiry . . . into the Causes & State of Gods Controversy with us." On 10 September 1679 the "Reforming Synod" was convened and after ten days had readied its result on *The Necessity of Reformation,* in effect a summary of all past jeremiads. "That God hath a Controversy with his New England people is undeniable," the delegates declared, "the Lord having written his displeasure in dismal Characters against us." They went on to prescribe the cures, calling for a "solemn and explicit Renewal of the Covenant," and, as a further antidote to waywardness, they devoted a second session in May 1680 to the adoption of a Confession of Faith, the first to be formally published in New England.[3]

The Synod's Confession was virtually a verbatim edition of the Declaration issued by the English Congregationalists at Savoy in 1658. This Savoy Declaration, in turn, was based very closely on Parliament's slight revision of the Westminster Confession. The essential doctrines are the same, except that Congregational polity is substituted for Presbyterian and the authority of the magistrates to interfere with the free exercise of conscientious religious convictions is denied. This same confession would also be adopted by the Connecticut churches in 1708, and it stood as the official symbol of American Congregationalism for nearly two hundred years.

Yet God's controversy only grew more intense. In 1684 the Bay Colony's

3. See Williston Walker, *Creeds and Platforms of Congregationalism,* pp. 367–439. Walker's careful editing and scholarly commentary make this work indispensable for the study of New England's major ecclesiastical deliverances from the Cambridge Synod of 1648 to the Saybrook Synod of 1708.

charter was annulled, and a year later the Roman Catholic James II became king. A consolidated "Dominion of New England," including also New York and New Jersey, was created, with the imperious Edmund Andros as royal governor. These plans, of course, went awry: King James fled, Andros was deposed, a Protestant monarch was settled on the English throne, and Connecticut and Rhode Island regained their former status. But the Bay Colony was rechartered in 1691 on vastly different terms; thereafter it had a royal governor and a franchise based on property rather than church membership. Toleration was imposed, and Anglicanism was provided a foothold in Boston. By this time the mantle of churchly leadership had fallen on the willing shoulders of Increase Mather (1639–1723), since 1664 the minister of Boston's Second Church and since 1685 president of Harvard College. He was aided by his brilliant son, Cotton (1663–1728), who in 1683 had become his ministerial colleague.

Before the Mathers were fully launched on their many-pronged campaign for renewing the churches and asserting the "rule of the saints," the entire clerical cause was embarrassed by the infamous witchcraft hysteria, particularly in Salem during 1692. This episode as a whole, despite its notoriety, does little to elucidate the Puritan mind of the age; but it did lead to chagrin and public remorse, which in turn reduced respect for the colony's religious leadership, especially in the eyes of the merchant class whose social and political importance were notably increased under the new charter.

Already in the 1630s the merchants had expressed doubt that the Bible as interpreted by the clergy made adequate allowance for the exigencies of a healthy commerce. In the Anne Hutchinson affair, oddly enough, the merchants had aligned themselves against the clerical party. With the need to expand foreign trade after the drying up of the Great Migration, old restrictions derived from the Pentateuch became increasingly burdensome. By 1691, as a self-conscious element in society, the merchants would welcome both the limitations of ecclesiastical power in the new charter and the improved mercantile relations with England. Against this background the two decades between 1690 and 1710 may be designated as a most critical period, a turning point in New England's intellectual and religious history.

Some of the events of this crisis period have already been suggested, notably the new charter. But others followed swiftly. In 1699 a group of Boston merchants led by John Leverett and William and Thomas Brattle issued their "manifesto" justifying the formation of a new church along "broad and catholick" lines. In this new and innovative Brattle Street Church, professors of Christian belief were to be given full communicant, not merely "half-way," status; all who helped support the minister were to have a voice in his call; the Lord's Prayer was to be used ritually in worship; and, as a final assault on the cherished Boston tradition, Benjamin Colman—a Harvard graduate with Presbyterian ordination obtained in England—was called to be pastor. As if to document the ascendancy of this new group in the colony's affairs, Increase Mather was removed from the presidency of Harvard in 1701, being replaced in 1707 by John Leverett himself (though a layman), with the two Brattle brothers also in important positions to influence the college's affairs. The clerical party suffered another rebuff in 1705 when the Mather-sponsored "Proposals" for a more effective connectional relation among the churches were rejected.

While these various events were signalizing the emergence of a distinguishable social ethos and intellectual tendency in the seaboard area, still other portents were appearing in the west. Out at Northampton, Solomon Stoddard (1643–1729) had also been attempting to heal the woes of a declining church by startling innovations of theory and practice. Neither "broad" nor "catholick" and in many ways more Calvinistic in spirit than most New Englanders, he called for the abandonment of church covenants, demanded more effective preaching, redefined the Lord's Supper as a "converting ordinance" which was open to all morally responsible "professors," and advocated a "presbyterial" organization to prevent local churches from wandering into doctrinal errors. In his eschatology he also accented the individualism of his approach by deemphasizing the holy commonwealth's role in God's plan for the church. He instead concentrated his revival preaching on each person's concern for the final judgment. He defended himself against Cotton Mather and other critics in two powerful volumes, *The Doctrine of the Instituted Churches* (1700) and *An Appeal to the Learned* (1709). By the time of his death his policies had won wide acceptance in western Massachusetts and Connecticut, five "seasons of harvest" had given practical vindication to his measures, and the place of Northampton in the annals of American Christianity had been secured by the ordination of his grandson, Jonathan Edwards, as his colleague and successor. Even before that ordination Stoddard had in effect begun New England's Great Awakening, thus proving that declension need not be permanent.

In Connecticut still other developments exhibited a parting of the ways between eastern Massachusetts and the rest of New England. Disturbed by the declining state of the colony's church life and its inadequate educational opportunities, three ministers in the old New Haven jurisdiction revived John Davenport's dream of a collegiate institution. After broadening their group to include other ministers of the colony and ripening their plans in consultation with the Mathers, they presented their proposed charter to the Connecticut General Court. Their petition was favorably received, and on 9 October 1701 the Collegiate School was duly chartered, with ten ministers as its trustees. After fifteen years of great instability, the infant institution finally ceased its peregrinations among various Connecticut parsonages and came to rest permanently in New Haven. As Yale University, the institution's influence would ultimately be measured in national and even world-wide terms; but its most important first fruits were strictly ecclesiastical and limited largely to the colony of Connecticut and its spiritual dependencies in the upper Connecticut Valley.

The College trustees at once became the most important ministerial gathering in Connecticut, and they soon busied themselves with the problem of the colony's deplorable religious condition. Most of the ministers shared the conviction of the Mathers that the answer to its ills lay in a stricter ecclesiastical constitution. Unlike the men of Massachusetts, they were able to carry their designs to fruition because of the absence of a strong merchant class to thwart them and because they were not only unhindered by a royal appointee as governor but had one of their own number, the Reverend Gurdon Saltonstall of New London, elected to that office in 1707. A year later the General Court ordered the churches of each county to send lay and clerical delegates to a synod for religious reformation, and in September of 1708 the men so appointed—including eight of the college trustees—met at Saybrook. A month later the result of their deliberations, the Saybrook Platform, was enacted into law.

The platform dealt decisively with two fundamental problems in ways that would have far-reaching consequences. In the realm of doctrine it adopted, almost verbatim, the Savoy Declaration, just as the Reforming Synod of Massachusetts had done in 1680; this placed the colony firmly in the Westminster theological tradition, a move which had already been indicated in the college regulations. In the realm of polity, on the other hand, it deviated from the old Cambridge Platform by instituting a semipresbyterian structure which provided for county consociations to enforce discipline and doctrine in the churches, ministerial associations to regularize ordinations and other matters, and a General Association of ministers to oversee the commonwealth's church affairs. For a century and a half the Saybrook Platform exercised a determinative influence in Connecticut affairs, making this commonwealth a stronghold of orthodox Puritanism, with Yale College as its intellectual center. The Platform's stand on polity also led to ever closer ties between the Connecticut churches and the Presbyterians of the Middle Colonies, who had organized their first presbytery in 1706. Probably no legal instrument in Connecticut's history was to have wider religious and cultural consequences. From it one may date the definitive emergence of two New Englands: a "maritime province," with Boston and Harvard College at its center, and a "Connecticut valley province," with Yale the chief institutional bulwark of its farflung parishes.

As New England stood at the threshhold of the eighteenth century, the religious situation as a whole exhibited a static quality which another outbreak of the French and Indian wars only intensified. For Massachusetts especially the situation is perhaps best summarized by an old aphorism which Cotton Mather had quoted in his survey of the Plymouth colony: *"Religio peperit Divitias, Filia devoravit Matrem; Religion* brought forth *prosperity,* and the *daughter* destroyed the *mother."* [4] In Connecticut order had replaced chaos but with no apparent revivification of spirit. In Rhode Island, where the fires of religious enthusiasm once had burned so brightly, a pluralistic status quo had won acceptance and, except for various controversies among the Baptists, the drift to quiescence was equally noticeable.

Such references to declension and a static situation, however, can easily be misleading; one must not regard the value judgments of contemporary Puritans or even less of the Great Awakening's champions as the last and only word. Even the unsympathetic report of the Anglican Society for the Propagation of the Gospel in Foreign Parts stated that New England in 1710 was the only well-churched area in the American colonies. A faithful, learned, and numerous clergy—now being trained at Harvard and Yale—was steadfastly if unsensationally serving its many territorial parishes. A large, prosperous, and remarkably well-educated population was organized in towns, governing itself without disorder and loyally supporting the churches. These were not insignificant accomplishments.

The dramatic flowerings of New England in Edwardsean theology, revolutionary activity, and Unitarian culture were as yet in the future, though the foundations were laid and intimations of things to come were already visible. Also on the horizon was the Great Awakening—and a new age of American revivalism. As for the "worldly Puritans" who were becoming more numerous and more outspoken, they, too, had been enriched by an important Puritan legacy. The commitment to useful labor, the sense of civic responsibility, the concern for lawful government, the passion for learning—these and many corollaries in the New England character had been central elements of puritan preaching since the beginning. By 1700

4. *Magnalia Christi Americana,* 2 vols. (Hartford Edition, 1820), 1:59. "There is danger," he went on to say, "lest the *enchantments* of this world make them to forget *their errand into the wilderness."*

this moral and practical message was becoming still more prominent. If zeal was now flagging, there were still many signs of vitality and promise. At least this could be said of the Bible Commonwealths. As for Rhode Island, it had been a world by itself from the earliest days and therefore deserves a chapter to itself.

11

RELIGIOUS DIVERSITY IN RHODE ISLAND

The commonwealth of Rhode Island and Providence Plantations has the longest name and the smallest area of any state in the American union, hence its name rather than its size is the better symbol of its vexed, often turbulent history. Conceived in Puritan "heresy" and maturing as a remarkable seat of religious pluralism, it provides both an invaluable insight into the "left wing" of the Puritan movement and in important anticipation of later American problems and solutions. After Roger Williams and Anne Hutchinson established settlements, Baptists and Quakers flourished in the area and used it as a base point for evangelism. Anglicans and Congregationalists also founded significant churches. Still later its tolerance made it a colonial center of Judaism, and eventually it would come to have more Roman Catholics, in proportion to its population, than any other state in the Union. All but these latter two developments are best considered in the context of Rhode Island's early history.

ROGER WILLIAMS AND THE FOUNDING

In the middle of January 1636 Roger Williams fled from Salem in the Bay Colony, made his way southward, and after grueling exposure to "winter miseries in a howling wilderness," finally found refuge among Indians whom he knew from his earlier ministry at Plymouth and with whom he would retain friendly relations all his life. Purchasing land from them, he and five other refugees settled at Sekonk, but when warned by Governor Winslow that this was Plymouth territory, they moved to the head of Narragansett Bay. Here they again purchased land from the Indians and planted a straggling settlement on the Great Salt River.

Late in 1638 Williams and twelve "loving friends and neighbors" joined together in a social compact whereby all promised to submit themselves "in active or passive obedience, to all such orders or agreements as shall be made for the public good of the body, in an orderly way, by the major consent of the present inhabitants, masters of families, incorporated together into a township, and such others who they shall admit into the same, *only in civil things*." (The italicized phrase appears in the second, but not the first draft of the instrument.) Naming the place Providence, Williams later wrote: "I desired it might be for a shelter for persons distressed for conscience." Equal shares of land were accordingly allotted to newcomers, though with special concern for refugees. Rhode Island, therefore, is justly remembered as a sanctuary of freedom, though in the seventeenth century Williams's community was only one of the several which caused men in the Holy Commonwealths to regard Rhode Island as a catch-basin for heresy and eccentricity, not even worthy of membership in the New England Confederation.

In the spring of 1638 another band of exiles had purchased, with the help of Williams, the island of Aquidneck in Narragansett Bay. This group was under the dominant religious influence of Anne Hutchinson (who had been expelled from the Bay Colony two years after Williams) and the astute political leadership of William Coddington, who would later become a Quaker. Nineteen persons joined in the following agreement: "We whose names are underwritten do here solemnly, in the presence of JEHOVAH, incorporate ourselves into a body politic, and as he shall help, will submit our persons, lives, and estates, unto our Lord Jesus Christ, the King of kings and Lord of lords, and to all those perfect and most absolute laws of his, given us in his holy work of truth to be guided and judged thereby." They laid out Portsmouth at the northern end of the island and chose William Coddington as "judge" of the colony. Dr. John Clarke served as physician and preacher to the settlement.

For a few months affairs proceeded smoothly in the new community. But the peacefulness ended with the coming of Samuel Gorton (1593?–1677), an extreme individualist whose religious radicalism went far beyond that of Mrs. Hutchinson. He had since 1637 worn out his welcome first in Boston, then in Plymouth, and before founding his own settlement at Shawomet (Warwick) in 1642 he would also spend some time in Providence and Pawtuxet. At this stage in his stormy career, however, he precipitated a revolt which put Coddington out of his judgeship and elected William Hutchinson (Anne's husband) in his place. Coddington and his followers, prominent among whom was John Clarke, withdrew to the south end of the island, where they established Newport on 1 May 1639. As governor of the new plantation, Coddington began immediate negotiations with his sympathizers at Portsmouth looking to a union of the two towns, which were consolidated under a common administration in March 1640. The next year Coddington tried to secure for Aquidneck a patent which would legalize his proprietary control of the island and make it an entirely independent jurisdiction. In this he was unsuccessful, but his ambitions were checked only when Roger Williams was able to draw the towns of the whole Narragansett area into a federation for mutual cooperation and support.

In 1643 Williams became convinced that if his colony were to resist successfully the encroachment of its enemies, it must have a stronger legal claim than was afforded by the uncertain title of an Indian deed. He went to England therefore and in 1644 published his classic defense of religious freedom, one of the greatest of Puritan books, *The Bloudy Tenent of Persecution for the Cause of Conscience Discussed.* With the assistance of Sir Harry Vane, he also obtained from Parliament in that year a patent authorizing the union of Providence, Portsmouth, and Newport under the name of "Providence Plantations." This patent fully empowered the inhabitants "to govern and rule themselves and such others as shall hereafter inhabit within any part of the said tract of land, by such a form of civil government as by voluntary consent of all or the greatest part of them, shall be found most serviceable in their estates and condition." [1]

An assembly composed of freemen from the four towns met at Portsmouth in 1647 and laid plans for a federal commonwealth. The preamble of their instrument of government declared that "the form of government established in Providence Plantations is DEMOCRATICAL, that is to say, a government held by the free and voluntary consent of all, or the greater part of the free inhabitants." The document closes with a ringing manifesto that reveals how Rhode Island too deemed itself a holy commonwealth.

> These are the laws that concern all men, and these are the penalties for the transgressions thereof, which, by common consent, are ratified and established throughout the whole Colony. And otherwise than thus, what is herein forbidden, all men may walk as their consciences persuade them, every one in the name of his God. And let the saints of the Most High walk in this Colony without molestation, in the name of Jehovah their God, for ever and ever.[2]

1. Rhode Island Historical Society, *Collections,* 4 (1838): 221–25.

2. Ibid., pp. 228–30.

The governing body possessed legislative as well as judicial functions. It was at first a primary assembly of freemen, but after 1650 it became a representative body with strictly delimited powers. The doctrines of religious liberty and the separation of church and state were jealously guarded.

In 1651 John Clarke and Roger Williams went to England again to counteract further efforts of Coddington, and this time Williams followed up his earlier tract on religious liberty, with a sequel, *The Bloudy Tenent Yet More Bloudy.* It was a reply to John Cotton's *The Bloudy Tenent Washed and Made White in the Bloud of the Lambe* (1647). Clarke also did his part for the cause, writing *Ill Newes from New England,* the story of how he and two other Baptists had been tried, fined, whipped, and imprisoned in Massachusetts for expounding their views there. When Williams arrived home in 1654, internal and external difficulties required his urgent attention, and he accepted the presidency of the colony even though he was tired and broken in health. A letter from Oliver Cromwell in 1655 urging him to take whatever measures were necessary to insure the peace and safety of the plantation had a salutary effect, and the next year Coddington himself freely submitted to the authority of the colony "with all my heart." When Williams retired from the presidency in 1657, the worst of the internal dangers were past.

It is well that they were, for the colony soon had to face threats from without. A land speculation company led by John Winthrop, Jr., of Connecticut and including members from Massachusetts and even Rhode Island itself, purchased in 1659 a tract of land in northern Narragansett and began to press vigorous claims to ownership. When this struggle was at its height, the Rhode Island patent was further imperiled by the restoration of Charles II to the throne in England. Rhode Island immediately recognized Charles as king and commissioned Dr. John Clarke, still in England, to act as its agent in securing royal confirmation of its patent. Despite Winthrop's efforts, Clarke succeeded in keeping the boundary between Rhode Island and Connecticut at the Pawcatuck River, where it had always been, and in gaining a royal charter (8 July 1663). Freedom of conscience had been included prominently in all of Clarke's presentations, in which the colony's historic stand on religion was reiterated:

> no person within the said Colony, at any time hereafter, shall be in any wise molested, punished, disquieted or called in question, for any differences in opinions in matters of religion, and do not actually disturb the civil peace of our said Colony; but that all . . . may from

> time to time, and at all times hereafter, freely and fully have and enjoy his and their own judgments and consciences, in matters of religious concernments . . . not using this liberty to licentiousness and profaneness, nor to the civil injury or outward disturbance of others.[3]

The charter was received in the colony with appropriate rejoicing and gratitude. Rhode Island no longer needed to fear the calumnies and encroachments of its haughty neighbors; it could become, on the contrary, an important nursery of several important Protestant traditions.

THE BAPTISTS

The church at Providence which was formed by Roger Williams and his fellow refugees is generally called the first Baptist church in America. In March 1639 Ezekiel Holliman, who had been a member of Williams's church at Salem, baptized Williams, probably by immersion, who in turn baptized Holliman and ten others. Williams seems to have accepted this method, because, like so many other radical Puritans both in England and America, he placed great emphasis on the conversion experience and on the strong New Testament testimony concerning believers' immersion. Regardless of the source of his views, however, they were not held long. Richard Scott, who later became a Quaker, wrote to George Fox of the next stage in Williams's spiritual pilgrimage:

> I walked with him [Williams] in the Baptists' way about three or four months, in which time he brake from the society, and declared at large the ground and reasons of it; that their baptism could not be right because it was not administered by an apostle. After that he set upon a way of seeking (with two or three of them that had dissented with him) by way of preaching and praying; and there he continued a year or two, till two of the three left him.[4]

Going even further, Williams left the ministry and denied the legitimacy of instituted churches altogether. In the corruption of the Middle Ages, he said, the church had lost its authority. "God's people are now in the Gospel brought into a spiritual land of Canaan. . . . Therefore, an enforced settled maintenance is not suitable to the Gospel as it was to the ministry of priests and levites under the law." Restoration could come only by a mighty

3. Ibid., pp. 243–44.

4. Quoted in Isaac Backus, *A History of New England, with Particular Reference to the Denomination of Christians Called Baptists,* ed. David Weston (Newton, Mass.: Backus Historical Society, 1871), 1: 189.

interposition of God—and to Williams the day of its coming was not far off.

From Williams's conviction that the church in his time lacked clear authority stemmed his further denial that governments had any legitimate right to regulate "the spiritual Israel" or to restrict anyone's freedom of conscience. Insisting that Old Israel was done and gone, Williams made his most extreme departure from the mainstream covenantal Puritanism of the Holy Commonwealths. He, like them, interpreted the Old Testament typologically; but to him "the former types of the land, of the people, of their worships, were types and figures of Spiritual land, spiritual people, and spiritual worship under Christ." After the coming of Christ, therefore, Old Israel was no longer a model for church *and* state, but only for the church.

In these respects he was more radical than the Quakers, with their increasingly well-ordered meetings and well-defined membership. As his later debates with the Quakers would reveal, however, Williams's thought retained the conservative and orthodox cast of his earlier years on many vital doctrines, especially that which held Scripture to be the only source of saving knowledge. His rationale for religious freedom, one may say in conclusion, was worlds removed from that of John Locke or Thomas Jefferson; and the same could be said for the various Protestant movements that gave Rhode Island its distinctive history. Of these perhaps none was to play a larger role in the colony and in the nation than the Baptists. Their complex story, moreover, provides an invaluable example of how controversy, schism, and evangelism became intrinsic elements in the long history of Baptist growth in America.

Rise of the Baptists in England

Historians generally concede that modern Baptists bear little direct relation to the Continental Anabaptists who arose as part of the "Radical Reformation" of the sixteenth century. They emerged rather from the left wing of the Puritan movement in England during the early years of the seventeenth century in what were actually two strands of development: an Arminian group called General Baptists because of their belief in a general provision of redemption, or unlimited atonement, and a more Calvinistic group called Particular Baptists because of their belief in particular election and limited atonement.

The origins of the General Baptists are associated with the name of John Smyth, a graduate of Cambridge who was serving as City Preacher in Lincoln when he became a convinced Separatist and assumed the leadership of a Separatist congregation at Gainsborough. To escape persecution they fled in 1607 (or 1608) to Amsterdam. Soon they were reasoning that if the Church of England were a false church, its baptism must also be invalid, and that only those who professed personal faith in Christ were the proper subjects of baptism. In 1609 they dissolved their previous covenant relationship to make a new start. Smyth baptized himself (by affusion) and then baptized all the rest. When Smyth showed inclinations to merge with the Dutch Mennonites, however, part of his congregation, led by Thomas Helwys, broke away. Becoming convinced that they had erred in fleeing persecution, they returned to England in 1612 and founded at Spitalfields (outside London) the first known Baptist church on English soil.

These Baptists continued to hold the Arminian theology they had espoused in Holland and, in spite of severe persecution, showed surprising growth. The General Baptist fellowship included five churches by 1626 and forty-seven by 1644. During the days of the Cromwellian Commonwealth they multiplied rapidly, and not even the repressive measures of the Stuart Restoration were able to prevent them from developing a corporate denominational life. A General Assembly was formed in 1671, an elaborate creed promulgated in 1678, and a program of church extension pushed in the western counties. Many Baptists of this persuasion migrated to America, mainly to Rhode Island, Virginia, and North Carolina.

The roots of the Particular Baptists, on the other hand, lie in nonseparatist Puritan Independency. In 1616 a congregation of this sort was formed in Southwark, near London, by Henry Jacob, who designated himself one of "the rigidest sort of those that are called Puritanes." In 1622 Jacob removed to Jamestown, in Virginia, and was replaced by John Lathrop. Because of severe persecution Lathrop and some thirty members of the church emigrated in 1634 to Scituate, in Plymouth Colony, and later planted themselves at Barnstable, on Cape Cod. The Southwark congregation meanwhile continued to grow—and divide. In 1633 one group withdrew because they were dissatisfied with the noncommittal attitude of the church toward the issue of separating from the Church of England. After another group of seceders had joined with these in 1638, they all came to the conclusion that baptism was not for infants, and two years later they adopted the view that baptism ought to be "by diping ye Body into ye Water, resembling Burial & riseing again." In 1641 they were all immersed—thus culminating a three-step process by which the administrator, then the subject, and finally the mode of baptism were successively investigated.

The independent Puritan congregation of Henry Jacob eventually spawned six other churches, five of which became Baptist. These all retained the Calvinistic theology of their forebears and remained more or less in fellowship with their Congregational cousins. In 1644 seven Particular Baptist churches of London joined in publishing their first Confession of Faith, which was replaced in 1677 by a longer confession modeled closely after the Westminster Confession. In 1689 a second edition was subscribed by 107 churches. The area of their strength outside London was Wales, and from here many Particular Baptists came to America. The first Baptist church in Wales, forced to emigrate after the Restoration of Charles II, became also the first Baptist church to establish permanent rootage in Massachusetts; it came with pastor John Myles to Swansea, in the territory of Plymouth Colony, in 1663. Welsh Baptists were most numerous in the Middle Colonies, and early placed their characteristic stamp on the churches of the Philadelphia Association, formed in 1707. Thus, while some Baptist congregations emigrated bodily to the New World, many individuals brought their sentiments with them or adopted them soon after arriving. Roger Williams was doubtless of the last category, but many who flocked to his Rhode Island haven were already convinced Baptists, mainly of the Arminian type.

Baptists in Rhode Island

After the withdrawal of Williams, the leadership of the Baptist church in Providence fell to Thomas Olney, who had been censured for "great error" at Salem in 1639. He was one of the original freeholders of Providence Plantations and a convinced Calvinist, though his leading laymen were General Baptists. The Arminians in this church followed the English General Baptists in believing that the laying on of hands was an apostolic practice requisite to the reception of the Holy Spirit and necessary to interchurch fellowship. Those who held to this controversial doctrine (and Roger Williams was among them) drew support from Hebrews 6:1–2, which lists it as one of the six "foundation principles" of Christianity: repentance, faith, baptism, laying on of hands, resurrection of the dead, and eternal judgment. Hence, the term "Six Principle Baptists."

The controversy over this point at Providence came to a head in 1652, when the church divided over the issue. The five-principle, Calvinistic faction was headed by Thomas Olney, who ministered to the group until his death in 1682. They represented the minority party, and since their losses were not replenished by new converts or immigration, they passed out of existence about 1720. The Six Principle, Arminian faction continued as the original church but accomplished little that is memorable either in the way of evangelism or wider social influence. They did not even have a meetinghouse until 1700. When Rhode Island College (founded in Warren, 1764) was moved to Providence in 1770, President James Manning became pastor of this church and brought it back to Calvinistic sentiments. The future history of the Providence church merged with that of the other churches of the Warren Association, which was formed through Manning's influence in 1767.

In Newport, Dr. John Clarke became the spiritual leader. Born in England in 1609, he had practiced medicine in London before coming to Boston in 1637 as a convinced Separatist. The time of his conversion to Baptist views is unknown, but a Particular Baptist church seems to have been formed in Newport in 1644, and he was its pastor until his death in 1676. Thereafter the church often languished under less able pastors, though it remained one of the few Particular Baptist churches in New England and kept contact with its counterparts in England. The Baptists of Newport, however, were even more contentious than those of Providence. In 1656 a Six-Principle church was formed out of adherents won by "missionaries" from Providence. A decade later an English Sabbatarian collected a large enough following to form a Seventh-Day Baptist church there.[5]

Baptist Expansion

There had been isolated opposition to infant baptism in Massachusetts since the days of Roger Williams at Salem. The first place where definite efforts were made to form a church, however, was at Rehoboth, where several withdrew from the Congregational church and were immersed in 1649 by John Clarke. After citation by the court in Plymouth the next year, they removed to Newport. In 1651, when Clarke and two other men from the Newport church accepted an invitation to Lynn, Massachusetts, they were arrested for holding an unauthorized religious meeting.

The net result of this incident was to publicize further the sentiments of the Baptists and win for them more sympathizers in the Bay Colony. In 1653 Henry Dunster, the first president of Harvard College, withheld his fourth child from baptism and had to resign from his post the next year. Before moving to the more tolerant town of Scituate, he associated himself with Thomas Gould, who soon became the recognized leader of the

5. For Christians bent on ordering their lives, worship, and churches according to God's express will, the Old Testament's Sabbath laws were not easily ignored. The Emperor Constantine had set aside Sunday as a day of rest in 321; but the fully developed idea of a strictly observed Christian Sabbath is a creation of English Puritanism, with Lancelot Andrewes, Nicholas Bownde, and Thomas Greenham as major early theorists. More literal and legalistic thinkers, such as John Trask (ca. 1573–163?), demanded a Seventh Day observance, and this view continued to find favor among some radically antitraditional Puritans.

Boston Baptists and the pastor of the church formed there in 1665. Being arraigned before the courts and sentenced to banishment, this little group withdrew to Noddle's Island for a time, but then returned in 1680 to erect a meetinghouse in the heart of Boston. By this time other Baptist churches had been formed in Newbury and Kittery, two Indian Baptist churches were in process of being gathered on Nantucket and Martha's Vineyard, John Myles's Welsh church was well established at Swansea, and there was a growing cluster of Baptist churches along the Plymouth–Rhode Island border. In 1717 both Increase and Cotton Mather indicated a degree of rapprochement by participating at a Baptist ordination in Boston.

Baptist beginnings in Connecticut stemmed from the influence of Rhode Island. Before 1705 there were only temporary preaching missions in Connecticut, but in that year a church was planted in Groton by the Reverend Valentine Wightman of Rhode Island. He remained pastor of that church till his death in 1741, and was succeeded by his son and grandson until 1841, so that the Wightmans became literally the patriarchs of Connecticut Baptists. A second church was formed in 1726 at New London by Stephen Gorton, also from Rhode Island, and from these two centers Baptist principles spread slowly into other areas of Connecticut.

It is often said that the first association of American Baptists (referring to the Particular tradition) was formed at Philadelphia in 1707. The Rhode Island Yearly Meeting of General, or Six Principle, Baptists, however, seems to have been in existence several years earlier. Including churches from Providence, Newport, and North Kingston, this association functioned in a purely advisory capacity and disclaimed any authority over the internal affairs of the churches. Growth was slow because all the churches were poor and feeble and travel was difficult; but in 1729 this association held what the youthful John Comer called "ye largest Convention yt ever hath been." Thirty-two messengers (eight ministers, three deacons, and twenty-one laymen) from thirteen churches (eight in Rhode Island, two in Massachusetts, two in Connecticut, and one in New York City) met at Newport on 21 June. In its early years the Rhode Island Yearly Meeting included nearly all the Baptist churches of New England except the Calvinistic churches of Newport, Swansea, and Boston. Although the body began to decline after the Great Awakening had revitalized Particular attitudes, it remained fairly strong throughout the eighteenth century and counted seventeen churches in 1764. Having changed its name to the Rhode Island Association, it has continued to eke out a meager existence. In 1955 the Association embraced five churches with 324 members; by 1965 the numbers had decreased to three churches with 96 members.

When the Great Awakening burst upon the scene in 1740, there were perhaps two dozen Baptist churches in New England—eleven in Rhode Island, eight in Massachusetts, and four in Connecticut—and an unknown number of small Baptist groups. None of them at that time were particularly strong or vigorous, and as a group they would not have a strong or sustained organic relation to the vast expansion of Baptist churches (in that sense the Philadelphia Association was to be far more important); yet, as we shall see in later chapters, a characteristic impulse from New England Puritanism would play a vital role in the development of Baptist strength in the southern states.

THE QUAKERS

Rhode Island was extremely important not only for Baptist history but for the early expansion of the Society of Friends in America. Before the opening of Pennsylvania to settlement, it was second only to the island of Barbados as a base of operations for Quaker missions in the New World. Within its safety they established a beachhead from which to carry their witness into the neighboring colonies. Conversely, the Quakers were important to Rhode Island, contributing to the political development of the colony perhaps more than any other group. Among the earliest converts were William Coddington, who served as governor successively of Portsmouth, Newport, Aquidneck Island, and Providence Plantations; Nicholas Easton, who served several times both as deputy governor and governor of the whole colony; and other leading citizens such as John Easton, Joshua Coggleshall, Walter Clarke, and Caleb Carr. A fruitful field for Quaker growth was also prepared by Anne Hutchinson, whose thought in several ways qualifies her as a proto-Quaker.

The Society of Friends arose in England out of left-wing Puritanism. As a movement, it exhibits the relentless movement of the Puritan-Reformed impulse away from the hierarchical, sacramental, and objective Christianity of the Middle Ages toward various radical extremes in which intensely individualistic and spiritual motifs become predominant. There were, to be sure, many evanescent sects and movements to the "left" of the Quakers—indeed, they often forced Quakers to define themselves more conservatively and to tighten the discipline of their societies. But the movement which looks to George Fox as its founder is overwhelmingly the most important and enduring manifestation of Puritan radicalism in either England or America.

George Fox (1624–91) was a weaver's son, born in Leicestershire and apprenticed as a shoemaker. He early evidenced a serious religious disposition, but as his spiritual anguish deepened, he could find no solace in the existing churches. He began to despair: "And when all my hopes in them and in all men were gone, so that I had nothing outwardly to help me, nor could tell what to do, then, oh then, I heard a voice which said, 'There is one, even Christ Jesus, that can speak to thy condition.' "[6] This experience offered him direct access to God, apart from all human mediation, through the gracious activity of the Holy Spirit.

In 1648 Fox began to witness to an inward spiritual faith in various public places, and sometimes in the parish churches ("steeple-houses") after the minister was finished with the service. Despite imprisonment, beatings, and the scoffing of mobs, he persevered, and his powerful witness, homely eloquence, and wonderful tenderness began to win followers to his way. The traditional date for the origin of the Society of Friends is 1652, when Fox brought "convincement" to a group of seekers in the household of Judge Fell and his wife Margaret of Swarthmore Hall in Lancashire.

The distinctive Quaker testimony is to the direct revelation of Christ to the soul, although this is not understood to be contradictory to or even apart from the revelation in Scripture. It does mean, however, that true revelation is an experienced reality. As the great Quaker theologian Robert Barclay (1648–90) put it in his *Apology for the True Christian Divinity*, "the stamp of God's spirit must be known by inward acquaintance." Fox made the same point:

> Now I was sent to turn people from darkness to the light, that they might receive Christ Jesus, for to as many as should receive him in his light, I saw that he would give power to become the sons of God, which I had obtained by receiving Christ. And I was to direct people to the Spirit that gave forth the Scriptures, by which they might be led into all truth, and so up to Christ and God, as they had been who gave them forth. . . . I saw that the grace of God, which brings salvation, had appeared to all men, and that the manifestation of the Spirit of God was given to every man to profit withal.[7]

Such a statement reveals the remarkable degree to which the early Quaker message belongs not only within a broadly defined Christian tradition but even within the narrower Puritan tradition, with its intensely Christocentric experientialism, its total reliance on the grace of God, and its emphasis on salvation. Mysticism and moralism were extremely peripheral or absent altogether. This message was nevertheless regarded as dan-

6. *The Journal of George Fox*, p. 11.

7. Ibid., p. 34.

gerous in a century when the conception of the Bible as a closed and static body of doctrine reached its zenith and predestination was a tenet of popular orthodoxy. It must be said, too, that Quaker teaching was feared because it undermined the establishment by minimizing the liturgical and teaching function of an ordained ministry, abandoning the idea of objective sacraments, and inspiring conduct which was attributed to the promptings of an inner voice. Most ominous of all to the authorities was the phenomenal missionary zeal which flowed from the Quaker conviction of the universality of the Holy Spirit's work.

In July 1656 the ship *Swallow* anchored in Boston Harbor. It became known quickly that on board were two Quaker women, Mary Fisher and Ann Austin, who had shipped from Barbados. The authorities moved swiftly. The women were kept on the ship while their belongings were searched and more than one hundred books confiscated. Although there was as yet no law against Quakers in Massachusetts, the two were hurried off to jail, stripped of all their clothing, and inspected for tokens of witchcraft. After five weeks, the captain of the *Swallow* was placed under a £100 bond to carry them back to Barbados. Two days after the ship left, another carrying eight Quakers docked in its place. The prison was ready—and for eleven weeks it was their home. But before they were shipped back to England, they had made at least one convert, Nicholas Upsall, who fled to Rhode Island. The Bay Colony then enacted a law providing that any shipmaster bringing a Quaker into the colony would be fined £100, that any colonist possessing a Quaker book would be fined £5, and that any Quaker coming into the jurisdiction would be arrested, whipped, and transported out of the colony without conversing with any person.

Thus barred from boarding any boat bound for Boston, the Quakers built their own. Robert Fowler of Bridlington, at the bidding of the Lord, built a small craft (the *Woodhouse*), loaded it with Quakers who felt impelled to missionary service in America, and (disclaiming any navigational skill) followed the guidance of God to New England. They landed at Newport on 3 August 1657. This so aroused the commissioners of the united Puritan colonies that they requested the officials at Providence to prevent the arrival and settlement of Quakers. But to this demand Governor Benedict Arnold returned a crisp negative. Rhode Island, he said, does not meddle with matters of conscience, and regards the reception of Quakers as less dangerous than "the course taken by you to send them away out of the country."

It was not peace, however, for which the Quakers had come to Rhode Island. They rejoiced in their freedom to "publish" in the Narragansett region, of course, but they also felt a mandate to tell their tidings in Massachusetts. Within a few weeks Mary Clark was in Boston to test the new law, and before long "twenty stripes of a three-corded whip, 'laid on with fury,' " and twelve weeks of prison silence testified that the statute was not a dead letter. Plymouth Colony was also "invaded," with the result that meetings were established at Sandwich and Falmouth, and by 1660 "the whole southern part of Massachusetts was . . . honeycombed with Quakerism," the Plymouth laws notwithstanding.

The Friends' dogged persistence in returning to preach in the very stronghold of Puritan orthodoxy prompted stronger repressive measures. In October 1658 Massachusetts took the final step, and under this law William Robinson, Marmaduke Stephenson, Mary Dyer, and William Leddra died on the gallows between 1659 and 1661. In the latter year a published notice of these atrocities came to the attention of King Charles II, who—unwilling to lose an opportunity to discommode the Puritans—ordered that all Quakers were to be sent to England for trial. No Quakers were sent to England, lest their testimony endanger Massachusetts' already precarious charter, but neither were any more hung, though punishment and deportation continued.

A new phase of Quaker expansion in New England as well as in other colonies opened with the visit of George Fox in 1672. Arriving at Newport on 30 May, he was entertained most cordially by Governor Nicholas Easton. He was accompanied by some of the most eminent Quakers of England, and the meetings which they conducted in Rhode Island gave a new lease on life to Friends all over New England. Fox describes one of the more momentous of his meetings:

> We went to Narragansett [North Kingston], about twenty miles from Rhode Island, and the Governor, Nicholas Easton, went with us. We had a meeting at a Justice's house, where Friends had never had any before. It was very large, for the country generally came in; and people came also from Connecticut and other parts round about, among whom were four Justices of the Peace. Most of the people had never heard Friends before; but they were mightily affected with the meeting, and there is a great desire amongst them after the Truth.[8]

Another result of Fox's visit was the arousing of Roger Williams to one of his last controversies. The old Seeker had never wasted any affection on Quaker "heresies," and now drew up fourteen propositions for debate with

8. Quoted in Rufus Jones, *The Quakers in the American Colonies,* p. 114. Cf. Fox's *Journal,* pp. 623–24.

the founding father himself. Though some seventy years old, he rowed alone the thirty miles to Newport, only to find that Fox had departed before the challenge reached him. Williams was obliged to debate instead with three other Quaker ministers who had remained behind. He published the result in *George Fox Digg'd Out of His Burrowes* (1676), in which he stood fast for strict biblical authority and condemned illuminism, pantheism, and the spiritualization of Christ. He was answered by Fox and John Burnyeat in *A New England Firebrand Quenched, Being Something in Answer unto a Lying, Slanderous Book, Entitled George Fox Digged Out of His Burrowes, Etc.* (1678). As usual in such disputes, both sides claimed to have the better part; but the practical result was to give wider dissemination to Quaker doctrines.

While Friends were taking increasingly larger part in the affairs of Rhode Island, they did not neglect the further publishing of the truth in New England. They ranged from Nantucket to New York, and as far north as New Hampshire. "Meetings" (the name used to designate a local group) were formed in many of these places, and their members were bound together in a remarkably homogeneous fellowship. As in England, so across the Atlantic traveling Quakers became "the bearers of ideas and ideals which formed a common stock of thought and aspiration, and without knowing it the native ministers shaped their message and formed their manner of delivering it under the unconscious suggestions supplied by their visitors, so that the Quaker in Dover and the Quaker in Sandwich were almost as alike in inward tissue as they were outwardly in cut of coat!"[9] In America the same unifying process was soon in evidence. Formal organizational structure began to take shape with the organization of Monthly Meetings in 1658, Quarterly Meetings about 1680, and a nascent Yearly Meeting at Newport in 1661.[10]

Quaker occupation of political office created many problems in Rhode Island, as it would later in Pennsylvania during the Indian and Dutch wars, because of the Friends' pacifism and aversion to oath-taking. In Rhode Island far more than in a heavily settled Quaker area like Pennsylvania, however, they compromised their principles so as to provide for armed defense, though they exempted conscientious objectors from military duties. During the eighteenth century, in fact, the Rhode Island Quakers were to lose much of their distinctive spirit and zeal, though their libertarian convictions stood the colony in good stead. It was the Quaker Stephen Hopkins, five times governor, who led the little colony in its prompt rejection of

9. Jones, *The Quakers in the American Colonies,* p. 140.

10. For Quaker activity as it moved into other areas, see pp. 192–93, 198, 206–12.

the Stamp Act, its call for a Continental Congress, and its acceptance of the Declaration of Independence, which he signed.

CONGREGATIONALISTS AND ANGLICANS

The first Congregational ministry in Rhode Island was carried on as a mission from the established churches of Massachusetts and seems to have begun around 1695 in Newport as a mission "to some who had desired it." In 1720 a church was gathered with Nathanael Clap as pastor. In 1728 a second church was formed. These two influential Congregational churches were served in distinguished fashion later in the century by Ezra Stiles, later president of Yale, and Samuel Hopkins, the disciple of Jonathan Edwards. In 1722 the Congregationalists also formed a church in Providence, erecting a meetinghouse a year later, and in 1728 ordaining Josiah Cotton, a descendant of John, as its minister. There was also a Congregational missionary to the Pequot Indians after 1733.

The beginnings of Anglican worship in Rhode Island were due to the Society for the Propagation of the Gospel in Foreign Parts, whose missionary assembled a small group in Newport in 1698. His successor, the Reverend James Honeyman, developed this field further, founded another church in North Kingston, and helped to obtain a minister for an Anglican group that had gathered itself in Providence. The society was also supporting a minister in Bristol after 1719. All four of these churches—the only permanent ones in the early period—were greatly encouraged between 1729 and 1731 by the lengthy visit to Newport of Dean George Berkeley, who on returning to England would earn world reknown as a philosopher. In later years Anglicanism would flourish in Rhode Island, becoming proportionately stronger there than in any other state.

THE RELIGIOUS SIGNIFICANCE OF RHODE ISLAND

In the full retrospect of history the place of Rhode Island in the development of American religion is anomalous in the extreme. An important chapter was undoubtedly written there, and the many historians who have dwelt at length on its tiny details are not simply lusting after eccentricity. Yet the influence of its many extreme and atypical modes of church life has been very small. Indeed, most of its supposed importance has been based on the most egregious kinds of misunderstanding. Rhode Island's chief religious significance arises from the fact that through geographical accident it became a place of refuge for Separatists, Baptists, Quakers, and other radicals whose controversial actions serve wonderfully to reveal the nature and full range of the Puritan religious impulse. By providing a very sharply defined reverse image of convictions dominant in Massachusetts and Connecticut, which were immensely influential, Rhode Island illuminates the intensely held and violently disputed religious issues of early New England. Yet in the colony itself these passionate little movements soon lost their intensity and frittered away. Roger Williams adopted an extreme theological position which made discipleship almost impossible; Anne Hutchinson moved on to an isolated death in New York; the propulsive power behind Baptist growth in America, or even its revival in Rhode Island, came from elsewhere; the Quakers accommodated to Yankee ways. The colony became a kind of composite dead-end street for its founding churches.

The other reason for dealing with early Rhode Island is essentially ideological and commemorative. It is the first commonwealth in modern history to make religious liberty (not simply a degree of toleration) a cardinal principle of its corporate existence and to maintain the separation of church and state on these grounds. This honor cannot be withheld. Maryland was formally chartered though not settled and organized at an earlier date, but the liberties it granted were not so clearly grounded in libertarian conviction and theory. On the other hand, Roger Williams's separatistic and radical route to a notion of "soul liberty" had almost nothing in common with the rationale by which the idea of religious liberty became operative in United States history. Williams's views were conceived in an "orthodox" Puritan context, based on an unusual form of scriptural interpretation, and clothed in an extreme doctrine of the Church. The Puritan mentality of Rhode Island's founding fathers, moreover, stands in an almost polar relation to the Enlightened conceptions of the "rights of man" which prevailed among the nation's Founding Fathers. The ground of Rhode Island's early liberties was neither practicality nor natural law philosophy; nor can it be interpreted simply as religious indifference.

Rhode Island's influence was limited by still other factors. Long after its early religious fires had cooled to the point of offering no offense to anyone, the state won a reputation for intractability and monetary irresponsibility which made it anything but exemplary or influential. It was the stormy petrel of the Confederation period (1783–87), it boycotted the Constitutional Convention, and it was brought into the Union by coercion after the basic American pattern of religious liberty and church-and-state had been formally established. Roger Williams and his confreres did, to be sure, express their convictions in both charter and statute. The history of the colony's early years is thus a welcome relief from seventeenth-century intolerance and a foretaste of latter-day American freedoms. Yet in view of the pragmatic way in which Americans have in fact resolved the problems of democracy, liberty, and order, Rhode Island seems to illustrate in an almost tragic way the political corollary of a dictum often voiced by historians of science, that premature discoveries are uninfluential.

12
EARLY PROTESTANTISM IN THE SOUTHERN COLONIES

VIRGINIA

Virginia was named for Elizabeth, the Virgin Queen, and it was an appropriate memorial to an immensely capable champion of England's cause in an age of religious and imperial conflict. During her reign the prayer book was carried by Martin Frobisher's expedition to the shore of Hudson's Bay and by Francis Drake's to the California coast. Then on 24 May 1607, four years after Elizabeth's death, the *Susan Constant,* the *Godspeed,* and the *Discovery* disembarked their motley cargo of 105 men on the low-lying shore of the James River, and an English colony finally took permanent root. What also had its American origin under these inauspicious circumstances was not the mere "germ of a church," as Leonard Bacon declared, but the established Church of England. And it was present not just because a chaplain had been put aboard, but because the leaders of the Virginia Company were convinced that Englishmen needed the church's ministrations and were dedicated to propagating the gospel in the New World.

Religious motives were hardly primary for the London merchants who supported this venture. Like most of the first settlers, they sought commercial profits; if possible, such treasure as Spain had been hauling out of Mexico and South America for nearly a century. In all seriousness they told Captain Newport of the *Susan Constant* that he must find a way to the South Sea, or a lump of gold, or one of White's lost colonists—or else not come back and show his face in England. As proud Englishmen they wanted to check the expansion of England's major rival, and as fervent Protestants they wanted to halt the advance of popery. But closely related to all these aims was a desire to evangelize the Indians, an obligation formally recognized in their own, and nearly every subsequent, colonial charter. The sealed instructions that went out with the colony, now carved on the monument at the site of the first settlement, point to still profounder convictions:

> Lastly and chiefly, the way to prosper and achieve good success is to make yourselves all of one mind for the good of your country and your own, and to serve and fear God, the Giver of all goodness, for every plantation which our Heavenly Father hath not planted shall be rooted out.

Another vital glimpse into the mind and will that underlay the Virginia Company's enterprise is provided by Sir Edwin Sandys (1561–1629), who more than any other exemplified its highest aims. The son of a Puritan-minded archbishop of York, and a student of Richard Hooker at Corpus Christi College, Oxford, Sandys had given much serious thought to the nature of the faith as well as the mission of the church. A long-time member of Parliament, he had angered James I by an attack on royal authority in 1614. Five years later he became treasurer of the Virginia Company and began to implement his ideals through a committee that was set up to codify the regulations for the colony, institute a form of government, appoint colonial officers, and define their duties.

Initially charged with the supervision of Jamestown's church affairs was Robert Hunt, sometime vicar of Reculver in Kent, selected by the colony's president, Edward-Marie Wingfield, and approved by Archbishop Bancroft as a man "not anywaie to be touched with the rebellious humors of a popish spirit, nor blemished with the least suspition of a factius scismatick," and described by Captain John Smith as "an honest, religious, and courageous Divine." Soon after landing, on the Third Sunday after Trinity, Hunt celebrated the colony's first Holy Communion, and thus began a ministry in Virginia to which the rest of his life was devoted. He survived the "starving time" which ran through the winter of 1609–10, and seems to have been a stabilizing influence during those early years when acrimonious dissension wracked the colony. He was among the ragged and sickly remnant who were stayed from abandoning the colony by the arrival of Governor De La Warr in 1610.

This new governor's first act was to lead them all to a service in the dilapidated chapel, where they heard from the clergyman he had brought with him a sermon on vanity and idleness. De La Warr also brought more substantial things: much-needed supplies and absolute powers of government authorized by a new charter and vested in him by the company. His compassionate nature and good judgment made his power a blessing to the distraught colony; but within a year, after seeing most of his people go down before the pestilence, and almost carried away by disease himself, he returned to England. The staggering colony was bolstered again in 1611 by the arrival of large and well-provisioned groups under Thomas Dale and Thomas Gates, who between them were to govern the colony until 1616. With Dale came still another clergyman, Alexander Whitaker, whose contribution to Virginia's spiritual welfare would be rich and manifold.

From Commonwealth to Royal Colony

Governor Dale figures strongly in the ecclesiastical history of Virginia because of his strict concern for *The Lawes Divine, Morall and Martiall* which Gates and William Strachey, secretary of the company, had drawn up. Here, in effect, was "divine" law for civil conduct and "martiall" law for the church—virtually the outline for a Holy Commonwealth. As put into effect by a tough-minded veteran of the Dutch wars like Dale (and later Samuel Argall), the parallel with Cromwell's Commonwealth in Old England becomes striking. Army officers were commanded to see "that the Almightie God bee duly and daily served" and that those who absented themselves from morning and evening prayers were punished. It was further ordered that "everie man and woman duly twice a day, upon the first towling of the Bell, shall upon the working daies repaire unto the Church to hear divine service," and that the Lord's day be given over even more to public and private religious exercises. Ministers were enjoined to discipline their flocks as well as to perform diligently a wide range of church duties. That these laws contemplated a far more settled community and a more numerous army than then existed is painfully obvious. But the fact remains that a period of Puritanic strenuousness was entered upon, and the colony for the first time began to show signs of stability. To the writer of *The New Life in Virginia* (1612), prospects were "good."

Complementary benefits flowed from Dale's founding of a second settlement at Henrico, a less ague-ridden and more easily protected tract fifty miles up the James River. The intervening lands were opened and the colony's economy began to shift from a communal to a more individualistic basis. The population increased slowly but steadily. As a result of this expansion a second parish was formed at Henrico and a "fair-framed Parsonage impaled for Master Whitaker." From this point the first and foremost "Apostle of Virginia" extended his influence. Most familiar of his many achievements are the conversion and baptism of Pocahontas.

After Governor Dale returned to England, the colony again fell on evil times, due most of all to the incompetent administration of Deputy Governor Samuel Argall (1617–18). In London opposing factions struggled for control of the company. These difficulties were finally resolved in favor of Sir Edwin Sandys, who then ordered the formation of a representative House of Burgesses in the colony (1619) and the repeal of "Dale's Lawes." Though it is certain that no Virginia governor was ever able to enforce such defiantly cross-grained legislation as William Strachey had conceived, it is highly significant that the men who took the oath of office and met in the choir loft of the Jamestown church as America's first elective assembly did not wish for more than slight modification of the "morall lawes." According to their enactments, idleness and gaming were still punishable offenses; immoderate dress was prohibited; and ministers were to reprove the intemperate, publicly if need be. There were fines for swearing, and excommunication and arrest for persistent sinning. Morning and afternoon services were required on Sunday, and neglectful persons were subject to censure. The governor set apart "glebes," or lands to support the church and ministers in each of the four parishes into which the colony had been divided. To promote evangelism among the Indians, each town was to educate "a certain number" of natives and prepare them for college. There was even talk of founding a missionary "university" at Henrico, and Sandys obtained company approval to set aside ten thousand acres for its maintenance. The project was premature, both from the standpoint of the company's condition and the Indians' readiness, and it was soon abandoned.

Disturbances within the home company, aggravated by general political difficulties in England, became even more serious after 1619. King James denounced the company as the "seminary of a seditious Parliament," and accused Sandys of contriving to erect in America a republican and Puritan state. In June 1621 James confined Sandys to the Tower (though he found it politic to release him the next month) and quashed the company's plans to present a still more liberal charter to Parliament. To make matters worse, the colony was ravaged in 1622 by a frightful Indian massacre which brought death to 347 colonists, reducing the population to 1,800 and the number of tobacco plantations from eighty to a bare dozen. In 1623 the king set about to destroy the company entirely. He appointed an investigating commission which reported on its woeful state, cited evidence of gross mismanagement, and recommended a larger measure of royal control. The company protested in vain, and on 26 June 1624 Virginia became a royal province. It probably would have lost its representative assembly as well had not James died the next year. His son and successor, Charles I, had less specific grievances, and therefore allowed it to continue. The next two decades were nevertheless marked by constant strife between the royal governor, the council, and the assembly. The most violent resentment was aroused when Charles permitted Maryland to be carved out of the Virginia grant and turned over to a Roman Catholic proprietor. Only with the appointment in 1642 of William Berkeley as governor did the colony affairs begin to settle down.

Yet "settled" is not the word for anything English in the mid-seventeenth century. In 1644 a second Indian massacre occurred, in which over five hundred people in outlying communities were killed. (This tragedy was followed by a treaty which lasted until 1676.) More serious were the distant rumblings of civil war in England. Governor Berkeley was, of course, a Royalist and a champion of the established church, and he took stringent measures to halt Nonconformist inroads on his colony. He was supported in these attitudes by the more wealthy and powerful planters. Strangely enough, Parliamentary sympathizers in the colony remained relatively quiescent, even after Charles I was beheaded in 1649. Berkeley was forced to resign in 1652, while a fleet of the English Commonwealth stood off the coast, but even then he remained in Virginia. In 1659, while the future of the government was still in doubt in England, the House of Burgesses *elected* him governor, a proceeding which in due course Charles II authenticated by appointment. During the turbulent years of the interregnum, therefore, Virginia experienced little of the mother country's violence.

The Anglican Establishment

The Stuart Restoration meant a return to royal control in Virginia. This provides a convenient occasion to survey the situation of the Church of England in the colony, especially since the relationships then in effect were to prevail without substantial modification until the Revolutionary War. A church settlement had been reached through three successive stages. From 1607 to 1619 the colony's religious affairs were guided by the Virginia Company, which framed its laws and sent out ministers in the capacity of chaplains. The rudiments of parochial government were present in this period, being modeled on traditional English practice. The establishment of the House of Burgesses in 1619 marks another stage, for then a representative body included ecclesiastical legislation among its responsibilities. The third stage begins in 1624, with the appointment of a royal governor who ruled with an appointive council and an elective assembly. Only during this last stage could Anglicanism be said to be established in Virginia; and even then, as elsewhere in America, it enjoyed only a partial establishment. A resident bishop—or even clear ecclesiastical jurisdiction—was lacking; organization of the clergy was informal; canon law was unenforced; and

Nonconformity was widespread. On the other hand, the ecclesiastical laws of England defined the religion of the colony; its support was guaranteed by law; parishes were created and divided by the assembly; and the governor exercised formal jurisdiction over many phases of church life, including the authority "to induct (a minister) into any parish that shall make presentation of him."

The fortunes—and misfortunes—of the church rested most directly on the vestry of the individual parish. In operation from the earliest times and officially recognized by 1643, these small trustee groups were elected in each parish to manage parochial affairs, most important of which were supervising the property and arranging for a ministry. By 1662, when they were made self-perpetuating, they had fairly established their practical rights to "present" a living to the rector, or (as was frequently done) to withhold this final action and keep the priest on a temporary basis. This gave the vestry a far larger control over local church affairs than a strict application of English law would have allowed. Such powers rendered almost nugatory the tradition and law which made the ministers responsible for discipline, because their tenure and livelihood were in nine out of ten cases dependent on the pleasure of a religiously tepid constituency. Since financial niggardliness often added to the minister's difficulties, such a situation almost guaranteed an equally tepid ministry. Except in a few more closely settled areas, priestly and pastoral labors were often sacrificed to the sullen performance of minimal duties, or to bickering for more regular payment of the meager support the vestry had promised. It may be that the unattractiveness of clerical livings in Virginia kept away the more indolent types, but it also failed to draw many selfless servants of the church. The seeds of many eighteenth-century difficulties were being sown.

No one was more concerned about the low tenor of religion in Virginia than James Blair (1656–1743). Arriving in Virginia in 1685, Blair served as minister at Henrico until 1694, at Jamestown until 1710, and at Williamsburg until his death. In 1689 he was appointed by the bishop of London as commissary for Virginia, the first such authorized representative in any of the colonies. As the highest ecclesiastical officer in Virginia, Blair's nominal powers were practically those of a resident bishop, and he exercised them rigorously, though tactlessly, in a futile effort to elevate the character of the colonial clergy. The interlocking interests of the assembly and the vestries, however, precluded any substantial result. He did not so much amend the existing state of affairs as point out its seriousness. His most lasting memorial is the college for which he secured a charter in 1693, naming it in honor of England's sovereigns, William and Mary. Located at Williamsburg, and eventually an institution of great usefulness, its early years under Blair's presidency were little more than a struggle for existence. It rarely had more than twenty students at one time, and was described by a contemporary as "a college without a chapel, without a scholarship, without a statute; having a library without books, a president without a fixed salary, a burgess (this right was included in the charter) without certainty of electors." [1]

The magnitude and liveliness of operations at William and Mary were but a reflection of Virginian Anglicanism at large. The first accurate knowledge of the church's extent comes from the year 1720. At that time there were forty-four parishes in Virginia's twenty-nine counties, each with a church and some of the larger ones with auxiliary chapels, so that the total number of places of worship was about seventy. Every parish had a parsonage, some including glebes of more than 250 acres; but only about half the churches were supplied with ministers, while lay readers performed services in the vacant parishes. Taken altogether, the state of religion in Virginia was low; and so it would remain until the Great Awakening began to shift the ecclesiastical center of gravity.

In the realm of theology and on the issues of church order so fiercely contended in England and New England, the Virginia clergy were not very vocal. Yet the colony's errand, in Perry Miller's important words, "was fulfilled within the same frame of universal references as the Puritans assumed. . . . In fact, professions of Virginia adventurers sound much like Massachusetts Puritans." [2] The leaders in England revealed this temper, so did the early governors, so did the first elected assembly, and, as it seems, so did the people, though for obvious reasons they had not been "winnowed" as were the early New England settlers. The clergy, of course, did not flout England's ecclesiastical laws, but in the early seventeenth century at least their theology was not contrary to "Dale's Lawes." Alexander Whitaker, Virginia's greatest early divine, was the son of William Whitaker, master of Saint John's and Regius Professor of Divinity at Cambridge, and one of of the university's most outspoken predestinarians. The judgments made by the son in 1613 reveal that he followed his father in theology. His *Good Newes from Virginia* declared that some of the company's leaders were "miserable covetous men," while the settlers they sent out were often drawn from the dregs of society. Too many, he said, "had not been reconciled to God nor approved of Him." Yet men like Whitaker were unable to change

1. Quoted in Charles C. Tiffany, *A History of the Protestant Episcopal Church in the United States of America*, ACHS, vol. 7 (New York, 1895), pp. 38–39.

2. Perry Miller, *Errand into the Wilderness*, pp. 99–101.

colonial policy; and in later years both the royal governor and the parish system precluded the recruitment and support of a rigorous ministry. Thus Virginia never felt the shaping power of institutional Puritan nurture, even in the early days. Accordingly, there are profound religious sources of the "Southern ethic" which gradually came to pervade an entire region.[3]

Religious history has a vital place in any explanation of the characteristic Southern attitudes toward work and leisure. Neither idleness nor the propensity to live by the sweat of another man's brow was ever encouraged by the Puritan doctrine of vocation. On the other hand, it is equally obvious that church life—or the lack of it—in early Virginia was decisively affected by the dramatic rise of tobacco culture after its introduction in 1619, and by the increasing dependence on African labor, which began in the same fateful year. The servitude of blacks was soon made involuntary, and slavery became a fundamental feature of Virginian culture, as it would in the other southern colonies wherever agricultural needs made the institution profitable. In 1667 Virginia lawmakers accelerated this development by making clear that "Baptisme doth not alter the condition of the person as to his bondage or freedom." Gradually, the colony's social structure and every major feature of its life began to be conditioned by the presence of a rapidly growing slave population. Commissary James Blair would report the fully developed fact in 1743: "From being an instrument of wealth, [slavery] had become a molding power, leaving it a vexed question which controlled society most, the African slave or his master." And by that time the same could be said of the neighboring colonies. For over a century, moreover, extreme unconcern for the religious nurture of the slaves was a feature of this social order, despite the professed aims of the society for the Propagation of the Gospel in Foreign Parts. In 1731 George Berkeley complained that American slaveholders held the blacks in "an irrational contempt . . . as creatures of another species who had no right to be instructed or admitted to the sacraments." [4] Thus by a complex process that has challenged historians ever since did political, economic, and ecclesiastical policy, plus slavery, immigration, soil, and sun, conspire to bring the "first South" into existence.

In addition to the emergence of a remarkably rural culture, topography accounted for still another feature of Virginia church life. Many long and wide river estuaries made the tidewater region a series of peninsulas, and

3. See David Bertelson, *The Lazy South*, p. 21; C. Vann Woodward, "The Southern Ethic in a Puritan World," *William and Mary Quarterly*, 3d ser., 25 (July 1968): 343–70. See also pp. 314–15, 699–702 below.

4. See Winthrop D. Jordan, *White over Black: American Attitudes toward the Negro, 1550–1812*, chap. 5, "The Souls of Men."

with the rise of immense waterfront plantations, the parish as it had been understood for centuries in western Christendom simply ceased to exist. A Virginia "parish" was sometimes sixty miles long: a vast, thinly populated territory which had some logical reality on a map, but little actuality for the hapless priest charged with the spiritual care of its scattered population. These economic and geographic factors also accelerated the process of class stratification. With tax-exempt councilors and the royal governor possessing wide authority over church and land policy, with self-perpetuating vestries controlling the local churches and dominating the House of Burgesses, and with slaves performing much of the colony's productive labor, the church became inescapably associated with social privilege. To be sure, there was a large degree of social mobility, and for whites the transition from plebeian to patrician status was sometimes accomplished in a single generation. But by and large, prevailing patterns of caste and class account for the church's declining popular influence.

Dissent in Virginia

Virginia's charter specified that her religious life was to be governed by the "ecclesiastical laws of England," and during the entire colonial period this policy was officially maintained. In 1629 Virginia was able to secure the ejection of Lord Baltimore and his Roman Catholic followers by demanding that they take the Oath of Supremacy. A law of 1643 required Nonconformists to depart the province "with all convenience." In that year three New England ministers were prohibited from responding to calls from Independent congregations in Virginia, and by 1649 several hundred Puritans had migrated to Maryland where milder laws prevailed. In March 1661/62 Virginia passed very stringent laws against Baptists and Quakers, and a year later John Porter was expelled from the assembly for being "loving to Quakers." In regard to the Baptists, this legislation seems to have accomplished its ends: not even their most aggressive antiquarians have found evidence of seventeenth-century congregations, or anything more substantial than occasional North Carolinian Baptists who said they had left Virginia.

Presbyterian ideas found some advocates among the Anglican clergy with whom vestments and ceremony carried little weight, but not to the extent of formal dissent. Before 1710 a few men with Presbyterian ordination even occupied Anglican parishes. Two definitely Presbyterian ministers, Josias Mackie and Francis Makemie, registered preaching points in Virginia (in 1692 and 1698 respectively), but their efforts were sporadic and no presbytery was organized.

Quakers seem to have been far more successful than any other Dissenters in resisting restrictive legislation. Friends were active on the Virginia coast after 1650, and a meeting was in existence there by 1662. When George Fox visited the colony in 1672, he addressed many large gatherings. His Journal reveals a whole network of Quaker relationships, and he is noticeably proud that many people of "quality" and authority were sympathetic. In October 1672 he wrote:

> So we passed all the day through the woods and bogs, and sometimes in to the knees, and at the night we made us a fire to lie by, and dried us. And the next day we passed through the woods and bogs and were sorely wet. . . . And the next day we had a precious meeting, for the people of that country (Somerton) had heard of me and us and had a great desire to hear me. . . . The 25th day we passed by water six miles, to a Friend's house called Thomas Goode where we had service. And on the 28th day we came about four miles where we had a meeting pretty large. . . . And there in this county they said the high Sheriff had an order to take me; but I met him by chance, and he took me by the hand and was very civil and courteous. And we passed about six miles by land and water to take in Friends for Maryland.[5]

Fox's account of his travels suggests the obstacles to evangelism everywhere in the South, and explains why Anglican and Nonconformist churches alike tended to be small, poorly supported, and isolated.

MARYLAND

The proprietary colony founded by Lord Baltimore in 1634 is remembered chiefly for the prominent place of Roman Catholicism in its founding and early growth (see chap. 21). After the Glorious Revolution, however, the colony underwent a gradual but fundamental transformation of its ecclesiastical makeup. In the later colonial period it was to become, with Virginia, one of the two places where Anglicanism was most thoroughly instituted. Seventeenth-century developments, however, made only a very small contribution to this result.

The Church of England

Compared to its strong position under state support in Virginia, the Church of England in Maryland maintained only a feeble existence during the entire Stuart period. An ordained Anglican minister served on the Isle of Kent under the Virginian William Claiborne, but when that island

5. *The Journal of George Fox*, pp. 645–47.

passed to Lord Baltimore, his ministry came to an end. There were also some loyal Anglicans among the first settlers; led by a lay reader, they held services in Saint Mary's during the early years, possibly using the same building as the Roman Catholics. Although a chapel was built in 1642, there is no record of an ordained Anglican clergyman in Maryland until 1650, and even then he had no settled relation to a church, making his living rather by trade. In 1676, when John Yeo sent to the archbishop of Canterbury a plaintive petition for an establishment of the Church of England, he reported that he had only two ministerial colleagues in the whole colony of over twenty thousand souls, and that "many Dayly fall away either to Popery, Quakerism or Phanaticisme." [6]

Despite this Macedonian call the situation remained unamended until King William III bore off the fruit of Goode's Rebellion and made Maryland a royal colony in March 1691. Soon after Governor Copley arrived, an "Act for the Service of Almighty God and the Establishment of the Protestant Religion" was passed. This act, like three others passed with the same intent in 1694, 1696, and 1700, was disallowed by the Board of Trade in London because it violated the English Act of Toleration. Finally, in March 1702, when the assembly accepted legislation written in England, the establishment of the Anglican church became a legal fact. But in the meantime many important actions had been taken. Close restrictions were placed on both Roman Catholics and Protestant dissenters, although the act of 1702 removed those which applied to the latter group. Thirty parishes were mapped out despite the small number of "conforming" Christians among the colony's twenty-five thousand people; vestries were organized in twenty-two of these parishes, and the number of ministers was increased to nine. An annual church tax of forty pounds of tobacco was levied.

Governor Francis Nicholson, who arrived in the summer of 1694, was far more energetic in his aid to the church, partly because he and subsequent governors were unhindered by local vestries of the Virginia type. He personally subsidized the building of churches and petitioned the authorities to send priests and a commissary. Both these pleas were answered: in 1697 there were eighteen clergymen in the colony, and in March 1700 Commissary Thomas Bray arrived for a brief but significant stay.

Bray had been appointed in 1696 as commissary of the bishop of London, and he immediately busied himself with the needs of the church in the New World by gathering libraries for use there. The most important results of his zeal are the two societies which he founded: the Society for the Promo-

6. Quoted from Maryland Archives, 5:129, 133, in Percy G. Skirven, *The First Parishes of the Province of Maryland* (Baltimore: Norman, Remington, 1923), pp. 30, 33.

tion of Christian Knowledge (SPCK), and the Society for the Propagation of the Gospel in Foreign Parts (SPG). Because their impact was felt throughout the colonies, especially where colonial governments offered little or no aid to the church, both of these agencies are discussed in the next chapter.

Of hardly less moment for the church in Maryland was the restoration of the proprietary charter to the Calvert family. Benedict Leonard Calvert became a member of the Church of England in 1713; when he died two years later, his son and heir, Charles, the fourth Lord Baltimore, received a charter substantially the same as that of 1632. These later Calverts provided very unimpressive governance, but the new arrangements did accent the social benefits accruing to conformity, and an Anglican constituency gradually arose among the landowning classes. This transition was facilitated by the steady waning of Puritan fervor among the Dissenters. Maryland's chief distinction derived from the fact that its laws and its prosperity provided better clerical livings than any other colony, and hence drew to itself a more dissipated and ease-loving ministry. During the eighteenth century, nevertheless, its church life would blend increasingly with the establishments in Virginia, the Carolinas, and Georgia, to create a unique tradition of southern Anglicanism.

Dissent in Maryland

Dissenters were from the first very numerous in the Calvert colony. When answering official queries regarding his conduct, the second Lord Proprietor stated in 1675 that "the greatest part of the Inhabitants of that Province (three of four at least) doe consist of Presbiterians, Independents, Anabaptists and Quakers, those of the Church of England as well as those of the Romish being fewest." In explaining how this situation came to be, he reported that he had found "very few who were inclyned to goe and seat themselves in those parts but such as for some Reason or other could not live with ease in other places. And of these a great part were such as could not conforme in all particulars to the several Lawes of England relating to Religion." [7] The same state of affairs was repeatedly lamented by Anglican ministers and missionaries in the colony, by none more eloquently than by Thomas Bray.

The strength of Maryland's Puritan population was demonstrated in several outcroppings of rebellion during the seventeenth century. The primitive state of the colony seems to have prevented any very effective or lasting organization among these groups, however. On the other hand, the presence of Roman Catholics neutralized or at least tended to moderate the

7. *Maryland Archives,* 5:267–68.

opposition of Dissenters to the Anglican establishment, with the result that after 1690 Maryland lacked the intra-Protestant contentions which were so prominent in Carolina and Virginia. This relative peacefulness was also reflected in the failure of non-Anglican Protestants to organize and maintain their church life until well into the eighteenth century.

THE CAROLINAS

Early Settlements

Unlike the men who combined to form the Massachusetts Bay Company or even the Virginia Company, the men who set their eyes on the vast territory south of Virginia showed scant interest in church affairs. Tangential to church history are the complicated proceedings by which a group of London adventurers and a coterie of court favorites became proprietors of this vast feudal barony in 1663. Although most of the eight original proprietors were Anglican in sympathy, they granted liberty of conscience to all who settled within their grant. Yet even this inducement was insufficient to overcome the unattractiveness of the area. A group of New England Puritans migrated to Cape Fear in 1663, but soon abandoned the site. Another group from Barbados made a similar attempt in the same area two years later, but they also withdrew. In 1669 a larger expedition of about 140 people under Joseph West left England in three ships, the *Carolina,* the *Port Royal,* and the *Albemarle.* After stopping at Barbados and Bermuda, they landed at Port Royal Sound, whence they moved north to the Ashley River and established Charles Town in 1670. Some commerce, largely in tobacco, was conducted quite apart from regulations by Puritan captains from New England, and by 1700 this district had a population in the neighborhood of four thousand.

The incompetence of the proprietary government became increasingly apparent. In the south the French and Spanish menace, together with the terrible Yamassee War, precipitated a crisis in the colonial administration that provoked the king to establish royal control in 1721. In the north the Tuscarora War, combined with many other signs of disorder and incompetence, led to the gradual assertion of royal control until proprietary rights were extinguished completely in 1729.

The Fortunes of the Church of England

For reasons not difficult to imagine, the church in any form had a very slender hold in the wild, sparsely settled and ill-governed expanses of early

Carolina. In the scattered settlements of the northern district there were no organized parishes with a settled ministry until well into the eighteenth century, though Saint Paul's in the Chowan precinct traces its origins to 1701. Before that date even missionary visitations were few and irregular.

John Blair toured the colony on behalf of the SPG in 1701, baptizing children and appointing a lay reader at three places where he was able to organize vestries. Since the people did not permit him to settle in one place, however, he returned to England when his funds were exhausted. The society was unable to send more missionaries until 1708, when two men were dispatched; these were replaced in a few years by John Urmiston and Giles Rainsford. Urmiston was suspended from the ministry for immorality and died in a drunken fit, but Rainsford later went to Maryland where he had a useful ministry.

The North Carolina Assembly passed an act establishing the church in 1701, but it was vigorously protested and speedily disallowed by the proprietors. In 1705, after Quaker members of the assembly had been expelled, a Vestry Act was passed. It too was nullified (by Cary's Rebellion), and not even half-effectively restored until 1741. By that time life in North Carolina had become more settled, and the royal government was as firmly in power as it could expect to be in that land of many uprisings.

In South Carolina the Anglican situation was somewhat better. The first church in Charleston, Saint Philip's, was built in 1681 of black cypress on a brick foundation. It was served by Atkin Williamson until 1696, when he was replaced as rector by Samuel Marshall. By 1723 there were thirteen parishes; and those in the more populous areas were fairly prosperous, boasting substantial buildings, comfortable parsonages, glebes of several hundred acres, and governmental guarantees of support. In more remote areas, the work sometimes languished for lack of a settled minister, though the society endeavored to supply missionaries for these parishes. The office of Commissary of the Bishop of London was established in 1707, and was usually occupied by men of energy and sagacity.

In 1704 the assembly passed two acts concerning religion, one requiring conformity to the Church of England, and the other a full-blown act of establishment. The latter, in addition to setting up parishes and providing for vestries and ecclesiastical taxes, authorized a lay commission to supervise clerical activities. This was a source of great discomfiture to the clergy. Samuel Thomas, who had come in 1702 as the first missionary of the SPG, returned to England in 1705 and called it to the society's attention, whereupon they pressured the bishop of London to send no more ministers to the colony until the obnoxious law should be repealed. The House of Lords and the queen were also led to condemn the act, and it was repealed by the assembly in 1706. The supply of ministers and missionaries was resumed, and many men of ability came to labor fruitfully in the colony. The Anglican clergy of early South Carolina was above average; even John Wesley, visiting Charleston during the Annual Visitation of 1737, found their religious life above reproach.

Dissent in the Carolinas

One result of Virginia's fairly stringent laws against Nonconformity was a gradual exodus of Dissenters to neighboring areas, including the Albemarle Sound region which ultimately became North Carolina. In this wild and unregulated area, Anglicans were a very small minority. Quakers seem to have been the most numerous; and when they were not temporarily outmaneuvered or disqualified, they played a significant role in the assembly. George Fox was the first missionary of any denomination in North Carolina. He spent a month among these people in 1672, healing the wife of a former governor, holding a disputation in another governor's house, visiting many Friends, and conducting several meetings. There were also Baptists and people of Presbyterian persuasion in the area, and no doubt even a number of New England Puritans; but for the most part these various groups were not organized into churches, and only resistance to acts for establishing the Church of England brought them to any kind of concerted activity.

In South Carolina, where life was somewhat more settled, Dissenters were also in the majority. William Sayle, the first governor, was a Puritan, and some in the party of ninety-three who came out with him seem to have been of Baptist persuasion. In 1683 Lord Cardross founded a settlement of Scotsmen, some of whom had Baptist leanings, while the Baptist tincture of another group led out of Somersetshire by Humphrey Blake in 1682–83 was even more pronounced. About this time a group of Baptists from Kittery, Maine, may also have arrived, although their minister, William Screven, seems not to have come until 1696. In any event, by 1700 there was a Baptist congregation in Charleston. A group of Huguenots formed a congregation in 1680. Quakers were fairly numerous here also, and one of their number, John Archdale, served as governor in 1694–95. Numerical preponderance notwithstanding, the strength of these scattered and disorganized groups in southern Carolina as elsewhere in the South, was potential rather than real. Their future would be heavily conditioned by immigration, revivals, and external organizational impulses.

In the South generally churches were weak and poorly organized. Except among the Roman Catholics of Maryland and in a few other places, the absence of a trained and dedicated ministry was paralleled by the lack of a religiously concerned laity. The sparseness of the population, the growth of the plantation system, the difficulty of travel, and the scarcity of towns or cities created other obstacles, while the diversity of religious views impeded those who desired to found churches. Help from across the seas was sporadic and meager until very late in the century, when certain governors and a few determined individuals began to awaken interest in England. The SPG repeatedly expressed its inadequacy for the awesome challenge. Often the effectiveness of such aid as came was vitiated by uncooperative vestries or the hostility of Dissenters. All told, it is remarkable that anything was done. There is no doubt, moreover, that the patterns of the seventeenth century go far toward explaining southern religious developments during the remainder of the colonial period.

Southern Anglicanism became a dominant tradition not by force of popular vitality, but because of governmental support and the social prominence of its membership. The prevailing theology in these churches drifted steadily away from the earlier Puritanism toward a mild, rationalistic Arminianism, while remaining firmly Protestant and strongly anti-Roman in spirit. For many, church membership came to be increasingly nominal.

By 1700 the enlightened ideas and attitudes marked out by John Locke and Archbishop John Tillotson were gaining ground, though this trend was, of course, by no means limited to southern Anglicans. The whole Atlantic community was involved. By the nature of the case, however, such views were ordinarily the concomitant of advanced education, cosmopolitan intellectual contacts, and therefore, to a certain degree, of social privilege. Because social privilege was not usual among Dissenters in the southern colonies, theological distinctions tended to enforce social distinctions. Since Anglican evangelism was weak and the dissenting churches were both poor and very feebly organized, one of the primary characteristics of the growing southern population was that it was unchurched. At the dawn of the eighteenth century, therefore, the religious situation in the South provided many reasons for the pious to hope that a Great Awakening would come.

13

THE MIDDLE COLONIES: DUTCH, PURITANS, AND QUAKERS

The "Middle Colonies" were fated to bear a bland and undignified name, one that would develop none of the loyalties of "the South" and connote nothing of New England's regional homogeneity. These in-between colonies are distinguished by neither a unifying social-political-economic outlook, nor a common religious tradition. Yet they do have a distinctive character, deriving from a cultural and religious pluralism which in some ways anticipated the experience of the future American nation. This multiplicity of heritages appeared early: in 1644 Governor Kiefft of New Amsterdam told Father Isaac Jogues that eighteen different languages could be heard on the island of Manhattan and its environs. The Dutch conquest of New Sweden added still another—indeed two more, for many settlers in that area were Finns. Then came the English conquest, followed by the parceling out of New Jersey with its congeries of diverse settlements, and finally the opening of Pennsylvania to immigrants from all parts of Europe. George Bancroft, who saw God's hand so clearly in American history, could well point to the Middle Colonies as a providential training ground where colonial settlers might rehearse the destiny of the United States as a sanctuary for peoples of all lands.

NEW NETHERLAND AND NEW YORK

Political Background

John Fiske found "something romantic in the fact that in the summer of 1609 the first founders of the Dutch, the French, and the English powers in America were pursuing their adventurous work but a few hundred miles from each other." In July of that year Champlain in a forest battle by the lake that bears his name was making the Iroquois the implacable enemy of France and the ally of the Dutch and English. A few months later, John Smith in a friendly parley was buying the tract of land on which Richmond now stands. And in September Henry Hudson, an Englishman in the employ of the Dutch East India Company, was steering his eighty-ton *Half Moon* up the majestic river that is named for him. His imagination, says Bancroft, "peopled the region with towns." Hudson's imagination—and perhaps even that of the romantic Bancroft—would eventually be outrun by reality, though not under a Dutch ensign.

The year 1609, in which Spain began to recognize the futility of further attempts to subjugate the Dutch, marks the beginning of the amazing commercial and imperial expansion of the Netherlands. All around the world its merchants, bankers, and seamen gained fame. It was appropriate, therefore, that they recognized Manhattan and the valleys of the Delaware, Hudson, and Connecticut as lands of promise. By 1613 they had a few trading houses on Manhattan, while a fort erected about this time on Castle Island (Fort Nassau, later Orange) was transferred in 1617 to the present site of Albany. After 1621 colonial affairs in America became the monopoly of the new Dutch West India Company. Two years later the first party of permanent settlers arrived at New Amsterdam and Fort Nassau, and established still other settlements on Long Island (Brooklyn), on the Delaware (across from the future Philadelphia), and on the Connecticut (near the site of later Hartford). With the appointment of Peter Minuit as director in 1626, New Netherland became a full-fledged colonial enterprise.

In contrast to the well-executed maneuvers of these early years, however, the subsequent history of New Netherland is a tale of misgovernment, internal dissension, and exceedingly slow growth. Perhaps the chief factor in its mismanagement was the unchecked authority of the governors, who in addition were not temperamentally or morally equipped to wield such extensive power. An equally great blunder was the adoption of decadent feudal methods, ostensibly to stimulate colonization. The large grants to "patroons" actually discouraged prospective settlers, while at the same time creating another divisive element in the colony. Large-scale immigration was also hindered by the West India Company's close restrictions on the fur trade, which was the chief source of wealth, by the inadequacy of the land and climate for producing the necessary agricultural staples, and by the relative prosperity of the mother country which made most Dutchmen satisfied to remain at home, despite vigorous efforts by all concerned to increase the flow of immigrants. Several charming Dutch communities and farms grew up in New Netherland, but only on the lower tip of Manhattan did anything like a real town come into being. In 1650, when New England's population had grown to thirty thousand, the Dutch colony numbered only about two thousand—and half of these were of British origin. In 1667 a glowing description of the colony (part of a futile plea that New Netherland be recovered from the English) could say no more than that it consisted of "two tolerably well built inclosed towns, one open town and fifteen villages, besides divers extensive Colonies, bouweries and plantations." It had a population at that time of about eight thousand souls, composing about fifteen hundred families.

England had never conceded the Dutch claims in North America, and after the Stuart Restoration (as part of a larger reorganization of her "empire") she determined to challenge her commercial rival. To this end a vast proprietary grant of the land between the Delaware River and the Connecticut, including also part of Long Island, Nantucket, and Martha's Vineyard, and even part of Maine, was deeded to James, duke of York, the brother of Charles II. The duke then sponsored the naval operation which secured New Amsterdam's peaceful surrender in 1664. Thereupon the Dutch holdings were divided, the duke of York retaining control only of New York, which he governed through a series of appointed deputies. Compared to Dutch rule the new government was liberal and humane, since by this time the economic advantages of religious liberty were generally conceded by colonial entrepreneurs; moreover, the conversion of James to Roman Catholicism in 1672 led him to seek toleration for his coreligionists. Compared with other colonies, however, the New York government was restrictive and arbitrary. The "Duke's Laws," approved by the Dutch deputies in 1665, perpetuated the feudalistic paternalism and class structure of the patroon era. The English were ousted by the Dutch temporarily in 1673–74; and when the duke of York regained control he appointed as governor Sir Edmund Andros, who reinstated the "Duke's Laws" and resisted appeals for representative local government.

New York hardly prospered under Stuart rule. In 1678 there were probably not over three thousand people in Manhattan, nor over twenty thousand in the whole colony. The great estates remained practically empty, with what settlers there were hugging the Hudson and eking out a meager agricultural livelihood. Wealth was concentrated in the hands of a few landed gentlemen, merchants, and fur traders. The heterogeneity of the population heightened the problems of government. The Dutch were not particularly good subjects of the English crown, and the Puritans on Long Island regarded the Catholic James and his deputies with grave suspicion.

Due to constantly shifting boundaries, there was little provincial loyalty or chance for a sense of community to develop. Only a tenth of the population was enfranchised; and although the townsmen succeeded in setting up an elective assembly in 1683, what progress it might have made was upset by Leisler's Rebellion and the Glorious Revolution in 1688. The feeble and disordered church life of New York, therefore, stood as the product of turmoil and discontinuity which did not abate until well into the eighteenth century.

Religious Developments

The religious factor in seventeenth-century New York was singularly weak, though in later years it came to be highly significant. This is basically explained by the ethos of New Netherland and not by the nature of the Dutch Reformed church, which was as noble and profound as any current of Christianity the age produced. It had manifested unity and unambiguous adherence to the Reformed tradition at the Synod of Emden in 1571. The ravages inflicted by Philip II of Spain had only deepened and strengthened its faith, and its universities and theologians had made the country a major center of Protestant influence. The Synod of Dort, convoked in 1618 to deal with the Arminian controversy, became a virtual ecumenical council of Reformed churches, and was the chief event in Reformed confessional history between the death of Calvin (1564) and the Westminster Assembly (1643). Even the Dutch princes were devoted champions of the Reformed cause.

The religious ferment of the mother country, however, is notably absent in New Netherland. In the first place, conditions in the homeland forced very few to emigrate for religious reasons; Holland was already the chief sanctuary for the persecuted in Europe. In the second place, the colony attracted those least likely to have burning religious motivations; it was only "a by-venture in a great scheme of combined money-making and state-craft." The Dutch West India Company did "establish" the Dutch Reformed church, but it was anything but conscientious in carrying out its commitments. Two lay *Kranken-besoeckers* (comforters of the sick) were sent out in 1626, but only in 1628—five years after the first settlers came—did an ordained minister finally arrive.

This was Jonas Michaelius. He found the 270 souls then at Manhattan to be "free, somewhat rough, and loose." Nonetheless, he organized a congregation and had fifty communicants at his first administration of the Lord's Supper. In addition, he held separate services for the French-speaking Walloons. His report on the situation is an invaluable historical source, but he had already left the colony in 1633 when Domine Everardus Bogardus arrived.

This second minister presided over the colony's religious life during its best years. He saw the old meeting place in a mill loft replaced by a wooden church, and it in turn by a stone church (1642). He quarreled constantly with Governor Kiefft, however; and when Peter Stuyvesant arrived in 1647, both men sailed for home to appeal their cases. Their appeal reached a higher court than they planned, however, for their ship was lost at sea. In 1642 a third domine, Jan van Mekelenburg, better known as Megapolensis, arrived to serve the manor of Patroon van Rensselaer, thus becoming the first Dutch minister on the upper Hudson. Here he also pioneered as a missionary among the Indians and helped the Jesuit Father Jogues to escape from the Mohawks.

The annals of the Dutch Reformed church in this province could be continued down to the time of the English conquest, but such a narrative would include only a dozen struggling congregations formed by some fifteen ministers whom the company sent out. Six of these men were in service when the English assumed control in 1664, but only three remained when the Dutch reconquered the region briefly in 1673. One had arrived from Holland during this period. At the request of the English governor the newly organized classes (or synod) in 1679 ordained Peter Tesschenmaeker, who lost his life when the French and Indians burned Schenectady in 1690. In the decade before the Glorious Revolution, there was much discussion of religious affairs, grandiose instructions from the king for the provision of churches and ministry, much popular clamor against official efforts to discredit the Dutch church and establish the English—but there was very little congregational activity. When the conservative Dutch clergy almost unanimously opposed Leisler's Rebellion, their relation to the people became even more distant.

With William III, the Dutch stadtholder, on England's throne, attempts to establish the Church of England were intensified. Such efforts were forestalled until 1692, when an ambiguous act was passed providing for the public support of religion in four of the province's ten counties (See pp. 215–16 below). Yet even this had little effect; though the first church officially incorporated under the new act was a Dutch church in New York City in 1696. By 1705 there were thirty-four Dutch congregations in the province, but most of them held only a few services a year, with seven ministers remaining in service of some twenty-three who had served since the English occupation. Perhaps the most promising circumstance in the situation was the important beginning that had been made among the Dutch migrants to New Jersey, where ultimately the "garden of the Dutch church in America" would come to flower in the next century.

PURITANS AND QUAKERS IN NEW JERSEY

Like several other American colonies, New Jersey began as an ill-fated County Palatine, with (in the imagination of Sir Edmund Plowden at least) all the feudal trappings of a medieval barony. In 1648 there appeared "A Description of the province of New Albion" dedicated to the "mighty Lord Edmund" and others. But nothing more permanent: the reality of New Sweden on the Delaware and of New Netherland to the east was substantial; yet so far as "New Jersey" is concerned, the lands between the Delaware and Hudson remained a wilderness. Peter Stuyvesant's conquest of New Sweden in 1655 did little to establish Dutch influence in the intervening territory. The patroonship of Pavonia (including Hoboken) was stillborn in 1630; and most of what few advances the Dutch made around Jersey City were lost in the Indian wars of 1643. When it came within the power of the duke of York to grant "Nova Caesaria" to Lord John Berkeley and Sir George Carteret (1664), he could give them an almost virgin land. Their *Concessions and Agreements* accepted the idea of religious freedom and provided for an appointive governor and council and an elective assembly.

Scattered settlements were made during the first decade, but the only one of much consequence for church history was the planting of "New Ark" in 1666 by the strictest of the strict Puritans from the New Haven jurisdiction. This marks the beginning of developments that eventually made New Jersey a major religious sanctuary. The trend took a decisive turn between 1674 and 1676, when a group of Quakers led by William Penn gained possession of Berkeley's share, "West Jersey." With its generous *Concessions and Agreements,* this colony became an attractive haven for both economic adventurers and spiritual pilgrims. After 1682 East Jersey came under similar proprietorship. The crowning of James II, the abortive formation of a vast Dominion of New England under Governor Andros, and the accession of William III made events in the Jerseys far more complex than a religious history can pause to unravel; but the development of two distinctive subprovinces nevertheless went forward. The patterns thus established existed long after 1702 when Queen Anne, at the request of the Jersey proprietors, unified the province as a royal colony.

East Jersey

Following the lead of Newark, East Jersey became predominantly Puritan. These were days when some men were in flight from the "great persecution" visited upon Puritans in Restoration England, when Baptists and

Quakers were kept on the move by legal and corporeal harassment, and when considerable numbers of New Englanders emigrated to new frontiers to found more strictly regulated Puritan communities. As ever, the lust for new land drew men on. One after another towns were founded: Shrewsbury, Perth Amboy, Middletown, Elizabethtown, Woodbridge—each of them conceived as a New Zion and enacting laws appropriate to that conception. Town and church were integrated; in each village the church was at the center, while homestead lands and outlying fields were drawn by lot. The East Jersey Assembly worked with the same ideals as the towns, though their diversity mitigated the rigor of their laws; nor could they often bend the royal or proprietary governments to their will.

Yet a new "New England" it remained until well into the eighteenth century. Thereafter, the encroachment of non-Puritan settlers, the inevitable decline of fervor in subsequent generations, and the antipathy of royal governors all served to turn these people from their original ways. In one sense, however, these threats to their ecclesiastical traditions brought them toward their most enduring contribution. Unfriendly circumstances impressed upon them the advantages of Presbyterian forms of church government, and as Presbyterians who retained their New England loyalties, during the Great Awakening of the eighteenth century they would give a second birth to Puritan influence in the Middle Colonies.

West Jersey

West Jersey was from the first a predominantly Quaker colony. George Fox, after his travels in New Jersey, had interested certain of his English followers in its possibilities, and William Penn took a prominent part in stimulating its settlement after the territory passed into Quaker hands. In 1675 the ship *Griffin* brought the first group under John Fenwick to Salem. Two years later another ship brought two hundred more who founded the town of Burlington. Still other ships followed, and within eighteen months fully eight hundred Quakers had arrived. By the time Penn received his Pennsylvania grant in 1681, there had come fourteen hundred, "many of them persons of large property and wide influence." Because most of the proprietors of New Jersey were Quaker, they also controlled the governorship, and awarded it in 1682 to Robert Barclay, the Scottish apologist and systematic theologian, though he remained at home and governed by deputy until New Jersey became a royal colony.

"Meetings" were organized at each new point of Quaker settlement, the first apparently started by Quakers from New England at Shrewsbury by 1670, followed by one at Salem in 1675. Burlington became the center of

Quaker organizational life; here a Monthly Meeting was set up in 1678, a Quarterly Meeting in 1680, and a Yearly Meeting in 1681. After 1686, the Yearly Meeting alternated between Burlington and Philadelphia, and only in 1760 was it removed permanently to Philadelphia.

West Jersey developed a way of life quite different from that of its Puritan neighbor and more nearly approximating that of Maryland, in part because of its fertile plains and river frontage. The retention of primogeniture and the Quaker insistence on marriage "within meeting" also conduced to the emergence of a strong class of large landholders, as well as extensive reliance on slave labor. With these influences came a conservative, aristocratic social structure to which family interrelationships and county government, rather than the town meeting, were basic. On the other hand, it was a society pervaded by Quaker piety and sobriety, from which emerged during the eighteenth century two of America's greatest Quaker leaders: John Woolman, the mystic and reformer, and Stephen Grellet, the preacher. Both of these men left memorable journals that witness to the enduring nature of the West Jersey tradition.

At the end of the century the proprietors yielded to a recommendation of the Board of Trade that a unified government under the crown be established. This was achieved by Queen Anne in 1702; and Lord Cornbury became the first royal governor a year later, serving jointly New Jersey and New York. The Instructions prepared for him and his successors took cognizance of New Jersey's religious traditions, which included liberty of conscience for all but "papists." Drastic property restrictions, however, made political life highly undemocratic, and this led Quaker landholders to support royal authority, while the townsmen and farmers of East Jersey became an increasingly vocal opposition. Fed by old Puritan convictions and strengthened by the immigration of large numbers of sturdy and devout Scotch-Irish, East Jersey became the seedbed of an aroused Presbyterianism before it rose up against royal authority. But this is an eighteenth-century story.

THE QUAKERS IN PENNSYLVANIA

William Penn and the Holy Experiment

The most exciting adventure in the settlement of the Middle Colonies was unquestionably the Holy Experiment of William Penn, which marks the convergence of religious, social, political, and imperial history in a particularly interesting way. Expressly formed as a Quaker venture in state-craft, it became something of a laboratory for testing the viability of those views. Because of Penn's methods of opening the land to settlement, it also became a populous antecedent of America's pluralistic society. Finally, the testing of both Quakerism and pluralism was made especially acute by Pennsylvania's extraordinarily strategic location between the Atlantic seaboard and the wilderness empire of the French and the Indians.

The nature of the Society of Friends lies at the heart of the experiment. This radical phase of Puritanism has been mentioned before, and its votaries have been observed in virtually every American colony. Often they were resisted or suspected; in some cases they sought (and found) the martyr's crown. The Quakers would have played a significant role in American history with only their New England or southern roots to sustain them, and they would have made a major contribution if they had been halted at the Delaware River in New Jersey. But with the founding of Pennsylvania their ideas and institutions assume decisive importance. To speak of Pennsylvania is to speak of the man who put upon it the stamp of his own genius to an extent that no other colony's founder was able to do.

William Penn (1644–1718) was the son of Admiral Penn (1620–70), conqueror of Jamaica under Cromwell and friend of Charles II and the duke of York, whom he also served. The younger Penn inherited and made the most of these advantages, but no capsule biography can indicate the depths and anomalies of his mind and spirit or the extraordinary range of his activities. For he was almost "all things": the pacifist son of a naval hero; the favorite of kings (Charles II and James II) who was also the friend of the philosophers John Locke and Algernon Sidney; the sometime student of Christ Church (Oxford), Saumur, and Lincoln's Inn who was also a Quaker convert, friend of George Fox, and author of a minor devotional classic, *No Cross, No Crown;* the devout adherent of a radical Protestant sect, democratic theorist, and champion of religious freedom who was yet an aristocrat, accused of Jesuitry and suspected of Jacobitism; the visionary idealist who was also the founder and longtime proprietor of the most successful colony in the British Empire. A practical man of affairs, yet truly a man of the spirit. His long life charts an important path across the terrain between the age of Puritanism and the dawning Age of Reason.

The modest success of colonization in New Jersey seems to have stimulated Penn's larger plans for a colony where religious freedom, representative government, cheap land, and strictly feudal proprietary arrangements would furnish a haven for poor and oppressed peoples, an example of enlightened government for the world, and a continuous source of income for the Penn family. His plans were carried out with amazing dispatch. In

1681 he persuaded Charles II to discharge a £16,000 obligation by making him owner and governor of a tract of land west of Delaware between 40° N. and 43° N. The ambiguity of the description left the status of the lower Delaware in doubt, but the next year the duke of York (although he himself lacked clear title to the area) deeded the western shore of Delaware Bay to Penn. By July 1681 his deputy governor had taken possession, and in the fall of 1682, after a harrowing passage during which a third of the passengers died of smallpox, Penn himself arrived at New Castle in the ship *Welcome*. Before the year was out, the Assembly had been called and Penn's Frame of Government adopted.

In the first year Philadelphia was laid out in the geometric criss-cross which was to be copied all across America. Nine months after Penn's arrival the town had 80 houses surrounded by 300 farms; when he returned to England in 1684 it had 357 homes. Many difficulties attended the development of political institutions, but the colony grew apace—as did its Quaker population. In 1699, as if to mark the end of the century, Penn himself returned. Quitrents had amounted to little more than a trickle, and his debts were vast; but his colony was thriving. Philadelphia was a "city" and the Society of Friends had become probably the most potent religious movement in the colonies outside Puritan New England. Before leaving Pennsylvania for a second time, Penn saw it invested with a constitution largely of its own making. There was now little to cloud its future but the incompetence of deputy governors, the constant harassment of royal officials, the decline of Quaker piety, and the threat of the French and Indians on the frontier.

Problems of Growth

During these early decades, the growth of Pennsylvania meant expansion of the Society of Friends, for the immigration was overwhelmingly Quaker. By 1700 there were over forty meetings, some of them very large and flourishing. They were organized as Fox would have desired into a Yearly Meeting and radiating groups of Quarterly Meetings, all under the "Canons and Institutions" issued by the London Yearly Meeting in 1668. In doctrine they agreed with George Fox's letter to the Assembly of Barbados (1671).

There were four developments, however, which darkened the prospect for unimpeded growth and prosperity. Two of these were external and implied serious threats for the future, while two were internal and more immediately troublesome. The first and most rudimentary to describe is the growth of a vigorous non-Quaker element. Immigration brought a steady stream of Scotch-Irish and various German groups to Pennsylvania, and while these did not become really formidable until later in the eighteenth century, they were a sizable minority before 1710. A second and perhaps more critical factor was the European War of the League of Augsburg, which broke out in 1688 when Louis XIV of France arrayed himself against a large coalition including England under William and Mary. The long series of conflicts thus generated gave impetus to German immigration, and more importantly, became part of the international struggle for empire which, as the years went by, brought French military pressures to bear on the Pennsylvania frontier in ways which would finally drive the pacifistic Quakers from their place of prestige and power.

Of a far different sort was the crisis brought on by the Keithian schism, a harsh jarring within the society itself. George Keith (1639–1716) was a brilliant Scotch Presbyterian who converted to Quakerism around 1663. He became a close friend and associate of Penn, and the headmaster of the school at Philadelphia (now the William Penn Charter School). Possibly he aspired to leadership of the entire Quaker movement upon the deaths of George Fox (1691) and Robert Barclay (1690). At all events, in the year of Fox's death he began a series of public attacks on the society, deploring lax discipline and doctrinal heresy. Since many of the objects of his broadsides were also magistrates, he was found guilty of sedition. In 1692 the Yearly Meeting found him guilty of "a mischievous and hurtful separation," and disowned him. After carrying his case to various other Quaker bodies, including the London Yearly Meeting, and being disowned by them also, he led the formation of a separate body of "Christian Quakers and Friends." These actions may have contributed to Penn's temporary loss of his proprietorship (1691–94), and the Keithians remained an active and long-lived element in the resistance to Penn's policies in the province. But Keith's sect as such fell to pieces very quickly, with Baptists probably drawing off its more strictly Puritan adherents. Keith himself entered the Church of England in 1700, took orders, and worked off his grudge against the Quakers by serving as the first traveling missionary of the SPG in America. After two years in America he returned to a living in Sussex, where he served until his death.

Keith's charges of disciplinary laxity and doctrinal deviation doubtless contained some truth. Formalism was creeping up on Quaker religious life, and many historic traditions were being compromised. Magistrates were resorting to force, the Scriptures were being neglected, the redemptive work of the historic Christ was being underemphasized, and increased reliance was being placed on immediate spiritual revelation. Had Keith proceeded with more charity and less vituperation, he might have been remembered as an important reformer. But his actions and attitude were a repudiation of the Quaker heritage; both the offensiveness of his manner and the crudity of his language bespeak highly compulsive behavior.

The final and by far the most critical development among the Pennsylvania Friends was the gradual and subtle transformation of the Quaker spirit, a change which has been designated as a shift in concern from the meetinghouse to the countinghouse. This can be noted in Penn himself, in both his actions and his theology; and there is little doubt that an awareness of this transition underlay the Keithian protest. But what was premonitory in 1700 became fully apparent during the next few decades, as Quaker merchant princes and political leaders continued to dominate the life of the city and the province despite the rapid growth of the non-Quaker population. In the midst of economic and political preoccupations they tended to lose hold of George Fox's early counsel: "My friends, that are gone, and are going over to plant, and make outward plantations in America, keep your own plantations in your hearts, with the spirit and power of God, that your own vines and lilies be not hurt." [1] One may see the trend illustrated in the return to Anglicanism by William Penn's own sons, or the tendency in Philadelphia for Quaker membership to become a birthright. The entire development reveals how the Quakers' rigorous ethical discipline conduced to commercial success. It also indicates the great difficulty of transmitting sectarian enthusiasm to the second generation. Finally, it shows the virtual impossibility of applying a perfectionist moral code to the whole gamut of human activity from personal behavior to international policy.

Despite difficulties and compromises the Pennsylvania Quaker community persisted for seventy-five years in its effort to guide and transform the world. Unlike the Mennonites, the Friends were too filled with Reformed optimism to forego the challenge. Only in the deepening crisis of the French and Indian Wars did they find it necessary to withdraw from public life and return to the vines and lilies of the inward plantation, thus bringing to a close the Holy Experiment. In 1756 the Quaker Samuel Fothergill reflected on the spiritual cost:

> Their fathers came into the country, and bought large tracts of land for a trifle: their sons found large estates come into their possession, and a profession of religion that was partly national, which descended like a patrimony from their fathers, and cost as little. They settled in ease and affluence, and whilst they made the barren wilderness as a fruitful field, suffered the plantation of God to be as a field unculti-

1. Quoted in Frederick B. Tolles, *Meeting House and Counting House, The Quaker Merchants of Colonial Philadelphia, 1682–1763*, p. 3.

> vated, and a desert. . . . A people who had thus beat their swords into plough-shares, with the bent of their spirits to this world, could not instruct their offspring in those statutes they had themselves forgotten.[2]

When in the 1750s the Philadelphia Friends relinquished the "world" and resumed their role as a "peculiar people," a new spirit of "Quaker tribalism" settled down over the life of the society. This new quietistic temper, even when it took a strongly humanitarian turn as it did in the life and thought of John Woolman, was almost as far removed from George Fox's Puritan enthusiasm as the worldly concerns of Quaker politicians had been.

Yet William Penn's Holy Experiment, the last great flowering of Puritan political innovation, with the City of Brotherly Love at its heart, was truly to become the "Keystone State" of American religious history. Facing Europe through Philadelphia's teeming harbor, with Pittsburgh at the gateway to the Ohio Valley and the great West, and astride the valleys leading into the southern back country, Pennsylvania was to become a crossroads of the nation. It would remain a world center of Quaker influence. The country's first presbytery would be organized in Philadelphia and a later influx of Scotch-Irish would keep the state a Presbyterian stronghold. For more than a century after its founding in 1707, the Philadelphia Association was a dominant force in the organization and expansion of the Baptists, and the national headquarters of the American Baptist Convention is still located there. The Protestant Episcopal church in the United States would be constituted in Philadelphia with that city's Bishop White playing a major role. Its toleration would allow the Roman Catholic church to lay deep foundations on which later immigration would build. For similar reasons the Pennsylvania Ministerium would become a key force in American Lutheranism. The German Reformed church also had its chief strength in this state, and its theologians at Mercersburg Seminary would write a brilliant chapter in the church's intellectual history. Moravians, Mennonites, Amish, Schwenkfelders, Dunkers, and other German groups, including Rosicrucians, would flourish there. During the early decades of the nineteenth century followers of Otterbein, Albright, and Winebrenner would first be marshaled in Pennsylvania; and from its western edge the Restorationist movement of Thomas and Alexander Campbell would be launched. In Philadelphia, too, the African Methodist Episcopal church—the first independent Negro denomination—had its origins. As the chief residence of Benjamin Franklin, the seat of the American Philosophical Society, and

2. Ibid., p. 4.

the birthplace of both the Declaration of Independence and the Constitution, Philadelphia also served as a symbol of the Enlightenment's vast contribution to American religion. Finally, it was in this province that all of these groups experienced the difficulties and discovered the possibilities for fruitful coexistence that American democracy was to offer. Within the borders of no other state was so much American church history anticipated or enacted.

14
THE EXTENSION OF ANGLICANISM

Outside of Virginia, Maryland, and the Carolinas, the Church of England during most of the seventeenth century was only a flickering and uncertain reality in the American colonies. In hardly a dozen localities was there a self-sufficient parish or a sustained ministry before 1700. Yet some of these little focal points of Anglican loyalty were in time to become important centers of influence.

BEGINNINGS IN NEW ENGLAND

The first place in New England where the flame burned for a while before it sputtered out was at Sabino Beach at the mouth of the Sagadohoc River in Maine. Here George Popham of the Plymouth-Virginia Company erected Fort Saint George in the fall of 1607; a church was built and Chaplain Richard Seymour conducted a ministry marked by many funerals. Calamity followed calamity, the weather proved "unseasonably cold," and the colony returned to England in the following year. For the next eight decades the history of Anglicanism in New England is a story of wandering ministers, occasional lay protests against Puritan claims, and a few abortive efforts to colonize Maine and New Hampshire: the Reverend William Blaxton "discovered" by Winthrop's party living alone with his books and his herb garden on Beacon Hill; Thomas Morton with his maypole and Indian maidens, his whiskey, gun, and fur trade, twice routed from Merrymount by Puritans; the Reverend John Lyford, of uncertain reputation, ejected after a brief, uneasy time at Plymouth, who, after faring little better at Cape Ann, finally moved south to less hostile environs; the brothers John and Samuel Brown, packed off to England by Governor Endecott for refusing to approve the congregational church order instituted at Salem in 1629. These incidents remain, and others like them—but not much more.

There were of course many other persons, perhaps hundreds of others, who, like the Brown brothers, would have welcomed the prayer book and an Anglican ministry. Such people grudgingly conformed to the New England Way while maintaining traditional usages in their private religious life, or else they drifted outside the influence of the church altogether. Since church party lines were indistinct in this early period, a large number of settlers no doubt tipped their loyalties the other way, and like many episcopally ordained ministers entered wholeheartedly into the churches of Massachusetts and Connecticut, whose nonseparation made them, in effect, "purified" extensions of England's church.

Only after the Stuart Restoration was the Church of England securely planted in New England. The first premonition of the change came in 1686, when Robert Ratcliffe brought the surplice and prayer book to Boston on the same ship which served notice on Massachusetts that her charter had been revoked. Ratcliffe began his ministry under the enormously unpopular Edward Randolph, secretary of Governor Andros's council, and his efforts were roundly condemned from every Puritan pulpit. When Andros arrived, he pressed plans for the erection of King's Chapel, commandeered Second Church for part-time Anglican use, and by other high-handed measures provoked a crisis which eventually erupted as the Massachusetts phase of the Glorious Revolution. The little congregation survived the ordeal, however, and entered upon nearly a century of modest growth. But because of its dependence upon the royal governor's retinue and the social prestige associated therewith, King's Chapel did not have a secure future. During the Revolution, when the rector and most other Tories had fled, it passed over into Unitarianism. As the "Old Stone Church" of present-day Boston, King's Chapel remains the oldest Unitarian congregation in America.

BEGINNINGS IN NEW YORK

Virtually the only seventeenth-century breach made by the Church of England between Boston and Chesapeake Bay occurred in the New York area. Anglican rites came with the English conquerors in 1664, but for thirty years this foothold consisted of no more than services conducted by the governor's chaplain in the old Dutch church within the fort on Manhattan. Since British immigration was exceedingly slight during these years, little more was needed. Even as late as 1695, 700 of New York City's 865 families were Dutch or French Reformed. There was also a scattered congregation of Lutherans, and a sprinkling of English Dissenters. These facts notwithstanding, Governor Benjamin Fletcher in September 1693 extorted from the reluctant assembly an act of establishment calling for six "good sufficient Protestant Minister[s]" to serve in New York City, Westchester and Queens counties, and on Staten Island. The studied ambiguity of the act's provisions was a deliberate flouting of the governor's wishes, and led to an endless series of conflicts in the colony.

The act received royal confirmation in 1696, and produced its first fruit in the same year, when a Dutch church was chartered in Manhattan. (At this time there were five Dutch ministers in service: at New York, Albany, Kingston, Long Island, and New Jersey.) This was followed in the next year by the chartering of Trinity parish, the first Anglican church in New York City. William Vesey (Harvard College, 1693), an Independent minister on Long Island, was elected by the vestry on condition that he procure episcopal ordination in England. The governor's grant of the "king's farm" in lower Manhattan was highly significant, for it eventually made Trinity the wealthiest parish in America. With the expansion of royal officialdom and of a closely related merchant class, this parish and its offshoots came to enjoy the status of establishment and social dominance during the remaining years of English rule. Outside Manhattan, varying degrees of indifference and dissent prevailed, though several Anglican churches in Westchester County and on Long Island survived.

BEGINNINGS IN PENNSYLVANIA AND DELAWARE

Although the original charter of Pennsylvania specified that Anglican worship might be set up in any community where twenty or more people desired it, no effort was made to introduce such worship until 1694. The first building for Christ Church, Philadelphia, was erected a year later; but services were held only occasionally until Thomas Clayton came three years later as the first regular incumbent. Shortly before his death in the plague of 1700, he wrote that "in less than four years' space from a very small number her community consists of more than five hundred sober and devout souls in and about this city." During these years the preponderance of Quakers in the colony was turned in a peculiar way to the advantage of the Church of England by the Keithian controversy which began in 1691 (see pp. 210–11 and 221–23).

Delaware was until 1701 a part of Pennsylvania. The first churches in the territory had been built by the Swedish Lutherans as early as 1638, when a log chapel was erected in Wilmington. In 1677 the Reverend John Yeo, who had pleaded so eloquently for an established ministry in Maryland, came from that colony to New Castle and with the governor's approval was appointed minister in the Delaware region. Because of cultural differences, the people here were not receptive to Anglican forms at first, but gradually as these circumstances changed they passed into the Anglican fold. The Old Swedes' (Trinity) Church in Wilmington, erected in 1698, abandoned the Swedish language in the next century and, along with the Old Swedes' (Gloria Dei) Church of Philadelphia and a few other Swedish congregations, gradually became Anglican.

THE MISSIONARY SOCIETIES

By the end of the seventeenth century it was fairly clear to any acute observer that lay initiative could not guarantee the future of Anglicanism in America, not even when dedicated laymen were royal governors and not even when the church was supported by official acts of establishment. In the midst of this growing awareness emerged a number of farsighted and energetic churchmen whose actions and organizational work greatly altered the colonial prospect for the Church of England.

The American Situation

Some idea of the strength of the English church in the American colonies at the close of the seventeenth century may be gained from the estimate of the Society for the Propagation of the Gospel that in 1701 there were forty-three thousand Anglican church members in all the colonies, of which twenty thousand were in Virginia, twenty thousand in Maryland, and one thousand in New York. Clergymen numbered in this year about fifty; twenty-five were in Virginia, seventeen in Maryland, and two or less in each of the other colonies. The description of the situation in the society's charter was not an exaggeration: "in many of our Plantacons, Colonies, and Factories beyond the Seas . . . the provision for Ministers [is] very mean," many places were "wholly destitute, and unprovided of a Mainteynance for Ministers, and the Publick Worshipp of God; and for Lack of Support and Mainteynance for such," and many English subjects were "abandoned to Atheism and Infidelity." [1]

Around the turn of the century a series of developments significantly altered the attitude of the Church of England toward the American colonies. The first of these was England's overall "imperial awakening," the dawning awareness on the part of statesmen and merchants that England's overseas possessions were not a meaningless string of feeble outposts but

1. C. F. Pascoe, *Two Hundred Years of the SPG*, 2 vols. (London: SPG, 1901), 1: 86–87. Cf. H. P. Thompson, *Thomas Bray*, p. 64.

an empire—sadly in need of organization and consolidation—but an empire nevertheless. This awareness begins to be noticeable during the Interregnum, deepens under Charles II and James II, comes more fully to consciousness under William III and Queen Anne, and finally overreaches itself under George III. The church, too, slowly became aware of the "empire."

During these years one may also observe the gradual realization of another important fact: that a comprehensive national church for all English Christians was an impossibility. This fact had been recognized officially well before the Act of Toleration in 1689, above all by the mass deprivation of Nonconforming clergy on that fateful Saint Bartholomew's Day in 1662 and the harsh, uncompromising administration of the Clarendon Code which followed. The flight of James II awakened interest in reconciliation for a time, with Archbishop Tillotson and Bishop Compton of London taking prominent roles. Basically, however, it was the Restoration policy which prevailed, and under Queen Anne, the High Church party was again in the ascendancy (1702–14). Its aims are apparent in the instructions to royal governors in America to seek acts of establishment wherever possible. The effects are visible in the efforts of Andros in Massachusetts and Fletcher in New York, as well as in the partially successful enactments in Maryland and the Carolinas. There may even be some connection between the designs of Governor Fletcher in New York and the organization of Christ Church in Philadelphia during a brief (1692–94) suspension of Penn's proprietorship.

Yet all of these measures were futile attempts to turn back the clock, and despite their desire for uniformity, more sensitive churchmen were beginning to see that the church must win its way not through coercive legislation, but by an appeal for personal commitment on the basis of a convincing presentation of Christian truth. In 1711 Colonel Lewis Morris, though a fervent Anglican who believed New England's population to be "the scum of the old," testified eloquently to this view. He was then in New York, but from 1738 to 1746 he was governor of New Jersey.

> If by force the salary is taken from [the people] and paid to the ministers of The Church, it may be a means of subsisting those Ministers, but they wont make many converts among a people who think themselves very much injured. . . . Whereas, let this matter be once regularly determined . . . and then the Church will in all probability flourish, and I believe had at this day been in a much better position, had there been no Act in her favor; for in the Jerseys and Pensilvania, where there is no act, there are four times the number of church men than there are in this province of N. York; and they are soe, most of

> them, upon principle, whereas nine parts in ten, of ours, will add no great credit to whatever church they are of; nor can it well be expected otherwise.[2]

Whether expressed in the terms of Colonel Morris or not, a vital feature of the times was the awakening of the missionary spirit, a closely related resurgence of moral concern, and the formation of various societies for the reformation of manners. No aspect of these movements is more important to Anglican history in America than that which created the "Venerable Society" to which frequent reference has already been made.

Thomas Bray and the SPG

English interest in North American missions was articulated early. The Society for the Propagation of the Gospel in New England had been founded in London and chartered by Parliament in 1649, in response to the labors of John Eliot (1604–90) among the Indians in Massachusetts. This work was severely curtailed after King Philip's War, and the responsibility for sponsoring Christian missions in the English colonies devolved on individual colonies, churches, and persons, or, rather haphazardly, upon the bishop of London. Henry Compton was the incumbent of this strategic post from 1675 until his death in 1713, except during the period of his rupture with James II (1686–89), and it was he who sent James Blair to Virginia in 1685 and appointed him four years later as the first commissary of the bishop in any American colony. In 1696, in an act fraught with significance for the future of Anglicanism in America, he appointed as commissary for Maryland the Reverend Thomas Bray, to whose energy and foresight both the Society for Promoting Christian Knowledge (SPCK) and the Society for the Propagation of the Gospel in Foreign Parts (SPG) may be attributed.

Thomas Bray (1656–1730) was born on a farm near the Welsh border. Attending All Souls' College, Oxford, as "puer pauper," he took his B.A. in 1678 and entered orders the same year. In his first pastorate at Sheldon, Warwickshire, Bray planned *A Course Of Lectures Upon the Church Catechism, in Four Volumes,* completing only the first volume (consisting of twenty-six lectures), which was published at Oxford in 1696. It secured for him not only considerable profit with which to finance his later ventures, but also the recognition of the bishop of London. Bray's interest in the teaching role of the church and his concern for the adequate equipping of

2. Letter to John Chamberlayne, secretary of the SPG, in *Documents Relative to the Colonial History of New York,* ed. E. B. O'Callaghan, 15 vols. (Albany, 1853–87), 5:321.

the clergy made him a natural choice for the task in Maryland. His first project was to organize a voluntary society to provide libraries at home and abroad; its first meeting in March 1699 marks the beginning of the SPCK. Although it was an unchartered organization, Bray's exertions resulted in the foundation of nearly forty libraries in the American colonies from Boston to Charleston. The largest, at Annapolis, Maryland, was one of the first semipublic lending libraries in the New World.

By December 1699 Bray was ready to sail for Maryland. Arriving in March 1700, he soon became convinced that he could promote the religious interests of the colony better in England; and less than six months later he was home again. Bray secured a royal charter for a second society, the Society for the Propagation of the Gospel in Foreign Parts, in June 1701, a date which became a watershed in the American history of Anglicanism, for the society from the first had powerful royal, political, and episcopal support. Archbishop Tenison himself officiated at the first meeting. The society became the chief means of extending the Church of England beyond the seas, and for the next eighty years, America was its almost exclusive concern. Its primary task lay in securing suitable men to serve as missionaries, thus preventing the dissolute dregs of the English clergy from gravitating to the unregulated colonial parishes. It helped support ministers in existing colonial parishes and sent itinerant missionaries to organize congregations where possible in colonies which showed little or no solicitude for Anglicanism. It also professed a concern for evangelizing the Indians and slaves. Finally, it sought to coordinate this farflung enterprise so as to make maximum use of the funds it could raise. Its records, and the reports of its missionaries, then as now, were an invaluable source of information on the fields, the sowers, and the harvest.

The impetus thus given was desperately needed even in the most favored colonies. Commissary James Blair reported in 1700 that more than half the parishes of Virginia lacked a ministry; yet through his efforts and with SPG aid all but two of these were staffed in the year of Blair's death (1743). In Maryland too the need was great, since the governors who followed Francis Nicholson lacked his churchly zeal. Governor Hart in 1714 secured approval for two commissaries, one on the eastern shore, another on the western, but neither the legislature nor the clergy wished to acknowledge the ecclesiastical jurisdiction of the bishop of London. Men and aid from the SPG made a great difference. The importance of SPG missionaries in the Carolinas has already been indicated.

In the northern colonies this new source of support had a still more decisive effect, as Anglican history literally began in some cases with the arrival of the first SPG missionary. The man to whom this honor fell first was the petulant ex-Quaker, George Keith, whose earlier accomplishments have already been noted. Keith's *Greater and Lesser Catechism* was published by the SPCK shortly after he entered the Anglican ministry, and in 1702 he was sent on an exploratory tour of the colonies, joined by John Talbot, chaplain of the ship on which he crossed. They traveled eight hundred miles from Maine to North Carolina, and accounted for the first formal Anglican "presence" in several colonies. In their wake came hundreds of others, 309 altogether, before the Revolution ended the enterprise. Since no detailed account can be given here of all their multifarious labors, some typical accomplishments and a few especially significant ones must suffice.

THE MIDDLE COLONIES

In New Jersey the visit of Keith and Talbot came almost simultaneously with the union of East and West Jersey as a single crown colony (1702). Talbot remained in Burlington, founding Saint Mary's Church and staying on as its rector. His High Church views and suspected sympathy with the deposed house of Stuart aroused much criticism, however, and during a three-year period he was kept from his church. His interest in missions nevertheless took him all over the province, and only a lack of ministers and money prevented him from establishing many permanent places of worship. Talbot was also prominent among those who urged the appointment of a bishop for America; he was even suspected of performing episcopal acts himself. In 1705 John Brooke arrived as missionary of the SPG and laid the foundations for Saint John's Church in Elizabethtown; by the time of his death two years later he was ministering at seven other stations across the fifty miles of his "parish." Thomas B. Chandler, a Yale graduate who was later put in charge of this cure, continued to organize the movement to obtain an American bishop. (He himself was later designated the first bishop of Nova Scotia.) During the three quarters of a century before the Revolution, New Jersey was served by forty-four SPG missionaries.

In Pennsylvania the unusually fruitful ministry of Thomas Clayton was continued with equal success by the Reverend Evan Evans, a Welshman sent out by the bishop of London. His ability to preach in Welsh helped to cement the ties of the many Welsh settlers in the Philadelphia area, and his sincere concern for spiritual matters allayed the suspicions of the many Quakers who still distrusted the institution which had caused them so much suffering in England. In Pennsylvania, as elsewhere, many "Keithian Quakers" proved most ready to conform to the Church of England. Evans remained in charge of Christ Church in Philadelphia for eighteen years, nurturing a strong, well-organized parish. He also introduced Anglican worship in seven other communities in the vicinity, baptized several hundred former Quakers, and helped to found churches at Oxford, Chester, and New Castle (Delaware), which were functioning permanently by the time of his retirement in 1718 to an easier living in Maryland. From the time of Keith and Talbot's visit until the Revolution, nearly fifty missionaries of the SPG served the Anglicans of Pennsylvania, though regular services were held in scarcely half a dozen places outside Philadelphia.

In New York the society was able to lend a similar kind of support, especially to outlying parishes in Westchester County and on Long Island. Fifty-eight missionaries were sent during the years before the Revolution. In addition, more Indian missions were attempted here than elsewhere, but due to weak official support they had very little success. Only after the fall of New France, with aid provided by Sir William Johnson, the northern superintendent of Indian affairs, was a small apostolate to the Mohawks carried out.

Higher Education in Pennsylvania and New York

Until the middle of the eighteenth century one of the chief hindrances to the prosperity of the Anglican churches in America was the inadequacy of its educational institutions. William and Mary existed to alleviate this situation, but for many reasons (not least of which was the tactlessness of its first president, James Blair) this college grew very slowly. In the Middle Colonies the needs were especially acute, and Anglicans were to figure importantly in two of the most promising responses to these needs, one in New York, the other in Philadelphia. By an interesting coincidence some constructive advice was provided to both of these efforts by the distinguished philosopher, George Berkeley, who between 1729 and 1731 took up residence near Newport, Rhode Island, while waiting for financial support to implement his own plans for an Indian college in Bermuda. After returning to England he became a generous benefactor of both the Harvard and Yale libraries, and through his most fervent American disciple, Samuel Johnson, the Anglican minister in Stratford, Connecticut, he made his own educational ideas felt. When Benjamin Franklin on behalf of the Philadelphia trustees requested Johnson to become president of their nascent institution, Berkeley's plans were forwarded, though Johnson himself declined the position. After receiving aid from various sources, the Philadelphia College and Academy finally gained a firm footing in 1754. The Reverend William Smith, an Anglican minister and educational theorist, was appointed provost, and under his leadership a new charter was obtained in 1755. In 1757 the first bachelor's degrees were awarded. What was to become the University of Pennsylvania was in existence.

By this time similar plans had been carried forward in New York, and here too Anglicans led the effort. Trinity Church was a kind of godfather of the project, though this very fact blighted the early years of the institution, on account of the opposition it aroused among non-Anglicans. The assembly approved a fund-raising lottery in 1753, and then in 1754 a royal charter was issued. In that year Samuel Johnson reluctantly left his Connecticut parish and assumed the presidency of King's College (later renamed Columbia). Now by another more direct channel Bishop Berkeley's educational ideas were instituted, and in 1758 King's College awarded its first bachelor's degrees.

Neither of these schools were church-related in the forthright way in which Harvard, Yale, William and Mary, and Princeton were, and such Anglican connections as existed at the outset soon became fairly tenuous. Yet in both places Anglicans were most prominent among the institutions' early supporters and in their faculties, and both institutions received modest royal patronage partly on that account. From both of them many prominent leaders of the Episcopal church would be graduated.

NEW ENGLAND

In the Puritan sanctuaries of New England the SPG made more impressive gains than in the other colonies, and it figured in one sensational triumph, though here as elsewhere the proportion of its efforts was modest. Congregations were widely scattered and usually so small that extensive support from the SPG was required everywhere except in the Boston area. Boston was the starting point for the missionary journey of Keith and Talbot, but the presence of King's Chapel there made their visit less significant than elsewhere. Some years later, the role of Puritan gadfly was filled in the unlikely person of a young Massachusetts-born, Harvard-educated layman of Jacobite tendencies and polemical disposition, John Checkley. Beginning around 1719 he wrote or edited a series of works that opened issues of theology and church order. In 1723–24 he even became the object of legal proceedings for libel. Naturally a spate of controversial publication followed, but Checkley remained steadfast in his views. Many years later he was ordained in England at the age of fifty-nine, whereupon he began a fourteen-year Anglican ministry in Providence, Rhode Island.

In the meantime the Anglican constituency of Boston was growing. In

1723 Christ Church was opened for worship, the historic "North Church" associated in American memory with Paul Revere's ride. Trinity Church was built in 1735 on a still larger scale, and all three Anglican churches as well as several in surrounding towns, notably Christ Church in Cambridge, showed considerable vitality until they were disrupted by the Revolution and the exodus of Loyalists. The dominant Anglican spokesman during these years was Dr. Timothy Cutler, rector of North Church during forty-two eventful years (1723–65). Cutler's forthright pronouncements suggest the degree to which Anglican growth in these years profited, first from the declining vitality and assurance of the older Puritan spirit, and then from widespread revulsion for the excesses of the new forms of fervency promoted by the Great Awakening. The growing prosperity and widening intellectual horizons of the Boston area also increased the attractiveness of the broad and liberal rationalism, the dignified worship, and the freedom from strict conceptions of church discipline which characterized eighteenth-century Anglicanism. In Rhode Island a similar process could be observed, though in that seat of sectarian dissension the Church of England became an even more attractive haven, especially in the areas where commercial growth was most marked.

In Connecticut the pattern of Anglican growth was very different, for in this "land of steady habits" the disparities of country and city were much less marked, the government was in colonial hands, and the Standing Order had been much more firmly knit together in accordance with the Saybrook Platform. Except for occasional individual representations, the colony's first public manifestation of Anglicanism was the services of Keith and Talbot in New London (1702). For the next twenty years the SPG made very small advances. Only one weak "parish" was in existence, at Stratford, founded in 1707 by a New York missionary but still without a building and usually without clergy. 1722 became memorable, however, as the year of the "great apostasy" in the New Haven area. The leader of this defection was Timothy Cutler, sometime Congregational minister in Stratford but since 1719 rector of Yale College, who seems to have been somewhat influenced by Checkley's polemics in Massachusetts. In close contact with him was a group of Yale graduates including Daniel Brown, the college's one tutor, Samuel Johnson, a former tutor now minister in West Haven, James Wetmore, minister in North Haven, and three somewhat less avid ministers in nearby towns. These men during a period of several years had been reading and discussing many works of Anglican divinity and recent philosophy that had been given to the Yale library by various English donors. They were fascinated by these broader, more urbane attitudes, and became correspondingly less committed to the stricter doctrines of New England theology. They also began to have serious doubts as to the validity of "presbyterial" (i.e. nonepiscopal) ordination. Finally, after stating their doubts to the college trustees, they were asked by the Reverend Gurdon Saltonstall, a trustee who was then also governor of Connecticut, to discuss their problems with a group of Congregational ministers. On the day after commencement (13 September 1722) this historic colloquy was held in the college library, but to no effect other than to strengthen the resolve of the incipient Anglicans, who very soon thereafter proceeded to England for ordination.

They returned within a year to New England. Cutler, now with an honorary doctorate from Oxford, began his long ministry in Boston; Johnson went to Stratford, where he completed the first Anglican church building in Connecticut and for two decades acted as "dean" of the small but slowly growing group of SPG missionaries serving congregations in Connecticut; Wetmore was sent to Rye (New York). By 1742 there were fourteen churches and seven clergymen in the colony; by 1760, thirty churches and fourteen ministers.[3] By 1775 there were twenty ministers and perhaps twice as many parishes or missions, but by this time the revolutionary spirit and the rising anti-British sentiment was gravely hindering Anglican growth.

The Anglican constituency in Connecticut, laity and clergy alike, was in several ways unique. More than any other in America it stood without official or governmental support, gained no social prestige or favor due to its religious affiliation, and suffered considerable harassment by the authorities of church and state, despite the colony's toleration law of 1708. Many of the clergy were native-born, Yale-educated "converts," firm in their convictions and generally committed to High Church attitudes on the church and sacraments, and to Tory views on governmental and colonial issues. They tended to be more conservative politically, and after the Stamp Act crisis of 1765, their Loyalism began to bring another kind of odium upon them. Had they not been reasonably inured to obloquy, the war would probably have eliminated their advances. As it was, they persevered, and during the difficult postwar years they were able to contribute very significantly to the formation of the Protestant Episcopal church in the United States.[4]

3. Included among this Connecticut group was also the minister to a small flock in Great Barrington, Massachusetts.

4. Among the missionary rectors of Connecticut was Samuel Seabury, a former Congregational minister of North Groton who after his ordination in England served as an SPG missionary in New London before moving to an extended ministry on Long Island. His son, Samuel, Jr., after attending Yale, also became an SPG missionary in New York, and after many vicissitudes was elected by the Connecticut clergy to seek consecration in England or Scotland. Successful in this effort, he returned in 1784 as the first Anglican bishop in the United States, thus gaining an old objective of Dr. Bray and a persistent goal of the SPG (see chap. 23).

GEORGIA

The last of the old southern colonies, Georgia was founded because of England's need to protect her other possessions from Spanish and French depredations. Also decisive, however, was a genuine philanthropic concern for the victims of poverty then being thrown into filthy debtors prisons. The event thus figured in the great European competition for American empire as well as in the moral and humanitarian movements arising in England after 1690. By an interesting series of interconnections, Georgia is also an important theater of activity for the SPG, the realization of a lifelong interest of Thomas Bray, and a direct product of his organizing activity. A recent biographer even asserts that "Bray may perhaps claim to have originated [Georgia]." [5]

Bray's active association with the SPG lasted only a few years beyond its founding, but in later years, as rector of Saint Botolph, Aldgate, in London, he carried on diverse works in education, composed a vast "martyrology" on the "encroachments and invasions of Popery," and became increasingly interested in moral and humanitarian movements. In this latter connection he came in contact with James Oglethorpe, a military hero of the War of the Spanish Succession who, as a member of Parliament, had instigated an investigation of prisons in which Lord Percival, a friend of Bray's, was also involved. In 1723 Bray had formed a group of Associates to administer a fund for the evangelizing of Negroes in America, and shortly before his death twenty-four new Associates were added with a view to combining and broadening their objectives. These Associates of the late Dr. Bray then worked in concert with other interested parties, including Thomas Coram, founder of London's Foundling Hospital, to obtain royal and parliamentary support for a colony between South Carolina and Florida, the highly touted earthly paradise of "Azilia."

King George II granted the Georgia charter in 1732, giving to a group of twenty-one trustees full proprietary rights to the vast pine-forested area between the Savannah and Altamaha rivers—and from their headwaters west to "the Great South Sea." Parliament also granted generous financial aid. With Oglethorpe in charge, the first company landed early in 1733. Savannah was founded, land was purchased from the Creek Indians, and in the first year over five hundred objects of charity entered the colony, to be followed during the next twenty years by a thousand more. As in Pennsyl-

5. Thompson, *Thomas Bray*, p. 100.

vania, moreover, the offer of haven to distressed Europeans was often accepted. In 1735 Moravians from Saxony arrived at Savannah, taking up lands which had earlier been offered to the harassed Schwenkfelders. The first of four contingents of the persecuted Salzburg Lutherans also came in that year, founding Ebenezer twenty-five miles up the Savannah, and later a New Ebenezer. Supported by the pietists of Halle and supplied by a remarkable series of pastors, Ebenezer became one of the few prosperous settlements in early Georgia, while also remaining a center of intense pietistic spirituality.

But Georgia as a whole did not prosper. The trustees ruled without a duly constituted governor or popular assembly; discontent was increased by the prohibition of hard liquor, slaves, and fee-simple land ownership, unrealistic regulations for the planting of mulberry trees, and general administrative ineptitude. Oglethorpe's two unsuccessful campaigns against Saint Augustine occasioned further hardship and wrangling, though his ambush of a Spanish attack on Saint Simon's Island seems to have vindicated the colony's worth as a buffer. In 1742 rum was legalized, in 1749 slavery was permitted, in 1750 fee-simple land ownership was provided; but to no avail. The trustees yielded up their charter in 1752, a year before it expired, and three years later John Reynolds, a naval captain, became the first royal governor. Georgia's population, which then consisted of two thousand whites and one thousand slaves, continued to grow very slowly, reaching eighty-two thousand by 1790. It remained the least populous and least prosperous of the colonies.

The religious history of Georgia is desultory and rather sad. Anglicanism was nominally favored and the trustees provided a chaplain. When their first appointee died, they sought and received a replacement from the SPG. He promptly returned to England, complaining bitterly about lack of cooperation from the authorities, yet the trustees were unable to amend the situation. Nor did things improve after the institution of crown colony government, despite the passage of an act of establishment in 1758. Of the long series of ministers who came and went, the predominant traits seem to have been extreme susceptibility to fatal disease, marked eccentricity, strong desires to serve elsewhere, or unusual faults of character. Aside from the Moravian and Salzburger settlements, Savannah, Frederica, and Augusta were the only three places of settled worship, and rarely were all three fitly supplied. Only Bartholomew Zouberbuhler, a Swiss-American ordained in England, conducted a long and fruitful Anglican ministry in Georgia in the years before the Revolution. Most notorious was the Reverend Thomas

Bosomworth, who left his station at Frederica to marry an already twice-wed Indian "princess" and later instigated an Indian outbreak. For extended periods the colony was without benefit of any Anglican clergy.

Yet Georgia has withal an illustrious colonial church history; great names abound. It was in this remote outpost that the famous Wesley brothers began their ministry in 1736 with such magnificent lack of success. Coming at Oglethorpe's urging, John began his ministry at Savannah, Charles at Frederica; and both of these men, still in the extreme High Church phase of their careers, at once instituted a legalistic, rubrically punctilious ministry to rapidly shrinking congregations who soon denounced them as papistic and unreasonable. Most objectionable were their insistence on baptism by immersion, and John Wesley's rigorous restriction of admission to the Lord's Supper. After four months Charles gave up and returned to England, but John endured a year and five months longer, his departure at that time being precipitated by a severe altercation involving a woman he seems to have loved and sought, the man she married, and her uncle who was the colony bailiff and "chief magistrate." What these troubles meant for the Wesleys' spiritual development is difficult to say, but there is much evidence that at least John Wesley's contacts with the Moravians and the Salzburgers both on shipboard and later in the colony were decisive for the spiritual quickening which was soon to set him upon his remarkable career (see pp. 242, 324 below). The Moravian Bishop Spangenberg almost deserves rank as a patriarch of Methodism.

The ship that bore the future founder of Methodism back to England crossed that which brought his friend and associate, George Whitefield, to Georgia. With Whitefield's arrival the church at Savannah experienced a new problem: it could no longer contain the multitudes who thronged to hear one of the greatest preachers ever born. But after a half-year he, too, returned to England to seek ordination and to raise funds for an orphanage he planned in the colony. After returning to America a year later and making a sensational preaching tour in the Middle Colonies (see pp. 271–72 below), he returned to Georgia to prosecute plans for his beloved orphan house, now named Bethesda and located nine miles from Savannah. During the next thirty years he gave $16,000 of his own money to the institution and raised over four times that amount. By 1770 plans to make it into a "university" were firmly afoot; but in that year Whitefield died, conveying Bethesda to his pious patroness, the Countess Huntingdon. The chaplain she dispatched failed to prevent the institution's breakup during the Revolutionary War; its inmates were dispersed and the buildings destroyed.

Dissent in Georgia during this period was even less organized than Anglicanism, except insofar as it be identified with the broad ministry of Whitefield himself, who after 1740 was replaced as minister of Christ Church in Savannah and gradually thereafter became estranged from the Church of England both in America and in the mother country. Before he died, this "Grand Itinerant" would put a more permanent mark on the Great Awakening and on American evangelical religion in general than any other single colonial figure. In filling this great role, however, he had to defy the Anglican establishments in virtually every colony; he was excoriated by the SPG missionaries who carried on the chief work of the Church of England in America. Both sought to win souls, rekindle piety, and plant churches, but they worked at opposite ends of the British religious spectrum. Perhaps the greatest irony lies in the fact that, whereas Whitefield's zeal led most of all to the strengthening of Congregational, Baptist, and Presbyterian churches, the SPG developed a clergy and constituency so fervently Anglican that its work was decimated by the Revolution and the exodus of the Loyalists.

15

THE GERMAN SECTS AND THE RISE OF PIETISM

Unfavorable connotations have accrued to the term "sect" until it is often understood as condescending and abusive. Nothing of the sort is intended here—or anywhere in this book. The word derives from *sequi* (to follow) not from *secare* (to cut); it thus emphasizes a group's response to a leader and not the group's existence as a tiny fraction or section of the whole. More important than etymology for the historian's usage of the word is Ernst Troeltsch's conception of a "sect" as a religious group which is gathered or called out of some natural organic group or state church on positively anticonformist grounds, sometimes by a charismatic leader, but as often by some principle of greater strictness, more singleminded dedication, or more intense abnegation of the world and its attractions. Often, even usually, the sect has as its main principle some aspect of the orthodox faith which is being lost or neglected. In this sense left-wing Puritan groups often showed "sectarian" tendencies even though circumstances, especially in America, sometimes made them comprehensive, inclusive and "churchly" in their stance, rather than exclusive.

One index of the fertility and fervor of the Reformation's underlying religious motivation was the luxuriant growth of sectarianism which accompanied it. Early colonial arrivals especially are worth close attention, because they illustrate a long-term process that was to be repeated over and over again on the American scene.[1] And none played a more prominent role than the various German groups who from early times made Pennsyl-

1. More extensive consideration is given to the characteristically American features of sect formation in chap. 29.

vania famous. Among the emigrants from Germany were also many Lutherans or Reformed people from inclusive state-church traditions, but they will be dealt with in the succeeding chapter. Our present concern is with those who came frankly and by intention as sectarians, some tracing their heritage back to the earliest Reformation years or even earlier, others moving in the more extreme vanguard of German pietism which was already taking shape in the closing decades of the seventeenth century. If they are treated here with brief reference to their future fate and not discussed in later chapters, it is only because space limitations make continuous references impossible.

Many types and degrees of radicalism flowered during the sixteenth-century Reformation, some rationalistic and antitrinitarian, some intensely biblical, some predominantly "spiritual." These radicals tended to agree on a number of points: (1) that the Christianity of the first century was ideal and that the institutional church had "fallen" from the pristine purity of that primitive age; (2) that the Roman Catholic church as well as the "magisterial reformation" placed too much emphasis on the sacraments, the priesthood, and dogma; (3) that the true Church is a visible community of disciplined saints, whereas the inclusive attitude of the Middle Ages had unwisely equated the church with the total society; (4) that the use of force and civil authority in religion were unchristian, and that all regulation of the church by the state was illegitimate; and (5) that the Christian should withdraw so far as possible from the "world," i.e. civil and social concerns. They were, in other words, more or less subversive of established conceptions of law and order in church and state alike. They were "revolutionary" in several senses of that word; at times their revolutionary subversion took the form of chiliastic judgment upon all existing society, while at other times their principles and leaders became allied with social rebellion (as in the Peasant War). In one historic case—at Münster in 1534—the sectaries established themselves in power with bloodshed and violence.

Within and throughout this larger left-wing movement there were certain groups which deserve and proudly claim the name Anabaptist (re-baptizer), though the major groups of Baptists in America are properly traced not to these Continental movements but, as we have seen, to the left-wing Puritanism of the English Reformation. Very prominent among the Anabaptists were two interrelated and enduring groups, one in Switzerland and southern Germany, where Zwingli's revolt from Rome had inspired an extremely persistent left wing; the other, in or near the Netherlands, rising some dozen years later from the work of Menno Simons (1496–1561). Menno strove to disengage this movement from violent forms of action and gradually had a great deal to do with molding a quiet and pacifistic type of evangelical Anabaptist movement.

THE MENNONITES AND AMISH

From the sixteenth to the late seventeenth century, regardless of who was in power, these groups led a harried existence, sometimes (as in Holland) enjoying intermittent toleration, though usually forced into semiseclusion. When offers of a haven in Pennsylvania began to be circulated, the combination of intolerance, wars, and economic uncertainty led a group of Mennonites from Crefeld (near the Dutch border) to migrate to America. Penn granted eighteen thousand acres to a group of six men, all Mennonites, on the condition that they plant a colony. The first group of thirteen families arrived in Germantown in 1683. Whether all were Mennonites is doubtful; probably many were Dutch Quakers.

In Germantown they met a remarkable attorney, scholar, mystic, and Lutheran pietist, Francis Daniel Pastorius (1651–1720). Pastorius was agent for the Frankfurt Land Company, an originally utopian group of pietists in Frankfurt-am-Main who had been granted twenty-five thousand acres, and he became agent for the Mennonite group as well. Until his death in 1720 he was one of the most fascinating and profound figures in Pennsylvania. As chief citizen of the town, Pastorius was mayor, clerk, schoolmaster, and assembly representative. In 1688 he joined three Friends in sending to the Monthly Meeting a protest against slaveholding, the first such action in the American colonies. The document was transmitted to the Yearly Meeting at Burlington, which quietly suppressed it.

Under Pastorius's leadership Germantown became a flourishing village. Because the location was ideal, the soil good, and the settlers industrious and peaceable, no special difficulties were encountered. In 1686 a common meetinghouse was built for Quakers and Mennonites, although by 1690 it proved more expedient for each group to hold separate services, and the former built their own place of worship in 1705, the latter in 1708. At first the Mennonites took an active part in governmental affairs, but as complexities increased they withdrew, leaving such matters to the Quakers and later the Scotch-Irish and Anglicans. They also virtually ceased to exert any missionary efforts despite their unusual freedom to do so. Under the pressure of an expanding population and attracted by the rich farm lands, especially after the arrival of brethren emigrating from Swiss communities, the Mennonites began their occupation of the rural areas of what is now Lancaster County. Gradually other Mennonites joined the movement westward.

their churches marking the westward flow of population along the way. After 1760 there was for half a century very little new immigration of Mennonites to America.

Toward the latter part of this colonial immigration period the Amish began to arrive in significant numbers. They were a more conservative group founded by Jacob Amman (1644?–1730?), a Mennonite preacher of Berne, Switzerland, who around 1693 urged stricter observance of earlier practices, especially that of shunning excommunicated members. After gaining a few additional adherents in Alsace-Lorraine and the Palatinate, the Amish began to emigrate to America in 1727, then in larger numbers during the 1740s. They settled first in Berks and Lancaster counties, but gradually they drifted by "colonies" farther west, always continuing to be more conservative in their religious life, manners, dress, and language than other Mennonites. Opposing the use of church buildings as the first step to ritualism, they used barns or dwellings instead. They also refused to form any general church organization, or to found any colleges. In the twentieth century their descendants still use hooks and eyes rather than buttons, eschew motorized farm machinery, and insist on educating their own children.

Later Mennonite Migrations

The successive seventeenth-century movements of Mennonites to the colonies and their gradual migration south into Virginia and Carolina, west into Ohio, Indiana, and even beyond into Ontario (Canada) by no means constitute all of Anabaptist history in America. Though it will not be possible to refer to later events in their proper place in this book, some indication of their nature is needed.

Between 1810 and 1830 large numbers of Mennonites came from Berne (Switzerland) to Ohio and Indiana, organizing many congregations there which were at first unaffiliated with the Pennsylvania groups. During the pre–Civil War period these and similar groups also migrated into other western states, frequently torn by schisms caused by the appearance among them of advocates of greater or lesser adherence to American Protestant practices. They took the revolutionary step of founding a college at Goshen, Indiana, in 1902. By force of numbers, and perhaps aided by a greater willingness to meet the demands of the American environment, these descendants of the Swiss Brethren of Zwingli's day gradually became the dominant element among American Mennonites.

In the midst of this process came a dramatic migration from southern Russia. Mennonites had been moving from Germany to unoccupied lands in southern Russia since 1786, when Catherine the Great, herself once an impoverished princess in Anhalt-Zerbst, welcomed German immigrants to the wasteplaces of her vast, undeveloped realm. The migration soon became a tide, and by 1870 there were two or three million Germans prospering in the Sea of Azov and lower Dnieper areas and enjoying a measure of protection from the Prussian government. Due in part to increasing difficulties under German laws, and to exemption from military service and other advantages granted in Russia, Mennonites joined this migration in considerable numbers. But by 1870, when the Russian Mennonites numbered from twenty to thirty thousand, the prospect that their special status would be discontinued led a large minority to another exodus. During the next decade many moved to Manitoba, while others chose the United States, especially Kansas. They soon founded another college and an important church publishing house. This immigration brought an important invigorating impulse to the older Mennonite community with which it became closely interrelated.

Even in the twentieth century Mennonites are withdrawn and largely rural. Their church discipline continues to be sectarian in practice: intergroup relations and many "modern" customs and fashions are still prohibited, plain attire prevails, and insurance, television, public athletic contests, and bathing beaches are often frowned upon. Ethnic ties are close, and old Mennonite families continue to people the church. From earliest times, to be sure, other Protestant groups and American culture generally have wielded a covert influence not only on their quaint customs and anachronistic regulations, but also in the areas of evangelism and Christian education. Later still, Fundamentalist and Holiness doctrines gained entrance. Yet the movement flourishes best where these influences are restrained. Indeed, the most conservative among the score of different Anabaptist church bodies in North America (usually those who are least interested in "new blood") are the very ones which show the greatest growth rate, with the Hutterites leading the list.

The Hutterian Brethren

The Mennonites were by no means the only branch of the early Anabaptist movement, though they are the largest group, both in America and elsewhere. In the great exodus of "Russian Germans" during the 1870s still another remnant made its way to the United States and Canada. This group was composed of the spiritual followers of Jacob Hutter, who was burned at the stake in Innsbruck in 1536, the same year in which Menno Simons renounced the Roman church. These "Hutterites" were chiefly Swiss who had fled to Moravia after 1526 to escape persecution. Here the Swiss Anabaptists prospered under the leadership of Balthasar Hübmaier. From this larger group Hutter led a secession of those who felt compelled to obey the apostolic practice of community of goods, and at Austerlitz in 1533 they organized themselves as a thoroughly communistic or communal society. By 1548 there were twenty-six such colonies in Moravia, and here their tradition became firmly rooted.

When their survival was endangered by the outbreak of the Austro-Turkish wars in 1593, the Thirty Years War, and Counter-Reformation activities, many of them made their way separately and in groups into Hungary. Within a century Austrian intervention had made their continued stay there impossible; and they moved again—this time into Wallachia (Romania), then under Turkish rule, where they were joined by Lutherans from Carinthia who had also been expelled by the Hapsburgs. When Russian armies invaded this territory in 1777, the Hutterites accepted an invitation to Russia. Their next move was in the early nineteenth century, after Czar Alexander I granted them crown lands on terms like those offered to the Mennonites. Under these circumstances they prospered materially, but their communal practices deteriorated until revived by certain leaders in the 1840s and 1850s. By 1879 the czar had withdrawn their special privileges. The entire reconstituted group, numbering less than 500, together with as many other noncommunal Hutterites (who organized themselves separately or affiliated themselves with the Mennonites) migrated to southeastern South Dakota. By World War I there were nineteen communities; by 1931, thirty-three; by 1950 they numbered 8,542 persons distributed in about ninety communities in the Dakotas, Montana, Manitoba, and Alberta. Showing the highest net reproduction rate of any modern population, and losses by apostasy of a mere 2.5 percent, they seemed likely to double their numbers in sixteen years.

The Hutterites have undertaken no significant evangelism since earliest days, and the family names that constitute the group now go back chiefly to the Lutherans who joined them in Transylvania. Three of these family names now embrace nearly half the present-day membership. Their growth indicates the degree to which they have prospered in the New World; but their unusual pattern of life and their isolation have also aroused bitterness and discriminatory legislation. Their chief impact has probably come through their testing of American ideals of religious freedom—a test in which America has been found wanting. It should be added, however, that they have greatly enriched our understanding of Anabaptist history by preserving through all their harrowing experiences a most remarkable *Chronicle,* which provides not only an illuminating account of this unique group, but a great deal of information on the Anabaptist impulse itself. Their quiet tenacity through the centuries is one of the marvels of church history.

The Mennonites, Amish, and Hutterites as a people are thrifty, industrious, and predominantly rural. The places they settled in Germany, Russia, and America have become garden spots. Yet because they lived together in groups, seldom moving into new areas as isolated individuals or families, they have perpetuated themselves and their faith despite their unpopular pacifism. "Perpetuation," in fact, is the word to describe their history. Well before they began leaving Europe they had lost their aggressiveness; they were the *Stillen am Lande*. Even in the mid-twentieth century one cannot but marvel at the degree to which the Mennonites have preserved their tradition. But it has been accomplished so quietly, so inoffensively, in a manner so withdrawn, that until fairly recently they have existed on the American scene more as a picturesque souvenir of Anabaptism than as an influence on the nation's religious life.

THE PIETISTIC SECTS

Sectarian groups similar in some respects to the Mennonites arose from later developments in Europe. Pietism as a distinct religious movement began to take recognizable shape in the later decades of the seventeenth century. It is an exceedingly difficult movement to define, however, despite the fact that few Protestant impulses have been fraught with larger or more enduring consequences. Described most simply, it was an effort to intensify Christian piety and purity of life. At the outset it also involved a protest against intellectualism, churchly formalism, and ethical passivity. With the passing decades this protest broadened; pietists also began to inveigh against the new forms of rationalism and the spiritual coldness of the Enlightenment. Pietism was thus a movement of revival, aimed at making man's relation to God experientially and morally meaningful as well as socially relevant. It stressed the feelings of the heart. It emphasized the royal priesthood and sought to revive the laity. It called always for a return to the Bible.

The Thirty Years War (1618–48) and the decades of political and military turmoil which followed created an immense need for reconstruction and church renewal. Against the background of war and dynastic conflict, pietism may be seen as a reaction from the scholastic period of Protestant Orthodoxy, during which the doctrinal implications of the Reformation were being carefully—some would say too carefully—worked out. This "Orthodox" movement was from the first highly rationalistic, showing great dependence on Aristotelian concepts and methods of theological argumentation, a tendency that was accentuated by the prominence of the continuing controversy with Rome, and between Reformed and Lutheran theologians. There is also a connection between the rationalistic confidence of Orthodoxy and the later emergence of intellectual trends associated with the Enlightenment, since both scholasticism and rationalism tended toward intellectualistic formalism and religious complacency.

Another important provocation of pietistic attitudes was Reformed doctrine itself, with its powerful emphasis on the remoteness and inscrutability of God and the awfulness of his predestinating decrees. In the face of this awesome teaching, questions of assurance were inescapable, and the practical solution was often to regard a conversion experience as a sign of election. This was the Puritan answer, and in this sense Puritans like William Ames were important forerunners of pietism. Ames's great Dutch pupil, Johannes Cocceius, was even more influential on the Continent. Similarly motivated were a whole group of German and Dutch theologians, such as Witsius and Vitringa. A less orthodox tradition stems from Jean de Labadie, leader of a quietist movement within the Dutch Reformed church, and some would see Theodore Untereyk, a Dutch disciple of Labadie, as the founder of the pietist movement. Thus there is much truth to the claim that the Dutch Reformed church was the "cradle of pietism."

Philip Jacob Spener (1635–1705) is usually cited as the father of pietism, however; and a brief glance at his career is instructive. Spener was in background and by explicit commitment a Lutheran, and he found in Luther a powerful witness to the kind of existentially relevant faith which he sought for himself and others. Yet as with so many other pietists, Christian experience concerned him more than doctrinal precision. He drew much inspiration from the mystically inclined Johann Arndt, who has been called the "second Luther" because his devotional classic, *Wahre Christenthum* (*True Christianity,* 1605–09), for three centuries almost rivaled Luther's Catechism in its influence. But Spener was indebted most immediately to his personal contacts and reading among the Puritan, Dutch, and German Reformed champions of a more "spiritual" Christianity. He had studied in Geneva and Strasbourg, and been a pastor in Strasbourg before coming to Frankfurt-am-Main in 1666. Here he sought to renew the life of his congregation not only by preaching and Bible study but by organizing *collegia pietatis* (spiritual societies) within it. In 1675 he published the first edition of his famous *Pia Desideria,* in which he explained his methods, defended his strict "pietistic" moral demands, and gave theological and biblical substance to his program of renewal.

A few short passages cannot expose the theological grounds of Spener's

"Heartfelt Desires" for the church, but they can indicate the spirit and aims of his classic work:

> Nobody can read Luther's writings with some care without observing how earnestly the sainted man advocated this spiritual priesthood, according to which not only ministers but all Christians are made priests by their Savior, are anointed by the Holy Spirit, and are dedicated to perform spiritual-priestly acts. Peter was not addressing preachers alone when he wrote, "You are a chosen race, a royal priesthood, a holy nation, God's own people, that you may declare the wonderful deeds of him who called you out of darkness into his marvelous light." [1 Peter 2:9]
>
> Every Christian is bound not only to offer himself and what he has, his prayer, thanksgiving, good works, alms, etc., but also industriously to study in the Word of the Lord, with the grace that is given him to teach others, especially those under his own roof, to chastise, exhort, convert, and edify them, to observe their life, pray for all, and insofar as possible be concerned about their salvation. If this is first pointed out to the people, they will take better care of themselves and apply themselves to whatever pertains to their own edification and that of their fellow men.
>
> As for me, I am very confident that if several persons in each congregation can be won for these two activities (a diligent use of the Word of God and a practice of priestly duties), together with such other things as, especially, fraternal admonition and chastisement (which have all but disappeared among us but ought to be earnestly prosecuted, and those preachers who are made to suffer in consequence should be protected as much as possible), a great deal would be gained and accomplished. Afterwards more and more would be achieved, and finally the church would be visibly reformed.[2]

Spener was later called to Dresden, and later still, in 1691, he accepted an invitation to Berlin from the Reformed prince, Frederick of Brandenburg (and later Prussia). Here Spener achieved the peak of his influence, inducing King Frederick to found the University of Halle and to appoint August Hermann Francke as pastor and professor there. Francke, and his son after him, made Halle the mecca of pietism and a worldwide evangelical influence. Under the leadership of Johann Albrecht Bengel, another influential school of pietism flourished in Württemberg.

2. Philip Jacob Spener, *Pia Desideria,* ed. and trans. Theodore G. Tappert (Philadelphia: Fortress Press, 1964), pp. 92–95.

With the passing decades pietist concern for the "experience" of regeneration, or the "new birth" steadily intensified. Constantly pietists raised the urgent question, "How do I know I am saved?" And they answered their question with an increasing tendency toward subjectivism. Their moral emphasis directed men to charitable concerns, and led to a great flowering of Christian philanthropy, the founding of schools, orphanages, and hospitals. They gave immense impetus to the Protestant missionary spirit. Less gloriously, pietism also tended to formalize its own legalistic code of "Christian behavior" in terms of a wide range of prohibitions on such practices as dancing, card playing, and even play or recreation in general. Within the church it sought to transform the minister's office, making him a shepherd of souls and a preacher of salvation, not simply an administrator of sacraments and a protector of pure doctrine. In developing the pious life the Lutheran pietists put great emphasis on the catechetical instruction of the young and the rite of confirmation. They encouraged Bible study and sought to organize *ecclesiolae* within the churches as means for Christians to deepen their piety and minister to one another. These "little churches" were not intended to be gatherings of the "saved" in contradistinction to the "worldly" church, but the separatistic tendency was always present, and under certain conditions it manifested itself.

Taken as a whole, pietism performed an immense revivifying role in all Protestant churches during the eighteenth century, not only on the Continent but in England and America as well. More controversial were the blows that it struck at liturgical worship, its depreciation of philosophical and doctrinal concerns, and its encouragement of legalistic moralism. In addition, its accent on the religious feelings combined with its denigration of theological rigor opened the doors to rationalism, even at the University of Halle. The charge that its stress on personal piety undermined the church's sense of community is ill-founded, but there can be no doubt that it unleashed centrifugal forces that soon resulted in separatistic movements. Some of these new groups, moreover, would enter the stream of American religious history. Methodism, which arose in the Anglican communion, is obviously the most important of these groups, but it is dealt with in a later context. Among the German pietists who emigrated to America in early colonial times, the most significant and revealing were the Dunkers and the Moravian Brethren.

The Dunkers

Earliest of the organized pietist groups in America was the Church of the Brethren, also known as Dunkers, Tunkers, or Taufers. Their founder was Alexander Mack (1679–1735), a radical Pietist who withdrew from the Reformed church of the Palatinate and in 1700 took refuge in Schwarzenau, a village in the county of Wittgenstein (Westphalia). Here eight years later he and seven others of like mind recapitulated a process familiar in Puritan history: they "covenanted and united together as brethren and sisters into the covenant of the cross of Jesus Christ to form a church of Christian believers." One of the seven, selected by lot, baptized Mack in the river Eder, after which he baptized the others in the same fashion. In many respects this group revived the ideas of the early Anabaptists, and for a time at Schwarzenau they advocated both celibacy and community of goods. They also practiced many primitive rites with biblical precedent: footwashing, the holy kiss after Communion, and the love feast. But their most distinctive practice was derived not from the Bible but from the work of the pietistic historian Gottfried Arnold, whose account of early Christian customs led the Brethren to insist on trine (i.e. thrice repeated) immersion, face forward, in a flowing stream.

The community at Schwarzenau grew with some rapidity during these years, as did another at Marienborn in the Palatinate, but later increasing intolerance caused the two communities to move, one to West Friesland, the other to Crefeld. In 1719 Peter Becker led the first of these to Germantown, and Mack followed with the other group a decade later. With these migrations the European history of the sect came to an end.

Becker did not reassemble his congregation in America until 1722, but within a year from this time two more congregations were formed at Coventry and Conestoga. Several others were formed during the next decade, but growth was slow and sporadic. Meetings were usually held in the homes of members. Later the Brethren moved west with the other Germans, and consequently suffered not only the normal adversities of a small group on a thinly settled frontier, but from the proselyting efforts of other sectarian prophets as well. By the time of the Revolution the Brethren seem not to have numbered over a thousand members divided among twenty congregations in eastern Pennsylvania, New Jersey, and Maryland, and in 1825 their number had only doubled. By 1882 they counted some fifty-eight thousand members in congregations strung all the way to the Pacific coast, but by this time the character of the sect had changed considerably.

The most famous Dunker in American history is probably the elder Christopher Sauer (or Sower, 1693–1758). Born in Germany and educated at the University of Halle, Sauer came to America in 1724. After farming for a while in Lancaster County, he moved in 1731 to Germantown where he practiced medicine. He established a printing press and began in 1739 to publish the *Hoch-Deutsch pensylvanische Geschichts-Schreiber*. In 1743 he issued a large quarto edition of Luther's Bible complete with the Apocrypha, the first Bible in a Western language printed in America. (The type was brought from Frankfurt.) He also established a papermill, an ink factory, and a type foundry (the first in America); and helped to found a high school in Germantown. The Sunday school cards which he printed for the Dunkers appeared many years before Robert Raikes introduced Sunday school work into England.

Of all the pied pipers of Pennsylvania, none was more colorful and disruptive than Conrad Beissel (1691–1768), who had been converted in the Palatinate and had joined the Dunkers at Schwarzenau, Crefeld, and finally in Germantown, where he was baptized by Becker. An ascetic at heart, Beissel soon withdrew to the wilderness and gathered around him a congregation which, after various vicissitudes, became the Ephrata Community. In this "Order of the Solitary" a seventh-day Sabbath was observed, the sexes separated, and a communal semimonastic economy inaugurated. Beissel was a gifted leader with a flare for the dramatic, and his venture soon became a widely publicized success. For a time, after the conversion of the gifted Reformed minister and theologian John Peter Miller (1710–96), the Ephrata Brethren posed a serious threat to Pennsylvania's German Reformed population; from the first it had drawn heavily from the Brethren and other groups of strong pietistic persuasion. But after 1768, when Miller succeeded Beissel as superintendent, the community began to fall on evil days; and after Miller's death it was disbanded. At its height the community was in its way a cultural center for all the Pennsylvania Germans.

The Moravian Brethren

The most important of the pietistic sects in America was the Renewed Church of the United Brethren. The *Unitas Fratrum* was an evangelical branch of the old Hussite movement which had flourished in Moravia and Bohemia in the fifteenth century. Virtually stamped out by the Counter-Reformation, it had maintained a tenuous clandestine existence until the early eighteenth century. By the time Christian David gathered together a few of the "hidden seed" and led them to a promised refuge on the estate of Count Nicholaus Ludwig Zinzendorf (1700–60) in Saxony, the *Unitas Fratrum* had retained its succession of apostolic bishops but lost almost everything else.

Gradually the settlement at Herrnhut (as they called it) grew. In the meantime, the count became increasingly interested in the Moravians and gradually identified himself with them, though seeking at the same time to convert them to the unique form of Lutheran pietism which he had developed after being trained in his youth at Halle. Zinzendorf considered their semimonastic, semicommunal brotherhood as an *ecclesiola* within the *ecclesia Augustana* (Lutheran church) even after he was consecrated their "bishop" in 1737. He also broke away from the almost scholastic legalism of Francke's latter-day pietism, with its negative moralism and its highly ritualized conception of the order of salvation. Zinzendorf's emphasis on God's love for man as revealed in Christ was recognizably Lutheran, but his intense concentration on the passion of Christ tended to alienate him from the stricter sort of Lutherans, as did his insistence that his type of community could be affiliated to virtually any Christian church. Evangelism was a major Moravian concern from the first, as it was for nearly all pietists, and it was this that brought them to America—to minister to the American Indians—very soon after they had been reorganized in Saxony.

The first party of Moravians destined for America sailed for Georgia in 1735 under the leadership of Augustus Gottlieb Spangenberg (1704–92). Their plans were to occupy lands made available by that colony's philanthropic trustees, and to evangelize the Creek and Cherokee Indians. Their second voyage to the same place is even more memorable, since it was then that Spangenberg met a brilliant English High Churchman who was also bound for Georgia to minister to the colonists and to convert the Indians—John Wesley. The passages in Wesley's Journal which describe the character of the Moravians are justly famous. By a succession of Moravian contacts Wesley would be brought to his notable "conversion." Spangenberg's party, meanwhile, was led from Georgia to Philadelphia by George Whitefield, in whose employ they settled at Nazareth, where the great revivalist hoped to found a school for Negroes. The Moravians were to construct the buildings; but as their theology clashed with Whitefield's increasingly firm Calvinism, the friendship turned to enmity, and the Moravians moved on to the lovely site which Zinzendorf himself—newly arrived in the colonies—named Bethlehem on Christmas Eve 1741. Nazareth was also purchased from Whitefield two years later.

The count had been banished from Saxony. Impelled by reports of the religious destitution of the Pennsylvania Germans, he had arrived there with hopes of founding for the Germans one communion that would transcend or avoid the confessional divisions of the Continent. Seven meetings of representatives from the various Pennsylvania German groups were convened to this end, and during the 1740s a few ministers fitfully remained committed to his Congregation of God in the Spirit. For a time Zinzendorf served the Lutheran church in Philadelphia; later, when dissensions arose, he founded the First Moravian Church there. He also helped organize the

Moravian congregations at Nazareth, Bethlehem, and a half-dozen other places. He made long trips into the Indian country, laid plans for extensive missions, and then went off for a long stay in London to organize the English province of his "church." In 1749 the English parliament formally granted the *Unitas Fratrum* special rights as an ancient Protestant Episcopal church.

By 1748 the impossibility of Zinzendorf's ecumenical idea was apparent, and the American Moravians began to steer a self-consciously independent course. There were then congregations in thirty-one localities; and about fifty Indian missionaries and itinerant preachers, with circuits ranging from Maine to the Carolinas, were being supported. At the heart of this whole American enterprise were the thriving semicommunistic settlements at Nazareth and Bethlehem, where over thirty industries and several farms were in operation. Between 1753 and 1763 a similar colony was begun at Salem, North Carolina, with southern responsibilities. These communities were by no means simply self-centered utopias. All of their surplus was contributed to the support of Moravian work in Europe and to their large missionary program among the American Indians. After the French and Indian Wars, however, the communal aspect of the Moravian settlements was gradually abandoned.

The Moravians never succeeded in entering American life as an influential church movement, despite the unique way in which they blended churchly and sectarian traditions. They were hindered at the outset by Zinzendorf's grandiose ecumenical projects, and then for a century they were cramped by the supervision of authorities in Germany. The border wars in the West from the 1750s through the War of 1812, and still later, President Jackson's removal of the Cherokees, brought tragedy and disruption to their Indian missions. They remained a relatively static movement, numbering about 3,000 in 1775, 8,275 in 1858, about 20,000 in 1895, and over 60,000 in 1965, scattered widely across the country, but still concentrated in Pennsylvania. Their largest influence in America probably came through the Wesleys, but more intrinsic to the *Unitas Fratrum* has been its characteristic form of pietism, its devotional literature, and a tradition of hymnody and church music that would make its mark on many churches in Europe and America.

The Schwenckfelders

Closely associated with the Moravians but by no means similar were the Schwenckfelders. Like the Moravians they claimed an old but attenuated tradition that linked them to Reformation times. Furthermore, the generosity of Zinzendorf provided an occasion for a reconstitution of both groups. But beyond this, the similarities cease. Where the *Unitas Fratrum* was hierarchical, highly organized, and rigorously doctrinal despite constant disclaimers, the Schwenckfelders continued to manifest their founder's quiet concern for inner spirituality.

Kaspar Schwenckfeld von Ossig (1489–1561), traditionally grouped among the "spiritual reformers," taught an inward, somewhat mystical faith. Unlike the "magisterial reformers" he emphasized the spirit rather than the letter, and spoke of a living word beneath and beyond the Scriptures. Unlike the Anabaptists, with whom he is sometimes linked, he was concerned not to restore the apostolic church, but to build the invisible church. Men of this type simply do not become organizers of tightly knit churchly institutions, or founders of sectarian communities. "The devotees of such a church," says Professor Bainton, "are bound to be rejected of men, and their only recourse is to make a cloister of their own hearts." [3] So it was with Schwenckfeld and his followers.

By the eighteenth century Schwenckfelders survived as scattered and unorganized spiritual communities in only a few areas of Germany. In the face of Roman Catholic pressure they drifted to Saxony and other Protestant states, and for eight years some of them gathered on Count Zinzendorf's estates. In 1734 this group was to take up a land grant in Georgia, but at Zinzendorf's behest they went to Pennsylvania instead. Here they were joined by other small groups who came via Denmark and the Netherlands; and in Bucks, Montgomery, and Berks counties they maintained an unostentatious but continuous existence. They did not consider themselves a church or denomination, nor did they attempt to erect any church buildings until the time of the American Revolution. At first they had recognized religious leaders—George Weiss to 1741, Balzer Hoffman to 1749—but the response was slight and almost no evangelism was carried on. In terms of impact or influence on American religious life the Schwenckfelders were not important. In 1895 they reported a total of six church edifices, all in Pennsylvania, with 306 communicants; in 1950, five churches with 2,400 members. They stand as representatives of a quiet phase of the Reformation, filling out the wide spectrum of early Pennsylvania's highly diversified church life.

3. Roland H. Bainton, *The Reformation of the Sixteenth Century*, p. 129.

16

THE GERMAN REFORMED AND LUTHERAN CHURCHES

The political history of the German-speaking regions of Europe in the centuries following the Reformation is an incredibly complex tangle, involving over two hundred independent or semi-autonomous states, episcopal principalities, and free cities, most of which bore some relationship to the Holy Roman emperor. Ecclesiastical division compounded these complications, not only because confessional loyalties deepened interstate hostilities, but also because doctrinal issues were fiercely debated. Lutheranism probably reached its greatest territorial advance by 1566. Some conquests came still later, but at that point the Roman Catholic powers began to make important recoveries. After 1560, moreover, Germany experienced a powerful surge of Reformed strength, with the Elector Frederick III of the Palatinate becoming the great standard bearer of this cause. Convinced that Reformed theology offered a more decisive alternative to Catholicism, he put his powerful duchy where it would remain for a century: squarely athwart the Roman Counter-Reformation. In 1562 he made the Heidelberg Catechism the confessional basis of his realm, and in due course other Rhineland provinces (Anhalt, Hesse, Nassau) followed the Palatine example. Bremen and the Hohenzollerns of Brandenburg responded to the same influences. A powerful "third force" emerged in Germany.

THE GERMAN REFORMED CHURCH

The distinct German Reformed tradition which came into existence both as a theology and as a political force naturally owed much to the Reformation in German Switzerland, above all to Zwingli and Bullinger of Zurich.

Yet in the family of Reformed communions it has a character of its own, expressed most compellingly by the pious, irenic, and experiential tone which Kaspar Olevianus and Zacharias Ursinus gave to the Heidelberg Catechism. In this confession one may also perceive the mediating influences of Luther's great associate, Philip Melanchthon. In German Reformed churches, moreover, the Lutheran liturgical tradition was never completely replaced by the thoroughgoing reforms of Zwingli, nor did the doctrinaire spirit, rigorous discipline, and dogmatic concern for ecclesiastical polity of "ultra-Calvinism" condition its church life as they did the Reformed churches of Holland, Switzerland, or France. Perhaps due to its proximity to Lutheran churches and universities, perhaps too because of the pre-Reformation German tradition, it also nourished an extremely fertile tradition of devotional writing and theological inquiry, a tradition, incidentally, that was of immense importance to Puritan divines in England and which, in turn, would be much indebted to reciprocal Puritan influences during the formative period of German pietism.

Between 1618 and the Peace of Westphalia (1648), when the Thirty Years War raged in Germany, these states—and especially the Palatinate—were terribly ravaged. Later in the seventeenth century dynastic conflict continued, leading among other things to French invasions of the Rhineland under Louis XIV, whose victories resulted in the temporary establishment of Roman Catholicism in the Palatinate, and the overturning of Protestant rule in Strasbourg. During the eighteenth century the competition of the great European powers led to four more devastating wars, which had as their counterparts the French and Indian Wars fought by American colonists. In this unsettled state of affairs serious economic dislocations and continual outbreaks of religious persecution led great numbers of harassed peoples of every religious affiliation to seek haven in America. Anabaptist and other sectarian groups had come earlier—they had been persecuted by everybody—but now they were joined by others: Reformed, Lutheran, and in much smaller numbers, Roman Catholics.

THE GERMAN REFORMED CHURCH IN AMERICA

The planting of the German Reformed church in Pennsylvania was one result of these upheavals. By 1730 it was estimated that the German Reformed church had fifteen thousand potential adherents in Pennsylvania. The bulk of the immigration came from the provinces of the Rhineland; indeed, so many Palatines came to America that the word became almost a synonym for "German." Many came as "redemptioners," indentured as servants for a stipulated length of time in repayment for their passage. Because very few of them moved as organized religious groups, they lacked a ministry. Like many others who came to America out of state churches in Europe, moreover, they were habituated to having ecclesiastical matters ordered by the authorities, and were ill prepared to take them into their own hands.

The primitive state of the country and the dispersion of the people were also obstacles to organized church life and the support of a regular ministry. These conditions at the same time provided a fine opportunity for various religious freebooters to impose themselves on the ill-informed and isolated settlements. Especially disruptive of the Reformed church were the various sectarian groups which abounded in Pennsylvania, notably Conrad Beissel's semimonastic community at Ephrata. When John Peter Miller, the highly gifted young minister at Tulpehocken, joined that colony in the 1730s, he took a good number of his parishioners with him into ascetic retirement. On the other hand, they could not be absorbed by Dutch Reformed congregations, as had happened in New Amsterdam, because most of these Germans were scattered far away from the Dutch in an unchurched wilderness. A "founder" of a German Reformed congregation, therefore, would be faced with a difficult task. At the outset, nevertheless, churches were formed, sometimes by devout laymen and at other times by ministers. The earliest congregation was gathered at Germantown in 1719, though it had no minister. John Frederick Hager and John Jacob Oehl ministered in succession among Palatines in the Hudson-Mohawk region. Henry Hoeger gathered a church at New Berne, North Carolina, Samuel Guldin in Berks County, and the Dutch minister, Paulus van Vlecq, at Neshaminy in Montgomery County, Pennsylvania.

John Philip Boehm (d. 1749) undertook his important work on foundations laid by van Vlecq. Coming to America as a schoolteacher and lacking ordination, he yielded to the insistent demands of the people he had been serving informally and accepted the pastoral office over three related congregations formed at Falckner's Swamp, Skippack, and White Marsh. Two years later his status was challenged by George Michael Weiss (ca. 1700–ca. 1770), the founder of the Reformed Church in Philadelphia (1727), who had been ordained in Heidelberg and sent out by the Church of the Palatinate. On the advice of the Amsterdam classis, Boehm was ordained by the Dutch ministers in New York in 1729, and thus reconciled to Weiss. These two continued to serve the Philadelphia area, while others carried the work beyond the Schuylkill out to Lancaster County and beyond. One important result of the Boehm-Weiss controversy, and of the latter's subsequent visit to Europe, was the Amsterdam classis's assumption of responsibility for the increasing number of Germans in Pennsylvania. In sending Michael Schlatter to work among the Germans of America, the Synods of North and South Holland performed one of the most important acts in the colonial history of the German Reformed church. But the decisive importance of this event can be comprehended only against a background of the more specific troubles that beset the church after the early years.

The arrival of Zinzendorf in America in November 1741 created a crisis for the Reformed church even as it would for the Lutherans. The count's ruling passion, as we have seen, was to form a "Congregation of God in the Spirit," among the hundred thousand Germans then resident in Pennsylvania. Each of the German churches, while retaining its individuality, would be lifted up to a higher unity in the new "Congregation." To a distracted and scattered church, it was a tempting prospect; and during the 1740s Reformed leaders participated in the count's "Pennsylvania synods," with John Bechtel, Reformed pastor in Germantown, and the layman Henry Antes playing prominent roles. Had the scheme succeeded, it is highly doubtful that the scattered Reformed peoples could have withstood the distinctive doctrinal tendencies of so strong-willed a man as Zinzendorf, or so tightly knit an organization as that of the *Unitas Fratrum.* But the plan collapsed after the seventh conference, by which time only the Moravians, Lutherans, and Reformed were participating.

It was into a church situation fraught with these actual and potential difficulties that Michael Schlatter (1716–90) came in August 1746. Born and educated in Saint Gall, Switzerland, he had worked as a teacher in the Netherlands, where he was ordained. After serving briefly in Switzerland, he offered himself to the Dutch synods as a missionary to the destitute German Reformed churches in Pennsylvania. Within three weeks of his arrival he had demonstrated not only his amazing energy, but his gifts as a conciliator as well, restoring harmony in a number of distracted congregations and inspiring renewed zeal in some of the more lethargic ones. He was installed as pastor of the united churches of Germantown and Philadelphia on 1 January 1747, and in this position he soon won enthusiastic commitments from the other ministers to cooperate in forming a coetus (or synod) the next year.

On 29 September 1747 four ministers and twenty-seven elders representing twelve churches convened in Philadelphia, the first organizational gathering of the German Reformed church in America. They adopted the Heidelberg Catechism and the Canons of Dort, and determined to meet annually for general oversight of the work. The coetus was somewhat handicapped in that it was not an autonomous judicatory in a fully presbyterian sense; the Dutch synods acting through the classis of Amsterdam retained a veto power over all its acts and did not grant it the authority to ordain ministers. Its organization was nevertheless a historic milestone.

Schlatter proved a tireless overseer of Reformed churches from northern New Jersey to the Great Valley of Virginia. In four years he traveled eight thousand miles and preached 635 times. In 1751 he estimated that in Pennsylvania there were thirty thousand German Reformed people gathered into fifty-three churches, yet among these churches there were only four settled ministers. So Schlatter embarked on a trip to Europe to solidify ecclesiastical arrangements in Holland, to plead for money, and to recruit ministers. He was highly successful, returning in 1752 with considerable missionary funds, the guarantee of a stipendium from Amsterdam in return for its supervisory rights, and six able young ministers. This closed the period of his greatest work.

Schlatter's subsequent usefulness was severely curtailed by his unfortunate involvement in the work of the [English] Society for the Promotion of the Knowledge of God among the Germans. He had prepared an appeal in Dutch and German to aid him in presenting the cause of the Germans in Europe; this was translated into English by the Reverend David Thomson of Philadelphia who then worked for the formation of the society. Schlatter, because of his passionate interest in education, allowed himself to be made superintendent of the society's "charity schools" in 1755. But the society's propaganda drew such an insulting caricature of Pennsylvania Germans and was so widely (and perhaps justly) suspected of having Anglicanization as its ultimate end, that the whole program became exceedingly unpopular. Schlatter resigned in disillusionment after two years, spent two ensuing years as a military chaplain, and in 1759 retired to private life.

Another critical aspect of the Reformed situation was the growing strength of an extreme pietist wing, the "new lights," who were encouraged by similar developments among the increasing numbers of Presbyterians in the area and by the ferment of the Great Awakening. For many so disposed, the attractiveness of Zinzendorf's proposals was heightened, as was that of various sectarian appeals. The rise of radical pietism also fostered a tendency to simplify the content of the traditional Christian teaching, to minimize Reformed doctrine, to disparage a regularly constituted ministry, to discourage concern with church order, and to make the conversion experience the essence of Christianity. Ironically, the leader of this movement, Philip William Otterbein (1726–1813), came to America in 1752 as one of Schlatter's most promising new ministerial recruits. He had been educated and ordained in Nassau under strong pietistic influence, and in his ministry there he had already become known for his strenuous views of Christian life and experience. After serving several parishes in Pennsylvania and Maryland with considerable distinction, he was called in 1774 to the Second Reformed Church in Baltimore. This was formed by a group which had seceded from the First Church out of loyalty to an enthusiastic lay revivalist. After long deliberation, Otterbein accepted. In Baltimore his strong pietistic tendencies, his convictions about the value of *ecclesiolae* in the church, and his growing doubts regarding Reformed dogmatics led him into close connection with the Methodist societies; and in 1784 he participated in the ordination of Francis Asbury as bishop of the Methodist Church in America. After two more decades he would finally become the founder of a "New Reformed Church," the United Brethren in Christ. This event belongs to a later phase of American church history, but it demonstrates the force and significance of the more extreme sort of pietism which was at work in the eighteenth century.

The tensions revealed by Otterbein's career were to be continuous problems for the German Reformed church throughout the eighteenth and nineteenth centuries, but they did not prevent the coetus from carrying on its work even after Schlatter's retirement. After 1772 this body began to ordain its own ministers, and in 1791, a year after Schlatter's death, it declared itself, though in a friendly way, to be independent from the Dutch synods. Two years later at a meeting in Lancaster attended by thirteen ministers, the first fully self-sufficient synod of the German Reformed Church in America was formed. The church at that time consisted of about thirteen thousand communicants, perhaps as many as forty thousand adherents, gathered in 178 congregations scattered between New York City and northern New Jersey, through Pennsylvania and Maryland, and on into the valley of Virginia, with a few congregations (but only one pastor) beyond the Alleghenies. The shortage of pastors and the lack of a seminary were the church's most critical handicaps. With little help now coming from either Holland or Germany, many members and whole congregations were lost to other churches, especially to the Lutherans, Presbyterians, and later still, to several more pietistic churches. In the nineteenth century, however, these institutional deficiencies would be amended.

THE LUTHERAN CHURCH IN AMERICA

In 1703 the Swedish Lutheran Provost Andrew Rudman, with two Swedish associates, proceeded by authority of the Archbishop of Uppsala to ordain a German graduate of Halle, Justus Falckner, and to commission him for service in the Dutch Lutheran church of New York. The incident illustrates the interweaving of the three main strands of Lutheran life in the early colonial period. A fourth strand might be termed "English," that stemming from the six Lutheran churches of London and the Lutheran chaplains at the Hanoverian court. The first three require separate discussion.

The Lutherans of New Sweden

Sweden's colonial adventure on the Delaware, conceived under King Gustavus Adolphus, led to the founding of Fort Christina in 1638; it was brought to an abrupt and inglorious end by the soldiers of Peter Stuyvesant in 1655. The Swedish colony holds little interest for the colonial historian except that it provides a starting point for one of the thirteen colonies and marks the introduction of that venerated American institution, the log cabin. But New Sweden commands the closer attention of the church historian because of its relation to the Anglicanism of the area, because of Swedish support for the German churches, and because immigration would restore Swedish Lutheranism to the American scene long after New Sweden was a memory.

In its early days New Sweden was served by a continuous line of ministers, some good, some bad, and at least one of them extraordinary. This was the Reverend John Campanius, the saintly apostle to the Indians, whose translation of Luther's Catechism into the Delaware Indian tongue antedates John Eliot's Indian Bible by several years. In 1690, however, when Andrew Printz, nephew of a former governor of that name, visited the thousand or so Swedish and Finnish people on the Delaware, he found them without ministers. When this news reached King Charles XI, he aroused the interest of the energetic Jesper Svedberg (later bishop of Skara, 1702–35), whose efforts resulted in the dispatch of a large supply of books including a printing of the Campanius catechism, and three new and capable young pastors, who arrived in 1697. One became pastor of Holy Trinity at Tranhook (the "Old Swedes' Church" at Wilmington, where a new building was consecrated in 1699), another of Gloria Dei at Wicaco (the "Old Swedes' Church" of Philadelphia, where a new building was consecrated in 1700), and the third was to make a survey for the king. For seventy-five years these and several other churches were supplied with learned and devoted ministers from Sweden. One of them was always designated as a "provost," with powers similar to those of a suffragan bishop. The doctrine and beautiful liturgy of the Church of Sweden was maintained; matins and High

Mass were celebrated on Sundays, and some of the ministers conducted both matins and vespers daily.

Concern for America lagged for a time due to Bishop Svedberg's declining vigor, but it was revived by Archbishop Jacob Benzelius. Provost John Sandin of the Swedish church helped to organize the Ministerium of Pennsylvania (1748) and two succeeding provosts, Israel Acrelius (1749–56) and Karl Magnus von Wrangel (1759–68), not only revitalized the parish life of the three thousand Swedish church members, but helped to further the work among the Germans. Acrelius is also remembered for his valuable history of these churches. Under Wrangel the Swedish ministers for a time virtually became a part of the Germans' Pennsylvania Ministerium.

The difficulties of maintaining Swedish tradition and culture in the midst of these complex circumstances became almost insuperable with the passing years. Because Swedish immigration, unlike the German, did not continue, the language problem became increasingly troublesome, and brought about an inevitable rapprochement between the Swedish and Anglican churches. For the same reasons, the forms, liturgy, vestments, theology, and constitution of the Church of Sweden were not projected into American Lutheranism at this time. Its chief contribution was a measure of stability and continuity during the critical years when support from Germany was very weak.

The Dutch Lutherans

The two oldest continuously existing Lutheran parishes in the United States (Saint Matthew's in New York City and First Lutheran in Albany) trace their origins to the small group of Lutheran laymen in New Netherland who organized a congregation in 1649 in order to call upon the Lutheran consistory in Amsterdam for a pastor. Even in the mother country, however, any church but the Reformed was allowed only by "connivance," so that a man could not be ordained for American service until 1657. When Pastor Johannes Gutwasser arrived, Governor Stuyvesant promptly had him arrested and shipped back to Holland. The struggling group of laymen had to await the more tolerant rule of the English. Even so, it was 1669 before the Amsterdam consistory had found a man who would or could accept a call to New York. The man who then came, Jacob Fabritius, was a quarrelsome eccentric who lasted only two years—though later he redeemed himself as pastor of the Swedish church at Wicaco. His successor, Bernardus Arensius, served until 1691—the year of Leisler's execution for rebellion, hence very troublous years for the colony—after which the New York–Albany congregation was pastorless for twelve years.

Justus Falckner (1672–1723) began his two decades of tireless activity in 1703. He had no more than begun when thousands of Palatines began to arrive in New York with only Joshua Kocherthal to minister to their spiritual needs. When Pastor Kochertal died in 1719, Falckner was left with the care of fourteen congregations strung from Albany to New Jersey. This proved more than one man could handle, and it remained for William Christopher Berkenmeyer (1686–1751) to bring some regularity into the churches of this sprawling area. Arriving in 1725, Berkenmeyer divided the vast "parish," and before he died, he was able to see five pastors serving the twenty-three congregations in his area. He also established rules for assuring an orthodox and duly commissioned ministry. In 1735, in order to settle a parish controversy in New Jersey, he convoked what some have considered the first Lutheran "synod" in America. True synod it was not, but Berkenmeyer did lay the foundations upon which the New York Ministerium would rest when it was founded just after the Revolution.

By 1750 it was clear that a new order of things was on the horizon in New York: the immediate future would see a German Lutheranism in the vast area over which Berkenmeyer presided. Even in Albany, where the Dutch had yielded to the English, the German language was being demanded, while in New York City Germans now outnumbered the Dutch and were causing a good deal of contention. The bulk of this new migration would go to Pennsylvania, and its ministry would come from the pietist center at Halle rather than from Amsterdam and Hamburg. Berkenmeyer viewed this invasion by pietistic *Schwärmer* as tragic, and his bias had a longlasting influence on the New York churches—doubtless prolonged by his son-in-law, Peter Sommer, who took over his work in the upper Hudson area and served until his death in 1795. But by the time of the Revolution, Halle men were numerous in New York too.

The Dutch Lutherans at least had the satisfaction of knowing that in matters of church order, the experience of the Netherlands would stand American Lutherans in good stead as they began the enormous task of organizing the Lutheran church in the wilderness, without benefit of sympathetic kings and state-church traditions, and in an ethos which was predominantly Puritan insofar as it was religious at all. The combined pressures of American democracy, the inescapable importance of the laity in so scattered a church, and the preponderance of various Reformed churches would cause basically presbyterian forms of government to be utilized by the Dutch Lutherans as the safest constitutional model. Formally adopted in New York in 1786, this constitutional pattern would also be followed in 1792 by the Ministerium of Pennsylvania.

The German Lutherans

The great exodus from the Palatinate and the other Rhenish provinces began in earnest during the first decade of the eighteenth century. Pastor Kocherthal of Landau (Palatinate) had led one party to Newberg (now Newburgh), New York, in 1708; and in 1710 he brought a larger group, numbering some three thousand. Queen Anne's promise of land near the Schoharie River was betrayed by the governor's desire for a colony that would produce tar and other products for the British navy, however, and a large proportion of the émigrés drifted away to other parts. Gradually, the New York–New Jersey region witnessed the emergence of a major German community with several congregations of Lutherans.

After 1712 the main tide of Lutheran immigration flowed into the immense haven created by William Penn. The Lutherans arrived in general somewhat later than the other German Protestant groups, their chief influx coming during the decade or so after 1735, and by this time they, like their predecessors, also pressed southward and westward from Pennsylvania. During the first three decades after the colony's founding only very few congregations had been formed, though a few Lutherans seem to have been among even the earliest German immigrants. Gloria Dei, the Swedish church at Wicaco, was for a long time the only well-established church in the area; it included the congregation at Germantown until that church achieved independent status. At New Hanover a congregation could trace its origins back to 1703. There were also services held in Philadelphia very early; but before 1730 the congregation was loosely organized and without a regular pastor. Three or four ministers and a number of unordained men of varying personal dedication served the southeastern counties. The situation here became desperate as more people, almost always without pastors and usually without schoolteachers, continued to arrive.

A turning point came in 1733. Pastor John Christian Schultze led a lay delegation from Philadelphia, New Providence, and New Hanover to Dr. Frederick Michael Ziegenhagen, the court chaplain in London, who, with others, finally aroused the authorities at Halle to the missionary needs of America. In an open letter the chaplain quoted the report of one of the laymen: "We live in a country that is full of heresy and sects. As far as our religious interests are concerned, we are in a state of greatest destitution; and our means are utterly insufficient to effect the necessary relief, unless God in his mercy may send us help and means from abroad." [1] What finally

1. Quoted in Henry E. Jacobs, *A History of the Evangelical Lutheran Church in the United States,* ACHS, vol. 4 (New York, 1893), p. 192.

seems to have bestirred the men at Halle was not cries such as these, nor the offer of a definite salary for ministers (which they had been demanding), but the arrival in Pennsylvania of Count Zinzendorf and his representation of himself as a Lutheran pastor.

Henry Melchior Muhlenberg (1711–87), whose destiny it was to be the chosen instrument of Halle's response to these needs, proved to possess gifts as far beyond imagining as was the difficulty of the tasks that lay ahead. He was born in Eimbeck (Hanover) and educated nearby at the new university in Göttingen. Guided chiefly by a theology professor there, he became firmly committed to a pietistic understanding of the faith. After helping to found an orphanage, he taught at the famous orphan house at Halle; at the same time he continued to develop his lifelong interest in music and languages. In 1739 he was ordained in Leipzig (Saxony) and began his ministry in a parish of Upper Lusatia, a few miles from Zinzendorf's estate. Only two years later, while visiting Halle, he was convinced by Johann Gotthilf Francke that he ought to accept the call to America, and after a two-month visit in London, he embarked for Charleston, South Carolina. On 23 September 1742 he went ashore, remarking in the first American entry of his journal on the tragic fact of Negro slavery: "This is a horrible state of affairs, and it will entail a severe judgment." He proceeded almost immediately to visit the Salzburger Lutherans at Ebenezer near Savannah, then began the journey north to his life's work.

Ecclesia plantanda (Let the Church be planted) was Muhlenberg's motto. He came with the highest credentials: as a deputy of the younger Francke at Halle, with the approval of the consistorium of Hanover (whose ruler was King George II of England), and bearing letters from the royal chaplain in London. Almost from the first it was evident that his "errand into the wilderness" was not merely to answer the call of three destitute congregations, but to work toward the ideal of a united, independent, self-sustaining church. During a career contemporaneous with a half-century of America's most tumultuous history, Muhlenberg became a denominational "founder" in a fuller sense than anyone except Francis Asbury, the Methodist, and Bishop John Carroll, the Roman Catholic, who began their American careers about the time that he ended his. Jacobs remarks that "the history of the [Lutheran church in America] from his landing in 1742 to his death . . . is scarcely more than his biography." [2]

Muhlenberg arrived in Philadelphia on 25 November 1742. Unheralded, unreceived, and alone, he rode through the mud to New Hanover—to discover that all three of the congregations whose call he was answering were

2. Ibid., p. 305.

now shepherded by others, the most formidable of whom was Zinzendorf, installed in Philadelphia. Within a month he was master of the situation, and was legally preaching in the carpenter shop in Philadelphia, the barn at New Providence (Trappe), and the half-built log chapel at New Hanover. Over the years his tact, patient firmness, and spiritual power had an ever deepening impact. Both in Pennsylvania and in Europe long pent-up potentialities were released, conflicts were healed, pastors and catechists were brought to America, congregations were rallied, and church buildings were erected or enlarged at Tulpehocken (1743), Providence (1745), Germantown (1746), New Hanover (1747), and Philadelphia (1748). The three huge volumes of his translated journal are one of the finest records extant of the frontier missionary, pacificator, preacher, teacher, pastor, and priest. The saga of his indefatigable ministry is capsuled in many an entry:

> June 10 [1747]. I set out from New Hanover with the schoolmaster, Jacob Loeser. Eight miles from New Hanover we stopped in at the home of an old man, one of the sect called Newborn, who had married Kasebier's widow some twenty years ago, and begotten with her five children, whom I had instructed and baptized at the mother's request without the father's consent. . . . In the afternoon we traveled four or five miles farther to the home of an aged God-fearing widow, who with her family and neighbors was anxiously awaiting us, desiring edification. The old widow had prepared herself with penitential prayer and exhibited a hunger and thirst for the Lord's Supper, which I administered to her after prayer and singing. . . . From there we rode nine miles farther and took lodgings with an old man of our congregation, who refreshed and edified himself with us in prayer and good conversation. . . .
>
> June 11. We rode nine miles farther to a place where the Lutherans and the Reformed had built a church together and where they were in controversy with one another. The members of both faiths are so intermarried in this country [and] occasionally the two parties have made trial of building a common church. . . . Our people elect as pastors the schoolmasters who have come of their own accord. . . . In general, such preachers are not only ignorant, but unconverted besides.
>
> June 13. Rode six miles farther up to the church [Stouchsberg, Berks Co.] and conducted preparatory and confessional service with the members of the congregation who desire to receive the Lord's Supper the next day.

June 14. Trinity Sunday. Preached on the Gospel to a numerous assembly, baptized several children, and administered the Lord's Supper to over two hundred communicants. . . . In the afternoon I rode nine miles in another direction to another congregation [Northkill, Lebanon Co.] and preached there to an attentive audience; also baptized several children, announced that Holy Communion would be celebrated there three weeks hence, and exhorted them to pray God for repentant hearts and hunger for grace and to devote the intervening time to true self-examination.

June 15–18. Instructed a number of young people who wanted to be confirmed and also visited various ones in the congregation with whom I spoke a word of edification.

June 19. We journeyed from Tulpehocken to the new city of Lancaster which is thirty miles away by road and arrived towards evening.

June 20. Visited several deacons and elders of the congregation and inquired concerning their spiritual and congregational condition.

June 21. First Sunday after Trinity. I preached in the congregation, catechized the young people, baptized children, and had the congregation elect a new deacon, one of the others having died. . . . In the afternoon had to ride twenty-two miles farther because I had promised to preach in Maryland on June 24. . . . [The trip was extremely difficult because of rainstorms and swollen rivers.]

June 24. The heavy rain continued. We went to the church where most of our people and also a few of those who were Zinzendorf-minded were present. Before we began divine services, I had them give me the church book and I wrote in it in English several brief articles to the effect that the subjects of His Majesty, George, in this country enjoy the free exercise of religion; that the Lutherans adhere to the Holy Word of the prophets and apostles, to the Unaltered Augsburg Confession and the rest of the symbolical books and have the Sacraments administered to them in a regular manner by regularly called and ordained preachers in accord with the Word and the Confessions; that they will not suffer open, gross, willful sinners against the holy Ten Commandments of God and the laws of the government to be considered among them as true members, and so on, etc., etc. I read this publicly to the congregation and explained it to them in the German language, and said that whoever desired to be such a Lutheran and member of the church and congregation, and to conduct himself in accord with these articles, should subscribe his name. The Lutherans who were present willingly signed their names, but when it came to the two or three Zinzendorfers, they refused to sign it and brought in their complaint. . . .

June 25. We rode several miles farther to a newly founded town [Frederick, Maryland] where lived a number of Lutherans who belonged to the congregation, but were unable to be present on the previous day on account of the heavy rain. Most of them signed their names to the articles in the church book and they also elected several from their midst as deacons and elders. . . .

June 26. We set out on the return journey. . . .[3]

The climax of Muhlenberg's early labors came in August 1748, when the need to ordain a minister and to consecrate Saint Michael's Church in Philadelphia brought together six Swedish and German pastors and twenty-four lay delegates. This meeting marks the beginning of the Pennsylvania Ministerium, the most important single event in American Lutheran history. It not only attended to the immediate business at hand, but outlined a synodical organization and prepared a book of common worship which drew upon the church's liturgical tradition.

At the second meeting of the ministerium the delegates showed a further sign of independence by electing an "overseer" for the united congregations; this office was filled briefly by Pastor Peter Brunnholtz of Philadelphia, then transferred to Muhlenberg, who occupied it for many years. The ministerium met annually through 1754, but obstacles were so great that the pastors grew discouraged and no meetings were held for five years. In 1760 it was revived under a new constitution, never to lapse again. This reorganization was due largely to the efforts of the newly arrived provost of the Swedish churches, Karl Magnus von Wrangel, who became during his years of American service (1759–68) Muhlenberg's closest friend and co-worker. During these years the German and Swedish churches were drawn into close cooperation, though they were not formally merged.

Almost as significant as the synodical organization was the written constitution adopted for Saint Michael's in 1762. Muhlenberg, in response to urgent appeals from the Lutherans of New York, had spent the summers of 1751 and 1752 ministering to the Dutch Lutheran church in New York City. This congregation was almost one hundred years old, and represented the church order of Amsterdam. The experience acquainted Muhlenberg much more fully with the details of church organization, and when he prepared (with Wrangel's help) the constitution for the Philadelphia

3. *The Journals of Henry Melchior Muhlenberg*, ed. Theodore G. Tappert and John W. Doberstein, 3 vols. (Philadelphia: Muhlenberg Press, 1942–58), 1:149–59.

church, he incorporated many of the provisions he had observed in New York. In this way the Amsterdam order was not only transferred to Pennsylvania, but became an important pattern for the organization of Lutheran congregations in America.

With these great formative actions in which Muhlenberg and the Swedish provost played so important a role, the main lines of Lutheran development were laid down in the area which would witness its greatest colonial growth. It was done none too soon, for the rate of immigration was increasing sharply. Twelve thousand Germans landed at Philadelphia in 1749 alone, and by 1771 there were eighty-one congregations in Pennsylvania and adjacent states, plus some thirty more in other parts of America. Lutheran churches, along with the Presbyterian and German Reformed, were being founded in the valley of Virginia and in North Carolina. Although in the face of the vast work to be done the resources were pitiably inadequate, not only had a start been made, but a decisive turn had been taken. Lutheran leaders were thinking in terms of an American church with an American ministry and an American future, not in terms of a transitory mission abroad on the part of representatives of the European churches. The actualization of this ideal, and solutions for many of the difficulties along the way, began to emerge early in the next century.

III
THE CENTURY OF AWAKENING AND REVOLUTION

Under the execrable race of the Stuarts [James I and Charles I] the struggle between the people and the confederacy of temporal and spiritual tyranny became formidable, violent, and bloody. It was this great struggle that peopled America. It was not religion alone, as is commonly supposed; but it was a love of universal liberty, and a hatred, a dread, a horror, of the internal confederacy [of an ecclesiastical hierarchy and despotic rulers] that projected, conducted, and accomplished the settlement of America. After their arrival here, they began their settlement, and formed their plan, both of ecclesiastical and civil government, in direct opposition to the canon and feudal systems.

John Adams, *Dissertation on the Canon and the Feudal Law* (1765)

What do we mean by the American Revolution? Do we mean the American war? The Revolution was effected before the war commenced. The Revolution was in the minds and hearts of the people; a change in their religious sentiments of their duties and obligations. . . . The people of America had been educated in an habitual affection for England, as their mother country; and while they thought her a kind and tender parent (erroneously enough, however, for she never was such a mother), no affection could be more sincere. But when they found her a cruel beldam, willing like Lady Macbeth to "dash their brains out," it is no wonder if their filial affections ceased, and were changed into indignation and horror. This radical change in the principles, opinions, sentiments, and affections of the people was the real American Revolution.

John Adams, *Letter to Hezekiah Niles* (1818)

By 1700 the colonial commonwealths of North America were becoming a prosperous extension of British provincial society, in which the prevailing outlook on life and the world was unmistakably conditioned by a Reformed and Puritan ethos. Yet the modes of institutionalizing this system of nurture were very uneven. In most of New England a regulated ecclesiastical and educational system was duly established. As the decades rolled by, the "southern ethic" came to reflect many similar emphases, yet more decisively it bore the marks of the steady expansion of chattel slavery. The Middle Colonies were anticipating the American future by dealing with the actuality of ethnic and religious pluralism. Yet all of these colonies were pervaded by an ideology which, though increasingly secularized, was Puritan at the level of both personal and social ethics.

Fundamental to this entire process of church extension and cultural modification was a great international Protestant upheaval, manifested in pietism on the Continent, the Evangelical Revival in Great Britain, and the Great Awakening in America, where its intrinsic relation to Puritanism was most marked. In New England it was an apocalyptic outburst within the standing order, a challenge to established authority. Everywhere it extended the range of gospel preaching; in the South it brought personal religion to the slaves for the first time. Everywhere it brought rancor and division along with popular enthusiasm and new theological depth. Everywhere it rejuvenated the politically potent elements of the Puritan ideology. Most important for the future of American Protestantism, revivalism itself became an institution, and two denominations, Baptist and Methodist, were set on a course that was to make them the nation's largest. Vital for the political future of the colonies, the Awakening also made the people aware of their common spiritual heritage, and of their existence as an American nation.

After the revivals had waned (as such things must), the imperial situation was suddenly changed by the British conquest of New France in 1759. With this external danger removed, the long maturing "American Revolution" almost immediately took political form. A familiar course of events involving a famous cast of Patriot heroes from James Otis to Thomas Jefferson began to unfold. And this epoch of political and military turmoil did not end until Jefferson entered the White House four decades later.

Accompanying these religious and political events was a wide-sweeping intellectual revolution—the Enlightenment. The Age of Reason had begun to create theological problems for the Puritans even before 1700, leaving Jonathan Edwards no less than Benjamin Franklin to struggle with its religious implications. It also provided a philosophical basis for the work of the Founding Fathers. The long preoccupation of Americans with government and politics, not to mention with the war itself, raised immense problems for the churches, bringing on, among other things, a prolonged religious depression. Yet the first "new nation" never for a moment lost the Puritan's sense of America's special destiny, and as if to demonstrate that God had not despaired of his chosen nation, the very year of Jefferson's inauguration was marked by revivals of religion in both the East and the West. Part III charts the course of these events from the first signs of a "great and general revival" through the War for Independence to the settled operation of the new federal republic.

17

THE SHAPING OF COLONIAL PRESBYTERIANISM

Episcopalian, Presbyterian, Congregational—the very names of these great Protestant church communions indicate the intensity with which questions of church order rose to prominence in the age of the Reformation. In England, along with related questions of worship, they proved to be more divisive than elsewhere. In the Netherlands, certain parts of Germany, Switzerland, France, and Scotland, on the contrary, the prevailing mode of governing the Reformed churches had been from the first "presbyterian." Though terminology naturally varied, this meant in broad terms that a hierarchy of judicatories (or church courts) similar to those developed in Calvin's Geneva came to be regarded as the only true gospel order. Above the local or congregational "session" were ranged in ascending order the "presbytery," the "synod," and the "general assembly," each with certain fixed responsibilities and usually with definite geographical boundaries. At each of these levels both ordained and lay elders were represented, with the higher courts exercising functions and authority traditionally ascribed to bishops in an episcopal system. Such a system stressed universality, catholicity, and uniformity, while it discountenanced particularism and "independency."

In England the proponents of presbyterian order gradually declined after a show of considerable strength in the earlier part of Elizabeth's reign. Their place was taken on the left by various forms of Puritan congregationalism, and on the right by Calvinistic episcopalianism. But during the Civil War and the early Commonwealth, when Presbyterians again rose to power in England, Scotland played a powerful role, and America became involved in the consequences. A brief consideration of the Scottish development is therefore an essential part of United States religious history.

Scotland in 1500 had been a weak, poor, and strife-torn cultural backwater, its politics polarized by French and English factions. Patrick Hamilton was burned for his Lutheran preaching in 1528 and George Wishart met a similar fate in 1546, with several martyrdoms in between serving to indicate the suffering and ineffectual state of Protestantism during that period. One follower of Wishart named John Knox (1505–72) was captured and sent to the galleys by the French. Later released, he became a royal chaplain in England under Edward VI. With the accession of Queen Mary (Tudor) he fled to Frankfurt, then to Geneva where he worked on the Geneva Bible, preached to other English exiles, and became a devoted disciple of Calvin. In 1558, the year Elizabeth became queen of England, Mary Queen of Scots (a Roman Catholic who also claimed the English throne) married Francis II of France. These events made the situation ripe for a nationalistic revolt, and Knox returned in the following year to ensure that his native land should also become firmly Protestant. By 1560, with strong English support, both ends were accomplished: papal power was abrogated, the Scottish Parliament adopted Knox's Calvinistic confession of faith, and the first General Assembly of the new Scottish Kirk was convened. Its *Book of Discipline* and Knox's *Book of Common Order* set up a presbyterian system of church government and worship for the entire kingdom.

What uncertainties remained in the situation were largely removed when Mary of Scotland was forced to abdicate in 1567. Her execution in 1587 at Queen Elizabeth's order removed still another threat to Roman Catholic recovery in both kingdoms. When Mary's son, James VI of Scotland, became King James I of England in 1603, the importance of Scotland's church for America was immeasurably increased. Its integrated and firmly established system of doctrine and order became extremely influential in the English Reformation during the decade after 1640, especially at the Westminster Assembly, whose formularies of doctrine, worship, and polity were enforced in both kingdoms—temporarily in England, to the present day in Scotland. After the Restoration (1660) Presbyterianism lost its vitality in England, but through force of example and by immigration, the Scottish church in later years became a very powerful influence in America.

During the seventeenth century immigrants of presbyterian inclination were so few and so scattered that only the Dutch churches could be said to have upheld this tradition in America—although they did so very incompletely, since they remained under the classis (presbytery) of Amsterdam until 1754. This situation began to change after the turn of the century, however. The Saybrook Platform (1708) revealed a persistent inclination of many New England Puritans, and frankly transformed the congregational independency of Connecticut into a connectional order that greatly increased its rapport with emergent presbyterian interest in the Middle Colonies. More significant was the influx of Scotch-Irish peoples, which began to reach sizable proportions after 1714, swelling to a tide later in the century. In this context a genuinely American form of presbyterianism began to take shape, but the process was not smooth, peaceful, or easy. Serious problems existed on every side and deep-seated theological and ecclesiastical issues had to be resolved.

ORGANIZING THE PRESBYTERIAN CHURCH

Men with presbyterian ideals and hopes had since the earliest years been scattered the whole length of the colonies from Londonderry, New Hampshire, to Charleston, South Carolina, in certain areas in considerable potential strength. Only after 1700 did the accentuated official pressures for Anglican establishments lead a few leaders among these groups to think of founding an inclusive organization. To this end a group of Presbyterian ministers met in Philadelphia in 1706 and organized the first American presbytery. The leader of this effort was Francis Makemie (1658–1708), a tireless Scotch-Irishman who was educated at Glasgow and ordained in Northern Ireland as a missionary to America in 1681. He had preached or organized churches in Barbados, Maryland, Virginia, New York (including Long Island), and New England. On good terms with the Mathers of Boston and the Congregationalists and Presbyterians of London, who in 1691 had united under the "Heads of Agreement," Makemie was ideally suited for bringing together various disparate elements at that first meeting. Associated with him on this occasion were one Scottish, two Scotch-Irish, and three New England ministers. Their congregations were even more diverse. The presbytery they organized was conceived more or less on the Scottish model, but it remained independent of any existing church. During its early years it drew most of its accessions from the scattered Puritan churches of Long Island, Delaware, and New Jersey, all of whom felt a need for interchurch connections similar to that which was to motivate the Saybrook Synod in Connecticut. They had no practical way of achieving this end save by joining the new presbytery. Common ties to the doctrinal formulations of Westminster facilitated their association. Thus a "New England" element gained an early preponderance in the nascent church.

But the increased immigration of Scotch-Irish, particularly to the Pennsylvania area, soon began to alter this ethnic balance, and by 1716 Presbyterian churches had become so numerous that there were three presbyteries—Philadelphia, New Castle, and Long Island—and a synod was formed. Seventeen ministers had been gained, bringing the total to twenty-five, eight of whom had come from New England, three from Wales, eight from Scotland, and seven from Ireland. The Presbyterian Church in America was now clearly in being, with a membership of at least three thousand distributed in forty or more churches; but its adversities were many. Only a few of its congregations were in compactly settled areas. Poverty and poor communications saddled them with difficulties on every hand. No American ministerial training was available outside of New England, and no adequate procedures for examining immigrant ministers or disciplining functioning ones were in force. There was increasing tension over the proper method of bringing some semblance of proper presbyterian order into this situation.

The questions which could not be postponed naturally affected both polity and doctrine. Specifically, how should disciplinary authority be vested in presbyteries and synods? What standards for approving ministers and ministerial candidates should be adopted? Above all, should subscription to the Westminster symbols be required, and if so, how? Around these interrelated issues definite factions or parties began to emerge, as they had already in the various British Presbyterian churches. The alignment in America tended to follow ethnic lines, with the Scots and Scotch-Irish, strongest in the New Castle Presbytery, demanding doctrinal subscription and stricter presbyterial discipline. At least as early as 1724 this presbytery required subscription to the Westminster Confession. In 1722 it deposed a minister because he bathed himself in a creek on the Sabbath. The New Yorkers and New Englanders, on the other hand, argued that the Bible alone was a sufficient rule of faith and practice.

In 1722 a compromise was reached which allowed some authority to presbyteries and synods; but the controversy continued. John Thomson, spokesman for the Scotch-Irish party, asserted that the American synod was utterly independent of every other judicatory on earth and hence responsible for its own purity and duty-bound to make the Westminster formularies its official confession and to require its ministers to subscribe. Jonathan Dickinson (1688–1747), Yale graduate, pastor at Elizabethtown, and leader of the antisubscriptionists, voiced the immemorial alternative: the purity of the church would be better safeguarded by a close examination of every candidate's religious experiences and strict disciplining of scandalous ministers. He pointed out the "glorious contradiction" of subscribing to Chapter 20 of the Westminster Confession, which calls God alone "Lord of the conscience," and then submitting to the rigid authority of the other chapters.

As the intensity of these disagreements increased, it became necessary to adopt some more explicit compromise; this was done at the Synod of 1729. Its fateful "Adopting Act" affirmed the idea of subscription, but with two important qualifications. First, refusing to make literal subscription to the Westminster standards a condition of ordination, it drew a distinction between essential and nonessential articles and allowed the examining judicatory to decide if a given candidate's scruples violated the intent of the confession. Second, it made the synod an administrative and not a legislative body; and then merely recommended the Westminster Directory on church government as a guide. These qualifications left quite uncertain the limits of orthodoxy, as well as the respective authority of sessions, presbyteries, and synods in the calling, examination, ordination, and installation of ministers. In general, it marked a victory for the antisubscriptionist party of Jonathan Dickinson.

The peace resulting from the Adopting Act of 1729 was, to say the least, an uneasy one. The two factions with their characteristic nostrums for saving the church remained at heart unpacified. The stability of the denomination was soon imperiled from another quarter by the emergence of a new group among the Scotch-Irish led by William Tennent, Sr. (ca. 1673–1746), an Irish-born Scotsman, ordained in the Episcopal Church of Ireland. Emigrating to America in 1716, he married a Presbyterian minister's daughter and was accepted without reordination into the Presbyterian church in 1718. He served churches in Bedford, New York, and Neshaminy, Pennsylvania. He was an excellent teacher, and by 1733 had trained three of his sons (Gilbert, John, and William) and Samuel Blair for the ministry. Since the elder Tennent fostered a very "experimental" form of evangelical Puritanism, his students were potential allies of Jonathan Dickinson. Such an alliance became more imminent when Gilbert and John Tennent took congregations in New Brunswick and Freehold, New Jersey. At the former place Gilbert was profoundly influenced by the Dutch Reformed pastor four miles away in Raritan, Theodore Jacob Frelinghuysen (1691–1748). Frelinghuysen, who deserves to be known as an important herald, if not the father of the Great Awakening, had come from the Netherlands in 1720. He taught the necessity of personal conversion and subsequent holiness of life, and enforced strict standards for admission to the Lord's Supper. The revivals which he fostered at Raritan were forerunners of the Great Awakening in the Middle Colonies.

When Gilbert Tennent took up his ministry in New Brunswick he was both rebuked and inspired by Frelinghuysen's success as a preacher of experimental piety, a pastoral counselor, and above all a converter of souls. Tennent adopted no new or unusual doctrines except that staple insistence of the New England Puritans which was so dramatically exemplified in Frelinghuysen: that a definite experience of regeneration followed by assurance of salvation was the indispensable mark of a Christian. Rededicating himself to the task of preaching and counseling with individuals, he made the conversion of sinners the chief end of his ministry. By 1729, Tennent's scattered congregations between New Brunswick and Staten Island began to show new signs of life. The Great Awakening had begun in the Presbyterian churches. In the meantime, John Tennent's church at Freehold was blessed with a quiet revival which, after that pastor's untimely death, was stimulated still further by his brother William's ministry.

By natural gravitation this new revival party among the Scotch-Irish tended to coalesce with Jonathan Dickinson's group, whose affinities were also with New England Puritanism. The alliance was further cemented by the elder Tennent's "seminary" at Neshaminy, established in 1726 for the training of his sons and others in the gospel ministry. This "Log College," as its enemies termed it derisively, performed a significant service during these critical years by turning out nearly a score of pietistic revivalists for the Presbyterian churches. Many of them made important contributions to the church generally, and to the Awakening in particular. It should be added in this connection that their revivalism was by no means the tumultuous type scouted by their critics. "Stirrings" and seasons of excitement there may have been, weeping of sinners under conviction there certainly was; but permanently changed lives were the goal toward which the immense energy and pastoral care of these men were directed.

While these advances were being made by the revival party, immigration from northern Ireland was slowly augmenting the strength of the subscriptionist, antirevival faction. This was a mixed blessing, even to that group, because religious life in Ulster had been at a very low ebb. It was still lower on the American frontier where most of them settled, and where poverty and distance placed additional obstacles in the path of their few and not overly fervent ministers. The church was again heading for a confrontation, though it came by degrees. One large step was taken in 1738, when the synod demanded that ministers without degrees from major universities submit to examination by a synodical committee. This struck directly at the Log College men. Other measures were designed with similar intent to keep revivalists out of the church, while various incidents witnessed to the rapidly growing strength of the subscriptionist party in the higher church courts, and their determination to deprive the presbyteries (notably that of New Brunswick) of their authority.

In November 1739 the tide was turned quite dramatically by the appearance in Philadelphia of George Whitefield (1714–70), who was now beginning his second missionary journey in America. He preached first in the Anglican church there, and then from the courthouse steps to vast multitudes. This spectacular beginning was followed by a series of meetings at many Presbyterian churches, which produced a strong resurgence of lay support for pietistic religion. This effect was widened and deepened after Whitefield returned from a visit to Georgia. During his wide itinerations, he also strengthened the relations between the Dickinson group of New Englanders and the Log College men, while these Presbyterians, in turn, gradually drew Whitefield away from Methodist-Moravian pietism toward a stricter Calvinism. The popular result of this activity was a great rejuvenation and numerical increase in the ranks of the revival party.

By the time the Synod of Philadelphia convened in May 1741, things had come to a hopeless pass. Gilbert Tennent's sermon at Nottingham, Pennsylvania, on "The Danger of an Unconverted Ministry," besides being an unauthorized intrusion on another presbytery, had touched the antirevival party at its sorest point. Whitefield's whirlwind campaigns had stirred other controversies. Both sides had hurled many unsubstantiated accusations at the other. It was too much to expect that any synod could long survive the rancor of such deeply divided factions. Gilbert Tennent was quite just in refusing arbitration by some British judiciary on the ground that nobody could agree on what the issue was. Even today there is disagreement on this point.

In retrospect, the historian can clarify matters, perhaps, by designating the question as to the place of the presbytery in the Presbyterian system as the *formal* issue. The Log College and New England men insisted that it had an unimpeachable authority in its own sphere and that the higher courts could not encroach legislatively upon it. The *material* issue concerned the place of revivalism in the Westminster tradition, or, put more broadly, the relation between doctrinal orthodoxy and experimental knowledge of Christ. The Tennent-Dickinson group was unanimous in its support of experimentalism, questioning the value of strict orthodoxy in the absence of personal religious experience. The issue of ministerial education which the Scotch-Irish party sought constantly to exploit was superficial, even irrelevant: as the past revealed even then, and as the future was to reveal more fully, both sides were determined to maintain an intellectual tradition and a learned ministry.

But issues were lost in the synod's turbulent proceedings. The Scotch-Irish group presented a protest against the "Brunswick-Party" which concluded with the assertion that "these brethren [!] have no right to be acknowledged as members of this judicatory of Christ." In rushing to sign it they discovered that they had a majority, whereupon they declared themselves to be the synod. The Log College men, thus ejected, withdrew after the closing prayer. The proceedings were illegal, but there was no recourse.

The "New Side," as the revival party was popularly known, responded to the need for regrouping their forces by organizing their churches into the Conjunct Presbyteries of New Brunswick and Londonderry. This body faced many difficult problems, not least of which stemmed from constant abuse by the "Old Side," but in general it conducted its affairs with diligence and decorum. It evidenced commendable openness to reunion and great evangelical zeal for converting the people then moving in large numbers into the western parts of Pennsylvania and Virginia. Jonathan Dickinson and the ministers of the New York Presbytery sought to heal the schism; and when that proved impossible, they united with the conjunct Presbyteries to form the Synod of New York in 1745. The new synod took its stand essentially on the Adopting Act of 1729, made ordination a responsibility of the presbytery, and took no specific action prejudicial to the Log College men. They stressed the need for educational, doctrinal, and experiential qualifications for the ministry, affirmed revivals as a work of God, and indicated their desire to see the church reunited. The moderate course taken by the new synod is exemplified in Gilbert Tennent himself, who in 1743 had accepted a call to the Second Presbyterian Church in Philadelphia. In this church built by Whitefield's supporters so that the great evangelist might have a pulpit in the city, Tennent pursued a more temperate ministry—so much so that some of his more enthusiastic followers became disappointed and moved off to the Baptists or the Quakers.

ESTABLISHMENT OF THE COLLEGE

The New Side's sense of responsibility for the future of Presbyterianism (could they have known how much it lay in their hands?) was shown further in their move to found a college. Initial actions in this direction were taken by the group of New Englanders led by Jonathan Dickinson, and they succeeded in overcoming Anglican opposition to the institution and secured a charter in 1746, the very year of the elder Tennent's death. It was, to be sure, a shaky instrument gained shortly after Governor Lewis Morris's death while the president of the council was serving *ad interim;* this possibly explains their decision to enlarge the board of trustees to include the Log College men. In any event, it was a foregone conclusion that Dickinson would be the first president. He was duly elected, and began in May 1747 to conduct classes for eight to ten pupils in his parsonage at Elizabethtown. The Reverend Caleb Smith served as tutor.

But within five months the president was dead. He was succeeded by another New Englander, the Reverend Aaron Burr, who had just married a daughter of Jonathan Edwards. The students moved to his parsonage at Newark. At this time their cause was favored by the appointment as governor of Jonathan Belcher, an admirer and friend of Whitefield, under whose patronage a new, less tenuous charter was obtained and the board of trustees enlarged. They immediately invested Burr with the presidency, but he too was carried away by an untimely death in 1757, though not before becoming the veritable founder of the institution. He had broadened the base of its support, located it at Princeton, and erected the spacious and beautiful Nassau Hall—at that time the finest college building in America. Burr was succeeded by his father-in-law, Jonathan Edwards, who died of a smallpox inoculation in 1758 before he had properly assumed the duties of his office. The next president, Samuel Davies, also died after two years; and in 1766 Samuel Finley, one of the seasoned leaders of the Log College group, had his term cut short by an early death. In two decades the College of New Jersey had devoured the best leadership of both the New England party and the Log College men.

The next presidential election at Princeton marked the end of the formative period. By now the institution was secure; with 120 students in attendance, it had become an educational mainstay of the entire region. For the church the next election was even more significant, but explication of this fact requires a brief résumé of the way in which the schism of 1741 was healed in 1758.

The outstanding characteristic of the period of schism is the phenomenal growth of the New Side. It had about twenty-two ministers in 1741, but had increased to seventy-three in 1758. More important, it had won the respect and enthusiastic support of the laity. The Old Side, meanwhile, had not even held its own, and its educational efforts had been feeble. In view of these facts, the New York Synod's strong desire for reunion speaks eloquently of their magnanimous spirit and genuine concern for the church as a whole. Gilbert Tennent's *Irenicum Ecclesiasticum, or A Humble Im-*

partial Essay Upon The Peace of Jerusalem, Wherein the Analogy between Jerusalem and the visible church is in some Instances, briefly hinted . . . Also a Prefatory address to the Synods of New York & Philadelphia (1749) and other conciliatory gestures indicate that overtures for peace were initiated almost entirely from the New Side. Finally, after committees had combed out the main obstacles, the reunited church met in Philadelphia with Gilbert Tennent as moderator. The terms of union were essentially those for which the New Side had stood: the attitude toward subscription was that of the Adopting Act of 1729, with some verbal modifications; presbyteries were charged with the examination and licensure of ministerial candidates; learning, doctrinal fidelity, and an "experimental acquaintance with religion" were affirmed as equally needful to the minister; revivals were approved as a blessed work of the Holy Spirit.

A reunion—especially on one-sided terms—rarely erases all the malice of the past, and many sharp words remained to be spoken. In 1761 schism even threatened again, especially in areas where the two parties overlapped, for there was much disagreement on the importance and knowability of "holiness" in the ministry, and cognate disputes occurred over the problem of ministerial discipline. Several of the Old Side ministers went over to Anglicanism as a result of their position on these matters. This, plus the fact that vast numbers of nominally Presbyterian immigrants continued to stream into the Middle Colonies, made it evident that the training of an adequate ministry was urgent. The College of New Jersey, therefore, occupied a position of paramount importance, and this made the choice of its president extremely crucial. Although the first five presidents had all been men of New Side sympathies, by 1768, with the Scotch-Irish influx reaching record proportions, it became eminently desirable that the next incumbent be a man who could attract and hold the support of the entire church. After a long series of factional maneuvers, the trustees' choice finally fell on the Reverend John Witherspoon (1723–94) of Scotland. After almost coercive supplications, long delays, and much vacillation, he finally agreed to come.

The choice was a fortunate one, and Witherspoon's acceptance a godsend. He was by any account an impressive man, and had already become a recognized leader of the evangelical cause in the Kirk of Scotland. He was also a man of considerable intellectual stature, conversant with the exciting philosophic developments of the "Scottish renaissance," and well prepared to take the burden of leadership in a church now stripped of many of its more capable men. As events were to prove, even his political ideals were admirably suited to a country that was hurrying toward its independence—and he would be the only clergyman to sign the Declaration of Independence. His temperament, moreover, made him an ideal instrument of reconciliation in a situation deeply in need of an irenic spirit. Finally, he was a Scot. This made him sensitive to the church's most pressing challenge, and enabled him to lead it to its greatest opportunity: ministering to the large and restless potentially Presbyterian tide of Scotch-Irish settlers who were altering the ethnic constituency of the Presbyterian churches.

In August 1768 the eminent Scotsman was joyfully received in Philadelphia, then escorted to Princeton to begin his duties, including that inevitable burden of American college presidents, fund raising. His successes were many and varied; and when he died a quarter of a century later, his college had assumed a prominent place in the new nation. It had also lost its grim reputation as a death trap for presidents. Within the Presbyterian church there had come significant changes traceable in large part to him, notably the passing of the New England tradition. Witherspoon's advocacy of the Scottish Philosophy, common sense realism, gradually eclipsed the Edwardsean New Divinity. At the same time the congregational emphasis of the Dickinsonian New Englanders lost its appeal, and Witherspoon made a large contribution to the constitution of 1788 and the formation of a General Assembly. The tendency to value religious experience more highly than doctrinal rectitude likewise abated. The acceptance of revivalism and insistence on the need for conversion remained, but in the days of the Enlightenment and the Revolution even these emphases began to fade until revived again in the new evangelical resurgence that would begin in the 1790s.

THE IMPACT OF IMMIGRATION

The Scotch-Irish

In the last analysis it was not a theologian or a college that changed the character of Presbyterianism in colonial America, but the arrival of wave upon wave of Scotch-Irish immigrants. For a half-century England had sought to attract Scotsmen to Ulster, and by the time of the Civil War it had succeeded in bringing in a hundred thousand or more. After 1660, however, the enactment of various repressive measures put the Scotch-Irish to flight. A few departed in the later years of the seventeenth century, but during the eighteenth century this trickle swelled to a tide. At certain periods the exodus was especially heavy: in 1717–18 because of a drastic increase in rents by Anglo-Irish landlords, in 1727–28 and 1740–41 because of poor harvests and the resultant famine, and in 1771–73 because of the decline of the Irish linen industry. The entire eighteenth century in Ireland is marked by unrest and rebellion due to English mismanagement, severe commercial restrictions on Irish industry lest it compete with English, and religious bigotry that deprived both the Roman Catholics of the south and the Presbyterians of the north from any part in government.

Resentment over these conditions combined with the tempting lure of opportunity in America to draw thousands of Scotch-Irish to the New World. Most of them came to Pennsylvania, which received in the later 1740s some twelve thousand immigrants each year. Some fifty thousand came during the 1770s, and perhaps five times that number during the whole colonial period, of which the large majority settled in the Quaker State. By 1776 Benjamin Franklin estimated their strength at three hundred fifty thousand, a third of the colony's population. Those who did not remain in Pennsylvania most often moved into adjacent areas: the Shenandoah Valley and the valley between the Alleghenies and the Blue Ridge in western Virginia, the back country of New Jersey, and western New York.

The Scotch-Irishman was, as historians keep saying, "the typical frontiersman," bold, courageous, lawless, individualistic, resentful of constituted authority, a hard drinker, a hater of Indians, and an inveterate "squatter" on land he had not bought. Historians also speak of his "rigid Calvinism" as if he were invariably a psalm-singing covenanter; but such was not the case. He had been twice uprooted. Both the migration to Ulster and that to America were made by people who were more restless than pious. And to America, at least, he brought with him little of his religious tradition and very few ministers. Although doubtless he carried a residual loyalty to the Scottish Kirk and a violent antipathy to anything Anglican, in America he and his companions constituted chiefly a mission field. This was the enormous challenge to the reunited Presbyterian church.

The challenge was accepted; and though the church was restricted in its work by its constitution and ministerial requirements, its accomplishment was immense. By 1788 the church consisted of at least 220 congregations, organized in sixteen presbyteries divided among four synods, with about 177 ministers serving this constituency. Bringing large numbers of these Ulster Scots into the church, however, resulted in a radical alteration of its character. "The future of the church belonged to the descendants of the Scotch-Irish . . . and before many years of the nineteenth century had passed, a Scotch-Irish party arose within the Church in whose eyes the New England group were interlopers, who had somehow crept into a Church that had always been essentially Scotch-Irish." [1] In this subsequent struggle

1. Leonard J. Trinterud, *The Forming of an American Tradition*, p. 227.

another type of New England influence would be confronted and another schism would be endured. But that is a nineteenth-century story.

OTHER PRESBYTERIAN CHURCHES

Not all Presbyterians of the Scottish tradition were willing to abandon the specific churches of which they had been a part in the home country. Remarkably, the Kirk itself—the established Church of Scotland—was not projected onto the American scene as were the state churches of England, Sweden, or Holland. This is explained in part by the fact that the Stuart kings after 1603 were primarily rulers of England, secondarily of Scotland. This made their Anglican relationships preeminent, and often led them to try to impose episcopacy on Scotland. After the Act of Union (1707) Scotland ceased to be an independent political entity. During the seventeenth century, moreover, except for those who had spent one or more uprooted generations in Northern Ireland, the Scottish people did not leave their country in great numbers. Nor was the missionary spirit strong during the eighteenth-century heyday of Scottish rationalism. Yet those dissenting groups which seceded from the state church of Scotland did succeed in perpetuating their traditions in America.

The first dissenting group to withdraw from the main line of the Scottish Kirk were the scattered Covenanters who after 1660 refused to accept Charles II and the Restoration settlement in Scotland; some of these "Old Dissenters" maintained this role even after the Glorious Revolution, on the ground that the church must not be subservient to the state. The Reformed Presbytery which they organized in 1743 became the Reformed Presbyterian Church in 1811; with some accessions and losses, this group has maintained itself in Scotland to the present time. Lay members of this group came to America as early as 1720; and in 1750 their first minister arrived, though not until 1773 was this lone itinerant joined by two others so that the Reformed Presbytery of America could be organized. This was accomplished the following year at Paxtang, Pennsylvania, near Harrisburg.

In 1733 the same issue in a somewhat different form arose in Scotland when Ebenezer Erskine led a group of Seceders out of the Kirk in protest against "lay patronage," the prevalent policy of allowing patrons or landholders to bestow livings on ministers without congregational approval. Such a system tended naturally to prefer the more complacent, urbane, and even worldly men of the "moderate" party in the clergy. The Associated Synod of the Secession Church, as it was called, grew rapidly, and in Scotland it counted over two dozen settled charges by 1747, when it divided over the propriety of religious clauses in the oath tendered to city officials (burghers). The two synods which resulted, "Anti-Burgher" and "Burgher," perpetuated themselves in Northern Ireland, and by 1753 the Anti-Burghers had formed an associate presbytery in the Susquehanna Valley of Pennsylvania. Because the issue dividing them was unreal in America, a Burgher minister was admitted in 1764 and the schism in the Secession church was healed, though in spirit the American Seceders remained in the more strict Anti-Burgher tradition.[2]

Because of the difficulties created in America by widely scattered constituencies, and because they shared the very conservative Covenanter spirit, the Reformed and Associate churches were gradually drawn together. A plan of union broached during the Revolution was consummated in 1782 by the formation of the Associate Reformed Synod. This church suffered several divisions and secessions over the years, yet the main body persevered. A few of the Seceders who balked at the merger maintained a separate existence until 1858, showing in the meantime a most remarkable vitality despite great obstacles. In that year they united with the Associate Reformed Church to form the United Presbyterian Church, which continued for a century, merging with the Presbyterian Church, U.S.A., in 1958.

The relative ineffectiveness in evangelism of the Covenanters and Seceders as compared with the larger Presbyterian body highlights the importance of the English, Welsh, and New England influences which from the first directed American Presbyterians to deeper and broader theological currents than those of Scotland, and turned its attention to essentially American problems. This contrast also suggests that the Northern Ireland experience had the effect of uprooting men from specifically Scottish concerns. When the Scotch-Irish began to put their mark on American Presbyterianism after 1768, their spirit was far different from that of the Scottish Dissenters.[3]

The issues that were seriously contended within the two groups—as well as the presuppositions of the controversy between them—betoken the same difference in spirit. While one argued about the continuing relevance of

2. The Anti-Burgher strictness is indicated by the fact that when the Secession was reunited in Scotland in 1820, the American Synod condemned the act as a sacrifice of principles and in 1832 joined two small protesting groups who had constituted themselves as the Associate Synod of Original Seceders. (Probably the most famous Anti-Burghers to come to America were Thomas and Alexander Campbell, father and son, who founded one of the main branches of the Disciples of Christ. See pp. 447–52 below.)

3. In 1821 the General Assembly of the Presbyterian Church, U.S.A. did make an overture for union with the Associate Reformed Church, whose General Synod was a delegated body that had lost its southern and western presbyteries. This merger proposal was railroaded through the General Synod against the prevailing sentiment of the constituency. Its ultimate result, therefore, was negligible, though a few large urban churches in New York, Philadelphia, Baltimore, and Washington were lost to the Associate Reformed Church.

the Scottish covenants, closed communion, and fine points of doctrine, the other was debating the importance of subscription to the Westminster symbols and the necessity of personal religious experience. In 1801 the latter group was willing to make drastic departures from traditional Presbyterian church order as laid down in the Westminster Directory, in order to co-operate with Congregationalism in the West. Even when the same questions were discussed by both groups (e.g. temperance, slavery, Masonry, or psalmody), the spirit and presuppositions were different. In one case we find a dissenting tradition desperately seeking to justify the issues that had brought it into being; in the other, an eclectic tradition bent chiefly on making a maximum Presbyterian witness in a new and rapidly changing environment. In both traditions and both attitudes there were important sources of strength and weakness, but only the historian of the future can evaluate their interaction and reciprocal influence in the decades following the merger of 1958.

For the colonial period, the important fact is that "American," rather than Scottish, Presbyterianism became the chief bearer of the Reformed tradition in the Middle Colonies. Of almost equal significance is the parallel fact that the Great Awakening enabled an emphatically revivalistic party stemming from the Log College and from New England to put a characteristic and enduring mark on this influential church.

18

THE GREAT AWAKENING IN NEW ENGLAND

Cotton Mather made his greatest bid for earthly immortality in 1702 with his *Magnalia Christi Americana,* a vast biographical and historical record of New England's founders which was also a call to his own generation to save themselves from the ruck of routinization. He did not perceive that his own Latin-larded writings were signs of the very trend he lamented. The ideal of a Holy Commonwealth standing in a national covenant with its Lord was fading. Mather's own defense of inoculations for smallpox was undermining the popular conception of pestilence as a sign of God's wrath. The Half-Way Covenant, though itself no proof of declension, documented the passing of churches composed solely of regenerate "saints." The Enlightenment, meanwhile, was eating away at the federal theology: the national covenant, once a mainstay of Puritan thought, was yielding to moralistic individualism. The first generation's fervently held convictions had become a formal doctrinal position upheld by an outmoded structure of Ramist *technologia,* to be passed from the notebooks of third and fourth generation preachers to those of the fourth and fifth, with few of any generation being able to invest it with relevance and ardor.

Having seen Samuel Willard's posthumous *Compleat Body of Divinity* (1726) drop stillborn from the press, a massive memorial to the previous century's achievement, Mather went to his grave in 1728 with small grounds for hope that a resurgence was on the horizon. Ironically, he never suspected that much promise was hidden in the Connecticut revivals of 1721 or in the periodic "harvests" of souls being reaped in the Northampton parish of his arch-antagonist, Solomon Stoddard. He was in communication with the pietists at Halle, but he could hardly foresee their potential impact on

America. Nor was Cotton Mather the only disappointed man. The ministerial utterances of the period—from pulpit and press—were equally gloomy.

In retrospect, however, we can see what these prophets of declension could not see. There would be a resurgence of pietism among the Dutch and Germans, traceable in part to New England's own theological hero, William Ames. John Wesley would inaugurate a great evangelical revival in Great Britain which would spread to America. George Whitefield, meanwhile, would become a tremendous engine of transformation in all of the colonies.

Although Jonathan Edwards was surprised in 1734 when a revival of religion became manifest in Northampton, that event was neither accidental nor strange; the soil had in many ways been prepared. In the first place, Puritanism was itself, by expressed intention, a vast and extended revival movement. Few of its central spirits had ever wandered far from a primary concern for the heart's inward response, and its laity inwardly knew that true religion could never be equated with dutiful observance. Even in years of most lamented declension the churches were informed by a carefully reasoned theology and warmed by a deeper faith than the jeremiads acknowledge. Far out in the Berkshires, for example, the little community of Westfield was blessed for a half-century by the ministry of Edward Taylor (1642?–1729), without knowing that posterity would consider his meditative poems and intricately wrought sermons to be the work of a literary and theological master. Taylor's first Preparatory Meditation on the Lord's Supper (1682), like the two hundred that followed, displays this animating spirit. It is also a prayer for personal awakening that could serve as an epigraph to the life work of Jonathan Edwards.

> What Love is this of thine, that Cannot bee
>   In thine Infinity, O Lord, Confinde,
> Unless it in thy very Person see
>   Infinity and Finity Conjoyn'd?
>   What! hath thy Godhead, as not satisfi'de,
>   Marri'de our Manhood, making it its Bride?
>
> Oh, Matchless Love! Filling Heaven to the brim!
>   O'rerunning it: all running o're beside
> This World! Nay, Overflowing Hell, wherein
>   For thine Elect, there rose a mighty Tide!
>   That there our Veans might through thy Person bleed,
>   To quench those flames, that else would on us feed.

Oh! that thy love might overflow my Heart!
  To fire the same with Love: for Love I would.
But oh! my streight'ned Breast! my Lifeless Sparke!
  My Fireless Flame! What Chilly Love, and Cold?
  In measure small! In Manner Chilly! See!
  Lord, blow the Coal: Thy Love Enflame in mee.[1]

Cotton Mather was himself a preparatory voice. Despite his ostentatious vanity and contradictory moods, he made memorable contributions as an historian, thinker, and defender of the new science, and also as a sensitive interpreter of the times who developed a theology and a conception of piety keyed to the increasingly individualistic spirit of his age. For all of his nostalgia, he called for a new kind of theology, and in *The Christian Philosopher* (1721) he attempted in his old age what the young Edwards was even then striving toward. He also sought to set Christian ethics and eschatology in a new and more promising direction without sacrificing what he considered to be the old orthodoxy. Nor were Taylor and Mather isolated exceptions.

PRELIMINARY STIRRINGS

The Great Awakening of New England began, as has been suggested, in Northampton, Massachusetts. But Jonathan Edwards, to whose preaching the first stirrings are usually traced, did not bring it into being. Nor, in plain fact, did it come suddenly. For sixty years Northampton parishioners had heard the solid and powerful preaching of Solomon Stoddard (1643–1729), and they had experienced five separate seasons of revival. Since the great man's death, they had heard his grandson's carefully wrought sermons. At first Edwards found his people "very insensible of the things of religion," but by 1733 he began to notice a change. Then late in 1734, while he was in the midst of a closely reasoned sermon series on justification by faith, the response began to accelerate. During the spring and summer it continued. "This town," he wrote in his original narrative letter to Benjamin Colman of Boston, "never was so full of Love, nor so full of Joy, nor so full of distress as it has lately been. . . . I never saw the Christian spirit in Love to Enemies so exemplified, in all my Life as I have seen it within this half-year." Edwards came to the only conclusion possible for him: it was a work of the Holy Spirit and a vindication of sound doctrine.

News of these remarkable providences of God quickly spread to the ad-

1. *The Poetical Works of Edward Taylor,* ed. Thomas H. Johnson (New York: Rockland Editions, 1939), p. 123.

joining towns; and showers of blessing were soon felt in these localities as well, especially in Suffield, South Hadley, and Hatfield in Massachusetts, and in East Windsor (where Edwards was born and where he had experienced his first revival), Lebanon, and New Haven in Connecticut. Before long there were similar visitations in towns along the whole Connecticut River valley and spreading slightly eastward as that river approached Long Island Sound. A recent student of these events stresses the importance of word-of-mouth transmission in this new fervency. "From Northfield to Saybrook Point, the religious stirrings of Northampton were known many months before Edwards sat down to write this *Narrative*."[2] He also points out its brief duration, and distinguishes it from the Great Awakening proper by calling it a "frontier revival." It was clearly on the wane in 1737, when Edwards's *Faithful Narrative of the Surprising Work of God* appeared, and it was past history in 1738 when he published the *Discourses* which had occasioned the revival four years earlier.

Yet neither the churches nor the ministers fell back into their former lethargy, and hopes for a new revival were fed by news from the Presbyterian awakeners in the Middle Colonies. Far away in Boston, and farther still in England and Scotland, prominent theologians and ministers were thrilled by the news and convinced that a new day of the Lord was at hand. Edwards himself became convinced that America was the chosen place for the Kingdom's coming, and he invited the great Whitefield to preach in Northampton.

"A GREAT AND GENERAL AWAKENING"

To have reckoned the revival as finished in 1738 would have been to reckon without George Whitefield—a gross miscalculation. The *Great* Awakening was still to come, ushered in by the Grand Itinerant. Whitefield had gradually widened his American circuit: in 1738 only Georgia had been favored, but in 1739, on his second visit to the colonies, he had made a triumphant campaign north from Philadelphia to New York and back to the South, ostensibly in behalf of his orphanage in Georgia. In the Middle Colonies his influence, then and later, extended beyond the British churches to the Dutch and Germans. Muhlenberg tells of a German woman who, after hearing Whitefield preach, asserted that she had never in all her life been so edified, though she understood not a word of English. And Muhlenberg himself was sometimes more drawn to "converted" ministers of other churches than to Lutherans who were not.

2. Edwin Scott Gaustad, *The Great Awakening in New England*, p. 20.

In 1740 Whitefield brought New England within his orbit, and at every place he visited, the consequences were large and tumultuous. Sailing from Charleston, South Carolina, to Newport, he landed on 14 September 1740, and on the following day (Monday) preached twice in the Anglican church. He recorded in his journal that there was "great Reason to believe the Word of the Lord had been sharper than a two-edged sword in some of the Hearers Souls." On Tuesday he preached again "with much Flame, Clearness and Power to still greater Auditories," before moving on to his greatest and most decisive triumph—a solid week of amazing activity at Boston. There were prayers at King's Chapel on Thursday morning; preaching to an overflow crowd at Brattle Street Church in the afternoon; preaching to a vast auditory in South Church on Friday morning, and to five thousand people on the Common in the afternoon. He preached on Sunday afternoon in the First (Old Brick) Church, and afterward outside to eight thousand who could not gain entrance. On Monday he preached to two large outdoor audiences; on Tuesday at Second Church, Wednesday at Harvard, and on the last day of this visit, he honored the "Great and Thursday Lecture" at First Church, where Edwards nine years previously had made his Boston debut.

Whitefield then extended his conquests up the coast as far as Portsmouth, and returned to bid farewell to thirty thousand Bostonians on the Common on 12 October. Leaving Boston, he journeyed out to Northampton, where he spent a few days with Edwards, preaching twice in the parish church while Edwards wept profusely. He then made his way to New Haven, where he found that at Yale, as at Harvard, "Light is become Darkness." After preaching on down the coast, he crossed over into New York on 29 October, thus concluding a whirlwind evangelistic tour of six weeks. Of the religious situation in New England he had a dim view: "I am verily persuaded, the Generality of Preachers talk of an unknown, unfelt Christ. And the Reason why Congregations have been so dead, is because dead Men preach to them." Concerning the effect of his own efforts he was more sanguine: "Dagon falls daily before the ark." Basically both estimates had a great deal of truth in them. Everywhere his preaching had had a sensational impact; and though he raised some suspicions at Cambridge and New Haven, he had at least effectively raised the Puritan churches from their "declension."

On meeting the Presbyterian Gilbert Tennent on Staten Island, Whitefield persuaded him to visit Boston in the near future "in order to blow up the divine fire lately kindled there." Tennent did as he was bidden, and in December continued the mission which Whitefield had left off in October, preaching in Boston with an outward success hardly less than

Whitefield's. Although Timothy Cutler, the former rector of Yale, now an Anglican priest at Christ Church in Boston, reported that "people wallowed in snow, night and day, for the benefit of his beastly brayings," most of the Boston ministers acknowledged the enlivening effect of his visit, and conceded that he was not the barbarian that the antirevivalists had pictured. In other towns throughout southeastern Massachusetts, Rhode Island, and southern Connecticut, the response to his three-month tour was much the same—great crowds, considerable tumult, many conversions, a heightening of revivalistic fervor, and an aftermath of violent controversy. Thus Tennent succeeded both in extending the revival and in deepening the animosities which Whitefield had left behind.

What Whitefield had done in the fall of 1740 and Tennent in the winter, James Davenport (1716–57) attempted to do in the following summer. If Whitefield and Tennent brought to the New England pulpit an unprecedented degree of explosive power, they seemed models of decorum in comparison with Davenport. Yet this young man was a New England product: born at Stamford, Connecticut, great-grandson of New Haven's founder John Davenport, graduate of Yale (1732), theological student of the highly respected Elisha Williams, and since 1738 minister of the old Puritan church at Southold on Long Island. From his youth he had been impressionable and imitative, and he had readily adopted Whitefield and Tennent as his heroes. In the summer of 1741 he determined to follow in their footsteps as awakener of New England. After a trial run at Easthampton, he began his assault on the southern coast between Westerly, Rhode Island, and New Haven. Everywhere he aroused resentment and opposition by his fanatical harangues and his arrogant attacks on "unconverted" ministers. A year later, after a similar foray, he was arrested at Stratford under Connecticut's new law against itinerant preaching, tried by the General Assembly at Hartford, adjudged mentally disturbed, and deported under guard to Long Island.

Now filled with the spirit of martyrdom, Davenport set out immediately for Boston, where after some days of wild and denunciatory preaching, he was again arraigned, declared *non compos mentis,* and expelled. His ill-starred career reached a height of fanaticism in March 1743, when he returned to New London to organize some of his followers into a separatist church. After ordering that wigs, cloaks, rings, and other vanities be burned, he then gave out a list of books to be committed likewise to the flames—works of piety by evangelical greats such as Flavel, Colman, Increase Mather, and others. In a frenzied ceremony down at the wharf, the books were burned, though someone spared the clothes. These excesses were Davenport's last. Heeding the counsel of two "New Light" ministers and apparently returning to a less febrile state of health, he published in 1744 his *Confessions and Retractions.* In 1748 he soberly took up parish duties among the Presbyterians of New Jersey, where he spent the few remaining years of his life. His return to favor among the more moderate revivalists was acknowledged by the New York Synod when they elected him moderator in 1754. He seems to have seen in retrospect that he had done the revival more harm than good by bringing discredit upon the more constructive labors of Whitefield and Tennent and all who had enlisted in its cause.

The chief events of the awakening were of two sorts: first, the whirlwind campaigns of the "Grand Itinerants," Whitefield, Tennent, and the highly unstable Davenport, followed by a large number of lay itinerants and clerical interlopers; second, the intensified extension of the preaching and pastoral labors of the regular New England ministers, now awakened to the power of personal evangelism. Historians have stressed the first of these because of the immense controversy it stirred up, but the latter was by far the more lasting and significant. The chief work of reviving New England was carried forward by the regular ministry, though many conceded the effectiveness of Whitefield's witness and viewed their own labors as an extension of his. Sometimes the stimulus of a revival was simply regular preaching by the parish minister, many of whom had been hoping for years for such a harvest. At other times one of New England's own itinerants, respected and sought after by his clerical colleagues, was the instrument of reviving a church. At still other times, one of the customary exchanges of pulpits by two ministers would be the occasion. More often it was a combination of these circumstances, but in and through all there was the atmosphere of revival—the general air of expectancy and the increasingly avid public interest in the literature of religious experience. So widespread were these manifestations that a brief account could be reduced to a simple list of the 150 New England towns touched by the movement. The important fact is that New England did experience a "great and general Awakening" during the years 1740–43. Even in Boston, where opposition was most vocal, chiefly in the persons of the Congregationalist Charles Chauncy and the Anglican Timothy Cutler, the revival party held a three-to-one majority among the settled clergy. By an interesting irony, their leader was Benjamin Colman of the prestigious Brattle Street Church, while Cotton Mather's son, Samuel, and his nephew, Mather Byles, took their stand with the Old Lights.

The Great Awakening in New England was not essentially different from the "frontier revival" of the preceding decade; but it nevertheless bore certain distinguishing marks. Flamboyant and highly emotional preaching made its first widespread appearance in the Puritan churches (though by no means in all), and under its impact there was a great increase in the number and intensity of bodily effects of conversion—fainting, weeping, shrieking, etc. But we capture the meaning of the revival only if we remember that many congregations in New England were stirred from a staid and routine formalism in which experiential faith had been a reality to only a scattered few. The ideal of a regenerate membership was renewed, while Stoddardeanism and the Half-Way Covenant were called into question. Preaching, praying, devotional reading, and individual "exhorting" took on new life. In spite of far more demanding requirements, the increase in church membership is estimated variously between twenty and fifty thousand.

Yet the other side of the phenomenon is equally important: the high pitch of religious excitement subsided. By the time of Davenport's New London debacle it was already past its apogee. The year 1743 was occupied with retrospective and highly polemical evaluations. Ministerial friends and foes of the revival held conventions in Boston to praise or blame, but their "testimonies" came after the fact. All things considered, however, there could have been no other result. The conversion experience as defined by the revivalists was a single soul-shaking experience; when assurance came, it brought release, and the emotion subsided. Without an infinitely large reservoir of susceptible sinners, the enthusiasm simply had to wane. In addition, there were widespread misgivings over the excesses of spirit. Davenport's recantation is perhaps an extreme but illustrative example. When further distractions were provided by the French and Indian War, and after 1763 by the declining state of Anglo-American relations, the revivals lost priority as a general concern in New England.

Equally certain is the fact that the Awakening had many far-reaching, even permanent, results. Consideration of the social and political legacy of the revivals must be deferred until the movement can be surveyed as a broad intercolonial phenomenon—indeed, the first such. But certain developments in New England provide a basis for this broader view.

CHANGE IN THE STANDING ORDER

In the long run the influence of Jonathan Edwards and the unfinished edifice of his thought is the most enduring result of the New England Awakening. For this reason it is the subject of the next chapter. Yet Edwards expounded a theological tradition that had deep popular roots; and its revival among the laity had important cultural results. A new and irrepressible expectancy entered the life of the churches. A national sense of intensified religious and moral resolution was born. Millennial hopes were kindled. The old spirit of the jeremiads was extinguished. Evangelicalism in a new key was abroad in the land, and its workings had a steady internal effect which was nowhere more apparent than in the Congregational churches.

It is difficult to see how Congregationalism could have survived the revolutionary epoch and emerged as a large New England denomination had it not benefited from the enlivenment which was a primary result of the Great Awakening. The most obvious sign of new life was an increase in membership, not vast (because owning the covenant became a more serious thing than ever) but considerable. Of equal importance was the increased seriousness among existing members and clergy. Edwards's powerful witness and his development of a distinct school of theology would help to nurture these results. For a century his influence would put its stamp on New England preaching, keeping the concerns of the Awakening alive in the pulpit even as the excitement ebbed away. Yet the price of concern was the perpetuation of extremely divisive controversies. Revival issues created antagonistic schools of Old Lights and New Lights, each claiming with obvious justice to be orthodox, and each insisting that it was the bearer of the authentic New England traditions. For a half-century and more "Old Calvinists" and Edwardseans would contend for control of local parishes, educational institutions, and other corporate enterprises of the churches. Such contention had serious negative consequences, in that it drove many peace-loving souls out of the churches and led many more to embrace milder forms of religion.

The Great Awakening thus became the single most important catalyst of that "Arminian" tradition which had been growing surreptitiously and half-consciously since the turn of the century. One can, in fact, regard Charles Chauncy's critique of the Awakening, *Seasonable Thoughts on the State of Religion in New England* (1743), as a primary document in the rise of Unitarianism. When this book appeared, both Harvard and Yale were considered seminaries of Puritan learning; but thereafter Harvard became increasingly a bastion of liberal thought, and its graduates became suspect wherever the Awakening had won acceptance. By the time of the Revolution, Harvard men generally were serving in the churches of the eastern seaboard, while Edwardseans predominated elsewhere in New England. In due course, the "broad and catholick" party against which Edwards had inveighed in 1734 was to be arrayed against the "New England Theology" which he fathered. The Anglican churches also benefited from the drift to liberalism, for they gladly offered refuge to those in flight from the doctrinal rigors of orthodoxy, the vigorous application of discipline, and the objectionable features of revivalism. As the nineteenth century dawned, however, the clear emergence of Unitarianism and a reconstituted Episcopal Church would lead orthodox Old Lights and New Lights to close ranks for the great task of evangelizing the new nation as well as the heathen beyond the seas. In this manner the Second Great Awakening grew out of the colonial revival.

The missionary spirit itself was a fruit of the Awakening—in America just as in Great Britain and Europe. Whitefield indeed was the very model of a missionary. In New England this spirit is especially apparent with respect to that foreign field which lay at home—the Indians. Jonathan Edwards figured in this campaign both personally at Stockbridge and through his celebration of the piety and missionary zeal of David Brainerd (1718–47), who had worked with Indians west of Stockbridge. Edwards preached Brainerd's funeral sermon and edited his autobiography. Dartmouth College grew out of another Indian enterprise; at the same time, its early years demonstrate the importance of the Awakening for the founding of colleges.

The rejuvenation of higher education was a field in which New England's efforts matched those of the New Light Presbyterians of the Middle Colonies. Eleazar Wheelock (1711–79), one of the most active promoters of the revival in eastern Connecticut, was one of the most ambitious of the educational pioneers. Wheelock was a graduate of Yale (1733) who served as minister of the north parish in Lebanon (now Columbia), Connecticut. He conceived a plan for educating Indian boys so that they could spread the gospel effectively to their own people. After gaining support for his project from Joshua Moor of Mansfield, he opened Moor's Indian Charity School in Lebanon in 1754 with two pupils. By 1762 he had some twenty students under his tutelage. Contributions were solicited in various parts of America and in Scotland and England as well, eventuating in a trust fund managed by a board under the chairmanship of the earl of Dartmouth. When in 1769 the province of New Hampshire invited Wheelock to transfer his school to Dresden (now Hanover) and to establish a college there, he complied, opening it to whites as well as to Indians. Dartmouth College, as it became known, was most influential in supplying the new churches of that frontier territory with New Light ministers, sending out some forty before 1800.[3]

At the already established colleges, the impact of the Awakening was

3. Brown University, established by Baptists as Rhode Island College in 1764, also furthered the emphasis on experimental piety and revivalistic fervor in New England; but its originating impulse stemmed from the Philadelphia Baptist Association and was less a direct institutional effect of the Great Awakening (see pp. 174, 317, 375–76).

somewhat different. Most consequential for Yale College was the process by which the revival interests of students gradually overcame the official hostility which had greeted the efforts of Whitefield, Tennent, and Davenport. "It was the beginning of what is known today as the 'Student Movement,'" wrote the historian of religion of Yale in 1901.[4] The expulsion of David Brainerd and others for their pious excesses had if anything a stimulating effect. By 1753 President Thomas Clap had been converted to the cause; and in 1757 the professor of divinity whom he had installed as preacher to the newly founded Church of Christ at Yale was rewarded by a revival. When Whitefield returned to New Haven for his fourth visit in 1764, he was invited to preach in the college chapel. So moved were the students that they urged President Clap to call the great preacher from the coach in which he was departing and persuade him to give them another quarter-hour of exhortation. By this time Yale and its graduates were assuming a role in the American evangelical movement that they would not relinquish for over a century.

THE REVIVAL OF SEPARATISM

The New England churches had been troubled by problems of fellowship since the stormy 1630s, when Roger Williams and Anne Hutchinson had raised the issue. The Half-Way Covenant had precipitated later divisions, while Baptists had never ceased to stir the waters. And now the Great Awakening again aroused these separatistic impulses. One of the earliest incidents was James Davenport's affair at New London, but others soon followed. The dissenters in these cases were "Strict Congregationalists," who objected to the semipresbyterian structure of Connecticut's Saybrook Platform and appealed to the old Cambridge Platform of 1648, which was more explicitly congregational. Above all, they insisted on evidence of regeneration as a condition of church membership. Because their withdrawal threatened to disrupt the uniformity of the ecclesiastical establishment, the Connecticut Assembly passed in 1743 a law which denied them the toleration granted to Baptists, Quakers, and Anglicans. Persecution followed, but failed to bring compliance; and "Separate" congregations were gathered in many towns. The statement of those who withdrew in Preston, Connecticut, delineates the most prominent issues:

> This Church is Caled the Seperate Church because [it] . . . Came out from the old Church in the Town. which caled its Self Partly

4. Cyrus Northrup, ed., *Two Centuries of Christian Activity at Yale* (New York: G. P. Putnam's Sons, 1901), p. 25.

> Congregational and Partly Presbyterial: who submitted to the Laws of the Governments to settle articals of faith; to govern the gathering of the Church, the settlement and support of its Ministers, building of meeting houses, Preaching, Exhorting &c: as also the Church Refuses the members should Improve there Gifts of Preaching and Exhorting Publikly &c: as also were offended at the Powerful opperations of the Spirit of God: and Did Not Make Saving Conversion the necessary termes of Communion: but admitted unbelievers to Communion: also made half Members: Baptized there Children, &c:—
>
> We bore our testimony to them and Came out from them: to Carry on the worship of God according to our Knowledg of the will of God: and gathered into Church order: and the Lord has graciously owned us ever sence.[5]

Here opposition is expressed not only to the ecclesiastical constitution which subjected the churches to governmental support and control, but also to the suppression of exhorting and testifying by awakened laymen, to Stoddardean views of the Lord's Supper and Half-Way Covenant terms for baptism, and to the denial of revivalistic doctrines of conversion and regenerate church membership.

Wherever there were Congregationalists there were likely to be persons of separatist inclination, and wherever the standing churches retained broad "halfway" standards of membership, movements for secession tended to accompany the revival. In Connecticut, where the standing order was rigorously upheld by law, about forty Separate churches were formed, most often in the less thickly settled eastern part of the commonwealth. In Massachusetts, where Congregationalism was also established, there were over thirty, most of them in the old Plymouth Colony area and around Boston and northward. In the outlying areas of Maine, New Hampshire, Vermont, and New York, Separate churches also appeared, though many of these had migrated from older regions. Even free Rhode Island witnessed some separations from its few Congregational churches. In all New England approximately one hundred Separatist congregations emerged from the revivalistic ferment. Due to inadequate leadership and strenuous official opposition, however, few of these separations achieved permanent status as Congregational churches. One notable exception is the United Church of New Haven, in which two separations from the First Church are merged, one of them having been occasioned in 1769 by a ministerial call to Jonathan

5. From the handwritten entry of the minister, Paul Parke, in the church record book (1747); quoted in Clarence C. Goen, *Revivalism and Separatism in New England: Strict Congregationalists and Separate Baptists in the Great Awakening*, p. 82.

Edwards's son. As this date indicates, separatistic agitation continued for decades.

THE BAPTIST REVIVAL

When the Great Awakening began, the Baptists were a weak and dispirited denomination, especially in New England. Even the famous old congregations in Boston, Providence, and Newport had become placid in manner and complacent in spirit. They bitterly resisted the ministry of the revivalists, denouncing Whitefield as "a second George Fox." They showed no awareness whatever that Baptists would be by far the greatest beneficiaries of the revivals in general and of the Separatist movement in particular. Yet many of the most zealous among the "awakened" came to regard Congregationalism—even in its classic Puritan form—as only a halfway house on the road to true and complete church reform. When conversion came to be viewed as the decisive Christian experience, infant baptism was an anomalous embarrassment. Among many revivalists, moreover, both baptism and the Lord's Supper ceased to be regarded as "means of grace" in the traditional sense of the term. When these tendencies were conjoined with doubts about established churches and tax-supported ministers, the road to a Baptist outlook was open. The ways in which Separate Baptist congregations came into existence were various. In some cases, a Separatist church accepted Baptist beliefs in a body; this happened at Sturbridge, Massachusetts, in 1749, and elsewhere in following years. In other cases, members of a Separatist church who had accepted believer's baptism withdrew and covenanted together as a Baptist congregation; this happened at North Middleborough, Massachusetts, in 1756. Perhaps most important, however, was the fact that for more than a half-century after the outbreak of the Great Awakening, there was a steady stream of individuals moving from New Light Congregational churches into organized Baptist churches where the fires of the revival remained alive much longer because no tradition of community inclusiveness tended to smother it. The shift to Baptist principles was also encouraged to some degree by laws which made it easier for Baptists to organize legally than for Strict Congregationalists; but the extent to which this was a real motive cannot be assessed.

Perhaps no single separatistic convert augured larger consequences for New England church history than Isaac Backus (1724–1806). Born into a devout Congregational family in Norwich, Connecticut, Backus was "brought to a saving knowledge of the truth" in 1741 at a local revival. The following year he united with the church of his fathers; but five years later he was among the group who formed a Separate church on Strict Congregational principles and refused, despite fines and jailings, to relinquish their convictions. In 1748 he accepted a call to minister to a Separate church at North Middleborough, where he became exceedingly disturbed over the question of baptism. After some vacillation he was baptized, but he refused to make believer's baptism a norm of communion. For five very troubled years during which one council of twenty-seven Separate churches (1753) and another representing forty churches (1754) met to adjudicate matters, Backus tried to conduct his church on the basis of mutual tolerance. Compromise produced nothing but strife and stricken consciences, however, and in 1756 he covenanted with five others to form a strict communion Baptist church. Thus began a half-century of distinguished service as pastor, evangelist, apologist, and historian in the cause of the Baptists and religious freedom.

Repeated experiences of this sort account for the remarkable Baptist growth in New England during the latter half of the eighteenth century. In 1740 Baptists had only eleven churches in Rhode Island, eleven in Massachusetts, and three in Connecticut. Thirty years later these states had twelve, thirty, and thirty-six respectively. In 1804 New England had 312 Baptist churches grouped in thirteen associations, besides the growing Freewill (or Arminian) connection and a number of unassociated churches. But these figures do not indicate the most portentous events, for they do not include the many Separate Baptist preachers who fanned out into the newer frontier areas, and those who began their amazingly productive missionary labors in the South.

TOWARD WIDER ASSOCIATIONS

The final factor to consider is the Great Awakening's unitive effects, which were felt in two distinct ways. Paramount was the way in which the renewed emphasis on Christian experience and the religious affections led to the recovery of an old aspect of Puritanism: an inclination to regard conversion and regeneration as a bond of fellowship that transcended disagreements on fine points of doctrine and polity. Whitefield, Tennent, and Edwards—Anglican, Presbyterian, and Congregationalist—felt themselves to be of one mind in their great undertaking. Similarly, the revivals led other American evangelicals to discover each other. Here was recompense for the controversy and acrimony which they had experienced so often and which, in fact, they could never long avoid.

Almost equally important was the geographical corollary to this discovery. Fellowship became not only interdenominational but intercolonial. In this regard Whitefield was unparalleled as an influence, yet many others widened their horizons through similar activities. Jonathan Edwards's move to the presidency of Princeton symbolizes both kinds of rapprochement and points to a new era of Protestant cooperation. Based on a wide and durable consensus, evangelicalism would become a powerful force in the future development of American culture.

Given the immense social consequences of the Awakening, it is unfortunate that historians have been almost totally unable to agree as to why it occurred. Few if any improvements have been made on the conflicting explanations advanced by Edwards and Chauncy in the mid-eighteenth century. It came to pass that the message of sin and redemption spoke with sudden and peculiar power to the condition of many New Englanders—though these sons of the Puritans seemed to be no more receptive during those years than other Protestants in Europe, Great Britain, and the more southerly parts of America. Efforts to establish political, social, and economic explanations have been conflicting and unconvincing. Revivals and conversions seem to have come to churches and persons in all areas and classes and walks of life. Given present limitations of knowledge, it is enough to say that in New England as elsewhere the revivals became a major means by which people of many diverse types responded to changing moral, religious, intellectual, and social conditions.

As for the social and political consequences of the Awakening, they are so important and so widely ramified that they can be discussed only in the context of the country's ongoing experience. Richard Bushman's observation summarizes the overall effect: "A psychological earthquake had reshaped the human landscape." [6] Many of the chapters which follow attempt to measure and describe the reverberations of that earthquake.

6. Richard L. Bushman, *From Puritan to Yankee: Character and the Social Order in Connecticut, 1690–1765*, p. 187.

19

JONATHAN EDWARDS AND THE RENEWAL OF NEW ENGLAND THEOLOGY

During the critical first decade of the eighteenth century, higher learning in New England underwent an important transition. In Massachusetts the age of the Mathers drew to a close, and Harvard was virtually refounded when "the great John Leverett" was installed as president in 1707. The path he marked out for the college would lead naturally to the tradition of William Ellery Channing and Ralph Waldo Emerson. Six years earlier, the leading divines of Connecticut had obtained a charter for another collegiate institution, and installed Abraham Pierson to lead it. The path they and he marked out, and which was set even more firmly after the apostasy of 1722, would lead to the tradition of Jonathan Edwards, the Dwights, Nathaniel William Taylor, and the Beechers. It is this latter tradition that concerns us here.

Connecticut's college was chartered on somewhat broader principles than Harvard had been; it would fit its students for "Imployment both in Church and in Civil State." Theologically and doctrinally, however, it was committed to conserving the Puritan heritage; to this end its founding fathers donated to the nascent seminary of learning forty ponderous tomes, the great bulk of them works by Alsted, Wollebius, and other Dutch, Swiss, or Rhineland theologians. The regulations of the institution prescribed the Westminster Catechism and William Ames's *Marrow of Sacred Theology* as guides to scriptural truth. Divinity was to be taught and defended by the sixteenth-century logical methods of Petrus Ramus. But within a couple of decades, the adequacy of this curriculum began to be questioned.

especially as new textbooks in science, logic, and ethics began to reflect the new world of thought created by Descartes, Newton, and Locke. Incongruities between the old learning and the new deprived the covenant theology of its power to inspire. Perry Miller's description of the situation is overdrawn but essentially accurate:

> The period becomes a complex of tensions and anxieties, in which, in sober fact, the die was cast. . . . This society had become a time-bomb, packed with dynamite, the fuse burning close. It was a parched land, crying for deliverance from the hold of ideas that had served their purpose and died.[1]

Two brilliant Yale students of those years, each of whom was to become a noted thinker and college president, exposed the fundamental nature of the problem. Both Samuel Johnson and Jonathan Edwards, moreover, each in his own way, were to mark out the main lines of a *via moderna.*

Samuel Johnson (1696–1772), born in Guilford of an old New Haven Colony family, was prepared for Yale by various of its earliest graduates. He was granted the B.A. degree in 1714, and during the next few years, as he studied the new English books which Jeremiah Dummer and other British benefactors had contributed to the college library, he broadened and modernized his thought. In retrospect he would refer to the old learning as "a curious cobweb of distributions and definitions," and his published *Works* include the youthful notebooks which demonstrate that this condescending judgment was not entirely unwarranted.

The initial instrument of deliverance in Johnson's case was Lord Bacon's *Advancement of Learning,* which he chanced upon shortly after graduation while keeping school in Guilford. After reading this old attack on scholasticism he found himself "like one at once emerging out of a glimmer of twilight into the full sunshine of open day." Thus illuminated, he turned with a still greater sense of discovery to other books in the library. In 1715, when student disaffection and disputes over the school's location led to a dispersal of the infant college, his opportunity to gain further light was increased. The students from upper Connecticut went to Wethersfield, a few others stayed at Saybrook, and some were under Johnson's care at Guilford. A year later, when New Haven was chosen as the future home of the college, he became a tutor along with his friend and classmate, Daniel Brown. By 1720, when Johnson accepted a call to the church in nearby West Haven, the trustees had pacified New Haven's rivals, put Elihu Yale's £500 gift to use, and installed the Reverend Timothy Cutler of Stratford as rector.

1. Perry Miller, *The New England Mind: From Colony to Province,* p. 484.

Institutional concord was soon followed by spiritual unrest. Johnson by now had not only been released from scholastic thralldom; his intellectual horizons had been widened by various English philosophers and cosmopolitan essayists. He also began to confront some of the newer Anglican divinity that was then being so reasonably and felicitously expounded. As old foundations crumbled, the problem of ecclesiastical authority began to bother him. Doubting the validity of his own ordination, he had to reexamine the question of episcopacy. Nor was he alone in the doubts created by his vicarious translation to the realm of English urbanity. A coterie of Anglican admirers had come into being in the New Haven area, with Rector Cutler at their head. Then in 1722 there occurred a great defection from Yale and the Congregational ministry, as the entire faculty (Cutler and Brown) and two ministers in the area, Johnson and James Wetmore of North Haven, announced their intention to seek Anglican orders in England.[2]

The incident is an important sign of the times. Johnson's dissatisfaction with the state of New England's theological and philosophical orientation illustrates the uneasiness of many thoughtful spirits who were feeling the impact of a new, scientifically ordered world view. In this connection Johnson is the most important of the Yale apostates, for he took his discovery seriously and became a comparatively effective disciple of Bishop Berkeley's unique idealistic system of philosophy. He also became a moderate Arminian in theology—which involved him in controversy with Jonathan Dickinson, Princeton's first president. In ethics Johnson took a rationalistic stand, defended natural law, and held morality to be "the same thing as the religion of Nature," not discoverable without revelation, to be sure, yet "founded on the first principles of reason and nature." Moral goodness consisted in a man's being what he is essentially. Johnson's social philosophy was antidemocratic, and with the years he became an outspoken Tory, viewing the extension of the episcopate to the colonies as an essential preventive to independence.

Johnson's sympathetic and admiring biographer opens his work with the observation that it would not have been worthwhile to write his life "had it been as barren of incident and historic interest as the lives of most clergymen." The remark is just. Had Johnson not been a participant in a sensational apostasy at Yale and the first president of King's College, he

2. Other men in the immediate group were John Hart of East Guilford, Jared Eliot of Killingworth, and Samuel Whittelsey of Wallingford, who remained in the Congregational ministry. They exemplify the prevailing restiveness as well as those who found greater security in the older Establishment. Brown died of smallpox in England. See pp. 224–25.

would be remembered only as a moderately effective advocate of Berkeleyan philosophy. Of Jonathan Edwards, however, the reverse is true. Edwards would be remembered if he had lived out his days in a peaceful parish; in fact, his largest claim to remembrance stems from words on freedom, sin, virtue, and God's purposes which were put to paper in remote frontier villages. His chief contribution is an enduring intellectual and spiritual reality, a monumental reconstruction of strict Reformed orthodoxy which is remembered for its exegetical insight, its literary power, and its philosophical grandeur.

The remainder of this chapter, therefore, is devoted entirely to Edwards. Later chapters will consider the New Divinity men who carried on the Edwardsean tradition, and the ways in which the New England Theology affected the Second Great Awakening. For the present we deal with the source, in the conviction that Bancroft's judgment is correct: "He that would know the workings of the New England mind in the middle of the [eighteenth] century, and the throbbings of its heart, must give his days and nights to the study of Jonathan Edwards."

THE EARLY DEVELOPMENT OF EDWARDS'S THOUGHT

Jonathan Edwards was born in East Windsor, Connecticut, in 1703, the fifth child and only son among ten daughters of the Reverend Timothy Edwards and his wife, the daughter of Solomon Stoddard. Both parents were persons of rare endowments, deeply concerned for the liberal education and spiritual nurture of their children. Jonathan entered Yale before he was thirteen, while the college was still fragmented. He received part of his education in Wethersfield and the other part in New Haven, where the unpopular Samuel Johnson was his tutor. By the time of his graduation in 1720, he may have discovered the new philosophy of John Locke, and the bent of his mind was becoming established. He stayed in New Haven two years to pursue theological studies. After he was licensed to preach in 1722, he served a Presbyterian church in New York for ten months, then returned to Yale as a tutor for two more years. By this time (1726) the immense fertility of his mind would have been apparent to anyone who could have read his private writings. In "Notes on the Mind" he had marked out, quite independently of Berkeley, the main lines of his lifelong commitment to an idealistic understanding of reality; in "Notes on Natural Science" and in other youthful writings such as his observation of spiders, he had shown his devoted concern for empirical data; and in his diary he had already revealed that passionate interest in religious experience which was never to leave him. In these early writings, indeed, one may find anticipations of nearly every theme he was to develop during his lifetime. Yet all of these interests were to remain utterly captive to the Reformed tradition as Edwards knew it through the Synod of Dort, the Westminster Assembly, and his Puritan forebears.

One of the remarkable facts of his intellectual history during this period is that, despite a very strong propensity to theological innovation, he seems almost completely untouched by the questions of ministerial authority that were perturbing Cutler, Brown, and Johnson. Perhaps this testifies to the fine example and nurture provided by his father, who had not sacrificed the affective dimension of the Christian faith to the aridities of dogma and polity. Nor can one discount the possibility that Edwards may have simply reacted negatively to tutor Johnson's personality (as most students seem to have done). Finally, one must consider at least the possible impact of his being called as a tutor in 1724 to help repair the shattered prestige of the college; because he now became an official defender of the college, was he not led to uphold the faith of his fathers?

Whatever the explanation, the fact is that Edwards's own conversion experience, as he describes it later in his *Personal Narrative,* involved a genuinely new kind of vision of God's visible glory in every aspect of the natural world. For his sense of nature's beauty there is no precedent among his Puritan forefathers, with all their talk of the "howling wilderness." Indeed, he even seems to move beyond the Enlightenment's characteristic attitudes. In this frame of mind he began his appropriation of Locke. As he undertook the serious study of theology, he was thus involved in the creative process of conforming his inherited Puritanism to a larger manner of apprehending the world.[3]

3. One may ask if passages like the following from his *Personal Narrative* should not be included in anthologies of preromanticism: "The first instance that I remember of that sort of inward, sweet delight in God and divine things that I have lived much in since, was on reading those words, 1 Tim. 1:17. *Now unto the King eternal, immortal, invisible, the only wise God, be honor and glory for ever and ever, Amen.* . . . Not long after I first began to experience these things. . . . I walked abroad alone, in a solitary place in my father's pasture, for contemplation. And as I was walking there, and looking up on the sky and clouds, there came into my mind so sweet a sense of the glorious majesty and grace of God, that I know not how to express. I seemed to see them both in a sweet conjunction; majesty and meekness joined together. . . . After this my sense of divine things gradually increased, and became more and more lively, and had more of that inward sweetness. The appearance of every thing was altered; there seemed to be, as it were, a calm, sweet cast, or appearance of divine glory, in almost every thing. God's excellency, his wisdom, his purity and love, seemed to appear in every thing; in the sun, moon, and stars; in the clouds, and blue sky; in the grass, flowers, trees; in the water, and all nature" (*The Works of President Edwards,* 4 vols. [New York, 1879], 1:16–17).

According to the custom of the day, however, tutoring was only an apprenticeship to the ministry, and in 1727 Edwards was ordained in Northampton as the junior colleague of his grandfather, Solomon Stoddard. Two years later Stoddard's death left him the full ministerial responsibility in a town that was becoming the most influential in western Massachusetts, and in a church to which his grandfather had already brought notoriety and prominence. Young Jonathan was now more observed and listened to simply by virtue of his situation.

He formally stepped onto a wider stage in 1731, when he accepted the invitation to deliver the "Great and Thursday Lecture" in Boston, thus giving an august body of Harvard men the opportunity to hear Stoddard's successor and at the same time to witness the result of a Yale education (perchance to discover that Timothy Cutler, now rector of Boston's Christ Church, had left little influence on at least one of his students). The sermon delivered by the light-framed, soft-voiced, twenty-eight-year-old divine spoke not to old controversies that had racked New England, but to the condition of the times—and thus, as it were, to future controversies. He stood before his elders, well aware of the "enlightened" drift of things, and called them to the faith of their fathers, castigating "schemes of divinity" that in any way mitigated the doctrine announced in his title: "God Glorified in the Work of Redemption, by the Greatness of Man's Dependence upon Him, in the Whole of It." Youth called age to its heritage.

Yet the distinctiveness of his utterance lay not only in its assertion that "reasonable" moderations of doctrine were "repugnant to the design and tenor of the gospel," but in two other characteristics: the terms and concepts of the old Puritan covenant theology were notably absent, and (to the discerning) the thought was invaded by concepts of the new learning. Here is Edwards's first public hint of high Dortian doctrines being maintained from a new perspective, one that in a complex way combined philosophical idealism and Lockean psychology. It is not surprising that the audience was troubled by his message. Beneath the urbane congeniality that had graced the ministers' meetings since the passing of the choleric Mathers, there was a growing conflict between the "Old-Style Calvinism" and the incipient rationalism that marked the men of more "free and catholick" temper. Lines of cleavage that were eventually to divide New England more deeply and irreparably than ever before were already forming, and the more perceptive listeners surely knew that the young successor to the "pope" of the western regions had taken a firm doctrinal position.

For two or three years after the Boston lecture Edwards carried on the usual round of pastoral duties without abnormal interruption. In 1734, in compliance with his congregation's wish, he published another of those subtly inclusive sermons that reveal so much of his thought to the discerning reader: *A Divine and Supernatural Light, Immediately Imparted to the Soul by the Spirit of God, Shown to be Both a Scriptural, and Rational Doctrine.* This sermon, too, defends something very much like "Calvinism," but in a very new and rational way. Also in 1734 he began a more ambitious project with the same objective: a series of sermons directed against the increasingly popular tendency toward Arminianism which was observable even in his own Hampshire ministerial association. Published in 1738 as *Discourses on Various Important Subjects, Nearly Concerning the Great Affair of the Soul's Eternal Salvation,* the leading one of which was on the doctrine of justification by faith, these sermons seem to have precipitated the "surprising conversions" in Northampton during 1734–35. As the revival spread elsewhere, Edwards's renown increased, although his involvement in these events was limited primarily to his own parish.

This continued to be the case even in the more widespread awakening that began in 1740. To be sure, he made a few sallies out of Northampton; and on one such occasion at Enfield he delivered the sermon "Sinners in the Hands of an Angry God," which for many Americans has been the only thing he ever produced.[4] If Edwards did not become an itinerant, however, his influence was widened by the many ministers and evangelists who visited his Northampton parish. In addition, nearly all of his publications between 1737 and 1746 dealt with central issues of the Awakening, and through these carefully qualified writings he emerged as the chief New England spokesman for a somewhat restrained type of revivalism. He also became one of the most important interpreters of religious experience and experiential religion in post-Reformation history.

APOLOGIST FOR EXPERIENTIAL RELIGION

During the revival period proper, Edwards published two works of extensive influence. The first of them was *A Faithful Narrative of the Surprising Work of God in the Conversion of Many Hundred Souls in Northampton, and Neighboring Towns and Villages* (1737), in which he

4. Actually there are fewer than a dozen imprecatory sermons among the more than a thousand for which manuscripts are extant. This sermon's popularity with anthologists indicates the journalistic level of interpretation by which Edwards has been victimized. Hell, of course, did have a place in Edwards's thought. Those who have internalized Auschwitz and Hiroshima may find the Enfield sermon less absurd than have many intervening commentators. But readers of even this chapter may discover that its precise place is a complex matter (see H. Richard Niebuhr, *The Kingdom of God in America,* p. 137).

combined minute detail and remarkable reserve in describing the marvelous and to him quite inexplicable (on the human level) works of the spirit that had constituted the frontier revival in 1734–35. He saw it, as he almost had to, as "an Extraordinary dispensation of Providence." He was grateful, too, that it was accompanied not by censorious behavior and emotional excesses, but by many signs of charity, moral reform, and a deep renewal of faith in those doctrines "that we account orthodox." A major aspect of the *Narrative's* influence stemmed from its masterly portrayal of the true Christian convert. Reading it today, we can easily understand how John Wesley, pondering its pages as he walked from London to Oxford, should have exclaimed, "Surely this is the Lord's doing, and it is marvelous in our eyes."

Many of the excesses for whose absence Edwards was grateful in 1737 did appear in the new outburst of revival fervor that accompanied Whitefield's visit in 1740. This fact gives special importance to Edwards's discourse delivered at Yale's commencement exercises in 1741: *The Distinguishing Marks of the Spirit of God, Applied to that uncommon Operation that has lately appeared on the Minds of many of the People in New-England: With a Particular Consideration of the extra-ordinary Circumstances with which this Work is attended* (1741). The heart of the matter is suggested in the subtitle, for Edwards defended those manifestations that were found so objectionable by most critics of the revivals (including the authorities at Yale who were still smarting from Whitefield's castigation of their coldness). After a discerning exegesis of his text (1 John 4) and a careful survey of the revival, he concluded that "we must throw by our Bibles, and give up revealed religion; if this be not in general the work of God." Yet he was not undiscriminating in his approval, and he granted both that persons might be saved without apparent bodily effects and that some of the physical manifestations might be demonic. Two years later, when Edwards reworked this subject into a full-length book, the opposition was stronger, and he altered his defense accordingly. In *Some Thoughts Concerning the Present Revival of Religion in New-England* (1742), he spoke not to a local situation but to all the world.

Charles Chauncy of Boston was not one to leave Edwards unchallenged, however. In his *Seasonable Thoughts on the State of Religion in New-England* (1743), Chauncy threw off his earlier reserve and in point by point refutation denounced the revival as a resurgence of the antinomian and enthusiastic heresies that had plagued the early Puritans. He provided at the same time a valuable mine of information on the screechings and agitations of persons overcome by powerful emotions, and poured special venom on Whitefield, Tennent, and Davenport for their role in arousing these horrendous passions. In conclusion, he laid bare the chief intellectual issue posed by the revival: "There is the Religion of the Understanding and Judgment, and Will, as well as of the Affections; and if little Account is made of the former, while great Stress is laid upon the latter, it can't be but People should run into Disorders."

Chauncy set the stage for the first of Edwards's great theological works, his "ultimate philosophy of the revival": *A Treatise Concerning Religious Affections* (1746). This book was ignored by Chauncy, who had written off Edwards as a "visionary enthusiast, and not to be minded in anything he says." It became, nevertheless, one of his most widely read treatises, and it remains one of America's profoundest inquiries into the nature of religious experience. It is a classic evangelical answer to the question, *What is true religion?* Edwards's thesis, directly stated, is that "true religion, in great part, consists in holy affections." The "affections" to Edwards are not simply the emotions, passions, or even the "will," but more fundamentally, that which moves a person from neutrality or mere assent and inclines his heart to possess or reject something. Love, therefore, "is not only one of the affections but it is the first and chief . . . and the fountain of all the affections."

Edwards's purpose in the book is to delineate the twelve signs of genuine piety and the rightly inclined heart. Under the First Sign he clarifies the basic point that holy affections are spiritual, supernatural, and divine. He even quotes John Smith, the Cambridge Platonist: "A true celestial warmth . . . is of an immortal nature; and being once seated vitally in the souls of man, it will regulate and order all the motions in a due manner; as the natural head, radicated [rooted] in the hearts of living creatures, hath the dominion and the economy of the whole body under it. . . . It is a new nature, informing the souls of men." This point is further developed under the Fourth Sign: "Holy affections are not heat without light; but evermore arise from some information of the understanding, some spiritual instruction that the mind receives, some light or actual knowledge." The argument culminates in the Twelfth and "principal" sign: "Gracious and holy affections have their exercise and fruit in Christian practice." In describing this practice, moreover, Edwards closes off the possibility of any kind of antinomianism by presenting it as that "which is universally conformed to, and directed by Christian rules," and persisted in to the end. On the other hand, he also closes the door to utilitarian legalism by insisting that "the first objective ground of gracious affections, is the transcendently excellent and amiable nature of divine things, as they are in themselves, and not any conceived relation they bear to self, or self-interest. . . . What makes men partial in religion is, that they seek themselves, and not God, in their religion."[5] Here was a defense of holy affections that could arouse true religion and at the same time present a stern rebuke to arrogant and censorious enthusiasts.

By the time the *Religious Affections* appeared, affairs in Northampton were moving toward a crisis. For one thing, Edwards was ill at ease under the lax standards for church membership sanctioned by the Half-Way Covenant, and even more disturbed by Stoddardean views on admission to the Lord's Supper—and he said so. He also ran into trouble with some respectable families when he proposed to discipline certain young people who had been circulating "bad books" (a manual for midwives). This antagonism was fully manifested in 1748, when Edwards's request to deliver a series of sermons on the qualifications for admission to communion was met not only by a firm refusal, but by a demand that he tender his resignation as minister. The tangled skein of events which culminated in a council that advised his dismission cannot be traced here, but on 1 July 1750, he preached his farewell sermon, an utterance whose quiet compacted strength still proclaims the man's greatness in a tragic hour. After dedicating twenty-three years of his life to Northampton, making it for a time a famous center of orthodoxy and revived spirituality, he was set adrift with a wife and seven dependent children.

Edwards was lifted from the anxieties of his expulsion by a call to Stockbridge, Massachusetts, a frontier town where the Society for the Propagation of the Gospel in New England (the so-called New England Company) and the Bay Colony's Board of Commissioners for Indian Affairs maintained a mission. Though hardly a promotion, the new post was not an exile. During the first years he was diverted by the necessity to foil the plans of those who at this early date were building the great American tradition of Indian exploitation. Although he also had to carry on a double ministry, to the whites and to the Indians, he now was free from many time-stealing distractions, and his most brilliant and understanding disciple, Samuel Hopkins, was in nearby Great Barrington. The Stockbridge years actually became the most productive in his life.

His first task was to conclude his elaborate answer to the "communion question" which had been brought to such a disheartening issue in Northampton. On this matter he had stated his case massively in 1749 with *A Humble Inquiry into the Rules of the Word of God, Concerning the Qualifications Requisite to a Complete Standing and Full Communion in the Visible Church.* This work, to put it mildly, left Northampton un-

5. Jonathan Edwards, *Religious Affections*, ed. John E. Smith (New Haven: Yale University Press, 1959), pp. 95, 188, 219, 266, 383, 393–94.

convinced; more troubling still, his cousin Solomon Williams of Lebanon, Connecticut, had ventured a full-scale refutation which now required and received a rejoinder: *Misrepresentations Corrected, and Truth Vindicated* (1752). Edwards's writings on this entire controversy were once very influential, but they have been slighted by scholars. Consistent with the stand taken in the *Religious Affections,* they are not extreme. The membership pledge he asked for was no more rigorous than the Anglican confirmation vow. Yet he did make a decisive break with the accepted principles of Stoddardeanism, and he cast a shadow upon the Half-Way Covenant. He accepted what his Congregational colleagues were unwilling to admit—that the Holy Commonwealth and its "national covenant" were gone, utterly dead. The church was living in a new age; it stood in a new relation to the world. He rejected the older view that New England's total corporate errand was part of God's design. His grandfather's easy identification of town meeting and church meeting was found wanting. The church, he was convinced, must be gathered out of the world. On this general point Edwards's influence, exerted through his books, sermons, and example, was decisive; and he has been called in truth "the father of modern Congregationalism." [6] No works document this aspect of Edwards better than those on the problem of church communion.

When Edwards turned from ecclesiastical controversy to an immemorial philosophical problem, the result was his most celebrated treatise: *A Careful and Strict Enquiry into the modern prevailing Notions of that Freedom of Will, Which is supposed to be essential to Moral Agency, Vertue and Vice, Reward and Punishment, Praise and Blame* (1754). The second installment of the vast revision of current thought on the moral and religious life which Edwards began in the *Religious Affections,* this was one of the literary sensations of eighteenth-century America, and it has continued to be the most seriously analyzed of all of his works. What metaphysical situation could be more exciting: the chief critic of Arminianism forging a weapon out of the very Lockean materials which "enlightened" theologians and deists had claimed as their own. In a word, Edwards insisted that this was an orderly universe; in Ramsey's nice phrase, "either contingency and the liberty of self-determination must be run out of this world, or God will be shut out." Said Edwards:

6. Alexander V. G. Allen, *Jonathan Edwards* (Boston, 1894), p. 270. Allen, of course, was writing in 1889, before liberal theology had transformed the denomination. We perhaps should now say "middle Congregationalism," which was primarily a nineteenth-century phenomenon, though its origins lay in the Great Awakening. After the Civil War it was progressively altered by influences best represented by Horace Bushnell.

> Yea, if once it should be allowed, that things may come to pass without a cause, we should not only have no proof of the being of God, but we should be without evidence of the existence of anything whatsoever, but our own immediately present ideas and consciousness. . . . If things may be without causes, all this necessary connection and dependence is dissolved, and so all means of our knowledge is gone.[7]

Not only do we set science at nought, but we make an absurdity of the biblical teaching of an omnipotent, omniscient God. For once Edwards indulged his sense of humor:

> In such a situation [where the deeds of men are not caused] God must have little else to do, but to mend broken links as well as he can, and be rectifying his disjointed frame and disordered movements, in the best manner the case will allow. The supreme Lord of all things must needs be under great and miserable disadvantages, in governing the world which he has made, and has the care of, through his being utterly unable to find out things of chief importance, which hereafter shall befall his system; which if he did but know, he might make seasonable provision for.[8]

God Almighty would become the Great Tinkerer who could not even know if "the incarnation, life, death, resurrection and exaltation of his only begotten Son" had provided "any tolerable restoration" of the divine economy.

Edwards did not leave his case in so generalized a state, however, but in a closely reasoned argument distinguished between moral and physical causation, going on to show that the determinations of the will are no exception to the general principle. This he does by rooting human choice in the motives that dominate the will. Man chooses as he pleases, not in indifference; the will is determined by the strongest motive. This is the link between our deeds and our nature, without which our acts would be utterly capricious and irresponsible. But this linking of human choices with human nature involves an inescapable determinism, because human nature is corrupted and depraved by sin.

Here we move out of the area of primary concern in the *Freedom of the Will* and enter the domain of Edwards's next Stockbridge treatise, *The Great Christian Doctrine of Original Sin Defended* (1758), which was going through the press at the time of his death. This work should be read as one

7. *Freedom of the Will*, ed. Paul Ramsey (New Haven: Yale University Press, 1957), p. 183. For the quotation from Ramsey, p. 9.

8. Ibid., p. 254.

with its predecessor, for the question of human motive so central in the former is resolved only in the latter, where the empirical and biblical basis for the doctrine of man's sinful nature is expounded. Edwards begins this work by describing in great detail the matrix out of which human motives arise. Proceeding inductively, he shows the inadequacy of the optimistic anthropology of the Arminians in accounting for the facts. "He invited [the disbelievers in Original Sin] to a reading of history, a realistic report of village gossip, and a frank inspection of the police blotter. He left each to judge for himself . . . how far disinterested love . . . rules the world." [9] The undeniable truth is that sin and death are everywhere.

Edwards followed this rehearsal with a long survey of the biblical evidence (parts 2 and 3), a marvelous testimony to his command of scriptural materials and an impressive exhibition of Old and New Testament exegesis. Here he heavily reinforced the empirical data, underlining again and again that it was through Adam that sin came into the world, and that his fate was the fate of mankind. Throughout the book Edwards wages a vigorous polemic against the English Unitarian John Taylor of Norwich, whose critiques of this doctrine were the most formidable and influential of the time, largely because of the high seriousness with which Taylor had dealt with the evidence of the Scriptures. Finally (part 4) Edwards deals with objections to the doctrine and states his own views, insisting at the outset that one must not ignore the plain evidence already presented. "It signifies nothing to exclaim against a plain fact." He concedes difficulties, even mystery, but insists that "fact obliges us to *get over* the difficulty, either by finding out some solution, or by shutting our mouths, and acknowledging the weakness and scantiness of our understandings."

The argument that bears the chief burden in Edwards's defense of the doctrine of Original Sin is his insistence on the unity of mankind in Adam. What is exciting here is not the bare doctrine—it is traditional Augustinianism, articulated most recently to Edwards's satisfaction by Johann Friedrich Stapfer, the eminent Swiss dogmatician—but the *way* in which Edwards stated it. Here again he brought forward the grand conception adumbrated in his youthful notes "On Being" and reiterated in his Boston lecture on man's dependence. The creation, he insisted, does not possess the absolute independent identity of the First Being.

> Nay, on the contrary, it may be demonstrated that even this oneness of created substance, existing at different times, is a merely *dependent* identity, dependent on the pleasure and sovereign constitution of Him

9. Perry Miller, *Jonathan Edwards*, p. 269.

> who *worketh all in all.* . . . God not only created all things, and gave them being at first, but continually preserves them, and upholds them in being. . . . It will certainly follow from these things, that God's *preserving* created things in being is perfectly equivalent to a *continued creation,* or to his creating those things out of nothing at each moment of their existence. . . . And I am persuaded, no solid reason can be given, why God, who constitutes all other created union or oneness, according to his pleasure . . . may not establish a constitution whereby the natural posterity of Adam, proceeding from him, much as the buds and branches from the stock or root of a tree, should be treated as *one* with him.[10]

This has been justly called the most profound moment of his philosophy. Its power is increased by his daring explanation of Adam's (and man's) fall as a fall from "original righteousness," wherein man was governed by a higher, supernatural principle, to a state of sin (or natural righteousness) where even man's "good" behavior never breaks out of the circle of self-interest. Since the Fall, man lives in darkness because the candle has been withdrawn; now only a "divine and supernatural light" can lead him to redemption and righteousness. Weighty as this part of his theology may be, however, it proved to be the most evanescent. Perhaps no doctrine Edwards developed was so ignored by his disciples. This development, in turn, is an aspect of the larger fact that the metaphysical foundations of Edwards's theology were not or could not be preserved by the New Divinity men who attempted to sustain the tradition. Amid the turbulent and untheological preoccupations of the revolutionary epoch, they turned to other forms of argument. It was not long, therefore, before both orthodox and liberal theologians of New England abandoned altogether the idea of the imputation of Adam's sin.

Not even the opus on Original Sin fully revealed the "rational system" which informed Edwards's entire life work. During his Stockbridge years, in fact, four years before *Original Sin* appeared, he wrote two other "dissertations" which serve even better to link his lifework with his youthful projects. As he concluded the work on Original Sin, he mentioned the manuscript of *The Nature of True Virtue* "lying by me prepared for the press," though the public was not to see it until seven years after his death. One who consults it now can see clearly how Edwards's highest thought moved out of the realm of Lockean psychology and into the great tradition of Christian Plato-

10. Edwards, *The Doctrine of Original Sin Defended,* in *Works,* 2:487–91. See also pp. 478–79, 481, 488–89.

nism. Appropriately, this is one of the few works in which he does not take a polemical stance. He frees himself from eighteenth-century moralism and expounds a doctrine of Being as the basis for understanding the nature of sanctified living. At the same time clarifying the "Twelfth Sign" of holy affections, he puts his central proposition clearly in the first chapter:

> Virtue is the beauty of those qualities and acts of mind, that are of a *moral* nature. . . . And therefore when we are inquiring concerning the nature of true virtue, viz., wherein this true and general beauty of the heart does most essentially consist—this is my answer to the inquiry: True virtue most essentially consists in benevolence to Being in general. Or perhaps to speak more accurately, it is that consent, propensity and union of heart to Being in general, that is immediately exercised in a general good will.[11]

The argument that the cordial consent of being to being is the definition of beauty and that spiritual beauty is the essential quality of true virtue, together with criticism of more restricted notions, provides the chief content of this fine contribution to the perennial discussion of moral philosophy. At the same time, however, its exalted conception of true virtue forcibly underlines both the fact and the tragedy of man's sinfulness.

These notions are put in a still larger and more clearly Neoplatonic frame in the posthumously published *Dissertation Concerning the End for which God Created the World* (1765). Shining through these sometimes laborious pages is a genuine mysticism, though a mysticism kept within bounds by Edwards's commitment to the Reformed doctrines of human depravity and irresistible grace. A passage like that which follows also explains why William Ellery Channing would later classify Edwards as a pantheist:

> The great and last end of God's works . . . is indeed but *one:* and this *one* end is most properly and comprehensively called, THE GLORY OF GOD . . . and is fitly compared to an effulgence or emanation of light from a luminary. . . . Light is the external expression, exhibition and manifestation of the excellency of the luminary, of the sun for instance: it is the abundant, extensive emanation and communication of the fulness of the sun to innumberable beings that partake of it. . . . It is by this that all nature is quickened and receives life, comfort and joy. . . . The emanation or communication of the divine fulness, consisting in the knowledge of God, love to God,

11. Edwards, *The Nature of True Virtue,* in *Works,* 2:261–62.

> and joy in God, has relation indeed both to God, and the creature; but it has relation to God as its fountain; and as the communication itself, or thing communicated is something divine. . . . as the water in the stream is something of the fountain, and as the beams of the sun are something of the sun. . . . In the creature's knowing, esteeming, loving, rejoicing in, and praising God, the glory of God is both exhibited and acknowledged; his fulness is received and returned. Here is both an *emanation* and *remanation.* The refulgence shines upon and into the creature, and is reflected back to the luminary. The beams of glory come from God, and are something of God, and are refunded back again to their original. So that the whole is *of* God, and *in* God, and *to* God, and God is the beginning, middle and end in this affair.[12]

This is a long quotation for a book of this sort, but it ought to be longer, for here is the true center of Edwards's rational account of the Christian religion, around which his earliest thoughts revolved and around which all his sermons, polemics, and treatises must be grouped. It defines the lines of force according to which his other writings arrange themselves.

The great *summa* which Edwards was planning when he died was, to be sure, conceived on another plan. It was to be a vast "history of the work of redemption"—a sacred history. Using facts and interpretations gathered for many years, he planned to consider all the parts of God's grand design in their historical order, "with regard to all three worlds, heaven, earth, and hell; considering the connected, successive events and alterations in each" so as to show "in the most striking manner the admirable contexture and harmony of the whole." [13] Edwards was here proposing to enlarge upon ideas that he had presented in an unpublished sermon series of 1739, "The History of the Work of Redemption," and in his published work *Union in Prayer* (1747). This treatise would expound Christian doctrine in the context of an account of physical nature, all of whose motions "tend to the striking at the appointed time . . . as in a clock," and of all human history, in which "all the changes are brought to pass . . . to prepare the way for that glorious issue of things that shall be when truth and righteousness shall finally prevail." It would also interpret Scripture in the light of actual events—including the American revivals—so that men might know the hour when God "shall take the Kingdom." He would thus clarify the opinion broached in his *Thoughts* of 1744: "What is now seen in America, and especially in New England, may prove

12. Edwards, *Dissertation Concerning the End for which God Created the World,* in *Works,* 2:254–55.

13. Edwards, Letter to the Trustees of the College of New Jersey at Princeton, 19 October 1757, *Works,* 1:48–49.

the dawn of that glorious day." [14] This work was never finished; but the sermon series, published in 1774, became Edwards's most popular book during the nineteenth century, especially among those with strong interests in biblical prophecies. Many scholars, therefore, have dismissed this work as little more than a "textbook for Fundamentalists." But it may yet be that Edwards will win a reversal of these judgments when it becomes possible to view his theology of nature and history as a whole. Regardless of that issue, the fact remains that he was speaking directly to that powerful millennial concern which the Awakening had accentuated and which in various forms became a prominent and distinctive feature of American thought on the nature, purpose, and destiny of the nation. Powerfully in the Great Awakening and repeatedly in later revivals, this old Puritan conception of the Redeemer Nation would be enlivened. It was on men's minds on the first Fourth of July, and in somewhat more secularized form it would become an enduring feature of American patriotic oratory.

EDWARDS'S INFLUENCE: SOME REFLECTIONS

The workman must be judged by what he did rather than what he might have done, though that is not easy when one of the most prodigiously productive thinkers of the age is cut down in mid-career. When Edwards was called in 1757 to the presidency of Princeton, he hesitantly accepted; but shortly after his installation he died of an unsuccessful smallpox inoculation on 22 March 1758. He was followed in a few months by his wife, who was buried beside him in Princeton. His works, of course, did not die. In a general way his categories, his statement of the theological problem, and his reconstruction of Reformed orthodoxy had a profound impact on Congregational and Presbyterian theology in America for more than a century. Yet as will be seen in chapter 25, he did not have a single disciple who was true to his essential genius. His three most dedicated followers, Joseph Bellamy, Samuel Hopkins, and Jonathan Edwards, Jr., were all men of another type and temperament. Even when they were true to the letter, they proved themselves to be of another spirit, at once more congenial to their age and less able to transcend it than Edwards had been.[15] What is still more surprising, the Edwardsean spirit was really never infused into the life and thought of his church (as was that of Saint Augustine, for

14. Edwards, *Union in Prayer,* in *Works,* 3:450–51; *Thoughts on the Revival,* in *Works,* 3:316.

15. See chaps. 25, "The New England Theology," and 26, "The Second Great Awakening in New England: Revival, Evangelism, and Reform."

example, whom he resembles in so many respects). He remained a kind of perpetually misunderstood stranger.

The explanation of this strange circumstance rests on two closely related facts. One, the more simple, is that no generation (least of all his own) has ever been able to read and consider Edwards's complete works. Two of his most essential treatises were published posthumously, as were some of his most crucial sermon series. The main body of his sermons has never been published, and the vast collection of "miscellanies" and notebooks into which he poured much of his heaviest exegetical labor and profoundest speculations have been only very incompletely published. To make matters worse, Edwards was not the kind of thinker who reveals himself fully in any one work; nor did he, like Augustine, Rousseau, or Wesley, lay bare his soul in a lengthy personal journal, autobiography, or "confessions."

Yet there is a second and deeper reason for the peculiar shape of Edwards's influence: his thought seems not to have achieved in its outward expression that inner unity which we know or suspect it had in his own consciousness. Hence his contemporaries (and much of his posterity) have confronted at least five distinct aspects of the man, and each of these aspects has been portrayed from time to time as the essential Edwards.

There is first of all Edwards the exegetical preacher, the man above all who has seemed to deserve the encomium: "the quintessence of Puritanism." His dedication to the minister's homiletical task has as its monument a thousand sermons in the rigorous tradition of his New England fathers, a body of exposition which in one arrangement could serve as a biblical commentary and in another as a system of divinity. A thoughtful Northampton parishioner might have beheld this Edwards. But in all but a few of these sermons only the scholar acquainted with Edwards's other works could discern the marks of a bold and original conception of the Christian faith.

Edwards the New England polemicist is bodied forth in a second cluster of writings on revivals and church order. These were occasional works, often on regional affairs and specific problems, and for this reason his larger views can be perceived only by the specialist who has an objective understanding of the events. Thirdly, we have Edwards the apologist for strict Reformed doctrine and "New Light" experientialism in a world that was making enlightened reasonableness the criterion of faith. What made Edwards such a conundrum to so many of his contemporaries was precisely his relation to the prevailing ethos—his positive evaluation of its leading ideas. Even his friends had no way of appreciating the audacity of a man who would champion John Locke (little better than a deist in many minds) and attack the blessed Isaac Watts (whom latter-day Puritans worshiped as the virtual successor to King David).

The fourth Edwards became fully public only after his death, when his dissertations on *True Virtue* and *God's End* were printed (1765). In them one beholds the Christian ontologist enraptured of Being in general. This Edwards, of course, was never completely hidden, yet most of his writing in this vein still lies unpublished in his notebooks. Even those fragments which have been published—like his remarkable speculations on the Trinity—remain simply potential elements of a full systematic statement. Yet these elements of his total vision of reality have, more than any others, placed Edwards in the lineage of Plotinus, Malebranche, and Spinoza, to name only a few. They have inspired most of the perennial interest in Edwards. Because he brought to this tradition a kind of Calvinistic unsentimentality, his religious philosophy maintains its power or even gains strength amid the rudest shocks of the twentieth-century experience.

Then finally we confront Edwards the sacred historian, dealing with God's disposition of the world through successive ages, from the Creation to his own times of millennial expectation. Aside from the Northampton people who heard his sermons, the public knew little more of this Edwards than appeared in his *Humble Attempt to Promote Union in Prayer* of 1747. The sermons of 1739 that make up the *History of Redemption* were posthumously published in 1774, while the lifelong development of his thought on scriptural exegesis, eschatology, and history was largely ignored until the critical edition undertaken in 1970. Only in our own time, therefore, can it be expected that a reasonably complete edition of Edwards's works will become available, and with it, the possibility for a fuller comprehension of his thought. The mid-twentieth century has already seen a renaissance of Edwards scholarship,[16] and the signs of the times point to its continuance.

16. In addition to the Yale edition of the *Works of Jonathan Edwards,* 4 vols. (New Haven: Yale University Press, 1957–72), see the studies of Edwards cited in Bibliography, sec. 18.

20

EVANGELICAL EXPANSION IN THE SOUTH

Between the Great Awakening and the Revolution some of the most momentous developments in evangelical Protestantism were taking place in the less established areas of the southern colonies. Here as nowhere else new Christian congregations were being gathered. To say this is not to imply that religious affairs elsewhere were static. In New England the "New Divinity" was gathering strength which would enable it, in due course, to redeem the promise of the early revivals. In addition to separations, a dozen new Congregational churches were being founded each year as New England's population grew. The continuing separatistic ferment was also creating new centers of zeal. At the opposite pole liberalism and Anglican churches were also gaining strength. All through the Middle Colonies, meanwhile, churches were ordering their institutional life and numerically outdistancing the many sectarian movements that had bulked so large earlier in the century. Here the Baptists pursued their most free and normal course. Here too the Presbyterians, Dutch Reformed, German Reformed, and Lutheran churches, though faced with staggering tasks, had the main problems of synodical organization more or less solved.

In the tidewater sections of the South the Church of England was slowly disengaging itself from its Puritan past, adjusting its message to the spirit of the Enlightenment, and regularizing its parish life. The ubiquitous Whitefield, to be sure, had left his mark, though much less indelibly than among the more religiously prepared peoples of the Middle and New England colonies. On his first brief visit to Georgia in 1738, he spoke to "the most thronged congregation . . . ever seen" in the colony, and influenced many "loose Livers"; but his efforts there were much restricted by the colony's very thin population. His second tour, which began in 1739 with sensational successes in Philadelphia, New York, and New Jersey, also involved a southern itinerary. Although he spoke as usual to some large groups, he found "no stirring among the dry bones" in the southern colonies. At Charleston he ran into especially strong resistance from his fellow Anglicans, and he found no other churches in which to promote a revival. In Georgia he was chiefly preoccupied with his ambitious orphanage project at Bethesda. Whitefield never failed to create some stir, but the chief work of evangelizing the South was to fall to those who used less grandiose methods and who were less dependent upon a large semicommitted constituency.

During these prerevolutionary decades a restless and expanding American population was rapidly creating new fields for missionary labor. The Piedmont, lying above the fall line of the rivers whose wide estuaries divided the tidewater tobacco country, was the first area to be occupied. Almost vacant during the seventeenth century, it began during the early decades of the eighteenth to be filled by former indentured servants, small landowners, and newcomers moving out from the coastal regions of Virginia and the Carolinas. After 1730 the valley between the Blue Ridge and the Alleghenies began to be settled by another stream of migrants, largely Germans and Scotch-Irish sifting down from Pennsylvania. By 1775 there were over two hundred Scotch-Irish communities strung all the way down to the Georgia uplands, and the way into Kentucky and Tennessee had been opened. Despite the fierce British and Indian wars on the frontier, the expansion of white settlements in the western border area was one of the phenomenal aspects of the revolutionary years, and with the coming of peace the westward migrations accelerated to both the Old Southwest and the Old Northwest.

The "Great Awakening in the South," as it has come to be called, was in fact not so much a revival as it was an immense missionary enterprise. Revivalism was the chief method of church extension, and its dynamic methods effected a radical transformation of the older religious groups in the area. Insofar as Old Side Presbyterians, Lutherans, Mennonites, or the earlier Baptist groups moved into these burgeoning frontier districts, they were not part of the "awakening"; in fact, they were often opposed to its emotional emphases. The future, however, belonged to the revivalistic groups who soon took the back country by storm.

THE PRESBYTERIANS

The New Side Presbyterians who were cut from the vine by the Philadelphia Synod in 1741 were emphatically evangelistic. Direct evidence of this concern was the decision of the New Brunswick Presbytery to ordain William Robinson and send him as a missionary to "western" Virginia and Carolina. This was to ignore the Old Side propensities of the Scotch-Irish who dominated the region and to invade a territory where four Old Side ministers of the Donegal Presbytery had already begun a widespread work. Robinson's itinerant ministry in the Piedmont and Valley districts during 1742–43 marks a new epoch in Presbyterian activity in that area. The popular response to his preaching was great—so great, in fact, that he inspired a whole series of Log College men to undertake similar visitations. These included John Samuel Blair, John Roan, Samuel Finley, Gilbert and William Tennent, and others.

The expansion of Presbyterianism in the South was to depend on this constituency, but for a time Hanover County, farther to the east, proved to be a much more fruitful field. Here among people untouched by established Anglicanism and quite ignorant of Whitefield's first Virginia visit, a devout and determined layman, Samuel Morris, had for several years been leading an enthusiastic, undenominational revival movement based on a few devotional or sermonic works and Luther's *Commentary on Galatians.* "Reading houses" were built, and their leaders had even been summoned to appear before the Governor's Council in Williamsburg. Until the arrival of Robinson this movement had called itself Lutheran, but thereafter it began to take on a more Presbyterian hue. Its denominational organization was furthered by Samuel Davies of the New Castle Presbytery, who, until called to the presidency of Princeton eleven years later, conducted an immensely productive ministry at many widely scattered preaching points. One may legitimately speak of his pastorate as the "Hanover County Revival," though in later years the Baptists would bear off much of its fruit.

These events concluded the Presbyterian phase of the Great Awakening in the back country. The extension of the church went on, though not swiftly. Physical obstacles were great, the number of qualified ministers few, and the people did not yearn for spiritual ministrations. Even the slumbering loyalty of the Scotch-Irish often proved unresponsive to the usual calls. By the time of the Revolution there were not a dozen settled Presbyterian ministers in the two Carolinas, and probably few more than that in Virginia. Their preaching, moreover, was limited in its appeal, and they did not try to reach the unchurched masses of Southern people. On the other hand, the Presbyterian church was strategically poised for responding to the home missionary challenge that would confront it in the trans-Appalachian migration after the Revolution. Its western presbyteries would open out into the "promised land" and make large contributions in spite of new and increasing difficulties.

THE BAPTISTS

If the Presbyterian phase of the southern awakening was a comparative failure, the Baptist phase was a remarkable evangelistic success as well as one of the most consequential religious developments in American history. In 1740 the Baptists were everywhere a relatively weak and scattered denomination; and in the South, where they are often thought to be as indigenous as the red clay itself, they were weakest and most scattered of all. But this picture began to change after the middle of the eighteenth century.

Early Baptist Life in the South

The most important center of Baptist activity in the American colonies was the Philadelphia area. The influences which decisively affected Baptist life in the eighteenth century radiated to the North and to the South from this central point. Two years after William Penn arrived in Pennsylvania, a Baptist church was gathered at Cold Spring in Bucks County. The church survived only a few years, but the men who were to lay the foundations for future growth were already in the field. One was Elias Keach, son of a leading Particular Baptist minister in England, who at the age of nineteen had come to seek his fortune in the New World. Though not even a professing Christian, Keach represented himself as a minister, and he was soon invited to preach. In the middle of his attempted sermon he confessed his imposture and was subsequently baptized and ordained.

By the end of 1688 Keach had organized at Pennepek a church composed of Baptists from England, Wales, and Ireland. At about the same time, Thomas Killingworth also arrived from England and gathered a church at Piscataway (or Piscataqua) in New Jersey. By 1691 these two men had formed two more churches in the area. Then in 1703 a congregation organized in Wales occupied a large tract of land in Delaware which became known as the Welsh Tract Church, and these five churches united in 1707 to form the Philadelphia Baptist Association. The provincial name of this body should not be allowed to hide its national scope. It soon attracted other newly organized Baptist churches to its fellowship, and by the middle of the century it embraced churches from Connecticut to Virginia. Its doctrinal platform was a slightly revised version of the Second London Confession of Particular Baptists (1677), which was in turn based on the Westminster Confession.

Although the early Baptists in the Middle Colonies were predominantly Particular (i.e. Calvinistic) with a strong Welsh element, the first churches in the South were formed by General (i.e. Arminian) Baptists from England.

This group began to settle in southeastern Virginia soon after 1700; by 1729 two churches had been formed, and possibly others. There were also Baptists living in North Carolina from earliest times, but there is no record of a Baptist church before 1727, when one was gathered in Chowan County by an emissary from the Welsh Tract Church. Although this church was soon scattered, another formed two years later in Camden County is still in existence. Its pastor after 1750 established a half-dozen other churches, including one in Virginia, and by 1755 there were sixteen churches in eastern North Carolina, reaching as far south as the Great Cohara. From these came a number of younger preachers zealous to extend the work.

These were all General Baptist churches; but while their evangelistic zeal surpassed that of any other group in the region, these churches were often established on a somewhat careless constitution, with loose discipline and no "conversion" requirement for baptism. There was, however, a "reformation" in the offing.

The response of the Philadelphia Association to two separate pleas for ministerial aid brought the first signs of rejuvenation. Two men were dispatched in 1752 to survey the field in Virginia, and in the next four years missionaries from the association effected reorganizations in nearly all of the old General Baptist churches in Virginia and North Carolina, while agents of the Charleston Association came northward for the same purpose. The result was that between 1752 and 1756 all but two or three churches were transformed into the Particular Baptist pattern. They dismissed many unconverted members (in some cases reducing the membership from over a hundred to fewer than a dozen), tightened discipline, adopted a Westminster-oriented confession, and fostered a spirit of unity. These reorganized churches in eastern North Carolina and Virginia joined to form the Kehukee Association in 1769. These Particular Philadelphia-oriented churches styled themselves "Regular" to distinguish themselves from the "irregular" Separate Baptists who began to flood the southern colonies after 1755.

The Coming of the Separate Baptists

The "missionary" work of the Philadelphia Association in the South consisted of little more than reorganizing the old General Baptist churches. But in the sixth decade the unchurched and rapidly filling back country of Virginia and the Carolinas received a new and much more dynamic influence: the Separate Baptists from New England, whose fervency and drive were destined to become determining factors in Baptist expansion throughout the South and the Old Southwest. The exuberant revivalism of the Great

Awakening in New England was transplanted to the southern back country by Shubal Stearns (1706–71) and his brother-in-law Daniel Marshall (1706–84). Born and bred in Boston, Stearns was converted in 1745 during Whitefield's second visit. He became a Separate New Light. In 1751 he was baptized at Tolland, Connecticut, and ordained as a missionary preacher to New England. After three years of this work he made his way to Opekon (now Winchester, Virginia), where he joined Marshall. His brother-in-law, a native of Windsor, Connecticut, had also been converted in 1745 and had withdrawn from the Congregational church. In 1752 he was a missionary among the Mohawk Indians on the upper Susquehanna River; but after eighteen months he made his way to Opekon, where he was baptized.

Stearns and Marshall now joined in the gigantic task of evangelizing the settlers who were streaming out to the southern frontier. After a brief period of only moderately successful labor, they received word that in the Piedmont section of North Carolina people were so hungry for preaching that they would ride forty miles on horseback to hear a sermon. This was tantamount to a divine summons. Late in 1755 Stearns led a company of fifteen (mostly his family and Marshall's) to Sandy Creek in Guilford (now Randolph) County, North Carolina, where they immediately constituted themselves into a church.

> Soon after the neighbourhood was alarmed and the Spirit of God listed to blow as a mighty rushing wind in so much that in three years time they had increased to three churches, consisting of upwards of 900 communicants, viz: Sandy Creek, Abot's Creek, Deep River. . . . [Sandy Creek] is a mother church, nay a grand mother, and a great grand mother. All the separate baptists sprang hence: not only eastward to wards the sea, but westward towards the great river Mississippi, but northward to Virginia and southward to South Carolina and Georgia. The word went forth from this sion, and great was the company of them who published it, in so much that her converts were as drops of morning dew.[1]

Under the leadership of the patriarchal Stearns, these three churches united in 1758 to form the Sandy Creek Association, which by 1760 included ten churches. John Gano of the Philadelphia Association attended their second meeting as an ambassador of the Regular Baptists and began an important process of rapprochement. He overcame the Separates' suspicions of "Regu-

1. Morgan Edwards, "Tour of . . . American Baptists in North Carolina," in George Washington Paschal, *History of North Carolina Baptists*, 2 vols. (Raleigh, N.C.: General Board of the North Carolina Baptist State Convention, 1930), 1:227.

lar" preaching by his own demonstration, while he himself went away convinced that the Separates "had the root of the matter at heart" even though they were "rather immethodical." Such mutual understanding had the future in it, though for many years there was much animosity and rivalry.

Stearns and Marshall were passionate evangelists, incredibly energetic, not a little eccentric, and rather extreme in their employment of emotional appeals. Both itinerated widely, and they inspired many converts to do likewise. Despite the antagonism of the Regulars their growth was little short of phenomenal. When fierce repressive measures by the government began in 1768, there were only five Separate churches; at the first meeting of the General Association of Separate Baptists in Virginia in 1771, there were twelve churches with 1,335 members. In 1773 there were thirty-four churches reporting 3,195 members, and the association divided again along the line of the James River. By the end of 1774 there were churches of the Separates in twenty-eight of the sixty counties of Virginia.

Political disturbances in North Carolina forced many dissenters to seek new homes in other states. Baptist work in the Piedmont also received a serious blow at the battle of Alamance (16 May 1771), not far from Sandy Creek, when Governor Tryon's militiamen crushed the Regulators for revolting against the eastern aristocracy.[2] But Separate Baptist expansion had already begun in South Carolina, though growth here was less rapid than in Virginia (seven churches in 1771, sixteen in 1789). In 1771 the far-ranging Marshall settled in Kiokee, Georgia, and gathered the first Baptist church in the colony. Shortly before his death in 1784, he presided over the initial meeting of the Georgia Baptist Association, formed with six constituent churches.

The Union of Separates and Regulars

The older Baptists and the newcomers naturally regarded each other with suspicion at first, the Separates objecting to the creedal rigor of the Regulars, the latter chary of the unrestrained enthusiasm of the Separates. The Regulars proved able to appreciate evangelistic success, however, while the Separates did tend to agree with the doctrinal substance of the Philadelphia Confession. Led by their common Baptist convictions, they broached merger in Virginia as early as 1767, although it was not consummated until

2. The Regulator movement of the Carolina back country (1765–71) was organized by small farmers to protect themselves, in the absence of duly constituted authorities, from lawless elements; but its supporters also had economic and political grievances not unlike those which led to Shays's Rebellion in Massachusetts (1786–87). It is perhaps not coincidental that Baptists were numerous in both of these discontented areas.

two decades later, when both parties felt it urgent to unite in order to press for the removal of all barriers to complete religious liberty. With the proviso that the Confession of Faith be received only "as containing the great essential doctrines of the gospel, yet, not in so strict a sense, that *all* are obliged to believe *everything* therein contained," the Virginia Separates and Regulars agreed in 1787 that these party names should be "buried in oblivion; and that, from henceforth, we shall be known by the name of the *United Baptist Churches of Christ, in Virginia.*" In North Carolina the Kehukee Association had been receiving both Regular and Separate churches for several years, and by this means the two groups gradually coalesced without any formal action.

Although the name of the Separates was buried, their influence was not. They put their characteristic stamp on much of southern Baptist life and thought. Revivalism was encouraged and meetings were often tumultuous. Their preachers held forth with a characteristic "holy whine" and encouraged all the extremer forms of religious expression. Far from the staid surroundings of New England, the behavioral extravagance of the Great Awakening was if anything exceeded. Because most of the ministers as well as most of their converts came from backwoods areas, restraints were lacking; intellectual sophistication was considered unnecessary and even undesireable. Yet the significance of these "primitive traits" is not nearly so great as some have tried to make it. More worthy of remark is the moral and spiritual discipline which the Separate Baptists brought to these unchurched areas. It was for laxity in these matters that they most often criticized the older Baptist churches, and at first they adopted very strict requirements—even to prescribing plainness of dress and speech in the Quaker manner. They compensated for their lack of education by close and serious searching of the Scriptures; this led some to revive the "nine Christian rites," many of which remind one of the German Dunkers: baptism, Lord's Supper, love feast, laying on of hands, foot washing, anointing the sick, right hand of fellowship, kiss of charity, and devoting children. Doctrinal concerns imbibed from the Regular Baptists served to check the aberrations of an uneducated ministry and helped to prevent preoccupation with trivial details or fantastic interpretations.

The general doctrinal position of the resulting Baptist tradition was distinctly Reformed, a modified version of Westminster; yet the prevailing distrust of rigid creedal definitions allowed considerable latitude for doctrinal differences. An Arminian or "free will" party persisted, as did a strict predestinarian party, with various "hard-shell," antimission, and "primitive"

Baptists stemming from the latter during the nineteenth century. Probably most of the preachers shared the feelings of John Leland, who came to Virginia from Massachusetts in 1776:

> I conclude that the *eternal purposes* of God, and the *freedom of the human will,* are both truths; and it is a matter of fact, that the preaching that has been most blessed of God, and most profitable to men, is *the doctrine of sovereign grace in the salvation of souls, mixed with a little of what is called Arminianism.* These two propositions can be tolerably well reconciled together, but the modern misfortune is, that men often spend too much time in explaining away one or the other, or in fixing the lock-link to join the others together; and by such means, have but little time in a sermon to insist on those two great things which God blesses.[3]

The net result was a blending of revivalistic and "orthodox" tendencies along the lines suggested by John Leland's compromise. Gradually the New Hampshire Confession (published in that state in 1833) came to express this majority view.

Finding a proper balance between local church autonomy and associational authority also exercised the Separates, and their love for local freedom counterbalanced the centralizing influences stemming from Philadelphia. That association seemed to regard itself competent to "determine the mind of the Holy Ghost" and enjoin upon its churches obedience to the commands of Scripture. It became a virtual denominational body, whose cohesiveness consisted in the willingness of like-minded churches to limit their independence. Something of the same advantage must have appealed to Stearns, whose background, it will be remembered, was in the semipresbyterianized Congregationalism of Connecticut. Facing the multiplication of members and churches, the Sandy Creek Association greatly reduced the autonomy of particular churches.

Backwoods converts, however, were not ready for such strict ecclesiasticism; and their dissatisfaction was doubtless a primary cause for dividing the Sandy Creek Association in 1770. It is noteworthy that the new Virginia body declared at the outset that it had "no power or authority to impose anything upon the churches, but that it [should] act as an advisory council, provided that all matters brought before the Association for advice be determined by a majority voice." Yet the retreat to radical independency did not go unchallenged; and the need to assert the rights of Baptists against

3. John Leland, "A Letter of Valediction on Leaving Virginia, 1791," in *The Writings of the Late Elder John Leland,* ed. Louise F. Green (New York, 1845), p. 172.

governmental discrimination gave rise to "connectional" sentiments, just as the union of Separates and Regulars was hastened by the necessity to make a common cause. The independent Separates readily saw the advantages of cooperative action in this instance and agreed to the formation of a General Committee to represent all the Virginia associations. After its ends were attained, the committee declined steadily, and in 1799 it was dissolved. Not until 1823 would a really representative body of Baptists in Virginia be formed.

This entire development points to the fact that the continuing concern for denominational order in the South was fostered mainly by the Regular Baptists through their connection with the Philadelphia Association. Early attempts by the New Englanders misfired; the pioneers who swarmed into the Separate Baptist churches via a highly emotionalized conversion experience were no more ready for a "presbytery" than for a pope. Nor would people who later overthrew a foreign despot and his church be anxious to thrust their necks into an ecclesiastical noose even of their own making. The influence of the Separates on Baptist ecclesiology, therefore, was *against* centralization—simply because of the character of their converts, who by sheer weight of numbers overwhelmed the older Baptist life in the South. The Philadelphia order eventually prevailed, but only because the more influential leaders in the East persistently pressed for its acceptance.

The surge of Baptist growth among the rural population in the South is not to be accounted for without considering the farmer-preacher, a figure rightly celebrated as one of the most important institutions in the westward expansion of the American people. This immensely effective servant of God was usually of humble agrarian origin, from a family on the move, living in a region where schools were nonexistent and hopes for "higher education" unheard of. He had in all likelihood been shaken out of his dreary agricultural routine by one or more visits from some itinerant evangelist. Under the force of an "awakening" sermon or a new convert's testimony, he had been "born again" and baptized. Recognizing gifts of preaching in himself and feeling a "call" to exercise them in the locality where he lived (or one to which he might be led), he would then gather a congregation and be ordained as its minister. Since the preacher did not leave his farm, the question of support did not arise—indeed, paying a minister might even be frowned upon—and since a home, barn, or shaded clearing would suffice for a meeting place, the poverty of his people scarcely hindered the work of his church. Thus churches sprang up and grew wherever people were. The Presbyterian revival in Hanover County collapsed after Samuel Davies went off to become president of Princeton, leaving no educated and ordained minister to succeed him in that remote area. The Baptists, on the other hand, continued to grow there and elsewhere, except in communities where the people, due to their church traditions or social status, were repelled by unrestrained religious enthusiasm, or where—as came increasingly to be the case—they were reached first by Methodist evangelists.

THE EMERGENCE OF METHODISM

Although John and Charles Wesley had come to Georgia in 1736 and been repulsed as inflexible High Churchmen, within fifty years they returned to America with power—not in person, except for Charles's brief visit in 1757—but through the ministry of their words and their followers. Between these two "Methodistic" manifestations lay the Wesleys' decisive confrontation with German pietism, out of which was born one of the most dynamic and consequential religious movements in modern times, a movement whose import would nowhere be more forceful and enduring than in America. To understand it, one must go back to the beginning in the rectory at Epworth, the rough country parish in Lincolnshire where Samuel and Susanna Wesley, but particularly Susanna, brought up their remarkable family. The Wesleys nurtured the eleven of their nineteen children who survived infancy in devout, thoroughly Anglican ways, even though both their fathers had been ejected from the church's ministry for Nonconformity in 1662. John was born in 1703, Charles in 1707. Both children were nearly lost in the burning of the rectory in 1709.

The two boys were well prepared for the university, and both distinguished themselves at Christ Church, Oxford. John was ordained in 1725 and made a fellow of Lincoln College in 1726. During the ensuing years both brothers were much preoccupied with their spiritual well-being, and they took prominent roles in a "Holy Club" at Oxford. Because of their emphasis on devotional reading, ascetic practice, and frequent communion, these rigoristic Anglo-Catholics (as we might term them now) were dubbed Methodists—and the name stuck even after their rigorism had become pronouncedly evangelical. George Whitefield (1714–70) also became a member of this club in 1735, only a year before he embarked on his sensational preaching career, and three years before he went to Georgia, where he succeeded to a degree on the scene of the Wesleys' resounding failure.

Upon returning to London from America in 1738, John Wesley pursued his search for peace with God, spending many hours with Peter Böhler, a Moravian missionary who continued the spiritual tutelage begun in Georgia.

He even joined a pietistic society that Böhler had organized in London. Then at about a quarter to nine on the evening of 24 May 1738, while attending an Anglican society meeting in Aldersgate Chapel and listening to a reading of Luther's Preface to Romans, Wesley's heart, as he said, "was strangely warmed." By 4 June his peace had become joy: "all these days I scarce remember to have opened the New Testament, but upon some great precious promise. And I saw more than ever, that the gospel is in truth but one great promise." In time his thought deepened and stabilized, but this experience transformed his career and provided the central theme of his amazingly powerful preaching. It is the clue to the conception of the Christian life that shaped Methodism. Not long after the world's first Aldersgate Sunday, John went to Germany, consulted with Count Zinzendorf, and visited at Herrnhut. On returning he began a serious study of the early English Reformers.

Three days before John's "conversion" Charles had been similarly changed. Thereafter he pursued a parallel career, less noted as a preacher than as the author or translator of over four thousand hymns, the best of which rank him with Isaac Watts in the annals of English hymnody. He would always remain more conservative than his brother, dubious about field preaching at first, and vigorously opposed to separatistic tendencies. Although Charles was not so deeply schooled in patristic theology as his erudite brother, he was equally influenced by the mystical writings of William Law, the nonjuring mystic and perfectionist who in turn owed so much to the German mystic, Jacob Boehme. Traditional motifs tended to figure more strongly in Charles's faith and conduct, and at his death in 1788 he was deeply perturbed by Methodism's imminent rupture with the established church.

Within a year of their conversion, the Wesleys were preaching in the fields at Whitefield's request, having decided that this was God's will by casting lots in the Moravian manner. For John, the discovery of his power as a preacher was a decisive personal event. When the brothers died a half-century later within three years of each other, the "Evangelical Revival" was a momentous British actuality, and a Methodist Church of over seventy thousand members was only a few legal steps from independent status. In that span of time John Wesley's itinerations carried him more than two hundred thousand miles in the British Isles, mostly on horseback. He aroused similar dedication in countless converts, and made Methodism a marvel of organization, with all its property vested in him personally. Societies dotted the British Isles, and in each of them "classes" under separate leaders were organized to enforce discipline and to nurture the group's religious life. The Puritan impulse, reshaped to answer eighteenth-century needs, was once again a transforming force in the land. Then in 1784 John Wesley took the decisive step of ordaining ministers for the orphaned Methodists of America, setting apart two superintendents to direct that work.

The basic theology of Wesleyan Methodism was expressed in the Forty-four Sermons, which John Wesley formally designated as normative. Further definition was provided by his *Notes on the New Testament* (a brief commentary clarifying his interpretation of key passages) and a condensed version of the Thirty-Nine Articles. The message was Reformed and Puritan in many of its major themes, above all in its moral emphases. Its stress on the sinner's penitential conflict was due in large part to the powerful influence of Moravian pietism.

Wesley's own theology, however, was profoundly wrought, thoroughly integrated, and, after 1740, remarkably stable. He took man's sinful state with entire seriousness and preached salvation through grace by faith; yet he was forcefully Arminian, stressing the universal efficacy of Christ's Atonement and assailing those who preached man's utter and helpless depravity. Denying the doctrines of irresistible grace and perseverance, he believed that men could both resist the Spirit and fall from grace. Wesley widened this breach with Calvinism still further with a doctrine of Christian perfection which is, nevertheless, his most original contribution to Protestant theology. In developing this distinctive phase of his theology, he drew upon many sources, including early Eastern Orthodoxy.[4] More important than such scholarly considerations, however, is the degree to which the life of every sincere Methodist became a quest for complete sanctification or holiness (i.e. sinlessness). Like Wesley, his followers believed that this "second blessing" of the Holy Spirit had been and could be attained. Justification of the sinner was absolutely essential to salvation, but sanctification was the "fullness of faith." Through a dynamic interaction of divine grace and human will the Christian could and should respond to the scriptural bidding, "Let us go on to perfection" (Heb. 6:1).

These "innovations" of Wesley led to his break with Whitefield, who took a strong predestinarian stand that led his pious patroness, Lady Selina, Countess of Huntington, to found a separate group of societies and encouraged the formation of a distinct Calvinistic Methodist church among the

4. For these assertions about Wesley's theology I am indebted to Albert C. Outler, ed., *John Wesley*, Library of Protestant Thought (New York: Oxford University Press, 1964), pp. 9, 10, 14, 251, 252. This volume of writings is an invaluable corrective, but it unduly minimizes Reformed, Puritan, Anglican, pietistic, and Roman Catholic influences that Cell, Schmidt, Piette, and other Wesley scholars have rightly stressed.

Welsh. Objections to Wesley's allegedly "papist" doctrines also arose among Calvinistic Anglicans who were loyal to the established church and even more vehemently among those, both in Britain and in the colonies, who were committed to the Westminster standards. Perhaps no anti-Wesleyan utterance became so well known and beloved—ironically, even by Methodists—as the hymn "Rock of Ages," written by the Anglican priest Augustus M. Toplady (1740–78):

> Should my tears for ever flow,
> Should my zeal no languor know,
> All for sin could not atone,
> Thou must save, and thou alone;
> In my hand no price I bring,
> Simply to thy cross I cling.

These doctrines became cardinal points of controversy whenever Methodists confronted the older Reformed theology, whether among Anglicans or among denominations of Westminster orientation in Great Britain and the colonies. Along with Methodism's highly organized and extremely centralized church polity, Arminianism and Perfectionism became the denomination's most distinctive features. Beneath all and through all, however, was the sustained Wesleyan demand for penitential conflict, conviction of sin, and the experience of regeneration. Among American Methodists especially there also developed a deep skepticism about the value of the more objective aspects of religion, whether doctrinal, liturgical, or sacramental. In many ways, nevertheless, Wesleyanism blended very easily with the other forms of evangelical revivalism that flourished in the eighteenth and nineteenth centuries. In England it also played a large role in stimulating a parallel resurgence of evangelicalism among the Anglicans.

EVANGELICAL ANGLICANISM IN AMERICA

In the colonial period Methodism per se was neither strong enough nor persuasive enough to have much effect anywhere except within the Anglican church, from which it had not yet separated when the Revolution came. Into this communion it infused a great deal of badly needed (though little appreciated) vitality. Between 1766, when the first American Methodist society was organized in New York, and the opening of hostilities with England a decade later, the movement had gained but 3,148 adherents. Twenty-five hundred of these were in the South, notably around Baltimore and in Brunswick County, Virginia, areas where Nonconformity had been prevalent from earliest colonial days. Francis Asbury, who as the first Methodist bishop in America would play a powerful formative role, was already active here in 1771. Certain permanent traditions of American Methodism began to develop from this time forward, but these trends will be discussed in connection with the formation of the independent Methodist church after the Revolution.

Of more immediate significance for the growth of organized church life in the southern back country was the work of a very small group of evangelical and revivalistic Anglicans who carried on a "counter-awakening" in the established church before Methodism had gained momentum. Devereux Jarratt (1733–1801) was unquestionably the most important of these men. Born in New Kent County near Richmond, Virginia, he had taken up the profession of schoolmaster. Although he had received very little evangelical nurture in his youth, he was brought to a "full persuasion" that he was a "stranger to God and true religion" while hypocritically feigning to enjoy the sermons of John Flavel which the mother of his pupils was wont to read aloud. Other reading and the counsel of some Presbyterians finally led him to vital faith and a decision to enter the ministry. Since his spiritual education, both personal and literary, had up to this point been Presbyterian, he had no other thought than to make that way his own. Further study, however, convinced him that Anglican worship and doctrine did no violence to his strict Reformed principles; and because he also saw in the established church a vast field for one with his views, he undertook the harrowing wartime adventure of seeking ordination in London. Upon returning to Virginia in 1763, he went to the vestry of Bath in Dinwiddie County, where a vacancy existed, and preached with ready acceptance. At the age of thirty-one he began a remarkable ministry that ended only with his death.

Jarratt's efforts to end the "carnal repose" of the people soon sparked a revival that burst the boundaries of his parish and county. After 1776 he was itinerating in a dozen counties of Virginia and North Carolina with a circuit from five to six hundred miles long. He carried on this work almost alone against the nearly unanimous opposition of the Anglican clergy. Even the one rector whom he won to his cause defected to the Presbyterians. When the Methodist preachers began to arrive in 1772, Jarratt cooperated with them closely and let his revival blend with theirs, partly to counteract Baptist inroads on his farflung flocks, but also because he accepted their protestations of Anglican loyalty, not realizing, as he said later, that he "jumpt out of the frying pan into the fire."

For some years this cooperation with the Methodists produced rich fruits. Many "Christian societies" were formed within Jarratt's large circuit; he cooperated with the Wesleyan revivals in the nearby counties of Brunswick and Sussex, and 1776 this combination was blessed by the most extensive revival in Jarratt's career. By the same token, it was the high point from which a steady decline of his evangelical Anglicanism can be measured. Deism, the Revolution, and religious factionalism decimated the movement's gains. After the war, however, the Presbyterians and, to a far greater extent, the Baptists and Methodists extended their conquests in the back country by following the great migration into the trans-Appalachian regions. They would thus continue the Great Awakening—or at least keep revival fervor alive when it flickered low elsewhere. For this reason the story of the frontier awakenings in the South is not only an important chapter in itself, but a prologue to the "Great Revival in the West," which is, in turn, a vital link between the colonial Awakening and the tumultuous events which shaped American evangelical Protestantism during the early nineteenth century.

21

ROMAN CATHOLICISM IN THE AMERICAN COLONIES

During the period of American exploration Roman Catholics in one way or another made their appearance almost everywhere. Earliest of all were the Norsemen who came to "Vinland." There is also a tradition—probably false—that Bishop Eric of Greenland visited Rhode Island in the twelfth century. Cabot, Verrazano, Estavan Gómez, and several others in the employ of England, France, or Spain explored the coastline in the sixteenth century. New York's harbor and river had been named for Saint Christobel and Saint Antonio eighty years before Henry Hudson saw them. The southern colonies, too, had a Roman Catholic "prehistory" associated with the extension of Spanish missions out of Florida into Georgia, Carolina, and as far north as Chesapeake Bay. New France made approaches from the north and west. Intermittent individual contacts occurred, sometimes accidentally, as with the Dutch rescue of Father Isaac Jogues from the Mohawks in 1643, sometimes intentionally, as with the brief visit to Boston by the French Jesuit missionary, Jean Pierron, sometimes officially, as with Father Gabriel Druillette's negotiations with Massachusetts on the problems in Maine. There are also military advances, particularly by the French in the Great Lakes–Mississippi basin. The long French and Indian Wars from beginning to end involved a hostile Roman Catholic presence in various areas, and they left an enduring legacy of heightened anti-Catholic animosity among colonial Americans. Aside from these developments there is also a Roman Catholic "nonhistory" written during this period by people (innumerable because unknown) who for any number of reasons drifted into various colonies where they forgot their church allegiance or were too far removed from the ministrations of any priest.[1]

In Maryland, however, Roman Catholics contributed a highly significant chapter in American church history; in fact, they built foundations that made Baltimore a virtual primatial see during the nineteenth century. Pennsylvania also acquired a considerable Catholic population, and New York for a time enjoyed some favoring circumstances, but outside these three areas the colonial history of the Roman Catholic church is almost non-existent.

RELIGIOUS FREEDOM AND POLITICAL TURMOIL IN MARYLAND

"Mary-land," wrote one of her early chroniclers, "may (without sin, I think) be called Singular." Nor did the writer sin—for this colony does exhibit many peculiarities. It was carved out of an existing crown colony (Virginia) and chartered anachronistically as a feudal barony in an age of entrepreneurial expansion. This generous grant was made, moreover, by the Protestant king of England to a Roman Catholic convert so that the founder's coreligionists might be free from the statutory disabilities they suffered in England. George Calvert, first Lord Baltimore, had become secretary of state in 1619, a post he was forced to resign upon espousing the Roman Catholic faith in 1625. He remained in royal favor, however, and shortly after his death in 1632 Charles I delivered the Maryland charter to his son, Cecilius Calvert. Governing through his brother Leonard Calvert, the second Lord Baltimore allowed freedom of religion to all Christians who settled in Maryland. Nothing in the charter itself can be interpreted as a guarantee of these rights, but the instructions prepared by the proprietor for the colony's governors are remarkably explicit. He asks them to see that "they suffer no scandal nor offense to be given to any of the Protestants, whereby any just complaint may hereafter be made." He also bids Roman Catholics to worship "as privately as may be," and not to discuss religious matters in public.[2]

Aside from the extremely liberal grant of proprietary authority the unusualness of the colony was more apparent than real. The grant itself was part and parcel of Stuart foreign policy, which was aimed at conciliating

1. Thomas Pheland makes the most of these scattered facts. He also claims that Myles Standish of Plymouth came from "an ancient Catholic family" and made "annual visits to the Kennebec settlements where the Catholic missionaries were located, presumably to perform his Easter duty" (*Catholics in Colonial Days* [New York: P. J. Kenedy & Sons, 1935], p. 121).

2. John Tracy Ellis, ed., *Documents of American Catholic History*, pp. 100–01.

the great Counter-Reformation powers. Neither James I nor Charles I gave wholehearted support to the Protestant forces in the Thirty Years War, not even to their kinsman in the Palatinate when his territory was invaded by the French. Charles I married the sister of Louis XIII of France, Henrietta Maria, for whom Maryland, by a fortunate *double entendre,* was named (Terra Mariae). Charles II and James II, of course, would go even further in this direction. The grant to Calvert, therefore, whatever else it may have been (a settlement of a debt or evidence of real sympathy for English Catholics), was a domestic corollary to the crown's international aims in this period.

The years from 1612 to the Civil War (1640) were for English Catholics generally the most satisfactory period between the reign of Mary Tudor and the Relief Act of 1778. Lord Baltimore's allowance of religious liberty was far ahead of its time, even if freedom for Catholics and a desire for profits were the motives. John Tracy Ellis rightly complains that many historians, including Charles M. Andrews, have been unduly niggardly in their recognition of the proprietor's openmindedness on religious matters. To what degree Lord Baltimore or Father White were influenced by the undeniably democratic implications of Cardinal Bellarmine's political philosophy is not clear.[3] Given the fact, however, that during these years the crown itself had shown, and was to show, amazing liberality in granting colonial charters to groups and individuals of the most radically Nonconformist stamp, the strategy of Lord Baltimore is not an idealistic breakthrough. Religious toleration in Maryland was the only conceivable basis upon which Roman Catholics could have obtained any rights at all. The Roman Catholic James II followed the same course both as ducal proprietor of New York and as king of England.

No other policy, moreover, would have given an incentive to immigration and settlement. This practical consideration influenced many proprietors during the seventeenth century, as is evidenced by the liberality shown in the Carolinas, the Jerseys, and Pennsylvania, not to mention Newfoundland (Avalon) for which George Calvert received a charter before becoming a Roman Catholic. In all these instances, principle seems to have blended with expediency. Only in Rhode Island and Pennsylvania did religious freedom have profound theological undergirding. Thus the common tendency to bracket Maryland with these other two colonies as "experiments in religious liberty" confuses as much as it clarifies. Maryland's toleration is best remembered as one more instance of English liberality during a

3. John Tracy Ellis, *Catholics in Colonial America,* pp. 325–26.

century when France and Spain ruled their empires without the slightest allowance for deviation from Counter-Reformation norms.

In the spring of 1634, when the *Ark* and the *Dove* had discharged their small company of sixteen to twenty gentlemen (all or nearly all Roman Catholic) and two or three hundred servants and laborers (predominantly Protestant), the town of Saint Mary's was founded on the Potomac. The settlement which gradually took shape was in a social and legal sense unique among English colonies: nowhere else was the manorial system with its attendant distinctions and privileges and with its aristocratic and seignorial life so fully established and realized. "At the beginning," wrote C. M. Andrews, "Maryland was no mere palatinate on paper; it was a land of actual manors, demesne lands, free-hold tenements, rent rolls, and quitrents. . . . Socially there was a great gulf fixed between the upper and lower classes."[4] The story of Maryland in the seventeenth century is that of the gradual but often violent breaking down of this system. Nevertheless, the colony prospered for many reasons: it was a healthful, pleasant site; its farm lands were lush and fertile; Leonard Calvert was farsighted and firm in his governing, and he avoided the terrible mistakes of Virginia. Diversified agriculture was practiced at first, but tobacco rapidly became the staple crop and the main base of the colony's economy. The resulting plantation system accorded well with the paternalism implicit in the Calverts' hopes for creating a medieval barony in America.

The extremely complex and tumultuous political development in Maryland during the seventeenth century can here be only briefly summarized. Her first difficulties arose over the territorial claims of neighboring Virginia. Quarrels over the possession of the Isle of Kent in the Potomac estuary near the Maryland shore led William Claiborne of Virginia to armed combat. This island had been an active parish of Virginia and had sent delegates to the House of Burgesses, but ultimately it was yielded to Maryland. Aside from these hostilities, Maryland's first decade was relatively peaceful; but its future was threatened both by the deterioration of royal authority in England and by the constant growth of Puritan strength in the colony itself. For two years after 1644—the "Plundering Time"—public order broke down almost completely while Richard Ingle and his men, incited by Claiborne, carried on their depredations, allegedly on behalf of Parliament. To preserve his province in this darkening situation the proprietor in 1648 appointed a Protestant, William Stone, to replace the lately deceased Leonard Calvert as governor. More firmly to establish the

4. *The Colonial Period in American History*, 2:297.

principle of religious liberty, he bound the new governor by a very specific oath not to "trouble, molest, or discountenance any person . . . professing to believe in Jesus Christ, and in particular no Roman Catholick, for or in respect of his or her religion, nor in his or her free exercise thereof . . . and to relieve and protect any person so molested or troubled." [5]

To the same end the Maryland Assembly on 21 April 1649 passed its celebrated Act Concerning Religion, putting the long-practiced policy of toleration in precise terms. Roman Catholics, though a minority in the colony, probably dominated the assembly by a small margin; and certainly proprietary pressure hastened the act's passage. Its concluding article contained the following stipulations:

> And whereas the inforceing of the conscience in matters of Religion hath frequently fallen out to be of dangerous Consequence in those commonwealths where it hath been practised . . . Be it Therefore . . . enacted . . . that noe person or persons whatsoever within this Province . . . professing to believe in Jesus Christ, shall from henceforth bee any waies troubled, Molested or discountenanced for or in respect of his or her religion nor in the free exercise thereof . . . nor any way compelled to the beliefe or exercise of any other Religion against his or her consent.[6]

These idealistic provisions were preceded by narrower and harsher articles: (1) that deniers of the Trinity receive the death penalty; (2) that the Virgin, Apostles, and Evangelists be not spoken of reproachfully; (3) that reproachful names for religious groups (papist, heretick, puritan, etc.) be not used; and (4) that the "Sabbath" or Lord's day called "Sunday" be not profaned.

This law in no way advanced the position taken by the Calverts from the beginning: it simply documented the assembly's support of past policy. Almost certainly the Roman Catholic deputies in the assembly supported it, and probably the more moderate Protestants did too, valuing the peace that such toleration promised to secure for the colony. The more fervent Puritans, wishing to impose their own principles, opposed it altogether and insisted on including the first article, which is an adaptation of a parliamentary statute then in force in England. Opportunity for Puritan revolt increased when Stone left the colony in 1651 and designated Thomas Greene, a Roman Catholic and a Royalist, as his deputy. Parliament, now firmly in Puritan hands, dispatched an investigative commission which

5. Maryland Archives, *Proceedings of the Council, 1636–67,* 2:210.

6. Maryland Archives, *Proceedings and Acts of the General Assembly,* 1:244–47.

temporarily deposed Stone and asserted its own authority. Baltimore retrieved the situation but soon faced new difficulties. Fired by social and economic grievances against Catholic magnates and manorial lords, the Puritans called an assembly in 1654 which repudiated the proprietor's authority and abrogated the Toleration Act. Aided by Roundheads from Virginia, they captured Stone and routed his forces at a battle on the Severn in 1655. The victorious Puritans then outlawed Roman Catholicism, plundered the estates of the Jesuits, forced all priests into exile, and executed at least four Roman Catholics. Lord Baltimore regained his proprietary privileges in 1657 only on condition that Josias Fendall, a Protestant, serve as governor in Stone's place.

After the Stuart Restoration, Maryland's political and religious affairs were hardly less troubled. In 1660 an antiproprietary party gained temporary control; other revolts occurred in 1676 and 1681, with deep-seated economic grievances and religious animosity figuring centrally in each. Finally in 1689, as the Maryland concomitant to the Glorious Revolution, an insurgent "Protestant Association" led by John Goode took control of the government and held power until 1691, when King William III vacated the Baltimore charter and made Maryland a royal province with Sir Lionel Copley as governor, the Calverts being allowed to retain their property rights. In 1692 the Church of England was formally established, though an approved law was not passed until 1702, and in 1695 the capital was moved to the Protestant town of Annapolis.

Maryland continued as a royal colony until 1715, when the Calvert heir was reinvested with a proprietary charter—two years after his father had led the family back into the Anglican communion. (The "Anglican phase" of the colony's church history has been considered in chap. 12 above.) Dissenters probably constituted the great majority of seventeenth-century settlers, but because of the diversity of these groups and their lack of solidarity except in times of civil conflict, they are treated in connection with various denominational narratives in subsequent chapters.

THE ROMAN CATHOLIC CHURCH IN ENGLAND AND IN MARYLAND

The church history of Maryland during the entire colonial period is closely related to the conflicts and difficulties of the Roman Catholic church in the mother country. In England its constituency was a persecuted and highly suspect minority, prospering slightly when royal favor or a turn in foreign affairs so conduced, suffering severely when events led to a resurgence of overt hostility, and inhibited always by the paucity of clergy, the absence of a regular hierarchy, and many social or political seductions to apostasy.

England might be said to have been constituted as a Roman Catholic mission field in 1570 when Pope Pius V excommunicated Queen Elizabeth and released Roman Catholics from allegiance to her. The massacre of Saint Bartholomew's Eve in France (1572) heightened animosity even more, and severe penal legislation was enacted in 1580 and 1585 against the practice of Roman Catholic religion by either laity or priests. Yet missionary work had already begun. A seminary in exile to train an English priesthood had been founded at Douai (Flanders) in 1568, and missionary priests had been entering England at least since 1574. In 1580 Edmund Campion and Robert Persons left the Jesuit residence at Saint Omer across the channel, and thus began the long, fruitful, but conflict-ridden English missionary campaign of the Society of Jesus. A year later (1581) Cardinal William Allen was made "prefect of the mission," and from time to time thereafter a cardinal was designated as "protector" of English interests. In 1622 Pope Gregory XV established the Congregation de Propaganda Fide to oversee the work of missions everywhere.

Although there were perhaps fifty priests in the English mission by 1610, it remained without episcopal supervision until 1623, when William Bishop was appointed vicar apostolic. Bishop died in less than a year, but set up subvicariates and archdeaconries whose heads formed the core of a "chapter" which exercised a measure of regulation in his absence. Bishop Richard Smith, who succeeded him, strengthened the chapter further. It needed what strength it had, for after 1631 English Catholics were again without resident supervision until James II allowed the consecration of a vicar apostolic who then consecrated three others. The realm was then divided into four districts, the American colonies being informally considered part of the London district until officially so designated in 1757. Since these men often led a harried existence, and since their clergy were often virtually the employees of various "recusant" families, a great deal of effective direction came from the English provincial of the Society of Jesus. This division of authority, when imposed on ancient rivalries of the regular and secular clergies, continued to disrupt Roman Catholic work in England for nearly two centuries. Pope Benedict XIV finally resolved the issue in 1753, though not even the pope could quiet the resentments building up against the Jesuits.

During the first decade in Maryland, the conduct of church affairs was entirely in the hands of Jesuit priests and a few lay brothers associated with them. They were, of course, responsible to the English provincial of their order. Andrew White and John Altham, who quietly joined the initial company as it passed the Isle of Wight, were thus able to renew the Jesuit mission in the Chesapeake area which had been attempted under Spanish auspices in 1570–72. From the start they were involved both in a parochial ministry to Roman Catholic colonists and in missionary activities among the Indians. Joined later by other Jesuit priests, these two carried on a very successful work in both directions, even converting a considerable number of the Protestant settlers. A church building was erected at Saint Mary's almost immediately, and by 1639 parish life had been established in at least four other centers. Work with the Indians also produced tangible results; and many converts were made among the Patuxents and the Piscataways, from whom the Jesuits also received large grants of land. Indian missions in Maryland, however, soon began to suffer from precisely the same difficulty that beset those in New England—the encroachment of settlers. The result was also very similar, except that in Maryland the vast land grants which the Jesuits received from the proprietor in return for settling lay brothers upon them provided material support for their church work elsewhere in the colony.

The leading spirit among these pioneer Jesuit missionaries was Father Andrew White (1579–1656), their superior until 1638 and justifiably called the Apostle to Maryland. Father White's career illustrates the life pattern of Roman Catholic priests of the English mission during these years. Born near London in Queen Elizabeth's reign, he was educated at Saint Albans College, which had been organized in Spain at Valladolid, and at the English College in Seville. He continued his studies at Douai and was ordained there in about 1605. He left for work in England, but after a year he was apprehended and banished. Father White entered the Society of Jesus, and after another season in England he took up a career as professor of scriptural studies and theology in Louvain and Liège, only journeying to England from time to time. By 1629 he had been contacted by Lord Baltimore with regard to an American colony, and he helped to advertise Maryland by writing a glowing declaration of the proprietor's intentions.

Within a month after the *Ark* and the *Dove* arrived in Maryland, Father White wrote a report to his superior general which has become the classic account of the journey and first days of the colony. His activities were diverse, encompassing regular pastoral duties at first, but also including increasing amounts of missionary work among the Piscataways. He was probably the first Englishman to reduce an American Indian language to writing, and after preparing a grammar and dictionary he also translated a catechism. For the English settlers, he sought to establish a college at Saint

Mary's. But this enterprise was shattered by Ingle's invasion of the colony in late 1644. In this anarchic period the Indian mission was laid waste, Father White and Father Thomas Copley were seized and sent back to England in chains, and the other three priests fled to Virginia. White was acquitted when tried, but he defied the rule of banishment and spent the remainder of his days in a quiet, semisecret ministry in England.

The energy and success of the Jesuits, however, had the same result in Maryland that it seemed to have in most other parts of the world. It antagonized the more numerous Protestants, very few of whom belonged to the dominant landed class, and who in any event objected to the evangelistic advances of Roman Catholicism. It also aroused the apprehensions of the proprietor, who shared (or was led to share) the somewhat Erastian attitudes of many leading Catholic families in England. Concerned about the growing discontent and fearful of a powerful ecclesiastical threat to the proprietary authority, the Calverts themselves began after 1641 to limit the activities and landholding privileges of the Jesuits. The first Lord Baltimore, while arranging for his colony, had sided with the Jesuits against the vicar apostolic, Bishop Richard Smith, who advocated expulsion of the order from England. Now a decade later the second Lord Baltimore also became involved in the church's jurisdictional conflicts. He sought to have the Jesuits replaced by secular priests or Franciscans, and even carried the matter to the Congregation de Propaganda Fide in Rome. It was finally adjudicated to his satisfaction by the general of the Society of Jesus in 1643.

Lord Baltimore's measures so severely curtailed the whole work of the church that by 1669 there were only two priests in residence, and only two thousand of the colony's twenty thousand inhabitants were regarded as faithful. In response to urgent requests from the proprietor in that year, several Jesuits and Franciscans were sent during the next decade, and the resulting Franciscan mission continued from 1672 to 1720. After 1650 the Jesuits were also active in neighboring provinces. In New York the administration of the duke of York and his Roman Catholic governor, Thomas Dongan (1682–89), provided a promising field of labor both among Roman Catholic Europeans and among the Iroquois. Maryland missionaries also carried on some early missionary work in Pennsylvania after its openness to all faiths became known.

The Glorious Revolution, as a name for the change of monarchs and the Parliamentary settlement of 1688–89, is an epitome of the Whig interpretation of England's history. From a Roman Catholic standpoint it was misnamed, because the accession of William and Mary ended many of the advantageous circumstances for Catholic missions in England and her colonies. Maryland did remain virtually the only stronghold of the Roman Catholic church, but even here the establishment of the Church of England and the enforcement of English law put Roman Catholics under serious disabilities. The period from 1692 to the American Revolution justifiably became known as the Penal Period, during which the church subsisted on a private, almost clandestine basis, while individual Catholics constantly were threatened or visited with legal actions. Since there were probably not more than three thousand Maryland Catholics in 1708, survival was a serious question. This small core nevertheless proved sufficient to guarantee the continuity of the Roman church in America, because its laity was a landed and moderately wealthy group which could sustain the church's work and was possessed of sufficient social prestige to withstand the seductions to apostasy that eighteenth-century circumstances would offer.

During this long and difficult period seventy Jesuit priests and at least seven Franciscans served in Maryland and adjacent areas, though often no more than two or three were in active service at one time. At Bohemia Manor, a vast tract of land in their possession near the Pennsylvania border which they cultivated with slave labor, the Jesuits maintained a rectory and chapel. In 1745 or 1746 they even founded a more substantial and long-lived secondary school than those at Saint Mary's (1650) and Newtown (1670), which had been established in more favorable times. At this institution several of the colony's most distinguished leaders, including John and Charles Carroll, received part of their education. In Maryland, at least, the Society of Jesus was spared the expulsion and confiscations it suffered in Portugal, Spain, Naples, and France. The Jesuits managed to survive partly through their successful resistance to the appointment of a vicar apostolic for the colonies, an appointment which, if made, would not only have aroused anti-Jacobite feelings among American Protestants and English officials, but would have brought the secular hierarchy's anti-Jesuit politics into play.[7] In Maryland, furthermore, they were able to stay on as secular priests; and in 1773, when Pope Clement XIV abolished their order, they made property arrangements for the future.[8] In any event, the American

7. Papal policy at this time still supported the deposed Stuarts as England's legitimate monarchs; the grandson of James II was a cardinal, moreover, and actively working for the suppression of the Society of Jesus. The vicars apostolic in London, including Richard Challoner, shared this disposition. American Catholics justly feared "anti-Jacobite" feeling, especially when Bonnie Prince Charlie led a rebellion against George II in 1745.

8. In 1801 the Society of Jesus was authorized in Russia, where the papal ban was not effective, and in 1805 American Jesuits affiliated with the order there. The society was restored worldwide by Pope Pius VII in 1814.

Revolution was soon to bring a new day of religious freedom, when Roman Catholic church life could be conducted above ground.

NEW YORK

The Roman Catholic history of New York properly begins only with the assumption of authority by James, duke of York, who in 1674, with Edmund Andros as governor, established a policy of religious toleration.[9] When Andros was recalled a few years later, his place was taken by the Roman Catholic deputy governor, Anthony Brockholles. From 1683 to 1685 Thomas Dongan, another Catholic governor, proved unusually successful both in maintaining domestic tranquillity and in countering the work of the French among the Iroquois in the West. At times he used English Jesuits to counteract the work of French Jesuits. Dongan also contributed to the work of his church by bringing a Jesuit as his chaplain to minister to scattered Catholics, and by inviting two others (Fathers Henry Harrison and Charles Gage) to extend such work in the colony. After the accession of James II, Andros returned to America with a commission to head a united government of New York and New England; but this plan met with determined resistance, especially in New England. When news of the king's flight was received, it collapsed completely. In New York Leisler's Rebellion and brief regime followed, and with it the violence of a bitter antipopery campaign that brought Dongan's earlier efforts to nought. The former governor, who since his retirement had taken up residence on Long Island, was forced to flee, as were the three priests whom he had admitted.

After the arrival of Governor Henry Sloughter in 1691, Leisler was duly tried and put to death, order was reestablished, and New York, like Maryland, was governed as a crown colony. Roman Catholic liberties were now categorically denied; and during the administrations of the more than thirty governors who served New York before 1776, the situation of Roman Catholics did not improve. In 1701 they were deprived of the franchise and rights of office; the Church of England was established in the lower counties; the Penal Laws were put in effect; and under Governor Bellemont "Jesuits and Popish Priests" were prohibited from entry. During a season of especially virulent anti-Catholic feeling in 1741, even a nonjuring Anglican priest was hanged. For seventy-five years Roman Catholics had no public place of worship in the colony, though occasionally the Mass was surreptitiously celebrated, as when the Jesuit priest Ferdinand Steinmayer (alias Farmer) of

9. The duke of York first gained the surrender of New Netherland in 1664, but the colony was reoccupied by the Dutch in 1673–74.

Pennsylvania would arrive incognito and convene a little congregation in the house of a devout German living on Wall Street. After the Revolution, this priest organized a congregation in New York City which became an important nucleus for further church activity when Roman Catholic immigrants began to flow into the growing city.

PENNSYLVANIA

In the proprietary domain of William Penn, including Delaware, Roman Catholics were less persecuted than elsewhere in the colonies, and quite naturally Catholics were from the earliest days among the diverse multitudes who immigrated. Father John Harvey, Governor Dongan's chaplain, visited the colony in these early years, and others followed. By 1700, in order to embarrass Penn in England, reports of the public celebration of the Mass were circulated. These threats seem not to have deflected the proprietor from his principles, but under Queen Anne the colony was finally required to enforce laws that prevented Roman Catholics from voting or holding office (1705). These laws prevailed in Pennsylvania as elsewhere until the end of the colonial period.

In 1729 Father Joseph Greaton of Maryland, after several years of mission work in Pennsylvania, took up residence in Philadelphia in order to minister to its Roman Catholics. In 1733 he was instrumental in having Saint Joseph's Church erected, the first completely public Catholic church in the English colonies. It sufficed for its English, Irish, and German constituency until 1763, when Saint Mary's was built. Meanwhile two German Jesuits arrived in 1741. One of them, Theodore Schneider, who had formerly been on the faculty at the University of Heidelberg, opened a school in Goshenhoppen outside the city; the other erected a stone chapel at Lancaster in 1742. Except for occasional outbreaks of hostility, public worship in these places was able to continue without molestation, as was the operation of a few other short-lived schools. In 1757 there were 1,365 persons, about two-thirds of them German, under the care of three Jesuit priests. The two colonial church buildings in Philadelphia, having survived the nativist riots of the nineteenth century and the ravages of urban change, still remain.

Outside of Maryland and Pennsylvania, where small islands of Roman Catholicism managed to survive either in public view or half in secret, Roman Catholic church history in the later colonial period is little more than a matter of rumor, unsubstantiated "tradition," and cautious inference. Only occasionally is there significant information about a fairly prominent individual, such as John Tatham (alias John Gray) of New Jersey, who gained some political prominence and whose house provided a refuge and convening place for occasional visiting priests. Even in Maryland Roman Catholics constituted not more than an eighth, probably only a twelfth, of the population. Richard Challoner, who was coadjutor to the vicar apostolic of the London district from 1741 to 1758, and vicar apostolic from 1758 to his death in 1781, gave this report in 1756 in connection with his continuing efforts to have a bishop or vicar apostolic sent to the colonies:

> There are no missions in any of our colonies upon the continent, excepting Mariland and Pennsilvania; in which the exercise of the Catholic religion is in some measure tolerated. I have had different accounts as to their numbers in Mariland, where they are the most numerous. By one account they were about four thousand communicants; another makes them amount to seven thousand, but perhaps the latter might design to include those in Pennsilvania, where I believe there may be two thousand. There are about twelve missionaries in Mariland, and four in Pennsilvania, all of them of the Society [of Jesus]. These also assist some few Catholics in Virginia upon the borders of Mariland, and in New Jersey bordering on Pennsilvania. As to the rest of the provinces on the continent, New England, New York, etc. if there be any straggling Catholics, they can have no exercise of religion, as no priests ever come near them; nor to judge by what appears to be the present disposition of the inhabitants, are ever likely to be admitted amongst them.[10]

A decade later Father George Hunter reported 10,000 adult communicants, and in 1785 John Carroll, who was then Superior of the American Mission, put the figures at 15,800 for Maryland, including 6,000 children and slaves. George Bancroft's estimate of 32,500 for the thirteen colonies and 12,000 for the formerly French population beyond the mountains follows the church's official estimate and represents the outside maximum. Committed adults would probably not have numbered more than a fourth or a third of this total—adequate justification for Bancroft's emphasis on the overwhelming Protestant character of colonial civilization. But however slender, these foundations proved to be a sufficient basis for renewing Roman Catholic church life when the Revolution brought substantial religious freedom to the new nation.

10. Edwin H. Burton, *The Life and Times of Bishop Challoner, 1691–1781* (New York: Longmans, Green and Co., 1909), 2:125–27.

22

PROVINCIAL AMERICA AND THE COMING OF THE ENLIGHTENMENT

George Fox's journal of his travels through the colonies from North Carolina to Rhode Island in 1671–73 leaves no doubt that its author and his hardy followers were making their way through essential wilderness. "A tedious journey we had through bogs, rivers and creeks, and wild woods where it was said never man was known to ride"—so he wrote of a day's trip beyond the Delaware. His traverse of New Jersey offered almost as little comfort:

> And we did pass with a second guide about 200 miles from New Castle, through many Indian towns and they helped us over a great river in a canoe and swam our horses over. And so we passed through the woods and bogs, and had lain many nights in the woods, and came to Middletown, a place in New Jersey, and were very glad when we got to a highway.[1]

Glad he had a right to be, for the impression left by his account is that the chief elements of American civilization were bogs, mud, and overflowing streams. What the "highway" was like we can only imagine. Such amenities as travelers found were as often given by Indian sachems as by the traditional refuges for wayfarers. Things were better on Long Island and in Rhode Island, to be sure; and if he had dared venture into the Boston area he could have seen a situation in which Puritan divines were already lamenting an excess of worldly comforts in Zion.

1. *The Journal of George Fox,* p. 619.

In another half-century, the picture everywhere would be remarkably altered. The roads were still bad—and getting mired to the hubs was to remain a basic American experience until well into the twentieth century—but in other respects the ways of English life were being impressed upon the wilderness by a half-million industrious people.

THE SHAPING OF A COLONIAL AMERICAN CULTURE

The most fundamental change, of course, was the remarkable rise in population from an estimated 360,000 in 1713 to 1,600,000 in 1760, and to nearly three million by 1776. This sensational growth resulted mostly from natural increase, for the predominance of farming together with the availability of land encouraged large families, and the colonists responded with gusto. Marriages were made early—an unmarried girl of twenty-one was "an antique virgin"—while families with a dozen children were common, and those with a score not rare. The other great factor in population growth was immigration. From England, Wales, Northern Ireland, Scotland, Germany, and many other areas the influx continued, making America even then the great melting pot of Western peoples and civilizations. Slavery accounted for 502,000 black Americans, 89.7 percent of them south of New Jersey, and they, too, were showing a natural increase not equaled elsewhere. As the foregoing chapters on religious history have made clear, moreover, this rapidly growing population included many elements of diversity besides that of nationality.

The mere fact of the colonies' growth in area and population involved still another diversifying process, in that the general subsistence economy of the early years soon yielded to many types of specialization. Agriculture itself was diversified. A few staples became predominant in the South: rice in South Carolina, tobacco in Virginia and Maryland. Baltimore and Philadelphia became great exporters of wheat and flour from their hinterlands. Accentuated by these adaptations to land and climate, but inevitable even without them, were other complicating developments. Most obvious were the growth of towns and cities with all their multifarious trades and activities, the emergence of much more clearly demarcated social classes, and the rise of clashing interest groups. The spirit of this burgeoning society was not feudal or traditional but fervently capitalistic and individualistic. The colonies were populated by individuals and groups, immigrants all, who were always beginning anew, even if they had left Europe in tears and with a determination to perpetuate its ways. America always destroyed preconceived designs, whether for Bible commonwealths or medieval baronies, and usually it assuaged the sorrow. Men and women, as in no other country, were on their own with their niches to carve.

From one end of the country to the other a Puritan emphasis on work and frugality gave impetus to the changes wrought by rising farm production and commercial growth. During the period of "salutary neglect" (1713–60), rising prices on the world market gave further inducement to international trade, while the very European wars that caused this price rise prevented England from implementing the prevailing theories of mercantilism. American produce found a wide market; American ships and traders were actively engaged in prosperous seaports from Salem to Charleston. A powerful gentry of merchants and landholders rose to social eminence and economic power in most of the colonies. In the South, where slavery fostered this trend, a closely knit but distinguished planter aristocracy had arisen; and it was already producing the kind of leadership later to flower as the "Virginia dynasty." In the coastal cities, on the other hand, a merchant class greatly increased its political and cultural importance, and set the tone of a middle-class society.

These transformations did not happen without tensions and turbulence. Both North and South, there was a strong tendency for economic factors to sharpen the cleavage between coastal areas, which often if not invariably retained preponderant influence in the colonial governments, and the so-called Old West, the long, uneven, and constantly enlarging region of back-country farmers. England's persistent refusal to solve the currency problems of the colonies heightened the tension, arousing especially sharp animosities over the issues of paper money and land banks. Indeed even aside from the conflicts which the expansion of slavery was preparing, there existed by 1760 a considerable basis for civil strife within the colonies, and these problems would remain during the succeeding decades even as the spirit of independence waxed stronger.

Beneath the discontent, however, the colonies as a whole were moving steadily toward a state of political and social self-sufficiency. In the middle of the eighteenth century real democratic freedom was still severely restricted by ecclesiastical establishments, aristocratic power blocs, restrictions on the franchise, and above all, by the extraordinary prevalence of chattel slavery; yet its advances were marked because land was easily obtained and class lines were fluid. A kind of middle-class democracy such as the world had never seen was developing. Increasing numbers of men were taking an active part in the legislative process. Except for the Anglicans, the English-speaking clergy of the churches was largely American-educated; the legal profession and a colonial judiciary were assuming form. An experienced class of leaders was emerging.

Signs of cultural self-sufficiency were becoming equally apparent by 1760. Homes of governors, planters, and successful merchants began to display the grace of distinctive architectural modes. Carpenters and cabinetmakers, freed from primitive limitations, began to study English books of design and to manifest a corresponding concern for aesthetic embellishment. Painted surfaces, fanlights, brass fixtures, gambrel roofs, and classical balustrades appeared. Meeting houses, too, lost their primitive severity and functional simplicity as Georgian towers and pilastered portals in the manner of Christopher Wren set off the newer church exteriors, and well-finished pews, chandeliers, and finely joined woodwork graced the interiors. In portraiture, the sturdy primitivism of itinerant limners gave way to the grander manner of Benjamin West, Gilbert Stuart, and John Singleton Copley. Even religious painting of traditional scope made its appearance in the work of Gustavus Hesselius.

By 1763 secondary schools had made Americans residing in the older, more settled regions the most literate people in the world, while New England possessed an educational system that was probably excelled nowhere. Six colleges from Hanover, New Hampshire, to Williamsburg, Virginia, provided an unusually broad range of possibilities for higher education, and three more would be added before the Revolution,[2] although some people still sought advanced training in England or Scotland. Ambitious publishing efforts had been undertaken in New England almost from the first. *The Bay Psalm Book* came from the press in 1641; and Samuel Willard's 914-page tome *A Compleat Body of Divinity, in Two Hundred and Fifty Expository Lectures on the Assembly's Shorter Catechism* set a North American record for size in 1726. For thirty-eight years after 1739 the press of Christopher Sauer and his son at Germantown issued a steady stream of German publications, including the famous Luther Bible of 1743. Johann Arndt's 1,388-page *Vom Wahren Christenthum* appeared in 1751. By the end of the colonial period there were over forty newspapers and over fifty public or semipublic libraries in existence.

Gradually taking shape beneath these signs of cultural maturity was a growing but unrebellious sense of common destiny. External factors con-

2. The following colleges were founded before the Revolution: Harvard (1636), William and Mary (1693), Yale (1701), the College of New Jersey at Princeton (1746), Philadelphia Academy (1751, later the University of Pennsylvania), King's College (1754, later Columbia), Brown (1764), Queen's College (1766, later Rutgers), Dartmouth (1769), and Hampden-Sydney (founded 1775, incorporated 1783).

tributed to this growth, notably the existence of an utterly alien and hostile Indian "civilization" beyond the frontier, resisting white encroachment and making frequent incursions on the westward-pushing white settlements. Ever since the New England Confederation of 1643, this peril had led the colonies to make common cause against mutual dangers. The menace of New France and New Spain accentuated that impulse. Because of these dangers and constantly improving economic interrelationships, the common history of these commonwealths, as well as their similar constitutional arrangements, became all the more important. Already one might speak of an English provincial culture that was characteristically American. The "American" himself would not become clearly aware of this fact until after 1763, when English rule was asserted over the former domain of the French, and when the king, the English Parliament, and the Board of Trade began to tighten their economic and political reins on a colonial empire which they had governed previously by such loose and haphazard methods.

The resentment and hardship resulting from these changed circumstances would lead, of course, to the War for Independence. Yet the "American Revolution" began when the first English settlers came to stay, and the complex process of colonial growth which went on for the next century and a half was just as decisive as the dramatic sequence of events that ensued between 1760 and 1776. Bernard Bailyn quite properly insists that "the Revolutionary ideology could be found intact—completely formed—as far back as the 1730s; in partial form it could be found even farther back, at the turn of the seventeenth century." [3]

No factor in the "Revolution of 1607–1760" was more significant to the ideals and thought of colonial Americans than the Reformed and Puritan character of their Protestantism; and no institution played a more prominent role in the molding of colonial culture than the church. Just as Protestant convictions were vitally related to the process of colonialization and a spur to economic growth, so the churches laid the foundations of the educational system, and stimulated most of the creative intellectual endeavors, by nurturing the authors of most of the books and the faculties of most of the schools. The churches offered the best opportunities for architectural expression and inspired the most creative productions in poetry, philosophy, music, and history.

A more specific element in the religious background was Puritanism itself, which even under Queen Elizabeth began to be a powerful factor in the transformation of English society and government. In this context the long-term American revolution should be seen as a great extension of the Crom-

3. Bernard Bailyn, *The Ideological Origins of the American Revolution,* p. xi.

wellian and Glorious revolutions. These relationships would be more readily perceptible to present-day Americans if by some accident of history the original colonies had peacefully matured as independent republics, and if generation after generation of Americans had studied the Mayflower Compact as assiduously as they now study the Declaration of Independence. With Jamestown or Plymouth Rock rather than Independence Hall as our point of focus, we would see first of all the way in which the Reformation heritage strengthened the colonist's conception of his "calling," or vocation, making him more serious, purposeful, and responsible in both his civic and economic roles. We would note in the second place the crucial susceptibility of Puritanism to transmute its power into secular impulses. This was due above all to the immense place of law (divine, natural, moral, and statutory) in its overall view. Law restrained man's sin, law humbled the sinner, law guided the saint and sinner alike in the quest for both personal holiness and an orderly society. The good man was a law-abiding man; that insistence remained even after the rapture of regeneration dropped from view. Puritanism, in a word, virtually sacrificed itself on the altar of civic responsibility. It helped to create a nation of individualists who were also fervent "moral athletes," with a strong sense of transcendent values which must receive ordered and corporate expression in the commonwealth. In this context a completely secularized son of the Puritans like Benjamin Franklin is quite as potent a symbol of the movement's lasting influence as his more orthodox contemporaries, such as Samuel Adams, Roger Sherman, and Patrick Henry.

The congregational method of governing churches, whether it stemmed from theological convictions (as in Massachusetts) or from New World necessities (as in Virginia) also strengthened the average American's desire for a voice in government, and gave him experience and competence in making his will known in an orderly and effective way. Put less abstractly, ecclesiastical localism prepared men to regard the social compact as the proper basis of government.

When joined with a pervasive antipathy to medievalism, ceremonial pomp, moral profligacy, ostentatious indolence, and aristocratic privilege, Puritanism became an even stronger factor in the formation of Whiggish attitudes. "No bishop, no king," James I had told the Hampton Court Conference in 1604. Samuel Johnson, the American Tory and Anglican convert, agreed: the colonies need a bishop, he said, if they are to remain loyal to England. In New England the people's memory of English kings was especially jaundiced, and the potency of Puritan teaching was unusually strong. It was no accident, therefore, that Boston became the chief thorn in the side of English authority. Attacks on the Stuart kings could be dusted off for service against the threat to liberty presented by Hanoverian kings and their corrupt court. Thus America, too, developed its radical opposition. Old Whig became New Whig. When seen in this large sense, Ralph Barton Perry's estimate of Puritanism's significance for the American tradition is eminently justified: "It is safe to assume that the influence of puritanism, in the broad Calvinistic sense, was a major force in the late colonial period, and that it contributed uniquely and profoundly to the making of the American mind when the American mind was in the making." And Edmund S. Morgan underlines the same point. "The Puritan Ethic as it existed among the Revolutionary generation had in fact lost for most men the endorsement of an omnipresent angry God. . . . The values and precepts derived from it, however, remained intact and were reinforced by a reading of history that attributed the rise and fall of empires to the acquisition and loss of the same virtues God had demanded of the founders of New England." [4]

"Declension" and secularization had put Puritanism's potential influence in jeopardy, to be sure, but this fact merely heightens the significance of the Great Awakening, which lifted the evangelical cause from its doldrums, revitalized the "dissenting" churches, threatened the established churches, aroused widespread suspicion of the SPG, focused attention on the threat posed by the possibility of an American bishop, and stirred up precisely those elements of the colonial population most unlikely to be fervent Loyalists on political grounds.

The Great Awakening wrote a crucial prologue to the political and ideological transformation that characterized the dramatic years between 1763 and 1775. This is not to say, however, that it was chiefly a response to social and economic pressures. Though young people may have been especially numerous among the new converts, it attracted or repelled people of every class and station, rural and urban, young and old, and in every region. And it did make forceful contributions to American self-consciousness. The leaders of the revival were the first to plan their activities in explicitly intercolonial terms. George Whitefield was perhaps the first "American" public figure to be known from New Hampshire to Georgia. He was heard by hundreds of thousands and left nobody noncommittal on his

4. Ralph Barton Perry, *Puritanism and Democracy*, pp. 18, 81. Edmund S. Morgan, "The Puritan Ethic and the American Revolution," *William and Mary Quarterly*, 3d ser. 24 (January 1967): 6.

merits; his death, which ended his seventh tour in 1770, was commented upon by the entire colonial press. Gilbert Tennent and Jonathan Edwards also achieved a large measure of intercolonial fame.

In his detailed study of the Awakening in Virginia, Professor Gewehr has emphasized the social and political implications of religious rejuvenation. It heightened back-country opposition to the religious restrictions of the royal government and conduced to a more thorough democratization of society. In a similar manner everywhere, the Awakening probably increased the willingness of people in all walks of life to open controversies, to criticize complacent dignitaries, to protest infringements of religious freedom, and to question accepted truths of constituted authorities. It also intensified the general tendency of the Reformed tradition—the religious heritage of three-fourths of the American people in 1776—to set bounds on the will of kings and the arbitrary exercise of governmental power. Above all, it awakened millennial hopes that a covenanted nation, repenting its sins and trusting in God, could become an instrument of Providence in realizing the Kingdom.[5] Taken as a whole, therefore, the religious foundations of colonial life were a powerful factor in American development. Few cultures are so intractable to purely secular categories of historical interpretation.

THE EMERGENCE OF ENLIGHTENED RELIGION

To speak of cultural maturation and growing evangelical self-consciousness is not, from the standpoint of religious history, to touch upon the only crucial developments taking place in provincial America. One of the greatest revolutions was going on quietly, even imperceptibly, in men's minds as they confronted the momentous issues of the Enlightenment. We have already mentioned how later Puritanism wrestled with this crisis of the European mind in its early stages. As early as 1710 John Wise opposed

5. See the final chapter of Wesley M. Gewehr, *The Great Awakening in Virginia, 1740–1790*. That the Great Awakening played a vital role in the American tradition there can be no doubt; but one must avoid exaggerated claims. Alan Heimert, in his *Religion and the American Mind from the Great Awakening to the Revolution*, attributes undue political influence to the predestinarian Awakeners and unduly deprecates the Arminian and liberal tradition that runs from Mayhew and Chauncy to John Adams as elitist and ineffectual. He ignores the liberal-Arminian party's influence upon the "power elite" of that day. Bailyn's work, cited in n. 3 above, provides a remarkably balanced and insightful account of Puritan and dissenting elements in the American revolutionary ideology.

The significant work of awakened Separates and Baptists in the cause of church disestablishment and religious liberty is thoroughly covered in Clarence C. Goen, *Revivalism and Separatism in New England, 1740–1800;* and in William G. McLoughlin's massive *New England Dissent, 1630–1833*.

the Saybrook Platform and the centralizing proposals of the Mathers with a natural law philosophy derived from Pufendorf. So clearly did he anticipate later revolutionary attitudes that his tracts were republished in the 1770s to bolster the Patriot cause. Samuel Johnson revealed another dimension of the new spirit in his well-reasoned break with the old Puritan order in New England. Most impressive, however, was the life work of Jonathan Edwards.

While still a very young man, Edwards read John Locke's *Essay Concerning Human Understanding* with more pleasure "than the most greedy miser finds when gathering up handfuls of silver and gold from some newly discovered treasure." A few years later he was dwelling with equal enthusiasm on the works of "the incomparable Mr. Newton." Then in his mature years, despite a career at the center of the Awakening—with all of its anti-intellectual tendencies—he infused the spirit of the Age of Reason into the faith of his fathers with a transforming sublimity equaled by no Reformed thinker of the century. He thus participated actively in the great spiritual transition that marks the end of a period when American culture was still recognizably medieval in its outlook and inner spirit, and the emergence of distinctly "modern" religious ideas. During the revolutionary era the American Enlightenment and its characteristic religious forms would flower even more luxuriantly—and with major political as well as eccelesiastical consequences.

The Rise of Rationalism

As with all large intellectual movements, the search for the origins of the Enlightenment leads into an infinite regress. The rise of the rationalistic spirit must be seen as an enlargement or continuation of scientific and naturalistic impulses which gained special boldness of expression during late medieval and Renaissance times as the intellectual heritage of antiquity was being rediscovered. There followed a long and involved series of theoretical, mathematical, and experimental efforts to explain the world of nature in a reasoned, orderly, and verifiable way. Modern science came into existence with epoch-making discoveries succeeding each other in several fields. But most earthshaking and provocative in the theological and philosophical sense was the transformation in cosmology demanded by the discoveries of Copernicus (1543), Galileo (1610), and Newton (1687), to name only the three most famous. Paralleling these scientific contributions was a series of equally disturbing philosophical statements such as those of Nicholas of Cusa (1440), Giordano Bruno (1584), and Descartes (1644). Most basically, Western man was now required to come to terms with an infinite universe in which the motions of known inanimate entities could be explained in terms of mathematically demonstrable laws. Alfred North Whitehead, his focus chiefly on the culminating work of Newton, has made a famous summation of the scientific achievements involved in this collective enterprise:

> The subject of the formation of the three laws of motion and of the law of gravitation deserves critical attention. The whole development of thought occupied exactly two generations. It commenced with Galileo and ended with Newton's *Principia;* and Newton was born in the year that Galileo died. Also the lives of Descartes and Huygens fall within the period occupied by these great terminal figures. The issue of the combined labours of these four men has some right to be considered as the greatest single intellectual success which mankind has achieved.[6]

Newton, the great terminal figure in Whitehead's sequence, was hardly a "man of the Enlightenment." He regarded his work as a defense of the Christian faith, and in later years he busied himself with elaborate exegesis of biblical prophecies. Yet the fundamental Newtonian ideas were soon reverberating through almost every corridor of Western thought. Reformulation became a necessity, with many social and political factors piling need on need; and "Enlightenment" is the name given to the vast and multifarious process of reconstruction that took place. Enlightenment thought, therefore, is not a well-defined systematic structure of consistent ideas. Its "productive significance," says Ernst Cassirer, its greatest analyst,

> is revealed not so much in any particular thought content as in the use the Enlightenment makes of philosophic thought, and the position and task it assigns to such thought. . . . Philosophy is no longer limited to the realm of mere thought; it demands and finds access to that deeper order of things whence all intellectual activity, like thought itself, springs.[7]

Philosophy becomes "the all-comprehensive medium" in which the principles of natural science, law, government, and religion are formulated, developed, and founded. The Enlightenment is thus not a doctrine, but a campaign for world renovation based on certain broad presuppositions which are informed above all by the achievements of the new science.

In this enormous task no one thinker was more important or more revealing than the man so often designated as America's philosopher, John

6. Alfred North Whitehead, *Science and the Modern World* (New York: New American Library, 1948), pp. 46–47.

7. Ernst Cassirer, *The Philosophy of the Enlightenment,* p. vii.

Locke (1632–1704). No one thinker so well exemplifies the Enlightened desire to take the thrust of scientific method, so central in Newton, and to apply it to all the agitated problems of the day: the operations of human understanding, the need for toleration, the nature and basis of civil government, and—most germane to the present study—the genius of the Christian religion.[8] In terms of subsequent thought, Locke is not so much a milestone as the designer of a large section of highway. He more nearly personifies the reigning spirit of the eighteenth century than any other thinker. His thought is guided by three great optimistic principles: that the chief end of man is felicity in this world and probably in the next; that man's rational powers, if rightly disciplined and employed, provide a means for solving the problems of life and attaining this felicity; and that the essential truths of such a view are so self-evident, and man himself so responsive to such evidence, that progress in human felicity is inevitable.

Still another reason for Locke's representative significance is that he was a champion of common sense, with unique gifts for gathering the presuppositions and implications of his age into an eminently reasonable system. He was also a moderate; and especially as a religious thinker does he exhibit these gifts, being opposed to antichristian or atheistic views and active in the controversy against the deists. He was in truth a *defensor fidei,* exuding intellectual confidence as he faced the perennial paradoxes of existence and the ancient mysteries of Christianity. No thinker better exemplified that confidence in man's mental powers which gives the Age of Reason its name. In the eighteenth century's "Deistic Controversy," in the debate over the nature of Christian morality, and in the ongoing contest with skeptics, there gradually came to prevail among the educated classes a climate of opinion in which moderate common-sense views prevailed. High-ranking churchmen as well as poets, essayists, and statesmen expressed this outlook. The effect of the Enlightenment on Christian thought thus became deep and pervasive. The central—indeed, almost the solitary—thesis of its religious message is expressed in the title of Locke's great work, *The Reasonableness of Christianity* (1695).

BUTLER, PALEY, AND THE SCOTTISH PHILOSOPHY

The history of British philosophy in the century after Locke can in no sense be reviewed here, not even the crucial developments linked with Locke,

8. Locke's treatises indicate this full gamut of concern: *Essay Concerning Human Understanding* (London, 1690; five editions by 1706), *Letters on Toleration* (1689–90), *Two Treatises of Government* (1690), *Some Thoughts Concerning Education* (1693), *The Reasonableness of Christianity* (1695), and *Paraphrase of Romans, First and Second Corinthians, Galatians, Ephesians* (1705–07).

Berkeley, and Hume, except to say that churchmen all over the world trembled when they faced what they regarded as the "skeptical" implications of David Hume (1711–76), particularly his critique of natural theology, the age's great stock in trade. (Hume saw fit to have his *Dialogues* on this subject published posthumously.) Churchmen were equally disturbed by the mechanistic psychology expounded by David Hartley in his *Observations on Man* (1749). Utilitarianism, materialism, and atheism seemed to be building great empires in European thought with weapons drawn from Locke.[9] Against these enemies Berkeley's theistic idealism was too subtle and too contrary to common sense to be an effective defense. At the other extreme were the champions of strictest orthodoxy who would brook no accommodation of modern ideas and the revivalists who often denied the compatibility of true religion and philosophical discourse altogether. There was thus great need for men who could provide intellectual defenses for a middle empire of reasonableness and a moderate sort of orthodoxy. From three sources came notable responses to this need: Bishop Joseph Butler (1692–1752), Archdeacon William Paley (1743–1805), and the "Common Sense" school of Scottish philosophy, led chiefly by Thomas Reid (1710–96) and Dugald Stewart (1753–1828).

Butler's celebrated work was his *Analogy of Religion, Natural and Revealed, To the Constitution of Nature* (1736), a closely reasoned attack on the deists in which he argued that the objections against the Christian faith apply equally to natural religion, and that given their common assumptions and the limitations of human reason, a prudent man will not abandon the church. Though far less impressive than his essays on ethics, Butler's *Analogy,* despite its skeptical tendencies and lack of positive argument or edifying content, was for a full century regarded as a major defense against infidel attack.

Paley's great contribution came toward the century's end. He provided a new and even more popular synthesis of empirical science and reasonable religion. Unlike Butler he wrote with marvelous clarity and with much greater confidence in the power of rational argument. Paley, too, wrote on ethics and political economy, taking what was often regarded as a dangerously utilitarian position; but he was most widely celebrated for two other efforts. One was in the extremely popular field of "Christian evidences," where his

9. These radical tendencies were an intrinsic element of the Enlightenment, and they became increasingly important with the passing years, especially in France, where Condillac did much to advance Lockean ideas. This may, indeed, be the movement's most essential phase. In provincial America, however, radical views had very few advocates. Peter Gay describes the "Era of Pagan Christianity" in *The Enlightenment: The Rise of Modern Paganism.*

book of that title (1794), supported by a companion work on Saint Paul (1790), became a classic. In these works Paley sought to demonstrate the reliability of the New Testament, drawing chiefly on the proof from miracles, but also marshaling other arguments to prove that the biblical writers were trustworthy witnesses. In his *Natural Theology* (1802) he supplied the English-speaking world with its best compendium of arguments for the existence and benevolence of Deity on the grounds of the design in nature. In this work he offered his famous (though unoriginal) argument that, just as we infer a watchmaker on discovering a watch, so we can infer an Almighty Designer when we study the marvelous designs of the human eye, a bird's beak, or a snake's mouth. His book, indeed, became a kind of rationalistic introduction to natural history. Paley summarizes the religious implications of the *saeculum rationalisticum* with unrivaled lucidity and comprehensiveness. He was widely imitated, and his message, directly or indirectly, reached millions of students, ministers, and churchgoers before he passed out of vogue.

Common Sense Realism (as it was often called) was a characteristic flowering of the Enlightenment and of the Scottish renaissance of the eighteenth century. It was developed by the Presbyterian Moderates who successfully controlled the established Kirk of Scotland and the four Scottish universities, which were then at the height of their influence and vitality, while the two great English universities were at the bottom of theirs. The founder and most creative contributor to this school of philosophy was Thomas Reid of Aberdeen and (later) Glasgow University; and his more systematic disciple, Dugald Stewart of Edinburgh University. The first great exponent in America was John Witherspoon, who left Scotland in 1768 to become president of Princeton.

The Scottish Philosophy, as it came to be called, sought to create first of all a position free from absurdity or unreasonable subtlety (faults that were laid to Berkeley and Hume despite the deep respect shown them). In other words, they tried to give solid metaphysical content to common-sense acceptances. In accord with their age they rang the changes on the greatness of Bacon and Newton, and they insisted on being scientific and empirical. They denounced the reduction of man's mental and moral powers to physical terms, however, and turned their empiricism inward with a view to clarifying the nature of man's faculties. In this enterprise they "discovered" the agency or genuine powers of man: first, a rational freedom that made man a genuine cause (not a complex reactor mechanism); and second, an ability to make self-evident moral intuitions (not simply pain and pleasure judgments). In addition, they discovered principles which were anterior to experience (thus in a way anticipating Immanuel Kant), and argued further that man experienced the objective world without the mediation of "ideas." They thus respected the ancient dualisms: mind and matter, subject-object, and Creator-Creation, by the same token escaping materialism, idealism, subjectivism, hedonism, utilitarianism, pantheism, and skepticism. Because they did accord with the "common sense" of things, the Scottish philosophers produced, in short, precisely the kind of apologetic philosophy that Christians in the Age of Reason needed. Above all they provided a wonderful philosophical corollary to the one thinker who vies with Hume as Scotland's greatest philosopher of the century, and who outdistanced all of them in concrete influence: Adam Smith (1723–90), Reid's predecessor in moral philosophy at Glasgow and the author of a treatise on the "Moral Sentiments," whose *Wealth of Nations* (1776) became the classic exposition of laissez faire capitalism.

That the Scottish Philosophy reached as large an audience as Butler or Paley is unlikely, since its best expositors wrote in accordance with the technical demands of their calling; but as digested and retailed by others, the Scottish Philosophy achieved a wider influence by far than any other school. It also broke down denominational barriers with amazing facility, becoming very popular in Great Britain, almost the official philosophy of France under the Restoration and July Monarchy, and a strong influence at the Roman Catholic University of Louvain. In America it would rise to dominance for longer or shorter periods among Unitarians, Congregationalists, Presbyterians, "American" Lutherans, and Episcopalians, as well as among many others whose church ties were tenuous. During the first two-thirds of the nineteenth century, at least, it was to become among American Protestants the chief philosophical support to theological and apologetical enterprises.

REFORMULATIONS IN THEOLOGY

Not many Christians, obviously, would or could go all the way with deists and the more extreme *philosophes*. Genuine radicalism did exist, but it was a small subcurrent in Britain and almost unheard of in the colonies. Various sorts of orthodox traditionalism, on the other hand, had strong popular support. But among many thoughtful liberals and moderates a distinct form of Enlightenment theology arose, though men differed as to which doctrines deserved attack or defense. The English Unitarian John Taylor of Norwich thought that the issue lay with the doctrine of Original Sin, and he directed a scriptural and rational barrage in its direction. The liberal Bostonian Congregationalist Charles Chauncy delivered his most vigorous salvo against the "limited atonement" and eventually went all the way to Universalism. The Anglican latitudinarian Daniel Whitby (1638–1726) considered the doctrine of predestination most in need of reformulation. Samuel Clarke (1675–1729) directed his attention to *The Scripture-Doctrine of the Trinity* (1712) and made recommendations for revising the Book of Common Prayer on this subject. Archbishop John Tillotson had anticipated Locke (who took much comfort in so prestigious a forerunner) by arguing for a redefinition of faith as intellectual assent. Yet many of these men, even to the radical Unitarian Joseph Priestly, were conservative in their views of scriptural authority and the centrality of miracles. Despite this diversity, there emerged a recognizable type of "enlightened" Christianity, several chief characteristics of which can be enumerated:

1. It was Arminian in its desire to emphasize or augment the human role in redemption. Man's freedom and goodness accordingly were posited, the possibility of falling from grace admitted, and the particular application of God's predestinating decrees denied.

2. It emphasized the simplicity of Christian faith and ridiculed the complexity of both medieval and post-Reformation dogmatics. Locke in a famous reduction noted only two "rules": believe in Jesus as Lord, and lead a virtuous life.

3. Ethics was the chief end of its advocacy. Archdeacon Paley argued that damnation in hell betokened God's goodness in that it roused men to lives of virtue. More profoundly, this interest turned most of the best minds of the time to the philosophical analysis of morality.

4. Due to its emphasis on simplicity and morality, "reasonable Christianity" tended to view any credence in the objective nature of the sacraments as superstitious, and to deprecate the ministry except insofar as it concerned itself with moral instruction.

5. Enlightened theology was usually exceedingly unhistorical, in that it mistrusted tradition and ignored the ways in which thought and belief are conditioned by the historical situation. It rather viewed reason as freeing man from history and its oppressive relativities. This, however, is not to deny that certain great thinkers of the Enlightenment really began what Ernst Cassirer called "the conquest of the historical world," a conquest which the nineteenth century would complete.

6. The idea of progress was given a prominent place in both secular and religious thinking. The typical thinker of the Enlightenment was optimistic about man and confident that his destiny on earth would involve a continual conquest of nature and ever greater human felicity. In Christian terms, this would lead to a postmillennial eschatology; that is, the kingdom of God

would be realized in history, whereupon Christ or his Spirit would in some sense return.

7. Man's relation to God, in the enlightened scheme of things, was increasingly understood in impersonal terms. "Deity" (a favorite word) was conceived as the Architect and Governor of the universe, who ruled from long ago and far away through immutable law, a *Dieu fainéant*. The enlightened man might say, "The earth is the Lord's and He made it," but he had trouble with "The Lord is my shepherd." He knew God as Power and Principle, not as a person capable of love and wrath. Enlightened piety, therefore, was rational, reserved, and law-centered. Its preachers were the surrogates of a Judge; their sermons, like a winter day, were short and cold.

Needless to say, not every person (or even every intellectual) of the age was "Enlightened" in precisely the manner just described. Each country also had its dissident voices: pietists, Methodists, and New Lights on the one hand; secular rebels, skeptics, pessimists, and precursors of romanticism on the other. The basic intellectual trend of the century, however, is unmistakable, and in the perspective of history the Enlightenment's overall accomplishment clearly constitutes a decisive modern rupture with the medieval tradition even though many continuities remained.

The influence of these new currents of thought in America was very strong. Yet the ultimate popularity of Locke, Butler, Paley, Reid, and Smith should not veil the hindrances to their advance in a country where Puritanism was still so lively a reality, and where the Great Awakening aroused such widespread concern for evangelical Christianity. Even in the "broad and catholick" party of Boston, whence came much of the opposition to the revivals, the wines of the Enlightenment were sipped with cautious moderation. As late as 1782 Charles Chauncy thought it wise to publish his defense of Universalism in London—anonymously. Yet the wines were sipped, and the inevitable result was an extension of rationalism. Under ambitious and forward-looking spirits like Cotton Mather the rational principle in the older Puritanism was given wider berth. It also became an integral part of the witness of the Old Calvinist, or Moderate, party in the years after the Great Awakening. The coming of John Witherspoon from Scotland to Princeton in 1768 initiated a similar tradition among the Presbyterians. In the Anglican clergy of the South the new theology also won numerous adherents. When Devereux Jarratt went to conventions of the Virginia ministers, he heard "some of the most sacred doctrines of Christianity treated with ridicule and profane burlesque."

Against this total background of theological and philosophical change, most of the men who were to become the new nation's founding fathers were led into essentially enlightened modes of understanding history, government, law, God, man, and destiny. This is as true for Ethan Allen of Vermont's Green Mountains as it is for George Washington of Virginia's tidewater. And from each of the three main sections of the country would come one man who by international standards represented the classical Enlightenment at its typical best: John Adams, Benjamin Franklin, and Thomas Jefferson. Each of these men sought to express the new rationalism with complete intellectual integrity. Each of them tried in a serious way, through a long and active career, to deal coherently with the separate but interrelated problems of man, God, nature, and society. Each of them exemplified in a unique way how the Puritan heritage, an emerging pattern of middle-class democracy, and the fresh influences of the Enlightenment were preparing the American colonies for a common and united destiny.

23
THE REVOLUTIONARY ERA

Seventeen sixty-three was a memorable year for Great Britain and her American colonies: the Treaty of Paris ended a half-century of conflict—at least for the present. Quebec and Florida were in English hands, the power of France on the North American continent was broken, and Spain was relegated to remote expanses beyond the Mississippi. The situation seemed to promise a new day for Anglo-American ambitions in the New World. Further enhancing this possibility, the Conspiracy of Pontiac in the West had been shattered. Yet neither in Europe nor in America did an Era of Good Feelings ensue. Quite to the contrary, the new situation entailed difficulties that in a dozen years resulted in open conflict, followed by eight years of declared war. With independence won, the new nation then entered upon another fifteen years or more of domestic uncertainty, conflict, and experimentation before the basic political forms of a democratic country had been established. It is this period as a whole—from 1763 to 1800—that the term "revolutionary era" is here meant to designate.

In political terms, the four decades between the end of the "Old French War" and the election of Thomas Jefferson as president of the United States divide with a minimum of confusion into four fairly definite eventful periods, each of them very familiar to most Americans:

1760–1775	A time of deteriorating relations with England and of growing sentiment for independence
1775–1783	A time of war, reorganization, and state-forming
1783–1789	The so-called Critical Period during which the problems of federalism were exposed, fiercely contended, and officially resolved
1789–1800	The Federalist Period in United States history, a period of crucial self-definition during which the problems of fed-

eral union under the Constitution and foreign relations of the new state were settled

In the events of these four periods the churches, their ministers, and their membership were, of course, actively involved.

RELIGION AND THE REVOLUTIONARY MOVEMENT

The years of mounting crisis found the churches implicated on both sides of every issue under debate, but in general they became increasingly identified with the Patriot tide of opinion and contributed powerfully to its rise. In terms of church affiliation, the chief strength of Loyalism lay in the Anglican clergy everywhere and in the Anglican laity of the middle and northern colonies. There was also considerable Tory sentiment among the wealthier Quakers, the older Lutheran clergy, and the leaders of the pacifistic German sects. In the South, however, the Anglican laity joined the Patriot cause and furnished much of its leadership. All in all, the Protestant disposition of the American people, regardless of how secularized their Puritanism had become, involved their viewing the king and English rule with suspicion. Their tribal memories of early persecution strengthened this hostility, while proposals for sending a bishop to America constantly reinforced it. In fact, the drift of American opinion during these years can hardly be explained unless one takes into account the deeply ingrained "antiprelatical" bias of all but a small percentage of the population. The Scotch-Irish, Scots, and Irish, as well as the fervent evangelical "dissenters" still suffering discrimination in Virginia and some other colonies, had more positive grounds for similar views. Parliament's solicitude for Canadian Roman Catholicism, shown in the Quebec Act (1774), provided additional provocation, while American Roman Catholics, on the other hand, had good reasons for wanting freedom from English disabilities. That the "Black Regiment" of colonial clergy addressing large, regular audiences from positions of great prestige was a major force in arousing the spirit of independence after 1761, was asserted at the time by both Tory and Patriot interpreters. Professor Bridenbaugh in his masterful history of the subject has heavily underlined the revolutionary potency of the "Great Fear of Episcopacy":

> For us of the twentieth century, it is very, very difficult to recover imaginatively a real understanding of the enormous effect of this controversy on the opinions and feelings of a pious, dissenting people grown accustomed to ecclesiastical self-government and currently engaged in a struggle to protect their liberties in the civil sphere. The

bad news or threats they read in every week's newspaper produced a cumulative effect like the rising crescendo of a bolero. The agitation over an American episcopate reached its peak by 1770, and the public had grown almost frenzied in the course of it.[1]

Far more important than the overt activities of ministers and church assemblies or the resentment of specific minorities were the factors stressed in the foregoing chapter on the longterm American Revolution, 1607–1776. This was the revolution in men's hearts, to which, in John Adams's view, the Declaration of 1776 gave only belated expression. And the source of its strength lay in the religious substratum, which was always Nonconformist, Dissenting, and Puritan in its basic disposition. For this reason the heroes and leaders of the radical opposition in eighteenth-century politics—John Milton, Algernon Sidney, John Locke, John Trenchard, Thomas Gordon, James Burgh—gained a vastly stronger following in America than in England. But much more than a simple dislike for the existing form of government and a desire for political independence developed in the minds of these people. A new conception of freedom and equality took shape, involving conceptions of God, man, human rights, the state, and history, which became inseparable from the Enlightenment's outlook on reality. On 4 July 1776, these conceptions became a cornerstone of the American political tradition; during this period they were given further embodiment in state constitutions (and in due course in the federal Constitution). In the words of the nation's Patriot heroes and Founding Fathers these ideas were woven into the very texture of American thinking. The American nation was born in the full illumination of the Enlightenment, and this fact would permanently distinguish it from every other major power in the world.[2]

The influence of the Enlightenment and its leading themes upon many thinkers and religious movements of the eighteenth century is evident, but after 1760 its political uses and implications came to be drawn upon with special fervor, and in this connection John Locke again became a much valued resource. His reasoned justification of the Glorious Revolution now became peculiarly relevant for the colonies as they strove to define their liberties and to limit the authority of Parliament and King George III. Government,

1. Carl Bridenbaugh, *Mitre and Sceptre: Transatlantic Faiths, Ideas, Personalities, and Politics, 1689–1775*, p. 313.

2. Only France would have a vaguely similar experience; but in that case the French Revolution merely engrafted the Enlightenment experience on a tradition that already included centuries of national glory. After 1800, moreover, a succession of kings, emperors, and republics would break and diffuse the influence of the Revolution. The rallying to General de Gaulle was hardly an evocation of 1789.

Locke had affirmed, is not absolute, but rather the result of a "social compact" made by free, equal, and independent men. It is instituted with the consent of the governed and should be reformed or replaced if it fails to fulfill its purpose. Permeating Locke's thought, of course, was an abiding confidence in natural law, which, though eternal and transcendent, was yet accessible to human reason whenever the mind was freed from bondage, superstition, and the passions. Such law controlled the relations of mankind as well as the natural order of things. Since man was a cosmopolitan constant in this scheme, Americans often saw themselves as sharing a common cause with the champions of republican principles in ancient Greece and Rome; and the Declaration of Independence would be addressed to a "candid world."

In one very important respect, however, Americans were participating in a fairly revolutionary departure from the traditional precepts of natural law. Reflecting a typical Puritan emphasis on inward experience, they shifted the emphasis from the *order* of nature and government to the reality of natural *rights*. In other words, they "interiorized" the significance of natural law and rendered it more man-centered, stressing human rights rather than cosmic order, the individual rather than the state, liberty rather than obedience. To a remarkable degree these solemnly proclaimed "rights" were the end product of centuries of English legal and constitutional history, clarified by the momentous revolutions of the seventeenth century and deepened by the Puritan's persistent emphasis on covenantal responsibility. In America, a generation of remarkable men thought through the implications of this political philosophy and invested it with new urgency and relevance.

After the military phase of the Revolution was accomplished, political issues again moved into the foreground, and problems of self-government rather than relations with king and Parliament now provided the occasion for controversy and creative thought. Enlightened motifs continued to prevail—perhaps above all a vast faith in written constitutions—but more than ever these motifs were modified by a realistic hardheadedness and an absence of illusion about the sinfulness of men. The *Federalist Papers,* published in 1787–88, as well as John Adams's defenses of the American constitutions, can be read as Puritan contributions to Enlightenment political theory.

In all the heated controversies of this period the churches were almost as much divided as the country. Liberalism in theology was by no means a concomitant of liberalism in social, economic, or political advocacy; nor was the orthodox host any more solidly conservative in policy. The theologically conservative Patriot heroes, Patrick Henry and Samuel Adams, showed more than average political radicalism. Daniel Shays's rebels of 1786 were probably more orthodox than their opposition. In Massachusetts generally, the more orthodox west stood opposed to the emerging Unitarianism of the Boston area where the ultra-Federalists would later make their last stand. The clergy, no doubt, held more conservative political views than their constituencies as a general rule, and after 1795 they became increasingly alarmed over the rise of the outspoken infidelity exemplified by Thomas Paine. By this time they were also disturbed by the declining state of the churches and the threat, in the person of Thomas Jefferson, of a president who was an articulate critic of "sectarianism" in religion and an eloquent defender of deism. Yet even in Connecticut, where President Timothy Dwight of Yale was exposing the errors of Jeffersonian infidelity, evangelical Baptists and Methodists together with High Church Anglicans were moving toward the Democratic Republican party in order to oppose the Congregational standing order. Theological-political correlations, in other words, are not easily established.

THE CHURCHES DURING THE REVOLUTIONARY ERA

The church-historical significance of this turbulent epoch is many-sided. First and most obviously, the churches experienced a period of distraction, disruption, and decline, for reasons that any political and military history of the period makes obvious. Second, the protracted political crisis extending from the Stamp Act furor to the election of Jefferson accelerated the advance of Enlightenment philosophy, natural theology, and secularized thought. It also gave priority to political issues, and hence to governmental or legalistic ways of conceiving traditional theological questions. In short, the age introduced modes of thought which in subtle ways contributed to theological transformation. Third, the churches were to varying degrees required to respond to the new political circumstances created by the War for Independence and the Treaty of Paris (1783). Some needed literally to reconstitute themselves, and nearly all experienced significant changes. Fourth, all religious groups were provided with new opportunities for increased vitality and growth by important adjustments of church and state relationships, adjustments which they, in turn, had helped to bring about. Established churches lingered in New England, to be sure, while social arrangements and Protestant pressure maintained "quasi-establishments" in most other regions; yet a new epoch in the history of religious freedom had unquestionably opened.

The Religious Depression

The revolutionary era was a period of decline for American Christianity as a whole. The churches reached a lower ebb of vitality during the two decades after the end of hostilities than at any other time in the country's religious history. In many ways the war itself began the process of decline: occasioning the flight of partisan ministers when opposing armies approached (Samuel Hopkins from British-occupied Newport, the rector of King's Chapel from encircled Boston); drawing many ministers into the chaplaincy (Timothy Dwight with the Continental army, Samuel Seabury with the British); or leading some into actual combat (the Reverend General Muhlenberg leading his brigade against Cornwallis at Brandywine; the aged Naphtali Daggett, professor of divinity at Yale, dashing off with his old fowling piece against the invaders of New Haven). In addition to these instances and hundreds like them, the more generalized disruption and occasional devastation wrought by the war left the churches disorganized and their members preoccupied by burning questions of a military or political nature.

As for the years after 1783 under the Articles of Confederation, historians have largely reinterpreted the state of the nation, finding its health considerably better than later Federalists would have had us believe. John Fiske's conception of a "critical period" is under a fair-sized cloud. But nobody has arisen to deny that it was indeed a "critical period" for the churches. Their difficulties were the product of distraction, attack, and apathy; and the greatest of these was apathy. A colonial people almost congenitally exercised with religious questions of all sorts—and possibly exhausted by or in reaction against the Great Awakening—became preoccupied for forty years chiefly with the problems of politics. When independence was achieved, social unrest flared up again, as in western Massachusetts, where outraged farmers under Daniel Shays resorted to armed force in 1786. After the federal Constitution had been ratified, unrest was translated into bitter partisan political struggle. When revolution in France and a new European war complicated the issues and aroused even fiercer passions, the churches had little opportunity for recuperation; and even if they had, the intellectual climate was too debilitating. By the end of the period, church membership had dropped both relatively and absolutely, so that not more than one person in twenty or possibly one in ten seems to have been affiliated; in many churches membership itself became increasingly nominal. Tory ministers fled; patriot ministers often had their labors interrupted. Most of the college faculties were scattered and their facilities appropriated for military use, disastrously affecting the recruitment and training of a clergy. "Enthusiasm" was widely spurned, and revivalism came to a temporary halt everywhere except in the remoter parts of the South.

The Spread of Religious Rationalism

One religious movement which enjoyed a season of popularity and great prestige during this era, in America as in France, was the cult of reason. Rational religion, or deism, is of course ancient, and even its modern renewal began early, often being dated from the appearance of Lord Herbert of Cherbury's *De Veritate* (1624). As the Enlightenment progressed, more and more thinkers came to accept its primary assertion that reason and scientific knowledge could supply all the necessary elements of religion and ethics, though many might concede that revelation was still needed by the masses. In America, to be sure, frank professions of pure deism were rare in the prerevolutionary period. Even the Arminians' cautious enlargement of the scope of man's reason and moral faculties was considered radical. Yet the growing enthusiasm for Newtonian cosmology and Lockean philosophy had broad effects, and "natural religion" flourished in alliance with "revealed religion" in the theology of many Christian rationalists. The trend is noticeable in the sermons of Anglicans like Timothy Cutler or Congregationalists like Charles Chauncy—not to mention those of Edwards.

In 1755 John Adams was deflected from a ministerial career by the forthright rationalism of a Worcester lawyer, and the religious views which he gradually formulated reflect this impact:

> One great Advantage of the Christian Religion is that it brings the great Principle of the Law of Nature and Nations, Love your Neighbor as yourself, and do to others as you would that others should do to you,—to the Knowledge, Belief and Veneration of the whole People. Children, Servants, Women and Men are all Professors in the science of public as well as private Morality. No other Institution for Education, no kind of political Discipline, could diffuse this kind of necessary Information, so universally among all Ranks and Descriptions of Citizens. The Duties and Rights of The Man and the Citizen are thus taught from early Infancy to every Creature.[3]

More outspoken and less respectful of "Christian principles" was Ethan Allen (1738–89), a self-educated rebel from the Great Awakening, hero of Ticonderoga, and controversial figure in Vermont politics. His long-gestated

3. Diary of John Adams, 14 August 1796, quoted in a very valuable context by Daniel Boorstin, *The Lost World of Thomas Jefferson*, p. 156.

work *The Only Oracle of Man* (1784) not only defended "natural religion" but attacked the Bible and "priestcraft" with sufficient boldness to earn Timothy Dwight's observation that it was "the first formal publication, in the United States, openly directed against the Christian religion." As Allen's life indicates, the war released many inhibitions, opening American minds not only to French liberalism and anticlerical thought, but to the larger and far more easily comprehended tradition of English rationalism. And of the English, none equaled the impassioned eloquence of Thomas Paine, the great pamphleteer of the war, whose *Age of Reason* (1794–96) became one of the period's most famous (or infamous) expositions of deism.

An American counterpart of Paine was Joel Barlow (1754–1812), a Yale graduate, sometime Revolutionary War chaplain, "Connecticut Wit," and patriotic epic poet, who later in his life went to France and became actively involved in the French Revolution. In his *Advice to the Privileged Orders* (1792), Barlow took forceful exception to Edmund Burke's negative *Reflections on the French Revolution,* and before he died he had become a thoroughgoing *philosophe.* Elihu Palmer (1764–1806), however, is most often remembered as the leader of those few Americans who thought deism or "Republican Religion" could be institutionalized in a more or less traditional way. After a brief career as a Congregational, Baptist, and then Universalist preacher, he became a devotee of the *philosophes,* and later, a friend of Paine. In 1794 he organized a "Deistical Society" in New York among a group of enthusiasts for the French Revolution, and after Jefferson's election in 1800 sought to enlarge its influence with a weekly paper, the *Temple of Reason.* These efforts won scant support and fierce opposition, perishing altogether in the surge of revivalism which was then beginning. But they dramatized for a while an unorganized impulse that had considerable popular rootage and distinguished intellectual leadership.

Thomas Jefferson (1743–1826) was unquestionably the most significant of the American rationalists, and his place in the history of American religion is exceedingly important because he was, as Saul Padover has said, "the St. Paul of American democracy,"[4] and because his philosophy of religion and his political theory form such a thoughtfully unified whole. Jefferson was also so important an architect of the United States' solution of

4. Saul K. Padover, ed., *Thomas Jefferson on Democracy* (New York: New American Library, 1967), p. 1. It is of interest in this connection to consider Jefferson's view of Saint Paul. In a letter of 1820 he contrasts the "lovely benevolence" of Jesus with the "charlatanism" which followed. "I separate, therefore, the gold from the dross; restore to him [Jesus] the former, and leave the latter to the stupidity of some, and roguery of others of his disciples. Of this band of dupes and imposters, Paul was the great Coryphaeus, and first corruptor of the doctrines of Jesus" (ibid., p. 121).

the church and state problem that some have seen this "solution" as the virtual establishment of his own theology. In content his theology was similar to that of Adams, Barlow, Palmer, and Paine, though Jefferson was more doctrinaire in his materialism than most of his American confreres and hence had more difficulty in stating his views of human freedom and moral responsibility. Because of the ferocious attacks against him by Federalist clergymen, he also became more bluntly anticlerical. Generally speaking, however, only an extensive essay could clarify the religious differences of the major Founding Fathers. They were all inhabitants of that "lost world" which Daniel Boorstin has delineated—a brief and beautiful flowering of confidence in man, education, and political institutions which Americans for over a century fervently and uncritically appropriated, and which all still honor even after seeing how far the country fell short of its founding principles.

Independence and Church Reorganization

If "Republican Religion" or deism gained ground for a while during the revolutionary era, the Church of England in America suffered a devastating blow. When hostilities ceased, "its fragments lay scattered from Portsmouth to Savannah." Outside of Virginia and Maryland and a few coastal cities in other states, the Society for the Propagation of the Gospel had provided the main body of clergy; and with the open rupture of relations with the mother country, most of its missionaries (who were Tories almost to a man) withdrew to areas held by British armies. Even in self-supporting parishes the incidence of Loyalism among the clergy was high. Two-thirds of Virginia's rectors left their parishes during the war. William White, the future bishop, was for a time the only Anglican priest in the whole state of Pennsylvania. Even Jacob Duché, who gave a moving invocation at the First Continental Congress, later joined the Tory exodus. At the war's end, there were but five priests in New Jersey, four in Massachusetts, one in New Hampshire, and none in Rhode Island or Maine. Nor was it only the clergy who remained loyal to the king. Among the Anglicans of New York, New Jersey, and Georgia, Loyalists were probably in the majority; and they were strong in Virginia, Massachusetts, and Maryland as well. Over seventy thousand of them left the country during the war or immediately after. A large part of those who were able to leave were merchants, wealthy landowners, or former royal officials, and since these classes were predominantly Anglican many very prominent parishes were depleted.

This was not the end of woe for the Church of England. Kings (Columbia) College and the University of Pennsylvania were all but severed from their Anglican origins. In every state where it had been established, church and state were separated—usually with surprising promptness, though in Virginia the basic disestablishment of 1785 was not fully achieved until 1799. By this legislation the Anglican churches lost much of their customary public or landed support. Finally and most seriously, in the very areas where its parish structure was strongest, Anglicanism was probably more pervaded by the extreme latitudinarianism of the Enlightenment than any other church body. This penetration began long before 1760, though it was considerably deepened during the revolutionary era, with the result that neither the large Patriot majorities in Maryland and Virginia, nor the fact that two-thirds of the signers of the Declaration of Independence were nominally Anglican, contributed much to the future restoration of the Episcopal church in America.

As a matter of fact the reverse is true. When the time came to rehabilitate the church, the most constructive leadership was provided by men from states where the Church of England had not been established. Connecticut, where Anglicans had been a suspect minority and often Tories, furnished the chief spiritual impulse. Fourteen of the twenty ministers who were still in the state when the war ended stood in a close relationship to the famous Yale "apostasy" of 1722; they had held their ground in an intensely theological environment, and they knew more clearly than the Anglican clergy of any other state what they wanted. Shortly after the peace treaty was signed, ten of these men held a secret conclave in rural Woodbury and made provisions for one of their number to seek consecration as a bishop. The man finally chosen was Samuel Seabury (1729–96), a strong-minded High Churchman, outspoken Loyalist, and sometime chaplain to British troops. Failing after almost a year's wait to obtain consecration in England, Seabury went to Scotland, and in November 1784 he was consecrated in Aberdeen by three nonjuring bishops.[5] On his return, America had its first Anglican bishop.

Elsewhere other plans were maturing. In Maryland certain actions had been taken during the war to preserve Anglican properties. On these foundations, Dr. William Smith, former provost of the College of Philadelphia, convened the clergy of the state at Annapolis in 1783. At this meeting the Protestant Episcopal Church was declared to exist, and Dr. Smith was chosen to seek consecration as bishop. In Philadelphia, William White, the Patriot rector of Christ Church, was also taking steps toward reorganization; and

5. The "nonjuring" bishops stood in the succession of "Jacobite" clergy who had remained loyal to James II and his heirs. They refused to swear allegiance to William and Mary after the Parliamentary settlement of 1689.

perhaps because he breathed the atmosphere of that politically conscious city, his ideas were dominated by the desire for a national church. Theologically he was vastly more latitudinarian than Seabury. In 1782 he published his proposal for organizing the church on a federal basis and for resorting to presbyterial ordination until an episcopate could be established. White also approached the Lutherans and Methodists, and in 1784 a Pennsylvania committee under his leadership, together with a more broadly based group from New Jersey, pressed for implementation of these plans. In due course a larger meeting, with delegates from the middle and northeastern states, proposed a general convention.

The convention met in 1785; and shortly afterward three states (New York, Pennsylvania, and Virginia) elected bishops, while White and Smith pressed ahead with their proposed revision of the prayer book. In the meantime Parliament had passed laws allowing the English bishops to consecrate an American. This they did in February 1787, Dr. William White of Philadelphia and Samuel Provoost, rector of Trinity Church in New York City, being the two candidates. As a result the United States had two episcopates: one Scottish, High Church, and Tory; the other English, latitudinarian, and Patriot. Nor was it obvious that the twain would meet, for Provoost considered Seabury a traitor to his country, while the Connecticut men as a group were suspicious of the other's doctrinal aberrations and concessions to the laity. What finally brought the two parties together was a request from Massachusetts that its candidate for the episcopate be consecrated by the three American bishops. With this issue before them, the convention of 1789 worked out the compromises that made union possible: Seabury acquiesced to lay representation in the convention and the omission of the Athanasian Creed but won approval for a separate House of Bishops; and though he thwarted the more radical proposals for revising the prayer book, he made good his promise to the Scottish bishops to incorporate elements of their communion liturgy. With agreement on these matters, the Protestant Episcopal Church in the United States came into existence. Perhaps the relatively desperate situation of the church accounts for the success of these negotiations, but this fact does not lessen the magnitude of the event. A quiet revolution had been wrought in the tradition of Anglican episcopacy, as monarchical institutions gave way to those of a democracy: lay representation, elected bishops, and strong vestries at the local level.

The Methodist predicament was entwined with the Anglican because it originated as a revival movement within the Church of England. Methodist Patriots in America were profoundly perturbed when in 1775 John Wesley published *A Calm Address to Our Own American Colonies,* in which he restated much of Dr. Samuel Johnson's *Taxation No Tyranny,* urging Americans to be grateful for England's beneficent rule. Public notice of this pronouncement did little to enhance Methodist popularity in the now openly rebellious colonies; and matters became still worse after the Declaration and the widespread imposition of loyalty oaths. Every one of Wesley's English preachers in the colonies returned to England except Francis Asbury (1745–1816), who since 1772 had superintended the American clergy. Even Asbury was greatly restricted in his activities, and for over two years he lived in virtual exile. Despite these adversities, the revivals in Virginia offset other losses, so that the four thousand members of 1775 had trebled by 1780. At the annual conference of 1778, for example, five old circuits were discontinued in Pennsylvania, Maryland, and New York, while six new ones were added in Virginia and two in North Carolina. By 1784, four-fifths of the country's fifteen thousand Methodists were located south of the Mason–Dixon line. Yet the status of the movement had before that year become increasingly uncertain: was it an independent denomination or not?

When the Revolution began, the answer to this question was unhesitatingly negative; and in England it remained so until 1791, the year of John Wesley's death. As the Anglican clergy began their exodus, however, and after widespread disruption of parish life in the South, pressure grew to make Methodism an autonomous church with a clergy authorized to administer the sacraments. The "Virginia brethren" were especially "warm for the ordinances." Proposals for American ordination were made in 1777 and 1778; and when in 1779 the Southern Conference appointed a committee with ordaining powers, it began to exercise them immediately in spite of remonstrances from Asbury and the societies of the North.

Methodism's year of decision in both England and America was 1784. In February Wesley executed for England the "Deed of Declaration," which vested the 359 Methodist chapels in a self-perpetuating Annual Conference of one hundred preachers. Then on 1 September he recorded in his diary the fateful decision concerning a ministry for America. "Being now clear in my own mind, I took a step which I had long weighed in my mind, and appointed Mr. [Richard] Whatcoat and Mr. [Thomas] Vasey to go and serve the desolate sheep in America." A few days later, Wesley, Thomas Coke, and James Creighton, all priests of the Church of England, ordained Whatcoat and Vasey. Thereafter Wesley, "assisted by other ordained ministers," also ordained Coke to be a superintendent in the United States. The three were then dispatched with this authorization: "Know all men, that I, *John Wesley,* think myself to be providentially called at this time, to set apart some persons for the work of the ministry in America." He acknowledged a departure from Anglican church order, but in an accompanying letter justified his decision on the basis of apostolic praxis and America's need, above all stressing concern for "feeding and guiding these poor sheep in the wilderness." His realization that "for some hundreds of miles together there is none either to baptize or to administer the Lord's Supper" put his scruples at an end. "I conceive myself at full liberty . . . and invade no man's right by appointing and sending laborers into the harvest." [6]

In September 1784 the three emissaries set sail, arriving after a stormy passage in November. The next month at Baltimore they convened the famous "Christmas Conference" for the great work of organizing the American church. Sixty preachers were present, thanks to Asbury's untiring efforts to notify the farflung circuits. "It was agreed," says Asbury, "to form ourselves into an Episcopal Church, and to have superintendents, elders, and deacons." Asbury and Coke were elected unanimously as superintendents, and Asbury was ordained successively as deacon, elder, and superintendent by the three English ministers, assisted by Philip William Otterbein of the German Reformed church in the last rite. With a few obvious adaptations to the American situation, including complete independence from Anglicanism, the discipline of English Methodism was adopted, as were the liturgy, prayer book, hymns, and Twenty-four Articles of Religion which Wesley prepared for his American brethren. The new church acknowledged themselves to be Wesley's "sons in the gospel, ready in matters belonging to church government to his commands." They also seemed to welcome his pruning away of "Calvinism, Romanism, and ritualism" from the Thirty-nine Articles.

An institution of great significance for America came into existence at this Christmas Conference. With Francis Asbury positively at its head, American Methodism would begin its great forward surge, just when the English movement was lapsing into formalism and stagnancy. Throughout the next century it would be the chief engine of evangelical Arminianism in this country. Expanding almost exclusively by domestic evangelism, it would exceed in its rate of growth all other large Protestant churches. By direct impact and negative reaction it would work large effects on nearly every other denomination, until by degrees it imparted its energy and spirit to American Protestantism as a whole. So complex and involved were these religious currents, however, that it is possible to evaluate the Methodist legacy only from a vantage point at the end of the nineteenth century. At

6. Diary of John Wesley (while in Leeds), quoted in J. M. Buckley, *A History of Methodists in the United States*, ACHS, vol. 5 (New York, 1895), p. 232.

the present time it is more important to note two fundamental aspects of the new church: its message and its structure.

The chief characteristics of the American Methodist message were its emphasis on personal religious experience, its legalistic views on Christian behavior, and its doctrinal simplicity. Each of these was an authentic Wesleyan tendency which came to be accentuated on the frontiers where Methodism flourished. The experience of regeneration and its penitential accompaniments were a requirement for church membership. The specific behavioral and moral demands laid upon the regenerate Christian were basically those of Puritanism, but they included prohibitions on alcohol and slaveholding. The doctrinal message rested on three primary points: (1) God's grace is free to all; (2) man is ever free to accept or reject it; and (3) the justified sinner, with the aid of the Holy Spirit, must seek the goal of "perfection" (i.e. freedom from willful sin). What made Methodism so dynamic an element in American Protestantism, however, was the remarkable institutions by which this message was spread and enforced.

Methodism from the first had been very strictly governed. Until 1784 every chapel in the connection (359 in the United Kingdom alone) was vested in Wesley himself, and even after that date (in America no less than in England) his will had almost the force of canon law. In the independent American church, the superintendent (or bishop, as he came to be called)[7] wielded more actual authority than any other Protestant official. Once elected, he could define the circuits which the traveling preachers were to cover and assign men to these circuits or to local charges as he saw fit. He appointed the presiding elders who in turn supervised the several districts into which the circuits were arranged. Thus he could marshal his men and resources in such a way as to make maximum gains in domestic missions. At the lowest level, meanwhile, was another crucial institution, the class meeting, or local unit of Christians who gathered weekly to strengthen each other by testimony, admonition, prayer, and joint study. They could also seek the licensing of a local lay exhorter when one with appropriate gifts was discovered. So long as it prospered, the class meeting was the institution which did most to guarantee that church membership was not merely a nominal affiliation.

With this message and this structure Methodism clearly met the requirements suggested by a recent historian of the frontier:

7. Asbury's use of the term "bishop" was contrary to the views of Wesley, who wrote Asbury, "For my sake, for God's sake, for Christ's sake put a full end to this!" Wesley to Asbury, 20 September 1788, *The Letters of the Reverend John Wesley, A.M.*, ed. John Telford (London: Epworth Press, 1931), 8: 91.

> A church with real hopes for success in the West should have been optimistic in its faith, with stress on the importance of the individual. It should have provided social and emotional content. It should have an organization adapted to the widely scattered [and one should add, constantly moving] western population. Further, it needed a clergy which could speak the language of the crude and hard-working West.[8]

The Congregational churches were not nearly so directly or drastically affected by the events of the revolutionary era as the Anglicans and Methodists. Outwardly their position was improved. The Anglican challenge was reduced by the taint of Toryism and by great physical losses. Congregationalism could ride the crest of patriotism, taking credit for having done much to foment the revolutionary spirit and having provided much institutional and theoretical groundwork for America's self-government. This was true, moreover, of both wings of the church. Jonathan Mayhew of Boston might be a spokesman for Arminianism, and Samuel Hopkins of Newport for "Consistent Calvinism," but they stood together as fervent Whigs, and neither had many Loyalists among his colleagues.

Such signs of prestige and prosperity, however, betray the internal facts of the matter. In actuality the Puritan ideal of which these churches were the custodians was being corroded by the Enlightenment's demand for simplicity and reasonableness. The "orthodox" churches were almost as thoroughly permeated by the tendency to rationalism and formalism as those which were professedly Arminian. Church membership became increasingly nominal. Revivals were sporadic and localized, and most of what "enthusiasm" there was, was channeled into the Baptist and Methodist churches.[9] Most ominous of all was the widening rift between liberals and conservatives, and hardly less serious, a division of the conservatives themselves into New Divinity men of Edwardsean stamp and the so-called Old Calvinists. Open schism in the Massachusetts churches would not occur until the next century, but the reorganization of King's Chapel and its antitrinitarian revision of the prayer book (1787) were signs of things to come.

For the Presbyterian church the revolutionary era involved a gradual severance of the bonds with Congregationalism that the Great Awakening had forged. In the years just before the war, they had united in a General Convention to resist the possible imposition of an Anglican episcopate on

8. R. E. Riegel, *America Moves West* (New York: Henry Holt & Co., 1947), p. 107; quoted by John L. Peters, *Christian Perfection and American Methodism*, p. 91.

9. After a few earlier visits by itinerant evangelists, Methodism was introduced into New England by Jesse Lee, who began a circuit at Norwalk, Connecticut, in June 1789. He preached at Fairfield, Danbury, and New Haven, and shortly afterward established a circuit in Rhode Island.

the colonies; but in theology, polity, and internal spirit they subsequently drew apart. The growth of Princeton, the coming of Witherspoon, and, above all, the very large migration of Scotch-Irish peoples during the 1770s hastened the process. At the end of the century, however, revivalism and the western missionary challenge would again draw the two churches together.

The single most positive response of the Presbyterian church to the needs of the time was constitutional. As the church grew in size, attendance at synod relatively decreased, indicating the inadequacy of the old structure. Finally in 1785 the church attacked the problem by appointing a committee to draw up a manual of discipline. There were also motions to reorganize the church and to prepare a new book of psalmody. Though badly attended as usual, the synod of 1786 continued these deliberations and appointed a new committee with Dr. Witherspoon as chairman. In 1787 a fierce debate raged over the committee's printed *Draught of a Plan of Government and Discipline,* and the perennial tension between the Scottish and New England factions was clearly visible. There was, nevertheless, some progress, and the synod of 1788 was able to approve a Plan of Government and Discipline, a Directory of Public Worship, and a slightly revised version of the Westminster Confession of Faith. The new constitution provided for a General Assembly, four synods (New York and New Jersey, Philadelphia, Virginia, and the Carolinas), and sixteen presbyteries. The presbyteries retained full powers of ordination. The church then had 420 congregations, 214 of which had pastors, 177 ministers, and 11 licentiates. Under its new constitution the church settled down to orderly democratic procedures, and the overall result was distinctly American. Scottish forms and precedents naturally predominated, but it was basically a compromise of the diverse traditions and influences that had flowed into the American Presbyterian church from many sources.

In the revolutionary period Baptists continued to profit from the revivalistic fervor infused into their ranks by the Separates. In New England they joined forces with the Calvinistic Baptists and almost completely overwhelmed the older Arminian Baptists of the area. In 1740 there had been only twenty-five Baptist churches in all New England: eleven each in Rhode Island and Massachusetts, and three in Connecticut. By 1790, in spite of the distractions of the times, these had multiplied to thirty-eight in Rhode Island, ninety-two in Massachusetts, fifty-five in Connecticut, fifteen in Maine, thirty-two in New Hampshire, and thirty-four in Vermont—a total of 266. Whereas only a half-dozen of the churches in 1740 had been Calvinistic, the vast majority in 1790 adhered to this theology.

In 1763 James Manning (1738–91), having graduated from the College of New Jersey (Princeton) the previous year, led the movement to establish a Baptist collegiate institution in Rhode Island. The Philadelphia Association had conceived this project and chose Rhode Island because they felt that a more liberal charter could be obtained there. Actually the charter as passed by the colonial assembly in 1764 was "liberal" in more ways than one. While it specified that a majority of the trustees and fellows were to be "forever Baptists," it admitted approximately one-third from other denominations. The college president was required to be a Baptist, but other officers and teachers, as well as students, were subjected to no religious tests. Manning began immediately with a group of young men in Warren, and graduated his first class of seven in 1769. The next year the college moved to Providence, secured additional instructors, and acquired the beginning of an endowment. During the war its faculty and student body were scattered and its buildings used for barracks, but it recovered speedily after the cessation of hostilities. In 1804 it assumed the name of Brown University in honor of its chief benefactors.

In the South, where revivalism continued even more vigorously, Baptists made larger and more important advances. Virginia alone had in 1790 almost as many churches (218) as all of New England, while the union of Separates and Regulars in 1787 left them poised to capitalize on the westward movement into Kentucky and Tennessee. In this entire process the Separate Baptists continued their aggressive advance, not only through personal and mass evangelism, but because of their ultimately successful fight against all forms of religious favoritism in Virginia. As this campaign gained momentum they were joined by the Presbyterians and Regular Baptists (who previously were content with toleration), and by many of the Old Dominion's greatest statesmen, most importantly Thomas Jefferson and James Madison—both nominal Anglicans.

With the coming of war, the rising tide of sentiment against the established church finally prevailed, and a series of enactments by the assembly eventually removed every vestige of religious inequality. In 1776 compulsory taxation for the support of the clergy was set aside, in 1785 the basic guarantee of religious freedom was enacted, and in 1799 the old glebe lands were returned to the public domain. In this long struggle, which in its later stages became a battle to enforce the First Amendment to the federal Constitution, the Baptist cause was ably led by John Leland and Reuben Ford.

America's many other denominations responded to the issues of the revolutionary era in ways so similar to those already described that details are scarcely necessary. The Dutch Reformed church, experiencing the inevitable difficulties, formed its own Coetus in 1748; then under the leadership of

Theodore Frelinghuysen it declared its freedom from Dutch control in 1755. (A small group of ministers wishing to remain under the aegis of the Classis of Amsterdam withdrew and formed the Conferentie.) The chartering of Queen's College (now Rutgers) at New Brunswick, New Jersey, in 1770 represented a further step in the direction of self-sufficiency. The next year the denomination was reunited, mainly through the efforts of John H. Livingston (1746–1825), a graduate of Yale (1762) and the last American to go to Holland for theological training and ordination. In 1810 Livingston became president and professor of theology at Rutgers, offices which he held until his death. His work in bringing together the Coetus and the Conferentie in a fully independent organization, as well as his decisive influence in shaping the constitution and preparing the hymnbook, earned for him the appellation "father of the Reformed Dutch Church in America." A fully autonomous Reformed Dutch Church in America did not come into being until 1792–94, however, when it organized itself along the presbyterial lines laid down by the Synod of Dort.

Lacking formal ties with a parent European body, the Lutheran church adjusted to the problems of the times with a minimum of trouble. Although Lutherans as a group were overwhelmingly behind the Patriot cause,[10] Muhlenberg, the patriarch, was a devoted subject of the house of Hanover, and he was therefore disinclined to involve the church in revolutionary or military activity. He found the singing of a *Te Deum* for a military victory not unlike celebrating an act of adultery which had evaded the law. His sons, however, took an intensely active part in the war and in the new republic. One left his pulpit to become a general in the Continental army, and another, who was prominent in politics, became the first Speaker of the House of Representatives.

Since the church itself had no organizational ties to sever, its structural adjustments were of minor importance, and the provisions of the constitution which had gradually evolved since the first synodical meeting in 1748 were formally entered in the minutes for 1781. This constitution was used also by the Synod of New York until its revision in 1792. There was no doubt a response to the American democratic spirit involved in the revision, which provided for lay voting. The most important influences were the subtle changes of attitude reflected in the liturgy published in 1786, which revealed the extent to which American evangelicalism and the Enlightenment had weakened the commitment of Lutherans to traditional liturgies.

10. The two chief German-language newspapers, the *Geschicht-Schreiber* of Christopher Sauer and the *Pennsylvanische Staatsbote* of John Henry Miller, were both critical of British rule.

Another sign of these broad cultural influences were the close ties established between Lutheran and German Reformed churches. As old confessional differences lost their force, the only differences perceived by the average layman were minor externals such as a preference for *Vater unser* (Lutheran) or *Unser Vater* (Reformed) in the Lord's Prayer, and variant ways of numbering the Ten Commandments. Hence many union congregations were formed, and in 1787 the two denominations joined forces in opening Franklin College in Lancaster, Pennsylvania, with one of Muhlenberg's sons as president. In 1818 these joint efforts were enlarged by plans for a joint evangelical seminary with no other doctrinal basis than that it should shield students from error and lead them to truth. This institution never did materialize; but in the previous year a joint Lutheran-Reformed *Gemeinschaftliches Gesangbuch* was published as a substitute for Muhlenberg's hymnbook of 1787.

But perhaps no single event illustrates the decay of historic Lutheran doctrinal standards so forcefully as the decision of the New York Ministerium in 1814 to replace Luther's catechism with a new one written by the synod president, Frederick Henry Quitman (1760–1858). Quitman (D.D., Harvard, 1814) was graduated from Halle after it had become a stronghold of rationalism, and his catechism is a monument to the enlightened theology of that age, "a skillful effort to Americanize German rationalism." He was a member of the New York Ministerium from 1796 until his death in 1832, its president for twenty-one years, and a learned student of later eighteenth-century German theology and biblical criticism.

For the Quakers the last half of the eighteenth century was doubly difficult. As pacifists they were subject to attack first for their principled inaction against the French and Indian menace, a dilemma which led them, after 1756, to abandon civil officeholding in Pennsylvania. As the revolutionary spirit grew, they were criticized both for the Loyalism they sometimes evinced and for their failure to aid the Patriot cause in any direct way. More seriously, their religious life, like that of the German "peace sects," proved highly vulnerable to the age's pervasive rationalism. The Quakers became a community withdrawn, but the withdrawal was chiefly social and political. Commerce became an even greater preoccupation than before (as it had for Dissenters in England ever since the Restoration), and gradually the intense evangelical fervor of George Fox was lost from view. Even the period's two greatest Quaker saints demonstrate this tendency. John Woolman (1720–72) exemplifies the movement of Quaker spirituality toward a generic form of mysticism and thus away from the christocentric piety of the seventeenth-century Friends, while the great humanitarian reformer, Anthony Benezet (1714–84), exemplifies a transition from piety to moralism very similar to that taking place in New England Puritanism during these same years.

CHURCH-STATE RELATIONS AND RELIGIOUS FREEDOM

It is ironic that a time of religious desuetude should also provide the circumstances for a resurgence of churchly activity in America, but such is the case—made doubly ironic by the fact that religious apathy contributed directly to the result. The "great tradition of the American churches," as it developed in the nineteenth century, depended upon—almost consisted of—(1) the reality of religious freedom, (2) the relatively distinct separation of church and state, (3) the growing acceptance of the idea of "denominationalism," (4) the rapid growth in favor of the "voluntary principle" in matters pertaining to church membership and support, and (5) the steady advance of patriotic piety, with its belief in the divinely appointed mission of the American nation. In the revolutionary era each of these aspects of the great tradition took on new importance.

Religious Freedom

The principle of religious freedom was formally recognized in at least two American colonies (Rhode Island and Maryland) at the time of their founding in the 1630s, though it survived only in the former. Later in the century it came to be recognized as well in the Carolinas, Georgia, New York, New Jersey, Delaware, and Pennsylvania, though Anglicanism was to receive some measure of public support in all but the latter two. Yet even where churches were established and undergirded by a parish system, as in Virginia, Maryland, Connecticut, and Massachusetts, the English Bill of Rights and toleration laws, coupled with the inescapable pluralism of the colonial peoples, brought about during the eighteenth century a continuous series of legal concessions. Baptists and Anglicans both made significant gains in Massachusetts; Baptists and many other groups were advancing in the South. By 1775 toleration verging on freedom had become a fundamental part of the long-term American revolution being enacted in the colonies.

Yet these libertarian trends accelerated during the revolutionary era, with the Virginia Declaration of Rights and the Declaration of Independence setting the pace. In every commonwealth a new spirit of liberty was evident —even Rhode Island's famous freedom was extended after Roger Williams's death by the removal of disabilities imposed on Roman Catholics. Toleration was granted to at least all Protestants in every colony. Most sensational of all, however, was the enactment of complete religious liberty in Virginia, where up to 1775 restrictions had been more strictly enforced than anywhere else. With the ratification of the federal Constitution (1787) and its first ten amendments (1791), the full range of Protestantism possessed liberties enjoyed nowhere else in the world. Roman Catholics suffered legal disabilities of various sorts, but in no other thoroughly Protestant land were they so free. At the same time humanists, deists, rational Unitarians, and persons with no professed religious beliefs were also at liberty to propagate their views and to aspire to (even to gain) the highest office in the land.

Separation of Church and State

Closely but not strictly coordinate with these new extensions of religious freedom was the disestablishment of churches. Most fundamental to this process was the federal Constitution itself, which in Article Six prohibited religious tests "as a qualification to any office or public trust under the United States," and the First Amendment, which stated that "Congress shall make no law respecting an establishment of religion or prohibiting the free exercise thereof." The ideals articulated in these provisions and the popular attitudes they reflected had already had effective results in the states where Anglicanism was established, though South Carolina experimented briefly with a constitution (1778) that established all forms of orthodox Protestantism. The most decisive acts of disestablishment were passed in Virginia, though here as in every other state but Rhode Island religious tests of one kind or another were required for state offices. Only in Massachusetts, Connecticut, and New Hampshire were the old colonial establishments continued. Even in the old Puritan strongholds, however, the era brought marked liberalization of old forms and great pressure for their complete elimination. New Hampshire disestablished the church in 1819. In 1817 Connecticut Baptists, Methodists, and Episcopalians joined other more political Jeffersonians to elect Oliver Wolcott of the Democratic Republican party to the governorship on an antiestablishmentarian platform. In 1818 the old charter was replaced by a new constitution providing that "no preference shall be given by law to any Christian sect or mode of worship." Two years later Maine came into the union, leaving behind its Massachusetts church-state heritage; and finally in 1833 Massachusetts abrogated what was left of its establishment by amending the constitutional provision which gave special privileges to the old congregational parishes, whether Orthodox or Unitarian. Beyond the original thirteen, no new state except Vermont allowed for any sort of an establishment.

Denominationalism

In one sense "denominationalism" is the most available term for the religious situation created in a land of many Christian churches and sects when none of them occupies a privileged situation and each has an equal claim to status as a Christian communion in the eyes of the law. In the United States, however, the term designates something more. It has theological dimensions, and especially among the mainstream churches of British origin, it very soon came to constitute a virtual ecclesiology (i.e. a theology of the Church). Denominational doctrine first of all repudiates the insistences of the Roman Catholic church, the churches of the "magisterial" Reformation, and of most sects that they alone are the true Church. This naturally leads to a repudiation of the idea that all Christians under any government must be comprehended in a single church. More positively, the theory affirmed an inclusive conception of the church, whereby each communion was respected, and, within limits, none was denied the right to the Christian name.

This form of ecumenicity was anticipated by the nonseparating Puritans; but it was first clearly formulated for a single country of diverse religious views by the small group of Congregational "Dissenting Brethren" who objected to the presbyterian inflexibility of the Westminster Assembly. The Evangelical Revival of the eighteenth century gave this view wide currency in England, and John Wesley stated it forthrightly:

> I . . . refuse to be distinguished from other men by any but the common principles of Christianity. . . . I renounce and detest all other marks of distinction. But from real Christians, of whatever *denomination,* I earnestly desire not to be distinguished at all. . . . Dost thou love and fear God? It is enough! I give thee the right hand of fellowship.[11]

What the Evangelical Revival did for England the Great Awakening did for America, with the antidoctrinal animus of the Enlightenment and the cohesifying force of patriotism furthering the process. In the 1780s Wesley's statement might seem somewhat extreme to most church leaders, but the resurgence after 1800 would lead to even more exaggerated versions of the theory.

Beneath American denominationalism lay a large Protestant consensus, Reformed and Puritan in spirit, which further prepared American Christians

11. John Wesley, "The Character of a Methodist," *Works* (1841), 8: 332–33; quoted in an important chapter on the subject by Winthrop S. Hudson, *American Protestantism,* p. 33.

to have done with establishments. This consensus also accounts for the almost complete absence of anticlericalism that differentiates the American from the French Revolution and helps to explain why innumerable ties between church and state were left unsundered. Each of the major Protestant denominations contributed to the total effort and each of them in some situations felt the advantages of the result. Baptists like John Leland, leading the assault on Anglican privilege in Virginia, could almost assume the language of Thomas Paine on this subject or see eye to eye with a deist like Jefferson. In Connecticut Baptists and Anglicans would become allies in such a cause. For these reasons, the victories for religious freedom and separation of church and state were by no means won by "left wing sects" battling against magisterial churchmen. Statesmen and *denominational* leaders solved the problems of American pluralism in the only way that was consonant with the ideals and necessities of the American Revolution.

Voluntaryism

The form of church life that resulted from these revolutionary developments depended on the voluntary support of a committed laity. This typically American arrangement was accompanied by certain other developments, even in the Roman Catholic church: a tendency to foster the democratically governed local church and to discount or oppose hierarchies and higher judicatories of the church, a concern for practical achievements rather than doctrinal purity, and a pervasive and growing disinclination for formalism in worship, intellectualism in theology, and otherworldly conceptions of piety and morality. Because the religious situation became more competitive, ministers were obliged to please their constituencies—and hence lost authority and status. Naturally there were many who viewed the future of religion and the churches with foreboding. Lyman Beecher gloomily confronting the election defeat of the standing order in Connecticut is the best known example.

Yet Beecher lived to rejoice in the revived evangelicalism which freedom seemed to inspire; he came to see the Church of God as the gainer in the transaction. Everywhere his enthusiasm was echoed; and this great chorus of approval arose, above all, because the revivals of the early nineteenth century brought to the churches a greatly increased measure of influence. Evangelical attitudes and assumptions very nearly became constituent elements of Americanism. Because many of the customary ties between religion and government had not been severed, moreover, evangelical Protestants were able to create a new sort of "quasi-establishment," or what Elwyn Smith has termed a "voluntary establishment." [12] In this system Jews and Catholics would feel the brunt of Protestant condescension and discrimination as well as the fierceness of nativist campaigns; yet opportunities would by no means be foreclosed to them. Roman Catholics would experience such continuous expansion of their church that "Americanism," as an enthusiastic Catholic movement applauding democracy and "voluntaryism," would finally engage the most serious attention of European Catholics and the pope himself.

Patriotism

Overarching all of the foregoing circumstances of the churches was the patriotic spirit which soon pervaded every aspect of the country's thought and feeling. When the Founding Fathers designed the new republic's Great Seal, they exposed their acceptance of an old Puritan idea that Providence had assigned a world mission to the American nation. In effect they reaffirmed the words Governor John Winthrop had uttered in 1630: "The God of Israel is among us. . . . We shall be as a city upon a hill." E PLURIBUS UNUM—ANNUIT CŒPTIS—MDCCLXXVI—NOVUS ORDO SECLORUM. With this sublimely confident and optimistic principle the Federal Union entered upon its destiny—a beacon to all peoples and a refuge for the oppressed. With the passing years a new kind of national feeling came into existence. The Union became a transcendent object of reverence, a stern author of civic obligations as well as a source of faith and hope. Americans became stewards of a sacred trust, while the country's statesmen, orators, and poets gradually brought a veritable mystical theology of the Union into being:

> Sail on, O Union, strong and great!
> Humanity with all its fears,
> With all its hopes of future years,
> Is hanging breathless on thy fate!

So would Longfellow hymn the national majesty. "The Union exists in absolute integrity," William H. Seward would declare; even if crucified, it must rise again, triumphant.[13] From the start both national reverence and Christian piety came to be seen as intrinsic elements in the religion of Americans. It thus became the duty of the churches to uphold the sacred

12. Elwyn A. Smith, ed., *The Religion of the Republic*, p. 155.

13. Paul C. Nagle, *One Nation Indivisible: The Union in American Thought, 1776–1861*, pp. 107, 216–17; see also by the same author *This Sacred Trust: American Nationality, 1798–1898;* and compare the statement by Alexis de Toqueville in the epigraph to Part IV, p. 386. The Latin in the Great Seal may be translated: ONE OUT OF MANY—[GOD] HAS SMILED ON OUR UNDERTAKINGS—1776—A NEW ORDER OF [OR FOR] THE AGES.

trust and yet avoid the temptations of idolatry; to remind men of the country's ideals and yet preach that the God of Israel is a Judge of all nations. But in decade after decade the supreme difficulty of that task would be exhibited. Patriotism would protect and enliven the churches, yet threaten their integrity.

So it was that the unique institutional and ideological heritage of colonial America passed through the turmoil of revolution—transformed but yet intact. Many long-hidden implications became explicit affirmations, while old informal working arrangements were enacted into law. The pragmatic compromises and undefined aspirations of the past became guiding principles of the first new nation.

IV

THE GOLDEN DAY OF DEMOCRATIC EVANGELICALISM

Upon my arrival in the United States, the religious aspect of the country was the first thing that struck my attention; and the longer I stayed there the more did I perceive the great political consequences resulting from this state of things, to which I was unaccustomed. In France I had almost always seen the spirit of religion and the spirit of freedom pursuing courses diametrically opposed to each other; but in America I found that they were intimately united, and that they reigned in common over the same country.

Religion in America takes no direct part in the government of society, but nevertheless it must be regarded as the foremost of the political institutions of that country; for if it does not impart a taste for freedom, it facilitates the use of free institutions. Indeed, it is in this same point of view that the inhabitants of the United States themselves look upon religious belief. I do not know whether all the Americans have a sincere faith in their religion, for who can search the human heart? But I am certain that they hold it to be indispensable to the maintenance of republican institutions. This opinion is not peculiar to a class of citizen or to a party, but it belongs to the whole nation, and to every rank of society.

Alexis de Tocqueville, *Democracy in America* (1835)

The Second Great Awakening began during the 1790s in New England with scattered renewals of piety in various towns. It then gathered momentum in the early decades of the new century. In the southern back country Baptists and Methodists kept the First Awakening alive and carried it over the mountains to the new settlements in the Old Southwest. But the most cataclysmic outbreaks of religious enthusiasm occurred in Kentucky at the great camp meetings of 1800 and 1801—most memorably at Cane Ridge. Thereafter revivalism became a steady feature of advancing Protestantism throughout the nineteenth century and into the early twentieth. But the antebellum period was the great time of evangelical triumph. These were the days above all when the "Evangelical United Front" took up the manifold causes of moral renewal, missionary advance, and humanitarian reform —with revival preaching almost always leading the way. Its aim was to bring the gospel to all America and to heathen lands abroad, but primarily it hoped to make America the world's great example of a truly Protestant republic. The institution by which this vast program was carried out was the interdenominational voluntary association, one society for each cause: missions, antidueling, Sunday schools, temperance, Sabbath-keeping, and any number of other worthy objectives. Less worthy were the attacks on Masonry, Mormonism, and Catholicism. Most decisive for the nation was the great crusade against slavery and the "Slavocracy," which is treated in Part VI.

Another sign of the reforming spirit was the rise of utopian socialism and the founding of communitarian ventures, some native, some originating in Europe, some fervently religious, others explicitly secular. In this experimental atmosphere, moreover, unconventional prophets and radical church reformers seemed always to find a following, and three memorable American contributions to world religion had their origin: Christian restorationism, led by Alexander Campbell; Seventh-Day Adventism, which grew out of the millennial furor aroused by William Miller; and above all, Mormonism. But there were many other sectarian movements which stayed within or only slightly transgressed the limits of evangelicalism. Despite controversies and schisms—or perhaps because of them—evangelical Protestant churches, with their message and methods tuned to the patriotic aspirations of a young nation, reached their high point of cultural influence.

24

THE EMERGENCE OF AMERICAN UNITARIANISM

Early in the spring of 1776, British officials in Boston recognized the hopelessness of their military situation, and on 17 March they withdrew their troops, little realizing that they were providing future Irish-Americans with a perpetual occasion for the joint celebration of Saint Patrick's Day and the British Evacuation. The army, about eight thousand in number, and more than eleven hundred refugees began their embarkation at four in the morning; in less than six hours, all were aboard, and before ten o'clock, they were under way. The flower of Massachusetts Anglicanism sailed with them, including Henry Caner, the aged rector of King's Chapel. When Caner's assistant departed in the following November, this church had perhaps the largest measure of religious freedom in the town; it was beholden to neither the Church of England nor that of New England. In 1777 the chapel building was "loaned" to the Old South congregation, whose meetinghouse had been made into a riding school by the British army; but after 1782 the remaining members decided to reactivate the church. As a lay reader they called James Freeman, a Harvard graduate of strong liberal tendencies, who in 1785 introduced substantial revisions in the Book of Common Prayer. When both Bishop Seabury of Connecticut and Bishop Provoost of New York refused to recognize the church as Anglican, Freeman was ordained by the senior warden on 18 November 1787, and "the first Episcopal church in New England, became the first Unitarian church in America." [1]

1. Francis William Pitt Greenwood, *History of King's Chapel in Boston* (Boston, 1863), p. 139. The open avowal of liberal sentiments was greatly encouraged by a visitor from England, William Hazlitt, father of the famous essayist and an active Unitarian. James Freeman (1759–1835) was a follower of Joseph Priestley and more radical than most Boston Unitarians of his time, a determinist ("Necessitarian") in metaphysics and a "humanitarian" in Christology.

The liberal "revolution" at King's Chapel between 1776 and 1787 was outwardly an isolated phenomenon. Yet it was symptomatic of spiritual changes in the Boston conscience that ran far deeper than men realized, and it proved a portent of other disruptions to follow. King's Chapel is especially valuable as a symbol because it points to the immense significance of Anglican latitudinarianism as the means by which the century's harsher forms of religious radicalism were transmuted into a benign, optimistic, and utterly respectable Christian rationalism. This Anglican response had an immense effect on the dissenting traditions in England, and both of these in turn continued to have a compelling effect on New England thought, an effect which the Revolution actually made more acceptable. In other words, the King's Chapel incident signalized the gradual maturation of a long continuing New England trend.

The "broad and catholick" party had emerged in 1699 with the formation of the Brattle Street Church (which would eventually keep Unitarian company with King's Chapel) and the election of John Leverett to the presidency of Harvard College. As this "catholicity" had assumed the lineaments of Arminianism, it had aroused the fears and defined the life task of Jonathan Edwards. As it waxed in strength, it had involved the New Divinity men in incessant debate which grew in intensity as the years passed. By the end of the war a self-conscious group of liberals proud of their role in the revolutionary cause had emerged; and by the end of the century more than fifty ministers announced their membership in it by forthright publication. Even at the time of James Freeman's ordination there were many Congregational ministers who half-consciously envied the freedom of that church's pulpit.

Arminianism flourished best in the "maritime province" of New England, those towns along the Atlantic coast from Longfellow's birthplace in Portland to Channing's in Newport. Indeed, such tendencies were becoming apparent even while the Mathers yet lived. During the early years of the republic this area was to be the stronghold of Federalism, implacable in its suspicion of France and Thomas Jefferson, warm in its regard for England and the settled order of things. The focus of its intellectual life was Harvard; but because of its orientation toward the sea and its commercial ties with England, a certain cosmopolitanism characterized its outlook. With an economic life constantly strengthened by a world at war, it had brought forth an impressive merchant aristocracy that preferred a religious stance looking out on wide contemporary horizons rather than back to old Puritan ideals. After the Tory-Anglican exodus, these aspirations affected the Congregational churches more than ever before.

At the same time, one must recognize that the churches of eastern Massachusetts were peculiarly open to these influences. As did all Puritan churches, they had a venerable tradition of respect for the light of reason. To the enlightened mind of John Adams it might seem that the first founders were "enthusiasts," but the more patient scholarship of a later day has shown how persistently the Puritans tended to make revelation rational. They did not understand God's truth as bare, dogmatic fiat.

> New England had never been of that mind: it had always assimilated doctrine within the nexus of a logical system. . . . Because man is still benighted, the defects of his reason are supplied by the Bible, in which he must believe, not because the content is reasonable but because the testimonies are convincing. Thus he becomes rationally persuaded of irrational mysteries, such as the Trinity, because, in a phrase originated long before the Reformation, the truths of revelation may be above reason but are not contrary to it.[2]

The church covenants of the early Puritans, moreover, were so simple as to allow of almost any interpretation. At Salem, where in later days the liberal faith was to flourish so verdantly, the saints of 1629 had said:

> We Covenant with the Lord and one with another, and doe bynd ourselves in the presence of God, to walke together in all his waies, according as he is pleased to reveale himself unto us in his Blessed word of truth.

Where New Divinity men had not moved in and revised these covenants, people could "walke together" into a theological world wholly removed from the covenantal faith of their fathers—and so they gradually did. In Massachusetts, where the Mather "Proposals" of 1705 had been defeated, there was no synodical or consociational means of hindering either the progress of liberal views or the ordination of liberal ministers. In the Bay area even the ministerial associations were weak, and that of Boston did not take measures for licensing candidates for the ministry until 1792. In such a context it is hardly surprising that the "self-evident truths" of liberalism would finally lead more than three-fourths of the hundred oldest churches of eastern Massachusetts away from their orthodox allegiance.

THE SHAPING OF A LIBERAL FAITH

In view of many foregoing observations on the Enlightenment, no detailed examination of New England's emerging liberalism is necessary; but a brief

2. Perry Miller, *The New England Mind: From Colony to Province*, p. 422.

survey of its central tenets may serve to make this movement less of an abstraction—especially since each of these tenets continually involved its adherents in serious biblical exegesis, strenuous theological endeavor, and much acrimonious argument.

A firm opposition to revivalism and the whole pietistic emphasis on a religion of the heart was a settled conviction with the liberals. As this opposition came into the open during the Great Awakening, it created a deep and longlasting rift in New England church life. Its leader during his long pastorate at the First Church in Boston was Charles Chauncy (1705–87), whose *Seasonable Thoughts* of 1743 still stands as the classic expression of this attitude. He and his colleagues also reshaped the old preaching tradition. The sermon became a well-styled lecture, in which the truths of religion and the moral duties of man were expounded in as reasonable a manner as possible. Sermons thus became a species of polite literature, to whose perfection the prose tradition of Addison and Steele was more important than the homiletical corpus of Puritanism. Reviews of published sermons frequently were critiques of syntax and style rather than of content. Social stratification began to emerge as a side effect, as unlettered people with little or no appreciation for Augustan periods drifted away from the liberal churches and found their way into the more popular societies of Baptists, Methodists, Universalists, and revivalistic Congregationalists.

Closely related to antirevivalism and almost inseparable from it was a deep-seated disinclination to regard a specific experience of conversion as essential to the Christian life. The liberals did not deny the possibility of conversions (even Channing traced his mature views to two decisive experiences), but only their necessity. In terms of old Puritan concepts these men also favored the Half-Way Covenant and the still larger concessions of the Brattle Street Church's manifesto, yet their aim was not (as it had been for the early advocates of halfway membership) to strengthen the baptismal covenant. They affirmed rather that the Christian life was a continuous rational process of self-dedication. A radical distinction between communicant and noncommunicant members was seen as undemocratic, illiberal, and anachronistic, especially since the Lord's Supper was regarded more and more as neither a sacramental "means of grace" nor a "converting ordinance," but as simple memorial.

The central doctrinal characteristic of the liberal movement was that which gave its early adherents the name "Arminian." They assaulted the Reformed or Westminster conceptions of God, man, and the divine-human relationship, stressing God's role as the Architect and Governor of the universe, though also placing an unmistakably Christian emphasis on his fatherhood. Yet this was a fatherhood bereft of awfulness and wrath, defined chiefly in terms of "benevolence," one of the chief marks of which was that men were not consigned to heaven or hell irrespective of their actual belief and willful deeds. Man was a free agent—John Locke, democratic statesmen, and later and less ambiguously, the Scottish philosophers had given assurance of that. Man worked out his own salvation and suffered his just deserts. God's grace and mercy were needed, to be sure; yet with regard to the nature of man and human ability, these liberal ministers showed perhaps a greater measure of confidence than any significant group of churchmen in the Reformed tradition. And what buoyed their confidence above all was the exhilaration of national independence, the economic and social advances of the American people, and the great destiny (already manifest) of this New World democracy. The idea prevailed widely that "this new man, this American" was a new Adam, sinless, innocent—mankind's great second chance. Nowhere was it given so well-rooted a Christian interpretation as among these New England liberals, whose ideas on man were far more determinative than the ideas about the Godhead which later won them the name "Unitarian."

Departures from traditional views on the Trinity were rare, cautious, and long-delayed. Conrad Wright is no doubt correct in saying that "Anti-Trinitarianism in New England before the Revolution was in a stage comparable to Arminianism before the Great Awakening." [3] Yet there were immensely influential English thinkers who led this way, above all, the Anglican Samuel Clarke, with his *Scripture-Doctrine of the Trinity* (1712), and the pro-American Unitarian Richard Price. These men, like their American followers, took what was then called the Arian position that Christ, though less than God, was more than man—a preexistent divine being. Only James Freeman of King's Chapel and a very few others went on to the Socinian, or "humanitarian" view that Jesus was a man with a special divine mission. In general, however, these liberal Congregationalists were probably not far in spirit from those leaders of the Protestant Episcopal church who quietly dropped the Athanasian Creed from the prayer book. Had the issue not been seized upon by their enemies, it might have lain dormant.

Liberal ideas concerning man's relation to God were to lead eventually to belief in universal salvation, or at least future probation,[4] but the early liberals were similarly cautious on this issue. That redemption is for all men is clearly implied in their ideas on the benevolence of the deity, but uni-

3. Conrad Wright, *The Beginnings of Unitarianism*, p. 202.

4. Belief in future probation involves the idea that man's life on earth is not the sole basis for his eternal destiny, but that after this life God carries man from strength to strength until (it was sometimes argued) all men shall behold the beatific vision.

versalism was seldom advocated. Chauncy seems to have begun his full-length exposition of the doctrine as early as 1750, but his manuscript was not published until 1784, and then anonymously in London. His fellow ministers never made universalism a prominent part of their preaching except insofar as they tended to ignore the doctrine of eternal damnation. It was left for the Universalists to take the initiative on these matters; but they were a movement utterly different in origin and in social background, so that even in the twentieth century, when all doctrinal distinctions have faded from view, these two New England movements of religious liberalism have only slowly begun to coalesce.

A final issue on which the liberals took a firm stand was that of religious freedom and complete congregational independency. While New Divinity men were busy devising new and more detailed church covenants, the liberals defended the old simple ones. When anyone proposed tests of orthodoxy, or—worse yet—insisted that closer organization of the churches was necessary, they were at the forefront of the opposition. They revived and applauded the early arguments of John Wise, who in 1710 and 1717 had brought natural law theories to the defense of true congregationalism, but abhorred Nathanael Emmons's thesis that "unity of sentiment among Christians [was] necessary to unity of affections." They felt that "harmony in the spirit" could be maintained without coercion, and that the idea of "heresy" was a relic of less enlightened ages. On the other hand, they rarely questioned the privilege of legal establishment which their churches enjoyed. Like their orthodox brethren, the liberals regarded a tax-supported church as essential to the preservation of morality and the regulation of society.

THE OUTBREAK OF CONTROVERSY

For two decades King's Chapel stood alone in its "Unitarianism," and ecclesiastical peace was maintained among Massachusetts Congregationalists despite the growing strength of Arminianism in the Boston area. Then just after the turn of the century, while camp-meeting religion was expanding in Kentucky and signs of a "Second Awakening" were stirring orthodox hopes in Connecticut, death jogged the wheel of fortune by removing two key divines in the Boston community. David Tappan, Hollis Professor of Divinity at Harvard, died in 1803, and in 1804, before Tappan could be replaced, so did President Joseph Willard. Both men were moderate Calvinists, much respected and widely mourned, whom it would not have been easy to replace under any circumstances. It became impossible to do so without controversy when Jedidiah Morse (1761–1826), minister in

Charlestown and an overseer of the college, forthrightly and publicly opened the doctrinal dispute by demanding that both appointments go to sound and orthodox men. Inflamed feelings erupted in many quarters. The governing boards of Harvard were seriously divided, and a long delay ensued; but Morse lost. Henry Ware (1764–1845), the minister in Hingham and a well-known liberal, became Hollis Professor in 1805. In 1806 Samuel Webber, another liberal, was elected president, to be followed in 1810 by John Thornton Kirkland (1770–1840), not only a liberal but a much more dynamic and far-seeing leader than Harvard had had since Leverett a century earlier. After Kirkland's election, three more liberals were appointed to the faculty, young John Quincy Adams among them, and the die was cast. Harvard was firmly in liberal hands.

But to have considered the issue closed would have been to reckon without Morse. A native of Connecticut and admirer of its church way, a graduate of Yale now ministering at Harvard's back door, he was not a man to ignore. A national reputation as America's leading geographer and an extremely large network of friends among both New Divinity men and the moderate Calvinists of his own persuasion made him even more formidable. Morse had come to the conclusion that the two orthodox parties must draw together in the present danger, and to that end he opened the long-drawn-out "Unitarian Controversy." His first decisive act was a published blast, *True Reasons on Which the Election of a Hollis Professor of Divinity in Harvard College was Opposed at the Board of Overseers* (1805); and he soon after founded the *Panoplist,* a periodical which was used as a sounding board for orthodox viewpoints. He then began engineering the coalition which in 1808 was to found a new and rigorously orthodox theological seminary at Andover, Massachusetts. Although there were many active participants in this ambitious undertaking, the seminary is undoubtedly Morse's most enduring ecclesiastical memorial. Andover almost immediately became a major rallying point for orthodoxy. Its faculty was brilliant and aggressive, its student body large and enthusiastic. In a few years its influence was being felt all across the country and in farflung mission fields abroad.

Yet not even the founding of this "West Point of Orthodoxy" satisfied the relentless Morse. In 1815 he aimed a blow at the standing order itself by publishing a chapter from Thomas Belsham's *Life of Theophilus Lindsey,* in which the bellicose English Unitarian recounts the progress of Unitarianism in America and quotes selected statements of the Boston liberals. Morse accompanied his reprint of some one hundred pages with a quotation of Belsham's radical creed, and strongly implied (as did a simultaneous review article in the *Panoplist*) that this creed was accepted by many respected Boston ministers. He concluded with a strident call to break off communion with the crypto-Unitarians. It was a charge which the accused could not ignore in silence.

Nor did they. Almost immediately the quiet and dignified young minister of the Federal Street Church, William Ellery Channing, made reply. In a manner befitting his nature and position he published an open letter to one of his ministerial colleagues, Samuel Thatcher of the Brattle Street Church, lamenting the rudeness and injustice of the attack. Samuel Worcester of Salem, "an inflexible Hopkinsian," hastened to reply, thus beginning a notable exchange of controversial tracts in which he published three and Channing two open letters during 1815. Channing was much more sensitive to the semantic problem than some of his opponents, and well aware of the emotional images conjured up by party labels. He pleaded that "earnestly desiring Christians" seriously try to gain "accurate ideas of the most important point in the present controversy."

> Let them learn the distinction between Trinitarianism and Unitarianism. Many use these words without meaning, and are very zealous about sounds. Some suppose that Trinitarianism consists in believing in the Father, the Son and the Holy Spirit. But we all believe in these; we all believe that the *Father* sent the *Son,* and gives, to those that ask, the *Holy Spirit.* We are all Trinitarians, if this is belief in Trinitarianism. But it is not. The Trinitarian believes that the one God is *three distinct persons,* called Father, Son, and Holy Ghost; and he believes that each is the only true God, and yet that the three are only one God. This is Trinitarianism. The Unitarian believes that there is but one person possessing supreme Divinity, even the Father. This is the great distinction; let it be kept steadily in view. . . . I am persuaded, that under these classes of high Unitarians many Christians ought to be ranked who call themselves orthodox and are Trinitarians. In fact, as the word Trinity is sometimes used, we all believe it. Christians ought not to be separated by a sound.[5]

Channing's definitive word, however, was delayed until 1819, when he used the occasion of Jared Sparks's ordination at an explicitly Unitarian church in Baltimore to deliver what became the manifesto of a new liberal faith, "Unitarian Christianity." The Baltimore sermon was recognized immediately for what it was intended to be: a comprehensive and forthright

5. William Ellery Channing, *Remarks on the Rev. Dr. Worcester's Letter to Mr. Channing on the "Review of American Unitarianism" in a Late Panoplist* (Boston, 1815), pp. 38–39.

proclamation of principles. Its publication quickly drew replies from the two most powerful defenders of orthodoxy at Andover Seminary.

The strongest formulation of the biblical argument from the orthodox camp was published by Moses Stuart (1780–1852), a disciple of Timothy Dwight and a former minister of the First Church in New Haven, who since 1812 had been revolutionizing American biblical studies as a professor at Andover. By 1819 Stuart had become a learned scholar of Hebrew with probably a larger command of German critical literature than any other American. President Kirkland had not allowed Andover to preempt the theological field, however, and by 1811 he had begun to gather the nucleus of a divinity school around Henry Ware. Andrews Norton (1786–1853) had become Dexter Professor of Sacred Literature in 1819, and in the same year he answered Stuart with *A Statement of Reasons for Not Believing the Doctrines of the Trinitarians.* This production grew with the passing years from an essay to a large book, reaching final form in 1833. Seen in its entirety, this long controversy documents a momentous transition in American Christianity. After Stuart and Norton had made their mark, it would be almost impossible for men to debate biblical matters without taking full account of historico-critical questions. Advancing scholarship in both camps would soon make Channing's manifesto of 1819 a somewhat archaic monument to enlightened rationalism.

In the meantime, however, the view of human nature set forth in Channing's Baltimore sermon had been challenged by Leonard Woods (1774–1854), whose *Letters to Unitarians* (1820) opened another famous debate. Henry Ware picked up his challenge, and the so-called Wood 'n Ware Controversy was underway. Woods was a graduate of Harvard (1796), who had studied theology with Charles Backus of Somers, Connecticut. Upon joining the Andover faculty in 1808, he had become the chief mediator between the Hopkinsians and the moderate Calvinists. Woods was also a forceful if somewhat uninventive champion of orthodoxy. Ware, on the other hand, displayed great acuity in his replies, thus fully justifying the confidence the liberals had placed in him. The debate extended for four years and ran to five good-sized volumes, two by Woods (besides the *Letters*) and three by Ware. Ware's central claim was that man was essentially good, and that "even in the worst men good feelings and principles are predominant." Despite admitted metaphysical difficulties in his own position he insisted that Andoverian theology was "immoral." Wood countered with biblical, empirical, and philosophical arguments drawn from the arsenal of the New Divinity men, especially Nathanael Emmons, of whose distinctive views Woods was a major champion. Taken together the volumes of this debate constitute one of the best theological discussions of human nature in American church history.

EMERGENCE OF A UNITARIAN DENOMINATION

While these theologians (and many others) were taking the issues to the court of public opinion, other institutional problems were being settled. Individual churches were coming down on one side or the other of the matter or, as frequently happened, on both sides—in which case a division would occur. Jedidiah Morse's church in Charlestown suffered a secession of liberal sympathizers in 1816. The First Church in Cambridge was also divided, with Abiel Holmes (father of the "Autocrat of the Breakfast Table") leading out the conservatives. In the Bay area many churches, Boston's First Church, for example, simply became Unitarian by gradual acceptance, without conflict, schism or change of covenants, and often without even a change of name. Park Street Church in the center of Boston—memorable for Peter Banner's fine architectural design—was organized in 1809 as a separately incorporated and gathered church, and it has remained a bastion of orthodoxy to this day. But the determining event of this sort was the 1820 "Dedham decision" of the Massachusetts Supreme Court. Written by Chief Justice Isaac Parker, a Unitarian, it held that the larger parish or religious society had the legal power to call a minister and retain control of the property, even if a majority of the communicant members of the church were opposed. With this precedent on record, a great many of the old territorial parishes of eastern Massachusetts moved into the Unitarian fold.

Unitarians meanwhile were not organizationally idle. The Boston Ministerial Association became a veritable Unitarian agency, and in 1820 Channing organized the Berry Street Conference as an informal advisory body for the Unitarian ministers of Massachusetts. There was considerable disagreement as to how much denominational form the movement should take; Channing favored a minimum, while Andrews Norton advocated a more definite and responsible organization. The American Unitarian Association, founded in 1825, was something of a compromise; it did assume certain denominational functions, yet its support from both churches and individuals was meager. Although at the time of its organization there were 125 churches under the Unitarian banner, most of them venerable, socially prominent, and conveniently grouped for collective action, the association was able to carry on little more than a modest propaganda campaign. The series of tracts which it published prior to the Civil War, however, is one of the most distinguished collections of denominational literature that any American church has produced.

Unitarians also expressed themselves in other less popular ways, however. One means was the learned journal, and in this field they were particularly successful. At the beginning of the century the *Monthly Anthology* (1803–11), published in Boston, pioneered in the field of literary journalism. It soon died, but in due time two other outstanding and long-lived journals emerged from its remains: the *North American Review* in 1815 and the *Christian Examiner* in 1824. The first of these was somewhat less religiously oriented, but both were outstanding for the wide range and high quality of writing they carried. The editors of these two journals alone constitute something of a hall of fame of the New England flowering: Edward Everett, William Emerson (father of the poet), George Ticknor, Jared Sparks, Richard Henry Dana, Henry Adams, James Russell Lowell, and Edward Everett Hale.

Harvard College also became essentially and conscientiously Unitarian. The divinity school which gradually took shape between 1811 and 1819 professed to be simply Christian; but its faculty and students were Unitarian and remained so with few exceptions during almost the entire nineteenth century. Although its faculty rarely numbered more than three full-time teachers, it naturally had a great deal to do with forming the mind of the Unitarian ministry. Until after the Civil War, moreover, the entire university was pervaded by the spirit of the movement. Most of its presidents and faculty were Unitarians, whether ministers or devout laymen, while the curriculum in almost all of its parts reflected the outlook and presuppositions of Unitarianism. Professors of rhetoric John Quincy Adams and Edward Tyrell Channing (William Ellery's brother), philosopher Francis Bowen, professors of modern languages George Ticknor, Longfellow, and Lowell, and even the distinguished professor of medicine, Oliver Wendell Holmes, were all consciously Unitarian and served to make Harvard a major force in the entire Unitarian movement. Add to this the immense literary output of two or three generations of early Unitarians, and it becomes clear that the "flowering of New England" which Van Wyck Brooks made a household word in America was chiefly a flowering of Unitarianism—though some of its representatives (as we shall see) were rebellious and unappreciative of their fathers' piety.

The "representative man" of Unitarian Christianity during the period when it provided the religious background for the American renaissance was unquestionably William Ellery Channing (1780–1842). Both for his contemporaries and for subsequent historians he was the Luther of the Boston reformation; and during his single forty-year ministry the Federal Street Church became, after Harvard, the central institution of Unitarianism.

Though he was to reject the New Divinity, Channing was grateful for his youthful nurture under the ministry of Samuel Hopkins in the Second Church of Newport, Rhode Island. He came to Harvard College at a time of religious desuetude, but nevertheless he looked back fondly to a conversion experience there which he traced to the Scottish thinkers and to Richard Price—who saved him, he said, from the materialistic implications of Locke. While employed as a private tutor in Virginia his religious commitment deepened further. He entered upon theological studies and in 1803 he was ordained.

From that time until his death, Channing's influence constantly increased, while his theological stance shifted from a softened form of Hopkinsianism to the "liberal faith" whose champion he became. Except for a few reviews, his large corpus of published works consists entirely of sermons, lectures, and addresses; and he died with a larger, more systematic presentation of his views still unwritten. Had he carried out this plan he would, no doubt, have set forth the broadminded consensus of his ministerial colleagues as to the Bible and its interpretation, miracles, God, Christ, and the mission of the Church. Channing perpetuated an essentially eighteenth-century outlook, yet he did so with a generosity of spirit, a disinclination for combat, and an openness to modern nuances that quite rightly led Emerson in his old age to look back upon him as the "bishop" of early Transcendentalism. In his Federal Street ministry he brought "convincement" and moral rededication to a wide range of socially prominent and intellectually distinguished men and women.

> It seems to me of singular importance [he proclaimed in 1830], that Christianity should be recognized and presented in its true character, as I have aimed to place it before you this day. The low views of our religion, which have prevailed too long, should give place to this highest one. They suited perhaps darker ages. But they have done their work, and should pass away. Christianity should now be disencumbered and set free. . . . It should come forth from the darkness and corruption of the past in its own celestial splendour, and in its divine simplicity. It should be comprehended as having but one purpose, the perfection of human nature, the elevation of men into nobler beings.[6]

His "perfectibilitarian" message brought self-confidence to those who heard him, but making them dissatisfied with the contemporary situation, it sent them into the world to reform society and renovate man's spiritual condition.

6. "The Essence of the Christian Religion," from *The Perfect Life* (1873), in Sydney E. Ahlstrom, ed., *Theology in America: The Major Protestant Voices from Puritanism to Neo-orthodoxy*, p. 208.

THE ANTEBELLUM UNITARIAN ETHOS

As a Christian denomination Unitarianism during its flowering time was inseparable from its cultural context. It belonged not only to a region, but in large degree to the upper social classes of that region. Unlike orthodox Congregationalism it seemed bound to the town and city streets that the early Puritans had marked out and settled. Its missionary efforts in the West were generally unfruitful. Meadville Seminary, founded in western Pennsylvania in 1844 jointly with the Christian Connection, never developed a constituency. Unitarian churches that prospered outside the Boston region were usually organized by migrating Yankees, and they retained the character of isolated colonies. Outside of maritime New England liberalism was more effectively spread by Alexander Campbell or the Universalists, or by impious freethinkers.[7] On the other hand, when Lyman Beecher left Litchfield, Connecticut, for a church in Boston, he felt like an alien. His revivalistic efforts gained no support or response from the people of status and learning, whom he himself identified as overwhelmingly Unitarian.

In New England's maritime province, however, Unitarianism did put its mark on a rich and distinctive culture; or, to put it another way, it articulated the moral and religious dimensions of that culture. But this was not a small or subservient role. No group of ministers so clearly earned the respect which Puritan tradition assigned to the clergy as did the Unitarians of this period. They were genuine moral and spiritual leaders, and the laity whom they influenced became a moving force in the social order in ways that were theologically congruent with the liberal faith. Unitarian preaching in an age of intellectual transition brought peace of mind to its hearers (too much peace, too little contrition, Lyman Beecher would have said); but it also encouraged philanthropy, humanitarianism, love of education and learning, and a strong sense of civic concern. Unitarianism thus gave meaning to certain fundamental aspects of the Puritan heritage which orthodoxy had had to abandon when it took up the banner of revivalism, perhaps because both revivalistic and rationalistic tendencies were latent in the original Puritan impulse. In any case, the guiding spirits of the movement, both lay

7. Among the several "Christian" movements that coalesce with Campbell's to make up the Disciples of Christ was one which had New England origins as well as a following in the West. This "Christian Connection" was founded chiefly by Abner Jones (1772–1841) and Elias Smith, two Vermont laymen who objected to the tenets of "Calvinism." Unitarians cooperated with the Connection in maintaining Antioch College in Ohio, and they later took it over entirely. Horace Mann played a vital role in saving the institution. See chaps. 27 and 29 on the Disciples and the Universalists respectively.

and clerical, despite the handicap of many elitist assumptions, were a beneficent and enduring influence in a dozen realms. No adequate history of the later Social Gospel can ignore them; and they must also be credited with providing the circumstances that prospered a large part of the American renaissance. The old remark that Unitarian preaching was limited to "the fatherhood of God, the brotherhood of man, and the neighborhood of Boston," has more rhyme than reason in it. Only the geographical reference is approximately true. Yet when Unitarianism's aspiring spirit was conveyed to the nation in the literary forms of Bryant, Longfellow, Lowell, and Holmes, it was accepted, loved, and learned by heart. It undoubtedly changed the minds of many without their knowing it. Emerson's words about "corpse-cold Unitarianism" and its "pale negations" are equally unsatisfactory. The Christian Unitarianism that flourished in the Boston area in the first half of the nineteenth century was a distinctive, cogently reasoned religious movement that conceived of itself with some justice as the modern cutting edge of Protestantism. Yet its originality should not be exaggerated; it owed much to its closest neighbor in spirit, the rationalistic theology of eighteenth-century Anglicanism, and to the liberal movements in English Dissent which took the same hue. It also drew heavily upon the philosophic resources of the Scottish renaissance; indeed, the Scottish Philosophy nowhere found a task so fitted to its genius as when it provided rational undergirding for this liberal urbane culture. Obviously it was imbued with the optimism of the Enlightenment and of American democracy; but just as obviously, it had inherited the church ways and moral fervor of Puritanism, as well as something of the corporate concern of the Holy Commonwealths. It was thus a unique blending of seventeenth- and eighteenth-century traditions, American and British.

In doctrine the Unitarian movement continued along lines drawn by the early Arminians. It remained fervently biblical. The standard Unitarian commentaries wrestled with every verse of Saint Paul; the "extremes" of German scholarship and philosophy were no more acceptable to Unitarians than to Andoverians; the new geology and Darwinism would be received with equal or even greater alarm. Trinitarian formulations faded from their sermons and treatises, to be sure; but the Holy Spirit was regarded as a divine influence, while Jesus Christ if not God was indeed Teacher and Redeemer. There were sharp disagreements among them as to Christ's precise nature and the meaning of his atoning work; tendencies to Universalism were strong. Natural theology assumed a more important place in their thought than it did among their orthodox assailants, and the idea of progress decisively controlled their idea of human history and Last Things. Beneath all was their conviction as to the perfectibility of man—or as Channing put it, man's "likeness to God."

The rationalistic and liberal bent of their thinking did not mean that they ceased to be evangelical. Andrews Norton nearly deserved the appellation he won as the "Pope of Unitarianism," and no American labored more zealously to ward off attacks on "the genuineness of the Gospels" (the title of his major work), the miracles, and the finality of Christianity. Historical relativism, forms of "pantheism," and subjective notions of revelation became the chief objects of his polemic. This theological disposition was widely shared, and it was clearly expressed by the American Unitarian Association in 1853, when it was seeking to dissociate itself from the ideas of Emerson, Theodore Parker, and the Transcendentalists. After reaffirming its profound belief in the supernatural element of Christianity, the Association made a declaration that was often criticized for its overwrought prose:

> We desire openly to declare our belief as a denomination, so far as it can be officially represented by the American Unitarian Association, that God, moved by his own love, did raise up Jesus to aid in our redemption from sin, did by him pour a fresh flood of purifying life through the withered veins of humanity and along the corrupted channels of the world, and is, by his religion, forever sweeping the nations with regenerating gales from heaven, and visiting the hearts of men with celestial solicitations. We receive the teachings of Christ, separated from all foreign admixtures and later accretions, as infallible truth from God.[8]

What particularly troubled the men who framed this effusive statement was that the emergence of transcendentalism seemed to fulfill a prophecy made by Moses Stuart in 1819, that Unitarianism was a halfway house on the road to infidelity. This embarrassing accusation was to loom large in the so-called Second Unitarian Controversy, which Emerson would help to precipitate. Before taking up that episode in American intellectual history, however, it is necessary to survey other immensely influential church developments, which, while contemporaneous with the emergence of Unitarianism, were of another spirit entirely.

8. *The Twenty-eighth Report of the American Unitarian Society* (Boston, 1853), pp. 22, 23.

25

THE NEW ENGLAND THEOLOGY IN DEMOCRATIC AMERICA

When Jonathan Edwards died in 1758, the Great Awakening in New England was a thing of the past. But short-lived flames continued to shoot up in various localities from time to time, especially during Whitefield's later tours. In 1763–64 a more general awakening took place. Contention over revival issues, moreover, was almost continual, with church separations an ever recurring result. As a consequence, the Puritan body ecclesiastic as a whole became seriously divided. Over the decades three quite distinct parties emerged.

Most numerous at the outset were the Old Calvinists, or Moderates, who cherished the traditional doctrine and polity of New England as it had gradually adjusted to changing American circumstances. They accounted themselves orthodox and resented the excesses of revivalism which had brought so much unrest to the established order. By no means, however, did they repudiate the Puritan conviction that a circumcision of the heart—regeneration—was essential to the Christian life, nor did they cease to hope that the Holy Spirit would descend with special favor on whole communities and nations. Until the turn of the century men of this stamp were predominant at Yale, as were others of a somewhat more liberal tendency at Harvard. Although for some years after the Awakening Moderates held the largest number of pulpits in western Massachusetts and Connecticut, they were by nature rather undistinguished in strictly theological enterprises, and they won few new recruits to succeed them in the ministry. Yet many of them were undeniably accomplished men who revealed their gifts in diverse ways. Among them were such distinguished leaders, for example, as Jedidiah Morse, minister in Charlestown, Massachusetts; David Tappan, professor of divinity at Harvard (1792–1803); Joseph Willard, president of Harvard (1781–1804); Thomas Clap, president of Yale (1740–66), who obtained a new charter for the college and moved to a middle position on revivals; Isaac Stiles (1697–1760), Clap's supporter in nearby North Haven, whose election sermon of 1742 has been called "the first public attack on the Great Awakening in New England"; and Isaac's son, Ezra Stiles (1727–95), an urbane and learned Congregational minister, after 1778 president of Yale, and possibly New England's most articulate and appealing Moderate. In 1761 he would look back on the "late enthusiasm" as a time when "multitudes were seriously, soberly, and solemnly out of their wits."

More liberal than the Moderates was a slowly growing party of "Arminians," as they were often called with no little inaccuracy.[1] Chiefly products of the "broad and catholick" culture championed at Harvard since Leverett's day, they usually went on to occupy pulpits in eastern Massachusetts. Charles Chauncy at Boston's First Church and the more radical Jonathan Mayhew at the West Church were most prominent. These serious and rationalistic ministers came only gradually to full consciousness of their divergence from the Reformed tradition. Social and intellectual ties kept them from a definitive break with the Old Calvinists until the disruptive events of the Unitarian controversy shattered the standing order in Massachusetts between 1805 and 1820.

The "New Divinity" men constituted a much more clearly delineated party. They acknowledged Edwards as their hero, and despite the distractions of Indian unrest, colonial wars, revolution, political upheaval, and religious dissension, they sought to establish their churches on strict principles of regenerate membership and on sharply defined (albeit new) standards of doctrinal orthodoxy. Almost all were graduates of Yale, and most of them were settled over churches in Connecticut and the Connecticut River valley. They were closely tied by teacher-student relationships, kinship, and marriage. Although they defended revivals and sought (with little success) to fan the fires of religious fervor anew, their concern with doctrine and metaphysics, their fondness for controversy, and their harsh and acrimonious

1. Named after the Dutch theologian Jacobus Arminius (1560–1609), whose views were condemned by the Synod of Dort (1618–19), Arminianism was a term used to designate almost any form of Reformed theology that modified the traditional doctrines of total depravity, limited atonement, or unconditional election and accentuated man's role in salvation. By the eighteenth century there were two major but not always clearly defined types of Arminianism, evangelical (with John Wesley as its greatest proponent) and rationalistic (with Daniel Whitby and John Taylor as representative advocates). The Arminians here referred to tended toward the latter type but often not decisively. Some may not technically have been Arminians at all. In America the term often was a synonym for "liberal" or "broad and catholic."

ways tended to hinder these efforts; and their churches were often beset by declining membership, factional troubles, or open schism. Moderates and liberals often dismissed them as a "metaphysical school," yet they persisted, and at the end of the century they were rewarded by a Second Great Awakening, just when eastern Massachusetts was being swept into the ranks of Unitarianism.

The contribution of the New Divinity men to this result was almost entirely in the realm of ideas. Building on the older Puritan divinity as it had been enlivened in the Awakening and set on a new course by Edwards, they maintained and extended the New England Theology. They thus contributed creatively to the single most brilliant and most continuous indigenous theological tradition that America has produced. The course of its development through a century and a half belongs in part to later chapters, but here we shall treat its growth in the difficult half-century after Edwards's dismissal from Northampton. Even in this formative period there were almost a dozen men who would deserve consideration in a general account, but four in particular merit special attention. Two of these, Samuel Hopkins and Joseph Bellamy, are in a special sense "Edwardseans" in that they studied with Edwards, became his personal friends, and dedicated themselves to developing and defending his doctrines. Closely associated with them is Jonathan Edwards, Jr., only thirteen years old when his father died, who studied under both Hopkins and Bellamy and who belongs to the inner circle. Nathanael Emmons belongs in a class by himself as a highly distinctive, almost eccentric theological genius, who in spite of personal idiosyncrasies belongs to the Edwardsean tradition. In the works of these men one may find many grounds for the complaint that they degraded Puritan theology by turning it into a lifeless system of apologetics. But it is equally important to perceive in these intricate theological reasonings a series of transmutations that form a bridge between the still recognizably Puritan outlook of Edwards and nineteenth-century American Protestantism.

Not the least of their achievements is the degree to which the New Divinity men kept alive a tradition of theological concern in the laity. Horace Bushnell described the services of his home church in rural Connecticut during "the Age of Homespun."

> There is no affectation of seriousness in the assembly, no mannerism of worship; some would say, too little of the manner of worship. They think of nothing, in fact, save what meets their intelligence and enters into them by that method. They appear like men who have digestion for strong meat, and have no conception that trifles more delicate can

> be of any account to feed the system. Nothing is dull that has the matter in it, nothing long that has not exhausted the matter. . . . Under their hard and . . . stolid faces, great thoughts are brewing, and these keep them warm. Free-will, fixed fate, foreknowledge absolute, Trinity, redemption, special grace, eternity—give them anything high enough, and the tough muscle of their inward man will be climbing sturdily into it; and if they go away having something to think of, they have had a good day.[2]

Evidence of such theological maturity abounds, even in the writings of a statesman like Roger Sherman. Governor John Treadwell of Connecticut (1745–1823) also published his views on various controverted points and earned serious responses from the divines.

ARCHITECTS OF THE NEW DIVINITY

Joseph Bellamy (1719–90)

Of the early life of this first and most undeviating of Jonathan Edwards's disciples, little is known except that he was born in Chesire, Connecticut, educated at Yale (B.A. 1735), and trained for a time in the Edwards household. He was ordained to the ministry at Bethlehem, Connecticut, in 1738, where he remained throughout his career. Here a revival began while he was still a candidate-preacher. He was, as Ezra Stiles put it, "highly carried away with New Lightism in 1741," and during the Great Awakening his talents were widely demanded. In later years, however, his attitudes were much moderated "by the friendly counsels of President Edwards, to whom he was greatly attached." Though called to the First Presbyterian Church of New York City in 1754, Bellamy chose to devote a full half-century to his Bethlehem parish, founding there what was possibly the country's first Sabbath school. He was much beloved for his pastoral care, and his home became a favorite resort of theological students, with more than fifty future ministers being trained there.

What Bellamy's parishioners, students, and readers received from his lips and pen was an ordered foundation in the polemical and dogmatic theology of the emerging New Divinity tradition. Edwards himself indicated his approval in a laudatory preface to Bellamy's *True Religion delineated; or experimental Religion, as distinguished from formalism on the one Hand, and Enthusiasm on the other, set in a scriptural and rational Light* (1750), a long treatise in which questions of law and gospel were extended into many

2. Horace Bushnell, "The Age of Homespun," in *Work and Play* (New York, 1864), pp. 387 ff.

other areas of systematic theology. In subsequent writings Bellamy took up problems of theodicy, the most notable of which was his discussion of God's wisdom in permitting sin. He also wrote several essays of varying scope on the question of "experimental religion," attacking "antinomians" on one side and advocates of an "external graceless [Half-Way] Covenant" on the other. In all of these works Bellamy was motivated by regret that in a land where in 1740 there had been "so general an outpouring of the Spirit" there were now "so many fallen away to carnal security, and so many turned enthusiasts and heretics."

Edwards probably would have been pleased with Bellamy's labors on behalf of orthodoxy and experimental piety, yet the changing times brought some very important shifts of emphasis. The most conspicuous of Bellamy's theological innovations was his concept of God as Moral Governor. This was, to be sure, an eighteenth-century commonplace, but in his hands it was prefatory to the most salient revisions of the Reformed tradition to be proposed by the New Divinity men. One of these revisions, and possibly the fundamental one, was the exoneration of God as the cause of sin through an emphasis on the divine *permission* of sin as the necessary means of achieving the greatest good in this best of all possible worlds. This was followed quite naturally by a muting of Edwards's argument for mankind's unity with Adam, which in turn opened the way for excising the idea of the imputation of Adam's sin. For Bellamy, man was sinful because he sinned. Another corollary was a redefinition of reprobation, according to which God's punishment of sin was not seen as an expression of holy wrath, but rather as an essential means of maintaining the authority of God's Law. Perhaps most famous (or notorious) of all was Bellamy's reinterpretation of the Atonement, whereby God was no longer considered an "offended party" receiving Christ's death as a "satisfaction" for man's infinitely evil ways and limited in its effect only to the elect. Bellamy rather took Christ's sacrifice as an outworking of God's love accomplished for the well-being of the universe.

In the last analysis, Bellamy carried his rationalism a long stride farther than Edwards; and his most characteristic doctrines sprang from his efforts to justify the ways of God to the enlightened conscience of his day. In a not too controversial sense he was the founder of the more popular and apologetic branch of the New England Theology, which would later include Jonathan Edwards, Jr., Timothy Dwight, and Nathaniel William Taylor.

Samuel Hopkins (1721–1803)

The founder of the stricter and more aggressive branch of the Edwardsean school nearly made his name synonymous with the New Divinity. The author of "Hopkinsianism" (or "Hopkintonianism") was born in Waterbury, Connecticut, and graduated from Yale in 1741. He was profoundly affected by Edwards's commencement sermon of that year (*Distinguishing Marks of a Work of the Spirit of God*), and spent eight months as a student in the Northhampton parsonage. From 1743 to 1769 he served as minister of a struggling frontier parish in what is now Great Barrington, Massachusetts. When his former teacher moved to nearby Stockbridge, Hopkins took full advantage of every opportunity for further conversation and fellowship. Forced from his charge when Tories and the well-to-do opposed his strict views of church membership and his Whig politics, he responded to a call from the First Church in Newport, Rhode Island. Here, where he served until his death, his native abilities were permitted to flower in a much larger and more influential ministry, despite an exile caused by the British occupation of Newport during the Revolution. American temperance, antislavery, and missionary movements owe a great debt to Hopkins's pathbreaking efforts. His chief influence and largest claim to remembrance, however, issued from his theological work, above all, from his two-volume *System of Doctrines* (1793). This was the first systematic theology to reflect the Edwardsean impulse, and his contemporaries had good grounds for placing Hopkins among the Reformed tradition's greatest divines. The least that can be said is that he did for the theology of the eighteenth century in New England what Samuel Willard had done for the seventeenth.

Hopkins's first work (in 1759) was an amplification of Bellamy's sensational proposal that "God's greatest and most glorious work is . . . to make sin in general, which is [the] greatest evil, the means of the *greatest* good." Others of Bellamy's new emphases were similarly carried over into Hopkins's system, and some of these were accentuated further—most importantly his virtual elimination of any idea of *original,* as distinct from *actual* sin. Yet in certain significant respects Hopkins put his own mark on the New England theology. Most memorable are his identification of sin and self-love, and his very forceful exposition of its Edwardsean corollary that true virtue consists in "disinterested benevolence," even unto complete willingness to be damned if it be for the greater glory of God. The metaphysical heart of Edwards's thought—his doctrine of Being—had no more prominent place in Hopkins's thought than it had in Bellamy's.

Probably larger in its effect on future church practice was the way in which Hopkins made the doctrines of total depravity and absolute divine sovereignty consistent with his entire moral and evangelistic enterprise. To do this in the face of growing Arminian criticism, Hopkins called "regeneration" an entirely imperceptible work of the Holy Spirit in which man is completely passive. "Conversion" was then made to rest wholly upon the active exercise of the human will, which leads to growth in positive holiness. In this dualistic view, regeneration lays a foundation "in the mind for holy exercises, for hungering and thirsting after righteousness"; while conversion consists in the volitional "exercises of the regenerate, in which they turn from sin to God, or embrace the Gospel." Against this background one can easily understand how Hopkins could work so large a moral and reformatory effect in the church, and yet be a champion of both revivalism and intellectualism. He combined strict views of covenanted church membership with a certain reasonableness about the criteria for regeneration. His most serious weakness—and it was well-nigh fatal to his tradition—was that he allowed himself to be dominated by the moral emphasis of his age and was overly concerned with detailed and acrimonious theological controversy. "In Hopkins, Calvinism was suffering from focusing attention on its enemies instead of on its God." [3]

Jonathan Edwards, Jr. (1745–1801)

The younger Edwards made only a small theological contribution beyond what was accomplished by Bellamy and Hopkins, but he did play a vital role in defending his father and his teachers. He is also remembered for developing the first full modern statement of the "governmental theory" of the Atonement in the New England Theology, though he must share these honors with Bellamy and with Stephen West, who had succeeded the elder Edwards at Stockbridge.[4] Edwards's *Three Sermons on the Necessity of the Atonement, and Its Consistency with Free Grace in Forgiveness* was published in 1785.

Actually the younger Edwards's career as a whole reveals more about the nature of the New Divinity tradition than anything he wrote. He was gradu-

3. Joseph Haroutunian, *Piety versus Moralism: The Passing of the New England Theology*, p. 62. As if to counterbalance his polemics, Hopkins wrote and edited a moving life of Edwards that drew on Edwards's own personal writings (1765), reprinted in David Levin, ed., *Jonathan Edwards: A Profile*.

4. The "governmental" or New England theory was also indebted to the thought of Grotius, the great Dutch theorist on international law. It interpreted Christ's infinite sacrifice as a demonstration of God's concern for legal government. Man's infinitely evil sin had to be expiated in the interests of moral order. This made sense to the revolutionary generation, which was deep in controversy over natural law, natural rights, and the nature of government. Stephen West (1735–1819) was a formidable thinker and a worthy successor of Edwards. Connecticut-born and Yale-educated (B.A. 1755), West studied under Timothy Woodbridge of Hatfield, Massachusetts, before taking up his lifetime pastorate at Stockbridge. In addition to his *Scripture Doctrine of the Atonement* (1785), he wrote treatises on *Moral Agency* (1772), and *Evidence of the Divinity of our Lord Jesus Christ* (1816). He also wrote a controversial work on the meaning of baptism (1794) and edited an autobiography of Samuel Hopkins (1805).

ated from Princeton in 1765, and remained there as a tutor until John Witherspoon began to expunge Edwardsean "idealism" after he had assumed the presidency in 1768. In 1769 Edwards was called to the White Haven Church, formed in 1742 out of a New Light secession from New Haven's First Church. This church, however, had reverted to the practice of the Half-Way Covenant in 1760. Edwards immediately demanded its abrogation, and his insistence on this point (as well as his unpopular metaphysical discourses) caused a portion of the church to withdraw from his ministry. This group organized itself as the Fair Haven Church in 1771, and maintained a separate existence until after Edwards left New Haven in 1795.

Edwards compensated for his rigor with neither great powers as a preacher nor a winning personality, so that his congregation finally dwindled to the point where his resignation was demanded. Had he not been one of New Haven's foremost supporters of the Patriot cause, and had not the famous Roger Sherman been one of his most devoted parishioners, the end would have come sooner. As it was, he followed in the footsteps of his father, moving first to a small frontier village (North Colebrook, Connecticut), then to a college presidency (Union College, Schenectady, New York), and very shortly thereafter to his final resting place. Perhaps his most significant labors were those in behalf of a closer alliance between the Middle States Presbyterians, among whom his father had died, and the consociated Congregationalists of Connecticut.[5] His fierce loyalty to the New England Theology, his strict churchmanship, his dry, doctrinal preaching, his profound incompatibility with the drift of popular religion in the revolutionary epoch—all of these make Jonathan Edwards, Jr., a fit representative of the Edwardsean epigone.

Nathanael Emmons (1745–1840)

The longest-lived of the New Divinity men was also the most intellectually independent and creative. Nathanael Emmons was a colorful personality, given to aphoristic expression and unusual opinions. He referred to his birth date in the Old Style of the Julian calendar, and died in Jacksonian America still wearing the knee breeches and buckled shoes of colonial times. As a student at Yale, he was deeply affected by his reading of Edwards's *Freedom of the Will.* After receiving his baccalaureate in 1767, he took postgraduate theological training first with Nathan Strong of North Coventry, for whom he mastered Willard's *Compleat Body of Divinity,*

5. The Plan of Union between these two groups was formally adopted in 1801, the year of Edwards's death. Union College itself was a cooperative venture on the part of Dutch Reformed, Presbyterians, and Congregationalists. See pp. 456–58.

followed by a far more influential stint with John Smalley of New Britain, Connecticut. Smalley was a disciple of Edwards, a student of Bellamy, and an ardent New Divinity man whose "scheme of sentiments" the young Emmons received "with great avidity." At his examination for licensure as a minister, this "novel scheme" of Smalley's was bitterly resisted by a minority, so that Emmons emerged, as he said, "in some measure a speckled bird." [6]

These speckles may have had something to do with the fact that Emmons was not called to a church until 1773. On the other hand, he was a hard man to please, for he had to be sure that the congregation would accept his didactic doctrinal preaching. "As soon as I entered into the ministry," he said (and his determination was fairly characteristic of his school), "I resolved to devote my whole time to the sacred work, without encumbering myself with the cares and concerns of the world." He once refused to replace a fallen bar on his fence, lest it start him down the road to worldly preoccupations. The way to keep church members in peace, he felt, "is to keep them interested in the great truths of the Bible." The necessary conditions were finally found in the completely rural parish at Franklin, Massachusetts, where for fifty-four years Emmons conducted a ministry according to his desires. Five very thick octavo volumes of his collected *Works* attest to the vigor with which he lived out his axioms. These tomes also help to account for the fact that eighty-seven students studied for the ministry under his care—and repaired his fences.

The theology which these students learned was forged in many controversies—against Arminians, Antinomians, Universalists, Unitarians, and the whole diverse band of eighteenth-century infidels. Nevertheless, it was steadfastly systematic, sermonic in form, and rational in structure, though neither intensely exegetical nor rigorously philosophical. Emmons professed to hold ontology in horror, and never expressed himself clearly on many very relevant metaphysical issues. His views were basically and professedly Hopkinsian, and his students did more to perpetuate that outlook than Hopkins's own. Yet Emmons's thought had a definite tendency, which he himself described as not "Calvinisticalish, Calvinistical, nor Calvinistic—but Calvinist." Emmonsism as a term arose later in reference to the extreme view of "the sole

6. The written protest of the Reverend Edward Eells objects to the New Divinity man's contention that man's rational faculties were unaffected by either sin (the Fall) or salvation. Emmons taught that the *imago Dei* was not upon Adam's understanding any more than on his fingers and toes, but upon his heart and will (Edwards Amasa Park, *Memoir of Nathanael Emmons: with Sketches of His Friends and Pupils* [Boston, 1861], pp. 39 f.). "Emmons was, by common consent, the boldest thinker and writer in the entire school," says George N. Boardman (*A History of the New England Theology*, p. 14).

causality of God" which became a key doctrine of his system. Holiness and sin consist in actions, or "exercises," of which God is the immediate agent; yet as introspection reveals, these exercises are willed, voluntary, and free. Sin is in the sinning; it springs neither from a prior disposition nor from a sinful nature.

Emmons was a highly original theologian who shaped every doctrine to his systematic needs. Yet it is not misleading to accept his own insistence that he chiefly extended and clarified the New England Theology. The future significance of these labors was, of course, increased by the great number of his disciples who entered New England pulpits; Leonard Woods, later on the faculty of Andover Seminary, was perhaps the most influential. Almost all of the New Divinity men, on the other hand, persistently exerted a kind of involuntary reverse influence. A famous example is the eminent educational reformer, Horace Mann, who grew up in Franklin under the stern preaching and imperious "rule" of Emmons. Mann looked back on his Christian nurture as a blight on his life; he consciously rebelled at an early age, and became a pronounced liberal in theology.

AN EVALUATION OF THE EDWARDSEAN SCHOOL

The New Divinity tradition has not been treated kindly by historians and theologians. Herbert W. Schneider found it "one of the most intricate and pathetic exhibitions of theological reasonings which the history of Western thought affords. The dialectic involved is so replete with apparently meaningless technical distinctions, and the literature of the movement is so controversial in spirit, that the few theologians who have taken the pains to pick their way through this desert have merely succeeded in convincing others that there are no signs of life in it." In a chapter entitled "The Decline and Fall," Schneider associates himself with "modern Protestants [who] are so thankful to be rid of the Puritan incubus that they point to these post-Edwardseans as the death agony of a monstrous theology which should never have been born." [7]

Joseph Haroutunian, a theologian of Reformed background, is almost as harsh, though his judgments are unusually penetrating:

> The profound tragedy of Edwards' theology was transformed into a farce by his would-be disciples, who used his language and ignored his piety. . . . Edwards' "true virtue" was buried under a mass of distinctions invented in order to make the church acceptable to men of secondary virtue. . . . Holy love faded into conformity to the moral

7. Herbert W. Schneider, *The Puritan Mind*, p. 208.

> law, and such conformity was not the measure and substance of "true virtue." Such bleak and cruel Calvinism was doomed in New England, when, with the opening of the new century, a humanized liberalism won the day, and introduced a new and softer note into the religious life of New England. . . . The difference between "Christians" and "moralists" [according to Emmons] is that the former believe a body of doctrinal truths, while the latter do not. Calvinism thus degenerated into a scheme of theology *plus* an independent set of "duties." Its holy fire was quenched, and its theological ashes lay exposed to the four winds. . . . The logic of Calvinistic piety was being transformed into a vast, complicated, and colorless theological structure, bewildering to its friends and ridiculous to its enemies. It was like a proud and beggared king, hiding his shame with scarlet rags and yellow trinkets.[8]

Jonathan Edwards himself is usually exempted from the more sweeping denunciations, but not always. Vernon Louis Parrington is typical of the once large but now diminishing group of undiscriminating interpreters, though few have misunderstood Edwards so utterly:

> Edwards was at the dividing of the ways; he must abandon transcendentalism or the dogma of total depravity. Instead he sought refuge in compromise, endeavoring to reconcile what was incompatible. Herein lay the tragedy of [his] intellectual life; the theologian triumphed over the philosopher, circumscribing his powers to ignoble ends. . . . The greatest mind of New England had become an anachronism in a world that bred Benjamin Franklin. . . . The intellectual powers were his, but the inspiration was lacking; like Cotton Mather before him, he was the unconscious victim of a decadent ideal and a petty environment.[9]

Having thus disposed of the founder of the New England Theology, Parrington simply dismisses the ensuing tradition without comment. Still other scholars, most notably Frank Hugh Foster, veer to the other extreme, not only lavishing superlatives on Edwards, but describing the work of his successors as a continuous ascent, with Nathaniel William Taylor and Edwards Amasa Park ensconced on the nineteenth-century summit. George N. Boardman regarded the best of these men as possessed of original power as thinkers, and he thought the power of the tradition itself "really a matter of wonder." [10]

8. Joseph Haroutunian, *Piety versus Moralism: The Passing of the New England Theology,* pp. 96, 130, 176, 127, 71.

9. Vernon L. Parrington, *Main Currents in American Thought,* 1:158, 162–63.

10. Frank H. Foster, *A Genetic History of the New England Theology;* Boardman, *History of the New England Theology,* p. 14.

In view of such radically conflicting judgments some concluding observations are necessary. The first is simply that Edwards no longer stands in need of merely qualitative defense. His reputation as America's greatest speculative theologian is fairly secure. It is not at all apparent that the Reformed tradition anywhere in the world has produced his equal between John Calvin and Karl Barth, or that America had a metaphysician of his stature until late in the nineteenth century. As the quotations from Schneider and Haroutunian indicate, Edwards can easily be disjoined from "Edwardseanism." Yet the successors of Edwards discussed in this chapter are his legitimate offspring, and the father, regardless of his greatness, must bear part of the burden of abuse. The historian of ideas may still consider the New Divinity of the eighteenth century as a single tradition.

The chief extenuating circumstance for the post-Edwardsean tradition as a whole is that it was a victim of the Enlightenment and the country's political concerns, whereas Edwards alone benefited from his proximity to the Puritans and from the religious support provided by the Great Awakening. He could more easily continue the perennial dialogue of philosophic Christians that reaches back to Saint Augustine and the early Fathers. But his disciples faced the difficult task of carrying on their labors when other ideas and aspirations had become dominant. After 1760 Americans were increasingly preoccupied by issues of government, law, trade, war, and nation-building—not theology. The New Divinity men, therefore, had to take up huge apologetical questions while performing their ministry in hostile parishes on the farflung edge of Anglo-European civilization. Nevertheless, they succeeded in doing what almost no one else in the Reformed tradition was then doing creatively: they maintained a dogmatic tradition and steadily developed it in the face of both revivalistic and rationalistic challenges to theological rigor. Never have theologians struggled against greater odds. Yet no one who reads their productions patiently can deny that they executed their task with brilliance. For the churches their works served as a highly effective sheet anchor during the period's political storms, enabling the New England religious tradition to move ahead again under the fair winds of the new century. Yet the metaphor may be too static—for these thinkers were, in a sense, at the helm, and in their way they charted a route through difficult seas. At the dawn of the nineteenth century, the churches which they influenced were no longer restricted to the intellectual categories of the sixteenth century. These men were by no means a provincial aberration: the Second Great Awakening in New England would not be their doing, but it did vindicate their steadfastness and should allow posterity to forgive them their contentiousness.

26

THE SECOND GREAT AWAKENING IN NEW ENGLAND: REVIVAL, EVANGELISM, AND REFORM

While Jedidiah Morse was mounting his first campaign against the Boston-Harvard liberals and working to form the orthodox coalition that would found Andover Seminary, he was in correspondence with fellow Yale alumni who were rejoicing in a spiritual renewal of their churches. As the new seminary became an actuality, its students and faculty knew that it was a strategic outpost of these resurgent churches. When Moses Stuart and Leonard Woods took up the cudgels against William Ellery Channing and Henry Ware, they also knew that they were no longer merely spokesmen for a disappointed New Divinity underground. Every one of these men, in fact, was already participating in the Second Great Awakening. "God, in a remarkable manner, was pouring out his Spirit on the churches of New England," said one of the revival's leaders and earliest historians. "Within the period of five or six years . . . not less than one hundred and fifty churches in New England, were visited with times of refreshing from the presence of the Lord." [1]

The years since the great ingathering of the first Awakening had been hard to understand. God seemed almost to have withdrawn his blessing from New England, and above all from those who most cherished "true" doctrine. There had been occasional local revivals since those great wonder-working days, especially in the years 1763–64. But at the end of the century, though the number of New Divinity men had grown from a small band to over a

1. Bennet Tyler, *The New England Revivals . . . from Narratives First Published in the Connecticut Evangelical Magazine* (Boston, 1846), p. v.

hundred, the main signs of refreshing seemed to come to Baptists and the invading Methodists, not to the churches of the standing order. It was then that the new revivals occurred, almost uniformly under the strictest preaching of the New Divinity, and the orthodox took new heart.

Just where they began or which came first will probably never be settled. Edward Dorr Griffin, so far as his "personal observation" was concerned, traced them to 1792, when he had come home from Yale as a theology student and seen his family and many kinspeople become "professors of religion." But the first phase of the Second Awakening proper took place between 1797 and 1801, when many towns from Connecticut to New Hampshire felt refreshing showers. "I saw a continued succession of heavenly sprinklings," wrote Griffin, "at New Salem, Farmington, Middlebury, and New Hartford . . . until, in 1799, I could stand at my door in New Hartford, Litchfield County, and number fifty or sixty contiguous congregations laid down in one field of divine wonders." [2] In 1800 the *Connecticut Evangelical Magazine* was founded to report and encourage the revival spirit. Then in 1801, just as it began to flag in the towns, it came to Yale to reward the earnest preaching of President Timothy Dwight. A third of the students (many of them destined for the ministry) were converted. Membership in the student "Moral Society" rose to unprecedented numbers in 1802; and Benjamin Silliman, the future "father of American science," wrote home that "Yale College is a little temple; prayer and praise seem to be the delight of the greater part of the students, while those who are still unfeeling are awed with respectful silence." [3]

This tardy but highly influential college revival won Dwight the undeserved credit for having begun the Second Awakening, though the religious interest in the college soon flagged, not to return with power until 1812–13 and 1815. But in 1807–08 it was felt in New Haven, after one of Dwight's protégés, young Moses Stuart, succeeded a stern and aging Moderate as minister of the First Church. In due course these revivals too became statewide, and soon they became almost continuous on a local basis, though more intense manifestations of the Spirit were felt in 1815–16 and in 1820–21. This last was especially powerful in New Haven, where Nathaniel William Taylor, another of Dwight's students, was Stuart's illustrious successor. In 1825–26 and in 1831 still other "displays of divine grace" occurred; but by this time a basic pattern had been set, and influences from great western revivals were flowing back into New England. For two or three generations the revival remained a characteristic feature of Congregational life.

2. Quoted in Charles Roy Keller, *The Second Great Awakening in Connecticut*, pp. 37–38.

3. George Park Fisher, *Life of Benjamin Silliman*, 2 vols. (New York, 1866), 1: 83.

Until western and Methodistic practices and a revised "New School" theology began to take hold in this later period, the Second Awakening was remarkably uniform in almost all of its appearances. In the first place, revivals came to the parishes of New Divinity men with a consistency that they could interpret only as a sign of divine favor. In the words of the Edwardseans, it was the preaching of "plain gospel truths, with which the people had long been acquainted, and had heard with indifference." These "plain gospel truths" were God's absolute sovereignty, man's total depravity, and Christ's atoning love.

> It has been no uncommon thing for the subjects of the work, whose chief distress and anxiety antecedently arose from a sense of their being in the hands of God, unexpectedly to find themselves rejoicing in that very consideration. . . . They have . . . apparently rejoiced in God's supremacy, and in being at his disposal, calmly leaving their case to his wise and holy decision.[4]

One feature of such preaching which certainly conduced to the awesomeness of the phenomena and to the calmness of the results was that the revivals were seen as in very fact God's work, not man's. The God who had spoken to Abraham was speaking in New England. The main street of any village led into Jerusalem the Golden. This was an exciting fact; yet the revivals were without the hysteria and commotion that had brought the Great Awakening into disrepute in many quarters, and which would soon be arousing similar opposition to the tumultuous camp meetings in the West.

That people were calm was indeed the second important feature of these revivals, and one for which the ministers unanimously thanked God. They were not marked by "outcries, distortions of the body, or any symptoms of intemperate zeal. . . . You might often see a congregation sit with deep solemnity depicted in their countenances, without observing a tear or sob during the service." The fruits of conversion, moreover, were incontestably shown in renewed spiritual seriousness and reformation of morals. This helps most to account for the sustained character of the Second Awakening, and shows that the clergy were not being simply prudish in their gratitude for the prevailing sobriety. Over and over again the effects on individual behavior were attested as permanent, while undue excess and the reaction it would have caused were rare. Very different from the first Great Awakening, the unbelievers (as young Silliman reported from Yale) were awed into "respectful silence" rather than provoked to antagonism and ridicule.

4. Tyler, *New England Revivals,* p. 59.

LEADERS OF THE PERIOD

For the most part these revivals were conducted not by sensational itinerants like Tennent, Whitefield, and Davenport, but by settled ministers within their own parishes. But this did not prevent the assertion of leadership by certain naturally dominant personalities whose memory enhances the history of more than revivalism. The more outstanding of these may be singled out for brief attention.

Timothy Dwight (1752–1817)

First by virtue of his unquestioned ability, by the prestige accruing from his presidency of Yale (1795–1817), and by his own personal assertiveness, was the grandson of Jonathan Edwards, Timothy Dwight. Born in Northampton, graduated from Yale (1769), and remaining there as a tutor, Dwight was sorely disappointed at not being made president of the college in 1777. He entered the army chaplaincy instead; following this, by laborious efforts he sought to establish himself as an epic poet of the new nation. Serving a pastorate at Greenfield Hill, Connecticut, Dwight also began to make his mark as a philosophical defender of the faith and as a hymn writer, extending the revolution begun by Isaac Watts with his departure from metrical paraphrases of the Psalms. ("I Love Thy Kingdom, Lord" is perhaps Dwight's most famous hymn.) Elected president of Yale in 1795, he set about making his administration memorable as a time of educational broadening and deepening, just as John Thornton Kirkland, his contemporary at Harvard, was to do. Also like the Unitarian leaders of Boston, Dwight was an ardent Federalist; politically he (and even more forcibly, his brother Theodore) would continue to ally with the Unitarian and Episcopalian Federalists of Boston and Essex County, even at the Hartford Convention of 1815.

But Timothy Dwight was not chiefly a political leader; his primary crusade was against infidelity and in behalf of true doctrine and experimental religion. This led him to undertake at Yale his four-year cycle of discourses on the Christian religion, expounding its nature, defending it against detractors, and pointing out at great length its moral implications. After six years of declaiming this "system" to unenthusiastic students through warm weather and cold, in greatcoat and mittens when necessary, his first collegiate revival finally happened. The lectures, first published in 1818 and often reprinted, became a major theological guide for a generation.[5]

5. *Theology Explained and Defended in a Series of Sermons*, 5 vols. (Middletown, Connecticut,, 1818–19). Reprinted in 5 vols. (London, 1819), in 2 vols. (Glasgow, 1822–24), in 4 vols. (New Haven, 1825; New York, 1829), et al.

Whether Dwight was an Old Calvinist or a New Divinity man has often been debated, but the question cannot be settled in those terms. He was neither. As the founder of the New Haven Theology, he begins a new trend that was carried to completion by Nathaniel William Taylor. In preferring the Scottish Philosophy to Locke and Berkeley, and in enlarging upon man's moral and intellectual agency, he was certainly not a strict Edwardsean. The first emphasis made him practical and commonsensical; the latter pointed him in the direction of a "system of duties" based on a utilitarian notion of happiness which was far removed from Edwards's conception of true virtue as love for Being as such. At no other point did the New England Theology move so decisively toward that unloved moral legalism which later Americans were to condemn and abandon.[6] Dwight represents, even if he did not shape, the tradition that would later be so roundly condemned by liberals as "Puritan."

Nathaniel William Taylor (1786–1858)

But such forward glances must not divert us from the immense evangelical energy that was loosed on New England and America by Dwight's devoted students, of whom none is more important than the real architect of the New Haven Theology, Nathaniel William Taylor.[7] After beginning his career as a reader and amanuensis for Dwight (whose eyesight was very poor), Taylor proceeded to an outstanding ministry at New Haven's First Church (1811–22). His most important services, however, were rendered as professor of theology at the Yale Divinity School, established in 1822 mainly to supply the swiftly increasing demand for ministers, but also to provide Taylor with a platform on a par with Andover. He presaged things to come by remarking that Leonard Woods's arguments against Henry Ware had set back the orthodox cause fifty years. In 1828 Taylor shocked some of the stricter Edwardseans with his *Concio ad Clerum,* an address before the General Association of Connecticut. But even then, and long before his death in 1858, "Taylorism" was a definite and recognizable point of view. In spirit the New Haven Theology, as it became known, remained distinctly Reformed, for Taylor would never concede that he had departed from the Westminster Confession; he professed his deep indebtedness to Dwight and his respect for Edwards.

6. If any one group can be credited with identifying Puritanism and moral legalism, it is Dwight and his immediate disciples. All Reformed theologies tend to be legalistic, but Dwight and his influential followers almost extinguished the idea of free Christian decision in a given situation or moral context.

7. Chronologically, Asahel Nettleton, the Second Awakening's most important itinerant evangelist, and Lyman Beecher, who did almost everything, were on the scene before Taylor; but Taylor's position as the chief successor to Dwight makes it logical to consider him first.

But more importantly, he gathered together the innovations of the intervening New Divinity, especially as set forth by Bellamy, based them firmly and knowledgeably on the Scottish Philosophy, and propounded a plausibly rationalistic "revival theology" for mid-nineteenth-century America.

Taylor's fundamental insistence was that no man becomes depraved but by his own act, for the sinfulness of the human race does not pertain to human nature as such. "Sin is in the sinning," and hence "original" only in the sense that it is universal. Though inevitable, it is not—as with Edwards—causally necessary. Man always had, in Taylor's famous phrase, "power to the contrary." As a free, rational, moral, creative cause, man is not part of the system of nature, at least not a passive or determined part. Preachers must confront sinners with this fact, and address them in the knowledge of it.[8] Unlike Leonard Woods, Taylor was consciously formulating a reasonable revival theology that could prosper in the democratic ethos of Jacksonian America. As these ideas gained acceptance with the passing years, revivals came to be understood less as the "mighty acts of God" than as the achievement of preachers who won the consent of sinners.

Bennet Tyler (1783–1858)

Not surprisingly, Taylor's views attracted opposition from many quarters. Leonard Woods, at whom they were to some extent aimed, turned from his battles with the Unitarians to a new controversy on this front. When Woods was joined by Bennet Tyler, the "Tyler-Taylor Controversy" became a New England conversation piece. Tyler was Connecticut-born and Yale-trained (1804), a former president of Dartmouth College (1822–28), and after 1828 minister in Portland, Maine. While on a visit to Connecticut in 1829, he opened a correspondence with Taylor in protest against the latter's *Concio ad Clerum.* The dispute became public, and the objections to Taylorism multiplied. In 1833 dissatisfaction with Yale had grown so strong that the conservatives founded the Theological Institute of Connecticut (later Hartford Theological Seminary) in East Windsor as a counterseminary, with Tyler as president and professor of theology. Here until his death he sought to build a bastion of what he thought was unrevised and uncompromised Edwardseanism.[9]

8. Worth noting in this connection is the fact that Taylor's alleged "Arminianism" is far more liberal than John Wesley's. He argues from the nature of man, not, as did Wesley, from the scope of Christ's atoning work and the generality of God's grace.

9. Perhaps the seminary drew strength from the fact that it was located in the very precincts where Jonathan Edwards had received his first intuitions of God's great glory. More material was the longstanding rivalry between the New Haven and the Hartford areas.

Asahel Nettleton (1783–1844)

Unsuccessfully sought for the first faculty of the new seminary in East Windsor was the evangelist Asahel Nettleton, a figure far more representative of the Second Awakening. Stirred during the early years of that revival, Nettleton was converted in 1801 and determined to spend his life in the foreign mission field. His health prevented that, but his peculiar abilities as a revivalist were discovered almost by accident when he was asked to interrupt his postgraduate theological studies at Yale to take an interim preaching assignment in eastern Connecticut. Aware that the first Great Awakening had produced its most enthusiastic and disorderly responses in this region, Nettleton adopted very sane and sober methods. His effectiveness was a minor sensation, however, and he was ordained as an evangelist by the Consociation of Litchfield County in 1811.

His next assignment was among the churches of western Connecticut, which were being decimated by the great "Yankee Exodus" to the West. So fruitful was his preaching, so self-effacing and cooperative was he, and so decorous and unsensational were his methods, that he was soon in great demand not only in Connecticut but in New York and elsewhere in New England. Yet his invariable success in calling sinners to repentance undermined the idea that a revival was the work of God, despite the fact that Nettleton himself insisted on understanding conversion in a thoroughly Edwardsean sense. He thus became another in the long succession of professional revivalists, adding to his powerful appeals from the pulpit a systematic approach to home visitation, personal conference, inquiry meetings, and follow-up instruction. After his health broke in 1820, his activities were much curtailed. He traveled abroad for a time, and from 1834 until his death he resided at East Windsor, lecturing occasionally at the new theological institute which he had helped to found.

Lyman Beecher (1775–1863)

If Nettleton was a self-effacing apostle who gravitated toward Tyler's camp, Lyman Beecher was a self-asserting apostle of Taylorism, who even in death lies side by side with his friend and theological hero in the old Grove Street Cemetery in New Haven. No other figure sums up in his own life the many facets of the Second Awakening and its enormous consequences for American history.

Beecher was graduated from Yale in 1797, having spent two years under Ezra Stiles and two under Timothy Dwight. He then remained another year to study theology. It was Dwight who converted him, turned him to the ministry, formed his mind, and won his undying admiration and perhaps exorbitant praise. When in 1798 he accepted his first charge, a Presbyterian church in East Hampton, Long Island, Beecher had already been "baptized into the revival spirit"—and no baptism ever had more persistent effect. In East Hampton he won a reputation both as a moral reformer (for a crusade against dueling) and as a revivalist. He was called in 1810 to the First Church in Litchfield, Connecticut, where he weathered "Mr. Madison's War" and the successful assault of Jeffersonians, Baptists, Methodists, and Episcopalians on Connecticut's ecclesiastical establishment.

Pursuing his career as a revivalist during these years at Litchfield, Beecher brought to fullness the conception that most distinguishes the evangelical resurgence of the next half-century: the intimate association of evangelism in its broadest sense with moral reform and social benevolence. As a reformer, he was especially active in the temperance movement. When he was called in 1826 to the Hanover Street Congregational Church in Boston, he brought the tactics of revivalism to the service of conservatism against the liberals and Unitarians. Thereafter he returned to the Presbyterian fold, and in 1832 he moved out west to become president of Lane Theological Seminary. The controversies and campaigns in which he and his numerous family later became involved will be treated in subsequent chapters. His autobiography, compiled with the aid of his children shortly before his death, provides an extraordinary picture of evangelical Protestantism in antebellum America.

THE FORMATION OF VOLUNTARY ASSOCIATIONS

One of the startling features of Professor Kenneth Scott Latourette's labors as an historian of the expansion of Christianity is his designation of the nineteenth century, despite all its distractions and temptations, as "the Great Century." The things which, to his mind, make it great in America take their rise with remarkable consistency from the evangelical enthusiasm aroused by the Second Awakening in New England. Most basic perhaps was a new kind of religious institution, the voluntary association of private individuals for missionary, reformatory, or benevolent purposes.[10] Usually these societies were chartered and governed independently, even when they

10. There were several precedents for this type of organization, such as the Society for the Propagation of the Gospel in New England, formed in 1649, which under the name of the New England Company still supports the education of Indians in Canada with the revenues from its ancient government grant. The SPG was a different type of organization, being more nearly an arm of the Church of England. Later in the eighteenth century the Evangelical Revival generated many voluntary associations in Great Britain.

had a nominal relation to some church body. Their membership grew wherever interest could be created, often on an interdenominational basis. Their activities were carried on without church or state control, and in most cases they were focused fairly sharply on one specific purpose. To give even a brief account of all the many cooperative agencies would require a large volume; but certain representative ones must be considered if the significance of the Second Awakening is to be grasped.

Missionary Societies

Both logically and chronologically prior was the Connecticut Missionary Society, formed in 1798 when the General Association of Connecticut (following a resolution of the previous year and the example of the Hartford North Association) voted to become the core of an agency "to christianize the Heathen in North America, and to support and promote Christian knowledge in the new settlements, within the United States." In 1800 the *Connecticut Evangelical Magazine* was founded to further the society's work and to promote financial support. A similar society and magazine were founded in Massachusetts, with Nathanael Emmons playing a leading role in the conduct of both. After the Congregational-Presbyterian Plan of Union in 1801, this kind of work was accelerated. In 1812–13 the two societies sent Samuel J. Mills, Jr., and John Schermerhorn on a remarkable tour to estimate the religious needs of the West, which led to the setting of still more ambitious goals. Finally, as the western populations grew and as the home mission movement expanded, the consolidated American Home Missionary Society was formed in New York in 1826. For two generations its missionaries were a major force in the development of the West, not only as apostles and revivalists, but as educators, civic leaders, and exponents of eastern culture. The reports of its missionaries, its fund-raising activities, and its publications, on the other hand, had a constant invigorating influence on the supporting individuals and churches in the East.

The foreign missions story is very similar, though it has somewhat more dramatic origins in the famous "Haystack Prayer Meeting." While seeking shelter from a summer shower one day in 1806, Samuel J. Mills, Jr., and a few fellow students at Williams College dedicated themselves to missionary service in the foreign fields. Later at Andover Seminary they and other interested students organized themselves more formally, and in 1810 they were able to enlist the official support of the newly constituted General Association of Massachusetts. Before the year was out a group of Connecticut and Massachusetts ministers had incorporated the famous and long-lived American Board of Commissioners for Foreign Missions.

Mills's poor health forced him into home mission work, but in 1812 a group of foreign missionaries did set sail for India under the auspices of the board. Two of the young missionaries, however, were unexpectedly converted to Baptist views, Adoniram Judson on board ship and Luther Rice shortly after arriving. Judson and his wife remained to begin a mission which led eventually to memorable achievements in Burma.[11] Rice meanwhile returned to America to sever their connection with the American Board, and to enlist American Baptists in organized support of foreign missions. Rice discovered or aroused considerable missionary interest, which was harnessed in 1814 with the formation of the General Convention of the Baptist Denomination in the United States of America for Foreign Missions —a name long enough to kill many an organization, but not this one, for it not only survived but became a major coordinating force among American Baptists until divided by the slavery issue.

No general history can chart the remarkable expansion of the work of these and other missionary societies in every part of the world, or trace the manifold ways in which the missionaries almost created the nineteenth-century American's image of "heathendom" and heavily influenced American foreign policy. But in countless ways the Haystack Prayer Meeting continued to have repercussions throughout the world. Perhaps more germane to our story is the way in which the work of these societies strengthened the home churches themselves. When one society representative was seeking a new charter from the Massachusetts legislature, he observed that "religion is a commodity of which the more we exported the more we had remaining." Certainly no evangelical labor undertaken by the churches had a larger rejuvenating effect than the foreign mission enterprise.

Publication and Education Societies

Closely allied to the missionary societies were a group of similarly organized associations for the promotion of Christian knowledge and education. Earliest of these were the Bible societies modeled on the English organization of 1804, the first of which appeared in Philadelphia in 1808. But in 1809 others were formed in Connecticut, Massachusetts, Maine, and New York. Then in 1816, after the idea of a national organization had been advanced in many quarters, the American Bible Society was organized. In less than four years it had distributed nearly a hundred thousand Bibles. For the work of distributing tracts a similar pattern developed: a highly successful English

11. Judson's lifelong work in Burma, which included pathbreaking language studies, translation of the entire Bible from Hebrew and Greek into Burmese, and the preparation of a massive two-way lexicon, illustrates the way in which both the piety and the scholarship of Andover Seminary reached around the world (see the excellent biography by Courtney Anderson, *To the Golden Shore*).

model, a series of well-functioning state associations in America, then an enlargement of scope and the emergence of a national society. In 1814 the New England Tract Society came into being, and nine years later it was transmuted into the American Tract Society. By that time it had already printed 777,000 tracts and was publishing a bimonthly magazine, a Christian almanac, and a series of children's books. In 1825 it became a truly national organization by merging with another New York society which had the same name and a similar history.

Education was as much an object of associative effort as the publishing of Christian literature. The foundation of seminaries signified the immense new demand for ministers resulting from the revivals and from America's westward expansion. These needs led also to corollary efforts in behalf of some kind of scholarship program. In that age, a pressing need was all it took to spark the creation of a new society. This one began at New Haven in 1814–15, when a charitable society for aiding indigent theological students was founded, along with a "female auxiliary." In 1826 this movement too achieved national form as the American Education Society. Its reports are a vital chapter in the history of American higher education.

Finally, and to some extent parallel to these other societies, came the Sunday school movement and its cluster of ascending organizations. Its English precedents included the famous work begun by Robert Raikes as early as 1781. In America, Philadelphia moved first, while in New England the Second Awakening soon stimulated a like response. The schools, of course, were organized locally, but the need for an adequate supply of literature and educational materials required a larger organization, and in 1824 the American Sunday School Union was organized. Because of its primary concern as a publisher, it acted from the first as something like a nondenominational tract society, though the predominantly Reformed cast of American Protestantism at that time kept it from being so ecumenical an endeavor as it might sound. In New England especially, the state organizations were for all practical purposes Congregational agencies.

Moral Reform

Antinomianism and moral license were always special horrors to Puritan piety, and Reformed preaching never neglected to stress radical amendment of behavior as a necessary concomitant and sign of true conversion. If one recalls the intense moralism in the theology of latter-day Puritans like Dwight, it goes without saying that the revivals led also to associations for moral reform. At Yale a Moral Society existed secretly among the students as early as 1797; but before long such societies were statewide, then nationwide —and anything but secret.

The first of the great moral crusades to emerge was that directed against intemperance, which was then very widespread. Puritans had never been abstemious: rum was a vital factor in the economy of early New England, and distilled spirits had long been a popular feature of marriages, funerals, ordinations, and meetinghouse raisings, not to mention private hospitality. Most of the early attacks on drinking (John Adams's assault on the taverns in his native town of Braintree, for example) rested on a civic or hygienic rationale. In 1811, when Lyman Beecher was awakening gradually to the need for a moral crusade on Sabbath-breaking, profanity, and intemperance, there was still considerable political reasoning involved. The "ruff-scruff" among whom the abuses were worst seemed to be infidels and Jeffersonians as well as reprobates. "Our vices are digging the grave of our liberties," Beecher cried, "and preparing to entomb our glory." Due largely to his labors the Connecticut Society for the Reformation of Morals was organized in 1813, and men like Beecher soon infused the movement with an evangelical spirit that transcended political party labels. In Massachusetts a parallel movement was launched by Jeremiah Evarts, a lawyer associated with Jedidiah Morse and intimately connected with the foreign mission cause. The Massachusetts Society for the Suppression of Intemperance resulted. Both societies encouraged the formation of local auxiliaries. The War of 1812 slowed these efforts but inspired plans for wider campaigns lest infidels, slaveholders, and backwoodsmen provoke still other wars. But when peace came Dwight took the lead in making drinking, not intemperance, the sin—and in demanding total abstinence. Beecher took the same stand in his *Six Sermons* on the subject. First published in 1826, this volume made a strong and persuasive case for temperance. It was many times reprinted and constantly quoted by other temperance leaders.

To further the cause, the American Society for the Promotion of Temperance was formed in Boston in 1826 by men active in the missionary movement. In 1829 Connecticut followed suit, and its temperance society within a year reported 172 branch societies with twenty-two thousand members. In 1836 the American Temperance Union was formed on a total abstinence platform. The extraordinary success of the temperance movement during the next two decades forms a familiar chapter in American social history. The Maine Law, passed under the leadership of Neal Dow in 1846, was the first statewide prohibition law, and as revised in 1851 it became the model for numerous other states.[12] But the relation of this success to the evangelical counterreformation springing from the Second Awakening is less often noted.

12. Similar laws were passed in 1852 in Vermont, Rhode Island, and Minnesota Territory; in 1853 in Michigan; in 1854 in Connecticut; and in eight other states by 1855.

As moral rigor increased in this field, so did it in others. The Sabbath was protected by an organization which became national in 1826. Dancing and theatergoing became increasingly suspect. Lotteries, which once had financed buildings for both Harvard and Yale and for innumerable churches, also fell under the ban. Obscenity and profanity came to be defined in far more rigorous terms, and in due course these evils aroused the crusading impulse of other moral reformers. Gradually Americans would come to identify Puritanism and blue-nosed Victorianism.

Humanitarian Interests

The first half of the nineteenth century was also the age of the humanitarian reformer, a time for assailing the status quo with a wide variety of campaigns and benevolences. Taken together, these many causes constitute a movement deeply rooted in the Puritan's compulsion to transform the world, the democratic American's conviction that men ought to be free, and the new Adam's soaring faith in human progress. Some sprang unmistakably from the enlightened ideals which were expressed in the Declaration of Independence and reinforced in the age of Jackson. Others were brought into being by the liberal Unitarians and Transcendentalists of eastern Massachusetts. Another important and characteristic pattern of humanitarian philosophy, however, was linked intimately with the Second Awakening; and it would produce as its ultimate classic Harriet Beecher Stowe's *Uncle Tom's Cabin*. But long before that work burst upon a nation already riven by sectional strife, the leaven of revivalism was doing its benevolent work. The service of the poor and unfortunate (*diakonia,* whence the word "deacon") is an immemorial obligation of the church, and the Puritans had taken it seriously from the beginning. At the end of the eighteenth and the beginning of the nineteenth century this work became increasingly the concern of voluntary associations of one sort or another. Characteristically (and fatefully) these societies brought women into the work of organized philanthropy, thereby setting off the woman's rights movement on a history of its own.

The physically handicapped provided another important incentive to action, and among the most famous resultant enterprises was Hartford Asylum for the Education and Instruction of the Deaf and Dumb. The initial impulse came from Dr. Mason F. Cogswell of Hartford, whose daughter was so afflicted. Cogswell turned to the Congregational General Association, and was encouraged to further action by Timothy Dwight, Benjamin Silliman, and Professor Jeremiah Day of Yale. The institution really came into existence when the Reverend Thomas Gallaudet of Hartford, a graduate of Yale and Andover, devoted himself to its cause. Gallaudet went to England and

France in search of technical knowledge and returned in 1816 not only adept himself, but bringing with him an accomplished protégé of the Abbé Sicard of Paris. Thereafter the Hartford Asylum became an important center for this special sort of education. Other kinds of sympathy led to other institutions: the Hartford Retreat for the Insane founded between 1822 and 1824, the General Hospital Society of Connecticut, and the movement for the new and reformed prison at Wethersfield. Unquestionably the most important issue of all was slavery, which already by 1817 had led to the founding of the Colonization Society. Indeed, the entire impulse for humanitarian and moral reform was inexorably converging on this nation-shaking question; but these are matters for later chapters.

The "American as Reformer" was by no means exclusively the child of revivalistic Protestantism. Men and women of every possible intellectual and religious persuasion undertook countless campaigns for various causes, and often joined forces. Unitarians, Transcendentalists, and belligerently secular reformers helped to advance this half-century's reforming impulse. The extent to which a vague and secularized Puritan transformationism underlies all of these characteristically American movements is difficult to say, but it would be hard to imagine the American's persistent "interferiority complex" [13] without the substructure of Puritan concern for amending the ways of this world and his "theocratic" insistence that God's moral government applies to societies as well as to individuals. During the early nineteenth century the Puritan began to gain his reputation as a meddlesome legalist, narrow-minded, joyless, and small-bored. But this stereotype needs correction. Even in an age when Puritanism was undergoing profound inner changes, it remained a creative and energy-releasing power. And that power was generated not only in New England, but ever westward as Americans restlessly pressed the frontier farther and farther from the Atlantic. In this vast inland empire the Puritan impulse would join with others, changing them and being changed, but always making its mark on American evangelical Protestantism as well as on the nation's life and institutions.

13. The term, for better or worse, was used by the elder Arthur M. Schlesinger, who by himself and through his many students made an immense contribution to the study of American reform impulses.

27

THE GREAT REVIVAL IN THE WEST AND THE GROWTH OF THE POPULAR DENOMINATIONS

After victory in the last French and Indian War, the English government, without much thought for enforcement problems, prohibited settlement beyond the Appalachian Mountains. Long before that, however, fur traders had penetrated those areas, and there was no way to prevent settlers from flowing into a land which Christopher Gist described in 1751 as "Watered with a great number of little streams and Rivulets, and full of beautiful natural Meadows, covered with wild Rye, blue grass, and Clover." By 1772 there were four settlements in the upper Holston Valley, in 1776 Kentucky County was erected, and during the Revolution George Rogers Clark led a contingent of western Virginians on his famous conquest of the British forts at Vincennes and Kaskaskia. By 1783, when the Treaty of Paris established the Mississippi River as the western boundary of the United States, the population of these settlements in Kentucky and Tennessee was approaching fifty thousand, with the chief areas of settlement in the valleys of eastern Tennessee, the Nashville basin, the limestone areas of Kentucky, and the Ohio River lowlands. A year later the people in the Wautauga area organized themselves, elected John Sevier as governor, and applied to Congress for recognition as a state. Though they were unsuccessful then, after eight years and nine conventions Kentucky achieved statehood, and four years later (1796) Tennessee was admitted to the Union, both with constitutions and bills of rights similar to those in other states. At the time of their admission, the two states had respectively 73,000 and 77,000 inhabitants. The settlers, most of whom were from Maryland, Virginia, and the Carolinas, were thinly scattered. Lexington, Kentucky, was the largest town, with 1,795 people in 1800, while Louisville, Frankfort, Nashville, and Knoxville all had fewer than 500. Even in 1810, when Kentucky boasted 406,501 people and Tennessee 261,727, the two areas had only 10 and 6.2 persons per square mile respectively.

It was a rude civilization dominated by the desire for land.

> The Indian understood when the "tall men came / Whose words were bullets" that he had to reckon with a people quite different from the pleasure-loving *coureurs de bois,* the peaceful Quakers, and the English traders. These grim backwoodsmen were not concerned, as the Jesuit fathers, with his salvation, or, as the traders, with his beaver, but came to kill his deer and occupy his land permanently. Under the circumstances, it is not surprising that the Indian fought the settler in buckskin.[1]

Between the rough tasks of expelling the Indians and subduing the wilderness, the frontiersman acquired a reputation for wild and lawless living. His barbarity never failed to shock the occasional easterner who ventured a visit.

> It may not be improper to mention, that the backwoodsmen, as the first emigrants from the eastward of the Allegheny mountains are called, are very similar in their habits and manners to the aborigines, only perhaps more prodigal and more careless of life. They depend more on hunting than on agriculture, and of course are exposed to all the varieties of climate in the open air. Their cabins are not better than Indian wigwams. They have frequent meetings for the purposes of gambling, fighting and drinking. They make bets to the amount of all they possess. They fight for the most trifling provocations, or even sometimes without any, but merely to try each others prowess, which they are fond of vaunting of. Their hands, teeth, knees, head and feet are their weapons, not only boxing with their fists, . . . but also tearing, kicking, scratching, biting, gouging each others eyes out by a dexterous use of a thumb and finger, and doing their utmost to kill each other, even when rolling over one another on the ground.[2]

Whether or not this traveler "reported rather more than he observed" and contributed to the romantic haze which soon enveloped the frontiersman,

1. Arthur K. Moore, *The Frontier Mind: A Cultural Analysis of the Kentucky Frontiersman* (Lexington, Ky.: University of Kentucky Press, 1957), p. 50.

2. Moore quotes the English traveler, Fortescue Cuming, ibid., p. 54.

the western settlers did speedily acquire an unequaled reputation for violence and heedless ways. The society to which circuit riders, farmer-preachers, and evangelizers of all kinds were to make their gospel appeals offered a challenge equal to any in the church's long history.

The religious life of the vast area did not simply remain dormant until one fine day in August, 1801, when the fires of revival suddenly sprang up at Cane Ridge in Bourbon County, Kentucky. The settlers did, to be sure, outrun the organized churches, but many were earnest and some were zealous in religious matters. It was said of the Scotch-Irish farmers that when crops failed and food was short, they could live off the Shorter Catechism, and this exaggeration could also be applied to many Baptists and Methodists. The most important single factor in the westward movement of popular piety was the extended "Great Awakening" in the southern back country. Because of the revivals (Presbyterian, Baptist, and Methodist in turn) there were among the migrants a significant number of strongly committed laymen who became missionaries without formal commissioning.

Each of these three denominations, furthermore, had certain important assets for the immense new work before it. The Presbyterians were strategically poised in western Pennsylvania, where the Redstone Presbytery had been formed in 1781. It soon gave birth to others in the Ohio Valley. Presbyterians had also penetrated the southern back country. The first Presbyterian preacher in Kentucky was David Rice, who in 1784 moved from Hanover County, Virginia, and organized at Danville the first church of his denomination in the state. Largely as a result of his labors, twelve other churches were organized by the next year, and the Transylvania Presbytery was formed. By 1802 two more presbyteries had been organized, making it possible to constitute the Synod of Kentucky. Their secure footing in the old Middle Colonies ensured the Presbyterians resources of money and personnel, while their hierarchical polity facilitated an organized missions program. Not least, they could appeal to the Westminster birthright slumbering in the consciousness of so many of the pioneers.

The Methodists were less solidly based in the East, but they had formed a highly efficient organization which was closely superintended by a man of amazing energy and foresight, Bishop Francis Asbury. They sent the first regularly appointed circuit rider over the mountains in 1782, and within nine years there were ten Methodist circuits in the new West: four in Tennessee, three in Kentucky, and three along the upper Ohio. By 1800 there were more than two thousand Methodists in Kentucky and Tennessee. Bishop Asbury himself took a personal interest in the growth of Methodism in the "Western Conference," as the tramontane area was called, crossing the mountains several times to confer with the preachers and minister to the churches.

The Baptists, on the other hand, were much more flexible than either of these two bodies; they opposed the idea of settled, educated, and paid ministers, relying instead on preachers who could move along with their migrating flocks. They were also well situated on the trails that led through the mountains. Daniel Boone himself was of Baptist background, and there were at least two Baptist preachers at Harrodsburg by 1776. Several others followed, and in 1781 the first church was organized at Severn's Valley. Within four years there were a dozen churches grouped in three associations, two of which were Regular (Elkhorn and Salem) and one Separate (South Kentucky). Efforts to unite these two groups were begun in 1793 and finally consummated in 1801. Though the 1790s were deemed "a period of spiritual dearth," a constant influx of settlers added to the number and size of Baptist congregations.

THE WESTERN REVIVALS

As providence would have it, the Presbyterian work in this new mission field was to have the most dramatic historical consequences. The first well-remembered actor in the drama was the Reverend James McGready (1758?–1817), a bold and uncompromising Scotch-Irishman whose family had moved from Pennsylvania to western North Carolina when he was a child. Showing great religious interest as a youth, he was sent back to Pennsylvania for theological studies under John McMillan, a Princeton graduate, and he was later licensed by the Redstone Presbytery. McGready ministered in Carolina until 1796, when he took charge of three parishes in southwestern Kentucky. At the Gasper River Church in July 1800, he and his associates gave decisive impetus to that great institution of western evangelism, the camp meeting, which may be defined as "a religious service of several days' length, held outdoors, for a group that was obliged to take shelter on the spot because of the distance from home."

Another Presbyterian who attended this Logan County revival was Barton Warren Stone (1772–1844). Born in Port Tobacco, Maryland, Stone had moved into western Carolina, where he was converted under McGready. In 1800 he was serving the small Cane Ridge and Concord churches in Bourbon County, Kentucky. Greatly impressed by what he saw at Gasper River, the more so because of his concern over the prevailing apathy in his own area, Stone adopted McGready's methods. After some preliminary revivals, he announced a great meeting to be held at Cane Ridge on

6 August 1801. When the day arrived, so did a great many ministers, including some Baptists and Methodists, and an unbelievably large concourse of people. The crowd was estimated at from ten to twenty-five thousand—and this at a time when nearby Lexington, the state's largest city, barely exceeded two thousand. This "sacramental occasion" continued for six or seven days and nights, and would have gone on longer except for the failure of provisions for such a crowd. When it was over, Cane Ridge was referred to as the greatest outpouring of the Spirit since Pentecost. It marks a watershed in American church history, and the little log meetinghouse around which multitudes thronged and writhed has become a shrine for all who invoke "the frontier spirit" in American Christianity.

The Cane Ridge meeting has challenged the descriptive powers of many historians, yet none has risen fully to the occasion. Critics and sensationalists then and since have dwelt almost exclusively on the rampant emotionalism and bodily agitations. Most of those who were caught up in the enthusiasm were never able to report it objectively. Barton Stone himself stated the basic fact: "Many things transpired there, which were so much like miracles, that if they were not, they had the same effects as miracles on infidels and unbelievers; for many of them by these were convinced that Jesus was the Christ, and bowed in submission to him." [3] One must first try to re-create the scene: the milling crowds of hardened frontier farmers, tobacco-chewing, tough-spoken, notoriously profane, famous for their alcoholic thirst; their scarcely demure wives and large broods of children; the rough clearing, the rows of wagons and crude improvised tents with horses staked out behind; the gesticulating speaker on a rude platform, or perhaps simply a preacher holding forth from a fallen tree. At night, when the forest's edge was limned by the flickering light of many campfires, the effect of apparent miracles would be heightened. For men and women accustomed to retiring and rising with the birds, these turbulent nights must have been especially awe-inspiring. And underlying every other conditioning circumstance was the immense loneliness of the frontier farmer's normal life and the exhilaration of participating in so large a social occasion.[4]

The physical effects of so drastic a conjunction of apathy and fervor, loneliness and sociality, monotony and miracle, could not have been mild. Critics thought they noted a greater increase of fleshly lust than of spirituality, and charged that "more souls were begot than saved"; while even the

3. "A Short History of the Life of Barton W. Stone Written by Himself," in *Voices from Cane Ridge*, ed. Rhodes Thompson, facsimile ed. (Saint Louis: Bethany Press, 1954), p. 68.

4. Nowhere in the world were farmers so scattered on their isolated homesteads as in America, and until the advent of the automobile, churches would continue to be their chief social bond.

most sympathetic observers conceded that camp-meeting conversions were not decorous religious transactions. Barton Stone devoted a whole chapter of his memoirs to a description of the outward manifestations of strong religious emotions; and this account by the meeting's leader merits extensive quotation, for it reveals his serious estimate of the very excesses that made Cane Ridge not only a landmark in the history of revivalism, but a cause of controversy and schism.

> The bodily agitations or exercises, attending the excitement in the beginning of this century, were various, and called by various names. . . . The falling exercise was very common among all classes, the saints and sinners of every age and of every grade, from the philosopher to the clown. The subject of this exercise would, generally, with a piercing scream, fall like a log on the floor, earth, or mud, and appear as dead. . . .
>
> The jerks cannot be so easily described. Sometimes the subject of the jerks would be affected in some one member of the body, and sometimes the whole system. When the head alone was affected, it would be jerked backward and forward, or from side to side, so quickly that the features of the face could not be distinguished. When the whole system was affected, I have seen the person stand in one place, and jerk backward and forward in quick succession, their head nearly touching the floor behind and before. All classes, saints and sinners, the strong as well as the weak, were thus affected. . . .
>
> The dancing exercise. This generally began with the jerks, and was peculiar to the professors of religion. The subject, after jerking awhile, began to dance, and then the jerks would cease. Such dancing was indeed heavenly to the spectators; there was nothing in it like levity, nor calculated to excite levity in the beholders. The smile of heaven shone on the countenance of the subject, and assimilated to angels appeared the whole person. Sometimes the motion was quick and sometimes slow. Thus they continued to move forward and backward in the same track or alley till nature seemed exhausted, and they would fall prostrate on the floor or earth, unless caught by those standing by. While thus exercised, I have heard their solemn praises and prayers ascending to God.
>
> The barking exercise, (as opposers contemptuously called it,) was nothing but the jerks. A person affected with the jerks, especially in his head, would often make a grunt, or bark, if you please, from the suddenness of the jerk. . . .
>
> The laughing exercise was frequent, confined solely with the reli-

> gious. It was a loud, hearty laughter, but one *sui generis;* it excited laughter in none else. The subject appeared rapturously solemn, and his laughter excited solemnity in saints and sinners. It is truly indescribable.
>
> The running exercise was nothing more than, that persons feeling something of these bodily agitations, through fear, attempted to run away, and thus escape from them; but it commonly happened that they ran not far, before they fell, or became so greatly agitated that they could proceed no farther. . . .
>
> I shall close this chapter with the singing exercise. This is more unaccountable than any thing else I ever saw. The subject in a very happy state of mind would sing most melodiously, not from the mouth or nose, but entirely in the breast, the sounds issuing from thence. Such music silenced every thing, and attracted the attention of all. It was most heavenly. None could ever be tired of hearing it.

Stone concludes by admitting that "there were many eccentricities, and much fanaticism in this excitement," but insists that "the good effects were seen and acknowledged in every neighborhood." [5]

GROWTH OF THE POPULAR DENOMINATIONS

The most important fact about Cane Ridge is that it was an unforgettable revival of revivalism, at a strategic time and a place where it could become both symbol and impetus for the century-long process by which the greater part of American evangelical Protestantism became "revivalized." The organized revival became a major mode of church expansion—in some denominations the major mode. The words evangelist and evangelism took on this connotation. A second consequence of this historic camp meeting and the great revival which swept across Kentucky, Tennessee, and southern Ohio during the next three years was the vitality which it poured into the participating churches. The future of the country's denominational expansion was in large part determined by the foundations laid during this period. Denominational growth began to reach a new order of magnitude, not only in the West, but in the East as well due to the stimulating effect of enthusiastic reports that soon drifted back to the older and more settled parts of the country. In the positive sense this development was primarily Baptist and Methodist, for Presbyterian leaders were repelled by the reports and began to take disciplinary action. From this time forward Presbyterian growth would lag far behind. A third consequence of the revivals was the

5. "Life of Stone," pp. 69–72.

rise of conflict and schism, from which the Presbyterians suffered most severely, though the Baptists sustained considerable losses as well. Finally, a new Christian movement, destined to become a large American denomination, came into being during these enlivening years.

The Methodists

No group prospered more in the West or seemed more providentially designed to capitalize on the conditions of the advancing American frontier than the Methodists. A small and highly suspect adjunct to Anglicanism before the Revolution, this church had begun its independent American history only in 1784. Since then its web of preaching circuits had come to cover almost the entire country. In 1789 even New England had been invaded. Yet the 1790s had generally been unencouraging, with almost as many years showing a net decline in membership as those which showed a gain. The hierarchical structure of the church was seriously challenged in 1792, when James O'Kelly of Virginia led out the "Republican Methodists" to become a separate movement. Cokesbury College, the first Methodist experiment in higher education, had burned to the ground in 1795. At the turn of the century there were probably not sixty-five thousand Methodists in the country, and Asbury's health was in serious decline. The General Conference at Baltimore in 1800, however, was the scene of a great revival among those in attendance—strangely synchronous with more tumultuous developments beyond the mountains—and as the preachers returned to their circuits the whole church began to feel and respond to the new impulses.

John Magee, one of James McGready's most vigorous aides in Logan County, was a Methodist. At Cane Ridge another Methodist, William Burke, seems to have preached with as powerful an effect as anybody else. After 1800 other men continued their tradition, and "because early Methodists did not turn their backs on groans and jerks," writes Bernard Weisberger, "they could slay their thousands while the other denominations counted their hundreds." Circuits were laid out both to create and to tap the religious potential of the Old Southwest; the circuit became an institution of the region, and the Methodist Episcopal church itself experienced a virtual second birth.

> When the century began there were 2,622 white Methodists and 179 colored in the whole western country; in 1812 there were 29,093 white and 1,648 colored, while the circuits had increased from 9 to 69. In 1830, instead of 1 conference west of the Alleghanies, there were 8, while the membership had grown from 30,000 to more than 175,000,

> and among these were nearly 2,000 Indians and more than 15,000 negroes.[6]

By 1844, when the church divided north and south, the Methodists had become the most numerous religious body in America, with 1,068,525 members, 3,988 itinerant preachers, 7,730 local preachers, and an incalculable number of regular hearers. Even in New England, where its progress was slowest, it had become the second largest denomination.

The most important factor in this amazing expansion was the system of circuits and preaching stations, and the disciplined, basically autocratic way in which they were laid out, staffed, and supervised. The country was subdivided into districts in 1796, each overseen by a presiding elder, and after 1808, with the enormously active, knowledgeable, and far-sighted William McKendree as bishop of the Western Conference, Methodists were in a position to evangelize a moving population. They had been in such a position from the beginning, as a matter of fact; but they became even more effective by virtue of a second factor—their appropriation of the camp meeting, which they made an instrument for satisfying both the social and the religious impulses of a scattered, though naturally gregarious, people. When other denominations abandoned it as leading to excess and division, the Methodists became its sponsors. Bishop Asbury was one of its most enthusiastic champions, and it became fully subject to the famous Methodist penchant for meticulous planning. Nothing was left to chance, from the scheduling of the meetings and their advertisement to the sharing of duties among the camp leaders and management of the camp services. From one end of the country to the other there were great Methodist conclaves, sometimes organized within a single circuit, sometimes for a whole conference, often serving as the annual conference itself. Due both to overuse and overorganization, however, they slowly lost their spontaneity and became decorous and formal. Cabins and two-storied residence houses replaced the tents, and by the 1840s the original impulse was dying. In later years the camp meeting became a resort, a place for an edifying vacation—an outcome shown in the multiplication of summer assemblies and Bible conferences, both denominational and interdenominational.[7] But during the early nineteenth century "harvest time," the camp meeting was a great engine of Methodist expansion and a very important part of the church's system.

A third factor which had been operative from the first was this church's

6. William W. Sweet, *Religion in the Development of American Culture, 1765–1840*, p. 119.

7. By the middle of the twentieth century at least one of these has become a "place not to miss" for those who followed Duncan Hines's advice to gourmets.

recruitment of its ministry from among the common people, and its continuing interest in the masses. Ordination was conferred only on well-proved preachers, with the result that ordained men were something of an elite within the system. But they were by no means a social elite. With little formal training to divorce them from the common idiom, they reduced the Christian message and its implications for life to the simplest possible terms, and preached it simply, directly, and forcefully. Peter Cartwright (1785–1872), most famed of the circuit riders and a great presiding elder of the West, scorned theological education, which he considered often even a hindrance in preaching the Gospel: "I have seen so many educated preachers who forcibly reminded me of lettuce growing under the shade of a peach-tree, or like a gosling that had got the straddles by wading in the dew, that I turn away sick and faint." The Methodists also made maximum use of informality, as Cartwright likewise made clear:

> The Presbyterians, and other Calvinistic branches of the Protestant Church, used to contend for an educated ministry, for pews, for instrumental music, for a congregational or stated salaried ministry. The Methodists universally opposed these ideas; and the illiterate Methodist preachers actually set the world on fire, (the American world at least,) while they [the others] were lighting their matches! [8]

The fourth factor, implied in Cartwright's statement, was the preaching of Wesleyan theology, sometimes described as "Arminianism set on fire." There is no justification for the conclusion of many historians (including the most fervent Methodists) that the Methodist message was a "democratic theology" or a "frontier faith." In the earlier part of the nineteenth century, at least, its theology was derived not from American democracy or the frontier but from John Wesley—a very different source indeed. The conference courses of study instituted in 1816 for prospective ministers in lieu of divinity schools were thoroughly Wesleyan in spirit. And the starting point of this theology (as of all Reformed theologies, whether "Arminian" or not) was the sovereignty of God and the depravity of man. No one spoke more forcefully of man's abject need for divine grace than Wesley, and the true Methodist demand for repentance—or, more often, penitential conflict—stems from the heart of the Puritan movement. Arminianism in this context meant not an optimistic view of human nature (as with the Boston liberals), but a reinterpretation of the strict Calvinistic understanding of atonement, grace, and the sanctifying work of the Holy Spirit. Had this not been the case, Methodism would never have been the moral force that

8. *Autobiography of Peter Cartwright*, ed. Charles L. Wallis, p. 64.

it was on the frontier. Decades of vulgar, simplistic theological polemic between Wesleyans and Calvinists ultimately forced both sides to exaggerate their distinctive tenets and banish subtlety from theological discussion. Revivalistic preaching thus in time worked its effect on Methodist theology, shifting the emphasis from "grace for all" to "human freedom," but there is no evidence that the new patterns of thought which emerged brought any increased effectiveness in preaching. In fact, one must insist that the force of primitive Wesleyan theology constituted a major factor in the Methodist explosion on the frontier.

German Evangelicals and United Brethren

The contagiousness of the Wesleyan appeal is further indicated by two other Methodistic movements that emerged at the same time among the German-speaking peoples, and which flourished under very similar circumstances. These served even more effectively to perpetuate the traditions of pietism and even to revive the earlier Anabaptist vision of an *ecclesia restituta.* The outstanding leader of this revival was Philip William Otterbein (1726–1813), a native of the Reformed duchy of Nassau in Germany, who in 1752 answered the call of Michael Schlatter for American missionaries. Already well known for his efforts to restore experiential religion, Otterbein extended his reputation during a series of five pastorates in America, the last, longest, and most eventful one in an evangelical German church in Baltimore. While in Lancaster, Pennsylvania, he also felt a notable deepening of his own experience of God's grace. His new perspective on the church gained significance in subsequent years, especially after his meeting with the Mennonite preacher Martin Boehm (1725–1812), and the Methodist Francis Asbury. In 1784 the attraction of these new contacts finally overcame his allegiance to the German Reformed church. During the famous Christmas Conference of the Methodist church in that year, he participated in the ordination of Asbury as general superintendent. The following year Otterbein set up rules for the government and devotional life of his own congregation, which in due course defined the character of a new pietistic, semi-Methodist German denomination in which "inward spiritual experience" became a requirement of membership.

This group progressed toward separation in 1789, when fourteen like-minded pastors (nine German Reformed and five Mennonite) met in Otterbein's parsonage and adopted regulations and a confession of faith adapted from the Apostles' and Nicene creeds. They stressed especially "the fall in Adam" and affirmed the importance of both the human will and the sanctifying work of the Holy Spirit in salvation. Particularly interesting are the passages which compromise the conflicting Reformed and Mennonite views on baptism, communion, and foot washing. What was emerging here was a new version of the same sort of religious impulse that a century before had created the Church of the Brethren in Schwarzenau, and which a century and a half before that had brought the Mennonite movement into being.

The final moves toward denominational independence came in 1800, when Otterbein and Boehm were elected bishops, and in 1815, when the first general conference of the United Brethren in Christ was convened, and a more complete discipline adopted. In the permissive American milieu, such an organization could develop rapidly; and by this time its preachers had made their way to wherever Germans were settling. Like the Methodist church, which continued to absorb many of its English-speaking younger people, it moved west. In 1810 the Miami (Ohio) Conference was formed, and there were congregations in Kentucky and Indiana as well.

While the leaven of pietistic and Wesleyan influence was bringing the United Brethren into existence, still another revivalistic movement was emerging among the Germans of eastern Pennsylvania. Its founder was Jacob Albright (1759–1808), who had been born and reared in the spiritual desolation of the revolutionary era. Stirred from his lethargy by a funeral sermon in 1790, he was converted some years later, and joined the Methodists. Gradually Albright became disturbed over the religious welfare of his German-speaking neighbors, for whom the church showed little concern, and in 1796 he embarked on a preaching career. Eventually he organized his scattered converts into locally led "classes," which were soon brought together in an essentially Methodistic "Evangelical Association." When a formal council in November 1803 officially declared its denominational integrity and acknowledged the leadership of Albright, a new religious body was on the American scene. At the first regular annual conference in 1807, though the movement was still very small (consisting of only three local preachers, five itinerants, and twenty lay leaders), they elected Albright as bishop and adopted as their official—though temporary—name "The Newly Formed Methodist Conference."

In structure, doctrine, and discipline, this movement was decidedly Wesleyan, and it would doubtless have integrated with the Methodist church had not that body repulsed it.[9] During the early decades of its existence, its "large meetings," protracted revivals, and enthusiastic employment of

9. In 1810 (two years after Albright's death) Bishop Asbury declined proposals of merger from "the Albright People." Pursuing thereafter an independent course, the group was greatly divided in the latter half of the century over Wesley's doctrine of complete sanctification.

emotionalism won the allegiance of numbers of America's westward-moving German population, until this very migration shifted the center of gravity of the group to the Old Northwest. In 1815 they began publication work at New Berlin, Pennsylvania, and their *Christliche Botschafter* (1836) became an outstanding German religious periodical. In 1853, however, they deemed it advisable to move the publishing house to Cleveland, Ohio. The Eastern Conference organized in 1838 the first "German Evangelical Missionary Society of North America," which was transmuted the next year into a general denominational organ for missionary endeavor. Although they had no schools before the Civil War due to a strong prejudice against education, they moved to establish several in the latter part of the century. In 1946 they effected a merger with the United Brethren, forming the Evangelical United Brethren Church, and finally, in 1968, this united church returned to the Methodist church, which now added the word "United" at the head of its corporate name.

The Baptists

Baptist growth in the West in the decades after Cane Ridge was almost as sensational as that of the Methodists, a resurgence that lifted the Baptists into a prominent position in American religious life from that time forward. As with other churches, the effects of this western revival also flowed back into the older churches of the East. The Baptist expansion also underlines again the fact that successful evangelism did not require a congenial "frontier theology," for Baptist preaching continued to be strictly Reformed in spirit. Adherence to the Philadelphia Confession was not so strict as the Regular Baptists had hoped, but the creedal basis on which Regulars and Separates of Kentucky united in 1801 was at least as Reformed in temper as, say, the Thirty-nine Articles of the Church of England. Since this historic compromise of Arminian and Calvinistic views set a pattern, it deserves to be quoted in full:

> We, the committees of the Elkhorn and South Kentucky Associations, do agree to unite on the following plan. 1st. That the Scriptures of the Old and New Testaments are the infallible word of God, and the only rule of faith and practice. 2nd. That there is only one true Godhead or divine essence, there are Father, Son, and Holy Ghost. 3d. That by nature we are fallen and depraved creatures. 4th. That salvation, regeneration, sanctification, and justification, are by the life, death, resurrection, and ascension of Jesus Christ. 5th. That the saints will finally persevere through grace to glory. 6th. That believers' baptism by immersion is

> necessary to receiving the Lord's supper. 7th. That the salvation of the righteous, and punishment of the wicked will be eternal. 8th. That it is our duty to be tender and affectionate to each other, and study the happiness of the children of God in general; to be engaged singly to promote the honour of God. 9th. And that the preaching [that] Christ tasted death for every man shall be no bar to communion [that is, deviation from strict Reformed teaching on "limited atonement" is allowed]. 10th. And that each may keep up their associational and church government as to them may seem best. 11th. That a free correspondence and communion be kept up between the churches thus united.[10]

Again it must be stressed that such a confession proclaimed not the "religion of democracy" or a "frontier faith" but a basically Calvinistic theology, with concessions made only to those whose interpretation of Christ's work was in the tradition of Jacobus Arminius—who was, after all, a Reformed theologian. The basic doctrinal differences between Baptists and Methodists, therefore, should not be exaggerated. But frontier preachers did precisely that in their constant efforts to evangelize or "proselytize" the people;[11] and in the highly competitive situation that ensued, they debated the issues of election, grace, and human freedom almost as frequently as the doctrine of baptism. In the early part of the century the effect of all this popular controversy was to widen the rifts that separated the denominations, as well as to work significant changes within them.

Like the Methodists, the Baptists had a long history of minority status everywhere except in Rhode Island. With the Great Awakening this began to change throughout the country, and the flourishing Baptist revival in the southern back country even gave Baptists political power, especially in Virginia. Of special strategic importance was the location of several very zealous congregations along the fringe of the old frontier, where they could reach the migrants streaming past their doors. In 1790 only 3,105 of Kentucky's 73,677 people were Baptists, and these were scattered in 42 churches with some forty preachers, of whom only nineteen were ordained. By 1800 these had increased to 5,110 members in 106 churches, which were organized into one Separate and two Regular associations. Then came the great revival, in which "all were visited and refreshed by the copious and abundant rain of righteousness which was poured over the land," and by

10. William W. Sweet, *Religion on the American Frontier: The Baptists, 1783–1830*, pp. 23–24.

11. "Proselytizing" was (and is) the term for the widely discountenanced but nevertheless very widely practiced policy of trying to win members from another denomination.

1803 Kentucky numbered 10,380 Baptists; by 1820, when Kentucky's population had climbed to 564,000, they had 491 churches with 31,689 members. In other parts of the Old Southwest, in the lower parts of the Old Northwest, and in the seaboard states, there was a corresponding development as the revival became a general national phenomenon.[12]

The proliferation of Baptist churches depended above all upon their spiritual vitality and their individualistic emphasis on conversion.[13] Yet they also were remarkably well adapted to the social structures (or lack of them) on the frontier. Baptists did not exceed Presbyterians in zeal, but they were unhindered by the bottlenecks to evangelistic work created by strict educational requirements and a rigid presbyterial polity. The genius of Baptist evangelism was also at the opposite pole from the Methodist insistence on order and authority. Its frontier hero was not the circuit rider but the farmer-preacher, who moved with the people into new areas. Unpaid, self-supporting, and hence financially independent, the farmer-preacher was usually a man who had heard the "call" to the ministry and got himself licensed to preach. In due course he would be ordained by a church, sometimes one which he had gathered himself. From such churches sprang other candidates for the ministry, and by this process the Baptists advanced into the wilderness, or moved back in among the unchurched multitudes of the older areas, without direction from bishops or synods, and without financial support from denominational agencies or special societies. On many occasions an entire church would move on to a new location, just as Lewis Craig's congregation moved from Virginia to become Gilbert's Creek Church in Kentucky in 1783. Baptist work was not as disorganized as all this may imply, however, for their regional associations fostered a spirit of unity, as well as a concern for discipline and doctrinal harmony.

Like the Methodists, the Baptists grew because they sprang from the most numerous class of Americans—the common people of the country and small towns—and they spoke to these people with simplicity and power, without pretense or condescension. Peter Cartwright tells of stopping on his circuit at Stockton Valley during his early years to make a preaching appointment in an old crumbling Baptist church:

> When I came there was a very large congregation. While I was preaching, the power of God fell on the assembly, and there was an awful shaking among the dry bones. Several fell to the floor and cried for

12. In 1812 the entire denomination registered 172,972 members in 2,164 churches with 1,605 ministers, having doubled in the previous decade.

13. On this individualistic emphasis on conversion and its later consequences, see Samuel S. Hill, Jr., *Southern Churches in Crisis*, chap. 5.

> mercy. . . . I believe if I had opened the doors of the Church then, all of them would have joined the Methodist Church.[14]

But Cartwright moved on, and the Baptists, having heard of his twenty-three conquests, sent three preachers to the place. The few scattered Methodists in the neighborhood then took alarm, he said, "for fear these preachers would run my converts into the water before I could come round." They persuaded Cartwright to return, and he was able to save his spiritual children only at the very brink of the creek, by a most desperate stratagem. Cartwright presented himself for Baptist membership, recounted his own Christian experience, and was received gleefully by the Baptist preacher. At the last moment, however, in the hearing of all, he declared that he still believed in infant sprinkling, thus forcing the Baptist to reject him publicly. At the sight of his rejection, his twenty-three converts returned to the Methodist fold. This story indicates the depths to which theological controversy descended, but it also illustrates the enthusiasm with which both Methodists and Baptists sought to bring wandering frontiersmen of every rank and station within the influence and discipline of their churches.

The Presbyterians

The Baptists and Methodists were the two great popular churches of the frontier; but this is not to deny the popular aims of the Presbyterians, who were among the first to work beyond the mountains, and in whose churches the revivals of 1800 and 1801 took place. Since the days of Whitefield and the Tennents they had been aggressive in their evangelism, but on the frontier they were beset with obstacles which they were unable to overcome. As legatees of a monumental dogmatic tradition, Presbyterians were committed to a concept of education and instruction. The doctrinal system of the Westminster formularies was ill-adapted to the simplifications of frontier preaching; it demanded a genuinely "teaching church," a catechetical system, sustained preaching, and a well-educated ministry. Faced with these realities, Presbyterians responded, with varying degrees of intensity, in one of two ways. In some cases, they modified their message, as the Separate Baptists had done, or adopted the New Haven Theology and even explicit forms of Arminianism. The other recourse was to break away completely from the doctrinal and educational restrictions of Presbyterianism. Because many chose the latter alternative, conflict and schism became characteristic features of Presbyterian history in this period and region. The new churches

14. *Autobiography of Peter Cartwright*, pp. 55–56.

thus formed became rivals of the Baptists and the Methodists due to their message, popular approach, and appeal.

The first division within the newly formed Synod of Kentucky was a direct aftermath of James McGready's revivals in Logan County. The men who had led this renewing work soon gained control of the Cumberland Presbytery (organized in 1802), which in 1806 was exscinded from the Synod of Kentucky on account of its revivalism, its waiving of traditional educational requirements for the ministry in order to meet more quickly the region's religious needs, and its growing tendency to depart from the Westminster standards (especially in regard to divine sovereignty and human ability). After the General Assembly unanimously supported the synod's action in 1809, the outcasts organized an independent Cumberland Presbytery, which in 1813 in Sumner County, Tennessee, divided in three and formed a synod. They adopted a revised, Arminian version of the Westminster Confession, and set in motion the Cumberland Presbyterian Church. During these early years the new group made extensive use of the camp meeting as an evangelistic instrument. By the time their own General Assembly was formed in 1829, they had presbyteries in Kentucky, Tennessee, Alabama, Mississippi, Arkansas, Indiana, Illinois, and Missouri—and missionaries from Pennsylvania to Texas. In 1906 most of the Cumberlands would be reunited with the Presbyterian church more or less on their own terms; but during the intervening century their growth was impressive, with their membership composed almost entirely of "converts won from Satan's dominions, and not of proselytes won from other churches." [15]

RISE OF THE DISCIPLES MOVEMENT

The Stonites

While these events were moving toward their final issue, Barton Stone and other New Light leaders of the Cane Ridge revival were coming under suspicion not only for indecorous churchmanship and low educational standards, but for heresy as well. Rather than stand trial, they withdrew and in 1803 organized the Springfield Presbytery. The degree to which these men had removed themselves from Reformed doctrine and Presbyterian polity was revealed in their *Apology for Renouncing the Jurisdiction of the Synod of Kentucky.* This document was so explicitly and violently critical of historic Presbyterianism that it was only a matter of time before

15. The reunion was facilitated by the larger body's revision of its doctrinal standards in 1903.

the New Lights realized the incongruity of their being in a "presbytery" even of their own making. In June 1804 they published the "Last Will and Testament of the Presbytery of Springfield," abandoned the "traditions of men," took the Bible as their only creed and law, and adopted for themselves the name "Christians." What they derived from the Scriptures was a decisively Arminian theology, a radically congregational polity, and a contractual conception of the ministry which all but dissolved the idea of ordination. The common charge that the Stonites were deists, Unitarians, and infidels in revivalistic guise is perhaps unjustified; but their doctrinal outlook was a compromise "somewhere between Unitarianism and orthodox popular Calvinism." [16] Of the six men who started the movement, two went on to the further excesses of the Shakers, and two returned to the Presbyterian fold, leaving only Stone and David Purviance in the role of "founders." Yet they had many followers, and the "Christians" grew rapidly in Kentucky. In southeastern Ohio they swept every Presbyterian church but two into their movement. Until 1832, when they coalesced with the followers of Alexander Campbell, they were a broad, extremely congregational, never precisely defined current in the moving stream of frontier revivalism.

Other Currents of "Reform"

Two or three much smaller currents were also flowing beside the "Christians," sharing their concern for return to the "primitive gospel." One of these was the so-called Christian Connection, a minority revivalistic movement among people of lowly station on the New England frontier. Strongly anti-Calvinistic in sentiment, it grew contemporaneously with the similar body of Freewill Baptists who were also strongest in Vermont, New Hampshire, and Maine; and many of its ministers had been ordained by Freewill congregations. At the beginning of the nineteenth century, the two groups contemplated merging, since both held similar doctrines, inclined toward primitivism, and practiced open communion. But as they expanded westward across New York State, the "Christians" began more and more to show Unitarian tendencies, which alienated them from the Baptists and turned them toward the Stonites—and occasionally toward the Unitarians.

Out of Virginia and North Carolina flowed still another "Christian" movement, this one of Methodist background. It arose from the revolt of "Republican Methodists" against the authoritarianism of the Methodistic system, especially as it was embodied so strenuously in Bishop Asbury. Led by James O'Kelly and Rice Haggard, by the end of the eighteenth century

16. William Garrett West, *Barton Warren Stone: Early American Advocate for Christian Unity* (Nashville, Tenn.: Disciples of Christ Historical Society, 1954), p. 82.

it had assumed the shape of a separate movement. After 1804 Haggard wielded considerable influence upon Stone, convincing him that "Christian" was the only proper biblical way to designate the true believer.

The Campbellites

The "Christians" and other closely related movements were soon to be overshadowed by still another offshoot of frontier Presbyterianism led by Thomas Campbell (1763–1854), a Scotch-Irish minister of the Anti-Burgher faction of the Secession church. On coming to America from northern Ireland in 1807, Campbell continued his ministry in western Pennsylvania; but after being censured by the Associate Synod of North America for laxity in admitting people to the Lord's Supper, he withdrew from it and began a private ministry to any who would hear and follow him. In 1809 this group organized itself as a nondenominational "Christian Association of Washington" (Pennsylvania). Taking Campbell's *Declaration and Address* as their statement of purpose, they also approved the now well-known maxim, "Where the Scriptures speak, we speak; where the Scriptures are silent, we are silent." For a time it seemed that Campbell, like Zinzendorf and Wesley before him, had no plans to organize a new denomination. His announced purpose was to promote Christian unity by preaching a simple gospel which would rise above denominationalism. But the arrival that same year (1809) of Campbell's aggressive and disputatious son Alexander (1788–1866) caused this irenic intention to be put aside. Before the year was out, the "Christian Association" had compiled a complete catechism and initiated a periodical to point out the "errors" of the existing churches. As was perhaps inevitable, only two years elapsed before a new denomination was virtually in existence, though at that time it consisted of only one country church of thirty members at Brush Run, Pennsylvania, with Alexander Campbell as its leader and pastor. In 1813 this independent denomination seemed to disappear for a time as it entered the Redstone Baptist Association; but this uneasy affiliation was to last only until 1827.

From the very beginning, it was perfectly clear to anyone with an attentive ear that the message of Brush Run was unique on the American frontier—in fact, on the American scene. It was equally obvious that the source of its uniqueness was the younger Campbell. What the disturbed Baptists were confronting was a complex of doctrines, usages, and historical interpretations which this young man had heard and adopted while a student in Scotland. Even in Glasgow Campell was so far estranged from his traditional church allegiance as to walk out of a Presbyterian communion service. The ideas which were churning within him then, matured by further thought and study in America, became the largest single formative influence on the whole group of "Christian Reformers" in the Ohio River valley. Several widely publicized debates and the circulation of his periodical the *Christian Baptist* (1823–29) made Alexander Campbell a man to reckon with. By any standard he is an important figure in American church history, a curious compound of the rationalistic theologian on one hand and the eccentric and legalistic sectary on the other. To deepen the paradox, Campbell's campaign for undoing denominationalism was the chief factor in the origination of a new denomination.

An effort to place Alexander Campbell must begin with the fact that his early nurture was in the Presbyterian Church of Scotland, where he learned the Reformed distrust of historical tradition and accretions in every aspect of church life. Like so many other "reformers," Campbell sought to reestablish the patterns of primitive Christianity as he conceived them. Although he also shared the Reformed emphasis on divine law, he broke decisively with Reformed-Puritan views by insisting on a far more drastic disjunction between the Old Covenant and the New than early covenant theologians had dreamed of. Discarding the typically Puritan adulation of the Old Testament, Campbell put his whole emphasis on the New Dispensation, finding the "law" for Christian life and worship in the New Testament. In its interpretation, moreover, he took silence to be as eloquent as specific injunction. Since musical instruments were not mentioned specifically as contributing to Christian worship, they must be banned; since there was no command to form missionary societies, they were not to be organized. On such grounds the Campbellite "reformers" developed a rigorous church order. Baptism was by immersion, for believers only, and necessary for the remission of sins; the ministry was in no sense above the laity, and not to be set apart by the title "reverend"; communion was to be celebrated on each Lord's Day (the word "Sabbath" was avoided as belonging to the Old Testament dispensation); the autonomy and self-sufficiency of the local congregation was primary, and all higher levels of ecclesiastical organization (if allowed at all) were regarded as purely informal and without authority. Worship was conducted in the free-church tradition of simplicity and informality.[17]

17. Alexander Campbell's ideas were drawn from the reform impulse stemming from John Glas (1695–1773) of Perth and his son-in-law Robert Sandeman (1718–71), who in 1730 led a number of "Old Scotch Independents" out of the established Kirk and into several separatist congregations. Glas was a fervent restorationist who advocated (in addition to congregational independency and the separation of church and state) a return to the early church's practice of weekly communion, believer's baptism by immersion, and a charismatic ministry. Sandeman came in 1764 to New England, where his doctrines excited several controversies with the Baptists and Congregationalists. After organizing several

But Campbell was not only a restorationist and a legalist; he was also a fervent exponent of eighteenth-century rationalism, a disciple of John Locke and the Scottish philosophers. Natural law concepts figured prominently in his ethical thought. An intellectualist bent determined his understanding of faith as the mind's assent to credible testimony, an emphasis which served powerfully to divorce his movement from the prevailing currents of emotional revivalism. This rationalistic note stands out in his views on baptism, which occasioned his ruptures first with the Presbyterians, then with the Baptists. For Campbell baptism was neither a gift of grace—a "sacrament"—as with the Roman Catholics or Lutherans, nor merely a symbol signifying God's redemptive act, as with the Baptists. It was the decisive, formal compliance of the believer with the command of Jesus, a washing away of sins, not a "mysterious" supernatural transaction.

Formation of the Disciples Denomination

The emergence of the "Christians," "Reformers," or "Disciples" as a distinct denomination, disengaged from both Presbyterians and Baptists, was not the work of the Campbells alone. Very influential was another Scotsman, Walter Scott (1796–1861). Upon graduating from the University of Edinburgh in 1818, Scott came to America as a school teacher. The next year he secured a position at Pittsburgh in the academy of George Forrester, the pastor of an independent Haldanean church which met in the courthouse. Forrester soon convinced Scott of the importance of restoring the pattern of the New Testament Church in every detail. The young teacher gradually became aware of other restorationist movements in America, such as that of Elias Hicks and Abner Jones in New England, James O'Kelly in North Carolina, and Barton Stone in Kentucky; and between 1821 and 1827 he drew close to that of the Campbells. In 1827 Scott was teaching school in Steubenville, Ohio, where he attended the meeting of the Mahoning Baptist Association, largely Campbellite even then, and soon to become expressly so. The vitality of the association was at such a low ebb that Scott was persuaded to become its traveling evangelist. This was a fateful appoint-

churches, he died at Danbury, Connecticut. In Scotland the "Glasites" or "Sandemanians" might have remained inconspicuous if their movement had not been invested with a new vitality at the end of the century by the work of the Haldane brothers, Robert (1764–1842) and James Alexander (1768–1851), of Edinburgh. Depressed by the cold "moderatism" of the established Kirk, these two wealthy laymen began a movement of evangelism which soon after 1794 (the date of their conversion) began to produce independent congregations bent on restoring the worship and ordinances of the early Christians. In their group the doctrines of Glas and Sandeman found fertile soil, and this is the circle of influence in which Alexander Campbell had moved when he was in Edinburgh.

ment, for he was then on the verge of his great "discovery" that the "restored gospel" he had long sought was an *objective* plan of salvation, in contrast to the subjective plan preached by the revivalistic groups. Scott's "restoration" can be dated quite exactly in 18 November 1827, when he preached at New Lisbon, Ohio, using the new plan of salvation for the first time.

> In this sermon he gave the invitation according to what he conceived to be the original pattern of the ancient gospel, and received his first convert, William Amend, whom he baptized immediately without asking for an experience, without having a church vote, at the end of the meeting that very evening. This was the exciting beginning of a new program of expansion for the Disciples of Christ.[18]

The objective plan which Scott preached with such effectiveness from that time forth was nothing more than Campbell's popular theology shaped to peculiarly practical, simple, and matter-of-fact conceptions. It had six points: faith, repentance, baptism, remission of sins, gift of the Holy Spirit, and life eternal. To make them even simpler, the last two were combined, and the whole scheme reduced to a "five-finger exercise" which could be comprehended even by children. This became a popular key to "the ancient gospel," at once simple, rationalistic, and authoritarian. In summary it was:

1. Faith consists in accepting the proposition (which Scott called "the golden oracle") that "Jesus is the Christ."
2. If faith is genuine, repentance follows logically (one may almost say, automatically), motivated by Christ's authoritative promises.
3. Baptism for the remission of sins is obedient response to the Lord's command, making one's commitment complete. These are the three things for a man to do.
4. The remission of sins is the fulfillment of God's promise, as are
5. The gift of the Holy Spirit and eternal life. These are the three things God does.

It was all as simple as that. And western folk liked its directness. Within a year the Mahoning Association, which in 1827 had received only thirty-four members while losing thirty-one by death, exclusion, and dismissal, increased from six hundred to sixteen hundred. And for the next thirty years Scott alone continued to "convert" a thousand people a year. In 1830, as an almost inevitable climax to this development, prompted by the agitation of Scott, the Mahoning Association dissolved itself as an unscriptural and

18. Dwight E. Stevenson, "Walter Scott and Evangelism," in *Voices from Cane Ridge*, p. 171. See also Stevenson's *Walter Scott: Voice of the Golden Oracle*.

unwarranted organization. The alliance with the Baptists was over after seventeen years of uneasiness. The "Campbellites" as a separate wing of Christian restorationism were an acknowledged reality.

Campbell meanwhile was making a name for himself and his movement through the pages of the *Christian Baptist,* as well as in his public debates, where he argued for believer's baptism against the Presbyterians, for baptismal regeneration against the Baptists, for Protestantism against Archbishop John Baptist Purcell of Cincinnati, and for Christianity against the agnostic Robert Owen of New Harmony. He also scourged the Mormons in a controversial volume that in part balanced the loss of Sidney Rigdon, the most outstanding restorationist evangelist in northern Ohio, to Joseph Smith's Church of the Latter-Day Saints. With men like Walter Scott playing similar roles in other associations, Campbellism speedily became anathema to the Baptists, especially in Ohio and Kentucky. Since the Baptists' specific condemnations expose the innovations of the restoration movement, they too deserve summary here.

1. They distinguish sharply between the Old and New Covenants and hence abolish the Law of Moses.
2. They hold conversion to be wrought through the Word alone without any direct operation of the Holy Spirit. Thus "faith" and "repentance" in their sense constitute regeneration.
3. They believe baptism should be administered on profession of belief that Jesus is the Christ, without examination of experience or consent of of the church.
4. They believe that baptism procures the remission of sins and the gift of the Spirit. It is thus man's obedience which alone can bring him within the purview of God's "electing" grace.
5. They believe that none have a special call to the ministry and that all baptized persons have a right to administer the ordinance of baptism [and the Lord's Supper].
6. They believe that the Christianity of the New Testament is simple and clear, with no element of mystery or mysticism. Creeds and enthusiasm, which obscure this fact, are therefore not to be tolerated.[19]

What Presbyterians, Baptists, and Methodists apparently faced during these decades of Disciple expansion was a remarkable projection into the Amer-

19. This list of Disciples "errors" is drawn from the widely adopted "anathema" of the Beaver Association (Baptist) of Pennsylvania in 1829, and from a similar pronouncement by the Tate's Creek Association (Kentucky) in 1830 (see Errett Gates, *The Early Relation and Separation of Baptists and Disciples* [Chicago: Christian Century Co., 1904], chaps. 9 and 10, especially pp. 92–93).

ican frontier scene of a popular, down-to-earth form of eighteenth-century Christian rationalism, a movement all the more striking because it was successfully propagated in the ethos of revivalism and by an adaptation of its methods. Its unusual prescriptions regarding the ban on musical instruments, its demand for weekly observance of communion, and its rejection of "unscriptural" interchurch organizations and agencies served only to set it farther apart.

Then in 1832 an event occurred which strengthened considerably the "Christian" movement in the West: the gradually realized similarity of the Stonite and Campbellite movements became the occasion for a merger, as far as their loose organizations allowed. There were some differences between the two. Campbell was suspicious of Stone's antitrinitarianism, while Stone was more lenient toward divergent doctrinal views, and feared that Campbell vaunted himself too much. These suspicions were little by little overcome, and representatives of the two groups who met at Lexington, Kentucky, in January 1832 agreed that they should become one.[20] During the months and years which followed, an increasing number of congregations implemented their agreement. Due especially to the dynamic leadership of Campbell and the evangelistic success of Scott, the Disciples entered a period of dramatic growth. Literally dozens of little periodicals spread their message and coordinated their activities. Zealous preachers brought lucid and simple sermons to hundreds of frontier communities, and by 1850 they could claim perhaps 118,000 adherents. After the Civil War the denomination would enjoy a still more dramatic growth, until by 1890 it counted 7,246 churches with 641,051 members. Then, as in the beginning, its chief strength lay in the border states and the Ohio River basin; but many new and seriously divisive issues were to arise during the intervening period.

RETROSPECT

Despite the temptation to be retrospective about frontier religion, any major effort of the sort must be postponed. The "frontier" in America is not a region, but a process, and the process began, as Frederick Jackson

20. Stone represented about eight thousand "Christians," while some five thousand Campbellites were represented by Raccoon John Smith. Though Stone had taken the initiative in these proceedings, the practical result was the absorbing of his followers into the more precisely defined and aggressively led Disciples movement. Some of the "Christians" refused to follow their leader, and gradually tended to identify themselves with the Hicks-Smith and O'Kelly movements as a "Christian Connection." This Connection entered an informal entente with Unitarians in the founding of Meadville (Pennsylvania) Seminary in 1844, but further merger never materialized. In 1929 what was left of it merged with the Congregationalists.

Turner insisted, with the arrival of the *Susan Constant* and the *Mayflower*. Contrary to his observations, the process did not halt even in 1893, but still continues in Alaska and elsewhere. Insofar as that great historian and his church-historical disciples provided a clue to the understanding of modern America, the events discussed in this chapter are but a part of a vast whole. Yet certain things are clear. The creativeness of the frontier, or rather, the power of the frontier to alter or refashion whatever came into it, must not be exaggerated. Gothic cathedrals, to be sure, were delayed for a while and even Georgian meetinghouses had to bide their time. Churchly decorum was not easily found, although all of these marks of civilization were exhibited as soon as time, effort, and money would allow. Borderland and semi-wilderness, in other words, remained just that; and religion inescapably bore the impress of this actuality.

Far more remarkable than the primitive and rudimentary aspects of frontier religion was the persistence with which the thought, institutions, and practice of Europe and the settled East crossed the mountains and penetrated the life of the newly settled areas. At this point, therefore, one can and must contradict the assertions of Turner, Sweet, and the other frontier enthusiasts. Turner minced no words in his assertion about democracy and the frontier:

> American democracy was born of no theorist's dream; it was not carried in the *Susan Constant* to Virginia, nor in the *Mayflower* to Plymouth. It came stark and strong and full of life out of the American forest, and it gained new strength each time it touched a new frontier.[21]

Church historians are always tempted to see a religious corollary, and speak of "democratic churches" and "democratic theology." Yet it would seem that here in the classic frontier experience, not to speak of Virginia and Plymouth, the opposite phenomenon is more striking. The continuing force of the Westminster Assembly behind all of these movements defies calculation. Equally remarkable is the way in which the deliberations of the London Baptists in 1677, or of the Philadelphia Association a half-century later, would shape Baptist articles of association in frontier Kentucky. Even more forcefully did the message and methods of John Wesley mold a movement continuing long after his death in an environment he could scarcely have imagined. Similarly, the restorationist proposals of the Haldane brothers

21. Frederick Jackson Turner, "The West and American Ideals," *Washington Historical Quarterly* 5 (October 1914): 245. Quoted in an important context by Henry Nash Smith, *Virgin Land: The American West as Myth and Symbol* (New York: Vintage Books, 1957), p. 295.

of Glasgow altered the church life and religious experience of thousands of American frontier farmers.

Slowly and inexorably the total American experience did put its mark on all of these impulses. And the frontier is, of course, an important part of that experience. The most crucial change in American religion to be linked to the great western revivals is the shift in America's denominational equilibrium which the revivals portend in part and bring about in part: most notably the growth of the Methodists and Baptists, the emergence of the Disciples, and the relatively slow expansion of the three denominations which were dominant in the colonial period—Congregational, Presbyterian, and Episcopal. In the Old Northwest, which was settled somewhat later than Kentucky and Tennessee, different eastern influences would come to bear, shaping quite a different frontier experience. The nation as a whole, meanwhile, was maturing in significant ways as a New World frontier of Western civilization.

28

PRESBYTERIANS AND CONGREGATIONALISTS IN THE OLD NORTHWEST: ADVANCE AND CONFLICT

In 1788 the founders of Marietta, Ohio, floated down the Ohio River in a flatboat named the *Mayflower* and on landing reenacted the arrival of the Pilgrim Fathers at Plymouth. The persisting influence of the British and the extremely unsettled state of Indian affairs, however, kept these hopeful beginnings from rapid fruition. The famous Northwest Ordinances of 1785 and 1787 had made excellent provisions for surveying the land and organizing local governments, but full-scale settlement could not proceed until after General Anthony Wayne's victory at Fallen Timbers in 1794. When settlers began to stream in, a large proportion of them were from Kentucky, Tennessee, and the western parts of the Old South, which meant that from very early times the southern parts of Ohio, Indiana, and Illinois would share many viewpoints with the Old Southwest, with the Hoosier State being most thoroughly affected by this influx.

From the beginning, however, historical as well as geographical circumstances set the Old Northwest, including upstate New York, markedly apart from the region south of the Ohio. The chief factor was the prominence of northerners, especially of New Englanders, among the settlers. Very early they had formed land companies to develop the tracts along the Ohio. Massachusetts made the most of its original sea-to-sea charter by obtaining land titles in western New York, while Connecticut was even more successful in staking out its "Western Reserve" in northern Ohio. This was the natural line of advance for migrants from New England's rock-strewn fields, and consequently the society and institutions of the Old Northwest took on a strong Yankee tincture. Timothy Dwight sensed this kinship with his homeland during his travels in New York; and the Methodist preacher Peter Cartwright quickly realized that when he left Kentucky for a northern circuit he was facing a new kind of challenge. Ohio became a state in 1803, with a population of about fifty thousand, and Indiana followed in 1816, after the War of 1812 had removed the harassments of the British and Indians. Although large numbers of settlers continued to come from below the river to these areas, as well as to Illinois (statehood 1818), the region retained its New England flavor. Even today, a traveler to towns like Oberlin or Beloit can observe the transplantation of New England that resulted from the great Yankee exodus.

CONGREGATIONAL AND PRESBYTERIAN EXPANSION

For the churches as well as for the nation generally, central and western New York was the proving ground for further westward expansion in the more northerly areas, providing a base of operations not dissimilar to that which the southern back country had provided for the Old Southwest. This New York challenge hastened the rapprochement of Presbyterians and the consociated Congregationalists of Connecticut. Schenectady Academy, started by the Dutch Reformed pastor Dirck Romeyn in 1785 and chartered as a college in 1795, provided the point of convergence when it became Union College and called Dr. Jonathan Edwards, Jr.—a Connecticut Congregationalist educated at Princeton—as its president in 1799. Though he met an untimely death in 1801, Edwards helped to institute the famous Plan of Union of 1801, whereby Presbyterians and Congregationalists agreed to combine their efforts for the winning of the western missionary field. In this "presbygational" arrangement, each group agreed to recognize the other's ministry and polity.[1]

The Plan was a large scale comity arrangement to allow Congregational and Presbyterian settlers in a given community to combine or to found a single congregation and to have a minister of either denomination. If the majority were Presbyterians who preferred their discipline, the church could be so organized even if the minister were a Congregationalist, and vice versa. Similar rules allowed congregations to affiliate with either a presbytery or a Congregational association. If a disagreement arose between pastor and

1. George M. Marsden, *The Evangelical Mind and the New School Presbyterian Experience*, p. 11.

church the matter could be referred to the presbytery or association of which the pastor was a member or, if this was not agreeable, to a committee consisting of equal representatives of each group. Arrangements for appealing cases were also made. As Williston Walker says, "it was a wholly honorable arrangement, and was designed to be entirely fair to both sides." But in its long-range institutional effect, the Plan of Union operated in favor of Presbyterianism, which because of its intrinsic connectionalism tended to absorb the more independent Congregational churches. Walker suggests still other reasons for Presbyterian strength:

> They were nearer the scene of missionary labor: their denominational spirit was more assertive than that of the Congregationalism of the day; their Presbyteries were rapidly spread over the missionary districts, and the natural desire for fellowship where the points of separation seemed so few led Congregational ministers to accept the welcome offered therein. Moreover, the doctrinal discussions of New England and the development of Connecticut consociationism had created a widespread feeling in the older Congregational churches that Congregationalism could not thrive in unformed communities.[2]

In doctrinal matters a reverse tide of influence was observable. Advocates of New England Theology were more fervent in evangelism because of their participation in the Second Awakening, and this led to their dominance among the Congregationalists participating in the Plan of Union. The rise of the great voluntary associations, above all the American Home Missionary Society (1826), further extended the New England influence in the West as graduates of Andover and Yale took up the missionary challenge in large numbers. By an ironic turn of fate, the Presbyterian church's absorption of Congregationalist missionaries vastly extended the influence of the New Haven Theology of Nathaniel William Taylor and the revised Hopkinsianism of Andover. It created a situation that was pregnant with controversy and schism despite the prevailing enthusiasm for a campaign to transform an uncouth frontier and bring it into a pious and well-behaved Christian republic.

In addition to their joint efforts, both churches continued to be independently concerned with evangelizing the West. The actual westward extension of the Puritan heritage proceeded most directly in centers where New England people simply gathered churches, called ministers, and organized associations in the time-honored way. Because of the high regard these

2. Williston Walker, *A History of the Congregational Churches in the United States*, ACHS, vol. 3 (New York, 1894), p. 318.

people had for each other's company, this became a fairly familiar pattern of advance, reaching far across the land to places like Beloit, Wisconsin (whose church was organized in 1838), and Minneapolis, Minnesota (whose church was organized in 1851 at Saint Anthony). The emergence of such "little New Englands" had a striking effect not only on the religious nature of the western communities, but also on their political, economic, and cultural life; for this reason, it constitutes a highly significant factor in any estimate of Puritan influence on American life.

The voluntary associations and the Plan of Union account for the largest extension of evangelical influences, however. Through these channels a steady stream of devoted missionaries, church founders, and educators moved westward. Sometimes, as in the case of Julian Monson Sturtevant (1805–86), they came from New England families who had moved west but who nevertheless sent their children "home" to Yale College for a liberal education. They then went to Yale Divinity School and the lecture room of Professor Taylor before returning to their western labors. But whether from the West or from New England, whether products of Yale Divinity or Andover, they became enthusiastic emissaries of eastern culture, education, and above all, the Christian gospel as it was understood in New England's Second Awakening. The record of their ministry is written in the multiplication of Congregational churches across the northern West. Estimates differ as to the number of churches of Congregational origin which became Presbyterian. Older estimates ran to more than two thousand, while a more recent study concludes that not more than six hundred ever placed themselves under the care of the General Assembly. Between 1807 and 1834 Presbyterian communicant membership as a whole grew from 18,000 to 248,000, and at the later date an "allied population" of two million was reliably reported. Modes of definition and computation vary, but nearly all accounts affirm the large degree to which missionary concern outweighed the denominational spirit in the early evangelizing of the Old Northwest.

BEECHER AND FINNEY

No single person better illustrates the methods and spirit of the great campaign mounted by the "evangelical united front" than Lyman Beecher. Already nationally famous for his great revival preaching, his campaign against Boston Unitarianism, and his work as a temperance reformer, Beecher was called in 1832 to become president of Lane Theological Seminary in Cincinnati, a Presbyterian school owing much to the philanthropy of Ebenezer Lane (a Baptist), the Kemper family, and Arthur Tappan (a wealthy layman of New York City who pledged $60,000 on condition that Beecher accept the presidency). Beecher did accept—mainly because he was convinced of the West's great significance in the future growth of the new nation. His *Plea for the West* (1835) is a classic statement of that widely held conviction; and though the need for "saving the West from the Pope" figured prominently in this manifesto, he also showed more liberal and far-sighted views:

> The West is a young empire of mind, and power, and wealth, and free institutions, rushing up to a giant manhood with a rapidity and a power never witnessed below the sun. And if she carries with her the elements of her preservation, the experiment will be glorious.

In this sense Beecher anticipates Frederick Jackson Turner's belief in the force of the West in determining the future cast of the emerging nation. Yet no man was more sure than he that the civilizing influence of New England was required to rescue the region from barbarism and license.

In Cincinnati, Beecher also became pastor of the Second Presbyterian Church, where his known affinities for the New England modifications of strict Calvinism immediately aroused the suspicions of the conservative Presbyterians. In 1835 Dr. Joshua L. Wilson placed three formal charges against Beecher: heresy, on the ground that he differed from the Westminster standards; slander, on the ground that he claimed to represent true evangelical Christianity; and hypocrisy, on the ground that he claimed to agree substantially with the Scriptures and the Westminster Confession. Despite the fact that the Presbyterian organizations of the region were controlled by conservatives, Beecher was acquitted by a large majority in both presbytery and synod. But these proceedings indicated that a long-standing source of tension in the Presbyterian church was beginning to erupt. It would be occasioned, as the Old Side protest had been of a century before, by an excess of New England influence.

Beecher represents the New England establishment responding with vigor to the new empire beyond the Hudson. But there was another, more tempestuous son of Connecticut who found his vocation in the West—Charles Grandison Finney (1792–1875), "the father of modern revivalism." Finney was born in Warren, Connecticut, but two years later his parents joined the westward trek, so that he grew up in small towns of Oneida and Jefferson counties in central New York. Returning to Warren for secondary schooling, Finney then kept school for a while. But in 1818 he began to practice law in Adams, New York, where he came under the influence of a young Presbyterian minister, George W. Gale (later to be founder of Knox College in

Galesburg, Illinois). Finney admired Gale personally, but disagreed violently with his theological views. Led by a personal reading of the Scriptures, the skeptical lawyer finally experienced a soul-shaking conversion in 1821, which he said brought him "a retainer from the Lord Jesus Christ to plead his cause." His career as a highly successful converter of souls began that very week on the streets of Adams. Refusing formal theological training but already evincing great power as a preacher, Finney was licensed—somewhat reluctantly—by the local Saint Lawrence Presbytery. Soon he was making news in the local papers, and before long he gained national attention by a series of spectacular evangelistic meetings in Rome, Utica, Troy, and other cities along the Erie Canal.

This is where the "new measures" with which Finney's name was to be linked took form. His speech was tough, direct, forceful—and inescapably popular. Like God, he was no respecter of persons: sinners were sinners. He prayed for them by name; and when occasion required he included in his prayers any persons, lay or clerical, who were notable by their absence or their opposition to his efforts. Finney also departed from the regular stated times for religious services and made extensive use of the "protracted meeting," which continued nightly for a week or more. He introduced the "anxious bench" to cull from the multitudes the almost-saved, so that they might be made objects of special exhortation and prayer, and encouraged women to testify in public meetings, despite Saint Paul's admonition of female silence in the churches (I Cor. 14:34). He also discovered the advantages of publicity, and as his followers became sufficiently numerous, he was able to make a "team approach" to prospective Sodoms. Nor did Finney mince words on his efficacy; in his *Lectures on Revivalism* (1835) he declared that a "revival is not a miracle, or dependent on a miracle in any sense. It is a purely philosophical [i.e. scientific] result of the right use of the constituted means."

Finney's emphasis on the human production of conversions was not the only point on which he strayed from strict Westminster standards. And far from concealing the fact, he proclaimed it. From the first he demanded that some kind of relevant social action follow the sinner's conversion, and in time this led to an even more disturbing emphasis on "entire sanctification." In Finney's theology sin was a voluntary act and theoretically avoidable, hence holiness was a human possibility. Even from the liberated ground of Taylorism, the Finneyite departures seemed bold and extreme.

So alarmed and critical were Lyman Beecher, Asahel Nettleton, and a number of others, that a conference of eight representatives of each party met 18–27 July 1827, in New Lebanon, New York, to discuss their differences. This meeting only heightened the rancor and perhaps signalized a renewal of the rupture in the American Reformed tradition which had been agitated periodically ever since the Great Awakening.

> I know your plan [declared Beecher] and you know I do. You mean to come into Connecticut, and carry a streak of fire to Boston. But if you attempt it, as the Lord liveth, I'll meet you at the State line, and call out all the artillery-men, and fight every inch of the way to Boston, and I'll fight you there.[3]

Finney, needless to say, was not intimidated; he went on to new successes at Wilmington, Delaware, and Reading and Lancaster, Pennsylvania, before moving on to New York City, where he held forth for over a year under the patronage of Anson G. Phelps. By this time Finney was essentially a free-lance revivalist. After another year of touring which included Boston, he returned in 1832 to New York to preach for a year in the Chatham Street Theater which Lewis Tappan and others rented for him. They called it the Second Free Presbyterian Church, for it had grown out of Finney's earlier ministry in New York; but even its "free-ness" was insufficient, and Finney soon withdrew to become an independent Congregationalist and minister of the Broadway Tabernacle which had been built for him. His tenure here was brief, however, since ill health and an intricate series of events connected with the antislavery movement led him in 1835 to accept an appointment as professor of theology in the newly founded Oberlin College. He also served as president of Oberlin from 1851 to 1866, and his dynamic presence made Oberlin a center of influence for revival theology, the "new measures," and a growing emphasis on perfectionism—all combined with an urgent sense of Christian activism.

Finney is an immensely important man in American history by any standard of measure. His revivals were a powerful force in the rising antislavery impulse and in the rise of urban evangelism. He was an influential revisionist in the Reformed theological tradition, an enormously successful practitioner, almost the inventor, of the modern high-pressure revivalism which, as it spread, would have important consequences for the religious ethos of the nation as a whole. Yet Finney was also an extremely divisive figure, and in the Presbyterian church the tensions created by his kind of ministry contributed to a recurrence of schism.

3. Forty years after the New Lebanon conference Beecher attributed these ringing words to himself, but Finney had no memory of them. Whether spoken then or not, they nevertheless reveal a common Eastern estimate of Finney's worth to the cause of religion. In any event Beecher later had to eat crow and invite Finney to Boston (see Beecher's *Autobiography*, ed. Barbara Cross, 1: 75).

PROBLEMS OF PRESBYTERIANISM

Despite the gains resulting from the Plan of Union, the Presbyterian Church during this period was beset with a number of problems, chief among which were a shortage of ministers for the western churches and sharp differences of opinion over theology, polity, and missionary methods. Pursuing an independent course for evangelizing the West, the General Assembly established in 1802 a Standing Committee of Missions. Before it was replaced by a Board of Missions in 1816, this body had sent out 311 itinerant ministers, usually for a two-month tour each. Follow-up efforts were poorly managed, however, and the results were disappointing. Competition from Methodists, Baptists, and Disciples was strong, especially among the southerners who were moving into the Old Northwest. The church's official membership reports, on the other hand, did show substantial Presbyterian growth in the country as a whole. At the beginning of the century there were an estimated 13,470 communicants in about 500 churches; in 1820, 72,096 members in 1,299 churches; and in 1837, 226,557 members in 2,865 churches. The most impressive growth took place in western New York and in Ohio, where the Plan of Union was functioning best. During the same period the percentage of churches with ordained ministers rose from fifty to seventy-five.

In the long run, the most important consequences of this period may have been the growing awareness of an acute ministerial shortage in the Presbyterian Church and the realization that Princeton College was in no position to meet the urgent need. With Andover as an example of what a theological seminary could do, various individuals and synods began to consider the problem. The man who finally emerged as the catalyst of this growing interest was Archibald Alexander (1772–1851). Grandson of a Scotch-Irish immigrant who had been deeply touched by the Great Awakening, Alexander had grown up in the Great Valley of Virginia, where he slowly came of a mind to enter the ministry. With only an "academy" education and informal theological training under the Reverend William Graham of Lexington, Virginia, he had become president of the struggling little Hampden-Sydney College in 1796. Ten years later he was a prominent Philadelphia minister, from which position he led the movement to found a seminary at Princeton. When in 1812 his efforts succeeded, the General Assembly asked him to be its first professor. He set the new center of conservative divinity on its course, and through his sons and pupils and their sons, the direction he gave the Princeton Theology prevailed for a century.

The theological history of Presbyterianism owes much to the fact that this powerful Scotch-Irishman sought and found the intellectual and doctrinal guidance he needed not in the Edwardsean tradition of New England (though the writings of Edwards had helped bring about his own conversion), nor in the New Divinity of the later Puritans, nor yet in the Scottish philosophical traditions of Witherspoon (though this element remained prominent as a conditioning factor in the Princeton Theology), but in the seventeenth-century scholasticism of François Turretin (1623–87), a stalwart defender of orthodoxy at Geneva, who above all attacked efforts to modify a strict doctrine of predestination and a literalistic view of scriptural inspiration. Until replaced in 1873 by the *Systematic Theology* of Alexander's admiring protégé Charles Hodge, Turretin's *Institutio Theologiae Elencticae* (Geneva, 1679–85; reissued in 4 vols. at Edinburgh, 1847–48) stood side by side with the Swiss Confessions and the Westminster formularies to provide both structure and content for the message which hundreds of the seminary's graduates carried across the land and into many foreign mission fields.

Especially as developed and defended by Charles Hodge, the Princeton Theology became the criterion of Reformed orthodoxy in America. When judged by these standards, Taylor's New Haven Theology was found utterly wanting, Andover's Edwards Amasa Park was attacked almost as violently, Hopkinsianism was viewed with suspicion or disdained altogether, Moses Stuart's biblical studies were held suspect, and even Jonathan Edwards was considered unduly venturesome. Yet despite its negative features, the Princeton Theology was a great positive force, affording theological substance wherever revivalism threatened to vaunt experience only, fostering education and the learned tradition, and striving desperately to provide a Christian message that was not simply an amalgam of folk religion and Americanism. In the West, however, it would ultimately precipitate an immense crisis.

The founding of other Presbyterian seminaries sharpened the approaching crisis. Responding to the same demand for ministers, the Synod of Virginia established Union Seminary at Hampden-Sydney in 1812 and won the support of the North Carolina synod in 1828. Later moving to Richmond, it became a virtual Princeton of the South. During the twenties still other seminaries were established in Tennessee, South Carolina, and western Pennsylvania. But the most consequential was Auburn Seminary, founded in 1821 by the Geneva Synod in western New York. Well supported and powerfully led, catering to Plan of Union churches and drawing many students from New England, Auburn soon became a strong theological counterweight to Princeton—serving, in fact, to magnify Princeton's role as the preserver of orthodoxy.

The schism between Old and New Sides which had rent the Presbyterian Church in the period of the Great Awakening had been healed in 1758, largely to the advantage of the revivalistic party of New Englanders and Log College men. The college at Princeton during its early years was molded to their ideals. With the great Scotch-Irish migrations which reached their peak just before the American Revolution, however, the balance of sentiment shifted away from the New Side. John Witherspoon's election to the presidency of Princeton in 1768 was one sign of this transformation, and Archibald Alexander's appointment to Princeton Seminary another. Yet theological views were not merely ethnic manifestations, and as an indigenous intellectual and theological tradition developed, Presbyterians gravitated to one pole or the other on various grounds.

One of these groups, known then and since as the "Old School," increasingly came to admire the church's traditional polity and took very seriously the Reformed tenet that matters of church order were within the divine law (*jus divinum*). To them the constitution of the church was not a structural convenience which could be altered to suit the circumstances; it was an article of faith. The hastily contrived arrangements of the Plan of Union were regarded as almost blasphemous; and the motley congeries of Congregational churches, elders, messengers, associations, and presbyteries which had resulted seemed a monstrous deformation of God's plan for his Church. Further incongruities were provided by the extra-ecclesiastical voluntary associations which were assuming the missionary and even the teaching role of the church. To many, the situation seemed so chaotic that within the church justice could no longer be done nor wise action taken.

By a natural grouping of tendencies, these Old School men also had grave suspicions about the new kind of revivalism that seemed to be breaking out everywhere in the years after 1800. Many, indeed, were suspicious of all revivalism, fearful of the growing emphasis on conversion and religious experience, and disturbed over the corresponding laxity with regard to doctrine and the sacraments. The Great Awakening in America and the Evangelical Revival in Great Britain, of course, had put an indelible mark on Presbyterian thought and practice. Even Old School thinkers like Alexander and Hodge reveal at every turn that they are part of the Great Awakening's progeny. But this was a matter of degree: some men put more emphasis on the baptismal covenant, or cherished decorum in church affairs, or found greater consolation in the doctrinal heritage of Reformed churches, or clung more fondly to tradition itself. To the extent that they leaned in this general direction, they resisted the movements that brought "new measures," new thoughts, and new constitutional arrangements into Presbyterianism.

What aroused Old School men most was the growth within the church of what they could only regard as heretical departures from the Westminster standards. The source of these departures was traced usually to New England theologians, especially to Samuel Hopkins and Nathaniel William Taylor, with Taylor being regarded as the more dangerous by far. Since the American Board of Commissioners for Foreign Missions and the American Home Missionary Society were both associated intimately with these New England trends, the Old School men interpreted the church's official support of these missionary agencies as outright propagation of error. The Plan of Union was to them an open gate through which alien ideas and practices entered the Presbyterian church. The only corrective was to establish definitively Presbyterian agencies and to make missions a responsibility of the church as a whole.

The conservative set of mind here described was common throughout the church at the opening of the century; it was observable even in Kentucky during the great revivals there. At the time of the frontier schisms, neither the Synod of Kentucky nor the General Assembly was inclined to compromise, and the Cumberland and Springfield presbyteries were allowed simply to go their way. But this pervasive immobility faded with the growth of the revival spirit, as Presbyterians beheld not only the sensational increase of Methodists, Baptists, and Disciples, but also the alarming inroads these groups were making on "good Presbyterian stock." Even more serious was the defection of whole congregations.

After 1800 the influence of Congregationalism began to create within Presbyterianism itself a "New School." It was at first a rather unorganized movement of those who valued the united work of the interdenominational societies, who worked harmoniously with the New Englanders and regarded them as fellow champions of evangelical Christianity, and who welcomed the additional strength that such an alliance provided on a thinly settled frontier where aggressive and vulgar rivals were advancing everywhere.[4] They by no means forsook Presbyterian principles as Barton Stone and Alexander Campbell had done; but they did feel that the urgency of the situation made stronger claims than the traditional forms of ecclesiastical government. They regarded the voluntary societies, even though interdenominational, as

4. I am, of course, using the word "vulgar" as it might then have been used. The degree to which Congregationalists and Presbyterians considered themselves the chosen means for bringing learning, culture, and religious sophistication to the frontier is difficult to exaggerate.

mighty evangelistic instruments; and like Taylor, Beecher, and Finney, they felt that "improvements" could be made in the traditional doctrinal system.

These improvements were first of all in the direction of simplicity: on the American frontier they were understandably embarrassed to confront their untutored hearers with the baroque intricacies of Westminster. Secondly, they wanted—like most other Americans east and west—a religious faith more obviously consonant with the Enlightenment ideals that had been woven into the nation's democratic faith. In its later eighteenth- and early nineteenth-century form, strict Calvinism, especially double predestination, seemed inadequate to this need, especially as interpreted by Turretin. Finally, perhaps most importantly, the obvious effectiveness of revivalism in winning people to the gospel seemed to demand theological revision. Both east and west, the Scottish Philosophy and the Enlightened principles of American democracy had obliterated so completely the meaning of the great Christian paradoxes that something had to give. Among New School men, Taylorism or Arminianism of some sort seemed the only recourse. Resistance to Finney's doctrinal revisions was so strong that he left the Presbyterian church. Even Taylor seemed too daring for many. But the general tendency of New School theology was undeniable and steady.[5]

SCHISM IN THE PRESBYTERIAN CHURCH

In a thoroughly connectional system like the Presbyterian, where any controversy could come to the highest court (the General Assembly) for ultimate adjudication, it was impossible that such inner tensions could be suppressed, especially when conservatism was rooted so deeply. Indeed, portents of future struggle had been evident ever since the Plan of Union was approved. They became more obvious after 1812, when the American Board of Commissioners for Foreign Missions was given official support, and especially so after 1826, when the American Home Missionary Society was formed as the chief instrument for furthering the Plan of Union. The heavily Scotch-Irish, rigorously orthodox Pittsburgh Synod in 1802 had converted itself into an every-member missionary society. Out on the marches Edward Beecher, Julian M. Sturtevant, and Theron Baldwin, all former

5. By 1906, when the main body of Cumberland Presbyterians was reunited with its parent body, the Northern Presbyterian church in effect committed itself to Arminianism, though, of course, many individuals dissented from this action. From among these dissenters came those who led another schism between 1929 and 1936. The Baptists meanwhile exhibited the same trend. By 1911, when the Free-will Baptists returned to the main body of Northern Baptists, the old Philadelphia Confession had become almost a dead letter. Indeed, the so-called New Hampshire Confession of 1833 won widespread approval for this very reason. So the tide was with the New School.

Congregationalists and former members of Yale's "Illinois Band" who had led in the founding of Illinois College, were accused of heresy in 1833, only to be exonerated by synod. In 1835 Lyman Beecher, who by then had made peace with Finney, was similarly accused and acquitted, though he was asked to publish for the record the arguments that had freed him from suspicion. The church was obviously moving toward a showdown.

What finally drew the issue to a head, ironically, was not a frontier revivalist at all, but an immensely respected pastor, biblical commentator, and theologian from the urban East, Albert Barnes (1798–1870). Having come fresh from Princeton Seminary to his first pastorate at Morristown, New Jersey, in 1824, Barnes five years later preached (and soon thereafter published) a sermon, "The Way of Salvation." Though Edwardsean in much of its argument, the sermon was critical of Westminster and clearly Taylorite in tendency, especially with regard to the doctrine of Original Sin. When Barnes was called the next year to the distinguished First Church of Philadelphia, therefore, the conservatives seized the occasion to raise all the troublesome issues that had been seething for so long. They charged him with heresy and ultimately brought the case before the General Assembly of 1831, where a New School majority sustained his call.

In 1835 Barnes reiterated his views in a new commentary on Romans.[6] Renewing its attack, the Old School carried their charges from presbytery to synod to assembly, and this time they succeeded in having him silenced. In a reversal of sentiment the next year, however, the Assembly restored Barnes to his pulpit. The General Assembly of 1836 then proceeded to approve the American Board in preference to the purely Presbyterian Western Foreign Missionary Society (an agency of the Pittsburgh Synod), and almost succeeded in blending the church's education and home mission boards with the interdenominational associations. More than that, it extended the policy of "elective affinity," which permitted separate liberal and conservative presbyteries (and even synods) within the same geographical territory. To make the issue even sharper, in 1836 the liberals joined with Congregationalists to establish Union Theological Seminary in New York City as an institution independent of all official church control. The strength of the New School party at this point is indicated partly by the fact that additional presbyteries dominated by their men had just been created in New York and Philadelphia, with the latter joined to the newly formed Synod of Delaware.

6. This was the first volume of Barnes's *Notes, Explanatory and Practical, on the Scriptures,* which became an immensely popular semischolarly series of expositions widely read by the laity and of special usefulness to Sunday school teachers. Hodge of Princeton and Stuart of Andover also joined this controversy with commentaries and articles on Romans.

Such drastic New School advances had the effect of consolidating conservatives, moderates, and neutrals of the Old School, to which Princeton Seminary now also gravitated. The southern Presbyteries, who were beginning to sense a growing antislavery spirit in the New School, were also predominantly of this party. As a result, the Assembly of 1837 was decisively in conservative hands. It acted with dispatch. First it abrogated the Plan of Union. Then in a sweeping unconstitutional act it made this abrogation retroactive, and without providing recourse or appeal to the judicatories concerned, proceeded to exscind from the church four western synods which had grown out of the union plan. In one blow 553 churches, 509 ministers and between sixty and a hundred thousand members were lopped from the rolls. In other actions, the General Assembly made the Western Missionary Society (an official board) its sole missionary agency, and warned the American Board of Commissioners and the Home Missionary Society not to encroach on Presbyterian work.

Immediately New School men rallied their forces, published a denial of heresy charges in the "Auburn Declaration," and made plans to press their case at the Assembly in 1838. When that body convened, however, a resolute and high-handed Old School moderator kept the New School forces at bay. Finally, the Reverend Nathaniel Beman, an old champion of Finney from the unexscinded Troy Synod, took charge of the New School elements present and led them to organize separately on the ground that they were the legal continuation of the General Assembly. During the years which followed, litigation both ecclesiastical and civil failed to heal the division, and ultimately two churches came into existence, the New School engrossing about four-ninths of the total membership.

RESURGENCE OF DENOMINATIONAL CONSCIOUSNESS

The years following the schism in the Presbyterian church saw a resurgence of denominational consciousness among all the groups that had figured in the events leading up to that development. In the South the secession crisis would soon bring Old and New Schools together in a separate Southern Presbyterian church. The Civil War and the continuing southern racial situation would give it a self-consciousness and corporate spirit that would show few signs of disappearance even in the mid-twentieth century.

In the North, where the New School was much larger, the two bodies prolonged their parallel labors for twenty-two years until their reunion in 1869. During the interim, the Old School showed slightly greater growth, largely because it faced fewer problems of reorganization, and because it was unaffected by the contemporary revival of Congregational self-consciousness in the areas where the Plan of Union had prevailed. During the period of separation, however, many Old School leaders came to regret the inflexibility which had occasioned the schism and to work for reunion.

The New School meanwhile experienced a Presbyterian awakening, perhaps chiefly out of the need to demonstrate the injustice of the exscinding action and to legitimate their claim to be a legal continuation of the old church. They were further prodded by dissatisfaction with the policies of the American Board of Commissioners for Foreign Missions, which despite large Presbyterian support had prevented a single Presbyterian mission field from developing. Professor Henry B. Smith of Union Seminary (New York) gave theological strength to the Presbyterian cause by transcending the older dependence on the New England Theology and the issues it aroused, and turning attention to broader and deeper resources, both contemporary and traditional. Domestic "Presbygationalism" also lost favor, and local churches increasingly declared themselves for one side or the other. During the period of separation (1837–69), the New School grew much more slowly than before, because whatever gains were registered in local congregations were often offset after 1837 by energetic Congregational evangelism. This meant that the steady westward flow of New Englanders no longer augmented New School Presbyterian churches.

The corollary to this development was the revival of Congregational interest in its own traditions and characteristic institutions. From 1830 on, Congregationalists were planting their own churches in Illinois, Iowa, Wisconsin, and Minnesota. In 1846 a Congregational convention in Michigan questioned the wisdom of the Plan of Union; and in 1852 a national convention of Congregational churches at Albany, New York, renounced it altogether, declaring it to be deleterious to the interests of their heritage in both theology and government. Two years later a Congregational seminary was founded in Chicago, with the encouragement of two of the denomination's most renowned historical scholars, Leonard Bacon and Henry Martyn Dexter. By the time the National Council was convened in 1865 for its historic deliberations, Congregationalism had become continental in scope, with about six hundred churches in a score of states and territories, strongest in New England but also to be found wherever migrating New Englanders had paused to work and prosper.

THE EVANGELICAL MAINSTREAM

The Old Northwest, needless to say, did not become a Presbyterian or Congregational preserve despite the civic and cultural leadership these two communions provided for the region. If one were guided by statistics alone, a discussion of the Northwest would concentrate upon the popular denominations treated in the previous chapter. In 1840, for example, when the Old and New School Presbyterians together numbered less than 250,000, the Methodists counted over 850,000 members and the Baptists over 570,000. These two churches were making their chief advances elsewhere, but they soon far outnumbered Presbyterians and Congregationalists even in Ohio, Indiana, and Illinois.

Such quantitative canons, however, obscure a fundamental phenomenon: the way in which these several denominations, all of them profoundly affected by the evangelical resurgence dating from the century's first decade, were forging a mainstream tradition of American Evangelical Protestantism. Theologically it was Reformed in its foundations, Puritan in its outlook, fervently experiential in its faith, and tending, despite strong countervailing pressures, toward Arminianism, perfectionism, and activism. Equally basic, and almost equally religious, was its belief in the millennial potential of the United States as the bearer and protector of these values. This mainstream would play a vast sustaining and defining role in the life of the nation during the entire nineteenth century. It would not gain unified institutional embodiment in anything more substantial than the World Evangelical Alliance, founded in 1846 and provided with an organized American branch in 1867. But many voluntary associations, including some which had helped to forge the evangelical united front, continued to advance important causes even after denominational self-consciousness reduced their power. Denominational rivalry, on the other hand, tended both to stimulate evangelism and to expose the existence of a common tradition. Despite the legal separation of church and state this American Protestant mainstream would enjoy the influence and self-confidence of a formal establishment.

These general observations, however, should not usurp the place of a summary observation on the overall contribution or impact of the evangelical advance in the trans-Appalachian West which has been described in this and the preceding chapters. The basic fact is that generalizations about the impact on frontier society of these churches—or of others yet to be discussed—cannot easily be made. Churches were not independent forces but complex cultural institutions which contained judges, doctors, educators, politicians, social reformers, and much else in their membership. Yet the churches functioned with enormous and unrivaled effect as organizing centers. To lonely, scattered people they brought vital fellowship and an intimate personal concern which shored up both individualistic and social aims of the people. In Scott Miyakawa's words, they functioned as informal institutions of adult education, giving practice, counsel, and direction in a society where very few other institutions were available.[7] Out of these impulses, moreover, came many of the collective efforts which led to the founding of other institutions, above all the myriad schools and colleges that soon were organized (they did not "spring up" as is so often said).

The church members also constituted reference groups for an unformed social order; with many admitted limitations, they thus provided standards of personal behavior, vocational stability, family responsibility, and civic concern which contributed significantly to the establishment of social peace, order, and the mutual acceptance of differing values. Had the missionary impulse been lacking, life on the frontier would have remained violent, lawless, disorganized, culturally barren, and out of touch with the subtler and profounder aspects of Western civilization much longer than was the case. Even in the area of race relations—with regard to Indians and Negroes—the most effective humanitarian impulses would be church-related though they would long be weak and half-hearted. There was much narrowness, bigotry, censoriousness, and petty factionalism in these evangelical churches. Some groups in the American population could only regard their very existence as a misfortune, and one can bring forward strong critiques of their sense of priorities. They were by no means exclusively beneficent in their works or their effects. Yet just as in the preceding century, when the East had been a frontier, they did answer to fundamental human needs, facilitating the efforts of men and women to make their life together more humane.

Our final conclusion regarding all of these social results—good, bad, and questionable—is that in one sense they are only side effects of efforts that were ineffable and beyond mundane measuring, for the missionaries and church founders came above all to minister the consolations of religion—to bring word of amazing grace to wretched souls. In what measure they succeeded in that primary task God only knows.

7. T. Scott Miyakawa, *Protestants and Pioneers: Individualism and Conformity on the American Frontier*, p. 215.

29

SECTARIAN HEYDAY

Revivalism has always provoked both praise and blame, but the concurrent waves of enthusiastic religion and sectarian strife which swept the nation in the early decades of the nineteenth century made judgments of its worth more extreme than ever. Robert Baird, an American Presbyterian who served as a missionary to Roman Catholics in Europe, held aloft the American ideals of freedom and "voluntaryism" as a banner for Europeans, and lauded revivalism for making Christian experience a bond of unity between churches that had been drawing farther apart ever since the Reformation:

> When viewed in relation to the great doctrines which are universally conceded by Protestants to be fundamental and necessary to salvation, then they all form but one body, recognising Christ as their common Head. They then resemble the different parts of a great temple, all constituting but one whole; or the various corps of an army, which, though ranged in various divisions, and each division having an organization perfect in itself, yet form but one great host, and are under the command of one chief.[1]

Almost simultaneously John Williamson Nevin was designating the "sect-spirit" as the Antichrist and condemning revivalism as the single most scandalous feature of American Christianity.

> We have reason [wrote Nevin] to stand upon our guard against the inroads of an unchurchly spirit. . . . It magnifies the inward and spiritual, and affects to call the soul away from a religion of forms and outward show. . . . It will know nothing of a real revelation of Christ in

1. Robert Baird, *Religion in America*, p. 220. Still a valuable account, as well as a near classic document of the epoch.

> the flesh. This is emphatically Antichrist. . . . The old Gnosticism has been long since shorn of its glory. But what is it but a more subtle phase of the same error to deny the existence of a real, historical *Church* in the world? Without a real Church we can have no real Christ. Let us beware of the Gnostic, unchurchly, Nestorian spirit. . . . Let us have no fellowship here with Antichrist.[2]

Later scholars show equally wide disagreement. Do we face a paradox, or simply confusion? The situation calls for interpretation.

First of all let us get the record straight. The most fundamental divisions in America's religious life are a direct inheritance from the Old World, whose Christian subgroups have simply been projected across the seas by immigration. Many American religious bodies, moreover, are simply regional variants or else parallel churches of different national origin, but within a single confessional communion. Still others have resulted for various reasons from the process of denominational division, not through sect formation. Yet America is undeniably the home of many sects, and evangelical ferment frequently did stimulate their formation. It is imperative, therefore, to establish a working definition of terms and to consider the role of revivalism.

As used here the term "sect" refers to a movement, almost necessarily small at the outset, which secedes from or forms the periphery of a more stable, socially adjusted, and often culturally dominant religious group.[3] Sect formation is thus usually an expression of alienation; it is a movement of people who are spiritually, socially, economically, educationally, or in other ways "disinherited." If not disinherited in this sense, the sect's following is at least in search of values, fulfillment, or fellowship that a dominant, socially acceptable church by its nature cannot ordinarily satisfy. It is usually "joined" by adult believers; and as soon as it begins to face the problems of nurturing children in its faith, it is threatened by extinction or stagnation, or it is gradually transformed into a movement or institution for which the term "church" or "denomination" is more appropriate, with sectarian withdrawal now becoming a potentially disruptive factor in its own organizational life. Sociologically speaking, Christianity was at first a Judaic and Roman sect; it became a "church," however, and thereafter was constantly confronted with the threat of secession by those who demanded a purer, more rigorous membership. Montanism, Novatianism, and Donatism are classic examples of such movements. American church history is

2. John Williamson Nevin, "Sermon on Ephesians 1:23" (15 October 1846), in *The Mercersburg Theology*, ed. James H. Nichols, pp. 75–76. See also the statement by Philip Schaff on p. 512.

3. On early sectarianism, see chap. 15 above.

replete with sects, some now extinct, others alive but stagnant, some dynamic, and others now become "churches."

Characteristically, sects take shape with some charismatic leader at their head; they have this leader's personality or some single, sometimes unusual, tenet (or cluster of tenets) as their reason for being. Personalities and heroes loom large in the origin of all kinds of movements, of course, but they are usually of crucial importance in sect formation. Finally, a sect is recognizably related to the movement whence it emerged; usually it accentuates a traditional tenet which it regards as in danger of being lost. Protestant sects, for example, almost invariably justify themselves with their own "correct" interpretation of the Bible; they frequently insist that the parent movement is apostate, and that they alone now confess the true faith. Because the Christian Church had persistently defined itself as a sect vis-à-vis the "world," it was inevitably haunted and challenged by sectarianism and other manifestations of spiritual discontent. For the same reason the study of sects and similar groups reveals much about the broader course of history.

When a movement's origins and structure have all the sociological or institutional characteristics of a sect except that its doctrinal stance represents a fundamental departure or that it seeks essentially different objectives, the term "sect" is probably inappropriate. But no alternative term has so far won acceptance, though the term "cult" is often so used. If a movement invokes new scriptures or another principle of authority, it is perhaps more appropriate to recognize the emergence of a new religion.[4] These distinctions, of course, are famously easier to make than to apply. But they do serve, nevertheless, to give some direction to historical investigations. This and the succeeding chapter are concerned with a wide variety of the "sect-like" movements which abound in American religious history.

REVIVALISM AND SECTARIANISM

By any standard of measurement, the United States during the first half of the nineteenth century provided a good setting for the emergence of many disruptive and revolutionary religious movements. It was a time of rapidly shifting social standards and institutional life. After the War of 1812 nationalism had a new birth, and with it came a unique blending of jingoism and Christian eschatology. Colonial traditions of rank and station

4. Cultic phenomena and related "religions," including Christian Science, are discussed in chap. 60; Mormonism in chap. 30. No accepted term exists for those divergent movements which encompass the population and political leadership of entire national, ethnic, or regional units (e.g. Arianism, Albigensianism, American Unitarianism, etc.). It is, in fact, well to realize that historical reality does not lend itself to neat classification.

fell to pieces in an "age of the common man." American political conservatives, even the "God-like Daniel Webster," were forced down on their hands and knees in the rough and tumble of the Log Cabin and Hard Cider campaign of 1840. Tumultuous population growth and the westward movement transformed the map and makeup of the country. Social and geographical mobility took on new meaning. Canals, railroads, textile mills, and the cotton gin led to or symbolized other transformations. Voluntaryism, freedom, and personal initiative brought the individual and collective aspirations of Americans to a new order of magnitude. The nation was on the make.

Yet there were frustrations of equal magnitude for those who were displaced by the new egalitarian order, and more drastically for those left behind in the race. Immigration, exploitation, dislocation, loneliness—and, very significantly, the financial panic of 1837—darkened the dream. Modern thought and the newer science, meanwhile, seemed to controvert one traditional belief after another. All these factors served to ripen the sectarian harvest.

Into and across this turbulent scene moved the great surge of evangelical revivalism. It was by far the dominant religious movement of the period, and it served in many ways to open channels for diverse kinds of innovation and disruption. Put most simply, the "new measures" weakened the old measures; traditional church ways were directly challenged. This wrenching occurred among old "magisterial denominations" like the Presbyterians as well as among the Baptists who in many areas (notably in Rhode Island and around Philadelphia) had lived down their sectarian past. On the intellectual level, revivalism also served mightily to undermine doctrinal moorings, emphasizing personal experience instead. It opened opportunities for exploiting a new kind of freedom. The cry went up against hierarchies, seminary professors, dry learning, "hireling ministers," unconverted congregations, and "cold" formalism. Geographic localities, congregations, ministers, and individual laymen assumed new prerogatives. Farmers became theologians, offbeat village youths became bishops, odd girls became prophets.

Beyond these general tendencies, America's kind of revivalism served to arouse other long-dormant but always latent forms of enthusiasm. Leland Jamison in an important essay has pointed to some of the more prominent ones:

> The real impact of revivalism is not to be measured in membership statistics or the number of new religious groups which it has historically brought into being. Rather, its significance lies in . . . the ideas, attitudes, feelings, dreams and hopes which revivalism helped to dis-

> seminate and to be expressed among the American people. . . . Here [in America], as probably nowhere else or ever in Christendom, people had the opportunity of implementing and institutionalizing various particular religious emphases, most of which were as ancient as the Bible itself.[5]

He singles out four of these emphases as especially prominent, stressing the close connection between revivalism and the first two, but pointing out that each of the four could and did arise quite aside from a revivalistic context:

> 1. *Perfectionism,* the doctrine that "perfect sanctification" or complete holiness and the "second blessing" were attainable or even necessary to the salvation of the converted Christian.
> 2. *Millennialism,* a doctrine of "last things," often based on precise and extremely individualistic interpretations of the apocalyptic books of the Bible, urging Christians to ready themselves and the world for the imminent coming of the Kingdom or Christ's second advent.
> 3. *Universalism,* the doctrine, diversely stated, that in Christ's sacrifice the ultimate salvation of all mankind had been accomplished or revealed.
> 4. *Illuminism,* the claim that "new light" or further revelation of God's purpose and nature had been given to men in these latter times and that such new teachings, whether simply modifications of received doctrine or revolutionary conceptions of religion, should be heeded. [The possibilities in this realm were obviously almost infinitely various.]

These dominant emphases, which appeared as often in combination as singly, were given still greater intensity by the willingness of converts to regard anyone who opposed or doubted them as perdition-bound, or to believe that the entire Church was now apostate and lost or, indeed, that it had been for centuries. These themes sometimes became so unanimously the preoccupation of whole denominations that little or no sectarian activity resulted; but when resistance developed, secessions and self-conscious new movements often followed.

Ancient Christian concerns were by no means the only ideas to come to the fore, however, nor was revivalism the only stimulant. Religious excite-

5. A. Leland Jamison, "Religions on the American Perimeter," in *The Shaping of American Religion,* ed. A. Leland Jamison and James Ward Smith, pp. 197–98. Peter Berger makes an exceedingly valuable classification of three leading sectarian motifs: (1) Enthusiastic (an experience to be lived), (2) Prophetic (a message to be proclaimed), and (3) Gnostic (a secret to be divulged), ("The Sociological Study of Sectarianism," *Social Research* 21, no. 4 [Winter 1954]: 467–85).

ment, for one thing, had a way of producing its opposite: disappointment, disgust, remorse, ennui, and even a sense of betrayal. An old associate of Finney put it eloquently in reporting on an earlier harvest of souls in western New York: "I have visited and revisited many of these fields, and groaned in spirit to see the sad, frigid, carnal and contentious state into which they had fallen . . . within three months after we left them."[6] Chronic ill health, disease, and accidents, as always, cried out for healing and assuagement. Socialistic and communitarian theories reinforced literalistic concern for the early Christian communism described in the New Testament (Acts 2:41–47). Mysticism and various forms of pantheism provided links to important philosophic trends of the time. Other interests, often with only remote Christian rootage or none at all, kept appearing and reappearing in different contexts. The discovery and popularization of "animal magnetism" (hypnotism) added a new dimension to popular conceptions of human consciousness. Lurking under America's puritanic Victorianism was a persistent and not sufficiently appreciated restiveness about sex and the monogamous family, a restiveness that the antinomian preaching of the revivals often heightened.

Certain of the new movements, especially among the communitarian experiments discussed in the succeeding chapter, found a place for almost every emphasis and minor theme we have just been considering. Not all of these can be illustrated in a survey history; but certain representative and influential movements require attention, not as an odd assortment of eccentricities introduced to provide comic relief, but as an essential part of the age and a genuine symptom of tensions latent in American life and religion.

PERFECTIONISM AND HOLINESS

John Wesley is unquestionably the greatest modern Protestant preacher of Christian perfection, the church he founded was its dynamic bearer, and the first half of the nineteenth century was American Methodism's greatest hour. Emerging as a semisectarian secession from Anglicanism during the later eighteenth century, Methodism had become by the dawn of the twentieth the largest Protestant denomination in America. The place of perfectionist preaching in this great success story was, however, anything but secure. During the 1820s and early 1830s its popularity definitely waned, after which a great perfectionist revival occurred, not only within Method-

6. Finney himself lamented "the awful declension" in Oneida County that had followed his successes there (see Whitney R. Cross, *The Burned-Over District*, pp. 257–58). Wave after wave of diverse religious excitements made New York State notoriously "burned-over."

ism, but after 1835, in the preaching of the country's greatest revivalist, Charles G. Finney, as well. In 1837 Phoebe Palmer of New York began her extraordinary career as the greatest among countless other Methodist propagandists for the doctrine. In the atmosphere of the antebellum years, therefore, advocates of the "second blessing" felt little need to secede from the Methodist churches. In 1860, however, when the Genesee Conference excommunicated one minister for his strident criticism of Methodism's laxity in these matters, the nucleus for a perfectionist sect was provided. And before the year was out, B. T. Roberts with fourteen other ministers and eighty laymen had brought the Free Methodist Church into existence. The event was premonitory of larger disruptions if and when the church's commitment to perfectionist preaching should decline, but only late in the century would the great Holiness-Pentecostal chapter in the history of American sectarianism be written.

Long before those far-off events, however, perfectionism found its place in many radically untraditional contexts, often in strange combination with other tenets. The most celebrated instance of organized perfectionism was John Humphrey Noyes's Oneida Community, but this "scientific" and closely regulated socialistic experiment had its origins in the radical evangelical perfectionism which flourished among the more enthusiastic preachers of the great revival sweeping the country in the early 1830s. Noyes belonged to a group of seceders from a "free church" which radical "new measures" men had founded in New Haven. With them were affiliated various other groups in New England. These "New Haven Perfectionists" were ostracized at Yale and by the leading churches, but they were moderate in comparison with other movements in New York City and Albany. Everywhere their extreme doctrines were disruptive; and when their assurance of being "beyond the Law" led them to take "spiritual wives," county sheriffs sometimes enforced the law of the land if not that of Moses. During the 1830s perfectionist emphases were becoming pervasive among the revivalists. As Timothy Smith has stressed, moreover, "Eastern and urban evangelism played the dominant role," whereas Western and rural revivalism was lagging.[7]

ADVENTISM

The teaching that the Kingdom of God is at hand is inescapably biblical, and although apocalyptic or chiliastic prophecy has put its mark on many chapters of church history, a distinctly new kind of concern for Christ's Sec-

7. Timothy L. Smith, *Revivalism and Social Reform in Mid-Nineteenth-Century America*, p. 59.

ond Coming arose amid the anxieties and evangelical enthusiasm of antebellum America, as the ancient doctrine became first an urgent popular expectation, and then a "great disappointment" which the Seventh Day Adventists slowly shaped into a stable sectarian witness. Later in the century, when millennialism had again become a widespread concern, Jehovah's Witnesses would begin their sensational ascent from obscurity to national and international prominence. In the meantime, millennial hopes and fears won a prominent place even in many of the large old denominations. All across the country Protestants were singing:

> Stand up, stand up for Jesus,
> The strife will not be long;
> This day the noise of battle;
> The next, the victor's song.[8]

William Miller (1782–1849) grew up on the frontier of upper Vermont. He was a radical Jeffersonian and a deist with something of the stamp of Ethan Allen upon him until conversion in a local revival made him a devout member of a "Calvinist" Baptist church. He tended a large farm and studied the Bible intently in a King James Version bearing Archbishop Ussher's chronology in the margins. Deeply concerned as to when Christ would come again, Miller pondered the Book of Daniel. Counting the days referred to in certain passages of this highly symbolic apocalypse (especially 9:24–27 and 8:14), making each "day" a year, and accepting Ussher's date for these events as 457 B.C. (see Neh. 2:1), he discovered that "seventy weeks" added up to the date of Christ's death (A.D. 33, according to Ussher) while "two thousand three hundred days" added up to A.D. 1843. He described his findings with fine New England bluntness: "I was thus brought, . . . at the close of my two-year study of the Scriptures, to the solemn conclusion that in about twenty-five years from that time [1818] all the affairs of our present state would be wound up." Confessing great diffidence, Miller feared to "go before the world" with his awesome news. In time he overcame his hesitations, however, and won wide acceptance as a revival preacher in Vermont, New Hampshire, and New York.

Miller was ordained as a Baptist minister in 1833 and published his lectures on the Second Coming in 1835; but he was not catapulted into national prominence until two years later when he was heard by Joshua V. Himes (1805–95), a minister of the Christian Connection whose Chardon Street Chapel in Boston was a favored meeting place for reformers and prophets

8. The hymn's author, George Duffield (1818–88), with his father a leader among the "New School" Presbyterians, was noted for his strenuous millennial preaching.

of all sorts (including early abolitionists). Himes was a born publicist and a lover of crowds and camp meetings. After 1839 he became Miller's promoter, a great organizer of millennial fear and fervor, the editor of two millennialist papers, and the compiler of a hymnbook, *The Millennial Harp.* Between 1840 and 1843 meetings were organized all across the country, with Miller himself lecturing over three hundred times during one half-year period. Despite warnings and condemnation from many quarters, thousands, no doubt hundreds of thousands, began to prepare for the Lord's coming. As in Reformation times, there was even a comet to heighten popular apprehension. Yet March 1843 and March 1844 passed by, and time still continued. Finally 22 October 1844 went by, the last definite date to be set by the movement's leadership. The mass movement collapsed amid a general feeling of betrayal, widely circulating charges of profiteering, and harsh disciplining in the Baptist, Methodist, and other revivalistic churches from which the millennial throngs had been chiefly drawn. Sick, discouraged, and cast out by the Baptists, Miller, who had never been as specific in his predictions as Himes, formed a little Adventist church in Vermont. He died without seeing any tangible result from his labors. But the leaven was now abroad in the land as never before. To the hard core of true believers who survived, the "Great Disappointment" was only a challenge.[9]

In 1845 a group of these convinced Adventists, including Miller himself, had convened in Albany and adopted a rudimentary organization along congregational lines. But they were by no means united. Some opposed evangelism, believing that the door was now shut, the Foolish Virgins were forever outside. Others were convinced that the millennial Great Sabbath had in fact arrived, and with it the time for jubilee and alms but not for work. In 1844, however, on the very morrow of the Great Disappointment, Hiram Edson, a New York farmer and staunch Millerite, had beheld a vision as he walked through a cornfield: the "cleansing of the temple" *had* actually been accomplished on the date forecast—but in heaven! Meanwhile, fraternization with the Seventh Day Baptists and further scriptural study led another group to accept the cruciality of observing the Seventh Day rather than the popish Sunday. New advocacy followed, and fierce disagreements on the state of the dead, the fate of the damned, the role of Satan, the nature of the Millennium, the Judgment, and the Atonement. Within a decade the once grand movement was reduced to a disorganized welter of Adventist controversy.

9. Leon Festinger et al., *When Prophecy Fails* (Minneapolis: University of Minnesota Press, 1956) is an important and fascinating study of group responses to apocalyptic disconfirmation, though he treats "Millerism" only in passing, pp. 12–23. See also Festinger's more general work *A Theory of Cognitive Dissonance* (Stanford, Calif.: Stanford University Press, 1962).

Yet out of this chaos emerged an agent of reorganization in the person of a slight teen-aged girl of Portland, Maine, the "Adventist Prophetess," Ellen G. Harmon (1827–1915). Converted to the movement in 1842 and soon extruded from the Methodist Church, she (like Edson) had her first vision shortly after the Great Disappointment, and therewith began her life's mission. After marrying James White, an Adventist elder, in 1846, the range of her activities increased. Given as she was to visions and transports—an estimated two thousand before she died—she poured out her version of the Adventist message in an endless stream of publications. Gradually she more or less absorbed the Edsonites and the Sabbatarians, gathering a reasonably united following that not only accepted her claims to be the "Spirit of Prophecy," but also her doctrinal teaching and her special views on health and diet.

In 1855 Battle Creek, Michigan, became the movement's headquarters when the Whites took up residence there. Five years later, a representative group took the name "Seventh-Day Adventists," incorporated the publishing house, and projected a general conference, which was duly organized in 1863. Soon Mrs. White's vegetarian protégé, Dr. John H. Kellogg, would begin his career—and eventually make Battle Creek the nation's breakfast cereal center. With fidelity to Mrs. White's nine-volume *Testimonies* as its chief unifying factor, the church continued to expand. In 1903, not long after returning from a ten-year mission in Australia, Mrs. White moved the central offices to Takoma Park, near Washington, D.C. Since her death in 1915 the church has continued its worldwide growth, using new communications media as they became available, displaying the largest measure of lay dedication of any church in America, and organizing extensive works of mercy, notably in the realm of health and medical care. At the same time, they have remained in almost complete isolation from all other churches. With the passing years their doctrinal stand has moved somewhat closer to that of general American fundamentalism, but any significant cooperation with these groups is prevented by the Adventists' extreme legalism, Sabbatarianism, and unusual doctrines on the Atonement, Satan, and the damned, as well as their strongly held views on health, medicine, and diet. Most distinctive of all is the special authority that they continue to show for the writings of Mrs. White.

UNIVERSALISM

Though not usually discussed in the context of American sectarianism, the Universalists are an important reminder of how an ancient "heresy" could be revitalized as a divisive force through the interplay of revivalism and the American social situation. The central Universalist contention, that "it is the purpose of God, through the grace revealed in our Lord Jesus Christ, to save every member of the human race from sin," has a long lineage. Richard Eddy's history of the denomination, in fact, devoted more pages to the documentation of its antiquity than to its American history.

The Universalist church in the United States was founded by John Murray (1741–1815), an Englishman of "high Calvinist" background, who had been brought into the Methodist movement by the preaching of John Wesley and George Whitefield. He was converted to Universalist teaching by James Relly (1720–ca. 1780), another British Methodist who, while remaining a Trinitarian of Calvinist tendency, had extended the logic of Wesley's proclamation of "grace to all" to mean that Christ's sacrifice had purchased salvation not only for the Elect but for the entire human race. Excommunicated in England, Murray reached American shores in 1770, preached in several states, and finally went to live in Gloucester, Massachusetts, where he had found a small group of Relly's converts. These he organized into the first American Universalist church in 1779. Murray was also present at the convention held six years later when an association was formed to gain Universalist liberties in Massachusetts, a right that was won in the courts in 1786. In 1793 a New England "Convention" began to meet. In the meantime spokesmen for similar but not identical views had organized groups in Boston, Philadelphia, New Jersey, and New Hampshire.

The definitive prophet of this movement was to be Hosea Ballou (1771–1852). Like several other early Universalist ministers, Ballou was of Baptist background, but was also influenced by the liberal sentiments of Boston Congregationalism, many of whose leaders (most notably Charles Chauncy) were arriving at Universalist views through an emphasis on the goodness of man and the benevolence of Deity. In 1804 Ballou published his *Treatise on the Atonement,* which displays a very strong biblical interest, deep evangelical conviction, and strong Rellyan influence. It departs from Murray in its shift toward Unitarianism and away from a substitutionary view of Christ's sacrifice. Ballou defended a "moral theory" of the Atonement, holding that Christ suffered for men but not instead of them. This revision had great effect on organized Universalism, which increasingly moved toward Boston Unitarianism in theology even while remaining socially and spiritually an entirely different sort of movement. The Universalists grew steadily in strength, established a weekly paper in 1819, and in 1831–41 (when it suffered a minor schism on the issue of future punishment) claimed over five hundred ministers. By the Civil War there were state conventions throughout most of the North, with district associations at a lower level and a very weak General Convention above. Tufts College (1852) and Divinity School (1869) in Medford, Massachusetts, became its major educational institutions, though there were several colleges and a seminary elsewhere.

The sect became a small denomination which throughout the nineteenth century was far more evangelical than is generally realized. Its leaders had the further satisfaction of seeing its chief tenet win acceptance not only in liberal constituencies but in revivalistic movements ordinarily considered conservative. On the frontier their views frequently found favor. Throughout this period it bore the marks of its sectarian origins, especially in New England, where it began as a revolt from the standing order by humble, unlettered people rather than by the intellectual and social leaders. Although in 1961 the Universalists would merge with the Unitarians in a new Association of Liberal Religion, their beginnings contrast sharply with the process by which the culturally dominant elements of Eastern Massachusetts gradually drifted away from their ancient moorings and became a separate denomination.

THE SWEDENBORGIAN IMPULSE

Of all the unconventional currents streaming through the many levels of American religion during the antebellum half-century, none proved attractive to more diverse types of dissenters from established denominations than those which stemmed from Emanuel Swedenborg. His influence was seen everywhere: in Transcendentalism and at Brook Farm, in spiritualism and the free love movement, in the craze for communitarian experiments, in faith healing, mesmerism, and a half-dozen medical cults; among great intellectuals, crude charlatans, and innumerable frontier quacks. When Emerson's *Nature* appeared anonymously in 1836, many thought that it was a manifesto from the Swedenborgian church; and in *Representative Men* Emerson not only paid homage to Swedenborg as the "last Father in the church," but also revealed essential aspects of his own world view. Bronson Alcott put Swedenborg in his hall of fame along with Plato, Plotinus, and Boehme. William James was linked with Swedenborgianism by birth (his father had been so attracted) and many interpreters have remarked on the continuities from father to son.

There are many clues to Swedenborg's amazing capacity to satisfy such varied yearnings, but first among them was his self-assured optimism and his sweeping comprehensiveness. He made the whole universe religiously intelligible, giving satisfaction to those who were surfeited with revivalism and narrow-mindedness. Swedenborg dealt with nearly every historic doctrinal issue, yet he pleased those who desired freedom from all ancient dogmas. Powerfully asserting the freedom of man and the promise of the times, he gratified those who would flee Calvinistic doctrines of sin, reprobation, and hell. And in all this he not only made the Bible his constant point of departure but gave a thrilling new impulse to biblical exegesis. Thus each of the major sectarian themes of the day—perfectionism, millennialism, universalism, and illuminism—had their place in his message. Its popularity, in short, is an essential guide to much that was new in America's great period of religious innovation.

Behind this immense ramification of influence, naturally enough, is the thought of an incredibly versatile religious genius, Emanuel Swedenborg (1688–1771). He was the son of Jesper Swedberg, an eminent Swedish theologian and bishop. After his university studies Swedenborg dabbled in poetry, turned to natural science, traveled widely in Europe, and then served brilliantly on the Council of Mines. In various capacities and through many publications he made memorable contributions in geology, anatomy, neurology, paleontology, physics, and astronomy. Then in his fifty-seventh year he announced his concern for religion in his book *The Worship and Love of God*. The vital turning point had been a vision in which God had directed him "to explain to men the spiritual sense of the Scripture." His first response was the *Arcana Coelestia,* an enormous eight-volume commentary on Genesis and Exodus in which nearly his entire system is expounded or foreshadowed. Before his death thirty more volumes had given scope and specificity to the "Heavenly Doctrines."

The central claim of Swedenborg is that the Lord had come again in accordance with John's vision in the Apocalypse: "And I John saw the holy city, New Jerusalem, coming down from God out of heaven" (Rev. 21:2). The Second Coming of Jesus Christ is made in the inspired Word of God through Swedenborg's disclosure of its spiritual meaning; it is thus a way of reading the Bible revealed in God's good time by most extraordinary means. "I enjoy perfect inspiration," said the Swedish seer in his strange, matter-of-fact way. "The inner sense of the Word of God has been dictated to me out of heaven." Swedenborg was himself an eschatological event.

Swedenborg's formal principle, his method of disclosing the Bible's spiritual meaning—as against the literal, historical sense of the letter—was a corollary of his doctrine of correspondences, which may be said to be his material principle. Emerson described this doctrine as "the fine secret that little explains large, and large, little. . . . Nature iterates her means perpetually on successive planes." In Swedenborg's system there are three distinct orders of being: the natural world of mineral, vegetable, or animal "ultimates," the spiritual, and the celestial. He described the Bible in terms of these same three degrees: "The Word in its bosom is spiritual because it descended from Jehovah the Lord, and passed through the angelic heavens; and . . . was in its descent adapted to the perception of angels, and at last to the perception of men." When interpreted through Swedenborg's special visions, the Bible clarified the correspondences that linked together the one system of God. Hence he could assert that "all heaven in the aggregate reflects the single man." On the other hand, such are the correspondences of the cosmos that every "ultimate," including man in all of his parts, corresponds to some higher reality. The Divine and the Natural are consubstantial in God and Man. All of this, moreover, has historical implications, for it means that the historic church and its old controversies are done and gone. In this new era of rational clarity there is hope for the heavenly conquest of hell. "The object of creation was an angelic heaven from the human race; in other words, mankind, in whom God might be able to dwell as in His residence." Swedenborg's ethic, naturally enough, was neither ascetic nor extreme. One need not renounce all to be saved; one must rather keep his loves—to God, neighbor, world, and flesh—in the proper order.

Taken as a whole the Heavenly Doctrines were gauged to attract persons of liberal and thoughtful tendency. Yet the more esoteric features of his writings also attracted more eccentric followers. Swedenborg's visions and his communications with famous men long dead encouraged emulation, while his unusual views on sex and conjugal love provided a rationale for defying laws and social conventions on marriage. His spiritual interpretations encouraged new views on health, healing, and sickness, and his disdain for tradition encouraged radicalism in every direction: in social and religious matters, and particularly in biblical interpretation. Swedenborg, in sum, meant many things to many minds.

Since he believed that his appeal was limited only to intellectuals, and that the New Church would manifest itself gradually, Swedenborg would not have been surprised at its slow growth. Whether he in fact intended to found a visible church organization is uncertain, even doubtful. But in England an institute for the extension of his reformation was organized soon after his death, and it spread from there to other countries. After bitter controversy among Anglicans between separatists and nonseparatists, the first New Church society in the world was founded in London in 1787. Its first apostle to America was James Glen, a rich planter from British Guiana who had been converted by a chance reading of Swedenborg's *Heaven and Hell.* Slowly small groups of intense and sometimes distinguished adherents were formed in Philadelphia, Baltimore, Boston, New York, and a few other places. The first General Convention, held in Philadelphia in 1817, reported seventeen societies, with a total of 360 members living in nine states. During the next few years the New Church seemed to be declining; but even when this trend was reversed, growth was very slow. It never has numbered even 10,000 members in the United States; but through articulate spokesmen, an active publication program, and the phenomenal appeal of its "founder," it has wielded an influence very disproportionate to its size. Swedenborgianism, moreover, has spread far beyond the institutional New Church. Indeed, the way in which Swedenborg stimulated or became associated with other deviations from mainstream Protestant impulses is the major aspect of his American influence.

SWEDENBORGIAN VARIATIONS

The first of the eccentric religious impulses with which Swedenborgianism became closely allied sprang from mesmerism or "animal magnetism" (i.e. hypnotism, somnambulism, and related phenomena). Friedrich Mesmer (1734?–1815) was an Austrian physician and astrologer who identified the force of the stars with electricity and magnetism; he was also a mystic and a born showman who during a long "practice" in Paris accomplished healings and many strange psychic phenomena. Due to this early association of "mesmerism" with magic and the black arts, and later with spiritualism, it was denounced and ignored by the medical profession, but for precisely this reason it flourished in the religious underground. Nowhere was it possible to find a more attractive basis for a Christian understanding (even a biblical theology) of these phenomena than in Swedenborg's writings. This fact had the double effect of attracting many doctors and pharmacists into the New Church, and of making Swedenborg a favorite resource of innumerable itinerant healers and quacks. Homeopathy or homeopathic medicine provides an important case in point. Both Swedenborg and S. C. F. Hahnemann (1755–1843), the originator of this medical theory, were intensive students of Paracelsus and held that disease was, essentially, a "dynamic aberration of the spirit." Hahnemann's accent on natural forces and spiritual healing explains why homeopathy spread through the New Church like wild-fire. Dr. Hans B. Gram, a Dane who had studied with Hahnemann in Germany, introduced the practice in America and soon became a New Churchman, and many others in the church also became very prominent in the "profession."

Homeopathy also was taken up in diverse ways by many other healers, including those who had animal magnetism in their quiver. Phineas P. Quimby of Portland, Maine, who tried in his way to evolve a scientific view of mental healing, did not stress these affinities, but Warren F. Evans, a former Methodist minister in that city, became an ardent Swedenborgian after being healed by Quimby. Evans published his views on healing well before Mary Baker published *Science and Health,* and with other disciples of Quimby he founded the New Thought movement. Such linkages to Swedenborg continue throughout the century, and as we shall see in a later connection, Christian Science itself may be usefully understood as a precisely formulated, highly organized, and authoritatively led instance.

Mesmerism and spiritualism were so intimately related that for several generations they were deemed to be virtually inseparable. It is by no coincidence, therefore, that Swedenborg, too, became implicated. In fact, there is some ground for seeing Swedenborg as the greatest medium in modern times and the New Church as the first spiritualist church. In 1818, when a spiritualistic phenomenon was described to William Schlatter (one of the early New Church leaders in Philadelphia), he was not at all incredulous and urged that the person be won for the New Church with a copy of Swedenborg's *Heaven and Hell.* Many similar but isolated instances followed. Then in 1845 a series of articles on the subject appeared in the *New Jerusalem Magazine.* The major outcropping of interest in intercourse with the other world, which came in 1848 with the Fox sisters' rappings, was not directly traceable either to Swedenborg or to the New Church; but it did conduce to so rapid a growth of spiritualism among Swedenborgian "liberals" that the New Church was threatened by schism in the 1850s and after.

The most widely read philosopher-theologian of spiritualism was Andrew Jackson Davis, the "Poughkeepsie Seer." Davis was an apprentice cobbler when an itinerant mesmerist found him an exceptionally apt subject. For a time thereafter he was a professional medium and exhibition piece of hypnotic marvels. Later, while under hypnosis and professedly in contact with Swedenborg and others, he gave lectures published with the aid of scribes as *The Harmonial Philosophy* (1852), which went through twenty-four editions in thirty years. Professor George Bush of New York University in his book *Mesmer and Swedenborg* (1847) did much to dignify these efforts by publishing an enthusiastic appendix on "The Revelations of Andrew Jackson Davis." A member of the New Church and convinced that Davis could not possibly have absorbed such wisdom by any other means than spirit-contact, Bush was doubly rejoiced. Actually Davis's works exhibit nothing that an intelligent person of his background and absorptive propensities could not have produced under hypnosis; and they serve admirably to illustrate the way in which Swedenborg's unitive thinking could be combined in the popular mind with both animal magnetism and many of the popular reform panaceas of the day, including socialism. This complex syndrome was even better illustrated by Thomas Lake Harris (1823–1906), a Universalist minister of New York who was much impressed by Davis, and also by the Utopian theorists Charles Fourier and Robert Owen. In 1850 Harris and an associate founded a short-lived cooperative community of spiritualists in Mountain Cove, Virginia, before returning to New York to found an independent Christian spiritualist church and a periodical to propagate Swedenborgian views. Yet he honored Swedenborg chiefly as a "forerunner" and in 1857 scandalized orthodox New Churchmen by publishing *The Arcana of Christianity,* wherein it was announced that to Harris had been revealed not merely the spiritual but the *celestial* meaning of Scripture. From this point he went on from excess to excess, even to the hour of his death.

SPIRITUALISM

Spiritualism both as an organized movement and as a vast congeries of commercialized disorganization stems from exciting events in the "burned-over district." In 1847 a Methodist farmer, John D. Fox, his wife, and six children moved into an old house in Hydesville, New York. True to rumors about the house, their peace was soon interrupted by strange rappings. During the following year the two youngest children, Katherine (age twelve) and Margaret (age thirteen), established contact with the rapper with the command, "Hear, Mr. Splitfoot, do as I do." A simple code communication was set up; the neighbors, sometimes in fear and trembling, flocked to see the marvels. Some time later an older married sister living in Rochester became a kind of manager of the sensation; and on 14 November 1849, Margaret Fox appeared for the first time in public with admission charged. Later in the year the Fox sisters were signed up by P. T. Barnum, and they soon became celebrities. The news spread rapidly, not least because Horace Greeley of the *New York Tribune,* long since a devoted follower of Fourier, became a fervent believer.

Soon countless other mediums began to make contact with the spirit world. Scoffers probably outnumbered believers, but investigations made by various persons of dignity and authority sometimes led to affirmative reports and enthusiastic discipleship on the part of the investigators. Séances and spiritualist societies became a common phenomenon all across the country. Various groups combined spiritualism and free love. Mesmerists, magicians, and fortune-tellers also discovered an important opportunity, with the result that a whole new era in American roadshow entertainment was opened. As was inevitable, the first simple feats of the Fox girls gave way to other marvels: table turnings, slate writings, mysterious appearances, and great feats of clairvoyance. Margaret Fox, meanwhile, had won the affections of Elisha Kent Kane, the arctic explorer and socially prominent Philadelphian. He even proposed marriage, and for a time, as his prospective wife, she left "the tables" behind to pursue a polite education. Before his death in 1857 they had been married in an informal "Quaker" ceremony, and Margaret subsequently claimed his name and received a small legacy.

Spiritualism was not merely commercialized entertainment, however. It was a religious force—for some it was a religion—and this was true long before the Hydesville rappings. There were always the bereaved and the remorseful who desperately needed and wanted to make contact with the departed—a fact that stimulated interest in spiritualism after each of the country's major wars. Mrs. Lincoln herself showed such an interest after her husband's assassination. Still others, having drifted away from the churches, now sought and found confirmation of their religious yearnings in an objective and "scientific" way. In the pre–Civil War period the actual denominational possibilities of the movement went unrealized, even though an increasing number of clergymen became interested. Because the mediums almost invariably stressed the general immortality of man, Universalists were especially attracted. For reasons already indicated Swedenborgianism added other incitements.

Because of its extra-ecclesiastical auspices and lack of doctrinal complications, spiritualism also appealed to liberals and anticlericals, and it often became affiliated with communitarian and reformist movements. The best-known example in this category was Robert Dale Owen (1801–77). Owen had been a freethinker and a proponent of his father's communitarian socialism, but in 1856, while serving as an American diplomat in Naples, he experienced occult phenomena in a decisive way. The year after his father died in 1858, Owen began writing the book that betokened his conversion. *Footfalls on the Boundary of Another World* (1860) became the most famous American defense of the movement's central conviction. Owen's fame even won him an invitation to read a paper in the White House, which led to Lincoln's classic remark: "Well, for those who like that sort of thing, I should think it is just about the sort of thing they would like." [10]

Since 1863 there have been several attempts to organize spiritualism as a

10. Quoted in Earl Wesley Fornell, *The Unhappy Medium: Spiritualism and the Life of Margaret Fox*, p. 118. See also Richard W. Leopold, *Robert Dale Owen*, pp. 321–39.

national denomination. The first effort collapsed within a decade, but a more permanent National Spiritualist Association was organized in 1893 (the year Margaret Fox died) on a loose congregational basis with a very liberal statement of principles. At this time it had about fifty thousand members and over three hundred affiliated organizations. In some cities, as in Boston, the Spiritualists achieved a fairly stable and respected denominational status, with an enlightened and liberal membership, a fine edifice in the Back Bay, and a well-edited paper, the *Boston Banner of Light.* Generally, however, the chief constituency has been a vast unorganized multitude which has ebbed and flowed with changing times and circumstances, but which reached its floodtide around 1870, when the movement claimed eleven million adherents. Spiritualism was not a "sect" in the usual sense of the term, yet it became a component in many kinds of sectarian revolt from the more traditional churches. It sometimes merged with various forms of occultism—as had astrology in ages past—to form an undercurrent of esoteric religion from which new movements would continuously arise. Its growth in America and elsewhere reveals a fundamental kind of religious uneasiness. In its popularity one may observe both the threat of modern science to traditional faith and the appeal to empirical confirmation of cherished hopes. It is thus a form of theological liberalism in which such eminent thinkers as Alfred Russel Wallace, Victor Hugo, and William James were seriously interested.

30

THE COMMUNITARIAN IMPULSE

"We are all a little wild here with numberless projects of social reform. Not a reading man but has a draft of a new community in his waistcoat pocket." The words are Emerson's, one of his most quoted observations, from a letter to Carlyle written in 1840.[1] As was so often the case, he spoke the truth. The United States was the Promised Land for both American and European communitarian planners, and the antebellum half-century was their great seedtime. Most of the new communities, of course, remained simply the ideas of "reading men," yet six score of them were actually founded, a few dozen of them became celebrated though transient successes, and, if we include Mormonism, one became a major American cultural force. Like sectarianism, however, this communitarian impulse is difficult to characterize, because these experiments were so often but the lengthened shadow of some charismatic leader; and as Max Weber observed, "Charisma knows only inner determination and inner restraint." Almost by definition, the innovators rejected codes and statutes, traditions and customs—and this they did with more than usual abandon in the open society of the young American republic. In many cases they not only founded new sects, but called them out of the world. Thus they challenged the individualism and conformity of the nation as well as the conventional views of the churches. Rare were the times, nevertheless, when these efforts were not motivated by a belief in Christian perfection and the conviction (as old as cenobitic monasticism) that a dedicated community provided the ideal conditions for attaining it.

Socialistic communities of one kind or another have had a long history in America. Even Jamestown before the advent of John Smith had its "com-

1. Carlyle in turn revealed his estimate of such efforts by referring to the founder of Brook Farm as a "Socinian minister who left the pulpit to reform the world by growing onions" (quoted in Charles Crowe, *George Ripley*, p. 69).

munitarian" phase. Necessity pushed our beloved "Pilgrim Fathers" to the same resort for a time. The Mennonites and other German sects often verged on such a social system, and some openly adopted it. The early nineteenth century brought another resurgence of this communitarian impulse, manifesting itself in the most diverse ways among both anticlerical freethinkers and Christian enthusiasts. In the events of the preceding chapter there were intimations of such an impulse, but in this chapter the communitarian movements themselves are considered, particularly those which are significant episodes in religious history. We begin with the Shakers, one of the earliest and most radical communitarian sects to organize, yet one which America took peculiarly to its heart—though only after it had become virtually extinct.

THE SHAKERS

The United Society of Believers in Christ's Second Coming (the Millennial Church) was brought to this country from England. Its founding spirit was Ann Lee Stanley (1736–84), who immigrated with eight followers (including her brother and her husband) in 1774. Mother Ann Lee's early life was one of almost unmitigated tribulation, culminating in the most remarkable exaltation. The daughter of one Manchester blacksmith and while very young the wife of another, she was unschooled and illiterate when she was converted by Jane and James Wardley, leaders of the so-called Shaking Quakers. (This sect, resembling the Camisards, may have been brought to England by refugees from the France of Louis XIV, and reinvigorated by the millennialist fervor of the Wardleys, who were also committed to various Quaker ideas.) Ann Lee seems to have outdone all others in the intensity of her piety; and after some years during which she suffered much distress and gave birth to four very short-lived children, her trances and visions convinced others and then herself that Christ's Second Coming would be in the form of a woman, and that she was that woman. She had also become convinced that sexual relations, ever since Adam and Eve, had been the root of all sin. Yet few people in England were persuaded by the little group of noisy worshipers and irrepressible preachers of which she was now the recognized head. Mistreatment, mob action, and imprisonment seemed to be their lot and only expectation—and so, they departed for America.

Even upon arrival in the promised land, poverty compelled a two-year dispersal of the little group. In 1776, however, they reconvened near Albany at what is now Watervliet, where economic difficulties led them to organize themselves in a socialistic Christian community, although communitarianism had heretofore had no part in their message. Mother Ann, now deserted by her husband, joined the company at its forlorn gathering place, but until 1779 they made no evangelistic advances. Then came an incident that would become the pattern for Shaker growth during the entire period of their greatest significance. In the aftermath of a revival in nearby New Lebanon, certain "New Light" Baptists who had been spiritually moved but left dissatisfied visited the Shakers and were further converted. As other people began seeking them out in ever greater numbers, the little community began a more concerted mission into communities where revivals had occurred. To those who wondered what to do with their reborn lives, the Shakers offered a meaningful answer. You have not left the world and the flesh, they would say, bidding the seeker to confess his sins to Mother Ann Lee and enter the true millennial church.

The Shakers made important gains during the Revolution despite their pacifism and British origins, and when Mother Ann died in 1784, capable leaders took her place. In the Harvard-Shirley area of Massachusetts they capitalized on the groundwork of a prophet who had recently preached very similar doctrines. Among Baptists they were especially successful. They made deep inroads on the newly formed Freewill Baptists, especially in New Hampshire, where one such congregation became the nucleus of a new Shaker community, and where many others were decimated by Shaker influence. Among the early Baptist converts was the Reverend Joseph Meacham, who in 1787 became the church's first American leader, an excellent organizer, and a powerful factor in the sect's expansion. By 1794 there were twelve communities: two in New York, four in Massachusetts, two in New Hampshire, one in Connecticut, and three in Maine. The community at New Lebanon remained the center of authority.

But the great harvest would be gathered when the Second Awakening created ideal conditions both in New England and in the West. The Shakers' most sensational coup was in Kentucky, when they carried off three former Presbyterians who had led the Cane Ridge revival. One of these, Richard McNemar, became the Shakers' outstanding western leader. Between 1805 and 1809 four new communities were founded beyond the mountains: two in Kentucky and two in Ohio. Two more in Ohio and one in Indiana were added later, and once founded these communities grew both in numbers and in extent. Union Village in Ohio came to embrace 4,500 acres. During its period of greatest size and vitality, between 1830 and 1850, the church as a whole numbered about six thousand persons living in nineteen communities.

The Shaker communities became one of the American marvels, visited by almost every systematic foreign observer. In a simple Yankee way these Shaker villages were, in fact, idyllic: the wants of life were fully, even abundantly supplied; the clean-lined functional buildings, spotless interiors, gracefully practical furniture, wonderful cattle herds, fine herb gardens, and perfectly tended fields all witnessed to organizational, social, and economic success. Within the community a straightforward, strait-laced, and peaceable but minutely regulated life went on, with duties clearly assigned, authority clearly demarcated, and the sexes separated so far as practicality would permit.

Shaker communities, however, were not conceived primarily as secular utopias, and it was only after the Civil War that economic and worldly considerations gradually became predominant—a trend which, with other factors, hastened their decline. By the century's end they had become a mere remnant. But during their great period the Shakers were an intense biblically oriented sect, millennialist in primary doctrinal concern and revivalistic in spirit. For them the Second Coming was a past fact, consummated in and through Ann Lee, who was a feminine incarnation as Jesus had been the masculine. Mother Lee was the "Second pillar of the Church of God," and the Shakers were the advance guard or the intercessory remnant whose example and prayers would ultimately lead all men into blessedness. They were thus universalists in their total view. In the moral demands they placed upon this remnant they were legalistic perfectionists: twelve classic virtues and four moral principles would bring men from the animal to the spiritual plane. Because the Kingdom was literally at hand, procreation was unnecessary, which accounts for their rule of celibacy, the only moral precept which they did not share with standard Protestant statements of Christian virtue.

In addition to this theology, which owed much to the revelations of Ann Lee, the Shakers were from the first spiritualists. They communicated with the departed, and for a decade or so after 1837 public séances were a very important part of their corporate religious life. At all times their worship was extremely important, regularly scheduled, and intensely communal, though Pentecostal gifts of speaking in tongues and personal testimonies had their place. The most distinctive feature of Shaker worship was the group dance, a legacy from the Camisards which, when accompanied by lively singing, could at times become quite frenzied. With due allowance for its special doctrines and practices, Shakerism was at once both an extraordinary embodiment of basic monastic motifs and a remarkable example of the special Christian emphases generated by revivalism. The Shakers were perhaps the single most influential source for the country's widespread interest in communitarian experiments during the early nineteenth century.

THE SOCIETY OF THE PUBLIC UNIVERSAL FRIEND

The earliest indigenous American communitarian experiment so closely resembled the Shakers in its origins and leading tenets that contemporaries spoke of deliberate imitation. At the outset, nevertheless, the two movements were quite independent. Jemima Wilkinson (1752–1819) was the daughter of a prosperous Quaker farmer in Cumberland, Rhode Island, who in 1776 was expelled from the local meeting because of her affiliation with the revivalistic "New Light" Baptists. Very soon thereafter, she emerged from a period of illness and visions as a Publisher of Truth in her own right, announcing that she had died to self and had been reborn as the Public Universal Friend, with a Christlike mission to preach repentance, otherworldliness, and preparation for death. A sense of millennial expectancy pervaded her pronouncements, but except for a strong emphasis on the virtues of celibacy, her message was a fairly conventional form of New School evangelicalism, as modified by her Quaker nurture and her reading of Fox, Penn, Barclay, and Penington. Far more sensational in that day was her itinerant preaching and the "personality cult" which she fostered. Mounted sidesaddle at the head of a small cavalcade of followers, she moved in ever-widening circles, first in Rhode Island, then in Massachusetts and Connecticut, and finally to eastern Pennsylvania.

By 1789 Jemima Wilkinson's "Universal Friends" were a recognized denomination of about two hundred members, many of them former Quakers, some of surprisingly high social station. Several local groups were meeting in Rhode Island, with others in New Milford, Connecticut, and Worcester, Pennsylvania. On this basis she projected an isolated community in western New York, which at that time was still an unsurveyed wilderness. In 1788 a settlement was begun on Lake Seneca, and within two years, by which time the Universal Friend was on the scene herself, her 260 followers were the largest community in the region. In 1794, due to land title problems and the encroachment of outsiders, they founded a new "Jerusalem" twelve miles farther west on Crooked (Keuka) Lake. Here as before freehold farms were laid out, and the Universal Friend, with her entourage of a dozen or more celibate women, was provided with a fine frame house, later replaced by still another, more ambitious one.

Evangelism ceased in this frontier outpost, but until her death in 1819 the Friend continued to minister to her society, preaching with particular effectiveness at services for the deceased. Despite growing internal dissension and continued land problems, meetings were held in Jerusalem more or less in the Quaker manner even after her death. A semblance of organization remained until 1863, and the last of her converts did not die until 1874. By that time the publicity of her community's pioneering had done its part to spur the region's rapid population growth. Out in the "burned-over district" as back in the East, however, the society suffered from the indistinctiveness of its leader's message and from the absence of strict communitarian organization. It gradually coalesced with the surrounding culture, leaving a great frame house on the hill overlooking the lake as a monument to Jemima Wilkinson's forceful personality.

GERMAN PIETISTIC COMMUNITIES

From the early eighteenth-century Ephrata Community in Pennsylvania to the controversial expansion of the Hutterites in the twentieth century, German Anabaptism or radical pietism has made a continuous contribution to the history of American communitarianism. The six hundred followers of George Rapp (1757–1847) who organized Harmony, Pennsylvania, in 1804 were in this tradition. They were extreme pietists who had separated from the established church of Württemberg. Their doctrine was characteristically strong in its anticipation of the millennium, universalistic, uninterested in evangelism, and after 1807 opposed to procreation and marriage. Like the Shakers the Rappites practiced auricular confession and set themselves on the road to perfection by close personal discipline in order that a pure remnant could be presented to God on the Great Day. In the social and physical sense Harmony became a famous success, a garden in the wilderness. And this was equally true of the new Harmony in Indiana to which they removed in 1815, or of Economy (in Ohio, near Pittsburgh) which became the "permanent" location of the Rappites ten years later.

In addition to the Rappites there were several other German sects who during the lifetime of their leaders maintained highly successful communities. Wilhelm Keil, a Prussian immigrant converted by the German Methodists and for a time a preacher in that connection, made a group of disaffected Rappites the nucleus of two flourishing communities: Bethel (in Missouri), which flourished as a supply post for the Oregon Trail, and Aurora (in Oregon), which was reached by a famous trek in which the coffin of Keil's son was borne across the plains. Though it perpetuated an extreme form of antisacramental pietism, Keil's group was characterized by much less doctrinal eccentricity than most.

Somewhat similar was the group of three hundred Quaker-like pietists led from harassment in Bavaria, Württemberg, and Baden to Zoar (Ohio) by Joseph Michael Bäumler (Bimeler) in 1817. Like the Bethelites (and later the Mormons), they were greatly aided in the economic sense by the American westward movement, in this case by the Ohio Canal. Although the community continued for some time after Bimeler's death in 1853, it finally was dissolved in 1898.

Still another group of this type was the Amana Society, or Community of True Inspiration. As lowly in its origins as the other German pietistic movements but more charismatic in its leadership, this group had been gathered in various places in the German Rhineland before the decision to migrate. In 1843 they founded Ebenezer near Buffalo, New York; then in the 1850s to gain more land and to escape urban seductions, they gradually removed to east-central Iowa, where they maintained a plain but thriving cluster of villages. In the late twentieth century they continue to prosper on their 25,000-acre holdings, though since 1932 as an incorporated cooperative.

UTOPIAN COMMUNITARIANISM

In addition to a wide variety of experiments in Christian communitarianism, the early decades of the nineteenth century witnessed the formation (and usually the early dissolution) of dozens of utopias which lacked sectarian or churchly aspirations, or were even antireligious. The most famous of these experiments was New Harmony, founded by Robert Owen (1771–1858), a Welshman, who had distinguished himself in Scotland as an industrialist with a passionate concern for the well-being of his labor force. Owen was also an amateur philosopher of deterministic persuasions who considered the social environment the decisive factor in personal development. He made New Lanark a model factory town; then discovering in 1824 that the Rappite property in Indiana was for sale, he acted on a long-considered plan to establish a true model of socialism in America.

On arrival in the United States, Owen continued to publicize his views, even lecturing once in the national capital to a large and distinguished audience that included President John Quincy Adams. He became more confident that America was socialism's promised land. A great many distinguished scientists, educators, and social dreamers (but far too few competent craftsmen) answered the call; and early in 1826 *New* Harmony was occupied. Owen was often dictatorial; his odd assortment of followers showed little capacity for maintaining peace and order in his absence; his sons (William and Robert Dale) were ineffective as his lieutenants. By 1827 Robert Owen was ready to confess that he had invested four-fifths of his fortune for naught. The community was dissolved. By 1830 nearly two dozen other Owenite groups had also come and gone. All of these communities rested their hopes on education, freethinking, and human idealism. They had only theory as an integrative force, and in the midst of American opportunity, freedom, and individualism, this proved, over and over again, to be an insufficient basis for communitarian success.

At least in theory a religious ingredient was present in the ideas of the French Utopian Charles Fourier (1772–1837). In Arthur Brisbane, Horace Greeley, William Henry Channing, and Parke Godwin, Fourier gained persuasive American propagandists; and within two decades about fifty ephemeral communities had testified to both the popularity and the impracticality of his proposals. All of these secular communities demonstrated what many a foreign observer had declared: that a community's failure was almost certain when its participants lacked the intense religious commitment which could repress individual inclinations and render paternalism agreeable. One might add that charismatic leadership was equally necessary—and this Owen and the American disciples of Fourier invariably lacked. Never were such observations borne out more strikingly than by the contrast between the Harmony of the Rappites and the New Harmony of the Owenites. Yet there was an intermediate type of community that occupies an important, almost legendary niche in American memory. These experiments were informed by fundamentally religious aspirations at least in their origins, though they were distinctly liberal, even radical, in their revisions of orthodox doctrine. Among many others, three that originated in the early 1840s are best remembered: the Oneida Community, the Universalist experiment at Hopedale, and Brook Farm.

The Oneida Community

The most successful, most widely publicized, and most ably defended example of evangelically inspired communitarianism in the United States was the Oneida Community founded by John Humphrey Noyes (1811–86). Although his background and training were not the usual ones for such a career, his story reveals with remarkable clarity how the evangelical fervor generated by a great revival could create a Christian radical. Noyes was the son of a well-to-do merchant, a first cousin of Rutherford B. Hayes, a graduate of Dartmouth, a convert in the great revival of 1831, and soon after that a divinity student at Andover and Yale. At Yale he was a troubler of the waters from the start. He was active in Garrison's abolitionism and in a separatistic revivalist church in New Haven. Most troubling of all, he declared that the Second Coming of Jesus *had* ended the Jewish dispensation in A.D. 70. For Noyes "salvation from sin" (perfectionism) was the only gospel for the present age. Barred from ordination on account of these views, he continued nevertheless as an unlicensed itinerant preacher, propagating his views by tracts and forging contacts with other perfectionist groups in New York City, Albany, Connecticut, and Massachusetts.

Noyes's social theory, ethics, and theology meanwhile took on more permanent structure. He came to view socialism as the means by which Christian love would bring in the Kingdom of Heaven on earth. Both personal experience and antilegalistic doctrines served to make him doubt the morality of exclusiveness in wedlock, and soon after his own "marriage" in 1838, he gathered various members of his family into a small perfectionist colony in Putney, Vermont, where he began to publish his views in a periodical that soon won new converts. When "complex marriage" was instituted in 1846, the surrounding community was scandalized, and in 1848 the group was obliged to flee, only to be reconstituted at Oneida in western New York. Here a large communal dwelling was built, and by 1851 the community had grown to 205, with farming and logging providing its economic support. Three years later they began what became an immensely successful manufacture of steel traps, and still later, after an allied community had been organized in Wallingford, Connecticut, they moved with equal success into the production of sewing silk and silver-plated flatware.

The community was increasingly rationalized in all that it did, becoming almost a model of efficient organization. This applied, of course, even to matters of love, sex, and marriage. Wives and husbands in the possessive sense were forbidden, as was "special love." Each adult was a spouse to every other adult; male continence was required and eugenics (or "stirpiculture") was systematically practiced; procreation (as distinguished from sexual "transactions") was made a matter of overt communal decision. Life was not ascetic or unduly arduous, cultural activities were encouraged, and the communal children were reared and educated in a progressive spirit. Descriptions of Oneida remind one of Brook Farm, though the philosophy was less elevated and practical affairs more under control. In a logical sense as well as in terms of its own tendency, moreover, it moved steadily toward secular communitarianism. Its concern for God's final judgment faded, and its perfectionism drifted from that of Finney to that of Channing. The Oneida Community, however, crashed head on into the most sacred institution in Victorian America: the monogamous family; and in the long run the cumulative effect of external criticism was more than it could withstand. In 1879 Noyes recommended the abandonment of complex marriage, and two years later he proposed that a joint-stock company be formed with shares distributed to members. The community became in due course a prosperous Canadian corporation.

Hopedale

Contemporary with Noyes's community and even less concerned with evangelical enthusiasms was the Hopedale Community set up by Adin Ballou, a Universalist minister. Ballou was an inveterate champion of reform causes, sympathetic to the views of Channing, Parker, and Garrison, as well as to those of the kinsman who had founded his denomination. He was also committed to actualizing God's kingdom on earth and convinced that a successful communitarian embodiment of "practical Christianity" would trigger a world movement. To this end he founded a periodical, devised a utopian constitution, sold stock in a company, and bought a farm near Milford, Massachusetts. In 1841 the experiment began, and for over a decade it flourished, adding acreage and buildings, promoting many reform causes, and winning fame as a "Christian republic." But its end occurred suddenly in 1856, when two members who had bought up three-fourths of the stock decided to liquidate the company. Like so many other communities, it yielded to the seductions of freedom and the lure of private enterprise.

Brook Farm

The forces that converge in Brook Farm are many and diverse. Without Immanuel Kant and post-Kantian philosophers, says one of the experiment's historians, the experiment would "very likely have never existed." But Transcendentalism and the small group of its leaders constituting the Hedge Club provided the major context. The immediate occasion was George Ripley's dissatisfaction with his Unitarian ministry at the Purchase Street Church in Boston, and his belief "that some practical application should be made of the fresh views of philosophy and life" which were turning the quiet club into a reformist cell. In deciding on this "practical application" the founders also drew inspiration and ideas from early experiments, notably Zoar, the Shakers, and the Rappites.

As at Hopedale, a joint-stock company was formed, and many shares were bought by philanthropic friends of the experiment. A pleasant but unfertile farm was bought in West Roxbury, and in April 1841 the Ripleys and fifteen others moved in, with Articles of Association to govern their common life. Nathaniel Hawthorne was on the committee for the Direction of Agriculture. In due course a printing press and means for woodworking and the manufacture of Britannia ware were added, and for three or four years these activities combined with a variety of progressive and excellently staffed schools kept the community economically viable. Conversation abounded, distinguished visitors came and went, and the community managed to maintain its morale. The *Dial* provided an invaluable platform for expounding the transcendental good news, though it was not published by or at Brook Farm.

The fateful turning point was in 1844, when the trustees following the lead of Ripley yielded to the cult of Fourier, which was then at its American apogee. In 1845 the Articles of Association were redrawn so as to convert Brook Farm into a Fourierist "phalanx." An ambitious program of industrialism was projected and construction of a large "phalanstery" begun. A new socialist paper, the *Harbinger,* began its brief four-year existence. When in 1846 the nearly completed phalanstery burned, bankruptcy threatened, membership declined, and in 1847 the entire property was transferred to a board of trustees for disposal.

Brook Farm's life was brief, but waves of the splash it made rippled to shore for a long time and often far away. Bronson Alcott undertook a still more ideal but even briefer experiment at Fruitlands in Harvard, Massachusetts (1843–44); Isaac Hecker and several others were led to the Roman Catholic Church for a peace that utopias could not give; and many who studied in its schools gratefully remembered Brook Farm as an enduring inspiration. Nobody seemed the poorer for having participated in its common tasks and partaken of its fervent, hopeful spirit.

THE MORMONS

During the summer of 1844, while the energies of Brook Farm were being redirected by the visions of Fourier, another more ambitious venture was in travail far away on the Mississippi. In Carthage, Illinois, Joseph Smith, Mormon prophet, Lieutenant-General of Nauvoo, and "King of the Kingdom of God," was murdered; and his followers were contemplating the horrors of still another "Mormon War." Two celebrated communitarian ventures were in crisis: for one it was the beginning of the end, for the other it was the real beginning.

This Joseph Smith, Jr., who came to the end of his tether in 1844, had lacked all of the advantages that led people to Brook Farm. His great adventure had begun less than two decades before in western New York. Yet he, too, was a New Englander with a measure of "come-outerism" in his family inheritance; he would in due course exhibit an almost uncanny sensitivity to the yearning and frustrations that underlay the religious turmoil of his age. While still in his twenties Smith would found a church which has outlasted or outdistanced every other sect and communitarian movement brought into being in America. While other movements floundered or slid into oblivion or stagnated, his shaped a regional culture-area of the United States, and in 1970 counts a membership of about three million people. Moreover, as Fawn Brodie has correctly insisted, "Joseph's was no mere dissenting sect. It was a real religious creation, one intended to be to Christianity what Christianity was to Judaism: that is, a reform and a consummation." [2] For the drama in its story no less than for its revelations of the American religious character, Mormonism deserves far more extensive and intensive consideration than any of its contemporary parallels.

Joseph Smith was born in 1805 under unpromising circumstances. His father was one of the many farmers who were finding the difficulties of farming in Vermont unsurmountable. In 1816 after several failures he moved his family to Palmyra, New York, in the Erie Canal boom country. But the boom passed them by. They continued to be failures at farming, and Joseph was no more successful in his treasure hunting and money digging. While engaged in this "work," in fact, young Joseph was once found guilty in a local court of being "a disorderly person and an imposter" for his use of a certain "seer stone." Between 1826 and 1830, however, this unschooled farmer's son with a disinclination for the plough changed roles. No longer was he simply the village necromancer who saw more wonder on Mulberry Street than anybody else: he became the "author and proprietor" of a new bible and the founder of a new religion.

The highly problematic order of events by which the book and the movement came into existence can no longer be precisely reconstituted, but it is known that within a year after his marriage in January 1827, Smith was rumored to have found some long lost treasure which would unlock the mysteries of the area's Indian history. Before long, he let it be known that the angel Moroni had appeared to him in a vision and had led him to a cache of golden plates inscribed in "reformed Egyptian" hieroglyphics, as well as a set of seer stones (Urim and Thumim) wherewith to read them. (Except within essentially ecstatic experiences no person beside Smith ever saw these plates; and soon after the translation was completed they were swept away by an angel.) Late in 1827 Joseph began translating with his wife as copyist—he on one side of a curtain, she on the other. In 1829, after three other copyists had filled in for Emma Smith, the task was completed; a printer was found and paid, and in March 1830 the Book of Mormon was put on sale.

Like the Old Testament Hexateuch, this book is primarily historical in form. It is a five-hundred-page account of the wanderings, vicissitudes, and

2. Fawn Brodie, *No Man Knows My History*, p. viii.

battles of America's pre-Columbian inhabitants: first, the Jaredites, who left the Tower of Babel and crossed to America in remarkable windowed, reversible barges only to extinguish their race in continuous intestine wars; second, the evil sons of Laman (Lamanites), who were the American Indians; and third, the good sons of Nephi, who after many battles were all but extinguished by the Lamanites. Finally, only Mormon and his son Moroni were left, and they buried their chronicles in A.D. 384 so that in God's good time their spiritual descendants could establish the Nephite stake in Zion before the Last Day.

Also like the Old Testament, the history is interspersed with sundry exhortations and many pronouncements on topics of doctrinal or social contention. Yet taken as a whole, the Book of Mormon, like the Mormon church itself, shows cohesiveness, structure, and purpose to such a degree that a certain kind of learning and a considerable measure of imagination (or inspiration) must be attributed to its author. The language resembles that of the King James Version of the Bible, and not a line of it requires one to posit either wholesale plagiarism or supernatural powers. The theories which attribute authorship to the Reverend Solomon Spaulding or to Sidney Rigdon are farfetched in the same way and for the same reasons as the Baconian views on Shakespeare are farfetched. As with Shakespeare, sources and influences can, of course, be traced; but the most remarkable fact is the entirely natural way in which the book is related to Smith's nature, to his purposes, and to the total social and spiritual situation of the "burned-over district" of western New York. The author apparently possessed absorptive powers far beyond the ordinary, a roving curiosity, boundless imagination, a facile, easygoing, uncommitted set of mind, and a keen sense of the religious needs of those who had been seared but not consumed, both by revivalism and by the various forms of dark and irrational eccentricity which swept over the land.

This familiarity with the religious situation is as important a factor as any other, though non-Mormon writers have minimized it. Joseph Smith may or may not have had a decisive religious crisis in which his agony over the multiplicity of sects led to the vision that made him a seer and prophet (his description of the event was written many years later). But he and other members of the Smith family certainly had experienced revival preaching, and he was familiar with a wide gamut of doctrinal contention. Universalism, Methodism, and skepticism had made their mark on his father; his mother was a seeker after cultic certainties; and in 1824 Joseph himself had heard a local preacher consign his dead brother to hell. He was also thoroughly at home with the King James Version of the Bible. About 27,000 words of the Book of Mormon were borrowed from that source, while the book as a whole as well as subsequent "revelations" would reflect not only its English style, but its heterogeneous structure.

Beyond these general and personal factors, there were other important regional concerns that Smith could not ignore: the increase of anti-Catholicism, the intense anti-Masonic movement which arose in western New York, and the question of Indian origins, provoked with special force around Palmyra by nearby Indian mounds and old palisaded forts atop certain hills.

Fawn Brodie, whose sympathetic and insightful account of Joseph's life and work is unequaled, has put the matter eloquently:

> Its matter is drawn directly from the American frontier, from the impassioned revivalist sermons, the popular fallacies about Indian origin, and the current political crusades.
>
> Any theory of the origin of the Book of Mormon that spotlights the prophet and blacks out the stage on which he performed is certain to be a distortion. For the book can best be explained, not by Joseph's ignorance nor by his delusion, but by his responsiveness to the provincial opinions of his time. He had neither the diligence nor the constancy to master reality, but his mind was open to all intellectual influences, from whatever province they might blow. If his book is monotonous today, it is because the frontier fires are long since dead and the burning questions that the book answered are ashes.[3]

A few isolated, atypical individuals can still read it as a religious testimony; a few dedicated historians can study it profitably as a help to understanding a bygone day. But not even loyal Mormons can be nourished by it as they were a century ago. At that time, before anthropology and archaeology had developed plausible alternatives to Joseph's mythic rendering of America's ancient past, the Book of Mormon brought a satisfying answer to many needs: it undercut sectarian pluralism and emotionalism with objectivity, moral legalism, a liberal answer to many old issues, a positive this-worldliness, and even a kind of rationalism that had grown, perhaps, out of Joseph's own disdain for frontier sermonizing. Fable or not, the Book of Mormon provided the kind of stability immemorially brought to Christianity by the Old Testament. Yet the book did not make Mormonism: Joseph did that from day to day as circumstances demanded; and after the mob at Carthage did him in, Brigham Young carried on, more soberly and with more concern for this world than the next, but not with less determination.

Within a month of the book's publication, six members of Joseph's un-

3. Ibid., p. 69.

organized following were baptized by immersion and formed into a church; within another month there were forty persons who acknowledged Joseph as "Seer, a Translator, a Prophet, an Apostle of Jesus Christ, and Elder of the Church through the will of God the Father, and the grace of your Lord Jesus Christ" (his official title). Thereafter a steady flow of revelations began to define the shape and goals of Mormonism. Sensationally administered healings of the familiar sort won some converts then as later; and a further crescendo of warnings about the impending Millennium added others. Five months after the church's founding, the Prophet announced that the New Jerusalem would be found out "on the borders by the Lamanites," and he sent a three-man party to look for land.

On their way, this group won over the most impressive convert so far received, Sidney Rigdon (1793–1876), an ex-Baptist who had become a major disciple of Alexander Campbell in Ohio. With true Restorationist rigor Rigdon had gathered a small following into a communistic colony near Kirtland, Ohio. The prospecting party soon baptized him and nearly his entire colony into the Mormon church; and sometime later (after Smith and Rigdon had met) the Prophet issued a revelation in the form of a Book of Enoch which commanded the gathering of an earthly "City of Holiness." Then came a momentous decision to move the church to Kirtland, which was said to be on the eastern boundary of the Stake in Zion. In January 1831, therefore, Mormonism's first westward movement began.

In Kirtland the "United Order of Enoch" took positive form, while many revelations brought the Rigdon-Smith constituencies under common authority. As in New York there was hostility from surrounding people, and on one occasion Joseph was torn from his home and tarred and feathered. But converts poured in, the economy was organized, surprisingly large loans were floated, and a stately temple was built and dedicated with festivities pervaded by pentecostal fervor. Though the panic of 1837 was on the horizon, a bank was organized and notes were issued with abandon. Then the bubble burst and the creditors swarmed in. Schism, rioting, fires, and other woes followed. Joseph, with those who would, fled to Missouri, choosing that remote land because since 1831 the most numerous colony of Mormons had been gathered there at the "crossroads of the West," where the indefatigable and ingenious Edward Partridge was chiefly responsible for receiving and allotting land to the steady stream of converts and seeing that the United Order functioned according to revealed regulation.

Unfortunately the western woes had been of far greater magnitude than those in Ohio. First the Mormons had been mobbed and harried out of Jackson County, near Independence. Finding less hostility in the counties north of the Missouri River, they settled there, and again began to prosper and multiply, yet only to arouse new hostilities. When Joseph went west in 1838, their situation was becoming precarious, and it must be said that he soon made it hopeless. On 4 July 1838 at a great celebration, Joseph delivered an oration which ended with a spine-chilling promise to wreak vengeance on his oppressors. Election day brought further violence, followed by the Prophet's infamous cry "I will be a Second Mohammed." In the bitter Mormon War the Stake in Zion was again desolated; and with Joseph in jail, the Latter-Day Saints were forced to move again, this time across the Mississippi into Illinois, where Nauvoo was founded on the river in Hancock County.

It was a most propitious time, for with the elections of 1840 in the offing, Whigs and Democrats outdid each other to win the fifteen thousand Mormon votes. Nauvoo was given a charter that made it almost an autonomous theocratic principality. Here Joseph forgot the woes and ignominy of New York, Ohio, and Missouri; he did great things and dreamed far greater dreams. Nauvoo became the largest and fastest growing city in Illinois as redoubled evangelistic efforts brought results especially among the urban poor of England, who began immigrating by the thousands. Under Illinois militia laws the Nauvoo Legion became a disciplined military force with Joseph in command; he was declared King of the Kingdom of God and became increasingly despotic. In a series of revelations in 1841–43, Smith introduced many new teachings which made Mormonism much more clearly a new religion and much less obviously Christian than it had been in 1830. More than ever Mormons were defined as a people apart.

His megalomania constantly growing, Smith announced his candidacy for president of the United States in the election of 1844. Yet again the horizon darkened; popular fear and jealousy mounted as Mormon apostates and dissidents published horrendous tales of polygamy, corruption, and lawlessness. At last the Prophet overreached himself by destroying the opposition press in Nauvoo without due process. The case aroused widespread agitation and when the Illinois militia threatened, Joseph and Hyrum Smith yielded themselves to the authorities. Finally, on 27 June 1844, the militia became a mob, moved upon the Carthage jail where the two leaders were awaiting trial, and lynched them in cold blood.

After this awful sacrifice Nauvoo was spared the worst kind of atrocities, but the Saints prepared to leave. Joseph had long been conceiving plans for a western empire, and now these plans were taken up by the main body of Mormons, who recognized Brigham Young as Joseph's successor. This fierce and sturdy disciple was a former Vermont Methodist who had been converted and made one of the twelve Apostles during the Kirtland period. Young had organized the exodus from Missouri, and now, after a brief period of preparation in Iowa, he led the Mormons in their famous trek to the place he chose in the Great Salt Lake basin. In July 1847 the first wagon train ended its hundred-days crossing. After a constitutional convention in 1849, the autonomous state of Deseret took shape on the outer rim of the Mexican republic as a church-regulated community. Within a decade ninety communities had been founded, most of them in the Salt Lake area, yet some three hundred miles north of the lake, and some as far south as San Bernardino, California. In most of these communities, the need for irrigation gave a functional base both to communitarian ideals and to the power of the church's leaders.

But the Stars and Stripes were borne to Utah in 1850, and the old conflicts were renewed, especially after 1852 when Young published Joseph's heretofore "secret" (but much discussed) revelation on "the order of Jacob," i.e. plural marriage. When in 1857 President Buchanan replaced Young with a non-Mormon as territorial governor, another "Mormon War" broke out, the most sensational incident of which was the Mormon massacre of a peaceful group of California-bound settlers. In 1879 the Supreme Court finally rendered its verdict against polygamy in the United States, ruling that religious freedom did not involve the right to subvert an institution upon which "society may be said to be built," and hence that the 1862 Act of Congress against bigamy was constitutional. The Edmunds Act of 1882 brought still more stringent political pressures to bear, to which an act of 1884 added economic penalties. Only in 1890, after long delays and various legal maneuvers, did the church revise its teaching on polygamy, thus opening the way to statehood, which was granted in 1896. By that time a strait-laced kind of prosperity and stability had replaced enthusiasm and millennial expectation as the leitmotiv of Mormon life. Creeping capitalism had taken over the communitarianism of the old Order of Enoch. Yet Mormon missionaries were abroad throughout the world, and in 1970 about three million people with greatly varying degrees of intensity accounted themselves Latter-Day Saints.[4] The church was growing and its people prospering.

4. Between 1840 and 1900 close to ninety thousand immigrants from abroad entered the church, most of them from England, but many from Scandinavia as well. At a much slower pace immigration has continued into the twentieth century. By this time, however, the accent has been placed on gathering converts wherever they live. In 1970 about twelve thousand missionaries were at work to this end in more than sixty-five countries all over the world.

As the dominant group in Utah, with much strength in surrounding states, and with Salt Lake City as their mecca, the Mormons constitute an important American subculture. Their movement has changed, in Thomas O'Dea's words, "from 'near-sect' to 'near-nation.'" They had not merely avoided becoming a small isolated sect, he continues, but "had developed so far away from that possibility that they almost became a separate nationality."[5] It was a remarkable monument to the visions of Joseph Smith, if not precisely to his vision. Even Young's achievements in the West rested on the Prophet's culminating accomplishment: "Utah had its roots in Nauvoo; without that seven years' experience in Illinois the development of the Great Basin . . . would not have been the same."[6]

Almost no one denies that the entire saga of Joseph Smith and Mormonism is a vital episode in American history. A vast literature, both hagiographic and critical, covers each phase of the movement's development. Yet the exact significance of this great story persistently escapes definition. It is certainly the culminating instance of early nineteenth-century sect formation, and at the same time that period's most powerful example of communitarian aspiration. On the other hand, the transformation brought about by numerical growth, economic adaptation, internal divisions, external hostility, and heroic exploits renders almost useless the usual categories of explanation. One cannot even be sure if the object of our consideration is a sect, a mystery cult, a new religion, a church, a people, a nation, or an American subculture; indeed, at different times and places it is all of these.

With attractive edifices on Brattle Street in Cambridge, Massachusetts, and in many other cities and suburbs, and with a reputation for conservatism in both personal ethics and social policy, Mormons sometimes appear to have become another white middle-class denomination with obvious Yankee origins. Yet they remain a people apart, bound to a very distinctive tradition that was brought into the world by a most unusual man. Their inner intellectual and spiritual problems cannot easily be shared with others. The problem of history—in the Book of Mormon itself and as it pertains to the people of that book since 1830—has been especially acute; and the fact of contradictory interpretations is inescapably felt by every his-

5. Thomas O'Dea, *The Mormons*, p. 115.

6. Robert Bruce Flanders, *Nauvoo: Kingdom on the Mississippi*, p. v. Nauvoo also inspired at least three other branches of Mormonism. One remnant survived in Texas until the Civil War; another maintained itself on an island in Lake Michigan until its leader, James Strang, was murdered in 1856. The Reorganized Church dating from 1852 won the allegiance of the Smith family and under the presidency of Joseph's son and grandson established itself in southern Iowa. As the lawful legatee it also holds property in Nauvoo and Kirtland. Its headquarters since 1921 has been in Independence, Missouri. Its membership in 1970 stood at about 170,000.

torian. In retrospect, nevertheless, the Mormons can be likened to a fast-growing hardwood towering above the sectarian underbrush of the burnt-over district: a witness to the possible social potency of prophetic religious ideas. Interpreted in detail, the movement yields innumerable clues to the religious and social consciousness of the American people.

V

COUNTERVAILING RELIGION

Puritan Protestantism forms properly the main basis of our North American Church. . . . We may never ungratefully forget that it was this generation of godly Pilgrims which once for all stamped upon our country that character of deep moral earnestness, that spirit of strong intrepid determination, that peculiar zeal for the Sabbath and the Bible, which have raised it to so high a place in the history of the Christian Church. . . . But while we thankfully and joyfully acknowledge this, we have no right still to overlook the fact that an unhistorical and unchurchly character has inserted itself into the inmost joints of our religious life. . . . Thus we have come gradually to have a host of sects, which it is no longer easy to number, and that still continues to swell from year to year. Where the process of separation is destined to end, no human calculation can foretell. . . .

The most dangerous foe with which we are called to contend, is not the Church of Rome but the sect plague in our own midst; not the single pope of the city of seven hills, but the numberless popes—German, English, and American—who would fain enslave Protestants once more to human authority. . . .

Let our watchword be: One spirit and one body! One Shepherd and one flock! All conventicles and chapels must perish, that from their ashes may rise the One Church of God, phoenixlike and resplendent with glory, as a bride adorned for her bridegroom.

Philip Schaff, *The Principle of Protestantism* (1845)

The prevailing spirit of the American nation during the antebellum decades was informed by a popular and patriotic version of the Puritan hope for the Kingdom of God on earth, as that notion had been freed of its medieval and aristocratic components. But this individualistic and evangelical outlook was not accepted by all America, and not everyone living in the United States was admitted to the elect company of true Americans. The most obvious outsiders were the black slaves and the red Indians—the latter being regarded until 1871 as a foreign power against whom one waged wars and made treaties of peace. In addition to these drastic cases, there were many subtle shades and degrees of exclusion. There was the South, which in a sense regarded the Constitution itself as a kind of treaty guaranteeing the perpetuity of the peculiar institution in its midst. There were Old School Presbyterians, Hard Shell Baptists, and other mainline Protestant conservatives who challenged prevailing concessions regarding man's free will and perfectibility. Lutherans, whose numbers were being rapidly swelled by immigration, were becoming increasingly dissatisfied with the theological and moral stance of the Protestant mainstream—especially when its actions were overtly nativistic. Equally unenthusiastic were various smaller groups whose often unusual tenets aroused the evangelicals to countersubversionary tactics: the Mormons, especially, but also for a time the Masons and various communitarian movements that challenged American taboos. The Jews were potentially in this category, but until after the Civil War they were too few in number to attract significant notice.

Most numerous and most easily isolated of all were the Roman Catholics, who by 1850 had become the largest denomination in America, and who continued to immigrate at an increasing rate. Because they resisted religious assimilation and were suspected of subservience to a "foreign potentate," they became the object of the most powerfully organized opposition, first by voluntary associations, and finally by a very strong, semisecret political party. The conversion of several well-known Protestant thinkers intensified the polemical spirit. Also viewed with suspicion were various Protestant groups —and not only Lutheran and German Reformed—who during these very years were becoming disenchanted with revivalistic evangelicalism and finding spiritual solace or aesthetic satisfaction in various aspects of the Catholic tradition. Least criticized were those romantics who were merely attracted to Catholic externals such as Gothic architecture and the celebration of Christmas. More controversial were those Episcopalians who took England's Oxford Movement seriously, for they impugned the entire Reformation heritage.

The rising interest in things Catholic, however, was sometimes expressed in the context of pronounced theological liberalism; indeed, Boston Unitarians were a common source of it. And this fact points to another truly major countervailing force in American religion—the emergence of new forms of religious modernism that were far more seductive than the rationalistic "infidelism" of Tom Paine. Emerson and the Transcendentalists stand out as proponents of the new spirit, but other equally radical groups existed outside of New England. Even in the orthodox churches themselves liberal theology and scholarship were being articulated and defended by men like James Marsh and Horace Bushnell. The chapters of Part V deal with the religious communions and new currents of thought which intruded upon the evangelical consensus, and with the Protestant opposition to these tendencies.

31

THE ATLANTIC MIGRATION AND LUTHERAN CRISIS

"Once I thought to write a history of the immigrants in America," wrote Oscar Handlin in 1951. "Then I discovered that the immigrants *were* American history." This widely shared discovery has given rise to basic reinterpretations of American culture in every period. Many of the ensuing revisions arose from a new awareness of the experience of immigration as a shaping influence on the spirit of this nation of movers. Anyone who has left behind the familiar surroundings and comforting associations of one community and begun to adjust to another has had at least a sample of the myriad migratory traumas that have formed the life style of this "nation of immigrants." It is the accumulated pain and sadness of more drastic departures from native lands and the tribulations of beginning again in an alien, often hostile, environment that makes the immigration residuum so important to the American character and to the religious institutions which served so many purposes in the process of adjustment. From John Winthrop's sad farewell to England in 1630 to the anguish of the latest refugee, the "uprooted" have been shaping the national life.

Immigration is also the source of this country's fabled diversity. In 1790 when the first federal census reported a population of 3,929,214,[1] 22.3 percent of the white population stemmed from non-British lands, while 700,000 slaves added a huge component of African origin. During the next three decades, when Europe was embroiled by the French Revolution and the Napoleonic wars, only 250,000 immigrants arrived on American shores; but

1. Richard B. Morris. ed., *Encyclopedia of American History* (New York: Harper & Brothers, 1953), p. 445 (taken from the census of 1790 as analyzed by the American Historical Association, *Annual Report*, vol. 1 [1931]). At this time the slave population was about 700,000 (17 percent) and the free Negro about 20,000 (0.5 percent).

then the tempo began to accelerate, and during the hundred years between 1832 and 1932 the influx would reach an altogether different order of magnitude.[2] Irish troubles occasioned the first wave; a great movement of Germans and Scandinavians dominated the next phase, and the "Great Atlantic Migration" would culminate after 1890 in a vast exodus of eastern European Jews, southern Italians, and Balkan peoples. Before the gates were closed over 40 million immigrants had cast their lot with the United States. Seen as a totality, this movement of European peoples is probably the greatest *Völkerwanderung* in human history. And it is scarcely surprising that in 1920, when the Bureau of the Census made its somewhat arbitrary breakdown of the population on the basis of "national origins," only 41 percent of the white population was of British or North Irish origin.

Underlying this extended upheaval was an industrial and agricultural revolution which all but destroyed the ancient peasant economy of Europe.

> The immigrant movement started in the peasant heart of Europe [writes Oscar Handlin]. Ponderously balanced in a solid equilibrium for centuries, the old structure of an old society began to crumble at the opening of the modern era. One by one, rude shocks weakened the aged foundations until some climactic blow suddenly tumbled the whole into ruins. The mighty collapse left without homes millions of helpless, bewildered people. These were the army of emigrants.[3]

In a brilliant chapter Handlin goes on to describe the process by which Europe as a whole, from Ireland to the Ukraine, from Norway to Sicily, was involved in a large insoluble agricultural crisis. It was worse in some lands than in others: Scandinavians, for example, never fled a famine-stricken land as did the Irish, while Germans and Italians never faced persecutions and pogroms as did the Russian Jews. As immigrants in America, therefore, these different peoples looked to the "old country" and conceived of the past with varied sentiments. They also faced the future with sharply contrasting attitudes, and the dynamics of Americanization varied correspondingly.

Supporting this great influx on the American side was the continuous expansion of industry, beginning with the growth of textile manufacturing and the canal and railroad building booms, and the opening of agricultural opportunities in the West. These developments naturally had as many conse-

2. The dates are not arbitrary. In 1832 the influx almost trebled that of any previous year, and not until 1932 did the figure ever fall below the 60,482 of 1832. Between 1845 and 1931 it never fell below 90,000. During six different years between 1905 and 1914 immigration went over the million mark. Between 1820 and 1950, 39,325,482 people migrated to the United States (ibid., pp. 446–47).

3. Oscar Handlin, *The Uprooted*, p. 7.

quences for the country's native stock as for the immigrants. Both alike suffered from industrial exploitation and unplanned urban growth. Both alike experienced the loneliness and isolation of life in a land of scattered farms and miserable roads. Everyone in America lived in the uncertainty caused by boom periods, financial panics, and depressions. Yet a major fact remains: the newcomers—whether they ended up in a city tenement or in a farmhouse—came in overwhelming proportion from the little agricultural villages of Europe. They were joined by a few political exiles, idealistic intellectuals, entrepreneurs, musicians, teachers, and priests; but in general they were not bearers of civilization. They came in many cases from countries rich in learned and artistic traditions, from lands and churches famous for their universities; but these they left behind. On the other hand, the home countries for a variety of reasons—resentment, indifference, or poverty—did little or nothing to assist the outwanderers. In America the immigrants had to begin anew, individually and in groups, to achieve their aspirations for culture and well-being. Religious institutions, therefore, often became a more vital factor than they had ever been before.

IMMIGRATION AND THE CHURCHES

Immigration has had from the first a decisive effect on the religious affiliation of Americans and the relative size of the various churches. The statistics of church membership, to be sure, are a notorious quagmire.[4] But even when full allowance is made for the known inadequacy of existing figures, certain drastic changes are manifest when one compares the ecclesiastical situation before and after the Great Migration.

At the end of the colonial period (1775) three large ecclesiastical blocs, all of British background, accounted for at least 80 percent of the Americans who could be regarded as affiliated with any church. They were distributed about evenly among the Congregationalists of New England, the Anglicans of the South, and the Presbyterians whose chief strength lay in the Middle Colonies. Small but influential Quaker, Baptist, and Methodist groups added two or three percentage points to the British Protestant total, while Dutch Reformed churches, strongest in New York and New Jersey, had over the years become very closely affiliated with the English-speaking population. Roman Catholics and Jews constituted at most 0.1 percent of the population. Because evangelism among the slaves had been widely neglected, the

4. The statistics developed and used by historians show wild variations; yet they tend to agree on the proportional relationships of various groups, which in turn tally with the census figures of 1790. Percentage figures are only estimates. On this problem see Winthrop S. Hudson, *Religion in America,* pp. 129–30.

largest non-British religious minority in the colonies may have been African, but investigations of its nature and strength have only belatedly begun.[5]

The Great Migration of the nineteenth century, as everyone knows, drastically altered the religious composition of the American people. Steady acculturation was naturally a major feature of the passing decades, yet by the twentieth century the United States had become far more than before a nation of religious minorities whose self-consciousness was by no means rapidly disappearing.[6] In 1926, by which time 40 percent of the population claimed a religious relationship, Roman Catholics were the largest single group (18,605,000), while the next three largest denominations—Baptist (8,011,000), Methodist (7,764,000), and Lutheran (3,226,000)—accounted for 59 percent of the Protestants. At that time Jews constituted 3.2 percent of the total population. Immigration, of course, was not the only reason for these radical changes in the American religious balance, but it alone had ended the possibility of speaking of the American churches solely in terms of a common British background. Other traditions had not only introduced new ranges of variety and color to the situation, but had also put serious pressures on the American tradition of equality and toleration. In successive chapters, therefore, the antebellum history of immigration and religion will be considered: first the Lutheran because of its contiguity with the foregoing accounts of Protestant resurgence, then the growth of Roman Catholicism and the hostile response of "native" Americans to this seeming threat, and finally the arrival and early development of Judaism.

THE LUTHERAN CHURCH

During the half-century after the Declaration of Independence, the Lutheran church in America experienced many remarkable changes and reversals. Having entered the new nation as an independent church, it encountered few organizational difficulties. In churchly matters the leadership and continuing influence of the elder Muhlenberg and his sons was a powerful stabilizing force. Furthermore, the process of Americanization was moving rapidly ahead. In 1807 the Ministerium of New York (presided over by Muhlenberg's son-in-law, a professor at Columbia) changed its official language from German to English. Yet with acculturation and the passage of time, the influence of the American Enlightenment (strengthened by patriotic fervor) made deep inroads on the faith of the founders, modifying the

5. Melville J. Herskovitz, *The Myth of the Negro Past* (Boston: Beacon Press, 1958) reveals the paucity of evidence. See pp. 698–705 below.

6. See Michael Parenti, "Ethnic Politics and the Persistence of Ethnic Identification," *Political Science Review* 61 (September 1967): 717–26.

firm but practical concern for the historic Lutheran confessions which Muhlenberg and Berkenmeyer had established in Pennsylvania and New York. This decline in vigor led to a gradual rapprochement with the Episcopalians. In 1797 the New York Ministerium made it an official policy not to recognize English-language churches in localities served by the Episcopal church, and in North Carolina there was sporadically a similar integration of activities. Mutual proposals for consolidation of the churches were heard from time to time.

Countering these accommodations, however, were strong undercurrents of sentiment and conviction that portended difficulty and conflict. In rural areas, and among those church leaders who tended to regard true piety and German culture as inseparable, a strong opposition to Americanization developed. The Pennsylvania Ministerium especially took strong measures to insure the perpetuation of the German language. Since men who held these views were also opposed to rationalism and imbued with the revival spirit, they drew closer to similarly minded leaders in the German Reformed church, with whom they were often closely tied by intermarriage, village associations, and joint worship in "union churches." Sharing the antidoctrinal temper of early nineteenth-century evangelicalism and insensitive to ancient confessional cleavages, they saw the separation of Lutheran and Reformed as a perpetuation of mere trivialities. Meanwhile, these men could observe the progress of unionism in Prussia, where Napoleon's invasions had aroused German longings for unity.

When the Ohio Conference of the Pennsylvania Ministerium was formed in 1812, this pan-German tendency was already apparent. In 1818 it took more definite form in the proposal of the two communions to found an "Evangelical Seminary" in conjunction with Franklin College, which they were already operating jointly. Though this seminary never got beyond the planning stage, it was chiefly intended to shield students from rationalistic error without an emphasis on creedal allegiances. The declining Lutheran consciousness is also visible in the Pennsylvania Ministerium's liturgy of 1818, in which most of the responsive, corporate, and ritual characteristics of Muhlenberg's liturgy were sacrificed. Even more illustrative of nonconfessional evangelicalism, both Lutheran and Reformed, is the *Gemeinschaftliches Gesangbuch* (Congregational Hymnbook) of 1817, from which much of the classical hymnody of both communions was eliminated.

Reaction

As a kind of intrusion on this nondenominational spirit came the tercentenary of Luther's Ninety-five Theses in 1817. This observance did not create harsh confrontations, since all the non-Roman churches accepted the

Reformer as a great religious hero; and Bishop William White responded warmly to the invitation given him to join the celebration in Philadelphia. As in Prussia, however, the occasion did underline the contrast of confessional and unionistic tendencies. These incipient difficulties became evident in 1818 when the Pennsylvania Ministerium proposed that a general synod be organized in order to provide a central advisory agency for the existing synods and such new ones as the westward expansion and immigration would bring into being. Yet indecision and divided opinion were to hinder these bold designs.

In 1817 three loosely organized territorial synods were in existence (Pennsylvania, New York, and North Carolina), and in 1818 Ohio was organized, followed in 1820 by Maryland-Virginia and Tennessee. In 1820 the delegates of these (Ohio and Tennessee not participating) drafted a constitution for the General Synod to accomplish the desired unification, but they could agree on no more than the Lutheran name to show their confessional consciousness, and they made no mention whatever of the historic standards of faith. Because New York declined to join until 1837, while Pennsylvania separated itself between 1823 and 1853, even this witness lacked sustained support from the two largest American synods. Thus in 1834 the General Synod only encompassed 20,249 Lutherans—which was 6,000 less than the Pennsylvania Ministerium alone.

During these dark years of the General Synod, however, Samuel Simon Schmucker (1799–1873), a brilliant young pastor in Maryland, determined to save it. And save it he did—first by persuading the newly formed West Pennsylvania Synod (1823) to join, and then by leading the movement to found a seminary at Gettysburg, which opened in 1826 with Schmucker as professor of theology. In all these endeavors he was spurred on by a desire to save his church from the corrosions of rationalism and indifference. To this end he wrote a professor's oath for the new seminary, demanding loyalty to the Augsburg Confession and to Luther's Catechisms. The ordination oath which he later drafted compelled "substantial" agreement with these standards.

Even in these early measures, however, and throughout the four decades of his career as a theologian and church leader, Schmucker was torn between a desire to hurl traditional Lutheran symbols against infidelity, and an equally strong or somewhat stronger desire to avoid doctrinal commitments which ran counter to his own pietistic background, the Reformed substratum of American Protestantism which he had studied at Princeton Seminary, or the interdenominational voluntary movements for evangelism and reform in which he vigorously participated. With the passing years he made more explicit his dissent from both the emphasis and the substance of the traditional Lutheran teaching on the sacraments and on many other matters. In a Reformation Day address in 1837, he defined the Lord's Supper as a "mnemonic ordinance" and "a pledge of his [the Savior's] spiritual presence and blessing on all worthy participants." [7]

The doctrinal basis thus laid down was probably the only kind of compromise on which anything could have been accomplished at that time, and upon it the General Synod grew and prospered. By 1839 it included 316 congregations organized into seven regional synods, varying in viewpoint from the extremely free attitudes of New York to a fairly rigorous confessionalism in parts of Pennsylvania. The General Synod had also established fraternal relations with many other denominations and voluntary associations, and was beginning to evince an anti-Catholicism that would spill over into nativism. Schmucker had also gained national attention in 1838 with his *Fraternal Appeal* for an "apostolic Protestant union." This ecumenical interest would lead him to take an active role eight years later in the founding of the World Evangelical Alliance.

It should not be concluded, however, that all was peace and concord. From the very first the General Synod had been roundly condemned by the Reverend Paul Henkel on strict confessional principles, and the Tennessee Synod which Henkel had helped to found embodied his protest in an ecclesiastical structure of considerable strength. The influence of Henkel's energetic sons and other associates also helped to keep the Ohio Synod from joining. There were other men in the Pennsylvania Ministerium who on similar grounds defended that synod's isolation. But ultimately of far greater significance than any of these factors were three new developments: the powerful Lutheran awakening in the churches and universities of Germany, the growth of indigenous dissatisfaction with American evangelicalism, and the immensely increased flow of non-English-speaking immigrants from Germany and later from Scandinavia.[8]

The first of these phenomena is too complex to be taken up here, except to note that important roles were played by tercentenary observances of the Reformation, a surfeit of rationalism, the rise of new spiritual and historical interests, and the emergence of many talented theological and ecclesiastical leaders. This "Lutheran awakening" began a process of theological re-

7. Quoted in Vergilius Ferm, *The Crisis in Lutheran Theology*, p. 111.

8. In references to the Lutheran Confessions and "confessionalism" the Augsburg (*Augustana*) Confession of 1530 is always primary. But in 1580, after fifty years of controversy, the Lutheran churches of Germany agreed to a "Formula of Concord" which together with other accepted "symbolic" documents was published in the *Book of Concord*. The first complete English edition of this book was published by David Henkel and others in 1851.

covery which was sustained during the entire century, until it finally joined with the so-called Neo-Orthodox impulse of the early twentieth century. Among the German Reformed, Philip Schaff became a brilliant but characteristic participant in a similar movement of recovery; and John W. Nevin drew much inspiration from it through private reading even before Schaff joined him on the faculty at Mercersburg Seminary. The "Mercersburg Theology," in fact, was a corollary to Lutheran developments. A similar spirit took hold at the same time in Scandinavia and other Lutheran lands, where parish life was often revitalized by movements which reasserted old pietistic ideals, or by other movements calling for a churchly renewal similar to that of the Oxford Movement in England. At all events, a marked shift in temper was very soon communicated to America, giving added impetus to an indigenous movement of Lutheran recovery. In the period after 1830 one notes almost everywhere an increasing denominational consciousness and a concurrent rise in church-historical interest.

Probably more important than these purely intellectual influences was the actual migration of Germans in the pre-Civil War period, and an equally large influx of Scandinavians beginning more or less at midcentury. The crescendo of German immigration was dramatic, as the following statistics reveal. In the period from 1821–30, 6,761 German immigrants arrived; in 1831–40, 152,454; in 1841–50, 434,626; and in 1851–60, 951,667. Not all of these people were Lutherans, to be sure; many were Roman Catholic, Reformed, "Unionists," adherents of various sects, completely unaffiliated, or (as with some exiles from the abortive revolution of 1848) bitterly anticlerical. But the impact on the Lutheran church in America was heavy, especially since many of the laity and pastors who came were deeply touched by the revival in Germany. They settled almost everywhere, but with a noticeable preference for northern states and border areas where slavery was not a prominent feature. When settlers came to places where the Lutheran church was already planted, they usually joined existing congregations, often drastically changing their character. In 1837 the New York Ministerium reversed its decision of 1807 and again made German an official language—and in this as in most other cases of the time, doctrinal concern tended to follow language. As the immigrants moved into the Old Northwest, thinly scattered bodies like the Joint Synod of Ohio were greatly augmented in numbers. Still farther west, many new synods, organized with the aid of the General Synod, soon became members of the larger body. Completely new and independent synods were also formed, some of them holding fraternal relations with the older synods, some not. Almost all of them took definite confessional stands, however; and their influence flowed back to the East.[9]

Lutheran Crisis

With the passing years two parties or tendencies became increasingly visible, one deeply affected by American evangelical ideas and practices, the other much more intransigently rooted in Continental ways and Reformation thought. After 1833, when Benjamin Kurtz (1795–1865) made the *Lutheran Observer* an outspoken defender of the "new measures" in revivalism, of Sabbatarianism, and of Schmucker's point of view generally, the tensions increased. The founding of Wittenberg College and Seminary in 1845 provided an important anchorage in Ohio for this "American" party, and Samuel Sprecher (1810–1906), during a long career as its president followed by a further term as a professor of systematic theology, did for the western flank what Kurtz did for the eastern. The conservatives, however, were also gathering strength and developing greater intellectual depth; and by 1849 three journals were upholding its cause, including the scholarly *Evangelical Review* published by Professor Charles Philip Krauth and others at Gettysburg Seminary. At the General Synod convention of 1850 Krauth stated the conservative position clearly; and in July of that year he published his manifesto in the *Evangelical Review:*

> Too ignorant have we been of our own doctrines, and our own history . . . and we have taken pride in times past in claiming a paternity in every reputable form of Christianity, and have denied our proper parentage, in our mendicancy for foreign favors. Shame that it has been so! . . . Let us go back to our father's house.

After 1840, on the other hand, Professor Schmucker became much more explicit and vigorous in his exposition of "American Lutheranism." Yet the contrary tide grew stronger after 1853, when the now increasingly confessional Pennsylvania Ministerium returned to the General Synod. The "American Lutheran" leaders seem to have decided at this point that the conservative strategy of slowly absorbing its opposition must be halted in some decisive way. The means chosen were almost melodramatic. An anonymous forty-two-page pamphlet entitled *Definite Synodical Platform* was sent out to the ministers of the General Synod in the autumn of 1855. It contained an "American Recension of the Augsburg Confession," a

9. The founding of these new synods will be taken up in a later chapter, since they gained their chief significance only during the post–Civil War decades.

highly polemical statement defending the deletion of "errors" from this historic symbol as well as from other confessional documents, and a proposal that in this revised form it be made a standard of faith for the synod. Nine traditional doctrines were condemned as remnants of Catholicism. Three of these (private confession, ceremonies of the mass, and exorcism of evil spirits) were regarded as so serious that retention of them would be a bar to fellowship. Six others were roundly condemned, including baptismal regeneration, the Real Presence in the Eucharist, the remission of sins through the Eucharist, and denial of the divine obligation of Sabbath observance. The last issue carried with it the whole question of the force of Jewish law under the New Covenant and the problems of Law and Gospel. By any standard, the Platform was a bold stroke. It made manifest what critics had been saying all along, that Schmucker's "American Lutheranism" was little more than another name for "modern American Puritanism." There was almost no chance that any peaceful settlement would result—and none did.

The decade following the issuance of the Platform brought a showdown. The General Synod now comprised over a score of regional synods, and each one had to face the issue or explicitly evade it before the convention of 1857. By that time, however, no action by the General Synod was necessary, because the "American Lutheran" plan had already been killed by the express disapproval of eight of the synods, including the influential Pennsylvania Ministerium and Professor Schmucker's own synod of West Pennsylvania. Yet the prevalence of "American Lutheranism" was clearly demonstrated by the fact that three synods in Ohio and Indiana unanimously adopted the Platform as their own, while six others indicated basic concurrence with its most outspoken claims. Six were noncommittal, equivocal, or silent. Most of those who opposed it did so less on theological principle than because they wanted ecclesiastical peace or less dogmatism. In not more than three synods could the resurgence of traditional doctrine be held clearly accountable for disapproval.

Peace, naturally, did not follow. In 1857 Dr. Kurtz led a small group of his sympathizers in the Maryland Synod into a new Melanchthon Synod which specifically rejected the "errors" condemned in the Platform. Its admission to the General Synod in 1859 brought a storm of protest. A year later, as part of the secession crisis and Civil War, the entire group of Southern synods formed their own general body on a fairly conservative basis, though their basic tendency and sympathy, like the views of their most distinguished leader, John Bachman of Charleston, were broadly evangelical rather than emphatically Lutheran. In the North a kind of "civil war" in the General Synod went on even during the national crisis. The break finally came in 1864 when the General Synod admitted the Franckean Synod, which had been formed in western New York in 1837 under the influence of Charles G. Finney's preaching. Since it professed no Lutheran ties at all, the Pennsylvania Ministerium withdrew, founded another seminary in Philadelphia, and issued a call to all explicitly confessional Lutheran synods in America to affiliate themselves with a new General Council. This organization became a reality in 1867. The Lutheranism of "Muhlenberg descent" was thereafter to move into separate channels.

Certain things were clear even in 1867. "American Lutheranism" as a dominating tendency was a thing of the past. Schmucker's chair at Gettysburg was filled in 1864 by one of his bitterest critics. In that same year the General Synod took a definite stand not for the Platform, but far more explicitly than ever before for the Augsburg Confession—and this despite the fact that it no longer included the conservative delegates from Pennsylvania and the South. The age of Schmucker's dominance was over.

In 1860 the General Synod's 864 ministers and 164,000 communicants comprised two-thirds of the Lutherans in America. Ten years later two competing organizations had replaced the unified church for which Muhlenberg had hoped. Yet in light of the total situation, the rupture seems as inevitable as the Civil War. In 1820 it would have been folly to propose a general synod on strict Lutheran principles. By 1860 it was no more possible for a church to be half Lutheran and half Puritan than for the nation to be half slave and half free. In both cases it was the end of an era.

The new era found its spokesman in Charles Porterfield Krauth (1823–83), the first professor of theology in the new seminary at Philadelphia and also a professor of philosophy at the University of Pennsylvania. Krauth, who was the son of professor Charles Philip Krauth of Gettysburg, became the chief defender of the General Council. In his early years he had tended toward "American Lutheran" views, but between 1841 and 1864, while serving as a pastor, he became imbued with the newer German theology. As he was drawn into the controversies of the day, he increasingly emphasized that Luther had led a *conservative* Reformation which was essentially at odds with the radicalism not only of the sectaries but of the Reformed tradition as well. Entering into the exciting historical research of the time, he came to regard the Eucharistic question as central in the Reformation. The doctrine of the Real Presence which Schmucker had dismissed Krauth defended as crucial. As only a few followers of the Oxford and Mercersburg movements had ever done in America, Krauth challenged the basic presuppositions of the prevailing Reformed and Puritan theology from the conservative side. In his magnum opus, *The Conservative Reformation and Its Theology* (1872), he synthesized a vast amount of German scholarship and consolidated his writings as a controversialist, producing one of the most influential books in American Lutheran history. The work also places him among this country's pioneers of Neo-Reformation thinking.

In time the scholarship and advocacy of men like Krauth would merge with similar influences flowing into American Lutheran life and thought through newer synods of more direct immigrant background, but these groups had barely begun their organized existence in the pre–Civil War years. Largely because of the way in which the Lutheran crisis was resolved, the older eastern synods and the newer German and Scandinavian synods would remain in contact. The General Council which sprang from a division in the church would in later years become a powerful agency of unification.

32

THE FORMING OF THE ROMAN CATHOLIC CHURCH

The Roman Catholic church has a longer history in America—even in the United States—than any other Christian denomination, and each of its several American beginnings has at least a tenuous connection with the present day. These ancient traditions notwithstanding, no major church in America experienced a more decisive break between its colonial phase and its development after the Revolutionary War. Unlike the Congregational, Presbyterian, Baptist, and Lutheran churches, whose patterns of development were established long before 1776, the Roman Catholic church began almost a second history in the national period. So incredibly large was the flow of immigrants that by 1850 Roman Catholics, once a tiny and ignored minority, had become the country's largest religious communion. The Revolution transformed the church's legal and psychological situation to such an extent that Roman Catholics could participate with few legal restrictions in a free democratic society such as the world had never seen, and for which neither Roman Catholic theology, canon law, nor ancient precedent provided much guidance. Indeed, the American cultural ethos in its totality constituted so drastic a break with tradition that even after decades of explaining by American bishops, it still remained an enigma to popes and curial officials in Rome. And at the end of the nineteenth century "Americanism" would become a serious doctrinal issue both in Europe and America.

THE ROAD TO INDEPENDENCE

For Roman Catholics as for all other American colonials the Treaty of Paris in 1763 marked the end of an epoch. Great Britain's resounding triumphs swept away the entire continental empire of the French and brought the Spanish Floridas under British rule. The perennial threat on the frontier was pushed beyond the Mississippi; Roman Catholics were no longer suspected as potential collaborationists, and tensions were eased. With regard to the ecclesiastical rule of Roman Catholics in British America, however, a new problem was created. Was a resident bishop to be sent, or could the diocese of Quebec be enlarged, or should regular visitations from Florida and Quebec be arranged, or should the old arrangements continue? Richard Challoner, after 1758 vicar apostolic of the London district with jurisdiction over the American colonies, persistently pressed the Vatican to provide closer regulation than he himself could exercise from afar. The Jesuits in the colonies, on the other hand, were deeply suspicious of anti-Jesuit sentiments among the bishops and cardinals in Rome and in other Catholic countries. Also aware of the uproar aroused by Anglican proposals for an American bishop, they warned against a move that would revive Protestant hostility. Challoner, in turn, interpreted these warnings as a Jesuitic maneuver, and dwelt on the tragedy of American Catholics being deprived of the sacrament of confirmation. In fact nothing was done to alter the old arrangements except that after the suppression of their society in 1773 the Jesuits were placed directly under Challoner's authority as secular priests.

In the meantime, relations between England and America were steadily deteriorating, and most Catholics apparently shared the outrage of their countrymen at Parliament's new taxes and tightened colonial administration. Charles Carroll of Maryland even entered into journalistic combat for the Patriot cause in 1773. Into this era of good feelings for Catholics, however, Parliament cast a bomb in 1774—the Quebec Act, which not only freed Quebec Catholics of the traditional oath of loyalty to the king and granted them full freedom of religion, but attached the entire trans-Appalachian territory north of the Ohio to Quebec. This provided new incitement to the rise of revolutionary sentiment, at the same time that it goaded colonists to another round of anti-Catholicism. So violent were the formal protests of the First Continental Congress, indeed, that future possibilities for Canadian participation in armed resistance were rendered out of the question. Had not the War for Independence begun, another season of domestic intolerance would undoubtedly have followed.

During the war, Roman Catholics seem to have participated in a way that justified Charles Carroll's signature on the Declaration of Independence. Few of his coreligionists could rejoice over their stakes in the British Empire. If they were Irish, as were many, they were not likely to have forgotten the treatment that England had meted out in the past. They had every reason to expect much improvement of their situation in an independent America where no one church could expect to dominate the others. Their participation in the war effort, therefore, was wholehearted. Tories among them were very few; and though a Loyalist regiment was raised during General Howe's occupation of Philadelphia, it was more than balanced by two Patriot regiments and an unknown number of volunteers in the Continental armies. The American alliance with Roman Catholic France and Spain provided additional motivation, as did the work of foreign volunteers like Count Pulaski.

ORGANIZING AN AMERICAN CHURCH

Neither freedom and independence nor the grant of civil rights in Maryland and Pennsylvania (where most Roman Catholics lived) solved the serious ecclesiastical problems that lay before the twenty to twenty-five ex-Jesuit priests who were serving in America in 1783. In 1784, therefore, they organized themselves into a "Select Body of Clergy," adopted a constitution regulating their affairs, and formed a corporation to administer the properties which the Society of Jesus had owned at the time of its suppression. This group also realized the importance of reestablishing their authority now that English jurisdiction was terminated, but here they faced a perplexing situation. Because they were aware of the strong hostility against the Society of Jesus still entertained at the Vatican, and because they worried about Protestant antipathies, they feared the appointment of an ordinary bishop and objected strenuously to the erection of a vicariate apostolic which would be in the jurisdiction of Propaganda in Rome.

A complicated series of maneuvers followed in which even Benjamin Franklin had a hand, since he desired to link American Catholics more closely to France, perhaps under a French bishop. But the United States government stated an explicit policy of noninvolvement in the affair. Finally in Rome on 9 June 1784, without the consultation of the American priests, the Reverend John Carroll was appointed superior of the mission in the United States. Carroll considered this arrangement unsatisfactory, for it placed severe limits on his authority, and he hesitated four months before accepting. Yet he and his colleagues were gratified that a French bishop had not been given the jurisdiction, and at least some of his fellow priests hoped that Rome would soon recognize the need for a regular diocesan arrangement. In any event, the man chosen for this arduous task was well fitted for the role.

John Carroll (1735–1815) was born into an old Maryland family distinguished for its material prosperity, its widely manifested civic responsibility, and its allegiance to the Church of Rome. As befitted his station, Carroll's father, a merchant in upper Marlborough, sent his son first to a Jesuit school at Bohemia Manor near the Pennsylvania border, and then in 1748 to the famous school conducted by the English Jesuits at Saint Omer in French Flanders. In the discipline and austerity of this academic and clerical world the boy found his vocation, and five years later he began his novitiate as a Jesuit. Upon completion of further studies he became a teacher in the school of his order at Liège. During the years which followed, however, an exceedingly disruptive series of events reached their climax, and the Society of Jesus was officially dissolved. In 1744 the long-smoldering opposition to the order had led to the condemnation of its missionary practices in China; then in 1759 it was expelled from Portugal. France, after various preparatory restrictions, proscribed it entirely in 1764, Spain followed suit in 1768, and finally, in 1773, Pope Clement XIV, a Franciscan, ordered its dissolution. After a tour of the Continent, Carroll returned to America in 1774, just as it was girding itself for armed conflict with England. He sympathized with this cause and even participated in an unsuccessful attempt to bring Canada into the Patriot camp. Thus doubly separated from traditional sources of authority, Father Carroll spent the war years as a priest in his home district, helping to secure the ex-Jesuit properties for the future work of his church in the new nation.

Like his distant cousin who had signed the Declaration of Independence, John Carroll was a convinced Patriot. As early as 1779 he assured an English correspondent that "the fullest and largest system of toleration is adopted in almost all of the American states; public protection and encouragement are extended alike to all denominations, and Roman Catholics are members of congress, assemblies, and hold civil and military posts as well as others." [1] Though firm in his attachment to the Holy See and orthodox in doctrine, he was remarkably progressive in practical matters, favoring a vernacular liturgy and expressing fierce dissatisfaction with both the political and the ecclesiastical attitudes prevailing in Rome. Before receiving word of his own appointment he expressed the hope that if America were to have a bishop, it would be "an ordinary national bishop in whose appointment Rome shall have no share." [2]

Carroll's new status as superior of the mission was far from that of "an ordinary national bishop." In fact, his very limited powers barely augmented

1. Carroll to Charles Plowden, 28 February 1779, in Annabelle M. Melville, *John Carroll of Baltimore*, p. 55.

2. John Tracy Ellis, *Catholics in Colonial America*, p. 426.

those he had been exercising. Quite clearly his authority was insufficient to assert and retain control of an undisciplined situation where congregations of Roman Catholics, north and south, were organizing and calling priests at their own pleasure. But four years later the pope responded to requests from the American priests and allowed them to elect a bishop. In 1790 Carroll went to England to be consecrated bishop of Baltimore and to obtain much-needed assistance for work in his vast, half-explored diocese. As he indicated in his first report, there were then about twenty-five thousand Roman Catholics in the United States, sixteen thousand of them in Maryland, seven thousand in Pennsylvania, fifteen hundred in New York, and two hundred in Virginia.[3] What remnants of Catholicity there were beyond the mountains Carroll had no way of knowing.

After his consecration Bishop Carroll began in earnest to order and to pacify the "Church Turbulent" which was in his charge. The first major event in the diocese's short history was the convocation of a synod in 1791, where his four vicars-general and sixteen other priests (of seven nationalities) gathered for the hard legal work of providing decrees to govern the church's affairs. They did their work impressively well, and the result "served as a happy model for all its successors." Aside from regulatory measures, however, Bishop Carroll had to make decisions—and to set precedents—with regard to one special problem which was to bring more consternation and tumult to the church during the ensuing sixty years than any other, namely, trusteeism. The American Roman Catholic equivalent of congregationalism, trusteeism was further evidence of the characteristic localism that in a practical way was to alter, at least temporarily, the traditional polity of almost every communion that moved onto the American scene. In many varying patterns and for a variety of reasons, nearly every early Roman Catholic diocese had to deal with the question. One case involving two fractious Irish Capuchins and a privately incorporated parish in New York City had already resulted in disgraceful public disturbances before Carroll became a bishop. In 1791, due to similar disruptions in Boston, he had to suspend two French-born secular priests. In Philadelphia he faced still another disturbing situation which stemmed from the founding in 1789 of Holy Trinity Church by a privately incorporated "German Religious Society of Roman Catholics," the first such expressly national congregation formed in the United States.

The reasons for the emergence of these "congregational" churches are obvious. Distances were great; priests were few; genuine piety searched

3. Carroll's Report to Cardinal Antonelli, in John Tracy Ellis, *Documents of American Catholic History*, p. 152.

for parish expression. Protestant examples were everywhere to be seen. The revolutionary spirit and American ideals encouraged ecclesiastical democracy. Moreover it became known that the American priests had been authorized to elect their first bishop. In a time when funds were lacking and when episcopal authority was weak or nonexistent, trusteeism was a way of providing a church for people who wanted one; in a time of ethnic tensions, it would get them a priest who spoke the right language. For such good reasons, and because he was a mild-mannered person, Bishop Carroll at first permitted or accepted these practices; but he did not live to deal with the many extreme cases where unworthy priests or trustees violated canon law, creating situations where bishops had no alternative but to use every legal sanction to eliminate the practice. Later bishops would reap the whirlwind.

More impressive and positive, though also fraught with present and future difficulties, was Bishop Carroll's chief stratagem for obtaining the priests he so desperately needed and for training the new American-born clergy that would ultimately have to be relied upon. To attain these ends he accepted the support of the Society of Saint Sulpice in France. Carroll's French contacts had been established during prerevolutionary days and had deepened during the war, but it was the outbreak of the French Revolution, with its attendant anticlericalism, that made available an invaluable reservoir of missionary zeal, educational talent, and administrative ability. During his visit to England and France in 1790, Carroll accepted the offer of Jacques André Émery, superior general of the Society of Saint Sulpice in Paris, to furnish not only priests, teachers, and some students, but important financial aid. In 1791 Charles François Nagot and three colleagues arrived in Baltimore and with little delay transformed the "One Mile Tavern" just beyond the town into Saint Mary's Seminary. The institution nearly collapsed at times, yet for nearly two decades it remained the primary seminary of the American Catholic church as its graduates assumed many positions of usefulness and prominence. The Sulpicians also opened Mount Saint Mary's College at Emmitsburg, Maryland, in 1808.

Before 1815 these teachers were joined by nearly a hundred other émigré priests from France. In 1817 Ambrose Maréchal, the rector of Saint Mary's College who had shortly before declined the see of Philadelphia, was made archbishop of Baltimore. When in 1808 another émigré, Benedict Flaget, became bishop of Bardstown, Kentucky, he took with him Jean-Baptiste David, who founded a seminary in the West and later succeeded Flaget as bishop. In the meantime Jean Dubois left the presidency of Mount Saint Mary's to become the second bishop of New York. Father François

Matignon was sent to pacify the disrupted church in Boston, where he was later joined by Jean-Louis Lefebvre de Cheverus, who served as bishop there until translated to the see of Montauban in France. Cheverus was later made archbishop of Bordeaux and a cardinal. In Bordeaux he was as fondly remembered for his gentle saintliness as he had been in Boston. Even Georgetown College, one of the favorite educational projects of Bishop Carroll, owed its reputation and almost its existence in these early years to the French priests who served as it teachers and administrators.

Few of these émigré priests played a more varied role than William Dubourg (1766–1833). After theological studies at Paris, Dubourg was ordained and entered the Order of Saint Sulpice in 1788. Fleeing the Revolution, he arrived in the United States in 1794, serving for a time as president of Georgetown College and later as the first superior of Saint Mary's College. In 1812 he was appointed apostolic administrator of Louisiana and the Floridas, and three years later he was consecrated bishop. Because the cathedral at New Orleans was in the hands of those who refused submission to the American hierarchy, he was forced to reside at Saint Louis, where he founded a college and a theological seminary as well as an academy which later became Saint Louis University. During his visit to Europe in 1815—when he was consecrated bishop of New Orleans—Dubourg also visited Lyons in France, and inspired a small group of laywomen with the need for missionary aid. Out of that seed grew the Society for the Propagation of the Faith, founded in 1822, which made a large and continuous financial contribution to church work in America. In 1826 Dubourg was transferred to the see of Montauban, in France, and in 1833 he became archbishop of Besançon.

Perhaps most eminent of all was the career of Ambrose Maréchal (1764–1828). Maréchal had entered the Sulpician Seminary in Orléans, but he sailed for Maryland immediately after his ordination in 1792. Here he served as a priest until 1799, when he became a teacher of theology first at Saint Mary's College of Baltimore, later at Georgetown, then again at Saint Mary's. Under Napoleon he returned to France for a time, but in 1812 he came back to his post in Baltimore, where he served until made archbishop. His years in that office—1817 to 1828—were stormy. There were disagreements with the Jesuits over ownership of the Whitemarsh plantation. Conflicts broke out continually over Irish and German resistance to priests of other nationalities. The issue of trusteeism erupted in several places. The Irish clergy were restive because of the obvious French dominance of the hierarchy. By exceeding his authority, Maréchal did take some measures to pacify the church, but he steadfastly refused to call a provincial council, preferring to keep his bishops isolated from each other.[4] On the other hand, he did succeed in reducing European intervention in American church affairs. And in 1821, he dedicated the fine cathedral of Baltimore which Benjamin Latrobe had designed and which Archbishop Carroll had begun.

The nature of the theological and spiritual influence of the Sulpicians on the Roman Catholic church in America is difficult to estimate. But the society was always known for its firm discipline and for its strict conception of orthodoxy rather than for its venturesomeness, and it is perhaps just to say that it propagated a similar spirit in America, where in any event the intensely practical necessities of an expanding church hindered the growth of theological profundity, a great tradition of learning, or even the ardent piety associated with Jean-Jacques Olier, the society's great founder. Here again a step taken by Bishop Carroll had a decisive impact on the church—in the immediate sense providing a source of priests and bishops when they were badly needed, but in the long run creating a very serious source of ethnic tension and jealousies that often sharpened trusteeship conflicts. Probably the most enduring legacy of the Sulpicians to the American church was their very conservative theological tradition.

The prominence of the Society of Jesus is another feature of American Catholicism which the church's first prelate, a Jesuit himself, tended to accentuate, though in no unusually overt manner. In America the former members of the Society of Jesus, who in fact constituted the main body of clergy in 1783, maintained their identity despite their official nonexistence. After 1805, capitalizing on the pope's recognition of the Society of Jesus in Russia, they reprofessed their vows and went ahead openly with their work, though there was no American province before 1833. During these early decades the college at Georgetown, opened in 1791, was the main center of their labor, but they made contributions as priests and bishops in every sector. It has been justly said that American Catholicism was "in its inception, wholly a Jesuit affair and [has] largely remained so." [5] What truth there is to this exaggeration is largely due to the success of the Jesuits of Carroll's generation in maintaining themselves and then in regaining a prominent place in the church's life.

It must be added, however, that Sulpicians and Jesuits were not the only orders at work in these early years. In 1806–07 Father Edward D. Fenwick

4. See Thomas F. Casey, *The Sacred Congregation de Propaganda Fide and the Revision of the First Provincial Council of Baltimore, 1829–1830* (Rome: Gregorian University, 1957), pp. 12–16; and the several works of Peter Guilday therein cited.

5. Thomas O'Gorman, *History of the Roman Catholic Church in the United States*, ACHS, vol. 9 (New York, 1895), p. 208.

and other Dominicans built the Church of Saint Rose of Lima in Washington County, Kentucky, and opened a novitiate that marks the origin of that order in the United States. The Dominicans also worked extensively as missionaries in the area; and in 1821 Father Fenwick was made the first bishop of Cincinnati. Women's orders, too, were at work. The Ursulines had been in New Orleans since 1727, and early in the nineteenth century they were carrying on their teaching work in New York and Boston. Outside of New Orleans the oldest convent in the United States is that settled by the Carmelites in Maryland in 1790; but the old established orders were not alone in advancing the course of education.

Notable in her own way was Elizabeth Seton (1774–1821). Widow of a well-to-do New York merchant and an Episcopalian, she became a Catholic soon after her husband's death in 1803. After a brief teaching experience in New York City, she went in 1808 to Baltimore, where, encouraged by Carroll and Dubourg, she opened an academy in a house adjoining Saint Mary's College. Moving to Emmitsburg a year later, she established Saint Joseph's Academy, and in order to staff it, founded the Sisters of Charity as a teaching order. In decades to come the American Sisters of Charity would make a major contribution as teachers and administrators of schools throughout the country. Mother Seton was beatified by the pope in 1963, and she may well become the first American-born canonized saint.

EXPANSION OF THE CHURCH

The trends established and the problems faced or created during the early years of a fully constituted Roman Catholic church in the United States have been the focus of our attention up to this point. This has perhaps obscured the major fact that the church actively ministered to the widely scattered faithful in the new country, as well as to the ever increasing numbers arriving through immigration. The most obvious index of this activity is the expansion of the hierarchy and the increase in the priesthood and membership. In 1790 Bishop Carroll had been alone with little more than an ex-Jesuit remnant. In 1799, however, he received a coadjutor bishop, Leonard Neale, a Marylander and Jesuit; then, more momentously, in 1808 Pope Pius VII erected Baltimore as a metropolitan see. Archbishop Carroll now was given four suffragan sees: Boston, Bardstown, New York, and Philadelphia. As nearly as the archbishop and his suffragans could determine, there were then eighty Roman Catholic churches, seventy priests and perhaps seventy thousand faithful in the United States, exclusive of Louisiana.

At Boston John Cheverus became the ordinary of a diocese that included all of New England but consisted of only three widely scattered congregations, one of which was the recently conflict-ridden Boston congregation of about seven hundred members. Cheverus was one of the few French émigrés who was deeply beloved by parishioners and non-Catholics alike; and the whole city mourned his departure when he returned to France in 1823. His successor, Benedict J. Fenwick, a Jesuit, took charge of a diocese that had grown only slightly to include eight churches served by three priests. Although his Boston membership was by then largely Irish, the great deluge still lay ahead.

The first bishop of Bardstown was Benedict Joseph Flaget, the Sulpician who since 1792 had been ministering in the West, at Vincennes and many other places. With a responsibility that at first included the entire trans-Appalachian region except the Louisiana Purchase lands, Flaget faced staggering problems. Yet aided by the Kentucky Dominicans and a small group of itinerant missionary priests (most of them French), he did much to organize the church life of old settlers and newcomers alike. The growth of his diocese was steady. In 1817 Flaget received a coadjutor, and the Dominican Father Fenwick was appointed to the newly erected see of Cincinnati with the Old Northwest as his charge.

The first bishop of New York was appointed in Rome and died at Naples in 1810 without ever seeing his diocese. His successor was another stranger to America, John Connolly, who did not occupy his unruly see until 1815. Until his death a decade later, Connolly's efforts to cope with the rising tide of Irish immigration were inhibited by bitter struggles with trustees and an acute shortage of clergy. In 1825 he had but ten priests for an estimated 150,000 Roman Catholic people. His successor, the Sulpician Jean Dubois, a former schoolmate of Robespierre, showed greater competence. Dubois founded a diocesan seminary, but because of his nationality he was doomed to even fiercer opposition from the trustees. It was not until 1837, when John Hughes, a former seminary student of Dubois's, was consecrated as coadjutor in New York, that the diocese gained a bishop fully able to deal with the rapidly growing Catholic population, serious trusteeship problems, and most ominous of all, the rising tide of anti-Catholicism. Orator, theologian, strenuous controversialist, and effective administrator, Hughes demonstrated the advantages and possibilities of a prelate who had been trained in the United States.

Philadelphia, the fourth suffragan see erected in 1808, had at that time and for some time continued to have the most substantial Catholic population in the country. Trusteeism raised greater problems here than elsewhere, and Michael Egan, a Franciscan who in 1810 became the city's first bishop, was unable even to assert his authority over the cathedral priests. The man appointed in Europe to deal with the Philadelphia diocese after Egan's death was Henry Conwell, the aged vicar general of Armagh in Ireland. Around him for a decade swirled the events of the Hogan affair, the *cause célèbre* of trusteeism, which finally did him in. William Hogan was a handsome priest who came from Ireland in 1819, the year of Conwell's consecration as bishop. He had been granted faculties as a priest in Saint Mary's Church by the interim administrator of the diocese, but these faculties were withdrawn after Hogan publicly ridiculed the new bishop. The trustees of the cathedral church supported the priest, who in turn intensified his attack, accusing the bishop of exceeding the canonical limits of his authority (as, indeed, several bishops had done). Hogan also urged Archbishop Maréchal to call a provincial council to rule on these matters; but he then outdid himself and forged a pastoral letter ascribed to Bishop Conwell. Conwell retaliated, admonishing the congregation and threatening Hogan with excommunication if he should exercise his faculties. Since Hogan, at the trustees' urging, did not desist, he was excommunicated in May 1822. The trustees then went still farther and published an "Address of the Committee of Saint Mary's Church of Philadelphia to their Brethren of the Roman Catholic Faith throughout the United States of America, on the Subject of a Reform of Certain Abuses in the Administration of our Church Discipline." They alleged intervention by "foreigners" sent among them by "the Junta or Commission directing the Fide Propaganda of Rome," and called for procedures allowing the "nomination and selection of our pastors from our own citizens." From among these pastors, moreover, bishops should be chosen. They went on to accuse the existing bishops of being "a disgrace to our religion," victims of "superstition and ignorance." Hogan and the trustees were, in effect, calling for an independent Catholic church of some sort.

In due course these events prompted a condemnatory brief, *Non sine magno,* from Pope Pius VII. Though it did not rule out benign trusteeship arrangements, it did declare Father Hogan's pastoral acts to be null and void. But even this did not end the affair. Hogan, after showing some reluctance, continued the struggle for a while, but he later resigned, became a lawyer, and was married in 1824. He died without the offices of the church in 1848. The trustees continued the conflict, however, by gaining the services of two other priests (Angelo Inglesi and then Thaddeus O'Meally) for another year. Thereupon the lay committee and the bishop worked out a compromise proposal for selecting pastors for Saint Mary's, which, together with a confusing counterdeclaration by the lay committee, found its way to

Rome. A decree of the Propaganda approved by the pope reprobated this agreement. Bishop Conwell was called to Rome and ordered not to return to his diocese. He did return, however, and was pardoned, but he was not allowed to exercise his episcopal functions. In his place Francis Patrick Kenrick (1796–1863) was appointed in 1831. Irish-born, educated in Rome, only thirty-four years old, and by nature a theologian rather than an administrator or man of action, Kenrick now faced the problem that had broken two bishops and left a vast diocese in undeveloped disarray. In addition to these problems, and in part because of them, he also would have to deal in future years with the infamous Know-Nothing riots of 1844, the most violent ever to occur in the United States. More suited to his nature was the direction of the seminary which he founded in 1835. Bishop Kenrick was transferred to the metropolitan see of Baltimore in 1851, where he served till his death. When he died he left to the church a large corpus of writing on dogmatic and moral theology, an English version of the Bible, and numerous treatises and controversial works on baptism, justification, the primacy of Peter, and other subjects.

THE FIRST PROVINCIAL COUNCIL OF BALTIMORE

Even prior to some of these events in the first four suffragan dioceses, other sees had been erected and other bishops appointed, and in these areas many of the same circumstances had been encountered. Some unaccountable decisions were made in Rome, such as the erection of a see in Virginia where there were scarcely enough church members to support a single priest. Good and bad appointments were likewise made: Bishop John England of Charleston being one of the greatest prelates ever to grace the church in America and Patrick Kelly of Richmond one of the least effective. Both came from Ireland, both faced trusteeism in one form or another.

In 1815 Archbishop Carroll died. His coadjutor, Leonard Neale, served as archbishop for two years until succeeded by Maréchal. While this French prelate was metropolitan (1817–28) the need for uniform regulations and procedures and the consequent pressure for a council of bishops most forcefully arose. But Maréchal refused to call one, and it was his successor, James Whitfield, who upon authorization from Pius VIII convoked the First Provincial Council for 4 October 1829.[6]

6. James Whitfield (1770–1834), fourth archbishop of Baltimore, was born at Liverpool, England, lived for a time in Italy, and when detained in France by the Napoleonic wars, was educated at Saint Irenaeus Seminary. Ordained in 1809, he continued on to England where he became for a time a Jesuit novice. In 1817 he departed for Baltimore to join his close friend and former rector of Saint Irenaeus, Ambrose Maréchal, then coadjutor to

It was an auspicious conclave in a critical period of American history. Its proportions were modest, but the actions taken as well as the trends observable in the country portended much. The canonical members of the council were the bishops, including coadjutors, of the sees in the province of Baltimore: Baltimore, Boston, New York, Philadelphia, Charleston, and Cincinnati (Richmond, which was vacant, was under the administration of the archdiocese of Baltimore). Also invited to be present were those bishops serving outside the province, and depending directly on the Congregation de Propaganda Fide in Rome: New Orleans, Saint Louis, and the vicariate of Alabama and Florida. In its collective letter to the Holy See, the council could rightly express thanks and something approaching amazement at the changes wrought in the state of the church during the past four decades. They could point to six "ecclesiastical seminaries," nine colleges, three of which were chartered universities, houses of Dominicans, Jesuits, Sulpicians, and of the Congregation of the Mission, thirty-three monasteries and houses of religious women of several congregations and orders, and, of course, a rapidly growing body of faithful laity which even then numbered over two hundred thousand. The Roman Catholic church had become a major force in American life.

Archbishop Neale of Baltimore. Under Maréchal, who was soon made archbishop, Whitfield was appointed first rector of the Cathedral of the Assumption in 1821, and as coadjutor and titular bishop of Apollonia on 8 January 1828. Maréchal died three weeks later, and on 25 May, Whitfield was consecrated as archbishop.

33

THE EXPANSION OF THE ROMAN CATHOLIC CHURCH

The first Provincial Council of Baltimore, held in October 1829, was an epoch-marking event in American Catholic history in the United States. In the first place, it was a considerable achievement in the realm of ecclesiastical administration, for its influence would be wide and long-lasting. It also revealed to non-Catholic Americans in no uncertain terms that the Roman church was a substantial, growing, and well organized reality. With Andrew Jackson enjoying his first year in the White House, the council occurred at an important time of transition in the nation's history; what historians have called the "early national period" was over. The "era of good feelings" and the day of presidential knee britches was yielding to the "age of the common man." Amid sharpening sectional conflict, a notable increase in the rate of immigration was also heightening ethnic tensions.

The Roman Catholic church was especially implicated in immigration, and in two ways. First, because very many of the immigrants were Roman Catholic, the challenge of reaching them with the offices and sacraments of the church was to make all of its earlier efforts seem like pioneering sorties. Second, because the American people, in any event defensive, self-conscious, nationalistic, and somewhat xenophobic, were ill prepared to receive so large a component of "strangers" into their midst, the church was also required to adapt itself to a new atmosphere of suspicion and overt attack. The present chapter is concerned chiefly with the first challenge; that which follows will take up the matter of antebellum nativism.

THE COMING OF THE IRISH

Even in the late colonial period the Irish had constituted a large (possibly the largest) proportion of the church's laity. Michael J. O'Brien has argued that his compatriots of the revolutionary era virtually won the war. But the uncertain estimates of colonial times yielded to firm statistical fact after the turn of the century, when increasingly large numbers of Roman Catholics from Ireland began their historic migration to the New World.

Why four and one-half million Irish came to America in the century after 1820 is no mystery. If there were ever any doubts, Cecil Woodham-Smith has removed them with her recent research and unforgettable historical account of "the great hunger." Life on the Emerald Isle had become unendurable as population pressure increased. Food was scarce, agricultural methods backward, prices and wages disastrously low, taxation heavy, and government by absentee English landlords unbelievably ruthless and intolerant. After the close of the Napoleonic wars emigration increased, especially among the class of more substantial farmers. As economic conditions grew worse, and as American factories and construction projects beckoned, still poorer people began to leave; and to accommodate their needs, the "immigrant traffic" grew as a means of providing mass transportation at minimum cost. During the 1830s, 200,000 Irish arrived in the United States. After 1845 a succession of cold, damp summers and a mysterious blight ruined the potato crop on which life itself depended, and as a result about 1.5 million died. What this meant for the villages of Ireland is suggested by the parish record in Donoughmore, County Cork, where the future American bishop, Dennis O'Connell, was born.

> December, 1847: This was the Famine Year. There died of famine and fever from November 1846 to September 1847 over fourteen hundred of the people and one Priest, Revd. Dan. Horgan. Requiescat in Pace. Numbers remained unburied for a fortnight, many were buried in ditches near their houses, many without coffins, tho' ther wer four men employed to bury the dead and make graves and [two], and sometimes four carpenters to make coffins. On this year also we were visited by the Cholera Mortis. 5 only died of it in this parish. [signed Michael Kane, Pastor] [1]

The exodus from Ireland became a desperate, frantic flight, involving about 780,000 people in all. By 1850 the census reported 961,719 Irish in the United States, and over 200,000 came in that year alone. In another decade the total figure had risen to 1,611,304.

Yet statistics can never capture the meaning of this terrible exodus and

1. Quoted by Gerald Fogarty, "The Life of Dennis O'Connell" (unpublished manuscript, Yale University, 1968). On the Irish catastrophe as a whole, see Cecil Woodham-Smith, *The Great Hunger: Ireland, 1845–1849* (New York: Harper & Row, 1962).

its painful sequel in the shantytowns of America's too rapidly growing cities, or the hardships and disrupted family life wherever there were back-breaking jobs at low pay on canal projects, railroad and dam construction, or anywhere else at the mudsill of the American labor market. Nor were the obstacles only hard work, poverty, and miserable living conditions, for the Irish had to face the contumely, prejudice, and insulting condescension of Protestant and Anglo-Saxon America. In this context the work of extending the Roman Catholic church proceeded.

Within the Roman Catholic church, tension between the Irish and Germans persisted during the entire nineteenth century. It underlay early trusteeship conflicts in New York, Buffalo, and Philadelphia, then reached its most critical stage in the latter half of the century, when the issues had involved the highest levels of the American hierarchy and become entangled in the internal and external politics of the Vatican. Ethnic hostility was thus vented within the church as well as against it. Yet the primary fact of Roman Catholic history in antebellum America, aside from its basic task of reaching the immigrants, is the vigorous entry of the Irish into the life of the nation and the church.

The first and most obvious effect of Irish immigration was an immense multiplication of the church's missionary problems. As it met and overcame these obstacles, the church experienced a phenomenal growth in numbers, reaching 1.75 million by 1850, and doubling this figure in another decade. In the process, a church originally largely Gallic in its leadership became and remained dominantly Gaelic. But such transformations do not usually come peacefully or without stress, and they did not in this case. Parishes revealed the conflict first, either through disagreements between Irish and French parishioners (as in Boston) or through the resistance of local trustees to a French bishop (as in New York).

In addition to disorderly manifestations by the laity, there were deep dissatisfactions among the lower clergy who, if Irish, resented the tendency of the hierarchy to award all the ecclesiastical plums to "foreigners." This is not to say that the French appointments were unwarranted or unjust. These men were, as Maynard has said, almost too good. "Men so learned, so able, so pious as Cheverus and Dubourg and Dubois and Flaget and Bruté and Maréchal simply *had* to be made bishops." [2] Such dispassionate judgments, however, could not come easily to those who had suffered real adversities in Ireland or America, who had come from humble circumstances, and who had received only such education as a raw young nation and a too rapidly expanding church could provide. And there were other grievances.

2. Theodore Maynard, *The Catholic Church and the American Idea*, p. 184.

Members of the higher clergy were known to speak in private (as did Maréchal) of *"la canaille irlandaise."* And Archbishop James Whitfield, a French-educated Englishman, revealed the same kind of prejudice in a letter to his friend Joseph Rosati, then bishop of Saint Louis. Speaking in 1832 of the empty see in Cincinnati, he urged that "an American born be recommended" and then added that "(between us in strict confidence) I do really think we should guard against having more Irish bishops." [3] In the midst of such attitudes peace and good will could hardly flourish.

Gradually the situation changed, however, in part because the Irish in the church exploited the same aptitudes that were making their political leaders a force to reckon with, and in part because of the sheer force of numbers. Not only was the overall increase due to immigration in their favor, but Irish-Americans were entering the priesthood and the religious orders in numbers far exceeding those of other nationalities. Furthermore, these men simply demonstrated their abilities. Outstanding among these was John Hughes, who in 1837 became the coadjutor of Bishop Dubois in New York, soon showed his superior talents for leading an harassed and growing church during turbulent times. Under these circumstances the Irish-American clergy gradually won their place in the church, and once they had attained a dominant position, they retained it successfully from that time forward except in sees which were tacitly reserved for Germans and a few other special cases. In the American church, unlike the ancient churches of Europe, these leaders would have to proceed without government aid or favor. Majority opinion in the nation would be hostile. Immigrant tides would roll in, and most of their constituency would be low on the social and economic scale. Yet the historic institutions of the church would rise—cathedrals, seminaries, colleges, monasteries, hospitals, and hundreds of parish churches—a tremendous testimony to the advantages of a free church in a free country and to their own ecclesiastical leadership.

GEOGRAPHICAL EXPANSION

If the Roman church's response to the challenge of immigration and the integration of wave upon wave of new Irish-Americans was one major fact of its growth during its first half-century in America, the geographical expansion of its jurisdiction was hardly less exciting. Frontier church history is usually considered a predominantly Protestant phenomenon. But the Roman Catholic church from the first carried on an active work in the West. The small remnants of French Catholicism in the upper

3. John Tracy Ellis, *American Catholicism,* p. 49.

Mississippi Valley provided the first incentive to western plans, and the work preceding and following the appointment of Bishop Flaget was a critical beginning. This organizational activity was extended into the Midwest and into the vast territory purchased from France in 1803. In New Orleans both the laity and the old clergy offered stout resistance to incorporation in the United States hierarchy, even preventing Bishop Dubourg from occupying the cathedral, but after 1818 peace and order were established. In 1821 Ohio was erected into a diocese; in 1826 upper and lower Louisiana were separated into two dioceses; and in 1837 Mathias Loras was consecrated bishop of Dubuque with jurisdiction over Iowa, Minnesota, and part of Dakota. In 1843 Minnesota and Wisconsin became dioceses. And so the process continued as each of the successive provincial councils meeting at Baltimore (1833, 1837, 1840, 1843, and 1846) recommended new sees and the men to occupy them.

The 1840s, however, were a decade in which the territorial extent of the United States itself was heatedly contested—and then vastly increased—by the annexation of Texas, the Mexican War, and the Oregon settlement. With regard to the war in which the "enemy" was a Roman Catholic country, the hierarchy was silent, though it approved some overt efforts to convince Mexican church leaders that the United States did not threaten them. Patriotism tended to tranquilize rather than exacerbate anti-Catholicism, however, and after the war Congress approved President Polk's recommendation that diplomatic relations be established with the sovereign of the Papal States. From 1848 until after the Civil War this representation was continued. More important for the church were the problems incident to a vast territorial gain in the Southwest.

In 1846, at a time when the Oregon question was still unsettled, a new stage in American hierarchical history was reached. A second metropolitan see was erected with the French-Canadian Francis N. Blanchet as archbishop, his brother as suffragan in Walla Walla, and another French-Canadian as bishop of Vancouver. In both fact and theory this province was at first an extension of the Canadian church. The first organized work in Oregon by the United States hierarchy was initiated in 1840, when Bishop Rosati of Saint Louis, having turned to the Jesuits, gave the assignment to Pierre Jean DeSmet (1801–73), a Belgian-born priest who had entered the Society of Jesus in Maryland in 1821. For thirty years DeSmet labored to extend and support the Northwest missions, making eight trips to Europe in search of aid, traveling over 250,000 miles, and even becoming a leading publicist of Indian missions. Led by DeSmet, the Jesuits conducted an extensive mission among the region's Indians. Their exploits, indeed, recall the history of their society in New France—both in its eventfulness and in its lack of enduring success. In 1852 the Jesuit mission in Oregon was abandoned. The Oregon province, nevertheless, became part of the American church after the territorial controversy with Great Britain was resolved.

Saint Louis was given similar status in 1847, with Nashville, Chicago, Milwaukee, Dubuque, and Saint Paul included in the province. The country now had three archbishops, yet Americans and immigrants steadily moved west, and before the century ended each of these cities except Nashville had itself become a metropolitan see. Saint Louis was by then a great ecclesiastical center, and one of the dedicated pioneers who had helped to make it so was Mother Philippine Duchesne (1769–1852).

Born in Grenoble, France, Philippine Duchesne had entered the Society of the Sacred Heart, a teaching order organized by Saint Madeleine Sophie Barat. Responding to the missionary needs that Bishop Dubourg had described, she won permission to go out to Saint Louis, where after 1818, in close collaboration with the Jesuits, she and her sisters founded several schools. She was over seventy years old when she took up work in Indian territory. Philippine Duchesne's career stands as a saintly example of the enormous educational work her order would perform in America.[4]

In the meantime, a vast area of former Mexican territory was added to the Union, a region with a storied Spanish past but, by the mid-nineteenth century, very little organized church life. In Texas, where nominal Catholics may have numbered ten thousand, Vicar Apostolic Odin, a Frenchman, was made bishop of Galveston in 1847. New Mexico, where possibly twenty-five thousand Catholics were being served by only nine priests under the bishop of Durango, was made a vicariate apostolic under the American hierarchy in 1850. Three years later the see of Santa Fe was erected and Jean-Baptiste Lamy (1814–88) was named to lead this picturesque desert diocese where Indian, Spanish, Mexican, and American traditions now crossed. The life of this remarkable French churchman is the subject of Willa Cather's *Death Comes for the Archbishop* (1926). California remained under the bishop of Monterey until 1853, when the archdiocese of San Francisco was constituted—and with this administrative act the continent was spanned. Considered as a whole, this ecclesiastical conquest was a

4. The Society of the Sacred Heart had been formed in the restorationist underground of Napoleonic France in collaboration with men who were working for the reorganization of the Jesuits. Philippine Duchesne was virtually a cofounder. First authorized in 1807 as *Dames de l'Instruction Chrétienne*, the society has always made education its primary mission. By 1935 the work begun in the United States by Mother Duchesne was an impressive subsystem of Catholic education that included seventy-two elementary and secondary schools and ninety institutions of higher learning (see Louise Callan, *Philippine Duchesne*).

stupendous achievement, though not because dioceses were drawn on a map, but because countless men and women yielded themselves to a task and to a command.

One era was concluded and another opened, a fact which was fittingly documented when the archbishop of Baltimore, Francis Patrick Kenrick, received papal authorization to convoke the first plenary council in America. On Sunday, 9 May 1852, the council was convened with the solemn procession into the Baltimore cathedral of the incumbents or proxies of six metropolitan and twenty-seven suffragan sees, an abbot, and the superiors of many religious orders and congregations. The Catholic population stood at an estimated 1.6 million, served by 1,800 priests in about 1,600 churches and mission stations. A fine Roman Catholic historian who himself at Sioux Falls, South Dakota, in 1896 became the bishop of a western diocese is entitled to a measure of pride in summarizing the accomplishments of the six decades since John Carroll had become the country's first bishop: "The world beheld the objective lesson of a growth and extension within half a century for the like of which we must go back to the earliest days of Christianity, when in the freshness of youth and vigor of apostolic zeal the church laid hold of the Roman Empire. . . . The era of plenary councils begins." [5]

THE CHURCH AND AMERICAN CULTURE

The first half-century of American Catholic history is not simply a story of geographic expansion and external organization. There is another remarkable dimension to the story, involving a different kind of pioneering—the adaptation of this rapidly expanding, multinational immigrant church to an individualistic democratic society. For this undertaking, guidance or example could scarcely be found in the church's experience since the age of the Emperor Constantine. Father O'Gorman's fervent reference to the "earliest days" of the church was warranted. As for the Curia in Rome, it seems not to have understood the distinctive character of American developments until well into the twentieth century, if then. Shaping an American Catholic church was an exciting venture, carried out on a grand scale by men who were often so involved in the multifarious details of their work that they did not know that they were ecclesiastical revolutionaries. Yet that something like an "American revolution" was accomplished in the Roman Catholic church as well as in society at large could not be

5. Thomas O'Gorman, *History of the Roman Catholic Church in the United States*, ACHS, vol. 9 (New York, 1895), p. 425.

hidden or suppressed. In the decrees of the First Plenary Council (1852) there are more than intimations of that fact, as the bishops dealt with the crosscurrents of language and national tradition which flowed through the American church. In their pastoral letter the bishops exhorted their vast flock: "Obey the public authorities, not only for wrath but for conscience sake. Show your attachment to the institutions of our beloved country."

The First Plenary Council was closely followed by the Civil War, during which the American sense of nationhood gained a new kind of profundity. Almost immediately after that appalling sacrifice of life and wealth, a Second Plenary Council was convoked in Baltimore by Archbishop Martin John Spalding on 7 October 1866. At the time, this was the largest formal conciliary assembly held in the Roman Catholic church since the Council of Trent; seven archbishops, twenty-eight bishops, three mitred abbots, and over one hundred twenty theologians were in attendance. They spoke in behalf of a church of over three million members which had almost doubled in size since 1852. Behind them lay not only the war and Lincoln's assassination but the encyclical of Pope Pius IX (*Quanta Cura,* 1864) and the sensational "Syllabus of Errors" which accompanied it. This comprehensive attack on modern thought and political liberalism had long since been "explained" in public by several American Catholics, yet it undeniably created difficulties for the council because the clear meaning of its reactionary denunciations could not be avoided. Despite this dilemma, the council fathers wished to express their democratic faith and their thankfulness for American institutions. The decrees of the council and the pastoral letter of the bishops were, therefore, "the nearest to a definition of Catholic Americanism that any official body of Catholics ever reached in the nineteenth century." [6] The only serious complaint about the American situation voiced by the council pertained to the laws by which some of the states, most pointedly Missouri, denied the right of the church to possess property.

The process of adjusting the structures and attitudes of a European church which had relatively little experience in conducting itself as a minority in a large democratic society resulted in an important two-way flow of ideas. Catholicism, on the one hand, commended itself to a surprisingly large number of American Protestants despite nativism and an old tradition of antipopery. Democracy, on the other hand, was interpreted to the church both by general experience and by theologians and church leaders, of whom the two most significant were, as it happened, converts.

6. T. T. McAvoy, *The Great Crisis in American Catholic History, 1895–1900,* p. 14.

CONVERSIONS TO ROMAN CATHOLICISM

The Roman Catholic church had successfully sought converts to its faith and discipline during the whole course of American colonial history. In fact, one source of the hostility directed against the early Jesuits in Maryland was their success in this regard. Toward the end of the seventeenth century the example of the later Stuart royal family gave rise to a considerable number of "Jacobite" converts, though the age of the Enlightenment coupled with many legal harassments had a contrary effect. Around 1800, a surfeit of "reasonable religion" and reaction from the French Revolution led to a widespread "romantic" reassessment of the religious heritage. In its wake came a new wave of Catholic interest. This impulse was often only aesthetic or sentimental, but it sometimes resulted in movements of Catholic renewal in the Reformation churches; and it also stimulated a great increase of conversions to the Roman church. The romantic revolution in religion is considered in a later chapter, but certain aspects of it loom large in antebellum Catholic history. In the words of one Catholic, it was "a time when great throngs of Americans began to flock to the Roman Catholic church despite bitterly intense propaganda and overt opposition." Between 1813 and 1893 the number of converts may have reached 700,000.[7]

Even if greatly exaggerated or almost balanced by an equally large defection from the church, such figures reveal an important fact of American religious life. They also point to a significant factor in the shaping of American Catholicism. Mixed marriages probably account for most of the losses and gains of the Roman church, but among the converts who attained some degree of public notice, the largest number came from the ranks of High Church Anglicans who were dissatisfied by the evangelicalism of the Protestant Episcopal church and who were carried forward by the implications of their own arguments on apostolic succession and "valid" ordination. After the Oxford Movement's *Tracts for the Times* began to appear, and especially after John Henry Newman's sensational conversion to Rome in 1845, there was considerable movement of Episcopalians toward Catholicism, about fifty of whom were priests or seminary graduates. The most publicized case was the conversion of a bishop, Levi S. Ives of North Carolina, in 1852.

Some of these converts attained considerable eminence as Roman Catholics, notably Edgar P. Wadhams, who in 1872 became bishop of Ogdens-

7. George K. Malone, *The True Church: A Study in the Apologetics of Orestes Brownson* (Mundelein, Ill.: Saint Mary of the Lake Seminary, 1957), p. 2.

burg, New York, after twenty-two years in the priesthood, and Augustine F. Hewit, one of the first Paulists and the successor of Father Hecker as superior-general of the congregation. Achieving the highest eminence of all was James Roosevelt Bayley, a relative of Mother Seton, who, like so many of his fellow Episcopal priests, turned to Rome during the 1840s. After serving in several positions in the appointment of Archbishop Hughes Bayley became bishop of Newark in 1853. His great ability as diocesan leader finally led in 1872 to his translation to the archepiscopal see of Baltimore.[8]

Among all the converts of the period, however, there were two men who best expressed the thoughts and feelings that lay behind this renewal of Catholic interest: Orestes Brownson and Isaac Hecker. By an interesting irony, both emerged from the Transcendentalist movement on the left wing of Unitarianism, and perhaps because of this fact, both men were especially eloquent interpreters of the reciprocal benefits of democratic ideals and Catholic faith.

Orestes Brownson

Orestes Brownson (1803–76) was a self-educated spiritual wanderer from rural Vermont whose pilgrimage brought him to the Church of Rome at the age of forty-two—but by a notoriously winding route. In 1822 he ended a youthful period of haphazard religious drift by entering the Presbyterian church; but within three years he had recoiled from its doctrinal rigor, and from 1824 to 1829 he was active as a Universalist preacher and editor. Enticed from that tie by the earnest arguments of Fanny Wright, the British-born freethinker and humanitarian reformer, Brownson entered a period of atheism during which the Workingman's party was his chief preoccupation. In 1831, deeply moved by William Ellery Channing's writings, he became a Unitarian; and after ministries in various places he burst onto the Boston scene in 1836, editing a reform journal and preaching to a Society for Christian Union and Progress which he organized in order to reach laboring people untouched by the regular churches. In the same year he published his *New Views of Christianity, Society, and the Church,* which together with his lectures and articles soon made him one of the most influential leaders of the emerging Transcendental movement. Deeply imbued with the romantic religious philosophies of France, Brownson became the leading American expositor of Benjamin Constant, Victor Cousin, and a group of Saint-Simonian thinkers.

8. The Oxford Movement and American Anglo-Catholicism are considered in more detail in their Episcopal context in chap. 38.

His radical Jacksonianism gave a sharp critical edge to his social prophecy, but the disgusting character and disappointing result of the 1840 presidential campaign diminished his political optimism and gradually religious perspectives again dominated his thought. In this context the French Saint-Simonian Pierre Leroux (1797–1871) became to him so sure a guide that Brownson would always regard him as, after Malebranche, "the ablest and most original philosopher France has produced." Leroux convinced him that human life and thought is a "joint product of subject and object," and that man's well-being and progress depend, therefore, on "communion"—with nature, mankind, and with God. For Leroux humanity was the means to communion with God; for Brownson the means slowly came to be understood as "the mediatorial life of Christ" (the "Providential man"), then more precisely the corporate church, and finally—despite the lifelong prejudices of a New Englander—the Roman Catholic church. On 20 October 1844, after a period of instruction under John Bernard Fitzpatrick, coadjutor-bishop of Boston, Brownson did as he had always done: he took the step to which his convictions had led.

Under the tutelage of Bishop Fitzpatrick he continued to publish *Brownson's Quarterly Review,* which he had founded in 1843 as successor to his *Boston Quarterly Review,* but he abandoned the line of thought that had led him to Rome, adopted the bishop's strictly traditional apologetics, and consigned all of his former friends and all other victims of Protestant "no-churchism" to the nether regions of hell. They, in turn, wrote off his last turn of mind as another example of his "vicissitudinary petulance" and struck him from their lists of Transcendental heroes. Brownson the Roman Catholic was still Brownson, however, as sure as ever that his convictions were based on unerring deductions from indubitable premises. In the midst of vigorous activity as America's foremost convert, he gradually reasserted his characteristic modes of thought, and for these reasons as well as for his impolitic criticism of parochial schools and of the Irish "rabble," he had soon aroused a Roman Catholic opposition which for the rest of his life would undermine his prestige and assault nearly every position he occupied.

In 1855 Brownson moved out of the Boston diocese to New York, but in this supposedly freer atmosphere his outspoken "Americanism" awakened the hostility of Archbishop John Hughes and many others, while his criticism of despotic rule in the Papal States and of even the idea of the pope's wielding temporal power aroused suspicions in Rome. Moving to New Jersey in 1857, he published *The Convert, or Leaves from My Experience,* which was, in effect, a declaration of intellectual independence.

Although to the end of his days this independence was limited by harassment and attack from all quarters, Brownson did nevertheless return to the lines of thought which had led him to Catholicism, augmenting themes derived from Leroux with an equally great responsiveness to the writings of the Piedmontese philosopher-theologian Vicenzo Gioberti (1801–52). Gioberti was a fervent champion of Catholic truth and Italian unity whom Brownson declared to be "certainly one of the profoundest philosophical writers of this century." A critic of modern romantic pantheism, he convinced Brownson that ontology, not psychology, is the proper starting point of human thought, and that Malebranche, not Cousin, was the greatest of French religious philosophers. Since Gioberti's works were put on the Index, largely because of his alleged "ontologism," Brownson was also tarred with that brush despite his efforts to "correct" Gioberti's errors.[9]

Combining these various emphases in his own way, Brownson became again a bold and distinctive thinker. He continued to believe that religion and politics were virtually inseparable and that Catholicism was a fulfillment of American ideals, though his dual commitment to Calhoun's constitutional thought and to the antirevolutionary school of Catholic thinkers (notably Joseph de Maistre) gave a very conservative organicistic tincture to his advocacy. In the country's great sectional controversy he held a strong "Southern" position even through the Dred Scott affair. Only in the campaign of 1860 did he become an antislavery Unionist—and remain so throughout the war, to the great irritation of Archbishop Hughes and many powerful members of the hierarchy. During these years Brownson also became more liberal on theological issues, a fact which he documented in his one systematic work *The American Republic: Its Constitution, Tendencies, and Destiny* (1866). This work shows the continuing hold of Leroux, Gioberti, and Maistre on his thought, but it is also a ringing affirmation of democratic ideals. Yet Pius IX's sweeping condemnation of liberalism in *Quanta Cura* and its accompanying Syllabus of Errors created difficulties for Brownson. It seemed to sustain the view of his Catholic critics and hence reduced the influence of his best political thinking.

Brownson's lifetime literary production was enormous, running to twenty large volumes in the collected *Works;* and almost to the end of his life, his powers of analysis and expression remained impressive. But his influence was small, especially after 1844, and especially among Catholics. His "Ameri-

9. Ontologism was a heresy which consisted of carrying the ontological argument to undue lengths, so as to assert that the primary or fundamental operation of intellect is the direct intuition of Being, identified as God. It was a view which nineteenth-century currents of philosophical idealism often encouraged.

canism," his hostility to the Jesuits, and his condescending attitudes toward immigrant culture offended Roman Catholics at every level. His harshly stated defenses of papal infallibility and the church's authority struck Catholics as impolitic and Protestants as outrageous. The acerbity of his attacks offended everyone. Perhaps a realization of these shortcomings had something to do with his discontinuance of his *Review* for a decade. After 1873 he did reassert the ultra-orthodoxy of his early Catholic period, but at his death disappointment and bitterness loomed large in his thoughts. Ten years later, in a fitting tribute to an immensely creative but unappreciated thinker, his remains were reinterred in the Chapel of the Sacred Heart at the University of Notre Dame.

Isaac Hecker

Isaac Hecker (1819–88) was a convert of Brownson's before either of them encountered Catholicism, and despite many differences, their later lives ran in parallel channels as interpreters and defenders of the Roman Catholic church in democratic America. Both of them were just as interested in changing the attitudes of their adopted church as the Protestantism they left behind.

Born in New York to a modestly situated family of German immigrants, Hecker was first a Methodist. Very early his concern for the plight of working men had led him to be active in the antimonopoly faction of the Locofoco Democrats. He attended a lecture by Brownson in 1841, and from this meeting grew other associations that took Hecker to Boston, Concord, and finally, to both Brook Farm and Bronson Alcott's utopian fiasco at Fruitlands. Intensely contemplative and religious by nature, Hecker was drawn to Catholicism for quite different reasons than was Brownson, though it was the latter's advocacy that triggered his own. He entered the Roman church on 2 August 1844, more than two months before his mentor, and in the following summer, along with two recent converts from the Episcopal church, he sailed for Saint Trond in the Netherlands for his novitiate as a Redemptorist. A year later he took his vows, and in October 1849 he was ordained.

Hecker had chosen to enter the austere and ascetic Congregation of the Most Holy Redeemer (Congregatio SS. Redemptoris), founded in 1732 by Saint Alphonsus Liguori "to preach the gospel to the poor." During the succeeding century the Redemptorists had spread rapidly into most European countries, and in the United States they were performing valuable services among German immigrants. Almost immediately upon his return to the United States in 1851, Hecker became an active member of a Redemptorist team of parish revival missioners that achieved outstanding success in almost every part of the country. Hecker was even one of the three nominees for the vacant see of Natchez.

The appointment of a new Redemptorist provincial in 1854, however, brought these activities to an end; and in the midst of the ensuing difficulties, a small group of young American members of the order (all of them converts) informally delegated Hecker to present their case to the order's rector major in Rome. This group desired to found a distinctly American house where the English language (rather than German) would be used, and which would have as its primary missionary concern American Protestants rather than immigrants. But the rector major of the order was of another mind. For having made the visit to Rome Hecker was charged with disobedience, and dismissal would have shortly followed had he not won powerful support in the papal Curia. At last, after seven anxious months of working and waiting, he and his four associates received from Pope Pius IX a dispensation from their Redemptorist vows and permission to organize a new congregation with a specific mission to non-Catholic America.

After his Roman triumph Hecker sailed for America in April 1858, and by July he had won Archbishop Hughes's approval of the "Program of Rule" for the Congregation of Missionary Priests of Saint Paul the Apostle (CSP). Except for the substitution of a voluntary agreement in place of vows, the rule provided for a religious life very similar to that of other orders, notably the Redemptorists. At first their work consisted largely of preaching missions to Catholic parishes; but in 1859, having been assigned a parish in (then) suburban 59th Street, they occupied their own convent and church in New York. In 1865 they founded the *Catholic World* (the church's first general monthly magazine) and soon afterward they began a tract society to distribute far and wide the appealing and highly intelligent apologetic literature for which the Paulist Fathers were rapidly becoming famous. In all of their work they sought to confront Protestant America not with the traditional type of polemic, but with the sort of positive and comforting message that characterized Father Hecker's two most widely read books: *Questions of the Soul* (1855) and *Aspirations of Nature* (1857). Through these books and countless other articles Hecker accomplished what Brownson with his fiery, dogmatic temperament never could: a genuinely persuasive portrayal of Catholicism as an answer to man's spiritual dilemmas and as a fulfillment and guarantee of democracy's highest ideals.

Even while commending his church to non-Catholics, Hecker and his Paulists became an extremely significant force within the Roman church as champions of a revised estimate of America, with its freedom, voluntary churches, and church-state separation, as an environment for Roman Catholicism. "Heckerism," to use a term that later gained controversial currency, became a recognizable point of view. Its foundation, of course, was a firm commitment to the dogmatic tradition; Hecker was not a "Minimalist" in doctrinal matters as was sometimes charged, and certainly not a Modernist. The closest he came to doctrinal revision was in the field of ethics, where he accented the "active" virtues rather than the "passive" emphasis of classic monasticism; and with regard to the Holy Spirit, where he stated his views so fervently that some suspected a depreciation of the instituted church. Like many American bishops, Hecker thought that the constitutions on papal infallibility of the Vatican Council of 1869–70 were inopportune and unnecessary. His greatest influence undoubtedly resulted from the Paulists' central campaign, which was at once reformatory and apologetic: to increase the rapport of the Roman Catholic church with democratic institutions and with modern modes of thought. Probably no nineteenth-century Roman Catholic in America so clearly foreshadowed the *aggiornamento* which Pope John XXIII would begin to call for when he became pope—on the centenary of the Paulists' founding.

When Hecker died in 1888 the Paulists were occupying their new church in New York, then the city's largest after Saint Patrick's Cathedral. The congregation continued to show modest but steady growth. At the turn of the century they numbered over 70 priests (in addition to novices and seminarians), and by 1965 this number had risen to 265. From the start, however, Paulist influence had never been a function of the order's size. During most of its first century it was a leading force in the "Americanist" movement in the church. Contributing much to Paulist effectiveness was the Apostolic Mission House founded in 1902 at Catholic University in Washington, D.C., to train priests for the apostolate to non-Catholic America. Its founder and rector was Father Walter Elliott (1842–1928), a Roman Catholic lawyer and Civil War veteran whom Hecker had won for the Paulist priesthood in 1867. Few did more than he to continue the congregation's spirit and aims after Hecker's death. Elliott also did much to extend Hecker's personal influence beyond the grave, with his *Life of Father Hecker* in 1891. The translation of this book into French made "Heckerism" the focus of international controversy. The dramatic series of events that constitute the great Americanism crisis, however, is the concern of a later chapter in this history.

34
ANTI-CATHOLICISM AND THE NATIVIST MOVEMENT

During the first half of the nineteenth century the Roman Catholic church in the United States ceased to be a persecuted, numerically insignificant body and became the largest church in the country. Due to this unexpected shift in the nation's denominational equilibrium, America experienced the most violent period of religious discord in its history. Local, state, and national politics became involved, and in a culminating phase of the struggle, a bitter and secretive form of anti-Catholic nativism reached the very threshold of national power. Never before or since have religion and American politics been more explicitly interrelated, nor has ethnic conflict reached such ugly dimensions.

The basic reasons for such eruptions are not altogether mysterious. The inner security of individuals rests upon a sense of group identity. Groups define themselves against other groups. People are also disturbed by rapid social change. When one of the transitional factors is a rapidly accelerating immigration rate which disrupts established group relationships, a strong response is likely to ensue. Xenophobia is thus latent in almost every self-conscious people, and especially near the surface in a country which has only recently achieved full national status and which is vigorously engaged on many fronts in asserting its special character and destiny.

Within the Roman Catholic church itself, ethnic tensions played an exceedingly active role. Even distinguished prelates heightened the unrest; and during the heyday of trusteeism these fears and jealousies flared up in a continual series of power struggles. From New York to Charleston, and as far west as Saint Louis and New Orleans, Americans beheld a bitter struggle between French, Irish, and German elements in the Roman Catholic church. When conflicts of such intensity could break out *within* Catholicism, it is scarcely surprising that more violent conflicts and fiercer disagreements should arise between this increasingly assertive church and the great body of non-Catholic Americans.

A full explanation of American nativism and anti-Catholicism, however, requires consideration of peculiarly American factors. The subfoundation of nativism was the militant religious tradition which had been a basic element of Anglo-American thinking since the days when Queen Elizabeth led the Protestant cause against Philip of Spain and all the allies of popery. This sentiment became still more explicit and fervent among the Puritans, who carried it in one form or another to all the American colonies. Here it was kept alive by the imperial threat of France and Spain. These attitudes nourished the view that the United States had a special responsibility to realize its destiny as a Protestant nation. Emotional revivalism intensified such views even as it emptied them of doctrinal content. Finally, to many Protestants who were distressed by intersectarian conflict, anti-Catholicism offered a motive for Protestant solidarity and reunion.

To this aggressive Puritanic impulse was added the characteristic bias of the Enlightenment, which was, if anything, more negative. To a *philosophe* like Thomas Jefferson, the Roman Catholic church was simply the most powerful—and therefore the most dangerous—institutionalization of medieval superstition, sectarian narrowness, and monarchical despotism in religion. This "enlightened" form of anti-Catholicism figured prominently in the denunciation of the Quebec Act by the First Continental Congress, and it persisted long after the revolutionary era.

Resting on these foundations was the somewhat rambling structure of the American Protestant "quasi-establishment," which was enjoying its heyday of public influence between 1815 and 1860. Its moral attitudes and basic teachings were honored by lawmakers, and dominated newspapers and textbooks. The faculties and curriculum of the public schools and even state universities were molded according to its specifications. Any threat to this establishment, needless to say, would be strenuously resisted. There were also social, political, and economic factors which intensified group conflict.

The social factor was probably foremost: urban concentrations of working people were an obvious intrusion on the traditional patterns of American life. America's middle and upper classes would have reacted with consternation even if this new segment of society had been drawn entirely from older American stock (as indeed it was in some areas). The disruption of America's agrarian dream could not but disturb even the most thoughtful and humane. Protestant reformers had for years been castigating the strong thirst for gin and the disorderliness of the "lower orders," but now immigration and the growth of cities added an identifiable brogue and a new religious dimension to the old problem.

Political fears enlarged and stimulated this intolerance. The Federalist–National Republican–Whig tradition of American conservatism was put under severe strain by the widening popular base of politics. Every immigrant ship at the wharf made the older political elites more apprehensive about the country's future. With the politically adept, ideologically united Irish strengthening the Democratic hosts of Jackson and Van Buren, it seemed that decency, order, justice, and sound social principles (i.e. a conservatively structured society) were doomed. Since the Democratic party was far better geared (both ideologically and organizationally) to mobilize the immigrant population, a strong temptation to exploit popular fears was placed before opposition aspirants, and many political leaders, as well as voters, quickly yielded.

It may be stated parenthetically that the political needs and the fears of a conspiracy against democratic institutions which brought nativism into the anti-Jacksonian camp also fostered the anti-Masonic movement. The Christian opposition to Masonry was of long standing; and in 1798, when Jeffersonianism and the "French mania" were undermining the Federalist order, Jedidiah Morse of anti-Unitarian fame had raised the specter of subversion by the Bavarian Illuminati. In 1827 the old antipathy for the Masonic Lodge broke out again when William Morgan of Batavia, New York, was abducted and apparently murdered for exposing lodge secrets. Even the Book of Mormon reflects this uproar.[1] With much aid from evangelical ministers, William Henry Seward of New York, Thaddeus Stevens of Pennsylvania, John Quincy Adams of Massachusetts, and many opponents of Jackson in other states harnessed the resultant anti-Masonism into an effective political movement. It proved powerless on the national level, and by 1831 its independent life was almost over; but its great popularity in several states provided considerable voting strength to the Whig party. Soon Mormonism itself became the object of sustained attack because it, too, seemed to subvert American democratic aspirations and to violate prevailing views of religious orthodoxy.

1. For references to secret societies in the Book of Mormon, see Helaman 6:18, 19–26; Ether 8:15–26, and many other passages. During the Nauvoo period, on the other hand, Joseph Smith showed a positive interest in the secrecy and ceremonial aspects of Masonry. In this respect he reflected a propensity of vast numbers of Americans who before long would be flocking not only to Masonic lodges, but to many other national lodge organizations and (in the colleges) to various secret fraternities. Lodges as such soon ceased to be an object of concerted criticism except from the Catholic and Lutheran churches. For many they seemed to satisfy social needs and a yearning for rites and ceremonies that Protestantism lacked. For many others they seem to have provided a religious alternative to the churches.

In the North a very similar countersubversionary campaign was directed against the "Slavocracy" on the grounds that it was the slaveholder's conspiracy with designs on ultimate governmental power. Anti-Masonry proved to be the most ephemeral of these crusades, yet the gravitation of all four toward the Republican party when it was formed points to the existence of a certain ground beneath them.

Finally, there were economic pressures. The influx of cheap labor brought an outcry, and often outright violence, from those who suffered from it—or thought they did. Later in the nineteenth century, neither the pope nor the American hierarchy of the Roman church could force German-American laborers to welcome Polish or Italian Catholic immigrants to their society or to their churches. In the twentieth century some of the harshest behavior toward Negroes and Puerto Ricans has come from the whites and blacks who were most imperiled by competition in the labor market. In the Jacksonian period, native American labor reacted to the Irish immigrants in a similar manner, making them objects of derision and aggression. To make matters worse, the immigrants were often jobless, and thus they began to fill the almshouses of coastal cities and to require a large proportion of the funds available for charity. By 1837 there were 105,000 paupers in the country, of whom perhaps half had immigrated recently. New York City alone in that year devoted $280,000 to their care.

In summary, it may be said that the lot of the immigrant has rarely been made easy by the receiving population, and that there were many factors in the American situation during the first half of the nineteenth century which conduced to make his plight harder than usual. Given the swiftly increasing immigration rate, these factors provided the materials for a sordid chapter in the nation's history. Yet it is equally important to bear in mind that most Americans favored immigration until the twentieth century, despite many campaigns to close the gates. One of the most remarkable facts about America's nativism was its inability to obtain significant supporting legislation. When successive showdowns came, the force of the movement proved illusory. Too many Americans, it seemed, always loved—or needed—the "foreigners."

ANTI-CATHOLIC AGITATION

Colonial history is full of overt and explicit anti-Catholicism. In the seventeenth century, as the Protestant obverse of Louis XIV's fierce dragonnades against the Huguenots, American Catholics faced disabilities in every colony, even Maryland. In some cases this legislation was supported by the very Huguenots who had fled France for their lives. After 1688 the principle of toleration emerging from the Anglo-American experience of religious pluralism gradually began to find practical expression, and the development of the idea of equality during the American Revolution produced further moderating effects. Even so, seven of the original thirteen colonies carried some kind of anti-Catholic legislation into the national period, the Bill of Rights notwithstanding.

Late in the 1820s, however, a new kind of anti-Catholic mood began to flow in American life, gradually changing its form and becoming increasingly political both in action and in ideology. Religious and political adventurers, profit seekers, publicity hounds, fanatics, opportunists, "joiners" of all kinds, and some men who in retrospect seem almost mad played their unseemly roles. Yet respectable church leaders did not avoid the fray, abetted by the great interdenominational voluntary associations and puritanical movements for temperance and Sabbath reform. Even the founding of the Evangelical Alliance in 1846 must be understood in this context. Horace Bushnell worked for its formation chiefly on anti-Catholic grounds, and he expressed his disgust when it adopted more positively evangelical aims. The Lutheran proponent of the alliance, Samuel S. Schmucker, also combined nativism with his desires for a "fraternal union" of Protestant churches, though in actuality the alliance took a very elevated stand on this issue. The essential unity of the "Protestant Crusade," however, and the peculiar ways in which it differs from colonial anti-Catholicism can be perceived only in a survey of its history down to the eclipse of the movement by the slavery issue, secession, and war.

As the immigrants kept coming and the Roman church kept growing, grave doubts about the future of American democracy began to displace the earlier optimism. During the 1820s, when the battle began to reach new heights of intensity and new depths of vulgarity, other catalysts besides immigration statistics began to have their effect. In 1827 Pope Leo XII announced a papal jubilee. In 1829 the First Provincial Council not only made the growth of American Catholicism manifest, but also castigated the King James Version of the Bible and encouraged the founding of parochial schools. In the same year the English Catholic Emancipation Bill provoked a tremendous outpouring of "No Popery" literature which quickly made its way into the United States and Canada.

As a result of such provocations, churches joined individuals in protest. In their pastoral letter of 1829 the Episcopal bishops warned of papist perils. The many evangelical periodicals founded to advance the Second Awakening gave increasingly more space to anti-Catholic writings. The very influential *New York Observer* (founded 1823) was particularly active in this cause, and it was joined in the next decade by a considerable brood of specifically nativist magazines. The *Protestant,* founded in 1830 by George Bourne, has the dubious distinction of chronological priority, though it soon gave place to the *Protestant Vindicator,* founded in 1834 by the Reverend William Craig Brownlee. This Dutch Reformed minister, who for several years had been the leading light in New York anti-Catholic circles, further augmented his influence in 1836 by helping to found the American Society to Promote the Principles of the Protestant Reformation. Organized along the interdenominational lines which had become standard for almost all evangelical and reformatory causes of the period, this was a voluntary association with a national agency and local auxiliary societies. The *Protestant Vindicator* became its official organ.

Roman Catholic publications naturally took up the gauntlet. The *United States Catholic Miscellany,* founded in 1822 by Bishop John England of South Carolina, was among the earliest—and most elevated. It was soon joined by vigorous papers in Boston, Philadelphia, and New York, and in 1827 the Catholic Tract Society was formed. Through these and many other channels the controversy was prosecuted in very strenuous terms, with the individual papers often reporting or featuring special debates between well-known figures. As the years went by, formal debates and recognizably theological discussion came to play an increasingly large role, but in the 1830s unprincipled exaggerations tended to preoccupy the Protestant forces, while desperate efforts at correction and contradiction were prominent in the Catholic papers. Bishops and priests had to take time off from the overwhelming problems of an immigrant church to deny (and somehow try to prove) that subterranean dungeons for the murder and burial of illegitimate babies were not standard furnishings in a Roman Catholic convent. So extreme was the tenor of this journalism that the highly inflammatory *Protestant* readily accepted as authentic and published a whole series of articles signed "Cranmer"—which turned out later to have been written as parodies of nativist writings by none other than John Hughes, later bishop of New York.

The horror literature, which often had a strong salacious appeal, found an even more popular outlet in book form. The first sensation in this category was published in Boston, where no Puritan raised a cry to have it banned. *Six Months in a Convent* (1835) purported to be the confessions of one Rebecca Theresa Reed, a well-known figure in Boston because of her uncertain connections with the Ursuline convent there. Despite a detailed answer by the mother superior, the book was widely praised in the Protestant press and became a best seller. Lurid though Rebecca Reed's account may have been, it seemed pale and innocuous when compared with Maria Monk's *Awful Disclosures of the Hotel Dieu Nunnery of Montreal* (1836), which was published (and in large part written) by a group of New York anti-Catholics, lay and clerical. Actually her popularity, as well as the public's credulity, had been seriously undermined by 1837 when her *Further Disclosures* appeared; and no small part of this undermining was accomplished by the even more transparent fraudulency of a companion piece, *The Escape of Sainte Frances Patrick, Another Nun from the Hotel Dieu Nunnery of Montreal,* published by an anti-Catholic competitor of the Maria Monk clique. Miss Monk (if we may call her that) had been quite forgotten by her former sponsors in 1849, when she died in prison after having been arrested for picking the pockets of her "companion" in a house of ill-fame. But her books continued to sell, reaching the 300,000 mark by 1860 and appearing in new editions after the Civil War (and in still another in 1960). It earned, as Professor Billington says, "the questionable distinction of being the 'Uncle Tom's Cabin of Know-Nothingism.' "[2]

But the conflict did not begin and end with mere words. In Boston, several years of mounting tension, punctuated by frequent outbreaks between Yankee and Irish workingmen and a great many anti-Catholic sermons, finally culminated on the night of 11 August 1834. A well-organized group burned the Ursuline convent in Charlestown which until then had been conducting a successful girls' school. The whole nation was shocked by this incident, and a flood of laments and disclaimers followed. Yet the remorse seemed to have been brief and limited. Men of prominence soon made plans for publishing Rebecca Reed's confessions, while the "meaner sort" made municipal heroes out of the men who were tried for arson and acquitted.

Lyman Beecher, whose sermons were at least indirectly related to the Ursuline tragedy, responded by publishing his *Plea for the West* (1834). It contains the substance of his fund-raising messages for Lane Theological Seminary in Cincinnati, of which he had been president since 1832. In this masterpiece of propaganda Beecher opens with a paean to the nation's destiny, an exposition of Jonathan Edwards's belief that the millennium would commence in America. But this exordium is followed by a 140-page tirade which depicts the pope and Europe's reactionary kings, with the Austrian emperor at their head and Catholic immigrants for agents, as engaged in an organized conspiracy to take over the Mississippi Valley.

2. Ray A. Billington, *The Protestant Crusade, 1800–1860,* p. 108.

> "The spirit of the age," which Bonaparte says dethroned him, is moving on to put an end in Europe to Catholic domination, creating the necessity of making reprisals abroad for what liberty conquers at home. . . . Clouds like the locusts of Egypt are rising from the hills and plains of Europe, and on the wings of every wind, are coming over to settle down upon our fair fields; while millions, moved by the noise of their rising and cheered by the news of their safe arrival and green pastures, are preparing for flight in an endless succession. . . .
> No design! How does it happen that their duty, and the analogy of their past policy, and their profession in Europe, and their predictions and exultation in this country, and their deeds, should come together accidentally with such admirable indications of design? [3]

Taking a cue from Samuel F. B. Morse, Beecher put nativism and anti-Catholicism on a common ideological footing; and as this mode of thinking grew more prevalent, the popular strength of the Protestant crusade increased, especially since "native American" organizations and papers were springing up in almost all of the eastern cities due to growing economic pressures, certain honest fears for the functioning of democratic institutions, and an irrational repugnance for aliens.

These years also mark the emergence of nativistic anti-Catholicism as an intensely relevant political force, with Samuel F. B. Morse playing a prominent role. A son of the anti-Unitarian controversialist Jedidiah Morse, but best remembered for his invention of the telegraph and very worthy of remembrance for his contributions to American painting, Morse is said to have been incited to enter the nativist campaign by a soldier in Rome who knocked off his hat as a religious procession passed by. The anonymous letters which he began writing to the *New York Observer* were republished quickly in a volume entitled *Foreign Conspiracy against the Liberties of the United States* (1834). Through many editions it purveyed the theory which Beecher found so convincing—that the Holy Alliance, through the pope, the Jesuits, and the hierarchy, was conspiring to subvert democracy by promoting Catholic immigration to America.

> What then shall be done? [Morse asked.] Shall Protestants organize themselves into a political union after the manner of the Papists, and the various classes of industry and even of *foreigners* in the country? Shall they form an Anti-Popery Union, and take their places among this strange medley of conflicting interests? And why should they not? [4]

3. Lyman Beecher, *Plea for the West,* 2d ed. (Cincinnati, 1835), pp. 72, 117, 129.

4. "Can the right with any propriety be refused to American Christians?" he asked in

Morse became a nativist candidate for mayor of New York City in 1836, but he was defeated because his Democratic background gave him no hold on the Whig vote. A year later, when Whiggery was placated, nativists carried the election.

More significant still was the widening of the political rift between 1840 and 1842 as a result of the school issue. In this crisis Bishop John Hughes took the initiative, demanding a share of public funds for Catholic schools and roundly condemning the Protestant character of existing instruction, particularly their practice of reading the King James Version of the Bible. Thwarted at every turn and ignored by the major parties, Hughes finally entered a Catholic party in the contest of 1841, and taught New York City Democrats a lesson by whittling away their margin of victory. Under Governor William H. Seward, state legislation such as Bishop Hughes had desired was finally passed, but in the city itself nativist political strength prevented Hughes from reaping much more than a reputation for crafty political manipulation and jesuitical argument. The bishop thus did much to bring New York City's "American Republican" party into existence, to guarantee its successes there, and to provide the basis for its expansion as a national movement.

In May 1844 violence erupted in connection with meetings called by the American Republican party in Kensington, a suburb of Philadelphia, and one nativist, George Shiffler, lost his life. This disturbance led to the wildest and bloodiest rioting of the entire crusade. Two Roman Catholic churches and dozens of Irish homes were burned, militia fired point-blank upon advancing crowds, a cannon was turned against the soldiers guarding Saint Philip Neri Church, and for three days mob rule prevailed in the city and its environs. The final toll was thirteen dead and over fifty wounded. Bishop Kenrick felt obliged "to suspend the exercises of public worship in the Catholic churches which still remain, until it can be resumed with safety."

When the same sort of hostilities under the same auspices threatened New York City a few days later, Bishop Hughes acted with his customary decisiveness. He stationed large numbers of fully armed men around every Catholic church, and by such a show of strength (which neither police nor militia had done in Philadelphia or would have done in New York), he prevented ominous nativist mass meetings from turning into anti-Catholic mobs. Thus again, ten years after the burning of the Ursuline convent in Boston, bigotry had resulted in violence.

---

a footnote—and answered affirmatively (Brutus [Samuel F. B. Morse], *Foreign Conspiracy against the Liberties of the United States*, rev. ed. [New York, 1835], pp. 125–26).

THE RISE AND FALL OF KNOW-NOTHINGISM

Before the memory of these tense days had faded, America had a new diversion which also had indirect anti-Catholic implications. On 25 April 1846, shots were exchanged on the disputed Texas border, and soon the nation was embroiled in the Mexican War. Nativistic anti-Catholicism declined in the period from 1845 to 1850 as Americans were swept up in the momentous issues of war and territorial expansion and as economic conditions improved. Despite an enormous rise in the flow of immigration, tempers cooled. Many northern evangelicals turned to attacking the war as a slaveholder's conspiracy. A number of fanatics including William Craig Brownlee retired or lost their prominence, to be replaced by the more respectable type of controversialist exemplified by Nicholas Murray, a Presbyterian minister in Elizabeth, New Jersey. The specifically Protestant element in the movement turned to more positive approaches, especially through existing missionary and educational agencies. Brownlee's intemperate society and journal were replaced by the far more constructive American Protestant Society and its *American Protestant Magazine*. In 1849 the American and Foreign Christian Union was organized with a program for diffusing "the principles of Religious Liberty, and a pure and Evangelical Christianity, both at home and abroad, wherever a corrupted Christianity exists." Its instruments were to be "light and love." Robert Baird's famous book *Religion in America* (1844) is a memorial of its relatively benign spirit. By far the most constructive of such organizational efforts was the Evangelical Alliance formed in London in 1846 by some fifty denominations of Great Britain and America.

While these religious developments unfolded, anti-Catholic sentiment broadened out through the middle and upper classes of "American" ancestry, becoming diluted but not disappearing as it blended with vague feelings of Anglo-Saxon pride and class consciousness. In the process, it helped to palliate Whig frustrations by providing something that looked like an "issue" to a party that had always had difficulty in finding anything more substantial than Clay's compromises, Webster's rhetoric, Tippecanoe, log cabins, and an intense distaste for Jackson. The almost incredible increase in immigration during the late forties and early fifties served meanwhile to give some basis to nativistic concern. It should be recalled that whereas the total immigration in the twenties was 128,452 and in the thirties 538,381, in the fifties it reached 2,811,554. Between 1850 and 1860, indeed, almost a third of the nation's population growth—from 23,191,000 to

31,443,000—was accounted for by immigration. Pauperism, labor-class rowdyism, and crime statistics showed that the country was facing a new kind of social problem, although immigration was merely the most easily exploited factor.

The impulse for nativism's sensational surge came from a secret "patriotic" society, the Order of the Star-Spangled Banner, founded by Charles B. Allen of New York in 1849 and reorganized by James W. Barker, a merchant, also of New York, in 1852. By 1854 internal difficulties and organizational kinks had been straightened out, and the entire "lodge" was set up on a federal basis with local, district, state, and national councils, each responsible for political decisions within its own jurisdiction. Only American-born Protestants without Catholic wives or parents were eligible; upon joining they swore to oppose the election of foreigners and Roman Catholics and to renounce other political ties. If a member advanced to the exalted second degree of the order, he was eligible for office in the order and for nomination by the order to public office. At this rank he had to swear that he would not appoint foreigners or Roman Catholics to public office and that he would remove them wherever it was legally possible. Upon initiation the member was introduced to all the glories of a secret lodge: grand titles, special handclasps, passwords, distress signals, and other types of mumbo-jumbo. George Washington's order, "put only Americans on guard tonight," was a favorite slogan. As a political entity, the body was called officially the American party; but because of their secretiveness and their frequent reliance on "I don't know," they were known popularly as the Know-Nothings.

As early as 1852 they exerted a real, though mysterious, influence in New York City politics. But the national Democratic victory which brought Franklin Pierce to the White House, allegedly on the strength of the "foreign" vote, spurred the Know-Nothings to greater activity during 1853 and 1854. In local and state elections in the spring and summer of 1854, they began to win sensational victories, sometimes snatching offices from unopposed candidates with write-in votes. By fall they were the rage of the day, and sent seventy-five men to Congress. In Massachusetts they won every state contest except in the House of Representatives, where one Whig and one Free Soiler won the right to sit with 376 Know-Nothings. In 1855 they also did very well in Rhode Island, New Hampshire, Connecticut, Maryland, and Kentucky; not much worse in Tennessee, New York, and Pennsylvania; and they very nearly carried Virginia, Georgia, Alabama, Mississippi, and Louisiana. A presidential victory and control of the national Congress appeared to be in sight for 1856.

The true sensation of 1856, however, was not a Know-Nothing sweep but the phenomenal strength of an even younger party, the Republican, which had come into existence in 1854. Ever more serious threats to national unity had been felt ever since the Mexican War and the Compromise of 1850 with its fugitive slave law. Then came the Kansas-Nebraska Act, which repealed the Missouri Compromise and provided for popular sovereignty in the new territories. Senator Charles Sumner said at the time that it was "at once the worst and best Bill on which Congress ever acted; the worst because it was a victory for the Slave Power, the best because it annuls all past compromises with slavery, and makes all future compromises impossible." Since the Know-Nothing party was at best a compromise on the slavery issue, its position did become impossible. At its national council of 1855 Senator Henry Wilson of Massachusetts, an abolitionist who had bored from within, led the party's northern delegates to repudiate the proslavery platform.

By 1856 Know-Nothing strength lay almost wholly in the South, where the party's unionism made it an expression of moderation. In searching for a standard bearer, they could find none better than the innocuous incumbent, Millard Fillmore, whom the Whigs also nominated. Fillmore had joined the Know-Nothing party for what political good it might do him, but he was little interested in nativism and went down to defeat essentially as a Whig. The Know-Nothing party survived only in Maryland and in a few other localities. As a political power it was dead, except for its continuing effect on the Republican party which absorbed—and held—most of the northern nativists as well as the main anti-Masonic remnant.

What explains the rise and fall of the political Know-Nothingism? Taking most obvious things first, it rose because two centuries of antipopery made a large part of the American population suspicious of Roman Catholics, and because immigration as well as many other social, economic, and political specters aroused fears of the foreigner. David Brion Davis isolates another important factor by noting how the Catholic stereotype, like that of Mormon and Mason, embodied "those traits that were precise antitheses of American ideals . . . an inverted image of Jacksonian democracy." [5] One may suggest a corollary to this insight: that the anti-Catholic attitudes of most participants in the antislavery movement were steadily heightened because the Roman Catholic hierarchy remained noncommittal on slavery and almost completely unrepresented in the abolitionist crusade. One subversive power seemed to be abetting the other.

Roman Catholic developments also conspired to aggravate American sus-

5. "Some Themes of Counter-Subversion: An Analysis of Anti-Masonic, Anti-Catholic, and Anti-Mormon Literature," *Mississippi Valley Historical Review* 47 (September 1960): 208; see also Davis's *Fear of Conspiracy: Images of UnAmerican Subversion.*

picions during these years. From Europe came persistent reports of the church's opposition to the revolutions of 1848, including its successful suppression of the Hungarian independence movement which had endeared itself to American hearts. This was brought forcefully to public attention in 1852 by the nationwide tour of Louis Kossuth, who had led that abortive revolt, and by many other anticlerical lecturers, sensationalists, and intellectuals, some of them in exile. These conflicts did not remain remote European questions, however, for the old trusteeship question flared up again in so virulent a way that Bishop Timon of Buffalo, New York, had to place a German church (Saint Louis) in that city under interdict in 1851. When John Hughes, now an archbishop, began agitation for legislation vesting all church properties in the hierarchy, the New York legislature reacted by passing in 1855 a bill requiring lay trusteeship. Then, as if to magnify both European reaction and the trustee problem in American eyes, Pius IX (who had just crushed a republican revolution in Rome itself) sent Monsignor Gaetano Bedini to the United States as a papal representative empowered to deal with the recalcitrant trustees. As an administrator of the Papal States, Bedini had helped to quell the upsurge of Italian liberalism in 1848. This role was exaggerated enormously by all the forces of anti-Catholicism in this country; but even if he had played no role at all in that affair, his coming would have been denounced as foreign intervention. His tour of the country in 1853–54 was a riot-ridden disaster which heads the list of Roman Catholic blunders during this period. Bedini probably stimulated as many Know-Nothing votes as any other single factor.

Despite all these very good reasons for the success of Know-Nothingism, one must not lose sight of the transitoriness of its triumph. It fell so swiftly and so resoundingly because, in the last analysis, the American people were more seriously divided by the slavery issue than by ethnic or religious issues. The latter issues were susceptible to a pluralistic settlement, the former was not; the country could be half "foreign," but not half slave. Had Senator Douglas decided one or two years earlier to run the Kansas-Nebraska Act through the gauntlet of the American conscience, political Know-Nothingism might be remembered as only a minor localized phenomenon. Yet at least two other factors also hastened its downfall: the continual eruptions of violence that accompanied campaigns in which nativists were active, and the inescapable contradiction between Know-Nothing methods—the sinister aspect of a large political party conducting its affairs in secrecy—and the anticonspiratorial ideals which most Americans honored.

The fall of Know-Nothingism was as abrupt as its rise. However deep Protestant convictions about the errors of Rome may have been (and they were held at least as firmly as Roman Catholic views of Protestant error), however thoroughly anti-Catholic attitudes were inculcated (and they were disseminated with a thoroughness that rivaled the indoctrination of Roman Catholics), Americans in general were not ready to deny both their moral heritage and their national ideals.[6] Know-Nothingism failed most completely in the Old Northwest, where immigrants and Roman Catholics were more familiar to native Protestant Americans because they mingled on equal terms and in about equal numbers.

Yet antagonism and conflict continued. Just as anti-Catholic nativism was a blight on the reformist movements of antebellum America, so it would be after the Civil War. Against a background of rapid social change, both nativism and anti-Catholicism (joined in due course by anti-Semitism) would again become ugly realities. Race relations would also deteriorate steadily. A nation of immigrants dedicated to the proposition that all men are created equal would again postpone the new birth of freedom. Americans were discovering that Crèvecoeur's "melting pot" was easier to conceive than to realize. Not everyone wanted to be melted.[7]

6. The parenthetical references in this sentence merely point to the stand-off in Catholic-Protestant relations that had prevailed since the excommunication of Luther (1520) and of Queen Elizabeth (1570). It would be another century before the "revolution" of Pope John XXIII would bring the Counter-Reformation to an end.

7. See the quotation from *Letters from an American Farmer*, p. 7 above.

35

THE EARLY GROWTH OF JUDAISM

In proportion to its numbers, the Jewish community in America was more profoundly revolutionized by nineteenth-century immigration than any other. A tiny group that numbered scarcely a half-dozen active congregations when the century opened grew eight-fold in as many years, largely due to the immigration of German Jews. By 1880 this group had not only achieved a most remarkable accommodation to the American scene, but had institutionalized a new and distinct stage in the history of Judaism.

Jews had been involved in American history from the start. At least two Jews were aboard the ships of Columbus, and one scholar has argued that the admiral himself was a wandering Jew. During succeeding decades other Jews undoubtedly found their way into the American empires of Spain and Portugal. Yet the year 1492 is remembered for other events—events that explain why "Spanish Jews" were rare in New Spain, and why the first American synagogue was founded in New Amsterdam. In 1492 the Moors were forced from their last foothold on the Iberian Peninsula, and in the same year the systematic persecution of Jews within Spanish domains began. The full significance of these events cannot be appreciated, however, without a brief digression on the dispersion of Israel.

THE LONG, LONG HISTORY OF ISRAEL

The dispersion of Israel might be said to begin in 722 B.C.E. (Before the Common Era), when the Assyrian hosts of Sargon entered Samaria, the capital city of the Northern Kingdom (Israel), and carried off thirty thousand of its people, leaving others to be taken captive in later years. When in 586 the Southern Kingdom (Judah) fell, Jerusalem was taken by Babylonians who during the preceding decades had overpowered both Assyria and Egypt. The famous Babylonian Captivity followed, while other Jews established refugee communities in Egypt and still others maintained a disorganized existence in Palestine. Babylonian dominance yielded to Persian rule in 538, when Cyrus the Great took Babylon, and Jews were allowed to return to their land.

Around the year 400 a great work of reconstruction was begun by these earliest of Zionists under Ezra and Nehemiah. They rebuilt Jerusalem and the Temple, and undertook as well a decisive reshaping of tradition, in which Jewish religion inevitably took on a less political and more priestly aspect. The Scriptures were given more definite form and status, and the Chosen People became a religious and cultic entity, a people of the Book more than an autonomous national state. The conquest of Palestine by Alexander the Great in 332 inaugurated an era of limited Jewish autonomy and religious freedom under Greek suzerainty, though this later had to be fought for again and wrested from the Selucid emperors who ruled in the Middle East after Alexander's death. The period of independence won by the Maccabees in 167 was cut short by the Roman conquest in 63 B.C.E., an event which marked the beginning of still another period of heavily qualified autonomy lasting until the destruction of the Temple by Titus and his Roman army in 70 C.E. (of the Common Era).

The historical period between the desecration of the Temple by the post-Alexandrian ruler Antiochus Epiphanes in 169 B.C.E. and its destruction by Titus was marked by outrage, factionalism, and bloodshed; yet in one governmental arrangement or another—as even the Christian New Testament reveals—the historic faith and worship of Israel was maintained. The impact of Hellenistic culture and religion was kept to a minimum, and Jerusalem held its place in Jewish aspirations and religious life. Not even disorganized vestiges remained after 135 C.E., however, for in that year the Emperor Hadrian put down a last desperate rebellion, renamed the city, and forbade Jews on pain of death to come within sight of Jerusalem.

With this ultimate disaster the *diaspora* (dispersion) became the fundamental circumstance of Judaism's continued existence. Yet because the dispersion of Israel had actually begun centuries before, notably during the Babylonian exile, by the opening of the Christian era Jews were gathered in various parts of the Middle East and in most of the cities of the Mediterranean world. In these scattered communities the synagogue, under the leadership of a rabbi (teacher), was the center of Jewish religious life; and in Hellenized areas the Scriptures were often read in the Septuagint version, a Greek translation made by Jewish scholars in Alexandria about 250 B.C.E. It was in Alexandria during the time of Christ that the philosopher-theologian Philo (ca. 20 B.C.E. to 42 C.E.) conceived his great accommodation of scriptural teaching and Greek (primarily late Platonic) philosophy.

The normative force that was to mold the Judaism of the coming centuries did not come from these Hellenized sources, however, nor even from the rabbinic tradition of Palestine, but primarily from those Jews who had found refuge in the Tigris and Euphrates region, the Babylonia of the ancient exile. Here under the lenient rule of the Persians they developed a way of life which produced the Talmudic commentaries on the Law. By 500 C.E. the huge Babylonian Talmud had taken definitive shape; the nature and rationale of Jewish isolationism and continuity were defined. "The law of the government is the law," they recognized; but with due allowances for alien rule, the possibilities for life under the Law of Moses were clarified and explicated. Judaism became more than ever a way of life according to the meticulously interpreted and rigorously applied provisions of the Torah. After 70 C.E. sacrifice and praise in the Temple at Jerusalem were a memory and a hope, as congregational worship in the synagogue, religious instruction by the rabbis, and above all the historic observance of Sabbath and holy days became the fundamental modes of Hebrew religion.

In the Roman Empire Jews were by no means accorded a secure place in society. Indeed, Roman laws governing their status, keeping them off the land, and limiting their occupations were to condition Jewish life in Europe for over a millennium. Yet life went on, and in every province of the empire Jews found a useful though precarious place. Those who found the restrictions unendurable drifted into regions beyond.

Then in the seventh century Islam exploded into the Levantine and Mediterranean world, expanding with dynamic, almost irresistible force. With Persia and the Byzantine Empire weakened, its sweeping conquests began under Omar (634–44). In a few decades the Ommiad Caliphate extended across the Persian Empire to the Indus River in India; and before the new century was very old, Arabia, Syria, Egypt, North Africa, and Spain were ruled from Damascus. Only at Tours in southern France in 732, the centennial of Mohamet's death, was the Moslem advance halted. In the vast realm of the Moslems the official laws against Jews were harsh, but they were so widely ignored that Jews on the whole lived a fuller and freer life under the Crescent than under the Cross.

In time a rich Jewish culture flourished at many points. Saadia ben Joseph (892–942), who as Gaon of Sura was in a sense the religious leader of Islamic Judaism, translated most of the Hebrew Scriptures into Arabic. His monumental treatise on philosophy and faith shows the remarkable degree to which Hellenic influences in Islamic thinkers were transmitted to the Jews. Spain gave rise to a particularly rich tradition. The philosopher and poet Solomon ibn-Gabirol (ca. 1021–58), whose great work *The Fountain of Life* was long thought to be the work of a Christian named Avicebron, carried Neoplatonic thought to exalted religious heights. Judah Halevi (ca. 1085–1140), born in Toledo, was one of its greatest and most versatile Jewish poets. Moses ben Maimon (Maimonides, 1135–1204), a native of Cordova who moved to Cairo, took his place with the Spanish Moslem Averroës (1126–98) and the Christian friar Thomas Aquinas (1225–74) in a great tradition of medieval philosophical theology that did much to extend the influence of Aristotle and Hellenistic rationalism.

Following the Spanish defeat of the Moors in 1492 the Jews were expelled from Spain by royal decree. They were expelled from Portugal in 1496, and the age of the Inquisition and the European ghetto began. Many Jews remained as real or apparent converts to Christianity, though they often persisted in private fidelity to the rites and faith of Judaism. But many of them —nobody knows how many—fled from Spain and Portugal to what refuge they could find in France, England, Germany, or even in eastern Mediterranean countries. In England these exiled *Sephardim* (as Jews of Iberian descent are called, see Obadiah 20) laid the foundations of the country's Jewish community. Holland, however, provided the best refuge, for Jews as for daring thinkers like Descartes and exiled English Puritans. During the seventeenth century, therefore, Jews participated in the great commercial conquests of the Dutch. They were investors in the trading companies which founded New Netherland in America; and in 1630, when the Dutch took Recife in eastern Brazil from the Portuguese, a number of Jews established residence there. When Portugal recaptured Recife in 1654, these Jews had to flee; and some of them came to New Amsterdam. With their arrival Jewish religious history in the United States begins.

JEWS IN THE BRITISH COLONIES

There were no rabbis or theologians among the early refugees from Recife; but since the only requirement for establishing a synagogue is the presence of ten adult males, this presented no problem. As soon as they could secure the right of public worship (the date is uncertain but 1685–95 seems probable) this Portuguese-speaking group formed the Congregation Shearith Israel (Remnant of Israel). By 1729 it had grown sufficiently to build a house of worship. With the passing years other Jews came to America, especially after 1740, when Parliament granted them naturalization rights in the colonies. Fifteen Jewish families came to Newport from Holland in 1658. Though this community may have died out, it later revived, and dedicated in 1763 the distinctive Touro synagogue designed by Peter Harrison of New Haven. Similar communities, largely Sephardic, grew up in other cities, including Charleston, Savannah, Richmond, and Philadelphia. But all of these groups were small: in 1773 the five hundred Jews in Charleston composed the largest such community in America. At that time there were only thirty Jewish families in New York, while other towns probably had even fewer. On the eve of the Revolution there was not a single rabbi in the American colonies. As late as 1800 all of American Jewry probably did not exceed two or three thousand.

Though small, and in some degree because it was small, the Sephardic community in the colonies was distinguished by a high sense of culture and a great competence in the ways of the world. Not all of these migrants were well-to-do; in fact, many were poor. But as a group with greater freedom than Jews anywhere in the world, they soon took a prominent place in colonial life. In manner and dress they blended in with the rest of the people. Although when the Revolution came, like colonials generally they were of divided opinion, yet they tended toward the Patriot cause, and one of their number, Haym Salomon, participated actively. Despite its adaptation to the American life style, this Jewish community retained a devoted concern for its religious tradition of "dignified orthodoxy." (Only two years after the first arrival in America, their brethren in Amsterdam had excommunicated the great philosopher Baruch Spinoza for his daring rationalism, his critical attitude toward the Scriptures, and his nonobservant conduct.) Though no rabbis were among them during the colonial period, the chanters took on the role of ministers and a highly literate laity preserved the teachings of their tradition.

JEWS IN THE NATIONAL PERIOD

The basic homogeneity of the American Jewish community did not long outlast the colonial period. The end of the eighteenth century saw a shift in the predicament of the Jews in northern Europe. A new kind of Jewish immigration began to flow into the United States as a result of these changing circumstances, and it had three quite decisive effects: it destroyed the unity and religious consensus of the existing congregations; it served to turn the Sephardic traditionalists in upon themselves and to enliven their attachment to ancient orthodoxy; and finally, it greatly augmented the number of Jews in the nation. An understanding of these factors and their interaction requires another brief historical digression on the *Ashkenazim*.

The name for Ashkenazic Judaism stems from the reference in Jeremiah 51 : 27 to the kingdom of Ashkenaz, which was probably in the neighborhood of Armenia, but in medieval rabbinical literature was interpreted to mean Germany. The designation was broadened by usage to include all of those Jews whose centuries-long heritage involved habitation in north European Christendom. These people had enjoyed something of a golden age of toleration under Louis the Pious (816–40), successor to Charlemagne; but after that, as the feudalization of Europe proceeded, society became "Jew-proof" and the ghetto with all of its concomitants became a characteristic institution. Regulations concerning these Jewish communities varied widely from one principality to another and from time to time, but isolation, persecution, and the communal existence which the laws required and which the ghetto made possible deepened the loyalty of Ashkenazic Jewry to the rabbinic tradition. As a result, its Judaism was at once deeper, narrower, and less cosmopolitan than that of the Sephardim; above all, its community life and its commitment to the Law was more intense.

With the rise of national states in the centuries after the Reformation, the Ashkenazic community itself came to be divided, though it was still unified by a strong commitment to Yiddish, Torah, and Talmudic study. Jews who moved or were forced eastward into Poland and later into Russia and the Slavic lands of the Holy Roman Empire experienced a fate very different from that of their brethren in the West. In these vast agricultural areas urban ghettos were rare, restrictions on Jewish movement and occupation were less confining, and the transformations wrought by modern commerce and industry were long retarded. The fervent piety and Orthodox ways of this eastern branch of the Ashkenazim did not enter into American history until the great migrations of the late nineteenth century. It is thus the western Ashkenazim in the more advanced German-speaking cultures that requires our prior consideration.

The Germany of 1800 was by no means the unified, heavily industrialized state that it was to become a century later. Social structures and economic life were relatively static. Antiquated taxation systems and inefficient modes of land division prevailed. After the crushing of revolutionary movements in 1830 and 1848, discontent was rife and emigration steadily increased. And since Jews continued to be harassed by many legal restrictions, they joined the exodus in increasing numbers. By 1840 the American Jewish community numbered 15,000; by 1850, 50,000; by 1860, 160,000; and by 1880, 250,000. Another estimate puts the nineteenth-century German immigration total at 5 million and the Jews among them at 200,000, with the largest number coming from Bavaria, where the anti-Semitic laws were strictest.

In the early years these Jewish immigrants were generally poor and very limited in education and social experience. Since they were for the most part unaffected by the newer movements of "emancipation," they were relatively orthodox in belief and observance. Mayer Klein remembered his early days in New York:

> The greater part of the Jewish young men went peddling. There were two or three Jewish merchants who supplied peddlers with "Yankee notions," which they called *Kuttle Muttle*. . . . There was a synagogue in New York called the "India Rubber *shul*" because it was principally upheld by peddlers whose stock in trade was mostly suspenders. . . . All those absent from home hurried to the city on a holiday, in order to be there for the service.[1]

As the quotation suggests, they usually took up the peddling and small merchandising for which their experience (or inexperience) fitted them. For the first time in fifteen centuries, life on the land was legally open to them; but naturally enough, few took the opportunity. Because various types of retail business became their most common occupation, they tended to gather in America's cities and growing towns. Taking advantage of a rapidly expanding country, they established themselves in all parts of the nation, perhaps even more frequently in the South, for example, than in New England. In San Francisco the first *minyan* of ten men was assembled as early as 1849.

Everywhere they adapted themselves with singular success, and the federal survey of 1890 revealed the remarkable fact that by then less than 2 percent were laborers or peddlers, almost half were in business, 30 percent were in clerical or sales positions, and 5 percent in the professions; 40 percent were employing at least one servant; 20 percent, two servants and 10 percent, three or more. Increasingly in later decades as those of higher income levels also immigrated, they tended to identify themselves as Germans, and often participated in literary and musical organizations. As they made the transition to American ways, this group made an invaluable cultural contribution to the country. Religiously considered, however, emigration from Germany to America involved traumatic changes, and traditional forms of observance came under tremendous pressures. Because this trend bore many similarities to European movements for emancipation, American Jews often sought guidance from the intellectual leadership developing in the cities of Germany. The leaders of Reform Judaism thus came to have a powerful influence on the generation or two of rabbis who provided spiritual leadership to synagogues formed by German Jewish immigrants.

What is known as the Enlightenment was chiefly a philosophical movement among the intelligentsia, though of course the economic, social, and

1. Quoted in Louis Wirth, *The Ghetto* (Chicago: University of Chicago Press, 1928), p. 154.

popular roots of this intellectual impulse were exceedingly important. As European rulers and governments became uneasy about the presence of compulsory ghettos and irrational restrictions on Jewish activity and dress, the laws were liberalized. Opportunities opened, and in ever-growing numbers the Jews themselves began to yield to the blandishments of reason and to the lure of political and cultural—though not necessarily religious—assimilation. German Jewry began to follow in the way of the Sephardim, even, at times, in the way of Spinoza. The real modern hero of the *maskilim* (the enlightened) was Moses Mendelssohn (1729–86). Born in the ghetto of Dessau, he very early made his way to the liberal Berlin of Frederick the Great, where he became a friend of the great poet and critic Lessing and won early fame as the "Jewish Plato." Mendelssohn published a German translation of the Pentateuch and became an ardent advocate of a philosophic approach to religion and a thoroughgoing acceptance of modern scholarship and German culture. Achieving prominence as he did just on the eve of the French Revolution and the Napoleonic liberations of Jewry, he made an enormous impact.

Mendelssohn remained—with whatever strain or inconsistency—an observant Jew; but many of the liberated Jews, especially young men of talent, found this very difficult. As they became involved in the liberal political movements aroused by the French Revolution and the revolutions of 1830 and 1848, the amount of nonobservance increased. Some men, like Karl Marx, moved far to the left. Others, like Heinrich Heine, Felix Mendelssohn (grandson of the philosopher), Augustus Neander (the great church historian and associate of Schleiermacher), C. P. Caspari (a strict Lutheran confessional theologian who went to Norway), and Julius Stahl (who became one of the great theologians and apologists for the old order in church and state) carried assimilation all the way to an enthusiastic adoption of the Christian faith.

These trends and difficulties gave rise to the movement for reforming orthodox rabbinic Judaism. Moses Mendelssohn's combination of emancipation and observance seemed impossibly contradictory. Many regarded the subjection of modern men to an utterly outmoded way of life as intellectually impossible or even morally wrong, yet the complete cutting of traditional ties was worse. Facing these alternatives, the Reform movement in Judaism as a broad scholarly, philosophical, and theological impulse gradually began to take shape in the synagogues of urban Germany. At first its concerns were external: demands to the governments of various principalities for a larger measure of freedom, and revisions in the modes of worship carried on in the synagogue.

The ceremonial revisions, which involved the introduction of vernacular worship, sermons, and congregational hymns as well as the elimination of messianic prayers, naturally impinged on old commitments and brought intense conflicts to the Jewish community. This in turn drove the leaders of the movement deeper into historical investigation of the Jewish past. A Society for the Scientific Study of Judaism (*jüdische Wissenschaft*) was formed, and a brilliant tradition of historical scholarship arose. Others turned to the philosophical and theological movements most prominent in the universities, showing great intellectual distinction in deploying the dialectical thought of Hegel and Schelling in a Judaic context. David Einhorn (1809–79), an important leader first in Europe then in the United States, clearly expressed the rationale for reform:

> Judaism has reached a turning-point when all . . . customs and usages as are lifeless must be abolished, partly with the object of retaining its own followers, partly to protect from moral degeneracy. In consequence of the insuperable conditions of life there has set in a violent antagonism between practice and religious conviction which will eventually cease to distress the conscience. The continuance of such a state of affairs would be the greatest misfortune that could befall Israel. On the one hand, the most important ceremonial laws are violated daily, laws which are still considered incumbent upon the Israelite; on the other hand, religious wishes and hopes are expressed in prayer which do not awaken the least response in the heart, and stand in absolute contradiction to the true spirit of Sinaitic doctrine. This must necessarily lead to one of two things, either that the religious sentiment will become completely dulled or take refuge in the bosom of some other faith. Experience has shown the futility of all attempts to breathe life into the obsolete and dead. . . . The evil which threatens to corrode gradually all the healthy bone and marrow must be completely eradicated. . . . Thus we may achieve the liberation of Judaism for ourselves and for our children, so as to prevent the estrangement from Judaism.[2]

Einhorn had been the chief rabbi of Mecklenberg-Schwerin and a leader of the movement in Germany; he had then gone to Pesth in Hungary until his congregation there was closed down after Kossuth's abortive revo-

2. Quoted in David Philipson, *The Reform Movement in Modern Judaism,* p. 347. Einhorn's commitment to German modes of thought was not easily exceeded; but other Jewish philosophers of religion such as Solomon Formstecher (1808–89), Samuel Hirsch (1815–89), and Solomon L. Steinheim (1789–1866) were more responsive to the ideas of Hegel, Schelling, and German romantic idealists, including the accompanying revival of Spinoza's thought. They also participated in the great movement of Jewish historical scholarship which Abraham Geiger (1810–74) had led in Germany. Geiger showed great originality in dealing with historical problems of the coexistence of Christianity and Israel.

lution. The words quoted above were spoken at his inaugural sermon at Baltimore in 1855. In the United States it was the conjunction of leaders of his caliber with large numbers of upward mobile German Jewish immigrants gathered in hundreds of recently founded synagogues which would provide the dynamics for a major episode in American religious history. Perhaps no feature of this German Jewish wrestling with the problems of modernity and tradition was more remarkable than the fact that an almost complete transformation of historic Judaism was accomplished in little more than a single generation.

THE RISE OF REFORM JUDAISM IN THE UNITED STATES

Social distance, linguistic and cultural differences, and conflicting ritual traditions made Sephardic-Ashkenazic relations difficult from the first. As early as 1802 the Congregation Mikveh Israel in Philadelphia had divided along these lines. In New York, where no separate Ashkenazic synagogue was established until 1825, long after German Jews had come to be a majority, leadership had remained in the hands of the Sephardim. But after 1840 rabbis who inclined to the Reform spirit began to arrive. By this time, too, the tide of German Jewish immigration began to reach its height, bringing to America increasing numbers of fully "emancipated" Jews and many liberal intellectuals. Except for a separation from the old Sephardic congregation in Charleston, the first explicitly Reform congregation in America was Temple Har Sinai, organized in Baltimore in 1842. It was followed by Emanuel in New York (1845), Sinai in Chicago (1858), and a whole wave of others. The changes that were initially effected in such congregations had usually to do with external reforms in the order of worship: the installation of organs, the use of mixed choirs, reductions in the proportion of Hebrew used in services, and seating by family groups. Yet in America as in Germany it was clear that even these alterations did such violence to the Law that ultimately a thoroughgoing revision in attitudes toward the Scriptures, the Talmud, and theology as a whole would have to follow. And the most important advocate and organizer of the American Reform movement in this crucial period was Isaac Mayer Wise (1819–1900).

The son of a poor school teacher, Wise was born in a small Orthodox Jewish community in Bohemia where life still followed its medieval patterns. He studied for certification as a rabbi both in traditional rabbinic schools and at the universities of Prague and Vienna. After two years as a rabbi in Bohemia, he came to the United States in 1846 and accepted the spiritual leadership of the Orthodox Congregation Beth-El in Albany, though his own ideas by this time were already markedly progressive. Wise began almost immediately to institute reforms which in 1850 led to a division of the congregation. A major cause of this schism was a controversy with a Presbyterian in which Wise won the approval of Theodore Parker, the Transcendentalist, but not of his own congregation. In fact, like Parker, Wise was becoming a free religionist, interested chiefly in the "permanent" elements of religion, not in its "transient" historical forms. A few years later he would publish a book on the origins of Christianity which showed how deeply he had been changed by modern modes of thought. Eight days spent in the national capital in 1850 completed his conversion, and, as his biographer observes, Washington became his Jerusalem.

In 1853 Wise became rabbi of Congregation Bene Yesherun in Cincinnati, where he immediately founded English and German weekly papers, *The American Israelite* and *Die Deborah.* Three years later, having led his congregation almost entirely away from traditional practices, he published his revolutionary *Minhag America* (American Ritual). In 1873 he achieved another goal by founding the Union of American Hebrew Congregations, a body which by 1880 "was closer to being the dominant organization in American Jewish life than any other organization has ever been." [3] Wise was also the animating spirit behind the founding in 1875 of Hebrew Union College in Cincinnati, and he served as its president until his death, thus fulfilling a longstanding ambition to provide modern American training for rabbis.

Wise was a voluminous writer and a learned man. He ventured widely in biblical criticism and the history of religions—and in *The Cosmic God* (1876), he exposed his deep commitment to a pantheistic theology rooted in German romantic idealism. Yet because his primary interests were practical and organizational, he did not try to produce a broad systematic work in theology. Indeed, his efforts often seemed chiefly designed to increase the social mobility of American Jews.

The more serious theological task was carried out with considerable distinction by Wise's son-in-law, Kaufmann Kohler, who also served as a professor at Hebrew Union College and later became its president. Kohler himself refers to David Einhorn as "the Reform theologian, par excellence." This liberal scholar, whose European career has already been mentioned, was the rabbi at Temple Har Sinai in Baltimore until his strong antislavery sentiments forced his departure at the outbreak of the Civil War. He made his chief contribution to American Judaism as leader of the more intellectual and radical group of Reform proponents, always avoiding ambiguity

3. Nathan Glazer, *American Judaism,* p. 39.

on even the most sensitive problems and following out the implications of his logic relentlessly. He abandoned the idea of a personal Messiah and the hope for Israel's political restoration, speaking instead of the Jewish people as the suffering servant whose hope was for a messianic *age* of charity and truth. This belief was accompanied by an almost complete rejection of the ceremonial law, the Talmud, and the whole tradition of rabbinic interpretation.

Judaism, Einhorn claimed, must be unfrozen and reinterpreted anew in such a way that the Jews might consider themselves no longer a "nation" alien until restored, but as citizens of various countries bound together only by the message of God and his will for all men. He called men to the "imperishable spirit" of the divine Law "whose spirit the Ten Commandments set forth exclusively." Einhorn's austere ethical monotheism seems to have been more deeply colored by the Enlightenment and less infused with romantic motifs than the prevailing thought of his colleagues in the Reform movement. Yet even he would probably have subscribed to the fervent testimony of Rabbi Bernard Felsenthal of Chicago:

> Racially I am Jew, for I have been born among the Jewish nation. Politically I am an American as patriotic, as enthusiastic, as devoted an American citizen as it is possible to be. But spiritually I am a German, for my inner life has been profoundly influenced by Schiller, Goethe, Kant, and other intellectual giants of Germany.[4]

Einhorn did not live to face the concrete issue of secular Zionism, but he probably would have opposed it, as Wise did. At the same time, he was ambivalent in his rejection of Israel's special peoplehood, and for all his radicalism he believed that Jews should retain their collective identity and not marry outside the faith.

The mature position of the Reform on the full range of issues in question was given clear and almost authoritative expression in an eight-point platform adopted at a conference of Reform rabbis meeting in Pittsburgh in 1885. Wise, who presided, called it a "Jewish Declaration of Independence," and David Philipson, the historian of the Reform movement, considered it "the most succinct expression of the theology of the reform movement that had ever been published to the world."[5] The document stated tersely that Judaism was "a progressive religion, ever

4. Eric E. Hirshler, ed., *Jews from Germany in the United States*, p. 51. Bernard Felsenthal (1822–1908) was in 1854 in Lawrence, Massachusetts, but after 1858 in Chicago.

5. Philipson, *The Reform Movement*, p. 355.

striving to be in accord with the postulates of reason" and capable of adapting itself to the advances of modern knowledge. In addition to disclaiming all national aims of Judaism, it disowned the parts of Mosaic Law which "are not adapted to the views and habits of modern civilization." Taking their place in the pluralistic society of America, the conference recognized "in every religion an attempt to grasp the Infinite One." Then in an important reflection of newer forms of thought, they spoke of "Christianity and Islam as daughter religions of Judaism with a mission to aid in the spreading of monotheistic and moral truth." "We consider ourselves no longer a nation, but a religious community," they announced, "and therefore expect neither a return to Palestine, nor sacrificial worship under the sons of Aaron, nor the restoration of any of the laws concerning the Jewish state." Their hope was for a "Kingdom of truth, justice, and peace among all men." The "mosaic legislation" was interpreted as "a system of training for the Jewish people for its mission during its national life in Palestine"; only its moral laws are binding in the present. Rabbinic regulations were dismissed even more summarily. Asserting the doctrine "that the soul of man is immortal," but rejecting ideas of bodily resurrection, heaven and hell, and everlasting punishment or reward, they concluded with a call for participation "in the great task of modern times, to solve, on the basis of justice and righteousness, the problems presented by the contrasts and evils of the present organization of society." [6]

By the time this declaration was published Reform Judaism had almost come to *be* American Judaism. In only three decades, in fact, Rabbi Wise had been able to witness an authentic "second tradition" grow up in his adopted homeland. By 1880, when the Jewish community numbered about 250,000, the Reform body was more lively and vigorous in the United States than anywhere else in the world, boasting a heavy preponderance of the country's 270 congregations and possessing "temples" of great prestige led by rabbis of impressive intellectual power and civic influence in New York, Charleston, Philadelphia, Cincinnati, and Chicago. The movement was bound together nationally not only by a conference of rabbis and an association of congregations, but by a host of other social, religious, and philanthropic organizations. In place after place the little burial and mutual aid societies that had usually marked the existence of a Jewish community had long since yielded to benevolent organizations and charitable institutions. Moreover, an optimistic esprit, a great feeling of confidence in human reason and good will, and a profound commitment to American freedom

6. Glazer, *American Judaism*, pp. 151–52.

pervaded the movement. Understandably, there was also a measure of pride and a sense of achievement; but it led to an equally generous spirit of philanthropy and civic duty.

Yet into this world of Reform Judaism broke two disturbing manifestations in the century's last decades; "the contrasts and evils" dimly foreseen in the Pittsburgh Declaration became increasingly apparent. The first of these events was the vast migration to America of Eastern Jewry. Projected from Eastern Europe by persecution and the disruption of long established ways of life, knowing little of either Spinoza or Moses Mendelssohn, speaking various dialects of Yiddish, and committed to Orthodox observance, these new immigrants would bring a deep and protracted *crise de conscience* to the existing Jewish community. Almost simultaneously, anti-Semitism, new forms of nativism, and the rise of crowded urban ghettos would reveal the dangers of regarding the United States as the Kingdom come.

36
THE ROMANTIC MOOD

"I have at the distance of half a mile, through a green lane, a forest," wrote Thomas Gray to his friend Horace Walpole in 1736, about six years before he began his famous "Elegy Written in a Country Church-yard." "The vulgar call it a common," he went on, but it is

> all my own, at least, as good as so, for I spy no human thing in it but myself. It is a little chaos of mountains and precipices; mountains, it is true, that do not ascend much above the clouds, nor are the declivities quite so amazing as Dover Cliff; but just such hills as people who love their necks as well as I do may venture to climb, and crags that give the eye as much pleasure as if they were more dangerous. Both vale and hill are covered with most venerable beeches, and other very reverend vegetables, that, like most other ancient people, are always dreaming out their old stories to the winds. At the foot of one of these squats ME (*il penseroso*), and there I grow to the trunk for a whole morning. The timorous hare and sportive squirrel gambol around me like Adam in Paradise before he had an Eve, but I think he did not use to read Virgil, as I commonly do.

More than a century and a half later Edmund Gosse would refer to this celebrated passage as "the first expression . . . of the modern feeling of the picturesque."[1] Given Gray's still obvious classical enthusiasms, one can hardly call it a bold announcement of a new spiritual epoch; yet it does mark an unmistakable shift of spiritual temper. More forcefully than Gray, moreover, other English writers would give substance to the change. James Thomson's *Seasons,* Edward Young's *Night Thoughts,* and Richardson's

1. Edmund W. Gosse, *Gray,* Englisn Men of Letters series (London, 1892), p. 16. We have already seen Jonathan Edwards's "new sense of glory" in this context, however (see chap. 19, n. 3).

novels seem almost to have made a heavier impact on the Continent than at home. And behind all of these loomed the titanic achievements of Shakespeare and Milton, whose reputations rose to new heights among the early romantics.

Of the several great alternations of mind and feeling which have convulsed Christendom since the age of the Reformation, none had larger consequences than the many-sided movement which, despite denials and confusion, is persistently named "romanticism." The concept has never been satisfactorily clarified, yet it points reliably and steadily to a broad phenomenon in Western culture, a pervasive mood which manifested itself in almost every realm of activity—literary, philosophical, political, artistic, and religious. And American religious history was involved in this variegated impulse at many points and in very divergent ways. The crisis, in fact, was especially severe for Americans because the most disturbing elements of the new sensibility were seldom indigenous; and they created very painful conflicts for peoples and churches with heavy commitments to Puritanism and the Enlightenment. The young nation was not only confronted by a whole galaxy of bold ideas and revolutionary attitudes, but at the same time it had to adjust itself to receiving influence from new quarters, for after 1815 the intellectual life of the European continent, especially of Germany, began to play an entirely new role in the United States. Scottish and English thinkers continued to perform an immense mediatorial function—Walter Scott, Thomas Carlyle, Samuel Taylor Coleridge, William Wordsworth, and Lord Byron were very widely read; but a major fact of modern intellectual history should be remembered: the nineteenth century was separated from the eighteenth not only by the age of Napoleon, but by the Rhine.

Yet "separated" is too strong a word. The Enlightenment had been an international movement, not simply French, however important France may have been in expressing the movement's genius. So with romanticism. Despite the primacy of Germany, its enthusiasms flowed back and forth across national frontiers with surprising ease.

In dealing with the history of romanticism it is probably more valuable to locate the period by the leading proponents of the new post-Enlightenment frame of mind than to add another definition to the world's overflowing store of abstractions. If this course is taken, there is only one person with whom the narrative can begin, and he is also the one whose works provided the most direct inspiration to those who continued the movement. By living and writing in the midst of the Enlightenment's flowering time, he also illustrates the perils of periodization and shows how the polarities and debates of one age fructify the future. In Jean-Jacques Rousseau, in fact, one finds the first major romantic, one might even say the movement's founder, among the *Encyclopédistes* and *philosophes* of the *ancien régime.*

ROMANTIC PRECURSORS

Jean-Jacques Rousseau (1712–78)

What was for Thomas Gray a moment of exhilaration through which the older voices of Milton and Virgil continued to speak became for Rousseau the passionate concern of an agonized lifetime. He is uniquely the source, the self-supplying fountainhead, of a new spiritual tendency in Western thought. A wandering son of Geneva, Rousseau was a music copyist by trade and a discerning writer on music. He is now most often remembered for the social and political theories announced in *The Social Contract* and related treatises, but the writings which contributed most to his fame while he lived and which did most to promote a major shift in later attitudes were those which criticized the artificialities of civilization and dealt with man's relation to nature, with human selfhood, and with the essence of true religion: *La Nouvelle Héloïse* (1761), *Émile* (1762), and his posthumously published *Confessions* and *Rêveries.* What Rousseau protests—through his own sin and spitefulness—is the goodness of man; through the buffeting of history that foils his every purpose he posits the freedom of man, and through the miseries of perpetual homelessness, the peace that comes from communion with Nature and with God. Out of some secret center of himself he came like a missionary to the eighteenth century, denouncing its spurious values and calling it to a larger vision of human possibilities. Yet he also wrote confessions that exposed his finitude and failure.

It was in *Émile,* however, ostensibly a tract on education, that he overturned traditional views of "natural theology" even before they had reached their ultimate rationalistic development in the work of men like William Paley. The "Confession of Faith of the Savoyard Vicar" is not another moralistic homily on natural law or an injunction to duty in the Stoic mode, but a fervent call, a sermon on a text from Rousseau which Friedrich Schiller took as his motto, *"Si c'est la raison qui fait l'homme, c'est le sentiment que le conduit"* (If it is by reason that man is made, it is his feelings that guide him).

Immanuel Kant (1724–1804)

Immanuel Kant, a professor of mathematics and natural philosophy in the University of Königsberg (East Prussia), was among the many who gained a new sense of man's active powers from a reading of *Émile,* and this discovery would begin to play a major role in the history of modern philosophy in 1772 when Kant was "awakened," as he said, from his "dogmatic slumbers" by David Hume's incisive assertion that the principle of causality was neither self-evident nor demonstrable, and by his consequent denial that experience by itself can ever validate or certify any inductive inference. Kant, of course, had never believed that induction could provide sure knowledge. He regarded empiricism as a form of skepticism, and to this degree he qualified his relation to the Enlightenment, especially as it unfolded itself in France. Kant was a rationalist; his "slumbers" were those of a man who trusts in the truly legislative and creative power of pure reason, believing that reason could discover truth out of its own resources. Now fully awake, he set out to determine for himself the nature and limits of human knowledge.

Kant accomplished his task in 1781, the year Cornwallis was defeated at Yorktown, with the publication of his famous *Critique of Pure Reason.* As he himself said, this was a "Copernican Revolution" in the realm of philosophy. It reversed the accepted order of human thought, not by making new calculations, observations, and objective discoveries, but by a thorough examination of man's way of dealing with the data. Words so famous should be quoted.

> Hitherto it has been assumed that all of our knowledge must conform to objects. But all attempts to extend our knowledge of objects by establishing something in regard to them *a priori,* by means of concepts, have, on this assumption, ended in failure. We must therefore make trial whether we may not have more success in the task of metaphysics, if we suppose that objects must conform to our knowledge. . . . If intuition must conform to the constitution of the objects, I do not see how we could know anything of the latter *a priori;* but if the object (as object of the senses) must conform to the constitution of our faculty of intuition, I have no difficulty in conceiving such a possibility.[2]

Kant's *Critique,* of course, created a ferment among thinkers, and he extended his influence in successive volumes on ethics, law, value theory, and religion. But underlying the entire Kantian argument are two central doctrines which continue as active elements of subsequent European (and American) religious thought. The first is the revolutionary idea summarized in the quotation above. Kant drew a distinction between the *phenomenal* and the *noumenal,* between the reality which man experiences and the

2. Immanuel Kant, *Critique of Pure Reason,* ed. and trans. Norman K. Smith (London: Macmillan & Co., 1933), p. 22. Passage quoted is from the preface to the 2d ed., 1787.

thing-in-itself. He then went on to demonstrate that man's knowledge, strictly speaking, is limited to the phenomenal world, and that the form or structure of such knowledge is conditioned by the nature of mind and the laws of thought. In this sense man does have a priori knowledge of reality, of *phenomena* though not of *noumena.* Kant's philosophy, therefore, enfranchises the mind, conceives of it as creative and active, as having a truly constitutive role in man's cognition of the world. Repudiating the notion of the mind as a mirror, a *tabula rasa,* or a receiver mechanism—a notion which flowed so ineluctably from Lockean premises and which had been so convincingly developed by Condillac in France—he substituted a notion of mind as a lamp which brings something *to* reality.

Yet Kant's franchise to reason was by no means the unlimited one which Leibnitz had provided (Hume had spoiled that possibility for him). He denied that man's knowledge can extend beyond experience: it cannot penetrate to the noumenal mysteries of God, eternity, and freedom, and it cannot prove or disprove propositions about this realm. Kant agrees with Hume that "natural theology" in its standard forms was a useless enterprise, a position that explains Kant's often quoted remark that he had to destroy reason to make room for faith. In his *Critique of Practical Reason* (1788), Kant developed another line of thought that compensated for what he withdrew and opened up an equally fertile area for further philosophical discussion. Here he insisted that man's moral nature and will testify to the existence of a divine reality, moral law, and human freedom. Wilhelm Windelband is surely not exaggerating when he asserts that "the compelling power which Kant's philosophy gained over the minds and hearts of men was due chiefly to the earnestness and greatness of its ethical conception of the world." [3] By the time of Kant's death, however, a group of young thinkers—most notably Fichte, Schelling, and Hegel—were building a new tradition of philosophical idealism. They not only drew on other "romantic" sources of inspiration, but also entertained more ambitious aims for philosophy than Kant's critiques had intended.

SOME EARLY ROMANTIC THEMES

One of the most exciting aspects of this new impulse was its appropriation of Spinoza's pantheistic conceptions. Several men contributed to this revival but most influential perhaps was Johann Gottfried Herder (1744–1803), who sought both to ward off the charge of atheism and to imbue

3. Wilhelm Windelband, *A History of Philosophy,* trans. James H. Tufts (New York: Macmillan Co., 1926), p. 573.

Spinoza's "mechanistic" monism with the dynamic sense of organic process. These bold notions were gradually infused with the emphasis on consciousness which Kant had licensed. Yet Kant's mysterious "thing-in-itself" receded, and reality was increasingly construed in dynamic idealistic terms as an interrelated organic whole. Subjectivity and objectivity were seen as interpenetrated aspects of the whole. With *becoming* the prime category under which nature, reality, reason, and history were understood, causal explanations tended to yield to teleological considerations.

Yet this recovery and transformation of Spinoza is only one aspect of the romantic flowering. Other streams of thought, scholarship, poetry, and art were also stimulated by a sense of surfeit with the static certainties and artificialities of rococo civilization. The dissatisfaction with formality and decorum which had also been characteristic of the pietistic revolt from the Age of Reason welled up anew, both with and without evangelical motivation. Poets, dramatists, and composers cast aside ancient rules and regulations, while critics applauded their new boldness in self-expression. A new vaunting of the subjective self—the feelings, the intuition, and the passions—was evident. Even "immorality" and freedom from convention became a badge of the new ideas. The ego asserted itself and the demonic was championed. Pascal's old dictum that the heart has its reasons which the mind can never know became a slogan. Nature in its wildness and unrestraint was a wellspring of inspiration. Where the Age of Reason had gloried in its geometrically patterned gardens, the new era reveled in the natural grandeur of mountains and forests. And pervading this entire impulse was an emphasis on spirit that accorded wonderfully with the new idealistic and antimechanistic trend of philosophy. It was a concept that could be blended with traditional Christian thinking about the Holy Spirit, but it was also connected with all the animating forces of man and nature. Because Europeans generally were responding to similar circumstances, the good tidings were proclaimed almost simultaneously in several countries. English readers heard the new message on nature, man, and God primarily in the works of Wordsworth, Coleridge, and—somewhat later—Emerson.

A New Emphasis on History

The discovery and enthronement of history was another major accomplishment of the age. The Enlightenment, of course, produced great historical writing. In Britain alone the classics of Gibbon, Robertson, and Hume attest to that. And Ernst Cassirer devotes an exciting chapter of his great study of the Enlightenment to its "conquest of the historical world." But the overall conception of history also underwent something of a romantic transformation that owed much to both Herder and Kant. The idealist philosophers tended to conceive nature itself in historical evolutionary terms. In the most obvious sense, this brought with it a marvelous stimulus to the historical imagination as well as the rebirth of historical scholarship. And for more than a century, this stimulus had a prodigious effect on nearly every academic discipline. Most controversial of all, a new age of biblical study was inaugurated with Herder's *Spirit of Hebrew Poetry* (2 vols., 1782–83). Knowledge and belief were "historicized." In the system to which Georg Wilhelm Friedrich Hegel dedicated his life (1770–1831), theology, philosophy, and logic itself were turned to the task of elaborating a dialectical view of all reality, natural, human, and divine. For this reason Hegel can be regarded as the philosopher *par excellence* of the romantic spirit.

Historicism had immense moral, legal, religious, and aesthetic implications. Not only could nations and institutions be "historicized" but also every presumed certainty, every belief and assumption, every law, every standard of judgment, every source of authority, and every sacred text. Each had its history. It might even be contended that all such things were historical without remainder. History could disrupt, destroy, and dismay. Yet its vision of the future could inspire and ennoble.

The new interest in history also aroused an intense interest in the past, nourishing the primal romantic instinct that "distance lends enchantment to the view." The remote, the bizarre, and the ancient acquired a new fascination even as historical research provided increasing gratification to the aroused curiosity. The ages which the Enlightenment had found so "dark" were now seen to be filled with grandeur, heroism, and beauty. For the eighteenth century, "Gothic" had been almost synonymous with barbarity, and the medieval stained glass of old cathedrals had sometimes been replaced to admit the clear light of day. The nineteenth century turned with enthusiasm to a Romanesque and Gothic revival, followed by a Greek and even an Egyptian revival. The new scholarship combined with pantheistic enthusiasm to discover profound expressions of truth in the religions of the pagan East—especially those of India. And when this created acute religious problems, it became the task of an historical approach to religion and theology to solve them. History, in short, became queen of the *Geisteswissenschaften* (sciences of the spirit); and because of its emphasis on the social context of human events, history stimulated the kind of studies which we now call sociology. Further, the belief that all reality is in a state of becoming set the stage for an evolutionary way of regarding all nature.

Here then in brief and unsystematic compass is the revolution of romantic idealism as it flowered first and most riotously in Germany, in part perhaps as a nationalistic reaction against an Age of Reason over which France had proudly presided. Magnificently summing up its meaning were the overpowering personality and works of Johann Wolfgang von Goethe (1749–1832). The gargantuan scope of his genius made him a virtual *homo universalis,* perhaps the last such: a revolutionary theorist in evolutionary biology, personification of historicism, novelist, dramatist and poet of classic stature, and philosophical thinker whose personal development through successive stages almost defines the periodization of German intellectual history during his lifetime. Born in Frankfurt, educated at Leipzig and Strasbourg, Goethe became famous in 1774 with the publication of *The Sorrows of Young Werther,* an epistolary novel of romantic despair which took Europe by storm. A year later he was invited to the court of Saxe-Weimar where, in various capacities, he spent the rest of his life. His final work, *Faust, Part Two,* made it clear that Weimar had become a shrine of deep religious significance: a dynamic and mystical pantheism, owing much to the thought of Spinoza, Herder, and Schelling, found its prophet in Goethe. What Rousseau's Savoyard vicar had suggested gains full expression in a view which understands Nature as instinct with the divine. Reason strives upward through its material forms to the organism in which it achieves consciousness. Man's spiritual life becomes a culminating reality.

A New Theology

For Christian thought, the comprehensive genius of the epoch and the "father of modern theology" was Friedrich Schleiermacher (1768–1834). When he suddenly achieved notice in 1799 with the anonymous publication of *Speeches on Religion to Its Cultured Despisers,* Schleiermacher was a little-known chaplain to a Berlin hospital. The son of an army chaplain, he received his education and seminary training in the schools of a small pietistic sect. At the University of Halle he became engrossed in the study of Kant, and later, in Berlin, he was associated with a brilliant circle of philosophical and literary personalities, leaders in the German romantic movement. In this environment he came to his central conviction that religion is a deeply experiential reality, a sense of the Infinite, an element of man's spiritual life without which aesthetic, philosophic, and ethical concerns were but empty husks. After leaving Berlin to proceed with his great translation of Plato and to lecture at Halle, he returned to Berlin in 1807 where he became a remarkably successful preacher at Trinity Church.

In 1810 he was appointed professor of theology in the new University of Berlin.

During the years which followed, Schleiermacher's thought deepened as he elaborated and applied his famous contention that the essence of all religion is a feeling of absolute dependence upon God, and that the religious consciousness is a primary object of theological inquiry. After some important work in historical criticism of the New Testament, Schleiermacher produced in 1822 his magnum opus, *The Christian Faith.* Reiterating his basic motif that living experience—an immediate awareness of God and of man's dependence on him—is the heart of religion and the source of all religious beliefs and institutions, he goes on in this work to distinguish Christian experience from the common element in all religion, on the basis that the person of Jesus Christ defines Christian dependence and awakens the awareness of sin and grace. On this central christological affirmation he reinterpreted Christian doctrine and elaborated his understanding of the Church as a community of such awareness. Thus at one stroke, Schleiermacher removed Christianity from the traditional arena of apologetics by establishing it as an experience which is *sui generis* and which can be understood only through itself. At the same time he transformed theology into an "empirical science" with its own data and its own mode of treating the data, though it must also be said that he simultaneously opened it to the objection that religious faith is only the psychological projection of one's own inner hopes and desires. It is difficult to overstate the crucial place which he occupies in the development of modern Christian thought, or to gainsay the assertion of his admiring colleague Augustus Neander, who is himself remembered as "the father of modern church history": "From [Schleiermacher] a new period in the history of the Church will one day take its origin." Only one qualification need be added: Schleiermacher inescapably stands with Hegel. The two together express the central dialectic of romantic religion.

THE RISE OF ROMANTICISM IN FRANCE

The *Sturm und Drang* of intellectual, literary, and religious transition which actually brought the "romantic movement" into existence was not exclusively a German experience. France could claim the patriarch of the spiritual revival, Rousseau. And it was the destiny of France to culminate the revolutionary process that Cromwell and George Washington had anticipated, and which is *the* great background event of all romanticism. But only after the violent changes wrought by the French Revolution, the

Napoleonic wars, and the Restoration did France undergo a spiritual renaissance similar to that in Germany. By then it had felt the effects of Madame de Staël's remarkable book *Germany* (1810), which remains one of the most contagious affirmations of the new spirit that has ever been written. The impact of her "gospel" would soon be strengthened by the work of her sometime lover, Benjamin Constant, whose semiautobiographical work *Adolphe* (1816) is an account of personal despair and torment reminiscent of Rousseau's *Confessions* and Goethe's *Werther*. Constant also wrote a five-volume work on religion in which he proposes that the religious sentiment is imperishable, even though it undergoes many successive transformations.

Among the Roman Catholic émigrés and others who had suffered at home during the Revolution, there was another group—one which made romantic enthusiasms and neomedievalism captive to the church. While Napoleon was at the height of his power, François René de Chateaubriand (1768–1848) published *The Genius of Christendom,* in which he developed a new apologetic based on the aesthetic and emotional satisfactions of traditional religion and chanted a magnificent poem to the splendors of the Christian tradition. Chateaubriand also gave brilliant expression to almost every other theme that romantic writers would exploit; but it was left for Louis Gabriel de Bonald (1754–1840) and Joseph de Maistre (1754–1821) to develop the full political significance of the Catholic revival. In the realm of political theory they sought to rally a return to the church around a loyalty to conservative institutions, particularly to the papacy. History and tradition, they insisted, not reason and science, were the keys to peace and social order. Felicité de Lamennais (1782–1854) was at first similarly motivated. Though repudiated by the pope, he attempted to achieve a rapprochement between the church and democratic institutions, assisted in his campaigns by two other romantic thinkers, Jean Baptiste Lacordaire (1802–61), and Charles René de Montalembert (1810–70), whose enthusiasm for the monastic ideal of the Middle Ages was especially remarkable. During Napoleon's last years and the early years of the Restoration, the romantics led a widespread return to the Roman church. Their hopes for a liberal (i.e. constitutional) monarchy were soon shattered, however, and the papal condemnation of Lamennais took the heart out of their ecclesiastical hopes and sharpened the antagonism between Catholicism and democratic aspiration in France.

In many cases only the historicism, the fascination with the Middle Ages, a fervent opposition to materialism, and an immense, often very nationalistic faith in progress were all that remained at midcentury. The historian Jules Michelet and the great man of letters Victor Hugo reveal aspects of this tendency in their long careers. The best instance of the routinization of the romantic spirit, however, is the "official" *spiritualisme* sponsored by Victor Cousin (1792–1867) who appeared on the somewhat jaded philosophical scene in 1815 as a lecturer at the École Normale. After various vicissitudes, he returned from exile with great éclat in 1828, fired by the new philosophical influences he had absorbed in Germany. Until his death under the Second Empire, Cousin was a dominant force in French philosophical education, suppressing the materialism of the *philosophes* and inspiring a great movement of historical research. Cousin's "Eclectic Philosophy" actually never strayed far from the safe and sound principles of his first love, the Scottish common-sense philosophy; yet, perhaps because of this very moderation, it had a provocative impact on the early Transcendentalists in America.

ROMANTICISM IN GREAT BRITAIN

Not long after Thomas Gray wrote the letter with which this chapter begins, Edward Young ruffled classical waters with his *Conjectures on Original Composition* (1759). In this vigorous critical work, twice translated in Germany, Young bade writers leave behind the "soft fetters of easy imitation" and "soar in the regions of liberty." Further, he used and evoked that great shift from mechanical to organic metaphor that became a hallmark of the transition from classic to romantic literature, and which in due course (to borrow M. H. Abrams's phrase) would transform critical literature from a wilderness of mirrors into a jungle of vegetation.

> An *Original* [said Young] may be said to be of a *vegetable* nature; it rises spontaneously from the vital root of genius; it *grows,* it is not *made; Imitations* are often a sort of *manufacture,* wrought up by those *mechanics, art* and *labor,* out of pre-existent materials not their own.[4]

Young had many followers, for discontent with the standards of Alexander Pope and the ideals of the Augustan Age was widespread. One of the more influential was Edmund Burke, who as early as 1756 had rejected neoclassic ideals in his essay *On the Sublime and the Beautiful.* But Burke was to be remembered far better for his success in turning the romantic revolt against the eighteenth century into an argument for conservative traditionalism. He applied the organic metaphor to the whole culture—to society, religion, and above all, to politics. Certain types of reform, such as conciliatory action

4. Quoted in M. H. Abrams, *The Mirror and the Lamp: Romantic Theory and the Critical Tradition* (New York: Oxford University Press, 1953), p. 199.

toward Ireland, India, or the American colonies, he defended as a kind of preservative pruning; but radical change of any sort was to him the equivalent of a blow at the roots. Burke's *Reflections on the French Revolution* (1790) was immediately recognized as a classic statement of the organic theory of the state and nation. As a critique of anticlericalism and revolutionary upheaval, his message became the broad, tolerant, typically British parallel to the impassioned Roman Catholic affirmations of Maistre and Bonald in France.

Samuel Taylor Coleridge (1772–1834)

In his religious outlook, Burke was in many respects a child of his century. Although he defended the established ecclesiastical system, he never reaped the full theological harvest of his basic presuppositions, and the significance of the *Reflections,* therefore, is not nearly so important a religious event as the publication in 1798 of the *Lyrical Ballads* by William Wordsworth (1770–1850) and Samuel Taylor Coleridge. Wordsworth's introduction, in particular, was a virtual manifesto. While its immediate preoccupation is literary, and its major assertions stem from his conception of poetry as an expression of feeling opposed not so much to prose as to science, there are vast implications in Wordsworth's definition of a poet as one who "rejoices more than other men in the spirit of life that is in him." Perhaps he and his fellow spirits felt threatened by science or jostled by the commercial world with its "getting and spending," but they nevertheless were advancing a theological cause. Wordsworth lapsed rather soon into a conservative and uncreative orthodoxy which contrasts almost inexplicably with his early fervor, but Coleridge carried out the revolution they had proclaimed together, and during his later "theological phase," he developed its full import for Christianity.

Not without reason did John Stuart Mill designate Coleridge and Jeremy Bentham as the master spirits of nineteenth-century Britain. What made Coleridge a major figure in British intellectual and religious life was not simply that he symbolized a point of view at the far pole from Bentham's utilitarianism, but that he was a powerful interpreter and champion of the spiritual life. His understanding of religion and theology, moreover, grew out of his own peculiarly vivid and painful spiritual journey. Coleridge was the British Schleiermacher, but not simply because he made the most of a brief sojourn in Germany. After his early enthusiasm for German literature deepened into a full appreciation of the idealistic philosophical tradition, the speculative and metaphysical side of his thinking was much enhanced. Plato, Kant, and above all, Schelling informed his ideas, and he began to identify himself with the "Platonizing divines" who had flourished in England before Locke's day. Convinced that "this dead English Church especially, must be brought to life again," he made Christian thinkers alive to the divine Reason. Coleridge called attention to the spiritual center of man's being and related it to the spiritual center of the universe. "The first range of hills that encircles the scanty vale of human life is the horizon for most of its inhabitants," he said; but he was one of those few who, "sounding the rivers of the vale . . . have learned that the sources must be far higher and far inward . . . [and] detected elements which neither the vale itself nor the surrounding mountains contained or could supply." [5] Though less systematically than Schleiermacher, he also related his speculations to Christian doctrine.

Coleridge's best remembered work, especially in America, was his *Aids to Reflection* (1825), which fended off the encroachment of science and materialism by making a sharp distinction between reason and the understanding. The understanding was merely sensuous, variable in every man, and restricted to a mundane concern for things and animal needs. A person living on its plane is a prisoner. But in Reason he detected the divinity of man. Reason was universal, the image of God in all men, providing insight into the harmony of man's essential nature with the attributes of God. Even the mysteries of the Christian faith were not closed to Reason, and Coleridge was able to justify an extensive apologetic for Christian doctrine which, though liberal, remained in contact with traditional Anglicanism. By espousing his version of Kant's doctrine of the practical reason, Coleridge could also attack the hedonistic ethic of the *philosophes* and inspire men with a passionate moral concern. In this spirit he developed optimistic views of a National Church, broad in membership and led by a "clerisy" constituted by the clergy and intellectuals of all denominations.

Thomas Carlyle (1795–1881)

The secular corollary to Coleridge was the Scottish thunderer and sage of Ecclefechan, Thomas Carlyle. Although he shared none of Coleridge's interest in traditional doctrines and ridiculed the opium eater's philosophy as "plaintive snuffle" and "transcendental moonshine," he could still refer to Coleridge as "a sublime man, who, alone in those dark days [of Carlyle's youth], had saved his crown of spiritual manhood; escaping from the black materialisms and revolutionary deluges, with God, freedom, immortality

5. The quoted phrases are from Coleridge's *Biographia Literaria,* chap. 12, where he discusses the concept of the "transcendental" and in due course gives a name to New England's romantic movement.

still his; a king of men . . . a kind of *Magus,* girt in mystery and enigma." But Carlyle more than Coleridge received his inspiration directly from Germany, and Goethe was "the Great Heart" who raised him out of the Slough of Despond. The spirit of Schiller, Goethe, Kant, and Fichte convinced him that English philosophy after Locke had ceased to be a philosophy of mind and had become merely a genetic history of what is in the mind, with "no word in it of the secret of our Freedom, of our mysterious relations to Time and Space, to God and the Universe." [6] With all these men Carlyle cherished an antipathy toward the church which rose at times to disdain; but from them (especially from Kant and Fichte) he gained that immense concern for duty and the moral will which gave such Olympian grandeur and prophetic force to his critique of the age. As a thinker, he was even less systematic than Coleridge; but his forceful language made his message contagious, and his scholarly historical and biographical works opened broad pathways into the land of his inspiration.

In America, for reasons not entirely clear, Carlyle's reputation was greatest of all. Frothingham was not exaggerating when he recalled in 1876 that "thirty-five years ago Carlyle was the high priest of the new philosophy . . . the dregs of his ink-bottle were welcomed as the precious sediment of the fountain of inspiration." [7] Needless to say, there were many other voices from across the Atlantic that conveyed the new spiritual stirrings to the land of the transplanted Puritans. Most difficult to measure is the quiet and steady influence of Wordsworth. Many aspects of the impulse have necessarily been slighted in this chapter—movements as diverse as the immensely popular blending of historical interest and romantic sentiment in Walter Scott's novels and narrative poems, the great poetic outpourings of Keats, Shelley, Byron, and Burns, and the massive historical and philological scholarship of the Continental biblical critics. Yet something of the spirit, breadth, and power of the total impulse has at least been suggested, and still other dimensions of the "romantic revolution" will become apparent in our consideration of America's diverse responses.[8]

6. John H. Muirhead, *The Platonic Tradition in Anglo-Saxon Philosophy* (New York: Macmillan Co., 1931), p. 130.

7. Octavius Brooks Frothingham, *Transcendentalism in New England: A History,* pp. 93–94.

8. American romantic movements are the concern of chaps. 37 and 38, which follow; but see also chaps. 31 and 33, on Lutheran and Roman Catholic developments respectively. Some aspects of Southern romanticism are treated in chap. 40. Liberalism, in large degree an outgrowth of romantic thought, is considered in chap. 46.

37

ROMANTIC RELIGION IN NEW ENGLAND

Just after the turn of the nineteenth century, Samuel Miller, a Presbyterian minister in New York who was soon to become professor of church history at Princeton Seminary, published his *Brief Retrospect of the Eighteenth Century* (1803). In this wide-ranging two-volume survey he remarks that "it would be improper to pass in silence the celebrated *Immanuel Kant,* Professor at Koeningsberg [sic], in Prussia"; but having heard that "the acutest understanding cannot tolerably comprehend [this profound and extensive system] by less than a twelve-month's study," he satisfies himself with a short secondhand report. Miller also took note of the new literary tendencies evinced by Edward Young, Oliver Goldsmith, Thomas Gray, and the "romantic" forgeries of James Macpherson and Thomas Chatterton. To Goethe he devoted two sentences; to Schiller, one sentence plus a footnote of warning that "such characters [as Schiller and Kotzebue created] ought never to have been exhibited at all," since they "undermine" the virtue of those by whom they are contemplated. Yet even Miller's mild interest in the newer trends of thought was then unusual in America. During these turn of century years the battles of rationalistic infidelity and revivalistic orthodoxy were a more immediate concern.

In Europe, on the other hand, these years witnessed one of the most amazing outpourings of innovative genius in history: Schleiermacher's *On Religion,* Friedrich Schlegel's *Lucinda,* Beethoven's *Eroica,* Chateaubriand's *Genius of Christianity,* Schiller's *Wallenstein* and Coleridge's translation of it, Novalis's *Hymns to the Night,* Wordsworth and Coleridge's *Lyrical Ballads,* Maistre's *Considerations on France,* Hegel's essay on Fichte and Schelling, and a dozen other epoch-making works. But the United States remained a land of romantic silence. One might say that the most promising "romantic" event of the period was the birth of Ralph Waldo Emerson in 1803, though the father of this promising infant viewed Europe's cultural flowering with no more enthusiasm than Miller.

In due course America would awaken from its dogmatic slumbers. The first new nation was becoming aware of its powers and determined to express its genius. Before long writers with less restricted tastes and bolder conceptions of the national spirit were making themselves heard. This meant that democratic individualism was abroad in the land; and individualists, because they think first of themselves, put neoclassical rationalism on borrowed time.

Washington Irving (1783–1859) is frequently credited with being the first to respond creatively. During an extended stay in Europe after 1815, he wrote *The Sketch Book of Geoffrey Crayon, Gent.* (1819), which included essays on "Westminster Abbey" and "The Mutability of Literature," and tales like "Rip Van Winkle" and "The Legend of Sleepy Hollow." Irving was the first American to gain an international reputation as a man of letters, and during the course of his life he turned his talent to all of the less speculative interests of the romantic movement: primitive lore, ancient legend, medieval life, Roman Catholic culture, and non-Western religion, including both Moorish culture and the life of Mohammed.

Yet anomalously or not, it was only in the land of the Puritans that American romanticism gained expression across nearly the full range of its possibilities. The historical explanation of this remarkable development involves no more than an extension of earlier narratives. Economic and social circumstances continued to encourage New England's literary and intellectual life in both the orthodox and liberal communities, as did a remarkably literate public, and the existence of support for libraries, colleges, seminaries and periodicals. And behind all of this was a learned tradition and a heritage of religious passion. New England's romantics belong first of all to the genus of religious enthusiasts, of which Puritanism was another, earlier species. The Edwardsean New Lights were an intermediate factor no less important for the Transcendentalists than was German pietism for Schleiermacher. Emerson stands in the tradition of Thomas Shepard and Jonathan Edwards as an awakener of the sleeping spirit.[1] In the field of religious scholarship and thought the orthodox showed slightly more creative energy; among the Unitarians, meanwhile, the lifting of old Puritan inhibitions about literature and art, as well as a larger measure of doctrinal freedom, provided many

1. The term "transcendentalist" is of uncertain origin and ambiguous in meaning. Kant gave currency to the term, but the early Transcendentalists were not rigorously Kantian. The term, whether used in ridicule or as finally accepted, indicated their concern for the higher use of Reason and its objects: the Good, the True, the Beautiful, the Divine.

advantages. Since the romantic gospel was in one sense a specific prescription for the spiritual paralysis brought on by a diet of common-sense rationalism, the "corpse-cold Unitarianism of Boston and Harvard College" (Emerson's epithet) was soon experiencing a Transcendental awakening.

THE EMERGENCE OF TRANSCENDENTALISM

The religious revolution carried out in antebellum New England is associated inescapably with Transcendentalism, but it arose with equal spontaneity outside of the Unitarian circles usually designated by that name. It was in fact but a distinctive American phase of a great alternation of mood and mind that affected most of Western Christendom. All the spiritual dissatisfaction created by the Enlightenment motivated its quest. All the social and economic forces that underlay the political revolutions in America and France conditioned its form. In a sense, therefore, its origins are unfathomable and its causes are beyond explanation. In a new and culturally underdeveloped country, and especially in a region where the Puritan tradition was, if anything, overdeveloped, the need for outside influence was great.

If fresh impulses had not come in from abroad, American religion and especially the later forms of Puritanism would have stewed much longer in their own juices. For this reason one can ascribe more than symbolic significance to the decision of four gifted New Englanders to pursue advanced studies at Göttingen University.[2] Every one of these students returned to America as at least a temporary apostle for those aspects of German intellectual life that had impressed him most. In their train came two accomplished German scholars to the Harvard faculty. In the meantime many men, both orthodox and Unitarian, were improving their linguistic equipment in growing recognition of German scholarship, while still others, in mounting numbers, followed the pattern of study in Germany. But the real source of excitement was the printed word: reviews and articles in the journals, first and always the great English romantics—Scott, Wordsworth, Coleridge, and Carlyle—but also the works of German and French writers, many of them in translation. In this realm the contributions of James Marsh were extremely important, especially his edition of Coleridge's *Aids to Reflection* (1829), accompanied by an extremely thoughtful introduction, and his translation of Herder's *Spirit of Hebrew Poetry* (1833). Though intended primarily to strengthen the orthodox cause, Marsh's works served almost im-

2. These were George Ticknor, Joseph Green Cogswell, Edward Everett, and (the next year) George Bancroft. Professor Levi Hedge sent to Bancroft his brilliant thirteen-year-old son, Frederic Henry, for precollegiate training—an equally momentous decision.

mediately to arouse the enthusiasm of the more restive elements in the Unitarian and later the Congregational ministry. During the 1830s this restiveness, strengthened by a convergence of many other influences, led to a continuous series of earnest discussions of recent literature and speculative thought in the *Christian Examiner*, the *North American Review*, and other journals.

The *annus mirabilis* was 1836. Not only did it bring forth an unusually stimulating crop of articles and translations, but it witnessed the appearance of Emerson's classic *Nature*. Though published anonymously and dismissed by some as the work of a Swedenborgian publicist, it was clearly a pivotal utterance. When implications of this essay were more clearly understood, Emerson became the acknowledged leader of what Convers Francis was to call the "German School" of American Unitarianism. In September of that year the Transcendental Club met for the first time at the parsonage of the most active of the insurgents, George Ripley (1802–80) of the Purchase Street Church in Boston. Also present were Bronson Alcott (1799–1888), Orestes Brownson (1803–76), James Freeman Clarke (1810–88), Ralph Waldo Emerson (1803–82), Convers Francis (1795–1863), and Frederic Henry Hedge (1805–90). All but Alcott were Unitarian ministers, as were seventeen of the twenty-six persons (including five women) who entered the club during its three or four years of activity. The publications of the club members would alone provide an outline for a literary history of the period, but it was a group which by its concentration of talent, zeal, variegated eccentricities, and intense libertarian convictions would have made history in one way or another in any age or clime. Together with the men and women whom they won to their banner, they constituted the Transcendental movement in New England. Simply because they were so active and so diverse it is impossible to trace here the complicated course of their interwoven careers. Happily the stature of Emerson and Parker as leaders of the movement's two major tendencies allows a simplified bifocal approach.

Ralph Waldo Emerson

Matthew Arnold once stated that Emerson had written the most important English prose of the nineteenth century. The philosopher John Dewey declared him to be the only American thinker worthy of being ranked with Plato. Yet the career of the Seer of Concord creates grave difficulties for every biographer and historian: an early life showing few signs of genius, a short middle period of brilliance during which the renowned intellect never quite disengaged itself from its parochial milieu, and an unnaturally long maturity—Emerson was already a "grand old man" by the time he was forty.

He was born in the parsonage of Boston's First Church; his father, the dignified and cultivated William Emerson, died eight years later, leaving Mrs. Emerson with six children under ten. At Harvard he received a formal classical education under safe Unitarian auspices, accomplished little that presaged extraordinary greatness, and graduated in 1821 in about the middle of his class. Most significant for him were the disciplined rhetorical training of Professor Edward Tyrell Channing (brother of the minister and a man to whom many New England writers were indebted) and the splendid lectures of his idol, Edward Everett, just returned from study and travel in Germany. Emerson kept school for a time, attended the Harvard Divinity School, and in 1829 was ordained as junior colleague of Henry Ware, Jr., at the Second Church in Boston. When Ware accepted a professorship at Harvard, Emerson became the church's pastor—but not for long. In 1832 misgivings about administering the Lord's Supper and a disinclination for public prayer led him to offer his resignation.

Emerson did not renounce the ministry at once, however, but supplied for a time in various churches when he was not otherwise occupied. In 1833 he began his lifelong career as a public lecturer with a series in Boston on natural history. By 1836, the year of *Nature* and the Transcendental Club, Emerson had arrived at his mature position, one which in future years he would perhaps modify, but would never significantly alter. That his views had revolutionary religious implications was only hinted in his plea for an indigenous American literature before the Harvard Phi Beta Kappa chapter in the following year. But in 1838, in his now famous address to the graduating class of the Harvard Divinity School, he cast aside the veil, revealed his accumulated distaste for the prevailing tradition, and announced the Emersonian alternative. Woven into the poetic phraseology of this manifesto were ideas on religion and the "sentiment of virtue" like nothing previously heard in America.

Opening with an evocative yet idea-laden hymn to nature, Emerson moves immediately into an exposition of his most fundamental metaphysical views. The phraseology is deceptive, but the heart of his "sublime creed" is made explicit: "the world is not the product of manifold power, but of one will, of one mind; and that one mind is everywhere active, in each ray of the star, in each wavelet of the pool; and whatever opposes that will is everywhere balked and baffled, because things are made so and not otherwise. . . . All things proceed out of the same spirit, and all things conspire with it. . . . The perception of this law of laws awakens in the mind a sentiment which we call the religious sentiment, and which makes our highest happiness. . . . By it the universe is made safe and habitable." Only against the background of this almost Spinozan monism can one discern the stark force of Emerson's harsh contribution to the controversy over miracles that was stirring the Unitarian churches: "The word Miracle, as pronounced by Christian churches, gives a false impression; it is Monster. It is not one with the blowing clover and the falling rain."

Nor was this all, for he called not for mere assent, but for a change of heart, a consent to Being reminiscent of Jonathan Edwards. "There is no doctrine of the Reason which will bear to be taught by the Understanding."

> It cannot be received at second hand. Truly speaking, it is not instruction but provocation, that I can receive from another soul. What he announces, I must find true in me, or reject; and on his word, or as his second, be he who he may, I can accept nothing. On the contrary, the absence of this primary faith is the presence of degradation.

With his primary faith thus stated, Emerson launched into an indictment of the New England tradition that shocked most of his contemporaries:

> Historical Christianity has fallen into the error that corrupts all attempts to communicate religion. It has dwelt, it dwells, with noxious exaggeration about the *person* of Jesus. Men have come to speak of revelation as somewhat long ago given and done, as if God were dead. The church seems to totter to its fall almost all life extinct. The prayers and even the dogmas of our church, are like the zodiac of Denderah, and the astronomical monuments of the Hindoos, wholly insulated from anything now extant in the life and business of the people. Historical Christianity destroys the power of preaching, by withdrawing it from the moral nature of man, where the sublime is, where are the resources of astonishment and power. . . . In how many churches, by how many prophets, tell me, is man made sensible that he is an infinite Soul; that the earth and the heavens are passing into his mind; that he is drinking forever the soul of God? Where now sounds the persuasion, that by its very melody imparadises my heart, and so affirms its own origin in heaven? . . . I look for the hour when that supreme Beauty which ravished the souls of those Eastern men, and chiefly of those Hebrews, and through their lips spoke oracles to all time, shall speak in the West also. The Hebrew and Greek Scriptures contain immortal sentences, that have been bread of life to millions. But they have no epical integrity; are fragmentary; are not shown in their order to the intellect. I look for the new Teacher that shall follow so far those shining laws that he shall see them come full circle; shall see their rounding complete grace; shall

see the world to be the mirror of the soul; shall see the identity of the law of gravitation with the purity of the heart; and shall show that the Ought, that Duty, is one thing with Science, with Beauty, and with Joy.[3]

With the Divinity School Address, Emerson became America's first "death-of-God" theologian, and it goes without saying that his efforts were not received with enthusiasm by the pillars of church and society. In a later day the address would be regarded as a Unitarian manifesto, ranking with Channing's Baltimore Sermon. At the time, however, the Harvard authorities and the more official custodians of "the Unitarian mind" looked upon it as an affront and a scandal. Nor were they slow to say so; but before considering the Second Unitarian Controversy, which erupted almost immediately, it is useful to consider more carefully the message which had been elaborated so unostentatiously in *Nature* and brought to such precise focus in the address, and which was to be explicated and applied in a long series of lectures, essays, and poems throughout the next forty years of Emerson's quiet but busy life. Such an interruption of the narrative might even be justified by the fact that Emerson himself withdrew from the conflict, retired to Concord, and left the ecclesiastical battle in the hands of more belligerent spirits while he became Transcendentalism's sage and seer until his death in 1882. Because every American lives with at least faded memories of words that were pressed upon him by uninspired (or perchance inspired) teachers in various school rooms, and because some of Emerson's themes have been woven into the fabric of American idealism, his version of the Transcendental evangel remains important. It is also surprisingly relevant.

The essential greatness of Emerson as a religious thinker stems from his acute sense of the modern spiritual situation, its fears, assurances, and hopes. He absorbed the full impact of the romantic movement, and in his capacious and meditative soul blended its special enthusiasms with what he called "the total New England." Yet his vision went far beyond his region. Like almost every American of his age, he was thrilled by the newness of this nation's history and ecstatic about its unique potentialities. "One cannot look on the freedom of this country, in connection with its youth," he said, "without a presentiment that here shall laws and institutions exist in some proportion to the majesty of Nature." The revolutionary quality in his unrestrained optimism was the radicalism of antitraditional individualism. Emerson was bitterly opposed to tradition as such and almost savagely critical of all existing ones. America, he said, "has no past: all has an onward and prospective

3. The address is given in *Theology in America*, ed. Sydney E. Ahlstrom, pp. 293–316. See also the introduction. In the above summary quotation only large omissions are indicated.

look." The past was not a building to be renovated for present living, but a quarry to be pillaged, as he himself pillaged the Western and later the Eastern intellectual traditions, transforming every element he appropriated into an instrument of his boundless hope.

Emerson was no more concerned with history than with tradition. The historicism of the age made no impact upon him. At no other point, in fact, are his relations with Plato and the Neoplatonic tradition more prominent than in his refusal to think historically or to rehearse ancient debates. His essay "On History" (1841) made this tendency explicit; in *Representative Men* (1850) his subjects become timeless symbols, ideal types rather than actors in human history. It was this disposition that drew him, as it had drawn Coleridge, to the "transcendental genius" of the seventeenth-century Cambridge Platonists, yet he ultimately rejected them because of what he could only regard as their bondage to Christianity. Religiously speaking, this rejection of history and heritage makes Emerson a new kind of romantic pagan, one who throws from the temple not only the money changers, but the priests as well, and with them their beliefs, creeds, and rituals.

Even Emerson's more positive doctrines are lifted out of their venerable contexts. Taking seriously his own call for an original relationship to the universe, he made his form of individualism a solvent for old dilemmas. His radicalism stems from the absolute way in which he defined and defended personal autonomy—his own, and that of anyone else who would fully realize himself as a human being. "Nothing is at last sacred," he would say, "but the integrity of your own mind." "Man's dazzling potentiality," in the words of F. O. Matthiesson, was the base of Emerson's credo, and both Thoreau and Whitman elaborated its implications in authentic ways.

Emerson made self-reliance the cardinal virtue. Yet because he understood the self as a microcosm of the All, the various aspects of his thought attain full expression only within the pantheistic view of man, nature, and God which frames his entire message. Naturally idealistic, he drew much from the Platonic tradition; yet he rejects its emphasis on permanent forms and seals his bond with the romantic's tendency to combine post-Kantian idealism with an enthusiasm for Spinoza and the mystic spiritualism of Emanuel Swedenborg. He also commits himself wholly to the organic metaphor: the identity of mind and nature was his first postulate, but he conceived of reality as a dynamic, creative process; growth was its primary feature.

These several tendencies led him to discover a community of spirit with the higher philosophy of India. Brahma and karma and other concepts of Oriental religion entered his thinking. The *idea* of a thing was more important to him than its materiality, yet he regarded no fact as profane—the

Each was taken up in the All, the system of Nature was identical with the Oversoul. This is the rationale behind the remark that Emerson saw sermons "not just in stones but in bean rows at Walden Pond and mud puddles on Boston Common." In this sense, one can say that his "self-reliance" was a kind of God-reliance. This persistent monism in Emerson's thought serves in turn to account for the most serious limitation of his thought, his nearly total unconcern for evil, pain, and death. Sin, despite his New England background, could mean little more to him than narrowness of view or blindness to Nature. The revival of religion which Emerson desired, in other words, would come only when men repented of their membership in the Party of Memory, forswore the sins of looking backward, joined the Party of Hope, and realized their participation in the Oversoul with confidence and optimism. There was a strongly implied corollary, moreover, that Americans were specially "elected" to be thus converted, and that in their response they would fulfill their country's destiny.

The Emersonian message was not a mere softening of traditional doctrines, but a dramatic and drastic demand for a complete recasting of religious life and thought. "Like all puritans, Emerson was an extremist." Some have argued that his was a benign and etherealized form of democratic individualism. Others have pointed to Emerson's parochialism, his puritanic suspicion of the theater, his perennial sermonic tone, his tendency to take the edge off of every sharp romantic insight, his insistence on reducing philosophic discussion to a popular, even a pedestrian, level. Still others have made of him chiefly a "literary" rather than a speculative figure. There is a great deal of truth in all of these observations. Yet they do not fully account for his obvious importance or explain why he is, with William James, peculiarly America's own philosopher. They fail to recognize that Emerson is in fact the theologian of something we may almost term "the American religion." Most important for our present purpose, none of these deprecations explains why such strident opposition should have arisen against him and those who came to share his outlook.

The opposition sprang into action almost as soon as what we now call American Transcendentalism began to make itself seen and heard. In the fall of 1836 Andrews Norton had taken strong exception to George Ripley's approval of new and more liberal views of biblical interpretation, particularly as these theories tended to minimize miracles as proof of scriptural authority. He grew more irate as champions of the "Newness" gave substance to Moses Stuart's old charge that Unitarianism was a halfway house on the road to infidelity. This tempest had by no means subsided when Emerson blew it up again with his demand at the Divinity School that ministers replace their "faith in Christ" with a "faith in man like Christ's." Again Norton was soon into the fray with an abusive public letter. A month after the address, Emerson's old colleague at Second Church, Henry Ware, Jr., now a professor at Harvard, asserted "The Personality of the Deity" in a public sermon. The Unitarian press took up the issue. In the following year Norton delivered and published his *Discourse on the Latest Form of Infidelity;* and this, in turn, involved him in a new public debate with Ripley into which leaped another who took the pseudonym Levi Blodgett. His real name was Theodore Parker (1810–60), and he was the largely self-educated son of a Lexington farmer. From the Harvard Divinity School he had come to be minister of the church in nearby West Roxbury. Around him swirled the second phase of the Second Unitarian Controversy.

Theodore Parker

Parker stepped into the fierce light of public controversy in the same year that Ripley resigned from the ministry. Invited to deliver the sermon at the ordination of Charles Shackford in the Hawes Place Church of South Boston on 19 May 1841, he chose as his subject, "The Transient and Permanent in Christianity." When his discourse was published, a clamor arose among the Boston clergy, including the more conservative Unitarians whom until this time Andrews Norton had tried in vain to mobilize. Christians of nearly every sort were scandalized by Parker's acceptance of German critical studies of the "historical Jesus," including those of the notorious Friedrich Strauss, and above all by Parker's insistence that Christianity did not depend on the actual existence of Christ at all. Theism, as he came to understand it, was "permanent," not historically rooted or "transient." With considerable goading from the orthodox, accusations and rejoinders again filled the Unitarian press. And the controversy grew in intensity rather than waned, because Parker did not retire to obscurity, leave the ministry, or even relinquish the name of Unitarian and Christian. In 1841–42 he gave public lectures in Boston which appeared in book form as *A Discourse on Matters Pertaining to Religion* (1842), followed in 1843 with his heavily annotated translation of DeWette's *Introduction to the Old Testament,* on which he had labored since divinity school days at Harvard. In 1844 he twisted the dagger in Unitarianism's wounded side by using his turn as "the great and Thursday Lecturer" at First Church to offer another succinct exposition of his views on Jesus. This audacity led to virtual ostracism by the Boston Association of Unitarian Ministers.

Parker advanced the battle the next year by accepting the invitation of a group of Unitarian laymen to preach regularly in the Melodeon Theater, an assignment which was soon regularized by their formation of the Twenty-Eighth Congregational Society. For six years after 1852, when the "Twenty-Eighth" moved into the spacious Music Hall, Parker exposed the full range of his ideas to the largest regular audience in Boston. His thought as now exhibited in a vast corpus of treatises, lectures, sermons, and occasional essays was always sharply phrased and activistic in the extreme. Yet he never achieved a reconciliation of the Transcendental fervor, the Enlightened absolutism, the positivistic interest in fact, and the humanitarian reformism that warred for supremacy in his soul.

At least as early as 1852 a decisive break between "Christian" and "theistic" Unitarians had occurred; and as Norton had long insisted, the critical issue was that of biblical authority. In 1853 the executive committee of the American Unitarian Association, "in a denominational capacity" so far as that was possible, separated itself from the errors of Transcendentalism and declared its faith in "the Divine origin, the Divine authority, [and] the Divine sanctions of the religion of Jesus Christ." Many of the younger men, lamenting this statement as the next thing to a creed, rallied to the more radical wing. Many of them, it must be added, were further attracted by Parker's stand on the slavery question, where his continuous decisive statements ranked him with Garrison and Phillips as a major force in arousing the New England conscience. The profound degree to which the Unitarian community was riven appeared in 1859, when Parker lay on his deathbed in Florence, Italy, and the assembled alumni of the Harvard Divinity School voted down a motion to convey their sympathy.

The Civil War temporarily quieted these harsh dissensions, but after the war they broke out again, and from 1865 to 1872 the Parkerites were excluded from the newly formed National Unitarian Conference. After 1867 many of them were active in the Free Religious Association, but gradually their position won recognition as legitimately Unitarian, even though they had by then adopted evolutionary doctrines and Social Darwinism—tendencies which actually made them more "humanistic" than "theistic" in Parker's old sense. By 1885 the theological faculty at Harvard was of their persuasion, and at the century's end Emerson's Divinity School Address and Parker's South Boston Sermon had been fully accepted into the official canon of Unitarian scriptures. Emerson's essays and poems, meantime, had become stock items of American literature as it was studied in the country's schoolrooms and parlors. There can be little doubt that both Emerson and Parker would have objected to being absorbed by the "genteel tradition"; yet the very existence of that mild and inclusive tradition testifies to the pervasiveness of the Transcendental influence in America.

Though always a minority in antebellum New England, Transcendentalists inspired many brilliant persons not mentioned here.[4] Several Transcendental Club members became involved in the celebrated communitarian project at Brook Farm, and some of these, in turn, becoming disenchanted, moved off in wildly various directions. George Ripley, a central figure in the early years, became a New York journalist; his wife entered the Roman Catholic church. Orestes Brownson had gone through a long series of conversions before his Transcendental phase; and in 1844, after several years as a radical social critic, he became a Roman Catholic, as did another brief sojourner at Brook Farm, Isaac Hecker. Bronson Alcott, more famous as the father of Louisa May and other "little women," was the movement's least practical, most contemplative member. Yet his mystical Platonism notwithstanding, Alcott made educational history with an experimental school for children in Boston. In him the "Newness" became most "transcendental." In James Freeman Clarke and Frederic Henry Hedge one best sees the Transcendentalist as a loyal and conservative Unitarian minister. Both men were also scholars of real significance who did much to establish the historical standpoint. Clarke's *Ten Great Religions,* like *The Religion of Asia* by Samuel Johnson, a more radical Transcendentalist, documents the new interest in Oriental thought and other world religions which Emerson, Thoreau, and Parker jointly inspired. Clarke further represented an important medium of transfer for the incoming German influence. As a professor first of church history and later of German at Harvard, Hedge was even more noteworthy as a transmitter of German literature, scholarship, and speculative thought. Appropriately, it is his translation of Luther's "A Mighty Fortress Is Our God" that Americans have usually sung. And Hedge's Dudleian Lecture of 1850 marks the transition from Enlightenment rationalism to romantic idealism in natural theology at Harvard. After the Civil War, he and Clarke were leaders in the effort to maintain Unitarianism as an explicitly Christian denomination. Together they represent the many ways in which Transcendentalism was a movement of church reform.

In a class by herself was Margaret Fuller (1810–50), a protégé of Elizabeth Peabody and the only woman to play a major intellectual role in the Transcendental movement. Her education was begun by her father and extended chiefly by herself, but she came to embody more aspects of the romantic spirit than any of her associates. A mystic by disposition, she was already wrestling with Spinoza and the debates of the German romantic

4. Among those not named or discussed in this chapter are Elizabeth Peabody, the educational reformer; Sampson Reed, the Swedenborgian; William H. Furness, biblical scholar and minister in Philadelphia; and George Bancroft, the historian.

idealists in 1832. A translator of Goethe's conversations and his defender against Puritanic critics, she was also a leading literary critic and the chief editor of the *Dial,* the movement's major periodical. She was a warm admirer of Mazzini and while in Italy served as a nurse in the Roman republican uprising of 1848. Her unique place in American intellectual history is made especially secure by her book, *Woman in the Nineteenth Century* (1845), which was the first thorough and mature treatise on feminism and sexual equality by an American. She married the Marquis Angelo Ossoli, a follower of Mazzini; but along with her husband and infant son, Margaret Fuller was lost in a shipwreck off the Long Island coast in 1850.

New England was not the only locus of Transcendental activity. Both James Freeman Clarke and William Henry Channing (a nephew of the minister) tried to establish outposts in the West, in Louisville and Cincinnati. Two other movements of idealistic thinking—the so-called Hegelian movements of Ohio and Missouri—also received considerable stimulus from one or another of the New Englanders, but they owed more to their German lineage, their pride in the post-Kantian tradition, and the active German intellectual life in Cincinnati and Saint Louis. Both groups showed great freedom in their use of Hegelian ideas and applied idealistic thought to a wide range of American problems—in education, science, law, religion, literature, social analysis, and politics. As befitted such westering intellectuals, most of them were, by American evangelical standards, fairly radical. The Ohio movement flourished earlier, with Moncure Conway, August Willich, and John B. Stallo as its leading thinkers. The more publicized Saint Louis group had its flowering after the Civil War, with Henry C. Brokmeyer, Denton T. Snider and William T. Harris as its leading lights and the *Journal of Speculative Philosophy* to disseminate its ideas.[5]

ROMANTIC INFLUENCES ON NEW ENGLAND ORTHODOXY

In 1894, when John White Chadwick published his fine historical study, *Old and New Unitarian Belief,* he could report that the hostilities of the Unitarian Controversy had waned; new trends in historical and philosophical thought had brought the old antagonists onto common ground; Harvard and Andover were contemplating merger. He felt an especially close sympathy with the Progressive Orthodoxy of the Congregationalists and the Boston University Theology of the Methodists. This phenomenon itself will

5. Thinkers as interesting as these deserve lengthier exposition, but see Loyd D. Easton, *Hegel's First American Followers: The Ohio Hegelians* (Athens, Ohio: Ohio University Press, 1966); and Henry A. Pochmann, *German Culture in America,* pp. 257–93, 639–58.

be taken up in a later chapter, but the origins of the rapprochement must be considered here. The heralds of this new spirit in Congregationalism were men like Moses Stuart, the professor of biblical studies at Andover Seminary, and his student James Marsh of the University of Vermont, who introduced to their American contemporaries some of the most important scholarly and speculative achievements of the time.[6] But the man who absorbed these impulses and by his unusual powers as a writer and preacher made himself virtually the "American Schleiermacher" was Horace Bushnell (1802–76).

Born near Litchfield, Connecticut, Bushnell "owned the covenant" at the age of nineteen in the little stone church of New Preston, where his family had moved in 1805. After receiving his baccalaureate from Yale (1827), he turned fitfully to teaching, commerce, and law, until a conversion experience of sorts led him to the Yale Divinity School. Here he occupied the liberal ground which Nathaniel William Taylor and the New Haven Theology had won; but he later confessed that it was Coleridge's *Aids to Reflection* and Schleiermacher on the Trinity that transformed his entire view of Christianity.[7] A further influence was the challenge presented by the North Church in Hartford where he served from 1833 to his retirement, ministering to an urban, socially aspiring congregation. Faced after his ordination by a controversy-torn parish, Bushnell tried to develop a theology of comprehension. He reshaped the New England Theology and the old Congregational understanding of the church so as to satisfy and yet awaken those "who believed in reform, self-improvement, and gentility, who were nervous and nostalgic about the faith of their fathers, who were affronted by Calvinistic accusations and bored by theology." [8] His congregation, like many others, was committed to American democratic optimism, repulsed by revivalism, concerned about the religious nurture of its children, and attracted to the social amenities and liturgical graces of Episcopalianism. Recognizing these eroded foundations, he entered upon his ministerial task.

Bushnell was a preacher more than a theologian; and his thought is practical and apologetic in purpose: he set out to fit the Christian message to the dominant presuppositions of his time by modifying those aspects of belief or practice which scandalized many educated Americans. His first and most famous work, *Christian Nurture* (1847), dealt with the problem of

6. Marsh's work has already been alluded to. Stuart translated an essay of Schleiermacher's on the Trinity, and even more importantly promoted much interest in German biblical scholarship during a long teaching career. See pp. 394–96.

7. Bushnell was influenced chiefly by genuine mediators between traditional Christian doctrine and the new romantic emphases. Hence Coleridge, Schleiermacher, and possibly F. D. Maurice counted for more than either Emerson or Parker. The Unitarian who meant most to him was the conservative Transcendentalist Cyrus Augustus Bartol of Boston's West Church.

8. Barbara Cross, *Horace Bushnell*, p. 157.

Original Sin, provided an escape from revivalism, and became the foundation stone for new approaches to religious education. Accepting the view of Hopkins and Taylor that "sin is in the sinning," he denied that children were lost in sin until visited by the Spirit in conversion; a person need never know a time when he had not been a Christian. Bushnell's intensely organic view of family, church, and nation led him to view nurture as the means of evoking the goodness of human nature. Conversion was ideally a gradual lifelong process of growth and deepening awareness. Such views opened Bushnell to the charge that he made Christianity a matter of natural development, but his actual teaching on grace and Atonement blunts the accusation.

A vital theological complement to these views was his *God in Christ* (1849), which consisted of a revolutionary "Dissertation on Language" and three theological addresses delivered at Harvard, Andover, and Yale. *Christ in Theology* (1851) was a point-by-point defense of the former, and hence an assertion of his own orthodoxy. His starting point in both books was the insistence that verbal communication is essentially evocative, symbolic, and social in nature.

> The crux of Bushnell's theory was not, as in the case of Emerson, the metaphysical status of language. . . . Bushnell's aim was to differentiate the logical and the poetic modes of language, to define the function of each, and to demonstrate the priority of poetic method. . . . Bushnell would replace a scientific, logical, mechanistic, or abstractive ideal of language with an aesthetic, symbolic, organic, literary one. . . . Rational speech is not the rule of language but a special case, and it goes wrong when it tries to be anything more.[9]

In effect, he made a literal appeal to scriptural and creedal statements impossible. Having thus robbed language of the precision which dogmaticians and heresy hunters had assumed it to possess, Bushnell went on to explain the doctrine of the Trinity in modalistic terms. He regarded Father, Son, and Holy Spirit as merely three different modes through which the ineffable One revealed himself to man. Bushnell called this an "instrumental Trinity," but its similarity to the Patripassian heresy of the Church's early centuries indicates his difficulty in asserting the real humanity of Christ. An uproar of criticism drove Bushnell to reconsider his views, and brought him in later years to stronger sympathy for the Athanasian doctrine of the Trinity.

9. Charles N. Feidelson, Jr., *Symbolism and American Literature* (Chicago: University of Chicago Press, 1953), pp. 151–52.

Even more offensive to his New England contemporaries was his revival of the moral influence theory of Atonement, first enunciated by Abelard and advocated by the Socinians and Unitarians. This view asserts that the sinner beholding in Christ the forbearance and forgiveness of God ceases his disobedience and distrust.

> My doctrine [said Bushnell] is summarily this; that, excluding all thoughts of a penal quality in the life and death of Christ, or of any divine abhorrence to sin, exhibited by sufferings laid upon his person; also, dismissing, as an assumption too high for us, the opinion that the death of Christ is designed for some governmental effect on the moral empire of God in other worlds,—excluding points like these, and regarding everything done by him as done for expression before us, and thus for effect in us, he does produce an impression in our minds of the essential sanctity of God's law and character, which it was needful to produce, and without which any proclamation of pardon would be dangerous, any attempt to subdue and reconcile us to God, ineffectual.[10]

In orthodox circles these works of Bushnell aroused a furor hardly less violent than Parker had created in the Unitarian community. Old Bennet Tyler turned from his assaults on Nathaniel William Taylor to decry this new source of error, while Bushnell's ministerial brethren in Hartford became increasingly reluctant to exchange pulpits with him. Finally in 1852, to forestall a prosecution for heresy which seemed imminent, Bushnell's church withdrew from the consociation. On this subject, however, as on the subject of the Trinity, his later views show a movement toward traditional doctrine, in this case, toward an acceptance of Saint Anselm's insistence that God was affected ("satisfied") by Christ's atoning sacrifice.

In *Nature and the Supernatural* (1858), Bushnell set forth his defense of religion and the Christian faith in comprehensive terms, unfolding a total view of the cosmos. Although he guards himself from pantheism, protects the special historical significance of Christ (still with small stress on his humanity), and recognizes the reality of miracles and spiritual gifts in New Testament times and his own, in this work Bushnell exhibits his most radical innovation: his very untraditional use of the word "supernatural." For him this category includes all that has life, every aspect of reality which is not caught up in the mechanical chain of physical cause and effect. In such a view, nature and supernature are consubstantial and interfused; man by definition participates in supernatural life, while (conversely) God is as-

10. Quoted in Williston Walker, *History of the Congregational Churches in the United States*, ACHS, vol. 3 (New York, 1894), p. 367.

serted to be immanent in nature. Taken together, nature and the supernatural constitute "the one system of God."

Much more could be said of Horace Bushnell, for his creative mind illuminated and enlivened many complex topics, almost always by the application of his basic views on the organic, corporate, or social nature of language, the Church, and man's everyday life in the family or the nation. The unity and coherence of his thought is one of the factors that contributed most to the steady expansion of his influence, which was large—larger perhaps than that of any liberal theologian in American religious history. On the "new" geology and Darwinian views of evolution as on women's rights and slavery he was conservative, and he aided the nativist cause. Yet his adoption of romantic notions of process and development facilitated an accommodation of evolutionary thought and opened into the Social Gospel of Washington Gladden. On two broad social issues, moreover, he was a pioneer. His essay "City Planning" (1864), as well as his active efforts in Hartford, make him "one of the most incisive proponents of the city that a national tradition may possess." [11] In his essay "Work and Play" and on many other occasions he also did much to alter older Puritan attitudes on leisure and recreation. Almost immediately his theory of language began to make its mark on liberal theologians; but he also won a conservative following, notably in the person of Edwards Amasa Park, the influential theologian at Andover Seminary. Park adopted Bushnell's paradoxical view of the "theology of the intellect and that of the feelings" with such vigor that he disrupted the cordial relations that had prevailed between Andover and the ultra-orthodox Presbyterians at Princeton Seminary. Bushnell's *Christian Nurture,* in due course, became a foundation stone of the religious education movement. His broad antisectarianism, his emphasis on religious experience, his flexible view of dogma, and his eloquent optimism all made him truly "the father of American religious liberalism." Through him the romantic movement made its entrance into theological seminaries and pulpits just as, in a more indirect though perhaps more pervasive way, Emerson brought it into the nation's schoolrooms and parlors.

THE BROADER REACH OF NEW ENGLAND ROMANTICISM

The foregoing section closed with references to the pervasive presence of Bushnell's and Emerson's thought in the churches, classrooms, and parlors of America—and one could say even more of their contribution to America's

11. Robert Wheeler, in an unpublished volume on the arts, leisure, and the city in later nineteenth-century America.

ways of understanding itself and expressing its ideals. But it would be grossly improper to speak of these two without considering the enormous influence of another group of New England writers, some of whom are seen as constituting the American Renaissance (Hawthorne, Melville, Thoreau, and Emily Dickinson, for example), others of whom are often demeaned as the "parlor poets" (Longfellow, Lowell, Whittier, Bryant, and Holmes), and still others who are remembered as the country's "classic historians" (Bancroft, Ticknor, Prescott, Motley, Palfrey, and Parkman). To consider these writers in proportion to their religious influence would require several chapters, for nearly all of them were very widely read. Persons they created in their fictions—Evangeline, Captain Ahab, Hester Prynne—became part of American history. Millions of people memorized their verse and cherished their wisdom. But one must simply give thanks for the historians and critics of American literature who have dealt with their works intensively.

These writers spoke to the central religious questions in diverse ways and for diverse audiences. Longfellow and Whittier seem almost deliberately to have assumed roles as lay preachers to the American people. And if Holmes's bidding, "Build thee more stately mansions, O my soul," lacked depth, Hawthorne, Melville, and Dickinson brought reminders of tragedy, terror, and human perversity. Even the most superficial of them broadened the American's awareness of his heritage and heightened his appreciation of both nature and Western culture. All of them wove romantic themes and insights into the fabric of the American's religion and self-understanding.

38

CATHOLIC MOVEMENTS IN AMERICAN PROTESTANTISM

The set of attitudes and convictions that give the romantic individual his characteristic identity in Western history was pervaded by religious concern. In this sense the Transcendentalists were true to their tradition. But the forms into which this concern was poured were almost infinitely diverse. Tridentine Catholicism, orthodox Protestantism, and rationalistic Freemasonry all felt its transforming influence. In Germany two roommates, both active in the early "romantic school," went their separate ways: Friedrich Schlegel to Metternich's Vienna as a Roman Catholic apologist for a restored empire, Friedrich Schleiermacher to the new University of Berlin as the liberal theologian of the Prussian Union. And in America, too, this variety was exhibited, Emerson moving to Self-Reliance, Brownson to Church-Reliance. That a return to historic traditionalism is a vital aspect of romanticism has already been illustrated in connection with the crisis in Lutheranism and the series of conversions to Roman Catholicism that included Brownson's. Two other American movements that exhibit this Catholic interest warrant particular attention, however: one of them is linked to an ancient university in England and the other to a new German seminary in Pennsylvania.

THE MERCERSBURG MOVEMENT

The most creative manifestation of the Catholic tendency in American Protestantism was the movement of theology and church reform which flowered for two or three decades after 1840 in the German Reformed church. This body had grown slowly but steadily since its separation from

Dutch Reformed jurisdiction in 1793. At that time it had consisted of twenty-two ministers, 178 congregations, and about fifteen thousand members, all organized into one synod. In 1819 this synod divided itself into eight classes (a classis is the equivalent of a presbytery), and in 1824 the Ohio classis organized itself into an independent synod. By the time a seminary was founded the next year, the denomination was perhaps twice as large as in 1793.[1] Its greatest strength remained in Pennsylvania though it was slowly spreading westward. Serious losses had been sustained due to the secession and continued proselytizing of two Methodistic groups (the United Brethren and the Evangelical Association) and to a schismatic "Free Synod," numbering about a hundred churches at the peak of its strength, which broke away in 1822 but returned in 1837. Further disruptions had occurred in 1823, when John Winebrenner, an extreme revivalist and antipedobaptist, withdrew to found the Church of God, a group that closely resembled the earlier Church of the Brethren. In each of these four instances the schismatics had protested against various types of church formalism in the name of revivalistic experientialism.

Since 1820 thoughtful leaders of the synod had been considering founding a seminary, and in 1825 a feeble school was opened in conjunction with Dickinson College, a Presbyterian institution at Carlisle, Pennsylvania. This school languished, however, and a move to York in 1829 did little to revive it. Stability was finally achieved through the receipt of large gifts of money and books from Germany, and in 1836 the seminary moved to Mercersburg, where it combined with Marshall College (founded as an academy in 1831). There among the lovely mountains of Franklin County, in the struggling educational center of a very small denomination, appeared one of the most impressive constellations of religious thinkers in American history.

The man chosen to guide the infant seminary during its first precarious years was Lewis Mayer, a self-educated, somewhat rationalistically inclined pastor. But the first really eminent figure was Friedrich Augustus Rauch (1806–41), a German-born graduate of Heidelberg and student of Carl Daub, who first distinguished himself as a teacher in the academy and then served as president of Marshall College from 1836 until his untimely death. His *Psychology, or a View of the Human Soul, Including Anthropology* (1840) was meant to be the first of a series in which he planned to bring the results of conservative Hegelian thought to the attention of the American people. Its influence on a wide range of American thinkers was considerable.

1. Statistics for 1825 are very incomplete; but the "mother synod" included eighty-seven pastors and reported 23,291 communicants at that time (Joseph Henry Dubbs, *A History of the Reformed Church, German, in the United States*, ACHS, vol. 8 [New York, 1895], p. 336).

Shortly before death ended Rauch's promising career, the synod in a most unusual course of action elected as his colleague John Williamson Nevin (1803–86), a Scotch-Irish Presbyterian, graduate of Union College and Princeton Seminary, sometime instructor at Princeton, and since 1828 professor of biblical literature at Western Theological Seminary (Presbyterian) near Pittsburgh. Although Nevin was known to be strongly attracted to the German Reformed church and its confessional standards, not even he could have foreseen the future that awaited him after accepting the call to Mercersburg in 1840. Before long, however, he was working out the implications of his decision. In 1841–42 he published a series of essays entitled *The History and Genius of the Heidelberg Catechism*, depicting that document as "the crown and glory of the whole Protestant Reformation." These essays mark the beginning of an American movement to recover the spirit and content of Reformation theology.

What this meant for the rampant New Measures of the revivalists who were making large inroads on German Reformed congregations as on other groups Nevin soon made clear with a forthright attack, *The Anxious Bench* (1843). A far more profound work, *The Mystical Presence; or a Vindication of the Reformed or Calvinistic Doctrine of the Holy Eucharist* (1846) further penetrated Reformation theology, charging that the sacramental practice of nearly all the "Calvinistic" churches of America had fallen from the views that reigned among the Reformed churches during the sixteenth century. Even in the Westminster formularies he found standards by which to weigh American practices and find them wanting. Singling out "modern Puritanism" as the chief villain, Nevin leveled serious criticisms at Jonathan Edwards and Timothy Dwight, and by no means spared American Episcopalians or even Professor Hodge and the Presbyterians in his indictment of spiritualistic, subjective, and memorial views of the Lord's Supper. In this controversy he provoked from Hodge the unexpected and damaging statement that on the Lord's Supper Calvin was virtually a "crypto-Lutheran," who had introduced "foreign elements" into Reformed sacramental theory in an effort to stand on better terms with the Lutherans. These compromises, said Hodge, had been expunged in the course of time as out of harmony with the true spirit of the Reformed churches.[2]

By this time Nevin was not alone on the Mercersburg faculty. Philip Schaff (1819–93) had left a promising career at the University of Berlin to replace Rauch in 1843. Schaff was an historian and theologian who like

2. See James H. Nichols, ed., *The Mercersburg Theology*, pp. 245–59. The Heidelberg Catechism which Nevin championed was written by Zacharias Ursinus and Casper Olevianus and published for the Church of the Palatinate in 1563. Reflecting both Lutheran and Reformed influences, it has had a strong mediating effect in the Reformed tradition.

Nevin drew much inspiration from Schleiermacher and from Augustus Neander. But his intellectual heritage was much richer than this. During his years in Germany he had been profoundly impressed by other movements of historical revival and churchly renewal. He had been confirmed after a conversion experience under Lutheran pietistic auspices, and he had felt the full impact of Hegelianizing church history and biblical study at Tübingen University, the more evangelical influence of Professor Tholuck at Halle, and the strict orthodoxy of Hengstenberg at Berlin. Gifted and amiable, Schaff was in a unique position to make an important mark on American scholarship and theology. In Nevin, moreover, he found an extraordinarily compatible colleague.

The Mercersburg professors articulated two fundamental convictions: (1) the person of Christ is the ultimate fact of Christianity, which makes Christology and the Incarnation the essential starting point of Christian theology; (2) the historical development of the Church reveals by its richness and diversity how the Christian faith fulfills and culminates every human or historical tendency, blessings which are lost when and if the Church becomes static and unresponsive to its history. Schaff drew out some of the implications of these attitudes in his inaugural address, *The Principle of Protestantism, as Related to the Present State of the Church.* Stressing the developmental principle, he shocked his audience by discussing the Reformation itself as a flowering of the best in medieval Catholicism. As expanded by Schaff and translated and published with an aggressive introduction by Nevin (1845), this work became one of the central manifestos of the Mercersburg Movement. Beside it, however, must be placed Schaff's very important work of 1846, *What Is Church History? A Vindication of the Idea of Historical Development.* Here he described the main schools of church history since the sixteenth century (orthodox-dogmatic, pietistic, and rationalistic) and placed himself with the new "historical school" that looked to Herder as its prophet, seeking not to impose present-day values on past events, but stressing the themes that unite past and present. The work is a milestone in the history of American historical theory.

These works on the nature and general tendency of church history set the keynote for the many scholarly articles and reviews that made the *Mercersburg Review,* at least during the years of Nevin's editorship (1849–53), one of the great theological journals of pre–Civil War America. In its pages one can trace the way in which their scholarship roved over the whole history of the Church, to greatest effect probably when they drew lessons from the early centuries and patristic writings, stressing subjects that Protestants had ignored, giving vitality to the doctrine of the Church as the body of Christ, and emphasizing its objective and visible character.

Because it was so forcefully advocated, the Mercersburg Movement provoked violent controversy from the very outset, but antagonisms were heightened during these years because immigration and other domestic anxieties were provoking America's endemic anti-Catholicism into overt acts of violence. In this atmosphere the charge of "Romanizing tendencies" was much more inflammatory than it otherwise might have been, and it was pressed with vigor by those who had been taught to regard Protestantism as purely a revolt from ecclesiastical authoritarianism and corruption. Other, complementary sources of unrest were the resurgent revivalism of the period and the practice of the mainstream denominations to carry out their programs through the great voluntary associations. The Mercersburg Theology tended to create difficulties for both simple anti-Catholicism and uncritical nondenominationalism. In an "era of strong feelings" ecclesiastical conflict was inevitable.

Dr. Joseph Berg, the influential pastor of the First Reformed Church of Philadelphia, threw down the gauntlet immediately after Schaff's inaugural address, calling the new professor before the synod for heresy. Schaff was exonerated—in large part because none of his assailants knew what the German Reformed standards were. In 1851 Berg left the denomination for the Dutch Reformed church and later became a professor at its seminary in New Brunswick, New Jersey. During the 1860s the promulgation of a new liturgy led to another round of bitter controversy, with Dr. J. H. A. Bomberger (1817–90), Berg's successor in the Philadelphia church, leading the anti-Mercersburg forces.

In his early days Bomberger had been something of an adherent of the Mercersburg view, but in Philadelphia he gradually exchanged these sympathies for a theological outlook that undergirded his active participation in the many interdenominational campaigns of the day. To gain institutional strength for his cause, he helped to found Ursinus College in Collegeville, Pennsylvania, and in 1870 he became its first president. As a professor of theology there, Bomberger was able to bring a more Reformation-oriented theology to the "Ursinus Movement" in the Reformed church and to avoid an open schism. In 1878 the General Synod formed a "peace commission" which gradually worked out the necessary liturgical and doctrinal compromises. The denomination continued to expand westward, and in 1907 the Ursinus School of Theology merged with the seminary which the Western Synod had founded in conjunction with Heidelberg College at Tiffin, Ohio, in 1850.

Continuous conflict within the denomination partly explains why Nevin shifted his responsibilities to the college after 1851—and why Schaff resigned from the seminary in 1863. During their years of collaboration, nevertheless, these two men put their mark unmistakably on the German Reformed church, and the attitudes they championed probably achieved widest acceptance in 1863, when the tercentenary of the Heidelberg Catechism was celebrated with a great convention in Philadelphia. Nevin and Schaff were largely responsible for the renewed interest in history shown even by their critics, for the awakening of sacramental concern in the church, for the return of their church to liturgical patterns of worship—unique among American Reformed bodies—and for a lively theological tradition carried into the twentieth century by a long succession of able thinkers.

Despite its profundity and intellectual force, the influence of the Mercersburg Theology was small. It ran counter to too many ingrained American attitudes. Yet it did reveal with startling clarity that the basically Puritan forms of church life which had become so pervasive in America could be subjected to searching criticism by men who still honored Calvin and treasured the Reformation's confessional heritage. And in a limited but important way, it did radiate beyond its proper denominational setting. American Lutherans were stimulated in their own process of theological and liturgical recovery not only by the scholarship of Nevin and Schaff, but by the Mercersburg insistence that American Protestantism would be impoverished and static until the great Reformed-Lutheran dialectic became an experienced theological reality. An Episcopal theologian like William Porcher DuBose of Sewanee was led to deepen his thinking about the Church. Bushnell was jogged by Rauch's *Psychology*. "Modern Puritans" and Presbyterians were forced to sharpen their historical instruments and reconsider the direction of their drift. And, of course, Schaff through his monumental labors as a church historian became an international figure, important also as an interpreter of America to the Germans and of Germany to the Americans.[3] Finally, the Mercersburg men—especially the ex-

3. A church-historical work should not neglect to mention the immense contribution of Philip Schaff in this area. His *Apostolic Christianity* (1851) was followed by three more books delineating the history of the Church to 1073, and later by two volumes on the German and Swiss Reformations respectively. (In the later eight-volume set the two volumes on the Middle Ages were contributed by his son, David Schley Schaff.) Schaff edited the series of *Nicene and Post-Nicene Fathers* (28 vols., 1886–1905) and the first edition of *The Schaff–Herzog Encyclopedia of Religious Knowledge* (3 vols., 1884). He was instrumental in founding the American Society of Church History, and he arranged for the writing and publishing of the American Church History series (13 vols., 1893–97). He was also active in the field of exegesis (an American edition of Lange's *Bibelwerk*, 25 vols.), of hymnology (*Christ in Song*, 1868), of symbolics (the monumental and indispensable *Creeds of Christendom*, 3 vols., 1897), and biblical translation (playing a leading role in the preparation of the revised version of 1881–85). Schaff's *America* (1854) is a major interpretation of the United States, as is his memorable essay on the Civil War (1865). Besides this, he was extremely active in the Sunday school movement, the Sabbath Committee, and the Evangelical Alliance. After leaving Mercersburg he taught at Andover Seminary for a time, but from 1870 until his death he taught at Union Theological Seminary in New York.

Presbyterian Nevin, who for a while teetered on the verge of Roman Catholicism—exposed a latent dissatisfaction with Puritanic evangelicalism that was fairly widespread. And because this yearning for more catholic forms of church life had always led many to Anglicanism, it was only natural that the Protestant Episcopal church itself would become a major locus of these strenuous controversies.

THE CATHOLIC MOVEMENT IN THE PROTESTANT EPISCOPAL CHURCH

Simultaneously with the coming of Nevin and Schaff to Mercersburg, the Episcopal church was also being agitated by the "Church Question." In this case, too, the chief provocation came from theological stirrings abroad. The entire Anglican communion, to be sure, had been in a state of unsettlement on the Catholic-Protestant issue for three full centuries, but special problems within the established Church of England now precipitated a genuine crisis.

English Precursors

The Oxford Movement began, according to Cardinal Newman, with John Keble's sermon on the "National Apostasy" on 14 July 1833, at a time when the church and state issue was much agitated. Close on the heels of the Reform Bill of 1832, which had greatly extended the franchise, Parliament had passed a bill to suppress ten redundant Anglican bishoprics in Ireland. Keble's sermon was a ringing call for an autonomous church, holy and catholic and worthy of its independence, a divine society sprung from heaven, not a plaything of politicians or a casual appurtenance of the people. When very soon thereafter he and a small group of colleagues in Oriel College set out to end the national apostasy, they stirred up the greatest storm the English church had experienced in almost two centuries.

Among the leaders of this group of determined reformers were the brilliant Richard Hurrell Froude (1803–36), John Henry Newman (1801–90), whose keen intellect made him the dominant figure in the movement until he became a Roman Catholic in 1845, and Edward Bouverie Pusey (1800–82), professor of Hebrew, who was destined to be the main stabilizing force in the loyally Anglican phase of the movement. They decided on an aggressive strategy of rallying all loyal churchmen, especially those with High Church sympathies, by a series of outspoken yet scholarly *Tracts for the Times*. In the very first tract, which appeared in September 1833, Newman put the matter squarely: "*Choose* your side, since side you shortly must, with one or other party, even though you do nothing." What his readers were asked to choose was a "Catholic" view of the Church, its ministry, and its sacraments. His movement was not primarily ritualistic or liturgical, but theological. Its chief emphasis was upon the objective, visible Church and its means of grace as the very ship of salvation; and upon the importance of historic episcopate to a valid ministry. Inseparably connected with these concerns was an insistence upon a return to the faith of the ecumenical councils of the "undivided church" and of the early Fathers. Because the movement was by no means simply intellectual, they also called all men to a renewed sense of Christian discipline, worship, and holiness—here again with an emphasis on the older Catholic literature and practice rather than that which Puritanism had informed.

The Oxford reformers were heard. Ninety tracts running to six volumes appeared between 1833 and 1841. And men did choose sides, even within the movement. Some followed Keble with his desire for an uncontroversial restoration of Caroline ways; others followed Pusey's concept of the Church of England as a catholic *via media* between Protestantism and Romanism; and a third, more restless party, moved away from the very idea of an autonomous Church of England toward submission to the pope. When Newman turned down this last road and followed it to the end, "the nightmare which had oppressed Oxford for fifteen years" (his own phrase) came to an end. But an immense struggle within the Church of England had only begun. And by this time, too, the noise of battle was heard elsewhere, perhaps most influentially in an "ecclesiological" movement of another sort which had been launched in Oxford's great sister university.

The Cambridge Movement stemmed from the Ecclesiological (later the Camden) Society organized at Cambridge University in 1837 to promote the appreciation of Gothic church architecture and other "ecclesiastical antiquities," both by the study of actual English churches and by documentary research. Its leaders were clergymen and fellows of various colleges, most of whom sympathized with the Tractarians. John Mason Neale (1818–66), now most often remembered for his translations of medieval and ancient hymns, was a founder and leading spirit. Between 1841 and 1870 the society's journal, *The Ecclesiologist,* became an enormously influential arbiter of the "laws" of restoring, building, decorating, and furnishing churches. And in due course its fiercely dogmatic confidence in the inerrancy of the medieval church emerged as a powerful force throughout the Church of England. As the society came increasingly to take up the cause of the Ritualist movement, it also worked a large effect on liturgical practice, championing medieval ways and divorcing the Church from the modern world. Because its demands were more superficial and aesthetic, its influence probably exceeded that of the Tractarians.

Romanticism and the Catholic Spirit

Viewed in perspective, the Oxford and Cambridge movements exhibit important differences; yet because they are complementary the Catholic movement as a whole becomes more obviously a manifestation of the same romantic currents which were moving Brownson, Bushnell, and Nevin during the same years. The frequency with which romantic feeling awakened a nostalgia for Catholic tradition is a commonplace, illustrated over and over again at high intellectual levels as well as in changing popular tastes. In America one notes the Spanish and Catholic interests of Ticknor, Irving, Longfellow, Prescott, and Parkman. In England these signs were also evident. The rediscovery of monasticism documented in Samuel Roffey Maitland's great work *The Dark Ages* (1844) is an English parallel to the work of Count Montalembert in France, revealing how both nostalgia and intense historical interest underlay the entire movement. Nor was it to end with medievalism and Gothic revival. In John Henry Newman most notably, the principle of development became both an argument for the Roman church as the proper bearer of catholicity and a means of understanding the history of dogma. Newman's historical studies of medieval English saints, moreover, were an immediate prelude to his final decision to submit to Rome.

Another "romantic" tendency, separable from the Catholic movement but often related to it, was a revival of philosophic idealism which brought with it a recrudescence of mysticism and Platonic thought as well as an interest in metaphysics, a pursuit which British empiricism had tended so long to suppress. The future of the English church during the early nineteenth century was, according to one English historian, "largely being moulded, not at Lambeth and Bishopthorpe, but at Rydal Mount and Highgate, by men [Wordsworth and Coleridge] who little dreamed that they were doing anything of the kind."

The Rise of Parties in American Episcopalianism

The predicaments of Anglicanism in England and in America during the early nineteenth century were different in the extreme. In England the national church had retained all its prerogatives, vested interests, encumbrances, and temptations. In the United States, the Episcopal was one voluntary church among others. The Revolution had left it "a church in ruins," but by 1792 the structures necessary for self-preservation were reconstituted: a united episcopate, a prayer book, and a federal system of government. Yet Episcopal historians agree that vitality was lacking during the early nineteenth century. The bishops made almost no visitations; the clergy were few in number, lax in their duties, and uninspired in their preaching. Rationalism, indifference, and suspicion were rife. Deprived of their glebe lands, the country parishes of Virginia languished in desuetude. Bishop James Madison busied himself almost exclusively with the affairs of William and Mary College, of which he had been elected president in 1790. At the state convention of 1812 only thirteen priests appeared; and the following year, when the fervent Evangelical Richard C. Moore (1762–1841) was elected bishop to succeed Madison, there were only seven. Chief Justice Marshall thought that the church was on the road to extinction. In the Middle Colonies the desolation was even greater, for here the Loyalist exodus had been largest and the odium of Toryism strongest. Bishop Samuel Provoost of New York had simply retired from his ecclesiastical vocation.

The most hopeful signs of life were visible where Anglicanism had never been taken for granted or publicly supported, as in New England—and particularly in Connecticut where the High Church (almost Nonjuring) tradition of the SPG and of Bishop Samuel Seabury still prevailed. In New England the Episcopal church also benefited from the dissatisfactions that arose among members of the "orthodox" Congregational churches, due in some cases to a distaste for the prevailing revivalism, in others to dislike for the doctrinal and disciplinary rigor of reawakened Puritanism. In eastern Massachusetts, where orthodoxy yielded to Unitarianism, the antipathy for Anglican Loyalism gave way to desires for social prestige, aesthetic satisfactions, and a church that resisted Transcendental radicalism.

The Evangelicals

The year 1811 is often designated as the turning point in American Episcopalian fortunes, because it marks the resurgence of both the Evangelical and High Church parties, neither of which at that time could look to more than a few parish ministers for vigorous leadership. In that year Alexander Viets Griswold (1776–1843) was consecrated bishop of the "Eastern District" comprising all of New England except Connecticut, an area with only sixteen priests and twenty-two feeble parishes. Griswold experienced a religious crisis at the time of his consecration and became thenceforth a dynamic preacher of experiential Christianity and a ceaseless visitor of his vast diocese. By the time of his death he had ordained well over a hundred priests and watched his original jurisdiction develop into five dioceses with a hundred parishes. In the meantime, Bishop Moore had similarly resuscitated the church in Virginia. In the more sparsely settled regions beyond the Appalachians, Bishop Philander Chase (1775–1852) went his stormy way, founding Kenyon College in Ohio, Jubilee College in Illinois, laying Episcopal foundations in such remote places as Michigan and New Orleans, and arousing concern for domestic missions.

As the years went by, these militant Evangelicals were joined by other strong bishops, notably William Meade of Virginia and Charles P. McIlvaine, who became Chase's successor in Ohio after having virtually turned West Point into a conventicle during his term as chaplain. Evangelicals were never able to gain a decisive majority in the House of Bishops in the antebellum period; but after 1840, when nativism added to the growing fear of the Tractarian movement, they were spokesmen for the church's most swiftly growing parishes, strong supporters of Episcopal home missions, and prominent figures in many interdenominational voluntary associations.

In matters of doctrine they met the other denominations on their own ground. Sin, justification by faith, and the experience of regeneration held an important place in their teaching, as did a strong sense of scriptural authority and a disinclination for arguments from tradition. In matters of parish practice, they were less decorous than the High Church leaders. Extemporaneous prayer, special night meetings for devotional exercise, and occasional revivalism were permitted, sometimes even encouraged. The sacraments were not accorded great significance or efficacy. Holy Communion was administered quarterly and understood in the subjective manner of the "modern Puritanism" so roundly condemned by John W. Nevin. The Real Presence was not asserted, the word "altar" was avoided (as it is in the prayer book), and the *Agnus Dei* was not sung. Evangelicals also opposed the doctrine of baptismal regeneration. Deeply suspicious of Romish tendencies, their church buildings, like their public worship, displayed an almost puritanic austerity: the pulpit dominated the "Lord's Table," crosses and candles were rare, and even Gothic architecture was suspect until the romantic revival made it popular. On questions of church order, however, fears of sacerdotalism and "priestcraft" did not exclude genuine gratitude for the heritage of the threefold ministry of deacons, priests, and bishops. Amid the perils of sectarianism and popery, they treasured the prayer book and the orderly worship it provided.

The High Churchmen

The High Church party could also look back to 1811 as memorable. In that year John Henry Hobart (1775–1830) became a bishop of New York, an office which enabled him to become perhaps the greatest religious leader the American Episcopal church ever produced. Hobart's background provides a cross-section of the British religious heritage in America. Of Puritan stock, his grandfather had become an Anglican after moving to Philadelphia. He himself was baptized, confirmed, ordained, and consecrated there at the hands of Bishop William White. Hobart was educated in the Calvinistic atmosphere of Princeton, where he imbibed an evangelical outlook which he never lost, while at the same time he sharpened his arguments for episcopacy. After parish experience in Hempstead, Long Island, and Trinity Church in New York City, he was made assistant bishop of New York in 1811 and bishop in 1816. For fourteen extraordinarily busy years he devoted himself to reconstituting his diocese, eschewing bigotry and arrogance in advancing the High Church cause. His preaching was accounted by many as unduly enthusiastic, even Methodistic. Yet Hobart demanded that his fellow Episcopalians claim their special heritage with resolution and confidence. To further this purpose he vigorously advocated a seminary, and later became a mainstay of the General Theological Seminary founded in 1817 and opened in New York City in 1819, where, as professor of pastoral theology and pulpit eloquence, he had great influence on a whole generation of students. In 1821 he also founded a college at Geneva, New York, which in 1860 changed its name to Hobart College. Episcopal tract, Sunday school, prayer book, and Bible societies owed much to his sponsorship and support, as did the *Churchman,* a journal which under the editorship of Samuel Seabury, Jr., became a semiofficial voice of the High Church party.

The centrality of Hobart's work in New York cannot be minimized; but the High Church movement was strongly fortified at many other important points. Theodore Dehon in South Carolina (consecrated 1812) and John Stark Ravenscroft in North Carolina (consecrated 1823) were both of similar mind; and during the next decade their party was to be augmented by aggressive bishops in New York, New Jersey, and Pennsylvania. As a result, the High Church party, both North and South, became a strong factor in the church.

The Impact of the Tractarian Controversy

The Tractarians at first created almost no stir in the land of the Puritans. They seemed dry, academic, and devoted to the malaise of a foreign situation. Even John Keble's collection of devotional poetry, *The Christian Year,* though first published in 1827, did not appear in America until Bishop Doane's edition of 1834. Newman's *Essay on Justification by Faith* (1838) broke the calm. Then in the following year when publication of the *Tracts* was announced, a tart exchange ensued. The *Churchman* favored this publishing venture; the *Gambier Observer* and other Evangelical journals opposed it. Needless to say, the younger Seabury's rather naïve hope "that no controversy may be awakened by [the project]" was far from gratified. Bishops Doane of New Jersey, Onderdonk of New York, and John Henry Hopkins of Vermont all praised the purpose of the Oxford reformers. After the appearance of Tract Ninety, however, Hopkins published *Letters on the Novelties Which Disturb Our Peace* (1842). Bishop Eastburn of Massachusetts went farther, denouncing the *Tracts* as "work of Satan" concocted by advocates of the Dark Ages and "followers of the Scarlet Woman." Bishop McIlvaine published a major treatise in the same general vein.

During this conflict the General Seminary in New York became a decisive force. Built up under the watchful eyes of Bishops Hobart and Onderdonk, it had become the church's strongest seminary—and after 1839 it was considered, as one convert to Rome remembered, "a little Oxford on this side of the Atlantic . . . in a little suburban appendix to New York City, known as Chelsea." Here the *Lyra Apostolica* of Frederick Faber (who went over to Rome in 1845), the works of Newman, Keble, Pusey, and the rest inspired a new concern for the Church, its ministry, and its sacraments. Along with this concern, of course, came a growing sympathy for the Roman Catholic church and even for the Council of Trent, with the result that there was soon a considerable (but disproportionately publicized) number of converts from among the seminary students. In 1843 Bishop Onderdonk ordained Arthur Carey, who frankly confessed his Tridentine tendency. This act sent a shudder through the church. The next year a committee of bishops visited the institution, interrogated the faculty, and finally acquitted it. But shortly after this vindication, a secret society for the propagation of "Romish views" was uncovered, and two students were expelled, one of whom later became a Roman Catholic bishop. In the America of the 1830s and 1840s, the seminary faculty was obviously only one among many sources of Catholic tendency; but General Seminary was then, and continued to be, the leading American center of both the older High Church and the newer Tractarian attitudes.[4]

The typically post-Tractarian Catholic tendency was more explicitly institutionalized by four students of the seminary who enlisted for service on the frontier under Jackson Kemper, missionary bishop for the Northwest. Led by James Lloyd Breck, they founded Nashotah House in Wisconsin in 1841 as a semimonastic center for study, worship, and evangelism. Breck later moved on to Minnesota, where in 1857 he founded Seabury Divinity School in Faribault. On these foundations and others of similar nature arose

4. The extent of Tractarian influence cannot be determined. Of the 1,976 men who were ordained between 1822 and 1855 at least 29 entered the Roman Catholic church. Some of them are discussed briefly on pp. 548–49.

a tradition of churchmanship to which the name "Anglo-Catholic" may be applied. This later movement bore little relation to the creative features of Cardinal Newman's thought, however, and it came to be increasingly recognizable for its emulation of nineteenth-century Roman Catholic practice, especially in the externals of architecture and worship. In America as in England a small Anglican monastic movement was initiated.

Catholic-Protestant Conflict

Works that drove so deeply into the heart of Evangelicalism as Newman's *Essay on Justification* and *Tract Ninety* (which sought to harmonize the Thirty-nine Articles with the decrees of Trent) inevitably drove men to more than a war of words. The Episcopal church did not simply grow quietly in two directions. Until the 1870s, moreover, the idea of comprehending these two deep-seated tendencies within a single church did not begin to win acceptance. Controversy quickly transformed the General Convention into a proving ground of party strength. Events of a formal nature, however, were neither momentous nor numerous. Official declarations of the General Convention or the House of Bishops were necessarily compromises, and they usually only reiterated a loyalty to the Bible, the prayer book, and the traditions of the Anglican communion. But a bitter party conflict did occasionally become public.

The most sensational developments had to do with the trials of the three most important leaders of the early Catholic movement, the Onderdonk brothers and Bishop Doane. Bishop Benjamin Tredwell Onderdonk of New York and his brother, Bishop Henry Ustick Onderdonk of Pennsylvania, were suspended from office in 1844, on charges of unchastity and unbecoming behavior in the former case, drunkenness and drug addiction in the latter. In 1852 Bishop George Washington Doane of New Jersey was much harassed, though never convicted, for questionable financial dealings in connection with the two schools he had attempted to found and foster. In all three cases the voting closely followed party lines, though the formal issues were hardly theological. Only slightly less sensational was the submission to Rome in 1852 of the bishop of North Carolina, Levi Silliman Ives, who had earlier encountered much criticism for his attempts to found a monastic community in his diocese.

As might be expected, the controversies provoked by the Oxford Movement were not resolved. Even in the Catholic party there was dissension, and a notable figure in the Nashotah tradition insinuated that the chief hindrance to the progress of Catholic principles in the Protestant Episcopal church came not from the Evangelicals but from the High Church party. It is true that this party showed little or no awareness of the special need for charity and moderation in a country where anti-Romanism was almost a birthright. At the same time, and possibly for the same reason, it had small evangelistic success despite its undeniable zeal.

THE MEMORIAL MOVEMENT

The closest these opposing forces came to a resolution of their contrarieties was probably in the person of the professed "Evangelical Catholic," William Augustus Muhlenberg (1796–1877) and the Memorial Movement which he sponsored. A great-grandson of the Lutheran patriarch, Henry M. Muhlenberg, he was baptized as a Lutheran but grew up in a thoroughly Anglicized Philadelphia family at a time when the Lutheran church was almost completely unresponsive to the religious needs of English-speaking people, especially in places where there were Episcopal churches. Young Muhlenberg was prepared for confirmation by the future missionary bishop, Jackson Kemper, and confirmed by Bishop William White of Philadelphia. After his ordination he served for a time in White's Philadelphia parish and in Lancaster, Pennsylvania; then in 1826 he accepted the charge of Saint George's in Flushing, Long Island. Two years later he became occupied exclusively with the Flushing Institute, a Christian preparatory school for boys, where during his eighteen years of dedicated work he became an American parallel to the famous Dr. Thomas Arnold of Rugby. Muhlenberg thus made a very large contribution in an area which would become an important adjunct institution of the Episcopal church—the private preparatory school. His interest in deepening the liturgical and devotional life of the school, moreover, led him to an "Evangelical Catholic" outlook of considerable breadth. He thus became at the same time —ironically—a founder of the ritualist movement.

Although Tractarianism appealed to him for a time, Newman's essay *The Development of Christian Doctrine* (1845) deflected him in another direction. Later he described his final decision:

> I was far out on the bridge, so to speak, that crosses the gulf between us and Rome. I had passed through the mists of vulgar Protestant prejudices, when I saw before me "The Mystery of Abomination." I flew back, not to rest on the pier of High Churchism, from which this bridge of Puseyism springs, but on the solid rock of Evangelical truth, as republished by the Reformers.[5]

5. Anne Ayres, *The Life and Work of William Augustus Muhlenberg* (New York, 1880), p. 173.

As it developed along these new lines, Muhlenberg's thought shows an interesting similarity to that of the Mercersburg reformers and their Lutheran parallels. But he was still, as he said, "in the Penumbra of Puseyism" when in 1846 he became rector of the new Church of the Holy Communion in New York City. Here in a Gothic structure designed by Richard Upjohn, complete with canopied altar, he introduced the weekly Eucharist, daily morning and evening prayer, antiphonal chanting, lighted candles, regular pews and kneelers in place of private box pews, and voluntary offerings instead of pew rents.[6] His church conducted a very successful apostolate among the poor, aided by the sisterhood of the Holy Communion, a deaconess society founded in this parish. Muhlenberg himself also led in the founding of Saint Luke's Hospital. In 1851 his short-lived journal, *The Evangelical Catholic,* began to explicate the full meaning of his reforms.

In 1853 his famous "Memorial" to the House of Bishops inaugurated a movement to make the Protestant Episcopal church on the one hand something more than a "church . . . only for the rich," and on the other, an instrument of Christian unity in America. This document raised the question whether the church

> with only her present canonical means and appliances, her fixed and invariable modes of public worship, and her traditional customs and usages, is competent to the work of preaching and dispensing the Gospel to all sorts and conditions of men, and so adequate to do the work of the Lord in this land and in this age.

The Memorialists suggested the extension of orders to sincere men, Episcopalians or not, who for all their zeal to fulfill the Great Commission, "could not bring themselves to conform in all particulars to our prescriptions and customs, but yet [are] sound in the faith, and who, having the gifts of preachers and pastors, would be able ministers of the New Testament." [7]

6. Pew rents, which involved a kind of property right, were passing out of use in this period. Abolishing them was also part of James Freeman Clarke's reform when he founded the Church of the Disciples in Boston (1841). Gothic church architecture was then coming into vogue, stimulated by Augustus W. Pugin in England (who became a Roman Catholic in 1834) and the English-born American Episcopal Bishop John Henry Hopkins's *Essay on Gothic Architecture* (1836). Richard Upjohn furthered the cause with his designs for Trinity Church in New York City. A New York Ecclesiological Society, imitating the English one, was founded in 1846. With the founding of the American Institute of Architects in 1857, the age of dogmatic commitment to "correct" Gothic "principles" began to yield to more improvisational attitudes; yet the Gothic revival contributed powerfully to the rising concern for environmental factors and professional design in church architecture (see Phoebe B. Stanton, *The Gothic Revival and American Church Architecture 1840–1856*).

7. Ayres, *Life of Muhlenberg,* pp. 263–67.

This would not only accomplish great good, but it would be an important step in cementing a central bond of unity among Protestant Christians. The church as a whole failed to accept the larger purpose of the Memorial, and its immediate result was little more than slightly larger liberties in the use of the prayer book; but some continuity could probably be traced between these efforts and the several major ecumenical proposals to be advanced by Episcopalians in the next century.

Muhlenberg exemplified the most productive forces in his church during the pre-Civil War years, especially those factors and appeals which account for the remarkable expansion of Episcopalianism in America's urban centers, where it grew by 46 percent in the decade before the war alone. He illustrates as well the process by which much of the Oxford Movement's advocacy gradually made a decisive mark on the faith and practices of the church, even upon those who were professedly evangelical. And finally, he serves as a reminder of the impact of romanticism. There were, to be sure, several other Episcopalians, like Caleb Sprague Henry (1804–84) of New York, who are remembered more explicitly as Christian Transcendentalists and as champions of Coleridge. Yet Muhlenberg adopted much of their spirit, including the proposal to make Anglicanism a means of uniting divided Christendom through a principle of comprehension.

The inner diversity of Episcopal life, however, must not obscure the fact that dissension and party rivalry were characteristic features of the church's history down to the 1870s when a minor schism in the church actually took place. The Reformed Episcopal Church was organized in 1873 in New York, after a secession led by George David Cummins, the assistant bishop of Kentucky. He was a strenuous Evangelical who desired more explicit checks on ritualism than the General Convention would enact. Because the convention of 1874 did take action against "Catholic" extremes, and also because the policy of allowing widely divergent views within the church began to gain increasing acceptance, the new church benefited from very few defections and grew very slowly, having but 8,700 members in 1954, and 7,085 in 1966.

In the mid-twentieth century the Protestant Episcopal church was still embroiled in questions of churchmanship. During this entire long period, however, there were many prominent Episcopalians, both lay and clerical, who adhered to neither of the two main parties that arose out of the Tractarian controversy. They were the moderates, the incipient Broad Churchmen. Pacific in spirit and socially concerned, they looked to Bishop William White of Philadelphia as a founding hero. Such men often embraced the new currents of Transcendental thought and the newer trends in historical biblical criticism. Tending toward theological liberalism, and after the Civil War drawing much sustenance from English Christian Socialists such as Maurice and Kingsley, this group would play a leading role in the American Social Gospel movement.

VI
SLAVERY AND EXPIATION

In the late 'fifties the people of Illinois were being prepared for the new era by a series of scenes and incidents which nothing but the term "mystical" will fittingly describe.

Things came about not so much by preconceived method as by an impelling impulse. The appearance of *Uncle Tom's Cabin* was not a reason, but an illumination; the founding of the Republican party was not an act of political wirepulling, but an inspiration; the great religious revivals and the appearance of two comets were not regarded as coincidences, but accepted as signs of divine preparation and warning.

The settlers were hard at work with axe and plough; yet, in spite of material preoccupation, all felt the unnameable influence of unfolding destiny. The social cycle, which began with the Declaration of Independence, was drawing to a close, and during Buchanan's administration the collective consciousness of men—that wonderful prescience of the national soul—became aware of impending innovation and upheaval.

Francis Grierson, *The Valley of Shadows* (1909)

That Western Christendom turned Africa into a hunting ground for slaves rather than a field for philanthropic and missionary endeavor is one of the world's great tragedies. That the New World became the chief arena for the European exploitation of slave labor is an extension of the same tragedy. That the United States—the first new nation, the elect nation, the nation with the soul of a church, the great model of modern democracy—moved into the nineteenth century with one of the largest and cruelest of slave systems in its midst with full constitutional protection is surely one of the world's greatest ironies.

Because European racial stereotypes were well formed and New World slavery widely institutionalized by the time England's colonies were founded, it is not surprising that the irony of Christian slave-keeping was rarely perceived during the seventeenth century. With the revolutionary generation's failure to put slavery on the road to extinction except in the North, where it did not exist in the full sense, the irony deepened. That the antislavery movement did not become an outspoken and powerful movement until the 1830s is thus one of the facts most in need of explanation.

The rise of abolitionism marks the beginning of the nation's central experience, its first truly fundamental moral encounter. Not surprisingly, this encounter led by steady steps to the country's *Volkskrieg,* the war that ended the old federal Union and brought forth on this continent in 1865 a new nation not really dedicated to the proposition that all men are created equal, but nevertheless one that could be led to put the right words in the Constitution. The antislavery movement did survive the war, moreover, and it did press on for Reconstruction; but given the wartime destruction of the South and the seemingly endemic racism of the human race, not even the finest evangelical leadership—and General Howard at the head of the Freedman's Bureau was that—possessed the requisite attitudes and will. So the southern churches, like American society from the beginning, made discrimination and segregation the basic pattern.

Yet one thing was new: the black churches replaced the invisible institution of slavery days and became a major means of preserving and giving voice to America's largest under-class. To this whole encounter from the rise of the humanitarian crusades through the ordeal of war and the failures of Reconstruction, all of the chapters in Part VI are related. In this sense they culminate all that had gone before and lead into the fundamentally new religious situation that came to prevail in the Gilded Age.

39

THE HIGH TIDE OF HUMANITARIAN REFORM

Nothing in America was safe from the reformer's burning gaze during the first half of the nineteenth century. Everything from diet and dress to the social structure itself—even the family and motherhood—were up for critical review, while panaceas and nostrums ranged from graham crackers and bloomers to free love and socialism. Crackpots and dreamers, sober philosophers and millennial prophets had their moment if not their day. In 1840 the Chardon Street Chapel of Boston was host to a convention of nothing less than the "Friends of Universal Reform," whose chairman was Bronson Alcott. By this time the great American epoch of political theory and constitution making was becoming legend. The victory at New Orleans had been won in 1815, and out of the new nation's exuberant self-assurance came a great surge of nationalism that made itself heard and felt over the cracker barrels in crossroads stores as well as in European halls of state. Men as sharply at odds as John Quincy Adams and Andrew Jackson heralded the new era. The old Federalist party yielded to National Republicanism. The Age of the Common Man was at hand. The future beckoned. It was, as Lewis Mumford said, America's "Golden Day." Why should not social reform and utopianism have their inning?

America did hear a new and authentic message in those antebellum years. The historical roots of humanitarian reform lay, first of all, in the Puritan's basic confidence that the world could be constrained and re-formed in accordance with God's revealed will. Revivalism intensified the nation's sense of millennial expectancy, and a doctrine of "disinterested benevolence" of Edwardsean lineage informed the Second Awakening's manifold activities, giving rise to the evangelical vision of a great Christian republic stretching westward beyond the Appalachians as a beacon and example for the whole world.

Enlightened rationalism, so inescapably associated with the nation's Founding Fathers, was another source of the prevailing optimism and the idea of progress which accompanied it. Because the War for Independence had conferred something like dogmatic status upon this sort of moral idealism, patriotic doctrines about man and history became stock components of Protestant preaching. Among the Unitarians philanthropic concerns were even more emphatically the order of the day. A "perfectibilitarian" like Channing praised the "devotion to progress" arising among his contemporaries and could count a score of reformers among his spiritual children. Transcendentalism, too, was in Channing's lineage. When Octavius Brooks Frothingham spoke of his own conversion to the new spiritual philosophy of Concord, he literally defined the movement in moral-reformist terms. "Not only was religion brought face to face with ethics, but it was identified with ethics." [1] Transcendental votaries in succeeding years would give fervent support to a dozen reform causes. Evangelicals, in the meantime, by no means yielded up perfectionism to Unitarians and Transcendentalists: for a century this doctrine had been a distinctive feature of Wesleyan preaching, and during the great revival of the 1830s it spread far beyond Methodism. After 1835 Finney and his following took up the same demand for holiness, calling for socially relevant Christian commitment as the proper sequel to conversion.

Timothy Smith's sweeping statement is essentially accurate:

> The Calvinist idea of foreordination, rejected as far as it concerned individuals, was now transferred to a grander object—the manifest destiny of a Christianized America. Men in all walks of life believed that the sovereign Holy Spirit was endowing the nation with resources sufficient to convert and civilize the globe, to purge human society of all its evils, and to usher in Christ's reign on earth. Religious doctrines which Paine, in his book *The Age of Reason,* had discarded as the tattered vestment of an outworn aristocracy, became the wedding garb of a democratized church, bent on preparing men and institutions for a kind of proletarian marriage supper of the Lamb.[2]

In the impetus which this gave to temperance, antislavery, and other moral crusades, the evangelical foundations for the social gospel of a later day were laid. Even when sectional tensions led many groups and individuals to avoid divisive issues, the seeds of social Christianity were being sown.

1. Octavius Brooks Frothingham, *Recollections and Impressions, 1822–1890* (New York, 1891), p. 50.

2. Timothy L. Smith, *Revivalism and Social Reform in Mid-Nineteenth-Century America,* p. 7.

PROBLEMS OF INDUSTRIALIZATION AND URBANIZATION

A distinctively new arena for early social reformism was provided by the poor and unfortunate, especially as they came to be clustered in the nation's cities. Urban poverty was a result of the steady growth of American industrialism after 1785 and, more markedly, after the War of 1812. Newly invented machines were rendering obsolete the old patriarchal economy in which each family supplied its own needs by handicraft and homespun, while the growth of the transportation system made possible steadily expanding markets. Between 1810 and 1860 American consumption of iron quintupled. As the overwhelmingly agricultural cast of American society began slowly to change, it changed most rapidly in New England, where farming had always been a struggle and where water power and the concentration of capital encouraged the rapid rise of factories. The result was a new kind of city, in which low wages, exhausting hours, and crowded living conditions became everyday facts of life. Before the "ten-hour campaign" swept the country in 1835, most laborers worked fourteen hours a day for an average of six dollars a week, while control of the factories and corporations gravitated to a small class of financiers. Women and children under twelve years of age worked the same long hours in the factories, and frequently whole families could be found in a single employ, though even this rarely secured enough income to maintain a decent level of existence. In 1829 the Boston Prison Discipline Society estimated that seventy-five thousand delinquent debtors, many of them owing only petty sums, were being held on this charge in unsanitary, crowded jails. Needless to say, the situation presented a compelling challenge to the country's idealists.

Caring for the poor and unfortunate had immemorially been the task of the church, but in America institutionalized responses to such needs had been few and weak. The pioneer hero of active church concern is the Boston Unitarian minister Joseph Tuckerman (1778–1840), described by his chief biographer (a Roman Catholic) as a veritable American Saint Vincent de Paul. A Harvard graduate and close friend of William Ellery Channing, Tuckerman moved in 1826 from his rural parish of Chelsea to become the first "minister-at-large" to serve Boston under the sponsorship of the Benevolent Fraternity of Churches, a Unitarian organization formed for the purpose of bringing a Christian ministry and charitable aid to the city's poor. During a decade of intense activity, Tuckerman became an effective social welfare worker, a crusader for his cause, and an influential theorist. Strong in his conviction that Christianity was a social principle and not merely a private pact with God, he became the first in a long and distinguished line of American apostles of the "Social Gospel." Not for half a century would his work be taken up in earnest by the American churches, but the concern was continual and rising.

The most remarkable living symbol of the era's rising concern for the underpaid and overworked working classes was that dynamic pilgrim and agitator, Orestes Brownson. Beginning his religious pilgrimage in Stockbridge, Vermont, and proceeding through the series of theological phases described in an earlier chapter, Brownson absorbed the socialistic sentiments of Robert Dale Owen, helped to form the Workingman's party in New York City, and by 1836, having come under the influence of Channing and then of Emerson, was ministering in Boston to his own Society for Christian Union and Progress. Perhaps no American before the Civil War testified more strenuously to the significant relationship between religion and social problems. Upon entering the Roman Catholic church in 1844, however, he began a long second career in which the problems of theology and Catholic apologetics became his primary concern.

THE REFORM CAMPAIGNS

The dominant tendency of early nineteenth-century reformism was not toward the creation of a new society by total revolution (except insofar as American democracy and Jacksonianism were "revolutions") nor primarily toward founding islands of communitarian perfection (though these were founded by the dozen). Following patterns set in England and in this country during the Second Great Awakening, most reformers dedicated themselves to specific campaigns. This did not prevent a given reformer from carrying several portfolios, and some men, like Lyman Beecher and Theodore Parker, put no limits on their interests. Though the diversified humanitarian movement was not nearly so closely linked to churches and church organizations as, say, the temperance crusade, church leaders of one sort or another frequently provided the initial impulse, ministers and dedicated laymen were often active agitators, and nearly all the campaigns were pervaded by appeals to "Christian principles." If the collective conscience of evangelical America is left out, the movement as a whole is incomprehensible.

Education

The most pervasive of all the crusades was that in behalf of education. Not always did it create the excitement of the more dramatic causes; but its results, if often prosaic, were far-reaching. Its vision of a better day rested on the conviction that the extension of knowledge would dissipate human misery. In this principle converged the Enlightenment ideals of Jefferson, founder of the University of Virginia, and the rationale of Harvard's Puritan founders. Idealists refused to be complacent in the fact that already America's high rate of literacy was probably unequaled anywhere in the world. More and better education was the cry. Some wanted it more Christian, others wanted it more secular; but the demand was sustained, and the hopes that rode upon it were high. The Reverend Samuel R. Hall of Concord, Vermont, founded and conducted a normal school, produced texts for most of the secondary curriculum, and worked steadily for better school laws. Graduates of Princeton and Yale flowed westward and southward in a steady stream, founding academies, colleges, seminaries, and universities, and staffing their faculties. This half-century was the great age of the church college, an age in fact when these church-related institutions virtually constituted American higher education.[3] Some state universities were in existence, to be sure, and more were being founded; but in view of the country's dominant Protestant ethos, and the fact that the clergy was still the leading intellectual class, these universities were rarely secular in spirit. A rather different approach was that of Josiah Holbrook, the enterprising founder of an "Agricultural Seminary" at Derby, Connecticut, who became an itinerant lecturer on scientific subjects in 1826. His mission expanded into an association of adults for mutual education which, as the American Lyceum, was imitated by many similar programs, all of which used the lecture platform to appease the appetite of a nation hungry for enlightenment.

Amid all this diversified interest, Horace Mann (1796–1859) stands out clearly as the age's most effective educational crusader as well as its outstanding philosopher of education. Like so many of his fellow reformers, Mann's family background included a strict orthodox upbringing. He grew up in the parish of Nathanael Emmons at Franklin, Massachusetts, but far from becoming a New Divinity man, he moved steadily during the course of his life toward a liberal form of Unitarianism. Dr. Channing's fervent exclamation when Mann took up his ultimate career as secretary of the Massachusetts Board of Education in 1837 reflected their common ideal: "If we can but turn the wonderful energy of this people into right channels, what a new heaven and earth might be realized among us!" Posterity was his client. His great *Annual Reports* (1837–48), no less than his

3. Of all the colleges and universities founded before 1860, 182, or only about 20 percent, survive. Of these 9 were founded before 1780, 25 before 1799, and 49 before 1820. About 90 percent of the pre-Civil War college presidents were clergymen.

creation of a public school system that became a model for many parts of the world, reflected this optimism and conveyed it to orthodox and liberal alike as a fundamental element of the American dream. Mann thus received, transmuted, and passed on an unquestioning faith (too unquestioning perhaps) in the wonder-working power of the schoolroom.

Dogmatic Puritanism was banished from Mann's mind, and the public education system he envisioned naturally made no place for it. When his famous *Seventh Annual Report* made this position explicit, it aroused orthodox wrath and endangered his project. But the determination to remake the world survived, as did the conviction that education, however nonsectarian, must instill the historic Protestant virtues. No humanitarian crusader reveals more clearly than Mann how the reform impulse sprang from and reflected back the evangelical conscience—including both its idealism and its cultural narrowness. In this respect Mann's great contemporary William H. McGuffey (1800–73) forged an even closer bond between Protestant virtues, national ideals, and literary values. Before the century's end over 120 million copies of his graded *Eclectic Readers* had helped to shape the American mind. Not far behind McGuffey's *Readers* in influence were the enormously popular works of instruction written by two New England ministers: Samuel G. Goodrich (1793–1860), known to several generations for his hundred or more "Peter Parley" books; and the prolific Jacob Abbott, whose literary creations "Rollo" and "Marco Paul" instructed American children in almost everything they could or ought to be curious about. The basic outlook and presuppositions of these dedicated men pervaded the nation's schools until well into the twentieth century, when a greater awareness of the country's pluralism required adjustments which are still in the process of being made.

Women's Rights

Rivaling education in its basic significance for the spirit and structure of American society was the crusade to gain fuller rights for women and to give them a larger role in the country's life. Unlike educational reform, however, this campaign encountered considerable resistance. The opposition can be traced in part to the Reformation's critique of monasticism and its concomitant exaltation of the family. Woman's place was in the home. Protestant churches also tended toward a strict interpretation of Saint Paul's demand that women be silent (I Cor. 14:34), and women lost their opportunity to be heard in the churches—except among the Quakers. During the eighteenth century and the early years of the Republic, the general legal status of women noticeably declined, in part, it has been suggested, as the price of their becoming "ladies." In the nineteenth century the time had come for feminist reform.

Margaret Fuller's *Woman in the Nineteenth Century* (1845) was the first full philosophic and historical statement of feminism by an American; but important steps had been taken long before that. One breakthrough resulted from the revivals, especially in the West, where Saint Paul's stricture was ignored, notably by Charles G. Finney's new measures. Another line of advance led through the many evangelical voluntary associations growing out of the Second Awakening. In these efforts the support of local women's groups came gradually to be almost essential. Various professions offered limited opportunities which a growing number of determined women grasped. In 1850 Oberlin, the country's first coeducational college, even granted a theological degree to a woman, Antoinette Brown, who after many difficulties was ordained three years later. A few daring pioneers broke into the medical profession.

But the chief avenue of advance was in education, where women served increasingly as teachers and headmistresses. Two women, each a feminist crusader in her own way, gained special renown for their lasting contributions in this field. Emma Willard (1787–1870), aided by her husband, spent a lifetime as lecturer, poet, teacher, textbook writer, and headmistress. Though "Rocked in the Cradle of the Deep" is her best-known production, she is more worthily remembered for the great "Female Seminary" in Troy, New York, which she founded in 1821. Mary Lyon (1797–1849) led a very similar life, culminating it with the founding of Mount Holyoke College for women in 1836–37. Like Mrs. Willard's seminary, it answered an immense need for the advanced schooling of girls and the training of future teachers. With greater intensity than at most such schools, the activities and ethos at Mount Holyoke were focused on the hope that every student would be brought to a personal knowledge of Jesus Christ. Emily Dickinson became one of the school's most celebrated failures in this regard.

Other significant contributions to the education of women were made by Matthew Vassar, a devout Baptist brewery owner who in 1861 provided an endowment of almost unprecedented size for the first true liberal arts college for women in America. Another subtle but effective feminist, who also did much to advance the work of women's education, was Sarah Hale, a sometime novelist, pious and practical, who for nearly a half-century held a position of unique influence as editor first of the *Ladies' Magazine* and then of Louis A. Godey's immensely successful *Lady's Book*.

The greatest, or at least the most ostentatious, point of feminist advance in the antebellum period was the result of women's involvement in the temperance movement, and then with greater force in the antislavery crusade. Not only did their presence gain attention in causes so notorious, but the antislavery movement itself became deeply involved in the struggle for women's rights. William Lloyd Garrison's insistence on this principle, when combined with other radical demands, led in 1840 to a schism in the abolitionist movement. Such activities did not prevent the organization of a separate feminist movement, however; and in 1848 the inevitable campaign was launched at a Woman's Rights Convention held in the home of Elizabeth Cady Stanton of Seneca Falls, New York. Though its progress before the war was not sensational, more liberal laws were passed in many states and women moved into far more prominent positions in American public life.

Prisons and Hospitals

The Reverend Louis Dwight became the leader of still another humanitarian cause when his work as an agent for the American Bible Society opened his eyes to the shocking conditions in the prisons he visited. Returning to Boston, Dwight became the chief inspiration and in due course the secretary of the Boston Prison Discipline Society. Through his influence the Auburn System (so called because of its initiation at Auburn, New York, in 1824) of cell blocks and group labor began to replace the Pennsylvania System of solitary confinement and solitary labor, in time providing the United States with prisons that were models for the whole world to observe. Alexis de Tocqueville, touring America in 1831, was impressed by the success of the Reverend E. M. P. Wells, the director of Boston's house of correction for children, in making his prison both educational and reformatory.

The most widely influential campaign for the proper hospitalization and care of the mentally ill was that of the indefatigable Dorothea Dix (1802–87), a remarkable spinster schoolmistress. Channing moderated her strict Puritan upbringing and aroused in her (as in so many others) a moral passion. With the aid of other reformers, she provoked the Massachusetts legislature in 1843 to improve and expand the Worcester hospital for the insane. Among her supporters in these efforts were Samuel Gridley Howe, already famous for his work in educating the blind, and Horace Mann. It was now left for Dr. Samuel B. Woodward (1787–1850) to make Worcester world-famous for humane treatment and for its successful cures. Miss Dix's vigorous ministry of compassion also contributed directly to increased national concern for the founding or improvement of mental hospitals.

The Peace Crusade

Most idealistic of all the reform campaigns was that which took its inspiration from the ancient dream of the prophet Micah—that men would beat their swords into ploughshares and their spears into pruning hooks. As in so many other crusades, the Society of Friends was at the root of the movement, articulating the doctrine of Christian pacifism. But it was not only among Quakers such as Penn, Woolman, and Benezet that the movement found its pioneers. The optimism of the Enlightenment influenced Benjamin Rush, Benjamin Franklin, and many others who saw little glory or value in war despite their involvement in the American Revolution. In William Ellery Channing the same streams of Christian moralism and rationalistic optimism ran together, as they did even more effectively in *A Solemn Review of the Custom of War,* written by the Reverend Noah Worcester in 1814.

The Massachusetts Peace Society was organized in Channing's own home in 1815, with Worcester as editor of its journal. Within a few years it had a number of local and state branches. But what stirred this organization into more than fitful activity was the organizing ability of two wealthy laymen, William Ladd of New Hampshire, a convert of Channing and Worcester, and David Low Dodge, who had independently organized a society in New York City. Through their joint efforts the American Peace Society was formed in 1828 along familiar lines. For a decade and more the society stimulated discussion of the evils of war and the possibilities of a "Congress of Nations" to avert it.

Soon, however, the Peace Society began to have battles of its own due to the pugnacious pacifists that it had won to its banner—notably William Lloyd Garrison, through whose influence it became involved in both the antislavery crusade and the struggle for women's rights. A further drift to radical nonresistance, pacifism, and anarchism took place with the accession of three communitarians: John Humphrey Noyes, Adin Ballou, and Bronson Alcott. In 1838 these forces routed the old leadership of the society and formed a new organization, the New England Nonresistance Society.

In 1846 still another organization, international in scope, was founded by Elihu Burritt, "the learned blacksmith" of Natick, Massachusetts. This League of Universal Brotherhood aroused considerable popular strength due to Burritt's tireless zeal in lecturing, writing, and organizing. By making a personal pacifist pledge a chief element of its program, it won a large and dedicated following. Yet both the motives and the effects of the peace movement were ambiguous. Before and during the Mexican War, for example, many prominent figures—James Russell Lowell and Charles Sumner, for example—voiced loud demands for peace, but such actions cannot be explained as simple devotion to pacifism. Sectional controversy was becoming the master fact of the times, and the peace movement's chief historical significance may well be its divisive role in the antislavery movement. In that irony, moreover, the tragic element of America's "golden day" stands revealed.

No one ever stated the hopes of the age with greater confidence and fervor than did that father of many reformers and crusaders, Lyman Beecher, in his sermon of 22 December 1827:

> The history of the world is the history of human nature in ruins. . . . It is equally manifest that this unhappy condition of our race has not been the result of physical necessity, but of moral causes. The earth is as capable of sustaining a happy as a miserable population. . . . A voice from heaven announces the approach of help from above. "He that sitteth upon the throne saith, Behold I make all things new." [Rev. 21:5] The renovation here announced is a moral renovation which shall change the character and condition of men. . . . It shall bring down the mountains, and exalt the valleys; it shall send liberty and equality to all the dwellings of men. Nor shall it stop at the fireside, or exhaust its blessings in temporal mercies; it shall enter the hidden man of the heart, and there destroy the power which has blasted human hopes, and baffled human efforts. . . .
>
> I shall submit to your consideration . . . that our nation has been raised up by Providence to exert an efficient instrumentality in this work of moral renovation. . . . The origin and history of our nation are indicative of some great design to be accomplished by it. . . . Who can doubt that the spark which our forefathers struck will yet enlighten this entire continent? But when the light of such a hemisphere shall go up to heaven, it will throw its beams beyond the waves; . . . it will awaken desire, and hope, and effort, and produce revolutions and overturnings, until the world is free. . . .
>
> Floods have been poured upon the rising flame, but they can no more extinguish it than they can extinguish the fires of Aetna. Still it burns, and still the mountain heaves and murmurs; and soon it will explode, with voices, and thunderings, and great earthquakes. And then will the trumpet of jubilee sound, and earth's debased millions will leap from the dust, and shake off their chains, and cry, "Hosanna to the Son of David."[4]

4. "The Memory of Our Fathers," in Beecher's *Works*, 4 vols. (Boston, 1852), 1:315–17, 324–28.

The apocalyptic tone and the catastrophic images, as it happened, would receive their partial validation in an unsuspected way. The Civil War would blot the clean white page which the reformers had reserved for future glories. The country faced a problem that humanitarian campaigns and vest-pocket utopias could not solve. The greatest moral crusade remained. The problem, of course, was slavery. When Horace Mann was appointed in 1848 to the seat of the late John Quincy Adams in Congress, he soon decided that a national role in educational reform was no longer open to him. Other business, ominous and utterly inescapable, was at hand. A whole nation gradually came to the same realization.

40

SLAVERY, DISUNION, AND THE CHURCHES

On 22 September 1862, with General Lee's army in at least temporary retreat, Abraham Lincoln announced to his cabinet that, in accordance with a solemn vow made before God on the eve of the battle of Antietam, he would issue an emancipation proclamation. Only twenty-eight years earlier, in October 1835, William Lloyd Garrison, the abolitionist leader, had been dragged through the streets of Boston with a rope around his body—in Massachusetts, the first of the independent colonies to outlaw slavery. Seventeen years before Garrison was hog-tied, the General Assembly of the undivided Presbyterian church had unanimously adopted a manifesto that declared the institution of slavery "utterly inconsistent with the law of God." [1] In 1861 the formal *Address* of the newly constituted Presbyterian Church of the C.S.A. declared in equally positive terms that "We have no right, as a Church, to enjoin [slavery] as a duty, or to condemn it as a sin." Such was the jagged course of events—paradoxical, ironic, tragic—that brought the American people through the most traumatic experience of its history. Between the beginning and the end a titanic drama was played out on a continental stage. Out of the culminating test of arms emerged a new nation, purged and scarred, deprived of innocence, and facing a task of "reconstruction" which after a whole century's passage would still be uncompleted. This ordeal is the crucial experience of the nation—and, not

1. This resolution of the General Assembly is often quoted out of context. It was in fact a full-scale compromise that conceded "hasty emancipation to be a greater curse" than slavery. Moreover, the same judicatory in the same 1818 meeting also voted to uphold the Lexington Presbytery (Kentucky) in its deposition of the Reverend George Bourne from the ministry for his antislavery views. But this only heightens the irony (see Andrew E. Murray, *Presbyterians and the Negro*, pp. 20–28).

less, of its churches. We do well, therefore, to explain this *crux,* this Cross.

There is a reason why. The Civil War has become enmeshed in the national self-consciousness not simply because of its enormous cost in carnage and death, but because it exposed a fundamental moral commitment which the nation has never been able to discharge. It tested whether Daniel Webster's vision of "liberty and union, now and forever, one and inseparable" was an oratorical ploy or a meaningful hope. In this sense the great sectional cataclysm was a "moral" war. It was not "moral" because one side was good and the other evil, nor because purity of motive was more pronounced on one side than on the other. It was a moral war because it sprang from a moral impasse on issues which Americans in the mid-nineteenth century could no longer avoid or escape. Had there been no slavery, there would have been no war. Had there been no moral condemnation of slavery, there would have been no war. Yet slavery had become a massive American institution, and the South, given its racial predicament, could not entertain emancipation: the peculiar institution was worth disunion. By 1860, on the other hand, the nation's always uneasy conscience had been aroused, and in the North it had been shaped into a crusade which could not accept either indefinitely continued compromise or peaceable secession. So war came. Its origins go back at least to Europe's almost simultaneous discovery of the African Gold Coast and the New World. Its aftermath still constitutes the country's chief moral challenge. Nowhere in Christendom was Negro slavery more heavily institutionalized, nowhere was the disparity between ideals and actuality so stark, nowhere were the churches more deeply implicated. Few subjects, if any, are so fundamental to American religious history.

The year 1619 has fateful significance, for it marked the institution of representative government, the introduction of tobacco culture, and the beginning of black servitude in white America. Slavery soon became an accepted fact of life in Virginia, as it had long since been in New Spain, and as in a few decades it would become in the other colonies, including those of the North.[2] Puritan and Yankee shipowners found equally strong economic grounds for cutting themselves in on the profits of the slave trade, a business far more inhumane than slaveholding. The complicity of the whole nation—in attitude and act—has been general from the beginnings to the present.

Yet very early there were also protests and denunciations. Perhaps the earliest in British America was a petition published in Pennsylvania in 1688

2. Slave labor was used to some extent in every colony. In 1775 the total slave population in the seven Northern colonies exceeded forty thousand. In East Jersey slaves made up 12 percent of the population, in Rhode Island, 6 percent (see Arthur Zilversmit, *The First Emancipation: The Abolition of Slavery in the North,* pp. 4–7).

by Francis Daniel Pastorius. In 1700 Judge Samuel Sewall of Boston published his *Selling of Joseph.* The Quakers made similar testimonies during these years though their relapse in New Jersey and elsewhere led to the publication of John Woolman's *Considerations on the Keeping of Negroes* in 1754. More outspoken and effective, however, was the Quaker Anthony Benezet, who in 1776 led the Society of Friends to expel its slaveholding members. And in 1775 a group of Philadelphia Quakers organized the country's and possibly the world's first antislavery society. During the next two decades similar organizations were formed in many states, including Maryland (1790), Virginia (1791), and Delaware (1794). John Wesley took over Benezet's view, and the Christmas Conference of 1784, from which American Methodism dates its formal origins, instituted measures to exclude slaveowners or dealers from membership. Later, where slavery took institutional root, the discipline was progressively relaxed in a pattern visible also among the Baptists, who have a similar history of forceful statements in the revolutionary period, followed by a steady accommodation of Southern practice. In New England the antislavery standard was also raised in the 1770s, most significantly by two strict Edwardsean divines, Jonathan Edwards, Jr., in New Haven, and Samuel Hopkins in Newport.

For the revolutionary generation antislavery questions were subordinate to other concerns, and the federal Constitution came to terms with the institution. Widespread moral uneasiness was exhibited, however, in the Constitution's provisions to end the slave trade, in the prohibition of slavery in the Northwest Ordinance of 1787, and in the fact that nearly every northern state had by this time abolished or provided for the gradual abolition of slavery. As the country matured, the questioning, lamentation, and protest continued, nurtured by Christian conviction and patriotic idealism. Objections were clearly spoken even in the South, where the institution was firmly entrenched. Between 1808 and 1831, in fact, Southerners were more important than Northerners in the antislavery movement.

In the midst of this state of affairs, the American Colonization Society was organized in 1817 with the support of many distinguished political leaders, Southerners John Marshall, James Monroe, and Henry Clay among them. Its purpose was to raise funds to remunerate slave owners and send free Negroes back to Africa. A paper was published and a farflung organization established. The response was wide; at one time over two hundred local auxiliaries were in existence with ministers and churches playing a prominent role. Yet however well-intentioned, the movement was a failure. It actually diverted criticism of slavery, accepted fully the notion of Negro inferiority, and became chiefly a means of ridding the country of free blacks. Even in its practical workings failure stood out everywhere: the rate of manumission was almost unaffected (only two hundred slaves were freed and transported in the first decade; possibly four thousand by 1860), while Liberia became anything but a radiating center of Christianity in Africa. The society in fact did little more than sow moral confusion; in Dwight L. Dumond's words, "it was a rationalization for the lazy intellect, a sedative for the guilty conscience, a refuge for the politician and the professional man." [3] Yet some of the greatest antislavery leaders in the country were associated with it: Benjamin Lundy, Lewis Tappan, Gerrit Smith, James G. Birney, Theodore D. Weld, Elizur Wright, and many others. The society served as an awakening force and as a transitional organization.

But in the 1830s there occurred a remarkable change, almost a revolution, in the nation's attitude toward the slavery in its midst. The transition which took place in this decade can only be compared to the transformation in American race relations during the 1960s. Inert pronouncements like that of the Presbyterians in 1818 or those of the many Southern antislavery organizations became acutely relevant. Slumbering acceptances awoke as existential realities; silence, indecision, or mere lip service became increasingly rare, both North and South.

THE NORTHERN REVOLUTION

In the North, where slavery was nonexistent, the experience of William Lloyd Garrison (1805–79) is representative. After a childhood filled with much hardship, followed by uncertain years as a printer's apprentice and editor, Garrison was running a little Baptist temperance journal when in 1829 he was converted to the antislavery cause by Benjamin Lundy (1789–1839). A New Jersey Quaker and the greatest of the precursors, Lundy had organized the Union Humane Society in 1815; and in 1821, as antislavery assumed preeminence among his varied reform interests, he founded the *Genius of Universal Emancipation.* Before the year was out Garrison was helping to edit Lundy's *Genius,* and he was soon jailed for libel. Upon his release he went back to Boston to found the *Public Liberator and Journal of the Times;* and in the first issue (1 January 1831) he took the stand that was to make him famous—and infamous:

> *I will be* as harsh as truth, and as uncompromising as justice. On this subject [of slavery] I do not wish to think, or speak, or write, with moderation. . . . I am in earnest—I will not equivocate—I will not excuse—I will not retreat a single inch—AND I *WILL* BE HEARD.

3. Dwight L. Dumond, *The Anti-Slavery Origins of the Civil War in the United States,* p. 17.

Never a colonizationist and no longer a gradualist urging emancipation sometime "between now and never," Garrison demanded abolition immediately. Yet he drastically reduced the useful effect of his zeal by his absolutism, his astounding lack of charity, his incapacity to understand the thought or predicament of others, his unyielding demand for women's rights within the movement, his fierce anticlericalism and increasingly radical religious views, his almost anarchistic pacifism, his repudiation of political action, and (after 1843) his demand for *Northern* secession on grounds that the Constitution was a diabolical compact. The extent of his influence on abolitionism will probably always be disputed; but there is little doubt that he did far more than any other man to heighten Southern opposition to emancipation. Yet Garrison was not alone; to the end he had a hard core of followers, some even more radical than he. In a strange way, moreover, his conversion coincides with a great resurgence of conscientious abolitionism in the North.

In 1831 the wealthy merchant Arthur Tappan formed a New York committee and began to move toward a national antislavery organization. A year later, Garrison and a small group of Bostonians organized the New England Antislavery Society on a platform of immediatism. Then in 1833 came the British Slavery Abolition Act, and on its heels the American Antislavery Society was organized in Philadelphia. Despite public opprobrium and fierce opposition, this group wielded an enormous influence in the crucial thirties, planning conferences and lectures, distributing tons of literature, and knitting together the many new reform groups that were springing up across the nation.

Gradually merging with this impulse was a movement linked to the revival activity of Charles Finney in the Old Northwest. In 1834 Theodore Dwight Weld, one of Finney's converts, brought the antislavery gospel to Lane Theological Seminary in Cincinnati, where after a long series of debates the students issued a ringing indictment of the Colonization Society. When their radicalism precipitated disciplinary measures by the seminary trustees, one vocal group of dissidents migrated to Oberlin. This college was then little more than a "bivouac in the wilderness," but under the leadership of Asa Mahan and later Finney himself, and with financial aid from the Tappans of New York, it soon became a center of both abolitionism and Finneyite revivalism.[4]

4. The linking of conversion and Christian commitment to a socially relevant cause is the clue to antislavery careers such as Weld's or Elijah Lovejoy's. John Gregg Fee (1816–1901) on coming to Lane Seminary long after the abolitionist exodus discovered this nexus for himself. Yielding to the entreaties of his most serious student friends, he says, "I saw that to

Just before the Lane debates James G. Birney (1792–1857), a former slaveholder and colonizationist, had moved to Kentucky, where he was converted to abolitionism by Weld. In 1835 Birney organized a short-lived antislavery society in Kentucky; but when mob action threatened, he moved to Cincinnati to publish a crusading journal. Various associates of Weld and Birney carried the work on into Indiana and Illinois. Then in 1837 the murder of Elijah Lovejoy in Alton, Illinois, sent an electrifying tremor all across the North. "A shock as of any earthquake," John Quincy Adams called it. Because Lovejoy died defending his fourth printing press, three others having been destroyed since his forced departure from Saint Louis, the event had the additional effect of demonstrating the ultimate incompatibility of slavery and freedom in the same country. The events in Alton brought Edward Beecher, then president of Illinois College, to a decision for abolitionism. From Beecher issued not only a dramatic narrative of the Alton riots, but in 1845 a series of articles on "organic sin" which gave evangelical abolitionism some of its major ethical and theological insights. Far away in Boston William Ellery Channing was also aroused; and at the Faneuil Hall protest meeting which he organized Wendell Phillips began his sensational career as a radical orator.

In this manner the antislavery axis of the Tappans, Garrison, Weld, Lovejoy, and Birney (who became secretary of the American Antislavery Society in 1837) transformed a despised and persecuted protest movement into a nationally organized crusade that by 1840 was far beyond the reach of catcalls and rotten eggs. In New England, New York, and the Northwest antislavery and evangelicalism had struck a close and powerful alliance that would soon wield great political influence. Among the factors contributing to this result was an equally profound transformation in the South.

THE SOUTHERN REVOLUTION

The decade of the 1830s brought a no less decisive change in the slave states than in the North. Perhaps the most important indigenous stimulus

embrace the principle [of abolition] and wear the name was to cut myself off from relatives and former friends. . . ." Yet one day, on his knees in a nearby woods, Fee consecrated himself with these words: "Lord, if needs be, make me an Abolitionist." He said that he rose from prayer that day "with the consciousness that I had died to the world and accepted Christ in all the fullness of his character as I then understood him." He went on to a life dedicated first to antislavery and then to the freedman, as the founding spirit of Berea College in Kentucky (see Fee's *Autobiography* [Chicago, 1891], p. 14; and the MS. biography of Fee by Robert Loesch [1966], Yale Divinity School Library, New Haven, Conn.). Gilbert H. Barnes in *The Anti-Slavery Impulse, 1830–1844* presents these matters better than any other study, but he does not cover the crucial period for the churches—from 1844 to 1861.

to the increasingly vigorous rallying of support for slavery in the South was the outbreak in August 1831 of the Virginia slave revolt led by Nat Turner, a black preacher and visionary. The report of at least fifty-seven white people dead spread a wave of fear and anger through the region and focused Southern attention on the new abolitionist movement—especially on the vituperative language of Garrison. During the winter of 1831–32, to be sure, the Virginia legislature did debate the slavery question, but the chief support for abolition came from the future West Virginia region, while open discussion of this sort soon disappeared altogether. More important than arguments were the measures taken to prevent the dissemination of antislavery literature. Advocates of emancipation were threatened or mobbed, and by 1837 not one of the many antislavery societies that had existed early in the century remained. Even the Colonization Society became suspect; and some of the country's most prophetic voices on the slavery issue had to move north.

The South was rapidly closing ranks. An elaborate "scriptural argument" had long since soothed Christian and Jewish consciences on slavery itself, but now a new kind of Southern nationalism began to take shape, and central to it was a romantic idealization of the "cavalier" tradition. Arguments that slavery was a "positive good" were rare up to this time, but after 1831 they gained more spokesmen and countless new believers. Professor Thomas R. Dew of William and Mary published the first systematic defense of slavery and the structure of Southern society in his review of the Virginia debates (1832). In this area, as in so many others, John C. Calhoun (1782–1850) became the region's leading defender. Before the Senate in 1837 he insisted that "Abolition and Union cannot coexist," then moved to "higher ground" with the declaration that, given the "two races," slavery was a "positive good." In the 1850s the published treatises of Calhoun, Edmund Ruffin, Henry Hughes, and George Fitzhugh would provide elaborate sociological defenses of Southern institutions, often coupling them with thoroughgoing critiques of industrial "wage slavery" in the North. Nor were these theoretical statements without some basis in fact. Eli Whitney's cotton gin, the development of upland cotton, the rising market for cotton, the westward extension of the plantation system, and the growing profitableness of slavery all served to undergird Southern confidence in its way of life.

THE IMPENDING CRISIS

This critical period was fraught with other vital developments. First and foremost was the acceleration of thought in the Western nations toward a larger understanding of human equality and freedom, a trend which erupted in the sporadic European revolutions of 1830. Legislative progress in England included the great Reform Bill of 1832, followed in 1833 by an emancipation act. By 1848, revolutionary repercussions were more severe and widespread, and one result was the abolition of slavery in the French Empire. The time for sweeping American outrage at the injustices of industrialism was not yet ripe, but in the emerging idealism there was almost no place left for serfdom, and even less for slavery. In this sense, Garrison's activity was only one unusually strenuous manifestation of a growing international tendency. It is impossible to imagine how this current of idealism could have been ignored or resisted anywhere in the Atlantic community. Indeed, the strangely retarded response of Americans, even of Northern Americans, is the situation most in need of explanation.

A second factor, peculiar to the American South, was a set of circumstances that prevented the free discussion of slavery and the elaboration of means to eliminate it gradually and peacefully. The basic factor was not the economic value of slavery (which was debatable in any case) but that the slaves constituted a huge nonwhite population numbering 700,000 in 1790 and at least 3.5 million in 1860. Slavery was, to be sure, a labor system, but more fundamentally it was considered an essential means of social control over a race which at that time was regarded by almost everyone (including most abolitionists) as an inferior branch of the human species. In the South the black-white population ratio made this "race problem" preeminent. In the resultant social order Western ideals of equality and freedom simply could not be accepted.[5] We are thus driven again to the moral issue. An increasing number of Americans could not condone slavery or rest at peace while it existed; other Americans could not contemplate life without it. Honorable, ethical, God-fearing people as well as self-seeking, egotistic opportunists and status seekers were on both sides. Social, economic, political, and psychological forces intensified feelings, sharpened disputes, clouded the fundamental issues, and consolidated existing fears and antipathies—but the moment of truth had to come.

In 1840 the American Antislavery Society broke in two. Women's rights

5. Slavery in all of its ramifying effects gave the entire social and moral order of the South its characteristic shape and spirit. The plantation economy, as U. B. Phillips insisted, was a "way of life." Eugene D. Genovese has further advanced our understanding of this way of life, emphasizing especially the way in which the dependence of the region's leaders made them violently intolerant of anyone and anything threatening to expose the full nature of their relationship to their slaves. Genovese also observes that it is not "the moral attack on slavery . . . in the world of the nineteenth century" that needs explanation, but its absence (see *The Political Economy of Slavery* [New York: Vintage Books, 1967], pp. 10, 33; and his foreword to Ulrich B. Phillips, *American Negro Slavery* [Baton Rouge: Louisiana State University Press, 1966], p. xix).

was the ostensible issue, though Garrison's insistence on nonpolitical moral suasion was the primary cause. Yet the breach was hardly disastrous, inasmuch as the antislavery movement was thoroughly politicized by 1840. Politicians and statesmen (some of them bunglers, some not) assumed new importance. By this time the Nullification Crisis of 1832–33 was past history and John Quincy Adams was midstream in his battle against the gag rule on slavery; Joshua Giddings from Ohio's Western Reserve had joined him. Weld, who had gone to Washington and set up "one of the most effective lobbies that the country had yet known," saw the facts clearly:

> Nothing short of miracles, constant miracles, and such as the world has never seen can keep at bay the two great antagonistic forces. . . . They must drive against each other, till *one* of them goes to the bottom. *Events,* the master of men, have for years been silently but without a moment's pause, settling the basis of two great parties, the nucleus of one slavery, of the other freedom.[6]

After 1840 events would continue to exert their polarizing pressure—but they would not be silent. Indeed, "irrepressible conflict" was an actuality long before William H. Seward uttered the words in 1858. Was not even Weld speaking of unavoidable war?

The annexation of Texas (1845), the Mexican War, legislation for the vast territory won from Mexico, fugitive slave laws, the Kansas-Nebraska Act, "Bleeding Kansas," the assault on Senator Sumner, the Dred Scott decision, the Lincoln-Douglas debates—such were the provocations. In this new context the nation's political life was inescapably transformed. The Liberty party had been founded in 1840 with Birney as it presidential nominee. No match for the Log Cabin and Hard Cider campaign, he garnered only 7,100 votes. But in the 1843 state elections, the party won 43,000 votes. Birney ran again in 1844 and had the enormous satisfaction of seeing 15,812 abolitionist votes in New York swing the state—and the nation—to Polk. Four years later the Liberty party passed its flickering torch to the Free Soil party. Thereafter political antislavery bided its time as the old party structure began to collapse. In the outrage over the Fugitive Slave Law and "Bleeding Kansas" the new "Republican" party was founded, gathered in the growing "antislavocracy" vote, and in the election of 1856 electrified the nation by carrying every Northern state but three. The Whig, Know-Nothing, and even the Northern Democratic organizations were being reoriented to other stars. In 1860 it would be Lincoln—and then secession.

6. Theodore D. Weld to James G. Birney, 22 January 1842; quoted in Dumond, *Anti-Slavery Origins,* pp. 91–92.

ECCLESIASTICAL INVOLVEMENT

The essential history of the years from 1840 to 1860 was not all written in Washington. Paralleling the political processes was a momentous series of events in the religious and moral spheres that made church history intrinsic to both Northern and Southern developments. More than ever the vision of the United States as a beacon to the world was moving men and women to action. The many voluntary associations for evangelism and moral reform became inseparable from the humanitarian crusades, including the most powerful of these, the crusade against slavery. The great fulcrum for moving the Northern conscience on these matters was the Second Awakening's blending of "modern Puritan" evangelicalism and patriotic idealism. The churches were slow in joining the antislavery cause, but they did most of the pioneering; and as the movement gained momentum the countless auxiliary organizations of mainstream Protestantism became radiating centers of concern and agitation. The national antislavery societies, now moribund and faction-ridden, were superseded by ecclesiastical organizations in which an antislavery "social gospel" was forging ahead, winning new leaders, trampling on compromisers, and bringing schism or conflict when the occasion demanded.

One of the profoundest contributions to this process did not appear until 1852, when the wife of a Congregational professor of Old Testament—and an able lay theologian herself—confronted the divided nation with *Uncle Tom's Cabin,* considered by one of its harshest and least comprehending critics as "perhaps the most influential novel ever published . . . a verbal earthquake, an ink-and-paper tidal wave." [7] Harriet Beecher Stowe was sure that God wrote the book—and in a way this was so, for no author was ever burdened with a more driving sense of Christian moral fervor. But there is much more in the book than ethical passion. Her picture of slavery, though artificial, was not overdrawn but on the verge of idealization; Simon Legree's New England origins gave a national scope to her argument, and though "Uncle Tom" was to become a twentieth-century term of abuse, her conception of the Negro's capacities was in advance of nearly all Southerners and most Northerners, including the abolitionists. She was by no means the first to enlist fiction for the antislavery cause. But no other storyteller matched her intuitions of the essential issue or knew so well how to touch the country's conscience.

7. J. C. Furnas, *Goodbye to Uncle Tom* (New York: William Sloane Associates, 1956), pp. 4, 7. In assailing the Uncle Tom image of the Negro, Furnas was ahead of most critics, but in seeing Harriet Beecher Stowe as an unusually virulent propagator of the image, he was wrong. Her view of the "political economy of slavery" was in advance of its times.

"Bleeding Kansas" also had its Christian history, for the churches in the East were active in defining the issue so as to lead men westward to save the Great Plains from slavery. Henry Ward Beecher raised money from his pulpit to provide rifles ("Beecher's Bibles") for the cause. Out of Kansas, too, came that Connecticut-born wanderer and Bible-reading son of the Puritans, John Brown (1800–59). Part prophet, part adventurer, he made himself the symbol of the irrepressible conflict; and even with his body moldering in the grave, the memory of his exploit at Harpers Ferry became a living component of Northern esprit during the war.

The same combination of moral certainty and evangelical fervor runs through the great hymns of the movement. As early as 1844 James Russell Lowell's explicit linking of biblical images and antislavery gave an apocalyptic meaning to "The Present Crisis":

Once to ev'ry man and nation
Comes the moment to decide,
In the strife of truth with falsehood,
For the good or evil side;
Some great cause, God's new Messiah,
Off'ring each the bloom or blight,
And the choice goes by for ever
'Twixt that darkness and that light.

Though the cause of evil prosper,
Yet 'tis truth alone is strong
Though her portion be the scaffold,
And upon the throne be wrong,
Yet that scaffold sways the future,
And, behind the dim unknown,
Standeth God within the shadow
Keeping watch above his own.

Two decades later, when the issue had been joined, Julia Ward Howe added her contribution to the Union's legacy. Beneath the throbbing rhythms of a "battle hymn" later generations have often missed the terrible import of her lines. Her eyes had seen the glory. A Day of Judgment was at hand.

But what of the South? How does one deal with the anomaly of its equally fervent religiosity, its equally strident moralism? Since the postrevolutionary revivals had made equally great—possibly greater—advances below the Mason-Dixon line, the impact of evangelicalism in this region requires comment, even though research on the subject has been remarkably sparse. But above all we must note the immense disparity between avowedly

Christian views on slavery in the North and in the South and recognize the degree to which culture conditions religion and ethics, especially when a racial factor is present. Northern righteousness (and self-righteousness) could flourish without serious racial hindrance; in the South it could not. In the North it was possible to examine, even to exaggerate the evil, as Weld did in his *American Slavery as It Is* (1839). In the South it was almost impossible and, in any event, illegal by 1839.

As to the social impact of evangelicalism or of the perfectionist demands stemming from Wesley's or Finney's kind of revival preaching, the most obvious differences spring from the Southern tendency to channel such demands against the weaker provinces of Satan's kingdom, or, in other words, to keep the work of the "evangelical united front" at the tasks which chiefly preoccupied it before 1830. They avoided what Edward Beecher saw as the enveloping "organic sin." Yet this is not the whole fact, for slavery was not ignored. Richard Furman's biblical argument was adopted by the South Carolina Baptist Association in 1822, and by 1841, when John England, the Roman Catholic bishop of Charleston, published his defense, this line of thought had sunk deep into the Southern consciousness and underlay all others. Theologians and laity alike learned to recite the standard biblical texts on Negro inferiority, patriarchal and Mosaic acceptance of servitude, and Saint Paul's counsels of obedience to masters.

Some controversy did break out on the question of the unity of mankind —with the more extreme racists adopting the theory of separate origins of the black race. In general this view was denied, however, and an obligation to Christianize the slaves was acknowledged. In fact, the evangelization of the slaves was prosecuted with increased vigor as the abolitionist attack continued. Revivalism also contributed its emotionalism and anti-intellectual mood to the politics of the era, and in doing so it probably contributed to the expression of extremist views, just as it had in the North. In a political sense this no doubt eased the way of the fire-eaters in their efforts to crush out the more reasonable moderates and commit the slave states to secession and independence, and insofar as this made war seem likely, millennial fervor probably made Southerners as well as Northerners willing to commit the issue to arms and the terrible judgment of God. But the full dimension of the churches' involvement in the era's sectionalism can best be appreciated when considered in a denominational context.

The Presbyterians

The Presbyterian church did not explicitly divide on the great sectional issue until after secession. But the Old School–New School division of 1837 can probably be regarded as the first great ecclesiastical South-North separation. When Calhoun lamented before the Senate in 1850 that "already three great evangelical churches have been torn asunder" by the slavery issue, he was thinking of the Presbyterian church as well as the Baptist and Methodist. The Old School's most solid strength lay in that third of its membership from the deep South, while the New School claimed most of the Presbyterians who were leading the "evangelical united front" in the North. Many of them, to be sure, were still fairly conservative on the slavery issue in 1837, but their susceptibilities were well known, and Lovejoy's murder later in that very year led many of them to cross the Rubicon.

By suppressing official discussion of the slavery issue, the Old School avoided schism until the secession crisis of 1860, though a few congregations were lost during the 1840s to an antislavery offshoot of the New School. In 1845 pressure from midwestern synods brought an end to the enforced silence by forcing a statement from the General Assembly—but this pronouncement acknowledged slavery as biblical, and bade slaveholders treat slaves as immortal human beings. The official position adopted in 1849 was that slavery was a civil institution which should be dealt with by legislatures rather than churches. Countless individuals and groups attacked this official stand—and for a time the seminary at New Albany, Indiana, was their center—but to the very last they were an outmaneuvered minority. In 1859 even the New Albany Seminary was brought under control of the General Assembly, which merged it with the new seminary endowed by Cyrus McCormick in Chicago. When in May 1861 the Old School General Assembly in the mildest of terms expressed its loyalty to the Union, schism followed. Southern commissioners met separately in Augusta, Georgia, in December, and declaring slavery to be the cause of disunion, they published a forthright defense of that institution and organized a new Old School denomination.

The New School was at first only slightly less conservative on slavery than the church which had expelled it. And because its leadership wished to demonstrate its true Presbyterianism at every opportunity in order to make the injustice of the expulsion more obvious, the Congregationalists, many of whom were ardent in the antislavery cause, tended to lose interest in Plan-of-Union arrangements and to reassert their own denominational tradition. Yet the New School's great numerical strength in areas where abolitionism was strongest, together with its very small Southern constituency, guaranteed that (unlike the Old School) it would at least hold the ground claimed by the General Assembly's deliverance of 1818. This much it did in 1846 and 1849, and it was goaded to go even farther when antislavery men, chiefly in Ohio and nearby states, began leading churches out of both the New and the Old School, forming the short-lived Presbyterian Free Church Synod (1847–67). This church, which at its height had about sixty-four ministers and congregations, explicitly denied membership to slaveholders, though of course its disciplinary measures had little exercise in states where slavery was forbidden by law.

In 1850 the New School General Assembly took the first steps toward a similar position by repudiating the view that slavery was a divinely sanctioned institution. In 1853 steps toward enforcement were taken, and tension increased until 1857, when the Southern presbyteries, with about fifteen thousand members, withdrew to form a separate church. After the war it merged with the Old School Church, South, and this united body has continued as the Presbyterian Church of the United States. In 1958, when it refused reunion with the northern church, the votes in its presbyteries correlated markedly with black-and-white population ratios in the respective districts.

The Methodists

The Methodist Episcopal church was indebted to John Wesley for two closely related characteristics that made a unified weathering of the antislavery controversy very unlikely. It was organized in an exceedingly strict and inflexible way, so that disagreements had to be formally resolved or generally agreed to be unimportant. Methodism, moreover, was not theologically oriented (as was Presbyterianism), and hence it placed far greater emphasis on visible matters of discipline. Due in large part to these factors it had modified Wesley's original regulations on slavery as it sought to extend its membership in the South. By 1843 there were 1,200 Methodist ministers and preachers owning about 1,500 slaves, and 25,000 members with about 208,000 more. The church's unity depended therefore on the strict enforcement of silence or neutrality on the slavery question, and for a half-century this proved to be possible.

At the General Conference of 1836, however, the evils of slavery were formally conceded, though "modern abolitionism" was also condemned in very forceful terms. This ambivalent act only incited the increasing number of Methodist abolitionists, but at the General Conference of 1840 they were again successfully throttled. Before long antislavery Methodists began to secede, organizing the Wesleyan Methodist Church in Michigan (1841) and the Methodist Wesleyan Connection in New York (1842–43). At the same time many other Methodists participating in unsanctioned meetings and conferences raised an outcry over the slaveholding of Bishop

James O. Andrew of Georgia and began to clamor for a division of the church. Everyone knew that the General Conference meeting at New York in 1844 would produce a dramatic confrontation of the opposing forces, though perhaps few could have guessed that this would be the last convention of a united Methodist Episcopal church for almost a century.

At the momentous gathering of 1844 the delegates were for almost a fortnight locked in profound debate over two distinct but inseparable issues. First and fundamental was the slavery question: how decisive a stand would be taken upon it, and how directly would the stand be carried out in terms of Methodist discipline? Closely related was the problem of interpreting the church's constitution adopted in 1808: how "democratic" was the church? Were the bishops creatures of the General Conference, responsible to it, and deposable by it? Should bishops retain the immense powers of appointment and control of agendas of annual conferences that they had traditionally exercised? Bishop Andrew's case and the ensuing debates joined the two issues. The Southern delegates were unanimously committed to a strong episcopacy. And when the conference did vote on sectional lines, 111 to 69, that Bishop Andrew "desist from the exercise of his functions," they made clear in a unanimous representation that they would take even his resignation as a sign that division of the church was necessary. The Northern delegates were equally adamant, for they knew that failure to discipline the bishop would result in Northern schism. Given the total situation, it seemed impossible to avert division or even a postponement of the controversy until 1848.

At this point the Southern delegation proposed that an amicable plan of separation be drafted, so that the two churches could at least remain in fellowship with each other. When this proposal won support, a nine-man commission was appointed to work out details of the plan. Three days later the commission presented its detailed proposals, which were to be effected if the annual conferences in the slaveholding states (including Texas) approved. Two general conferences were to replace the present one, state boundary lines would be mutually respected in church extension, clergy could choose their affiliation, the publishing concern and other properties would be equitably divided. After brief debate came a nearly unanimous vote, the negatives chiefly motivated by fears that the plan was unconstitutional. Bishop Leonidas Hamline seemed to express the prevailing sentiment: "God forbid that they should go as an arm torn out of the body, leaving a point of junction all gory and ghastly! Let them go as brethren beloved in the Lord, and let us hear their voice, responsive, claim us for brethren." On this strangely conciliatory basis the conference was adjourned.

Immediately afterward the Southern delegation reconvened to prepare an address to their fourteen annual conferences, asking them to send delegates to a convention in Louisville on 1 May 1845, if they so desired. When they all complied, the Methodist Episcopal Church, South, was brought into existence. Since the South had dominated the episcopacy and gained acceptance for slavery in the discipline, almost no constitutional changes were necessary. The church went about its way in the old manner, continuing its work with alacrity. In 1846 it reported 459,569 members (124,961 of them "colored") and 1,519 traveling preachers. In 1848 it duly elected a fraternal delegate to the Northern General Conference.

In the North, however, the spirit of brotherly separation quickly evaporated. Charges of unconstitutionality were hurled, abolitionists (now deprived of an easy bone to chew) were furious, officials of the publishing concern were outraged by the violence done to their empire, and many delegates began to have second thoughts. In the 1848 General Conference, therefore, the South's delegate was rebuffed and the Plan of Separation voted, though with heavy opposition, to be "null and void." Though this act was entirely ineffectual, it was rightly interpreted as extremely ungracious. But some grounds for complaint existed. The boundary settlement took no cognizance of some "Northern" conferences which extended into "slave" states, but had not been given time to vote before the Southern church had organized itself. Consequently a "gory and ghastly" border warfare had, by 1848, already begun. Since the legal actions requisite to dividing the publishing concern had not been carried out, the Southern church took legal action, and in 1851 and 1854 was awarded a *pro rata* division. Not until 1872 did the Northern church redress the actions of 1848 by sending a fraternal delegate southward. In the meantime it identified itself increasingly with Northern sentiment on slavery, war, and reconstruction.

The Baptists

The experience of the Baptists in the schisms brought on by sectional strife differed from that of the other denominations primarily because its polity was so distinctly congregational that the chief national agency was in theory no more than a cooperative agency of the churches, a "General Convention . . . for Foreign Missions." Founded in 1814 to support missionaries who had unexpectedly been converted to Baptist views while enroute to Burma, the convention met triennially, after 1832 in conjunction with the new Home Missionary Society and others. During the 1830s it successfully avoided the slavery issue. In 1839–40 the Foreign Missions Board formally declared its neutrality, and in 1843 it was supported in this by the convention's vote. In 1841 Southern delegates and Northern moderates, being still in a majority, had been able to oust Elon Galusha, a vice-president on the board, replacing him with Richard Fuller, a South Carolina minister; and three years later both the General Convention and the Home Board convened and adjourned with the same coalition in control. Francis Wayland, the moderate president of Brown University, was elected president of the convention. In this series of events, Baptist history parallels that of the Methodists, and it continued to do so.

By 1844 abolitionism had gained in both numbers and stridency in the North, while the South became equally demanding of respect for its situation. In state conventions both North and South popular pressures steadily mounted, and before the year was out both mission boards were faced with decisions deliberately thrust upon them by the South. In October the Home Board declined to appoint as a missionary the nominee of the Georgia Baptist Convention, James E. Reeves, who was stated to be a slaveholder. Two months later the Foreign Board took the same ground when petitioned to state its policy by the Alabama Baptist Convention.

The Southern response to these two decisions might have been predicted. Long dissatisfied with the Home Board's neglect of the South and Southwest, leading Southern Baptists welcomed the slavery issue as an occasion for instituting a more distinctly connectional polity. The Virginia Baptist Foreign Mission Society took the lead, addressing a call to "all our brethren, North and South, East and West, who are aggrieved by the recent decision of the Board in Boston." A consultative convention set for 8 May 1845 at Augusta, Georgia, was to decide on the type of organization to be formed. On that date 293 delegates from nine states convened, and after only a few days' deliberation, the Southern Baptist Convention had a constitution and a "provisional government." Dr. W. B. Johnson of South Carolina was president of the organization he had done so much to found and shape. After 27 December 1845 the convention had a charter under the laws of Georgia. The first regular triennial session held at Richmond in 1846 ratified these labors and with great enthusiasm began an ambitious project of consolidation and extension.

The Southern Convention was a new departure for American Baptists. It was frankly denominational in spirit and scope, designed by men who did not hesitate to speak of the Baptist "Church" (in the singular). It could undertake multiple tasks and organize appropriate boards as it saw fit. In this very important sense it objectified what had long been latent in the Southern Baptist tradition—what its historians have referred to as a "centralizing ecclesiology." But one cannot discount the long-term basis for hierarchical and authoritarian modes of social organization which were engendered both by slavery and by the major intellectual defenses of it. The same tendency is evidenced by Southern Methodists in their struggles over ecclesiastical polity, and to a lesser degree, by the strict views on polity of the Presbyterian Old School.

The Southern Convention also bore the marks of the "society" type of organization which had preceded it: in basic essentials it was, like a hundred or so earlier Baptist societies both large and small, a fund-raising agency: its membership consisted of those "who contributed funds, or are delegated by religious bodies [usually churches] contributing funds." Its main innovative feature was its power to carry out such "benevolent objects" as it determined to be necessary, though missions were its primary interest at the outset. Theologically, therefore, it was very different from a Presbyterian synod, the Episcopal House of Bishops, or a Roman Catholic provincial council. That it gradually took on the functions of all of these and came in some ways to wield an authority that equaled any of theirs is a major anomaly. Even during the remaining antebellum years these constitutional innovations became a divisive factor, and after the war they would be so again. The slavery issue was now excluded from convention activities, however, and a period of growth and activity ensued. During its first fifteen years, the Southern Convention's membership grew from 351,951 to 649,518.

The old General Convention, meanwhile, was refashioned under President Wayland's leadership according to contrasting principles which reflected the extreme congregationalism which the Great Awakening had intensified and which the influential New Hampshire Confession of 1833 clearly expressed. This "American Baptist Missionary Union" was composed of individual memberships only, with provisions to exclude proslavery members.

Undivided Churches

No church in either its local or its collective manifestation could long escape the disruptive impact of the moral issue which the abolitionists belatedly thrust into American life. In the Presbyterian and Methodist churches, for example, events marched forward with a steady inexorable step that trampled individual and corporate loyalties. Schisms in two highly structured churches of the socially dominant Protestant mainstream, with large constituencies in both regions, anticipated the national rift. The Baptists were in a somewhat different category. Though they also had a nationally dispersed membership, the division of 1845 had occurred within a coordinating agency of a denomination in which state and local loyalties had always been paramount.

The Disciples of Christ very closely resembled the Baptists. But these ultracongregational followers of Barton Stone and the Campbells had not yet even developed the sense of cohesion which leads to the founding of national missionary societies. Indeed, "Stonites" and "Campbellites" only began to blend their traditions in 1832. There was thus very little that the slavery issue could really divide except local congregations. Moreover, the border-state mentality which prevailed in the chief areas of Disciple strength greatly reduced the divisive impact of abolitionism, and even of the war itself. As the Disciples expanded northward and southward, characteristic attitudes did take shape and schisms with social and sectional overtones would occur, but not until the postwar era.

American Judaism can be similarly classified, since its basically congregational polity made institutional division almost out of the question. During these years of controversy the Reform was growing very swiftly, both North and South, with largely German Jewish leadership. Perhaps because it was so enthusiastically bent on identifying with American life, its views on slavery tended to vary from place to place according to the prevailing views. When Rabbi David Einhorn took an antislavery stand in Baltimore he was forced to resign. Isaac M. Wise and the institutions over which he presided at Cincinnati remained neutral. Efforts by individual Jews to gain public prominence were rare, although Judah F. Benjamin's dedicated service in the legal, state, and treasury departments of the Confederacy are an outstanding exception.

Another group of churches escaped division chiefly because they did not have a constituency in both regions. The Congregationalists were the most prominent in this group, but Unitarians, Universalists, and many other small groups were in a similar situation. In the North these churches contributed powerfully to the antislavery movement, and with the passing years they became increasingly unified in their witness. The Texas question and Mexican War, however, sharpened the cleavages in the Congregational antislavery movement; and in 1846 a group of radicals—mostly New School Congregationalists—met in Albany to protest against the compromised position of the evangelical voluntary associations. They organized the American Missionary Association on evangelical *and* abolitionist principles, and began rapidly to expand its work, especially in the West and Upper South, but also in the British West Indies and among fugitive slaves. After 1865 they became the major educational agency at work in the South. Still other churches were undivided because for ethnic or doctrinal reasons they were withdrawn or isolated from the country's problems. The Mennonites are one good example, the Mormons another.

The Lutheran, Episcopal, and Roman Catholic churches constitute a final category. These three large churches for all practical purposes remained undivided until secession created two sovereign nations, despite the fact that each of them had relatively large constituencies in both regions, and each contributed vigorous polemicists to both sides in the slavery controversy. Their separate histories are dissimilar, but certain resemblances remain: in each case a combination of ecclesiastical, theological, and social factors prevented a head-on collision within the church. For example, Lutheran synods, like Episcopal and Roman Catholic dioceses, tended to be organized on a territorial basis, so that extreme views often did not meet at this level. For Lutherans, moreover, a truly "national" echelon was virtually nonexistent, since the General Synod, which often took a strong antislavery stand, had little more than advisory or coordinating functions. Hence each territorial or ethnic synod came to terms with the issue much as did other segments of the population. The single significant exception was the Franckean Synod which in 1837 organized itself in western New York as a separation from the Hartwick Synod. Antislavery figured prominently in its rationale, along with temperance, Sabbatarianism, Finneyite "new measures," and dissatisfaction with the Lutheran confessions. The Lutheran synods organized by new immigrant groups were for the most part in free territory, and they tended to oppose slavery, though they naturally preferred not to commit the church on what they regarded as secular political issues.

The general conventions of the Protestant Episcopal church did, of course, provide an opportunity for controversy; but the church was at no point threatened by schism or even seriously torn by the slavery issue. Even its own historians have found the church's extraordinary passivity difficult to understand, but the explanation probably lies in the fact that Episcopalians were generally conservative and for good reason rather well satisfied with the status quo. The church, moreover, was already very deeply aroused by issues stemming from the Oxford Movement. Separate dioceses could and did adapt themselves to local conditions.

The official position of the Roman Catholic church in the antebellum period was that slavery as a principle of social organization was not in itself sinful, though in 1839 Pope Gregory XVI had reiterated the church's condemnation of the slave trade. Bishop Francis P. Kenrick sought to interpret the church's teaching in his *Theologia Moralis* (3 vols., 1840–43) and from 1851 until his death in 1863, as archbishop of Baltimore he occupied the most influential post in the American hierarchy. But his teaching shows a persistent failure to clarify the differences between the actual American form of slavery and that which the church had condoned. He has been justly accused of equivocation. "Kenrick seemed to have been satisfied to let conditions remain in *statu quo*," writes a careful student of his ethics.[8] American Catholics as individuals expressed the full range of opinion on slavery; but the church took no official position. The successive Pastoral Letters of the assembled bishops between 1840 and 1852 remained silent on the nation's moral dilemma. Only in 1840 was there an ambiguous, indirect allusion to the nation's political parties—an admission that the hierarchy was divided. When the war came, the church maintained this stance, while bishops and archbishops North and South kept contact with Rome and with each other so far as circumstances would allow.

RETROSPECT ON THE ROAD TO WAR

Democratic government and involuntary servitude began their uneasy coexistence in America soon after 1619. Moral doubts about the peculiar institution arose almost as soon. Yet slavery extended its hold until the social order of an entire region was shaped by its dependence upon the bondage of a black race in its midst. The early witness of the churches and the access of egalitarianism in the years of the Revolution deepened the anomaly of slavery in the land of the free. After 1800 broadening democratic processes and evangelical resurgence intensified the sectional aspect of the conflict, until in the 1830s an acceleration of activity rapidly drove the nation toward its moment of truth. As intellectual communication and mutual confidence deteriorated, political rivalry deepened. Controversy became endemic and irrepressible. The federal Union itself came to be regarded in the South not as a beneficent source of strength but as a threat. Those who counseled compromise and moderation lost their adherents in both sections as the impasse became increasingly stark. In this hardening of attitudes the churches were a powerful factor. They provided the traditional recourse and appeal to the Absolute. They gave moral grandeur to the antislavery cause and divine justification for slavery. In the North the churches did much to hold the party of Lincoln on its antislavery course despite the efforts of local politicians, especially in the cities, to stress lesser, more immediate issues. The drastic step of secession followed immediately the Republican victory in the presidential election of 1860. On 4 February 1861, delegates of six

8. Joseph D. Brokhage, *Francis Patrick Kenrick's Opinion on Slavery*, pp. 239, 242.

states of the Deep South convened at Montgomery, Alabama, to organize the Confederate States of America. Not long after Lincoln's inauguration, on 12 April 1861, with the firing on Fort Sumter in Charleston harbor, the terrible war began.

41

THE CHURCHES AMID CIVIL WAR AND RECONSTRUCTION

To Leonidas Polk, the Episcopal bishop of Louisiana, the justice of slavery, a state's right to secede, and the necessity of Southern nationhood were as certain as the multiplication table. Having already declared his church in Louisiana to have "an independent diocesan existence," and having signed the call to organize a separate Protestant Episcopal Church of the South, he laid aside his episcopal duties when the guns of Sumter sounded and entered the Confederate army as a major-general. "I believe most solemnly," he confessed in June 1861 to his dear friend, Bishop Stephen Elliott of Georgia, "that it is for constitutional liberty, which seems to have fled to us for refuge, for our hearth-stones, and our altars that we strike. I hope I shall be supported in the work and have grace to do my duty." [1] Far away in Newport, meanwhile, Thomas March Clark, the Episcopal bishop of Rhode Island, addressed a farewell service for the state militia as they left for the war. "Your country has called for your service and you are ready," he declared. "It is a holy and righteous cause in which you enlist. . . . God is with us; . . . the Lord of hosts is on our side." He closed with a prayer bidding divine protection for the soldiers "now going forth to aid in saving our land from the ravages of sedition, conspiracy, and rebellion." [2]

In this manner did God go to battle in America, sustaining hearts, inspiring hopes, and justifying anger. And so through the long dark years he led on. The words that came to Julia Ward Howe on a sleepless night in the autumn of 1861 before the fighting had really begun became, as it happened,

1. William N. Polk, *Leonidas Polk: Bishop and General,* 2 vols. (New York, 1893), 1: 325.

2. Quoted in Chester F. Dunham, *The Attitude of the Northern Clergy toward the South, 1860–1865,* p. 112. Quotations from denominational spokesmen which follow are from this valuable work unless otherwised indicated.

the crusader's hymn of the Union, but the literal content of her verses would not have prevented the Confederacy from adopting it:

> I have seen him in the watch-fires of a hundred circling camps;
> They have builded him an altar in the evening dews and damps;
> I have read his righteous sentence by the dim and flaring lamps;
> His day is marching on.
>
> I have read a fiery gospel, writ in burnished rows of steel,
> "As ye deal with my contemners, so with you my grace shall deal";
> Let the Hero, born of woman, crush the serpent with his heel,
> Since God is marching on.[3]

Southerners were equally certain that God willed their defense of liberty, hearth, and altar; and they shared the hymn's sense of ultimate apocalyptic urgency. Nor did four years of war dim their conviction that they were fighting God's war, though defeats and exhaustion gave them less and less occasion to proclaim their faith in God's justice-dealing power.

In April 1865 at a Thanksgiving service after the fall of Richmond, the Reverend Phillips Brooks, the future Episcopal bishop of Massachusetts, lifted his voice in prayer:

> We thank Thee, O God, for the power of Thy right arm, which has broken for us a way, and set the banners of our Union in the central city of treason and rebellion. We thank Thee for the triumph of right over wrong. We thank Thee for the loyal soldiers planted in the streets of wickedness. We thank Thee for the wisdom and bravery and devotion which Thou has anointed for Thy work and crowned with glorious victory. . . . Thou hast led us, O God, by wondrous ways. . . . And now, O God, we pray Thee to complete Thy work.[4]

After a few weeks no more prayers for military victory would be needed.

Volume after volume could be filled with the same bloodthirsty condemnations, the same prayers for aid from the Almighty, the same self-righteous benedictions. The statements above are chosen from Episcopal spokesmen not because that church was more extreme, but because it praised itself and won the suspicion of others for its neutrality on the great issue of the day. In other communions the language was even more self-righteous. The Southern Presbyterian church, for example, formally resolved in 1864

3. Julia Ward Howe, *Reminiscences, 1819–1899* (Boston, 1899), pp. 269–76, stanzas 2 and 3 in original draft.

4. A. V. G. Allen, *Life and Letters of Phillips Brooks*, 1: 531.

that "we hesitate not to affirm that it is the peculiar mission of the Southern Church to conserve the institution of slavery, and to make it a blessing both to master and slave." [5] This church's Pastoral Letter of 1865, written after slavery was overthrown and the Confederacy done, spoke out on this "question of social morality" more vehemently than ever:

> When we solemnly declare to you, brethren, that the dogma which asserts the inherent sinfulness of this relation [slavery] is unscriptural and fanatical . . . that it is one of the most pernicious heresies of modern times, that its countenance by the church is a just cause of separation from it (I Timothy 6:1–5), we have surely said enough to warn you from this insidious error as from a fatal shore.[6]

In the North, the *Methodist Magazine* in 1864 took the contrary view:

> We must take the moral, the sacred, the holy right of our struggle up before the throne of God. We must accustom ourselves to dwell before the divine throne, clothed in the smoke of our battles. . . . We have a right to plead and to expect that God will let his angels encamp about our army; then he will make our cause his own—nay, it is his already.[7]

Although the extremity of feeling and conviction expressed in these quotations was a continuous feature of the entire sectional crisis, yet for violence of statement and ultimacy of appeal, the clergy and the religious press seem to have led the multitude. "We have been accustomed to observe, for years past," wrote an Illinois Baptist editor as he reflected on the exchanged periodicals that came to his desk, "[that] the most violent and radical pro-slavery men in that quarter [the South] were ministers." Chester Dunham's research on the Northern clergy makes it clear that these extreme views were reciprocated. Both in the North and in the South, moreover, the ministers had the largest and most regular audience, not only at Sunday and weekday meetings, but through a vast network of periodicals. By 1865 the official Methodist papers alone were reaching four hundred thousand subscribers. Even more important was the fact that in an age of great evangelical fervor, the clergy were the official custodians of the popular conscience. When the cannons roared in Charleston harbor, therefore, two divinely authorized crusades were set in motion, each of them absolutizing a given social and political order. The pulpits resounded with a vehemence and absence of restraint never equaled in American history.

5. Quoted in Paul H. Buck, *The Road to Reunion*, p. 60. This from a church that had justified its separation from the Northern church on grounds that otherwise "politics would be obtruded on our church courts"!

6. Thomas C. Johnson, *History of the Southern Presbyterian Church* (New York, 1894), p. 426.

7. Quoted in Dunham, *The Attitude of the Northern Clergy*, p. 205, passim.

Recognizing the churches' large role in dividing the nation, we may return to Calhoun's famous last words with advantages that he lacked. Was not the snapping of ecclesiastical cords to which he referred in 1850 more than a useful illustration for his oration? Were not these church divisions demonstrations that the nation's conscience was already in twain? William Warren Sweet, the church historian, posits an even deeper involvement. "There are good arguments," he says, "to support the claim that the split in the churches was not only the first break between the sections, but the chief cause of the final break." [8] In 1864 Professor R. L. Stanton of the Presbyterian theological school at Danville, Kentucky, gave substantial support to the same theory in his book *The Church and the Rebellion.* The South's rebellious defiance of lawful authority, he said, was born "in the Church of God." He also implicated Northern "doughface" preachers who by defending "southern rights" encouraged the growth of secessionism. And his conclusions are supported by recent research. "As its greatest social institution," writes Professor Silver,

> the church in the South constituted the major resource of the Confederacy in the building and maintenance of civilian morale. As no other group, Southern clergymen were responsible for a state of mind which made secession possible, and as no other group they sustained the people in their long, costly and futile War for Southern Independence.[9]

The main facts must be kept in mind. Churchmen played leading roles in the moral revolutions that swept the North and the South in opposite directions between 1830 and 1860. Between 1846 and 1860, churchmen gradually converted the antislavery movement into a massive juggernaut, and dedicated the South to preserving a biblically supported social order. To these opposing causes, moreover, they transmitted the overcharged intensity of revivalism, carrying it even to the troops when war finally came. Nor were the preachers repentant. "We are charged with having brought about the present contest," declared the Northern Methodist Granville Moody in 1861. "I believe it is true that we did bring it about, and I glory in it, for it is a wreath of glory around our brow." [10]

8. William W. Sweet, *The Story of Religion in America,* p. 312. Henry Clay on the eve of his death in 1852 also thought this was the case: "I tell you, this sundering of the religious ties which have bound our people together I consider the greatest source of danger to our country" (in an interview reported in the *Presbyterian Herald,* published at Louisville; quoted in Dunham, *The Attitude of the Northern Clergy,* p. 2.

9. James W. Silver, *Confederate Morale and Church Propaganda,* p. 101 (the book's final paragraph).

10. My own reading of sermons and tracts suggests that Moody's statement was typical rather than extreme, and that in 1861 it could have been uttered in either section of the country.

THE CHURCHES DURING THE WAR

Once disunion was a reality, the sovereign ecclesiastical fact was the division of the churches. Those with international connections of one sort or another remained in some kind of indirect communion with each other, but even they functioned as churches in separate nations and professed their patriotism in unquestionable terms. The Episcopal Church, C.S.A., brought much obloquy upon itself by formally changing the Book of Common Prayer; but all churches, in effect, did as much. At a meeting in 1862, the General Synod of the Lutheran church—bereft of its Southern synods—appointed a special committee to apprise President Lincoln of its wholehearted support, characterizing the "rebellion" as most wicked, unjustifiable, unnatural, inhuman, oppressive, and "destructive in its results to the highest interests of morality and religion." [11] The Southern Presbyterians who had with equal vigor insisted on the neutrality of the church on all "political" issues, including slavery, shifted their ground. In 1862 they expressed their deep conviction "that this struggle is not alone for civil rights and property and home, but also for religion, for the church, for the gospel, for existence itself." [12] Monotonously the same positions were formally taken or practically demonstrated in virtually every church.[13] Even the Roman Catholic church provided powerful champions of both causes, though every bishop of its eleven small Southern dioceses was born outside the South.[14]

Not only did the churches attest their loyalty to their respective governments and armies through sermon and prayer, but they actively participated in the war effort by bringing a Christian ministry to the soldiers and by organizing noncombatant support among their constituencies. Of all these wartime activities, the chaplaincy was the most time-honored. The United States War Department authorized one ordained and denominationally certified chaplain per regiment, giving each the grade of private; and in

11. Henry E. Jacobs, *A History of the Evangelical Lutheran Church in the United States*, ACHS, vol. 4 (New York, 1893), p. 452.

12. Johnson, *Southern Presbyterian Church*, p. 427. After the war the Southern Presbyterian church most categorically disavowed this wartime stand and reasserted the doctrine of the "nonsecular character of the church" and that its relation to any and all governments was *de facto*, not *de jure*.

13. The Missouri Synod Lutheran church may be the only exception among major denominations, in part because its headquarters were in a border state, but also because it was theologically opposed to pronouncements on sociopolitical issues.

14. Three Roman Catholic bishops of the C.S.A. were born in the North, three in Ireland, and four in France, including Archbishop Odin of New Orleans (see Benjamin J. Blied, *Catholics and the Civil War*). After the war nativistic Radical Republicans made much of the fact that the pope was the only sovereign power to have recognized the Confederate government. In fact, this recognition consisted of no more than the pope's addressing Jefferson Davis in a letter of 1863 as "Your Excellency."

1862 it authorized their assignment to hospital duty as well. The Confederacy made similar arrangements. To this challenge the denominations responded with alacrity, the Northern Methodist church alone providing nearly five hundred chaplains, the Southern Methodist and Episcopal churches about two hundred and one hundred respectively. Other churches, North and South, showed proportionate concern. In light of the disruptions wrought by the war the number of chaplains who volunteered was remarkably high, though the men in service always felt that they were hopelessly few to do the work at hand.

Chaplains performed heroic duties in many circumstances, in battle and behind the lines, and won countless tributes for their services to the sick, the wounded, and the dying. As in no other American war, they also carried on their preaching ministries with astounding success, as their great revivals won many converts even among the highest ranking officers. In these revivals as well as in their pastoral work and many other tasks, the chaplains were often joined by clergy of the locality. The diary of a Southern Methodist chaplain, John B. McFerrin, gives a vivid picture of this ministry:

> The Federals occupied Chattanooga, and for weeks the two armies were in full view of each other. All along the foot of Missionary Ridge we preached almost every night to crowded assemblies, and many precious souls were brought to God. After the battle of Missionary Ridge the Confederate army retreated and went into winter quarters at Dalton, Ga. During these many months the chaplains and missionaries were at work—preaching, visiting the sick, and distributing Bibles, tracts, and religious newspapers. There was preaching in Dalton every night but four, for four months; and in the camps all around the city, preaching and prayer meetings occurred every night. The soldiers erected stands, improvised seats, and even built log churches, where they worshiped God in spirit and in truth. The result was that thousands were happily converted and were prepared for the future that awaited them. Officers and men alike were brought under religious influence. In all my life, perhaps, I never witnessed more displays of God's power in the awakening and conversion of sinners than in these protracted meetings during the winter and spring of 1863–64.[15]

So continuous were these manifestations of piety that William Wallace Bennett could devote an entire book to "the Great Revival" in the Southern armies. Most remarkable of all was the "revival on the Rapidan" which

15. Quoted in Gross Alexander, *History of the Methodist Episcopal Church, South,* ACHS, vol. 11 (New York, 1894), p. 72.

deeply affected the army making its mournful way from the bloody struggle at Gettysburg in July 1863. Underlying these great evangelistic successes, of course, was the unusually homogeneous religious tradition of the South.

The voluminous reports of the Christian Commission amply show that the Union armies were also responsive to the revival spirit. A missionary's report from General Sherman's army as it paused on the long road to Atlanta provides an authentic picture of the war's religious side:

> When we found that the army [of General Sherman] was to be at rest over the Sabbath, appointments were made in different brigades for two or three services to each preaching Delegate. I had an appointment in the Baptist church in the morning, and at General Howard's headquarters, in the woods, in the afternoon. . . . It was too late now to look for help. I took off my ministerial coat, and for one hour with the mercury at ninety degrees, worked with might and main. When I had swept out the straw, cleared the rubbish from the pulpit, thrown the bunks out the window, pitched the old seats down from the loft, arranged them in order on the floor, and dusted the whole house over twice, it was time for service. . . .
>
> In the afternoon I rode over to the Fourth Corps, four miles away. General Howard had notified the regiments around of the service. Two of his division commanders were present, and Brigadier-General Harker, whose promotion was so recent that the star had not yet supplanted the eagle on his shoulder. This was the last Sabbath service which this manly, modest, gallant officer attended. Five weeks later, in the charge at Kenesaw Mountain, he was shot dead. That Sabbath in the woods I shall never forget;—the earnest attention of all to the theme,—"The safety of those who do their duty, trusting in God,"—and the hearty responses of the Christian men, and the full chorus in the closing hymn, "When I can read my title clear." But the most effective sermon of the day was by the General commanding the corps, given upon the piazza of his headquarters, surrounded by his staff, his division commanders and other general officers. Nothing could be more natural than the turn of the conversation upon religious topics. The General spoke of the Saviour, his love for Him and his peace in His service, as freely and simply as he could have spoken in his own family circle. He related instances of Christian trust and devotion and triumph. Speaking of the high calling of chaplains, and the importance that they should always be with their regiments at the front, he told us of his visit to Newton's division hospital the night after the battle of Resaca, where he found

a fair-faced boy who could not live till morning. He knelt down on his blanket and asked if there was anything he wanted done for him. "Yes," said the boy, "I want somebody to tell me how to find the Saviour." "I never felt my ignorance so much before," said the General. "Here was a mind ready now to hear and act on the truth. What if I should give him wrong directions? How I wished I had a minister's training." And then he told us what directions he gave, and of the prayer, and of the boy's smile and peace,—appealing now to me and then to his generals, if it was not right and beautiful; and so, under the pressure unconsciously applied by their superior officer, with lips all unused to such confession, they acknowledge the power and grace of God.[16]

Estimates of conversions among the military during the war vary wildly between one and two hundred thousand; but even if certain, such information would only tell part of the story, for the "religious interest" reached untold numbers of men who could never become a chaplain's statistic. In the last analysis the vast tomes compiled by the religious emissaries to either the Blue or the Gray—so replete with stories of impromptu worship services, of mass meetings by torchlight, and of individual conversions of the living and the dying—could be interleaved one with another without distorting the overall picture. One can hardly deny the assertion of J. William Jones, a chaplain all the war long in Lee's Army of Northern Virginia, that "any history of that army which omits an account of the wonderful influence of religion upon it—which fails to tell how the courage, discipline and morale of the whole was influenced by the humble piety and evangelical zeal of many of its officers and men—would be incomplete and unsatisfactory." [17] One would only wish to apply it more generally. A fervently pious nation was at war, and amid the carnage and slaughter, amid the heroism and weariness, men on both sides hungered for inspiration and peace with God. Dedicated men and women on both sides responded to their hunger with wide-ranging ministries. On both sides the soldier's sense of duty was deepened, his morale improved, his loyalty intensified. More cynical commanders and more despairing men might have been less sure that the Almighty was with them and that victory must surely come. They might have felt a stronger impulse to compromise. Perhaps piety lengthened the war. Cer-

16. Lemuel Moss, *Annals of the United States Christian Commission* (Philadelphia, 1868), pp. 498–500. The General Howard whom Moss mentions is O. O. Howard, later head of the Freedman's Bureau. Howard University is named for him. On the Confederate side during these same weeks, the biography of General Polk contains very moving accounts of his private baptismal services for Generals Hood and Joseph E. Johnston (Polk, *Leonidas Polk*, 2: 329–30).

17. J. William Jones, *Christ in the Camp; or, Religion in Lee's Army* (Richmond, Va., 1888), pp. 5, 6. A densely printed book of 624 pages.

tainly it deepened the tragedy and made the entire experience a more enduring scar on the national memory.

ORGANIZED PHILANTHROPY IN THE NORTH

In the North a vast special ministry to the armies was organized through the Christian Commission which was formed early in the war in a manner similar to dozens of other evangelical voluntary associations. It was pervaded by a piety that owed much to the great "businessman's revival" of 1857–58. Local groups began forming soldier's aid societies as soon as hostilities began; but the task of coordinating these diverse impulses was begun by Vincent Colyer, a New York artist who had rushed to Washington after the first battle of Bull Run out of interest in a religious mission to soldiers. He soon prevailed upon the YMCA to call a convention to put such work on a solid footing, and at this meeting in November 1861 the Christian Commission was established, with George H. Stuart (1816–90) as permanent chairman. Stuart was a deeply religious Philadelphia banker who devoted his whole life to evangelical missionary agencies. During the war his talents at arousing the interests of others made the commission a major religious force in the Union armies.[18] It raised money and enlisted volunteer workers to aid the military chaplains, and in many other ways performed spiritual and charitable tasks. The provision of reading materials was one major concern, because the soldiers' hunger for the printed word was insatiable. Vast numbers of Bibles, tracts, and books were given away, and portable lending libraries circulated.

The printed certificate earned by every "delegate" of the Christian Commission made very clear, however, that other kinds of service were also performed:

> His work will be that of distributing stores where needed, in hospitals and camps; circulating good reading matter among soldiers and sailors; visiting the sick and wounded, to instruct, comfort, and cheer them, and aid them in correspondence with their friends at home; aiding Surgeons on the battlefield and elsewhere, in the care and conveyance of the wounded to hospitals; helping Chaplains in their ministrations and influence for the good of the men under their care; and addressing soldiers and sailors, individually and collectively, in explanation of the

18. See George H. Stuart, *The Life of George H. Stuart,* ed. Robert Ellis Thompson (Philadelphia, 1890). The role of America's intensely evangelical businessmen as public servants and philanthropists has not begun to receive the study it deserves.

> work of the Commission and its delegates, and for their personal instruction and benefit, temporal and eternal.[19]

The Christian Commission also made a special effort to arrange speedy communications between soldiers and their families and to provide soldiers with special "luxuries" of the sort that families would want to send. For its total work it raised nearly $3 million in cash and marshaled many more millions' worth of supplies and services. Over five thousand volunteers were enrolled in its work. To countless men and women it provided the experience of a lifetime.[20]

More directly relevant to the Northern war effort was the Sanitary Commission, an equally large and somewhat more revolutionary service organization intended chiefly to augment the work of the army's medical bureau. This organization came into being during the summer of 1861 largely through the efforts of Henry W. Bellows (1814–82), the enormously energetic minister of All Souls Church (Unitarian) in New York City, who continued to lead the agency throughout the war, with Frederick Law Olmstead as general secretary. In the sequence of events leading to its formation this organization resembled the Christian Commission. First, several newly founded local societies were coordinated. Supporters then accomplished the difficult task of convincing the president and other government officials that their service was needed; and finally, they recruited volunteers and funds.[21] The commission did not seek to take over military functions, however, as its sponsors made clear in their appeal for government authorization:

> The general object of the [Sanitary] Commission is through suggestions reported from time to time, to the Medical Bureau and the War Department, to bring to bear upon the health, comfort and morale of our troops, the fullest and ripest teachings of sanitary science, in its application to military life, whether deduced from theory or practical observations, from general hygienic principles, or from the experience of the Crimean, the East Indian, or the Italian wars. Its objects are purely advisory.[22]

Through its two hundred agents it sought persistently to expose problems of sanitation, drainage, preventive medicine, faulty diet, rest camp needs, hospital mismanagement, etc. In the Vicksburg campaign it rushed fresh

19. Moss, *Annals*, p. 542.

20. In addition to Moss's *Annals*, see Edward P. Smith, *Incidents of the United States Christian Commission* (Philadelphia, 1869).

21. These remarkable achievements are described in Charles J. Stillé, *History of the United States Sanitary Commission* (Philadelphia, 1866).

22. Linus P. Brockett, *The Philanthropic Results of the War in America* (New York, 1864), p. 39.

vegetables to Union troops threatened with scurvy, thus directly contributing to the military action. In short, it served as a vast composite Florence Nightingale, and was an essential component of the war effort.

The Western Sanitary Commission, organized in Saint Louis by another dynamic Unitarian minister, William G. Eliot, aided the Sanitary Commission in its work, and the two groups developed methods for cooperating with the Christian Commission in 1862. Taken together, these organizations played a major role in the long struggle to bring humane care to soldiers everywhere in the world. After the war Henry Bellows remained interested in "sanitary reform" until his efforts, together with the campaign of Clara Barton, led to American signing of the Geneva Convention and the organization of the American Red Cross.[23]

A third major concern of organized philanthropy was the increasing number of freed slaves. Freedman's relief societies were organized in most of the major Northern cities, with $150,000 being raised during the first year in New York, Boston, and Philadelphia alone. A particularly strong impetus was given to these efforts after the so-called Draft Riots in New York City during July 1863, when many free Negroes fell before angry mobs. Through the efforts of these early societies, moreover, Congress was persuaded to establish the Freedman's Bureau (3 March 1865) in order to discharge this enormous national responsibility more adequately. It was in the context of postwar reconstruction, however, that these activities attained their greatest significance.

In the meantime many of the older associations, including even those in foreign missions, continued their wide-ranging activities, most of them on increased budgets. The American Bible and Tract Societies and the YMCA responded with special vigor, launching large fund drives and distributing thousands of Bibles, tracts, and edifying books. They even succeeded in reaching Confederate troops, though similar organizations were formed in the South for the same purpose. The Methodist Society was the largest and most active agency for supplying literature to Confederate troops; but the Southern Baptist Convention reported in 1863 that it had distributed five million pages of tracts.

Accompanying this total work of charity was the amazing surge of fund raising which went forward at all levels. Every town and church was in-

23. In 1863 J. Henri Dunant of Geneva published *Souvenir de Solferino,* a vivid account of the horrors of that Italian "victory" of Napoleon III. He also spurred the movement to adopt an international code of warfare and to establish an agency of mercy. In 1866, the year in which the Red Cross was organized in Switzerland, Henry W. Bellows became president of an American auxiliary committee for these purposes. The American Red Cross, however, was not organized until 1884.

volved. Through the ladies' aid societies that were formed everywhere, women assumed a new role in local churches and, as a result, in national life. Innumerable local ministers also became involved as never before in public and secular undertakings. Throughout the land a philanthropic revolution occurred. Early in 1864, in order to stimulate further generosity in connection with the Metropolitan Fair being held in New York in behalf of the Sanitary Commission, Linus P. Brockett published his important little book, *The Philanthropic Results of the War in America.* After describing the manifold philanthropies, local, regional, and national, which the war had stimulated, he presented a statistical table showing contributions that totaled $212 million in the North alone—and more than a year before the end of the war. Quite rightly he contends that "neither in ancient nor modern times has there been so vast an outpouring of a nation's wealth for the care, the comfort, and the physical and moral welfare of those who have fought the nation's battles or been the sufferers from its condition of war." [24] Brockett might have said more, for this outpouring raised the charitable and missionary plans of the churches to a new order of magnitude. It extended the American reformer's conception of the possible, and because its effects were enduring, it opened a new philanthropic era in American history. On this same theme one must add that the churches, not only on account of their role in stimulating this philanthropy, but because of their entire involvement in sectional controversy and war work, were permanently altered in their public stance and in their attitudes toward social affairs. Like the nation as a whole, they would never again be the same.

INTERPRETING THE WAR

Palm Sunday, 9 April 1865, was the day of silent guns at Appomattox. Lee surrendered the Army of Northern Virginia while Jefferson Davis and his cabinet fled southward. On 17 April, just before leaving Raleigh, North Carolina, to treat with General Johnston for peace, General Sherman received word by telegraph that Abraham Lincoln had been assassinated on Good Friday. He died on Saturday. America did its best to celebrate the paschal feast on Sunday. By 26 May all Confederate armies had laid down their arms. The "close of the Rebellion" was proclaimed by President Andrew Johnson on 20 August 1866; and this was recognized as the official date by act of Congress on 2 March 1867. The Constitution of the United States, as interpreted before God's throne in the court of war, was again the law of the whole land. But what, in fact, had happened? A million casualties;

24. Brockett, *Philanthropic Results of the War*, p. 150.

six hundred thousand dead. For what had they died—if anything? And what —if anything—did it all mean?

The answers were no more easily given then than they are now, though intense feelings were registered and numberless statements made. In the South there was relief and dejection and smoldering rage. In the North—as Lincoln's funeral train made its way to Springfield—the exultation that might have burst forth yielded to relief and dejection and smoldering rage. The grief of the two sections differed greatly: that of the South was far more deeply etched, while that of the North was modified by victory and relatively large grounds for hope.

Father Abram Ryan, sometime free-lance chaplain to Confederate troops, whose spirit, as someone said, shall "keep watch over the Stars and Bars until the morning of the Resurrection," put his pen to paper a few days after Lee's surrender.

> Furl that Banner! furl it sadly!
> Once ten thousands hailed it gladly,
> And ten thousands wildly, madly,
> Swore it should forever wave;
> Swore that foeman's sword should never
> Hearts like theirs entwined dissever,
> Till that flag should float forever
> O'er their freedom or their grave!
>
> Furl that Banner, softly, slowly!
> Treat it gently—it is holy—
> For it droops above the dead.
> Touch it not—unfold it never,
> Let it droop there, furled forever,
> For its people's hopes are dead!

Ideologically many Southerners never transcended this kind of nostalgic resignation. They might work to restore their personal situation, but their hearts were with the Lost Cause, filled with memories of military valor and a half-mythic past. "Our people have failed to perceive the deeper movements under-running the times," said Sidney Lanier, their greatest poet. "They lie wholly off, out of the stream of thought, and whirl the poor dead leaves of recollection round and round, in a piteous eddy that has all the wear and tear of motion, without any of the rewards of progress." [25] The major religious corollary of this memory-laden view would be a firm attachment to

25. Quoted in Buck, *Road to Reunion*, pp. 31–32.

the evangelicalism of antebellum days and a refusal to admit the relevance of issues raised by modern thought. Its ecclesiastical results will be the subject of the two succeeding chapters.[26]

In the North Walt Whitman spoke to a nation's grief for the Captain whose lips were "pale and still":

When lilacs last in the dooryard bloom'd,
And the great star early droop'd in the western sky in the night,
I mourn'd, and yet shall mourn with ever-returning spring.

Ever-returning spring, trinity sure to me you bring,
Lilac blooming perennial and drooping star in the west,
And thought of him I love.

. . . .

In the dooryard fronting an old farm-house near the white-wash'd palings,
Stands the lilac-bush tall-growing with heart-shaped leaves of rich green,
With many a pointed blossom rising delicate, with the perfume strong I love,
With every leaf a miracle—and from this bush in the dooryard,
With delicate-color'd blossoms and heart-shaped leaves of rich green,
A sprig with its flower I break.

. . . .

Coffin that passes through lanes and streets,
Through day and night with the great cloud darkening the land,
With the pomp of the inloop'd flags with the cities draped in black,
With the show of the States themselves as of crape-veil'd women standing,
With processions long and winding and the flambeaus of the night,
With the countless torches lit, with the silent sea of faces and the unbared heads,
With the waiting depot, the arriving coffin, and the sombre faces,
With dirges through the night, with the thousand voices rising strong and solemn,
With all the mournful voices of the dirges pour'd around the coffin,
The dim-lit churches and the shuddering organs—where amid these you journey,
With the tolling tolling bells' perpetual clang,
Here, coffin that slowly passes,
I give you my sprig of lilac [27]

26. The cult of the Lost Cause not only encouraged retention of "the old-time religion," but led to the near transfiguration of Robert E. Lee—and other similar phenomena.

27. These, of course, are but a few isolated passages drawn from a much longer poem.

As men looked through their grief and sought the meaning of the war, the old theological presuppositions of the "crusades" usually sufficed for most. Even for the learned, the categories of judgment and punishment were often sufficient, though they were invoked with more assurance in the victorious North.

One of the most articulate theologians of Southern Presbyterianism was Robert Lewis Dabney (1820–98). A professor before the war, he had served as adjutant under Stonewall Jackson, and remained for nearly two decades in Virginia and Texas as a major spokesman for his denomination and his region. In lectures, sermons, published works, and in the deliberations of his church he expounded his convictions. The war, according to Dabney, had been "caused deliberately" by abolitionists who "with calculated malice" goaded the South to violence in order to revolutionize the government and "gratify their spite." "I do not forgive," he declared of the Northern Presbyterians. "What! forgive those people, who have invaded our country, burned our cities, destroyed our homes, slain our young men, and spread desolation and ruin over our land! No, I do not forgive them." He yearned for a "retributive Providence" that would demolish the North and abolish the Union.[28]

Henry Ward Beecher was moderate compared to Dabney. He counseled compassion for the generality of Southerners. Yet he minced no words in his indictment:

> I charge the whole guilt of this war upon the ambitious, educated, plotting political leaders of the South. . . . A day will come when God will reveal judgment and arraign these mighty miscreants, . . . and every maimed and wounded sufferer, and every bereaved heart in all the wide regions of this land, will rise up and come before the Lord to lay upon these chief culprits of modern history their awful witness. . . . And then these guiltiest and most remorseless traitors, these high and cultured men with might and wisdom . . . shall be whirled aloft and plunged downward forever and ever in an endless retribution.[29]

While Beecher painted his graphic picture of the Last Judgment with primary attention to Southern leaders, a more widely held view regarded the whole region as the proper victim of God's wrath. Theodore Thornton Munger, the distinguished pastor-theologian of New Haven, did not allow

28. From *A Defence of Virginia* (1867) quoted by William A. Clebsch, "Christian Interpretations of the Civil War," *Church History* 30 (1961): 4.

29. From an address delivered in Charleston on 14 February 1865, when the Stars and Stripes were restored to Fort Sumter. Presiding over the ceremony was General Robert J. Anderson, who as a major had surrendered the fort in 1861.

his liberal doctrines of progress to soften his conviction that divine retribution had already been accomplished. Indeed, they served to harden him to the plight of the South. In his essay on "Providence and the War," written two whole decades after Appomattox, Munger explained the "divine logic" by which the South had been punished "for its sins," with the North as the "sacrificing instrument." [30] Not only had a deathblow been dealt to a diabolical slave state so that America could realize its destiny, but justice had also been done in more detailed ways. That the war's carnage was felt chiefly in the South was the main fact, but within this lay a justification for Sherman's long march and Sheridan's devastation of the Shenandoah Valley. Munger even saw God's cunning in the failings of General McClellan, since his vacillations precluded a sudden Northern victory and made sure that the whole South would suffer the brunt of a long war.[31]

In the last analysis Dabney and Munger did little more than deck out the gut reactions of popular extremism in the trappings of theology. Other men, fortunately, revealed profounder theological grounds for understanding America's ordeal. Less confident in their knowledge of God's purposes, more aware of the ambiguity of historical events, less assured of their own or their region's moral purity, these men searched for a way of seeing the entire tragedy—its triumphs and its defeats—as primarily meaningful for the American people and nation as a single corporate whole. To them fire eaters and abolitionists alike were unacceptably self-righteous.[32] With greater or lesser confidence in their vision of America's destiny, they sought to bring all Americans first to penitence and reformation, and only then to reconciliation. Of the considerable number of thinkers who contributed to this view, three are outstanding. One was a Northerner and, oddly enough, Munger's hero, Horace Bushnell. The second was a German immigrant who spent his prewar years just above the Mason-Dixon line at Mercersburg, Pennsylvania, Philip Schaff. The third was born of Virginia parentage in Kentucky and grew to manhood in the proslavery climate of southern Indiana and Illinois, Abraham Lincoln.

Bushnell's great contribution stemmed from the two central concerns of his life. First, he stressed the organically *social* nature of human existence and hence the necessity of understanding the war as a single experience of

30. Munger professed a great indebtedness in these matters to Elisha Mulford, whose book *The Nation* (1870) he regarded as a supreme American contribution to political science. "The War," said Mulford, "was not primarily between freedom and slavery. It was the war of a nation and the Confederacy. Confederation, in its attack upon the nation, is in league with hell" (p. 340). Mulford's was an eloquent adaptation of the idea of the state which was developed in the German historical school.

31. See Clebsch, "Christian Interpretations of the Civil War."

32. William Lloyd Garrison was an exception. He by no means believed in the purity of the North.

one corporate being. It was a *Volkskrieg* in which the *nation* was purging itself and realizing its unity. Then out of his long meditations on the nature and meaning of expiation and vicarious sacrifice, especially as instanced in the Crucifixion, he sought to understand the suffering and sacrifice of war. In one case as in the other, the expiation of corporate sin and guilt opened the way for atonement (at-one-ment). Bushnell wrote his treatise *The Vicarious Sacrifice* as the nation bled on the battlefield; he delivered it to the publisher while the people were mourning Lincoln's death. He dared to think that the war could be good in some way akin to the way in which Good Friday was good.[33]

Philip Schaff had published a brilliant interpretation of America in 1854–55, but a visit to Germany after the war occasioned a long address explaining the significance of America's great tragedy. He, too, understood the war as a judgment on the centuries-long complicity of an entire nation in the sin of slavery. Like Bushnell, too, Schaff saw the possibility of a new and redeemed sense of nationhood rising out of the death and carnage. Reflecting his Hegelian heritage, however, he interpreted the war in a larger sense as having readied America for its great role in the cause of human freedom. Schaff felt grateful to have participated in an experience of world-historical significance.[34]

By a general consensus the Gettysburg Address and the Second Inaugural are Lincoln's supreme statements on the meaning of the war. In the latter especially he expounded the duty, destiny, and present woe of the "almost chosen people" from whom he would so soon be separated. We can apprehend even in these few words the astounding profundity of this self-educated child of the frontier, this son of a hard-shell Baptist who never lost hold of the proposition that nations and men are instruments of the Almighty.

> Both parties deprecated war; but one of them would *make* war rather than let the nation survive; and the other would *accept* war rather than let it perish. And the war came.
>
> One eighth of the whole population were colored slaves, not distributed generally over the Union, but localized in the Southern part of it. These slaves constituted a peculiar and powerful interest. All knew that this interest was, somehow, the cause of the war. To strengthen, perpetuate, and extend this interest was the object for which the insurgents would rend the Union, even by war; while the government claimed no

33. See especially Bushnell's "Our Obligations to the Dead," delivered at Yale at a gathering to honor those who had fallen (*Building Eras in Religion* [New York, 1881], pp. 319–56).

34. *Der Bürgerkrieg und das Christliche Leben in Nord-Amerika* (Berlin, 1865). A translation was published in the *Christian Intelligencer* 37, nos. 9–20 (1866).

> right to do more than to restrict the territorial enlargement of it. Neither party expected for the war, the magnitude, or the duration, which it has already attained. Neither anticipated that the *cause* of the conflict might cease with, or even before, the conflict itself should cease. Each looked for an easier triumph, and a result less fundamental and astounding. Both read the same Bible, and pray to the same God; and each invokes His aid against the other. It may seem strange that any men should dare to ask a just God's assistance in wringing their bread from the sweat of other men's faces; but let us judge not that we be not judged. The prayers of both could not be answered; that of neither has been answered fully. The Almighty has His own purposes. "Woe unto the world because of offenses! For it must needs be that offenses come; but woe to that man by whom the offense cometh!" If we shall suppose that American Slavery is one of those offenses which, in the providence of God, must needs come, but which, having continued through His appointed time, He now wills to remove, and that He gives to both North and South, this terrible war, as the woe due to those by whom the offense came, shall we discern therein any departure from those divine attributes which the believers in a Living God always ascribe to Him? Fondly do we hope—fervently do we pray—that this mighty scourge of war may speedily pass away. Yet, if God wills that it continue, until all the wealth piled by the bond-man's two hundred and fifty years of unrequited toil shall be sunk, and until every drop of blood drawn with the lash, shall be paid with another drawn with the sword, as was said three thousand years ago, so still it must be said "the judgments of the Lord are true and righteous altogether."
>
> With malice toward none; with charity for all; with firmness in the right, as God gives us to see the right, let us strive on to finish the work we are in; to bind up the nation's wounds; to care for him who shall have borne the battle, and for his widow, and his orphan—to do all which may achieve and cherish a just, and a lasting peace, among ourselves, and with all nations.

In this inspired document do we not see Lincoln's central convictions on the Union, the nation under God with its moral purpose; the great testing of its central proposition by an ordeal of blood; and the way of charity to a new birth? [35]

Whether Lincoln could have led the United States along the path marked out in his last great utterance no one will ever know. Certainly he would

35. See William J. Wolf, *The Almost Chosen People: A Study of the Religion of Abraham Lincoln,* a major contribution.

have run into difficulties of massive proportions. The vindictive positions of Munger and Dabney lived on in too many war-embittered hearts to give charity much of a chance.[36] And the nation's endemic racism stood squarely athwart the freedman's opportunity for genuine freedom.

Very soon after peace was established, still a third, and more assimilable interpretation of the war began to appear, a view which would ultimately predominate. One may call it the "sentimental view," though not without recognizing its many positive, even noble aspects. It arose, in part, because the more extreme forms of postwar animosity simply ran counter to the whole spirit of the national memory and the national hope. Lincoln himself had appealed to "our bonds of affection" in his First Inaugural. "The mystic chords of memory, stretching from every battlefield, and patriot grave, to every living heart and hearthstone, all over this broad land, will yet swell the chorus of the Union, when again touched, as surely they will be, by the better angels of our nature." And this in due time they did, though not by accepting the judgment of that "great tribunal, the American people" as Lincoln had hoped in 1861, but over more battlefields and many, many more graves. In growing numbers people tired of sectional invective.

A more responsive chord was struck by the ladies of Columbus, Mississippi, who in 1867 placed flowers over the fallen Blue as well as the Gray. Francis Miles Finch, a Yale graduate and attorney, called attention to their deed with verses which became the folk poem of Memorial Day. Millions of Americans, North and South, decade after decade, learned it by heart—and took it to heart.

From the silence of sorrowful hours
The desolate mourners go,
Lovingly laden with flowers,
Alike for the friend and the foe:—
Under the sod and the dew,
Waiting the judgment day;
Under the one, the Blue
Under the other, the Gray.

. . . .

So with an equal splendor
The morning sun rays fall,

36. Washington Gladden, the future Social Gospel leader, was among the few that counseled moderation even after Lincoln's assassination. He pointed out that Booth got little or no applause in the South. But Gladden admitted that his words were very coldly received, affecting the course of the nation about as much "as the chirping of the swallows on the telegraph pole affects the motion of the Twentieth Century Limited" (*Recollections* [Boston: Houghton Mifflin Co., 1909], pp. 147–53).

With a touch impartially tender
  On the blossoms blooming for all.

. . . .

No more shall the war-cry sever,
  Or the winding rivers be red.
They banish our anger forever
  When they laurel the graves of the dead:—
    Under the sod and the dew
    Waiting the judgment day;
    Love and tears for the Blue
    Tears and love for the Gray.

Memorial Day took its place in the American calendar not as an occasion for waving the bloody shirt but as a day of reconciliation.[37] It joined Independence Day and Thanksgiving as a time when the American's love for his country was blended with the solemnities of religion. In villages and cities it became a day for invocations, benedictions and hymns, Finch's poem, the Gettysburg Address, and patriotic orations—a day for flags and flowers, a "Decoration Day" in the nation's cemeteries. A unique American way of remembering a *civil* war emerged. Sentiment celebrated its conquest of logic as the country traveled the "road to reunion." Battle flags were returned; joint observances were held at great battlefields; and in 1874 Senator L. Q. C. Lamar of Alabama delivered his famous memorial oration in honor of Charles Sumner. In his words the illustrious Senator from Massachusetts speaks from the grave: "My countrymen! know one another, and you will love one another." [38]

Ironically, however, the Centennial Year 1876 witnessed not only a tumultuous national celebration, but the great sellout of Reconstruction, a "victory" of reconciliationism in which the freedman was left to his own tragically inadequate devices. America's moment of truth regarding the issue at the bottom of the crisis was postponed until the centennial years of the Civil War and Reconstruction. Thus collapsed Lincoln's profound hope that the Union of an "almost chosen people" —made "more perfect" in the Constitution and given a new birth in the agonies of war—would assume the moral burden laid upon it by the Almighty.

37. The origins of this American holy day are obscure, but on 30 May 1865, with much national publicity, James Redpath led a group of Negro children to put flowers on the Union graves near Charleston. The Grand Army of the Republic (Union veterans) pressed for the day's regular observance. In 1873 New York led the states in making it a legal holiday.

38. Sumner, one of the most adamant and powerful of the Republican Radicals in the Senate, had died in 1874. Lamar became the first ex-Confederate in a cabinet post.

RECONSTRUCTION AND THE CHURCHES

When the war ended, two weary armies rapidly disbanded, the victors marching home in ordered array to cheering multitudes, the defeated making their way as best they could amid desolation and ruin. With the tasks of peace at hand, the two sections remained as desperately at odds as before. Indeed, the chasm between them was wider than ever. For most Southerners reconstruction could mean only one thing: to put back the pieces so far as possible in the way they were in 1860, *status quo antebellum.* "They stacked their arms but not their principles," said one Northern Presbyterian editor. As Merton Coulter put it, they hoped to do for their way of life what all the king's horses and all the king's men could not do for Humpty Dumpty. Most Northerners, on the other hand, regarded restoration of the old regime in the South as precisely the solution to be avoided. They might differ on theories and strategies, but they agreed that the cause for which Union soldiers had fought and died should not suffer eclipse. There would be a "new South" in a new and stronger Union.

But the war had also created a "new North," and in this transformed region social and political problems arose with such speed that Reconstruction soon became a task for the left hand, then for neither hand, and finally not even for the lips. At both of the political party conventions of 1876 "Grantism" was repudiated. Two relatively unsmirched candidates were placed before the electorate, though the Democrat, Samuel J. Tilden, was not untainted by associations with the Tweed Ring in New York, while the Republican (and former major-general), Rutherford B. Hayes, had freely exploited Ohio's anti-Catholicism in running for governor there. A disputed election followed, in which Hayes (in any case not a radical reconstructionist) finally became president after an involved series of political maneuvers had resulted in the Compromise of 1877. The result is well known: with Federal military support withdrawn, the remaining Republican governments in the South collapsed; the "Solid South" emerged again, effectively keeping the Negro from the polls by legislation, party organization, and the Ku Klux Klan. With "home rule" accomplished, the South embarked on a course of its own, becoming reconciled to the North in certain respects, yet remaining profoundly separate in its own mind and memory and in its own distinctive religious history.

Between the early ardor and the later relaxation, the United States passed through one of its most crucial—and fateful—crises, an unprecedented time of testing when the nation was weighed and found wanting. A long, bloody war, to be sure, was the worst possible preparation for a profound moral encounter; and perhaps the same racial impasse that had made armed conflict inevitable also made a just reconstruction impossible. For these reasons the "tragic era" is of maximum importance to the moral and religious history of the American people. Yet its treatment by historians has been apologetic and evasive. Like the political historiography on the period, the conventional church-historical accounts need revision. In both cases the prevailing interpretation is seriously discolored by the fact that it was shaped amid a resurgence of crusading Anglo-Saxonism during the turn-of-century decades. Northern Protestant historians with their commitments to temperance, Sabbatarianism, nativism, and immigration restriction were overtaken by the same realization that Kenneth Stampp ascribes to the historical profession generally: their basic views on ethnic and racial issues "were *precisely* the ones that southern white men had been making about Negroes for years. And in their extremity, the old middle classes of the North looked with new understanding upon the problems of the beleaguered white men of the South." [39]

On the other hand, there is an equally important church-historical corollary to Stampp's observation, for the churches had provided the major institutional context in which the antislavery impulse could thrive during the war and Reconstruction, and they provided a place for its survival during the succeeding decades, when even old radical journals like the *Nation* and *Harper's Weekly* accepted the Compromise of 1877, and when the "best men" lost interest in the freedman. Yet by the time of the War with Spain this reforming zeal had lost its force. The Social Gospel itself would almost forget the South and the freedman—despite its debt both in method and theory to the antislavery movement, and even though the plight of the blacks would actually reach its nadir in the "Progressive Era."

During the period of Reconstruction (which in one sense began as soon as Union armies made substantial inroads on Confederate territory) the Northern Protestant churches were a mainstay of the Radical program. They regarded themselves, in fact, as the custodians of the moral factor in the entire sectional crisis, and with the coming of peace they remained the chief popular support for the political leaders who wished to prevent a compromise. This involved them inescapably in the Republican strategies which were designed to prevent or delay the rise of a politically potent South. Yet the needs of the freedman and a grim determination to reform the South best explain why the churches made Reconstruction an extension of the

39. Kenneth M. Stampp, *The Era of Reconstruction, 1865–1877* (New York: Random House, Vintage Books, 1965), p. 19.

antislavery crusade, and why they won powerful bases of support among agrarian as well as industrial constituencies. The most influential of church papers, the *Independent* of New York, put the matter in a way that no doubt satisfied the overwhelming majority of its seventy thousand subscribers: "These venomous [Southern] masters should be put under tutors and governors till the time appointed. A freedman's bureau is less needed than a rebel's bureau." [40]

Resisting this "Radical" program were the Democrats, who had a party to rehabilitate, and a small group of Republican moderates such as Henry Ward Beecher. These men were congenial to President Johnson's program of restoring the Union expeditiously—on the theory that secession had been illegal. Republicans, seeking to hold their party together, tended strongly to the opposite pole; and under the leadership of Thaddeus Stevens and Charles Sumner they advocated a far more complete and detailed reconstruction. Soon thoroughly at odds with the president, and piling up great majorities in the congressional elections of 1866, these Radical Republicans took the federal power into their own hands, overriding presidential vetoes, administrating the "conquered provinces," and controlling the readmission of states to the Union. As the party of principle, they won massive support in the Protestant churches until a combination of flagging fervor, stubborn Southern resistance, new distractions, and the rising spirit of reconciliationism led to widespread abandonment of Radical aims.

During the Reconstruction decade, however, exalted principles were more easily formulated than implemented. The Grand Old Party learned that social structures, immemorial folkways, and the legacy of slavery could not be transformed by governmental fiat or by the general run of civil servants. Yet the almost classic Southern version of Reconstruction's barbaric failures is faulty. Despite devastation and depression, agrarian recovery and industrial advance were achieved. The Bureau of Refugees, Freedmen, and Abandoned Lands, established in 1865 and extended over President Johnson's veto in 1866, never did fulfill the freedman's hope for a place on the "abandoned lands," yet in some states it did ease his transition from one form of bondage to another. In the end the Bureau, like so many other noble plans, became a victim of political interference, weak leadership, and racist presuppositions.

The whole cause of civil rights, nevertheless, was greatly and permanently advanced by the Civil Rights Act of 1866 (also passed over a veto) and three great amendments to the federal Constitution which probably could not have been passed at any later period. The Thirteenth Amendment, which

40. Vol. 17, no. 871 (August 1865): 4; quoted in Dunham, *The Attitude of the Northern Clergy*, p. 234.

abolished slavery, was passed to the states and ratified in 1865; the Fourteenth, which incorporated the principles of the Civil Rights Act and forbade the abridgment of any citizen's privileges or immunities, was passed in 1866 and ratified in 1868; and the Fifteenth, which guaranteed to all citizens the right to vote, was passed in 1869 and ratified in 1870. As every American knows, the provisions of the latter two amendments, even after a century, were very ineffectively enforced. Yet in the epoch-making court decisions and civil rights struggles since the end of World War II the Reconstruction Amendments played a vital role. In 1968, the Supreme Court cited the Civil Rights Act of 1866 in an open-housing case. Unless one simply accepts the idea that the United States was meant to be a "*Herrenvolk* democracy," the statesmen and private citizens who led the struggle for a real reconstruction deserve something better than *Gone With the Wind.*

That the Reconstruction Radicals were fiercely partisan cannot be denied; but equally undeniable is their consistent concern for civil rights, a concern that had been shaped in the abolitionist movement. The ideals and temperament of that crusade are clearly represented in the character of Thaddeus Stevens (1792–1868). Born in poverty in rural Vermont, reared by a pious Calvinistic Baptist mother, and educated at Dartmouth, Stevens became an eminent Pennsylvania lawyer and iron manufacturer. He had cast his lot with the antislavery cause in 1823, and in 1848 he went to Congress as a "Conscience Whig," an office which he held until his death. As the leader of the Republican Radicals he was, during the early postwar years, the freedman's most undeviating champion and the South's most implacable foe; in addition, he was perhaps the most powerful man in American politics. In 1850 the Southern Speaker of the House, Howell Cobb, recognizing a formidable opponent, had described him in words that remind one of William Lloyd Garrison's opening editorial in the *Liberator:*

> Our enemy has a general now. This man is rich, therefore, we cannot buy him. He does not want higher office, therefore, we cannot allure him. He is not vicious, therefore, we cannot seduce him. He is in earnest. He means what he says. He is bold. He cannot be flattered or frightened.[41]

It is unrewarding to explain the motives of a man like this in terms of social status, economic gain, or other concerns. What Stampp says of Charles Sumner, Stevens's powerful colleague in the Senate, seems equally true of

41. Quoted in Fawn Brodie, *Thaddeus Stevens: Scourge of the South* (New York: W. W. Norton & Co., 1966), p. 110.

Stevens himself: "To deny the reality of his moral fervor and humanitarian idealism is to deny the reality of the man himself." [42] The same could be said of many Radical leaders.

So intense was the commitment of most Northern Protestant churches to the congressional Radicals that even their most questionable effort—to impeach the president in 1868—won widespread support. The Methodists, meeting in general conference at the time of the trial before the Senate, set aside an hour of prayer in order that "corrupt influences" might be brought to an end. They also believed that even Southern Methodist church property should be confiscated. It is altogether possible, moreover, that if General Grant had not proved so ineffective as president, some measure of idealism and moral integrity might have pervaded reconstruction activity during the crucial years from 1869 to 1877. As it happened, corruption, indecision, and scandal became so widespread that many of the most ardent and most capable reform leaders were drawn away from the "Southern question."

While churchmen brought support to Reconstructionists in Washington, they also attempted through ecclesiastical channels to aid the newly freed blacks. Hundreds of relief associations for this purpose were organized in the towns and cities of the North, some as early as 1861. To coordinate this work the United States Commission for the Relief of the National Freedman was formed in 1863 by a merger of five of the larger city organizations, followed by the American Freedman's Union Commission, organized in 1866 to embrace a still larger range of such societies. After 1869 much of its activity ceased, as Congress took increasing control of reconstruction and freedman's aid, and because denominational societies were proceeding independently. The Northern Presbyterians organized their freedmen's committee in 1864; the Methodists their much more vigorous Freedman's Aid Society in 1866, and other churches did likewise.

By far the most effective of these church-oriented agencies for the freedman was the American Missionary Association, founded at Albany in 1846 by the merger of several small societies of Congregational origin who shared a missionary commitment to nonwhite peoples and a strong antislavery bent. By 1860 its 112 abolitionistic home missionaries outnumbered its workers abroad, and at the war's end it had 528 missionaries and teachers at work in the South. After the war the AMA also helped to implement joint projects for founding and staffing schools in the South, a philanthropic effort which marshaled millions of dollars and supported thousands of teachers and school administrators for work among the Southern blacks. One of the noblest and least recognized chapters in Reconstruction history was written by these

42. *The Era of Reconstruction*, p. 102.

poorly paid educators, most of them women, as they struggled amid penury, ridicule, hostility, and sometimes outright violence to demonstrate their faith in the nation's ideals and in the Negro's natural capacity to enter fully into American life.[43] Shortcomings there were—cultural condescension and curricular inflexibility, to name two—yet at no other point did the old antislavery impulse so clearly reveal the moral quality of its motivation.

Gradually, however, the sheer magnitude of the task, the hostility of Southern whites, and the decline of fervor even among leaders of the denominational agencies caused many projects to be abandoned. This trend continued with the steady deterioration of the Freedman's Bureau, the end of official reconstruction in 1877, and the catastrophic rulings of the Supreme Court in 1883 which declared crucial sections of the Civil Rights Act of 1875 unconstitutional. Nevertheless a limited number of institutions, such as Lincoln University in Pennsylvania, Morehouse College and Atlanta University in Georgia, Talladega College in Alabama, Tougaloo University in Mississippi, Hampton Institute in Virginia, and Fisk University in Tennessee, all founded or supported by the churches during these years, managed to survive. Prior to 1900, "practically all of the faculty members of Southern Negro colleges were idealistic educational missionaries who had been educated in Northern colleges."[44] The decision of George Peabody of Massachusetts to create a $3.5 million trust fund for the furtherance of Southern education gave great impetus to the cause, and with the Reverend Barnas Sears, president of Brown University, as its general agent until 1880, this fund accounted for much of the later advance in black education made in the South. In 1882 John F. Slater of Rhode Island created another million-dollar fund for similar purposes.

Support for radicalism and aid to the freedman were not the only efforts at reconstruction undertaken by the churches. Their most direct attempts were strictly ecclesiastical. The three large denominations which had divided over the slavery issue projected plans for displacing the Southern branches of their denominations. Because the Southern "schismatics" had in fact proclaimed slavery as God's will with far more absolutism and unanimity than the Northern churches had shown in their opposition, they were now simply considered disqualified. On 27 July 1865, the *Independent* again voiced the majority view: "The apostate church is buried beneath a flood of divine wrath; its hideous dogmas shine on its brow like flaming fiends; the

43. In 1870 the president of Talladega College (Alabama) was shot and killed by a mob. Southern aid and protection could be gained only for trade schools, and this but grudgingly until after World War I.

44. John S. Brubacher and Willis Rudy, *Higher Education in Transition* (New York: Harper & Brothers, 1958), p. 75.

whole world stands aghast at its wickedness and ruin. The Northern church beholds its mission." But it was one thing for religious journalists to behold a mission and quite another for Northern churches to carry it out. Although some large churches actually did at one time or another use the opportunities provided by military or radical reconstruction to "occupy" Southern churches, their successes in winning a new black membership or in forcibly reuniting their denominations were exceedingly modest. Only the Northern Methodists made significant gains among the freedmen, but this new black membership was organized in a separate jurisdiction with its own hierarchy.

The only successful reunion efforts carried out by the larger denominations were those of the Episcopal and Roman Catholic churches, where a diocesan polity and a record of ambivalent moderation on the central issues allowed the "Southern solution" to be carried out in appropriate territories of the united church. In 1861 the dioceses of the Confederacy, led by Bishops Stephen Elliott of Georgia and Leonidas Polk of Louisiana, had organized a Protestant Episcopal Church, C.S.A. No changes of doctrine, polity, or liturgy were made in the South, except for a few political references in the prayer book and the consecration of a new bishop in Alabama. The Northern church, meanwhile, merely noted the absence of Southern representatives at the 1862 meeting of the General Convention (a meeting which issued a mildly controversial declaration for the Union). When it next met three years later, unity was restored with a minimum of bitterness. In a formal sense the Roman Catholic church could not divide, inasmuch as the Holy See was outside and above the conflict. Yet as a practical matter bishops, clergy, and laity acted as if they were loyal citizens of two different nations. When hostilities ceased, the hierarchy resumed its normal functioning, and in the Plenary Council of 1866 all of the country's dioceses were represented. Neither of these churches, however, sought to press reconstructionist policies on their Southern dioceses.

Southern Baptists, Methodists, Presbyterians, and Lutherans, on the other hand, with one voice proclaimed their loyalty to the Lost Cause, accepted or arranged for the transfer or separated status of Negro "members," and in some cases even won accessions among whites in the loyal border states where slavery had once existed. In the small Protestant Methodist church the Northern conferences coalesced with the Southern. Presbyterians in the North meanwhile followed the wartime example of the Southerners, and in 1869–70 found occasion to end the Old School–New School schism which had riven the church in 1837. Because the South as a whole thus went its religious way, the chief new ecclesiastical development of the era was neither reconquest nor reunion of the alienated regions, but rather the rise of independent Negro churches, Baptist or Methodist. These churches played a significant role during Reconstruction days when the Federal army, the Freedman's Bureau, and the Union Leagues utilized them to strengthen Radical Republican power. But after 1877 they, too, became a part of the "Southern solution" (segregation, subservience, and tenantry), not to emerge as a "radical" social force again until the 1950s, and then with slow and uncertain voice. These churches grew apace during the later nineteenth century, however, and gradually developed a distinctive religious ethos which traditional denominational allegiances could neither submerge nor alter. Through a long and bitter century they became the chief bearers of the Afro-American heritage.

42

THE RISE OF THE BLACK CHURCHES

Enslavement and emancipation in changing proportions, though always with the emphasis on bondage, have pervaded the entire history of the African in America. From the earliest times there were sporadic manumissions and escapes; and heavily qualified emancipation during the revolutionary era led to the rise of a partially free black community in the North. But the Civil War was the great time of transition, though the accidents of military strategy made even that a drawn-out process—beginning with the Federal occupation of the Sea Islands of South Carolina seven months after the fall of Fort Sumter and ending only after the final Confederate surrender in 1865. Then began a remarkable period in American religious history. Out of the shambles of Southern civilization and amid the violence of Reconstruction, the freedmen undertook the tasks of church organization. Black Baptist churches were the first to be organized, and these congregations then began to form wider associations. The two African Methodist churches of the North also moved very early toward their newly freed constituency. The "invisible institution" of antebellum days thus became visible—and not only visible, but the chief institution of the freedman. By the century's end there were 2.7 million church members in a black population of 8.3 million.

This astonishing growth calls for explanations of several sorts, but obviously primary—for chronological reasons if for no other—is a degree of familiarity with the nature of black religious life under slavery. Some consideration of certain aspects of this history has already been given in chapters on the early South, the Great Awakening, the Revolution, the antislavery movement, and the Civil War; but a brief discussion of black religion and the rise of Negro Protestantism (as well as the questions pertaining to that distinction) is reserved for this chapter.[1]

THE CHRISTIANIZATION OF THE AMERICAN NEGRO

On exceedingly rare occasions a slave brought to America was a Moslem or showed signs of Islamic contacts; but almost never had the blacks encountered Christianity except through the Europeans who bought and sold them. Bondage constituted their introduction to Western civilization. Virginia, the major slave colony, could in 1670 safely legislate that "all servants not being christians" who were brought into the colony by sea were to be slaves for life.

It was well established by this time that baptism need not be followed by the manumission of slaves, but colonists remained reluctant to convert or catechize blacks. The notion that Negroes were not included in God's scheme of redemption probably justified the inaction of some, but others no doubt found it easier to justify the enslavement of heathen than of fellow children of God. The Society for the Propagation of the Gospel, from its founding in 1701 throughout the century, constantly admonished its missionaries to work among the slaves, and they in turn admonished the laity. Bishops of London admonished both clergy and laity. The Society of Friends continued to testify, as George Fox had done, that "Christ by the grace of God tasted death for every man"; and beginning with John Woolman in the mid-eighteenth century one can trace a continuous Quaker testimony against slavery. But reluctance among the chief slaveholders and opposition from many others (including Quakers) tended strongly to limit the effects of evangelistic zeal; and the early missionary efforts of Anglicans and Quakers usually expired after some modest program of instruction or even a school had begun. "Amid the blare of trumpets rallying Christians to the work of God," writes Winthrop Jordan, "one can easily detect the shuffle of dragging

1. My efforts can be regarded as no more than preliminary. Only the incitements of the mid-twentieth century awakened historians from their dogmatic slumbers with regard to Afro-American history. Until then efforts to understand the Negro's past had been minuscule, and specialists in religion were proportionately more remiss than the others, considering the importance of the churches in Negro life and the uniqueness of black religion. The American Church History series edited by Philip Schaff during the 1890s omitted histories of the African and Colored Methodist Episcopal churches as well as of the Negro Baptist churches. As late as 1970 no scholar had produced a religious history of the American Negro that even pretended to replace Carter G. Woodson's *History of the Negro Church* (1921), though E. Franklin Frazier shortly before his death had improved the situation with a brief overview adapted from lectures delivered in Paris in 1953, *The Negro Church in America*. Many important monographs have been written by both black and white authors, to be sure; but the amount of work yet to be done is awesome.

feet." [2] Outside New England, where slaves were few, ministers or catechists were in any case in such short supply that most of the white population was an almost equally needy mission field.

Only with the Great Awakening did a break in the Southern religious situation begin to occur. The preachers of that tumultuous revival upset the established order in many ways. They spread abroad a confidence in the people that made them harbingers not only of the Revolution but of abolitionism. Preaching sin and salvation to the slaves, they broke with the decorous Anglican efforts of the past. They offered no simple catechetical exercises on the Ten Commandments, no homilies of the virtues of obedience to masters and patience in suffering and toil. "The blessed Savior died and shed his blood as much for you as for your master, or any of the white people"—such was the Presbyterian "new light" that Cary Allen brought to the slaves of Virginia. "[He] has opened the door of heaven wide for you and invites you all to enter." [3]

Neither George Whitefield nor the American revival preachers raised direct questions about the institution of slavery, though New Divinity men like Jonathan Edwards, Jr., and Samuel Hopkins even did that. But these preachers did raise for the first time the revolutionary implications of equality before God. Whitefield was even blamed for the 1741 "arsonist-plot" in New York. And Samuel Davies, who would later be president of Princeton, very explicitly defended the slave's equal ability to appropriate the gospel:

> Your Negroes may be ignorant and stupid as to divine Things, not for Want of Capacity, but for Want of Instruction; not through their Perverseness, but through your Negligence. From the many Trials I have made, I have Reason to conclude, that making Allowance for their low and barbarous Education, their imperfect Acquaintance with our Language, their having no Opportunity for intellectual Improvements, and the like, they are generally as capable of Instruction, as the white People.[4]

As the American experience gradually undermined old views on the necessary, God-given stratification of society, such views would gain new significance.

Carter Woodson rightly placed "the Dawn of the New Day" in the Chris-

2. Winthrop D. Jordan, *White over Black: American Attitudes toward the Negro, 1550–1812*, p. 180. See also pp. 190–91 above.

3. William Hill, "Reverend Cary Allen," *Presbyterian Quarterly Review* 9: 76–77; quoted by Susan Solomon, "Evangelicalism and Moralism in the Eighteenth-Century South" (seminar paper, Yale University, 1969).

4. Quoted in Jordan, *White over Black*, p. 188.

tian history of the American Negro in the later eighteenth and early nineteenth centuries, after the Revolution had lifted most hindrances to freedom of religion.[5] There is a monumental irony in this observation, however, for these very decades between 1790 and 1815 were the time in which the cotton gin, new breeds of cotton, and westward expansion were giving the American slave system those features that made it "the most awful the world has ever known." [6] Descriptions of camp meetings, weeping sinners, great conversions, and rhythmic song must never blot that fact from view. Slavery shaped not only the political economy of the South, but its whole culture. Insofar as absolute power corrupts absolutely, the Southern white was reduced in his humanity by his lordship over the blacks he bought, sold, and raped. Harriet Beecher Stowe illustrates this point in the first ten pages of her great novel, which she first planned to subtitle, "The Man That Was a Thing." The slave, in turn, to make his own life endurable, had to act out the stereotype of childish immaturity by which his masters justified the system—in the process alienating himself from his blackness. Where the sin was in this unlovely picture—and what the sins were—was not a question on which an itinerant revivalist would have the last word.

During these years, nevertheless, the Baptists and Methodists did begin their active programs of evangelization, being aided in their efforts by mobility, fervent experientialism, and straightforward preaching. Bishop Benjamin T. Tanner of the African Methodist Episcopal church vividly contrasted the evangelistic methods which accounted for the changed religious spirit in the South—for whites and blacks alike:

> While the good Presbyterian parson was writing his discourses, rounding off the sentences, the Methodist itinerant had traveled forty miles with his horse and saddle bags; while the parson was adjusting his spectacles to read his manuscript, the itinerant had given hell and damnation to his unrepentant hearers; while the disciple of Calvin was waiting to have his church completed, the disciple of Wesley took to the woods and made them re-echo with the voice of free grace, believing with Bryant, "The groves were God's first temples." [7]

Under such auspices a considerable number of black preachers were ordained, some of them to very successful ministries. Occasionally it was even

5. Woodson, *The History of the Negro Church*, chap. 2.

6. Nathan Glazer, introduction to Stanley M. Elkins, *Slavery: A Problem in American Institutional and Intellectual Life* (New York: Grosset & Dunlap Universal Library, 1963), p. ix. Elkins overdraws the Sambo image, though his cautious comparative use of the Nazi concentration camp is instructive.

7. Quoted in Woodson, *The History of the Negro Church*, pp. 97–98.

possible to organize Negro congregations. That of the Baptists at Silver Bluff, South Carolina, between 1773 and 1775 is credited as the first. Scattered historical evidence indicates that a dozen others had been formed by 1800—most of them Baptist, but a few Methodist or Presbyterian.

After the Revolution considerable activity took place in the free or partially free black communities of the North; and by 1821 two independent African Methodist Episcopal churches had been formed.[8] In virtually all of the slave states, however, there were laws to restrict the slave's freedom of assembly, so that the usual practice was to compose local churches of both white and black members, allotting special seating to the blacks, who often outnumbered white members. In 1790 the Methodist church reported 11,682 "colored" members, almost a fifth of the church's total; and the Baptists at that early date are generally believed to have converted many more. Statistics are inconclusive, but diverse reports from scattered parishes support the view that these two groups were far more successful than the Episcopal, Presbyterian, and Lutheran churches.

When the antislavery movement shifted to a new level of intensity, the South took a much more defensive stance than formerly, with the result that after 1830 the benefits of Christianization became a common argument in the justification of slavery. The churches, therefore, were spurred to renewed efforts of evangelism. During the last decades before the war this emphasis on missions to the slaves was especially strong among Southern Methodists, who devoted $1.8 million to the cause between 1844 and 1864, partly due to the influence of Bishop William Capers of South Carolina in promoting this mission.[9] The Baptist and other churches also increased their efforts, but just how effectively the mission was carried out is difficult to say. In ideal circumstances the instruction or religious understanding of slaves probably approached that of the whites, but in areas of dense black population and on large "industrial" plantations, slaves were far less adequately churched—if at all.

If the rise of abolitionism had a positive influence on Negro evangelism, Nat Turner's slave insurrection in Virginia in 1831 had the opposite effect. Turner was a Baptist exhorter with strong visionary tendencies, and since there had also been significant religious overtones in Gabriel Prosser's plot of 1800 and Denmark Vesey's attempt in 1822, fear of further rebellions led to increased resistance to the preaching activity of free Negroes, the separate assembly of black congregations, and the spread of literacy among the slaves.

8. See pp. 708–09 below.

9. In the year of Capers's death (1854) $25,000 was spent for this effort. The twenty-five plantation missions served by thirty-two preachers then had ten thousand black members, one thousand white (Gross Alexander, *History of the Methodist Episcopal Church, South*, ACHS, vol. 11 [New York, 1894], p. 117).

Given the combination of these factors—the sheer vastness of the task, the prohibitions on public assembly, and restrictions on the extension of literacy among the slaves—only the most incomplete kind of Christianization could be carried out. One ex-slave described the situation when he said that "the colored folks had their own code of religion, not nearly so complicated as the white man's." [10] On the other hand, it would be unrealistic to exaggerate the complicatedness of the white man's religion. What developed, in fact, were intermingled streams of folk piety with distinctive Baptist and Methodist elements apparent in the religious life of each race. In many areas, especially in the Deep South where planters were more commonly Methodist or Baptist, ministers were cheered by the encouragement they received and by the large number of converts.

The Methodists had an advantage because their annual camp meetings in August, after the crops were in, were the social event of the year. Provision was often made for both blacks and whites to stay in some country grove for several days of rousing religion. U. B. Phillips gives a typical report from one Georgia preacher in 1807, one that shows incidentally how the greater receptivity of the blacks gratified the preachers.

> The first day of the meeting [Tuesday], we had a gentle and comfortable moving of the spirit of the Lord among us; and at night it was without intermission. However, before day the white people retired, and the meeting was continued by the black people. [After describing the mounting fervor on Wednesday and Thursday, he continues.] Friday was the greatest day of all. We had the Lord's Supper at night, . . . and such a solemn time have I seldom seen on the like occasion. Three of the preachers fell helpless within the altar, and one lay a considerable time before he came to himself. From that the work of convictions and conversions spread, and a large number were converted during that night, and there was no intermission until the break of day. . . . On Saturday we had preaching at the rising of the sun; and then with many tears we took leave of each other.[11]

Almost everywhere, but particularly in areas where Baptist or Methodist labors were fairly intensive, a kind of semi-independent religious life developed among the slaves. Black preachers and exhorters would continue the work, and in areas where slaves were relatively more numerous they often had charge of worship services on Sunday. Where whites were numerically

10. Quoted in E. Franklin Frazier, *The Negro in the United States*, p. 343.

11. Ulrich B. Phillips, *American Negro Slavery* (Baton Rouge: Louisiana State University Press, 1966), pp. 316–17.

predominant, slaves were usually assigned a segregated place in the church of the area. The so-called invisible institution took shape as the slaves combined their understanding of the Bible and their conceptions of life and the world with their suppressed yearnings for freedom from toil and bondage. This is the substance of Frazier's important observation that revivalistic Protestant Christianity became the chief means by which the African slave—bereft of his native culture, language, and religion—defined and explained his personal and social existence in America.

This religion also provided the only means at hand to preserve such vestiges of his African past as had not been utterly extinguished in the successive stages of the slave system. The spirituals, for example, reflect the way in which Bible stories and the gospel message could be invested with intense meaning. They were songs of faith and hope, not coded protest songs nor celebrations of specific events. In their otherworldliness, in their vision of jubilation and plenty "over Jordan," they expressed the same hope that was sung in the white churches, among the German pietists, and in Wesley's England. They also expressed the reality of work-weariness and bondage, with the slaves' condition giving such songs a kind of authenticity that was lacking in socially prominent white Protestant churches when similar hymns were sung. In addition, the theology of the spirituals shaped the religious experience of the singers. Individuals locked in the most awful corporate sin ever perpetrated by one race upon another came to a conviction of their little sins, then, in the fullness of time, they were "borned again." Whether this climactic event was explained in the predestinarian terms of the Primitive Baptists or the Arminianism of the Methodists (distinctions by no means lost on even the most lowly), a new life in Christ was hopefully begun. An eloquent example of this experience is provided by Mortimer ———, who recounts the beginnings of his life as a Christian in slavery days:

> One day while in the field plowing I heard a voice. . . . Again the voice called, "Morte! Morte!" With this I stopped, dropped the plow, and started running, but the voice kept on speaking to me saying, "Fear not, my little one, for behold! I come to bring you a message of truth."
>
> Everything got dark, and I was unable to stand any longer. I began to feel sick, and there was a great roaring. I tried to cry and move but was unable to do either. I looked up and saw that I was in a new world. There were plants and animals, and all, even the water where I stooped down to drink, began to cry out, "I am blessed but you are damned! I am blessed but you are damned!" With this I began to pray, and a voice on the inside began to cry, "Mercy! Mercy! Mercy!"
>
> As I prayed an angel came and touched me, and I looked new. . . .

I again prayed, and there came a soft voice saying, "My little one, I have loved you with an everlasting love. You are this day made alive and freed from hell. You are a chosen vessel unto the Lord. Be upright before me, and I will guide you unto all truth. My grace is sufficient for you. Go, and I am with you. Preach the gospel, and I will preach with you. You are henceforth the salt of the earth." . . .

About this time my master came down the field. I became very bold and answered him when he called me. He asked me very roughly how I came to plow up the corn, and where the horse and plow were, and why I had got along so slowly. I told him that I had been talking with God Almighty, and that it was God who had plowed up the corn. He looked at me very strangely, and suddenly I fell for shouting, and I shouted and began to preach. . . .

When I had finished I felt a great love in my heart that made me feel like stooping and kissing the very ground. My master sat watching and listening to me, and then he began to cry. He turned from me and said in a broken voice, "Morte, I believe you are a preacher. From now on you can preach to the people here on my place in the old shed by the creek. But tomorrow morning, Sunday, I want you to preach to my family and neighbors. So put on your best clothes and be in front of the big house early in the morning, about nine o'clock."

The permanence of this conversion is suggested by the narrator's concluding lines, spoken in the 1920s: "Ever since that day I have been preaching the gospel and am not a bit tired. I can tell anyone about God in the darkest hour of midnight, for it is written on my heart. Amen." [12] How this experience differs from that of Saint Bernadette of Lourdes is not easily stated. Even more interesting here is the obviously great similarity of the master's piety to that of the slave. Religion of this sort and music of this sort did not come out of an African past, but they did enable the slaves to find some kind of personal and social replacement for African modes of life and thought.[13]

12. Clifton H. Johnson, ed., *God Struck Me Dead,* pp. 15–18.

13. The question of African survivals in Afro-American culture has been heatedly debated, and religion is the sphere of life in which the most important continuities have been alleged (see Melville J. Herskovits, *The Myth of the Negro Past* [New York: Harper and Brothers, 1941]). My own inclination is to follow Frazier, Fauset, and others in discounting Herskovits's extreme claims. I find the distinctive characteristics of the American Negro's religion more parsimoniously explained as an adaptation of evangelical Christianity shaped by the special needs and conditions of black people in white America. The best case for continuities with an African past is made with regard to rhythmic and musical expression and the Afro-American's pronunciation and inflection of English. Frazier refers to the question in several books: so does Arthur H. Fauset, *Black Gods of the Metropolis,* pp. 1–8.

THE PASSING OF THE OLD ORDER

When war broke out, white fear of widespread slave revolts naturally increased—and a consequence of that fear was a heightened concern for the slave's religious welfare. The rationale as always included the view, more hoped for than demonstrated, that religion would aid in "securing the quiet and peaceful subordination of these people." [14] And in 1863 the loyalty of four hundred slaves on a North Carolina plantation was attributed to regular religious instruction that included Saint Paul's admonition, "Brethren, let every man wherein he is called abide therein with God." At the same time, a Richmond paper asked quite frankly, "May we not hope and pray that large numbers will be savingly converted to Christ, thus becoming better earthly servants while they wear with meekness the yoke of their master in heaven?" [15]

These well-worn determinations could not be carried out with regularity, however, simply because the war so utterly disrupted the normal means of religious work. Ministers went off as chaplains or soldiers, or sought other employment for lack of support. Candidates for the ministry were in similar straits, with the result that accessions to the ordained ministry were drastically reduced in all churches. Even the lifting of prewar restrictions on the use of black preachers was of little avail. And when Federal troops were expected, or the force of combat was actually felt, the situation became worse.

To make matters even more critical, the slaves themselves became increasingly aware of the issues at stake in the war, so that they could not be encouraged to minister to each other. Needless to say, there are many accounts (and even more postwar stories) of old Negro preachers whose prayers always included the petition, "Protect our massa far away"; but just as many observers reported the tendency of slaves to pray for President Lincoln's armies, and to sing songs of freedom and the Promised Land with a jubilant hopefulness that suggested not a heavenly but an earthly fulfillment. The number of flights to Union armies when the situation permitted confirms Booker T. Washington's reminiscences:

> As the great day drew nearer, there was more singing in the slave quarters than usual. It was bolder, had more ring, and lasted later into the night. Most of the verses of the plantation songs had some references to

14. A plea published in November 1862 by the South Carolina Conference of the Methodist Church, quoted by Bell I. Wiley, *Southern Negroes, 1861–1865* (New Haven: Yale University Press, 1938), pp. 98–99.

15. Ibid., p. 99.

> freedom. True, they had sung those same verses before but they had been careful to explain that the "freedom" in these songs referred to the next world . . . now they gradually threw off the mask and were not afraid to let it be known that the freedom in their songs meant freedom of the body in this world.[16]

Thus a basic result of the war was the gradual breakdown of the customary partially integrated but paternalistic ecclesiastical system of the Old South. By 1865 it was in a state of nearly total collapse.

At the start of the Civil War, despite fears and difficulties, somewhere between an eighth and a sixth of the South's slave population of approximately four million may have been affiliated with one or another of the churches in at least a vague way. In terms of formal membership about 225,000 of these were Methodist and 175,000 Baptist. By hearsay and song, however, vital elements of biblical religion had spread much farther—how far, or how deeply, no one will ever know. But when the black population of the South was emancipated from the formal restrictions of slavery, it soon became evident that the freedmen constituted a very special kind of home mission field, one in which the Christian faith was a widely apprehended reality. Both the circumstances of its propagation and the conditions under which it was appropriated and extended gave it a character of its own. The religion of the invisible institution, therefore, required very little modification when it became possible for blacks to organize churches under the new arrangements for life and labor that Southern Redeemers provided.

BLACK CHURCH ORGANIZATION

With the coming of peace the churches one by one went their separate, segregated ways. The Colored Primitive Baptists were organized in 1866. The first entirely Negro state convention of regular Baptists was organized in North Carolina in that same year. Since Baptist polity conduced to the formation, on a local basis, of literally countless black congregations (many entirely new and many by separation), other state conventions soon followed. These in turn gradually achieved various regional consolidations, until, by stages, a national foreign missions convention was organized. Finally, in 1895, the National Baptist Convention was formed at Atlanta, Georgia, though many local churches remained independent.[17] Following the same trend, the

16. Booker T. Washington, *Up from Slavery* (New York: Doubleday, Page & Co., 1901), p. 19.

17. Twelve years later the NBC was divided in a dispute over the control of property and the administration of the publishing house at Nashville. The larger faction was incorporated in 1915 as the National Baptist Convention of the U.S.A., Inc.; the other kept the old name,

Cumberland Presbyterian Church divided in 1869, about a fifth of its hundred thousand members withdrawing to form a "Colored" church of the same name. Five years later the main body of Southern Presbyterians, after almost a decade of extreme vacillation as to policy, made provisions for Negro members, already gathered in separate congregations, to form an autonomous Colored Presbyterian Church. The mother church continued to raise funds in very modest amounts for the aid of its churches and schools.

The Methodists, meanwhile, had achieved a much firmer organization in four different churches. In 1866 the Southern Methodist church released its Negro membership so that it could form a Colored Methodist Episcopal church in 1870.[18] In 1866 the Northern Methodist church, whose wartime additions of southern Negro membership had been large, also made provision within its structure for a separate Negro conference with its own bishop.[19] The larger part of black Methodism, however, came to be included in two older African Methodist Episcopal churches which had been formed in the North well before sectional controversy had taken possession of the country.

The African Methodist Episcopal Church was formed in Philadelphia after two decades of friction between white and black Methodists in that city. Richard Allen (1760–1831), a manumitted layman, had founded Bethel Church for Negro Methodists in 1793, and was ordained a deacon (the first of his race in American Methodism) two years later. Because jurisdictional disputes after 1814 only intensified Negro dissatisfaction, the AME Church [Bethel] was organized; and in 1816, at its first General Conference, Allen was elected bishop. Twenty years later it had about seventy-five hundred members, and about three times that in 1860. In the meantime it had founded the first Negro magazine in America (1841) and acquired Wilberforce University in Ohio (1856).

In New York a similar controversy in the John Street Church led its black members to found Zion Church in 1801. Due in part to the undesired inter-

---

without the "Inc." In 1893 the Colored Baptist Association of the South could claim about 1.5 million communicants. The relative size of the two NBC's has remained fairly constant:

	1920	*1970*
NBC	1,000,000	2,670,000
NBC, Inc.	2,000,000	5,500,000

For a history of the NBC see Owen D. Pelt and Ralph Lee Smith, *The Story of the National Baptists.*

18. In 1954 for social and legal reasons it changed the term "Colored" to "Christian." According to Frazier, a similar move of middle-class members to eliminate the word "African" from the AME church failed because of lower-class objections (*The Negro Church in America*, p. 78).

19. In 1939, when the three main branches of predominantly white Methodism were reunited, this Negro conference was constituted as a separate nonterritorial "Central Jurisdiction," which then became a serious source of controversy.

ference of Bishop Allen, this group announced itself to be the nucleus of another national church in 1821—the African Methodist Episcopal Church Zion, electing James Varick (ca. 1750–1827) as its first bishop. Because it was seriously plagued by controversy and schism, the AME Zion church numbered only five thousand members on the eve of the war. As Union armies moved into the South, both of the AME churches began missions among the freedmen which they sustained with outstanding success during the years that followed. In 1896 the AME church claimed 452,725 members and the AME Zion 349,788, both of them considerably outdistancing the Colored church of Southern Methodist lineage (129,383) as well as the Northern Methodist church's Negro Conference (246,249).[20]

The foregoing statistics and organizational details may seem wearisome and routine, yet they reveal some frequently overlooked dimensions of Protestant church history. Most important perhaps is the massive participation achieved during four turbulent decades by the independent Negro churches despite poverty and oppression. The fact of 2.7 million church members in a black population of about 8.3 million suggests that the pervasiveness of evangelical religion among the slaves must have been far greater than church records indicate.[21] It becomes apparent that Christianity answered to deeply felt needs of a people for whom emancipation had been a less than glorious boon. The churches were the chief means by which a structured or organized social life came into existence among the Southern freedmen. The little churches of the rural South were a psychological and social necessity—the more so because they institutionalized the only area in which a fair measure of Negro freedom remained. The success of this ecclesiastical effort, moreover, demonstrates the inadequacy of the "Sambo" interpretation of slavery's effect on the race. Given the opportunity, blacks showed immense resourcefulness in church organization. If the result did not meet the classic standards of Western ecclesiology, it was because American racism prevented blacks from "classic" forms of participation in the general society.[22]

20. The AME Zion church had a more democratic polity, with lay representation in annual conferences and elected rather than episcopally appointed presiding elders. For some reason it became especially strong in North Carolina.

21. "In the South, at least, practically every American Negro is a church member. . . . A proscribed people must have a social center, and that center for this people is the Negro church" (W. E. B. DuBois, *The Souls of Black Folk*, p. 143).

22. The large political function of many black churches during Reconstruction is undeniable. Northern Reconstructionists often encouraged their organization, but often with strong evangelical and educational purposes as well. After the end of Reconstruction, as part of the larger pattern of enforced white supremacy, this political activity was suppressed.

THE ROLE OF THE BLACK CHURCHES

From the days of emancipation until the mid-twentieth century, the church was by far the most important black institution after the family. Considering the effects upon family life of centuries of chattel servitude and the ways in which the American caste system has interfered with its "normal" development, one could even make a strong case for the unqualified priority of the church. The church has consistently been the chief agency of social control, though in urban contexts its hold was gradually weakened. The churches also gave the first impetus to economic cooperation among Negroes, published the most influential periodicals, and aided Negro education as actively as any other institution.[23] Finally, the churches were a badly needed refuge in a hostile world. There is more pathos than humor in the reply of a rural Alabama Negro who was asked to indentify the people in the adjoining community: "The nationality in there is Methodist." [24] The church was in a sense a surrogate for nationality, answering to diverse social needs and providing an arena for the exercise of leadership. Far more than for whites, the black church served other than strictly religious needs. After 1877, as Jim Crow laws, intimidation, and political suppression steadily intensified, this function of the church increased in significance. More than ever it became a vital means of preserving a sense of racial solidarity.

Virtually every major authority, whether black or white, seems to agree that despite poverty and poignant limitations, the local church was for good or ill the primary element of the American Negro's nineteenth-century heritage.

> The Negro Church [says Frazier in a representative passage] has affected the entire intellectual development and outlook of Negroes. This has been due both to the influence of the Negro church which has permeated every phase of social life and to the influence of the Negro

23. Even sixty years after emancipation the Southern states had made only the tiniest contribution to the public education of Negroes. Fourteen of the eighteen Southern states had an aggregate of only thirty Negro high schools in 1910, at which time only half the country's blacks were literate. Institutions founded by Northern white and Southern black churches chiefly to train a ministry provided most of the existing opportunities for primary, secondary, and higher education. These impoverished schools labored against almost insuperable odds, yet their students did become the leaders of the Southern Negro churches (see Richard Bardolph, *The Negro Vanguard*, pp. 98–111). The AME *Church Review*, edited by Benjamin T. Tanner until he became a bishop in 1888, was the leading Negro magazine (see August Meier, *Negro Thought in America, 1880–1915*, p. 44).

24. Quoted and commented on by Frazier, *The Negro Church in America*, p. 44.

> preacher whose authoritarian personality and anti-intellectualism has cast a shadow over the intellectual outlook of Negroes.[25]

Yet the institution about which such sweeping assertions are made was in its outward aspect a very humble thing. It was usually a plain, ramshackle structure serving a small neighborhood in the Southern countryside. (Until World War I, we must recall, nearly 90 percent of the Negroes in the United States lived in the South, and two-thirds of them were rural.)[26] Regardless of denomination each of these little congregations—or often a group of them—was being led by a very modestly educated minister. In most cases he had no more than elementary schooling. Yet as a member of the only profession open to a Negro, in charge of the blacks' only free institution, he was a very important man, "the greatest single influence among the colored people of the United States," in the judgment of James Weldon Johnson.[27]

In his early book *The Souls of Black Folk,* W. E. B. DuBois stresses the minister's importance: "The Preacher is the most unique personality developed by the Negro on American soil. A leader, a politician, a 'boss,' an intriguer, an idealist—all of these he is, and ever, too, the center of a group of men, now twenty, now a thousand."[28] Yet strangely absent from this list of roles is the central one: the conductor of prayer and praise, above all, the preacher—the man who had to proclaim the gospel and apply the law, and yet do so without ever addressing the primary fact of black existence, white supremacy. Against this background Johnson could characterize the preacher as the one "who instilled the narcotic doctrine epitomized in the Spiritual, 'You May Have All Dis World, But Give Me Jesus.' "

The black clergy was by no means unanimously submissive, however. Henry Turner (1834–1915), a former slave who became the first black chaplain in the Union army, was a member of the South Carolina legislature until blacks were expelled in 1868. As early as 1874 he became an advocate of emigration to Africa, and later, as a bishop of the AME church, he was a leading spokesman for that cause, as was another AME bishop, Jabez P. Campbell. His emigration schemes had little effect, but his attacks on injustice were strong and widely heard. "A man who loves a country that hates him," he declared, "is a human dog and not a man." The Constitution he declared to be "a dirty rag, a cheat [and] a libel." After the Supreme Court's

25. Ibid., pp. 41–42.

26. From 1790 to 1910 this ratio is remarkably constant. After 1910 the percentage of Negroes outside the South and in cities everywhere steadily mounts.

27. Quoted by William H. Pipes, *Say Amen, Brother! Old-Time Negro Preaching: A Study in Frustration,* p. 3.

28. DuBois, *The Souls of Black Folk,* p. 190.

fateful Civil Rights decision of 1883, Turner was so disgusted with the United States that he advised blacks "to return to Africa or get ready for extermination." [29] Francis Grimke, minister of the prestigious Fifteenth Street Presbyterian Church in Washington, D.C., continuously protested the nation's abandonment of Reconstruction ideals, and in 1909 he and his brother Archibald were active in arousing black resistance to Booker T. Washington's accommodationist policies. Another minister in the nation's capital, Alexander Crummell, led the struggle for Negro rights in the Episcopal church. Crummell also attacked the larger problem of Negro equality, though, like DuBois, always with a somewhat elitist emphasis on higher education and talented black leadership. In 1897 he and Grimke were among those who formed the forty-member American Negro Academy for the promotion of science, literature, and the arts.

But undeniably, the tendency of the Negro clergy to compromise was pronounced. Although they were by no means agents of the white overlords, as some have suggested, they did show considerable complacency about the status quo, and were very ineffective in the movement to displace Tuskegee Institute as the symbol of the Negro's place in American life. Between 1890 and 1915, the years of his almost sovereign influence, Booker T. Washington had a firm hold on the black clergy's loyalty; and by and large his influence was salutary, for he awakened ministerial concern for this-worldly problems. But Washington, though raised as a Baptist and at home in the Bible, was privately disdainful of the Negro clergy's outlook even as he solicited its support.[30]

The disdain for the preachers attributed to Washington as well as the retrospective criticisms of the churches made by Frazier and Johnson are directed primarily at the prevailing theology, which is seen as retarding the Negro's advancement in American society. To a degree the charge is unjust, given the overwhelming fact of white supremacy and the limited sphere in which the ministers could practice their gifts for leadership. In the realm of belief and piety, moreover, it is essential to recognize that this nineteenth-century heritage of the black church was above all an integral—though segregated—part of the evangelical tradition which underlay nearly all Southern and much Northern Protestantism. When the "invisible institution" that had been shaped in the days of slavery merged after the war with the more traditional forms of the instituted churches, it still bore the

29. Edwin S. Redkey, *Black Exodus: Black Nationalist and Back-to-Africa Movements, 1890–1910*, pp. 41–42.

30. Samuel R. Spencer, Jr., *Booker T. Washington and the Negro's Place in American Life* (Boston: Little, Brown and Co., 1955), pp. 65–66, 139.

marks, as Paul Radin has observed, of "the somewhat barren Christianity that prevailed in the antebellum South." [31]

The anti-intellectual heritage was only another name for endemic revivalism, which as it developed in the Negro church may have involved an evasion of reality; but the basic forms of religious experience and the content and style of rural preaching were very similar whether the church was "colored" or white.[32] Both groups lacked a social gospel, both came to terms with the status quo, both evaded the larger corporate sins, and both failed to do what they could to rectify a cruel social order. The fault in a general sense lies with evangelicalism—not with the black church. In a less negative spirit, one might also observe that the black church showed at least equal concern for intellectual improvement and higher education.

Despite all the obvious similarities that grew out of the common cultural situation of whites and blacks in the rural South, historians have convincingly insisted that there were very significant differences as well. Louis Lomax's statement on this question is representative:

> In classical cultural terms there is no difference between the Negro Baptist Church and the Baptist Church proper. In folk terms, however, there is. Not only do we Baptists have a way of preaching and singing, but there is a meaning to our imagery that is peculiar to us.[33]

The preaching does have a folk idiom of its own—and in many cases it is expressed in a distinct dialect of the English language. There may also be a different rhythmic sense in the music, whether vocal or instrumental, and certainly different gestures and body movements. But it is Lomax's final

31. Foreword to *God Struck Me Dead,* ed. Clifton H. Johnson, p. viii. When the twentieth century precipitated a crisis in the Southern churches, the white churches were as profoundly stricken as the black.

32. A comparative study of black and white preaching in the rural South or of black and white Pentecostal preaching in the twentieth century, with close attention to content and nuance, seems not to have been made. The peculiarities of Negro preaching do not stand out in the collections of sermons made by May, Pipes, and Johnson. In one case as in the other, the real heart of the sermon—when the Spirit was truly working in the preacher—showed the same ecstatic stress on the joy of being in the Lord, of knowing that the life of sin and death was done and gone, of rejoicing in the still greater bliss to come. Nonverbal aspects of worship may vary, but rhythmic singing and freely responding congregations were not reserved for the blacks alone. In 1968, moreover, when the funeral of Martin Luther King, Jr., was televised, millions of evangelical Protestants living all over America, and especially those in the South, could truly participate in every element of the service—the hymns, the anthems, the sermon, and the prayers—as though they were there in the Ebenezer Baptist Church of Atlanta.

33. Louis E. Lomax, *The Negro Revolt,* p. 46. For an early formulation of this concept of the "invisible institution," see George F. Bragg, *History of the Afro-American Group of the Episcopal Church* (Baltimore: Church Advocate Press, 1922), p. 39. On the concept of "black religion" as a distinct element in Negro church life, see Joseph R. Washington, Jr., *Black Religion: The Negro and Christianity in the United States,* though the book as a whole is overly dogmatic.

point, on the "meaning to [the] imagery," that is most basic. The key terms of the faith—salvation, freedom, the Kingdom of God, and others—do carry different connotations in the black experience, and they always have. More generally, a certain mournfulness qualifies joy and jubilation just as it does in the spirituals and in the "blues." Long before Emancipation, moreover, black Christians had found strength and hope through their own special identification of themselves as God's Israel, as a chosen people being led out of bondage.

Christian faith and "black religion" became inseparable elements of piety, belief, and aspiration. It was a composite result that stemmed from the American Negro's extraordinary situation: back of him no heritage but slavery and a rumor of Africa which was in effect but an unknown void. Free but not free in the present. Only vague intimations of America's great future destiny, but in any case no confidence that he could participate in its bounty. In the church and through religion these tragic circumstances were made to cohere.

43

THE SOUTHERN WHITE CHURCHES AFTER THE WAR

The desolation of the South as it pulled itself together for the years of peace and survival has always been a challenge to the descriptive powers of men. Even unsympathetic Northern travelers discovered their literary inadequacies. Almost every reason for tears, uncertainty, and hopelessness was to be found: death, hunger, social dislocation, political disorder, racial fear, violence, conscious hate, and subconscious guilt. Pervading the desolation was a memory of military valor which defeat had not paled; and at a still deeper level, a haunting idealized picture of the prewar way of life. Beneath all was a tragic racial heritage, as old as the region itself. This fact had risen up in the 1830s to take possession of the Southerner's mind and soul, and it never again receded to a point where it could be either complacently accepted or rationally evaluated. This indeed is the "burden of Southern history"—as heavy a burden as any sizable portion of Western Christendom has ever borne.

Emancipation merely changed the forms of the South's dark heritage, not its content; and Reconstruction, for one turbulent decade, exposed the magnitude of the region's problems. Then gradually by dint of great exertion, these problems were covered over again for a long season—with the diverse instrumentalities of white supremacy holding down the lid. In the present chapter we consider the major ecclesiastical and religious accompaniments of these events, and in some cases the prewar developments that led to them. This will involve primarily an account of the Methodists and Baptists who, about evenly between them, accounted for 90 percent of Southern church membership (in several states more nearly 95 percent), almost twice the strength (47 percent) of these two communions in the nation as a whole. Receiving more support than dissent from the region's other denominations (among whom Presbyterians, Disciples, evangelical Episcopalians, and Lutherans predominated), these two vast movements virtually constituted the South in its religious aspect. Guided by a ministry which for the most part moved from the grassroots to leadership without benefit of seminary training, the two churches both reflected and defined the region's moral tone; they gave their blessings to the "peculiar institutions" that replaced slavery, inveighed with more consistent vigor against card playing and dancing than against racism or the unpunished murdering of recalcitrant blacks, and led the general run of people to prize the values and practices of the "old-time religion" rather than to ponder the forces that were reshaping modern civilization. (In 1893 the Southern Presbyterian Assembly made dancing a valid ground for excommunication.) The South, in short, followed the exhortation of a Mississippi Methodist preacher during the last days of the war: "If we cannot gain our *political,* let us establish at least our *mental* independence." [1] It came to pass, therefore, that the Civil War, far from collapsing the South's religious tradition, actually rejuvenated this unique component of Western Christianity and guaranteed its existence for at least another century.

The three great evangelical churches which comprised nearly 95 percent of the Southern church membership—Methodist, Baptist, and Presbyterian—decided to maintain their separate existence in the postwar era, as did the much smaller Lutheran church. Their decision provided the Lost Cause with its own altars. The black chattel which had formerly been permitted a subservient place in these churches was encouraged to organize itself separately, and nine-tenths of the ex-slaves became Baptists or Methodists in independent churches whose history is considered in the preceding chapter. The Episcopal and Roman Catholic churches each reunited at the national level in 1866, at the General Convention of the former, and at the Second Plenary Council of the latter. At the diocesan level, however, these churches adopted the developing practices of segregation, serving their small Negro memberships separately. With no significant exceptions whites and blacks moved into separate ecclesiastical worlds and, as we shall see, into quite distinct "religious" worlds as well.[2] Not only would they worship apart from each other, but piety itself would take different paths and develop characteristic forms.

In a larger, and still more tragic sense, the Southern white churches, on whom the region's intellectual responsibilities necessarily fell, came to rest on old solutions and practices. Modern religious proposals were associated

1. Kenneth K. Bailey, *Southern White Protestantism in the Twentieth Century,* p. 1.

2. On the distinctiveness of black religion and theology see chaps. 42 and 62.

with abolitionism and other Northern errors. Efforts to grapple with issues raised by scientific and scholarly advances were repressed, while poverty and the absence of independently endowed seminaries and universities precluded the emergence of significant intellectual encounter. One must agree, indeed, with two assertions of Samuel S. Hill's recent analysis: that the churches of Dixie were pervaded by "a peculiar variety of evangelical Protestantism which has not flourished anywhere else in Christendom over a long period," and that "the entire region's maturation" was conditioned by the "prevailing state of religious affairs." [3] It was after the war, moreover, rather than before, that the real distinctiveness of this heritage became manifest.

THE METHODISTS

"If America is ever ruined," declared Joseph Cook, the Boston lecturer and preacher, "the Methodist Church will be to blame. For she is the strongest and most influential Church on the continent of America today." [4] A vast exaggeration if taken literally, Cook's statement is nevertheless relatively close to the truth as applied to the South. By seceding from the most tightly organized church in America at the much publicized General Conference of 1844, the Methodist Episcopal Church, South, became the chief ecclesiastical standard bearer of the Southern cause.[5] Firmly rooted amid the planters of the black belt, famous for its successful evangelism among the slaves, and having rid itself of old Wesleyan condemnations of slavery, it was by far the most acceptable and most powerful church in the South. Because its defenses of the "peculiar institution" were unstinting, and because its support of the Confederacy was as remarkable as the Unionist solidarity of Northern Methodism, the war's end found it prostrate. In the meantime, the Northern Methodist church, Bishop Edward R. Ames leading the way, invaded the South as Union armies cleared the way, occupying churches, proselytizing members, leading off the blacks, and unsuccessfully encouraging other Northern churches to do likewise.

Southern Methodism was roused from its apathy by the so-called Palmyra Manifesto, issued in June 1865 by an informally gathered group of Missouri Methodists. Encouraged by this strenuous call for reorganization, the bishops convened a General Conference in New Orleans in 1866, and in defiance of Northern proposals for reunion, Southern Methodism quite literally sprang to life. It repudiated the political heresies of the Northern church, added four new bishops, provided for the separate organization of its remaining

3. Samuel S. Hill, Jr., *Southern Churches in Crisis*, p. xii.

4. Quoted in Hunter D. Farish, *The Circuit Rider Dismounts*, p. 1.

5. The Baptists soon followed in 1845; New School Presbyterians in 1857; Old School Presbyterians and Lutherans in 1861.

Negro membership, and in 1870 revised its constitution to permit lay delegates to attend its conferences. In the face of postwar moral laxity, it called its membership back to Wesley's concern for sanctification and began to reestablish every aspect of its institutional life. Despite the woes of Reconstruction, the church was blessed "with a perfect blaze of revivals," and in fifteen years it had doubled its membership. Speaking now as a custodian of the Lost Cause, it quickly won back the dominant place in Southern life it had held in antebellum days. In 1866 its membership rolled past the million mark, to reach 1,443,517 by 1906. Missionary efforts of modest size were maintained in China, Japan, Brazil, Mexico, and among the American Indians of Oklahoma and Texas. Only the Southern Baptists showed comparable evangelistic vigor.

Accompanying this rapid expansion of Methodist membership were various limited types of institutional growth. In nearly every state academies and colleges were founded or reorganized—though state universities were often opposed. But the culminating achievement of nineteenth-century higher education in the South was the project for a central university and seminary in Nashville. This was founded in 1873 and endowed by Commodore Vanderbilt with a half-million dollar gift which he increased to a million dollars by 1876. As a result of the unusually broad and enlightened leadership provided by Chancellor Langdon Cabell Garland and Bishop Holland N. McTyeire, Vanderbilt began almost immediately to exert a kind of normative influence on higher education in the South, although a majority of both bishops and members were opposed to its founding and suspicious of its probable influence. Anti-intellectualism remained strong and militant. So precarious was the infant university's reputation in 1878 that the trustees had to cut short Professor Alexander Winchell's visiting lectureship in zoology and "Historical and Dynamic Geology" because the Darwinian tendency of his teaching was too dangerous.[6]

Yet Southern Methodism was leaving many old landmarks behind. In 1876 its bishops accurately declared that "a more homogeneous ecclesiastical community does not exist on the American continent." The nature—and the price—of this homogeneity needs to be noted. With the increasing affluence

6. Winchell's book, *The Pre-Adamites*, had appeared that year. At its next meeting, the Tennessee Conference of the Methodist Episcopal Church, South, commended the university trustees for having "the courage to lay its young, but vigorous, hand upon the mane of untamed speculation, and say we will have no more of this science." As the university grew, tensions developed between the Methodist bishops and the Board of Trust; and in 1910 the General Conference initiated a campaign to regain control of the university. This led to a long court battle which in 1914 finally resulted in the school's independence (see Edwin Mims, *History of Vanderbilt University* [Nashville, Tenn.: Vanderbilt University Press, 1946], pp. 100–05, 291–318).

of its membership, the old bias against fancy dress, fine church edifices, organs, and choirs was passing away. A strong middle- and upper-class constituency was developing, at the same time that the church was losing contact with the urban poor. (Statistics showed that the bigger the city, the smaller the percentage of Methodists.) As will become evident in a later chapter, the extreme demands and activities of the Holiness movement thus soon became an embarrassment, and its more strenuous advocates were either suppressed or forced into secession.[7] As the Winchell case revealed, moreover, the serious intellectual problems posed by modern science and scholarship were being most inadequately dealt with. Finally, active efforts with regard to the two major social issues of the South, the rise of industrialism and the intensification of racial segregation, were being sacrificed to an increasingly legalistic militancy on dancing, tobacco, alcoholic beverages, gambling, card playing, and theater going.

The "social gospel" in the South was largely a Methodist phenomenon, to be sure, but it was for the most part an outgrowth of the New South movement expounded by the Methodist layman Henry W. Grady and the Reverend Atticus G. Haygood (1839–96), president of Emory University and later a bishop. Haygood's Thanksgiving sermon of 1880 "The New South," followed in 1881 by his book *Our Brother in Black,* gave clerical support to Grady's vision. He bade Southerners forget a legendary past, face their responsibilities to the Negro, and bring in a great industrial future. Above all he was thankful that slavery was gone forever, and that whites and blacks were learning (and demonstrating) the advantages of work and thrift.[8] Haygood was a natural choice as agent for the Slater Fund for Negro education, and in this capacity he performed a considerable service. His life reveals the way in which the old forms of Methodist piety were playing out without being supplanted by thoroughgoing theological reconstruction.[9] Declining health and frustrated ambition led Haygood into alcoholic disrepute during his later years.

THE BAPTISTS

The national unity of the Baptists had been sundered by the slavery issue in 1844, and in the following year the Southern Baptist Convention was

7. On the Holiness and Pentecostal churches, see chap. 48.

8. Booker T. Washington would provide the black corollary to these doctrines with his famous Atlanta Exposition address of 1895. See pp. 712–13, 1070–71.

9. One outstanding exception was John B. Robins, who showed a significant awareness of both social and intellectual issues in his *Christ and Our Country* (1889), a response to Josiah Strong's *Our Country.*

organized with great enthusiasm at a meeting in Augusta, Georgia. A year later, with a constitution that provided for a degree of centralization without precedent among Baptists, the Southern Baptist Convention began its independent history. Led by aggressive men and infused with the rising fervor of the Southern cause, it enjoyed extraordinary growth. In the next fifteen years its constituency contributed seven times more to the missionary cause than it had given to the General Convention's work in the preceding forty years. Dissatisfaction with the old convention's nearly exclusive concern for Northern home missions had created pressure for a separate Southern organization even in the 1830s, and it was in this area that the new Southern Convention scored its most remarkable successes.

When the secession crisis came, the Southern Convention's response was immediate and unconditional. Baptist soldiers were disproportionately numerous in the armies, while the whole gamut of work carried out in the North by the Christian Commission was undertaken with an equal measure of concern among Baptists in the South. To support its foreign missionaries the appropriate board even worked out a system for running long-staple cotton through the blockade, selling it at very high prices in England, and then conveying the funds by secret commercial channels to Asia and Africa. With the collapse of the Confederacy, however, the Baptists, like the Methodists, were at first overcome by apathy and hopelessness. Men wondered if the convention *could* be revived. By 1866 Reconstruction had intensified Southern desires for autonomy, and a policy of continued separation from the North was decided upon. At the same time, Negro Baptists very rapidly moved off into churches and associations of their own, encouraged to do so both by Southern whites and by federal Reconstruction policies. This encouragement had heavy political overtones, for black congregations were often used to strengthen the Republican party, and as a result, Southern Baptists refused to contribute substantial financial aid and educational assistance for Negroes until after the turn of the century.[10] Nevertheless, beginning in 1866, the convention's history is one of continued growth in domestic membership, foreign missions, and other benevolent enterprises. The election of the remarkable Dr. I. T. Tichenor as general secretary of the Home Mission Society in 1882 was especially important for the attainment of these ends. By 1890 the convention reported 1,101,714 members. Small foreign

10. Various plans to provide institutes for black ministers were launched in the 1880s, but without success. In 1895 a more ambitious "New Era Plan" was organized in most states (with the cooperation of the Northern Convention), but by this time the Negro churches were disinclined to white tutelage, and the support of state district supervisors for institute programs was soon discontinued.

mission fields in West Africa, China, Japan, Brazil, and Mexico added about 3,500 more.

Poverty, agrarian backwardness, and terrible educational deficiencies prevented the Baptists, even more severely than the Methodists, from coming to terms with the main intellectual currents of the later nineteenth century. Anti-intellectualism was a corollary of revivalism; opposition to higher education and theological seminaries was powerfully evident almost everywhere. Despite this opposition, Southern Theological Seminary had been founded at Greenville, South Carolina, just before the war (1859). Like all other Southern institutions its financial situation was considerably weakened during the Reconstruction period, but in 1877 it began a second and extremely useful phase of its history after receiving further support and moving to Louisville, Kentucky. Even here, however, divisive elements among Southern Baptists worked havoc with its academic program.

Since early colonial days Baptists had been seriously divided in one way or another, but the emergence of the missionary movement and the founding of the General Missionary Convention in 1814 had raised new divisive forces: a widespread, popularly based opposition to organized evangelism, the practice of founding "unbiblical" societies, and a related concern for education. When Alexander Campbell's advocacy added strength to dissenting views during his Baptist years (1813–30), antimissionism became a powerful new force, usually among the poorest and least educated elements of the constituency, who felt threatened by eastern money-raising organizations and their relatively well-educated emissaries. In backward sections of the South, therefore, the condemnatory exclusivism of this "Hard-Shell" movement gained very effective grassroots leadership, notably that of Daniel Parker (1781–1844). Though born in Virginia, Parker was a product of the Georgia frontier who later worked in Tennessee, Kentucky, southern Illinois, and Texas. With great skill and power he expounded the chief convictions of the "anti-effort Baptists," above all, their extreme predestinarian "antinomianism," their belief that God needed neither "new-fangled" societies nor the corrupting influences of higher learning to advance the gospel in the world. Parker himself also developed certain doctrinal innovations that made him the chief prophet of the "Two Seed" predestinarian Baptist sect.[11]

11. In 1820 Parker began his attack on Baptist missionary efforts with the publication of a pamphlet, *A Public Address to the Baptist Society*. In 1826 he stated his "Two-Seed-in-the-Spirit" doctrine in another pamphlet. This Two Seed theology was an exaggerated and eccentric form of predestinarianism: two seeds were planted in Eve, one by God (good seed), the other by Satan (bad seed). The election of individuals is determined by their "seed," and

This type of extremist advocacy led to the organization in state after state of separate congregations and associations of "Primitive" Baptists. They made great headway in Tennessee, Alabama, Georgia, Kentucky, North Carolina, and Virginia, and very significant inroads in western states. By 1846 antimission Baptists numbered at least sixty-eight thousand, or about 10 percent of the country's total Baptist population. Throughout the century their preaching hindered the organized work of Baptists, North and South, and won acceptance for Hard-Shell doctrines among countless persons and churches who never became affiliated with Primitive Baptist associations. Their outspoken witness undoubtedly more than compensated for the Arminian tendencies advanced by the Freewill Baptists, but the "compensations" were sectional, since Freewill Baptists flourished chiefly in the North, predestinarians in the South.[12]

During the postwar half-century Baptists in the South continued to divide on these issues, and the Southern Baptist Convention was torn by still another movement that developed enormous disruptive power within its churches. This was Landmarkism, a type of "high church" movement which stressed not the "episcopal succession" so dear to High Church Anglicans, but the "Baptist succession." Landmarkers believed that since the time of Christ, baptized (immersed) believers had continued to pass on the true church by immersing others in Baptist congregational contexts in an unbroken succession—a trail of blood—even during the Dark Ages when the Antichrist occupied the papal throne. In Reformation times, according to this theory, Baptists had broken into the open again as a diversified international movement. The local Baptist congregation, therefore, was an apostolic institution with a continuous history.

Baptists had formulated variations on this doctrine for centuries, but in antebellum America, in the Southern Convention, as the nation rushed toward civil war amid a great outpouring of intensely subjective revivalism, James R. Graves (1820–93), editor of the *Tennessee Baptist,* articulated the matter anew in a way that gave rise to a powerful, well-organized movement.

---

neither missionary societies nor anything else can do anything about it.

During his two-year stay in Illinois (1829–31), Parker published the *Church Advocate,* a monthly paper. His lifelong efforts led to the founding of churches in several states—chiefly in the South and in the middle region. In 1890 the "Old Two-Seed-in-the-Spirit Predestinarian Baptists" numbered 12,881; but by 1945 the membership had declined to 201 and the number of churches to sixteen.

12. Primitive Baptists numbered 121,347 in 1890, but Hard-Shell tendencies were far more pervasive than these figures suggest. Freewill Baptists, gathered chiefly in two organizations, numbered 100,000, with their chief strength in the North, especially in northern New England, where there were 16,000 communicants in Maine alone (cf. W. W. Sweet, *Religion on the Frontier: The Baptists, 1783–1830,* p. 66).

At the heart of Graves's argument was a doctrine of the Kingdom which allowed a syllogism to do the work of historical research: the Kingdom has prevailed; the Kingdom must always have included true churches; Baptist churches are the only true churches; therefore, Baptist churches have always existed. After presenting his case in various contexts between 1848 and 1851, Graves finally saw his Cotton Grove Resolution formally adopted at a mass meeting in Bolivar, Tennessee, in 1851—along with an injunction to refuse fellowship with all other churches. In 1854 he published a tract by James M. Pendleton entitled *An Old Landmark Re-Set,* whereupon the movement got its name.[13] Then in 1855 he republished G. H. Orchard's *Concise History of Foreign Baptists* (1838) in which the historical documentation is presented.[14] The stage was set for a great resurgence of Landmarkism as the woes of Reconstruction brought doubt and uncertainty to many Baptist Southerners.

In some respects this resurgence of extreme localism, exclusivism, and opposition to supracongregational agencies strengthened old Hard-Shell tendencies, but it also provoked a fierce controversy over Baptist history that wracked the denomination for half a century. Throughout the 1880s and 1890s attacks on the work of the home and foreign missionary boards continued, accompanied by demands that the convention abandon its character as a society of financial donors to become a genuinely ecclesiastical association of local churches. When the showdown on this latter proposal came in 1905, most of the extreme Landmarkers seceded from the church. In the meantime, they loosed a steady flow of criticism upon all who cast doubt on even the historical facts of the succession theory. This kind of strife reached its peak in the Whitsett controversy.

William H. Whitsett (1841–1911), appointed professor of church history at Southern Seminary in Louisville in 1872, was a German-trained scholar whose careful research into Baptist origins contradicted Landmark theory.

13. Pendleton's *Church Manual* (1867) and *Christian Doctrines* (1878) also had wide influence on Southern Baptist faith and practice.

14. G. H. Orchard was a Baptist minister in Steventon, Bedfordshire, England, whose book *A Concise History of Foreign Baptists* appeared in 1838. James Robinson Graves added a bombastic introduction praising church history but insisting that for seventeen hundred years none had been written, because existing histories covered the years from 300 to 1600 only by telling the story of the Antichrist, "the scarlet harlot riding on the beast with seven heads and ten horns, . . . drunk with the blood of saints." "It is 'high time' for the history of the Church of Christ to be written," he went on, "the world has quite long enough wondered [sic] after the Beast, and the Church of Christ left in the obscurity of the wilderness" (pp. ix, xi). What Orchard did (with enormous dependence on Mosheim's old ecclesiastical history) was to chart the history of antipedobaptist doctrines as they had been held by a long succession of heretical groups (Novatian, Donatist, Paulican, etc.). He then connected these sects with the Baptist emergence in the Reformation period.

Although Graves and his followers were critical, open conflict did not ensue until the 1890s, when Whitsett's appointment to the seminary's presidency coincided with the publication of his findings in *A Question in Baptist History* (1896). Landmarkers now opened fire in earnest, with Thomas T. Eaton, a Louisville pastor and editor of the *Western Recorder*, assuming the role left vacant by Graves's death. The threat to the seminary's support became so great that in 1898 Whitsett resigned.[15] His more discreet successor, E. Y. Mullins, actually continued to uphold Whitsett's views on Baptist history; and due to his strenuous efforts and intellectual force, the rising tide of Fundamentalism did not submerge the seminary, even though the South became the great stronghold of anti-intellectual and antiscientific religion. Among Baptists in the South, however, the message and spirit which Graves represented had an immense and pervasive influence. A century after the Landmark testimonies began to be widely propagated, both local practices and collective policies of the Southern Baptist Convention still exhibited signs of their influence: the closing of the Lord's Supper to all but Baptists (often even to those of other Baptist congregations), and a general willingness not only to refuse fellowship with other denominations but to deny them the name of Christian.

In the rupture of Southern Baptist interdenominational relations Graves was also very influential. In his *Tennessee Baptist* he mounted a vituperative campaign against the popular rival, Methodism. These diatribes were then circulated as tracts, and finally as a widely read book, *The Great Iron Wheel; or, Republicanism Backward and Christianity Reversed* (1856). Graves ridiculed the Methodist church as an infant pseudochurch no older than its oldest living bishop (seventy-two years in 1856)—and in fact (on Landmark principles) no church at all, but "an Antichristian organization," a miserable granddaughter of "the woman clothed in scarlet who put the saints to death." "If the Methodist E. Societies are churches of Christ, scriptural organizations, Baptists are not. The former or the latter are manifestly in *gross error.*" The editor of Orchard's *History,* needless to say, had little doubt as to which was the case.

Methodists, not surprisingly, replied vigorously to such charges—indeed their Book Concern was accused of burying the South and West with tracts, periodicals, and books. And Graves's chief assailant was none other than "Parson" William G. Brownlow, who was to gain fame a decade later as

15. Whitsett was in fact the second major casualty. The German-trained biblical scholar and historian of religions, Crawford H. Toy, had resigned from Southern Seminary in 1879, due to the unacceptability of his research. Rigorous historical scholarship was virtually excluded from Southern Baptist seminaries during the next half-century or more.

Tennessee's Reconstruction governor. Brownlow could be as vituperative as any man, and before the year was out he had answered Graves's assault in kind. In *The Great Iron Wheel Examined; or, Its False Spokes Extracted* (1856) he refers to Graves's paper as a "low, dirty, scurrilous sheet," and persists in that general spirit for over three hundred pages, defending Methodism from slander and in turn slandering the Baptists: "How do they enter the Church? They come in *backwards*, or, if the reader please, *wrong end foremost!* They *back into the Church*, as a goat retreats from its adversary, which, if not an insult to God, is not in accordance with good breeding." Brownlow also (quite rightly) accused Graves of filching his indictment of Methodism from Fred A. Ross, a New School Presbyterian of Alabama, whom Brownlow designated (erroneously) as a "man of color." In a concluding chapter he expounded his total approval of Southern Methodism's defense of slavery, urging Elder Graves to break his silence on this subject or get back to Ohio's Western Reserve where he had come from. Taken together, the two books reveal many major facets of Southern church life—especially, perhaps, the process by which Southern Baptists were pressed to positions and attitudes that left them in many ways alienated from the mainstream of American evangelicalism of which they had long been so important a part.

Southern Baptists (both within the convention and outside it) moved into the twentieth century, nevertheless, with great vitality and expansive force. Because of this rapid Baptist growth, Methodists by 1906 had to surrender their place as the region's largest Protestant communion. Westward expansion, especially in California, would modify the convention's overall "Southernness," though not its conservatism and zeal. The struggle with liberalism in the North would bring to the Southern Convention some accessions of conservative Baptists from that region. And because Southern Baptists were so numerous and so singlemindedly committed to traditional forms of evangelical piety, doctrine, and personal ethics, they became, despite their separatism, a major force in the great Protestant campaigns for Prohibition and immigration restriction, as well as in the Fundamentalist assaults on evolution.

OTHER DENOMINATIONS

In 1890 the Methodists and Baptists, together numbering between 4.5 and 5 million members (approximately half of them Negro), defined the moral and religious ethos of the region. Next in size was the Disciples denomination, with about two hundred thousand members. In interpreting their own unique Campbellite origins, the Disciples were considerably divided among themselves, however, and in chapter 48 consideration is given to the process by which a group of very conservative "Churches of Christ" gradually separated themselves during the postwar half-century, largely in the South. As a denomination, Disciples of all types tended increasingly to blend into the overall evangelical scene, even when they occasioned ecclesiastical conflict and rivalry.

The Presbyterians in 1890 numbered about 190,000, including the small Cumberland church (strongest in Tennessee) whose piety and church life was more closely related to the South's evangelical mainstream than that of other Presbyterian bodies. The Presbyterian church, nevertheless, exerted a disproportionately large influence in Southern affairs on account of the social prominence of its members, its extreme inner cohesiveness, and its demand for a learned, doctrinally orthodox clergy. The war and reconstruction experience had terminated the New School–Old School rift both organizationally and spiritually, but not until 1882 were even a nominal sort of fraternal relations established with the Northern church. In the meantime almost all of its approximately fourteen thousand Negro members drifted away to other affiliations, just as they did among the Episcopalians and Lutherans. The Cumberland Presbyterian church, on the other hand, organized a separate "colored" church in 1869.

The Southern Presbyterian church, therefore, became the prime embodiment of the white establishment in the New South. Even in 1961 its leading historian reprimands his church for being satisfied if in a typical small Southern city the Presbyterian church can draw its membership from the managerial class, leaving wage earners to the other churches and the newer sects. Because of the intensity with which it insisted on its own peculiar doctrine of the "spirituality of the church," moreover, it formally removed itself from popular social and economic concerns.[16] Its membership was little involved in the great political movements that sought to express and harness agrarian discontent. On the racial issue they stood with "the better class of whites" who, in Professor Woodward's terms, adopted the "conservative" view, favoring white supremacy but not Negro degradation.[17] Yet toward the turn of the century, the Presbyterians too followed the drift toward segregation and racism.

In Presbyterian seminaries the Princeton theology of Charles Hodge, as

16. Ernest Trice Thompson, *The Spirituality of the Church: A Distinctive Doctrine of the Presbyterian Church in the United States*, p. 38.

17. C. Vann Woodward, *The Strange Career of Jim Crow* (New York: Oxford University Press, 1960), p. 29.

adapted for Southerners by Henry Thornwell, continued to be the accepted norm. Its chief expositor and defender was Robert Lewis Dabney, the totally unreconstructed professor of theology at Union Seminary in Virginia. In 1883 Dabney accepted a professorship in moral philosophy at the University of Texas in Austin, where he also helped to found another Presbyterian seminary. In the meantime he played a vigorous role in the widely publicized heresy trial of James Woodrow (1828–1907). This uncle of future President Woodrow Wilson had come to the Presbyterian seminary in Columbia, South Carolina, as professor of science and religion, a subject area which was itself controversial. Woodrow soon heightened the controversy by indicating a cautious willingness to accept the theory of evolution as a "not unreasonable interpretation of the Bible." A public address in 1884 brought his views into the open, and two years later the General Assembly by a vote of sixty-five to twenty-seven recommended his dismissal. In 1888 the General Assembly acted still more decisively and made this conservative position official by adopting a positive deliverance on Genesis, Adam, and evolution. On the great intellectual dilemma of the age, therefore, Southern Presbyterians showed their solidarity with the dominant faction among the Northern Presbyterians, and with Southern Protestantism generally.

Three very small denominations, the Lutheran, Roman Catholic, and Episcopalian, each in its distinctive way, tended to dissociate themselves from the chief theological tendencies of the Southern Protestants, though their institutional life fully reflected the dominant social presuppositions of the region.[18] Almost all of Southern Lutheranism was involved in a confessional movement that was leading them toward a larger awareness of Lutheran unity. Southern Roman Catholics were spared many of the internal problems of immigration. Except in Louisiana, however, they were a small minority in a hostile environment. For both reasons they tended to support the "Americanists" in the church. The bishop of Little Rock, Arkansas, Edward Fitzgerald, cast one of the two votes, and the only American vote, against the constitution on papal infallibility at the First Vatican Council in 1870. Socially the Episcopal church was in a situation very similar to that of the Presbyterians. Widespread concern for questions of high or low churchmanship and for the intellectual freedom of their seminaries at Alexandria, Virginia, and Sewanee, Tennessee, saved them from much of the environing obscurantism. In William Porcher DuBose (1836–1918), moreover, the South could boast—though in fact it largely ignored—one of the

18. In 1890 Episcopalians, Roman Catholics, and Lutherans each numbered between forty and forty-five thousand members in former slaveholding states. The main Lutheran synod merged with the Northern churches in 1918.

most profound American theologians of the period. DuBose was almost a living stereotype of "classic" Southern upbringing, yet the combination of evangelical fervor and Anglo-Catholic modernism which he expounded in several major works was remarkably attuned to the scholarly developments and philosophical interests of his age.

SOUTHERN PROTESTANTISM AT THE CENTURY'S END

The war with Spain, inadequate though it was as an expression of the martial spirit that Theodore Roosevelt personified, marks an end to the post–Civil War era. Imperial acquisitions in the Caribbean and the Pacific led to the nationalization of Southern attitudes on race. The freed Negro's situation reached its nadir as other domestic issues came to the fore: industrialism, urban political corruption, the "new" immigration, and Prohibition. In the age of Progressivism Southern and Northern Protestantism again joined hands as the need for an "evangelical united front" became manifest. Yet the situation within the dominant churches of the South remained fundamentally unchanged. Jim Crow was at the peak of his career. "Denomination mattered little, for support for the racist creed ran the gamut from urban Episcopalians to country Baptists." [19] The intellectual revolution of the nineteenth century had made only a small impact on prevailing attitudes, and because religious liberalism and troublesome scholarship had few champions and no appreciable constituency in the South, the Fundamentalist controversy remained for several decades a Northern affair. As late as 1927 only 4 percent of the Southern Methodist clergy were seminary graduates and only 11 percent had college degrees, while 32 percent had no more than an elementary education. It is most improbable that the Baptist situation was any better. In the Negro churches it was very much worse. With few exceptions, moreover, Fundamentalism reigned unchallenged in the denominational colleges and seminaries throughout the region. Their predominantly rural and small-town constituency made the Southern churches the strongholds of social patterns and ways of thought that were increasingly anachronistic. These churches could and did marshal public opinion on a wide range of social questions and enforce those forms of the Puritan ethic that had begun to assume a characteristically Southern tone in the early colonial period. Yet what Rufus B. Spain says of the Baptists could be applied generally: "Their significance in Southern life consisted not in their power to mold their environment . . . [but] in supporting and perpetuating the

19. David M. Reimers, *White Protestantism and the Negro*, p. 29.

standards prevailing in society at large." [20] When joining forces with Northern Protestants, they could be an awesome power in the land. Nationalism and the urgencies of war (whether against Spain or Germany) could divert popular attention, veil the facts, and stave off the impending crisis. Yet a rendezvous with the twentieth century could not be postponed indefinitely.

20. Rufus B. Spain, *At Ease in Zion: Social History of Southern Baptists*, p. 214. On the characteristic Southern forms of the Puritan ethics, see pp. 184–85, 190–92, 713 above.

VII
THE ORDEALS OF TRANSITION

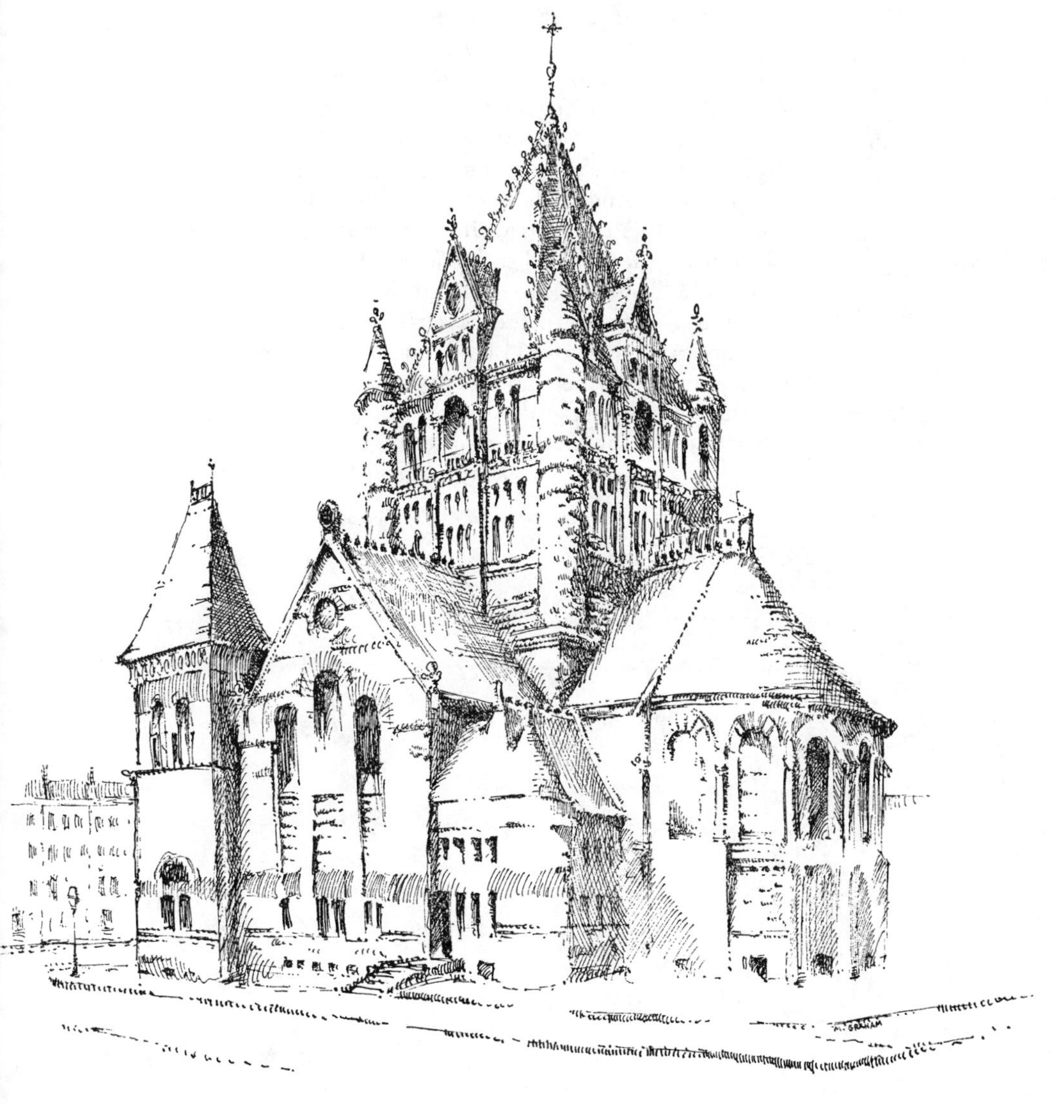

That the rapid changes now going on are bringing up problems that demand the most earnest attention may be seen on every hand. Symptoms of danger, premonitions of violence, are appearing all over the civilized world. Creeds are dying, beliefs are changing; the old forces of conservatism are melting away. Political institutions are failing, as clearly in democratic America as in monarchical Europe. There is a growing unrest and bitterness among the masses, whatever be the form of government, a blind groping for escape from conditions becoming intolerable. To attribute all this to the teachings of demagogues is like attributing the fever to the quickened pulse. It is the new wine beginning to ferment in old bottles. To put into a sailing-ship the powerful engines of a first-class ocean steamer would be to tear her to pieces with their play. So the new powers rapidly changing all the relations of society must shatter social and political organizations not adapted to meet their strain.

Henry George, *Social Problems* (1883)

A strange formlessness marks the half-century which follows the Civil War. The term "postbellum America" lacks the specificity of "antebellum America." One explanation for the difficulty is that evangelicalism was no longer calling the tune—or more accurately, that fewer people were heeding the call. The several ordeals to which the country was subjected during these decades of rapid change partially explain this circumstance. Primary, perhaps, was the great social and economic revolution that brought the urban and industrial situation to an acute stage without a corresponding revolution in government and politics. Compounding these social problems was a drastic shift in immigration patterns that put the old Protestant Establishment, already divided by memories of the Civil War, in a far more threatened position. This led to another recourse to nativism, to a revival of the immigration restriction movement, and to varieties of political reform that were less committed to democratic ideals than to keeping the "best men" in power. The Indian problem was turned over to the churches; the Supreme Court gutted the Civil Rights Act; and the Republicans gave up even their nominal role as protector of the freedman.

Another problem which affected the churches directly was America's belated and hence unusually harsh confrontation with many revolutionary forms of modern thought, most notably historical criticism of the Bible and Darwinian evolutionary theory. In this situation many champions of scholarship and science appeared, and there were newly endowed seminaries as well as wealthy congregations to give them a hearing; yet conflict on a large scale between liberals and conservatives ensued. Churches were seriously divided and various sectarian secessions occurred.

In this controversial context crusades of diverse sorts were organized, in part, it would seem, to heal or hide the disunity of the churches. Temperance and foreign missions easily commanded the largest attention, though Dwight L. Moody's great revival campaigns received much publicity. An increasingly shrill accompaniment to these crusades was the renewed emphasis on America's world mission. Josiah Strong as spokesman for the Evangelical Alliance coupled his strong interest in urban problems and home missions with a call to his country to assume its imperial duty to Anglo-Saxonize mankind. "My plea is not, Save America for America's sake, but, Save America for the world's sake." By 1898 widespread acceptance of such thinking had provided a pious major premise for the logic of a war with Spain, and beyond that for America's entrance into the commercial and political affairs of the world.

44

URBAN GROWTH AND THE PROTESTANT CHURCHES

When Fort Dearborn was incorporated as the village of Chicago in 1833, it was an ugly frontier outpost of seventeen houses. By 1900, though still ugly, it was a sprawling western metropolis of 1,698,575 people—the fifth largest city in the world. Chicago became the most dramatic symbol of the major social trend of the post–Civil War era: the rise of the city.

Within a generation after the Civil War the United States was transformed from a predominantly agricultural to a manufacturing nation. By 1890 the factory had outdistanced the farm as the country's chief producer of wealth, and by 1920 the population's center of gravity had shifted decisively to the city. Making the transition were dozens of new metropolitan centers besides Chicago. Nor was this only a western phenomenon; old eastern cities like Boston, Philadelphia, and New York expanded with startling speed.[1]

This social and economic revolution was accompanied by the final phase of the great Atlantic migration, which brought European peoples to these shores in such numbers as to dwarf all previous immigration. Whereas the pre–Civil War peak came in 1854 with 427,833 immigrants, nearly twice that number arrived in 1882; and in 1907 the all-time high of 1,285,349 was reached, a figure that exceeded by several hundred thousand the total number of immigrants to the thirteen colonies between 1607 and 1776. Between 1860 and 1900 about 14 million people arrived, and between 1900 and 1920 that many more. Since no more than one-third of these went into farming or related activities, the already teeming cities had to make room for the rest. Here they would usually carry out the immemorial tasks of new immigrants

1. Between 1860 and 1890 Boston grew from 177,840 to 560,892; Philadelphia from 565,529 to 1,293,697; and New York from 1,080,330 to 3,437,202.

at the lowest level of the social and economic order. Living together in congested quarters, yet close to old-country friends and customs, they challenged the absorptive powers of the metropolis and added still another problem to the many that were already plaguing the older social and governmental structures.

America's transformation also brought profound intellectual consternation to many sensitive participants in the process. One social analyst remarked in 1889 that "an almost total revolution has taken place, and is yet in progress, in every branch and in every relation of the world's industrial and commercial system." At about the same time Henry Adams shuddered before the awful power of the dynamo and wondered if his whole generation was not "mortgaged to the railroads." As corporations grew stronger, counter-organizations of farmers and workingmen were formed. Individualism in the old sense became a liability for all but the industrial and banking tycoons.

> As the network of relations affecting men's lives each year became more tangled and more distended, Americans in a basic sense no longer knew who or where they were. The setting had altered beyond their power to understand it, and within an alien context they had lost themselves. In a democratic society who was master and who servant? In a land of opportunity what was success? In a Christian nation what were the rules and who kept them? The apparent leaders were as much adrift as their followers.[2]

The moral dilemmas of industrialism, moreover, were compounded by problems created by science, scholarship, and the philosophic speculations of the age. Pervading all was the fundamental difficulty of evaluating urban civilization itself and weighing its values in the light of the nation's agrarian past. For the churches shaped by frontier evangelism these questions were especially acute. The post–Civil War decades were indeed "the critical period in American religion." [3]

THE CHURCHES AND THE CITY, PAST AND PRESENT

Commercial and maritime necessities spurred the growth of American cities almost from the beginning; and churches in these "cities in the wilder-

2. David A. Wells, "Recent Economic Changes," in *The Nation Transformed: The Creation of an Industrial Society*, ed. Sigmund Diamond (New York: George Braziller, 1963), p. 41. See also Robert H. Wiebe, *The Search for Order* (New York: Hill and Wang, 1967), pp. 42–43.

3. Arthur Meier Schlesinger, "The Critical Period in American Religion, 1875–1900," *Proceedings of the Massachusetts Historical Society* 64 (1932–33): 523–47.

ness" began to experience some characteristic urban problems even in the seventeenth century. The founding in 1699 of the Brattle Street Church in Boston, for example, clearly evidenced the growing self-consciousness of a merchant community. After the passage of a century the problems of urbanization had multiplied to the extent that the minister of this very church, the Reverend Joseph Stevens Buckminster, expressed gratitude on Thanksgiving Day that the country had an inexhaustible supply of unsettled western lands. It seemed to him then that the escape they offered from the city's festering problems was the only sure hope for American democracy. Though a stout Federalist addressing a congregation of stout Federalists, Buckminster shared Thomas Jefferson's agrarian ideal.

In many respects, however, westward expansion only enlarged the economic role of the cities, with the result that complications deepened in the older centers of population. Sixteen years after Buckminster gave thanks for rural America, the Unitarian ministers of Boston had felt obliged to form a "Benevolent Fraternity of Churches" and to call Joseph Tuckerman as "minister-at-large" to direct a program of social work among Boston's poor. Discovering that chapels and preaching were not enough, Tuckerman became one of the country's first Christian social welfare theorists and a forerunner of the Social Gospel. Yet urban growth soon created far larger problems than cooperative social work could solve. Remorselessly the population patterns changed. Buildings deteriorated, factories encroached, old residential areas decayed, tenements arose, peaceful streets became crowded thoroughfares. When the constituency of old "downtown" churches moved out into new residential neighborhoods, the church itself often followed, perhaps selling the old building to another congregation composed of in-migrants. Later, this church too would follow "its people" to some more favorable location. The changing ownership of church buildings thus documented the demographic history of the city, while the successive locations and edifices of a single congregation recorded the upward social mobility of its membership.

Such trends, tragically enough, meant that congregations which were involved in this struggle for survival were often in a poor position to undertake a program of evangelism in their own neighborhood. In the old location they became financially incapable of a wider social ministry. If they moved, such social problems became geographically and morally remote; if they stayed, the characteristic forms of Protestant church life prevented them from establishing cordial relations with the church's new neighbors unless they were of similar social status. In a church already moving up the social scale, the sermons tended toward greater intellectual sophistication, the music had a similarly restricted appeal, and parish programs increasingly answered to middle- and upper-class needs. In such congregations, proper sewing-circle conversation and the niceties of holding a teacup were effective bars to evangelistic outreach.

Urban change thus had two particularly devastating consequences. In the first place, large elements of the new urban population had no contact with any Protestant churches. This was especially true of the English-speaking peoples of Protestant background who were moving in ever-increasing numbers from the countryside to scattered locations in the cities. Immigrants were not so prominently handicapped, because their ethnic or linguistic isolation often led them to the churches of their fellow nationals, who more often than not were Roman Catholic, Jewish, Eastern Orthodox, or Lutheran. The liturgical worship and church life of these denominations tended to hold congregations together despite the upward mobility of some members. In the second place, urban growth created a serious cleavage in city population in relation to religious affiliation. The people who could afford churches were well churched; those who could not were unchurched—and hardly cared, or even regarded church people as their economic oppressors. Josiah Strong, the general secretary of the Evangelical Alliance, in two heavily documented books, *Our Country* (1885) and *The New Era* (1893), piled statistic on statistic to demonstrate the dramatic exodus of Protestant churches from the growing sections of American cities.

THE PRINCES OF THE PULPIT

Inanition, flight, and class segregation were by no means the only features of urban Protestantism in the Age of Enterprise. Large and wealthy urban churches offered opportunities not only to architects, artists, and musicians, but they also created the context for a new kind of minister whose merits and importance has often been underestimated. The oratorical style of these men finds little favor in the twentieth century; but all across the nation they did address the age's many moral and intellectual dilemmas with considerable intellectual power. Aiming to be understood by an active, socially prominent laity, they carried out an important task of mediating Christianity to the modern world. It was a time when science seemed to undermine the Christian message and when many people doubted the relevance of the church in an industrial-commercial environment. Faced by a widespread yearning for ethical and ideological anchorage, the great preachers took up the task of defending and interpreting the Christian tradition anew. In what they said there was no universal agreement. Some of these wealthy congregations were led by revivalistic Presbyterians, others by radical Unitarians. But there was a discernible central tendency which can be traced to the influence of the new "progressive" theologians making their impact in several centers of learning. Most prominent among the many preachers who set new patterns in the city churches were Henry Ward Beecher (1813–87) of Plymouth Congregational Church in Brooklyn, and Phillips Brooks (1835–93) of Trinity Episcopal Church in Boston.

Beecher, the fourth son of Lyman, graduated from Lane Seminary in 1837 and for ten years afterward followed the revivalistic tradition of his father in various Indiana churches. Coming to the newly formed Plymouth Church in 1847, by the charm of his personality and the force of his oratory he soon attracted a congregation of great size and wealth. From the first Beecher chose to minimize doctrinal differences, demanding nothing of his members save personal loyalty to Christ. Displeased by criticism of his theology, he led his congregation out of the Congregational denomination in 1882, proclaiming himself a free man with obligations to none. He often addressed himself to topics of the times, including the whole gamut of contemporary social and political issues: slavery, reconstruction, immigration, taxes, women's rights, civil service reform, and municipal corruption. In addition, he sought to expound a meaningful Christian accommodation of evolutionary theories, biblical criticism, and the cultural values of the city as such. He edited two widely read journals, the *Independent* (1861–63) and the *Christian Union* (1870–81), and contributed regularly to both the religious and the secular press as well. His sermons were published weekly in the *Plymouth Pulpit* (after 1859), while successive volumes of sermons and lectures reached a nationwide audience. He also delivered the Lyman Beecher lectures on preaching at Yale for three years straight (1872–74), compiled *The Plymouth Collection of Hymns and Tunes* (1855), and wrote a novel that dealt with changing religious values (*Norwood,* 1687). Neither his advertising testimonials in behalf of Pears's Soap, nor a great scandal arising out of his indiscreet attentions to Mrs. Elizabeth Tilton seriously diminished his public.

The broad churchmanship of Phillips Brooks is another example of ebullient confidence in liberal theology and American culture. "The spirit of man is the candle of the Lord," Brooks never tired of telling the Boston congregation to whom he preached for a quarter of a century (1869–93). To him the whole of mankind was the family of God, and the goodness and nobility of men as children of God was the essential article of his faith. His optimism kept him as untroubled by the inequalities of American life as were his self-satisfied parishioners. He found evidence of God's goodness in the thought that each class had its peculiar blessings and privileges. Like Beecher, his ethic rested more on the social assumptions of an earlier age than on those of the new industrial society. He believed that suffering caused by poverty and injustice was for the most part deserved, but that they were, in any event, only temporary problems which the natural harmony of God's purposes would certainly dispel. Suspicion of heresy notwithstanding, Brooks became the Episcopal bishop of Massachusetts in 1891. He published ten widely read volumes of sermons, along with a volume of *Essays and Addresses* and his *Lectures on Preaching* delivered at Yale in 1877.

These two princes of the pulpit were in a class by themselves, envied and emulated the country over. Yet each of them had strong rivals even in his own city: George Angier Gordon at Boston's Old South Church, and T. DeWitt Talmadge at Central Presbyterian in New York. In New Haven, Theodore Munger and Newman Smyth, both nationally eminent, held forth in two historic Congregational churches standing side by side on the city green. Rare was the city, especially in the North, that could not boast one or two of these great downtown churches with their carriage trade constituency and impressive buildings. Because they spoke with thoughtfulness and learning, the ministers of these churches did succeed in keeping a remarkable number of America's great men of business and public affairs active in the work and support of the church. Because of the accommodating nature of their message, on the other hand, they often contributed to the "inner revolution" of the epoch by transforming Christianity into a benign and genteel form of religious humanism. This dilemma is considered in greater depth in chapter 46, which deals with the "golden age" of theological liberalism.

PROTESTANT INNOVATION AND TRADITION IN THE CITY

One major explanation for the uneven effectiveness of urban Protestantism during this period was the fact that the churches, like the various institutions of civil government, were slow to overhaul their basic strategies and organization. The half-century before the Civil War had been the age of the nonsectarian voluntary associations, but rising denominational self-consciousness and other factors began to make serious inroads into these institutions even before the war. The conception of the church itself as a mission society began to win increasing allegiance. These shifts in rationale and method, in turn, led to several decades of disorientation during which cooperative home missionary efforts were reorganized. Only in 1908, with the founding of the Federal (later National) Council of Churches, was the full transition more or less accomplished.[4] In the meantime, the long-established tendency to emphasize the rural frontier's missionary call was not broken. The West,

4. On the reorganization of Protestant interdenominational cooperation, see pp. 802–04 below.

both as myth and as reality, was a more compelling lure than the city, and it continued to be the chief concern of home missions agencies. As Professor Handy has pointed out, the new city problems "were unfamiliar to a Protestantism that had flourished in small-town America, and the missionary movement was slow in regrouping its forces and reorienting its thinking."[5] Even when efforts were begun, the middle-class, frontier-oriented mentality of those in charge put its mark on the tactics employed and sharply circumscribed their effectiveness. Rural people were moving to the city in great numbers, but these arrivals tended to bring with them the patterns of congregational life which they had known in the past. In the absence of denominational or interdenominational planning, like-minded groups simply organized congregations as best they could with little concern for other groups or for the needs of the city. Within each denomination, therefore, there were often a variety of churches for different areas of the city and different types of people, most of them following the predictable patterns of America's small towns and rural areas, except that social stratification often became more pronounced.

An increasingly important aspect of congregational life during these decades, and also an invaluable instrument for reaching new members, was the Sunday school. This movement, like so many others, had British origins, and during the antebellum period it had become a vital element in the work of the Evangelical United Front. As a coordinating agency for many regional associations, the American Sunday School Union had been founded in 1824. Thereafter wide-ranging organizational and publication activities were carried forward. The Sunday school became a familiar American institution, and in many congregations the "Bible class" overshadowed the regular Sabbath worship. On both the local and the national level the evangelistic possibilities of these educational means were exploited, especially during the urban revivals of 1857–58.

During the post–Civil War years the movement experienced still another forward surge. Not surprisingly, Dwight L. Moody had a hand in it. Moody inspired the wealthy Chicago produce broker and real estate man B. F. Jacobs to reinvigorate the Sunday School Union. Jacobs's talents got results, and at the convention of 1872 he gained the adoption of a uniform lesson plan, whereby the same lesson, graded for different ages, could be studied and taught on each Sunday in all the participating churches. The plan encouraged interdenominational teachers' meetings, the expansion of supporting publications, and the foundation of teachers' institutes all across the

5. Robert T. Handy, *We Witness Together: A History of Cooperative Home Missions*, pp. 16–17.

country modeled on the Moody Bible Institute of Chicago (1886). Revivals and revivalists would come and go, but the Sunday schools remained as a strong stabilizing force in the churches. In small towns and large cities they attracted dedicated lay leaders of great ability, helping to set the tone and temper of American Protestantism and providing an effective means of reaching the unchurched and unaffiliated—adults as well as children. Although they necessarily mirrored the country's values, the Sunday schools did produce a pious and knowledgeable laity on a scale unequaled anywhere in Christendom.

In addition to these more traditional forms of congregational life, however, there were four very diverse but yet distinctly innovative forms of urban concern that became especially important during the postwar period, though they all had had earlier origins. The best known of these is the Social Gospel movement (see chap. 47). The other three are more clearly related to problems of evangelism.

Least heralded were the slum-oriented efforts of the Salvation Army, its offshoot, the Volunteers of America, and a diverse group of rescue missions, many of which were founded by Holiness and Pentecostal sects. (As parts of a distinctive Christian movement these groups are considered in chap. 48.) Far more extraordinary in their special adaptation to city needs were the Young Men's and Women's Christian Associations. Supported by the philanthropy of wealthy church members and catering to the needs of the many unattached young people who were moving to the city, the YMCA and YWCA entered upon their half-century of greatest vitality and usefulness during the 1870s. Though traceable to eighteenth-century experiments in Germany, the history of the YMCA among English-speaking peoples begins with a society formed in London by George Williams on 6 June 1844. By 1851 there were twenty-four such organizations in Great Britain, and in that year one was formed in Montreal and another in Boston. In 1855 the first YWCA was organized. The next year a New York YMCA was formed, and by 1860 there were some 203 associations with about twenty-five thousand members in all North America. During the Civil War the YMCA gave itself largely to the work of the Christian Commission among the soldiers, but afterward it returned to its ministry in the cities. Emphasizing Christianity in practical work, it had four major departments of endeavor: physical, educational, social, and religious. In the first of these fields the YMCA was a pioneer, fostering athletic recreation and defending the values of "play" in the face of much puritanic criticism. Its religious department, at the same time, was so powerful a force that the YMCA functioned not simply as an ecumenical service agency, but virtually as a church and as a Protestant denomination for the many young men and women who owed their Christian commitment to its Bible classes and religious services. All in all, the "Y" was one of the most remarkably functional church agencies of the period.

The fourth great strategy of Protestant advance in the city—and by far the most publicized—was nondenominational professional revivalism. The old methods pioneered by Whitefield, developed by Methodist camp meetings, and further refined by Finney became the major instrument of the urban churches in reaching out beyond the narrow circles of personal acquaintance to penetrate the anonymous mass of city folk who, in their uprooted loneliness, longed for the old-time religion. Revivals also offered a measure of excitement to break the monotony of urban existence, just as camp meetings had performed that function on the frontier. Indeed, the revivalists provided theatrical entertainment to people who regarded the theater itself as sinful. Its country-born practitioners knew these inner yearnings, and the successful ones were masters at appealing to them. Thus from Keokuk and Peoria to New York and Boston, revivalism constituted the single largest response of evangelical Protestantism to the challenge of the urban frontier.

THE GREAT REVIVALISTS

Dwight Lyman Moody (1837–99), like so many of those to whom he preached, was a village-born lad who despite a meager education had made good in the city. At the age of eighteen, leaving his widowed mother at the homestead in Northfield, Massachusetts, he sought his fortune in the Boston shoe store of his uncle. Between 1854 and 1856 Moody sold shoes, enjoyed Boston, listened to his uncle's pastor, discovered the Bible, and "accepted Christ"; in 1856 he became a church member. His conversion was quiet, simple, and unemotional, yet it eventually reordered his entire life. In September 1856, Moody moved to Chicago.

"Chicago hustled!" says one writer, and so did Moody. His energy and enthusiasm soon won him a reputation as a salesman in the shoe trade, but the business world could neither claim all of his immense gifts nor corrode the memory of his religious experience. Joining the Plymouth Congregational Church, Moody rented four pews which he filled each Sunday morning with whomever he could collect on the streets and in the boardinghouses. Taking charge of an out-of-the-way mission Sunday school in North Market Hall, he gathered a membership of fifteen hundred—mostly urchins and drifters whom he picked up off the streets and out of the gutters and cellars of the Sands district north of the Chicago River. And out of this motley group was formed in 1863 the Illinois Street Church, independent and nondenominational. Moody was equally successful in enlisting the support of wealthy friends such as John V. Farwell, B. F. Jacobs, George Armour, and Cyrus McCormick.

In 1861 he gave up business to devote himself entirely to the Lord's work, first as an independent city missionary, during the Civil War as an agent of the Christian Commission, and after the war as president of the Chicago YMCA, where he had been active since his arrival in the big town. One of Moody's first services to the YMCA was as chairman of its Visitation Committee, a capacity in which he indulged his soul-winning zeal to the fullest, visiting over six hundred families in one year—a "new model circuit rider in the urban wilderness." After twelve years in Chicago, Moody was a civic fixture. He was the "drive wheel" of the Chicago YMCA and a remarkable fund raiser after fires in 1868 and 1871 twice destroyed its building. His church was also influential, and although he had begun to preach, he had as yet done nothing to acquire the fame which was soon to be his.

Then between 1867 and 1872 four decisive events occurred. Through Harry Moorehouse, a Plymouth Brethren preacher from England, Moody discovered the love of God for sinners, a message which had been lacking in all his previous experience. In 1870 he persuaded Ira David Sankey (1840–1908) to join him as a chorister in his evangelistic endeavors. The next year, in New York, Moody had some kind of a reconsecration experience which literally set him on fire with a "passion for souls." Finally, in the spring of 1872, while in England on business for the YMCA, Moody was asked to substitute in a London pulpit. After his sermon four hundred people responded to his closing invitation. It was a sign from heaven: here was his life's work.

The first great campaign of the Moody-Sankey team was in Great Britain, where during 1873–75 they must have reached between three and four million hearers. Then it was America's turn. In Brooklyn the transport company laid down additional trolley tracks to accommodate the crowds seeking passage to the Rink, a five-thousand-seat auditorium. In Philadelphia John Wanamaker fitted out a Pennsylvania Railroad freight warehouse for a two-month campaign. After that they began a famous series of campaigns from New York to Saint Louis, and on to the Pacific coast. With listeners in the millions, converts in the thousands, their hymns on every lip, their names a household word, Moody and Sankey rejuvenated the revival. As Bernard Weisberger has put it, "Moody made clear what he had known all along: the American-born, middle-class urbanite of his day was still a villager under the skin. Using the methods and the money of big business, Moody reconciled the city and the old-time religion to each other." [6]

Dwight Moody's message was a simple and relatively innocuous blend of American optimism and evangelical Arminianism. Holding aloft his Bible, he assured his hearers that eternal life was theirs for the asking, that they had only to "come forward and t-a-k-e, TAKE!" This done, his follow-up instruction was short and to the point: "Join some church at once." Which church did not matter.

> Moody preached a gospel with but one center, God's saving act in Jesus Christ, and one goal, the conversion and salvation of the sinner. All other ends were secondary. . . . Public morality was to be improved through saving individuals. The church was a voluntary association of the saved.[7]

Nowhere in his message was there much help for the thinker who was seriously disturbed by the moral problems of industrialism or the new intellectual dilemmas of the nineteenth century. His optimism was revealed in his confidence that individual conversions would solve every personal and social problem. Charitable works were not an end in themselves, but a means of reaching individuals with a message of redemption.

Just as significantly, the campaigns of Moody and Sankey furthered the mounting tendency to convert the traditional message of Protestant Christianity into something dulcet and sentimental. The United States had embarked upon the most extravagantly sentimental period in its history, and through song and sermon across the land, the professional revival teams wove this sentimentality into the warp and woof of American Protestantism. The same mood suffused the new style of "Christian art." Biblical scenes by the German painter Johann M. F. H. Hofmann acquired enormous vogue, while the religious publishing houses and Sunday school suppliers laid the groundwork for twentieth-century America's unbounded enthusiasm for the pictures of Warner E. Sallman. Thus a new pattern was set for revivalism, and in the process, a prophetic faith was transformed into a sentimental moralism. Perhaps in these subtle (or not so subtle) nuances and emphases lies the chief import of the new revivalism.

After Moody's retirement in 1892 no figure of equal stature appeared on

6. Bernard A. Weisberger, *They Gathered at the River: The Story of the Great Revivalists and their Impact upon Religion in America*, p. 206.

7. Robert S. Michaelson, "The Protestant Ministry in America: 1850 to the Present," in *The Ministry in Historical Perspectives*, ed. H. Richard Niebuhr and Daniel D. Williams, p. 256. Conservatives were often critical of Moody's openness, notably his accepting the young British liberal, Henry Drummond, not only as a friend but as a co-worker.

the urban revival scene.[8] His mantle in a sense was conferred on J. Wilbur Chapman and Reuben A. Torrey, though these men never achieved his wide appeal or impressive results. But two other men continued his work on a grand scale: Samuel Porter Jones (1847–1906) and Benjamin Fay Mills (1857–1916). Sam Jones was a product of rural Georgia who turned from a bibulous past in 1872, became an itinerant Methodist preacher, and was known before long as the "Moody of the South." His revivals were a significant factor in the urban recovery of the Methodist Episcopal Church, South, especially after E. O. Excell joined him as chorister and gospel song writer. Jones began his attacks on the typical vices and shortcomings of city life, but his emphasis was radically practical. "If I had a creed," he declared, "I would sell it to a museum." [9] Sanctification he equated with a resolve to live by the mores of rural Georgia in the wicked city. No man documented so tellingly the long road away from John Wesley's theology which American Methodism had traveled during its first century of independent life.

Mills was of a different sort altogether. Not only was he an important link between America's revival tradition and the Social Gospel, but he made important innovations in revival techniques. His background was Old School Presbyterian, but he was ordained into the Congregational ministry in Minnesota in 1878. After nine years as a parish minister, he entered the field of professional evangelism. His chief distinction is the development of the highly successful "District Combination Plan of Evangelism." More than anyone up to his time, Mills marks the full accommodation of revivalism to the arts of business and administration. Nothing was left to chance: finance and organization were carried out in advance, and a city was attacked simultaneously in various precincts and by central meetings. Decisions were recorded on cards which were then distributed to the cooperating churches. All church meetings not connected with the revival were canceled, and, if possible, the entire city was encouraged to declare Wednesday a "midweek Sabbath" by closing all of its businesses. Ample press coverage was sought and usually secured. Then, with all these matters prearranged, Mills would mount his campaign on the city and its sins. One of the anomalies of his

8. Moody suffered a heart ailment in 1892 which curtailed his activities considerably. During the last years of his life he founded numerous institutions to perpetuate his witness: the Northfield Seminary for Young Women (1879), the Mount Hermon School for Young Men (1881), the annual student and Christian workers conference at Northfield, and the Bible Institute for Home and Foreign Missions in Chicago (1886). These were financed not only by Moody's affluent friends, but by the not inconsiderable returns on his and Sankey's hymnbook, which went through numberless editions during its long period of popularity (see James F. Findlay, Jr., *Dwight L. Moody: American Evangelist, 1837–1899*).

9. William G. McLoughlin, *Modern Revivalism: Charles Grandison Finney to Billy Graham*, p. 300. My indebtedness to this history is great, especially on Moody's successors.

success was that his message, and hence the meaning of his conversions, was so generalized that Christian Scientists, Unitarians, and Roman Catholics saw no incongruity in signing his cards. In theology Mills moved steadily toward a Bushnellian liberalism and gradually lost favor among evangelicals. In 1899 he left revivalism for the Unitarian ministry.

By the second decade of the twentieth century, it remained only for cheaper, simpler men with gaudier personalities and fewer scruples to bring the revivalistic movement into disrepute. Mannerisms of the theater and the music hall were combined in Knowles Shaw. The growing tendency to emphasize statistics was characteristic of Rodney "Gipsy" Smith, who not only made news on the number of "decisions" he secured, but indicated to his sponsors that he could produce converts for $4.92 apiece. The most spectacular champions of the sawdust trail, however, were the ex-baseball player, Billy Sunday, and his chorister, Homer A. Rodeheaver (1880–1955)—a team, incidentally, that cut conversion costs to $2.00 a soul when they finally got their system working.

William Ashley Sunday (1863–1935) was, like Moody, a farm boy, "a rube of the rubes," as he himself put it. Born in Iowa into a family ravaged by many tragedies, he gained prominence in 1883 as an outfielder for the Chicago White-Stockings. Three years later, after being converted, he began to amend his life. When Bible study classes at the Chicago YMCA aroused his interest in Christian work, he quit baseball to become an assistant secretary at the YMCA in 1891. Two years later he took a job as organizer on the revival team of J. Wilbur Chapman, who at that time was still something of a class-B attraction, touring only the smaller cities of the nation. In 1895 Chapman retired to a Philadelphia pastorate and recommended Sunday as his successor. Billy's debut in Garner, Iowa, was modest; but by 1900 he was able to hire his own musician and to require towns to erect pineboard tabernacles for his meetings. As he developed his innate abilities for vaudeville, he drew larger crowds, and by 1904 he could demand that expense monies be raised before he arrived. After securing Rodeheaver as a great trombone-playing song leader in 1909, he conducted a revival in Spokane, breaking into the 100,000-population circuit for the first time. From then on the team's average improved; and by 1917, the peak year, the average population of the revivalized cities was 1,750,000. This was the major league indeed. Sunday's box score in New York that year showed a total attendance of 1,443,000 for the ten-week campaign. Converts numbered 98,264.

Sunday's phenomenal success was due in no small part to his talent for dramatization before audiences. Accompanying his contortions, furniture smashing, and partial undressing was an unbroken torrent of words. What the church needed, he shouted, was fighting men of God, not "hog-jowled, weasel-eyed, sponge-columned, mushy-fisted, jelly-spined, pussy-footing, four-flushing, Charlotte-russe Christians." Similar language was turned against the familiar sins of the world: high society, worldly amusements, filthy habits, pliable politicians, liberal preachers, trashy immigrants, and especially the "booze traffic." Every man who was not a teetotaler was a "dirty low-down, whisky-soaked, beer-guzzling, bull-necked, foul-mouthed hypocrite." Not only did he define sin almost solely in terms of individual moralism, but he garbled the distinction between the sin and the sinner in a way that simply fostered the self-righteousness of his middle-class audiences.

The "altar call" was, of course, the climax and goal of the revival service. Professional evangelists had made the decision increasingly easier, so that by Sunday's time any "decent American" could painlessly respond. The burden was easy and the sawdust trail was wide. His invitation on the twelfth day of his New York campaign was typical. "Do you want God's blessing on you, your home, your church, your nation, on New York? If you do, raise your hands." . . . "How many of you men and women will jump to your feet and come down and say, 'Bill, here's my hand for God, for home, for my native land, to live and conquer for Christ?' " Then Rody and the choir began their musical accompaniment, and a sea of humanity surged forward—one out of every ten in that audience of twenty thousand.[10]

The high tide of mass revivalism in the trappings of vaudeville came during the decade preceding America's entry into World War I. In 1911 there were 650 active evangelists in the field and 1,200 part-time campaigners. Between 1912 and 1918 they staged at least thirty-five thousand revivals; and according to one careful estimate, the evangelical churches spent $20 million a year on "professional tabernacle evangelism" during the peak years from 1914 to 1917. But decline was inevitable. Already in 1915 Alfred and Kilmer Ackley had asked Billy Sunday to throw a few crumbs their way, pleading that the "evangelistic situation for the little fellow this season is going to be mighty hard." [11] With American doughboys in Europe, the nation's attention was diverted to less theatrical concerns for a time. In the war's complex aftermath, America's religious climate changed, and professional evangelism suffered a temporary relapse which some historians, perhaps hopefully, interpreted to be its demise. Even so, the movement had etched a deep mark on American evangelical Protestantism.

10. William G. McLoughlin, *Billy Sunday Was His Real Name*, pp. 261, xvii–xxix; see also Weisberger, *They Gathered at the River*, pp. 240–49.

11. McLoughlin, *Billy Sunday*, p. 261.

45

PROTESTANTISM AND THE LATER IMMIGRATION

Next to rapid urban expansion, probably no historical development of the later nineteenth century had a heavier impact on the spiritual self-consciousness of the American people than the demographic revolution produced by immigration. Its relatively greatest impact on the population occurred between 1851 and 1860, but the peak volume of the influx did not come until the years between 1901 and 1910. In its totality, the Atlantic Migration involved a much longer period of time and the movement of over forty-five million foreigners. It was during the post–Civil War half-century, however, that the American people felt the full impact—though not really the full import—of the country's ethnic and religious pluralism. Two brief tables reveal both the varying volume of the influx and the diversity of its origins. These bare statistics inevitably leave many vital facts veiled (for example, the ethnic makeup of the exodus from the composite Austro-Hungarian Empire), but they give unmistakable evidence of the new order of magnitude which immigration assumed in the later nineteenth century.

Total Immigration to the United States, by Decade

1821–1830	143,439
1831–1840	599,125
1841–1850	1,713,251
1851–1860	2,598,214
1861–1870	2,314,824
1871–1880	2,812,191
1881–1890	5,246,613
1891–1900	3,687,564
1901–1910	8,795,386

Total Immigration to the United States, by Decade (cont.)

1911–1920	5,735,811
1921–1930	4,107,209
1931–1940	528,431
1941–1950	1,035,039
1951–1960	2,515,479
1961–1970	3,321,677
WORLD TOTAL	45,154,253

Total Immigration by Country, 1820–1969

Europe:	
Austria	3,769,854
Germany	6,906,465
Great Britain	4,777,727
Ireland	4,712,680
Italy	5,149,119
Norway	852,891
Russia	3,346,455
Sweden	1,266,127
Other Europe	4,812,326
TOTAL EUROPE	35,593,649
America:	
Canada	3,941,858
Mexico	1,547,771
West Indies	1,033,386
Other America	1,784,847
Total America	7,307,862
Total Asia	1,429,020
Total Countries not Specified	458,781
WORLD TOTAL	44,789,312

Source: Department of Justice, Immigration and Naturalization Service, *Annual Reports.*

THE INNER HISTORY OF IMMIGRATION

No statistical table can reveal the billions of tears that were shed in the course of that massive uprooting; numbers cannot register the pain of severed human ties, nor the cumulative nostalgia, nor the anguish of loneliness in a strange land. Yet the tears and anguish are part of the American heritage, even though their full significance will never be known. Ever since John Winthrop and his party saw the English coastline sink from view in 1630, the entire religious life of America has been conditioned by two inescapable concomitants of the immigration experience. One of these consists of the tenacious ties to European culture and church traditions which the immigrant brought with him to this country, which he transmitted to his children, and they to theirs. The other, which became more drastic as the United States developed its own distinctive ways, is the confrontation with a new culture and the desire to appropriate the life and ideals of the country with whose destiny the immigrant has cast his lot. Between these two loves, desires, and needs, there could only be conflict, tension, and gradual resolution. The diary-letters of a young bride sailing away from Norway with her husband convey something of the grief that millions of emigrants could never banish:

> April 26 [1862] And now the last glimpse of Norway. It may be somewhere near Arendal, but it's far in the distance like a blue mist; nothing more. I am heavy-hearted. A silent prayer for comfort in my deepest sorrow and for strength and courage.
>
> April 27 (First Sunday after Easter). The captain led the worship. My heart was still heavy. My thoughts were with you, my dear ones, and of services at home. I could see you all in church. You know I was never absent—and now! O merciful God!
>
> Today my last glimpse of Norway. I shall never see my beloved homeland. O God of Mercy, my fatherland! O forgive me for causing my dear ones this anguish! O God, do not forsake us! Be our comforter and give us patience and strengthen our faith.[1]

Later, when settled on a farm in Iowa—her husband away fighting in the Union army—she tried to convey the meaning of it all to her parents:

> I have often thought that I ought to tell you about life here in the New World. Everything is so totally different from what it was in our beloved Norway. You never will really know what it's like, although you no doubt try to imagine what it might be. Your pictures would be all wrong, just as mine were.[2]

1. Theodore C. Blegen and Pauline Farseth, eds., *Frontier Mother: The Letters of Gro Svendsen* (Northfield, Minn.: Norwegian-American Historical Association, 1950), p. 14.

2. Ibid., p. 39.

After making the initial adjustments, immigrant parents would shed other tears at the sight—or even the thought—of their children taking bolder steps into the new world, many of them compusively cutting away every reminder of their "foreign" background, especially when under the pressure of nativistic movements. Pastors and church leaders felt the same tensions, needless to say, but their response was complicated by the impossible task of adjusting current practices to the needs of both those who were in the throes of rapid Americanization and those who had just arrived from Europe. To the degree that the foreign traditions and ways of life contrasted sharply with American habits and typical American religious practices, the problems were intensified. Only much later, when the membership and leadership were in the hands of a real or figurative third generation, would a balanced and noncompulsive attitude toward European and American cultures be possible. Even then, the workings of Hansen's law—that the third generation tries to remember what the second generation tried to forget—would complicate matters.[3]

TYPES OF RELIGIOUS RESPONSE

Few of the world's innumerable churches and religious traditions have avoided America entirely, and at the height of the Great Migration the diversity was so great as to preclude a detailed account in a general history. In this chapter, the Protestant immigrants are considered; discussions of Roman Catholicism, Judaism, and the ancient Eastern churches will appear in later chapters. Rather than undertaking a wearisome chronicle of the immigrant churches in all of their variety, however, one may describe five major types of accommodation to the American religious situation.[4]

The first category includes those immigrants who were merely nominal members of some state church in Europe, or simply unaffiliated, or anticlerical by conviction (as was fairly often the case with certain ethnic groups, especially if they came from industrial cities). Such people neither founded new churches nor sought out existing ones on arrival, but they made an important contribution to the history of American secret societies during their nineteenth-century heyday. They thus aggravated the old hostility of

3. Marcus L. Hansen, *The Problem of the Third Generation Immigrant* (Rock Island, Ill.: Augustana Historical Society Publications, 1930).

4. This typology will reveal why no statistical estimate of Protestant affiliations in America can be attempted. Father Gerald Shaughnessy, *Has the Immigrant Kept the Faith?* (New York: Macmillan Co., 1925) adduced a fairly affirmative answer for Roman Catholics; but his problem was relatively simple. For Protestant immigrants one can do little more than hazard a guess that they did *raise* the incidence of church membership in the United States.

the churches to such organizations, and they often divided ethnic groups into two factions: the "church people," and those who gratified their needs for ritualism and social contacts in the Masonic order, or in dozens of other flourishing lodges, some ethnically oriented, some not. Of course, they also constituted a ripened home missions field.[5]

A second type consists of the immigrating sectarians, those who recently or in the immemorial past had expressed their dissatisfaction with comprehensive state churches by forming more rigorously disciplined communities of their own. The Mennonites are a classic example; and their history in America was profoundly altered in this very period by a large migration of German Mennonites from Russia. Having fled Germany earlier in the century to escape military service and other impediments, they were confronted in 1870 by the czar's revocation of their privileges in Russia. Given the alternatives of compromise or emigration, many of them found America's promise of peace and plenty decisive (as did even larger numbers of non-Mennonite Germans in Russia). Settling chiefly in the Midwest, from Kansas to Indiana, this group soon became the largest element in the General Conference Mennonite Church, which is somewhat more moderate in its belief and discipline than the older Mennonite church of Pennsylvania background.

Similar in many ways to the professed sectarians were many other deeply religious immigrants who were, in European terms, incipient sectarians, deeply dissatisfied with the formalism, the moral laxity, or the doctrinal indifference of an established church. Because their attitudes toward the church of their fathers were thus distinctly negative, they were eager to identify with the American free-church tradition. Their numbers were further increased by the active evangelism of various American churches. Two German-speaking Methodistic churches, the Evangelical Association and the United Brethren in Christ, were thus able to make large additions to their membership. Similar growth occurred among Baptists, Methodists, Presbyterians, and Congregationalists, who in various ways conducted active foreign-language evangelism, followed by organizational provisions for special ethnic conferences or synods of Germans, Scandinavians, Slovaks, Hungarians, and others. Walter Rauschenbusch's father, for example, was a professor in the "German Department" maintained by the Baptist theological seminary in Rochester, New York. The Congregationalists showed a special solicitude for the non-Mennonite Russian Germans whose churches

5. Despite its obvious importance, the "lodge" as an American social and religious institution has been inadequately studied. The existing literature is largely designed either for polemical or defensive purposes.

in the Upper Midwest had adopted a congregational polity and set up a college and seminary at Yankton, South Dakota.

The fourth and fifth categories are constituted by those extremely numerous immigrants who belonged to various European state churches, and who wished to continue these affiliations in America. Most difficult to number are those of the fourth category. Their native loyalties simply led them to some branch or diocese of their home church. Great numbers of Anglicans, Presbyterians, Dutch Reformed, Lutherans, and others followed this course. Somewhat more visible are those of the fifth type who for various reasons organized new autonomous churches. They treasured the confessional heritage of their birth, and the churches they founded maintained close ties with a mother church in the old country, though only rarely did they receive substantial aid. Linguistic considerations were often an important factor in their choice. A great many in this category, however, were also church reformers of a sort, who used the opportunity for a new beginning in America to introduce important changes in liturgy, discipline, polity, and even doctrine. Because vigorous, new, and in some cases very large church bodies were brought into existence in this manner, three instances, the Christian Reformed Church (Dutch), Evangelical Church-Union of the West (German), and various Lutheran developments, merit more detailed consideration.

The Christian Reformed Church

The largest of several strictly "Reformed" churches in the United States, aside from the two large Presbyterian churches, is the Christian Reformed Church formed by a tiny group of Dutch immigrants in Zeeland, Michigan, on 8 April 1857. The decision of this frontier nucleus stemmed from dissatisfactions with the existing Dutch Reformed tradition which had been manifested almost simultaneously in both Holland and America. In the mother country a spirit of dissent rising during the revivals of the 1820s had by 1834 led to actual secession and the formation of a doctrinally strict free church, which in 1892 would be merged with another and larger secession. In America, Solomon Froeligh and four other ministers led a similar secession in 1822, forming the True Reformed Church. This group united in 1889 with the Christian Reformed Church of America, which at that time consisted of nearly ten thousand families, and by 1970 the church had about 400,000 members, most of whom are descendants of later nineteenth-century Dutch immigrants living chiefly in Michigan and nearby states. With a well supported church-school system and a strong intellectual and theological tradition nourished by Calvin College and Seminary in Grand Rapids, Michigan, the denomination has become perhaps the country's most solid and dignified bastion of conservative Reformed doctrine and church discipline.

German Unionists on the Frontier

The Evangelical Church-Union of the West (*Evangelischer Kirchenverein des Westens*), an immigrant church contemporary in its development with the Christian Reformed, represented the contrary tendency. This church founded on the Missouri frontier came closer than any other in America to achieving the union of Reformed and Lutheran confessions for which the king of Prussia had striven in 1817. In the mid-nineteenth century, Germans constituted perhaps a quarter of the population of the Saint Louis–Southern Illinois area; and they exhibited the full range of possible religious attitudes from ultra-orthodox Lutheran to anticlerical rationalist. Among them was a sizable number of pietistic evangelicals of both Reformed and Lutheran backgrounds, who in 1840 convened near Saint Louis to found a loosely organized union of pastors and laymen. In 1866, after the modest success of their early efforts, they made extensive constitutional changes in their polity, providing for a full-time president and a democratic synodical structure.

Nonsectarian and irenic in spirit, they always avoided a strict confessional basis for their synod, and at first authorized the use of both Luther's and the Heidelberg catechisms for instruction. In 1847, however, they showed their growing consensus by issuing their own Evangelical Catechism, based on both of the older catechisms but inclining in spirit toward the former. This Union catechism was "the ripest theological fruit" of the Union's early years. In 1862 they published an abridged version which was accepted as defining the church's official theological position. Even more important to the actual nurture of the members was the 242-page commentary on this Small Catechism written by Professor Andreas Irion (1823–67), a fervent, mystical product of Württemberg pietism with strong philosophical interests, whose early death robbed the church of an original "Union theologian."

Counting 122 pastors in nine different states at the time of reorganization in 1866, the synod steadily extended itself as German immigration continued to pour into the Midwest. Later, joined by four other churches of a similar nature, it became the Evangelical Synod of North America. In 1934, when its membership had reached 281,500, it further expressed its unionistic principles by merging with the German Reformed church, which then also included two Hungarian "classes." This process would be carried still further in 1957, when the Evangelical and Reformed church merged with the Congregational Christian church to form the United Church of Christ.

The New Shape of Lutheranism

If the Christian Reformed church represents the immigrant's doctrinal rigorism, and the German Evangelical Union his unionistic propensities, the Lutherans who poured into the country by the million in the period between the Civil War and World War I may be said to represent the entire span, from the strict confessionalism of the Missouri Synod (organized in 1847) to the moralistic revivalism of the Franckean Synod (organized in 1837 with probably more indebtedness to Charles G. Finney than to Martin Luther). Precisely this diversity had precipitated the crisis of 1855–69 and led to the division of the older eastern Lutheranism into two opposed formations, the confessional General Council, and the General Synod with its broader "American Lutheran" platform. By 1918, after the quadricentennial of the Reformation had been duly celebrated, a far more orderly situation would prevail, and the path to confessional fellowship among the Lutherans of America could be discerned. Between 1869 and 1918, however, lay the great immigration epoch of the church.

No Protestant communion was so thoroughly transformed by the later nineteenth-century immigration as was the Lutheran. Three million immigrants came from the diverse provinces of Germany, perhaps a half of them at least vaguely Lutheran, 1.75 million from Scandinavia, nearly all of them at least nominally Lutheran, and a heavy scattering of others from Finland, Iceland, and various parts of the Austro-Hungarian empire. They settled in every section of the country, in cities and on farms, but, of course, overwhelmingly in the North. It is hardly surprising that a communion which numbered a scant half-million in 1870 had almost quintupled by 1910, by which time they were outnumbered only by the Roman Catholics, Methodists, and Baptists.

Such an influx naturally contributed to the steady western expansion of the older Lutheran organizations, the General Council, the General Synod, and the United Synod of the South, though the latter two were hindered by their emphasis on the English language and by their lack of confessional concern. Most important for the reception of the immigrants were the independent new churches which the immigrants formed themselves. Oldest of these were the Buffalo Synod and the Missouri Synod, both of which date their American origins to 1839. One group of about a thousand had left Prussia because they could not accept the Prussian Union of 1817, when the king had celebrated the Reformation by forcibly uniting the Lutheran and Reformed into a single state church. Led by Johannes A. A. Grabau of

Erfurt, they founded churches chiefly in the Buffalo, New York, area and around Milwaukee. Grabau held an extremely strict conception of Lutheran doctrine, a "high church" conception of ordination, and a very authoritarian understanding of the ministerial role. His alleged "Romanizing" tendencies soon brought his synod into conflict with other Lutheran bodies which, coupled with Grabau's ineffective leadership, led to the Buffalo Synod's loss of many of its ministers and members to other bodies. It remained very small until the time of its absorption by merger in 1930.

Equally strict confessional Lutherans from Saxony, centered in Missouri, figured most prominently in the controversies with Grabau, and they enjoyed an almost completely different destiny. They, too, had left their homes out of dissatisfaction with the state church, above all its rationalism and its indifference to vital religion. Led by Martin Stephan, a brilliant preacher from Dresden, they established a Lutheran "Zion on the Mississippi" around Saint Louis and in Perry County, Missouri. Though less than seven hundred in number at first, and though beset by the nearly disastrous necessity of deposing "Bishop" Stephan, they were able as the years went by to gather an ever increasing number of German immigrants into their fellowship. In 1847 they formed the "German Evangelical Lutheran Synod of Missouri, Ohio, and Other States" and by the time of World War I they had become the largest single synod in American Lutheranism. This remarkable growth was due to many factors, not least of which was the synod's situation in the heartland of German immigration. But the chief factor was the intense confessional loyalty of the Missourians, and the powerful esprit and evangelical zeal of its members, both ministerial and lay. Behind this zeal lay the intellect, erudition, piety, and personality of Carl F. W. Walther (1811–87), who very early made Concordia Seminary a strong center of influence. For a half-century he almost achieved an identification of his life and soul with that of his beloved synod.

Walther was the son and grandson of Saxon pastors, and a graduate of Leipzig University. He had served as minister for a time before joining the Stephanite exodus, but by this time his independent Luther studies, his readings in the literature of pietism, and his deep attachment to the Lutheran confessions had made him thoroughly dissatisfied with the easygoing status quo of the Saxon church. In America, after the expulsion of Stephan, Walther became the struggling colony's theological rallying point. And before many years his journal *Der Lutheraner* became a powerful influence among Lutherans throughout the country. As a preacher, professor, and theologian, Walther put an indelible mark on the life and faith of the

Missouri Synod. Though two or three others might contend for the honor, he is probably the most influential figure in nineteenth-century Lutheranism in America.

The two predominant features of Walther's thought were pietism and confessionalism. Whatever else the Christian faith might be, it certainly involved a personal knowledge of forgiveness and justification by God's redeeming grace through faith in Christ; the rationalistic understanding of faith as simply "assent" was deficient. Yet his confessionalism stood opposed to all tendencies to reduce faith to feeling, as many pietists and, later, the romantic disciples of Schleiermacher tended to do. Another prominent aspect of Walther's thought was his emphasis on the "rule of faith" (*regula fidei*), which in fact constituted his resolution of the century's great struggle with historical relativism. He insisted that the Christian was committed to the testimonies of the Church given in the ecumenical creeds and the confessions of the Lutheran Reformation. The Gospel would be robbed of its power if it were not understood and preached in the light of this historic witness. Even among confessional Lutherans Walther stands out sharply for his attack on the prevailing tendency to consider a legalistic system of morality as the "essence of Christianity." In his most widely read work, *The Proper Distinction Between Law and Gospel* (published posthumously in 1897), Walther reveals himself as a truly "Neo-Reformation" thinker, for he insists upon this distinction as the central problem of theology.

In general Walther's views had the effect of isolating his synod from other Lutherans: against the Buffalo Synod and all other advocates of "high church" views, he committed the Missouri Synod to congregationalism and a "low" transfer theory of the ministry. In defining the Church he emphasized pure doctrine and greatly broadened the area in which clear theological consensus was demanded; as a result, controversy of all sorts became the lot of Missourians. Finally, he was led to so strong an emphasis on "grace alone" that he was widely accused of being a crypto-Calvinistic predestinarian. Out of this contention arose the most decisive controversial issue in later nineteenth-century American Lutheranism. Though many other factors were involved, this controversy did most to disrupt a burgeoning confessional entente—the Synodical Conference—which at its height included, under Missouri leadership, a large group of Norwegians and Germans in a great northern-swinging arc from Missouri to Ohio.

Isolation did not mean stagnation, however. Programs of parochial and higher education were instituted almost immediately; and Concordia Seminary at Saint Louis was set on its way to becoming one of the largest and most intellectually rigorous in the country. Missouri's sense of purpose and missionary zeal attracted new German immigrants, including many German-trained pastors; its explicitly conservative theological position also appealed to many pastors and congregations from older Lutheran bodies. Very soon "Missouri" anomalously designated a national church.

In the meantime other German Lutheran churches or synods were being formed in the West. The oldest in a strict sense, and soon to be one of the largest, was the Joint Synod of Ohio, which had begun as a conference of the Pennsylvania Ministerium, but had separated from its parent in 1818 and begun its steady process of growth and subdivision. Columbus, Ohio, became its headquarters and the seat of Capital University, its seminary and main college. In the Upper Midwest, chiefly in Wisconsin, another group of small synods took shape, the most important of which was the Wisconsin Synod organized in Milwaukee in 1850 by men sent out by missionary societies of the Prussian Union church. Gradually the explicitly Lutheran position of this synod was made clear, and Wisconsin soon began to coordinate its work with two other similarly minded synods in Michigan and Minnesota. By 1872 this group had moved far from its unionistic origins to an extremely rigorous kind of confessionalism. Its component synods even withdrew from the General Council to join Missouri in the still more rigorously confessional Synodical Conference.

Intertwined with these, and with many early congregations of the Missouri Synod, was another set of missionary impulses stemming from the great center at Neuendettelsau in Bavaria, which the eminent theologian, liturgical reformer, and missionary leader, Wilhelm Loehe, had made into an influential missionary agency. Though at first merely interested in extending the work of the church in the New World, men of this orientation grew fearful of the Missouri Synod's extreme congregationalism and strict demands for absolute consensus on all matters of doctrine. In 1854 they founded the so-called Iowa Synod, though like the Missouri, Ohio, and Wisconsin synods, it was by no means restricted to a single state. In fact, after 1895 "Iowa" even included an affiliation with the Texas Synod, a group which itself illustrates still another type of Lutheran origin in the United States. Organized in 1849, it had grown out of the response of the Saint Chrischona mission center near Basel, Switzerland, to the plea for pastors from German settlers in Texas.

By the diverse processes which have been sketched here with a few broad strokes, Lutheranism became a lively and extremely complex religious influence among the new German population of the country. Yet even this diversity among the Germans by no means reveals the whole fact, for during the same years, Scandinavian immigration reached flood tide, bringing nearly two million people to America, nearly all of whom were at least nominally Lutheran. The largest group was Swedish, whose earliest congregation was founded in Iowa in 1848. At first they affiliated themselves with the Synod of Northern Illinois, where ties with the General Synod actually established a sentimental relationship with the Old Lutheranism of New Sweden on the banks of the Delaware. In 1860 a separate Scandinavian synod was formed in this area, adopting the name Augustana (Latin for Augsburg) to proclaim its more explicit confessionalism. Ten years later the Danish-Norwegian elements in this synod went their own way, and the Danes later separated from the Norwegians as well. Between 1873 and 1884 the Swedish Augustana church also suffered the secession of a revivalistic, free-church element which formed the Evangelical Mission Covenant Church in 1884. Otherwise, Swedish Lutheranism during its entire first century was chiefly characterized by steady but relatively slow growth and nationwide expansion. Its greatest strength developed in Minnesota, though Rock Island, Illinois, remained the seat of its seminary and publishing house. Swedish people showed an unusual wanderlust, however, and the Augustana church became more national in scope than other Scandinavian synods.

Norwegian Lutheranism, by contrast, had an extraordinarily complex history during the same period. A strongly pietistic synod had formed in Wisconsin as early as 1846 and more or less on this foundation a synod named for the leader of Norway's religious awakening, Hans Nielsen Hauge, took form in the Upper Midwest, especially in Wisconsin and Minnesota. Another more confessional group, which also stood in closer relation to the Church of Norway and the theological tradition of Royal Frederick's University in Oslo (Christiania), was centered in Iowa, particularly at Luther College in Decorah. This group in its early years worked closely with the Missouri Synod until the predestination controversy shattered the arrangement and divided the "Old Norwegian Synod." Between these two divergent groups was still a third "moderate" group consisting chiefly of those who had been in the Scandinavian Augustana Synod. In 1900 they joined with several other small center groups to form a "United" Norwegian church.

Danish and Finnish groups showed similar tensions and tendencies. Among the Danes two small churches grew up, one of them closely identified with the traditions of the Church of Denmark. These "happy Danes," as they were called, were also profoundly touched by the folk church and romantic high church ideas of the great Danish theologian, reformer, and hymn writer, N. F. S. Grundtvig. The "gloomy Danes," on the other hand, were of a more pietistic persuasion. Both of these Danish churches were strongest in the Midwest; yet both were severely handicapped by the sparsity and dispersion of those Danes who came to America. The Finns were similarly handicapped, and were more seriously, though similarly, divided. The largest group was in effect an extension of the Church of Finland. More inclined to extreme congregationalism and to pietistic emphases were those who followed the church reformer Lars L. Lästadius. In America they founded a separate Finnish Apostolic Lutheran Church in 1873. To the right of center, still another small Finnish group, the National Evangelical Lutheran Church, has grown up since 1900. Though at first a child of the Evangelical Society in Finland, it was led both by institutional factors and by a doctrinal disposition to emphasize free salvation and to deemphasize the proclamation of God's Law. It has gravitated toward the Missouri Synod .

The foregoing highly simplified account at least suggests the immense complexity of Lutheran institutional history, though it scarcely makes it crystal clear. At one time there were sixty-six independent church organizations. Yet the statistic alone is deceptive, for beneath this multiplicity—which was accounted for chiefly by linguistic differences, geographical separation, and varying degrees of Americanization—was an underlying unity of faith and practice which was probably unequaled among America's large communions except in the Roman Catholic church. Even the General Synod, where "American Lutheranism" had made its largest inroads, was steadily moving during these decades toward an understanding of the faith which was rooted in the Augsburg Confession, while the same loyalty kept the more pietistic synods in communication with those who maintained a closer tie to European state-church traditions. Furthermore, all of these groups felt a moral obligation to develop as inclusive a Lutheran fellowship as possible, and they constantly sought means of intersynodical coordination. Because of these centripetal tendencies the General Synod and General Council were able to bring several of the newer churches into the circle of their fellowship, while most of those who considered the General Council's discipline too lax found their way into the Synodical Conference which was organized in 1872 at Milwaukee with Professor Walther of the Missouri Synod as its first president.

Mergers and extensions of fellowship were a constant feature of the post–Civil War half-century. In 1917–18 a whole series of momentous reunions were consummated. In 1917 Norwegian Lutheranism with two or three small exceptions united to form a single Norwegian Lutheran Church, and a year later, stimulated in part by moves instituted during the four-hundredth anniversary of the Reformation, the General Synod, the General Council, and the United Synod of the South came together in the United Lutheran Church of America. The Iowa and Ohio synods established pulpit and altar fellowship, while in the same year the National Lutheran Council was formed, giving nearly all Lutheran bodies outside the Synodical Conference a basis for increased fellowship and collective endeavor. From that time forward the movement of the Lutheran churches toward full participation in the American religious life rapidly accelerated. In 1967, as a penultimate step, the Lutheran Council in the U.S.A. was formed as a coordinating agency for over 95 percent of the country's Lutherans.[6]

6. While the reader has these relationships in mind, it may be appropriate to mention certain other steps in the movement toward Lutheran unity. In 1930 the Ohio, Buffalo, Texas, and Iowa Synods came together to form the American Lutheran Church, and in the same year this new church also joined with nearly all of the midwestern Scandinavian churches in a looser federation named the American Lutheran Conference. Out of this conference came the associations from which grew the great merger of 1960, whereby the American Lutheran Church merged with the Norwegian church and the larger of the two Danish churches to form The American Lutheran Church. This act created the first corporate union of large churches of both Scandinavian and German background. Soon afterward, in 1962, another similar union took place, by which the United Lutheran Church in America, Augustana (Swedish), the other Danish church, and the largest of the Finnish churches came together as the Lutheran Church in America. Since the more conservative Synodical Conference continued to exist, 95 percent of the once widely scattered Lutheran family had been brought within three rooms—connected by many doors and corridors, and well covered by a common confessional roof. The Lutheran Council in the U.S.A., formed by these large churches, had among its objectives both present-day cooperation and the achievement of future consensus (see John H. Tietjen, *Which Way Lutheran Unity?*).

46

THE GOLDEN AGE OF LIBERAL THEOLOGY

The nineteenth century was the "Great Century" in Christian history: so stands the assertion made, repeated, and substantiated in great detail by Kenneth Scott Latourette, America's most widely read church historian.[1] Yet his description of activity, fervor, popular strength, and global expansion is only half the story. The long epoch from the Second Awakening to the war with Spain was also a century of great tribulation, an "ordeal of faith" for churchgoing America. In an almost paradoxical manner, the religious impulse known as "liberalism" belongs to both sides of the century's picture. On one hand, it dealt responsibly with the social, moral, ecclesiastical, and above all, the theological issues of the crisis. On the other, it did so with such graceful ease and with such readiness to accommodate the spirit of the age that its effects were ambiguous. Alfred North Whitehead was even led to say in retrospect that "liberal theology . . . confined itself to the suggestion of minor, vapid reasons why people should go to church in the traditional way." [2] Viewed as a whole, however, American liberal theology was an impressive intellectual movement, and one that tends to confirm the idea of the Great Century.

The immediate background of liberalism's golden age was a profound social transformation which put the traditional content of preaching and teaching under severe duress. To these problems were added the intellectual difficulties provoked by scientific discoveries, religious scholarship, and per-

1. Kenneth Scott Latourette, *A History of Christianity,* chap. 45. His title for this section of the volume is "The Great Century: Growing Repudiation Paralleled by Abounding Vitality and Unprecedented Expansion."

2. Alfred North Whitehead, *Adventures of Ideas* (1933); quoted by Sidney E. Mead, *Reinterpretation in American Church History,* ed. Jerald C. Brauer.

vasive shifts in moral and religious attitudes. On the intellectual level the new challenges were of two sorts. First, there was a set of specific problems that had to be faced separately: Darwin unquestionably became the nineteenth century's Newton, and his theory of evolution through natural selection became the century's cardinal idea. But the struggle over the new geology was a vital rehearsal in which new conceptions of time and process were absorbed. Historical research meanwhile posed very detailed questions about the Bible, the history of doctrine, and other world religions. Accompanying these specific problems was a second and more general challenge: the rise of positivistic naturalism, the cumulative result of modern methods for acquiring knowledge. In every discipline from physics to biblical criticism, myth and error were being dispelled, and the result of this activity was a world view which raised problems of the most fundamental sort. Are deterministic principles as applicable to human activities as to the natural world? Are all moral standards and religious beliefs simply behavioral adaptations of the most intelligent vertebrates? Are the Bible, the Christian faith, and the Church to be understood as having their existence entirely within history? Granted these naturalistic challenges, are Christians to save their faith by resort to the unbiblical solutions of romantic subjectivism and idealistic pantheism? These questions constitute the dilemma of America's postwar churches. We do well, therefore, to begin our consideration of the responses with those who considered scientific positivism itself to offer the most viable religious option.

CHALLENGES TO TRADITION

Organized religious radicalism had never flourished in the United States. Elihu Palmer failed almost completely in his efforts to institutionalize a religion of reason during the revolutionary epoch. As for the "Religion of Humanity" launched by the French positivist, Auguste Comte (1798–1857), its failure to develop a following in America was even more resounding, though there was a flurry of interest in Fourier's utopian notions. The one form of radical religion to show a little continuous life had its domestic origins in Transcendentalism. This movement for "Free Religion" had only a brief independent existence, though it did attain a certain continuity through its impact on the Unitarian tradition. Its martyr-hero was Theodore Parker, who died prematurely in 1860.

In 1865, when the National Unitarian Conference was organized with a constitution specifically committing the denomination to the "Lordship of Christ," the radicals of the membership felt themselves excluded. Almost immediately they laid plans for organizing a Free Religious Association;

and in 1867 at their first convention in Boston they elected Octavius Brooks Frothingham (1822–95) as their president. Two years later the movement acquired a semiofficial organ when Francis Ellingwood Abbot founded the *Index* as a weekly journal. Abbot (1836–1903) had been a conservative Unitarian whose views began to shift leftward soon after his graduation from Harvard in 1859. As a seminary student, and later as a Unitarian minister in Dover, New Hampshire, his highly rationalistic and antiauthoritarian "scientific theism" began to take form, and for fifteen years he remained the chief philosophic figure in the movement. Acclaimed as the first American theologian to develop a system of religious thought in complete consonance with Darwinian evolution, Abbot was, however, too extreme to be popular, and his scientific emphasis alienated the Transcendentalists. He also organized the National Liberal League for the total separation of church and state and diverted much of the Free Religious Association's energies into that abortive campaign,[3] with the result that, in the 1870s, Frothingham became the movement's chief spokesman.

Frothingham, a very proper Bostonian by birth, was converted by Parker from a conservative Unitarian ministry to abolitionism and radical religion. During and after the Civil War he was a popular preacher in New York City. His book *The Religion of Humanity* (1872) best expresses the movement's effort to formulate a free and scientific religion for the American people. "The new Liberal Church," he declared, "has a consistent scheme of thought; it goes to the mind for its ideas; it admits the claim of spontaneity; its method of obtaining truth is rational; the harmony it demands is harmony of principles—the orderly sequence of laws."[4] Yet even Frothingham was unable to reach beyond a narrow circle of intelligentsia.

What Frothingham lacked, however, was possessed in great measure by Robert Green Ingersoll (1833–99), "the Dwight L. Moody of Free Religion," to borrow Abbot's label. Ingersoll had been a colonel in the Union army, a highly successful trial lawyer, and a political figure best remembered for the "Plumed Knight" oration with which he nominated James G. Blaine as Republican presidential candidate in 1876. The son of a conservative Protestant minister, he devoted his mature life to the cause of agnosticism in religion: "The rebellion of his boyhood became the crusade of his lifetime."[5] He made up for the very limited appeal of the Free Religious Association by ranging up and down the country, holding spellbound the many

3. The 1870s were a time of harsh interfaith contention and of controversy on the church-state question. Abbot's special target was the intensely evangelical National Reform Association which was working for a new Christian preamble to the federal Constitution.

4. Octavius Brooks Frothingham, *The Religion of Humanity* (New York, 1873), pp. 16–17.

5. Ralph Henry Gabriel, *The Course of American Democratic Thought*, p. 179.

auditors who paid admission to hear his eloquent attacks on the clergy, the Bible, and the Christian faith. By 1880 there were very few Americans who did not recognize him as the nation's most outspoken infidel and a scourge of the churches. Beneath the rhetoric and the diatribes was a completely naturalistic message of confidence in man and hope for the future, derived more specifically from Thomas Paine and the earlier rationalism than from either Comte or Darwin.

Ingersoll left more than a trace on the religious life of a generation of Americans. Untold thousands found solace in their infidelity due to the glowing rhetoric of the widely reprinted oration which he delivered at his brother's grave. By such means free religion of various sorts reached far beyond the boundaries of organized movements. Social Darwinism, the philosophy of Herbert Spencer, and popular forms of naturalism also gained adherents without any kind of pseudoecclesiastical sponsorship. It was, in fact, with precisely this general tendency, coupled as it so often was with a distaste for evangelical revivalism, that liberal theologians felt obliged to deal. The obligation led directly to specific questions, however, and one of the first of these had to do with the earth's own history.

Genesis and Geology

Scientific speculation as to the origins and history of the universe was one aspect of the intellectual ferment of the age, but it was not nearly so troublesome as the "new geology" that had been developing ever since James Hutton of Edinburgh had published his *Theory of the Earth* in 1788. By the time of Sir Charles Lyell's *Principles of Geology* (1830–32), it had become an organized scientific endeavor based, as he said, on the uniformitarian doctrine "that all former changes of the organic and inorganic creation are referrible [sic] to one uninterrupted succession of physical events, governed by the laws now in operation." In Lyell's works, moreover, the biblical account of Creation was called in question not only on geological grounds, but because of the fossil record which the rocks preserved. Controversy, needless to say, ensued.

In America the battle over Genesis would have been more sharply drawn than it was had not the country's leading geologist, Benjamin Silliman (1779–1864), sought to harmonize conflicting views. While a student at Yale, Silliman had been converted by the preaching of President Timothy Dwight. After graduation he was selected by Dwight to be a science professor, and dispatched to Edinburgh for advanced study. Although he returned as a man committed to a uniformitarian understanding of science, in 1836 he also argued that the Bible was not a scientific textbook, urging that the Hebrew word for "day" in the Creation story should be interpreted loosely as "aeon." Edward Hitchcock, his pupil, who became a professor and then president of Amherst College, took a still more positive stand in his important work *The Religion of Geology* (1851). An eminent geologist himself, Hitchcock explained the earth's long history as a further revelation of God's constancy and glory. Many problems remained, but in New England at least the Silliman-Hitchcock compromise opened the way to more constructive thought on the relations of science and religion. These relatively advanced views were accepted by only a very small minority, however, for most Americans knew little and cared less about scientific method. Indeed the great alienation of large sectors of American Protestantism from the newer forms of modern thought had begun to accelerate with the revivals of 1800, while the surging westward movement and the advances of anti-intellectual revivalism made matters worse with each passing decade. Only in limited circles did the general type of solution advanced by Professor Hitchcock win acceptance.

The matter could not stop with geology—in part because of the fossil record and in part because geological estimates of the earth's great age made developmental theories of biological evolution increasingly plausible. In fact, a very strong tradition of evolutionary speculation already existed. Lamarck had announced his theory in 1801. Romantic nature-philosophers had given further encouragement to developmental views, and the historical movement also accentuated the idea of process, struggle, and emergent novelty. Herbert Spencer, who was to become the greatest popularizer of Darwinian notions in both Britain and America, had long been defending a view of cosmic progress from homogeneity to heterogeneity. By 1857 the time was so ripe for a theory of natural selection that it was formulated almost simultaneously by two remotely separated men.

In 1858 at a historic meeting of the Royal Society, two papers on the origin of species were read: one by Charles Darwin, the other by Alfred Russel Wallace. In the following year Darwin's *Origin of Species* appeared —the most important book of the century. After a decade of fierce controversy, Darwin in 1871 published *The Descent of Man,* in which he drew the human species within the same encompassing hypothesis. Never since the scientific revolution completed by Newton had the humanistic and religious traditions of the West been confronted by a greater need for adjustment and reformulation.

The Response to Darwin in the United States

Darwin did not expect or hope that his theory of evolution through natural selection would be acceptable to more than a small circle of specialists, but he sent a copy of *The Origin of Species* to the most famous of all American naturalists, Louis Agassiz (1807–73), hoping to be credited "for having carefully endeavored to arrive at the truth." The great paleontologist and glacial theorist, however, had by this time become chiefly a popularizer, a dogmatic philosopher of nature, and a museum organizer, and his rejection of Darwin was well-nigh absolute. Reaffirming his allegiance to the French zoologist Cuvier, Agassiz took his stand for "special creationism" as an explanation of both the fossil record and present state of all living things. Genesis, in his view, told of only one among many occasions of God's creative intervention in the world. At other times and places God had created other species and other human races. Although Agassiz showed considerable liberty in his interpretation of Scripture, he became, for obvious reasons, the white knight of the anti-Darwinians.

Fortunately for American science, Agassiz no longer held the respect of the four or five Americans most qualified to give a scientific evaluation of evolutionary theory. Asa Gray (1810–88), a colleague of Agassiz at Harvard, had publicly insisted on the single origin of plant and animal species even before Darwin's book appeared, and in March 1860, in the *American Journal of Science* (a journal founded by Silliman), Gray's favorable review appeared. Further support came from William B. Rogers, James Dwight Dana, and Jeffries Wyman, with the result that Agassiz began to lose the allegiance of his own students. The appointment of Charles William Eliot as Harvard's president in 1869, despite the opposition of Agassiz and many others, marked a turning point in American science.

Only after 1869 was the real impact of Darwinism felt in the American churches, partly because of the vast distractions of the Civil War and Reconstruction. The first response, naturally enough, was opposition, but this clerical resistance chiefly revealed the prevailing incapacity to grasp the dramatic transformation in world view that evolutionary theory occasioned. During most of the eighteenth century, Western Christendom had been engaged in a drawn-out encounter with the Enlightenment, including among other things, Newtonian physics, rationalism, and deism. This intellectual challenge had been almost magnificently surmounted. The firmament had been made to declare the glory of God. As the whole creation was conceived as a hymn to God's benevolent governance, the natural religion of the *philosophes* found its place in even the most revivalistic of evangelical theologies: any Christian could look out of his kitchen window and behold a demonstration of God's marvelous design. Sun and clouds, trees and grass, seeds, cows, dogs, and insects—even manure—were all harmoniously interacting for man's well being! But after Darwin, what did the backyard reveal but a relentless struggle for existence, a war of all against all, with blood dripping from every bough, and man involved in the struggle not only against the locusts, but against other men, even other races of man, with victory for the fittest. No wonder that opposition to evolutionary doctrines arose. In this struggle, moreover, the Unitarian friends of Agassiz, having invested largely in the goodness and dignity of man, would join hands with the most strenuous conservatives. The Reverend Andrew Preston Peabody, a countercandidate for Harvard's presidency in 1869, was not far from Charles Hodge of Princeton Seminary when it came to attacking Darwinism.

Charles Hodge, in fact, soon published what many regarded as the orthodox repudiation. In his *What Is Darwinism?* (1874) he correctly isolated the essential factor, natural selection, and pronounced it to be in flat contradiction to the doctrine of an omnipotent, omniscient Creator. Christians, he insisted, must account for the facts in some other way. Professor Randolph S. Foster of Drew Seminary (later a Methodist bishop) took a lower route—one that was to be much more heavily traveled during the coming century—and sought to laugh evolutionary theory out of court: "Some future pup, Newfoundland or terrier, in the finite ages may," he said, "write Paradise Lost. . . . Therefore a pig is an incipient mathematician." Behind both Hodge and Foster lay a fundamental conviction that three decades later would still underlie Billy Sunday's confession that he did not believe "in a bastard theory that men came from protoplasm by the fortuitous concurrence of atoms."

There were serious Christian thinkers, however, who saw the conflict in less drastic terms, and by an unusual coincidence the two most impressive among them collaborated closely: George Frederick Wright (1838–1921), fervent evangelical, biographer of Finney, amateur geologist of distinction, and professor of science and religion at Oberlin; and Asa Gray of Harvard, America's most distinguished botanist and an amateur theologian adhering to a conservative Nicaeanic understanding of Christian orthodoxy. Issuing from the collaboration of these two men were the separate essays later published in Gray's *Darwiniana* (1876). In all of these essays, from his first review of Darwin to his more theological works, four important points stand out:

1. A deep respect for Darwin's empirical and theoretical contributions to the problem of species, and sharp criticism of dogmatic repudiation of the idea of evolution
2. A recognition that Darwin's theory lacked an explanation of variations (such as the science of genetics would later supply)
3. An insistence that scientific investigation continue without impediment

4. A conviction that Darwinian theory did not contradict Christian doctrine; that regardless of Darwin's or Spencer's beliefs, God's purpose in the Creation could be understood in evolutionary terms; and that orthodox views of man's sinfulness found corroboration in Darwin.

Darwin explicitly dissented from Gray's belief in divinely directed beneficent variations, but Gray's friendship with Darwin, as well as his demand for scientific autonomy, continued.[6]

During the 1870s President James McCosh of Princeton University and President Paul A. Chadbourne of Williams College added their prestige to the rapprochement of theology and evolutionary theory. Both thinkers introduced non-Darwinian elements which preserved the idea of beneficent design. They also strengthened the doctrine of progress by accenting Gray's idea that Divine Providence acts "*through* all time" rather than "*from* all time." More exuberantly optimistic than any was the prolific apologist for Darwin and Spencer, John Fiske (1842–1902). As early as 1872 Fiske had expounded a blend of evolution and idealism in his *Cosmic Philosophy*. Twelve years later, he ended his work *The Destiny of Man* with a hymn in which the full religious potentiality of evolutionism found expression. It deserves extended quotation as a prime example of the optimistic heights that nineteenth-century naturalism could reach:

> The greatest philosopher of modern times, the master and teacher of all who shall study the process of evolution for many a day to come, holds that the conscious soul is not the product of a collocation of material particles, but is in the deepest sense a divine effluence. According to Mr. Spencer, the divine energy which is manifested throughout the knowable universe is the same energy that wells up in us as consciousness. Speaking for myself, I can see no insuperable difficulty in the notion that at some period in the evolution of Humanity this divine spark may have acquired sufficient concentration and steadiness to survive the wreck of material forms and endure forever. Such a crowning wonder seems to me no more than the fit climax to a creative work that has been ineffably beautiful and marvelous in all its myriad stages.
>
> Only on some such view can the reasonableness of the universe, which still remains far above our finite power of comprehension, maintain its ground. There are some minds inaccessible to the class of considerations here alleged, and perhaps there always will be. But on such

6. Gray also continued his friendship with Alfred Russel Wallace (1823–1913), whose religious views were closer to his own than Darwin's. Wallace also shared William James's interest in psychical research and spiritualism.

grounds, if on no other, the faith in immortality is likely to be shared by all who look upon the genesis of the highest spiritual qualities in Man as the goal of Nature's creative work. This view has survived the Copernican revolution in science, and it has survived the Darwinian revolution. Nay, if the foregoing exposition be sound, it is Darwinism which has placed Humanity upon a higher pinnacle than ever. The future is lighted for us with the radiant colours of hope. Strife and sorrow shall disappear. Peace and love shall reign supreme. The dream of poets, the lesson of priest and prophet, the inspiration of the great musician, is confirmed in the light of modern knowledge; and as we gird ourselves up for the work of life, we may look forward to the time when in the truest sense the kingdoms of this world shall become the kingdom of Christ, and he shall reign for ever and ever, king of kings, and lord of lords.

When men outside the church could speak in this manner of Darwinism, it goes without saying that many other liberal Christian thinkers would sing evolutionary theophanies as well. Horace Bushnell never could accept the "development theory," but his chief biographer, Theodore Thornton Munger, in the prestigious pulpit of New Haven's North Church, made up for his hero's lack. And the minister of the neighboring church on the New Haven green, Newman Smyth, after spending long hours in the Yale biological laboratories, described his findings with equal fervor in *Through Science to Faith* (1902). Undoubtedly, the two successive ministers of Plymouth Church in Brooklyn did more than most others to popularize the "New Theology." Henry Ward Beecher was a fairly cautious pioneer. But Lyman Abbott (1835–1922), a bolder exponent, in *The Evolution of Christianity* (1892) sought to show that "in the spiritual, as in the physical, God is the secret and source of light." Accordingly, Abbott spoke of the evolution of the Bible, the Church, Christian Society, and the Soul.

In at least two areas of thought, the debate over evolutionary theology pointed to much larger issues than the origin of biological species or the descent of man. With new urgency it posed the question of "species" in general, that is, it reopened the ancient debate over the "essential nature of things" which had been at the heart of Western philosophy since the time of Plato. Many of the classic structures of traditional theology, as well as the post-Newtonian schemes of natural theology, were thus disrupted. The static yielded to the dynamic; stability to flux. History and Becoming emerged as dominant categories of thought. In this way Darwin's works underlined what had been implicit in the great romantic conceptions of the historical reason. The relativistic implications of history—natural history and human history—stood revealed. From this trend stemmed the second great problem: the forms of developmentalism traceable to historical scholarship. Here indeed lay the burning question of the age. Fossils and unimaginably remote developments in the plant or animal kingdoms were academic abstractions compared with the direct impact of historico-critical studies on the Holy Bible and sacred doctrine. Liberal theology in this realm occupied its most important ground, while Fundamentalism arose to repulse the invader.

The Impact of History

The writing of history is as old as the Old Testament; but in the nineteenth century it took on new vitality and in many ways transmitted this vigor to religious thought. In theology as in biology, a dynamic view of the past challenged traditional notions in at least five ways:

1. "Uniformitarian" principles were applied in the interpretation of past events to the exclusion of miracle and divine providence. As a consequence, the history of the Jews, the life of Jesus, and the rise of Christianity were treated no differently than "secular" events. Three famous studies, one in each of these subject areas, appeared in a single year (1835): Wilhelm Vatke's history of Israel's religion, David Friedrich Strauss's *Life of Jesus,* and Ferdinand Christian Baur's work on the place of the pastoral Epistles in the life of the early Church.

2. The Scriptures themselves were interpreted in the same manner as other important historical documents. Julius Wellhausen's questioning of both the Mosaic authorship and the literary unity of the Pentateuch (1878) made the implications of such methods fully manifest; and in New Testament criticism the results were even more troublesome. Nor could the problem be escaped by giving conservative answers to specific questions (such as the date of Daniel or the authorship of Second Peter), for the method itself undermined the idea of the Bible as the verbally inerrant Word of God.

3. Historical theology came into its own as a discipline; that is, anxiety about specific doctrines (such as the Atonement or the nature of Christ) came to be resolved by the scientific study of that doctrine in the history of Christianity. To the discomfiture of many, doctrinal truth seemed to depend on the "assured results" of critical scholarship. Some liberal scholars even insisted that the content of the faith had to be reduced to those few simple tenets which had been accepted in all times and places. This notion reached its fullest expression in 1900, when Adolph von Harnack, the great historian

of dogma, in his famous lectures on the essence of Christianity, rested his case on a few central precepts of Jesus.

4. Comparative religion as an historical science was involved in each of the foregoing matters to a certain extent, notably in such questions as the relation of Hebrew religion to its ancient neighbors, or the Apostle Paul's indebtedness to Greek thought and the oriental mystery cults. In these pursuits many of the major disciplines for studying the history of religions were first developed. But it was the Western discovery of the great "higher religions" of the Orient, above all Hinduism and Buddhism, that raised the more difficult questions, because these highly philosophical religions possessed an intrinsic appeal for an age already imbued wih idealistic philosophy and pantheistic theology. In Emerson's "Brahma" Americans savored the forbidden fruit in their parlors. Highly enthusiastic historical accounts raised more direct theological questions, above all, how is one to demonstrate the superiority and finality of Christianity? Even disclaimers raised the specter of religious relativism.

5. "Historicism" was a culminating and summary feature of the trend. This term is often used to designate two different philosophical positions, though they could be entertained together or separately. The first was basically an acceptance of the contextuality or interrelatedness of all human activities, thoughts, and concerns, and hence the insistence that all things human were inescapably historical. There is no nonhistorical vantage point for man, only the history of changing conceptions of absoluticity. There are no self-evident axioms in philosophical matters, only the history of changing views of self-evidence. The intellectual bedrock of today was the slimy ocean bottom of yore, and perhaps the mountaintop of tomorrow. In other words, "historicism" could refer to an all-encompassing relativism. Whether it was expounded by G. F. W. Hegel, Karl Marx, William Graham Sumner, or Ernst Troeltsch could make a vast difference in its social and religious implications, yet a disturbing insistence on the historicity of all things remained.

"Historicism" could also refer to the new kind of fatalism or determinism which historical studies induced—the conviction that what was, had to be; what is, must be. The nature of history's inexorable march was, of course, interpreted differently: some positivists thought in terms of physical causality rather than in terms of human action; Henry Adams could speak of a physics of history; Hegel early in the century and Marx in his train gave "dialectical" interpretations to the historical process; William G. Sumner as a "Social Darwinian" would take his cues from biological evolution. Some were pessimistic; others unbelievably hopeful. Yet by all of these men, chance and historical contingency, as well as freedom and human spontaneity, were regarded as extremely limited or entirely illusory. For weal or woe, man's fate was sealed.

In the end, regardless of how these five tendencies were used or interpreted, historical modes of thought became a powerful factor in the intellectual life of the age. Inasmuch as the categories of genetic explanation underlie geology and evolution as well, we may crown Clio, the muse of history, as the intellectual monarch of the century. Aided and abetted by other forces, this monarch very nearly succeeded in determining both the strategies and the content of liberal theology.[7]

The intellectual challenge with which liberal theologians grappled was awe-inspiring in its magnitude. From every sector the problems converged: the Enlightenment's triumphant confidence in science and in nature's law, the multiform romantic heresy that religion was essentially feeling or poetic exaltation, that nature was a cathedral and communing in it a sacrament; the disruption of the Creation story and the biblical time scale; the evolutionary transformation of the old notion that the world's orderliness bespoke God's benevolent design; the historical criticism of the Bible, the relativization of the Church and its teachings, the denial of human freedom and moral responsibility, and even the abolition of those eternal standards by which right and wrong, the false and the true were to be judged. All this had to be faced, moreover, in the new urban jungles of the Gilded Age, where Americans seemed to be chiefly bent on getting and spending and laying waste their powers. Never in the history of Christianity, it would seem, was a weak and disunited Christian regiment drawn into battle against so formidable an alliance, under such unfavorable conditions of climate and weather, and with so little information on the position and intent of the opposition. In such terms, at least, we must seek to understand the achievement of America's liberal theologians.

THE VARIETIES OF RELIGIOUS LIBERALISM

The response of American Christianity to its crisis was as varied as its denominational texture. Roman Catholicism was so deeply involved in

7. Principal A. M. Fairbairn of Oxford described this historical revolution in an immensely influential work: "The most distinctive and determinative element in modern theology is what we may term a new feeling for Christ. . . . But we feel Him more in our theology because we know Him better in history. . . . The old theology came to history through doctrine, but the new comes to doctrine through history; to the one all historical questions were really dogmatic, but to the other all dogmatic questions are formally historical" (*The Place of Christ in Modern Theology* [New York, 1894], pp. 3–4).

fending off the attacks of nativists and in solving its own institutional problems that the "modernism" of Europe which had provoked several major papal condemnations was almost—though not entirely—unknown. Lutheranism, too, was deeply engaged in solving the problems of immigration and church founding; synodical consolidation and confessional controversy were the main themes of its history. In the predominantly rural South, where the modern university and the German-trained seminary faculty were almost unknown, the response was negligible. And in countless congregations in the mainstream of American evangelical Protestantism, urban as well as rural, the older anti-intellectual patterns of revivalism held sway. The grappling with modern ideas obviously went on elsewhere.

In terms of denominations as a whole, only a few general statements can be made. Congregationalism, especially in the Northeast and in urban churches, now proved to be the most fertile soil for liberalism, just as it had been when Unitarianism struck down its roots. In Methodism, where religious experience rather than doctrine was the major concern, the liberal cause became almost as pervasive, and in Northern Methodism as nowhere in the nation it penetrated to the grassroots. In the Protestant Episcopal church, where the Enlightenment had made large inroads and where the evangelical resurgence had been rather restricted, liberalism also grew strong—except where it was countered by Tractarianism. The Northern Presbyterian church, the Northern Baptist Convention, and the Disciples of Christ all made important contributions to the liberal movement. These three were profoundly divided on the issues, however, and hence they were torn by the Fundamentalist controversy far more violently than other denominations.

Because the challenges to which the liberals responded were primarily intellectual, the seminaries were naturally crucial to the movement's development. Here again the importance of the Northeast was dramatized, for Harvard, Yale, and Union Theological Seminary (New York) played leading roles, and contributions of hardly less significance were made by Andover and Bangor (Congregational), Colgate, Rochester, and Crozer (Baptist), the Episcopal Theological School in Cambridge, Boston University (Methodist), and Lane Seminary (Presbyterian). After John D. Rockefeller's princely contributions to the University of Chicago, its Divinity School (Baptist) quickly became a great midwestern center of liberalism, around which Congregational, Disciples, and Unitarian faculties were also gathered. So dynamic and accomplished was its faculty, and so great a regional need did it fill that Chicago remained throughout the first third of the twentieth century probably the country's most powerful center of Protestant liberalism. From all of these seminaries came a long line of distinguished parish ministers. The wealthy urban congregation was enjoying its heyday; and the "princes of the pulpit" had their hour, reaching memberships of great power and influence and attaining a high level of intellectual distinction. Indeed, liberalism was the last major impulse in American intellectual history in which the pastor-theologian played an extensive role.

The era when these seminaries and their eminent graduates in parish pulpits made theological liberalism a continuous and coherent movement extends for more than two long generations. William Newton Clarke (1841–1912) had served in the parish for two decades when he became a professor at Colgate Seminary in 1890; his most distinguished student, Harry Emerson Fosdick (b. 1878), wrote an autobiography that reflected on his long ministry in the parish and seminary in 1956. Newman Smyth (1843–1925) entered the ministry only after serving in the Union army, published his most substantial book, *Christian Ethics,* in 1892 and his autobiography in 1926. The liberal movement maintained its inner unity through two wars and amid vast social changes.

Because the wide dispersion of liberal leadership and the absence of outstandingly influential American liberal theologians (aside from Emerson and Bushnell, whose careers belong to an earlier epoch) preclude concentration on individual studies in a general discussion of this sort, a review of the situation by denominations is probably most illuminating. Among the Congregationalists, liberals were legion in both seminaries and churches. In fact, this denomination's corporate stance underwent a nearly complete transformation between its basically traditional Burial Hill Declaration of 1865 (affirmed during a memorial assembly at the cemetery at Plymouth) and the liberal Kansas City Declaration of 1913. The spirit of Bushnell presided over this quiet revolution, but many men of national eminence furthered it. With the one important exception of Edwards Amasa Park, the entire Andover faculty led the way. At the Yale Divinity School the "new theology" did not become prominent until around the turn of the century and then chiefly through the work of an impressive group of biblical scholars: Harper, Bacon, and Porter. After World War I the Canadian Baptist and renowned pacifist D. C. Macintosh made Yale a center of empirical, realistic theology. Two other theologians with strong philosophic interests and wide influence were Louis French Stearns of Bangor Seminary and Eugene W. Lyman, who taught successively at Bangor, Oberlin, and Union theological seminaries. Reaching wider than any was Charles M. Sheldon, a pastor of Topeka, Kansas, who turned to the sentimental novel—and with *In His Steps* (1896) became a major apostle of not only the Social Gospel but of the broader liberal movement as well. The work of other pastors (Beecher, Smyth, Munger, Gordon, and Brooks) has already been mentioned.

The Presbyterian Church (North) also provided the liberal movement with both scholarly and popular leadership. Union Seminary of New York was the center from which radiated the influence of William Adams Brown, one of the movement's most widely read systematic theologians, A. C. McGiffert, an impressive historian of doctrine, and C. A. Briggs, the country's leading Old Testament scholar. Besides these intellectuals, the Presbyterians also claimed one of the era's most popular writers, Henry van Dyke, whose fiction and poetry were American parlor favorites for two generations, especially his famous Christmas story, "The Other Wise Man." He also wrote two extremely effective apologetical works: *The Gospel for an Age of Doubt* (1896) and *The Gospel for a World of Sin* (1899).

Among Methodists liberalism gained its most coherent philosophical expression in the idealistic "personalism" of Professor Borden Parker Bowne of Boston University. In later years A. C. Knudson at the Boston University School of Theology became personalism's chief systematic theologian, while his energetic contemporary Bishop Francis J. McConnell led the denomination in ecumenical affairs and as a social actionist.

The Baptists, like the Presbyterians, were preponderantly conservative. In several seminaries and many pulpits, however, extremely influential liberals made their mark not only upon the denomination but far beyond. Walter Rauschenbusch of Rochester Seminary, the Social Gospel leader, is now best remembered, but two other men made a much broader impact on their times. William Newton Clarke's *Outline of Christian Theology* (1898) became the most widely used of liberal texts in systematic theology. In rather sharp contrast to Clarke's modified evangelicalism was the far more radical speculation and scholarship of Shailer Mathews of the Chicago Divinity School, and somewhat later, the critical historical studies of his colleague, Shirley Jackson Case. Closely allied with the Baptists at Chicago were an influential group of Disciples of whom the philosopher, psychologist of religion, and theological radical Edward S. Ames, and the biblical scholar Herbert L. Willett were the most eminent. Immeasurably more influential was Charles Clayton Morrison, who in 1908 founded the *Christian Century* and made it a potent ecumenical, socially oriented journal.

In the Episcopal church, William P. DuBose of the Sewanee seminary (Tennessee) was probably his church's greatest theological mind. No Southerner of the period equaled his richness and depth of thought; yet his moderate, tradition-oriented liberalism was not widely noted, possibly because Catholic-Evangelical conflict consumed so much Episcopal energy. The

Broad Church movement, however, did raise up at least one impressive liberal thinker, William Reed Huntington of New York, whose work *The Church Idea* (1870) remains a major ecumenical document. Phillips Brooks of Boston's Trinity Church was by all odds the most popular voice the Episcopal church has ever had. Brooks's influence was given a second life by the very widely read two-volume biography by Professor A. V. G. Allen, who in other ways as well made historical studies an evocative vehicle for liberal theological themes. *The Continuity of Christian Thought: A Study of Modern Theology in the Light of Its History* (1884) is Allen's most brilliant achievement.

Finally, the Unitarians, who had been the American vanguard of liberal Christianity, continued, though with less élan than formerly, to provide important and intellectual leadership. Francis Greenwood Peabody of Harvard achieved wide attention as the first seminary professor of social ethics. Minot J. Savage, the minister of Boston's West Church, wrote a major work on *The Religion of Evolution* (1876). But more important than individual instances was a major theological trend which John White Chadwick described in 1894: "The fifty years which have gone by since Channing died in 1842 have seen great changes. . . . The critical results which Parker reached and which his brother Unitarians could not endure, are now the commonplaces [not only of the Unitarians but] of the progressive orthodox." [8] As the century's turn approached, a kind of religious peace became manifest in New England. With the new historical, philosophical, and religious attitudes as common ground, Andover Seminary even returned to Harvard, where for over two decades the joint faculty achieved great distinction and influence.[9]

The chief proponents of liberalism in all of these denominations came from diverse backgrounds, yet most of them traced their roots to pious families where evangelical nurture had prevailed. Their spiritual history often resembled that which William Newton Clarke revealed in his moving personal account *Sixty Years with the Bible* (1912): "I am one of the men who have lived through the crisis of the Nineteenth Century, and experienced the change which that century has wrought. . . . Thus I am entering into the heritage of my generation, which I consider it both my privilege and my duty to accept." They usually studied in Germany or in American seminaries where Continental theology and scholarship was favorably regarded. Most of them had wide ecumenical sympathies, yet very few had cut loose from

8. John White Chadwick, *Old and New Unitarian Belief* (Boston, 1894), pp. 31–32.

9. In 1908 Andover Seminary moved to Cambridge, adjacent to the Harvard Divinity School; but in 1925 the virtual merger of the schools was voided in the courts. Andover then merged with the Baptist seminary in nearby Newton, leaving its faculty and most of its students at Harvard.

denominational loyalties. Although they took diverse positions on the social issues of the day and were often motivated by different concerns, several common themes and tendencies characterize their work.

The Nature of Liberalism

Liberalism was, first of all, a point of view which, like the adjective "liberal" as we commonly use it, denotes both a certain generosity or charitableness toward divergent opinions and a desire for intellectual "liberty." Liberal theologians also wished to "liberate" religion from obscurantism and creedal bondage so as to give man's moral and rational powers larger scope. In this broad sense, liberals could be linked with a long Christian tradition extending from Abelard and Erasmus through Locke and Paley to Channing and the Transcendentalists. Actually, however, the "liberalism" of the nineteenth century was a positive and structured movement, not merely a vague tendency or an indefinite state of mind. Whether it was called the New Theology, Progressive Orthodoxy, Modernism, or some other name, it had a fairly definite doctrinal content.

In the language of historical theology, liberals were Arminian or Pelagian. With regard to human nature, they emphasized man's freedom and his natural capacity for altruistic action. Sin, therefore, was construed chiefly as error and limitation which education in morals and the example of Jesus could mitigate, or else as the product of underprivilege which social reform could correct. Original Sin or human depravity was denied or almost defined out of existence. As their predecessors of the Enlightenment had done, liberals tried to avoid deterministic conclusions by arguments for the creative and autonomous nature of the human spirit.

A strong emphasis on ethical preaching and moral education accorded with the liberal view of man. Ethical imperatives became central to the Christian witness, and the Sermon on the Mount was often regarded as the heart and core of the Bible. On the other hand, liberals tended to slight traditional dogma and the sacraments. Baptism came to be considered as an initiatory formality or as a dedicatory rite for parents, while the Lord's Supper was usually given only memorial significance and its importance to public worship was minimized. The sacramental character of ordination and of preaching was likewise deemphasized.[10] In New England, by the same token, the traditional covenants of membership were forgotten or revised, and because liberals were usually nondenominational in spirit, the theologi-

10. Preaching is sacramental when the preached Gospel of Christ's redeeming work is believed to be a means of grace and a mark of the Church. Liberals usually found it easier to preach duties and laws than to proclaim Good Tidings. To many critics this was the central issue: Does one have Good News (Gospel, Evangel) to preach?

cal controversies and church divisions which had raged in former times were lamented as evidences of superstition and spiritual immaturity. Interest in the reunion of Christendom correspondingly flourished, with heavy emphasis on the scandal of the Church's being divided over essentially dead issues. To most liberals, however, the Reformation's blow to "medieval thralldom" was a providential boon, so that anti-Catholicism could still flourish, and sometimes did. Francis G. Peabody, despite his wide ecumenical interests, thought that the whole "Faith and Order" movement for church reunion was a hopeless throwback to a darker age.

Because of their revised estimate of man's nature and their tendency to interpret the entire evolutionary process as ultimately for mankind's benefit, liberals were fervently optimistic about the destiny of the human race. Supported by the apparent success of democratic governments and the evidence of scientific and technological advances, their confidence in the future outran even that of the Enlightenment's apostles of progress. The Kingdom of God was given a this-worldly interpretation and viewed as something men would build within the natural historical process. For them, in Reinhold Niebuhr's striking phrase, "History was the Christ."

Their interest in history caused the liberals to go even farther, radically altering the meaning and significance of revelation. The Old Testament was interpreted chiefly as a record of Jewish history, religiosity, and growing moral earnestness that culminated in the life and message of Jesus. The New Testament was placed in the same context, and the main aim of scholarship was to clarify the religion of Jesus. Because the New Testament consists exclusively of the history and testimony of the post-Easter church, it created many problems for liberals. Paul the Apostle became a very troublesome saint. On the divinity of Jesus and the inspiration of the Scriptures, therefore, widely divergent views arose. The dominant tendency was in the direction of a benign naturalism, although it was veiled by an extremely pious and time-honored vocabulary. Hence Jesus' divinity sprang from the fact that he spoke the most sublime truths and proclaimed the highest and (probably) the final religion. Creeds and dogmas about these matters were "human constructions" subject to evolutionary development and interpretation. Time had purged them of much error, and the process was still going on. The Bible thus had authority because, judged by standards outside of it (historical, philosophic, scientific, and experiential), it deserved to be so regarded.

Liberals tended strongly to monistic ways of construing many traditional problems of theology and philosophy. Wishing to see unity in all things rather than disjunction, they preferred to combine or merge the romantic inclination to see man and nature as alike infused with divinity and the

Darwinian tendency to relate man to the natural world in a scientific way. Similarly, man and God were brought together. Liberals dwelt much more on the immanence of God than on his transcendence. As Bushnell had argued, the natural and the supernatural were consubstantial, observable in almost all forms of being. The supernatural and the spiritual tended to be identified; and the spiritual in turn was identified with consciousness—the conative, intellectual, emotive side of man. Finally, the ancient disjunctions between the subjective and objective, between the mental world and the "real" or "objective" world, were minimized philosophically by theories of reality which stressed the ideal nature of things and by intuitional or idealistic theories of knowledge. Not all liberals, by any means, believed that such matters were crucial, but when they did venture into philosophical realms, they usually regarded Plato, Kant, Hegel, Schleiermacher, Coleridge, and various mystical philosophers as very important and reliable guides.

A revised estimate of the purpose and power of religious education gave practical expression to so many articles of the liberal consensus that it must be singled out as a vital element of the movement's essence. Within the older Sunday school movement this new cause took a prominent place in the liberal understanding of church reform. The founding of the Religious Education Association in 1903 and the International Council of Education in 1922 gave it organizational focus; but the new educational philosophy probably owed most to George A. Coe, Harrison S. Elliott, and William C. Bower, all of whom were deeply interested in the psychology of religion, learning theory, and "progressive" views of education. The methods of Froebel and Pestalozzi were blended with John Dewey's social pragmatism, while Bushnell's *Christian Nurture,* republished by Luther A. Weigle of Yale in 1916, became the classic expression of the movement's underlying faith in the potency of education in the formation of Christian character.

Major Types of Liberalism

In the foregoing exposition of the liberal consensus, certain elements of dissent have been only faintly indicated. There were, however, fundamental disagreements on two large issues: on the nature of religion, and on the source of authority, which is to say, on the nature of revelation.

On religion the issue was twice drawn. In one school were the moralists who, like Rauschenbusch, insisted on "the fundamental truth that religion and ethics are inseparable, and that ethical conduct is the supreme and sufficient religious act." [11] This group's boundaries went far beyond the Social

11. Walter Rauschenbusch, *Christianity and the Social Crisis* (New York: Macmillan Co., 1907), p. 7.

Gospel movement, however, to include thinkers with almost no concern for public affairs. In the other school were those who, with varying emphases, placed ethics within the context of a more comprehensive effort to deal with the general phenomenon of religion. Within this second school, furthermore, was another very marked division. One subgroup included those who stood in the tradition of Schleiermacher and William James (not to mention the Puritans and John Wesley), who put great value upon "being religious" and upon analyzing religious feeling. For them the religious consciousness and Christian experience were central, and in philosophy they often tended to intuitionism, subjectivism, and mysticism. Among them were Bushnell and many more or less romantic thinkers. Newman Smyth's "garland for Schleiermacher," *The Religious Feelings* (1877), is a fine representative of this position. The second subgroup was less interested in experience (though they might treasure it deeply and build upon it) than in metaphysics and the philosophy of religion. Josiah Royce and Bowne were outstanding examples of this tendency in the early period; but after World War I, as part of the "realistic revolt" from idealism, Macintosh and Henry Nelson Wieman represented a new philosophic tack. Throughout the period, each of these three major points of view on religion (ethical, experiential, and philosophical) continued to receive effective expression.

On the issue of revelation, thinkers parted ways over interrelated questions as to the authority of Scriptures, the Church, and formal creeds. Related to all of these concerns was the question of Christ's nature and mission. Here as in the controversy over religion, two distinctive tendencies emerged. The "Evangelical Liberals" were those determined to maintain the historical continuity of the Christian doctrinal and ecclesiastical tradition, except insofar as modern circumstances required adjustment or change. Biblical study remained central, "Back to Christ" became a familiar slogan, historical study of Christian doctrine was vigorously pursued, and theology was carried out so far as possible in the traditional context and vocabulary. The term "Progressive Orthodoxy," chosen by the faculty of Andover Seminary for its published manifesto in 1884, very accurately expresses the purposes of the Evangelical Liberals. Since the vast majority of churchgoing America shared these purposes, the spokesmen for this cause won a wide audience. W. N. Clarke, W. A. Brown, and Rauschenbusch were among the most widely known.

The term "Modernistic Liberalism," on the other hand, may be used to designate a much smaller group of more radical theologians, men who took scientific method, scholarly discipline, empirical fact, and prevailing forms of contemporary philosophy as their point of departure. From this perspective they approached religion as a human phenomenon, the Bible as one great religious document among others, and the Christian faith as one major religio-ethical tradition among others. With varying degrees of concern for the traditional topics of systematic theology, and with more or less sympathy for their native religious heritage, they sought to salvage what they could of traditional belief, piety, and ethics. Emerson could be regarded as a prototype. Perhaps the best example of a modernistic school was that which flourished at Chicago, where men like Mathews, Case, Ames, Wieman and their colleagues for several decades worked out the implications of such a stance in almost every branch of the seminary curriculum. William James and Josiah Royce are more famous examples.

THE SIGNIFICANCE OF LIBERALISM

During the later nineteenth century a self-conscious and intellectually distinguished movement of theological liberals gained many eloquent proponents in the Protestant churches. Yet its influence is very difficult to estimate. Even the author of a book on *The Impact of American Religious Liberalism* has great difficulty in defining its "impact"—not because the movement was without effects, but because its legacy was all-pervasive.[12] It is impossible to determine whether the people it influenced were called back to the faith, or whether they were merely assured that their minimal beliefs constituted the essence of Christianity. The single most vital fact, therefore, is that the liberals led the Protestant churches into the world of modern science, scholarship, philosophy, and global knowledge.[13] They domesticated modern religious ideas. They forced a confrontation between traditional orthodoxies and the new grounds for religious skepticism exposed during the nineteenth century, and thus carried forward what the Enlightenment had begun. As a result, they precipitated the most fundamental controversy to wrack the churches since the age of the Reformation.

Aside from performing this immense educative role, the liberal movement also made significant scholarly contributions. Most important were its manifold labors in the fields of religious history, social and psychological analysis, comparative religion, educational theory, philosophy of religion, and sys-

12. Kenneth Cauthen, *The Impact of American Religious Liberalism*. This is not criticism of an important book to which my distinction between evangelical and modernistic liberalism is indebted.

13. "Modernism" performed a similar function in the Roman Catholic church during the same years, but its impact in America was slight (see pp. 836–41 below).

tematic theology. By sustained effort and creative thought, the liberals made a new place for religion in the modern world.[14] Because they remained in touch with the historical and romantic movements, they gave religious expression to the dynamic aspects of life and stood off the moral, social, and philosophical oversimplifications of scientific positivism. By raising problems for dogmatism, on the other hand, the liberals greatly enlivened the ecumenical movement.

It would be hard to deny that in doing these many things they sometimes stripped away the Church's spiritual armor. Often incredibly naïve in their evaluations of man, society, and the national destiny, they did little to prepare Americans for the brutal assaults of the twentieth century. In this respect they laid the groundwork for tragedy and disillusion. One can accept H. Richard Niebuhr's harsh summary of their outlook: "A God without wrath brought men without sin into a kingdom without judgment through the ministrations of a Christ without a Cross." [15] In the face of many difficulties, however, they maintained standards of scholarly rigor, intellectual honesty, and moral responsibility that their successors often failed to appreciate. In the later twentieth century renewed demands that Christians be "honest to God" would enhance their reputation. To be sure, they may have been overly optimistic about human nature, but they were not fatuous; and those who entered the Social Gospel movement were effective critics of the American social order.

14. These frequent references to the "modern" are not casually made (see Arthur C. McGiffert, *The Rise of Modern Religious Ideas.* Richard Ellmann and Charles Feidelson in *The Modern Tradition: Backgrounds of Modern Literature* (New York: Oxford University Press, 1965) pursue the question provocatively, yet affirm that "the modern awaits definition."

15. *The Kingdom of God in America,* p. 193.

47
THE SOCIAL GOSPEL

When the Social Gospel movement began and when it came to a close are much disputed questions. But nearly everyone agrees that it was more fully represented by Walter Rauschenbusch than by anyone else, and that it gained classic utterance in 1907 with the publication of his *Christianity and the Social Crisis*. Let us read, then, the final page of this book, where the "lonely prophet" discloses his vision of God's coming Kingdom:

> If the twentieth century could do for us in the control of social forces what the nineteenth did for us in the control of natural forces, our grandchildren would live in a society that would be justified in regarding our present social life as semi-barbarous. Since the Reformation began to free the mind and to direct the force of religion toward morality, there has been a perceptible increase of speed. Humanity is gaining in elasticity and capacity for change, and every gain in general intelligence, in organizing capacity, in physical and moral soundness, and especially in responsiveness to ideal motives, again increases the ability to advance without disastrous reactions. The swiftness of evolution in our own country proves the immense latent perfectibility in human nature.
>
> Last May a miracle happened. At the beginning of the week the fruit trees bore brown and greenish buds. At the end of the week they were robed in bridal garments of blossom. But for weeks and months the sap had been rising and distending the cells and maturing the tissues which were half ready in the fall before. The swift unfolding was the culmination of a long process. Perhaps these nineteen centuries of Christian influence have been a long preliminary stage of growth, and now the flower and fruit are almost here. If at this juncture we can rally sufficient religious faith and moral strength to snap the bonds of evil

> and turn the present unparalleled economic and intellectual resources of humanity to the harmonious development of a true social life, the generations yet unborn will mark this as that great day of the Lord for which the ages waited, and count us blessed for sharing in the apostolate that proclaimed it.[1]

This passage deserves close analysis not because it is extraordinarily difficult, but because beneath its blossoming rhetoric are three assertions which reveal the essence of the Social Gospel, a movement which has been widely hailed at home and abroad as the most distinctive contribution of the American churches to world Christianity.

The primary point of Rauschenbusch's conclusion is underlined by his central figure of speech: "now the flower and the fruit is almost here." The "great day of the Lord for which the ages waited" is at hand. The Social Gospel was a form of millennial thought; yet it was also an authentic "gospel" bringing good tidings of great joy to the people. Rauschenbusch's grounds for joy constitute the second point: "the immense latent perfectibility in human nature" has been revealed by the swift evolution of our country and by the progress that has been accelerating in Christendom ever since the Reformation. His third point is the moral demand, driven home by two conditional sentences that bracket the passage: men must gain control of social forces; the "bonds of evil" must be broken; and finally—and here is the insistence that makes the Social Gospel a movement in the churches—religious faith and moral strength must be directed toward these last great social tasks.

The Social Gospel must be understood as a transitory phase of Christian social thought. It was a submovement within religious liberalism, with a certain view of man and history governing its rationale. It reflected and depended upon the singular spirit of confidence and hope that prevailed for only a few decades before the Great War and the Great Depression shattered the mood. Historians can record its rise and describe its aftermath, but efforts to see its persistence or revival during the 1930s involve serious distortions. Similarly, a single set of social problems stirred its passions: the urban dislocations occasioned by America's unregulated industrial expansion. The Gilded Age was a prerequisite. In this context its moral message consisted almost exclusively in applications, mild or severe, of the idea that the doctrine of laissez faire required Christian modifications. The Iron Law of Wages so dear to classical economics must be qualified by the Great Com-

1. Walter Rauschenbusch, *Christianity and the Social Crisis* (New York: Macmillan Co., 1907), p. 422.

mandment. Between employer and employee brutality and conflict must yield to compassion and mutual respect. Even in this light, however, the historical problem of dealing with the Social Gospel remains very great, as four other important considerations will make clear.

SOME PRELIMINARY CONSIDERATIONS

In one sense, the Social Gospel was anything but new. The major element in America's moral and religious heritage was Puritanism, with its powerfully rooted convictions that the shaping and, if need be, the remaking of society was the Church's concern. American Protestantism was born in Holy Commonwealths and Holy Experiments. The Second Great Awakening and the great "theocratic" campaigns of the Evangelical United Front had intensified this tendency. Antebellum revivalism, in fact, was pervaded by concern for social reform and, beyond that, by the hope for a sanctified citizenry that would make this republic a model for the whole world. Lyman Beecher and Charles Finney were so fascinated by this vision that they almost forgot their quarrels about the "new measures" in revivalism. Unitarians and Transcendentalists also caught the contagious reforming spirit. During most of the nineteenth century, moreover, the professor of Christian morals and political economy became a stock figure in American colleges and universities. Until a very late date these men inculcated the old medieval principle that social, economic, and political theory is properly a branch of Christian ethics, a principle that the Social Gospel was to reaffirm.

The antislavery movement came to life within this matrix and gradually ate away the prevailing apathy and hostility in the churches. By 1860 Lincoln had at his back a crusading evangelical Protestantism so fervent that at times he feared it would trample him with the vintage that the grapes of wrath had stored. Abolitionism, with its hymns, slogans, and prophetic zeal, was a decisive prelude to the Social Gospel. Both were characterized by a readiness to harness the churches and a tendency to subordinate every other interest of the church to the one great national policy question of the day. The line from Theodore Dwight Weld and Elijah Lovejoy to Washington Gladden and Walter Rauschenbusch must never be ignored.

A second consideration is that by no means all opponents of the Social Gospel believed that public affairs and social questions ought to be put aside when a minister entered the pulpit. Even a social conservative like Henry Ward Beecher made freedom to speak out on social issues a condition of his accepting the call to Plymouth Church in 1847. During worship services in his church, Beecher not only "auctioned" slaves and raised money for Bleeding

Kansas, but with the Bible before him, citing appropriate texts, he preached and published sermons on the whole gamut of social questions, including the problems of poverty and labor relations that worried the Social Gospelers. Although he took the opposing stand on nearly all of the issues, the social orientation which Beecher established at Plymouth Church enabled his successor, Lyman Abbott, to defend quite different economic views from the pulpit and to become the virtual chaplain of Theodore Roosevelt's Progressivism. This change in social outlook, moreover, did not involve Abbott in any basic departure from Beecher's form of the "New Theology." In other words, liberal preachers like Beecher (and at reduced scale they were legion) belong in the prologue to Social Gospel history despite their ideological opposition to men like Rauschenbusch.

Another phase of social protest that flourished during the Social Gospel's heyday was Populism and the great agrarian crusade. It, too, had a religious orientation. Its dominant leader was the Great Commoner, William Jennings Bryan, who was also the Joshua of American Fundamentalism. "Would you crucify labor on a cross of gold," he had shouted—at a time when Pastor Rauschenbusch was equally agonized by society's crucifixion of the poor. Yet historians never include Populism in the Social Gospel movement, for it lacked both an urban orientation and the presuppositions of theological liberalism. The same criteria apply to the varied activities of the Salvation Army and, somewhat later, to the Pentecostal rescue missions and similar institutions which brought the church into living contact with city slums.

Liberalism and the Social Gospel movement must not be identified, however, because liberalism often encouraged complacency and self-satisfaction. It throve mightily among the most socially conservative classes of people. The Social Gospel, on the other hand, was always a prophetic and unpopular impulse. Although it became a large and powerful minority in the early 1920s, even then its intradenominational battles were often bitter, and many were lost. Social Gospelers were usually theological liberals; but the statement cannot be reversed.

A third consideration involves the question of the Social Gospel's originality. Is it the most distinctive American contribution to world Christianity as is so often alleged? The facts are confusing. Although its Puritanic concern for the commonwealth is, as we have seen, embedded in an indigenous tradition which is unique, almost every major new element of the Social Gospel betrayed enormous indebtedness to two major foreign impulses. From Britain came a legacy of inspiration drawn from the Christian socialism of Charles Kingsley, Frederick D. Maurice, John Ruskin, William H. Fremantle, and the architects of Fabian socialism. From Germany came nearly its entire biblical and theological grounding, as well as the historical view of economic theory by which the social statics of *Manchesterismus* was to be overthrown. The key figure for the Social Gospelers as for so many other liberal theologians was Albrecht Ritschl (1822–89), whose Jesus-centered, antimetaphysical theology of the Kingdom of God provided the movement's chief integrative idea. Adolph von Harnack, the most famous of Ritschlians, formulated many of these views even more appealingly, especially through his disparagement of vain scholastic speculation and the exceedingly simplified ethical principles which he defined as the "essence of Christianity." And after Ritschl had come the rising Social Christian movement in Germany and Switzerland, not to mention the advanced social legislation of the new German Empire.[2] British and German developments, in short, provided a vital prologue to American Social Gospel history.

The final preliminary consideration calls attention to the opposition which the Social Gospel faced—the villain in the plot, as it were. What the Social Gospel had to combat was above all the American's basic contempt for poverty, the "hard shell of sanctified realism" fostered by the Puritan ethic in both its pious and secularized forms. This attitude had nothing to do with the immemorial assumption that a certain amount of poverty was inevitable, or with the notion of a Great Chain of Being which made the lowly an essential element in the Creation. The Puritan doctrine of vocation avoided a static interpretation of the dominical words, "You have the poor always with you" (Matt. 26:11). Because God called nobody unto mendicancy and inactivity, those who begged and did not work either were being or ought to be punished for their sins. Even in the complex urban surroundings of New York in the 1870s Henry Ward Beecher was willing to make this proposition axiomatic:

> Looking comprehensively through city and town and village and country, the general truth will stand, that no man in this land suffers from poverty unless it be more than his fault—unless it be his *sin*. . . . There is enough and to spare thrice over; and if men have not enough, it is owing to the want of provident care, and foresight, and industry, and frugality, and wise saving. This is the general truth.[3]

William Lawrence, a Massachusetts Episcopal bishop, reduced this "gospel of wealth" to two "positive principles": "that man, when he is strong, conquers Nature," and that "in the long run, it is only to the man of morality

2. Karl Marx is a special case. His impact on German social and sociological thought extended far beyond socialist organizations. But in the Social Gospel movement, as in American thought generally, Marxian influence was slight and heavily filtered, even among the Christian socialists on the Social Gospel's left wing (see James Dombrowski, *The Early Days of Christian Socialism in America*).

3. Quoted by Sidney E. Mead, *The Lively Experiment: The Shaping of Christianity in America*, p. 160.

that wealth comes." Beyond this, of course, lay "the privilege of grateful service" and Christ's "precepts on the stewardship of wealth." [4] One could fill book after book with similar hard-shell quotations, from orthodox, liberal, and secular spokesmen alike, all of them anxious, it would seem, lest someone accuse them of being "soft on poverty." Yet only when this attitude was called in question could American Protestantism produce the Social Gospel.

Two new circumstances served to intensify the American's prevailing hardness of heart. Simplest of these was the powerful evidence that Andrew Carnegie's faith in America's "Triumphant Democracy" had its warrants: "The old nations of the earth creep at a snail's pace; the Republic thunders past with the rush of the express." Carnegie's statistics were impressive; and his own rags-to-riches life story was more convincing than anything Horatio Alger was writing.

But the common view of poverty and wealth was given even greater plausibility during the Age of Enterprise by the doctrine of evolution through struggle and natural selection of the fittest. Darwin learned from Malthus, and the Malthusians, in turn, learned from Darwin. Social Darwinism thus gave the stock ideas of the Puritan ethic a new potency and the added dignity of "scientific" support. Herbert Spencer with enormous confidence extended Darwinian theories of development to human societies, and in the United States he won to his banner a Broad Church Episcopal minister of Morristown, New Jersey, named William Graham Sumner. In 1872 Sumner abandoned the pulpit for an academic podium at Yale, where he exchanged liberal Christianity for conservative Spencerianism, first as a professor of political economy, then increasingly as a sociologist. In these roles Sumner used his evolutionary determinism to bludgeon soft-hearted reformism and governmental intervention of all types (plutocratic as well as democratic). What little hope he saw for mankind he vested in a stern work-oriented moralism and the evolutionary process. Like a Henry Ward Beecher minus every shred of religiosity and teleology, Sumner made the task of the Social Gospel more difficult.

PREPARATORY DEVELOPMENTS

During the years after the Civil War, many Christian spokesmen in a variety of places began for the first time in American history to express serious doubts that the organized selfishness of a free enterprise economy would automatically solve the country's problems. Less theoretically, they openly

4. "The Relation of Wealth to Morals," in *Democracy and the Gospel of Wealth*, ed. Gail Kennedy (Boston: D. C. Heath & Co., 1949), pp. 68–76.

lamented the fact that the laboring man was rarely understood and almost never defended in the Christian churches. Andover Seminary's famous journal, *Bibliotheca Sacra,* opened its pages to social commentary in 1866, and in 1868 it printed a series of articles entitled "The Natural Theology of Social Science," in which Professor John Bascom of Williams College criticized the conservatism of the Protestant pulpit. Bascom had no more sympathy for the poor and improvident than his contemporaries, but he did question the competitive principle, and advocated giving the workingman a "pecuniary interest" in the enterprises for which they worked. Later, after serving as president of the University of Wisconsin, he moved in his *Sociology* (1887) toward the more forthright "Kingdom theology" of the Social Gospel. Among Bascom's students was Washington Gladden, who in later years would earn his title as "the father of the American Social Gospel."

Two other pioneers of the movement merit brief mention, the first, a sensational preacher, widely known at the time but soon forgotten; the second, a typical champion of the workingman. Joseph Cook was an Andover graduate and an Orthodox Congregational minister who gained fame between 1875 and 1895 for his strenuous efforts to defend the Christian religion against biblical critics, evolutionists, and free thinkers. Cook was also a politically conservative enemy of vice and corruption of the fairly standard type. Less typically, he was concerned with working conditions, low wages, and child labor. Because his Monday Lectures in Boston attracted some of the largest audiences in that city's history, the Social Gospel's best historian can say of him that he "probably did more than any other individual or group in bringing the social implications of Christianity to the attention of Americans." [5]

The Reverend Jesse Henry Jones was a Boston Congregationalist of quite another order. As founder of the Christian Labor Union (1872–78) and editor first of *Equity: A Journal of Christian Labor Reform* (1874) and then of the equally short-lived *Labor-Balance* (1877), he defended a labor theory of value, advocated socialism, and made strident attacks on Henry Ward Beecher's truce between God and Mammon. Yet Jones was not simply a social radical with an ordination somewhere in his past. In his book *The Kingdom of Heaven* (1871) he envisioned a perfect Christian society of separate socialistic communities. As Professor May remarks, he was of a type that is "common in the unfrequented byways of American social science. Religious radicals, spinning plans for a perfect society out of their reading of the Gospels and prophets or out of their own troubled consciences." [6] The

5. Charles H. Hopkins, *The Rise of the Social Gospel in American Protestantism,* p. 39.

6. Henry F. May, *Protestant Churches and Industrial America,* p. 79.

views of such men had little to do with American realities, but their spirit was an important recurring ingredient of the Social Gospel, especially valuable as a reminder that the country's avid interest in utopian socialism during the antebellum period had some long-range effects.

Other Social Prophets

In addition to these anticipations of the later Social Gospel, a tradition of social criticism and "muckraking" opposed itself to the practices of the "robber barons" and the degeneration of political ethics that set in with the Grant administration. Civil service reform, government regulation of business, and antitrust legislation were its chief aims, and its accomplishments included the Civil Service Act, the Interstate Commerce Commission, and the regulatory legislation of the Progressive Era. With these later achievements the Social Gospel movement would have an especially close relationship. Contemporary with this eminently respectable reform tradition, however, were three more distinctive prophets who are related in special ways to social Christianity: Edward Bellamy, Henry George, and Lester Ward.

Bellamy (1850–98) was the son of a Baptist minister who during his short life moved from his father's faith to a "religion of solidarity" that took its inspiration in about equal measure from Christian liberalism, Transcendentalism, and Auguste Comte's "Religion of Humanity." "Living in the narrow grotto of individual life" he was "greedy of infinity." He yearned for a social order that would transcend the idea of "personality as an ultimate fact." Growing up in the industrial town of Chicopee Falls, Massachusetts, Bellamy became intensely aware of the "barbarity" and "monstrous cruelty" which were parts of the town's daily life. As a newspaper writer he vented some of his views, and as a novelist still others; but his reputation rests almost entirely on his novel, *Looking Backward* (1888), in which he portrays the socialistic perfection of the nation in A.D. 2000. It soon became a best seller, and Nationalist Clubs began to be organized to bring about Bellamy's imagined world just as the Social Gospel was gaining self-consciousness as a movement. Both Bellamy's social organicism and his futuristic orientation became indispensable elements in the social optimism of the age.

Henry George (1839–97) "exploded into fame" nine years before Bellamy with his *Progress and Poverty* (1879)—so searing in its indictment of the American social system, so fervent in the millennial hope that it offered, that in America its author became the emotional equivalent of a Karl Marx. His panacea was the single tax, and around this program grew up a tight phalanx of orthodox followers, many of them from organized labor. Far more contagious and far broader in its influence was his root-and-branch critique of the American economic system and the theory that underlay it, as well as his enraptured vision of a perfected America. His religious passion and his tender concern for every human being put George in the Social Gospel tradition. In 1886, when he ran for mayor in New York with both the Roman Catholic Father Edward McGlynn and Walter Rauschenbusch supporting him, he revealed his true force in American life as an awakener of the slumbering Christian social conscience. Although he died suddenly during his second New York mayoralty campaign, the hundred thousand mourners who filed past his bier paid homage to the powerful way in which he had taken economic theory out of obscure treatises and academic halls, making it a weapon in the social and political conflicts of a nation in crisis.

Lester Ward (1841–1913), unlike Bellamy and George, esteemed himself a scientist rather than a prophet or visionary. He was the first American to write a comprehensive sociological treatise, and his importance for the Social Gospel lies in the fact that in his sociology Ward challenged the reigning views of Sumner and Spencer. Though as interested as they in a cosmic scientific synthesis, and equally naturalistic in his premises, Ward distinguished human purposive action from all other natural processes, and attacked those Social Darwinians who used evolutionary theory to support the businessman's opposition to state intervention, charity, and all other "artificial" devices to preserve the "unfit" in the economic struggle for survival. For him sociology was an applied science to aid whole societies in bettering their condition. Ward was a liberal in politics; unlike George, he favored Populism and Bryan, and was "anxious to throttle the money power." He was too irreligious to affect the Social Gospel directly, but he did put on the record a formidable critique of Sumner's "biological sociology."

THE SOCIAL GOSPEL

During the last two decades of the century the movement to awaken the social conscience of the churches moved far beyond the sporadic and uncertain forays of the 1860s and 1870s. It deepened the intellectual foundations of its work, broadened its focus, vastly increased its following, and began to make a positive impact in some theological schools, on certain major denominations, and no doubt, on the prevailing opinions of churchgoing America. Since these changes did not bring agreement in methods and aims, subdivisions of the movement took shape, some conservative, others moderate, still others frankly socialistic. Without becoming a hopelessly unreadable catalogue of names and dates, however, no brief account can touch on all of the many socially concerned Protestants who took part, or the myriad organizations which perpetuated these diverse impulses, or the innumerable projects, experiments, publications, and conventions which marked the movement. The account which follows will concentrate on a few of the most outstanding and representative leaders.

In the annals of the Social Gospel Washington Gladden (1836–1918) undoubtedly deserves first mention. He was among the earliest to be awakened, and he continued to be active until World War I. His gradual progress from abstract moral protest to a specific critique of American economic institutions typifies that of the movement as a whole, near whose ideological center he consistently remained. Gladden was reared on a farm near Owego, New York, and educated at Williams when Mark Hopkins was president and John Bascom a professor. After private study with Moses Coit Tyler, he entered the Congregational ministry in 1860. He was even then a pronounced liberal in theology, and he soon became an admirer of Bushnell. Throughout his life, Gladden was a popular expositor of the New Theology, writing three widely read books, *Who Wrote the Bible?* (1891), *How Much Is Left of the Old Doctrines?* (1899), and *Present Day Theology* (1913). In all of these works he showed his indebtedness to the leading liberal theologians and scholars, but unlike most of them he saturated his liberalism with social concern. His specifically Christian leverage came more from an appeal to the Great Commandment than from a legalistic interpretation of the "social teachings" of Jesus.

Very early in his career Gladden became interested in the struggles of labor and capital. After several brief pastorates and a few years as a religious journalist, he began in 1875 an important seven-year ministry at Springfield, Massachusetts, an industrial city where he soon had an opportunity to express his sympathy for unemployed workers. From 1882 to 1914 he served with great effectiveness as minister of the First Congregational Church of Columbus, Ohio. Adding thirty more to the six books he had already published, and lecturing far and wide, Gladden became one of the country's most influential clergymen. During this period he also pursued his analysis of the nation's economic situation, digging deeper into labor problems and the details of taxation, and gaining experience which formed the background for his insistence that the churches do more than attack personal sin and public corruption.

Over the years Gladden's criticism of American free enterprise became more severe. Though he never became a socialist, he did advocate public ownership of utilities and cooperative management of many industries. Among his most constructive works were *Tools and the Man* (1893) and

Social Salvation (1902), both first presented as Beecher Lectures at Yale. His theology of social action, however, was very simple: he demanded that the churches concern themselves with social injustice, and that they help bring the economic aspects of American life under the laws of God's kingdom by example and by advocacy.[7] Yet this was no small matter in the Gilded Age, and Gladden is justifiably remembered as a major awakener of the American Protestant social conscience.

Francis Greenwood Peabody (1847–1936) represented the Social Gospel cause in another vital arena, the seminary. He had been deflected from the normal career of a Boston-born, Harvard-educated, Unitarian minister by a year at the University of Halle in Germany. When he was made a professor at the Harvard Divinity School in 1880, he very soon instituted what was probably the first systematic course in "social ethics" to be taught in an American theological school. Peabody understood himself to be living in "the age of the social question," and to promote an intelligent response, he implemented a program of undergraduate and graduate instruction in the subject at Harvard. His published volumes of chapel sermons and many treatises extended his influence far beyond his own university. *Jesus Christ and the Social Question* (1900) went through many editions and was translated into three languages. Rauschenbusch considered it, along with Shailer Mathews's similar work, to be definitive on the subject.

In theology Peabody drew heavily upon the tradition which Schleiermacher had inspired in Germany. His social advocacy was relatively conservative, with a strong emphasis on cooperatives, insurance, enlightened philanthropy, good planning, and a social security system on the Prussian model. In all of these areas, moreover, Peabody believed strongly in the value of factual knowledge. The Social Ethics department which he founded had an important library, introduced seminar methods, and laid the groundwork for future work in sociology at the university. Peabody also stands out as an important exception to the Social Gospel's prevailing lack of interest in Negro education and racial questions; and he is among the very few Americans of that period whose words on these matters could be read without embarrassment a half-century later. In addition, his career illustrates the two-way process by which liberal theology, historical studies, and the Social Gospel served for a time to bring Unitarianism back into the mainstream of American religious thought.

7. Like most Social Gospel men, Gladden advocated interchurch cooperation. In *The Christian League of Connecticut* (1883) he presents a fictional scenario of churches working together to face social problems in a factory town. Many socially minded ecumenical leaders testified to its influence.

Social Science for the Social Gospel

The Social Gospel, needless to say, did not consist solely of biblical exegesis and theological elaboration; indeed those are the two elements it most definitely lacked. It was always chiefly concerned to find out the truth about society, and on the basis of that knowledge to chart programs for ameliorating the country's social woes. To this end it drew political science, economics, and sociology to its service and, whenever possible, sought to provoke in all social scientists a regard for the ethical implications of their work. In the fertile exchange of ideas that resulted, two social scientists, Richard T. Ely and Albion W. Small, are important not only for their efforts to advance the Social Gospel as a movement in the churches, but for their contributions to the conduct of their disciplines in America.

Richard T. Ely (1854–1943) grew up in rural New York State in a strict Presbyterian environment; but in the course of his life he became an advanced liberal in theology, an Episcopalian, a strenuous critic of neoclassical economic theory, and a strong advocate of reform in America's urban-industrial system. After a college education divided evenly between Dartmouth and Columbia, Ely went to Germany from 1876 to 1880 for advanced study. He spent a year in philosophy at Halle, then went to Heidelberg for a Ph.D. in economics. As a result of this experience he became—and remained—an admiring disciple of Karl Knies, the historical economist, Johann Bluntschli, and Rudolph von Ihering, all of whom repudiated the alleged laws of classical economics and emphasized the prior importance of differing cultural contexts, historical developments, national needs, and political realities. They underlined both the fact and the desirability of human solidarity, insisting that economic theory must deal with national culture as a whole. The relativistic implications of such doctrines are obvious, but these were counterbalanced by an emphasis on the need for goals in economic, social, or legal thinking. These historical theorists stressed normative considerations even as they exposed the unexpressed ethical presuppositions of classical or absolutist theories. Throughout his life, therefore, Ely was to oppose those who took "Back to Adam Smith" as their motto. Identifying himself with "the ethical school of economists," he insisted that it aimed "to *direct* in a certain definite manner, so far as may be, the economic, social growth of mankind. Economists of this school wish to ascertain the laws of progress, and to show men how to make use of them." [8]

On returning to the United States, Ely was appalled both by the way economic theorists ignored the cultural, religious, and ethical norms of the

8. Richard T. Ely, *The Social Aspects of Christianity* (New York, 1889), p. 122.

nation, and by the widespread ignorance of alternative economic theories, Continental accomplishments in social reform, and the nature of the labor movement. During the next decade, while a professor at Johns Hopkins, he published books on each of these subjects, steeping all of them in his intense moral concern. In *Social Aspects of Christianity* (1889) he developed in more detail his understanding of the bearing of Christian ethics on social questions. With this book he became one of the most widely read of all American economists. To promote his large aims for America he led in the formation of the American Economic Association in 1885, also serving for a decade as its secretary or president. Through his participation in Episcopal social agencies and in many other conferences and commissions, as well as through his many writings, he became not only a "representative man," but an extremely influential theorist.

Albion W. Small (1854–1926) filled a very similar role as a reform-minded sociologist. He grew up in a pious New England Baptist home, attended Colby College in Maine and the Baptist Seminary in Newton, Massachusetts, and then proceeded to Germany, where at Leipzig and Berlin he became a convinced defender of the "historical school" in social thought led by Gustav Schmoller and Wilhelm Roscher. In later years he would add to this commitment a deep appreciation for the more positivistic sociological methods of Gustav Ratzenhofer and Ludwig Gumplowicz, thus becoming an important American pioneer of equilibrium theory in social relations.

After returning to America, Small became professor of political economy, then president of Colby College, gaining in the meantime his doctorate at Johns Hopkins. In 1892 he was called to the new University of Chicago to organize the sociology department. As the first person in the country to occupy a chair in this discipline, he played a major role in training the first generation of American-educated sociologists. His understanding of social science was, like Ely's, very comprehensive, involving an intense concern for its philosophic ground and its ethical implications. He believed that "the most worthy work of men is the effort to improve human conditions":

> If I am not mistaken, the most earnest seekers after God are . . . growing more and more in contact with the development of a science . . . of God's image, or the science of human welfare. . . . The ultimate value of sociology as pure science will be its use as an index and a test and a measure of what is worth doing.[9]

9. *General Sociology* (Chicago, 1905), quoted in Cynthia Eagle Russett, *The Concept of Equilibrium in American Social Thought* (New Haven: Yale University Press, 1966), pp. 61–62; Albion Small, *The Significance of Sociology for Ethics* (Chicago, 1902), p. 4.

For these reasons, he was consistently critical of Sumner and Spencer, but very appreciative of Lester Ward. And through his active participation in many important conferences called by Social Gospel leaders, Small was able to keep empirical questions and the need for organized sociological knowledge before their minds.

The Apogee of the Movement

Josiah Strong (1847–1916) was the dynamo, the revivalist, the organizer, and altogether the most irrepressible spirit of the Social Gospel movement. Though of orthodox upbringing, he became an admirer of Bushnell's theological leadings; but more importantly, he came to regard the new industrial city as the central crisis for the nation and the church. In 1885, when Strong was a minister of the Central Congregational Church of Cincinnati, he expounded his views in what was almost certainly the most influential Social Gospel book of the nineteenth century, *Our Country: Its Possible Future and Its Present Crisis.* He then implemented his conviction that concerted interchurch action was necessary by convening an Interdenominational Congress at his church in Cincinnati, inviting many of the country's most outstanding social Christian spokesmen to attend. Future meetings and a series of urban surveys were projected. At once Strong became a national figure, and his appointment as general secretary of the almost moribund Evangelical Alliance in 1886 gave him an opportunity to maintain the momentum of these projects. In 1887, 1889, and 1893, other congresses were held, all of them large, well-publicized, and followed up by publications and local conferences. The last of them, held at the Chicago World's Fair, had an especially powerful impact.

Two major results of these efforts were a revitalization of the country's main interdenominational agency and the focusing of ecclesiastical concern on the city. The Alliance meanwhile gave Strong a platform from which to proclaim his enormous confidence in America's destiny under Protestant leadership. That his fervor reached almost jingoistic proportions is undeniable, and there were also more than intimations of Anglo-Saxon racism in his message. In these respects he was clearly a spokesman for the "Protestant Establishment." Yet he was more than merely that, for he showed untiring concern for urban evangelism and for a linking of "fact and faith" in the churches' approach to industrial questions. Surveys and statistics informed his diagnoses and his prescriptions. When his advanced social views forced him out of the Alliance in 1898, he immediately organized the League for Social Service (later to become the American Institute of Social Service), which took social research and public education on social affairs as its primary tasks.

Strong's confidence in applied science and in guided evolution was boundless. His nationalism and his defense of imperialism have become almost infamous. Taken as a whole, however, his views were those which constituted the core program of the Social Gospel movement. In fact, without Strong's contribution, the very term "movement" would hardly be warranted. The latest and most thorough student of his work, moreover, rightfully stresses the way in which Strong's program parallels that of the political Progressives.[10] Josiah Strong, finally, almost personified the movement's culminating phase: the organization of an interdenominational agency of national scope. Certain other aspects of the movement need to precede an account of this chain of events, however.

Divergent Voices

Social Christianity could by no means be kept entirely within the liberal Protestant boundaries marked out by men such as Strong or Gladden. The writings of Marx no less than the old native American tradition of utopian socialism made that unlikely. And indeed a considerable number of more radical spirits soon were heard, and a few new organizations were formed. These radicals were colorful personalities whose exploits and bold ideas frustrate the historian with space limitations, yet a few representative types may suggest the range of their accomplishments.

Among the most impressive was William Dwight Porter Bliss (1856–1926), a Congregationalist become Episcopalian, a follower of George, Bellamy, and British Christian Socialism, who in 1890 gave up his parish ministry in Boston and founded the Mission of the Carpenter, a socialist congregation which in turn became the nucleus for other organizations and activities, including a newspaper, *The Dawn*. In 1897 Bliss also published a huge and valuable *Encyclopedia of Social Reform*. More than any other prominent Christian reformer of the period, he anticipates the "secularized" urban mission of some mid-twentieth century activists. After 1906 Bliss became an active member of the Christian Socialist Fellowship as well as of the Socialist party.

The Minneapolis Congregational minister, George D. Herron (1862–1925), had an even more unusual career. Bursting on the scene in 1890 as a dynamic preacher, within three years he had won himself an endowed chair in applied

10. See Dorothea R. Muller, "The Social Philosophy of Josiah Strong: Social Christianity and American Progressivism," *Church History* 28 (1959): 183–201.

Christianity at Iowa (Grinnell) College. A social critic from the first, Herron gradually became an outspoken socialist, though of a mystical, utopian sort; and between 1896 and 1900 his views were the inspiration for an unsuccessful communitarian experiment in Georgia. Suddenly in 1901 his influence in the American churches was ended by his divorce, his marriage to the daughter of his chief patroness, and accusations of his being a "free lover." Before his permanent departure for Italy, however, he played a brief but active role in the Socialist party, even giving the nominating speech for Eugene V. Debs at the party's Chicago convention of 1904.

Not surprisingly, the most durable impulses were those that led to more or less thoroughgoing versions of socialism, whether Marxian or Fabian. These movements possessed a degree of discipline and the guidance of a tradition. At that time, moreover, socialist leaders such as Henry D. Lloyd, Lawrence Gronlund, and even Eugene V. Debs showed a surprising measure of religious openness. The loosely organized Christian Socialist Fellowship, founded in 1906, affiliated itself with the Socialist party, which in the startling election of 1912 drew almost a million votes despite Wilson's and Roosevelt's competitive bidding for the progressive vote. Out of this milieu the Presbyterian minister Norman Thomas, the Episcopalian Bernard Iddings Bell, Professor Vida Scudder, and many others emerged as eloquent public figures.

Walter Rauschenbusch

If Josiah Strong typified the organized mobilization of social concern in the churches, Walter Rauschenbusch (1861–1918) typified its passion and its soul. Nearly every fundamental motif of the Social Gospel, including a strong interest in socialism, came to expression in his works. In theology, biblical interpretation, and church history he consistently expounded the major liberal themes. He subjected the American social order to informed analysis and found it wanting. He awakened compassion for human suffering and proposed realistic reforms. He delineated the key concept of the "Kingdom of God on earth" with persuasive clarity. And finally, he overcame apathy and pessimism with a stirring vision of the coming Kingdom. At one stage in his career Rauschenbusch was, as Winthrop Hudson has shown, a "lonely prophet," but before his death in 1918 and for almost a decade thereafter, his growing reputation justified H. Shelton Smith's assertion that he was "the foremost molder of American Christian thought in his generation." [11] Because of his most atypical insistence on the power of the "kingdom of

11. Winthrop S. Hudson, *The Great Tradition of the American Churches*, pp. 226–42; Hilrie Shelton Smith, *Changing Conceptions of Original Sin*, p. 199.

evil," he is also one of the few liberal theologians who could still be read after wars and depressions had dimmed men's vision of a perfected social order.

Rauschenbusch was born in Rochester, New York, where his father, an immigrant missionary, was professor in the Baptist seminary's "German Department." Except for his high school years in Germany, he was educated in Rochester; and he taught church history in the seminary from 1897 until his death. The decisive experience of his life was his eleven-year ministry (1886–97) to a German Baptist congregation situated in the proximity of New York City's notorious Hell's Kitchen. In that blighted district "an endless procession of men 'out of work, out of clothes, out of shoes, and out of hope' wore down the threshold and wore away the heart of the sensitive young pastor and his wife." [12] Out of that experience came the Rauschenbusch whom America remembers. His Social Gospel career began almost immediately, during Henry George's mayoralty campaign of 1886. With Jacob Riis he labored for playgrounds and for better housing. The friendships he forged with a small company of other Baptist ministers grew, with the addition of a few non-Baptists, into the Brotherhood of the Kingdom, a fellowship that between 1893 and 1915 became an influential nucleus of devoted social concern, especially through its publications.

In his own denomination and among the movement's leading spirits, Rauschenbusch had become a well-known Social Gospel leader even before the century's turn. But in 1907, while he was on leave for a year of study in Germany, *Christianity and the Social Crisis,* the book that made him nationally famous, was published. Here in seven simple but eloquent chapters the whole Social Gospel was expounded: the social message of the Old Testament Prophets, the "social aims of Jesus," the subsequent decline of social concern in the church, the "present crisis" and the church's stake in it, and finally, "What To Do." Ringing through the whole is Rauschenbusch's doctrine of the Kingdom, a disparagement of older forms of piety and traditional theology, a thoroughly instrumental conception of the church, and an insistence that religion and ethics are one and inseparable. *Christianizing the Social Order* (1912) was more concerned with prescribing reforms for America's capitalistic system, which he deemed to be only "semi-Christian."

Then in 1917, and despite his conviction that "theology is the esoteric thought of the church," Rauschenbusch published *A Theology for the Social Gospel,* first presented as the Taylor Lectures at Yale. With the World War now undermining his hopes for the Kingdom of God, he found reason

12. Hopkins, *Rise of the Social Gospel,* p. 216. He quotes Ray Stannard Baker, *The Social Unrest* (1910).

in this book to formulate more forcefully a doctrine of the "Kingdom of Evil." Having been stunned by the readiness of Americans to locate this kingdom exclusively in Germany, he traced the ultimate cause to "the lust for easy and unearned gain" of the "imperialistic and colonizing powers." He called for a "restoration of millennial hope," and declared that "after the war the Social Gospel will 'come back' with pent-up energy and clearer knowledge." He saw the "Christianizing of international relations" as the most acute sphere of concern.[13]

As it happened, military victory in "the War to End Wars" did stimulate social Christianity in America and lead to a great expansion of its machinery in the early postwar years. But we must first consider the prewar process by which the Social Gospel won an official, institutionalized place in American Protestantism.

Institutionalizing the Social Gospel

In 1907, when Rauschenbusch wrote the final lines of his first book (quoted in the opening of the present chapter), the fortunes of the movement he championed justified his enthusiasm. Josiah Strong, to be sure, had been routed from his commanding position in the Evangelical Alliance, but other agencies had been created. In 1901 the Episcopal and the Congregational churches both formed commissions to deal with labor issues; and in 1903 the Presbyterian Church (North) called Charles Stelzle to a "special mission to workingmen," and under his dynamic leadership its Department of Church and Labor became an outstanding success. In 1908 the Northern Baptists took a first step toward formal recognition of the movement, while the Methodist Church (North) went much further, making the Federation for Social Service an official agency and adopting as a church the very liberal "Social Creed" which the Federation had prepared. By 1912, when the Men and Religion Forward Movement was launched as an interdenominational campaign to win three million Americans to the church, a dozen other denominations had taken cognizance of the Social Gospel. The Social Service division, in turn, became the most active element in the Forward Movement.

At the same time that these advances were being made, the most portentous step of all was taken. Due largely to the efforts of the social action elements in several large denominations, the Federal Council of Churches was formally organized. Since the days of Josiah Strong's rejuvenation of the Evangelical Alliance, a series of important preparatory organizations had

13. Walter Rauschenbusch, *A Theology for the Social Gospel* (New York: Macmillan Co., 1917), pp. 4, 15, 224.

been formed, one of them being Strong's own privately sponsored League for Social Service. In 1894 the interdenominational Open and Institutional Church League was formed, and for a number of years Elias B. Sanford directed its campaign for enlarging the scope of unified social service work. Six years later Sanford also did much to found the National Federation of Churches and Christian Workers, a voluntary association based on precedents set in New York City in 1895. Its greatest achievement was to organize the Interchurch Conference on Federation which met with official delegates from twenty-nine denominations in Carnegie Hall, New York, in November 1905.

The Carnegie Hall Conference, besides issuing several statements on social issues, unanimously approved a plan of organization which, when adopted by denominations, would constitute the Federal Council of Churches of Christ in America. The proposed doctrinal basis was made brief and broad: no more than a reference in the preamble to "the essential oneness of the Christian Churches of America, in Jesus Christ as their Lord and Saviour." In Philadelphia in 1908 delegates from thirty-three denominations formally brought the Federal Council into existence. Although it possessed only advisory powers—or perhaps because of that fact—it turned to social issues at its first meeting, adopting a lengthy report on "The Church and Modern Industry" which clearly stated the church's responsibility for extending and applying "the principles of the new social order." This report also included a statement which virtually incorporated the Social Creed of the Methodists, including its bold assertion of the rights and objectives of the laboring man.[14] A Commission on the Church and Social Service was also established, with the liberal Presbyterian leader, Charles Stelzle, as "voluntary" secretary. One of its first tasks was an investigation of the Bethlehem steel strike in 1910. In its report it condemned both the twelve-hour day and the seven-day week as "a disgrace to civilization," chiding ministers, as well as Christians generally, for aloofness from labor's problems and aims. The Federal Council thus began very early to establish a tradition of outspoken liberal advocacy which would survive both the World War and the "normalcy" which followed. Genuine ecumenical aspirations went into its founding and continued to inform many of its actions, but there is no denying the statement of its veteran general secretary in 1933 that throughout its existence the Federal

14. Many years later the last surviving delegate to that meeting described the mood in which this report was adopted: "Most vivid in my memory is our singing of Frank Mason North's hymn 'Where Cross the Crowded Ways of Life' after the presentation of his report. Most of us had tears running down our cheeks" (Samuel McCrea Cavert, *The American Churches in the Ecumenical Movement, 1900–1968*, p. 56).

Council's animating force had "come from men who were wrestling with the practical tasks of the churches in what was becoming a hostile or increasingly unaccommodating social order." [15]

In the Federal Council social Christianity finally won its place and gained a platform in American Protestantism. Yet because the council was founded through the efforts of men committed to the Social Gospel, it failed to become an authentic voice of Protestants. Underlying this circumstance was the hard fact that most American Protestants were conservative evangelicals who, despite massive provocations to change, strove chiefly to maintain the faith and practice of yore. They regarded the Social Gospel and the Federal Council as dangerous enemies.

On the other hand, the basic political thrust of the Social Gospel was by no means radical. In 1912, for example, its adherents probably avoided the Socialist Debs overwhelmingly, splitting their vote between Wilson and Roosevelt. And therein lies the essential fact: they supported the liberal impulses of the times. One might even revise D. C. Somervell's *mot,* and refer to the Social Gospelers as "the praying wing of Progressivism." To assert this parallel between the two movements, however, accentuates rather than diminishes the movement's significance. A major development of the period was the growing awareness that social change demanded new forms of social action and new conceptions of government. The Square Deal and New Freedom alike betoken the nation's shift. In the reinterpretation of old social orthodoxies and in the storming of old conservative bastions, the Social Gospel movement simply took churchgoing America as its field of action and sought to convert the self-oriented Christian consciousness into one that was neighbor-oriented.[16] In reaching this wide and influential audience the movement played an important national role.

15. Charles S. Macfarland, *Christian Unity in Practice and Prophecy* (New York: Macmillan Co., 1933), p. 53. The social emphasis of the Federal Council was greatly heightened by the fact that other cooperative concerns of the churches were at that time still being dealt with through other agencies such as the Foreign Missions Conference (1907) and the Home Missions Council (1908).

16. Rauschenbusch stated the matter tersely: "The social movement is the most important ethical and spiritual movement in the modern world, and the social gospel is the response of the Christian consciousness to it. Therefore it had to be" (*A Theology for the Social Gospel,* pp. 4–5).

48

DISSENT AND REACTION IN PROTESTANTISM

American evangelical Protestantism was extraordinarily well adapted to the popular ideals and patterns of American life. Patriotism, manifest destiny, Anglo-Saxon self-confidence, the common man's social and economic aspirations, peaceful community life, the Declaration of Independence, and the Constitution—all were accommodated and supported in its capacious system of beliefs. During the later nineteenth century, however, at least five religious groups were left unsatisfied by this mainstream tradition, and some were openly hostile.

Most obvious were those like Robert Ingersoll, Henry George, Edward Bellamy, Francis E. Abbot, and Clarence Darrow, who left the church despite their sometimes strong religious interests, becoming outspoken advocates of agnosticism, socialism, free religion, or at least total disestablishment. More moderate but similarly perturbed were the liberals and Social Gospelers, who sought to adapt Christian faith and practice to more urgent modern needs. A third group included those whose ethnic background or particular claims (or both) were not part of the old Protestant mainstream. Mormons, Christian Scientists, Mennonites, Unitarians, and other divergent movements belong in this category, but it consisted chiefly of Negroes, Jews, Roman Catholics, Lutherans, and a few other large communions that consciously resisted wholesale assimilation or were refused the opportunity. The fourth group was a vast interdenominational movement of those who protested against innovation in religion. Most of its adherents were troubled by the decline of the old-time religion with its accent on conversion; but their bonds were chiefly doctrinal. Whether rich or poor, educated or illiterate, rural or urban, Baptist or Presbyterian, they were troubled by the advance of theological liberalism and the passing of Puritan moralism. Fundamentalism is a name for the movement which its own leaders adopted and used.

The fifth and final group effected a more distinct separation from mainstream Protestantism than most Fundamentalists sought. A desire for a rebirth of life in the Spirit often led its adherents to schism and sectarian withdrawal. Its chief doctrinal concern was sanctification, and the "gathered" communities which it founded were Holiness or, if more radical in their innovations, Pentecostal churches. Finding its adherents chiefly among the disinherited and the uneducated, this movement was primarily a protest against birthright church membership and a Protestantism that had settled for a religion of conformity, middle-class respectability, and self-improvement. Since the Wesleyan emphasis on Christian perfection was very prominent in its teaching, the Methodist church was deeply involved in the attendant strife. Many of these sectarians, however, came to share the Fundamentalist's concern for biblical inerrancy, and Christ's Second Coming often loomed large in their thought.

All of these groups and movements have been considered elsewhere in this history, but the present chapter is chiefly concerned with the development of the latter two, which are such distinctive forms of evangelicalism that most Europeans regard them, along with baseball and wild-west movies, as American creations. Both of these movements are, in one sense of the term, conservative, yet they share a kind of radicalism that is unmistakably new. They arose in part because historical relativism and positivistic science threatened the heretofore unchallenged certainties of Scripture and dogma, and in part because materialism and religious indifference were infecting society as a whole. Popular attitudes were changing; social and ecclesiastical structures were being transformed; many old landmarks of church life were passing away. Equally irritating to them was the assertion of liberal theologians that orthodoxy itself could be "progressive." Yet the new trends affected much more than doctrine: just as lace, jewelry, and cosmetics were enticing the ladies, simplicity in the churches was yielding to organs, ornate furniture, and comfortable pews, while the passion for vital Christian experience of sin and salvation was giving way to secular optimism. Even the clergy seemed vulnerable to the "inner revolution" of the Gilded Age.[1]

In charting the response to this new ethos, we begin at the most popular pole, where laymen who had almost no contact with the history of ideas rose up almost spontaneously against the prevailing religious ways and identified them with the great apostasy foretold in Scripture. Arthur T. Pierson in 1900

1. See Thomas C. Cochran, *The Inner Revolution*, chap. 1.

had no doubt that this was *the* culminating impulse among the evangelical "forward movements of the last half century." He described in detail "a general consensus of opinion that we are now on the threshold of that crisis, unparalleled in the history of the Church and the world, concerning which Christ bade us to 'watch and pray.' "[2]

RADICAL ADVENTISM

In the ensuing revival of millennialism the old Adventist bodies grew apace. The Bible was searched with renewed intensity for signs of the times; and champions of many new readings of "prophecy" arose. But of all the new chiliastic movements, the most successful and certainly the most publicized in subsequent years was the Jehovah's Witnesses. In its early years, the group embodied a vehement, thoroughgoing protest against the prevailing order. The bold, even lawbreaking, "publishers" of its message proclaimed that Satan's three great allies were false teachings in the so-called churches, the tyrannies of human governments, and the oppressions of business. They also attacked the pretensions of orthodox Christianity and questioned its two most central doctrines, the deity of Christ and the depravity of man. They appealed to the poor, outraged middle-class communities by violating their Sabbath quiet laws, and shocked "human governments" by refusing pledges, salutes, and military service to the devil's cohort.[3]

The founder of this movement (it is expressly not a "church") was Charles Taze Russell (1852–1916), a haberdasher from Allegheny, Pennsylvania, whose independent Bible studies led first to highly successful preaching, then, about 1872, to the organization of his followers. The intricacies of his interpretation of prophecy cannot be given here; but its central point was that the Millennial Dawn had come. The Second Advent had already occurred (in 1874) and the end of all things was slated for 1914; hence the famous slogan of the early Russellites: "Millions now living will never die." But Russell did die in 1916, and his successor, Joseph F. Rutherford, was not only less specific in his dating of the Last Days, but more effective as an organizer and propagandist. After his death in 1942, Nathan H. Knorr became president, and under his leadership the Witnesses' immense publishing enterprises, missionary training schools, and evangelism programs became still more efficient and farflung. By 1965 the Watchtower Bible and Tract

2. Arthur T. Pierson, *Forward Movements of the Last Half-Century* (New York, Funk and Wagnalls Co., 1900), p. 409.

3. Between 1940 and 1943 the persistent refusal of Jehovah's Witnesses to perform patriotic rites brought three important civil liberties cases to the Supreme Court. In 1943 the Court upheld their right to such refusal.

Society, with headquarters in Brooklyn, counted over a million "publishers" of its message in nearly every country of the world, more than three hundred thousand of them in the United States. Yet because of their exclusivism and proselytizing tactics, as well as their doctrinal departures on the Trinity and the means of salvation, Protestants generally have denied them fellowship.

THE RISE OF DISPENSATIONAL PREMILLENNIALISM

While highly individualistic adventist schemes of this sort were advancing at an unabashedly popular level, another similar movement of far more significance to the major church bodies was clarifying its testimony and more quietly gathering adherents. Several historians, in fact, would virtually *define* Fundamentalism as the creation of an interdenominational group of evangelical ministers, predominantly Presbyterian and Baptist, who after 1876 convened a series of annual meetings for Bible study, and who later organized two widely publicized Prophecy Conferences: in 1878 at Holy Trinity Episcopal Church in New York, and in 1886 at Farwell Hall in Chicago. The leaders of this group also met for fellowship and study at the annual Niagara Bible Conferences (so named for their most frequent place of meeting).

Animating this new impulse was a two-fold conviction that the whole Christian world, including the United States and Canada, was falling into apostasy and heresy so deeply and so decisively that it could only mean the approach of the Last Days; and that, therefore, nothing was more direly needed than preaching of the hard facts drawn from God's Word. The body of doctrine on which these men gradually converged, however, was more than "the precious doctrine of Christ's second personal appearing." They searched out God's whole "pattern for the ages," and gradually, a distinct system of dispensational premillennialism unified this intense "bible study" movement and informed its conferences.

The idea of successive divine dispensations is, of course, immemorial, being implicit in the very terms Old and New Testament. The Swiss Reformer Heinrich Bullinger developed the idea of God's dealing with man through successive covenants, as did the Anglo-American Puritans and the great Dutch theologian of the covenants, Johannes Cocceius. But the modern form of this system, especially the radical separation of the present "age of the church" from the coming "Kingdom," had its effective origin in the teachings of John Nelson Darby (1800–82).

Darby was born in London and educated in Ireland for the bar, but instead he became a priest in the (Anglican) Church of Ireland in 1825. He soon became deeply distressed by political interference in ecclesiastical affairs. Yet finding the contention-ridden Dissenting churches no better than established Anglicanism, he became convinced of the "ruin of the church." By 1828 he had joined the Plymouth Brethren, and he soon became the foremost promoter of this new movement, traveling incessantly throughout Europe, calling men to separate from ecclesiastical "systems" and worldly pretensions and to carry on in simplicity while awaiting Christ's secret return. Darby believed that Christ would rescue all true Christians before the Tribulation soon to befall the earth, including apostate Christendom, just prior to His Coming in glory to establish His Israelitish Millennial Kingdom. Gradually he developed a periodization of all time and declared a radical distinction between the future of Israel and that of the Church. This overall scheme became known as dispensationalism.

Disagreements over this scheme and other matters split the Brethren in 1849 into the Open and Exclusive branches, the latter and much larger branch led unofficially by Darby. Many Brethren, as well as their writings, made their way to North America; and Darby himself joined them on seven different occasions between 1862 and 1876. Relatively few converts were won to Exclusive Brethrenism, but many Protestants, to Darby's consternation, accepted dispensationalism or parts of it while remaining within their denominations.[4] Very soon, moreover, various American dispensationalists began to elaborate and "improve" upon Darby's never very precisely defined scheme. Of special importance in this effort was James H. Brookes (1830–97), a Presbyterian minister in Saint Louis who was under strong Plymouth Brethren influence even before he became the leading force in the Niagara Conferences, and who edited a widely read dispensationalist magazine. Dwight L. Moody was also significantly impressed by Brethren teachings, and through him and others many dispensationalist notions (if not the complete system) persistently appeared in the Student Volunteer and Laymen's Missionary movements. Yet nowhere did Darbyism fall on more fertile ground than when it reached Cyrus Ingerson Scofield.

Scofield (1843–1921) was born of Episcopal parents in rural Michigan, but reared in Tennessee where he served in the Confederate army. Entering the legal profession in Kansas after the war, he acted for a time as United States attorney in that state, but later moved his practice to Saint Louis. Here he

4. In 1964 the United States had eight groups of Plymouth Brethren, identified by as many numerals and differentiated chiefly by their principles of fellowship within an otherwise commonly held body of beliefs. Plymouth Brethren 2, the largest group, claimed 15,000 of the total membership of 33,250.

experienced a religious conversion in 1879, became a pupil of James H. Brookes, and soon entered the ministry. In 1882 Scofield accepted a call to a small Congregational church in Dallas, Texas, where he served until 1907, except for eight years (1895–1902) at the "Moody Church" in East Northfield, Massachusetts. After 1907 he propagated his scheme of dispensations and covenants by lecturing and through his Correspondence Bible School (which after his death continued as the Dallas Theological Seminary). The true monument to his lifelong efforts, however, is the Scofield Reference Bible, first published in 1909, but further amplified with the aid of various associates in 1919. For over half a century this Bible, with its explanations and annotations, has been a faithfully used resource of conservative Sunday school teachers, preachers, and churchgoers. It expounded the normative form of American dispensationalism, and for millions of people in diverse denominations its dogmatically phrased annotations became an indispensable guide to God's Word. In its time, few religious books equaled its influence, and the publication in 1966 of a new edition, revised by a committee of sympathetic dispensationalists, gave the book an extended term of influence.

At the heart of the matter, for Scofield as for rival interpreters, were two major themes: a "pattern for the ages" consisting of successive dispensations (usually seven in number, with the Millennium being the "Great Sabbath") and a radical distinction between Jews and Christians. Scofield understood these dispensations to be marked by, but not identical with, God's successive covenants:

1. *Innocency:* the Edenic covenant with Adam before the Fall
2. *Conscience:* the Adamic covenant, after man's expulsion from the Garden
3. *Human Government:* the Noahic covenant, after the Deluge
4. *Promise:* the Abrahamic covenant with God's chosen, Israel alone; all other peoples remaining under Human Government
5. *Law:* the Mosaic covenant with Israel, extending through the ministry of Jesus to the Jews, until the crucifixion in which Jew and Gentile both participate
6. *Grace:* the covenant of grace in and through Christ, to Jews and Gentiles individually until Christ's Second Coming
7. *The Fullness of Time, or the Kingdom:* the Millennium when Christ shall restore the Davidic monarchy of Israel and rule for a thousand years.

Dispensationalist literature is complex and generalizations are risky, yet the movement's distinctiveness seems to arise in part from its dual insistence on strict inerrancy and a unitary view of the Bible. Hence both Old and New Testament apocalyptic texts (especially Daniel and Revelation) are interpreted as parts of one divine plan, with the result that Old Testament ideas on the course of history play a dominant role. This is accompanied by a clear distinction between God's plans for Israel and for the Church, at least this side of eternity. The more common view has seen the Church as a new Israel, in which case New Testament eschatological ideas become dominant. On its own premises dispensationalist exegesis is difficult to assail. In this light one may see why the controversies were and are heated.

Dispensationalism, however, was much more than a partitioning of history, for its real appeal depended on its doctrinal foundations. In the first place it insisted undeviatingly on the absolute verbal inerrancy of the Bible as the "inscripturated" Word of the unchanging eternal God; every word and phrase was deemed capable of revealing not merely data for the historian and philologist, but divine truth. Its extensive use of typology, its commitment to numerology, and its dependence on highly debatable (not to say fanciful) interpretations of some obscure apocalyptic passages have led many to insist that its interpretation is anything but literal. Yet its repudiation of historical criticism was well-nigh total, except insofar as it was driven to textual problems in the original languages. During the nineteenth century it took little or no cognizance of geological or astronomic calculations, retained Archbishop Ussher's old dating of the Creation around 4000 B.C., and therefore placed the beginning of the seventh millennium around A.D. 2000.

The theological context of dispensationalism tended to be markedly Reformed or "Calvinistic." Methodists, for example, with their strong commitment to Arminian theology, found the atmosphere unappealing even though dispensationalists affirmed the characteristic American evangelical moral code and placed heavy emphasis on the experience of conversion. In a more general sense, however, this new system of prophecy aroused strongest resistance among American Protestants by denying what most evangelicals and all liberals firmly believed—that the Kingdom of God would come as part of the historical process. They could not accept the dispensationalist claim that all Christian history was a kind of meaningless "parenthesis" between the setting aside of the Jews and the restoration of the Davidic Kingdom. This claim aroused violent reactions because it provided a rationale for destructive attitudes and encouraged secession from existing denominations. Especially objectionable was the tendency of dispensationalists to look for the Antichrist among the "apostate churches" of this "present age."

As dispensationalist teachings developed, each system had many refined qualifications to meet as many equally refined objections, with the result that a whole new theological vocabulary came into being. This terminology, though alien to many deeply versed Christians, became the mark of a large band of Fundamentalist advocates, carrying with it many conceptions that earlier conservatives had never heard of. To many denominational traditionalists the new conceptions, far from being "fundamentals," were fundamental heresies. Name calling did not stop infiltration, however, and in 1927 the president of Princeton posed a question in his official report that was anything but merely rhetorical: "Shall Princeton Seminary . . . be permitted to swing off to the extreme right wing so as to become an interdenominational Seminary for Bible School–premillennial–succession fundamentalism?" This question leads us to consider the third level of Fundamentalist unrest, where Princeton Seminary played a leading role for over a century.

Presbyterianism and the Princeton Theology

Dispensational premillennialism was a vital factor in giving Fundamentalism a measure of interdenominational cohesion and esprit. It also gave a common body of theory to the many Bible study institutes which sprang up in every part of the country as training schools for missionaries and evangelists.[5] But the main forces of American conservatism did not believe that the Christian Church was a parenthesis. Indeed because they loved their denominations—often unduly—and wished to preserve them from liberal inroads, their resort was not in new schemes of scriptural interpretation but

5. The first Bible college—later named the Nyack [New York] Missionary College—in the United States was founded in New York City in 1882 by A. B. Simpson, a former Presbyterian who in 1881 had founded the Christian and Missionary Alliance for the purpose of extending missionary work at home and abroad. (The Alliance has since then virtually become a denomination, with a strong Pentecostal tendency, encompassing more than a thousand churches in North America and a still larger constituency abroad.) A more influential school, however, was the Moody Bible Institute, which accepted its first students in 1889 under the auspices of the Chicago Evangelization Society, thus realizing a dream of Moody and Emma Dryer, who had operated a school of "Bible work" in the Chicago slums for sixteen years. The general idea of preparing "gapmen" to fill the breach between the laboring poor and the organized church gripped Moody during his revival activity in England. Ignoring charges that he was competing with seminaries and the professional clergy, Moody set out to "fit laymen" for the "practical work" of "learning how to reach the masses" (see James F. Findlay, Jr., *Dwight L. Moody: American Evangelist, 1837–1899*).

The Bible Institute of Los Angeles was founded in 1907 under R. A. Torrey (1865–1928), who had been the first head of the Moody school. Many other more strictly denominational schools were also established, so that by 1961 the number of Bible institutes and colleges had swelled to 194 in the United States and 54 more in Canada. In 1947 an accrediting association was formed, and by 1960 half of their number were degree-conferring colleges. About two-thirds of the institutions are denominational, the Churches of Christ and the Baptists controlling about two-thirds of these. In all, about twenty-five thousand day students and ten thousand others were enrolled in 1960. They provide nearly all the ministers for various small conservative denominations and many for the larger ones, and are a powerful factor in sustaining a Fundamentalist constituency in American and Canadian Protestantism (see S. A. Witmer, *The Bible College Story: Education with Dimension*).

in shoring up old schemes; not in new doctrines, but in the official confessions and the writings of their own church Fathers.

The resultant Fundamentalist controversy occurred to a degree in all churches, though it was minor where liberalism was weak or nonexistent (Southern Baptist) or predominant (Congregational), or where doctrinal concerns had always been secondary (Methodist). A tripartite division in the Episcopal church—among high, low, and broad churchmen—reached schism-producing levels of acrimony in this period, but led finally to the acceptance of a live-and-let-live policy, whereby dioceses or parishes could move toward any of the prevailing options.[6] Lutherans were preoccupied with their own special problems, though by no means in the isolation often ascribed to them. In some denominations the intellectual life had been so neglected by conservatives that the need for a new apologetic was very tardily recognized. When they did awaken, moreover, they discovered that their seminaries and great urban pulpits were in the hands of the enemy. It is this total circumstance that made Princeton Theological Seminary so important—not only for Presbyterianism, but for all the denominations that honored the Reformed tradition, and even for some that did not.

The centrality of Princeton and the Presbyterians was, of course, not accidental. Presbyterians were widely dispersed in the nation and often socially prominent. They also had a long tradition of learning and theological concern. Very soon after its founding in 1812, therefore, Princeton Seminary's leadership was recognized by conservatives in all denominations (even among conservative Unitarians when Transcendentalism arose in their midst). The Old School–New School controversy strengthened this reputation, and during the troubled decades which followed the reunion of northern Presbyterianism in 1869, Princeton's power increased as the former New School seminaries drifted away or closed their doors.[7] The Princeton Theology, expounded for a half-century by Charles Hodge and published in systematic form both by him and by his son, won acceptance far and wide as the strength and stay of embattled conservatism. And during the 1880s this dogmatic tradition gained further support from Benjamin B. Warfield (1851–1921), who brought great theological and historical prowess to the

6. A small schism did disrupt the Episcopal church in 1873 when Bishop D. G. Cummins of Kentucky led out an evangelical faction that organized the Reformed Episcopal Church, which held to conservative evangelical positions. More important was the General Convention's 1874 decision for "comprehensiveness" precipitated by James DeKoven, an Anglo-Catholic who insisted that he either be tried for heresy or be left unrestricted by church regulations.

7. Union Theological Seminary (New York) declared its independence from Presbyterian control in 1892. Auburn Seminary joined forces with Union in 1939. In 1932 Lane Seminary merged with the Old School seminary which was founded in 1829 in Chicago with endowment from Cyrus McCormick.

defense of the Reformed tradition, and a new rigidity into the doctrine of scriptural inspiration. Each of Warfield's great interests, Reformed doctrine and biblical inerrancy, provided a major theme in the "Fundamentalist Controversy" that raged within Northern Presbyterianism.

The always latent doctrinal question had been sharply posed as early as 1874, when Dr. David Swing, a prominent Chicago minister, despite acquittal by presbytery, left the denomination rather than face further judicial proceedings over his view that "a creed is only the highest wisdom of a particular time and place." In 1892 the General Assembly responded to a widespread demand for revisions of the Westminster Confession. The results were far short of those sought by the church's liberals, but they revealed that Presbyterians were approaching the American Protestant norm on double predestination and the salvation of infants. In order to accommodate Cumberland Presbyterian views in the merger of 1906, the church went still farther in this direction, taking an Arminian position on man's free will—a traumatic event for many Old School thinkers.

In questions pertaining to biblical inerrancy, on the other hand, the denominational majority was intransigent. During the 1880s the General Assembly on several occasions affirmed the strictest possible views, and in 1892 it issued the famous Portland Deliverance, which made official the Hodge-Warfield doctrine that the "inspired Word, as it came from God [that is, in the 'original autograph'], is without error." This position was reaffirmed in 1893, 1894, 1899, and then most decisively in 1910, when the assembly made it the keystone of the Five Points that were to be regarded as "essential and necessary" doctrines of the church. The other four points in this formulation—which with slight variations would ring through many Fundamentalist testimonies during subsequent years—affirmed the Virgin Birth, the "Satisfaction Theory" of the Atonement, the Resurrection "with the same body," and the miracles of Jesus.

Nor were these empty gestures. The deliverances of the 1890s were all directly connected with a series of sensational heresy cases which resulted in the extrusion of three of the country's very greatest Christian scholars from the Presbyterian ministry for neglecting to take a strict "doctrine" of inerrancy as the starting point for their biblical scholarship. Two were Old Testament men, C. A. Briggs of Union Seminary (New York) and Henry Preserved Smith of Lane Seminary, while the other, A. C. McGiffert, also of Union Seminary, was an historian of the early Church who dealt with the New Testament literature. Each of them faced the issue head-on, Briggs most vigorously; but the preponderance of strict conservatives in the General Assembly was overwhelming. The first two were dismissed for heresy in 1893 and 1894; McGiffert reluctantly resigned from the Presbyterian ministry in 1900. Fundamentalism reigned in the denomination, and it would continue to reign, at least officially, for another quarter-century, though both scholarly and social pressures tended to modify the working theology of many ministers and church leaders.

A few men boldly persisted in proclaiming their liberalism, Henry Van Dyke (1852–1933) being especially outspoken. As a poet, short story writer, and literary critic, he is remembered as a very proper Victorian, but he was also a talented preacher, theologian, and controversialist. The son of an Old School minister and sometime moderator of the Presbyterian church, he was educated at Princeton College and Seminary. Up to that time he was a conservative, and very critical of the "vituperative theology" emanating from Germany. But a year in Berlin and studies under Isaak Dorner moderated his views. After becoming minister of the Brick Church on Fifth Avenue, he was a leader of the movement to revise the Westminster Confession. As for the famous Five Points, he declared one to be nonessential and the other four unbiblical; and he defended his judgment that the orthodox position on "prenatal election" was a "horrible" doctrine. In two widely read books, *The Gospel in an Age of Doubt* (1896) and *The Gospel in a World of Sin* (1899), he gave eloquent voice to a mediating theology that was remarkably attuned to the mood of the age, yet warmly evangelical. The popularity of his works demonstrated that he was not a solitary prophet. His literary fame and his position after 1899 as a professor of English at Princeton University rather than as a professor of theology in a seminary saved him from heresy proceedings.

Announcing the Fundamentals

The desire to arrest the drift from old moorings led to one other major event in the history of pre–World War Fundamentalism—an event, some would say, that gave the movement its name. Two wealthy Los Angeles laymen, Lyman and Milton Stewart, desiring to advance the cause of true religion in some decisive way, created a $250,000 fund in order that "every pastor, evangelist, minister, theological professor, theological student, Sunday school superintendent, YMCA and YWCA secretary in the English speaking world" might be given twelve substantial booklets in which the theological issues of the day would be addressed. These essays were to be written by a distinguished group of conservative Protestant theologians from Great Britain, Canada, and the United States. With Amzi C. Dixon, Louis Meyer, and Reuben A. Torrey serving in turn as editors, *The Fundamentals* began appearing in 1910, and before the twelfth volume had been issued three or so years later, a total of three million booklets had been distributed.

The books had at least two important effects. First of all, by enlisting the efforts of eminent spokesmen such as James Orr of Scotland, Bishop H. C. G. Moule of Durham (England), Benjamin Warfield of Princeton Seminary, and President E. Y. Mullins of the Southern Baptist Seminary in Louisville, a great interdenominational witness was achieved. It is not inappropriate to say that the Fundamentalist *movement* was launched. This was done, moreover, with dignity, breadth of subject matter, rhetorical moderation, obvious conviction, and considerable intellectual power. If they had appeared in routine periodicals, few if any of these four-score articles would have been long remembered; yet historians of Fundamentalism have deprecated them unduly. The conservative case was firmly and honorably made. The other important feature of the project was the way in which it created a kind of *entente* between two fairly incompatible conservative elements: a denominational, seminary-oriented group, and a Bible institute group with strong premillennial and dispensational interests. Since dispensationalism was highly esteemed by both the patrons and editors of the project, its message was prominent in every booklet, with R. A. Torrey, A. T. Pierson, Arno C. Gaebelein and even Scofield himself contributing one or more essays. Between these two groups there was a deep gulf, just as a cleavage of another sort and vintage separated Baptist and Anglican authors. Despite clashing interpretations of countless scriptural passages, however, the authors succeeded in forging an uneasy alliance to defend the doctrine of the Bible's literal inerrancy. The impact of this project, unfortunately, was interrupted in 1914 by a man-made Armageddon, but when peace had been established among nations, theological and ecclesiastical warfare would be resumed with even greater vehemence.

THE HOLINESS REVIVAL

Because certitude and peace are found in diverse ways, religious unrest takes many forms. In the premillennial movement Methodists were notable for their rarity. In the great surge of interest in Christian perfection and complete sanctification, on the other hand, the Wesleyan legacy was primary.[8] During the Gilded Age the Methodist churches, North and South,

8. John Wesley had insisted that the doctrine of Christian perfection was "the grand depositum which God has lodged with the people called Methodist." He set forth his views most definitively in the fourth edition of his *Plain Account of Christian Perfection* (1777) which he then incorporated in the *Discipline* of 1789. Believing that Christ died for all and that the doctrines of election and predestination distorted the faith, Wesley distinguished between the experiences of justification and sanctification, insisted that "justified persons are to go on unto perfection," and felt confident that some Christians, through grace, would experience perfection or complete sanctification in this life as a culminating event in their spiritual development (see John L. Peters, *Christian Perfection and American Methodism,*

were swept by a great Holiness Revival, and the preaching and practice of this doctrine led to religious manifestations which most Methodist leaders tended to discountenance as disruptive and unseemly. Repression, in turn, led to defiance of discipline and then to outright secession. What had first been jubilantly welcomed as a Pentecostal blessing turned Methodism into a battleground; and out of the ensuing conflict a new denominational impulse emerged, much as Methodism itself (and before that, Puritanism) had arisen in the Church of England. As this newly released evangelical energy extended into foreign missions, its impact became literally worldwide. By World War I, however, the new current had itself divided into two distinguishable branches, one relatively moderate, the other extreme. Both branches prospered at cultural levels that hid their significance from the major middle-class churches, but their success nevertheless merits close historical scrutiny.

The first perfectionist secession, the Wesleyan Methodist Church of 1843, had been a by-product of the antislavery crusade, and it had been followed by the Free Methodist Church in 1859–60. But these were relatively minor incidents in the great surge of perfectionism that swept almost every denomination after 1835 and figured prominently in the great revival of 1858. Soon after the war, when the momentum of this movement was renewed, Methodists, North and South, were in the vanguard as before. A distinct "Holiness Revival" can be traced from the celebrations of Methodism's American centenary in 1866, and a year later a "Holiness camp meeting" at Vineland, New Jersey, was attended by such stirring results that the National Camp Meeting Association for the Promotion of Holiness was organized. Year after year its work was extended, and its conquests in Methodist circles were impressive. Many bishops rallied to the cause, as did the first presidents of the newly founded Drew Seminary and Syracuse University.

In a sense, however, the successes were too great, for many nondenominational Holiness associations were formed, and in these circles a separatistic "come-outer" movement began to arise during the 1880s. By 1888 there were 206 full-time Holiness evangelists in the field, though most of them lacked regular assignments from ecclesiastical superiors. An independent press was also flourishing, and many autonomous ministers were gathering independent congregations in all parts of the country, some in the rural South, most

p. 33 et passim. See also pp. 324–26 above). The basic notion of going on to perfection was, of course, not new with Wesley. It was fundamental to Eastern Orthodox and Roman Catholic ethics, very prominent in most monastic movements, and in another form, a major theme in William Ellery Channing's Unitarianism. What most distinguished Wesley's version was his stress on two distinct works of grace and two equally distinct and separated personal experiences; both regeneration and sanctification were climactic events.

of them in the northern and far-western cities. Especially as they worked among the urban poor, these ministers discovered, as had the Salvation Army long before, that the needs of converts virtually required the organization of independent churches.

In the face of these trends Methodist bishops began to grow apprehensive. Theologians meanwhile became alarmed by the degree to which faith-healing, premillennialism, and other radical conceptions were gaining ground wherever Holiness flourished. Perhaps the most basic aspect of the antagonism, however, was the gradual drift of Methodist church practice away from the old Wesleyan landmarks and toward the sedate forms of middle-class Protestantism. The climax came in 1893 and 1894, when the truce between the Methodist churches and the Holiness associations ended. Secessions and expulsions became common during the turn of century decades. Since perfectionists are almost by definition censorious in their judgments of the worldliness of others, subschisms continued to occur.

Even as a disintegrative tendency accelerated, the need for coordination and fellowship led to new kinds of reintegration within the Holiness movement. Gradually an ordering process began to dissipate the chaos of competing evangelists, independent congregations, and loosely organized nondenominational associations. The result was by no means a single denomination, but two tendencies did become noticeable: the moderate one which the term "Holiness" designates, and a more extreme alternative, which adopted the name "Pentecostal." The Church of the Nazarene best exemplifies the more moderate tendency; the Assemblies of God the more radical. Each is also the largest of its type.

The Church of the Nazarene came into existence in 1908 at Pilot Point, Texas, when two predominantly urban northern groups, the Association of Pentecostal Churches, whose center of gravity was New York and New England, and the Church of the Nazarene which stemmed from the work of Phineas F. Bresee [9] in Southern California, joined forces with the Holiness

9. Bresee (1838–1915) also became the new church's first general superintendent. His career was remarkable. Born in western New York, he grew up in Iowa, where he was "converted" in 1856. A year later he was assisting on a Methodist circuit, and in 1861 was ordained an elder. When only twenty-three he was assigned to a fine church in Des Moines and made an editor of the Iowa Conference paper. He was respected as a leader of his church in the area. During the winter of 1866–67 Bresee experienced complete sanctification. Moving to California in 1883, he became minister of the First Methodist Church in Los Angeles, as well as a presiding elder and a prominent civic leader. With the arrival of a hostile bishop, however, the Holiness movement ran into determined opposition, and in 1895 Bresee left the Methodist church rather than abandon a mission to the poor which he was conducting. This very mission could probably be regarded as the nucleus of the later Church of the Nazarene (see T. L. Smith's excellent history *Called Unto Holiness*).

Church of Christ, a consolidation of rural southern congregations stretching from Tennessee to Texas. The components of this new church were rather diverse, for each was itself a federation with a complex history. Yet the action taken at Pilot Point dramatized the uniformity of conviction within this widespread Holiness Revival. It also revealed a trend away from interdenominational associations toward a more denominational understanding of the movement, and away from extreme congregationalism toward a connectional conception of the church that owed much to Methodism.

Future years brought mergers with other equally complex groups. Nazarene evangelism, meanwhile, won many converts. Yet the church retained a character of its own. It gloried in the grace that was free to all men, and especially in the "second blessing" that came to the sanctified. On this score there is much truth to their claim that they adhere to Wesley's "grand depositum" with greater fidelity than mainline Methodism. In polity, the church reflects the overwhelming preponderance of Methodists among its early leadership, though it has introduced a larger measure of congregational autonomy and democratic government. From the first it has been a church of simple dedicated people who were eager to carry the gospel and a strict perfectionist code of morals to the strata of society which the older denominations were unable to reach despite the valiant efforts of their home mission boards. In theology they were, of course, conservative; and they were suspicious of higher learning. Nearly all of them were in a technical sense Fundamentalists, yet their passions and goals were oriented not so much toward doctrinal purity as toward true Christian experience. Social mobility would affect them as it did all other American groups; and by 1969, when they numbered 350,882 members, their primitive fervor was considerably attenuated and their interest in education much increased. Some Nazarenes were even thinking of reunion with the church that had treated perfectionism with such hostility in the 1890s. In this respect the Church of the Nazarene is a remarkable American instance of a nearly full sectarian cycle.

Pentecostalism and the Assemblies of God

Most Pentecostal churches are, like the Nazarenes, unions of like-minded groups that received their initial impulse from Methodism and the Holiness Revival. Yet their historian does not exaggerate when he states that through this movement "a new element was introduced into the religious life *of the world.*" [10]

Charismatic gifts had, of course, come to many in times past, not least to Saint Paul and the converts he addressed in his epistles. In revivals of all

10. Irwin Winehouse, *The Assemblies of God*, p. 11. Italics mine.

ages in church history, including the Holiness Revival, people had experienced the "latter rain" spoken of by the prophet Joel (2:21–32) and referred to by Saint Peter in the classic Pentecostal passage (Acts 2:1–20). And on 1 January 1901, the gift of the Spirit came to Agnes N. Ozman, a student in Bethel Bible College, recently founded in Topeka, Kansas, by Charles F. Parham, a prominent Holiness evangelist. From this event can be traced a powerful movement which by 1970 was claiming a worldwide membership of over eight million. Soon most of the other Bethel students began to speak languages which they could not understand. A period of quiescence and ridicule followed, but after Parham's gifts of divine healing became known in 1903, the movement spread to various scattered Holiness groups.

In 1906, via Texas, Pentecostalism reached Los Angeles. A great outpouring of the Spirit came to the Azusa Street Mission, which under the leadership of the black minister William J. Seymour became a radiating center of Pentecostalism. From Azusa Street the message was soon carried to all parts of the country. When the news reached North Carolina and the Holiness movement consolidated by A. J. Tomlinson in the area around Cleveland, Tennessee, the result was especially momentous. In 1908 Tomlinson himself received the baptism of the Spirit, whereupon the Pentecostal seed was soon sown in Alabama, Georgia, and Florida.[11] So it went in other directions as well, though it moved chiefly where Holiness movements were prospering, attracting in the process many more non-Methodists, usually Baptists, than had the earlier forms of perfectionism, and planting the seed for much future contention on the issue of connectional as against congregational church polity.

Speaking with tongues is not the only distinctive feature of the churches in this fellowship. A strong belief in divine healing, a distrust of medical care, and an extremely Puritanic code of personal behavior are other marks. From the start, moreover, Pentecostalists were also theological conservatives, and in all phases of the Fundamentalist controversy they took a clear stand for scriptural infallibility. Their Methodist lineage, however, aligned them with Holiness groups in resisting the attempts of more distinctly Reformed denominations to make predestination one of the Fundamentals. They thus added a large militant faction to the Arminian wing of Protestant conservatism. The movement was also deeply marked by dispensational premillen-

11. Of the approximately two hundred religious groups named the Church of God, five have their headquarters in Cleveland, Tennessee, a common origin in A. J. Tomlinson, and a general emphasis on justification by faith, being born again, sanctification, baptism of the Holy Spirit, speaking in tongues, fruitfulness in Christian living, and a strong interest in the premillennial Second Coming of Christ. Forty-four Protestant denominations are attributed to Tomlinson's work.

nialism; from the start it has interpreted the Pentecostal outpouring as a fulfillment of prophecy and a sign of the Last Days. The imminence of Christ's return is therefore believed and taught.

As the movement grew, the need for some kind of coordination became more and more apparent, especially to support missionaries already being sent to foreign lands by local groups. Almost the only persons to have some view of the whole movement, or a large part of it, were the editors of a growing number of periodicals, so it was appropriate that one of these, Eudorus N. Bell, who published *Word and Witness* in Malvern, Arkansas, should initiate organizational measures. In December 1913, Bell issued a call for all "saints who believe in baptism with the Holy Ghost" to meet in April 1914 in Hot Springs, Arkansas, for the purpose of providing means to coordinate and propagate Pentecostalism more effectively.

Three hundred enthusiastic delegates from every region of the country convened at the appointed time, and after three days of devotional services, they displayed remarkable unanimity in adopting a preamble and a statement of organizational purpose and in electing an executive presbytery. This presbytery was first intended to be merely a permanent committee to guide the affairs of autonomous local assemblies which would send delegates to an annual council, but it became the executive agency of a new fellowship, the Assemblies of God. The two leading periodicals were merged and moved to Findlay, Ohio, where within four months they had a joint subscription list numbering twenty-five thousand. A school was also founded, with former editors Bell and J. Russell Flower on the faculty. Bell was also president of the Incorporated General Council, and Flower was its secretary.[12]

By similar processes other Pentecostal organizations were formed, most notably the black movement which also stemmed from the Azusa Street outpouring and attained a membership as large as that of the Assemblies.[13] In 1949, when the Pentecostal Fellowship of North America held its second convention, it could claim eight denominations with a total membership of one million.[14] Two decades later Pentecostalists in the United States numbered over 1.5 million. By this time they had demonstrated an amazing ca-

12. Bell had gone to Stetson College in Florida, then to the Baptist Seminary in Louisville, before going to the University of Chicago Divinity School for his B.D. He was a Baptist minister when he received the baptism of the Spirit in 1908, and a year later he became a Pentecostal minister in Malvern. Flower was Canadian-born but had grown up in Illinois. In 1913, when the Pentecostal movement was confronted by the rapid spread of a "Jesus Only" form of Unitarianism, the Assemblies of God lost 156 ministers, including Eudorus Bell, in a great defection.

13. The place of Pentecostalism in the black churches is considered in chap. 62 below. The Pentecostal awakening is surely an important instance of the direct influence of Afro-American religion on American Christianity.

14. John Thomas Nichol, *Pentecostalism*, p. 217.

pacity for both rural and urban evangelism. Inevitably, the sectarian cycle was also in evidence.[15] They were holding well-organized world conferences, and actively participated in the National Association of Evangelicals and were represented by two small Chilean churches in the World Council of Churches. They had become interested in advanced theological education, and had begun to experience internal dissension because of these accommodationist tendencies. As if to dramatize this trend, Oral Roberts, who rose to national fame as a Pentecostal preacher, healer, and television sensation, had become a Methodist in 1965.

In the later sixties, however, a surprising renewal of charismatic religion would take place—and not only among the usual constituencies but in the very movements and age-groups that were most animated by counter-cultural aims. But this revival is treated below (p. 1086, n. 6) in connection with its broader social context.

The Churches of Christ

Around the turn of the century, when the Holiness and Pentecostal revivals were flourishing, still another expansive form of conservative Protestantism was differentiating itself from its more staid and accommodating parent denomination. The Churches of Christ, which at their request were counted separately in the federal religious census of 1906, were related to the Disciples of Christ much as the Holiness churches were to Methodism. Indeed, they considered themselves the only true restorers of the New Testament Church, and hence the only faithful followers of Thomas and Alexander Campbell, who had inaugurated the Restoration movement a century before.[16]

The state of affairs formally documented by this religious census had been slowly developing for a half-century, with Alexander Campbell's opposition to missionary societies and instrumental music nearly always the ostensible points of contention. Underlying these tensions, however, were economic and social cleavages. Conservatives were most numerous in the poor rural areas of the South where rustic forms of church life remained, and where a piano

15. In a class by itself is the International Church of the Foursquare Gospel founded in 1927 by Aimee Semple McPherson (1890–1944). The declaration of faith professed by its ninety thousand members contains the Pentecostal distinctives, but her flamboyant ministry, her masterful fund-raising capacities, and the $1.5 million Angelus Temple which she built in Los Angeles make it a very atypical denomination. At her death the board of directors conveyed the leadership to her son.

16. In 1809 Thomas Campbell had pointed the road away from sectarianism with his *Declaration and Address.* The leaders of the Cane Ridge revival of 1801 wrote *The Last Will and Testament of the Springfield Presbytery* in 1804; Alexander Campbell preached his *Sermon on the Law* in 1816; and representatives of Stonite and Campbellite parties in the "Christian" movement merged their efforts in 1832.

was a snobbish luxury. They were unspoiled by either middle-class manners or a seminary-educated clergy. In some broad sense these dissenters were Fundamentalists, especially on the question of biblical inerrancy and closely related issues, but for the rest, they were immured behind a Campbellian wall, going their own way without cooperation, consultation, or coordination with anyone but themselves, and as a result, they were relatively insulated from millennialism, perfectionism, and glossolalia. Most of their controversies and doctrinal questions involved points that only other Restorationists could understand.[17] So radically congregational were they, moreover, and so opposed to hierarchies and human creeds, that they could make their secession official only by publishing lists of local churches which were in fellowship—or by a statistic in the Census Report. So it was that literal allegiance to Alexander Campbell's program for transcending Christian division resulted in one of America's most robust examples of rigorous exclusivism.

Neither apartheid nor the refusal to form official missionary agencies, however, prevented the Churches of Christ from expanding. They have proselytized with great earnestness and vigor, while demonstrating sufficient flexibility to keep the allegiance of socially mobile members desiring fine church buildings, good (but noninstrumental) music, graded Sunday schools, church-connected colleges, and well-educated preachers. They have become the most dynamic large denomination in the South, and have developed considerable strength in other sections and abroad.[18]

SUMMARY

No aspect of American church history is more in need of summary and yet so difficult to summarize as the movements of dissent and reaction that occurred between the Civil War and World War I. Even the reasons for the difficulty are obscure, though they surely are related to the differences be-

17. This is not an innocent or hasty assertion. Despite their persistent demand for unity, the Disciples have found it very difficult to participate in ecumenical discussions unless they abandon their "landmarks." This applies with special force to the ultraconservative Churches of Christ. Of the nine critical issues that cause dissension within the Churches of Christ and separate them from other conservative Disciples, few if any have any important place in the controversies of other Christian churches, Catholic or Evangelical (see James DeForest Murch, *Christians Only: A History of the Restoration Movement*).

18. Numbering only 159,688 members in 693 churches in 1906, they had probably exceeded 2 million members in 16,500 churches by 1969. By this time they had spread across the entire land—though the 4 churches in North Dakota must be compared with more than 2,000 in Texas. Four liberal arts colleges began to have an influence on the denomination's intellectual and theological attitudes (see Edwin S. Gaustad, "Churches of Christ in America," in *The Religious Situation: 1969*, ed. Donald R. Cutler, pp. 1013–33).

tween this period of ferment and that which preceded the Civil War. The postwar era lacked the spiritual foundation provided by an aggressive and self-confident Protestant majority against which even Shakers, Mormons, and Oneida perfectionists, not to mention Roman Catholics and Jews, could orient themselves. After 1865 the problems of Reconstruction, urbanization, immigration, natural science, and modern culture destroyed the great evangelical consensus, leaving a situation wherein dissenters were merely angry and frustrated. Increasingly, conservatives and liberals simply lost contact with each other, both culturally and religiously. Social and economic factors also seem to loom larger as divisive forces. Even the patterns of anti-Catholicism reflected this change, in that nontheological factors became predominant.

The older middle-class churches, whether countrified or urban, often exhibited a kind of birthright complacency even when they rejected liberal theology. These staid and predictable church ways alienated many and simply failed to attract others—who then sought religious solace where more earnestness and old-time fervor prevailed. Others reacted directly against theological departures from tradition and sought to reverse the tide of "apostasy" within their own communions or by joining more militant groups. Whether these conflicts, secessions, and new church formations were occasioned by doctrinal or more institutional forms of discontent, they all revealed deep fissures in Protestantism which wartime patrioteering could briefly close over, but which would open again and widen disastrously in the years after World War I.

49

THE "AMERICANISM" CRISIS IN THE CATHOLIC CHURCH

In 1898 a book appeared in Paris with a provocative question in its title, *Father Hecker, Is He a Saint?* The author, Charles Maignen, a Vincentian priest, answered this question with a shrill negative. But his attack was only one element of a great campaign being waged against the perils of "Americanism." The American founder of the Paulists, more than a decade after his death, had become a vital factor in a French ideological conflict which shook the Third Republic down to its hastily constructed foundations. That the matter had still wider implications is suggested by the fact that the imprimatur for this polemic was issued not by the archbishop of Paris, but by Monsignor Alberto Lepidi, master of the Sacred Palace at the papal court in Rome—who was also having an English edition prepared. In the United States, meanwhile, an equally acrimonious controversy was involving the entire Roman Catholic church, from several very prominent archbishops down to many parish priests and laymen. Ultimately it would take a papal encyclical to quiet the international waters; but by that time a major chapter in American church history would have been enacted.

"Americanism" in one or another of its manifold forms has always been a problem for the rest of the world; and many Europeans, both before and since King George III, have wrestled with its mysteries. As noted in earlier chapters, both John Carroll, the first American bishop, and Orestes Brownson reflected the antitraditional impact of American conditions in their proposals for the Roman Catholic church. Father Hecker's special concern for the American problem became a matter for direct papal action. In this sense the "Americanism crisis" has very early origins and a long eventful prehistory.

The climax of this long development occurred in the two last decades of the nineteenth century—decades that were no less critical for Protestants and Jews, and for similar reasons. In addition to a complex of issues more or less peculiar to the Roman Catholic church, the crisis involved many major aspects of the national experience; but the basic circumstance was increasingly rapid growth—in overall size, in ethnic diversity, and in administrative complexity. And behind all was the steady pressure of Catholic immigration and American nativism.

The decade of the 1850s marked a new order of magnitude in the history of American immigration (see table, p. 749 above), and it understandably resulted in the high tide of political Know-Nothingism. During the Civil War, however, American Catholics had loyally identified themselves with the sections in which they lived. The war thus underlined the truth of what the older group of Anglo-American Catholics had always insisted, that membership in the Roman church did not preclude participation in American life and a sharing of the nation's culture. It is very significant that the overt anti-Catholicism of the 1840s and 1850s passed from the American scene, even though many grounds for contention remained.

With the return of peace, the Second Plenary Council held in Baltimore in October 1866 proceeded with the task of unifying the ecclesiastical discipline of the reunited church. The presence of seven archbishops and thirty-eight bishops and the council's recommendations for two metropolitan sees and ten new dioceses testified to the church's rapid growth. The optimism that pervaded this great assembly as well as the sense of identification with the national purposes that it expressed was put to the test three years later, when Pope Pius IX convoked an ecumenical council in the Vatican to deal with the question of papal infallibility. Most of the American bishops regarded further definition of this doctrine to be inopportune, and they made no secret of their opinions during the long deliberations that ensued. Only one American bishop stayed to register his opposition, but they all returned home with a new apologetic burden to bear in democratic America.[1] Their known disposition, moreover, probably had some bearing on the decision of Rome to convoke the Third Plenary Council of the American hierarchy in 1884.

The agenda for this great ecclesiastical assembly was crowded with technical questions having to do with the jurisdiction of bishops, clergy, and religious orders, as well as many matters affecting relations between the Vatican

1. Bishops Edward Fitzgerald of Little Rock, Arkansas, and Luigi Riccio of Cajazzo registered the only two negatives in the final vote on the council's constitution on papal infallibility.

and the American church, such as the procedures for naming or translating bishops, and the kind of supervision of American affairs which the Congregation de Propaganda Fide would continue to carry out. The need for a separate system of parochial schools was also stressed. In response to the pleas of the Americans, Archbishop James Gibbons of Baltimore, rather than a Roman prelate, was named as the apostolic delegate to the council. Also evidencing the fact that the church was not "foreign" were many fervently patriotic statements by those bishops who were most convinced that American circumstances were ideal for the flourishing of the Catholic church. There is little doubt that both the size and the decisions of the Plenary Council made many American prelates feel a need to demonstrate the church's solicitude for the spirit of American democracy

Nor did the growth of the church during the three postwar decades contradict the optimism expressed in 1884. By 1895 the number of dioceses had risen to seventy-three and the number of provinces to fourteen. The Catholic population rose from about 3 million in 1860 to about 7 million in 1880 to an estimated 12.5 million in 1895.[2] While the attendant problems of expansion accumulated, however, the Vatican was beset by many difficulties of its own.

THE EMBATTLED CHURCH OF ROME

Not since the Reformation had the Roman Catholic church been more seriously threatened than it was during the later nineteenth century. In 1870, without even allowing the Vatican council a decent adjournment, the armies of a united Italy, having long since taken possession of the Papal States, entered Rome and stripped the pope of his last vestige of temporal power, leaving him a prisoner of the Vatican until the Concordat of 1929. In 1878 an angry Roman mob impeded the funeral procession of Pope Pius IX and almost succeeded in throwing his bier into the Tiber. In France, meanwhile, the friendly regime of Napoleon III collapsed into the fierce anticlericalism of the Paris Commune, which was in turn followed by the Third Republic, in which the church's legal stake depended on a declining royalist tradition that would finally break down between 1904 and 1907 in the tumults of

2. These estimates are interpreted in Thomas O'Gorman, *A History of the Roman Catholic Church in the United States* ACHS, vol. 9 (New York, 1895), pp. 493–500. The concluding portion of O'Gorman's history on the 1865–95 period is a remarkable instance of the uneasiness that was widespread in the church. He devotes many pages to a defense of the church's modes of jurisdiction and the problems of "foreign" Catholics, but, despite his own involvement in the events of the day, gives no account of the controversies that preoccupied both the American hierarchy and the Vatican.

the Dreyfus affair and a harsh renewal of anticlerical legislation. Bismarck, on the other hand, followed his French victories with a campaign against Roman Catholic power in the newly proclaimed German Empire, while the multinational Austro-Hungarian Empire lumbered on, its rulers treating the church with a kind of cynical utilitarianism, as nationalistic minorities added anticlericalism to their diversified appeals for support. Everywhere in Europe the urban working classes—as Marxist and anarchist advocacy strengthened their self-consciousness—were singling out the church as the keystone of an outmoded social order. Even in Bavaria, where Catholic romantics had made Munich a center of revival, these tendencies were visible. In America, immigration steadily increased ethnic tensions within the church itself, while nativists of assorted hues conducted an anti-Catholic *Kulturkampf* of their own. "Americanism" became a critical issue during the years when the American Protective Association was at the height of its influence.

The American Problem

An institutional crisis usually involves conflict between radically opposed proposals for present and future action. The Roman Catholic Americanism crisis was no exception. The crisis, as we shall see, was a complex of at least a dozen interconnected questions, but it is punctuated by the clash of two opposing groups or factions. Inevitably, the largest was a traditional party that simply assumed Catholicism and the American way of life to be fundamentally at odds. Pope Pius IX with his detailed Syllabus of Errors (1864) had provided support for such a stand, and Leo XIII, surprisingly, would bolster this support in the 1890s. All that conservative Catholics hoped for, therefore, was a kind of mutually advantageous truce between two hostile cultures. Most militant in this regard were the Germans. Strengthened by the immigration of seven hundred thousand of their countrymen between 1865 and 1900, supported by powerful agencies in Europe, and possessing a rich and deep theological tradition, they were strong enough in many areas to be highly self-conscious. Yet at the same time they were a defensive minority in an Irish-dominated church. The Midwest was their stronghold, and Milwaukee, Chicago, and Saint Louis were powerful centers of influence. Polish Catholics tended to be of a similar mind, though they were not numerically strong.[3]

3. Though small in the 1880s, the Polish minority would soon become large. The peak of Polish immigration came in 1912–13 when 175,000 arrived; during and after World War II 100,000 would arrive. Numbering 5 million by 1960, the Polish constituency had joined the Irish, Italian, and German as one of the four largest in the church. It had 500 priests, 7,000 nuns, and supported 585 elementary schools (See Aloysius J. Wycislo, "The Polish Catholic Immigrant," in *Roman Catholicism and the American Way of Life*, ed. Thomas T. McAvoy, pp. 179–87).

Allied with these groups was a large body of conservatives (clearly a majority) among the Irish clergy, who had so long defined themselves by their opposition to Anglo-Saxon culture that anything but the most utilitarian kinds of participation in American life seemed to imply a betrayal of their heritage. Indisputably at the head of this group was Archbishop Michael A. Corrigan (1839–1902), a former professor of dogmatics at Seton Hall (New Jersey) and a stern administrator of the New York archdiocese. Corrigan's constant adviser and supporter was the bishop of his suffragan see in Rochester, Bernard McQuaid (1823–1909), an older former president of Seton Hall whose great cultivation and intelligence did little to moderate either his theology or his ecclesiastical tactics. He was confident and articulate, and his parochial school system and seminary stood as models for the nation.

Among the Americanists four men consistently played leading roles. Chief among them was the archbishop of Baltimore, James Gibbons (1834–1921), after 1886 a cardinal. As the nominal primate of the American church he avoided a stridently partisan role, yet on almost every issue his very powerful influence was exerted in the progressive cause. Far more active was John Ireland (1838–1918), the outspoken and enormously energetic archbishop of Saint Paul. Metropolitan of a vast, rapidly growing midwestern province, he irritated eastern bishops by advertising western opportunities and even by arranging colonization projects with the railroads. His enthusiasm for the American system was boundless; his confidence in the nation's destiny well-nigh absolute. More avidly than any other American prelate, he sensed the advantages of full Roman Catholic participation in American politics and social affairs. He tended to the Republican party, for example, chiefly to prevent the Democrats from taking Catholics for granted. Having been sent to France by Bishop Cretin of Saint Paul for nearly all of his education, he remained a close observer of European affairs and never allowed his Americanism to be narrow or jingoistic. The other two leading Americanist voices were John J. Keane (1839–1918), the bishop of Richmond who became the first rector of Catholic University of America in Washington, D.C., and Monsignor Denis O'Connell (1849–1927), rector of the North American College in Rome, a later rector of Catholic University, and bishop of Richmond. Though occupying less lofty positions in the church, they made innumerable contributions, especially O'Connell, who served as a kind of Americanist agent at the Vatican.

Cardinal Gibbons was born five years after his father emigrated, but the other three Americanist leaders were born in Ireland to families which had felt the force of that island's woe. With deep personal memories of poverty and insecurity, they all showed marked solicitude for the immigrant and the laboring man. They were committed to democratic institutions and the full-scale participation of Catholics in American life, yet they also considered the theoretical questions of the day with a thoughtfulness not usually expected of ecclesiastical dignitaries. All four were more or less consciously moving along lines marked out by Father Hecker and the Paulists; and this commitment gave coherence to their advocacy on the whole complex of issues which are here brought under the single rubric of Americanism. So constantly interlaced were these controversies, however, that in the account which follows, chronological ordering must yield to a thematic discussion.

The German Campaign

The place to begin is with the conflict between Irish and German Catholics which had erupted repeatedly during the earlier struggle with trusteeism. After the Civil War, when many areas and, in some cases, whole dioceses became predominantly German, these tensions took on the character of cultural conflict. Not only were the Germans in general in a more favorable economic situation than the Irish, but they, like their Lutheran compatriots, were convinced that the Christian message could be safely conveyed only in their mother tongue. Despite Protestant resistance, they founded German-language parochial schools, accused the Irish of compromise and doctrinal laxity, and sought to end the subordination of German-speaking Catholics in the hierarchy and in the parochial organization of cities.

Several aspects of this problem as well as other questions relating to monasticism were raised by the arrival of the German Benedictines under Boniface Wimmer, who had already played a leading role in the reestablishment of his order in Bavaria. Receiving encouragement and land from Bishop Michael O'Connor of Pittsburgh, Wimmer founded Saint Vincent's Abbey in 1846. When the question of exempted status for this institution arose, conflict with the bishop occurred. Through their powerful friends in Bavaria, the Benedictines prevailed in Rome, and in 1855 the pope authorized a self-governing Benedictine congregation in America, naming Wimmer its abbot. Thereafter still other monasteries were founded, most notably in Minnesota, where Saint John's Abbey under its powerful abbot was soon creating problems for another Irish prelate, Archbishop Ireland of Saint Paul. Ireland seemed to share Father Hecker's reservations about traditional monasticism, and he made no secret of his displeasure at having semi-autonomous monasteries in his own province. At the installation of Thomas O'Gorman in Sioux Falls, South Dakota, in 1896, he publicly advised the new bishop to keep his diocese free of such institutions.

Not all Germans were monks; but nearly all of them drank beer, and Abbot Wimmer himself complained that only fanaticism could require monks to drink water. (Not even the Trappists do that, he maintained.) When Bishop O'Connor sought to close Saint Vincent's brewery, the abbot was also able to get papal authorization for its continuance. The incident, aside from the question of jurisdiction, aggravated a long-smoldering moral dispute. Before 1900 the Irish prelates generally and those of Americanist leanings in particular tended to be fervent temperance advocates. Interested as they were in the social welfare of their constituency, they saw the Irishman's drinking habits as a serious disability. The temperance controversy did not involve fundamental theological issues, but it caused much irritation and ill-feeling, and it continued to be a divisive factor until the political activities of the Protestant-dominated Anti-Saloon League and passage of the Eighteenth Amendment gradually created a nearly unified Catholic opposition to political prohibitionism.

Riding the crest of a great Catholic renaissance that was proceeding on the Continent, the Benedictines, on the other hand, agitated for far more than breweries. They reenlivened a monastic ideal that many had regarded as outmoded; their seminaries defended a rigorous theological tradition which gave prestige to German Catholicism. Through their influence in Europe, moreover, they won financial support from the Ludwig Missionsverein in Bavaria and the Leopoldinen Stiftung in Austria, and joined with others to convince powerful European Catholics that funds for missionary work among the Germans must bypass the Irish-dominated American hierarchy. As these efforts led to or coalesced with two other important developments, the "German question" assumed considerable significance in America.

Peter Paul Cahensly was a dedicated Roman Catholic businessman of Limburg-an-der-Lahn in Nassau who in 1871 organized the Saint Raphael Society to aid and protect German immigrants. Through these activities he also became linked with Catholic missionary movements in other countries. In 1890 the international convention of Saint Raphael Societies prepared a document which in the following year was presented to the Holy See. This memorial grossly exaggerated immigrant losses to the church and pleaded for arrangements that would make the institutions of the American church (parishes, schools, seminaries, bishops, etc.) formally multilingual and multinational. It also requested a cardinal protector in Rome to supervise the work of the Saint Raphael societies. In this way "Cahenslyism" brought European support to an American movement organized by the Germans to achieve the same ends.

The basic cause of dissatisfaction among German Catholics in America was the subordinate position to which their priests, parishes, and schools seemed to be relegated by the English-speaking (Irish) hierarchy. German priests in Saint Louis petitioned against these practices, but in 1886 the issue was drawn more sharply when Father Peter M. Abbelen, vicar general of the Milwaukee archdiocese, with the support of Archbishop Heiss, presented in Rome a memorial pleading not only for equal parochial status for German churches, but for regulations that would assign German laity to these churches regardless of parish boundaries. When the contents of this memorial became known, considerable public furor arose; but the counterstatement of four eastern archbishops and the representations of Ireland, Keane, and O'Connell, who happened to be in Rome, contributed to the memorial's rejection in 1887. German Catholics continued to resist and to criticize nearly all the projects and activities of the Americanist bishops.

Against the background of ethnic rivalry, the other old issue of public education and parochial schools continued to simmer. In fact, one of the irritations behind the Abbelen memorial was the silence of the Irish bishops in the Midwest when Wisconsin's Bennett Law of 1889 was passed, forcing all children to attend schools in their own districts rather than consolidated Catholic schools and requiring the use of English in all major subjects. Archbishop Ireland was a special irritant, not only because he advocated the use of English in churches and schools, but because he had publicly praised the work of the public schools, despite the demands of the last Plenary Council (1884) that parish schools be founded wherever possible. Ireland doubted that parochial schools were worth the outlay required, and he seemed convinced that the welfare of the immigrant would be improved by a free public educational system. For these reasons he tried to work out a scheme for the cooperation of church and state in education, the so-called Fairibault Plan, whereby the town took over parochial schools, paid approved Catholic teachers, and allowed religious education after school hours. By dint of extraordinary efforts and another trip to Rome in 1891, he gained papal permission for this plan, but Protestant opposition doomed it in any case. Here again was a perennial issue which remained alive to the end of the century and long after.

The school issue had only incidental ethnic overtones, and nearly all of the remaining issues divided "liberals" and "conservatives" on other grounds, a fact revealed very clearly by the agitation over the founding of Catholic University in Washington, D.C. Except within certain religious orders, American priests had usually received advanced training at the University of Louvain in Belgium or at the Propaganda College in Rome. In 1884, however, the Plenary Council had approved the founding of a university in the United States. Their decision resulted partly from the promise of a $300,000 gift, but it owed much to the eloquent plea made at the council by John

Lancaster Spalding, the learned and philosophic bishop of Peoria. The opposition was strong: Bishop McQuaid in Rochester, Archbishop Corrigan in New York, and the Jesuits all feared a rival center of Americanist influence, and it took all that Spalding, Gibbons, Ireland, and Keane could do to win the assent of Pope Leo XIII. In 1889, its constitution approved, the pope appointed Bishop Keane of Richmond as rector. During the ensuing seven years Keane made the institution a powerful progressive force, but in 1896 his sudden removal from office came as a stunning blow to the liberal cause.

Keane's undoing as rector was probably related to still another matter on which he, Gibbons, and Ireland took a stand during his years of tenure: the church's relations with Protestantism. All three men clearly followed Father Hecker and the Paulists in seeking to improve relations and to open some kind of dialogue. In 1890, therefore, Keane accepted the invitation of President Eliot of Harvard to deliver the annual Dudleian Lecture in the college chapel. Bishop McQuaid refused to give him permission to address the Catholic Club at Cornell, however, and many conservatives were outraged not only by the act itself but by his very irenic lecture. When in 1893 the World Parliament of Religions was held in conjunction with the Chicago World's Fair, both Keane and Cardinal Gibbons participated, Gibbons even leading a recitation of the Lord's Prayer in the Protestant version at the opening session. On this occasion the conservative outcry was even more violent.

That this outcry did not remain simply a domestic controversy was due in part to still another incident connected with the world's fair. In Rome there had long been strong pressures for the assignment of an apostolic delegate to the United States, but because they were sensitive to Protestant charges of Catholic subservience to a "foreign potentate," and because they remembered Archbishop Bedini's catastrophic tour in 1853, the American bishops had always resisted such an innovation. The appointment of Archbishop Gibbons as apostolic delegate to the Plenary Council of 1884 was one result of their tact in this area. In 1892, however, the pope sent Francesco Satolli as a personal representative bearing certain memorabilia of Columbus to the Columbian Exposition. Satolli stayed on in America, and in due course he was invested as apostolic delegate and, after the termination of his office, was made a cardinal. His unfavorable estimate of the Americanists was almost certainly an element in the rising resistance to their program that became evident in Rome.

In the meantime a cluster of other issues was coming to a head, and Satolli became involved in them as well. These problems had to do with the economic predicament of immigrants, particularly the many Catholics employed as laborers in industries where working conditions required cooperative protection, organized bargaining, and political activity. In this context the question of secret societies arose. The Masonic order was, of course, anathema to European Catholics, and Pope Leo XIII had issued a new encyclical (*Humanum Genus*) on the subject in 1884. Conservatives naturally urged obedience to the letter, and Bishop McQuaid would even have banned the Ancient Order of Hibernians. The Americanists, however, were wont to recognize that societies such as the Odd Fellows, the Knights of Pythias, and many other similar lodges performed essential social and economic functions.

This issue soon was complicated by the emergence of the Knights of Labor as the country's first large labor union. Because its founder, Uriah Stevens, was addicted to secret practices and rituals, and because the counteractivity of employers almost made secrecy a necessity, the Knights of Labor undeniably was, among other things, a secret society. Archbishop Taschereau of Quebec took the lead as conservatives not only urged obedience to the papal encyclical, but sought explicit condemnation of the Knights. As usual it fell to Gibbons, Keane, and their cohorts to prevent this blow from falling on the American labor movement with its heavy Catholic constituency. In 1886, the very year in which the union was involved in a critical test of strength, they met with Terence Powderly, then head of the Knights and also a Catholic, and, having determined that the secret oath had been discontinued, they then convinced all but two of the American archbishops to oppose condemnation. Due to this lack of unanimity, the issue was referred to Rome, but a year later, while Gibbons himself was in Rome, he personally and successfully averted the embarrassment which condemnation would have brought.

Closely related to the labor issue was the problem of Henry George and the economic theories which he had expounded with such great effect in *Progress and Poverty* (1879). The Knights of Labor had absorbed much of his thought, and in 1886 they supported his campaign for mayor in New York, where Archbishop Corrigan had a very satisfactory arrangement with Tammany Hall.[4] To compound matters, one of George's most eloquent supporters was Father Edward McGlynn, a very popular parish priest. The Archbishop disciplined the priest and sought to have George's book put on the Index for its unorthodox views on property; and only when Gibbons pleaded that the

4. In 1894 Archbishop Ireland himself entered Archbishop Corrigan's province, campaigned for the Republican party, and used his influence to have a liberal priest rather than Bishop McQuaid elected to the New York State Board of Regents. McQuaid's public condemnation of this invasion was so severe that he was reprimanded by the pope.

church not proclaim itself an enemy of the poor was this extreme action avoided, though the pope did publicly condemn socialism. After an extended consultation with the apostolic delegate, Father McGlynn had his excommunication lifted in 1892. McGlynn subsequently attested his utter concurrence with Pope Leo's encyclical *Rerum Novarum* (1891), with its famously liberal but antisocialistic espousal of the workingman's cause. The George affair, in fact, seems to have helped precipitate the encyclical, and it may be more than a coincidence that two months after the reinstatement of McGlynn, Pope Leo issued his celebrated encyclical to the French church, calling for a Catholic *ralliement* to the Republic.

THE CRISIS

As it happened, Pope Leo's *ralliement* and the question of Catholicism in the French Republic provided the setting for the final climactic stage of the Americanism crisis. The ideological and theological questions at stake were in the strictest sense of the term fundamental. The very presence of the Roman Catholic church in the United States posed the bedrock question as to how a huge ecclesiastical institution, which had emerged from the wreck of the Roman Empire, slowly structured itself according to principles of canon law, consolidated its authority during fifteen centuries of tumultuous European history, and defined its faith at the Councils of Trent and Vatican I, was to be regulated in a pluralistic democratic state in which churches existed as one kind of voluntary organization among others, and in which its members were scattered at random so far as their social, economic, and political relationships were concerned. The successor of Innocent III, Boniface VIII, and Pius IX faced a situation such as Western Christendom had never before presented to a pope. In the United States, moreover, was a thoughtful and articulate group of prelates and theologians, as well as a considerable body of laity, who were convinced that their country provided an excellent, possibly even the ideal, circumstance for the church to accomplish the transition to a modern social order. Archbishop Ireland had proclaimed this conviction in a stirring oration at the Plenary Council in 1884:

> There is no conflict between the Catholic Church and America. I could not utter one syllable that would belie, however remotely, either the Church or the Republic, and when I assert, as I now solemnly do, that the principles of the Church are in thorough harmony with the interests of the Republic, I know in the depths of my soul that I speak the truth. . . .

> Republic of America, receive from me the tribute of my love and my loyalty. . . . *Esto perpetua.* Thou bearest in thy hands the hopes of the human race, thy mission from God is to show to nations that men are capable of highest civil and political liberty. . . . Believe me, no hearts love thee more ardently than Catholic hearts, . . . and no hands will be lifted up stronger and more willing to defend, in war and peace, thy laws and thy institutions than Catholic hands. *Esto perpetua.*[5]

He stated the essence of this message again and again in his visits to France—almost a second homeland to him—and he repeatedly made his views known in Rome.

Then in 1891 Father Walter Elliott published his famous *Life of Father Hecker,* a ringing panegyric, so filled with Hecker's own writing as to make it a kind of *apologia pro vita sua* as well. All of Hecker was there: not only his fervent insistence that America must become Catholic to realize its destiny fully, but also his views on the Holy Spirit, on the active and the passive virtues, and the statements that had provoked the charges of "minimism" and pro-Protestant heresy. The book appeared, moreover, just when the international convention of Saint Raphael Societies in Lucerne was memorializing the pope with a most extreme statement of the German charges against the American church leadership and a demand for division of the hierarchy. Their petition was denied in Rome, but Archbishop Ireland and many others—including some congressmen—inveighed against it, accusing "foreign powers" of interfering with American internal affairs.

Against this background—as well as that provided by all the other controversies discussed above—Pope Leo XIII in 1895 addressed an encyclical to the American church, *Longinqua Oceani.* This remarkable document, in the traditional manner of such statements, contains warm felicitations to "the young and vigorous American nation, in which We plainly discern latent forces for the advancement alike of civilization and Christianity." Other praise follows, but "the prosperous condition of Catholicity" is attributed above all "to the virtue, the ability, and the prudence of the bishops and clergy"; and the "main factor, no doubt" is said to be "the ordinances and decrees of your synods," for it had been an early insistence of Pope Leo that a plenary council be convened in order to regularize the country's ecclesiastical arrangements. Then follows the famous reservation which American anti-Catholic diatribes have never ceased to quote. Despite the obvious prosperity of American Catholicism,

5. Quoted in James H. Moynihan, *The Life of Archbishop John Ireland,* pp. 33–34.

> it would be very erroneous to draw the conclusion that in America is to be sought the type of the most desirable status of the Church, or that it would be universally lawful or expedient for State and Church to be, as in America, dissevered and divorced. The fact that Catholicity with you is in good condition, nay, is even enjoying prosperous growth, is by all means to be attributed to the fecundity with which God has endowed his Church, in virtue of which unless men or circumstances interfere, she spontaneously expands and propagates herself; but she would bring forth more abundant fruits if, in addition to liberty, she enjoyed the favor of the laws and the patronage of public authority.[6]

Still later, in explaining his recent establishment of an apostolic delegation, he makes a related statement that must have rankled many: "We have wished, first of all, to certify that, in Our judgment and affection, America occupies the same place and rights of other States, be they ever so mighty and imperial." In the paragraphs which followed, other recent controversies were recalled by specific references: to respect for bishops and "mutual charity" among them; to moderation and respectful language in widely circulating periodicals; to the right of "the working classes . . . to unite in associations for the promotion of their interests," but on the other hand their duty to shun both those which have been openly condemned by the church and "those also which, in the opinion of intelligent men, and especially of the bishops, are regarded as suspicious or dangerous." As to social life in general, "unless forced by necessity to do otherwise, Catholics ought to prefer to associate with Catholics, a course which will be very conducive to the safeguarding of their faith." Elsewhere there were the expected admonitions to morality and religious duty; but it was, all told, an unusually—perhaps unexpectedly—severe and conservative message to have come from the author of *Rerum Novarum* and *Au Milieu des Sollicitudes.* One wonders if in 1895 the pope would have sent Ireland on a speaking tour of France as he had in 1892. Beyond speculation are the facts that in 1895 O'Connell was removed from his post at the American College in Rome, and in 1896 Keane was replaced as rector of Catholic University.

Whatever their response to such questioning, the progressives continued to press their cause. In 1897 Elliott's biography appeared in France, with a rousing introduction by Archbishop Ireland and a preface by the Abbé Felix Klein, a professor at the Institut Catholique of Paris. Klein stated that "probably no book in the last fifty years has cast so luminous a beam on the present

6. John Tracy Ellis, *Documents of American Catholic History,* pp. 514–27.

condition of humanity, on the religious development of the world, on the intimate relationships of God and the modern soul, or on the present-day requirements for the advancement of the Church." Ireland, in his introduction, confessed that Hecker's was the most salutary influence in his own life, proclaimed him "the ornament and jewel [*joyau*] of the American clergy" and a man for the priests of the future to take as their model.[7] As in America, so in France: the book was both praised and condemned. From pulpit and press attacks were mounted by royalists and extreme theological conservatives who had important connections in the Vatican, which at that time was also a vortex of many reactionary pressures.

Then the Spanish-American War broke out, with the United States attacking one of the old imperial powers to which Pope Leo had alluded in *Longinqua Oceani*. Factions were pressing their claims in the Curia; speculation and rumor were providing grist for adventurous journalists. Not surprisingly, therefore, the pope reserved the question of Americanism for an encyclical, and on 22 January 1899, a few days before Archbishop Ireland arrived in Rome with hopes of staving off a conservative pronouncement, *Testem Benevolentiae* finally appeared. It was an important—even an epoch-making—document. Never before or since, as Monsignor Ellis says, has the orthodoxy of the Roman Catholic church in the United States been "called in question," though it must be added that rarely has heresy been more ambiguously assigned. Yet this very ambiguity probably heightened the long-term effect of the encyclical. The document does, to be sure, say that "certain things are to be avoided and corrected"; on the other hand the pope's wording gave good grounds for progressives to accept Cardinal Rampolla's assurance that the encyclical's real purpose was to quiet the French. It refers to the French translation of Elliott's *Hecker,* and makes clear that various doctrines are in error, without asserting that either Hecker or any Americans had taught these doctrines. It also commends religious orders and the so-called passive virtues. Its tone is well conveyed in its concluding summation:

> Hence from all that we have hitherto said, it is clear, Beloved Son [the letter was sent to Cardinal Gibbons], that we cannot approve the opinions which some comprise under the head of Americanism. If, indeed, by that name be designated the characteristic qualities which reflect honor on the people of America . . . there is surely no reason why we should deem that it ought to be discarded. But if it is to be used . . . to commend the above doctrines, there can be no doubt but that our

7. Walter Elliott, *Le Père Hecker, Foundateur des "Paulistes" Americains* (Paris, 1897), pp. ii, xxxix, xl, lv.

> Venerable Brethren the Bishops of America would be the first to repudiate and condemn it, as being especially unjust to them and to the entire nation as well. For it raises the suspicion that there are some among you who conceive of and desire a church in America different from that which is in the rest of the world.[8]

All considered, it is hard to avoid the conclusion that the pope sought a general pacification in *both* America and Europe (especially in France), and that he was also giving a tangential rebuke to modernism wherever it might be advancing.

Modernism is the usual Roman Catholic term for the movement condemned by Pope Pius X in the encyclical *Pascendi Gregis* of 1907. The movement aimed, in the words of its greatest representative, Alfred Loisy, "to adapt the Catholic religion to the intellectual, moral, and social needs of the present time" (roughly 1890–1910). Basically modernists sought "to face and accept the general development of modern scientific knowledge, and, in particular, the results of biblical and historical criticism. . . . And it was from this approach that they proceeded . . . to broach wider philosophical and theological questions." [9] Given the near conjunction and vague overlapping in content of *Testem Benevolentiae* and *Pascendi Gregis,* the question of modernism's strength in America is often raised. In fact, conservatives often accused the progressives of modernism. When the Catholic University church historian Thomas O'Gorman was made a bishop in Archbishop Ireland's province, critics made reference to his having studied under Louis Duchesne, a French historian whose critical methods aroused consternation in many quarters. The same critics found fault with several of Bishop Keane's statements and with Bishop John Lancaster Spalding's effusive idealism, which sometimes verged on the "ontologism" of which Brownson had been accused.

These complaints did address an undeniable liberal current. Cardinal Gibbons and many others, for example, approved of Salvatore di Bartolo's

8. Ellis, *Documents,* pp. 553–562. The specific doctrines condemned in *Testem Benevolentiae* were (1) that "the Church ought to adapt herself [and] . . . show some indulgence to modern, popular theories and methods"; (2) that some ancient doctrines should now be suppressed or passed over; (3) that individuals may decide how the church should adjust to changing circumstances; (4) that a larger liberty of individual interpretation should be introduced into the church; (5) that the promptings of the Holy Ghost can be rightly discerned without the help of external guidance; and (6) that natural virtues are more to be extolled than the supernatural virtues.

9. In *Providentissimus Deus* (1893) Pope Leo had taken a very conservative position on critical studies of the Bible; and in 1907 Pope Pius X condemned "modernism" in *Pascendi Gregis* and published a comprehensive Syllabus of Errors (*Lamentabili Sane*). Alfred Loisy (1857–1940), who was expelled from the church in 1908, is quoted in Alec R. Vidler, *The Modernist Movement in the Roman Church,* p. 6.

limitation of biblical inerrancy to dogmatic issues—only to have this work placed on the Index (1891). Far more publicized was the case of Father John A. Zahm, a professor at Notre Dame University. During the very years when the Americanism agitation was at its height, the Holy Office ruled that his pro-Darwinian *Evolution and Dogma* (1896) could not be translated into other languages, and for a time threatened to put it on the Index. Zahm was, in effect, silenced. And in 1898 Father George Zurcher of Buffalo, New York, had his *Monks and Their Decline* placed on the Index. But these incidents were relatively isolated.

Three basic facts remain. First, despite the liveliness of many liberal tendencies, the essential demand of modernists (for a doctrinal or theological accommodation of modern science and critical studies) had few if any explicit defenders in the United States. American "liberals" were not doctrinal reformers. In fact, even the most outspoken Americanist prelates (Ireland, for example) held firmly to traditional views. The same could be said for Cardinal Gibbons's very widely read apologetic work *The Faith of Our Fathers* (1877). Except on the church and state question, their "liberalism" tended to be practical, not doctrinal.

Second, during the half-century after the Civil War, the faith, practice, church order, theology, and scholarship of American Catholicism was firmly in conservative hands. Knowing themselves to be supported in Rome, the great majority of the bishops and clergy saw no great threat and some obvious things to admire in "Americanism," though specific controversies often provoked bitter feelings and harsh words. The term "crisis" may indeed be too strong, unless it be applied to a profound inner contradiction between tradition and modernity that even most Americanists only dimly saw, and that would become widely recognized only in the later twentieth century.

Third, the doctrinal pronouncements of Leo XIII and Pius X had a distinctly stultifying effect on Roman Catholic intellectual life everywhere in the church. Americans, says Father Ong, "were so chastened . . . that they turned more industriously than ever to developing 'know-how' and letting theory be." [10] One great period of American ferment was over, and another was not to begin until 1958, when Pope John XXIII inaugurated a new epoch in Roman Catholic history.

In 1908 Pope Pius X at last terminated the mission status of the American church. Shortly after that, the World War gave the hierarchy further occasion to organize itself to deal with the urgent problems of the nation. Rapid social change, two wars, a depression, continued immigration, and a virulent

10. Walter J. Ong, *Frontiers in American Catholicism*, pp. 21–22. See also his *American Catholic Crossroads*, chap. 3.

renewal of nativism provided American Catholics sufficient occasion to exercise their practical bent. In the mid-twentieth century, however, many circumstances, both national and international, would enhance the reputation of the Americanists; and in the light of this new situation, church reformers like Hecker, O'Connell, Keane, and Ireland would be remembered not as defeated semiheretics, but as foresighted pioneers.

50

THE PROTESTANT ESTABLISHMENT AND THE NEW NATIVISM

"The halcyon years of American Protestantism" is the phrase used by a sensitive historian reflecting on his own experience as a minister during the closing decades of the nineteenth century.[1] In view of the social and intellectual turmoil that wracked the nation in that period, the name seems ironic, or perverse, or both. Yet his judgment is sound, and the explanatory fact of the matter is that liberalism's wrestling with evolution and historicism, like the Social Gospel's anguish over the inhumanity of industrialism, involved only a small troubled minority of the nation's vast Protestant host. In the slowly changing yet tradition-bound mainstream of American evangelicalism, Darwin and Wellhausen were remote heretics to be ridiculed or condemned by every itinerant revivalist. As for poverty, slums, and strikes—a rabble of foreigners, drunkards, anarchists, and Roman Catholics were the troublemakers. If the "money power" was behaving indecently, it was the fault of a corrupt few with aid from conniving politicians—and then there were the Jews. In any case, Protestantism derived its power and had its firm foundations far from the teeming multitudes.

The ascendant Protestant tradition was becoming increasingly homogenized. Revivalists could be nonsectarian without cramping their style. The hard edges of doctrinal polemic were directed against Catholics and the more extreme liberals, while hymnody, religious journalism, Sunday school study aids, and popular devotional literature covered over the old differences that had divided British Protestantism into Baptists, Episcopalians, Quakers, Presbyterians, Congregationalists, and Methodists. This composite entity was the "Protestant Establishment" which enjoyed special prestige and many

1. Gaius Glenn Atkins, *Religion in Our Times,* chap. 2. A fine retrospective volume.

privileges even though it was not supported or regulated by the government. The absence of a regular Catholic chaplain in the army until the Civil War and in the navy until 1888 is symbolic of the situation. This legal arrangement rested, of course, on colonial foundations which had not been destroyed by the American Revolution. The antebellum evangelical crusades had strengthened them. Then after the Civil War, especially during the 1870s, a minor revolution in church-state relations had actually strengthened the legal status of Protestantism in state after state, putting roadblocks in front of the Roman juggernaut, and routing the pagans who would keep religion out of the public schools. Rutherford B. Hayes had used these issues in Ohio along the route to the presidency. Garfield was a quondam preacher. And in 1896 either a Democratic or a Republican victory would have brought a testifying evangelical to the White House. The "common-core Protestantism" which was emerging by no means lacked internal variations; yet the developing consensus was highly relevant for American culture and for later church unity movements.

THE EVANGELICAL MAINSTREAM

Numerically and theologically, two vast, widely dispersed communions, Methodist and Baptist, provided the popular base of American Protestantism. Both of them had been relatively small fringe groups in 1800, but they had grown to denominations that numbered, respectively, 4,589,284 and 3,717,969 by 1890. The Presbyterians, though displaced from their proud position of other days, were next with 1,231,072 communicants. There were also 750,000 Christians and Disciples of Christ, and 540,000 Congregationalists. Many small groups and sects shared similar views, but even leaving these less influential bodies aside, the mainstream denominations constituted 80 percent of American Protestantism, and about 55 percent of America's religiously affiliated population in 1890. The figures themselves are relatively mute, however, unless various unifying factors are noted.

The distinguishing mark with deepest roots in the past was the basic Reformed or Calvinistic lineage of these bodies. Except among the Episcopalians, most of them accepted as virtually axiomatic the radical program of church reform that had been developed in Switzerland and elsewhere on the Continent, then matured with particular importance for America in Scotland and England. To England's long Reformation travail was owed the additional fact that Puritanism laid the chief foundations of American religious life in nearly every colony. This meant an even greater intensification of Reformed radicalism and a tendency to see the menace of popery at every turn. To be sure, many of the proudest hopes of the early Puritans had been shattered even during the seventeenth century, but their moralism and strict views of private behavior, as well as their conviction that America was a model for the world, remained.

Beyond the Reformed and Puritan legacy, American evangelical Protestantism had for the most part accepted as an essential part of its being the ideas and practices of revivalism. Puritan piety provided the basic theology for this great strategy of church extension, but the hero-founder of the tradition in America was George Whitefield. After him it was enthusiastically adopted by the Congregationalists, Presbyterians, Dutch Reformed, and other groups of colonial American strength; but no groups did so much to bring the revival spirit to every farm, way station, village, and city as the Methodists and the Baptists.

The crucial doctrine of revivalism was that which made a specific conversion experience the essential mark of a true Christian. This emphasis accounts for the radically individualistic accent of revivalism and its large role in extinguishing the Puritan's concern for the Holy Commonwealth as a whole. Concentration upon the individual sinner led inexorably to a preoccupation with exceedingly personal sins. The resultant erosion of social ethics was noted even in colonial times, but the full effect of this tendency was not manifest until after the Civil War, when the rise of huge corporate entities began to complicate the moral life of nearly all Americans. As exemplified in the preaching of Moody and Sunday, revivalism tended to become socially trivial or ambiguous to the point of irrelevance. It was precisely these tendencies which made pious Christians like Rauschenbusch so harsh in their judgments of evangelicalism.

Another element which became almost symbiotic with revivalism was Arminianism, a doctrinal tendency whose name stemmed from an intramural dispute of the Netherlands Reformed church but whose propagation in America owed most to Wesley and the Methodists. Because an emphasis on man's free will was intrinsic to revivalism, the doctrines of unconditional election and limited atonement lost their vitality. Practice of the "new measures" led to "New School" theology. By the end of the century double predestination was the pet doctrine of only the Hard-shell Baptists, a declining number of Old School Presbyterians, and a few smaller groups. In 1906, upon receiving back the Cumberland Presbyterians after a century of separation on this issue, the Presbyterian Church (North) formally revised the Westminster Confession to an Arminian reading; and by 1911 most of the Freewill Baptists, after an even longer separation, found the offending doctrine too weak to prevent reunion. As God's predestinating decrees passed from favor, the floodgates of emotionalism and sentimentality in religion were opened, with the result that the doctrine of human depravity was also threatened with inundation. Because revivalists so often addressed interdenominational audiences, moreover, nearly all doctrinal emphases tended to be suppressed, not only by the famous spellbinders, but by the thousands upon thousands of local ministers and now-forgotten regional itinerants. Gradually a kind of unwritten consensus emerged, its cardinal articles being the infallibility of the Scriptures, the divinity of Christ, and man's duty to be converted from the ways of sin to a life guided by a pietistic code of morals. Revivalism, in other words, was a mighty engine of doctrinal destruction. "Are you saved?" became the central question of American Protestantism; and more and more it came to mean, "Have you decided to be saved?"

In conjunction with these distinctly theological or ecclesiastical features, other "secular" convictions had taken on religious coloring. The ideas of democracy and the rights of the common man strengthened Arminianism, encouraged the development of democratic, laity-centered polities, and further minimized ancient distinctions that had marked off the status of the clergy. More basic was the almost universal American conviction that the United States had a mission to extend its influence throughout the world. To mainstream Protestants a denial of America's manifest destiny bordered on treason. Translated into theological categories, this meant that the American was characteristically a "postmillennialist." He believed that the Kingdom of God would be realized in history, almost surely in American history. His thought was also strongly tinctured with perfectionism. To orthodox New Englanders this had been heresy when they heard it from the lips of William Ellery Channing, or from the Methodists, or from Charles G. Finney; but the old heresy became the new orthodoxy as American idealism soared to new heights during the nineteenth century. Progress was both a personal and a social fact. And this change did not witness so much to an augmented conception of grace as to a profound shift in the prevailing notion of human nature.

Professor Mead points out that the United States had two religious heritages, one denominational and divisive, the other patriotic, rooted in the Enlightenment, and unitive: "The high degree of amalgamation of these two faiths took place in the decades following the Civil War." [2] The cumulative effect of these several factors was that American evangelical Protestantism came to resemble nineteenth-century Methodism in nearly every way except with regard to its hierarchical form of church government. This may have been why Theodore Roosevelt said that he never felt so sure that he was

2. Sidney E. Mead, *The Lively Experiment*, pp. 135–36.

speaking to a typical American audience as when he addressed a Methodist gathering.

The great reservoir of Protestantism lay in the middle-class churches of rural and smalltown America until long after 1920, when the census finally revealed that most Americans were city dwellers. And because the steady movement of people to the city had a continuous shaping influence on urban Protestantism, the chief characteristics of the mainstream heritage are nowhere better seen than in the individual churches of this rural reservoir. They were not, of course, strictly identical. Keepers of community social registers could make the subtle distinctions for which their antennae were attuned. There were also significant regional differences. Sociology rather than theology explains most of the variations. Yet the institution as such assumed classic, recognizable, highly predictable lines.

The American Protestant congregation of the later nineteenth century was a friendly place which fitted naturally and securely into the needs of the community. A newcomer there would be greeted by some local variant of the unique American greeting, "Howdy stranger." If he came somehow to the wrong church and the greeting was cool, he would find another where the people put him at ease, where the forms of prayer and praise came in accents familiar to his ears, where the minister "fitted in" and gave understandable sermons, where the hymns and the choir put no new demands on his musical tastes, and where the social converse after Sunday services and on many other weekday occasions—for men, women, and children alike—would be free of jarring notes or unexpected demands.

Perhaps nothing better expressed the piety pervading these institutions than the new hymnody which swept much of Isaac Watts, the older Reformed "psalms," and even much of British Methodism's fine treasury into disuse and oblivion. In their place came the gospel tunes of the new piety: "What a Friend We Have in Jesus" (1868), "Jesus Keep Me Near the Cross" (1869), "Blessed Assurance, Jesus Is Mine" (1873), "Softly and Tenderly Jesus Is Calling" (1909), "I Come to the Garden Alone/While the Dew Is Still on the Roses" (1912), and hundreds of others, fitted to attractive tunes, lilting and easily syncopated or sweetly sentimental, rich in simple harmonies and sliding chromaticisms. Heard once, they would be remembered forever. Few ties were there that bound American Protestants so firmly together in a common popular tradition.[3]

The popularity and friendliness of these church ways exacted a price,

3. The Broadway musical *Say, Darling* (1958) contained a nice scene in which supposedly hardened New York theatrical producers are holding auditions. When the script calls for a revival hymn, they all reveal their midwestern origins by joining in every stanza and the refrain of "Let the Lower Lights Be Burning."

however, for in drawing like to like they accentuated the social stratification of Protestantism. A prime characteristic of the ancient parish systems of Christendom, including those of Puritanism, was broken: judge, merchant, mechanic, and servant no longer had a common religious nurture. Although many denominations covered the whole social spectrum, this was rarely the case for a single congregation. Because each congregation had its characteristic constituency, a nation of socially mobile people developed patterns of church membership which were a radical departure from anything Christendom had seen. Abraham Lincoln's progress was typical: from a hard-shell Baptist background, through a "good" marriage and a successful law practice, to regular attendance on Presbyterian preaching. Yet the "progress" in Lincoln's case, as in millions of others, was by no means a matter of sheer social expediency; many such changes were required by maturing tastes and deepening intellectual interests. Denominational interchangeability was a feature of common-core Protestantism, and the movement of individuals within the system served to accentuate its overall homogeneity. The same end was served by the intense denominational rivalries which ensued. From 1870 to 1905 there was not a single large church merger in the country. As in commercial competition, the accent was on marginal differentiation.

The message and teaching of this increasingly homogeneous religious tradition and the attitudes it inculcated were closely adapted to what Americans wanted to hear and highly conducive to complacency and self-righteousness. The prophetic note tended to get lost. The sins most universally condemned were the middle-class "don'ts" applicable to any would-be self-made man. Positively, there was a "gospel of wealth" for the rich and a "gospel of work" for everyone. Henry May has stated the case accurately: "In 1876 Protestantism presented a massive, almost unbroken front in its defense of the status quo." [4] The leaders of the Social Gospel, whose history Professor May was writing, were an exception, but a numerically small one.

On more strictly ecclesiastical issues the prevailing bias was anticlerical in the good-natured American sense ("the minister should be a good fellow and one of us"), and antiliturgical in that it vented both an American love for spontaneity and a deeper anti-Catholic animus. Most pervasive of all was an anti-intellectual set of mind which was easily transferred from doctrinal or theological matters to more general areas. Theologians, intellectuals, professors, and the literati were rendered suspect. Richard Hofstadter in his *Anti-Intellectualism in America* points to revivalistic Protestantism as a primary source of this attitude; and a recent church historian makes the same case in more sympathetic terms:

4. Henry F. May, *The Protestant Churches and Industrial America*, p. 91.

> The "simple gospel" proclaimed by the American churches is not essentially a matter of rationalism or liberalism, but of grace for all. Nearly all the factors . . . contributing to the nontheological spirit of our faith are much older and run much deeper than the liberal tendency to discount the importance of dogma. The emphasis on simplicity is in part a Christian application of democracy. Our preachers have often quoted a saying attributed to Abraham Lincoln: "God must have loved the common people, he made so many of them." So the accent in our preaching has been not so much propositional as personal—an effort to commend to all men the Friend of Sinners.[5]

In such an ethos the troublesome facts and ideas propounded by the leading scientists, scholars, and philosophers of the nineteenth century were kept at safe distance or dismissed as unchristian. When an idea like biological evolution finally became almost axiomatic for large segments of the educated public, a wide sector of the religious community was still reacting with defensive ferocity. Revivalistic anti-intellectualism thus became one very important source of the Fundamentalist's anger and sense of betrayal. Already in the later nineteenth century this alienation was demonstrated by various movements of reaction which grew in strength with the passing decades, but these forms of dissent would have arisen sooner and with more disruptive force had it not been for the signs that the political and cultural power of Protestantism was being threatened.

THE RISING TIDE OF RACISM

After the Civil War, American fears of subversion had been turned, on a sectional basis, against Radical Republicans or the Southern "Redeemers" rather than against Catholics and foreigners. But in the Gilded Age the alarming increase of immigration and the growing concentration of unassimilated minorities in the cities provoked a revival of nativism. For at least three reasons, moreover, the new forms of countersubversion were often less theological and far more crassly racist. Because the old Puritan roots of antipopery were being steadily eroded by cultural compromises and liberal theology, nativism tended to lose its doctrinal animus and to become a function of folk Protestantism or secular prejudice. Evolutionary thought, meanwhile, brought a semblance of scientific support to old notions of "Nordic" superiority. These changes served to draw Northern attitudes on race closer to those which had received definitive formulation in the South. A growing consensus as to the "errors" of Radical Reconstruction was accompanied by

5. Ronald E. Osborn, *The Spirit of American Christianity*, p. 115.

an acceptance of Jim Crow laws. There was also widespread agreement that immigrant "hordes" were threatening the American dream.

The overt manifestations of this rising tide of racial pride, hostility, and fear were diverse. As usual, the country's "indigenous foreigners," the Indians, were among the first to feel the brunt of the white man's power. The most sensational aspect of the white man's dealings with the Indian, nearly to the end of the century, was continued armed conflict, a series of skirmishes and minor wars that became intrinsic to the American myth of the Wild West. Less celebrated were the efforts of missionaries, humanitarian reformers, and some government officials to create the conditions for peaceful coexistence, but even these well-meant efforts were seriously impaired by paternalism, racial stereotypes, sentimentalism, corruption, and very little awareness of the degree to which the cultural integrity of Indian life had already been hopelessly undermined.[6]

Another direction in which the new nativism was felt was foreign affairs. And as in the days when Puritan preachers had roused Queen Elizabeth to imperial action, so again the Protestant ministry proclaimed America's destiny in the world:

> "It seems to me that God, with infinite wisdom and skill, is here training the Anglo-Saxon race for an hour sure to come in the World's future. . . . The time is coming when the pressure of population on the means of subsistence will be felt here as it is now felt in Europe and Asia. Then will the world enter on a new stage of its history—*the final competition of races, for which the Anglo-Saxon is being schooled.* Long before the thousand millions are here, the mighty centrifugal tendency inherent in this stock and strengthened in the United States will assert itself. Then this race of unequalled energy, with all the majesty of numbers and the might of wealth behind it—the representative, let us hope, of the largest liberty, the purest Christianity, the highest civilization—having developed peculiarly aggressive traits calculated to impress its institutions upon mankind, will spread itself over the earth. And can any one doubt that the result of this competition of races will be the survival of the fittest?" Is it not reasonable to believe that this race is destined to dispossess many weaker ones, assimilate others, and mould the remainder, until in a very true and important sense, it has Anglo-Saxonized mankind? [7]

6. On missionary work and other involvements of the churches in the Indian question, see pp. 861–62, 1052, n. 21 below.

7. Josiah Strong, *The New Era; or, The Coming Kingdom* (New York, 1893), pp. 79–80, including a quotation from *Our Country: Its Possible Future and Its Present Crisis* (New York, 1885), p. 222.

These are not the words of an editorial writer for some jingoist newspaper: they were written in 1893 by the general secretary of the Evangelical Alliance, Josiah Strong, quoting in large part from *Our Country,* the book that had made him famous eight years before. No longer an obscure Ohio minister, he was now defining the world role of American Protestantism in his book *The New Era; or, The Coming Kingdom.* Strong reveals in this passage the gifts that made him a leader of the evangelical chorus which provided background music for the war with Spain.

But Strong was not only an imperialist. A long chapter in *The New Era* also elaborated the racist nuances of the passage just quoted. He described the providential way in which the Christian church stood on Hebrew, Greek, and Roman pillars, and, granting that each of these three peoples was supreme in the characteristics required for its role in history, he then went on not only to show how "all three unite in the one Anglo-Saxon race," but how this thrice-blest race reached still loftier heights. First, "The religious life of this race is more vigorous, more spiritual, more Christian than that of any other." Second, "The intellectual powers of the Anglo-Saxon" have created not only the world's greatest literary heritage, but the language which is better suited than any other to become a world language. Third, just as Rome possessed unequaled genius for law, organization, and government, "in the modern world the Anglo-Saxon occupies a position of like preeminence."

The Statue of Liberty was dedicated in 1886, between the publication of these two widely read books, but one can only imagine Strong and the readers he influenced wincing in disbelief as they read the lines of Emma Lazarus on the monument's base:

> Give me your tired, your poor,
> Your huddled masses yearning to breathe free,
> The wretched refuse of your teeming shore,
> Send these, the homeless, tempest-tost to me,
> I lift my lamp beside the golden door!

Yet the further fact must be faced: the American's attitude toward the foreigner was fundamentally ambivalent. Some have insisted that the national ideal of cosmopolitan optimism runs counter to human nature, while others have said that the doctrine of human equality was walled in by Anglo-Saxon pride. However formulated, the ambivalence remains. "We are the Romans of the modern world," declared the elder Oliver Wendell Holmes in 1858, "the great assimilating people." Yet forty years later John Fiske formulated a law that won some acceptance: "No ingenuity of legislation or of constitution making can evolve good political results out of base human material." Even the lines of Emma Lazarus vacillate between the masses "yearning to breathe free" and a condescending reference to "the wretched refuse of your teeming shore." American Protestantism in its best moods was capable of genuine charity, but in its average performance and typical expression, it strengthened nativism, contributing in many ways to extreme manifestations of intolerance, and even providing leadership for nativist organizations. But only a review of the way in which the period wrestled with this problem can show the difficulty of making an historical judgment.

THE "NEW" IMMIGRATION

The immense increase in European emigration during the later nineteenth century was not a single uniform movement of peoples. Americans at the time and architects of immigration laws in the 1920s all recognized that between 1880 and 1890 the ethnic makeup of the influx underwent a rather dramatic change. Northern European immigration tapered off, while that from eastern and southern Europe mounted at an unprecedented rate and remained dominant down to the closing of the gates in the 1920s (see tables, p. 750 above). Numerous economic and cultural factors dramatized the change. Because the old immigration tended to include a large proportion of people who were not utterly destitute, it had distributed itself fairly widely across the country with an urban-rural balance that roughly approximated that of the nation. But the "new" immigration, overwhelmingly constituted as it was by the dispossessed, the persecuted, and the poverty-stricken from less developed countries, moved largely to the mines, the iron range, and the cities where jobs were most available. There were related contrasts in literacy and educational level, and, of course, obvious differences in dress, cuisine, language, and customs that tended to heighten the native American's awareness of "foreigners." Finally, there were marked religious differences. The "old" immigration, except during the Irish famine years, was about evenly divided between Roman Catholics and Protestants, though it included a considerable minority of German Jews, articulate rationalists, and religious radicals. The "new" consisted largely of Roman Catholics, Jews, and members of various Eastern churches; but even here important differences were apparent: the piety of Italian and Portuguese Catholics differed from Protestant norms far more dramatically than that of the Irish and Germans; the Orthodox Jewry of eastern Europe contrasted sharply with the increasingly sedate ways of Reform Judaism; the Eastern Orthodox churches, when noticed at all, seemed like so many odd historical relics. Most of the newcomers, moreover, tended to hold jobs where wages and working conditions were bad, and to live in ethnic enclaves. The immigrant's presence thus became identified with the gravest social problems of the age.

In light of all these circumstances, it is not surprising that the half-century after 1880 witnessed another tidal wave of intolerance and racist venom. A specifically theological rationale is far less apparent in this period than in the antebellum "Protestant Crusade," but its religious relevance remains very great. And Protestants, speaking and acting self-consciously as such, ministers and laymen alike, played an active role in bringing about the culminating accomplishment of the later nativism: the virtually complete restriction of immigration. This legislation in the 1920s would eventually mark an epoch in American history.

THE REVIVAL OF NATIVISM

The last recorded meeting of the Grand Executive Committee of the Order of United Americans, largest of the early nonpolitical nativist associations, was held during the Civil War. The Know-Nothing party had by that time collapsed, a victim of the sectional issue. And for some years after the war nativism languished. Men remembered Irish heroism on the field of battle. The absorptive powers of the Union seemed stronger than ever. Yet the Gilded Age was not a time for prejudice to die or for virtue to flourish; in Roger Burlingame's phrase, it was a time of "moral paralysis." Nor was insensitivity to the doings of the Politicos and the Robber Barons the only form which moral complacency took, for widely accepted principles of laissez faire economics and conservative Social Darwinism made complacency a public virtue. "Getting ahead in the world" was the thing that mattered; the Self-Made Man was the idol and the rags-to-riches myth the animating vision for a nation of people on the make. Against this tradition, though often subtly a part of it, was arrayed a celebrated band of reformers whose continuing efforts would culminate in the era of the Muckrakers, the Progressive movement, the New Freedom of Wilson, and the New Nationalism of Theodore Roosevelt. Their counterparts in the churches were the leaders and adherents of the Social Gospel. Yet even among the men and women who led this reform tradition and who seem to represent conscience incarnate, surprisingly few were sensitive to the moral implications of ethnic, racial, and religious prejudice. Indeed it appears that most of them (Josiah Strong, Lyman Abbott, and Walter Rauschenbusch as well as Theodore Roosevelt) were victims of such prejudice. Protests against overt intolerance or its underlying assumptions took a very subordinate place in the reformist literature of both the Progressive and Social Gospel movements. As for Populism or the tradition of agrarian radicalism, neither its anti-Semitism nor its anti-Catholicism was ever far beneath the surface.

Nativism, antipopery, and anti-Semitism, therefore, resumed their place in American life. As the Grand Old Party wearied of the Bloody Shirt, its leaders took up the cry. President Grant found occasion to assail parochial schools; running for governor in Ohio, Rutherford B. Hayes declared the Democrats to be subservient to Rome; Garfield blamed the railroad violence of 1877 on foreign radicals. The Reverend Samuel Burchard's famous outburst against the party of "Rum, Romanism, and Rebellion" revealed an important stream of Republican thinking. During the 1880s when cities like Boston and New York got their first Irish mayors, these nativistic sentiments grew. In the same spirit the Order of the American Union was formed on the old Know-Nothing model around 1870, its membership open to all Protestants regardless of birth. Although it fell to pieces after an exposé in 1878, subsequent events would revive the impulse. The Grand Army of the Republic, the veterans organization, served the same end.

The discovery of the "immigration problem" as an object of social concern added fuel to these fires, especially when accompanied by the ideas of cultural "solidarity" so dear to Richard T. Ely and the "historical school" of economic thought. By these means both humanitarian concern and economic "science" could be turned into antiforeignism. Reformers could champion labor unions and their interest in stopping the flow of "cheap labor." In this way the views of men as diverse as Henry George and James Blaine could converge.

Then in May 1886 came the Haymarket Affair, in John Higham's judgment "the most important single incident in late nineteenth-century nativism." [8] In the hysteria which followed, a short-lived "American party" was formed, as were a group of secret and "patriotic" fraternal organizations which were at once antiradical, anti-Catholic, and anti-Semitic. The most important organized expression of these fears was the American Protective Association (APA), formed in 1887 by Henry F. Bowers, a paranoid crony of the mayor of Clinton, Iowa, who had been defeated by the Irish labor vote. Members of its secret councils were sworn never to vote for a Catholic and if possible never to hire or strike with one. By 1890, when the APA held its first national council, it was flourishing from Detroit to Omaha, and although

8. John Higham, *Strangers in the Land: Patterns of American Nativism, 1860–1925*, p. 54. In May 1886, when the entire country was troubled by labor unrest, a bomb exploded amid Chicago police who were moving in on a meeting of anarchists in Haymarket Square. The furor over the legal disposition of the accused kept the issue alive for over a decade.

it accomplished almost nothing in terms of actual political or legislative action, it did serve to revive grassroots anti-Catholicism in many areas, especially after its reorganization under William J. ("Whiskey Bill") Traynor during the depression of 1893. As American nationalism heightened in the 1890s, the APA emphasized the subservience of Catholics to a "foreign potentate." In 1893 Traynor even fomented a bogus "Popish Plot" by publishing a false encyclical. In its singleminded concentration on Catholicism the APA neglected other "foreigners"; it even rallied much support among Protestant immigrants.

Anti-Semitism of one sort or another is much older than Christianity, but there can be little doubt that over the centuries Christians added a new kind of depth and intensity to it. Yet due to the Puritan's defiant rejection of popery and his identification with Israel, a softening of attitudes occurred which later American ideals were to foster. In addition, Jews were rare in the United States until very late in the nineteenth century. Longfellow's elegy "The Jewish Cemetery at Newport" struck a responsive chord with its tribute to all the Ishmaels and Hagars who have been "mocked and jeered, and spurned by Christian feet." Americans had, of course, appropriated the traditional literary stereotypes from Shakespeare, Walter Scott, and Dickens, but as Oscar Handlin observes, "Until the 1930's . . . there was no anti-Semitic movement in the United States that was not also anti-Catholic." [9] The Jew served, along with other foreigners, as the scapegoat (Lev. 16:20–28) for a vast variety of curses that many Americans would be rid of: city dwellers, peddlers, bankers, non-Protestants, non-Anglo-Saxons, anarchists, freethinkers, etc. What is important after the 1880s is that the Jews are explicitly included in antiforeign attacks, while previously this had rarely been the case. Again, the Haymarket Affair presents itself as a decisive incident.

The principles of racism added further ammunition to the arsenal of American nativism. Up to this time, race theories had been applied only to the Negro, and then rather crudely, and usually in apologies for the institution of slavery and the Southern way of life. In general, however, racist notions had been throttled by the prevailing confidence in the assimilative and reformatory power of American Protestant culture. This confidence was buoyed by evolutionary optimism, the conviction that emigration was a winnowing process which brought the best and strongest to these shores, and a Darwinian environmentalism which saw American institutions as shaping these raw materials.

Gradually during the decades after 1880, however, urban corruption and

9. Oscar Handlin, *Race and Nationality in American Life* (Boston: Little, Brown and Co., 1957), p. 43.

social strife began to undermine the American's confidence and to raise racial questions. The tendency was especially noticeable in New England, where Anglo-Saxonism was strongest and Yankee dominance was most acutely threatened. James Russell Lowell struggled, though in vain, to maintain the antiracist radicalism and the anglophobia of his abolitionist days; but other cultural scions of New England's "Indian Summer" lacked even the restraining power of antislavery memories. Henry Cabot Lodge studied the Anglo-Saxon law; then as the "scholar in politics" worked in Congress to preserve his race, after 1895 making direct political use of Gustave le Bon's views on the tragedy of "racial" crossbreeding. President Francis A. Walker of MIT argued that, far from being superior peoples, America's newer immigrants were "beaten men from beaten races, representing the worst failures in the struggle for existence." Walker also perceived that the older American stock, as its birthrate declined, was being displaced by "the Latin and the Hun," whom he considered impervious to America's shaping power.

To this growing body of theory two other important scientific ideas were in due course added. America's leading eugenicist, Charles B. Davenport, pointed to the "biological issue," insisting that the admission of "degenerate breeding stock" was one of the worst, most suicidal sins that a nation could commit. William Z. Ripley of MIT in *The Races of Europe* presented the "anthropological issue," classifying Europeans into three races: Teutonic, Alpine, and Mediterranean, each with its characteristic physical constitution. The task of organizing this growing body of theory into an elaborate social argument was assumed by Madison Grant, a New York patrician, sportsman, and zoologist, whose book *The Passing of the Great Race* (1916) is perhaps the classic of American racism. It held the Teuton to be "the white man *par excellence,*" and maintained that races cannot crossbreed without suicide or reversion, thus providing a "scientific" rationale for preserving racial purity and restricting immigration.

When Grant's book appeared, his beloved Teutons (German and English) were at war with each other, and American entry would soon require of him a revised edition. Yet the war undeniably aided the nativist cause in two vital respects, by giving strength to the immigration restrictionists, and by reviving the campaign for "100 percent Americanism." Until 1917 every effort of the Congress to pass a literacy test had foundered on the presidential veto—Cleveland's in 1897, Taft's in 1913, and Wilson's in 1913—but in 1917 Wilson's second veto was overridden. The way lay open for still greater victories under Harding, Coolidge, and Hoover. Anglo-Saxonism would be weak at the League of Nations, but strong on Capitol Hill.

The drive on "hyphenated Americanism" was in part an opportunist use of the national emergency to achieve Anglo-Saxonist ends. In this sense such acts as Iowa's ban on speaking foreign languages (even on the telephone) extended a policy that many states had been implementing ever since the late 1880s. All over the country the behavioral and linguistic norms of the Anglo-Saxon were steadily enforced, often violently, with or without formal legislation. Labor leaders, civil service reformers, and champions of clean government all found such tactics convenient. The war and its aftermath are the concern of a later chapter, but it must at least be noted here that nativism, anti-Catholicism, and anti-Semitism prepared the ground for both the Immigration Restriction League and the Anti-Saloon League. They were prominent and functional features of the Protestant Establishment in America during the last troubled decades of its hegemony.

51

CRUSADING PROTESTANTISM

The idea of the crusade is essentially medieval and Catholic in its connotations, but the Reformation, despite Luther's misgivings and Anabaptist refusals, soon unleashed crusades of its own. Zwingli died in battle. William the Silent, Gustavus Adolphus, and Cromwell all led armies in the Lord's name. And in antebellum America, the Evangelical United Front with unparalleled enthusiasm launched many of its own nonmilitary crusades against the forces of evil—most unitedly against popery, most dramatically against slavery. It is hardly surprising that in the decades after the Civil War fervent men and women, especially in the North, should strive again to awaken the Protestant host. And so they did, with "Onward, Christian Soldiers" [1] and the "Battle Hymn of the Republic" setting the cadence.

The diversity of these organized efforts was extreme. Some were dramatic and new, others were commonplace attempts to solve old problems. Those born of anxiety and fear—such as the nativist movement—contradicted both Christian and national ideals; others were conceived in confidence, charity, and hope. Some failed, others succeeded. To make matters still more complicated, they varied widely in their impact. Some of the boldest campaigns only illustrate a transient mood; some of the most humble had lasting effects on the country as well as on the churches.

Perhaps the strongest underlying cause of this renewal of organized activity was an awareness of momentum lost during the period of war and reconstruction and a half-conscious desire to counteract the gaping cleavages between North and South, East and West, country and city, liberals and fundamentalists. Rejuvenation, unification of spirit, and cultural leadership would at once be achieved. Beneath all, without a doubt, was the basic

1. The Anglican High Churchman Sabine Baring-Gould (1834–1924) wrote this greatest of Victorian crusading hymns in 1865. Arthur S. Sullivan (1842–1900) wrote the music to which it is usually sung.

conviction that the church's message of salvation and righteousness was for the healing of the nations.

Among the less exalted movements was an interdenominational effort to revitalize the Sunday schools with a new kind of youth organization. In 1881 Dr. Francis E. Clark, a Congregational minister in Maine, founded the Christian Endeavor Society. Within six years there were more than seven thousand self-managed local societies with a half-million members, and by 1900 "Christian Endeavor," with its exciting international conventions and good organization, had become not only a significant ecumenical force, but had inspired emulation in almost every denomination not participating. The church had gained a new and effective means of nurture and extension, and youth had gained more distinct recognition.

More traditional in its method and aims was the Sabbatarian movement. Sabbath-keeping was a fundamental feature of Reformed religion, but industrialism and immigration had made heavy inroads upon the prevailing Puritan practices. Both old and new organizations sought to stem the rising tide of laxity, creating a furor, for example, by protesting the plan to keep the Centennial Exposition of Philadelphia (1876) open on Sundays so that workers on the six-day week could attend. It was opened, but without machine exhibits in operation. In 1893, the pressures for Sunday opening of Chicago's Columbian Exposition overwhelmed all Sabbatarian objections. The declining fortunes of Sabbatarianism do not accurately reflect the influence of evangelicalism in the nation, however, for there was widespread resistance within the churches to the Puritan conception of Sabbath keeping. Not only liberals looked back to the gloomy Sabbaths of their youth with sad revulsion and, like Richard Ely, wondered why—in light of Christ's word that the Sabbath was for man (Mark 2:27)—his father could piously sacrifice whole hay crops to the summer rain. Frances Willard of temperance fame was equally critical in her recollections of joyless, lonely Sundays on the Wisconsin farm where she grew up. But Protestant alarm over the decline in church attendance on the Sabbath did not become prominent until the 1920s.[2]

THE MISSIONARY IMPULSE

"One of the distinctive tokens of the Christianity and especially the Protestantism of the United States," writes Professor Latourette, "was the fashion

2. Despite its limited success, Sabbatarianism was by no means dead. All during the twentieth century its advocates were waging a strenuous, if losing, battle against the forces of urbanism, recreation, and leisure. Only after World War II did these reformers begin to encounter opponents who would defend their Sunday behavior by turning to the courts.

in which it conformed to the ethos of the country." The energy and organizational resourcefulness of the American evangelical churches were another such token; in fact, they were a wonder of the world. By 1893 Philip Schaff had long since turned from his early hostility, influenced in part by his work as a secretary of the Evangelical Alliance, in part by his historical studies. American writers from Robert Baird in *Religion in America* (1844) to Josiah Strong in *Our Country* (1885) exhausted the language in expressing their enthusiasm and hope for the future of "Anglo-Saxon" Protestantism. For foreigners and natives alike, it was the activity, the bustle, and the lay support of the churches which seemed so distinctively American.

Nowhere was this activism more evident than in Protestantism's diverse missionary enterprises. These had begun almost immediately in the seventeenth-century colonies from Virginia to New England, with "foreign" missions to the Indians and "home" missions to increasingly scattered European settlers and their descendants. During the Interregnum Puritans had already chartered one society for this purpose, and a half-century later, Anglicans founded the famous SPG. The Second Awakening in America spawned a whole family of state, regional, and national societies. The American Home Missionary Society was of greatest domestic importance, while the American Board of Commissioners for Foreign Missions led the way abroad. Despite Presbyterian involvement in both of these interdenominational agencies, the Presbyterian General Assembly inaugurated home mission work of its own in 1802, and the Old School faction pressed this line of approach to the extent of dividing the denomination in 1837. After the schism, even the New School yielded to the rise of denominationalism, as did the reunited Northern Presbyterian church after its formation in 1869.

Among the Congregationalists the new forms of denominational self-awareness had direct and important consequences for home missions. They held their first national conference in two centuries in 1852 at Albany, and after proceeding by regular steps to organize themselves, in 1871 they formed a national council which thereafter prosecuted a fairly vigorous program of extension. By the end of the century the denomination stretched from coast to coast and had founded new seminaries at Chicago (1855) and Berkeley, California (1866).

Baptist growth was largely due to the semispontaneous expansion of the farmer-preacher system; but missionary societies were also organized in Massachusetts (1802) and in New York (1807). In 1814 a new General Missionary Convention was organized, inspired largely by the missionary efforts of Luther Rice. Among the Baptists, however, there was much suspicion of centralized authority, strong theological misgivings about "societies" in particular, and many doubts about missionary work in general. In fact, the antimission spirit helped to give birth to two new Baptist denominations: the Two-Seed-in-the-Spirit Predestinarian Baptists in the 1820s and the Primitive Baptists in the 1830s. But evangelism was inextinguishable, and Baptists, North and South, grew rapidly as the country expanded westward. The Disciples of Christ shared Baptist misgivings about extracongregational institutions like the societies, and they spent much energy (and newsprint, for they did not doubt the legitimacy of unofficial denominational journals) debating the implications of the New Testament church model for the present day. The missions controversy among them boiled on throughout the century, but evangelism continued nevertheless; and by 1865 this communion was poised for its greatest half-century of growth and geographic expansion.

Methodism had easily accepted the idea of home missions. Itinerant preachers were in fact a fundamental element of its polity, and circuits and bishops were added, North and South, as occasion demanded. Voluntary missionary societies performed a relatively unimportant role. After 1835 the Protestant Episcopal church conducted its home missionary labors chiefly as a church, appointing missionary bishops over remote or thinly populated districts.

In terms of church organization, perhaps the most important missionary development of the century was the gradual process, already alluded to, by which evangelism was made the task of the denomination as a whole, every member thus being at least theoretically a participant. At the heart of the change was a conception of the Church-as-mission which served to channel denominational self-consciousness and competitiveness while at the same time permitting closer control of the missionaries in doctrinal matters. Less commendable but certainly evident were the desires of denominational leaders for wider authority and the need, when zeal was flagging, to gain at least the financial support of every church member, regardless of his personal enthusiasm for the cause.

The end of the Civil War with its great burst in American population growth and accelerated westward expansion led to a resurgence of missionary activity. Baptist, Methodist, and Presbyterian churches were most successful in these efforts, in large part because so many of them migrated, and because they were the most natural affiliation for the average unchurched but nominally Protestant American. But all denominations continued to extend themselves—usually by methods developed on earlier frontiers. It is not necessary, therefore, to weary the reader with a sequence of denominational histories on the trans-Mississippi West. But in the West was also the Indian, and missionary heroes and martyrs had their roles in this momentous confrontation just as did General George Custer. A century later, the problem of tarnished reputations arose in their case as much as in his.

The Indian and American Culture

During the decades after the Civil War the predicament of the American Indian demanded a shift in government policy. In 1871 Congress gave up the fiction that Indian tribes were independent powers, abolished the treaty system, and recognized that the Indians were in fact wards of the state. In retrospect, one can see that a process of cultural disintegration which had been set in motion by the European migrations of the sixteenth and seventeenth centuries was entering a critical stage. President Grant's announcement of a "peace policy," therefore, opened a new epoch in American Indian relations. The Indian reformer—after being ignored for so long—began to be heard. Helen Hunt Jackson culminated a long crusade with a stinging report to the nation, *A Century of Dishonor* (1881), and a powerful sentimental novel, *Ramona* (1884), while Senator Henry Laurens Dawes of Massachusetts marshaled the necessary congressional majorities. Conquest and removal yielded to a search for some means of "solving" the problem, whether by assimilation, protected isolation, or—it was advocated by a few—extermination.

Until the Civil War, Christian missions had been almost the only American institutions to deal constructively with the situation, although even they, like the Spanish and French, had always unabashedly sought to convert the Indian to Christianity and, in varying degree, to reshape his way of life according to Western norms. The Quakers and Episcopalians had been very vocal in their criticism of what passed for government policy, and when scandal and corruption in the Indian Service became a national disgrace, President Grant threw the doctrine of church-state separation to the winds and literally parceled out the task to the denominations. In their hands it largely remained until the Dawes Act of 1887 launched a new policy of individual land allotments that was frankly assimilationist in its intention though it became chiefly distintegrative in its effects. The churches also exerted considerable influence through the Board of Indian Commissioners, which functioned in an advisory capacity from 1869 to 1933; but public apathy and prevailing attitudes led to another long period of drift and neglect.[3] With the coming of the New Deal in the 1930s new efforts to reconstitute viable tribal life would be attempted. Yet in the 1970s the problem

3. Armed conflict aside, the inexorable force of white-red intercultural contact has been too little considered in discussions of missionaries, churches, and the Indian question (see Robert F. Berkhofer, Jr., *Salvation and the Savage: An Analysis of Protestant Missions and American Indian Response, 1787–1862;* Loring B. Priest, *Uncle Sam's Stepchildren: The Reformation of United States Indian Policy, 1865–1887;* R. Pierce Beaver, *Church, State, and the American Indians;* and Bernard W. Sheehan, "Indian-White Relations in Early America: A Review Essay," *William and Mary Quarterly* 26 [April 1969]: 267–86).

remained much as it had a century before. Although the churches by then were in no position to be active participants, their earlier search for ways to bring the Indian into the mainstream of American life was by no means discredited.

Missions and Empire

Against this general background there were two major movements of combined pioneer settlement and missionary enterprise that had specific consequences for American expansionism. Most exciting were the exploits of the early missionaries to Oregon, an area which the British Hudson's Bay Company had kept very much for itself until 1834. In that year two Methodists, Jason and Daniel Lee, started a small mission there, which probably induced the American Board to follow their example. With the support of the board, Samuel Parker and three others made the trek west in 1835, to be joined later that year by Dr. Marcus Whitman (1802–47), a physician, the Reverend Henry H. Spalding, their wives, and a few other volunteers. They founded two missions in southeastern Oregon, and in 1838 they were assisted by the Reverend Cushing Eells, a graduate of Williams College and Hartford Seminary who had also been sent out by the American Board. Dr. Whitman died at Indian hands in 1847 along with his wife and a dozen other settlers. But by that time he had already made his famous trip back East in 1842, where his interviews with the president and the secretary of state probably stiffened American demands for Oregon. In returning to his mission as part of the great migration of 1843, he had again influenced future events by urging this company not to abandon its wagons at Fort Hall (Idaho) but to press on and open the road to Oregon. Eells, however, remained active in the ecclesiastical and educational life of the Northwest until his death in 1893. He was a missionary among the Spokane Indians for a decade and helped to found or strengthen six congregations and three colleges in the region.[4]

The American Board's semi-imperialistic projects in Hawaii belong in almost the same category as its earlier work in Oregon, since Hawaii, too, was ultimately annexed (1898) and made a state of the Union (1959). Both are examples of "foreign" missions that were, quite literally, domesticated.

Located about 2,100 miles west of California and 3,400 miles east of Japan, the Hawaiian (Sandwich) Islands became known to the West only when Captain James Cook reported his "discovery" in 1778. A subsequent slow but steady increase in Western contacts gradually altered the native Polynesian culture and undermined a fairly stable form of feudal monarchy.

4. On Roman Catholic missions on the upper Missouri and in Oregon, see pp. 544–45 above.

The decisive event was the arrival in 1820 of a party of New England missionaries and three American-educated Hawaiians sent out by the American Board. Aided by later arrivals, these Americans had unexpected "success" in Christianizing a large majority of the natives, including numerous chiefs and members of the royal family. They were also successful in introducing diseases that decimated the native people (only 10 percent of the population was "native" by 1920), in developing the islands' economic potential, and in introducing constitutional reforms that finally led to the overthrow of Queen Liliuokalani in 1893 and the proclamation of an independent republic as the prelude to annexation. By this time the Yankees' economic feudalism had replaced the old order.

As immigration continued, Filipinos, Portuguese, and diverse Americans brought Roman Catholicism almost to numerical equality with Protestantism, while the very large influx of Japanese (43 percent of the population in 1920), Chinese (9 percent), and Koreans introduced a large non-Christian element. During the years preceding the American Board's discontinuance of support in 1863, however, the missionary achievement was considerable. They reduced the native language to writing, provided the basis for an educational system, and introduced viable modern forms of government and lawmaking. Nowhere else under the American flag, or any other flag, have the Orient and the Occident met and blended with such goodwill and amity.

HOME AND WORLD MISSIONS

In the actual conduct of "home missions" the most important transformation came about not in the West but in the East, not on the frontier but in the city. Here was a crisis that required two drastic adaptations. In the first place, the traditional individualistic emphasis on soul-saving came up against the fact that whole classes and ethnic groups needed saving. Even the most conservative denominational home mission boards had to concede that poverty, ignorance, and alienation posed problems with which rescue missions, revival campaigns, and Salvation Army methods could not cope. Next to the WCTU, the home missions movement was the most significant route by which social Christianity penetrated the conservative evangelical consciousness.

In the wake of this realization followed the second great adaptation: the resort to cooperative interdenominational planning and working. Charles L. Thompson (1839–1924) of the Madison Avenue Presbyterian Church in New York was a leader in both respects. After reorganizing his own denomination's board of home missions in the years after 1898 and developing relationships with parallel work in other churches, he had the satisfaction in 1908 of presiding at the organizational meeting of the Home Missions Council. Within a decade thirty-five boards were affiliated, and the Southern Baptist Convention was the only major evangelical denomination not represented. Its problems were vast, its resources and powers small, and the popular appeal of its cause could never match that of foreign missions during this period. But it did make important social surveys, develop methods of cooperation, and by joint promotional efforts, lay foundations upon which to build after World War I had enlarged the "home front" role of the churches.

"The Evangelization of the World in This Generation"

The closing two decades of the nineteenth century witnessed the climactic phase of the foreign missions movement in American Protestantism. This new surge of interest was due, above all, to the stimulus and inspiration of Dwight L. Moody, whose warm, optimistic evangelicalism shines through every phase of the activity which followed and was reflected in the hundreds and thousands of young men and women who committed themselves to the cause. The other essential contribution to this activity was that of the YMCA, which had, in fact, figured strongly in Moody's own life. This contribution can be traced to the YMCA's remarkable and spontaneous advance in American colleges and universities during the post–Civil War decades. At the YMCA convention of 1877 in Louisville, due largely to the zealous work of a student at Princeton University named Luther DeLoraine Wishard (1854–1925), the Intercollegiate YMCA movement was launched, with Wishard as corresponding secretary. His vigorous efforts brought the number of participating college associations from 21 to 96 in 1880, and to 258 by 1887. By this time the YWCA had also established a working relationship in a hundred or so women's collegiate associations.

The next stage involved Moody directly, first in a series of revivals at Princeton, Yale, Harvard, and Dartmouth that repeated his successes in Britain at Edinburgh, Oxford, and Cambridge. The meetings in England had resulted in the conversion of Charles T. Studd and Stanley Smith, who went on to careers in Hudson Taylor's famous China Inland Mission. It was Wishard's hope that a similar interest in foreign missions could be aroused in America. Climaxing the American college revival in 1886 was Moody's historic invitation of mission-minded college students to a month-long summer session at Moody's school in Northfield, Massachusetts. It turned out to be an occasion beyond anyone's dream, and before it was over an even hundred—the Mount Hermon Hundred—had taken the pledge to become foreign missionaries.

By the time of the next summer school, the number had reached twenty-one hundred (sixteen hundred men and five hundred women). President Seelye of Amherst called it the greatest missionary uprising in modern times. In 1888 the Student Volunteer Movement was organized, its almost unbelievable expansion due to the gifted leadership of another student, John R. Mott. Mott (1865–1955) was born of Methodist parents in New York State but brought up on an Iowa farm. In 1888 he was serving as the head of the YMCA at Cornell University. He was destined to become the leading American ambassador of missions and ecumenism for almost a half-century, and from 1890 to 1915 he served as the national college secretary of the YMCA. His impact on American Christian students during those years was phenomenal, and in due course the student community of the whole world became his parish.

The work among students was itself evangelism—a home missions work of sorts. But the growing student movement in turn gave impetus to the formation in 1906 of the Laymen's Missionary Movement, with a devout layman, John B. Sleman, providing the connecting link. The LMM owed its origins to a series of meetings held at Fifth Avenue Presbyterian Church to commemorate the "Haystack Meeting" at Williams College from which the American foreign missionary impulse had sprung. After long hours of prayerful discussion of a moving talk by J. Campbell White, the fifty men present resolved to set up a Committee of Twenty-Five to make plans for propagating missions and gaining financial support for the SVM's campaign to "evangelize the world in this generation." In 1908 the annual interchurch conference of foreign mission boards formally recognized the movement's "spontaneity and timeliness [as] evidence of the hand of God." Under the early leadership of Samuel B. Capen and, later, with J. Campbell White as general secretary, a large general committee and a network of subcommittees began its work: spreading the movement to Great Britain and Canada, organizing visits to mission fields followed by speaking tours in America, inaugurating education programs in local churches, and above all, stimulating generous gifts to the foreign missions cause.

The thousands of laymen awakened by the movement also became powerful agents in other crusades and campaigns during the World War and the twenties, illustrating what has always been the most important aspect of the entire foreign missions impulse: its reflex effect on the life and church activities of Christians at home. The missionary on furlough was the great American window on the non-Western world. Through him, the aims of the missionary movement, as well as the cultural stereotypes which underlay it, became fundamental elements of the American Protestant's world outlook. India, Africa, China, and Japan came to be regarded as spiritual provinces of the American churches from the Nebraska plains to New York's Fifth Avenue. Even in foreign policy the effects of this vast reservoir of popular interest and affection were registered. Statesmen could not treat these great "mission fields" as diplomatic pawns. The missionary's knowledge and experience also guided the State Department, and in due course missionary families furnished countless sons (John Foster Dulles being only the best known) to the diplomatic service and related scholarly pursuits.

The Crisis of the Missions

Alas, every movement has its crisis and the work of these mission-minded laymen was no exception. From the start the Laymen's Missionary Movement had been criticized as an escape and evasion. "Evangelization," so the critique ran, had come to mean no more than "presenting" Christ to the world so that prophecy might be fulfilled and a premillennarian expectation of the Second Coming provided. As early as 1911, Joseph E. McAfee, a Presbyterian with experience in urban home missions, defined the crisis:

> If the missionary maintains that the individualistic method is ultimate, and represents an individualistic scheme of salvation as final and complete, he runs counter to approved world tendencies and repudiates a social theory which schools of thought in all civilized lands are successfully establishing.[5]

By such a declaration the mission question was fatefully merged with the Fundamentalist controversy, and in this sense it points to larger aspects of the Protestant dilemma. But of more immediate concern to the development of missions was the remarkable degree to which McAfee's "conclusions" on missionary policy were adopted by the churches during World War I. The SVM itself would embrace a broader view of service at its convention of 1918, and thereafter the rift between liberal and conservative views widened year by year as increasing support accrued to a social and philanthropic rather than a narrowly evangelistic view of the Church's mission among non-Christians. The fact of crisis became undeniable; the "halcyon years" had blown up an unexpected tempest.

The ensuing debates made explicit what McAfee had implied. It began

5. Joseph E. McAfee, *The Crisis of Missionary Method* (New York, 1911), p. 37. The issue which McAfee raised was central to the entire mission enterprise of the churches; it even posed the problem of the American Redeemer Nation's relation to the rest of the world. Inevitably, therefore, the debate intensified, finally coming to a head in 1932 with the immensely controversial report of an appraisal committee headed by the Harvard philosopher William Ernest Hocking, *Re-thinking Missions: A Laymen's Inquiry after One Hundred Years.*

to appear that the foreign missions revival may well have arisen as a half-subconscious effort to divert Protestants from intellectual problems and internal dissensions by engaging them in great moral and spiritual tasks—only to have deeper problems and dissension reappear. And so it would be in the greatest and most unified of all Protestant crusades—that for temperance, a campaign whose successes and failures, far more than those on far away mission fields, would affect almost every aspect of national life.

THE GREAT TEMPERANCE DEBATE

The "temperance movement" (as that most intemperate of reform impulses is usually called) hit America in three major waves. The first shared the great victories of the Evangelical United Front and the humanitarian crusades during the antebellum era. The famous "Maine Law" was passed in 1846, and in another decade thirteen northern and western states had followed suit. Yet these victories were fleeting; when the Civil War ended, only Maine and Massachusetts were in the dry fold, and the latter soon wandered out. To recoup these losses the Grand Lodge of Good Templars launched the Prohibition party in 1869. It gained attention slowly, and despite the broad vision of its leadership, it never became strong.

The really effective revival of the movement occurred five years later, through a sensational series of demonstrations and "pray-ins" that has not inappropriately been referred to as the Woman's Revolution. It all began on 24 December 1873, when Eliza Trimble Thompson of Hillsboro, Ohio, led more than seventy determined women from a prayer meeting to one of the town's liquor vendors. Though followed by hundreds of townspeople, they did no violence; but on one side or the other of the swinging doors they prayed, sang, pleaded, and in other ways besought the proprietor to close and desist. During succeeding days they dealt similarly with the twelve other saloons in town, and achieved almost complete (though impermanent) success. By this time, with wide press coverage and surprising public approval, the Woman's Crusade had begun to spread throughout Ohio and then to other states. In Minnesota the Singing Hutchinsons of abolitionist fame lent their talents to the cause, singing Julia B. Nelson's new battle hymn:

> And where are the hands red with slaughter?
> Behold them each day as you pass
> The places where death and destruction
> Are retailed at ten cents a glass.

Within a year the crusade lost steam, and its long-term results were in one sense small, for the great losses in liquor tax revenue reported during 1874 were soon matched by new gains. But the crusade did revitalize the temperance movement—and at the same time summoned women to a new role in public affairs. "That phenomenal . . . uprising of women in southern Ohio " declared feminist Mary Livermore, "floated them to a higher level of womanhood. It lifted them out of a subject condition where they had suffered immitigable woe." In November 1874 at Cleveland, delegates from seventeen states, many of them active in church missionary societies or "veterans" of war work in the Sanitary and Christian commissions, organized the Women's Christian Temperance Union. To the crucial post of corresponding secretary they elected Frances Willard, the woman who for two decades would not only make the WCTU her lengthened shadow, but who made it also the greatest women's organization of the century.

Frances Willard, as most Protestant school children once well knew, was born on 28 September 1839 to westering Vermonters then living near Rochester, New York. The family soon moved on to Oberlin, Ohio—where the child developed a lifelong distaste for Charles Finney's fearsome sermons—and then in 1846 further west to Wisconsin. Frances grew up on an isolated farm near Janesville under the stern rule of an ultra-Methodistic father. In later life she remembered standing on a rainy day huddled with her brother and sister in a barn doorway and exclaiming, "I wonder if we shall ever know anything, see anybody, or go anywhere." As it happened, she did all three, and by a fairly direct route. She went away to schools in Milwaukee and Evanston. After graduating in 1859, she spent the next decade teaching in various schools, serving as secretary to the Methodist Centenary Fund, and traveling in Europe and the Middle East for twenty-eight months. Shortly after her return she became president of the Evanston College for Ladies. When the College became part of Northwestern University, she was appointed its dean, but finding that arrangement unsatisfactory, she resigned in 1874. By that time she was already a vice-president of the Association for the Advancement of Women, and before the year was out she was elected an officer in the organization with which her name will always be linked, the WCTU.

The union's early years were marked, as she herself said, by an ideological conflict "which became distinctly outlined under the names: 'conservative' and 'liberal.' " Its first president, Annie Wittenmyer (who in 1888 would also oppose Willard's efforts to get women accepted as delegates to the Methodist General Conference), led the conservatives, championing a focus on the single issue of prohibition. Dissenting from this narrow conception of the

WCTU, Frances Willard resigned and in 1877 worked for a time on the evangelistic team of Dwight L. Moody. She disagreed with his policy as well, and after heavy western support brought her to the union's presidency in 1881, she began to implement her own ideas: a vigorous membership campaign, endless speaking tours to propagate the cause, spectacular annual conventions, a major emphasis on women's rights, including the vote, expansion of the union's concern for a wide range of social issues, including the traffic in young prostitutes which prudery had heretofore kept from public discussion, and finally, the development of diverse political strategies to gain these ends. Her success in carrying out this vast "Do Everything" program owed most, perhaps, to her amazing gifts of leadership; but it also depended on the way in which the WCTU, like Willard herself, remained committed to the ideals and spirit of evangelical Protestantism and to her shrewd policy of resting the whole cause on the two institutions where woman's "place" was assured: the home and the church.

Under Mrs. Hayes and Mrs. Garfield the WCTU had entered the White House almost immediately, leading one statesman to remark that at presidential receptions "the water flowed like champagne." But Frances Willard was disappointed when Garfield reneged on his preelection political commitments to temperance, and in 1884, having been spurned at the conventions of both major parties, she led the union to support the Prohibition party. Here she won a minor triumph, and she was plausibly accused of having diverted enough Republican votes in New York to elect Cleveland! Lest the lesson be forgotten, the union also developed its techniques of pressure politics and practiced them with an effectiveness never before equaled in America. By 1896 Frances Willard had become sympathetic to both Populism and the rising demand for urban reform. She commended both Henry George and Edward Bellamy to her ladies, having turned from "Gospel Politics" to "Gospel Socialism." And after failing to unite the Populist and Prohibition parties under a banner that included temperance and woman's suffrage, she was working with other thoroughgoing critics of the status quo to create a single great reform party. But by this time her health was failing. Even more ominously for one with her vision, the Anti-Saloon League had been founded; and soon after her death in 1898, the WCTU gradually became little more than the woman's auxiliary of that single-minded engine of political manipulation.

Before considering the league's place in Protestant history, however, it is well to underline the degree to which the union's later leadership hid the actual Frances Willard beneath a sentimental legend of Saint Frances of the White Ribbon. Americans generally, including church historians, have almost forgotten the single most impressive reformer to have worked within the context of the evangelical churches. When she died, someone observed that the death of no other woman except Queen Victoria could have so stirred the world. Frances Willard had given American womanhood a new place in society and in the churches. And beneath her zeal was the burning evangelical faith which she had always communicated with such unparalleled effectiveness. She could be inspired by anyone who sought holiness, from Marcus Aurelius to Emerson, and she was an eclectic in theology; but Christianity was her bridle. "I am a strictly loyal and orthodox Methodist," she said, and then in the idiom of her times, "Like the bee that gathers from many fragrant gardens, but flies home with his varied gains . . . so I fly home to the sweetness and sanctity of the old faith that has been my shelter and solace so long." In this spirit she made the WCTU a vast national organization with lively, growing roots in and amid the parishes of every state and territory. She succeeded, moreover, in making it the chief exception to the rule of evangelical social complacency during the "halcyon years."

The Third Wave of Temperance Reform

In Oberlin, Ohio, a town famous for its role in the antislavery crusade, the Anti-Saloon League was organized in 1893 as a church-oriented direct action political pressure organization. Due to the efforts of an Iowa Methodist minister, Alpha J. Kynett, the league was organized on a national basis two years later at a convention in Washington, D.C. Hiram Price, a former Republican congressman from Iowa, was elected president, and Wayne B. Wheeler, an Oberlin alumnus, was superintendent. Within a few years they had paid agents in nearly every state and an efficient staff in the national office. The league was well financed by men of wealth—S. S. Kresge was one of its most generous patrons—and before the goal of a constitutionally dry United States was reached, the league had spent $35 million. It had but one aim: to get dry laws, the drier the better, the more stringent and sweeping the better. Unlike the Prohibition party and the WCTU, it had no diversionary purposes and cared little or nothing about a politician's morals or political principles so long as he voted dry. It used hard-driving, tough-minded methods, and they worked. "We have got to kill the Anti-Saloon League and then lick the Republican and Democratic parties," declared the Prohibition party's presidential candidate in 1908; but by then the would-be slayer was all but slain. Although only three states had stood squarely in the dry category in 1903 (Maine, Kansas, and North Dakota), two-thirds of the states had taken action by 1916, and three-fourths of the population was living under some kind of prohibition law.

The campaign for an amendment to the Constitution was launched in 1913, and Superintendent Wheeler's machine began to roll immediately, heading first for the primaries, then for the congressional elections of 1914. When the House assembled, a dry majority was seated. Then came the bonanza—war—giving nativists a rationale for harassing the German brewers. After American entry into the war, a great stress on saving fuel (alcohol) and using grain for bread advanced the cause further. Finally on 18 December 1917 the Great Day came: the Eighteenth Amendment cleared the House 282 to 128, and with surprising speed received overwhelming approval in the states (only Connecticut and Rhode Island failed to ratify). On 16 January 1919, with Nebraska's ratification, the Noble Experiment began. Its history, of course, belongs to the twenties, but some consideration of the churches' role in its prewar preparation is called for.

The dry crusade in its third and triumphant phase was chiefly the work of the Anti-Saloon League; and Wayne Wheeler repeatedly insisted that the league was simply "the churches [and the "decent people"] organized against the saloon." But one can be more precise: Methodism, North and South, gave the league its unanimous institutional support and supplied most of its most militant leadership. The Baptists and Presbyterians, North and South, were not far behind. Support came from everywhere, including at first some important Roman Catholics, but it was basically the last great corporate work in America of legalistic evangelicalism. Every major historian of the campaign, moreover, emphasizes other nontheological factors that identify this form of Protestantism more exactly. Most obviously it was rural or small-town; and its ancestry was British. Its deepest antipathies were directed toward city dwellers, foreigners, and Roman Catholics. Bigotry and nativism were often dry. Alphonso Alva Hopkins expressed a familiar combination of attitudes in his *Profit and Loss in Man* (1908):

> Our boast has been that we are a Christian people, with Morality at the center of our civilization. Foreign control or conquest is rapidly making us un-Christian, with immorality throned in power.
>
> Besodden Europe, worse bescourged than by war, famine and pestilence, sends here her drink-makers, her drunkard-makers, and her drunkards, or her more temperate but habitual drinkers, with all their un-American and anti-American ideas of morality and government; they are absorbed into our national life, but not assimilated; with no liberty whence they came, they demand unrestricted liberty among us, even to license for the things we loathe; and through the ballot-box, flung wide open to them by foolish statesmanship that covets power,

their foreign control or conquest has become largely an appalling fact; they dominate our Sabbath, over large areas of country; they have set up for us their own moral standards, which are grossly immoral; they govern our great cities, until even Reform candidates accept their authority and pledge themselves to obey it; the great cities govern the nation; and foreign control or conquest could gain little more, though secured by foreign armies and fleets.

As one feature of this foreign conquest, foreign capital has come here, and to the extent of untold millions has invested itself in breweries, until we are told that their annual profits at one time reached about $25,000,000 yearly, sent over seas to foreign stockholders, who shared thus in their conquest of America, while to them, in their palaces and castles, American Labor paid tribute, and for their behoof American morals were debased, the American Sunday surrendered.[6]

By no means all temperance reformers and enemies of the saloon shared this syndrome. Kresge was chiefly interested in an efficient laboring force. Jack London lamented ruined lives, including his own. Socialists attacked a pernicious industry. Jane Addams spoke as a compassionate social worker. Yet few things Frances Willard said to the WCTU won more immediate criticism from the rank and file than her suggestion that poverty caused alcoholism, even though she also admitted the orthodox point that excessive drinking often caused poverty. Because it did give focus to so many fears and hopes, the temperance movement united Protestant Americans as nothing else ever had or would. By the same token, however, it diverted attention from many other social concerns and left the churches ill-prepared for great calamities that were in the offing.

6. Born in Burlington Flats, New York, Alphonso Alva Hopkins (1843–1918) began in 1868 a long career as a lecturer and writer on temperance and economic topics. For three years he was vice-chancellor and professor of political economy at American Temperance University (Tennessee), and in 1882 he ran as a Prohibition candidate for governor of New York. His *Profit and Loss in Man* (New York: Funk and Wagnalls Co., 1908) elaborated the themes which he explored in *Wealth and Waste* (1896).

VIII
THE AGE OF FALTERING CRUSADES

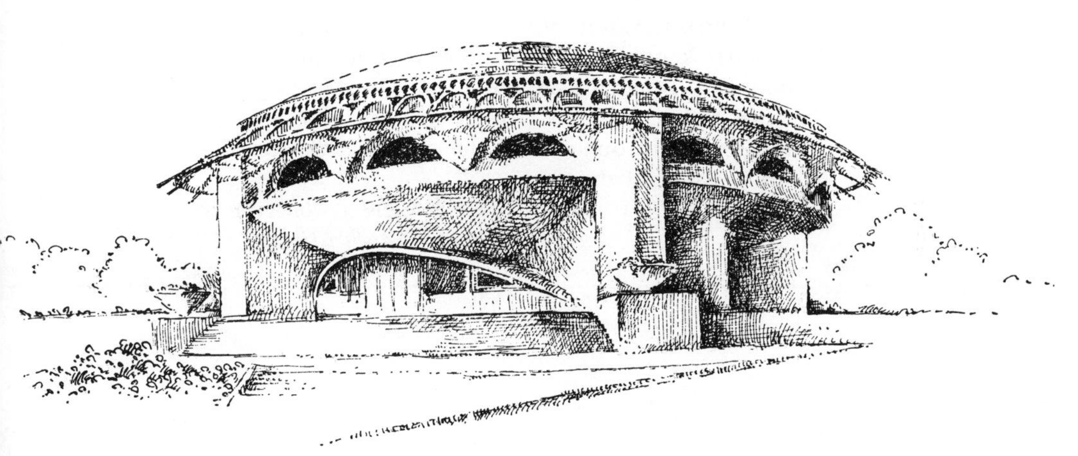

I can remember, for I am a little older than the present century, when the first automobile rolled down the main street of my native village. . . . And I remember when the first motion picture invaded the town. No one took them seriously at first; it was useless to condemn them. They were too obviously innocent at that time, and though a few men of great imagination foresaw some of their serious consequences for business, morals, education, and religion, the great majority accepted them for no better reason than that they were inevitable. . . . What has speed to do with justice or cheap entertainment with kindness? Even to this day there are religious spokesmen who claim to disregard purely "secular" inventions. . . . But everyone knows by this time that these instruments have changed not only *how* we express ourselves but *what* we believe and do.

These innovations were products and signs of similar changes in our minds, of new discoveries, new history, new ideals, changed philosophies. . . . The range and focus of our interests have been revolutionized. Our religion itself, our love of the eternal, has yielded to the pressure of the times.

Herbert Wallace Schneider, *Religion in Twentieth-Century America* (1952)

Wartime excitements and postwar deflations of spirit have provided the rhythms for the religious climate of the United States during the greater part of the twentieth century. The rise of fascism in the thirties and the cold war after 1945 filled in the intervals. Yet beneath these alternations, a steady acceleration of uncontrolled economic growth, population movement, and governmental expansion had brought the United States by the later 1960s to a state of advanced technocratic crisis compounded by yet another war. Nor was this due only to critical developments within America's traditional households of faith. The old consensus about the country's destiny also collapsed; many came to doubt that the Redeemer Nation was capable of redeeming anybody, and wondered if it was capable of saving itself from urban rot, environmental pollution, racist conflict, poverty, and countercultural disaffection. Having become a victim of individualism, exploitation, and world-policemanship, the United States had become somehow the Old World—a lesson for less ravaged countries on the wages of sin.

The chapters which deal with this twentieth-century course of events are divided into two parts. The five chapters of Part VIII are chronologically arranged, proceeding by periods from the war with Spain through the years of religious revival which followed World War II. In Part IX the late modern development of six major religious traditions and communities is followed from their late nineteenth-century situation down to their rendezvous with the sixties. This decisive decade is then surveyed in the final chapter.

A view of the general religious situation down to the election of John F. Kennedy as president reveals the trend which this victory of a Roman Catholic candidate symbolizes: the crumbling of the Protestant Establishment and the emergence of more genuine pluralism. The crumbling, however, did not occur in November 1960; its origins lay far back in early English decisions on colonial immigration policy and their later reinforcement by the Declaration of Independence with its declarations of equality. Yet the twentieth century also played its role in the process through a complicated series of actions and reactions: Prohibition, the revival of the KKK, immigration restriction laws, the Depression, the New Deal, and the election campaigns of Al Smith (1928) and Franklin Roosevelt (1932). Perhaps most basic were a set of value conflicts that reached an extreme phase during the twenties: the problems of the city, the revived Fundamentalist controversy, the implications of jazz, cocktail parties, and the movies. Rural America took its stand—and lost. And such experiences profoundly changed the ideals and inner character of all minorities, including white Protestants. Catholics and Jews gained a new place in American society, while black Americans migrated in large numbers to the cities.

Yet the Crash and the Depression did more than contribute to pluralism —they brought out new elements in every religious tradition, especially, perhaps, new kinds of critical thinking about the religious implications of the nation's domestic distress and the darkening political situation abroad. Those turbulent years also revealed that America's reservoirs of bigotry and fanaticism were by no means empty. Then with the war came a return to loyalty, cooperation, and relative singleness of purpose.

After World War II there was no return to the twenties, because the rising affluence was part of a social revolution out of which arose a new kind of industrial society. In this new ethos the hard edges of American religious life were corroded by a strange revival that had no precedent in American history. Unappreciated at the time was the degree to which the old-time religion was relegated to subcultural status. Even less appreciated was the degree to which the postwar concern for peace of mind was a foretaste, though an insipid one, of the radical theology which would grow out of the harsher confrontations that began to accumulate after President Kennedy's assassination in November 1963.

52

THE LITTLE WAR AND THE GREAT WAR

The Great War of 1914–18 left Europe shattered. The best part of its manhood was "missing in action." *La belle époque* was a tear-stained memory. The old order was gone. And more. When the retrospect of a half-century was at hand, historians would see that European civil war, that suicidal carnage, as the threshold of a post-European age in *world* history. Christendom might regain at least the outer semblance of health for two decades, or three; but the internal injuries sustained at the Marne, the Somme, and Tannenberg would not heal. World War II and all that came with it, before and after, would administer the coup de grace.

For Americans World War I was "over there"—a long, long way from Times Square. On the home front only a very few seemed to comprehend the tragic dimensions of the holocaust. During the twenties their numbers increased as participants and observers began to expose the reality and its aftermath. But only with the coming of the Great Depression did a fairly wide range of thinkers begin to see that bourgeois civilization was deep in crisis. And not until a quarter-century after that did the idea of a "post-Christian" world begin to dawn on the popular consciousness. All the more need, therefore, to approach the Great Crusade from the vantage point of the halcyon age—and to march into it, as it were, in the ranks of the Men and Religion Forward Movement, singing "Onward, Christian Soldiers." But before that, a glance at the Spanish-American rehearsal.

IMPERIAL AMERICA

Manifest Destiny as an American idea is probably as old as the "sea to sea" charters of the earliest colonies. The Puritan's sense of divine mission soon added a spiritual dimension to these grandiose ideas—a dimension that grew in importance after 1776, when nationalistic ambitions superseded the apocalyptic visions of an earlier day. In the antebellum decades evangelical dreams of a vast Christian republic brought prophetic certainty to the idea. Manifest Destiny became the catchword of an epoch.

John Quincy Adams, no less than John C. Calhoun, thought in continental terms. The vision extended not only "from sea to shining sea" but for some enthusiastic spirits from the snowy wastes of the Arctic to the tropical charms of the Isthmus. Journalists, railroad publicists, congressmen, and preachers exhausted the English language on the themes of America's destiny—until the question of slavery in the territories plus Northern fears of an enlarged "slavocracy" darkened the dream. For a quarter-century after the Civil War, Americans had other preoccupations. But in the 1890s the dream was enlivened again, partly because a kind of North-South comproise had been achieved, partly to hasten that process, and, of course, partly because a wide sector of the public anticipated real benefits from imperialism. With the Mexican and Canadian borders stabilized, men looked beyond the sea—especially to the Caribbean, the Pacific, and the Far East.

Behind these new impulses was advocacy of many kinds. Captain (later Admiral) Mahan was insisting on sea power as a condition of greatness, and his kind of logic led to acquisitions in Samoa and the annexation of Hawaii. Professor John W. Burgess and the Reverend Josiah Strong were proclaiming the destiny and duty of Anglo-Saxon civilization. Missionaries called for government furtherance of evangelism to the heathen, while nativists preached the liberation of oppressed peoples from Roman Catholic thralldom as a simple act of charity. With the horrors of the Civil War now gilded in memory, men like Theodore Roosevelt and others much less reserved celebrated the ennobling effects of war. Expansionism, in short, was popular—and perhaps *most* popular when surviving remnants of Spain's tottering empire hung nearby like ripened fruit.[1]

In 1896 William McKinley was elected president with a Cuban independence plank in his platform, while Bryan and the Populists during the ensuing years hammered for action, raising the threat of a "Free Cuba–Free Silver" campaign in 1900. Not only for this reason, however, is the election of 1896 one of the great revelatory events in American religious history. As in no other election, both candidates virtually personified American Protestantism. Both William Jennings Bryan and William McKinley

1. The fruit had been both near and ripe for a long time, to be sure; and during Cuba's unsuccessful Ten Years War of 1868–78 the United States had had sufficient provocation. But at that time the country was sated with war.

were reared in pious homes, educated in denominational colleges, and guided throughout their lives by the traditions and practices of evangelicalism. Yet the policy options they put before the nation in their campaigns were drastically at variance. McKinley took his stand for business, sound money, the tariff, and the myths of the city and the self-made man; Bryan for the farmers, laborers, and debtors, free silver, socialistic experiments, and the myths of rural virtue and the honest yeoman. In different ways each was at once nostalgic and forward-looking. Together they dispel the notion that Protestantism prescribed a specific program for America.

With regard to Cuba and Spain, the seemingly inevitable occurred in April 1898, when the president's war message to Congress expressed his pious hope that "our aspirations as a Christian, peace-loving people will be realized." As it turned out, America loved "the splendid little war" (19 April–12 August 1898), despite the gross mismanagement and ravages of disease in the armed forces. They also loved the gloriously simple victory of Commodore Dewey in the Philippines. "It was a little war," reflected Teddy Roosevelt a bit ruefully, "but it was the only one we had."

The churches reflected the American consensus—and then proceeded in the limited time available to convert the war into a crusade and to rationalize imperialism as a missionary obligation. President McKinley himself set the prevailing tone. To a meeting of fellow Methodists, he confided his deepest convictions:

> I am not ashamed to tell you, gentlemen, that I went down on my knees and prayed Almighty God for light and guidance more than one night. And one night late it came to me this way. . . . There was nothing left for us to do but to take them all and to educate the Filipinos and uplift and civilize and Christianize them and by God's grace do the very best we could by them, as our fellow men for whom Christ also died.[2]

E. L. Godkin, the anti-imperialist editor of *The Nation,* was probably correct in his judgment that McKinley's own denomination was the most strident of the churches. "The fervent Methodists, at the beginning of the war, resolved that it was going to be a righteous and holy war because it would destroy 'Romish superstition' in the Spanish West Indies." [3] "This war is the *Kingdom of God coming!*" declared the *California Christian Advocate;* and its cry was echoed widely in the Protestant press. "Coming to poor Cuba—the sunrise of a better day for the Philippines! . . . Oppres-

2. Charles S. Olcott, *The Life of William McKinley* (Boston: Houghton, Mifflin & Co., 1916), 2:110–11.

3. *The Nation,* 11 August 1898, p. 105; quoted by Kenneth M. MacKenzie, *The Robe and the Sword: The Methodist Church and the Rise of American Imperialism,* p. 66.

sion, cruelty, bigotry, superstition, and ignorance must down, and give a Christian civilization the right of way." [4] Reflecting on the results of past experience in Hawaii and China, the *Pacific Advocate* minced no words: "The cross will follow the flag. . . . The clock of the ages is striking." Though of another mind himself, Gaius Glenn Atkins remembered the same pervasiveness of the martial spirit in the Protestant churches. Even in Massachusetts, where the Anti-Imperialist League led by Senator George F. Hoar had its greatest strength, Atkins was in a minority in his own Congregational church.[5] Kipling's words on "The White Man's Burden" became for a season the battle hymn of the republic. Never have patriotism, imperialism, and the religion of American Protestants stood in such fervent coalescence as during the McKinley-Roosevelt era.

For American Catholics, whose church during these very years was deeply involved in a severe institutional crisis, the war created special difficulties. Just when strenuous efforts were being exerted in Rome to prevent a papal condemnation of "Americanism," the United States ignored sweeping Spanish concessions and the conciliatory efforts of the pope—then declared war on one of the oldest and most steadfast Catholic powers in the world. Yet the action revealed the nation's dominant mood, and Catholics in general offered their wholehearted support to the nation's leaders. Most Irish tended to identify Cuba's predicament with that of Ireland, and some spoke out strongly for a war of liberation. On the question of American imperialism Catholics again followed the prevailing views. What conflict there was arose over the disposition of Catholic properties in the new American empire—and on this matter the policies carried out won greater satisfaction among Catholics than among Protestants.[6]

ON TO A BIGGER CRUSADE

The churches moved from the little war to the Great War essentially without breaking the gait established in the 1880s and 1890s. Liberalism and the Social Gospel advanced in the spirit of Progressivism. The Fundamentalist controversy intensified; secessions of the disinherited from "common-core Protestantism" continued. Several new cooperative agencies were formed, and church-sponsored crusades followed one after another, while businessmen and perfected forms of promotionalism accounted for both the successes

4. Ibid., p. 72.

5. Gaius Glenn Atkins, *Religion in Our Times*, pp. 188–89.

6. See the careful study of Frank T. Reuter, *Catholic Influence on American Colonial Policies, 1898–1904* (Austin, Tex.: University of Texas Press, 1967).

achieved and the limitations revealed. In 1911 the greatest prewar crusade of all was launched: the Men and Religion Forward Movement, with its across-the-board program for revitalizing the churches.

Even the peace movement enjoyed an unusually favorable Indian summer climate. Meetings were well attended and membership lists grew. "The times were so ripe," remembered John Dewey in 1917, "that the movement hardly had to be pushed." [7] Thirty-odd organizations and foundations were working for the cause, and in February 1914 Andrew Carnegie added another through his $2 million endowment for the Church Peace Union, showing his optimism by giving directions for alternative use of the funds should peace become "fully established." The Catholic Peace Conference in Liège and the Twenty-first International Peace Congress in Vienna, both scheduled for the summer of 1914, were canceled, however, by the outbreak of hostilities.

Archduke Francis Ferdinand, heir to the Hapsburg throne, was shot in Sarajevo on 28 June 1914. The sabre rattling of July was followed by the drums of August—the death march of the old order in Europe. Americans at the time thanked "the foresight exercised by our forefathers in emigrating from Europe." President Wilson urged strict neutrality. "We have nothing to do with this war," he insisted; its causes "can not touch us." Wilson even urged movie audiences not to reveal partisan views when newsreels were shown. But this was a futile admonition—as well bid the skylark not to sing. The flexing of national muscle begun in 1898 was still having its effect, and Theodore Roosevelt was still abroad in the land. The president himself was a fervent admirer of England, and he cooperated from the start with Britain's efforts to control the seas. By 1916 American commerce with Germany had fallen from $169 million to $1 million. Allied propaganda poured in, and the situation was aggravated by the sinking of the *Lusitania* in 1915 and all the diversely interpreted events that led to the raw, rainy day, 2 April 1917, when the president went before Congress to declare that a state of war existed.

But that was not all, for he went on—what else could he do with the knowledge of five hundred thousand Germans, four hundred thousand French, and two hundred thousand English dead on the Somme?—to proclaim a holy war. "It is a fearful thing," he said, "to lead this great peaceful people into war, into the most terrible and disastrous of all wars. . . . But the right is more precious than peace, and we shall fight . . . for a universal dominion of right by such a concert of free peoples as shall bring peace and safety to all nations and make the world itself at last free." Looking back on

7. *New Republic* 11:297; quoted in Ray H. Abrams, *Preachers Present Arms*, p. 8.

his decision, he would reaffirm this purpose: "We entered the war as the disinterested champion of right." Early on Good Friday morning (6 April) Congress did his bidding. This was not *Realpolitik*—very few Americans and no policy makers acted out of long-term concern for the nation's security—it was but a slightly revised version of a classic American sense of its chosen task in the world. William Leuchtenburg states the case:

> American entrance into the war cannot be seen apart from the American sense of mission. The United States believed that American moral idealism could be extended outward, that American Christian democratic ideals could and should be universally applied. . . . The culmination of a long political tradition of emphasis on sacrifice and decisive moral combat, the war was embraced as that final struggle where the righteous would do battle for the Lord.[8]

Wilson, on the night before he asked for war, expounded for a friend the awful domestic consequences of putting the world *and the nation* on a "war basis." If we join with the Allies, he said,

> It would mean that we should lose our heads along with the rest and stop weighing right and wrong. It would mean that a majority of the people in this hemisphere would go war-mad, quit thinking and devote their energies to destruction. . . . A declaration of war would mean that Germany would be beaten, and so badly beaten that there would be a dictated peace, a victorious peace. It means . . . an attempt to reconstruct a peacetime civilization with war standards, and at the end of the war there will be no bystanders with sufficient peace standards left to work with. There will be only war standards.[9]

These were strong words, but events as they unfolded did not reveal Wilson as softheaded. Neither the nation's excesses, the overall military accomplishments, nor the complexities of peacemaking can be reviewed in detail here, however. Our purpose is to consider the religious aspects and consequences of the war; yet this alone is a vast subject, for like any traumatic national experience, this one had great transforming power. The churches discovered that in passing through the war they left one century behind and entered another. The experience, moreover, had both spiritual and institutional dimensions.

8. William E. Leuchtenburg, *The Perils of Prosperity, 1914–32* (Chicago: University of Chicago Press, 1958), p. 34.

9. From Wilson's conversation with Frank Cobb of the *New York World*, as reported by Maxwell Anderson (Samuel Eliot Morison and Henry Steele Commager, *The Growth of the American Republic*, 2 vols. [New York: Oxford University Press, 1956], 2:466).

PREACHING THE GREAT CRUSADE

For a full century before the coming of war Germany had been America's tutor in the arts and sciences as well as in philosophy and theology. Educational institutions from the kindergarten to the graduate school seminar had been reshaped. Social and political theory, many leading ideas of the Social Gospel, and even the concept of academic freedom had been enthusiastically championed by thousands of men who had studied in German universities and research institutes. So deep did this influence penetrate that the president of the Hartford Seminary Foundation resorted to Wilhelm Hermann's *Ethics* and Johann Kaspar Bluntschli's theory of military force to justify the United States' entering the conflict.[10]

Yet despite such deep intellectual indebtedness, the outbreak of hostilities began almost immediately to sunder old attachments. Traditional distrust of "entangling alliances" at first inclined Americans against involvement. In his campaign of 1916 President Wilson was somewhat surprised that his having "kept us out of war" provided his liveliest argument for reelection. Churches of all types conspicuously supported the peace movement.[11] Running against the old isolationistic sentiment, however, was a rising demand for preparedness, ever more outspoken support for the Allied cause, and, among some prominent leaders including Theodore Roosevelt, a positive glorification of war. To advance the war cause the National Security League, the American Defense Society, and other similar groups were organized—some of them even arranging for military training camps for civilians. These organizations flourished especially in the East among Americans of "Anglo-Saxon" descent, and they won increasing support from clergy of the denominations with strong and clear British rootage—Presbyterians, Congregationalists, Methodists and, most outspokenly, Episcopalians.

The steady pro-Allied pressure applied by many prominent spokesmen no

10. W. Douglas MacKenzie, *Christian Ethics in the World War* (New York: Association Press, 1918), pp. 23–24. Bluntschli was Swiss, but he was educated in Germany and was a professor there during his most influential years.

11. The Irish were not naturally disposed to spring to England's aid; and very early Cardinal Farley of New York returned from Europe with the diagnosis that all of the nations at war (perhaps especially France) were suffering justifiably for their abuse of the Roman church in recent years. England's brutal suppression of the Easter Rebellion in Ireland in the spring of 1916 further aroused Irish doubts about England's Holy Cause. German-Americans were also indisposed to accept the British interpretation of the war, and both intellectuals and church leaders (Lutheran and Roman Catholic) voiced their views. Under Pope Benedict XV the papacy was officially neutral, but diplomatic relations with France had been suspended since 1904, and Vatican sympathies tended to lie with the Central Powers. Wilson rejected the pope's peace proposals (summer 1917) as yielding too much to Germany.

doubt encouraged Wilson, despite obvious risks, to follow a policy that from the very first did not deny Britain the benefits of her naval superiority; and as the war settled down to a grim test of strength on the western front, he would not entertain "a single abatement of right" lest other "humiliations" ensue. Having settled upon this course, incidents such as the *Lusitania*'s sinking in 1915 with many Americans aboard were certain to happen. When they did, the stridency of anti-Germanism increased. The nation, therefore, was almost solidly behind the declaration of war when it came, and by this time the peace movement had been reduced to its hard core among the Quakers, Mennonites, and other conscientious objectors. Even these groups were subjected to such powerful patriotic pressures that many individuals defected.

Ray Abrams, who wrote in the isolationist atmosphere of the 1930s, has often been accused of exaggerating the wartime response of the churches in his *Preachers Present Arms*. But no successful refutation has been forthcoming—nor is one likely to appear. The simple fact is that religious leaders—lay and clerical, Jewish, Catholic, and Protestant, through corporate as well as personal expressions, lifted their voices in a chorus of support for the war. Every hideous term and image of the Allied and American propaganda offices found its way into official pronouncements. Even the Federal Council of Churches fell in line: "The war for righteousness will be won! Let the Church do her part." And indisputably, the church *did* her part. Randolph H. McKim, from his pulpit in the national capital, managed to pack all the standard crusading images into a single paragraph:

> It is God who has summoned us to this war. . . . This conflict is indeed a crusade. The greatest in history—the holiest. It is in the profoundest and truest sense a Holy War. . . . Yes, it is Christ, the King of Righteousness, who calls us to grapple in deadly strife with this unholy and blasphemous power.

Amid such displays of chauvinism the Congregational theologian George Holley Gilbert declared that "this thought of divine favoritism looks strange indeed in the light of the twentieth century. We expect to find it among uncivilized peoples; it is part of the narrow intellectual outlook of barbarians." But Gilbert was not chiding his American brethren of the cloth; he was referring to the *Gott mit uns* of the kaiser, or (as the urbane Henry Van Dyke referred to that ruler), the "Potsdam Werewolf." "If the Kaiser is a Christian," echoed Courtland Meyers from Boston's Tremont Temple, "the devil in hell is a Christian, and I am an atheist."

Nor was it only the kaiser who came in for such violent language. Many refused so limited a target. Francis Greenwood Peabody, who had experienced his own religious awakening at the University of Halle in the 1890s and in 1910 had extolled the German intellectual heritage in connection with the opening of a Harvard-Berlin university exchange program, now found the German people "untamed barbarians." Newell Dwight Hillis, minister of Beecher's Plymouth Church in Brooklyn, spoke favorably of a plan for "exterminating the German people . . . the sterilization of 10,000,000 German soldiers and the segregation of the women." That Germans were all "swinish Huns" became a cliché of the American pulpit. With a remarkable combination of these views, Henry B. Wright, a warmly evangelical YMCA director and sometime professor in the Yale Divinity School, provided a Christian meditation for young soldiers with qualms about bayonet drill: "In the hour of soul crisis the [YMCA] Secretary can turn and say with quiet certainty to your lad and my lad, 'I would not enter this work till I could see Jesus himself sighting down a gun barrel and running a bayonet through an enemy's body.' " The Unitarian Albert C. Dieffenbach was equally sure that Christ "would take bayonet and grenade and bomb and rifle and do the work of deadliness against that which is the most deadly enemy of his Father's Kingdom in a thousand years." And so one could continue quoting bloodthirsty Americans from the books and magazines that, shelf on shelf, gather dust in any large American library.[12]

The basic message of such wartime offerings could be and was filtered through almost every kind of doctrinal net. Shailer Mathews, the Social Gospel scholar of the Chicago Divinity School, made his book-length plea in the context of an extreme theological modernism. Mathews's central concern was the nature and interrelation of two great social forces, religion and patriotism. He argued for their substantial identity, but only after making clear that "the real expression of democracy in religious thinking is outside the field of orthodox theology. . . . Only where the spirit of democracy is working is there creative religious thinking. Only there is the union of patriotism and the religion of tomorrow. For in democracy alone can the immanence of God be expressed in the terms of human experience." He then expounded "the moral values of patriotism" in terms of America's destiny: "Our patriotism dares to glory in its outlook and its hopes because it knows that the triumph of our land is the triumph of the cause of a better humanity." Mathews believed that a conscientious objector should be spared persecution, "provided he does not speak with a German accent," but his positive moral counsel was unambiguously militant: "For an American to refuse to share in the present war . . . is not Christian." "A religion which will keep its followers from committing themselves to the support of such

12. Abrams, *Preachers Present Arms*, pp. 58, 55, 104, 105, 109, 70, 68, 31–32, 76, 100, 115, 150.

patriotism is either too aesthetic for humanity's actual needs, too individualistic to be social, or too disloyal to be tolerated." In a final chapter he expounded the manifold ways in which religion could serve patriotism, purging German influences from the country's teaching of sociology, history, political economy, and psychology, strengthening the people in times of trial, and above all, giving fervor and direction to the nation's moral life. The aims he proclaimed were an international extension of the Social Gospel and a world of democratic nations living in peace and justice. The first step in the achievement of these ends was the total defeat of the kaiser, the destruction of German *Kultur,* and the reeducation of the German people. He bade Christians, however, to oppose a "punitive" treaty and to encourage "the beginnings of a League of Nations . . . [that] already exist." Mathews thus concluded on a note of high idealism, but down to his final peroration he painted a world picture in solid blacks and whites and did his utmost to make religion an intrinsic component of national solidarity.[13]

At the opposite end of the theological spectrum, the conservative premillennialist S. D. Gordon of New York added a volume on "the deeper meaning of the war" to his long series of "Quiet Talks," attempting to fit Germany and the kaiser into his reading of the various "prophecies" that point to the Last Days. He found them, of course, and put special stress on the narrative of Moses, Joshua, and Amalek in Exodus 17:8–16. Germany in 1914, therefore, becomes "the modern Amalek through which Satan was renewing his old ambitious attempt. . . . The Satanic fingerprints are unmistakable. . . . The bloody footprints are beyond dispute." [14] They betray the Beast. Mathews, who was well aware of these interpretations among the organizers of the "prophetic conferences," dismissed their "fantastic expositions of scripture," their identifications of the kaiser as the Antichrist, and their predictions of war tanks found in the Hebrew prophets. He even condemned them for sapping "the springs of national courage" and leaving all to Christ and the angels. More remarkable, however, is the convergence of value judgments among modernists and premillennialists—and their agreement that in one sense or another, the war on earth was linked up with a war in heaven.

Speaking from what could be regarded as a rather central position in the evangelical Protestant doctrinal spectrum, W. Douglas MacKenzie, president of the Hartford Seminary Foundation, worked out what can fairly be designated as another characteristic rationale in his book *Christian Ethics in the*

13. Shailer Mathews, *Patriotism and Religion* (New York: Macmillan Co., 1918).

14. Samuel Dickey Gordon, *Quiet Talks on the Deeper Meaning of the War* (New York: Fleming H. Revell Co., 1919), pp. 52–57.

World War (1918). Like Mathews and a great number of other theologians who expressed their patriotism through ethical treatises, MacKenzie took great pains to counter the pacifist position which he himself had once supported. His argument, however, contrasted sharply with Mathews's message of religio-patriotic solidarity. He agrees with the German theologian, Isaak Dorner, that the nation-state, though a human institution, rests "on a divine basis," and hence must use physical force to restrain selfish and vicious men in order to secure the ends for which it exists. "Literal obedience to the outward phraseology [of the Sermon on the Mount] would actually cause the death or suicide of one institution after another." "In an unmoral world it is the moral duty of the State to use force." On the other hand, he sees on the horizon a time when even "the mightiest empires shall be brought under the control of a new international system" and justifies the war on the ground that a League of Nations will bring in a "new era in the moral development of humanity." Avoiding bloodthirsty maledictions of Germany, he contrasts it to the Allies in absolute terms: "The overthrow of German militarism will not only sweep away the supreme obstacle, but will compel the more rapid fulfillment of the age-long dream of seers and saints."

There were, of course, a few American pacifists who were not deflected from their stand. Those who came from the traditional "peace churches," Mennonite, Quaker, etc., suffered many public insults, but they were legally allowed to accept alternative forms of noncombatant service. The American Friends Service Committee (organized 1917) filled two important functions, assisting conscientious objectors at home and sending relief workers abroad. Christian Scientists also organized a service force.[15] Due to the enormous public pressures for loyalty, the workings of the Espionage Act, and the strong demands of most denominational leaders, dissenting views were only very rarely expressed. Even so, almost every communion had some representation among the several hundred who voiced conscientious objections to the war—or, as in most cases, to *all* wars. After a fairly rigorous survey Abrams documented seventy "nonconformist" ministers in the various non-German, nonpacifist churches. Most of them were socialists or showed pronounced Social Gospel leanings; Unitarians, Universalists, and Congregationalists made up slightly more than half of his list, while none came from the South or from

15. In October 1914 the Mother Church solicited funds for the relief of Christian Scientists in Europe, an act which began their War Relief Fund. By 1915 the fund had widened its range of giving to non-Christian Scientists, and in 1917, with United States entry into the war, a Camp Welfare Committee was organized to meet the needs of inductees. All told, the church contributed $2 million through the War Relief Committee, of which $300,000 was devoted to Christian Science literature and its distribution, while the remainder went for housing, rest centers, recreation, salaries of workers, transportation, clothing for refugees, and knitted garments for military personnel.

the Roman Catholic church. Nearly all of them paid dearly for their antimilitaristic scruples.[16]

German-Americans of almost every religious hue also became the objects of suspicion, discrimination, and in many cases, even of violence. There were almost no signs of overt resistance among them, even though a great many, probably a majority, of them doubted that the Allied cause was an unambiguous holy crusade. Walter Rauschenbusch spoke for the many German-Americans during these years who recognized the near inevitability of American involvement. Given the breakdown of world order and Germany's "excessive power," he could justify the United States' course of action and conscientiously support his government. In his 1917 Taylor Lectures at Yale, however, he held that "the ultimate cause of the war was the same lust for easy and unearned gain which has created the internal social evils under which every nation has suffered. The social problem and the war problem are fundamentally one problem." On other occasions he pointed to great evils on both sides and suggested that Germany "has not been the only power seeking geographical and economic expansion." He recoiled from the "war spirit" and "spiritual psychosis" that militarism was fomenting in America. When Algernon Crapsey, an Episcopalian liberal who had earlier gained national renown in a heresy trial, "demanded" that he clarify his stand in a public statement, Rauschenbusch dissented from the prevailing logic of American church leaders: "You assume that powers with such discordant interests as the present allies can be combined in a perpetual league. . . . You offer a Utopian scheme as a justification for emasculating and hog-tying one of the great parts of humanity. . . . I am afraid of those who want to drag our country in to satisfy their partisan hate, or because they think universal peace will result from the victory of the allies." [17]

In 1922 William Adams Brown reviewed the churches' work during the war. He admitted that one of their main responsibilities had been "to keep alive the international spirit, the spirit of brotherhood and good will, and in time of war to prepare the world for the healing tasks of peace." Yet he also knew from his experience as secretary of the General Wartime Commission that in this regard they had failed. "The fact remains," he said, "that in the heat of the struggle the judgment of many a minister did not conspicuously rise above that of the average citizen. The Universal note, so signally sounded by Israel's prophets in times of similar crises, was less in

16. Abrams, *Preachers Present Arms*, pp. 21–23, 35, 177, 92.

17. *Rochester Herald*, 23 August 1915; quoted in Dores R. Sharpe, *Walter Rauschenbusch* (New York: Macmillan Co., 1942), pp. 378–79.

evidence than we could have desired. Yet, thank God, the note of brotherhood was never entirely absent." [18] This is a just and accurate statement.

THE WARTIME WORK OF THE CHURCHES

As might be expected of groups so unquestioningly in support of American involvement in the war, the churches did everything in their power to strengthen the military effort. This involved them in two quite different campaigns: a ministry to the armed forces in the training camps and overseas, and participation in the countless tasks of the "home front."

When war was declared, the religious forces of the nation were unprepared. The military chaplaincy was moribund, and civilian agencies for ministering to soldiers and sailors, except for the YMCA, which at least stood ready as a national institution with interdenominational support, were almost nonexistent. As early as 8 May 1917, however, the Federal Council of Churches called a meeting in Washington to organize the General Wartime Commission, a coordinating agency consisting of official delegates of thirty-five different religious organizations including the Federal Council itself, the Home Missions Council and several other cooperative federations, the YMCA, YWCA, American Bible Society, and a representative group of Protestant churches.

This commission, in turn, created a Committee of One Hundred to carry out its tasks, with two Presbyterians, Robert E. Speer and William Adams Brown, as chairman and secretary. It included the heads of the large and aggressive war agencies which each denomination or group of related churches (such as the Lutheran) had organized. The committee thus was admirably suited to carry out its responsibilities as a source of reliable information, a liaison between the government and the churches, and a support for the military chaplaincy. Because morale was high and the need for cooperation great, the committee demonstrated the social potentialities of organized Protestantism in an unprecedented way. As changing needs required, it created as many as twenty-five subcommittees for various tasks. One of the most important of these was that which organized the Interchurch Emergency Campaign for funds—not only to meet the $300,000 expenses of the commission itself, but also to supply the far vaster needs of individual denominations. Least practical and most forward-looking was the Committee on the War and Religious Outlook, which, with Brown as chairman, sought to

18. William A. Brown, *The Church in America*, pp. 94–97. He is less severe in *A Teacher and His Times* (New York: Scribners, 1940), pp. 223–50.

evaluate the significance of the amazing release of ecclesiastical energy precipitated by the war and to lay plans for harnessing this power for postwar works of peace.

The chief contributions of cooperating churches were in answer to the perennial needs of armies. Once the War Department had improved the status of the chaplaincy, problems of recruitment and training ensued. A chaplain's school needed staff and support. Each denomination instituted procedures to gain chaplaincy volunteers sufficient to the ratio established by Congress of one for each twelve hundred men, and a joint commission was created to screen these ministerial candidates. The draft laws allowed seminarians to continue their theological studies so that a shortage of clergy would not develop, but each denomination, nationally and locally, did what it could to provide auxiliary ministries wherever military training was being conducted. Added to these needs was the enormous demand for Bibles, tracts, and general reading matter, as well as recreation facilities and rest centers at home and abroad. In response, the Red Cross, Library Association, American Bible Society, YMCA, and the newly constituted War Camp Community Service became major distributing agencies for Protestants. Particularly vital was the YMCA, which, with its agents in military uniform, became a semiofficial agency of the War Department to operate canteens and perform related services. The Salvation Army played a similar, less official role.

Jews and Catholics had less difficult organizational problems for obvious reasons, yet parallel agencies of coordination and direct activity were quickly formed or assigned wartime tasks: the Jewish Welfare Board, the Young Men's Hebrew Association, the National Catholic War Council, and the Knights of Columbus. For these groups, too, the wartime experience was to have an enduring impact, even though it was less complex, in one case for reasons of size, in the other because of existing institutional unity. In mobilizing Jewish resources the YMHA served a function like that of the YMCA among Protestants, while the Jewish Welfare Board coordinated other aspects of the task, including the arrangements for chaplains.[19] The great Roman Catholic fraternal order, the Knights of Columbus, appointed Patrick H. Callahan chairman of a new committee on war activities[20] and responded

19. There were about 200,000 Jews in the armed forces (48 percent of those in the army being in the infantry), about 10,000 commissioned officers, twenty-five chaplains—and about 2,800 fatalities. The Jewish Welfare Board was organized in April 1917 by representatives of other Jewish agencies, with Colonel Harry Cutler of Providence, Rhode Island, as chairman. It had 500 workers in 200 different places at home, and 178 in 57 centers overseas. After the war, the board turned its attention to the development of community centers in the larger cities.

20. Callahan was a Louisville industrialist who since 1914 had been head of the Knights' Commission on Religious Prejudices, an agency to counter nativist attacks.

almost immediately to the needs for recreational and religious facilities, especially in southern military camps far from Catholic population centers. Later they would carry their work overseas. In several campaigns for funds the Knights raised over $14 million, and by Armistice Day they had nearly two thousand secretaries in active service. That it received over 80 percent of the Catholic share in the United Fund Drive of 1918 indicates its centrality in Roman Catholic war work.

The formation of the National Catholic War Council, however, had a more lasting impact on the church as a whole. It was organized at a large general convention gathered in August 1917 in Washington, D.C., where sixty-eight dioceses, twenty-seven national organizations already members of the American Federation of Catholic Societies, and the entire Catholic press were represented. As chairman of the council's Committee on War Activities, Father John J. Burke, then editor of the Paulists' *Catholic World,* began a long career as a shaper of Catholic social and political policy. When the council's large executive committee proved too cumbersome, the archbishops placed the council's administration in the hands of four bishops. During the war, the council undertook very much the same tasks as the Protestant General Wartime Commission, among other things, arranging for the recruitment, training, and supervision (under a chaplain-general) of about a thousand military chaplains. Probably the most important side effect of the council's many activities was that it ended the neutrality or abstention of the bishops on specific questions of public policy. In 1919 the Wartime Council was reorganized as the National Catholic Welfare Council, and thereafter the bishops assumed a new position of responsibility for national leadership in the realm of social affairs.

As a result of the gargantuan effort of America's religious forces, over eleven thousand civilian service personnel accompanied the armed forces in Europe, while an uncounted but far larger contingent served in and around the military camps and stations at home. Another important consequence was the unprecedented cooperation of Protestant, Catholic, and Jewish organizations, as well as nondenominational or completely independent agencies like the Red Cross. The United Fund Drive of 1918, for example, set an American fund-raising record with a yield of $200 million. All across the land, local congregations became rallying points for volunteers and organizational centers for war work. For denominations that were too small to maintain their own war agencies, the Protestant commission became a channel between willing hands and military needs.

American religious institutions, however, did not limit themselves to evangelistic and charitable ministries, but plunged directly into the war work. Ministers were steadily supplied with government propaganda, and they made their pulpits an important point of emission. Both directly and indirectly they labored to gain enlistments in the armed forces, and they hung service-star flags in their sanctuaries. Liberty Loan drives were conducted in the churches. Despite all of this activity, the English-born Presbyterian and sometime chaplain and war correspondent Joseph H. Odell stirred the nation in February 1918 with an article in the *Atlantic Monthly* entitled "Peter Sat by the Fire Warming Himself," in which he castigated the passivity of the churches! Needless to say, fervent and violent rebuttals soon found their way into print. The response of Methodist Bishop W. F. McDowell revealed their prevailing tone: "We do not intend that any church shall have more stars in its service flag than we have." All in all, the judgment of W. W. Sweet will stand: "At least for the period of World War I the separation of church and state was suspended." [21]

ARMISTICE AND THE "NEW ERA"

On 11 November 1918 the news arrived: the war was over! A false report had sent the nation into a delirium of joy four days before, but President Wilson himself penned the three succinct sentences of this authentic report:

> My Fellow Countrymen: The armistice was signed this morning. Everything for which America fought has been accomplished. It will now be our fortunate duty to assist by example, by sober, friendly counsel, and by material aid in the establishment of just democracy throughout the world.

Jubilation reigned across the land, not always with sobriety. The "supreme obstacle" to the new era of international order was a battered ruin. The great opportunity was at hand. Only five days before, however, the Republican party had won control of both houses of Congress in the midterm elections. And all too soon the desire for "normalcy" would submerge the deep resolves that had been expressed since 1914. But before this trend could be discerned, the Protestant churchmen who had experienced the wartime triumphs of cooperative action resolved to find means for maintaining its momentum. In this access of euphoria a whole cluster of fund-raising campaigns were launched—all of them inspired by the astronomic attainments of wartime drives.

On the expected advent of a new era of world order, democracy, and peace, nearly every ethical and religious justification for American entry into

21. William Warren Sweet, *The Story of Religion in America*, p. 402.

Europe's war had rested. Almost every personal statement and official church pronouncement advancing the cause of war had anchored the argument in some plan for an international agency to outlaw war. What role, then, did the churches and the Presbyterian messiah in the White House play when the moment of truth arrived?

Even as churchmen were charting their ambitious campaigns, President Wilson, his selected peace commissioners, and a large group of technical experts were aboard the *George Washington,* moving toward their fateful rendezvous in Europe. These delegates of the American nation, and most assuredly their leader, were inspired by an even vaster vision: the delivery of Europe from the tyranny of history, the making of a world in which democracy would be safe and all peoples secure from war. But in one case as in the other, human nature and human history would soon reveal the undependability of visions. Indeed, the treaty and the League of Nations which Wilson hoped for were already doomed. The Wilson government had not made the relinquishment of the older Allied agreements a condition of American entry; Wilson's summons for a Democratic Congress in 1918 had not been heard by the electorate; the Republican party was alienated and hungry for power. Outraged by Wilson's decision to ignore the Senate in appointing his peace commissioners, powerful men like Henry Cabot Lodge and William Borah were determined to block Wilson's expected demand for unqualified American support. Finally and decisively, the American people had not been converted to a sense of international responsibility. Having been so long diverted from normal peacetime pursuits and pleasures, they were more isolationistic than ever. The long bombardment with war propaganda had probably served to cheapen and degrade popular idealism.

As for the churches and their memberships, the evidence is ambiguous. Robert M. Miller's careful canvass of both the denominational press and the official deliberations of the major churches has shown that by and large the attitude of ecclesiastical leaders was ideologically continuous with their wartime attitudes. Having supported a war to crush the Hun, they favored the treaty's harsh terms. "Within ten or fifteen years clerical criticism of the Treaty of Versailles became as common and as fashionable as denunciations of liquor, but in 1919 and 1920 only a very small minority of churchmen found the peace unjust." [22] On the other hand, approval of the treaty's harshness was accompanied by overwhelming support of the League without crippling reservations. According to every available index, whether editorials, official resolutions, or pronouncements by recognized spokesmen, the Protestant churches supported the League. Even after its defeat they continued

22. Robert M. Miller, *American Protestantism and Social Issues, 1919–1939,* p. 318.

throughout the twenties to advocate American participation in the World Court and similar efforts to implement the idea of international order. As might be expected, the Federal Council of Churches—not to mention the Church Peace Union—was overwhelmingly in support, even to the point of sending five delegates to Paris to convey this message to the president in person. Wilson hardly needed their assurance, however; and since only 15 percent of the Senate was irreconcilably opposed to the League, it may be that support was not needed there either. Even the American people would have accepted American participation in 1919. News of the League's final defeat in the Senate was greeted in the religious press and in various ecclesiastical assemblies by a wave of outrage and disappointment, and by unspecific charges that men in high places were putting politics before principle. What was lacking during the critical months was not support, but presidential statesmanship. When that failed, the road to "normalcy" and national irresponsibility was open.

53

THE TWENTIES: FROM THE ARMISTICE TO THE CRASH

The decade of the twenties is the most sharply defined decade in American history. Marked off by the war at one end and the Depression at the other, it has a character of its own—ten restless years roaring from jubilation to despair amid international and domestic dislocation. It has also had a bad press, whether viewed from the Right or the Left. To conservatives it has always been the Jazz Age, a lamentable season of excess, ballyhoo, and moral degeneration. To liberal and radical interpreters, especially if they felt the pain of the Depression and the thrill of the New Deal, it was simply the culminating expression of bourgeois decadence, a demonstration that a social order dominated by businessmen was bankrupt. Religiously oriented critics of all parties have usually spoken of these ten years as a tragic display of obscurantism, superficiality, complacency, and futile conflict. What has been lost to mind is the fact that the twenties were an exciting time of social transformation, intellectual revolution, and artistic triumph.[1]

In the decade after the Armistice modern technocratic America came of age and began to be conscious of its newly released potentiality. The United States became an urban nation not only in statistical fact but in its dominant mood.[2] The movies, the radio, and the automobile became commonplace. The standard of living took a great jump forward; leisure and play became the right of the many rather than the privilege of a few. Vacations with pay,

1. In 1950 *Life* magazine looked back at the twenties with amused condescension: "It is startling to find the old headliners still looking as chipper as they do in these pictures taken in the past few months—startling and pleasant. They were the life of the party and everyone loves them, even though it was not a party that the nation can afford to throw again" (2 January 1950). It may be that the 1960s provide the standpoint for a more sympathetic judgment.

2. The census of 1920 revealed that for the first time *most* Americans (51.4 percent) lived in "cities" of 2,500 or over.

golf, tennis, and spectator sports entered the American way of life. In Jack Dempsey, Babe Ruth, Knute Rockne, Paul Whiteman, Lowell Thomas, Rudolph Valentino, Charlie Chaplin, and, far above them all, in Charles A. Lindbergh, the nation found heroes cut from new kinds of cloth. The newly franchised American woman made her brazen appearance. And accompanying these highly visible cultural innovations were vast economic changes stimulated in part by national advertising and the mass media, but also reflecting important developments in technology, finance, and business organization. Given these circumstances, conflict was inevitable. Furious controversies, great debates, and wild fulminations were the order of the day. And nearly all of this conflict is part of the nation's religious history, either because the churches were active participants or because events impinged on their life.

THE PEACETIME CAMPAIGNS OF THE CHURCHES

Most appropriately, the first great peacetime campaign of the churches—Protestant, Catholic, and Jewish—received its impetus directly from the war. The United War Work Campaign directed by John R. Mott was conceived while the last great Allied advance on Germany's western front ground to its close. At their final victory banquet the campaign leaders listened to Mott's oration on "the Largest Voluntary Offering in History." He told them with unrestrained enthusiasm how "the entire American people—the rich and the poor, the members of all parties, races, and religious faiths—had united their gifts and sacrifices, and rolled up the vast sum of $200,000,000." Mott dwelt at length on the obstacles to success: hurried organization, high taxes, the competition of the government's Fourth Liberty Loan (itself a tribute to the newly developed art of high-pressure salesmanship), the congressional elections of 1918, the influenza epidemic, the "false" and then the "true" peace celebrations which, all across the nation, had disrupted the launching ceremonies, and finally, the very fact that the campaign had united the efforts of seven separate organizations and hence lost the power to capitalize on special interest groups. He did not exaggerate, however, in speaking of a "great triumph" and in insisting that "there has been nothing like it in the history of campaigns." [3] The event indicates the mood of America as it contemplated the return of peace and the discharge of three million soldiers.

Strictly in the realm of ecclesiastical history, the most important effort to propel wartime fervor and newly learned organizational techniques into the postwar situation was the Interchurch World Movement.[4] Professor Wil-

3. John R. Mott, *The Largest Voluntary Offering in History* (privately printed, 1919).

liam Adams Brown, who called it "the religious counterpart to the League of Nations," gives an inside account of the meeting at 25 Madison Avenue, New York City, on 17 December 1918, which had been called by the Board of Foreign Missions of the Southern Presbyterian church:

> No one who was present in the upper room on that momentous December day when the Interchurch World Movement was born can forget the thrill of expectation which stirred those who had gathered there. They were men of long experience—secretaries of church boards, professors in theological seminaries, veteran workers in the cause of home and foreign missions, and they knew the weaknesses and limitations of the bodies they served to the full. But they had seen a vision—the vision of a united church uniting a divided world; and under the spell of what they saw all things seemed possible. Difficulties were waved aside, doubters were silenced. In the face of an opportunity so unparalleled there seemed but one thing to do, and that was to go forward.[5]

What they attempted was a grand peacetime crusade which would unite all the benevolent and missionary agencies of American Protestantism into a single campaign for money, men, and spiritual revival. Included in its scope were every phase of church work, domestic and foreign. In the words of its own general committee, it was to be "a cooperative effort of evangelical churches . . . to survey unitedly their present common tasks and simultaneously and together to secure the necessary resources . . . required for these tasks." A lavish prospectus, expensive offices, and elaborate promotional plans featured the movement's launching. Work went ahead to analyze worldwide needs, to inaugurate a broad educational program, to instruct the churches in wise planning and management of these vast responsibilities, to recruit personnel, and above all, by united efforts and modern methods, to raise astronomic sums of money, not only for the central agency itself, but for all the financial campaigns underway or to be launched by participating denominations.

On the eve of the big campaign in April 1920, they issued a nationwide bulletin concerning "the biggest business of the biggest man in the world":

> Christ was big, was He not? None ever bigger.
> Christ was busy, was He not? None ever busier.
> He was always about His Father's business.
> Christ needs big men for big business.

4. See Eldon Ernst, "The Interchurch World Movement" (Ph.D. diss., Yale University, 1967) for a valuable interpretation of this great campaign.

5. William A. Brown, *The Church in America*, p. 119.

Three hundred million dollars was their first goal, but this was later raised to five hundred million and finally to a billion dollars. With such goals the result was perhaps inevitable; but a number of special factors help to explain the movement's collapse, not least the nation's postwar surfeit of idealistic financial campaigns. The prominence of liberal social thinkers among its leadership aroused already embattled conservatives to undermine the effort, and both Northern Presbyterians and Northern Baptists voted to withdraw their support in 1920. The obvious presence of Social Gospel tendencies also alarmed many potential donors, though the widely publicized pro-labor report of the commission set up to investigate the great steel strike actually appeared after the movement had begun to fall apart. Finally, a postwar resurgence of denominational loyalty left the IWM stranded, unable to meet even 15 percent of its indebtedness for expenditures. The "friendly citizens" outside the churches on whom the IWM's share of the take was to depend apparently lost their solicitude for the institutional church after the nation's martial spirit evaporated.

The Interchurch World Movement, a victim of its dreams and its overhead, failed completely and distributed its debts to the cooperating churches, who paid them in full. In financial terms the denominational campaigns were relatively more successful. By 1922 not less than $200 million in strictly denominational funds were raised or pledged, though the churches also suffered from excessive costs, unpaid pledges, and the general postwar letdown. In the qualitative sense, however, there was probably more loss than gain, for the promotional spirit that underlay these gigantic efforts corrupted and weakened the spiritual fiber of the churches. The methods used were artful, mechanical, and pragmatically effective; but the hard sell had a corrosive effect. It revealed the enormous toll of the wartime amalgamation of patriotic and religious objectives.

An excellent expression of this effect is William Adams Brown's *The Church in America, A Study of the Present Condition and Future Prospects of American Protestantism* (1922), an informative work by a great systematic theologian, a professor at Union Theological Seminary, and the liberal thinker most often praised for his great concern for the church. Yet the book rests its case on the utilitarian judgment that "American Protestantism contain[s] within itself the principle of improvement which warrants our hope that it will prove the unifying and inspiring influence which American democracy needs." [6] For Brown as for many others, the war seemed in retrospect to have been a tremendous stimulus to American piety, especially among Protestants. Never had the churches been better attended, never had

6. Ibid., p. 11.

so many members been busily involved in the country's life and work, never had the general public's judgments of religion been so affirmative or their generosity with money more apparent. Yet events were to reveal that these exhilarating experiences led the churches directly into the complacent culture-protestantism of the 1920s. The Great Crusade ended its march at the lawn socials of normalcy.

The indexes of denominational vitality show a prevailing downward trend for the next ten years.[7] Church attendance declined, not only in economically depressed rural areas, but throughout the country. The Foreign Missionary Conference of North America reported that only 252 students had offered themselves for foreign service in 1928, as against 2,700 in 1920. The income figures for the major mission boards also took a generally downward trend despite the nation's booming prosperity. Most serious of all, though almost impossible to quantify, was a pervasive thinning out of evangelical substance, a tendency to identify religion with the business-oriented values of the American way of life. Because of this prevailing spirit neither the widespread adoption of the Social Gospel by Protestant ministers nor the many social pronouncements of denominational assemblies had much popular impact.

All considered, however, "normalcy," "complacency," and "religious depression" do not adequately account for the many violent encounters of the twenties. One wonders if any decade was *less* normal, for it was a time of crisis for both the Protestant Establishment and the historic evangelicalism which undergirded it. It was the critical epoch when the Puritan heritage lost its hold on the leaders of public life, and when the mainstream denominations grew increasingly out of touch with the classic Protestant witness. Secular provocations, moreover, tended to speed up this estrangement—and this was especially true of the Red Scare.

RADICALS AND IMMIGRANTS

The Republican victory in the congressional elections of 1918 revealed an electorate surfeited with progressivism, sacrifice, and grand ideals. The war's enormous heightening of patriotic Americanism had also reduced the general tolerance for nonconformist behavior. Given the rise of world communism and the legacy of prewar nativism, therefore, the Red Scare was hardly a surprising response to the rash of strikes, bomb throwing, and radical advocacy that broke out after the Armistice. Nor were church members exempt from the pervasive hysteria. When the deportation of radicals was being

7. Robert T. Handy, "The American Religious Depression, 1925–1935," *Church History* 29 (March 1960): 3–16.

proposed in 1919, Billy Sunday, who rarely failed to offer his conservative Protestant audiences the views they held most dear, offered a simpler solution. "If I had my way with these ornery wild-eyed socialists and IWW's, I would stand them up before a firing squad and save space on our ships." As for Reds, he would "fill the jails so full . . . that their feet would stick out of the windows." The vast promotional campaigns of the churches also supported the nation's anti-Red hysteria. Over and over they depicted religion as a valuable bulwark against radicalism.[8] Even the IWM voiced a remarkably agrarian version of the American dream and expressed alarm at its subversion, while rural America took a strong (if not quite its last) stand against an emergent urban civilization. Most Protestants, therefore, tended actually to accept, internalize, and perpetuate the major theories that animated the Red Scare.

On the other hand, church-related social action committees and many other persons and agencies provided more than their share of leadership in opposing the great witchhunt and demanding justice for the accused. The same can be said of their stand on the great *causes célèbres:* the Sacco-Vanzetti case in Massachusetts, the Mooney-Billings case in California, and the Centralia affair in Washington, all of which involved the criminal conviction of radicals under questionable circumstances. The postwar bearers of the Social Gospel not only opposed the illiberal spirit of the times, but often became themselves the objects of suspicion and censure.

The Roman Catholic church faced a totally different situation. Its constituency was heavily foreign-born and urban, deeply implicated in the labor movement, and frequently bore the brunt of nativist activities. The so-called Bishops' Program of 1919 was entitled "Social Reconstruction: A General Review of the Problems and Survey of Remedies," and in so many words it was a call for a social welfare state. During the twenties, therefore, Roman Catholicism exerted a mildly liberal influence in national affairs. That Jews were also associated with liberal and radical causes gave many Protestants added inducement to campaign for immigration restriction.

When Attorney General A. Mitchell Palmer was winning wide popular applause for deporting aliens by the hundreds, legislative action on immigra-

8. "If the United States is to be one nation, with common feeling, language habits, customs and moral and spiritual attitude, the Americanization must center around the largest racial group, the old white stock. . . . The rural people, the agriculturists, have the least admixture of foreign blood of any portion of the population. . . . If American life is to have a tone, this tone must come not from the cities with their varied and heterogeneous racial groups, but from the villages and country districts. It is the task of the churches to see that this tone continues one of Godliness and pariotism, high ideals and clean living" (*New Era Magazine,* September 1919, p. 522).

tion was not hard to get. Woodrow Wilson, in one of his last presidential acts, declined to sign a bill setting 3 percent quotas based on the 1910 census; but under Harding the new Congress acted quickly and passed a bill in May 1921. In 1924 a still more stringent measure was passed, gauged to preserve the existing demographic balance, and thus to favor those countries which few wished to leave.[9] It was a "Nordic victory"—and it brought a long, colorful epoch in American history to a close. The country had somehow lost confidence in its assimilative powers. Nor did action stop with restriction, for many states passed laws which excluded aliens from a wide range of professional work, while suburban housing regulations, extralegal procedures, and new institutions like the increasingly numerous golf and country clubs accomplished the same ends. During the "tribal twenties" many colleges and even prestigious universities became noticeably restrictive in their admission policies.

More ominous still was the rapidly expanding activity of the Ku Klux Klan. It had been revived in 1915 by William J. Simmons, a camp-meeting revival convert and sometime preacher who retained the anti-Negro aims of the old Klan but soon broadened its scope to include anti-Catholicism and anti-Semitism. The Klan thus became a distinctly Protestant organization with chaplains and specially adapted hymns. "Never before," observes John Higham, "had a single society gathered up so many hatreds." [10] With agricultural depression, urban "immorality," and liberal religious ideas adding to popular discontent, the membership campaigns of the KKK became more successful, in the North as well as in the South. After 1921 D. C. Stephenson of Indianapolis rose to such prominence that he threatened the authority of Hiram Wesley Evans, the Texas dentist who had bought out Simmons's interest in the Invisible Empire. By 1923 the Klan had reached its peak of nearly three million members, and it was wielding great political power in a half-dozen states.

All of these campaigns—against radicals, immigrants, Negroes, Catholics, and Jews—revealed deep Protestant misgivings, and they elicited much overt support and participation in the churches. Compared with the problems of Prohibition, however, every public issue of the period took second place. Prohibition was *the* great Protestant crusade of the twentieth century—the last grand concert of the old moral order.

9. According to the 1924 law, quotas were to be computed on the basis of 2 percent of the 1890 population. Further restrictions were put in effect in 1927 and 1929.

10. John Higham, *Strangers in the Land*, p. 289.

PROHIBITIONISM'S INTEMPERATE BATTLE

The aim of the Anti-Saloon League had always been to extricate the dry cause from its bondage to an obscure third party and a vast regiment of unenfranchised women. It had set out to organize the five hundred thousand crucial "public opinion makers" of the country and to get dry commitments from politicians at any and every level in the nation—from village councils in Kansas to the president of the United States. With the WCTU functioning as a women's auxiliary, the league was marvelously successful in giving direction and power to a rising tide of temperance sentiment in the nation.[11] Yet from the start it functioned as a semi-ecclesiastical movement, with denominational leaders in prominent positions and with local churches providing place and occasion for itinerant lecturers and tract distribution. Its leaders recognized that church membership lists constituted the real key to the situation. Virginius Dabney accurately refers to it as "virtually a branch of the Methodist and Baptist churches," [12] but he neglects to emphasize the fact that with the exception of German Lutherans and Episcopalians, American Protestantism constituted an unprecedentedly solid phalanx that included evangelicals and liberals, Social Gospelers and conservatives, Democrats and Republicans. With remarkable unanimity the denominational press endorsed the antisaloon campaign.[13] Paul A. Carter does not exaggerate in calling the dry cause "a surrogate for the Social Gospel." The gaining and maintaining of Prohibition became *the* crusade and *the* panacea for a whole generation of Protestants.

The great "Dry Messiah" of the decade was the Southern Methodist bishop, James Cannon, who reached the pinnacle of his crusading career in the election of 1928, when he played a key role in shattering the Solid South. James Cannon, Jr. (1864–1944) was born in Maryland, reared in the Southern Methodist church, and converted while a student at Randolph-Macon College. He entered the Methodist ministry in 1888 after taking a B.D. from Princeton Seminary, an M.A. from the neighboring university, and a wife from the household of Randolph-Macon's president. At age twenty-nine he became principal of a struggling academy for girls in Blackstone,

11. The organization of "Dry Power" in the 1912–28 period makes the "Black Power" of the 1960s seem very amateur indeed.

12. Virginius Dabney, *Dry Messiah: The Life of Bishop Cannon*, p. 35.

13. Many Episcopal leaders and parishes enlisted in the crusade, especially outside the cities and in the South. Scandinavian pietistic Lutherans also joined in. Roman Catholics, though they had participated in the league's founding, dropped out as the crusade became more intemperate and nativistic. The northern and southern wings of the Democratic party were at odds on the issue.

Virginia, which at the time of his resignation in 1918 (to become a bishop) was a firmly established institution. In the meantime he had hitched his destiny to the Anti-Saloon League, helping to organize the Virginia branch in 1901 and becoming its president in 1904. In 1914, when a massive referendum victory brought statewide prohibition to Virginia, Cannon became a national figure and a dominant force in the Democratic politics of the South.

With such single-minded leaders at the helm the Prohibition movement marched to victory. In 1900 only about 24 percent of the population was living in dry territory; but in 1906, 40 percent. In 1913 the Webb-Kenyon Law provided the first great victory at the federal level by prohibiting the sending of liquor into dry states. By the time of Wilson's war message there were twenty-six prohibition states in the Union. More than half the population lived in no-license territory. After war had been declared against the kaiser, anti-German sentiments could be marshaled for a final assault on the "Beer Barons" with the alleged wartime needs for alcohol and flour as a rationale.

In 1917 came the deluge—or more accurately, the great drought. A tremendous effort by the league in the congressional elections of 1916 yielded the requisite number of dry victories. The Eighteenth Amendment was passed and sent to the states for ratification, and other legislation soon followed. In 1918 laws were passed prohibiting the manufacture and sale of alcoholic beverages after 30 June 1919. The country was, in effect, dry without the Eighteenth Amendment. Then in October 1919, the amendment now ratified, Congress passed the Volstead Act as an enforcement measure, repassing it immediately over Wilson's veto, 176 to 5 in the House, 65 to 20 in the Senate. Prohibition became a fact on 16 January 1920.[14] Billy Sunday, who had for years been satisfying customer demand for his famous "booze sermon," held a mock funeral for John Barleycorn. Yet keeping John in the grave was a major Protestant task of the twenties.[15]

The greatest threat came in 1928, when the Democratic party's presidential candidate was Alfred E. Smith, a wet Roman Catholic from New York City

14. Twenty-seven states were dry when Congress passed the amendment, but the ratification of the necessary thirty-six came more easily than expected. It was politically easier in many states to ratify the amendment than to vote and enforce a dry law. In addition, dry sentiment was growing, and ultimately only two states—Connecticut and Rhode Island—failed to ratify the amendment. The total votes cast in the lower houses of the forty-six ratifying states was 3,782 to 1,035. Votes on the amendment in the House of Representatives, both yeas and nays, were about evenly divided between the two parties.

15. Each of the fifteen hundred federal agents, for example, would have had to prevent the liquor traffic along twelve miles of the international boundary, over two thousand square miles of American territory, and among seventy thousand people!

who personified rural America's image of urban evil. Bishop Cannon and the Anti-Saloon Democrats were outraged, and on election day they broke the Solid South. Yet there was irony in that Protestant victory. The Dry Messiah could speak of "the kind of dirty people you find today on the sidewalks of New York . . . the Italians, the Sicilians, the Poles, and the Russian Jews." [16] But Al Smith, as he sang of those sidewalks, was forging a new Democratic coalition. The Crash provided a final blow, and after 1929 Prohibition's fragile supportive structure in American culture and politics collapsed. The election of 1932 would bring FDR to the White House and seal the doom of the Eighteenth Amendment. The temperance movement's greatest failure was its inability to accomplish an enduring reform.[17] In no previous crusade had the solidarity of Protestantism been so unbroken, its passion so aroused. Indeed, so great was the investment that the trauma of repeal would leave Protestantism itself transformed. This larger result, however, was due to the way in which the twenties also fomented strictly religious confrontations.

RELIGIOUS AND THEOLOGICAL MOVEMENTS

On the popular level a dominant theme of American religion was exhibited by a new wave of best sellers, often conservative or noncommittal on social issues but preoccupied with practical personal problems of health, harmony, and successful living. The genre was old, but it had its first great flowering in the twenties.[18] In 1922–23, when the Red Scare was waning, the French prophet of personal power through positive thinking, Émile Coué, made his American tour. He soon had thousands attending his institutes—and many more thousands repeating his famous formula: "Day by day, in every way, I am getting better and better." "Multitudes of people," said Harry Emerson Fosdick in his *Twelve Tests of Character* (1923), "are living not bad but frittered lives." And he, together with his immensely popular rivals Emmet Fox, Glenn Clark, and Ralph Waldo Trine, won millions of readers by providing inspirational paths to victorious living, con-

16. One of Cannon's campaign utterances in 1928; quoted in Dabney, *Dry Messiah,* p. 188. After 1928 Cannon was involved in two ecclesiastical trials, one civil trial, three congressional hearings, and at least two libel suits. The accusations ranged from adultery and stock market gambling to the wartime hoarding of flour. He was "acquitted" in every case, but his influence as the Dry Messiah was negated as he became a symbol of puritanic hypocrisy.

17. Given the nation's prevailing sentiment, a regulatory system that allowed the sale of beer and wine and put hard liquors under a government dispensary system, perhaps with rationing, might have endured.

18. Later developments of positive thinking and aspects of its background are considered in chaps. 60 and 61.

structive thinking, being in tune with the infinite, pushing to the front, and being a real person.

The decade's most popular work on Jesus was *The Man Nobody Knows* (1925), written by advertising executive Bruce Barton, who gives the Man from Nazareth front rank among the world's business organizers.[19] Not only was President Coolidge declaring that America's business was business, but many were expounding the religious corollary. "The sanest religion is business," wrote Edward Purinton in the *Independent* in 1921. "Any relationship that forces a man to follow the Golden Rule rightfully belongs amid the ceremonials of the church. A great business enterprise includes and presupposes this relationship." This presupposition, it must be added, was safely held, for businessmen were at the apex of their public esteem in these golden years before the Crash. They had also become key elements in the promotional strategies and financial planning of the churches. Ministers meanwhile increasingly adopted the life styles and value systems of their more successful parishioners. Russell H. Conwell preached his "Acres of Diamonds" six thousand times before he died in 1925, reaching millions of listeners and readers with his amazingly frank equation of being rich and being good. He became a philanthropist on the proceeds.

Liberal theology in the more formal sense also flourished in the postwar years. Its defenders participated vigorously in the ecumenical movement, aroused the social concerns of many interchurch agencies at home, and developed new responses to the changed intellectual climate of the times. The liberalism of the twenties was thus by no means a static continuation of nineteenth-century attitudes. Most noticeable, perhaps, was the eclipse of philosophical idealism, the trend toward more realistic, more scientific, more empirical ways of thinking. The pragmatism of William James figured in this development, for it was directed against the various forms of idealism which at the turn of the century had been the mainstay of the "genteel tradition" in religion and morals. Yet James was a subjectivist himself, and his classic, *The Varieties of Religious Experience,* became a popular apologia for religion. Faith that "worked" was true; given the "will to believe," it would work. Neither James nor Emerson would have been happy about it, but both of them figured prominently in the popular peace-and-harmony books of the period. Men like John Dewey and others of the "Chicago school," on the other hand, turned the pragmatic arguments into secular channels, above all toward social and educational problems.

The new currents of philosophical realism had an even more direct impact

19. Unbelievable as it may seem, the volume's epigraph was the query of the boy Jesus when he was found in the temple, "Wist ye not that I must be about my Father's *business?*"

on theology. In this context, Douglas Clyde Macintosh (1877–1948) and Henry Nelson Wieman (b. 1884) were especially influential. Macintosh came to Yale from Canada and carried his pacifistic refusal to bear arms in defense of the Constitution to the Supreme Court. He lost the case and never became a U.S. citizen, but his defense of the reasonableness of Christianity won wide attention. God, for him, was an objective, verifiable reality; and the essentials of the Christian faith could be established quite apart from any historical evidence. Macintosh was a moral optimist for whom salvation was within human grasp:

> As a result of acting intelligently on the hypothesis of the existence of a God great enough and good enough to justify our absolute self-surrender and confident, appropriating faith, there comes a religious experience of spiritual uplift and emancipation in which, as a complex of many psychological elements, there can be intuited empirically, or perceived, the operation of a Factor which we evaluate and interpret as divine, because of its absolute religious and spiritual value. It is here then, and not in traditional creeds or sacred books as such, that we find revelation.[20]

Eight years later he stated the realist case even more tersely:

> I will not mince words in this connection. . . . If in proclaiming the Christian gospel we can predict and promise that whosoever will fulfill the prescribed conditions of repentance and faith . . . will experience ethico-religious salvation, then it cannot be denied that there is in the Christian message a nucleus of essentially or potentially scientific generalization.[21]

Wieman, like Macintosh, was a critic of subjectivism and a champion of empirical theology. He was far less concerned with religious experience, however, and drew much inspiration from the metaphysics of Alfred North Whitehead. From 1927 to 1947 he was perhaps the dominant figure at Chicago, but several of his colleagues added much to the institution's fame (and notoriety) as a center of "modernism." Edward Scribner Ames, chairman of the Chicago philosophy department and minister to the University Disciples Church, became the country's most widely read psychologist of religion. Shirley Jackson Case carried positivistic methods into scholarship on the New Testament and the early Church; and Gerald B. Smith defined Christianity almost entirely in terms of social concern. In the spirit of these

20. *The Pilgrimage of Faith in the World of Modern Thought* (Calcutta, 1931), pp. 223–24.

21. "Empirical Theology and Some of Its Misunderstanders," *Review of Religion* 3 (May 1939): 398.

men and their many influential students, realism became the new watchword of religious liberalism.

A natural corollary of these trends was a growing dissatisfaction with the older type of Sunday school instruction, its accent on evangelism, its uncritical use of the Bible, and its lack of interest in scientific educational theory. In response to this uneasiness the Religious Education Association had been organized on an interfaith basis in 1903. John Dewey was a charter member, and the development of progressive theory in secular education was a constant spur to its work.[22] Due to the energetic direction of Henry F. Cope (1870–1923), the association's impact was enormous; and it became even greater through the participation of many of its members in the International Council of Religious Education, where churches were directly represented. As early as 1904 George A. Coe (1862–1951) had provided a basic programmatic statement in his *Education in Religion and Morals,* followed in 1917 by *A Social Theory of Religious Education,* in which reverence for personality and democratic life are the key principles. The other great theorist of the new views was Coe's successor at Union Seminary and Columbia, Harrison S. Elliott (1882–1951), who placed even more confidence in discussion and fellowship as instruments of moral and religious education.[23] In 1940 he would forthrightly ask, *Can Religious Education Be Christian?* By that time various countercurrents were leading Christian educators to the opposite question: Can Christian education be religious? But in 1928, at the movement's zenith, Gerald B. Smith could say with complete justice that in religious education as nowhere else "we see the direction in which religious thinking is moving."

The Social Gospel must be seen as another well-traveled road, however, for the prevailing complacency of the twenties did not prevent spokesmen of the church or denominational conclaves from "speaking out" on public issues with monotonous regularity. According to its closest student, "The most striking single fact which comes out of intensive reading in the denomination weeklies for the year 1920 is that their pages were filled with articulate and vigorous social criticism." [24] In that year, despite the Red Scare, the Interchurch World Movement report on the steel strike of 1919 was published,

22. The great American pioneer in scientific psychology, G. Stanley Hall, had in 1882 already announced views on religious nurture and child development which were to have widespread effects in later years (*Princeton Review* 58 [1882]: 32). Horace Bushnell, however, was the movement's American patriarch, and his *Christian Nurture* (1849) was its primary inspiration.

23. As early as 1908 Elliott had addressed an essay to the question, "What Does Modern Psychology Permit Us to Believe in Respect to Regeneration?"

24. Paul A. Carter, *The Decline and Revival of the Social Gospel,* p. 19.

and it probably received more publicity than had any similar findings in the preceding half-century. The same sources reveal persistent criticism of isolationism and support of the League of Nations despite the countercurrents exposed in successive national elections. In large part this development was a reaction from the churches' uncritical role in World War I; and this remorse deepened as evidence of the war's failure to resolve the world's problems accumulated. Harry Emerson Fosdick, who had enthusiastically "presented arms" in 1917, took a vow that he would never again come to the support of war. But it is also true, as Professor Carter has emphasized, that again the churches were simply providing biblical texts and "Christian" arguments for a secular trend that had put a Quaker in the White House and made a former conscientious objector prime minister of Great Britain.[25] Pacifism was in fact so popular in the late twenties and early thirties that serious concern for totalitarian threats to world peace were long delayed.

The ecumenical movement also made strong advances during these years. At home interdenominational cooperation continued to expand along lines laid down before the war, as the Federal Council of Churches, serving as a central coordinating agency, gained steadily in membership. And the movement had set even larger international goals. The vision of church reunion had been awakened at the great missionary conference held at Edinburgh in 1910 and discussed at three smaller international conferences, one just before, one during, and one just after World War I. Out of these, in turn, came the invitations that led to the historic Stockholm Conference of 1925, where six hundred delegates from thirty-seven countries, including some from the Eastern Orthodox churches, laid the foundations for the ecumenical Life and Work movement, which urged a unified Christian approach to the world's social problems. While these arrangements went forward, another movement animated by concern for the issues of faith and order among Christendom's divided churches gathered momentum. Charles Brent, the Protestant Episcopal missionary bishop in the Philippines and a delegate to Edinburgh in 1910, provided the impetus that finally led in 1927 to another historic ecumenical gathering, at Lausanne, Switzerland. Out of these two major elements the World Council of Churches would be formed in 1948; but even in the 1920s Americans played important roles in world ecumenism, offering a strong witness to their own practical concerns and receiving, in turn, a deepened awareness of traditions and theological issues that were rarely encountered at home.

Yet notes of liberalism and church unity by no means dominated the religious scene. What brought a sense of discovery and progress to some brought

25. Ibid., pp. 136 ff.

anxiety and a sense of betrayal to others. The great disorienting forces of the decade aroused a "silent majority" of deeply disturbed conservatives. We must turn our attention, therefore, to circumstances that threw American Protestantism into a state of disarray from which it would never recover.

THE FUNDAMENTALIST CONTROVERSY

The theological issue at stake in the twenties was, of course, immemorial, and it had aroused intense conflict for a century. After the wartime moratorium on internal conflict was lifted, the old issues were rekindled. This militancy took two distinct forms: first, as an effort to prevent public schools and universities from teaching scientific theories which were deemed incompatible with traditional interpretations of the Bible; and second, as an effort to block the advance of liberal theology and modern scholarship in the churches. Of these two movements, the former has received far more publicity, shed far more discredit on the churches, and won remembrance among many who know little or nothing of the church-oriented struggles. The latter, on the other hand, constitutes a more intrinsic element of ecclesiastical history and requires more detailed consideration.

Of Men and Monkeys

In the course of a few days in July 1925 two million words of newspaper reportage were telegraphed from Dayton, Tennessee. The occasion for this historic flood of publicity was the confrontation of William Jennings Bryan and Clarence Darrow at the trial of John Scopes, who was under indictment for teaching evolution contrary to the laws of the state. The trial itself bore more resemblance to a camp meeting (or a prize fight) than to a legal process, and the State Supreme Court of Tennessee rejected its finding on a technicality. In an age of ballyhoo it became something of a national joke. Scopes was no Galileo, only a recent college graduate struggling through his first year of high school teaching, yet the event exposed fears that pervaded every section of the country. It pointed to a poignant dilemma of American evangelicalism.

The trouble in Tennessee began, appropriately, on a farm; and, as Ray Ginger remarks, "with a sincere effort to do good." [26] George Washington Butler was perturbed by the spread of modern scientific teachings, and as a member of the Tennessee legislature he proposed "An Act prohibiting the teaching of the Evolution Theory in all the Universities, Normals, and all other public schools of Tennessee." Because he had many sympathizers, and

26. Ray Ginger, *Six Days or Forever? Tennessee v. John Thomas Scopes*, p. 7.

because even those who championed better education did not wish to risk a fight on this issue, the Butler Act was passed. Yet Tennessee was not unique in its efforts to hold back the advance of science and learning. Oklahoma's law in 1923 was the nation's first. Bryan himself helped draft the anti-evolution resolution passed by the Florida legislature later that year. Mississippi passed a law in 1926, and Arkansas in 1927, and in Arkansas a case came into court as late as 1966. In Louisiana and North Carolina similar measures were defeated by only a small margin.

This campaign to halt the teaching of evolution and kindred theories in the schools was not only a movement of the rural South. Ministers of great city congregations in the North also provided leadership. Through the World's Christian Fundamentals Association led by William Bell Riley of the large First Baptist Church in Minneapolis, the Fundamentalist movement gained nationwide scope. At the association's ninth annual convention in 1927—with representatives of several allied organizations present—it made plans for a coordinated approach to all state legislatures. Its publications, special conferences, and organized efforts served not only to unify the movement, but to keep it oriented toward the premillennial dispensationalism being advanced in many churches and Bible institutes. Especially in its efforts to gain anti-evolution laws in the states, it was supported by the Bible Crusaders of America, almost the personal agency of a single wealthy founder, George F. Washburn of Florida. From Wichita, Kansas, Gerald B. Winrod led his Defenders of the Christian Faith. The existence of many of these organizations depended on a single dynamic leader; yet they did maintain contact with a vast constituency of conservative Protestants and win countless local victories. In the process, no doubt, innumerable Americans were convinced that modern science was not only incompatible with Christian orthodoxy, but destructive to the moral order. Despite local successes, however, conservatives could not gain organizational control in the various denominations. It was this circumstance that underlay the second major phase of the Fundamentalist controversy.

The Battle within the Churches

The Fundamentalist controversy, properly speaking, was not fought out in courts of law and legislative halls but within the churches. It was, in fact, a struggle for ecclesiastical control whose intensity varied in direct proportion to the strength of theological liberalism in a given denomination, unless (as in the cases of Congregationalism and Northern Methodism) the liberals were unassailably strong. The situation remained relatively peaceful among the Lutherans and in the southern churches, especially in the Southern

Baptist Convention, where liberals constituted no threat.[27] It was disputed with greatest fury among the Northern Presbyterians and the Northern Baptists, with the Disciples of Christ perhaps the next most agitated.

The Presbyterian church, because of its closely knit polity and its rigorous doctrinal tradition, had already been deeply riven in the later nineteenth century. After the war, conflict broke into the open again with William Jennings Bryan playing an important role. Presbyterian withdrawal from the Interchurch World Movement and mounting conservative criticism of the Presbyterian New Era Movement were more than straws in the wind. During the war (1916) the General Assembly had required ministerial candidates to subscribe to its Five-Point Deliverance of 1910, and this gave conservatives leverage for future battles.

The chief provocation to renewed conflict was provided, oddly enough, by a Baptist, Harry Emerson Fosdick, who had come to Union Seminary in New York first as a student, then in 1908 as a professor. Shortly after the war he became a regular "guest preacher" at the First Presbyterian Church of New York. In that role he made known his objections to the exclusivistic tactics of ultraconservatives, especially among the premillennialists who were increasing their strength in the foreign mission fields. "Shall the Fundamentalists Win?" he asked in 1922 in a widely read article in the *Christian Century*. In terms of concrete acts the answer returned, "We will if we can." First they attempted to expel this liberal Baptist from his Presbyterian pulpit. This was accomplished—though with an untoward result. Fosdick's next call, to the Park Avenue Baptist Church, led directly to John D. Rockefeller's offer to build an interdenominational church on Morningside Heights, and in 1931 Fosdick was installed in that great architectural and institutional eminence.

During the next fifteen years Fosdick was the nation's most influential Protestant preacher. For countless tourists the chance to hear Fosdick in Riverside Church fulfilled a life's ambition. Meanwhile, a whole generation of Presbyterian preachers were forced to quote from his many books with the innocent introduction, "As someone has said . . ." Their reticence stemmed not from the Fosdick affair, but from the furor provoked by the Auburn Affirmation of 1924. This statement, signed by over twelve hundred people, condemned the denomination's official biblical literalism and the extraconfessional character of the Five-Point Deliverance. In the next few years it became increasingly clear that moderate forms of evangelical liberal-

27. In the Episcopal church there were several widely publicized cases involving individual priests, but Catholic-Evangelical tensions continued to provide the chief doctrinal controversy.

ism were acceptable to at least a narrow majority in the church, but this fact only increased the violence of Fundamentalist attacks.

Inevitably, Princeton Seminary moved to the center of this theological conflict, as its brilliant professor of New Testament, J. Gresham Machen (1881–1937), provided intellectual leadership for the conservative cause. Machen's *Christianity and Liberalism* (1923) even after a half-century remains the chief theological ornament of American Fundamentalism. His thesis—like the book as a whole—was uncompromising and crystal clear, stating that "despite the . . . use of traditional phraseology, modern liberalism not only is a different religion from Christianity but belongs in a totally different class of religions." By the late 1920s, however, Machen's refinement of the old Hodge-Warfield position on scriptural inerrancy was being challenged in the seminary itself. This fact finally led in 1929 to a reorganization of the seminary and to three secessionist moves by the conservatives: first, the formation of Westminster Seminary in Philadelphia, then the organization of an independent foreign missions board, and finally, the founding of the Orthodox Presbyterian Church as a new denomination.[28] All of these actions, it must be added, were accompanied by much debate, many polemical publications, and harsh personal recriminations. But the steady drift of sentiment in the denomination (among laity, ministers, and theologians) was toward a broadened evangelicalism and away from the strict, propositional orthodoxy that had held sway at least up to 1916, or even 1922. That the denomination was seriously scarred (as indeed it had been by the schisms of 1741, 1805–10, 1837, 1857, and 1860) nobody denied.

In the Northern Baptist Convention the Fundamentalist controversy involved wider extremes than among the Presbyterians. On one hand, the Baptists' anticreedal congregationalism left the way more open to theological departures. An unusually large number of leading liberal theologians were Baptists—Clarke, Rauschenbusch, Fosdick, Mathews, and Macintosh, to name only the more prominent. And financially independent Baptist seminaries such as Newton, Colgate, Rochester, Crozer, and, above all, the Chicago Divinity School made the denomination famous for its sponsorship of learning. On the other hand, the prominence of anti-intellectualism and revivalism had produced a membership (both clerical and lay) that was unresponsive to the problems created by scholarship, science, and social change. Baptists thus provided the chief leadership for the more important national

28. After an Independent Board of Missions had been barred from the church, the new denomination was formed (1936). The word "orthodox" was added only after litigation required a change of corporate name (1939). By that time the new conservative church had itself divided (1937)—premillennialism having been a major divisive issue. On the earlier phase of this struggle see pp. 813–15.

Fundamentalist organizations and were prominent in premillennialist circles. They also founded more conservative "counter-seminaries" than any other denomination.[29]

As in the Presbyterian church, Baptist conservatives succeeded in leading their denomination out of the Interchurch World Movement in 1920. Of larger future significance, however, was the preconvention conference of that year at which Fundamentalists consolidated their forces. Out of this grew the National Federation of Fundamentalists of the Northern Baptists, with John Roach Straton of New York, Jasper C. Massee of Brooklyn, and Amzi C. Dixon, editor of *The Fundamentals,* leading its many-pronged assault on modernism and evolution. William Bell Riley meanwhile guided the Baptist Bible Union toward similar ends. Due to the efforts of these organizations, most of the annual meetings of the Convention were torn by violent debates. Three issues predominated: the need for a formal declaration of doctrine, heresy among foreign missionaries, and liberalism in the seminaries. On all these matters conservatives scored victories, but they were invariably qualified and in some cases rendered almost nugatory by amendments. At the end of the decade the denomination was very much where it had been in 1920.

During the bottom years of the Depression something like denominational peace prevailed among Northern Baptists. As many historians of Fundamentalism seem not to have realized, however, the peace was only temporary.[30] During the 1930s conservative revivalistic Christianity would flourish. The number of Bible institutes grew from 49 in 1930 to 144 in 1950; radio evangelists prospered (most sensationally, Charles E. Fuller's "Old Fashioned Revival Hour" emanating from Los Angeles), and independent Fundamentalist congregations became increasingly numerous. In 1932, as the chances for asserting the Fundamentalist program in the Convention grew slimmer, the General Association of Regular Baptists was organized, and by 1946 it had grown to include five hundred churches. A second secession occurred in 1947, when the Conservative Baptist Association was formed, though it was

29. In the Boston area, where Newton Institute was showing signs of liberalism, A. J. Gordon had led off in 1889 with a Missionary Training School (in Boston), later Gordon College and Seminary (in Wenham, Mass.). In Chicago, Northern Baptist Seminary was founded in 1913 to counter the influence of the university divinity school; and in 1925 Eastern Seminary took up this role vis-à-vis Crozer Seminary in Philadelphia. The latter two retained a relationship to the convention, however. The nondenominational Moody Bible School in Chicago, like its sister institute in Los Angeles and Scofield's school in Dallas, was frequently attended by Baptist conservatives who had strong premillennial and dispensationalist convictions.

30. Norman K. Furniss, in *The Fundamentalist Controversy, 1918–1931,* revealed this tendency to premature obsequies in his concluding pages. This is surprising, since by 1954, when his book appeared, Fundamentalism was enjoying a rather sensational resurgence of influence and power.

not at first a separatistic organization. By 1969 it had become a strong Fundamentalist body with affiliated seminaries, a large foreign missionary society, and 315,000 members.

The restorationist movement which looks to Barton W. Stone and the Campbells as its founders had even less organizational structure than the Baptists to give focus to the Fundamentalist controversy. By 1906 its most conservative elements, largely in the rural South, had already separated themselves as the Churches of Christ, but even in the 1890s the remaining (and larger) part of the denomination had begun to be polarized. Among churches where magazine editors wielded extraordinary influence and power, the *Christian-Evangelist,* edited in Saint Louis by James H. Garrison, upheld the cause of moderate inclusivism and emphasized the Disciples' traditional concern for Christian unity. Setting a stricter restorationist tradition was the *Christian Standard,* edited by Isaac Errett from 1866 to 1888. Sharply accentuating this trend between 1893 and 1912 were the weekly columns of John W. McGarvey. He demanded baptism by immersion and the older methods of biblical study while inveighing against open membership, ecumenism, and a more centralized church order.

At the heart of this controversy, however, was the issue of liberal theology and biblical criticism, especially as it had been defended and propagated by Herbert L. Willett, a professor of New Testament at the Chicago Divinity School and for thirty years an indefatigable participant in denominational controversies. Willett supported the Divinity School and the Disciples House affiliated with it, encouraged those who would extend its scholarly ideals in other colleges and seminaries, urged the revision of Sunday school materials, and advocated participation in the ecumenical movement. As the possibility of halting or reversing these several trends diminished, the conservatives took the important step in 1927 of organizing the North American Christian Convention. No formal separation took place, but two quite distinct fellowships arose and the denomination's leading historian would subsequently speak of the conservatives as constituting a second group of "Churches of Christ." [31]

The Fundamentalist controversy neither began nor ended in the twenties, but that decade did witness the climactic confrontation of American evangelical Protestantism and modern thought. After the decade's turmoil the more extreme forms of doctrinal conservatism would continue to grow, notably among the Pentecostalists. Yet it would occupy an increasingly restricted place in the nation's life. Certain large denominations would continue to resist the advance of science and biblical criticism, but they would

31. Alfred Thomas DeGroot, *New Possibilities for Disciples and Independents, with a History of the Independents, Church of Christ Number Two.*

never again be able to alter the content of scientific education or hinder serious scholarship except in institutions they controlled. Hereafter Fundamentalism was in retreat.

THE CRISIS OF THE PROTESTANT ESTABLISHMENT

The Protestant churches of America did not lose their historic hegemony during the troubled twenties, but they were made sharply aware that their ancient sway over the nation's moral life was threatened. Even as modern religious ideas steadily advanced or as concern for social issues increased, the churches tended to lose their capacity to shape and inform American opinion. The debacle of Prohibition functioned both as evidence and cause of the churches' loss of authority in a culture where urban values became primary. The decline of the Puritan Sabbath despite strenuous campaigns in its behalf, the emergence of new attitudes toward recreation despite old Puritanic suspicions of play, and the expansion of the amusement industry served meanwhile to weaken the disciplinary aspects of church membership. Modern thought and social change were slowly bringing down the curtains on the "great century" of American evangelicalism.

A greatly diminished hold on the country's intellectual and literary leadership was another important sign of change. This meant in turn that ministerial candidates were turning to other vocations. Nor were they dissuaded from this decision by the assorted hypocrites and boobs that marched through Sinclair Lewis's *Elmer Gantry*. Dr. Arrowsmith's vocation seemed a more effective means for saving Main Street from Babbittry.[32] Offended as much by the obscurantism of the Fundamentalists as by the cultural accommodations of the churches, intellectuals, young and old, were leaving the church—with H. L. Mencken piping the tune and providing the laughs. "Every day," he said, "a new Catholic church goes up; every day another Methodist or Presbyterian church is turned into a garage." "Protestantism is down with a wasting disease." [33] And Mencken thought he knew why, though he ignored matters of urban ecology and spoke chiefly of regions where Catholics were scarce.

> Any literate plowhand, if the Holy Spirit inflames him, is thought to be fit to preach. Is he commonly sent, as preliminary, to a training camp,

32. Sinclair Lewis was the first American author to receive the Nobel Prize, in 1930. *Elmer Gantry, Dodsworth, Babbitt, Arrowsmith,* and *Mainstreet* all appeared in the 1920s. *The Good Earth* (1931) by Pearl Buck received the Pulitzer Prize in 1932, and the Nobel Prize in 1938. For her views on missions she was much criticized by Presbyterian conservatives.

33. From a review of Wilbur C. Abbott, *The New Barbarians,* in *Prejudices,* 5th ser. (New York: Alfred A. Knopf, 1926), p. 157.

> to college? But what a college! You will find one in every mountain valley of the land, with its single building in its bare pasture lot, and its faculty of half-idiot pedagogues and brokendown preachers. One man, in such a college, teaches oratory, ancient history, arithmetic and Old Testament exegesis. This aspirant comes in from the barnyard, and goes back in a year or two to the village. His body of knowledge is that of a street-car motorman or a vaudeville actor. But he has learned the clichés of his craft, and he has got him a longtailed coat, and so he has made his escape from the harsh labors of his ancestors, and is set up as a fountain of light and learning.[34]

More disturbing than the revolt of highbrows and middlebrows were more readily experienced social realities. Immigrant "hordes" were corrupting the old ways of life and upsetting the political order. New methods and ideas were invading the schools. The cities were ruling the nation. Hard work and sobriety were no longer honored. New temptations were disrupting the family and leading youth astray. Any number of public statements reveal the unsettlement and despair which many American Protestants inwardly felt. But none, oddly enough, better revealed the underlying pathos than Hiram Wesley Evans, the Imperial Wizard of the Ku Klux Klan. His lengthy defense of the Klan's course of action, published in the *North American Review,* deserves extended quotation and close reading.

> Nordic Americans for the last generation have found themselves increasingly uncomfortable and finally deeply distressed. There appeared first confusion in thought and opinion, a groping hesitancy about national affairs and private life alike, in sharp contrast to the clear, straightforward purposes of our earlier years. There was futility in religion, too, which was in many ways even more distressing. . . . Finally came the moral breakdown that has been going on for two decades. One by one all our traditional moral standards went by the boards, or were so disregarded that they ceased to be binding. The sacredness of our Sabbath, of our homes, of chastity, and finally even of our right to teach our own children in our own schools fundamental facts and truths were torn away from us. Those who maintained the old standards did so only in the face of constant ridicule.
>
> Along with this went economic distress. The assurance for the future of our children dwindled. We found our great cities and the control of much of our industry and commerce taken over by strangers, who stacked the cards of success and prosperity against us. . . .
>
> So the Nordic American today is a stranger in large parts of the land

34. "Protestantism in the Republic," ibid., pp. 104–05, 115.

his fathers gave him. . . . Our falling birth rate, the result of all this, is proof of our distress. We no longer feel that we can be fair to children we bring into the world, unless we can make sure from the start that they shall have capital or education or both, so that they need never compete with those who now fill the lower rungs of the ladder of success. We no longer dare risk letting our youth "make its own way" in conditions under which we live. . . .

We are a movement of the plain people, very weak in the matter of culture, intellectual support, and trained leadership. We are demanding . . . a return of power into the hands of the everyday, not highly cultured, not overly intellectualized, but entirely unspoiled and not de-Americanized, average citizen of the old stock. Our members and leaders are all of this class—the opposition of the intellectuals and liberals who held the leadership, betrayed Americanism . . . is almost automatic.

This is undoubtedly a weakness. It lays us open to the charge of being "hicks" and "rubes" and "drivers of the second hand Fords." We admit it. . . . Every popular movement has suffered from just this handicap, yet the popular movements have been the mainsprings of progress, and have usually had to win against the "best people" of their time.[35]

For Roman Catholics, Eastern Orthodox, Lutherans, Jews, Negroes, and other large groups who often bore the brunt of nativistic intolerance, the twenties were also decisive, but in very different—even opposite—ways; and later chapters will deal with these developments. For most churchgoers in the Protestant mainstream, however, the promise of American life—despite jazz, flappers, speakeasies, and gangsters—seemed never to have been greater.

Then in October 1929, the Crash. And in the darkening months and years that followed, the Depression. The promise evaporated. But during the hard times there came no great revival of religion such as had followed the panic of 1857. Indeed, for a long time there were not even many signs of popular social reformism; long addiction to make-believe delayed the general awareness that a national catastrophe would require a national solution. In due time an upsurge of realistic self-awareness would occur. A renewal of theology was also in the offing, even a considerable expansion of church membership, and after another great war, a religious revival. But the renewal would take place on a smaller stage, and the revival would be utterly discontinuous with America's earlier awakenings. In retrospect, it becomes clear that the decade of the twenties marked a crucial transition in American religious history.

35. "The Klan's Fight for Americanism," *North American Review* 213 (March–April–May 1926): 33–63; quoted by Richard Hofstadter, *The Age of Reform: From Bryan to FDR* (New York: Alfred A. Knopf, 1956), pp. 293–94.

54

THE THIRTIES: FROM THE CRASH TO PEARL HARBOR

The thirties, in effect, began with the Crash and ended with the outbreak of World War II. But in American memory this tumultuous decade always passes under the name of the Depression or the New Deal, and it is inextinguishably associated with Franklin Delano Roosevelt. His solemn predecessor in the White House, who presided over almost a third of the decade, is a leftover of the twenties. Under whatever name, the thirties were momentous times. Heinz Eulau ventured to say that the New Deal's impression on the American experience "in the long run can only be compared with the birth of the nation itself and the fratricidal blood-letting of the Civil War." [1] During these years the third great stride in the formation of the federal Union was taken; and the American people as a whole participated in this time of turning—in its sufferings and satisfactions, in its verbal and physical conflict, and in its profound discoveries.

THE IMPACT OF THE DEPRESSION

Like every great experience of any people, the Depression had wide-ranging religious ramifications. Moral tradition and church affiliation counted heavily in the politics of the day. Theological issues underlay several of the most heated controversies, while churchmen often led the corresponding crusades. And of course the churches were filled with echoes of the decade's momentous debates on the responsibilities of government for social welfare and the issues of war and peace. Just as the spiritual and intellectual life of

1. "Neither Ideology nor Utopia: the New Deal in Retrospect," in *The New Deal,* ed. Bernard Sternsher (Boston: Allyn and Bacon, 1960), p. 168.

the nation was matured by the decade's hard lessons, so were the churches forced to deeper levels of understanding. It would be no exaggeration to apply Professor Eulau's strong statement about the New Deal to the American religious experience of the thirties. Hence this chapter will deal with its institutional and social implications, while the next will consider its impact on theology.

Without doubt, much that went on in the churches followed immemorial custom. Clergymen went their rounds, baptizing, marrying, and burying—and preaching on Sundays according to their style. Controversies over the Atonement or the inerrancy of Scripture waxed and waned; liberals and conservatives continued the struggles of the previous decade. Among both Northern Presbyterians and Northern Baptists, controversies that had intensified during the twenties resulted in open schism. Among Roman Catholics the gap between social conservatives and progressives widened. Sectarian movements arose and strange new cults came into existence—some for the rich, others for the poor. On revisiting "Middletown" in 1935, ten years after their first survey, the Lynds found the "same serious and numerically sparse Gideon's band" inside the churches.[2] Yet they thought that the congregation looked older on the average, and we know now that baptisms were less frequent, since the population increase was only half as great as during the preceding decade. It was not a time for great confidence in the future. In the western dustbowl there were more prayers for rain; and as the decade wore on, prayers for world peace became more numerous everywhere. In other words, the historian's old problem of change and continuity also pertains to the thirties. Consequently, many developments of these years are dealt with in other more thematic chapters. The emphasis here will be upon the newer movements that arose most directly out of this decade's particular experience.

The Crash came as a shock to many Americans—like a "firebell in the night" to denizens of an allegedly fireproof building. Many wanted to believe that it was a false alarm, that prosperity was just around the corner. But there was no mistaking the Great Depression as actuality. It broke the mood of the twenties once and for all. The national income dropped from $83 billion in 1929 to $40 billion in 1932, while the number of unemployed began to approach fifteen million in early 1933.

> Fear, hunger, and finally desperation became the inevitable facts of life in an emergency that had no precedent in United States history. Across

2. Robert S. and Helen Merrell Lynd, *Middletown in Transition* (New York: Harcourt Brace, 1937); quoted in Frederick L. Allen, *Since Yesterday*, p. 156.

> America and across class lines spread privation. Men stood on bread lines, selling apples on street corners, sleeping in subways and parks and city incinerators. Armies of homeless youth roamed the land while relief agencies, running out of money and morale, had to stand helplessly by while thousands suffered. Violence erupted in some communities, as men chose to steal rather than watch their children starve.[3]

Americans of every type sought and found scapegoats and panaceas; racist attitudes and ethnic animosities intensified; class antagonisms sharpened. Political and religious views gravitated to the extremes; and demagogues, often with the Cross of Christ on their banners, began to gather their followers. Old popular beliefs collapsed, confidence in the redemptive power of the American way of life faltered, the "religion of business" lost votaries in droves, faith in automatic progress evaporated.

Yet amid these fallen idols a many-sided revival of spirit also occurred. Realizing that the whole country was in trouble, Americans gained a new kind of national self-awareness. Mutual distress drew people together. As neighbor discovered neighbor, a great many Americans found a new sense of solidarity. A nation of rugged individualists found reasons for group activities; laborers, farmers, small business men, the aged, and many others banded together. Ethnic and racial ties became more meaningful. And this sense of urgency ineluctably took on a religious aspect.

The nation by no means fell to its knees in penitence and supplication—though there were jeremiads enough. Among the Fundamentalists and in the Holiness and Pentecostal churches, something like a revival took place, perhaps because the Depression so enlarged their constituencies among the disinherited. Between 1926 and 1936 for example, the Church of the Nazarene grew from 63,558 to 136,227 and the Assemblies of God from 47,950 to 148,043, and this at a time when the large mainstream denominations were experiencing a drastic decline in congregational giving and were barely holding their own in membership. Most pointedly ecumenical was the process by which various "Fundamentalist" churches, due largely to their dissatisfaction with the liberalism and the social actionism of the Federal Council of Churches, felt a need for federation. This impulse led to the formation of the highly combative American Council of Churches in 1941 and the less exclusivistic National Association of Evangelicals in 1942–43.

In the older denominations a convergence of these factors—declining vitality, national awareness, ethnic solidarity—led to several important church

3. David H. Bennett, *Demagogues in the Depression: American Radicals and the Union Party, 1932–1936*, p. 4.

mergers. Southern and Northern Methodists ended their old alienation, drew in the smaller Protestant Methodist Church, and in 1939 formed a reunited church. The two African Methodist churches were not included, however; and even the black conferences of Northern Methodism were segregated in a Central Jurisdiction. Four smaller German churches—the old German Reformed, the Evangelical Synod, the Evangelical Church, and the United Brethren—held merger discussions. But they discovered too great a difference between the first two, whose origins were in the Reformation, and the latter two essentially Methodistic bodies, which had sprung from the Second Awakening revivals between 1800 and 1810. As a result, two separate mergers were carried out, producing the Evangelical and Reformed Church in 1934 and the Evangelical United Brethren Church in 1946. Of a similar nature was the merger in 1931 of two churches with very different origins, the Congregational churches of old New England background and the so-called Christian churches which had come together out of three separate secession movements between 1790 and 1810.[4] Perhaps coincidentally, all nine of these merging groups would merge again after World War II. The United Church of Christ was formed in 1957 to include the Congregational-Christian and Evangelical-Reformed groups. In 1968 the United Methodist Church was broadened to include the Evangelical United Brethren.

The Social Gospel Revival

As the fact of social catastrophe was gradually driven home to churchgoing America, Prohibition, Sabbatarianism, and the questions of personal morality occasioned by the rise of the movies and "ballroom" dancing yielded to larger issues. In significant portions of the church leadership the Social Gospel was revitalized. At their national meeting of 1931 the Northern Baptists had already virtually endorsed what the New Dealers would later propose. In 1932 the Northern Presbyterian Committee on Social and Industrial Relations reported to the General Assembly that the country faced "an emergency of unprecedented magnitude" that had been brought on by "incompetency and wrong-headedness." They went on to raise questions about the capitalistic principles "upon which it was assumed general prosperity was based." Episcopalians received even sterner warnings from the *Church-*

4. The oldest element in the "Christian churches" was the so-called Christian Connection which had withdrawn from the New England standing order under the leadership of Abner Jones and others; the second, led by James O'Kelley, had left the Methodist church to protest its hierarchicalism; the third was made up of followers of Barton W. Stone who chose not to merge with Alexander Campbell's very similar but more narrowly defined Restoration movement. These three had subsequently agreed to articles of union (see Robert Lee, *The Social Sources of Church Unity*, p. 112).

man, the denomination's most steady advocate of social Christianity. Its diagnosis would have justified far more thoroughgoing reforms than the New Deal would ever undertake.

In no large denomination were social concerns more forcefully expressed than among the Methodists. In 1932 the Committee on the State of the Church delivered to the General Conference a wholesale condemnation of the social order and the acquisitive principle on which it was based. Its semiofficial Federation for Social Service consistently took positions in advance of most other American church agencies, due to the strenuous leadership of such men as Professor Harry F. Ward of Union Seminary and Bishop Francis J. McConnell. In 1934 the National Council of Methodist Youth at its first national convention endorsed socialism, chided the New Deal for its halfway measures, and circulated a pledge that began: "I surrender my life to Christ. I renounce the Capitalist system . . ." In nearly all the churches, one could note how periodicals, special policy committees, and general deliberative bodies showed an increased willingness to speak out on social issues in a distinctly critical manner. Utopian platitudes about industrial peace and international order gave way to a more realistic concern for proximate causes of economic distress and the actualities of power.

When denominational pronouncements went to such lengths, the Federal Council of Churches naturally went as far—or farther. In 1932 it drastically revised the social creed which it had adopted in 1912, now affirming the need for government action and social planning. In early 1933 the *Christian Century* complained that the president-elect would probably be as hopelessly conservative as Hoover had been. Later in the year, after FDR's famous "hundred days," Benson Y. Landis, a leading Congregational social actionist who had also played a major role in the Federal Council, published his trenchant book *The Third American Revolution.* Is the New Deal, he worried, "more the expression of provincial America than of international cooperation"? Is its concentration on economic recovery "the enemy of revolution"? Yet he was proud that the "federal government was applying many of the policies which the churches [or "liberal churchmen," for he also used this more accurate term] had advocated for two decades." [5]

Interdenominational groups bent on a more radical critique of the status quo were also active. The Fellowship of Reconciliation, founded during World War I to strengthen the pacifist witness, shifted its interest markedly toward social affairs after 1928, when it absorbed the Fellowship for a Christian Social Order; and by 1933 it was so committed to the cause of labor that it had to poll its membership on the question of using force when

5. Benson Y. Landis, *The Third American Revolution,* pp. 128–33.

social justice was at stake. Despite constant tension on this question it gave strong support to liberal and socialistic policies. The Fellowship of Socialist Christians, in which Reinhold Niebuhr was a leading voice, was formed in 1930; its manifesto of the following year spoke frankly of "class struggle" and warned that "class war" would result if the inequities of the social order were not removed. In the early thirties it was highly critical of Roosevelt's kind of "whirligig reform" and contemptuous of liberals who would merely patch up the old system. As with the earlier Social Gospel, however, racial inequities had a minor place in most protest literature of the period. Few seemed to share Niebuhr's grimly realistic view that "the white race in America will not admit the Negro to equal rights if not forced to do so. Upon that point one may speak with a dogmatism which all history justifies." [6]

In November 1936 the United Council for Christian Democracy was formed in order to coordinate liberal and radical groups in the various churches and to organize such groups in denominations that lacked them. But by this time questions of pacifism and violence were dividing the coalition, first with regard to industrial class conflict, then later over matters of defense and foreign policy. The Depression unquestionably obtained for Social Christianity a voice in the churches which it had not had before. The men who felt deeply about issues and who wanted reform—or even social revolution—found agencies and platforms in the churches where they could speak, organize, publish, and act. How positive a response they got from the rank-and-file membership is another question. The revival of social concern and the great increase in liberal pronouncements by church groups of various types seems not to have brought Protestant churchgoers to a position in advance of the American electorate, though it probably brought many to a broader understanding of the issues and of the need for social change.

The Conservative Response

Social conservatism, sometimes of an extreme sort, continued to flourish in the great middle-class denominations in which liberal advocacy was most audible. Few active parish pastors rose to prominence in the social reform agencies. Angry rebuttals and expressions of mass displeasure greeted the Federal Council's new social creed, and in many churches there were organized countermovements. In 1935 James W. Fifield, the ultraconservative minister of a large and well-financed Congregational church in Los Angeles, organized Spiritual Mobilization to promote the cause of Christian individualism. In 1936 the Layman's Religious Movement was launched to perform

6. *Moral Man and Immoral Society* (New York: Charles Scribner's Sons, 1932), p. 253.

a similar service in the Methodist church. In the South the tradition of ecclesiastical silence on social issues (aside from Prohibition) was so strong that conservatives rarely had cause for complaint. The Southern Baptist Convention in 1938 termed the American economic system the "best in the world." "There ought to be no room for radical Socialism and for atheistic Communism in the United States of America, and the widespread propaganda now carried on in their interest should be as speedily as possible and in every way possible prevented and counteracted." [7] In pietistic or revivalistic churches in all parts of the country the counsels of patience, prayer, and belt-tightening usually prevailed. How men voted was regarded as a private civic affair.

Robert M. Miller, who surveyed all of the Protestant periodicals, gained the distinct impression that in 1932 almost all of them were favorable to Hoover. In 1936 they were for Landon, though less distinctly. Comparing their advocacy in 1928, 1932, and 1936, he found it very clear that Protestant editors were far more inclined to support candidates on the issues of Prohibition or Catholicism than on unemployment and hunger. The *Literary Digest* poll of 21,606 clergymen in 1936 revealed that 70.22 percent of them were opposed to New Deal policies. A poll conducted in 1936 showed that a majority of Protestant church members voted for Landon in the Roosevelt landslide. Interestingly, it also showed that Congregationalists were 78 percent for Landon and Southern Baptists 65 percent for FDR.[8] The evidence seems to support the generalization that, outside the Solid South, the economic well-being or social status of church members had more effect on their voting than their church's pronouncements.

Both North and South, moreover, the times were leading many to believe that President Roosevelt's emergency measures were not the answer the country needed. Adding greatly to the uneasiness of churchgoing Americans of all classes was the continued advance of those changes in manners and mores that had made the 1920s a nightmare for rural America. Despite the Depression, urban civilization continued to make its conquests. Jazz, dancing, feminism, and the Hollywood star system mocked the older moral standards, both Catholic and Protestant. Hard times notwithstanding, the automobile continued to transform traditional modes of living and loving. Sabbath-keeping was losing ground. All over the country racketeers and bank robbers seemed to prosper—even if Bonnie and Clyde and Dillinger were shot down. With millions hungry, the government was destroying livestock and

7. Quoted in Robert M. Miller, *American Protestantism and Social Issues, 1919–1939*, p. 118.

8. Ibid., 117–23.

ploughing under corn. WPA workers leaned on their rakes; hoboes and tramps were everywhere; prosperity manifested itself very slowly. The times seemed out of joint.

In this decade of desperate responses Protestant-Catholic relations were put under serious strain by the very fact that the resounding Democratic victories of 1932, 1934, and 1936 rested on the coalition that Alfred E. Smith had begun to forge in 1928. A new era in American power relationships was at hand. Among the many signs of this changing balance was the fact that only 8 of the 214 federal judges appointed by Harding, Coolidge, and Hoover were Catholic, as against 51 of 196 under Roosevelt. Nor were Protestant feelings assuaged in 1939 when the President sent Myron Taylor as his "personal representative" to the pope. With the Jewish vote in crucial urban areas also breaking the hold of the Protestant Establishment, anti-Semitism became sharper and more explicit.

Between 1929 and 1933, furthermore, the precarious state of Prohibition was a major source of Protestant anxiety. In this cause the churches had achieved unprecedented unity; and in this crusade they had triumphed. Yet now they beheld the great victory being undone by scorn, racketeering, and nonenforcement. Then with Utah's ratification of the Twenty-first Amendment in December 1933 came the dreaded calamity: Repeal. It was the greatest blow to their pride and self-confidence that Protestants as a collective body had ever experienced. Not even the comforting charm of FDR's fireside chats could prevent many from believing that only drastic reversals could save the country from aliens and radicals.

In the midst of this swirling contention about America's proper course of action at home and in the world, a religious movement with ostensibly no other interest than "changed lives" became for a time a strong, even sensational, conservative force. Its founder and charismatic leader was Frank Buchman (1878–1961), a Lutheran pastor of pietistic background. Buchman was a "Lecturer in Personal Evangelism" at Hartford Seminary en route to the World Disarmament Conference in Washington, D.C., when he received from God a commission to convert the world—through a program of Moral Re-Armament (MRA). Even on that trip he was using a strategy that his so-called Oxford Group or First-Century Fellowship would always employ, whether on the college campus or in the world's capitals—that of concentrating on the successful, the "up-and-outers," the people with prestige, influence, and power. By organizing "houseparties" in comfortable or lavish places, on the theory that "good food and good Christianity go together," he would gather like-minded people and in an informal way bring them through the "Five C's" (confidence, conviction, confession, conversion, continuance) to a "God-guided" life under the "Four Absolutes" (honesty, purity, unselfishness, and love).

During the twenties, amid much controversy Buchman developed followings not only at various eastern colleges in the United States, but in China and Britain as well (like Saint Paul, he had a chronic itching foot). During the 1930s, with Queen Marie of Romania and many other dignitaries as patrons, the movement became famous (or notorious) the world over. The tension-filled atmosphere of those years also politicized the pious evangelicalism that Buchman had absorbed from Moody and the Student Volunteer Movement. Anticommunism became a major theme in the increasingly thronged MRA assemblies, as did its reverse, a friendliness to fascism. Buchman revealed both his political attitudes and his missionary strategy in an interview in 1936:

> I thank heaven for a man like Adolf Hitler, who built a front line of defense against the Anti-Christ of Communism. Think what it would mean to the world if Hitler surrendered to the control of God. Or Mussolini. Or any dictator. Through such a man God could control a nation overnight and solve every last bewildering problem.[9]

During World War II MRA gained a more favorable image through its patriotic efforts, but by this time it had become a rich and complex organization and had lost the intimacy that accounted for its early strength. In the postwar era the applicability of its slogans and the health of its founder would decline together. Conservative evangelicals, however, would continue to use strategies very similar to those of early Buchmanism, especially in their college and university work.

Demagogues on the Right

Frank Buchman was hardly a demagogue in the usual sense of that term, though he was an elitist with great faith in simple formulas. In the later 1930s he organized vast MRA mass meetings tinged with conservative social ideology and far removed from traditional revivalism. Much more potent were various religio-political movements of the Right which, during these years, were being organized for the first time in American history. Most of them showed at least some influence from European fascistic and corporatistic thinking, though a certain continuity with Populism was even more in evidence, especially its addiction to radical monetary panaceas. Also visible was the racist and nativist bigotry which had motivated the Ku Klux Klan.

9. Walter Houston Clark, *The Oxford Group: Its History and Significance*, p. 16.

Gerald B. Winrod (1898–1957), a Baptist evangelist and militant premillennialist with headquarters in Wichita, Kansas, saw himself as the man to rally the Fundamentalist host. Honored in that constituency during the 1920s as the organizer of the Defenders of the Christian Faith to combat the spread of evolutionary teaching in the schools, he now towered above his many midwestern rivals. Through the *Defender Magazine* he was by 1938 reaching into a hundred thousand households. After 1933 he began to wage war on Roosevelt's "Jewish New Deal," and after a trip to Europe in 1934 he became more respectful of Hitler and more pronouncedly anti-Semitic. For his services to religion he was made an honorary doctor of divinity by Los Angeles Bible Institute in 1935. His aspirations to national leadership were groundless, for he was soundly beaten in the primary for the Kansas senatorial nomination in 1938. But throughout the thirties he nourished a huge constituency on a diet of bigotry and fear, as well as Fundamentalist theology, rugged individualism, and anticommunism.

Vying with Winrod was the less orthodox William Dudley Pelley, who published *Liberation* magazine and founded a college for the study of "Christian Economics" in Asheville, North Carolina. His Legion of Silver Shirts, organized in 1933, never amounted to much, despite its gaudy uniforms. And although Pelley's campaign for the presidency in 1936 as the Christian party's candidate was also a total failure, his pro-Nazi and violently anti-Semitic propaganda did its part to enlarge the "paranoid" element in the country. His religious message was a mixture of theosophy and astrology (see chap. 61, n. 7), but he wanted to disfranchise Jews and allow only Protestant Christians to lead the country. After Pelley ran afoul of the law, the "I AM" movement of Guy and Edna Ballard cut in on the Silver Shirts' constituency until it, too, ran into legal difficulties in 1941. Like Pelley, the Ballards stressed theosophical doctrines, but they added an emphasis on healing, personal self-fulfillment, and success that appealed to people in higher income levels. They also gave an elitist and "100 percent American" tone to their teaching and attacked every threat to the status quo. The huge public meetings which they sponsored in city after city took on heavy political overtones.

More significant than Winrod, Pelley, or the Ballards—not to mention dozens of lesser "apostles of discord"—was Gerald L. K. Smith (b. 1898), whom H. L. Mencken rightly judged to be the greatest oratorical "boob bumper" of his time. Wisconsin-born and relatively well-educated, Smith was a successful minister in Indianapolis until he took a church in the South for his wife's health. In Shreveport, Louisiana, as minister of the largest Disciples of Christ congregation in the state, he soon established a reputation for oratorical gifts and reformist interests. Then after the elections of 1932 he became one of Huey Long's chief lieutenants. He was especially active in promoting the Share-Our-Wealth Society and other schemes by which the Louisiana Kingfish sought to gain a national constituency. After Long's assassination in 1935, Smith delivered a memorable funeral oration and transferred his political base to Michigan. He was an orator in need of an organized cause when he allied himself and the Share-Our-Wealth Society with the Union party, a party which was at that time little more than the radio audience of the decade's greatest church-related demagogue.

Charles E. Coughlin was born in Hamilton, Ontario, in 1891 and grew up in a lower middle-class Irish Catholic environment. After distinguishing himself in college and seminary, he was ordained in 1916 and moved to the Detroit area in 1923. There he soon distinguished himself again as a preacher and parish organizer, especially after being assigned to a new church in the suburb of Royal Oak which was to be a shrine to the recently canonized Saint Theresa of the Little Flower. His work in that cause gained him local prominence as a radio preacher—and in 1929 the Crash provided a major topic for his sermons. Industrial management and the Hoover administration soon felt the brunt of his impassioned attacks. Coughlin also began to develop a distinct point of view on social matters which drew, first, on the papal social encyclicals of 1891 and 1931, persistently emphasizing their criticism of unchecked free enterprise and their openness to the idea of the "corporate state." Beyond this, however, Coughlin followed his own intuitions as to what would gain a response from his Depression-hit audiences. In 1932 the message was "Roosevelt or Ruin," but by 1934 he had cooled on FDR (who in turn had given very little attention to Coughlin's monetary nostrums). By 1936, with 145 clerks handling the mail and money that was pouring in from his ten million weekly listeners, Coughlin was in strident opposition to the New Deal and searching for a national political constituency.

The "sixteen points" of his Union for Social Justice summarized a reasonably coherent position. The key demands were for "nationalizing public necessities," replacing the Federal Reserve System with a "Government owned central bank," and allowing the government to facilitate the unionization of all laborers. They were not far removed from the "Blueprint for Economic Planning" which Catholic oil executive Michael J. O'Shaugnessy had proposed, or from the spirit of Pius XI's *Quadragesimo Anno,* or, indeed, from the ideas that underlay the National Industrial Recovery Act of 1933. But Father Coughlin's actual influence stemmed from his amazing capacity to manipulate the rhetoric of hate and fear. His basic opportunism is revealed by the senior partners he chose for the Union party: Dr. Francis E. Townsend's old age revolving pension movement, Smith's Share-Our-Wealth Society, and the farm refinancing reform movement that Lynn Frazier and William Lemke of North Dakota were rallying. With Lemke as the presidential candidate, with discontented urban Catholics, old people, and impoverished rural Protestants being held together by anti-Semitism, fears of atheistic communism, the lure of cheap money, and the oratorical power of Coughlin and Smith, the party hoped to be an influential factor in the election.

To entertain such hopes in 1936, however, was not to reckon with FDR. The Union party's campaign organization, moreover, soon fell into nearly total disarray. Roosevelt lost only Maine and Vermont, while the Union party garnered 892,378 votes and promptly fell to pieces, though not without some retrospective satisfactions. It had exceeded the 873,000 Socialist votes that Norman Thomas had garnered in 1932 and far surpassed Thomas's 188,000 votes in 1936. What may be most significant was the movement of the country's "protest vote" from the Left to the Right.[10] The election result hardly justified the alarm Sinclair Lewis had shown in his novel and play *It Can't Happen Here* (1935). But if a well organized Union party had faced a less formidable opponent than Roosevelt, it might have rallied the vast discontented audiences of its demagogues with heavy political effect. Of more enduring significance is the fact that ever since those years, the religio-political Right has remained a potent factor in American public affairs.

FACING THE DICTATORS: PEACE OR WAR?

The election of 1936 also marks the return of foreign policy issues to haunt the American scene. Japan had begun its occupation of Manchuria in 1931 and by 1936 was extending its control in China proper. Italy had fallen to the fascistic blandishments of Mussolini in 1922, and in 1936 its conquest of Ethiopia was being completed. Hitler had risen to power in Germany even before Hoover left the White House, and in 1936 he occupied the demilitarized Rhineland. In July 1936 the rising of the Nationalists had brought civil war to Spain. Franklin Roosevelt confessed in private that the situation was blacker than any he had ever known—though the isolation-

10. See Bennett, *Demagogues in the Depression*, pp. 263–72. Coughlin received very little official Catholic support and was opposed by many prelates, editors, and intellectuals in the church. Ideologically these several demagogic leaders drew more on America's nativist, antisubversionary, and populist traditions than on the fascistic "Extreme Right." Embattled Fundamentalism, aroused Catholic anticommunism, and deep dissatisfaction with the New Deal were also basic components.

istic disposition of the American people required him to minimize his concern. In the face of alarming events the basic commitments of Americans to peace and nonintervention were put to the test. Intellectual neutrality among the harsh alternatives of Soviet communism, the stricken democracies, and the rising dictators was impossible. Indeed, men like Winrod, Pelley, G. L. K. Smith, and above all, Father Coughlin, had abandoned neutrality. Anti-Semitism, extreme nationalism, and frantic anticommunism dominated their oratory. Other voices were declaring Western civilization to be at the crossroads—and calling America to rally to the democratic cause.

The effect of all this on the leadership of the mainstream Protestant churches was traumatic. Their remorse for the excessive militarism exhibited during World War I had led to a widespread commitment to dogmatic Christian pacifism. In 1929 the Federal Council of Churches had greeted the United States Senate's consent to the Kellogg-Briand Peace Pact with jubilation: "Let church bells be rung, songs sung, prayers of thanksgiving be offered and petitions for help from God that our nation may ever follow the spirit and meaning of the Pact." [11] Countless Protestant ministers had sworn that they would never again support a war. Three of the most prominent preachers (Fosdick, Ernest F. Tittle, and Ralph W. Sockman) were taking pacifist positions, many wondered if even police forces could be justified, and among radicals the question of justifying violence in the class struggle became divisive. The Fellowship of Reconciliation flourished in such an atmosphere, especially in the seminaries. The Oxford Union peace pledge was gaining countless signers in the universities. Undergirding this fervency were two almost contradictory assumptions: that civilized nations would not again resort to war, and that the United States could with a clear conscience ignore the aggressions of the dictators.

As the world situation darkened, however, the pacifist consensus began to weaken. What had been an almost academic debate on the legitimacy of always turning the other cheek began to yield to the question of collective security versus nonintervention. And this new phase created the anomaly of Christian socialists and Social Gospel liberals, because of their pacifism, joining voices with the Silver Shirts and Father Coughlin in a demand for isolation, neutrality, and America First. The anomaly proved unbearable for many Christian spokesmen but reasonable to as many others. In the churches the result was especially cacophonous and even divisive, perhaps because they felt obliged to speak when they did not even have a consensus to report, much less a clearly formulated Christian position. Editorial staffs, unofficial groups,

11. *Federal Council Bulletin,* February 1929, p. 24. The Peace Pact of Paris had been signed in August 1928; it was approved by the United States Senate in January 1929.

and official church agencies were split. Even peace groups such as the Church Peace Union and the World Alliance for International Fellowship offered contradictory counsel.

The arguments, needless to say, did not always rest securely on logic or biblical exegesis. Phobias and irrational loyalties also gained voice or sought rationalization. Easterners tended to be less isolationistic than westerners. Jews regarded Hitler as diabolical; anti-Semites considered him farsighted and wise. Germans, Italians, and Irish saw little reason for aiding Britain or France; Anglo-Saxons usually inclined to the Allied cause. Catholics tended to support Franco in Spain, as well as his allies, and, following the pope, to consider communism as the world's chief threat. And so the "debate" continued even after Hitler's invasion of Poland. In 1940 Roosevelt in his campaign for a third term still pledged to keep our boys at home. As for the churches, Professor Miller had good grounds for a negative judgment:

> History affords no sadder tale than the impact of [these] events . . . upon the followers of the Prince of Peace in America. . . . The response . . . was pathetically confused, halting, divided, and uncertain. It is a heartbreaking record of alternating deep despair and naive optimism, of timid vacillation and blind dogmatism. . . . To put it bluntly, confusion over war and peace seemed more starkly extreme in the Protestant churches than in American society as a whole—and this is a damning comparison.[12]

Then on Sunday, 7 December 1941, a Japanese decision brought America's indecision to an end. The New York Philharmonic Symphony's broadcast of Schubert's *Unfinished Symphony* was interrupted by the solemn announcement that Pearl Harbor had been treacherously attacked. America was at war—and the Depression decade passed into history. In a strict sense it did not pass away, however, for the decade of the "third American Revolution" had made a permanent mark on the mind and face of America. Especially important for Protestantism was a remarkable renewal in theology which had a quickening effect in the seminaries and churches. An examination of Neo-orthodoxy, therefore, can illuminate the inner meaning of the decade's adventure.

12. Miller, *American Protestantism and Social Issues*, pp. 333–34.

55

NEO-ORTHODOXY AND SOCIAL CRISIS

When events at Pearl Harbor embroiled the United States in World War II, the circumstances were as unambiguous to most Americans as such things ever are. Without warning or immediate provocation a "peace-loving nation" had become the object of sudden, carefully planned aggression. It was in President Roosevelt's words a day that would "live in infamy." Furthermore, the ideological grounds for a declaration of war could not possibly have been less ambiguous. Faced by Hitler's enormities, Mussolini's unprovoked aggression in Ethiopia, and their joint contribution to Franco's victory in Spain, the rhetoric of justification was virtually unassailable from a democratic standpoint. Yet the churches did not "present arms" with the disgraceful lack of charity and proportion they had displayed during World War I, nor were they so naïve and vainglorious when it came to talk of peace and the United Nations. What has been called "the Protestant search for political realism," had not been entirely in vain. A sense of the sinfulness of man, the finitude of nations, the actualities of power, and the limitations of American virtue was more in evidence.

Within the leadership of the Protestant churches another change was apparent: Fundamentalism had lost the support of the great "moderate middle" which even during the twenties and thirties had remained latently if not aggressively conservative in its doctrinal stand. Gradually a new way of conceiving biblical authority and the doctrinal tradition had taken hold. It was no longer necessary for "orthodox" Christians to regard scientific freedom, biblical criticism, urban mores, and the critique of social or economic structures as inimical to their faith. And in one case as in the other, the Neo-orthodox movement in theology was an essential aspect of the transformed situation. If one looks to the remarkable way in which theology and theologians loomed up during the forties in the nation's moral, intellectual, and cultural life, again Neo-orthodoxy becomes essential to an adequate explanation. The cultural and religious revolutions of the 1960s and the still more circumspect view of the churches toward American imperialism and the war in Vietnam are also relatively inexplicable if Neo-orthodoxy is not taken into consideration. This intellectual phenomenon of the thirties, therefore, deserves fairly detailed consideration. Although its heyday was relatively brief, it involved a major reassessment of the Church's entire tradition. It was by no means a unified movement, and its influence in the denominations varied greatly. But its overall impact was powerful.

PREPARATION IN EUROPE

For over a century the American churches had been profoundly stimulated by Continental scholarship and theology, especially as it took shape in Germany. On religious liberalism German influence had been especially strong. It was only natural, therefore, that Americans should also respond to the new currents of thought which were evoked by the military and cultural catastrophe of 1914–18. This meant that some attentive Americans very soon began to share in the discovery of a whole literature of religious prophecy which had been widely ignored during the halcyon decades of the nineteenth century. Voices from the underground such as Sören Kierkegaard and Fëdor Dostoevski were heard again, and now their demand for a deeper kind of Christian earnestness was better understood.

There was also a parallel line of secular prophets, men like Schopenhauer, Jacob Burckhardt, the historian and philosopher of culture, and, most piercing of all, Friedrich Nietzsche, who either sadly or triumphantly had proclaimed the decadence of bourgeois culture, the coming of the "mass man," the end of Western civilization, and the death of God. From his listening post in Basel, Switzerland, Burckhardt had seen the Franco-Prussian War as premonitory of the new caesarism:

> The military state must become one great factory. Those hordes of men in the great industrial centers will not be left indefinitely to their greed and want. What must logically come is a fixed and supervised stint of misery, glorified by promotions and uniforms, daily begun and ended to the sound of drums. . . . Long voluntary subjection under individual *Fuehrers* and usurpers is in prospect. People no longer believe in principles but will, periodically, probably believe in saviors. . . . For

this reason authority will again raise its head in the pleasant twentieth century, and a terrible head.[1]

During the ensuing decades, however, the cultural climate in Europe and America was not responsive to Nietzschean prophecy. Except among the socialists, profound social and spiritual criticism had a small audience. Not until after the Great War of 1914 did the full tragedy of Western history stand exposed. Oswald Spengler's *Decline of the West* may not be an enduring classic, but in 1918 it could not easily be ignored. Also in 1918 Karl Barth, an obscure Swiss pastor, sent into the world a commentary on Saint Paul's Epistle to the Romans. In its enlarged edition of 1921 this became a veritable "bombshell on the playground of the theologians" (as Karl Adam, a Roman Catholic, put it). Its impact derived from the evangelical intensity with which Barth drove home the Kierkegaardian axiom as to "the 'infinite distinction' between time and eternity." [2] Addressing the predicament of the preacher on Saturday night, he proclaimed God's transcendence. He turned with a new seriousness to the Word of God, a Word from beyond all human possibilities. He attacked every effort to accommodate the faith: the scholars who treated the Scriptures as so many runes to be deciphered, the liberals who merely provided an ideology for the middle classes, and the social Christians who made the Christian ethic a platform for reforming the world. With an immense and constantly growing emphasis on the victory of Christ, he called men back to the "strange world of the Bible." He also called attention to the classic theology of the Reformation. Then in the 1930s he began to publish his monumental *Church Dogmatics*.

In the meantime, the "theology of crisis," or dialectical school, had developed an articulate following: Georg Merz and Friedrich Gogarten in Germany and, most important so far as America was concerned, Emil Brunner of Zurich. Brunner was in fact much more than a mediator of Barthian views. Having studied in the United States and taught in England, he sensed the American situation better than Barth and made a very important impression as a guest professor at Princeton Seminary in 1938–39. Through his quickly translated and widely read books he was until after World War II the most influential of the European dialectical theologians.

Yet the theology of crisis was only one facet of the theological renaissance then stirring Europe. Equally basic was the increasing seriousness in evan-

1. Burckhardt to F. von Preen, 1872, quoted in Karl Löwith, *Meaning in History* (Chicago: University of Chicago Press, 1949), p. 24.

2. Karl Barth, *The Epistle to the Romans*, trans. Sir Edwyn Hoskyns, 2d ed. (New York: Oxford University Press, 1933), pp. 10, 27 (preface). The prefaces to the first six editions are an interesting commentary on the book's reception—and significance.

gelical exegesis of the Old and New Testaments. The playground of the biblical scholars had also had its bomb: Albert Schweitzer's *Quest of the Historical Jesus* in 1906, followed in 1912 by *Paul and His Interpreters.* Taking the form of critical surveys of the previous century's massive scholarly efforts to discover the historical Jesus, the young Strasbourg professor (who would later become famous as a Kant scholar, theologian, philosopher of civilization, authority on Bach and baroque organs, and medical missionary to Africa) pronounced the liberal tradition of New Testament study a failure. In effect, he found the scholars peering down the 2,000-year-long shaft of history and seeing their own bourgeois faces reflected from the bottom of the well. Schweitzer, on the contrary, saw the New Testament pervaded by an intense apocalyptic concern that ruled out liberalism's optimistic view of the Kingdom of God.

Schweitzer himself never joined the "school" which he founded, but the decades which followed were marked by a constantly growing current of scholarship and exegesis that took seriously his basic contention. Christian hope was revived as a living doctrine. (In 1954, to the great irritation of many liberals, it would be the theme of the World Council of Churches Assembly in Evanston, Illinois.) In a more general way, studies of the apostolic preaching began to replace the quest for the religion of Jesus. Barth himself was responding to this broad impulse. Among many others were Martin Dibelius, Karl Ludwig Schmidt, and the young Rudolf Bultmann, whose *Jesus and the Word* (1926) was a study of the synoptic gospels which gave new clarity to a postliberal conception of the *Kerygma* (message, proclamation) of the New Testament community. During the next four decades, by means of ever more intense scholarship as well as by theological interpretation, Bultmann would give added meaning and clarity to a wonderfully succinct sentence in his first chapter: "When we encounter the words of Jesus in history, *we* do not judge *them* by a philosophical system with reference to their rational validity; *they* meet *us* with the question of how we are to interpret our own existence." [3]

A third stream of renewal is commonly designated as the "Luther renaissance" though actually its interests were far broader. Theodosius Harnack, father of the famous historian of dogma, stands close to its source in the mid-nineteenth century. Karl Holl of Berlin, an outspoken critic of Adolf von Harnack and Ernst Troeltsch, was also important. Werner Elert at the University of Erlangen articulated another subcurrent. Destined to be best

3. Rudolf Bultmann, *Jesus and the Word* (Charles Scribner's Sons, 1958), p. 11. Bultmann's theology would not begin to have wide influence in America until after his controversial work on demythologizing of 1941—and hence not until after World War II.

known in America was the Swedish impulse stemming from Lund University. All of these scholars and theologians were determined to deepen the liberal notion of Luther as merely a pioneer of intellectual liberty. In 1900 Einar Billing of Lund had already published his corrective *Luther's Doctrine of the State*. Most influential of all were Bishop Anders Nygren's historical study of the Christian doctrine of love, *Agape and Eros* (1930, 1936), and Bishop Gustav Aulén's study of the Atonement, *Christus Victor* (1930). One of the remarkable results of the Luther renaissance was the way in which the Reformer became an intensely relevant contemporary theologian again. Other scholars, meanwhile, were performing a similar office for John Calvin—and at the same time giving new relevance to the issues that had long divided the Lutheran and Reformed traditions.

A fourth trend to be noted was the new urgency being given to "social Christianity" in many quarters. An uneasiness about the social situation of the church lurked in all of the views under discussion, but in some men it became a dominant concern. Appalled by the apostasy of Europe's working classes, incensed by official unconcern for social injustice, and considerably affected by the Marxian analysis of the modern economic order, a new breed of theologians tried to undo the churches' long commitment to middle-class values. There was, to be sure, a Continental "social gospel" to build on; indeed, the American movement of that name owed more to Albrecht Ritschl than to any other theologian. But the newer movement wished to be free of liberal theological assumptions, to be more existentially evangelical, and, above all, to be more realistic in assessing the waning "Protestant Era" in European civilization. For Americans none of these men would become so well-known and influential as Paul Tillich. H. Richard Niebuhr expounded Tillich's critique in an important essay of 1930, and two years later he published a translation of Tillich's *The Religious Situation*. The impact of this cluster of influences helps to explain why the theology of crisis in America led not to a decline, but to a revival of the Social Gospel's historic concerns.

British contributions to the changing theological climate were considerable though less influential than their quality warranted. Scotland, due to its many contacts with the Reformed family of denominations on the Continent and in North America, had a larger impact than England, especially through scholarship and translations pertaining to the Calvinistic tradition.[4] Anglican theology, meanwhile, tended to preserve its insularity and to concern itself with the tensions inherent in its ambiguous Reformation heritage—especially

4. Two Reformed theologians in England, P. T. Forsythe (1848–1921) and John Oman (1860–1939), did move from liberalism to profound reappropriations of classical theological insights; yet both of them were only belatedly discovered in the United States.

as these had been reawakened in 1928 by Parliament's rejection of a new revision of the Book of Common Prayer. In William Temple (1881–1944), however, there arose one monumental exception. As archbishop of York and later of Canterbury, Temple became an influential world figure. As a theologian he sought to expound the Christian faith in relation to man's scientific knowledge, moral light, and rational powers. In *Christus Veritas* (1924) and in his famous Gifford Lectures, *Nature, Man and God* (1934), he revealed his indebtedness to Alfred North Whitehead and to the liberal Catholicism of Bishop Charles Gore (1853–1932). His importance was not chiefly due to his philosophical apologetics, however, but to the compelling way in which he, as a church leader in England and as a major voice in the ecumenical movement, united a strong social concern with a profound conception of the Church. "Let the Church be the Church," the resounding slogan of the 1937 Life and Work Conference, can stand as an epitome of Temple's most enduring impact on America.

Temple's influence also serves to underline the importance of the ecumenical movement for American theology throughout these decades. In innumerable committees, commissions, and conferences of that worldwide movement, a wide range of American church leaders and theologians had their decisive personal confrontation with European theology and with church traditions that had previously been left out of consideration. They learned, for example, that Barthianism was not simply German fundamentalism. They also became church reformers in a new sense. Paul A. Carter rightly reminds us that the American delegates who came to the Oxford Conference "talking about *our churches*" went home "talking about the Church." [5]

THE AMERICAN RESPONSE

To most Americans of the 1920s, the notions of "crisis" and "despair' could arise only in the frightened and diseased minds of those who stalked the remote European ruins, the world of yesterday—or in the minds of expatriate intellectuals who preferred the ruins to the world of Cal Coolidge. Yet this façade of confidence began to crack with the passing years. As hope for peace and world democracy guttered out, the American dream was increasingly interrupted by nightmares. T. S. Eliot published *The Waste Land* in 1922 and *The Hollow Men* in 1925. In 1923—the year of Hitler's Beerhall *Putsch*—Professor Lee M. Hollander of the University of Texas brought out a volume of selections from Kierkegaard in an obscure bulletin series of the University of Texas. David L. Swenson of the University of Minnesota

5. *The Decline and Revival of the Social Gospel, 1920–1940*, p. 195.

was able to review it discerningly and perhaps to lay plans for the translation projects and further essays that were to make him virtually the father of American Kierkegaardian studies.

In the meantime, what is in retrospect recognized as American Neo-orthodoxy began to take shape piecemeal. The contributors came from all over; some traveled widely, some stayed at home, some were refugees from Hitler. Some of the new voices witnessed to conversions of one sort or other; many had radically changed their minds. They drew their inspiration from thinkers of the most diverse sorts and from many lands; they were themselves provoked to new kinds of thinking by Russian Orthodox, Jews, Roman Catholics, and Protestants of all sorts, by ancient Greek tragedians and by contemporary atheists. They spoke as confident heralds or as self-questioning diarists, as historians, exegetes, or systematic theologians. They were troubled by diverse problems: social injustice, political and churchly utopianism, routine complacency, and ecclesiastical passivity. Some protested against apostasy and heresy; others condemned orthodox pride. Yet to take account of all these variations would result in either a sterile catalogue or a long book. In a single chapter one can only discuss a few of the more influential thinkers and make some effort to represent their major theological interests.

Walter Lowrie (1868–1959), a Philadelphia-born and Princeton-educated Episcopalian, was rector of Saint Paul's American Church in Rome from 1907 to 1930. Liberal theology had saved him, like so many others, from skepticism; but the introduction to his translation of Schweitzer's *Mystery of the Kingdom of God* (1925) marks a transition that gradually deepened into fullscale revolt as he began to contact the dialectical theologians and to immerse himself in the German translations of Kierkegaard. In 1932 came his major outcry—with one of the century's longest titles: *Our Concern with the Theology of Crisis, the Fundamental Aspects of the Dialectical Theology Associated with the Name of Karl Barth, Appreciatively Presented with the Query Whether It Be Not Our Only Positive Possibility, The Crisis of Society and of the Church Understood as the Crisis of the Individual before God.* Kierkegaard looms larger than Barth in this book, so the groundwork was well laid for Lowrie's great lifetime achievement as a biographer of Kierkegaard and translator of a dozen of his works.

Douglas Horton (1891–1968) was an American-born Congregationalist who, after an education in four countries, was serving as a parish minister in the Boston area when he chanced upon an early volume of Barth's essays on the Harvard Divinity School new-book shelf. He determined that very afternoon to translate the work—and in 1928 appeared *The Word of God and the Word of Man,* Barth's first book in English. Thirty years later Horton, then dean of the Harvard Divinity School, reflected on that early experience:

> It was a generation ago that I ran across the German text, published under the title *Das Wort Gottes und die Theologie*. . . . Only those who are old enough to remember the particular kind of desiccated humanism, almost empty of other-worldly content, which prevailed in many Protestant areas in the early decades of this century, can understand the surprise, the joy, the refreshment which would have been brought by the book to the ordinary and, like myself, somewhat desultory reader of the religious literature of that time. To question evolutionary modes of thought in that day was something like questioning the Ptolemaic theory in the time of Copernicus, with the stupendous difference that Copernicus seemed at first to shut the transcending God out of the world and Barth seemed immediately to let him in.[6]

In addition to these and many other Americans who contributed to the rise of a new theological temper in America, two Germans who came to America permanently made especially vigorous contributions. Wilhelm Pauck (b. 1901) entered the University of Chicago Divinity School as an exchange student in 1925 and stayed on as a professor of historical theology in that great center of liberalism. In 1931 he published an informative and enthusiastic study of Barth. Pauck's many students moved on to faculties elsewhere inspired by his vast learning and, above all, by his expositions of Reformation theology. Paul Tillich (1886–1965) began his enormously influential second career as a professor at Union Theological Seminary in New York in 1934. Though basically a speculative religious philosopher in the German idealistic tradition, Tillich's strong ontological interests were powerfully informed by existential thought, a modified Marxian analysis of the Western cultural predicament, and a conviction that the church's middle-class orientation was a fatal shortcoming. His wide interests in art and culture and in the problem of history were vital factors in the great renewal of interest in theology which he stimulated even among intellectuals who had decided that that "ghostly enterprise" was void of interest and relevance.

The Niebuhrs

Despite all the varied contributions that make up the phenomenon of American Neo-orthodoxy, the fact remains that its dynamics, nature, and purposes are best revealed in the lives and works of Reinhold Niebuhr (1892–

6. Douglas Horton, Foreword to Karl Barth, *The Word of God and the Word of Man* (New York: Harper & Brothers, Torchbooks, 1957), pp. 1–2.

1970) and his brother H. Richard Niebuhr (1894–1962). Both men were born in Missouri, educated in the college and seminary of the German Evangelical church in which their father was a minister; both did further study at Yale.[7] After varied service in their own denomination—Reinhold for thirteen years as a pastor in Detroit, Richard as a professor and college president—they both entered upon careers as professors of ethics, Reinhold at Union Theological Seminary (New York) in 1928 and Richard at the Yale University Divinity School in 1931. For more than a quarter-century both men, with many congenial if not always like-minded colleagues, made these two institutions lively and influential centers of theological ferment.

The two brothers were by no means identical in interest or tendency. Richard was more a theologian's theologian and a moral philosopher; Reinhold was more involved with practical problems in social ethics. Yet both were learned historians, deeply concerned with the whole course of Western thought, and both brought formidable analytical powers to the theoretical questions of the day. Despite differences in approach they both also dealt with the problems raised on one side by the historicity and finitude of man, the social accommodation of the Church, the temptation to absolutistic moral judgments; and on the other side by the threat of moral emptiness and formality, the dangers of human arrogance, and the menace of idealistic naïveté. Although neither was an apologist for Christianity in the overt manner of, say, Archbishop Temple, both demonstrated the profundity and relevance of Christian views far more effectively by involving a whole generation of readers and listeners in their creative reexamination of the heritage and in their realistic relating of this heritage to contemporary dilemmas.

In 1937 H. Richard Niebuhr reversed his earlier judgment of Jonathan Edwards. With "Sinners in the Hands of an Angry God" in mind, he spoke of Edwards's "intense awareness of the precariousness of life's poise, of the utter insecurity of men and mankind which are at every moment as ready to plunge into the abyss of disintegration, barbarism, crime, and war of all against all, as to advance toward harmony and integration. He recognized what Kierkegaard meant when he described life as treading water with ten thousand fathoms beneath us."[8] This was a considerable change of mood from Niebuhr's first major work. In *The Social Sources of Denominationalism* (1929), he had followed Adolf von Harnack in seeking to liberate traditional Protestantism from "that strange interpretation of the faith which

7. Hulda Niebuhr, a sister, was also an influential professor of Christian education at McCormick Theological Seminary in Chicago. The mother of these three distinguished children was very appropriately awarded an honorary doctor's degree by Lindenwood College in 1953.

8. *The Kingdom of God in America*, pp. 137–38.

has prevailed since the days when Greek disputants carried into it the problems and methods of Greek philosophy." [9] Even at this date, however, he had participated in certain intellectual movements that prepared him for his future role as a Neo-orthodox prophet. D. C. Macintosh, Niebuhr's mentor at Yale, was a vigorous realist who demanded an objective basis for religious faith. The sociological analysis of religious institutions which liberal scholarship encouraged also began to shake the ground beneath the feet of many confident churchmen. Indeed, Niebuhr's *Social Sources of Denominationalism* worked to the same end. Using the insights of Marx, Weber, and Troeltsch, he exposed the changing historical involvements of the Church, showing how class, race, nationality, and economic factors had divided the churches, and how deeply involved in middle-class presuppositions was the American religious mainstream.

In the same year, 1929, Reinhold Niebuhr published his *Leaves from the Notebooks of a Tamed Cynic* and revealed that his burgeoning protest had roots trailing back to 1915. Here he did not merely condemn specific social abuses and industrial cruelty; he pointed to a more ominous kind of handwriting on the wall, finding the current faith in religious education "the last word in absurdity." Then came the Crash—after which many Americans began to raise doubts about the positive identification of Christian hope and the national dream. But in 1932 (the year of Franklin Roosevelt's election) both brothers again issued important books. Richard Niebuhr published his translation (with an introduction) of Paul Tillich's *The Religious Situation,* a very sober statement, deeply informed by Marxian analysis of the values of middle-class civilization. Reinhold Niebuhr, meanwhile, published *Moral Man and Immoral Society,* his single most important book and probably the most disruptive religio-ethical bombshell of domestic construction to be dropped during the entire interwar period—the major document in that "Protestant search for political realism" which Donald Meyer has so brilliantly described. Niebuhr distinguished between the ethical potentialities of individuals and organized groups and insisted that both in criticism and in advocacy the severe limitations of the latter be kept in mind. Labor unions, corporations, and sovereign states, he said, are *by their nature* all but completely incapable of altruistic conduct. Social ethics, therefore, require a dialectical rather than an absolutistic moral stance. Given the immensely practical bent of American Protestantism and the staggering policy

9. *The Social Sources of Denominationalism,* pp. 11–12. Harnack, the great historian of Christian dogma, had stated this view of early doctrinal controversies in his famous lectures on the essence of Christianity in 1900 (published in English as *What Is Christianity?* in 1901).

questions of the Roosevelt era, one may wonder if the degree to which American Neo-orthodoxy's history is enmeshed with the biography of Reinhold Niebuhr does not prove that a revision of the Social Gospel was the primary purpose of the movement.

Reinhold Niebuhr's views were further developed and explicated in a long series of important books and countless articles and reviews during the next quarter-century; but they took their basic shape in *The Nature and Destiny of Man* (1941–43), which was first delivered as the Gifford Lectures shortly after the outbreak of World War II. Throughout these years Niebuhr attacked the idea of progress and the notion that "history is the Christ." He saw man as "at once saint and sinner," as both creature and creator, as in and yet transcending history. Above all, he sought to make men fully aware of the depths of human sinfulness. Critics who found his message more prophetic than evangelical could hardly be denied their point; but no American did more to transform the old liberal Social Gospel movement and to demonstrate the relevance of biblical insights and Christian affirmations.

Two more books of great prescriptive value were published in 1935. Reinhold Niebuhr's *Introduction to Christian Ethics* appeared, with its famous Niebuhrian critique of the "illusion of liberalism that we are dealing with a possible and prudential ethic in the gospel." "The ethic of Jesus," he insisted, "does not deal at all with the immediate moral problem of every human life. . . . It transcends the possibilities of human life . . . as God transcends the world." Almost simultaneously, Richard Niebuhr joined Wilhelm Pauck and Francis P. Miller to issue what was in effect a Neo-orthodox manifesto to the churches: *The Church Against the World.* Niebuhr in his essay dwelt characteristically on the need of the Church, not to march out to battle (it had been marching to too many drums), but to withdraw from the world's embrace awhile and find itself, to rediscover its gospel, and then perhaps to fulfill its mission. Characteristically, during the 1930s and 1940s he was emphasizing the need for the Church to realize itself as a confessing community—an idea that would be more fully expounded in his classic, *The Meaning of Revelation* (1941).

Before proceeding to the constructive task of that book, however, Richard Niebuhr had to settle his accounts with the American church tradition, and that he did profoundly in *The Kingdom of God in America,* a masterpiece of reassessment in which the prophetic stance of Puritanism and Jonathan Edwards, as well as the great evangelical enterprises of the nineteenth century, were appreciatively reconsidered. Liberalism was then weighed and found wanting. In this book Harnack yields to Jonathan Edwards as a major source of Niebuhr's thought, and so it remains to the very end.[10] Nowhere is the living relationship of *Neo*-orthodoxy and *Paleo*-orthodoxy better illustrated—unless in Reinhold Niebuhr's continual invocations of Saint Augustine.

Annus Mirabilis

An account of the Niebuhrs must not be allowed to veil other vital aspects of the Neo-orthodox resurgence, though it has already led past the movement's most remarkably productive year, 1934, the year, let us not forget, in which Hitler settled down to the *Aufbau* of a national socialist state in Germany; the year, too, when the murder of Kirov set off the great purge trials in Russia. Not inappropriately, therefore, Reinhold Niebuhr published his *Reflections on the End of an Era* and delivered the Rauschenbusch Lectures on Christian ethics.[11] But other very important writings expanded the scope of the movement. Walter Marshall Horton of Oberlin Seminary published his *Realistic Theology,* a forceful work that described both a collective and a personal change of mind. The Methodist theologian Edwin Lewis of Drew Theological Seminary expanded an earlier essay, "The Fatal Apostasy of the Modern Church," into a book-length *Christian Manifesto* which underlined the same point. George W. Richards of the German Reformed Seminary of Mercersburg memory struck a very important note with *Beyond Fundamentalism and Modernism, The Gospel of God.* In the same year he and Elmer G. Homrighausen brought out the first volume of Barth's sermons in translation, an important event considering the degree to which the new movement championed a restoration of the preaching office in the church.

From this time forward books, articles, visits, and ecumenical conversations become so numerous that detailed narration becomes impractical. But taken together they do constitute a collective transformation of the theological situation: the beginning of a distinctly postliberal period in American theology. In 1939, when a series of autobiographical articles by the country's leading theologians appeared in the *Christian Century* (since its refounding in 1908 the chief organ of interdenominational liberalism), a genuine change of mood was made manifest.[12]

10. Compare *The Kingdom of God in America* (1937), pp. 113–16, with *Radical Monotheism* (1960), pp. 37–42.

11. They were published as *An Interpretation of Christian Ethics* (1935).

12. The difference which the passage of seven years had made is revealed by comparing this series with the volume of essays *Contemporary American Theology,* ed. Vergilius Ferm (1932).

THE ESSENCE OF NEO-ORTHODOXY

Neo-orthodoxy was not greeted with joy in every quarter. To countless liberal preachers and theologians it seemed merely an erudite form of the very Fundamentalism that they had shaken off in the bolder days of their youth.[13] To the more learned Fundamentalists, on the other hand, Karl Barth's theology (not to speak of American Neo-orthodoxy) was but a confusing form of modernism, especially dangerous because it had cut itself loose from religious experience, natural theology, philosophic rationalism, and a propositional view of biblical revelation. Because they perceived no return to a strict doctrine of scriptural inerrancy, they could take little comfort from the changes occurring in the old liberal seminaries. Given these claims and counterclaims, it is important to make some generalizations about the new movement as a whole.

The first step toward such a general view of Neo-orthodoxy must be a recognition of its doctrinal diversity, which was at least as great as that of the Orthodox Presbyterians and Pentecostalists bound together in the Fundamentalist movement. The translators of Kierkegaard alone included Lutherans, Anglo-Catholic Episcopalians, and Quakers. Participation in a movement of theological reform did not mean the relinquishing of other commitments on the historic points of controversy—the Church, the ministry, baptism, and Eucharist, predestination, and free grace. Neo-orthodox theologians differed from liberals, however, in regarding these questions as important, even as crucial. They differed from Fundamentalists and the older conservatives in that they wished to face them directly in the new context provided by contemporary thought and the ecumenical movement.

In the second place, Neo-orthodoxy was a critical movement, an attack on certain prevailing assumptions of liberalism. Neo-orthodox theologians criticized with special vehemence liberalism's optimistic doctrine of man and hence its doctrine of historical progress. The radical historicity and finitude of all things human must not be ignored, they said; nor should the opaque aimlessness of human history be minimized. The small solicitude of the universe for man must be recognized. The tragic sense of life must be apprehended. Closely related was an assault on both the great romantic doctrine that the religious and/or moral consciousness provides the proper starting point of theology and the philosophical idealism that often figured in theologies of that sort. The genteel tradition must go; metaphysics cannot do duty for the revealed Word of God. The Word, moreover, cannot be reduced

13. See Henry N. Wieman et al., *Religious Liberals Reply*.

to a literal concern for the teachings of Jesus and the virtual abandonment of Saint Paul's witness to the Christ. Man needs and the New Testament brings more than new rules, they would say. This critique as a whole adds up to the single complaint that theological liberalism left men spiritually naked and morally unprepared in an age of depression, despair, and international violence. Certainly not all liberals were as naïve as this critique suggested, but an aggressive new movement is not always fair, and Neo-orthodoxy was no exception.

In the third place, the essential consensus of Neo-orthodox theologians was not in specific doctrines, but, primarily, in a sense of urgency and a demand for moral and intellectual humility. The renewed interest in Kierkegaard was no accident. Just as such medieval theologians as Aquinas, Averroës, and Maimonides (Christian, Moslem, and Jew) were united by a commitment to Aristotelian rationalism, so Neo-orthodox thinkers responded affirmatively to the existentialism of the Catholic Gabriel Marcel, the atheist Jean-Paul Sartre, the Jew Martin Buber, or the Spaniard Miguel de Unamuno and his classic, *The Tragic Sense of Life* (1912).[14] This existential mood may have had more to do with their distaste for an ethic based on the rules of Jesus than with their exegesis of the New Testament, though the revival of evangelical exegesis did make their attack double-barreled. In any event, a situational-contextual "love ethic" became the positive part of a widespread critique of legalism and code morality. The existential commitment also made them suspicious of ambitious metaphysical systems, natural theology, and natural law concepts.

Neo-orthodoxy was pervaded by a dialectical mood; paradox and the contradictions of history figured strongly in its expositions. Hegel, Marx, and Kierkegaard in various ways supported this tendency, but not in any single way. The best explanation of this dialectical tendency may well be their further consensus as to the all-enveloping nature of human history. Neo-orthodox thinkers stressed the problem of historical relativism not because they liked it, but because they could not escape it. They were heirs of the whole historical movement. Everything had its history: every religion, every idea of the "absolute," every doctrine, every moral principle, every book of the Bible, every planet and solar system, every star—and every man. Small wonder that every problem didn't "come out even." Antinomies, paradoxes, and contradictions were conditions of existence. So the existential, historical,

14. They were well aware of their great remove from scholasticism, however; which is to say that their existentialism virtually assumed the critical work of Immanuel Kant. Time and again they affirmed their Kantian lineage. At the same time Roman Catholic theologians with various non-Catholic allies were developing a strong Neo-Thomist movement.

and dialectical moods mingled—to the consternation of Americans who wanted their theology simple and straightforward.

Despite all, however, Neo-orthodoxy was pervaded by a hopeful mood. It was neither cynical, pessimistic, nor nihilistic. Due to its concern for social issues, it absorbed the positive spirit of the New Deal. It never counseled resignation or passivity. Theologically it also recovered an eschatological sense of hope, one that rested on faith in the God who was beyond, beneath, and above all human possibilities. Because it did not rest its ultimate faith in human arrangements, it could bear—or even advocate—the shaking of cultural foundations.

Also partaking more of mood than of doctrine was Neo-orthodoxy's deep respect for the scientific, scholarly, and artistic achievements of men. Its great difference from fundamentalistic conservatism lay in its respect for these diverse activities. Indeed, Neo-orthodox thinkers not only continued the liberal attack on obscurantism in the churches, but made major contributions to the critical study of Scriptures, the sociological understanding of religious institutions, and the historical enterprise as a whole. Reformation and Puritan studies were especially meaningful to them; and they rescued many movements, writers, and thinkers from oblivion or obloquy. The newer tendencies in painting, music, and literature were not merely accepted, but explored for their theological significance.

Finally, in two ways Neo-orthodoxy undeniably did have positive doctrinal implications. For many, the doctrine of the Church, so slighted by liberals and fundamentalists, assumed a central place due to the convergence of several factors: (1) the new emphasis among biblical scholars on the message and tradition of the New Testament community; (2) the full scale emergence in both Roman Catholic and Protestant traditions of a liturgical movement that criticized many aspects of medieval ceremonialism and sought to restore the Reformation's emphasis on the corporate role of the laity in worship; (3) the persistent way in which the ecumenical Faith and Order movement revealed questions of the Church, the sacraments, and the ministry as key factors in the dividedness of Christianity; and (4) Neo-orthodoxy's own critique of culture-protestantism and its demand for a prophetic church that would recognize its continuity with the New Testament community and, therefore, its distinctness from the world in which it proclaims the Word and to which it ministers. It would be wrong, of course, to say that there was a Neo-orthodox doctrine of the Church; but the movement did much to make ecclesiology a major object of concern.

The other doctrinal effect of Neo-orthodoxy was its overall revival of interest in theology per se, and hence in the great ages of theological construction. The new concern for "biblical theology" was perhaps primary, above all the full restoration of Saint Paul as the first Doctor of the Church. Yet the early Fathers, the early councils, Saint Augustine, and, above all, the master theologians of the Reformation also gained new currency. Nor was it simply that they became objects of historical attention (though that they emphatically did) but that they were taken seriously rather than dismissed in the liberal manner as outmoded stages in the evolution of pure religion.

All considered, there are many reasons for regarding Neo-orthodoxy as an ambiguous prelude to the theological radicalism of the 1960s. Yet the interest in traditional doctrine which the movement stimulated—especially when Karl Barth was being heeded—did undeniably lead to a revival of supernaturalistic ways of thinking. And because they ignored many intellectual difficulties, Neo-orthodox theologians have been justifiably accused of putting down only a very thin sheet of dogmatic asphalt over the problems created by modern critical thought. Rudolf Bultmann was to protest this very tendency in 1941 with his call for "demythologizing" the biblical message. The implications of this protest, however, would not be exposed until well after the mid-twentieth century.

THE SCOPE AND DURATION OF NEO-ORTHODOXY

Neo-orthodoxy was primarily an intellectual movement. Like many another theological reform movement (from Aquinas through Luther to John Henry Newman and Rauschenbusch) academic professors played a dominant role in giving it shape and force. Its leaders were highly articulate, and in due course they set in motion a tidal wave of published articles and books which broke over the beaches of liberalism and cultural complacency with considerable effect. Due to the practical bent and anti-intellectual propensities of the American clergy, however, enduring changes in American parish life could result only as seminary graduates moved into the churches as ministers and denominational leaders. The distractions of the Great Depression followed by the terrible disruptions of World War II greatly retarded this movement to the grassroots, but even so, its influence was considerable. A new note of evangelical urgency became noticeable even among great liberal preachers like Harry Emerson Fosdick and Ernest Fremont Tittle. The widely read *Christian Century* reflected the movement's spreading influence. Christian education boards in nearly every denomination where liberalism had made deep inroads were subjected to demands for revised lesson materials, and in the Northern Presbyterian church forces were set in motion which led to the election of a new board and the launching of a totally reconceived educational program.

Neo-orthodoxy achieved its most direct influence on the churches precisely in the area where men like Reinhold Niebuhr had made their most original contributions—with a reshaped Social Gospel. The dire condition of the economy and a steady succession of international crises had in any event made a quantitative increase of social concern almost inevitable. But Neo-orthodoxy gave men a more realistic awareness of institutional power, social structures, and human depravity. It made men at once more biblical in their standpoint and less utopian in their advocacy. Most important, perhaps, it built bridges that opened communications not only with modernists who had all but decided that Christianity was obsolete, but also with conservatives who had all but decided that true Christians must repudiate modern modes of thought and action.

56

WORLD WAR II AND THE POSTWAR REVIVAL

The peace settlement after World War I was the prelude to a tragically unsettled twenty years in European history. And the United States participated in that unsettlement, actively or passively hastening the political crises, intensifying the underlying economic disaster, and sharing the period's drastic ideological impasse. On Sunday, 7 December 1941, therefore, as a result of Japan's assault on Pearl Harbor, Americans awoke to the massive irony of national consensus in the actuality of war. In a day the situation had changed. What had been confused became clear. The great debates were at an end. An "army" of pacifists dwindled to about twelve thousand (or about 1 percent of those who registered for the draft). About $4 million was raised during the war to support various forms of alternative service.

The churches shared in this *renversement;* whether Protestant, Catholic, or Jewish, they showed no reluctance in supporting the national effort. All became engaged in the characteristic tasks of war, providing about eight thousand chaplains, raising money and volunteers for war service agencies, distributing Bibles, prayerbooks, and devotional literature, maintaining contact with servicemen, consoling and aiding those left behind.[1] Even with the provocations which Hitler provided, however, the churches did not repeat the unrestrained capitulation to the war spirit which had left them disgraced after 1918. Many factors help to explain this change, but most important by far was the chastening experience of the decade 1925–35. In theological terms, Neo-orthodoxy is a large part of the explanation.

1. The government in turn showed its solicitude for religion by maintaining a uniformed chaplain corps (one chaplain for each twelve hundred men), building over six hundred interfaith chapels in training camps and posts, and providing many lesser services.

In more practical terms, one further effect of the social transformations wrought during the interwar decades was a distinct decline in the relative moral force of the churches. They simply were not as important a factor in the molding of public attitudes as they had been in 1916. The pulpit and church press had lost their preeminence among the mass media. Most conservative evangelicals had become committed to being noncommittal on public issues, while modernists, with their deemphasis of "divine" sanctions, had undermined the authority of the churches to speak on any issue. On the institutional plane, cooperative interchurch agencies had become so extensive that the war itself had nothing like the innovative impact of the 1916–18 experience. As the war dragged on, however, and especially as it drew to a victorious close, signs of increased religious interest multiplied. Events soon made clear that a revival was in the offing.

THE REVIVAL AND ITS SOCIAL SOURCES

The religious depression of the twenties had sunk to new depths after the Great Crash of 1929. Unemployment and hunger proved inconducive to a revival of popular religion, though they did cut away much superficiality and self-assurance from American church life. With the return of national confidence under the New Deal, something like an upturn in ecclesiastical prosperity also became noticeable. The collapse of European order, the rise of Hitler, and other ideological challenges led Americans to a new concern for their national heritage, including its religious tradition. Wartime mobilization interrupted the movement of renewal which Neo-orthodoxy had inspired, yet the anxieties of scattered families and the social dislocations of the "war effort" did stimulate an unmistakable rise of interest in religion. "There are no atheists in the foxholes," was the word from the theaters of military action. In millions of blue-star and gold-star households and in thousands of home churches the same could be said. In this sense, the "postwar revival" began long before the fighting ceased.

The atomic bombs, the final surrender, and the return of peace mark a new era in world history. Every major aspect of human affairs was involved, and American religious life was no exception. Yet three basic reminders seem essential to an understanding of American religious history during the fifteen-year period which ensued.

Most basic for the United States, which alone among the Western nations would experience a resurgence of religion during these years, was the dawn of an "age of affluence." After nearly two decades of depression and war, the nation's unsatisfied demands for the things of this world could now be supplied. The industrial expansion begun during the war accelerated afterward, making it possible between 1947 and 1957 for Americans to earn 2.6 trillion dollars and yet divert only 160 billion to savings and 290 billion to taxes. Along with these economic changes came an equally momentous transformation in the balance, structure, and dynamics of American life. By 1950 two-thirds of the American population had moved into metropolitan regions. In a great crescendo of migration, Negroes and Puerto Ricans moved into the inner cities. Orchards, woods, and open fields yielded to the bulldozer to accommodate an expansion of suburban population that was three times greater than that of the central cities. In the meantime, the mechanization of agriculture, the improvement of roads and automobiles, and the postwar explosion of the television industry tended to bring vast areas which were still statistically "rural" into a quasi-suburban ambiance. Due to a trend to organize industry and business on a national basis and a large numerical increase in managerial personnel, geographical mobility became as prominent a feature of the new industrial society as social mobility. The organization man, the "lonely crowd," and the suburban status seeker became new features of the religious situation.

As a direct result of these social trends, virtually all of the churches were confronted with vast new responsibilities for "home missions." Migrants from the farms, villages, and inner cities of America were populating a vast new suburban mission field. Many of them were moving around within this "field" with unprecedented frequency—either because a pay raise enabled them to occupy a slightly more expensive housing development, or because opportunities for white collar promotions often involved transfers to other parts of the country. Problems of adjustment and anxieties over status and "acceptance" were ever-present. Churches were obviously the sort of family institution that the social situation required.

The chief international accompaniment of this sensational increase in national production and per capita income was the cold war, the postwar confrontation between what was usually referred to as the "Communist bloc" and the "free world," but which meant chiefly the emergence of the USSR and the U.S. as the colossuses of world politics. A corollary of this development was the collapse of the old European empires and the rapid emergence of new nations in Africa and Asia. Between 1950 and 1953, moreover, the United States was deeply involved in a hot war in Korea. The chief religious result of the international standoff was twofold. Consciously and subconsciously, with and without governmental stimuli, the patriotism of this "nation with the soul of a church" was aroused. Being a church member and speaking favorably of religion became a means of affirming the "American way of life," especially since the USSR and its Communist allies were formally committed to atheism. The other side of this process—and to a degree its result—was a long drawn out repetition of the Red Scare of 1919–20. Senator Joseph McCarthy of Wisconsin had his heyday, and being an active church member became a way to avoid suspicion of being a subversive influence. It seemed understood that a church member would not be a serious critic of the social order.

In a rapidly changing intellectual and spiritual environment, there also arose an urgent need for the consolations of religion that was quite independent of prudential considerations. Grave international uncertainties became more oppressive in the dawning age of nuclear fission. New scientific views forced adjustments of older conceptions of the natural world. A profoundly altered social system brought changes in moral values that robbed old habitudes of their comfort.

Against this background of rapid change American religious communities of nearly every type (Protestant, Catholic, and Jewish; churches, sects, and cults) were favored during the postwar decade and a half by an increase of commitment and a remarkable popular desire for institutional participation. This popular resurgence of piety was a major subject of discussion in newspapers, popular magazines, and learned journals. Many books were published—some critical, some laudatory, some analytical. Publishers' lists, book sales, even the juke boxes and disc jockeys provided evidence of a change in public attitudes. In 1957 the Census Bureau reported that 96 percent of the American people cited a specific affiliation when asked the question: "What is your religion?" [2] And the statistics of church membership revealed that this always religious nation was in fact becoming affiliated at an increased rate.[3]

Church Affiliation in the Twentieth Century

Year	*Percentage of Total Population*
1910	43
1920	43
1930	47
1940	49
1950	55
1956	62
1960	69
1970	62.4

2. Winthrop Hudson, *Religion in America,* p. 383.

3. Roy Eckardt, *The Surge of Piety in America,* p. 22; augmented from *Yearbook of the American Churches.* Church membership statistics are notoriously inaccurate, but the basic trend is clear. See also Winthrop Hudson, "Are the Churches Really Booming?" *Christian Century* 72 (1955): 1494–96.

Accompanying this numerical growth was a very distinct increase in church attendance and even more remarkable acceleration of church-building construction.

Postwar Church Construction

Year	*Amount Spent*
1945	$ 26,000,000
1946	76,000,000
1948	251,000,000
1950	409,000,000
1954	593,000,000
1956	775,000,000
1958	863,000,000
1959	935,000,000
1960	1,016,000,000

These figures are not corrected for monetary inflation, and the reader must bear in mind the degree to which depression and wartime restrictions had held back church construction for over fifteen years. To a large extent, moreover, the churches were responding to needs for new churches created by the great postwar migration to suburbia. The increased tempo of construction provides evidence, nevertheless, of remarkable willingness by Americans to support local religious institutions.

Monetary support, increased church attendance, and even membership growth are by no means unambiguous demonstrations of religious commitment in the historical sense of that term. But the problem of interpreting the phenomenon is put in clearer light if five distinguishable but overlapping types of revival are recognized:

1. An accent on new forms of the civil religion which had always been a constituent element in American patriotism
2. A vast increase of popular interest in generalized forms of religion which, though discontinuous with the older revival tradition, were rooted in a long and lively American tradition
3. A resurgence of traditional evangelical revivalism which was also linked with serious intellectual efforts to update the older "fundamentalist" theology
4. The penetration into many congregations of a movement for liturgical renewal
5. A theological revival which was in fact a continuation of the Neo-orthodox impulse.

These separate, contemporaneous revivals must all be borne in mind if the religious character of the postwar "surge of piety" is to be understood.

THE ENLIVENED CIVIL RELIGION

Writing in the middle fifties about America's "triple melting pot" (Protestant, Catholic, and Jew), Will Herberg spoke of the American way of life as "the characteristic American religion, undergirding life and overarching American society despite indubitable differences of religion, section, culture, and class." [4] More important for the country's actual religious life was the propagation of a new form of patriotic piety that was closely linked to the "cold war." Finally, there seemed to be a consensus that personal religious faith was an essential element in proper patriotic commitment. In all of these modes, religion and Americanism were brought together to an unusual degree. This was especially true of the 1950s, when President Dwight D. Eisenhower served for eight years as a prestigious symbol of generalized religiosity and America's self-satisfied patriotic moralism. The president even provided a classic justification for the new religious outlook. "Our government," he said in 1954, "makes no sense unless it is founded on a deeply felt religious faith—and I don't care what it is." [5]

This "piety on the Potomac" was not limited to the president's private life, however, nor even to the prayer breakfasts and other religious activities in which many members of the Eisenhower administration participated. In the halls of Congress a whole series of legislative enactments actually extended the previous century's "quasi-establishment" of religion, with proponents of these measures sometimes showing a utilitarian conception of religion far more crass than the president's. When in 1954 the phrase "under God" (as used by Lincoln in his Gettysburg Address) was added to the Pledge of Allegiance, this important American pledge of loyalty came to include a theological affirmation which millions of American humanists could not honestly make. In 1956 the venerable statement, "In God We Trust," was raised from the semiofficial place it has had since 1865 as a device on our coinage to become the country's official motto. Such patriotic uses of religion were also employed by the American Legion in its organized Back to God move-

4. Will Herberg, *Protestant, Catholic, Jew,* p. 77. Characteristic of white analyses of the 1950s, this work shows almost no awareness of race or of Black America as a "melting pot" by itself.

5. *Christian Century* 71 (1954), quoted in *Christianity Today,* 8 May 1961. The postwar form of civil religion debased the older tradition which had reverenced the Union as a bearer of transcendent values and summoned citizens to stewardship of a sacred trust. See Bibliography, sec. 8, especially the works of Paul C. Nagel.

ment, and by countless other organizations. Yet they were not forced upon an unresponsive people by a few pious political leaders. Given the temper of the electorate, it is more likely that even impious congressmen found it expedient to vote for God.

PEACE OF MIND AND THE PLACID DECADE

The most characteristic religious feature of the period had little to do with either church membership or patriotism. The generalized kind of religiosity which predominated in the postwar years had "faith in faith" as its material principle and pious utilitarianism as its leading characteristic. Peace of mind and confident living were the promises it held out in the "age of anxiety," especially to those who were caught up in the stress and busy-ness of the business world and/or the insecurity and tensions of residential life in suburbia. The religion which answered to these needs was in fact a transdenominational phenomenon with a long and distinctive history. So important is it that a later chapter is devoted to harmonial religion in America; but we must at least take passing note here of some of the major peace givers.

The first to establish himself as a postwar best seller was Joshua Loth Liebman, a Reform rabbi of Boston. His *Peace of Mind* (1946) was not simply another work of inspirational mind-cure, but a thoughtful adaptation of Freudian insights to problems of personal composure. Liebman accomplished his ends so effectively, moreover, that his successors would not be able to ignore the rising public interest in depth psychology.[6] At the far pole from

6. This psychological genre, due to its semireligious function and appeal, would also be immensely popular, as Harry A. Overstreet's *Mature Mind* (1949), Smiley Blanton's *Love or Perish* (1956), Erich Fromm's *Art of Loving* (1956), and Eric Berne's *Games People Play* (1964) would demonstrate. Dr. Blanton popularized Freudian conceptions with great effectiveness and avoided Peale's simplism (see Donald Meyer, *The Positive Thinkers,* chaps. 21–23).

Another popularizer who cashed in on the interest in psychology and analysis was Lafayette Ronald Hubbard (b. 1911), a native of Helena, Montana, who in 1940 organized the Hubbard Association of Scientologists International. In recent years he has divided his time between a mansion in Sussex, England, and an oceangoing ship. Scientology (or dianetics), which was brought to popular attention in 1950 by Hubbard's best seller, *Dianetics: The Modern Science of Mental Health,* purports to be "the common people's science of life and betterment." Based on a theory of the brain as a virtually perfect calculating machine, it helps a preclear ("one who is discovering things about himself and who is becoming clearer") to become a clear ("one who has straightened up this lifetime") through sessions with a trained "auditor," who uses an "E" meter or "truth detector." Although some scientologists claim only to raise the I.Q. and develop personality, others have claimed the ability to cure all psychoses, neuroses, psychosomatic illnesses, coronary diseases, arthritis, and other ailments. In December 1963 scientology became the source of much controversy in Australia, with the state of Victoria setting up a special board of inquiry. In August 1968, despite considerable opposition, a World Congress of Scientology composed of delegates from twenty countries was held in London. In 1963 it was reported that there were fifty to a hundred thousand practicing scientologists in the United States.

Rabbi Liebman both in theology and in literary manner was a Presbyterian minister of Washington, D.C., whose posthumously published sermons gained a response so huge that a mass-audience movie of his life, *A Man Called Peter,* was also produced.[7] Within this range a great many others made highly varied efforts.

All of these writers and preachers, however, were but as forerunners to Norman Vincent Peale, the inspirationalist who indeed reached the height of his powers in the fullness of time. As minister of the Marble Collegiate Church on Fifth Avenue in New York, Peale moved into the field with such astounding success and with such a keen awareness of the potentialities of the mass media that he almost created a crisis in American Protestantism. He was as important for the religious revival of the fifties as George Whitefield had been for the Great Awakening of the eighteenth century. His "new measures" aroused as much criticism as Charles Finney's had in the nineteenth century. Although he by no means brought about the postwar renewal of religious interest, he rode its crest, and more than any other, he set the tone and guided the interests of the popular revival. When Peale's *Guide to Confident Living* (1948) and *The Power of Positive Thinking* (1952) succeeded in reaching a reading audience of millions, Monsignor Fulton J. Sheen had almost no recourse but to produce his own *Peace of Soul* (1949), and Billy Graham his *Peace with God* (1953). Then in 1955 Anne Morrow Lindbergh topped them all with her *Gift from the Sea,* a remarkable little book addressed to those Americans, especially housewives, who were distraught with the emptiness of their lives.[8] Ignoring the specific institutional appeals that Peale, Sheen, and Graham were wont to make, she drew on the timeless resources of mysticism. Her book in many ways looked beyond the revival. And this may indeed be a sign of her profundity, for during 1957 and 1958 historians and social critics began to speak of that phenomenon in the past tense.

THE REVIVAL OF REVIVALISM

Popular evangelicalism had been making a slow retreat for a century, but it still flourished in all parts of the country, especially among those who were least affected by modern intellectual currents. In rural areas, particularly in the West and South, in small towns, and in many of the older urban neighborhoods, the more revivalistic denominations and sects held intact the old-

7. Peter Marshall, *Mr. Jones, Meet the Master* (New York: Fleming H. Revell Co., 1949); Catherine Marshall, *A Man Called Peter* (New York: McGraw-Hill Book Co., 1951).

8. *Gift from the Sea* (New York: New American Library, Signet Books, 1957), p. 54.

time religion with its accent on experientialism, pietistic code morality, gospel hymns, and simple preaching. Dwight L. Moody would have found himself at home in these constituencies, while they in turn longed for the kind of national leadership which Moody—or even Billy Sunday—had provided. Against this background we consider the rise of Billy Graham, the handsome and strangely solitary hero who answered this mid-twentieth century longing for a restoration of revivals to their former glory.

William Franklin Graham was born in 1918 near Charlotte, North Carolina, the son of a strict, revival-favoring dairy farmer who belonged to the very conservative Associate Reformed Presbyterian Church (General Synod). Billy was converted at a revival led by Mordecai F. Ham in 1934, and in 1936 he entered Bob Jones College (then in Cleveland, Tennessee), only to transfer a semester later to the Florida Bible Institute near Tampa, where he underwent a deeper conversion, was rebaptized, and ordained as a Baptist minister. In 1940 he enrolled in Wheaton College (Illinois), and after receiving his B.A. in three years, he began a combined parish and radio ministry in the Chicago area in close association with the Moody Bible School and men who were organizing the National Association of Evangelicals and the Youth for Christ movement. As a field representative for the latter, Graham began after 1945 to establish his reputation as a preacher and evangelistic team leader, but it was a Los Angeles tent-meeting revival in 1949 which catapulted him into national prominence.

By 1956 the Billy Graham Evangelistic Association (incorporated, 1950) was using almost all available mass media—advertising, television, radio, paperback books, and cinema—and had an annual budget of two million dollars. Graham had become a rallying point for the National Association of Evangelicals, and he was doing much to alleviate the identity crisis of conservative evangelicalism. He made all Americans aware of the fact that the urban revival tradition in America was anything but dead.[9] At the same time, however, Graham's well-organized "success" served to conceal the degree to which time had eroded the old mainline constituencies to which Moody and Sunday had appealed. To be sure, it was his policy not to undertake his citywide crusades unless supported by local church councils; [10] yet his huge audiences did not come from the mainstream Protestantism to

9. It is surprising that so knowledgeable a Methodist as W. W. Sweet in his *Revivalism in America: Its Origin, Growth and Decline* (1944) should have ended his book with a kind of funeral sermon—"Revivalism on the Wane." There were no doubt hundreds of local revivals in progress on the day his book was published, especially in the South. Had there not been, the career of Billy Graham would have been impossible.

10. This policy estranged the ultraconservative evangelicals, though Graham's pronouncements on social and political issues were sufficiently individualistic, pietistic, and conservative to keep this estrangement to a minimum.

which Moody had preached. The chief source of Graham's strength was the conservatives within the larger Protestant denominations or in churches opposed to the ecumenical movement.

An important key to this "neo-evangelicalism" of the postwar years is the National Association of Evangelicals. It was founded in 1942 by a group of diverse conservatives who were dissatisfied with the politically oriented and rabidly exclusivist American Council of Churches which Carl McIntire had organized during the preceding year. Though agreeing with McIntire that conservatives needed to counter the Federal Council of Churches with some corporate expression, many evangelicals wanted a less divisive and more constructive association.[11] The NAE, therefore, replaced the moribund agencies of the old Fundamentalist movement and drew into its increasingly diversified activities a growing number of churches. By 1956 it claimed over a million and a half members, and spoke ambiguously of "service connections" with ten million more.[12] Though at this time the editor of the association's official organ estimated that half of the country's sixty million Protestants were still of Fundamentalist tendency, the actual membership of the NAE was heavily shaded toward the Holiness and Pentecostal churches, and only a quarter of its constituent elements exceeded twenty thousand members, while four members made up over two-thirds of its total.[13] It did, nevertheless, give a voice to conservative Protestants on questions pertaining to church-state relations, radio time, the military chaplaincy, and similar matters. It also gave something like denominational status to the "third force" in American Christianity. An additional measure of cohesiveness resulted from the founding in 1956 of *Christianity Today,* a fortnightly magazine of news and opinion edited by C. F. H. Henry, a former professor of New Testament at Northern Baptist and Fuller seminaries. By 1967 the magazine claimed 150,000 paid subscribers.

Still another aspect of this "new evangelicalism" which gained public notice during the fifties was its effort to overcome the powerful anti-intellectual and antiscientific spirit that had discredited the older Fundamentalism. This did not involve much (if any) modification of the movement's commitment to scriptural infallibility or its emphasis on the conversion experience. Nor,

11. McIntire had already been involved in a complex series of schisms among ultraconservative Presbyterians, many of whom were offended by his vituperative emphasis on anticommunist militancy. The NAE did not admit whole denominations that belonged to the Federal Council of Churches, but it would admit disaffected subdivisions thereof.

12. Louis Gasper, *The Fundamentalist Movement,* pp. 38–39.

13. The four largest member churches were the Assemblies of God (400,000), the Church of God of Cleveland, Tennessee (200,000), the National Association of Free Will Baptists (400,000), and the Church of the Four Square Gospel (88,000).

for the most part, did it involve an effort to transcend the many serious doctrinal issues that divided the "third force." But it did result in a considerable body of critical and apologetic literature attacking modernism, exposing Neo-orthodoxy as but another form of modernism, and defending conservative theology as a rational option for modern man. Less learned was its running critique of the World Council and the National Council of Churches as doctrinally lax, pro-Catholic, institutionally aggressive, and—on economic and political issues—too outspokenly in support of liberal causes. This concern for social issues betokened a highly significant shift among Protestant conservatives—a departure from the doctrine that the only proper concern of the church was the salvation of sinners. The tendency of "evangelicals" to align themselves with conservative, nationalistic, and racist politics had been noticeable in the interwar period, but it became more obvious and more nearly "official" in the postwar period.

By the end of the 1950s it had become clear that the old fundamentalist controversy was by no means a thing of the past. Conservative "evangelicalism" was a rapidly growing force in American Christianity. It included both a vast, inchoate multitude of earnest Christians and a much more dynamic and exclusivistic "third force." The churches in the latter category—chiefly those discussed in an earlier chapter on dissent and reaction—increased their membership from 400 to 700 percent during the two postwar decades, as against 75 to 90 percent for the older Protestant denominations. Yet these conservatives continued to be deeply troubled by the ways in which scholarship, science, technology, and rapid social change were destroying the old religious landmarks. Most of them had broken with the mainline denominations between 1890 and 1920 when liberalism and the Social Gospel were responding to new intellectual and social forces, and they remained committed to the individualism and morality of that bygone era. Both their consequent tendency toward conservatism in politics and their immense emphasis on foreign missions reflect their alienation from the domestic American scene.[14] In 1965 only 308,370 of the 1,040,836 Jehovah's Witnesses lived in the United States, while three-fourths of the Seventh-Day Adventists were overseas. Pentecostalism was surging in Latin America. During the later 1960s the situation of conservative evangelicalism in a pluralistic "nation of minorities" would have to be defined again in times of even greater urgency. It was becoming a major—and little understood—subculture. As if to confound supercilious observers, moreover, evangelicals, especially those who

14. See William G. McLoughlin, "Is There a Third Force in Christendom?" *Daedalus* (Winter 1967): 43–68; and Henry P. Van Dusen, "The Third Force's Lessons for Others," *Life*, 9 June 1958.

stressed charismatic gifts, would in the late 1960s experience a revival that made striking headway in new constituencies. Youthful, socially concerned "Jesus people" would even play a distinct kind of counter-cultural role.

THE MOVEMENT FOR PARISH RENEWAL

Practical concern for the worship and the religious life of local congregations had not been a major problem for most Neo-orthodox theologians. But after the war a pronounced awakening took place in this area, not just in abstract theological terms, but with concrete proposals for renewing worship, awakening the laity to its priesthood, invigorating the preaching office, and reforming parish education. In many ways the reformers sought to halt the inroads of patriotic piety and success-oriented religion. In this work the seminarians educated under Neo-orthodox auspices performed a vital function both in parishes and in denominational offices, though perhaps their most comprehensive achievements were made in the area of Christian education. In several denominations, notably the Episcopal and the Northern Presbyterian, an entirely new lesson system for all ages was prepared and instituted.

The postwar years also witnessed a rather remarkable flowering of the so-called Liturgical Movement. Its origins can be traced to the romantic religious revival of the nineteenth century in both Great Britain and on the Continent among both Roman Catholics and Protestants. In the twentieth century a long-developing movement of liturgical reform in several Benedictine abbeys began to take on ecumenical implications due to the surprising way in which major emphases of the Catholic tradition and those of the Reformation began to merge, as they had once abortively done in the work of Philip Schaff and John W. Nevin at Mercersburg Seminary.[15] Corporate worship was subjected to serious rethinking, as were the liturgical relationships of word and sacrament. Culminating the development was a renewal of concern for the royal priesthood and the active participation of the laity in the worshiping community. In this context the worshiping parish came to be a central fact of the Church's presence in the world. The effects of this

15. Dom Prosper Guéranger (1805–75), abbot of Solesmes and leader of the Benedictine Order's return to France, was one major source of renewed interest in worship. More directly pertinent to the United States was the restored abbey at Metten in Bavaria. From it came the founders of Saint Vincent's Abbey in Pennsylvania, and from Saint Vincent's, in turn, came the founders of Saint John's Abbey in Minnesota, which became almost the national center of the movement. Behind its work, and of special theological importance for the twentieth century, was the liturgical and theological pioneering of the Benedictine abbey at Maria Laach in Germany (see pp. 1012–15).

new emphasis became prominent not only in the so-called liturgical churches (Catholic, Episcopalian, and Lutheran), but in various branches of the Reformed tradition as well. Church building, which was proceeding at an unprecedented rate, thus became not only a major means of expressing the country's architectural renaissance, but a visible expression of a theological movement. Stone, concrete, and glass were often enlisted in the protest against the trivialization of the gospel. The slogan of the Faith and Order movement, "Let the Church be the Church," was taken to heart in many localities.

THE CONTINUATION OF NEO-ORTHODOX THEOLOGY

Many of the men who had inaugurated the Neo-orthodox period in modern theology—whether they were European or American—lived to produce some of their most important works in the postwar period. Karl Barth, for example, not only continued to add volumes to his monumental *Church Dogmatics,* but he saw these great works translated into English. After the war, American seminarians could study the powerful christological interpretations of the "later Barth." Paul Tillich also brought his *Systematic Theology* to completion. Reinhold Niebuhr never accepted Barth's extreme conception of God's otherness nor Tillich's strong philosophical interest, but he, too, continued to address public issues in his characteristic dialectical way. In 1959 he published *The Structure of Nations and Empires: A Study of the Recurring Patterns and Problems of the Political Order in Relation to the Unique Problems of the Nuclear Age.* At a quarter-century's remove, it became an important sequel to *Moral Man and Immoral Society,* which had first established his reputation as a realistic analyst of politics and international relations.

H. Richard Niebuhr was even more significantly active, counterbalancing, as always, the theological fashions of the time. His *Christ and Culture* (1951) again exhibited his dual interest in social forces and prophetic theology in a masterly discussion of the available options in relating the church to the world. In 1960 he published his *Radical Monotheism and Western Culture,* the last book he was to see through the press before his death in 1962. The revolutionary implications of this short work make it in fact a requiem for the Neo-orthodox period, and an opening into the secular theology and nonreligious interpretation of Christianity for which the 1960s would be remembered.

During the postwar decade and a half no new theologians arose either to eclipse the public eminence or to challenge the leading ideas of the older generation, though there did ensue a considerable extension of themes and methods that had come to prominence during the two previous decades. The World Council of Churches also inspired considerable groundbreaking in an international context, above all, on the nature of the Church.[16] In the United States the most provocative new concern of religious thinkers was the place of the Negro in American society. But this issue did not result so much in new thinking as in the activation of old ideals. President Truman's executive order desegregating the armed services (1950) and the Supreme Court's famous decision on the schools (1954) provided the basic response to the rising tempo of black demands. In focusing Protestant attention on civil rights, the National Council of Churches played a major role. Probably the most important religio-ethical event of the decade came in 1957, when the National Guard of Arkansas stood off the assault of a few black children on the segregated Central High School of Little Rock. Since that confrontation—which finally led President Eisenhower to order the army into Little Rock—neither the country as a whole nor the churches have been able to keep the question of racial justice in a closet. But only in the 1960s, in a radically altered context, would these questions begin to be squarely faced. Before long a new theology and a new ethics—and a new breed of thinkers and doers—would gain popular attention. Reformers would speak of secularity, poverty, political power, economic priorities, and Marx, often without awareness of how Neo-orthodox realism had led the way.

During 1958 and 1959, in any case, discerning observers began talking about the postwar revival in the past tense. By 1960 this view was generally accepted. The significance of the postwar revival, however, is not adequately indicated by an observation that it ended. More important is the fact that it failed to sustain human religious needs. The churches by and large seem to have done little more than provide a means of social identification to a mobile people who were being rapidly cut loose from the comfort of old contexts, whether ethnic or local. Yet with new multitudes entering their portals almost unbidden, the churches muffed their chance. Put more analytically, the so-called revival led to a sacrifice of theological substance, which in the face of the harsh new social and spiritual realities of the 1960s left both clergy and laity demoralized and confused. A loss of confidence occurred. Quantifiable aspects of the situation (church membership, attendance, and giving; seminary enrollments; demissions from the clergy, etc.) began to register decline. Thinkers who for some years—or decades—had been speaking of the "death of God" and of a "post-Christian era" began to

16. Claude Welch, *The Reality of the Church*, provides both an example of and an introduction to these ecclesiological concerns.

be heard. Forces of cultural change, subtle, pervasive, and ineluctable—far less tangible than wars, depressions, and political campaigns—were altering the moral and religious ethos. The postwar revivals came more and more to be interpreted as the epilogue to an epoch.[17] Americans began to sense the dawn of a new age in their spiritual history, a time of reorientation and beginning again, in which the past experience and present situation of every tradition would be opened for reexamination.

17. See Martin E. Marty, *Second Chance for American Protestants.*

IX
TOWARD POST-PURITAN AMERICA

Genuinely radical monotheism has . . . affirmed not only all mankind but all being. It has involved men not only in battle against the wrongs that afflict men but set them into conflict with what is destructive and anarchic in all accessible realms of being. Its religion has found holiness in man, but also in all nature and in what is beyond nature. It has believed in the salvation of men from evil, but also in the liberation of the whole groaning and travailing creation. Its science has sought to understand men, yet for it the proper study of mankind has been not only man but the infinitely great and the infinitely small in the whole realm of being. Its art has reinterpreted man to himself but also re-created for man and reinterpreted to him natural beings and eternal forms that have become for him objects of wonder and surprise.

Radical monotheism as the gift of confidence in the principle of being itself, as the affirmation of the real, as loyalty—betrayed and reconstructed many times—to the universe of being, can have no quarrel with humanism and naturalism insofar as these are protests against the religions and ethics of closed societies, centering in little gods—or in little ideas of God. But insofar as faith is given to men in the principle of being itself, or insofar as they are reconciled to the Determiner of Destiny as the fountain of good and only of good, naturalism and humanism assume the form of exclusive systems of closed societies. A radically monotheistic faith says to them as to all the other claimants to "the truth, the whole truth and nothing but the truth," to all the "circumnavigators of being" as Santayana calls them: "I do not believe you. God is great."

H. Richard Niebuhr, *Radical Monotheism and Western Culture* (1960)

America has endured many crises, but the moment of truth which the country began to experience in the 1960s was made uniquely critical by the convergence of several developments. Most serious were the military and domestic events that led to a loss of that kind of corporate commitment that a nation of unusually heterogeneous minorities desperately needed. This loss of national self-assurance was made more poignant by the declining incidence of dedication to the moral and doctrinal message of the churches and to the religious institutions that had sustained these traditions. An increasing awareness of public violence and environmental overexploitation, meanwhile, extended popular misgivings to the economic and social system itself, and thus also to the entire educational enterprise. The idea of America as a Chosen Nation and a beacon to the world was expiring. The people had by no means become less religious, and their sense of moral urgency was, if anything, heightened. Yet unmistakably at the heart of the prevailing anxiety was the need for reexamining fundamental conceptions of religion, ethics, and nationhood.

The chapters of Part IX deal with major aspects of this developing crisis. They first trace the more recent history of Judaism and Catholicism, and the whole course of the ancient Eastern Churches in America. In all of these contexts the new awareness of pluralism and the changing situation of the Protestant establishment is observed. This theme is then given additional emphasis by an account of black religion and the rise of the militant protest movement. In this chapter the centrality of America's racial dilemma is exposed. Two chapters are also devoted to two major streams of "harmonial religion" which have a long American history but which were enlivened almost simultaneously by Mary Baker Eddy's *Science and Health* in 1875 and Madame Blavatsky's *Isis Revealed* in 1877, and which after World War II gained increasing attention from religious seekers in all walks of life. During the 1960s these ancient religious traditions became highly significant elements of the American scene, in part because of the widespread rejection of the exploitive and competitive stress of the Puritan ethic and the questioning of Judaeo-Christian beliefs. Also very apparent was a serious awakening of interest in perennial forms of mysticism and various streams of Eastern religion.

How these and many other developments converged in the decades of the sixties and seventies is the explanatory task undertaken in the concluding chapter, wherein some grounds are given for the view that the great Puritan epoch in America's spiritual history was drawing to a painful and tumultuous close.

57

TWENTIETH-CENTURY JUDAISM

President Harding's signature on the immigration restriction act of 1921 marked the end of one period in American history and the beginning of another. As rendered more decisive by the acts of 1924 and 1927 and by President Hoover's executive order of 1930, this policy reversal was also a turning point in the history of American Jewry—as of many other ethnic groups. Mass immigration became a thing of the past; ahead lay only varying modes of Americanization for different immigrant groups in the population.

The generation before 1920 had, of course, experienced the deluge; nearly two million Jewish immigrants had arrived between 1870 and the outbreak of World War I. During the four postwar years a quarter-million more had come. After 1925 the American Jewish community's future was linked no longer to Ellis Island but to New York City, where half the country's Jews resided, and to the other cities of the country—the larger the city the greater the proportion of Jews. The Jewish population continued to grow, from nearly 3.5 million in 1917 to 4.2 million in 1927 to 4.5 million in 1937 to perhaps 5.5 million in 1964.[1] The number of Americans naming Yiddish as their mother tongue, however, reached its peak of 1,222,658 in 1930, and this fact points to what is perhaps the major shaping force in twentieth-century Judaism. Without the great influx of Yiddish-speaking Orthodox

1. The change in immigration volume was sharply defined: in the seven years before 1914, 656,400 Jews entered the country; in the seven years after 1924, only 73,378. Only about 170,000 Jews came to the United States during the twelve years between Hitler's rise and fall. Between 1933 and 1943 there were 341,567 unfilled places in quotas from Germany and countries it occupied, and 900,000 unfilled places from other quotas during these years; but the regulations were so strictly enforced that refugees could not claim these places. The political pressures against admitting Jews came chiefly from veterans organizations, "patriotic" societies, and overtly anti-Semitic movements.

Ever since the Jews in czarist Russia were divided nearly in half by the restoration of Polish and Lithuanian independence after World War I, American Jews have been the largest national Jewish community. Before the war the Russian Empire extended westward to the German border and the Baltic Sea.

Jews from Eastern Europe, not even the Hitlerian Holocaust nor the founding of Israel would have had the impact they later did.

FROM EASTERN EUROPE TO THE AMERICAN GHETTO

Certainly no religious group in America was more thoroughly transformed by the later immigration than the Jewish community. The Reform rabbis who announced their spiritual emancipation in the famous Pittsburgh Declaration of 1885 spoke for most of the approximately 250,000 Jews then associated with the synagogues (or temples) of America. There were two small exceptions, however. One was the small group of synagogues along the East coast with a few thousand members who maintained the "dignified Orthodoxy" of the old Sephardic tradition. The other exception was the larger and rapidly growing group of East European Jews. As early as 1852 they had organized a synagogue in New York City, and after the czarist pogroms of 1881–82 their rate of immigration had been steadily increasing. They were also fleeing from poverty and intensified persecution in various regions of the rambling Austro-Hungarian Empire and Romania. And after 1918 the plight of Jews in most of these areas became still worse. Hence the number of synagogues grew from 270 in 1880 to 533 in 1890 (with over 130 in New York City alone), to 1,901 in 1916 and 3,100 in 1927. These dramatic changes are not merely quantitative, however, for the new immigration came quite literally from a world of its own—the world of Eastern Ashkenazi Orthodoxy, a vast "nation" numbering from six to eight million at its height. These people were gathered in rural villages and urban ghettos, in the midst of a dozen other dominant nationalities in the huge, backward, predominantly agricultural region extending from the Baltic Sea to the Black Sea. By the time Hitler's Third Reich had been smashed in World War II this vast Jewish world had been almost utterly extinguished; but its history and character are vital to American religious history because 90 percent of those who emigrated came to the United States.

The Yiddish (*jüdisch*) language of these Eastern Jews, though spoken with many local variations, was a medieval German dialect written in Hebrew characters and containing various Hebrew words. As this fact betokens, German Jews had been moving eastward for a long time. In fact, a slow trickle had begun at latest in the thirteenth century, and it gradually increased in volume century by century due both to new legal restrictions in Germany and to encouragement from Polish or Russian rulers. After the defeat of Napoleon, however, most of Poland and Lithuania fell under Russian rule, and Jews were limited to a "pale of settlement" that tended to keep them out of Russia proper. The nineteenth century also brought great distress—persecution, famine, inequitable conscription laws—and most basically, a gradual collapse of the old peasant economy in which the trades and vocations of Jews had taken an important place. With the rise of industrialism a movement to the city had begun, with heavy de-Judaizing consequences.[2]

Yet until the 1880s the old ways of Orthodox observance were maintained, especially within the defined limits of each agricultural village (or *shtetl*), where a genuinely communal existence could continue. Here, where the gentile world did not intrude on Torah-centered living, the Sabbath could truly be a foretaste of heaven. The old system of nurture assured the raising up of new students of the Scriptures, the Talmud, and the rabbinic commentaries. The more promising students could be sent on to some respected center of studies for further training. Given a common language, moreover, great revivals of piety could take place, as they had since the mid-eighteenth century when Hasidism, with its joyous mystical devotionalism, had arisen.[3] It is not surprising, therefore, that on arrival in America these Jews would try to re-create the old institutions and, if possible, found a synagogue where the familiar dialect would be spoken. In old age, even if they had "made it" to a life of affluence and comfort, they would cherish their memories of life in the *shtetl*.[4]

Until the later nineteenth century the ghetto—an urban quarter where an observant Jewish life could be lived—had not figured strongly in American life. The migration of Eastern Jews changed that, and in every large northern city ghettos arose, but on the most massive scale in New York, "the Promised City." The immediate problem was survival in the intensely competitive atmosphere created by the cresting tide of the new immigration. It was solved through merchandizing in street and store, through innumerable

2. Lodz, the Russian Manchester, was a village with 11 Jews in 1793; a city with 98,677 Jews in 1897 and 166,628 in 1910. Warsaw's Jewish population numbered 3,532 in 1781; 219,141 in 1891. Along with urban life came contact with Western philosophical and social ideas which often undermined Jewish modes of life and belief.

3. Hasidism was a pietistic movement founded by Israel Baal Shem Tob (1700–60), a mystic, cabalist, and healer who, with the aid of several equally dedicated disciples, attracted numerous followers, first in the Polish Ukraine, then more widely. By the early nineteenth century half of Eastern Jewry, especially the poor and uneducated, were profoundly affected. By intention Hasidism was Orthodox, even intensely so; but due to its emphasis on the divine immanence and on communion with God, it tended to threaten those who stressed only rabbinical study and strict observance of the Law. To the oppressed it brought a message of God's love, a sense of joy, and a gift of hope that was reflected both in worship and in daily life.

4. After World War II a group of anthropologists through interviews with immigrants in America developed a remarkably colorful and detailed account of Eastern Jewish village life (see Mark Zborowski and Elizabeth Herzog, *Life Is with People: The Culture of the Shtetl*).

crafts and trades, and, above all, through "the great Jewish métier"—the making of clothes. The Jewish home and family became a workshop. As one reporter on the New York ghetto commented:

> You are made fully aware of it before you have travelled the length of a single block in any of these East Side streets, by the whir of a thousand sewing-machines, worked at high pressure from earliest dawn till mind and muscle give out together. Every member of the family from the youngest to the oldest, bears a hand, shut in the qualmy rooms, where meals are cooked and clothing washed and dried besides, the livelong day. It is not unusual to find a dozen persons—men, women, and children—at work in a single small room.[5]

Yet the household was held together and a measure of self-respect retained. As the garment industry became more organized, so did labor. And the old emphasis on education remained. All of these factors made the Jewish "ghetto" a place of rapid turnover, social change, and religious unrest.

JUDAISM IN THE TWENTIES AND THIRTIES

In 1927 probably 80 percent of the Jews in the United States were of Eastern European origin and Orthodox in background. They or their parents had been arriving in the country for over a half-century; but they were no longer crowded into the teeming ghettos of New York and a few other larger cities. Most of them (nobody agrees as to what percentage) had improved their economic status and were now living in houses or apartments of residential areas. Ordinarily these neighborhoods were also predominantly Jewish, but strict Orthodox observance was gradually yielding to a reliance on close-knit family life, participation in Jewish organizations, the best possible education of children, and close attention to economic advancement in a rapidly expanding country. The obvious success of preceding immigration waves, the German Jews in particular, provided both example and grounds for hope.

Genuinely Jewish communal life still went on in the old areas of first settlement, where kosher food stores and restaurants, Yiddish and Hebrew newspapers, and Orthodox synagogues of every description could still be found. But all of this was now carried on at a reduced scale. The important fact was that most Jews in America, including most of the latest immigration wave, were either becoming alienated from their religious heritage, or had already become so. Especially in the second generation, Jews were drifting

5. Quoted in Moses Rischin, *The Promised City: New York's Jews, 1870–1914*, p. 61.

away from the synagogue by the thousands. A survey made of New York City youth in 1935 revealed that 72 percent of the young Jewish men (between the ages of fifteen and twenty-five) and 78 percent of the women had not attended services for a year, and 89 and 94 percent not in a week. In other large cities the situation was probably not different. Two-thirds to three-fourths of these young people had probably had some kind of Jewish education during their school years; but only a tiny fraction had been schooled with Orthodox thoroughness. A larger percentage had been influenced by the Yiddish school movement which was socialistic, antireligious in spirit, and, after 1929 especially, inspired by the militant "proletariat" of the garment industry. Secular Zionism attracted others.

Undoubtedly, most young Jews were chiefly involved in the basic process of Americanization, for the public schools and secular universities played a major role in translating them into the professions (at three times the rate for non-Jews) and into white-collar occupations. In this context, Orthodox schooling and strict observance seemed to be a hindrance, irrational or meaningless once the bonds of thoroughly Jewish communal life were broken. The story—sometimes agonizing, sometimes exhilarating—of how the edifice of strict observance could be suddenly or protractedly toppled has been told many times; but the classic account is Abraham Cahan's autobiographical novel *The Rise of David Levinsky* (1917). Cahan shows how the process could begin even during a young boy's rabbinical training far away in Russia, and then accelerate rapidly in New York City. He confessed that "the very clothes I wore and the very food I ate had a fatal effect on my religious habits." "If you . . . attempt to bend your religion to the spirit of your new surroundings, it breaks. It falls to pieces." His decision to shave his beard became a traumatic turning point in his life.[6] American Jews were rapidly becoming an ethnic rather than a religious minority in America.

Forces were at work, however, which would maintain or even strengthen the solidarity of American Jews. One of these factors was the anti-Semitism which had first emerged in the 1870s and then been persistently fanned by nativistic organizations and the immigration restriction movement. In these campaigns Jews were marked off for discrimination on vaguely racial grounds

6. Abraham Cahan, *The Rise of David Levinsky,* pp. 110–11. In real life Cahan became the publisher of the *Jewish Daily Forward,* the most widely read Yiddish paper in the world. He was an outspoken liberal leader of Yiddish-speaking America. The world he lived in is memorably described in Hutchins Hapgood, *The Spirit of the Ghetto* (1902) with drawings by Jacob Epstein and additional commentary by Harry Golden (New York: Schocken Books, 1965). Michael Gold describes the next generation in the ghetto in *Jews without Money* (1930).

or for contradictory linkages with the urban "money power," social radicalism, commercial aggressiveness, and freethinking. Zionism was in part a response to anti-Semitism and persecution, and it, too, became an agent of solidarity.

Zionism, in one or another sense of the term, had been an intrinsic element of Jewish hope ever since the Babylonian Captivity of the sixth century B.C.E. It was renewed after the destruction of the Jewish commonwealth in 70 C.E. and the end of temple worship in Jerusalem. During the nineteenth century more than one movement of emancipation through colonization in Palestine had been set in motion by Jews in Eastern Europe. Most notable was Judah Pinsker's Love of Zion movement with headquarters in Odessa.[7] The effective origins of modern Zionism, however, must be traced to the zeal of Theodore Herzl (1860–1904), a completely secularized Jewish journalist of Vienna. After witnessing the degradation of Alfred Dreyfus in Paris in 1895, Herzl was converted to the Zionist cause, and in 1896 he published his manifesto *Der Judenstaat* (the Jewish State). As the sole solution of the anti-Semitic problem he demanded an international treaty-supported act of indemnification; and despite the hostility of Orthodox leaders, Reform Judaism, socialists, and emancipated Jews of great prominence, the first Zionist Congress was held in Basel in 1897. Other congresses followed and Herzl became a renowned international prophet and diplomat. In America the response to Zionism was immediate, and a federation was organized in 1898 with Rabbi Stephen S. Wise of New York as secretary.[8] Yet the opposition was also strong. The German Jews, often wealthy and thoroughly Americanized, saw Zionism as challenging a major tenet of their faith and as jeopardizing their status in the United States. The conference of Reform rabbis consequently stood in firm opposition. Labor leaders and socialists regarded Zionism as bourgeois, escapist, romantic, and chauvinistic. Orthodox leaders saw it as a secularist misunderstanding of Jewish hope.

Yet gradually Zionism began to gather a certain inchoate strength, chiefly among those of the Eastern Jewish poor who had been unattracted by labor radicalism. After 1903 "Zionist socialism" began increasingly to attract the

7. Emma Lazarus (1849–87), the Jewish poet, famed for her lines on the Statue of Liberty, wrote one of the more popular Zionist anthems ("O for Jerusalem's Trumpet Now"). Several American Christians also projected settlement plans. One which resembled earlier Negro colonization schemes was prepared by the Reverend William E. Blackstone of Illinois, signed by J. P. Morgan, J. D. Rockefeller, Philip D. Armour, and others, and submitted to President Harrison in 1891.

8. Wise was in many ways atypical, however. He declined a call to Temple Emanu-El—the New York "Cathedral of Judaism"—and in 1907 founded the Free Synagogue, which was very similar in spirit to the nonsectarian Ethical Culture Society which Felix Adler had founded in 1876. Both Adler and Wise were active social reformers, though Adler dissociated himself from Judaism almost completely.

workers.[9] Around the same time an allied federation of Orthodox Zionists was formed, and a few distinguished and scholarly supporters from the Reform group rallied to the cause. Still others came from the newly emerging movement of Conservatism, notably its spiritual father in the United States, Solomon Schechter, who left England to become head of the Jewish Theological Seminary in 1902. In the meantime the "official" Federation of American Zionists began to take shape, and by 1920 it had become the movement's chief organized focus amid a large number of other Zionist orders and associations. In 1925 the United Palestine Appeal was established to aid the cause.

The thirties brought other, more important stimuli, and a more complete sense of solidarity among American Jews than they had ever shown or known before. The largest and most horrible cause was Adolf Hitler and the rise of the Third Reich in Germany. Closer at hand was the emergence of militant anti-Semitism in the United States, incited most popularly by Father Charles E. Coughlin, the radio priest at the Shrine of the Little Flower near Detroit, but advanced as well by the reorganized Ku Klux Klan, the German-American Bund, Protestant Fundamentalist Gerald Winrod of Kansas, the Silver Shirts, and a number of other secret and semimilitary terrorist organizations. As a result, the leaders of the three great "Jewish defense agencies"—the American Jewish Committee, the American Jewish Congress, and the Anti-Defamation League—came to appreciate the significance of Zionism. By 1935 the Jewish National Fund had raised $5 million for the purchase of land in Palestine. The number of American Jews involved in Zionist groups rose from 150,000 in 1930 to 400,000 in 1940. As the world moved closer to World War II, especially after Great Britain's pro-Arab White Paper of 1939,

9. The destiny of Golda Mabovitch was hardly typical, but her life sheds light on the American movement. Born in Kiev, Russia, in 1898, she came with her parents at the age of eight to Milwaukee. During her high school years she became interested in the Labor Zionist movement, and soon she was teaching in a Yiddish school and working with a group of intense Zionists. In 1917 she married Morris Myerson, with whom she sailed to Palestine in 1921 and joined kibbutz Merhavia, ten miles south of Nazareth. (They had a son and a daughter but eventually separated; he died in 1951.) After moving to Jerusalem, Mrs. Myerson began a long and distinguished public career. By 1928 she was secretary of the Women's Labor Council, and soon thereafter she assumed a lifelong role of leadership in the Jewish Labor Party (Mapai). As a department head in the Jewish Agency for Palestine (1946–48) she made a major contribution to the establishment of a Jewish state through her highly successful fund raising in the United States. After statehood she served as ambassador to the USSR (1948–49), as minister of labor (1949–56), and as minister of foreign affairs (1956–66). When in 1956 Ben-Gurion requested cabinet members to take Hebrew names, she chose Meir, which means "illuminates." After succeeding Levi Eshkol as prime minister in 1969 she pursued a hard line against Israel's foes. While on a state visit in October 1969 she paid a nostalgic visit to her elementary school in Milwaukee. The pupils of the school, all of them black, greeted her by singing in Hebrew the Israeli national anthem.

and with the Jewish community in Palestine genuinely threatened with extinction, a great majority of American Jewry began to sympathize with the Zionist cause.

The basis of this new solidarity in the American Jewish community was not "religious" in the historic Judaic sense, nor was it Torah-centered. Challenged on an ethnic basis, they responded as an ethnic group. A certain nontraditional religious element was present, however, and this would have large consequences for the postwar revival. Equally important to these later developments were gradual changes taking place in the older forms of American Judaism and the rise of specific new movements.

THE DIVISIONS OF JUDAISM

Orthodox Judaism was the most important sector of Judaism, if for no other reason than that it was overwhelmingly the largest, its numbers having grown to between 1 and 1.5 million by 1937. The constituency of Orthodox Judaism had always been relatively unprosperous, and its places of worship were unpretentious. It had also been slow to organize on a national basis. But for a few remnants of Sephardic Orthodoxy (chiefly in New York City) it would have been almost leaderless and without an effective link to the non-Jewish world. Rabbi Henry Pereira Mendes of the old Spanish and Portuguese synagogue in New York did provide some leadership, however, and in 1898 he organized the Union of Orthodox Jewish Congregations. Four years later the Union of Orthodox Rabbis was formed, a group instrumental in founding the Rabbi Isaac Elchanan Theological Seminary in New York City. On this foundation Yeshiva College, later University, was built. In this institution and in similar ones elsewhere a new English-speaking Orthodox rabbinate was trained, who in 1930 organized the Rabbinical Council of America. The Young Israel movement (founded in 1912) gave further scope to such activity.

Due to these organizational efforts the continuity of Orthodoxy was assured; indeed, it showed remarkable vigor and adaptive power. By the time of World War II the major problems of transition had been solved. Steps had been taken to eliminate aspects of Orthodox worship which often made disaffiliation from the synagogue a first step toward Americanization. Some of the intellectual concerns of the Reform were also entertained. In the mid-1950s it was estimated that about half of the country's 5.5 million Jews were religiously affiliated, and that about a third of them were associated with somewhat over seven hundred Orthodox synagogues. Orthodox strength was declining, but not rapidly.

In Reform Judaism the opposite tendencies were observable. During the period 1885 to 1915 it had become increasingly disengaged from historic normative Judaism. Many congregations had adopted the forms of liberal Protestant worship and had even shifted their public services to Sunday. Of considerable significance for this Americanizing tendency was the fact that Hebrew Union College and Seminary, the intellectual center of the Reform, was isolated in Cincinnati, whereas the great concentration of Eastern European immigrants, with whom the future of American Judaism necessarily lay, were concentrated in other larger cities, particularly in New York. During and after World War I a number of forces began to reverse the assimilationist tendency, notably the increasing responsibilities of immigrant aid, the gradual movement of upward-mobile Eastern Jews into Reform congregations and the Reform rabbinate, and finally, the process by which anti-Semitism, fascistic harassment at home, and Nazi terrorism abroad combined to awaken the Reform's slumbering concern for Judaism. Intellectual trends and world-historical developments were also undermining the rationalistic optimism of the older theology. The Reform, in other words, underwent a chastening very similar to that of Protestant liberalism; and out of this experience came a rediscovery of the power and existential relevance of prophetic religion and those very Jewish attitudes which the Enlightenment had quite summarily rejected. Before World War II the full significance of these various forces could not be appreciated, but during the postwar decade important shifts in temper and practice were very much in evidence. This awakening to the values of the tradition seems to have helped the Reform to maintain its hold on about a third of the religiously affiliated Jews. In 1955 they were gathered in slightly more than five hundred congregations, many of them exceedingly prosperous. By this time, however, a newer religious movement was threatening their primacy in the American Jewish community.

Conservative Judaism has claimed the title of "authentic American Judaism"—a claim that need not be adjudicated here. Less controversial is the quip that it is "the lengthened shadow of Jewish Theological Seminary in New York." This school was founded due to serious dissatisfactions with the Reform trend, and because a number of Jewish leaders in New York recognized an educational responsibility for the vast numbers of immigrants who were pouring into the city. Nothing much came of the school, however, until 1902, when Solomon Schechter (1850–1915), a great Romanian-born scholar, powerful teacher, and deeply religious thinker, came from Cambridge University to become its president. Around him were gathered a learned faculty of biblical, talmudic, and historical scholars who made the institution a famous center of Jewish studies.

In substance the "Conservatism" that took shape in America was very similar to the secession from radical Reform led in late nineteenth-century Germany by Zechariah Frankel. Its hope was to unite American Judaism; and in the long run this aim may be realized. In the near term, however, a new and distinctive religious impulse began to be institutionalized. In 1913 Schechter led in the founding of the United Synagogue of America, a federation of congregations sympathetic to the school's objectives and paralleling the Rabbinical Assembly of America, which had been in existence since 1901 as a uniting bond of the school's graduates. Gradually a new Judaic movement came into existence, one that more or less accepted the Reform's openness to scientific research and its demand that Judaism continue as in the past to reinterpret its fundamental loyalty in terms of changing historical circumstances. In public services, too, certain desires for change were accommodated: mixed choirs, family pews, organ music, and the like. As the platform of the United Synagogue made clear, however, its objectives also included genuine efforts to preserve the tradition. Among its aims were—

1. to assert and establish loyalty to the Torah and its historical exposition;
2. to further the observance of the Sabbath and dietary laws;
3. to preserve in the service the references to Israel's past and the hopes for Israel's restoration;
4. to maintain the traditional character of the liturgy with Hebrew as the language of prayer.[10]

Not asserted as an "aim" but important as a fact was the tendency of the professors at the seminary to expound the Bible and the rabbinical writings essentially in the traditional manner and not to engage in the higher criticism of the Scriptures or to wrestle with modern problems of observance. This was to create a rift between the Conservative rabbis and their congregations, because it forestalled the nominal purpose of the movement, namely, to reinterpret and adjust the Law to the realities of the American scene. The movement helped to maintain the continuity of Judaism under circumstances of great difficulty and transitional stress, however, and it shaped a form of Judaism that was well adapted to American religious needs. A half-century after Schechter's arrival in the United States, Conservatism embraced 450 rabbis and over five hundred synagogues.

"Reconstructionism" also had Jewish Theological Seminary as its point of origin. Some interpreters, in fact, see it as a radical extension of Conservatism's interest in the "totality" of Jewish experience. By extending its concern to Jewish art and culture it sought to attract those who desired no participation in any kind of synagogue. Far more than Conservatism, moreover,

10. Rufus Learsi, *Israel: A History of the Jewish People*, p. 206.

Reconstructionism owed its organized existence in America to one man, Mordecai M. Kaplan (b. 1881). Kaplan was born in Russia and raised in the traditions of Orthodoxy. After coming to New York and attending City College, he became an Orthodox rabbi. His advanced studies, especially in philosophy at Columbia University, led to a change in his religious outlook, which came strongly to resemble the naturalism of John Dewey, Edward Scribner Ames, and Horace Kallen. Kaplan became an instrumentalist in religion; God was a name for man's collective ethical ideal. In 1918 he founded the Jewish Center in New York and set up a broad cultural program. During the 1920s he also served as a professor at Jewish Theological Seminary, where the convergence of scholarly studies and the secular cultural interests of Zionist students gradually gave content and purpose to his developing ideas. In 1934 he published his diagnosis and prescription, *Judaism as a Civilization,* in which he expounded not only his philosophical views, but a program for utilizing the study of Hebrew history, culture, and language in order to win back the loyalty of religiously alienated Jews.

In actuality, Kaplan was providing a rationale for the Jewish center movement which had been making considerable advances during the twenties and would continue to do so during the thirties. The centers were taking over functions similar to those assumed by the old German Jewish YMHA's and YWHA's and by various settlement houses that had been founded in immigrant communities. But in most cases these institutions had become little more than middle-class recreation centers. Even though occasionally connected with a synagogue, they were less interested in Judaism than in "Jewishness." It was precisely this broad tendency that Kaplan wished to provide with a deeper self-understanding and purpose. But because his "rationale" contained important elements that offended each of the three main movements in American Judaism, it never served as a unitive force. Organizationally it has become instead a very small and unpromising federation of a half-dozen or so Reconstructionist synagogues.

Kaplan's significance, however, was very great. He personified the major conflicts and uncertainties of his tradition and gave voice to the unarticulated conviction of many that Jewishness was a significant and sufficient basis for assuring the survival of the Jewish people in America, and, negatively, that Judaism, to the degree that it was Torah-orientated, would be an instrument of alienation. Kaplan's philosophical views became increasingly unattractive to intellectuals who had witnessed or endured the holocaust which began in the very year his book appeared. Yet he was deeply sensitive to popular needs as well as to modern religious trends. After the postwar religious revival had waned, his views would again be regarded as relevant.

JUDAISM IN THE AGE OF AFFLUENCE: THE POSTWAR REVIVAL

Will Herberg in 1955 commented on the great transformation of Judaism which had occurred largely within the last quarter-century:

> American Jewry first established itself in this country as an ethnic-immigrant group. . . . But unlike the rest, it somehow did not lose its corporate identity with advancing Americanization; instead . . . it underwent a change of character and turned into an American religious community, retaining, even enhancing, its Jewishness in the process.[11]

This participation of Judaism in the postwar "upswing in religion" is what Nathan Glazer has called "the Jewish Revival." [12]

The postwar revival probably had a more marked effect on Judaism than on any other religious faith in America. Nowhere had disaffiliation and alienation been so prominent a religious trend during the first three decades of the twentieth century as among the Eastern Jews who had entered this country since 1870. After 1945, however, neither Protestantism nor Roman Catholicism experienced so marked an increase in formal religious identification and institutional support. For a generation the process of denationalization was almost brought to a halt. The Jewish response, of course, bore many similarities to that of Americans in general, except that Jewish needs were, if anything, more poignant. In universities and residential areas alike they were awakened to a new kind of ethnic self-awareness which was accompanied by an unmistakable return to religious affiliation. Jewish ethnicity and religiosity, of course, have always been famously tangled, and new snarls were created by the establishment of the republic of Israel in 1948 and the subsidence of domestic intolerance in the 1950s. But a trend was clear.

That the future of this trend rests largely with the Eastern Jews is one of the truisms of American Judaism, but two other factors are almost equally vital. This first was documented with special force by Marshall Sklare in his *Conservative Judaism,* though it was anticipated by Louis Wirth's study, *The Ghetto,* in 1928. Both of these sociologists emphasize the fairly consistent pattern of movement by which Eastern Jews first took up their American abode in urban ghettos where, so far as possible, they reproduced the life they had left behind. Then gradually the more upward mobile members of the second generation, who were offended by such milieux and by the unedifying cacophany of synagogue worship, led a steady outward movement to "areas

11. Will Herberg, *Protestant, Catholic, Jew,* p. 172.

12. Nathan Glazer, *American Judaism,* p. 106.

of second settlement." These areas also became "Jewish neighborhoods," but in a more generalized and outwardly "American" way. Even the rabbi of an Orthodox synagogue would, in the American mode, take on increasingly professional ministerial functions, and worship would be made more orderly and decorous. The religious losses during this phase of Jewish Americanization, however, were enormous. It was the great "secularizing time" during which the foundations were laid for a highly significant "humanist" sector in the American population.[13]

In the postwar "age of affluence" the broad reaches of metropolitan suburbia became the "third area of settlement," and in this environment the return to institutionalized religion was largely made. Leaving behind vast inner-city neighborhoods to new in-migrants (largely Negro and Puerto Rican), Jews now joined other ethnic minorities as part of the suburban "lonely crowd" which David Riesman so memorably described. In this environment, fertile with its own anxieties and insecurity, Jews had to solve their problems of religion and child nurture in constant encounter with Roman Catholics and Protestants—who then, as earlier, were generally far more faithful in their formal religious obligations. In 1947 a national public opinion poll showed that 18 percent of the Jews attended services once a month, as against 65 percent of the Protestant respondents and 85 percent of the Roman Catholics. In addition to all the other religious pressures of postwar America, it may be legitimately supposed that status consciousness, the special pressures of "suburbanized Americanization," and the ordinary comforts of conformity have at least no less impact on Jewish modes of life than on others. Emulation, thus, is at least one factor in the revival.

A second factor of large importance has been underlined by Will Herberg through his invocation of "Hansen's law," the formulation of the great immigration historian, Marcus Lee Hansen: "What the son wishes to forget, the grandson wishes to remember." [14] Herberg saw a relation between the succession of generations and the dynamics of religious revival. Stressing certain anxieties which seem to be inherent in the process of Americanization, he interpreted the *second* generation, in its desire for acceptance and outward

13. John Courtney Murray speaks of the familiar three faiths plus this "humanist-secularist" sector as America's four great "conspiracies" (see John Cogley, ed., *Religion in America* [New York: Meridian Books, 1958]). Jews have provided this "fourth faith" with many of its finest defenders ever since the days of Felix Adler and Stephen Wise. Horace Kallen in his *Secularism Is the Will of God* (1954) gave strong expression to it.

14. Quoted in Herberg, *Protestant, Catholic, Jew*, p. 186. Even the distinguished writers who during the postwar decades made the "Jewish novel" a major genre in American literary history tend to substantiate Hansen's law (see Irving Malin, *Jews and Americans*, which considers Delmore Schwartz, Saul Bellow, Philip Roth, Bernard Malamud, Leslie Fiedler, and others).

acculturation, as striving to cast off every habit or custom that would remind others of its "foreign" origins. By the thoroughly Americanized *third* generation, however, these insecurities are less sharply felt; they are replaced, in fact, by a certain nostalgia for ancestral tradition and perhaps a measure of guilt and shame for having abandoned it. A general shift in national religious mores supported this trend by applauding affiliation with any one of democracy's "three great faiths." Over and above such popular encouragement is a value-oriented desire for meaning, inspiration, and moral guidance in a world where many of the older assurances seemed empty or fatuous. It is this last dimension of the revival that theologians and other serious religious thinkers have addressed.

Theological renewal was a prominent feature of the entire Atlantic community after the devastations of World War II. Jews, whose participation in this shattering experience had been the most tragic of all, made a large intellectual and artistic contribution, one that both responded to and developed the tendencies of thought expressed in other traditions. Leo S. Baeck, Franz Rosenzweig, Martin Buber, and Abraham Heschel are at least partially representative of these intellectual currents.

Rabbi Leo S. Baeck (1873–1956) was a profound spokesman for the tradition of Reform universalism whose great book *The Essence of Judaism* (1905) nevertheless sought to define the special vocation of the chosen people. Having endured the concentration camps of the Third Reich, he emerged after World War II as a peculiarly effective interpreter of Judaism for the postwar generation. Sensitive to the tensions of modern culture and profoundly aware of man's creatureliness, Baeck sought to combine a concern for man's religious consciousness with the conception of Judaism as fundamentally a religion of commandment. It is in deeds of moral dedication, despite the immensity of the task and the this-worldly hopelessness of the hope, that he finds the essence and strength of Judaism.[15]

If Baeck can be said to speak in a manner that is especially congenial to Reform Judaism, Franz Rosenzweig (1886–1923) and Martin Buber (1878–1965) developed themes more properly associated with Conservatism, though Buber especially can be said to speak to all men, and he has undoubtedly had a larger influence on Christian thought than any other Jewish thinker

15. In his strong ethical emphasis, Baeck, like many of his contemporaries, was deeply indebted to Hermann Cohen (1842–1918), the famed Neo-Kantian philosopher of Marburg University, especially to his posthumous *Religion of Reason Out of the Sources of Judaism* (1919). The Marburg school was firmly antimetaphysical, logical, and disinclined to concede authority to particular historical movements. Cohen shared this cosmopolitan outlook despite his self-conscious Jewishness.

of the twentieth century. Buber was born in Vienna, where, before going to the university, he lived with his grandfather and became thoroughly steeped in the Hasidic Judaism of Galicia, acquiring the mystical interests that colored his thought to the end. In later years Wilhelm Dilthey, Kierkegaard, Dostoevsky, and Nietzsche became important to his social and religious outlook, yet he never abandoned his role as an interpreter of Judaism. Like Rosenzweig, with whom he collaborated on a new translation of the Scriptures, he was also a brilliant participant in Jewish-Christian dialogue.[16] Rosenzweig's *Star of Redemption* (1921) and Buber's classic *I and Thou* (1923) are masterly statements of an existential and dialogical understanding of both human relationships and the divine-human encounter. Of the two, it was Buber who for a very wide range of thoughtful Americans—Jewish as well as gentile—contributed to the developing seriousness with which religious commitment was taken.

In the United States it was perhaps Abraham Heschel who addressed these several concerns most effectually. Heschel was born in Warsaw to a distinguished Hasidic family and educated at the University of Berlin on the eve of Hitler's takeover. He worked unflaggingly in Poland, England, and after 1940 in the United States to combine rigorous historical research with a fervent affirmation of traditional Judaism—though always with the dual emphasis on legal observance and inner piety that is the hallmark of Hasidism. Probably no Jewish thinker of his time so nearly warrants comparison with Karl Barth, the great scholar-theologian of Protestant Neo-orthodoxy. Intensely alert to social issues, deeply aware of the need to address the religious predicament of all men (not just Jews), and constantly involved in interfaith discussions, he nevertheless constantly strove to make biblical religion a vital reality and to lead modern Jews toward a serious encounter with their classic tradition.[17]

As in Protestantism and Roman Catholicism, so in Judaism there is a vast chasm between serious religious thinkers and American congregational life. Practicality and social activity predominate at the local level. Yet it would be wrong to let matters rest at that. Later developments would show that the

16. Jewish-Christian dialogue has been an important aspect of modern religious thought ever since the Enlightenment. Hegel's dialectical conceptions were a spur to the enterprise, as was the rise of the history of world religions. A translation of Rosenzweig's profound exchange with Rosenstock-Huessy has recently been published (*Whom Money Cannot Buy* [University, Ala.: University of Alabama Press, 1969]). In recent years Christians have been forced to ask if some of the most fundamental motifs of classic Christian nurture do not conduce to anti-Semitism and ethnocentrism.

17. See Fritz A. Rothschild's systematic anthology of Heschel's huge corpus, with an introduction, *Between God and Man: An Interpretation of Judaism* (New York: Free Press, 1959).

"Jewish Revival" was a significant *religious* phenomenon. Glazer, for example, though accurate in many of his judgments, overlooks those Jews who shared his dissatisfaction with prevailing trends of the mid-fifties:

> The pattern of middle-class respectability becomes the pattern that all Americans wish to follow. . . . The synagogues have become "synagogue centers" . . . Mordecai Kaplan's view of the future of Judaism has triumphed. . . . The Jewish law is now (except in Orthodox congregations) generally neglected, and the rabbi is no longer called upon to act as judge and interpreter. He can keep himself busy running his expanded synagogue and school and going to interfaith meetings.[18]

Again, as in Protestantism and Catholicism, even in the deepest reaches of darkest suburbia there was a countervailing revival—a revival against the revival, as it were—which did get beneath the superficialities of mere religious interest and peace-of-mindism. Even Herman Wouk's popular novel *Marjorie Morningstar* (1955) shows how a middle range of awareness came to many twentieth-century Jews who had lost touch with their heritage. And there were many others whose external religious observance was accompanied by great intellectual and moral seriousness.

Yet the postwar mood and the trend to religious affiliation would change in unexpected ways. For one thing, Jews, like other Americans, would discover that the religious revival had provided very feeble preparation for the social and spiritual tumult of the 1960s. In addition to these violent domestic confrontations, secularization, increased social mobility, and the decline of anti-Semitism tended to erode the Jewish sense of particularity. College students in considerable numbers repudiated the establishment's culture, constituting themselves, as it were, in a new category of "fourth generation" Jews. The rate of interfaith marriages rose so markedly that the question of the "vanishing Jew" became a subject of public debate. Radical secularists compounded the problem with denials of the possibility for theological inquiry "after Auschwitz." The situation of Judaism—as indeed of nearly all traditional forms of organized religion—would become unexpectedly critical.[19]

18. Glazer, *American Judaism,* pp. 116, 124–25.

19. For a penetrating survey of contemporary Judaism, see Jacob Neusner, *American Judaism: Adventure in Modernity* (1972). He stresses how support of the great national organizations is a major mode of Jewish identification and finds that "checkbook Judaism" is everywhere the norm (p. 15). His analysis of the meaning and implications of modern Zionism is a vital element in his conclusion that the "distintegration of the archaic religious and ethnic unity of the 'holy people' [is] the most important Judaic testimony about what it means to be a modern man" (p. 153).

58

THE ANCIENT EASTERN CHURCHES IN AMERICA

The Federal Council of Churches at its organization in 1908 was a Protestant agency, in effect a successor to the Evangelical Alliance. By 1961 its character had been fundamentally transformed: the Greek, Romanian, Russian, Serbian, Syrian, and Ukrainian Orthodox churches, as well as the Armenian church and the Polish National Catholic church had become active members and were asking that their historic views be recognized in the council's pronouncements. Winthrop S. Hudson could rightfully observe that this broadened participation had "effectively deprived the Protestant community of its one surviving institutionalized symbol." [1] On the other hand, this fact also symbolized the emergence of the "ancient Eastern churches" as an important component of American Christianity. The ecumenical participation of the Eastern churches, hesitatingly begun in 1927 at the Lausanne Faith and Order conference, was explicitly recognized as an invaluable enrichment at the 1963 conference in Montreal. At that Faith and Order assembly the Orthodox delegation for the first time involved itself at every level of discussion and shared responsibility for the final reports.[2]

For most Americans, nevertheless, these churches had been—or still are—a closed book. A Greek was a restaurateur, not a bearer of a rich and ancient Christian tradition. A Russian is variously suspected as White or Red. The historic testimony and ways of about one hundred thousand Unitarians or

1. Winthrop S. Hudson, *American Protestantism*, pp. 169–70. In 1950 the Federal Council was reorganized as a consolidated interchurch agency and renamed the National Council. In 1948 the World Council of Churches had been formed in a similar manner.

2. The encyclical *Unto All Churches of Christ Wheresoever They Be* issued by the Holy Synod of the ecumenical patriarch in January 1920 no doubt helped prepare the road to Lausanne.

four hundred thousand Christian Scientists or a handful of surviving Shakers are better known, even in many seminaries, than the faith and practice of America's nearly three million Orthodox.[3] Following the same pattern, most histories of American Christianity devote only three or four pages to the subject.[4] In the future, however, these churches may have an important role to play—not only due to the antiquity and richness of their heritage, but because they did not participate in the tumultuous events that have separated Catholics and Protestants since the Reformation. In a way, the long silence of Orthodoxy increases its ecumenical potential. Most markedly will this be true if the movement for a unified American Orthodox church achieves its end.

The ancient Eastern churches naturally had a long pioneering period in the United States, a time of small and isolated beginnings. The records of the early Virginia Company note that a certain "Martin the Armenian" came out to the colony in 1618–19, but not until 1866 was the first Orthodox parish in America organized, in New Orleans. The real expansion of these churches is a twentieth-century development, the years 1900–14 being a particularly important time of organization and reorganization. Only after World War II, in a manner somewhat similar to the Roman Catholics and Lutherans, have the Orthodox begun to experience the full implications of Americanization. They themselves began to point out the futility and inutility of making the church an agency for the perpetuation of Old World ties, languages, and folk traditions; and their impact on American religious life and the thought of the nation began to be felt. Essential to an understanding of this impact is a brief consideration of the historical background of the Eastern churches.

A GLANCE AT THE EARLY HISTORY

One astute historian has declared the "formal principle" of Eastern Orthodoxy to be "its tenacious adherence to the old," and nearly all of its own theologians also emphasize the unbroken continuity of their church and its undeviating commitment to the first seven ecumenical councils of the "undivided" Church. Elsewhere in Christendom, the Orthodox tend to see only

3. In 1944 the Greek archbishop of New York claimed 5 million Orthodox in the U.S., but this is little more than a totaling of nominally Orthodox ethnic groups. According to the 1936 federal census, there were only 100,000 effective Russian members and 189,000 Greek members. These figures are no doubt too low, but not exceedingly (see n. 19 below).

4. In 1936 a typical work on American religion would allot chapters to six kinds of Protestantism and three kinds of Judaism, plus Unity, Theosophy, and Spiritualism—and include nothing on Eastern Orthodoxy (Charles S. Braden, ed., *The Varieties of American Religion*). Winthrop S. Hudson's *Religion in America* (1965) is an exception to the pattern of neglect.

defection and unauthorized innovation, considering themselves to be the organic continuation of the apostolic Church, or in Bulgakov's phrase, the "elect from among the elect." [5] In terms of developmental logic, moreover, this claim is well supported: the patriarchs of Jerusalem and Antioch do indeed stand in a venerable succession. Yet the anomaly and perhaps the tragedy of this commitment is the fact that by the time John of Damascus (ca. 675–749), the last of the great Eastern Fathers of the Church, had rendered the teachings of the councils into semisystematic form, the Church was no longer undivided.[6] During the fifth and sixth centuries, the so-called Lesser Eastern churches, from Syria, Armenia, and Egypt on to Persia and India had separated themselves, partly for cultural and political reasons, but also out of dissatisfaction with certain doctrinal tendencies of the councils.

By the time the "Seventh Pillar" of Orthodoxy had been raised at the Council of Nicaea (787), not only had the Asiatic and African churches gone their ways or fallen under the sway of Islam; but the Western church under the bishop of Rome had long since developed its characteristic form, shaped and inspirited by Augustinian theology, Benedictine monasticism, and a rigorously unified hierarchy. In the West Greek became an almost unknown tongue. And the separation deepened with the passing centuries as each area endured its own vicissitudes.[7] Limited exchanges of influence would continue, and at the Council of Florence in 1439 a reunion was even temporarily achieved. Yet so distinctive did the Greek and Slavic church tradition become, that in 1846 a Russian theologian could declare that "all Protestants are Crypto-Papists," and that for Western Christians "a passage to Orthodoxy seems like an apostasy" from their past, their science, their creed, and their life.[8] A half-century later Adolf von Harnack, the great German historian of dogma, would exhibit the liberal Protestant view of "Eastern Catholicism":

> There is no sadder spectacle than this transformation of the Christian religion from a worship of God in spirit and in truth into a worship of

5. "Not the whole of the human race belongs to the Church, only the elect. And not all Christians belong, in the fullest sense, to the Church—only Orthodox" (Sergius Bulgakov, *The Orthodox Church,* p. 18).

6. The Seventh Council, to be sure, met long after John's death, in 787; but in approving the veneration of icons, it took a position he had defended. The Seventh Council is peculiarly vital to the Eastern Orthodox churches, who celebrate the final victory for holy images in 843 as "the Triumph of Orthodoxy."

7. Although A.D. 1054 is the traditional date of the Great Schism, political, cultural, and religious differences were already perceptible in the lifetimes of Saint Augustine (354–430) and Saint Benedict (480–543). During the seventh and eighth centuries Islam not only conquered vast regions of the Eastern church, but of the Western church as well—in North Africa and on the Iberian Peninsula.

8. Alexis Khomiakov, quoted in Timothy Ware, *The Orthodox Church,* p. 9.

> God in signs, formulas, and idols. To feel the whole pity of this development, we need not descend to such adherents of this form of Christianity as are religiously and intellectually in a state of complete abandonment, like the Copts and Abyssinians; the Syrians, Greeks, and Russians are, taken as a whole, only a little better. . . . As a whole and in its structure the system of the Oriental Churches is foreign to the Gospel.[9]

Since 1900 prejudice has declined and knowledge increased, but Western noncomprehension of the Eastern churches is still very widespread.

THE CHARACTER OF ORTHODOXY

Aside from their utterly different historical experience since the sixth century at latest, the Orthodox churches are distinguished by a strong propensity for Neoplatonic metaphysics, especially its confidence in reflection and its reliance on human consensus as a pathway to knowledge. Given this intellectualist traditionalism, Christ, the Trinity, and Redemption are defined in very complex philosophical terms.[10] The distinctive world of thought that lives on in the Eastern churches was thus a product of the Hellenistic age that extends from Alexander the Great to Constantine the Great. These five or six centuries were pervaded by an awareness that the old political and religious traditions had crumbled, and hence by a search for new grounds of certainty. Among both Christians and pagans one notes a rise of asceticism, mysticism, and pessimism, a despair of patient inquiry and social reconstruction, a desire for infallible revelation and for salvation *from* the world, a turning to mystery cults and religious ideas from Egypt, Anatolia, Syria, and Babylon. For many people religion replaced politics as a primary concern.[11]

Into this Hellenistic world came the Christian gospel, preached and accepted by men who in varying degrees were part of that world of thought, and who proceeded to formulate the implications of Christianity in the philosophical terms of the day, and by means of those same terms to distinguish Christian teaching from pagan speculation. In the East doctrinal expression became increasingly Platonic and mystical in spirit. The West, during the ensuing centuries, maintained the letter of the early councils (with some very

9. Adolf von Harnack, *What Is Christianity?* (New York: G. P. Putnam's Sons, 1901), pp. 204–05, 210; see also pp. 187–210.

10. The great controversies on the Trinity and the Person of Christ were essentially Eastern and with two exceptions "all the great writers and teachers of that wonderful age of theological dialectics were in the Greek Church" (Walter F. Adeney, *The Greek and Eastern Churches* [New York: Charles Scribner's Sons, 1908], pp. 1–2).

11. See Gilbert Murray, *Five Stages of Greek Religion* (1925; New York: Doubleday & Co., Anchor Books, 1955). I have paraphrased some passages of chap. 4.

controversial exceptions); but unlike the Eastern churches, it lost touch with the religious spirit and nonjuridical attitudes that had informed them.[12]

As in many other churches, worship provides a vital key to the nature and spirit of Orthodoxy. Any sympathetic observer of the Divine Liturgy will sense (and "sense" is the word) the otherworldly glory which pervades the place and ceremony, whether in a great cathedral or in a remodeled building bought from some now departed Protestant congregation. To the Orthodox the sacraments are sacred mysteries, not logical riddles, and this, too, will be borne out by all that is done, seen, and heard. The Eucharist is the constituting reality of the church; and when it is celebrated locally, the whole church in its fullness is present—as, indeed, the icons attest. Especially striking to most Westerners are these icons that bedeck the churches, especially on the *iconostasis* (icon wall) separating the chancel and the nave—and the kisses bestowed on them by each entering believer. The icons, in fact, do suggest the essence of Orthodoxy, for these stylized images are, in the words of Ernst Benz, "a kind of window between the earthly and the celestial worlds" through which each beholds the other.[13] In the same way, the church itself is an icon of heaven, while man ("in the image of God") carries the icon of God within himself. Christ is the New Adam—in and through whom the original image of God is restored.

The Westerner (especially if Protestant) may be surprised, or even repelled, by the casual way in which believers participate in these glories (the men ambling out for a smoke in the middle of the service, for example); yet another fundamental aspect of Orthodox religion is its blending with the common life as a kind of "natural religion" of the people. Nationality and religion became inseparable aspects of existence. If the civil government was destroyed or hostile, the church through its clergy spoke for the people. Au-

12. The sharpest controversy between the Eastern and Western churches had to do with the primacy, infallibility, and ecclesiastical authority of the bishop of Rome, and derivatively other questions of ecclesiastical polity. In Eastern Orthodoxy the ecumenical patriarch of Constantinople is *primus inter pares,* though he shares a position of special honor with the three other ancient patriarchates (Alexandria, Antioch, and Jerusalem). After the Fall of Constantinople in 1453, the patriarch of Moscow assumed a very high but never precisely defined honor. There are also twelve autocephalous churches, at least four autonomous churches, and several other provinces that in various ways depend on one or more of the above jurisdictions. All but those in the last category elect and consecrate their own bishops or patriarchs and adjudicate all ecclesiastical conflicts. Remaining in communion with all of the autocephalous churches is the chief criterion of a church's "orthodoxy" or legitimacy, though many great churches (e.g. the Russian and the Greek) for longer or shorter periods have lacked such acceptance. By comparison, the Church of Rome is far more unified and far more given to precise juridical regulation of authority and practice. Among other controversies with Rome, the most celebrated are those pertaining to the procession of the Holy Spirit from the Father (East) or from the Father and the Son (West) and to when and how the miracle of the Eucharist takes place.

13. Ernst Benz, *The Eastern Orthodox Church: Its Thought and Life*, pp. 5–19.

tochthonous religion of this sort could outlast centuries of persecution and foreign rule. On the other hand, a church with these strengths was very poorly adapted to the realities of mass immigration and the situation of ethnic minorities in the United States. Confusion and ecclesiastical inattention were often the rule. In the mid-twentieth century, therefore, institutional division remained a dominant characteristic of Orthodoxy's vast constituency in America. Over a score of Orthodox and other Eastern churches share this American experience, but only a few of the more representative ones can be considered here.

Russian Orthodoxy

In 1448, just five years before Constantinople fell to the Turks, a Russian council of bishops elected its own metropolitan. In 1472 Czar Ivan the Great married Sophia, niece of the last Byzantine emperor, and proclaiming Moscow to be the Third Rome, he declared Russia to be the protector of Orthodox Christendom—a grand consummation of the mission to the Slavs begun by Saints Cyril and Methodius in 863. In 1741 under Peter the Great the landing of Captain Vitus Bering on Kayak Island symbolized another vast missionary and imperial achievement—a reach beyond even the distant limits of Siberia. The first permanent settlement in Alaska followed in 1784, and a decade later the Holy Synod dispatched ten monks to establish a mission there. So successful was their evangelism that an Alaskan diocese was created in 1799 and Joasaph Bolotov, the mission's head, was consecrated as bishop—only to drown on his return trip. Finally in 1840 Ivan Venyaminov (1797–1879), "the greatest Russian missionary of the nineteenth century," became Alaska's first resident bishop. In 1848 he built at Sitka the Cathedral of Saint Michael which still stands.[14] In 1868, a year after the United States acquired Alaska, Venyaminov (an archbishop since 1850) became metropolitan of Moscow and primate of Russia. In this capacity he strengthened the Alaskan diocese by separating it from its Siberian province (1870) and by moving the see to San Francisco (1872). At this time the diocese numbered twelve thousand communicants—making it one of the most thriving Indian missions to be established north of Mexico.

The next major change in Russian church affairs came in 1891, when the membership of this Russian church in the United States was suddenly enlarged by an event that also required the extension of the diocese to include the entire country. This large accession of members consisted of Ruthenian

14. Serge Bolshakov, *The Foreign Missions of the Russian Orthodox Church*, p. 86; Chauncey Emhardt et al., *The Eastern Church in the Western World*, p. 52.

"Uniates" who had emigrated from the Carpathian area of central Europe.[15] In America they objected to the loss of special concessions granted in Europe (e.g. the right of priests to marry), and Father Alexis Toth of Minneapolis led a secession movement for a reunion with the Russian church which ultimately involved about 120 parishes, many of them in mining and steel areas of Pennsylvania and Ohio. By 1909 half of the membership of the Russian church consisted of this and other similar transfers. Some of these churches gained diocesan status as a separate Carpatho-Russian church in 1938. In response to still other developments, Archbishop Tikhon Belavin transferred his see from San Francisco to New York in 1905. Up to this point the Russian church provided what general Orthodox oversight there was—not only for the Russians, but also for other Orthodox groups that were emigrating in large numbers from Russia, Central Europe, and the Balkans. By 1916 this constituency was approaching a half-million, with Ukrainians the largest element everywhere but in the Far West.

After World War I the religious leadership of the Third Rome was shattered, primarily by dissension resulting from the Communist "reorganization" of the church. In 1918 the Romanians in America organized separately; they were soon followed by the Serbs, and in 1922 by the Greeks. In 1927 both the Ukrainians and the Syrians withdrew from Russian jurisdiction, but they were quickly overtaken by various kinds of factionalism. The Syrian Orthodox attained unity in 1933. The Ukrainians, on the other hand, remained divided among four different jurisdictions in addition to the Carpatho-Russian diocese. The Russian Orthodox church as well was rent by bitter controversies after the "exarchate" of the patriarch of Moscow gained control of the New York cathedral in 1925. The vast majority of Russian Orthodox in America resisted this jurisdiction, however, and since 1924 had been organized in a manner that made them more nearly an autonomous church than any other Orthodox communion in America. In 1970 the patriarch of Moscow healed this schism and declared the reunited church to be autocephalous. By this time, Saint Vladimir's Seminary in New York had become an important intellectual force not only among Russians, but in the world ecumenical movement. John Meyendorff and Alexander Schmemann,

15. Ruthenians (Latin for Russians) are in effect Ukrainians or Russians who were living in areas governed by Poland or the Austro-Hungarian Empire. "Uniate" constituencies were those which at various times (notably by the Council of Brest in 1596) had been brought under the authority of the pope, but with permission to use Eastern liturgical rites and to continue certain other practices. Similar constituencies do or did exist from Lithuania through the Middle East to India. They often lack strong popular support and hence constitute a Roman thorn in the Orthodox side. On the other hand, their existence conduced to a measure of flexibility in the Roman church.

and before them George Florovsky, have become important twentieth-century interpreters of the Orthodox tradition.[16]

Greek Orthodoxy

The largest single Orthodox constituency in the United States is the Greek, though the history of the Greek Orthodox churches in the United States is relatively brief. The great migrations from Greece, the Mediterranean islands, and Asia Minor began in the 1890s, reached a peak between 1900 and 1910, and continued unabated down to the restriction laws of the 1920s. By 1940 perhaps five hundred thousand had come. The first parish in New York was organized in 1891, and many others followed in other parts of the country. The church grew only very slowly, its overall expansion hindered by the overwhelming predominance of male immigrants (95 percent between 1899 and 1910) who often returned to Greece, by the violent polarization of royalists versus Venizelists both in Greece and in America, and by the absence of any fully recognized ecclesiastical authority in the United States until 1930. In that year the ecumenical patriarch in Constantinople arranged to have Metropolitan Athenagoras of Corfu undertake the difficult task of restoring order to a long embattled constituency. In this the new archbishop eminently succeeded; the price of order, however, was a drastic centralization of power in the new archbishop of North and South America. Other bishops, now without dioceses, served as his assistants. In 1949, after Athenagoras had been flown to Istanbul in President Truman's airplane and enthroned as ecumenical patriarch, Archbishop Michael was appointed. Under Archbishop Michael (1950–58) a still larger measure of order and advancement was established in the archdiocese, which increasingly became the recognized spokesman for the Greek minority in the United States. Under Archbishop Iakovos, who was appointed in 1959, the basic organization of the church was not altered, but far more aggressive efforts to meet the needs of an essentially English-speaking constituency were inaugurated.[17] Early efforts to found seminaries had fal-

16. See Alexander A. Bogolepov, *Toward an American Orthodox Church: The Establishment of an Autocephalous Orthodox Church*, p. 100. The Albanian Orthodox Church in America is also technically a Mother Church, but its constituency of about twelve thousand is too small to assume full antocephalous status. In her *Guide to Orthodox America*, Anastasia Bespuda lists 336 parishes in the Russian Orthodox church, 32 in the Patriarchal Exarchate, and 89 in the Russian Orthodox Church Outside of Russia, an international jurisdiction organized in Europe by exiles who hope for a return of the old czarist order. The reported membership in 1970 for these three churches was, respectively, 700,000, 160,000, and 60,000.

17. These adjustments to the American scene were much needed; with only 2.3 percent of the third generation Greeks being able to speak Greek, Americanization was obviously proceeding rapidly. This situation is due in no small part to the unusually high ratio of men to women among Greek immigrants (193 to 100, as against, for example, 115 to 100 among Russian immigrants), (see Constantine

tered, but in 1937 another was founded in Pomfret, Connecticut. Under more favorable conditions it was moved to Brookline, Massachusetts, in 1947. In 1968 the church had gained a liberal arts college; and by 1970 the Holy Cross School of Theology had graduated 321, founded an important theological journal, and become a flourishing center of Orthodox study.

AMERICAN ORTHODOXY IN RETROSPECT

In the history of Eastern Orthodoxy in the United States four features stand out. First and most obvious is its multiethnical character. Its constituency, in the language of its own canon law, has almost a dozen "Mother Churches" in Europe; but of these some have almost expired, others are suspected of having lost either their freedom or their orthodoxy, and almost all are entirely incapable of offering material support to their American counterparts. Given this practical motherlessness, the second feature becomes explicable; namely, that serious conflicts have ensued within almost every ethnic group, and in many cases separate jurisdictions have been the result. The Greeks were long riven by royalist-democratic issues in their homeland. Among the Ukrainians there were five separate groups, among the Russians (until 1970) three, and even the little Albanian group was divided in two.

The third feature has to do with the fact that Orthodox religion, due to its close identification with the land, culture, language, folk customs, and political structures of a specific country, does not easily follow the immigrant to a religiously neutral republic. Even greater difficulties stemmed from the hurly-burly of a rapidly changing industrialized and pluralistic social order. Religion and ethnicity could not long remain coterminous in the face of social mobility, geographical scattering, public education in the English language, and an inherited reliance on a hierarchy immobilized in the Old World and without autonomy in the New. As a result, these ethnic minorities were often "Orthodox" in the same way that countless unaffiliated Americans identify themselves as "Protestant." Due to the lack of a unified hierarchy and of strong missionary methods, the vast Orthodox constituency in America—estimated in purely ethnic terms as exceeding five million—has been waning steadily ever since the Great Migration ceased.[18]

Volaitis, "The Orthodox Church in the United States as Viewed from the Social Sciences," *Saint Vladimir's Seminary Quarterly* 5 [1961]: 74, 77). For other statistics and detailed accounts of Greek-American ecclesiastical turmoil, see Theodore Saloutos, *The Greeks in America*.

18. Federal census figures tend to be about a fourth as large as official claims. According to L. M. Gray's analysis in *Commonweal*, 13 April 1932, three fourths of baptized Orthodox children are inactive by age sixteen. Among those of the Greek Orthodox church who were baptized and actively church-related at age

Important for the future of the Orthodox churches in America was a fourth feature: their noticeably increased attention to the problems of an Americanized constituency during the quarter-century after World War II. Among the Russians this was especially marked, in part because this church had been in vigorous, even brilliant dialogue with Western thinkers since early in the nineteenth century, and in part because it most nearly approached ecclesiastical autonomy. In the largest group of all, the Greek, on the other hand, such concern was less evident. Very early in the century Archbishop Tikhon (later to become patriarch of Moscow) gained authorization for an English liturgy for his jurisdiction, which then included members from seven or eight language groups. Such liturgies and English language preaching have since become widespread in the Russian, Syrian, and Albanian churches, as has lay participation in parish affairs or at even higher organizational levels. In 1927 Metropolitan Platon of the Russian church drew up a plan for a unified autocephalous American Orthodox Church, complete with a proposal that the Syrian Archbishop Aftimios be president of the synod of bishops. But this plan also came to naught. Whether the grant of autocephalous status to the Russian church in 1970 would conduce to future unification was at best uncertain. In the meantime the Standing Conference of Canonical Orthodox Bishops, founded in 1960 with Archbishop Iakovos of the Greek church presiding, filled many important functions. Through eight commissions and regular meetings it began to deal with contemporary problems in a concerted way. In 1971 the Greek church began work on an English liturgy despite strenuous opposition.

THE SEPARATE EASTERN CHURCHES

"Is it not tragic," asks Professor Schmemann, "that one of the main reasons for the rejection of Orthodoxy by almost the whole non-Greek East was its hatred for the empire? . . . This was the price the Church paid for the inner dichotomy [of the union of church and state] under Constantine." [19] In less than a century after the condemnation of Monophysitism at the Council of Constantinople (553), the Syrians and Copts would greet their Mohammedan conquerors almost as saviors. The Lutheran historian Rudolf Sohm asks and answers a similar question regarding the pope's leadership of the secession of Western Christendom: "Was there any power in the Church

fifteen, half were in churches other than the Greek Orthodox (see Donald Atwater, *The Christian Churches of the East*, 2 vols. [Milwaukee: Bruce Publishing Co., 1948], 2:148–55).

19. Alexander Schmemann, *The Historical Road of Eastern Orthodoxy*, p. 157.

ready and able to withstand the Empire, and to defend the self-government of the Church through a supreme spiritual head against the ruler of the world? That was the great place in the world's history which was filled by the Bishop of Rome." [20] Nobody need be told what issued from the Roman bishop's rebellion from the empire's temporal authority; but the story of the Eastern churches has been lost in the shadows of imperial, Islamic, and Orthodox history. It is perhaps fortunate, therefore, that America possesses reminders of the great spiritual empires that once stretched from the Mediterranean south to Nubia and Abyssinia and east to Persia, India, and China. Even these vast ecclesiastical realms were not united in their opposition to Constantinople, however.

"No decree of a council has ever destroyed a powerful heresy," writes Adeney, who then points out how the Council of Ephesus (431) gave Nestorianism its opportunities for eastward expansion. Theological centers developed in Byzantine Syria at Edessa and in Persian territory at Nisibis where the disfavor of the empire was a boon. Perhaps as a concession to Zoroastrianism, the Nestorians moderated their Hellenistic asceticism and allowed priests to marry. Yet they remained true to the basic witness of the Patriarch Nestorius, and even truer to Theodore of Mopsuestia, who was, in fact, chief theologian of the christological tendency which Nestorianism emphasizes—the humanity of Jesus, the importance of his earthly life, and his brotherly concern for mankind. They also perpetuate Nestorius's objections to the veneration of Mary as the Mother of God, forbid icons in their churches, and strongly object to the doctrine of purgatory.

In 498 the head of the Nestorian church took the title "Patriarch of the East," and with headquarters at Seleucia and Ctesiphon began sending missionaries to the Far East over the caravan routes. At its height this church was said to have had 80 million members—which seems improbable. Yet heavy blows were to fall; and ultimately Islam, Ghengis Khan, and Tamerlane would reduce the Nestorian church to a few scattered remnants. In 1551 one of these remnants east of the Tigris appealed to Rome for the consecration of a dissident bishop. Julius III obliged, and subsequently these so-called Chaldeans became a kind of Uniate church. In 1843 the Kurds massacred four thousand Nestorians, and in 1915 a small group that had taken refuge in Anatolia was driven into neighboring countries by the Turks. It was due to these woes in the Middle East that a few Nestorians began emigrating to the United States in 1911. In 1940 the 119th patriarch of the Church of the East and Assyrians (Mar Eshai Shimun XXIII) took residence in the United

20. Rudolf Sohm, *Outlines of Church History*, pp. 60, 65.

States among the 3,000 or so of his coreligionists in this country. All over the world perhaps as many as 250,000 other Nestorian faithful have in some way recognized his authority.

The Nestorian offshoot dating from the Council of Ephesus formulated the doctrine of the Person of Christ so succinctly that new fears arose: in correcting Nestorius, had Saint Cyril of Alexandria led the council too far in the opposite direction? At the so-called Robber Council, also held at Ephesus (449), these fears were substantiated, for it approved the extreme position of Eutyches that the person of Christ was of one nature only, that the body of Christ was by union with the divine made different from that of other men. This "monophysite" doctrine was so widely unacceptable that the emperor convoked another council at Chalcedon (451), whose formulations unambiguously stated the doctrine of two natures, the divine and human, in one "person," which has ever since been accepted both in the Orthodox and the Roman churches as well as in the major Reformation churches.

In Syria and Egypt, however, Chalcedon met massive opposition. This led to the formation of separate national churches, which launched very successful missionary ventures of their own. The Monophysite cause was least disputed in Egypt, and under the patriarch of Alexandria it vigorously extended itself southward to Nubia and Abyssinia. Bishop Jacob Al Bardi, a former monk, became the great apostle of Syrian Monophysitism, to whose credit also falls the great Syriac version of the Bible. Ultimately this church, like that of the Nestorians, reached out through Mesopotamia and Persia to India, where the church of Malabar (Kerala) still perpetuates the Jacobite tradition. They suffered from the same great invasions as the Nestorians, however, and by 1900 their numbers (aside from Malabar) were reduced to 150,000, gathered chiefly in Mesopotamia but with a scattering in and around Damascus and Jerusalem. In the 1890s the intensity of Turkish persecution forced many of them into flight, and some came to America.

Still a third area of Monophysite strength was the so-called Gregorian Church of the semiautonomous Kingdom of Armenia, which never really accepted the Council of Chalcedon and in 491 finally anathematized it. This stand was formalized in its national council of 535, a date deemed so important that the Armenian calendar was reckoned from it. In addition to the common woes of Middle Eastern Christians, the Armenians finally had visited upon them the terrible Turkish massacres of 1895, when a hundred thousand or more were slain, most of them Gregorians or modern Protestant converts. The rest of the nation scattered; but in the United States the Armenian Apostolic Church became the largest and most prosperous of the Monophysite churches. Organized in 1899, in 1970 it consisted of about

275,000 members and nearly ninety congregations divided into two jurisdictions, one under the catholicos in Soviet Armenia, the other with its head in Lebanon.

Among the many who since the 1890s have escaped the violence and economic dislocations of the Middle East by emigrating to the United States, there were still other thousands who belonged to Monophysite churches. The Syrian Jacobites in America, probably not exceeding ten thousand in number, are organized under the jurisdiction of the patriarch of Syria in three separate churches. In 1970, when the Ethiopian Orthodox Church dedicated its headquarters in New York, it claimed ten thousand members. On a few feast days even a group of scattered members of the Malabar Church of India celebrate the liturgy together in New York City.

In the context of American religious history as a whole, these several separated Eastern churches obviously do not loom large. But they do pose the question of group existence and demonstrate the tenacity of certain forms of doctrinal commitment. They are thus living witnesses to the substantial nature of such controversies as the often ridiculed "battle over an iota" which agitated the Council of Nicaea in A.D. 325.[21] By the same token, all of these Eastern churches, including the Orthodox, exhibit the process by which the ancient Graeco-Roman religious legacy was transmitted to European Christendom. In this sense, even the most battle-scarred of these churches are reminders of theological issues which are intrinsic to a definition of Christianity.

21. The reference is to terms current in the Arian controversy: *homoöusion* and *homoiusion,* which characterized the Son of God respectively as being "of one substance" with the Father, or as "like" or "similar to" the Father.

59

ROMAN CATHOLICISM IN THE TWENTIETH CENTURY

Before Pope Paul VI had taken his stand athwart the tide of Roman Catholic reform, even before the Second Vatican Council and the revolutionary pontificate of John XXIII, and well before the United States elected a Roman Catholic president, the Jesuit scholar-theologian Walter J. Ong observed that "American Catholicism is in a state of intellectual and spiritual crisis." [1] He was pointing to the profoundly transformed social situation which no longer allowed Roman Catholicism to regard itself as an "immigrant faith." In the age of affluence presided over by Dwight D. Eisenhower, a vague, homogenizing civil religion had supplanted the old forms of interfaith strife. The Protestant Establishment was passing into history and a new age of pluralism was at hand. Though there were still vast untapped potentialities for bigotry and intolerance beneath the surface of the American mind, Roman Catholics had to abandon the defensive posture that constant immigration and wave after wave of nativism had provoked. Standing on the threshold of a new period of participation and responsibility, Catholics were justifiably pondering the circumstances that had brought about this change in their situation.

THE "NEW" IMMIGRATION OF CATHOLICS

During the later nineteenth century the main ethnic tensions in the church had arisen between the English-speaking Irish majority and a large, highly self-conscious German minority with great strength in the Midwest. After 1880, however, this situation began to be altered by a steady stream of immigration from eastern and southern Europe. By 1920 there were about 3.3

1. Walter J. Ong, *Frontiers in American Catholicism: Essays on Ideology and Culture,* p. 2.

million Americans of Italian parentage and about 3 million Polish, as well as many Hungarians, Portuguese, Croatians, Bohemians, and Ruthenians. During the intervening half-century the church had faced difficult problems of expansion as these poor, unskilled, and often illiterate people formed separate ethnic enclaves, usually in the cities. In their basic religious attitudes the new immigrants varied widely, but the total phenomenon had an enormous impact on the situation of Catholicism in America. Most obvious were the flamboyant celebrations of a new galaxy of saints' days. More basic were vast institutional problems involving schools, seminaries, hospitals, and convents, as well as agencies for immigrant aid. Less tangible, but equally important, was the way in which immigration prolonged the church's role as a protector of new Americans and thereby prevented it from assuming the constructive role in public affairs which "Americanist" leaders like Archbishop Ireland had long advocated.

For the Italians who came to America the church had always been an accepted fact of life amid the grinding poverty of the cities and villages of Sicily and southern Italy whence most of them came. Since the quest for national unity and social reform had led to open conflict with the papacy, the church was often associated with oppression, and relatively benign forms of anticlericalism were fairly widespread. Although in the Italian quarters of America the parish church did become a major agency of cultural identity and continuity, in neither the old nor the new country was the attachment marked by strong popular fervor; and even a proud historian concedes "some truth" to the view "that the Italian immigrant has not been generous toward his Church." [2] The presence of roughly five million Italian-American Catholics in 1960 indicates that apostasy was relatively rare. But in America, where economic opportunities beckoned, there was a relatively small movement of men and women into the priesthood and religious orders, and little avidity for the financial sacrifices that parochial schools required. Very few Italians have entered the hierarchy or become prominent church leaders in other ways. The great preponderance of men—over a million of whom returned to Italy between 1900 and 1916—also contributed to this circumstance. In urban politics the Italians and the Irish have frequently been at odds, but the kind of religious intensity that led German Catholics into ecclesiastical conflict has rarely been manifested, even in New York where nearly a quarter of the nation's Italians lived.[3]

2. Juvenal Marchsia, "The Italian Catholic Immigrant," in *Roman Catholicism and the American Way of Life*, ed. Thomas T. McAvoy, p. 175.

3. In 1930, 1,700,355 out of a total of 4,651,195 Italian-Americans lived in New York, a number that then exceeded the population of Rome. About 3.5 million Italians immigrated between 1900 and 1925.

Arriving in only slightly fewer numbers than the Italians were the Polish, but the fervency of their devotion to the Catholic church contrasted sharply. Repeatedly invaded, dismembered, or partitioned out of existence, and constantly menaced by Protestant Germany or Orthodox Russia, Poland has linked its national identity with Roman Catholicism for centuries, and never more devotedly than during the century of Russian repression preceding World War I. In America the parish church and the parochial school became a surrogate for the unfettered national existence that had been denied them since the Congress of Vienna in 1815. For first generation immigrants the Polish language "became the cornerstone that would maintain solidarity. They firmly believed that when the language was lost—all was lost." [4] In this spirit, whether in small farming communities or in the cities where most of them gathered in closely knit neighborhoods, they made great personal sacrifices for the institutions that would maintain their cultural heritage. During the nineteenth century they had been too few in number to affect the course of the Americanism controversy, but as their number passed the five million mark—as it did by 1950—over eight hundred identifiably Polish parishes constituted perhaps the largest self-conscious ethnic group in the church. Only after World War II, despite another considerable influx of émigrés, did urban change and the ineluctable processes of acculturation gradually disperse the great Polish communities that had arisen in Chicago, Buffalo, Detroit, Milwaukee, Cleveland, and many other cities.

The latest major Roman Catholic constituency to achieve large numerical importance and a degree of self-consciousness was in fact the oldest element in the American population—older than Virginia's first families, older even than the Spanish conquerors through whom the Spanish language and Catholicism became enduring elements of their culture. In 1970 the Spanish-speaking population of the United States numbered about nine million—though transients, illegal entrants, those with non-Spanish names, or Puerto Ricans who were erroneously counted as blacks may add up to another million. The largest part of this minority (about 60 percent) is constituted by Mexican Americans, most of whom have migrated during the twentieth century, and who live for the most part in Texas, the Southwest, and California. The other main component stems from Puerto Rico (about 20 percent), and to a much lesser extent from Cuba and other Spanish-American countries. They are concentrated heavily in the New York metropolitan region and in other eastern cities, notably Miami with its many Cuban émigrés.

About 95 percent of this Spanish-speaking population is at least nominally

4. Aloysius J. Wycislo, "The Polish Catholic Immigrant," in McAvoy, *Roman Catholicism and the American Way of Life*, p. 183. In 1897–1904 the Polish National Catholic Church, led by Father Joseph Hodur, gave form to such dissent.

Roman Catholic. (In a decade or two Puerto Ricans may become the largest Catholic group in New York City, since the Irish and Italians are gradually moving out of the city.) Yet because Spanish-speaking peoples, regardless of origin, tend to come from the least churched classes and areas of their respective countries, share a common tendency to anticlericalism, and have usually been extremely poor, their participation in Catholic church life has been very slight. Almost never have they on their own initiative formed and supported parish churches as so many other immigrant communities did, and the number of men entering the priesthood in the United States has been very small. Due to various ethnic tensions, moreover, existing parish churches, even when favorably situated, have been unable to extend an adequate ministry. The most effective work has been accomplished by various monastic orders and by special diocesan projects; but even these efforts, whether in Los Angeles or New York, have often been ambivalent in their cultural aims and hesitant to mobilize activistic programs. The institutions of Catholicism, therefore, have not played the crucial roles in the acculturation of these minorities that they have for other immigrant groups.

Protestant evangelism, on the other hand, has found a surprisingly strong response among both Mexicans and Puerto Ricans. As in Latin America generally, the Pentecostalists have been especially successful; and in these fervently evangelical contexts Spanish Americans have produced their own clergy and given relatively strong financial support to their churches. These churches, though rarely concerned with social issues per se, have through their nurture and moral discipline conduced to a pronounced pattern of upward mobility among their members. Yet the basic ecclesiastical problems of this minority are social and economic in origin; and only in the 1960s, when black militancy provided an important model, and in the 1970s, when a protracted strike by grape pickers in California became a national catalyst, did Puerto Rican and Mexican Americans begin to develop a kind of solidarity and militancy that could awaken the nation and its churches to their plight as grossly underprivileged minorities.

The Maturation of the Catholic Minority

The unsensational yet revolutionary process that underlay the new situation of most Roman Catholic Americans was social mobility, a function of modern society which had always been especially pronounced in the United States. For individual Catholics it had always gone on—though at a slower rate due to the repressive attitudes and actions of the Protestant majority. But for Catholic church members as a group it had been greatly retarded by a constant incoming tide of immigration which actually reached its peak in the early twentieth century. For this reason, World War I and the immigration restriction legislation of the 1920s had especially drastic consequences, the first of which was a virtual stabilization of the relative size of the Protestant and Catholic communities. From 1916 to 1955 the membership of 128 Protestant bodies increased by 94.2 percent, the Roman Catholic church by 92.4 percent. The following table reveals the steady but relatively similar increases in the percentage of the total population in the two groups: [5]

	Protestant	*Roman Catholic*
1926	27.0	16.0
1940	28.7	16.1
1950	33.8	18.9
1955	35.5	20.3
1958	35.5	20.8

The second consequence was that after 1930 the accultarative process had a more enduring effect; due to the sudden cessation of immigration, the Catholic community as a whole was transformed. The disruptions of the American social order wrought by the Depression and the New Deal, then by World War II, and finally by America's great postwar "industrial revolution" greatly accelerated the normalization of the country's vast Catholic minority. It could no longer be categorized as an "immigrant faith." Will Herberg described the situation in 1955:

> Increasingly the great mass of Americans understand themselves and their place in society in terms of the religious community with which they are identified. . . . The only kind of separateness or diversity that America recognizes as permanent, and yet also as involving no status of inferiority, is the diversity or separateness of religious community. . . .
>
> All this has far-reaching consequences for the place of religion in American life. . . . For being a Protestant, a Catholic, or a Jew is understood as the specific way, and increasingly perhaps the only way, of being an American and locating oneself in American society. . . . Not to be a Catholic, a Protestant, or a Jew today (1955) is for increasing numbers of American people not to be anything, not to have a *name;* and we are all, as Riesman points out, "afraid of chaotic situations in which [we] do not know [our] own names, [our] brand names." [6]

5. Will Herberg, *Protestant, Catholic, Jew,* p. 160.

6. Ibid., pp. 36–40. Herberg quotes David Riesman, *Individualism Reconsidered* (Glencoe, Illinois: Free Press, 1954), p. 178. Herberg does not deal with Negroes as a distinct community, except in passing. He also ignores the many humanists whom Duncan Howlett identified as a group in *The Fourth American Faith.*

It is this maturation of the American Roman Catholic minority that America was experiencing in the 1950s. Essential to our understanding of how it could result in the "crisis" to which Father Ong alludes, however, is an account of the major phases of the Catholic experience during these twentieth-century decades.

THE LEGACY OF THE AMERICANISM CONTROVERSY

When the century began, the church was faced with the warning issued by Pope Leo XIII in 1899 in his encyclical on "Americanism." *Testem Benevolentiae* was an ambiguous document, but coming at a time when it could hardly be dissociated from a series of stern papal moves against "modernism," the encyclical had a dampening effect on creative thought and churchmanship in America. It tended to heighten the constant temptation of Americans to concentrate on practical matters. The Progressive Era went its way, therefore, without creating many important positive responses to the social and theoretical challenges of the day.

Catholics were extremely active and remarkably effective in attaining positions of power and influence in the Democratic party, especially in the cities. Political activities, in fact, were woven into the web of religious charitable institutions that sheltered people from an alien world. As Daniel Moynihan has written, Catholic politicians "never thought of politics as an instrument of social change—their kind of politics involved the processes of a society that was not changing." [7] Politics were conceived in essentially conservative terms—as a device for taking the risk and uncertainty out of urban life. In labor relations a similar situation obtained. Since Roman Catholics were the largest element among the country's genuinely distressed workers, they were a mainstay of unionism. The hierarchy had tended to view unionization efforts with favor; and during the 1880s Cardinal Gibbons stirred up considerable nativist wrath by defending Henry George, the Knights of Labor, and various nonmasonic secret societies when the Vatican threatened condemnation. In the realm of social and economic theory, however, the hierarchy did little more than indicate a general approbation of labor unions so long as they were not socialistic, hostile to religion, or given to violence. Priests who actively identified themselves with social reform and labor radicalism were very rare. Father Thomas J. Hagerty did work with socialist unionists, and in 1905 he was one of the architects of the IWW, but he had left the priesthood in 1902. Father Thomas McGrady of Kentucky also de-

7. Nathan Glazer and Daniel P. Moynihan, *Beyond the Melting Pot,* p. 229. See also David J. O'Brien, *American Catholics and Social Reform: The New Deal Years,* pp. 30–33.

fended socialist policies, but in 1903 when his bishop asked for a retraction, he left the church.

First in the mind of most Catholic leaders were the problems of reaching the immigrant and strengthening an independent Catholic educational system. Opposed to socialism and an environmental analysis of poverty, the church concentrated on the rescue and rehabilitation of individuals, and by 1910 it was operating nearly twelve hundred charitable institutions. "Though lip service was paid to Leo XIII's *Rerum Novarum,* leading Catholics for nearly two decades [after its publication in 1891] failed to emphasize its meaning: they expounded it as a 'bulwark' of the *status quo* and not as a charter of social justice." [8]

In matters of theology and philosophy, the church was in general even less adventurous. Seminaries and institutions of higher learning were providing only the minimum essentials for the priesthood and laity despite the great social and intellectual transformations which were in progress. Handbooks and compendia sufficed. The "Sulpician tradition" of the nineteenth century perpetuated itself uncreatively.[9] The Thomistic revival promoted by Pope Leo XIII made slow advances. The vast problems of history, culture, science, and the social order—realms in which nineteenth-century thinking had left a revolutionary legacy—were left not only unresolved but unapproached. Even among the leaders of Americanism few went beyond a call for accommodating the church to American ways, and those who did were warned against dangerous innovations in Pope Leo's encyclical. Hecker and Brownson won few disciples; and Father John A. Zahm of Notre Dame University, whose *Evolution and Dogma* (1896) attempted a rapprochment with Darwinism, was silenced. Though founded in a moment of educational idealism, the Catholic University of America lacked the resources to become the great center of learning of which its founders had dreamed.

WORLD WAR I AND THE TWENTIES

The later years of World War I saw the beginnings of at least a partial resurgence, particularly in the realm of social thought. In this sense the war's effect on Roman Catholic thought was quite the reverse of its effect on Prot-

8. Aaron I. Abell, "Preparing for Social Action: 1880–1920," in *The American Apostolate,* ed. Leo R. Ward, pp. 18–19.

9. "Sulpician tradition" is simply a term to designate the tradition in which the continuing influence of the French Sulpicians was strong. Without denying the sacrificial contributions of the many Sulpicians who came to the United States and who served with distinction as professors, priests, and prelates, one may suggest that rarely during the nineteenth century were their intellectual efforts distinguished or imaginative.

estantism, for only then did the Catholic bishops of the country begin to exercise direct responsibility for thought and action in the social field. In August 1917 a General Conference of Catholics representing sixty-eight dioceses and twenty-seven national Catholic organizations created the National Catholic War Council with a large representative executive committee. Administrative responsibility was assigned to four bishops, and John J. Burke, former editor of the *Catholic World* and founder of the Chaplain's Aid Association, was appointed chief director of operations. After the Armistice, this group continued to function, its attention now turned to problems of citizenship, education, rehabilitation, and postwar social problems.

In February, 1919, the Administrative Committee of Bishops published an almost epoch-making document: "Social Reconstruction: A General Review of the Problems and a Survey of Remedies." It was written largely by Father John A. Ryan, who had been widely known as a progressive since 1906 when he published his treatise *A Living Wage,* justifiably remembered as a major contribution to the minimum wage law movement. In the superheated years of the postwar Red Scare and the revived Ku Klux Klan, the "Bishops' Program," as it came to be known, was far more often attacked than defended, even by Catholics. The program was, nevertheless, the first expression of Catholic social progressivism to be given at least semiofficial status in America. This was a triumph for Ryan, who a few years earlier, while he was a seminary professor in Saint Paul, Minnesota, had complained that he could not name five bishops in the country who had spoken out for social reform. Progressives were soon to be disappointed, however, for "not a single remedial or transforming proposal in the Bishops' Program was adopted [in the United States] during the 1920s." [10]

Yet movement in this direction did not cease. In 1919 the War Council was reconstituted as the National Catholic Welfare Council with a similar organization, with Burke as executive director and with Ryan as director of the Social Action Department. Though certain bishops strenuously objected to its encroachment on their authority, and still others to the liberal hue of its pronouncements, the National Catholic Welfare Conference (its name was changed to avoid misunderstanding) rapidly became the most effective agency in the country for acquainting Catholics with the social doctrines of Leo XIII. After 1920 it also provided the largest support given to the rural life movement led by Father (later Bishop) Edwin V. O'Hara.[11] In these and

10. Aaron I. Abell, *American Catholicism and Social Action: A Search for Social Justice, 1865–1950,* p. 204.

11. O'Hara became director of the Rural Life Bureau of the NCWC in 1920 and the first executive secretary of the National Catholic Rural Life Conference in 1923. During the first half of 1922 the council was in suspended ani-

many other efforts the National Council of Catholic Men and a parallel organization for women, both coordinated by the NCWC, became channels of communication to the Catholic laity and a valuable means of gaining support for various projects and programs. The scope of the NCWC's concern became well-nigh total, ranging from the publication of scholarly monographs to Father Burke's personal negotiations with the revolutionary government of Mexico in 1928.[12] In all realms its social consciousness was evident; and despite the fact that it was organized as a voluntary and unofficial agency with whose advocacy bishops frequently disagreed, it performed an important service in shaping Catholic thought and bringing it to bear on American problems.

The idealistic fervor frequently found in the NCWC or in the rural life movement, however, was not contagious. The 1920s was by no means a period of vital and adventurous advance for the Roman Catholic church. Its parishes, like the local congregations of other faiths, were invaded by the complacency of the times. Even more unfortunate was the defensive stance forced upon the church by the organized bigotry of the Ku Klux Klan and and the anti-Catholic hostility promoted by the temperance crusade and the campaign for restricting immigration. Drawing all of these impulses to a focus was the bitterly fought national election of 1928, when the Democratic nomination of Governor Alfred E. Smith of New York dramatized the "reli-

---

mation because Pope Benedict XV had withdrawn his approval. Pius XI reversed this decision. In 1923, to avoid confusion as to the organization's authority, its name was changed to the National Catholic Welfare Conference.

12. During the years of Spanish rule the church had become a powerful force in Mexican life. It owned much of the land, controlled the educational system, and enjoyed many legal immunities. After independence was gained in 1822, a series of Mexican governments sought to divest the church of much of its power and privilege; and with the outbreak of revolution in 1910 an especially bitter struggle began. The most determined persecution was carried out by Plutarco Elías Calles (1924–28), who even promoted the founding of a schismatic church. Catholics, in turn, organized the Liga de Defensa de la Libertad Religiosa, which engaged in boycotts, protests, and propaganda. When Calles moved to crush all resistance, the so-called Christero Rebellion erupted. Father John J. Burke held private discussions with President Calles at Veracruz in the spring of 1928, and a truce of sorts was signed in June of the following year; but hostilities resumed in December 1931. So persistent was Mexican anticlericalism that in 1937 Pius XI promoted the establishment of the Seminario Nacional Pontificio in Montezuma, New Mexico.

Many American Catholics were dismayed by the widespread apathy of their countrymen towards religious persecution in Mexico, and they were particularly alienated by President Roosevelt's refusal to become involved, even though he was given further provocation in 1938 by Mexico's nationalization of the petroleum industry. During the Roosevelt years, when Mexican secularization of education was at its peak, Josephus Daniels, the American ambassador to Mexico (1933–41), became the focus of controversy. Although a devout Methodist who in no way sympathized with Mexico's religious persecution, he provoked the wrath of many Catholics with certain of his statements on education. Daniels did, however, work quietly and effectively for greater religious freedom in Mexico (see E. David Cronon, *Josephus Daniels in Mexico* [Madison, Wis.: University of Wisconsin Press, 1960]).

gious issue" in politics as no event heretofore had done. Smith at this stage of his career proclaimed a humane, undogmatic liberalism that had grown out of his experience of New York's Lower East Side. He also stated in no uncertain terms how he could, as a Roman Catholic, take the oath and carry out the functions of the presidency as he had already done as governor of New York. Despite bitter and often fiercely bigoted opposition, he drew a large popular vote (40.7 percent), gained more votes than the Democratic party had ever before received, altered the trend set in the Democratic debacle of 1924, and laid important groundwork for the kind of majorities which Franklin Delano Roosevelt would marshal in 1932 and 1936. In this sense Smith played an important role in American Catholic history. He also revealed an important fact about the social liberalism of Ryan, Burke, and the Bishops' Program: that it was not merely the facade of an inevitably reactionary constituency.[13]

The immigration legislation of the 1920s made the decade the end of an epoch for Catholics. Nativism, Al Smith's defeat, and American indifference to anticlericalism in Mexico helped to maintain old Catholic attitudes during the decade. But the 1930s would see a turning of the tide—greater acceptance in public life, more concern in the church for national problems, and the beginning of a long process of adjustment to a situation in which the newly arrived immigrant no longer determined the church's basic stance.

DEPRESSION AND THE NEW DEAL

The New Deal was, in one sense, an enactment of the Bishops' Program; and Catholics contributed much to the electoral majorities of Roosevelt and the congressmen who made the social welfare state an actuality. On the other hand, the fact that Catholics came to constitute about two-thirds of the American union membership accentuated the labor movement's basic conservatism and weakened the advance of socialist ideas. The sympathy shown for laboring people by both the higher and lower clergy served meanwhile to maintain the goodwill, confidence, and Christian fidelity of the laboring classes far more effectively than has the Roman Catholic church on the Continent, the Anglican church in England, or mainstream Protestantism in the United States. In America the church has continued to draw its clergy and its prelates from the ranks of the working class. In the 1940s Archbishop Cushing of Boston, in an address to the CIO, could report that not a single bishop or archbishop of the American hierarchy was the son of a college graduate.

13. Gerhard Lenski's studies in Detroit bear out the view that Catholics tend to support social welfare legislation more than do white Protestants (*The Religious Factor*, pp. 135–42).

The Crash and the Great Depression were, of course, the efficient causes of increased popular support for social reform during the 1930s. For Roman Catholics as for other Americans the travail of unemployment and economic collapse stimulated a resurgence of both thought and action. A powerful additional stimulus was provided in 1931 by *Quadragesimo Anno,* the great encyclical on social reconstruction with which Pope Pius XI commemorated the fortieth anniversary of Pope Leo's *Rerum Novarum.* In that very year, in fact, the hierarchy itself petitioned the government to assist the unemployed and to reform American economic life along lines suggested in the Bishops' Report of 1919. One of its first fruits in America was the publication in 1935 by the Social Action Department of the NCWC of a programmatic pamphlet, *Organized Social Justice—An Economic Program for the United States Applying Pius XI's Great Encyclical on Social Life.* Prepared under Father Burke's direction and probably written in large part by Father Ryan, it was signed by 131 other prominent Catholic social thinkers. Ryan called it "the most fundamental, the most comprehensive, and the most progressive publication that has come from a Catholic body since the appearance of the Bishops' Program." [14] Touched off by the Supreme Court's invalidation of the National Industrial Recovery Act, it declared for a constitutional amendment to effect those same purposes. Its objective was a "new economic order," wherein the chaos and violence of the existing system would yield to integration under government auspices along industrial and occupational lines. Lamenting "the inadequate organization of some of the most important social classes," it called for fuller unionization of labor, the expansion of farmer and consumer cooperatives, and some creative way of organizing the urban middle classes, probably on vocational lines. Over and above these structures, the federal government would function somewhat in the manner suggested by the NRA.

Some Catholic theorists, such as Father Aloysius J. Muench (later bishop of Fargo) and Father Francis J. Haas of Catholic University (later bishop of Grand Rapids), argued that fuller unionization, probably under government auspices, must precede further organization. Haas, indeed, blamed the Depression itself on the fact that only 10 percent of American labor was unionized. Generally speaking, social thought based on the encyclicals tended toward the idea of the corporate state.[15] But the influence of "Encyclical

14. Abell, *American Catholicism and Social Action,* p. 251.

15. In corporatistic theory the state takes an active role to assure social justice and harmony by organizing and regulating all the major elements of society, including both laborers and employers. Mussolini's reorganization of the Italian social order was frequently seen as exemplary. "It is manifestly in the pontifical teachings," a textbook would declare, "that a Catholic statesman like Salazar, Prime Minister of Portugal, has found the inspiration that made it possible for him to lift up his country from an abyss of confusion and misery,

Catholics" was often modified by conservative business interests, pragmatic city politicians, humanitarian reformers, and old-line unionists. By far the most widely known of all the "Encyclical Catholics" was Father Charles E. Coughlin, the "radio priest" of Royal Oak, Michigan, who has already been discussed in connection with the politics of the 1930s. After his break with FDR, however, Coughlin began getting his signals from strange corners of the political universe and ceased to be a Catholic thinker in any significant sense. On election day in 1936 it became evident that his vast radio audience was not a political following.

THE NEW CATHOLICISM

That the situation of the Catholic in American life was changing was indicated by the passing of Coughlin as the nation's great "radio priest" and the ascent of Monsignor Fulton J. Sheen to that role. Sheen had made his mark as a defender of the Thomistic viewpoint in 1925, but not until the 1940s, as the reigning celebrity of "The Catholic Hour," did he become widely known as a preacher and as an extremely evocative apologist for a total Catholic world view. Claire Booth Luce and Henry Ford II were only the most prominent of the many converts who responded to his boldly expressive yet basically conservative social and theological views. After the war, when Peale and Graham were the popular Protestant voices, Sheen continued to demonstrate that Catholicism had become a live option for many religiously inclined Americans.[16]

Within the church itself there were also stirrings that anticipated not only a time when Catholicism would occupy an undisputed place as one of America's "three great faiths," but when Christians generally would have to redefine their relationships to the secular order. One of the most appealing leaders of this new breed was Dorothy Day (b. 1899). A former Socialist who had become a Catholic, Day set out in 1932 as a journalist and social worker to refute the Communist charge that Catholicism was indifferent to

---

and lead it to order and well-being" (Daniel A. O'Connor, *Catholic Social Doctrine* [Westminster, Md.: Newman Press, 1956], p. 81).

16. Fulton John Sheen was born in El Paso, Illinois, in 1895. He was educated in Catholic institutions, and after his ordination in 1919 he completed his education at the Catholic University of America and at Louvain (Ph.D., 1923). Sheen served as a member of the faculty of the Catholic University of America (1926–50), as national director of the Society for Propagation of Faith (1950–67), and as bishop of the Rochester Diocese (1967–69). (He had been consecrated titular Bishop of Caesariana and auxiliary bishop of New York in 1951.) Bishop Sheen achieved his greatest fame as preacher on NBC's popular "Catholic Hour" (1930–52) and on the radio and television program, "Life Is Worth Living" (1951–57). His numerous publications, which have ranged from *God and Intelligence* (1925) to *Guide to Contentment* (1966), have been read by millions of people of all religious faiths.

the social aspirations of labor. Her monthly paper, the *Catholic Worker,* first issued in 1933 (appropriately on May Day), soon achieved a phenomenal circulation of over a hundred thousand. She persistently gave papal social doctrines their most liberal, even radical interpretation. Intellectually and spiritually her movement owed much to the personalism of Emmanuel Mounier in France, with its emphasis on individual charity and direct participation, and to the liturgical thought of Virgil Michel, with its accent on the priesthood of all Christians.

Most directly influential was her teacher and collaborator, Peter Maurin (b. 1877), a French expatriate who lived for a social order that would truly recognize the image of God in every person. Convinced of the intrinsic inhumanity of industrial society and accepting the proposals of the English distributists (G. K. Chesterton, Hilaire Belloc, and Eric Gill), he sought in every possible way to mitigate the depersonalizing effects of the factory system. The lay apostolate which the Catholic Worker movement inspired was thus marked by intense sacramental piety, self-abnegation, and prayer. It involved itself directly in the plight of the poor and the unemployed, opening houses of hospitality in thirty cities, founding in 1936 a farming commune, participating in strikes, counteracting the Communists directly with a Christian philosophy of labor, and opposing the reactionary activities of the "Christian Front." [17] The broad program for social reconstruction which Dorothy Day and Peter Maurin inspired would still be a strong but subdued Catholic force in the 1960s, when nuclear testing, race relations, capital punishment, urban problems, and militarism had become national preoccupations.

Closely related to the Catholic Worker group in origin and spirit, though far less hostile to the industrial order itself, was the Association of Catholic Trade Unionists, formed in 1937 with the direct aims of supporting the CIO and the cause of responsible industrial unionism and helping Catholics to function effectively in the labor movement. As this work was augmented by dozens of labor schools which drew upon a wide array of talent for giving systematic instruction, Roman Catholics gained new prominence in the nonpolitical leadership of the labor movement.

More broadly influential than either of these labor-oriented movements in giving direction and intellectual force to "liberal Catholicism" in America was the magazine *Commonweal,* which was founded in 1924 by Michael Williams (1877–1950), a layman who guided its policy until 1938, when

17. The Christian Front was an alliance of ultraconservative and anti-Semitic elements that had been prominent in Father Coughlin's movement until the Union party's debacle of 1936.

Edward Skillen and two associates took over its direction. The long-term effect of their broad and vigorously liberal advocacy was to make "Commonweal Catholicism" a meaningful social position.

Like the Catholic Worker movement by which it was much influenced, Commonweal Catholicism found the American economic and social order in many ways unchristian. But Commonweal Catholics rejected the distributists' solution, for they believed that the industrial order could gradually be made compatible with a personalist Christian democracy. Asserting that Christian industrialism had not failed, but had never been tried, Commonweal Catholics found in the papal encyclicals a program which would supplant competition with cooperation by bringing workers and owners into a mutual community of interest. Laborers were to form unions, share in profits, and participate in the management of industries, which were to be decentralized. This approach, it was contended, would escape the twin evils of egoistic individualism and bureaucratic socialism. The attention of Commonweal Catholics, however, was frequently diverted from the full program to the immediate first steps required by it. The focus was on the struggle of indigent groups seeking to unionize rather than on plans to widen the worker's voice in management. The result was often an advocacy not immediately distinguishable from that of non-Catholic liberals, yet *Commonweal*'s success in keeping the newly suburbanized church at least somewhat aware of the inadequacies of the nation's social system was no small achievement.

The revitalization of Roman Catholic thought was not restricted to social theory, however. The post-Depression years also witnessed important changes in other areas of concern. Most apparent and perhaps earliest was a long overdue response to the admonition given by Pope Leo XIII in his *Aeterni Patris* (1897) that Saint Thomas Aquinas be taken more seriously as a theological and philosophical norm. Probably no thinkers did more to extend Thomistic influence in America than two Frenchmen, Etienne Gilson (b. 1884), a great scholar of medieval thought, and Jacques Maritain (b. 1882), a prolific convert whose works began to be widely published in America during the 1930s. Both men spent much time lecturing and teaching in the United States and Canada. Fulton J. Sheen also contributed to this movement. Having felt the rejuvenating influence of Neo-Thomism at Louvain, Sheen published in 1925 his *God and Intelligence in Modern Philosophy: A Critical Study in the Light of the Philosophy of Saint Thomas,* with an introduction by G. K. Chesterton, the English convert, who in his own journalistic manner also did much to advance the Thomist cause. Aided by many translations from European theologians and by increasingly mature scholarship at home, Neo-Thomism became a self-conscious and critical tradition, showing far greater sophistication and depth than the scholasticism which had dominated the manuals and handbooks. It also became a philosophic mainstay of Anglo-Catholics; and secular thinkers, too, found it attractive, most notably President Robert M. Hutchins of the University of Chicago, and Mortimer Adler. The so-called Humanist movement in literary criticism led by Professor Irving Babbitt of Harvard also appealed to Saint Thomas and Aristotle as bulwarks against romantic irrationalism.

During and after World War II still other influences, some of which had been gestating for decades and even centuries, began to be felt, among them an accentuation of the realistic and existential dimensions of Thomism such as Maritain had advanced in a moderate form. For others this shift showed itself in a renewed interest in Saint Augustine, or Pascal, or Sören Kierkegaard, or contemporary French thinkers such as Gabriel Marcel and Emmanuel Mounier. Inevitably, too, the profound critique of traditional philosophy carried on by logical positivists, scientific empiricists, and the English analysts introduced a certain caution in the use of language and speculation, especially in those realms where modern physics and historical studies weakened or invalidated the presuppositions of medieval Aristotelianism.

Far more important theologically than this process of philosophical tempering were three less strictly philosophical impulses that began increasingly to be felt: a renewed concern for the Church as the Body of Christ, a revival of biblical studies, and an awakened historical consciousness. The third of these was half-implicit in the second, and the first two were much implicated in what is known, rather ambiguously, as the liturgical movement; but they may advantageously be discussed separately.

The Rediscovery of the Church

To speak of the Church's "rediscovering" itself is, to be sure, only a manner of speaking; what the term designates is a new awareness of the corporate nature of the *ekklesia* (assembly) of God and its status as an organic entity, the Body of Christ, in which men are, in the Pauline phrase, "members one of another." In America, where atomistic or individualistic conceptions of the Church were so widespread (in both Protestantism and in the Roman church), this new emphasis was almost radical. Its most significant modern roots were probably in the thought of the great nineteenth-century German theologian, J. A. Moehler (1796–1838); they were taken up effectively by Karl Adam and given enormous practical significance by the liturgical movement. Especially after the issuance of Pius XII's momentous encyclical on the subject (*Mystici Corporis,* 1943) the movement functioned as a quiet but effective leaven in the practical and intellectual life of the church. One of its most pronounced effects was its promotion of serious concern for the place of the laity. In 1959 Professor Leo R. Ward could say that this new attitude toward the layman, though "hardly yet out of the baby stage," was, except for the church's emergence from its "ghetto-period," the most important new direction to be observed in contemporary American Catholicism.[18] Ramifying in almost every direction, the "lay apostolate" came increasingly to be felt in social action, retreat centers, interracial relations, and local parishes. Mitigating "spectator attitudes," it was giving the laity a deepened sense of participation in the life and work of the church.

Biblical Renewal

The real or supposed hesitancy of the Roman church to encourage Bible reading by the laity was increasingly put to rest in the twentieth century. The encyclical *Spiritus Paraclitus* of Benedict XV (1920) was one factor, the inevitable effects of the revision of church thinking another; but perhaps most influential was the advocacy and action of men such as Father Pius Parsch, leader of the *Bibelbewegung* in Austria (who made his personal discovery of the life of Jesus and the world of the Bible while a chaplain in World War I). American bishops such as Edwin V. O'Hara of Kansas City, and influential parish priests such as Monsignor Hellriegel of Saint Louis made forthright biblical preaching an important part of their ministry. That this "Bible movement" was paralleled by a revised attitude toward scholarly study of the Scriptures promised even larger consequences. Dating in one sense to an encyclical of Leo XIII in 1893, but gathering new momentum after Pius XII's epoch-making *Divino Afflante Spiritu* of 1943, this scholarly "revolution" rapidly brought Roman Catholic scholars into the midst of the biblical renaissance so prominent in Protestant thought during this period. Not only was a whole range of critical questions opened to research, but biblical theology took its place as a formative factor in Catholic thinking, often giving it a strong "evangelical" spirit and serving simultaneously as an important corrective to scholastic modes of theological expression.

Historical Consciousness

The great nineteenth-century resurgence of interest in history had left Roman Catholics relatively untouched, especially in America. "Modernism" was, to be sure, such a movement, but it had been condemned; and

18. Leo Ward, *Catholic Life, U.S.A.: Contemporary Lay Movements* (Saint Louis: Herder & Herder, 1959), p. 7.

the papal admonition on "Americanism" had made Roman Catholics in the United States doubly wary. After World War II, however, a distinct shift in attitude became evident. It resulted not only in far more serious historical research, but in a heightened awareness of the way in which the past inheres as a vital reality in the present. The renewed appreciation for Cardinal Newman's approach to "the development of Christian doctrine," and the reconsideration of "tradition" which began to emerge from ecumenical discussions were other manifestations. Perhaps most provocative of all was the comprehensive evolutionary theology of Father Pierre Teilhard de Chardin (1881–1955), the great Jesuit paleontologist whose works received widespread attention after his death.

Liturgical Renewal

Infusing the renewed interest in both the laity and the Bible and partaking also of the new historical concern was the many-sided liturgical movement, which began to put its mark on parish life and worship during the 1950s. The origins of this movement are traditionally seen in the efforts of the French Benedictine Abbot of Solesmes, Dom Prosper Guéranger (1805–75), to reappropriate the Church's full liturgical heritage. On the eve of World War I, Abbot Ildefons Herwegen of the German Benedictine Abbey of Maria Laach began the labors which were to make this institution a world center of the movement. Soon after the war the first of Romano Guardini's many works began to appear in Germany. The Augustinian Father Parsch carried on the work in Austria while still others advanced it in Belgium and France.

Since Benedictines were by far the most prominent in this work, it was natural that Saint John's Abbey in Minnesota should become the center of the movement in America. It was there that Father Virgil Michel, after studies in Europe, founded the pioneer organ of the liturgical apostolate in the English-speaking world, *Orate Fratres* (later renamed *Worship*). The Liturgical Press at Saint John's has also provided a steady flow of literature on the subject. Without doubt, however, the most powerful impetus to the renewal of worship stemmed from Pope Pius XII's encyclical *Mediator Dei* (1947), in which the implications of the Church as the Mystical Body of Christ were expounded in liturgical terms.

The liturgical apostolate was an effort to make the total worship (*leitourgia,* service) of the Christian Church a living reality in the believer. This involved an awakening of concern for the world and fellow men, for the corporate reality of the Church, for the biblical sources of faith, for a deeper and more relevant theology, and above all, for the involvement of the laity in a lively and meaningful way. Most centrally, the renewal of liturgical concern was directed toward the Great Prayer of the Church, the Mass, the Holy Eucharist. The need arose not only for intensified study in the seminaries, but for a deepening of the laity's understanding through the publication of English translations of the missal, for the encouragement of congregational participation, for the reconceiving of liturgical ceremony and church architecture to make this possible, for the wider use of the vernacular and preaching in worship, and for the renewal of private devotional life. Another aim was to increase among the faithful the actual reception of Holy Communion rather than mere regularity in attending Mass. Some indication of the movement's impact is provided by the fact that whereas in the 1920s English missals for the laity were being sold only a few thousands per year, during the 1950s the number in use rose to many millions. The real fulfillment of the movement's aims came in the 1960s after the Second Vatican Council made sweeping liturgical reforms. Yet even before that these several trends began to open up channels of conversation between long-separated churches and faiths.

THE NEW AGE OF THE CHURCH

This chapter began by describing a dispirited church: the new immigration was overwhelming its institutional structures, "Americanism" was deflated and liberal thinking intimidated. Yet almost all that followed has dealt with new signs of promise: progressive organizational reform, creative responses to the Depression, and a series of awakenings and renewals led by a generation of impressive thinkers, scholars, and reformers of church life. It is ironic, therefore, that during the later 1950s the church should have been disturbed by the problem of intellectualism: not the excess of it (though voices in high places did complain of this), but the dearth. Through widely disseminated public statements it became known that former president John J. Cavanaugh of Notre Dame, the eminent historian of American Catholicism, John Tracy Ellis, and the Jesuit theologian Gustave Weigel were alarmed by the fact that Catholics were lagging far behind the national average in science, scholarship, and other forms of intellectual leadership. Then in 1958 appeared *The Catholic Dilemma,* by lay sociologist Thomas O'Dea, who had been asked to study the situation. His book not only confirmed the facts, but suggested that the causes lay in long established Catholic patterns of formalism, authoritarianism, clericalism, moralism, and defensiveness. The appearance of his book in the very year in which Pope John XXIII began his memorable pontificate thus illustrates the coincidence of reformist thinking on both sides of the Atlantic.

In 1959 the recently elected pope proclaimed Elizabeth Seton, the American-born convert from the Episcopal church, a "venerable servant of God." He also took occasion to say of the American Catholic church that its "time of development" was past and its "full maturity" at hand. And in the following year Monsignor Ellis made those words the text for a very important essay. The "heroic age" of the American church, he said,

> is now a matter of history, and we stand on the threshold of another act in the ceaselessly unfolding drama of the Church's life in this land. . . . Today's world and today's America have a right to expect from the third most numerous body of Catholics in the universal Church . . . a positive contribution to a remedy for the ills that beset them in the atomic age.

Pointing out how unprepared they had been for the social upheavals of the twentieth century, primarily because "Catholic energies had been concentrated on the frantic race to keep ahead of the immigrant flood," Ellis called Catholics to a "realistic and constructive" approach to their responsibilities "within a pluralistic society." [19]

The circumstances that account for the transition which Ellis dramatizes are diverse. Most tangible were the end of the immigrant "flood" and the movement of Catholics into more favorable places in American social and economic life. A corollary to this change was the decline of suspicion and hostility among non-Catholics. Yet there were also the important inner changes that this chapter has touched upon, the several simultaneously developing movements of discovery and renewal which were made more profound by the adversities of war, economic distress, and tumultuous social change. One may even speak of the adversities of affluence. All of these developments were preparing the ground for "Pope John's Revolution." This fact could be only dimly apprehended in 1958 when the elderly John XXIII began his short but illustrious pontificate. Yet as the new pope's profoundly gracious personality began to be manifested, all of these reform movements were enlivened. Just about four centuries after the Council of Trent, the Counter-Reformation epoch in Western Christendom virtually came to an end. Within the church the influence of John's two great encyclicals, *Mater et Magistra* (1961) and *Pacem in Terris* (1963), would combine with the many-sided work of the Second Vatican Council (1962–65) which he convoked. Together they would release responses to the modern world which had been stifled for a century. In the United States hardly a village or city neighborhood failed to experience a transformation of interfaith relation-

19. John Tracy Ellis, "American Catholicism in 1960: An Historical Perspective," *American Benedictine Review* 11 (March–June 1960): 1–20.

ships. The church itself, meanwhile, was shaken by forces of change more powerful and fundamental than those which had been advanced by the Protestant Reformation.

The remaining chapters of this book all deal with the diverse ways in which the moral and religious life of Americans has been profoundly shaken during the twentieth century, and in a more drastic way since the 1960s. And Roman Catholicism, with the largest single religious constituency in the nation, has been deeply involved in this onrush of modernity. In fact, it has been more severely shaken than any simply because its doctrines, social attitudes, and institutional structures had been progressively rigidified after the Reformation, again after the French Revolution, and still again by the Vatican Council of 1869. With a large independent school system, and with a clergy and teaching force that was for the most part educated all the way to the doctorate within that system, it had separated itself from many general problems. The impact of the Second Vatican Council could not possibly have been gradual and mild, even though it did release much energy and enthusiasm. One may even wonder if many of the bishops at the Council understood the full scope of the transformation they were initiating.

In 1969 when lay journalist John O'Connor reported on his tour of the new movements and the new modes of action and worship that flourished all across the country, he entitled his report *The People versus Rome: Radical Split in the American Church.*[20] He was not exaggerating, for conflict was intense and consternation widespread. Priests and religious were complaining of oppression and demanding their rights—even their right to marry. The laity called for a voice in church affairs, and women, in and out of orders, were asking to be freed from a caste system. Married couples complained about regulations on birth control and abortion imposed by a celibate clergy. Eminent moral theologians, meanwhile, continued to stress the claims of conscience despite the firm language of the encyclical *Humanae Vitae* (Of Human Life) issued by Pope Paul VI, in 1968. This last-mentioned subject of contention was especially serious in that it was linked to the world's population explosion and hence to ecological issues. Some observers

20. "Rome is under siege again," wrote O'Connor. "Today it is Rome as center of an ecclesiastical establishment that is being besieged. . . . And the assailants are neither Goths, Huns, nor Yanks, but Roman Catholics themselves, priests and laymen, conditioned for too long to a velvet-gloved Renaissance terror, but now determined that the church of their childhood, the church as it is now understood, will in their lifetime be radically renewed. . . . For one camp the church is a movement to fully humanize man as a brother of Jesus in history and the Christ of faith. For the other the church is an institutionalized sanctuary where one can feel alone with God" (*The People versus Rome: Radical Split in the American Church,* pp. ix, xi).

even rank the encyclical's significance with that which excommunicated Martin Luther. Thomas O'Dea in *The Catholic Crisis* made a carefully measured understatement:

> The reception of the encyclical of Pope Paul VI on birth control testifies to the breakdown of two long-standing pillars of popular Roman Catholicism: mistaking fear of sex for spirituality, and mistaking subservience to authority figures for membership in the *laos theou* [people of God].[21]

These controversies became facts of everyday life during the years after 1965, though, of course, not only for Catholics. Less susceptible to wide public discussion but equally revolutionary were corresponding movements in theology and philosophy. The full significance of these difficulties, however, became inseparable from other larger changes, moral, social, and political, that were slowly being felt in the nation as a whole.

21. Thomas O'Dea, *The Catholic Crisis,* p. vii. For a profound and thorough history of Catholicism and birth control, see John T. Noonan, Jr., *Contraception: A History of Its Treatment by the Catholic Theologians and Canonists.*

60

HARMONIAL RELIGION SINCE THE LATER NINETEENTH CENTURY

"If we tire of saints," wrote Emerson in his profoundly confessional essay on Emanuel Swedenborg, "Shakespeare is our city of refuge. Yet the instincts presently teach, that the problem of essence must take precedence of all the others." He goes on to quote from a Persian poet: "Go boldly forth, and feast on being's banquet." And with these words he is well prepared to discuss the great Swedish mystic as a Representative Man, the seer whose insights "take him out of comparison with any other modern writer, and entitle him to a place, vacant for some ages, among the lawgivers of mankind." Emerson also names the great predecessors in this mystic succession: Plato, Plotinus, Porphyry, Boehme, Fox, Guion, and others. This list of heroes, to be sure, does not identify a narrow party, but it calls attention to a tradition that enjoyed a powerful revival in the nineteenth century, one with which he emphatically associated himself. And it merits clarification as a major force in modern religion.

Harmonial religion encompasses those forms of piety and belief in which spiritual composure, physical health, and even economic well-being are understood to flow from a person's rapport with the cosmos. Human beatitude and immortality are believed to depend to a great degree on one's being "in tune with the infinite." Specific instances of such religion frequently have very unusual features: charismatic founders, complicated institutional structures, secret doctrines, or elaborate rites and rituals. Despite their distinctive characteristics, however, these religious movements possess a kind of harmonial kinship among themselves. Their fundamental claims involve a persistent reliance on allegedly rational argument, empirical demonstration, and (when applicable) a knowledge of the "secret" meanings of authoritative scriptures.[1] Even those of very recent origin show similarities with the syncretistic religions that were challenging Judaism and Christianity two millennia ago, and many claim an even more ancient lineage.

Despite the problem of definitions and boundary lines, this chapter deals with certain major modes through which this tradition has found expression in America. This is emphatically not done, however, as a concession to a few odd people "who also believed." Harmonial religion as here conceived is a vast and highly diffuse religious impulse that cuts across all the normal lines of religious division. It often shapes the inner meaning of the church life to which people formally commit themselves. As earlier chapters have indicated, some of its motifs probably inform the religious life of most Americans. During the 1960s, moreover, one could note a steady growth in the strength of this general impulse, while those closely related but more esoteric forms of religion discussed in the next chapter seemed to thrive even more vigorously.

THE SCIENCE OF HEALTH

Phineas Parkhurst Quimby (1802–66) was a blacksmith's son born in Lebanon, New Hampshire, who later established himself in Belfast, Maine, as a clockmaker. Though successful in this trade, he began in the early 1830s to be impressed by the psychic dimensions of disease, attended some of New England's earliest demonstrations of "animal magnetism," and later became a traveling mesmerist himself, using an hypnotic subject to make diagnoses and prescriptions.[2] His success in healing led him to abandon mesmerism and to search for the "one principle" that would explain such cures. He finally concluded that disease was an error of the mind. After 1859 Quimby lived in Portland, Maine, treating the sick with great success and further developing his theories. His mature thought emphasized that man was a spiritual being, that the wisdom common to all men is God in man, and that

1. Modern forms of pantheism, for example, generally employ a rationalistic apologetic, as does mysticism in its main tradition. Occultist movements point to empirical evidence such as communications with the dead or fulfilled prognostications. When scriptural support is desired, these movements tend to find allegorical and other secret meanings that "transcend" the literal import of given passages.

2. Animal magnetism, mesmerism, hypnotism, and somnambulism had, under various names, figured in the history of religion, magic, and occultism long before Mesmer and Puységur began to control and explain the phenomenon in the later eighteenth century. Charles Poyen had become convinced of its value in 1832 while studying medicine in Paris; and after coming to New England in early 1836, he soon became a leading practitioner and defender of the new "science." In 1837 he published in Boston his *Progress of Animal Magnetism in New England*. The resultant furor naturally stimulated interest in faith healing. (Mary Baker Eddy, for example, regarded animal magnetism as a rival.) In 1899 Sigmund Freud would also gain valuable therapeutic insights from hypnotic work being done in Paris.

the soul, thus, stands in an immediate relation to the divine mind. He was interested in the Bible, used the terms "Christian science" and "science of health," and said his healings were similar to those of Jesus.[3] Yet Quimby would be all but forgotten had he not healed a very remarkable woman in 1862.

Christian Science is one of at least five large and easily differentiated religious movements that bear the stamp "made in America." (Mormonism, Seventh-Day Adventism, Jehovah's Witnesses, and Pentecostalism are the others.) Statistically it is the smallest of these, yet it is the institutionalized part of a huge popular movement involving millions of people who in largely unorganized ways resolve their personal problems through almost the same form of harmonial religion. Because Mary Baker Eddy was for many years a religious seeker of this sort, it is probably more important to trace the troubled course of her long life than the relatively uneventful history of the church she founded.

Mary Morse Baker (Eddy) (1821–1910) was born on a farm in Bow, New Hampshire.[4] She grew up in a relatively pleasant and normal household, but spinal and nervous ailments made her unable to attend school regularly. Yet her education was not neglected; and by her twelfth year she was writing verse, as she continued to do off and on throughout her life, and pondering matters of life, death, and immortality. Everything we know of her early years makes them an understandable prelude to an adult life of ceaseless search for health, religious certainty, and communion with God on the one hand, and for attention and fame on the other.

In 1836 the family moved to a farm in the more populous town of Sanbornton Bridge, where she became a member of the Congregational church and in 1843 married George Washington Glover, an old friend and neighbor. He died a year later, forcing her back to a frustrating nine years in Sanbornton Bridge as an impoverished and dependent widow. Her nervousness, chronic ailments, and signs of infantilism returned in acute form, especially after the birth of a son in September. Morphine certainly and possibly mesmerism were also resorted to without more than temporary avail. In 1853 she ended her widowhood to begin a miserable twenty years as the wife of Dr. Daniel Patterson, an itinerant dentist. For the next decade her health deteriorated further as they moved from place to place. She departed for Portland as an invalid in October 1862, and after being treated by Quimby, she almost immediately became vigorous enough to climb the 182 steps of

3. Horatio W. Dresser, *History of the New Thought Movement* (New York: Thomas Y. Crowell, 1919), p. 35.

4. This account of Mrs. Eddy and Christian Science is based in large part on my article, "Mary Baker Eddy," in Edward T. James, ed., *Notable American Women*, 3 vols. (Cambridge, Mass.: Harvard University Press, 1971).

the city hall tower. Thereafter she studied with her healer, praising him in print and expounding his theories in public lectures. But in 1866, while living in Lynn, Massachusetts, she received the crushing news of Quimby's death. Hard on this tragedy came the famous incident from which she herself, many years later, would date the birth of Christian Science. She slipped on the ice and hurt her back—but "on the third day," after reading the words of Matthew 9:2, she arose from her bed, healed.

Perhaps in the next few months it came to her that she must carry on in Quimby's place. In any event, at the age of forty-five, she became a woman with a vocation as teacher and healer. The decade 1866–75 was a time of homeless wandering, contention, estrangement, poverty, and intermittent exultation, lived out in a religious and cultic subculture now almost unrecoverable. In 1870 she returned to Lynn and formed a partnership with one Richard Kennedy, whom she had won to her views two years before. "Dr. Kennedy" began practice as a healer while Mrs. Patterson conducted her school.

Although this partnership soon collapsed, Mrs. Patterson seems to have gained from it a clarified sense of mission. She now began to see herself and her theories within the larger vision of a Christian Science church. In 1875, therefore, she bought an unpretentious house in Lynn, which became the "Christian Scientists' Home," and on 6 June she held the first public Christian Science service. In the fall she brought out the first edition of *Science and Health.* A Christian Science Association was formed in 1876, and in 1879 the Church of Christ (Scientist) was formally chartered. In 1881 she obtained a charter for the Massachusetts Metaphysical College. In the same year, following a disruption in her following which climaxed a series of defections and lawsuits, a faithful remnant ordained her as pastor, and a few weeks later, at the age of sixty, she moved her church to Boston. Asa Gilbert Eddy, whom she had married in 1877, helped her in these new ventures until his death in 1882.

Her college soon opened its doors in a house on Columbus Avenue; and by 1889 she would have received perhaps $100,000 in tuition for teaching the lower and higher elements of her science to at least six hundred students. The chief clue to her success was her capacity for transforming run-of-the mill students, the great majority of them women, into dedicated followers who would go out across the nation as practitioners of Christian Science, organizing societies where they could. In 1886, when the National Christian Scientist Association was founded, the church was a nationally significant phenomenon. In 1882 it had consisted of one fractious fifty-member congregation; in 1890, twenty churches, ninety societies, at least 250 practitioners, thirty-three teaching centers, and a journal with a circulation of ten thousand. It was a unique institution, and at its heart was the college on Columbus Avenue with an intense little lady on the lecture platform. Her hold on a rapidly growing constituency was a marvel of the times.

The written word was also a major instrument for propagating Christian Science. In 1883 Mrs. Eddy founded the monthly *Christian Science Journal* to which she contributed regularly until 1889. In 1898 the weekly *Christian Science Sentinel* was added, and in 1908, the great daily newspaper, the *Christian Science Monitor. Science and Health,* meanwhile, was not allowed to languish. After the third edition of 1881 new editions appeared with dizzying speed, reaching a total of 382 before her death. By 1891 this personally controlled and very profitable publication had sold 50,000 copies and by 1910, 400,000.

Growth during the decisive decade of the 1880s caused many changes in the church's organizational structure, of which none was more significant than Mrs. Eddy's decision to seclude herself, first to a house on Commonwealth Avenue in Boston, then two years later to "Pleasant View" on the outskirts of Concord, New Hampshire, with a view of the distant hills where she had been born, and finally, in 1908, to a mansion in Brookline, Massachusetts. During the last nineteen years of her life, she was to visit Boston but four times, not even attending the dedication of the Mother Church in January 1895, nor of its vaster "Extension" in June 1906. She concentrated on the long-range problem of creating a fixed and enduring institution, and the result was a sharp concentration of ecclesiastical power. In 1889 Mrs. Eddy surrendered the charter of her college, and in 1892 she "disorganized" the National Christian Science Association. In the meantime, the Boston church itself was reorganized, and Mrs. Eddy gained control through twelve "Charter Members" and twenty "First Members" of her own selection. Christian Scientists everywhere were then invited to apply for membership. The Mother Church thus took the place of the national association. The whole organization was crowned by a self-perpetuating board of directors appointed by Mrs. Eddy. Measures were also taken to limit the independence of branch churches: pastors were replaced by "readers" on three-year terms, while assigned passages from *Science and Health* and the Bible supplanted preaching as the central element of public worship. Unauthorized expositions of the faith were forbidden. Even before 1910 an "authorized" version of Christian Science history was in existence; and since then great quantities of historical source material have been removed from the public domain and sequestered in the church's archives.

During her last years, Mrs. Eddy could claim not only an amazingly devoted following but also wealth, power, and fame. Yet her life was anything but peaceful. As her health declined and attacks of renal calculi grew more frequent, morphine had to be administered at regular intervals. Darkest of all was her continuing dread of malicious animal magnetism (MAM), the destructive streams of telepathic influence which she had dreaded ever since the turbulent 1870s. It now became necessary to have a coterie of students around her to ward off the mental malpractice of real or imagined enemies. Only death brought relief from the pain, insecurity, and lifelong fears. It came on 3 December 1910: "Natural causes—probably pneumonia," said the medical examiner. She was eighty-nine years old. After modest ceremonies she was buried in Mount Auburn Cemetery, Cambridge, Massachusetts. Her estate was valued at well over $2 million, nearly all of which she left to her church. She had made no special provision for the succession of authority, but the board of directors readily assumed control. Mrs. Eddy's desire to have things stay as she left them was in this way gratified.

Besides a church structure, Mrs. Eddy left behind a body of doctrine, which is set forth primarily in *Science and Health with Key to the Scriptures*. She had, like Swedenborg, "discovered the key" which unlocked the previously hidden meaning, the "spiritual sense," of the inspired Word of God. Her book is thus an authoritative interpretation of the Bible. She insisted on the divine origin of her discovery: "the spiritual advent of the advancing idea of God as in Christian Science" was "unquestionably" the Second Coming of Jesus. The basic postulate of Christian Science, variously stated, is that God is All, the only Being, Mind. Man—the real man, not the seeming or "mortal man"—is a divine reflection of God. The so-called objective world of the senses is unreal, or mere "belief." "Matter and death are mortal illusions," as are sin, pain, and disease.

Christian Science, however, was not primarily a philosophy or a theology, but a "science of health." Mrs. Eddy began by training doctors of a sort, and the history of Christian Science down to 1910 can be understood as a continuous effort to explain the phenomenon of healing in specific metaphysical, religious, and biblical terms, and to give ecclesiastical structure to the result. The church appropriately marked the centenary of Mrs. Eddy's "discovery" with a volume of testimonies, *A Century of Christian Science Healing* (1966). In practice Christian Science has also focused on peace, comfort, and success in this life; indeed, worldly affluence is held to "demonstrate" its truth. The idea of God as Love did figure in Mrs. Eddy's thought, but humanitarianism, philanthropy, or social ethics did not have a prominent place. Christian Science can thus be described only in somewhat paradoxical terms: it can inspire lofty morals and the religious fervency of classic pantheism, yet it more ordinarily manifests itself as a this-worldly, health-oriented immaterialism and as a dogmatic denial of medical and pharmaceutical science, of many public health measures, and hence of a scientific search for knowledge.

At the same time, it must be seen as growing out of a great religious disquietude that was spreading through New England—and the rest of America—during Mrs. Eddy's lifetime. Her dissatisfaction with evangelical revivalism and orthodox dogmatism was shared by the Universalists, Spiritualists, Transcendentalists, and Swedenborgians as well as the mesmerists, faith healers, and health seekers with whom her life was entwined. Even thinkers such as Emerson and William James, who lived in quite a different intellectual world, shared much of her unrest and developed views that have important similarities to hers. Certain social trends are also relevant. The growth of cities seems to have created new anxieties to which these forms of religion brought a meaningful message. Christian Science and its competitors also gave a religious role to women which American Protestantism had characteristically denied.

Of the many new religious impulses which emerged amid these shifting circumstances, Christian Science was the most clearly defined and best organized. It proved attractive in ever-widening circles, especially to women. Of large American denominations it came to have the highest percentage of urban, female, and adult membership, and probably the greatest wealth per capita. By 1906 the federal religious census showed a membership of 85,717; by 1926, 202,098; by 1936, 268,915.[5] Its size in later periods can only be estimated, but it would appear to have leveled off between .2 percent and .25 percent of the national population. Because of its cultic sobriety and nonemotional concern with health and well-being, its status, character, and size are not likely to change rapidly.

Mrs. Eddy and her message have undoubtedly brought health, serenity, and prosperity to many people. She dramatized a new approach to religion and biblical interpretation, and she clearly stimulated much interest in the ministry of healing which the Protestant churches had virtually abandoned, despite its prominence in the New Testament. During the early years of her ministry at least, she performed a great service by reducing the number of Americans who were exposed to an unregulated and largely uneducated medical profession. During a critical age of transition in Western conceptions of body and spirit, physiology and psychology, health and sickness,

5. Christian Science has made considerable advances in Great Britain, Australia, New Zealand, Switzerland, and other countries whose social development parallels that of the United States.

she and her church also demonstrated the importance of will, mind, and religious faith for personal health and well-being.

Yet the largest significance of Christian Science lies neither in its sensational growth before 1930 nor in the durability of its authoritarian ecclesiastical structure, but in its clear revelation that Americans in large numbers were developing a new kind of religious interest. "A new continent has arisen . . . in the wide world of human thought and life," wrote one observer in 1911, while other writers spoke of a "new age in religion." [6]

NEW THOUGHT

The religious leadership of this "new age" was by no means conceded to Mrs. Eddy. Even while she lived, a strident group of Quimbyites challenged her directly. Both before and after 1910, moreover, many others sponsored parallel movements, criticizing her dogmatism, denouncing the authoritarianism of her church, and expounding modifications of the underlying theory. The term New Thought came to designate this variegated impulse. Besides Quimby, its adherents also honored Charles Poyen, the French mesmerist, Andrew Jackson Davis, the "Poughkeepsie seer" (a healer with Swedenborgian overtones in his message), and many others, including of course, Swedenborg himself. The first effective publicist of these views was Warren Felt Evans (1817–89), a man with New Church ideas who was healed by Quimby in 1863. A year later he championed Swedenborg in *The New Age and Its Messenger,* followed by *The Mental Cure* (1869), *Mental Medicine* (1872) and several other works. Evans was a thoroughgoing idealist who also showed a considerable interest in occultism and what he called "esoteric Christianity." For a time he maintained a healing sanatorium in Salisbury, Massachusetts. But his greatest distinction, according to the chief historian of the movement, "lies in the fact that he was the first of a long line of exponents of New Thought ideas and methods to set them forth in published book form." [7]

New Thought began to take organized shape in the 1880s when Julius A. Dresser and his wife came to Boston, opened a controversy with Mrs. Eddy on the Quimby question, and began a competitive movement of mental healing. It soon had many followers. The Church of the Higher Life was founded in Boston, while numerous periodicals took up the idea in various places across the country. The term "New Thought" began to win acceptance

6. John Benjamin Anderson, *New Thought: Its Light and Shadows, an Appreciation and a Criticism* (Boston: Sherman, French & Co., 1911), preface.

7. Charles S. Braden, *Spirits in Rebellion: The Rise and Development of New Thought,* p. 92.

after 1890 with the founding of a periodical of that name and with the organization of the [Boston] Metaphysical Club in 1895 and the International Metaphysical League four years later.

The movement's basic spirit is suggested by the constitution of the International New Thought Alliance, organized in 1915: "To teach the infinitude of the Supreme One, the Divinity of Man and his Infinite possibilities through the creative power of constructive thinking and obedience to the voice of the Indwelling Presence, which is our source of Inspiration, Power, Health, and Prosperity."

Two years later the alliance published a comprehensive set of "Affirmations" which constitute an almost classic summary of this form of harmonial religion.

We affirm the freedom of each soul as to choice and as to belief. . . .

The essence of the New Thought is Truth, and each individual must be loyal to the Truth as he sees it. . . .

We affirm the Good. . . . Man is made in the image of the Good, and evil and pain are but the tests and correctives that appear when his thought does not reflect the full glory of this image.

We affirm health. . . .

We affirm the divine supply. . . . Within us are unused resources of energy and power. . . .

We affirm the teaching of Christ that the Kingdom of Heaven is within us, that we are one with the Father, that we should judge not, that we should love one another. . . .

We affirm the new thought of God as Universal Love, Life, Truth and Joy.[8]

On this broad platform a host of preachers, healers, writers, organizers, and publishers took their stand, reaching out into every corner of the land.

People who left the Christian Science church but not the main lines of its teaching were a strong element in the New Thought movement. Many apostates simply continued to practice, teach, and preach on their own; but others founded churches. Augusta Stetson, the leader of an extremely prosperous Christian Science church in New York City until she was excommunicated by Mrs. Eddy in 1909, was among the first of these. Annie C. Bill led another dissenting movement out of Christian Science just after Mrs. Eddy's death. Then in 1929–30 her Parent Church, as it was called, abandoned its old allegiance entirely, and with Mrs. Bill's *Science and Reality* as its textbook, became the Church of the Universal Design.

Another very consequential exile from Christian Science was Emma Cur-

8. Dresser, *History of New Thought*, p. 211.

tiss Hopkins, who was for a time editor of Mrs. Eddy's *Journal*. In 1887 she founded her own Christian Science Theological Seminary in Chicago and soon made it a major fountainhead of New Thought. Through a woman she healed, her influence also reached Nona L. Brooks in Colorado, who with two other women founded the Divine Science movement in Denver. Mrs. Hopkins in her old age also had a strong influence on Ernest S. Holmes, who with his brother founded a flourishing Religious Science movement in Los Angeles.

Most successful of all these offshoots was the Unity School of Christianity founded in 1889 in Kansas City, Missouri, by Charles and Myrtle Fillmore, who also received the harmonial message from Mrs. Hopkins. After dedicating themselves to this cause in 1892 they gradually became its major exponents in the Midwest. Their magazine *Thought* (earlier *Christian Science Thought*) was a vital part of an immense publishing enterprise that would claim two million correspondents. The main themes of Unity theology, a modified form of Christian Science, are expounded in Mr. Fillmore's two widely circulated books *Christian Healing* (1912) and *The Twelve Powers of Man* (1930). Unity does not deny the material world or emphasize self-help so strongly as to jeopardize or inconvenience the lives of its adherents. On the other hand, Fillmore could push his notion of latent human power to the edge of occultism:

> The spiritual ethers are vibrant with energies that, properly released, would give abundant life and health to all God's people. The one and only outlet for all these all-potential, electronic, life-imparting forces existing in the cells of our body, is our mind unified with the Christ mind in prayer.[9]

As this statement suggests, prayer lies at the center of Unity's extensive communications network. The need for prayer attracts potential converts, while an elaborate computerized system which sends out seven hundred thousand answers a year gains and maintains the movement's vast constituency. The Unity School has never stressed institutional development; but even so there are over five hundred local Unity Centers in which "members" hold regular services. Conventions take place annually, and lavish headquarters designed by the founders' son have been built outside Kansas City. Only in a very loose sense, however, could this organization be considered a church or religious body. In 1970 Unity was under the executive management of the founders' grandson, Charles Fillmore, a graduate of the University of Missouri School of Journalism. The emphasis now was on the central

9. Quoted by Charles S. Braden, ed., *Varieties of American Religion*, p. 150.

institution and the effective maintenance of a system for reaching and helping as many correspondents as possible. Despite turbulent and revolutionary changes in the public's religious outlook, the inward flow of six thousand letters a day indicated that Unity's message still answered the needs of America for peace of mind and inner harmony.

POSITIVE THINKING

As early as 1831 Alexis de Tocqueville had said of American preachers that "it is often difficult to ascertain from their discourses whether the principal object of religion is to procure eternal felicity in the other world or prosperity in this." Even while Tocqueville toured the country, the major exponent of religious self-reliance, Ralph Waldo Emerson, was shaping the Transcendental gospel which he would soon be teaching the nation. The tougher and profounder elements in Emerson's thought make it almost blasphemous to link his name with positive thinking, yet the continuity of popularized Transcendentalism and later expositions of utilitarian piety is unmistakable.[10] William James's writings, too, especially as developed in "The Will to Believe," were also easily vulgarized. They seemed to justify religion on grounds of its personal utility, for its "cash value." His pragmatic apologetic for religion thus became a vital element in the inspirational literature of the twentieth century.

In tracing the lineage of the "positive thinkers," Donald Meyer singles out Dr. George Beard, a New York neurologist, as the pioneer diagnostician of the malaise which had to be cured. Beard's *American Nervousness* (1881) described nervous exhaustion as an inevitable concomitant of industrial society:

> The force in the nervous system . . . is limited; and when new functions are interposed in the circuit . . . there comes a period, sooner or later . . . when the amount of force is insufficient to keep all the lamps actively burning.[11]

Such negative thinking, however, could not prevail in the land of Emerson and James. "Neurasthenic" Americans demanded and received in abundance a more hopeful message. Kate Douglas Wiggin's *Rebecca of Sunnybrook Farm* (1903) and Eleanor Porter's *Pollyanna* (1913) gave optimistic counsel in fictional form, and a vast stream of sentimental novels carried the message

10. When *Science and Health* was published in 1875, Emerson's neighbor and fellow spirit Bronson Alcott provided Mary Baker Eddy almost the only positive encouragement she received from a major American intellectual.

11. See Donald Meyer, *The Positive Thinkers*, chaps. 21–23.

to an older audience. Ella Wheeler Wilcox reached into ordinary households with her sentimental stories, novels, poems, and autobiographical writings. "Laugh and the world laughs with you;/ Cry and you cry alone" are undoubtedly her best known lines—and they suggest the tone of her counsel. In the 1920s Émile Coué and his autosuggestive proposals had a brief triumph in America, and in later years the novels of Lloyd C. Douglas had a very similar impact, especially *The Magnificent Obsession* (1929), which as a popular film reached an even wider audience. Other New Thought advocates, meanwhile, provided a more theoretical literature.

The patriarch of the modern health and harmony tradition is Ralph Waldo Trine (1866–1958), whose parents, if indeed they did so christen their son, must be credited with prophetic powers, for no man so successfully adjusted the great Ralph Waldo's message to the needs of troubled Americans. Trine stated the substance of his philosophy and religion most specifically in the two best sellers with which he, in effect, opened his career: *What All the World's A-Seeking, or, The Vital Law of True Life, True Greatness, Power, and Happiness* (1896); and *In Tune with the Infinite, or, Fullness of Peace, Power, and Plenty* (1897). In the latter volume, his "classic," he puts the matter succinctly:

> The great central fact of the universe is that Spirit of Infinite Life and Power that is back of all, that animates all, that manifests itself in and through all; that self-existent principle of life from which all has come, and not only from which all has come, but from which all is continually coming. . . . The great central fact in human life . . . is the coming into a conscious, vital realization of our oneness with this Infinite Life, and the opening of ourselves fully to this divine inflow. . . . In essence the life of God and the life of man are identically the same, and so are one. They differ not in essence, in quality; they differ in degree.[12]

This "mighty truth," said Trine, "is the golden thread that runs through all religions." The differences between them are laughable absurdities. Buddhists, Jews, and Christians can worship "equally as well" in each other's temples:

> Let us not be among the number so dwarfed, so limited, so bigoted as to think that the Infinite God has revealed Himself to one little handful of His children in one little quarter of the globe, and at one particular period of time.[13]

12. Ralph Waldo Trine, *In Tune with the Infinite* (New York, 1897), pp. 11, 16, 13.

13. Ibid., pp. 205–07.

Through fifty eventful years, in dozens of books and countless articles he wrote in this vein, making practical applications of his basic doctrine, showing its resources for personal peace, power, and plenty. Yet he always remained a frank and consistent champion of generic universal religion as the key to these benefits.

Looking about him in 1897, noting the popular reception of his works as well as those of many rivals and, no doubt, aware of the surging expansion of Christian Science during these years, Trine could speak with confidence of the "great spiritual awakening that is so rapidly coming all over the world, the beginnings of which we are so clearly seeing in the closing years of this, and whose ever increasing propositions we are to witness during the early years of the coming century." He then invoked the master spirit of his thought: "How beautiful if Emerson, the illumined one so far in advance of his time, . . . were with us today to witness it all!"

In effect, a new genre of American religious literature had been created—one that by 1960 would have become as common as aspirin. Between 1900 and 1960 writer after writer found himself "in tune with Trine," as did millions of readers. So mighty was the stream of this optimistic inspirational literature, in fact, that it is almost unwise to speak of individual writers; the books seem almost to have written themselves. Yet certain practitioners of inspirational art revealed not only unusual gifts for attracting readers, but developed personalized varieties of the genre. Especially eminent are Emmet Fox (1886–1951), Glenn Clark (1882–1956), and E. Stanley Jones (b. 1884).

Fox was ordained as a minister in the Church of Divine Science, and for years his "congregation" in New York City filled first the old Hippodrome, and later Carnegie Hall. Of the popular writers, Fox stood most clearly in true New Thought tradition, hitting his peak with *The Lord's Prayer* (1932), *The Power of Constructive Thinking* (1932), *The Sermon on the Mount* (1934), and *Make Your Life Worthwhile* (1942). His message was that "things are thoughts," evil a false belief, and external reality an "outpicturing of our own minds." He was exceedingly technique-oriented, and given to a vocabulary that was strange to those unacquainted with Christian Science and New Thought literature. The broader interests of Glenn Clark are revealed in such best-selling books as *The Soul's Sincere Desire* (1925); *The Lord's Prayer, and Other Talks on Prayer, From the Camp Farthest Out* (1932); *I Will Lift Up Mine Eyes* (1937); and *How to Find Health Through Prayer* (1940); though Clark is distinguished by his radical confidence in the mental healing of physical ailments. He even diagnosed the World War I influenza epidemic as due "to a great inflooding of wrong thinking and wrong feeling of entire nations." Jones, an influential Methodist missionary in India, was by no means merely an "inspirationalist," yet such works as *Victorious Living* (1936), *Abundant Living* (1942), and *The Way to Power and Poise* (1949) have proved beyond doubt that liberal theology, deep respect for other world religions (especially modern Hinduism), strong ecumenical interests, and active participation in Methodist church life by no means need keep a man from publishing a large literature on personal peace and power.[14]

Other more practical teachers moved away from devotional themes to a much more explicit, even crass, concern for wealth and success. In this field the prolific Orison Swett Marden (1850–1924) had once been the undisputed leader. While he lived, he was one of the most widely read American writers. His "classic" treatise, *Pushing to the Front: or, Success Under Difficulties* (1894), was translated into twenty-five languages, and his *Success Magazine* attained a phenomenal circulation of nearly a half-million. In 1928 fifty-one of his books were in print. Bruce Barton dealt with the same themes, but Marden was without a true successor until Dale Carnegie's meteoric rise as a teacher of friend-winning and business success.[15]

Applied psychology was yet another very practical interest that for obvious reasons had always flourished in these circles. Indeed, the notion of functional illness had figured strongly in New Thought literature long before depth psychology entered American folkways. The most important pioneers in this field were two clergymen, Dr. Elwood Worcester and Samuel McComb of Emmanuel Episcopal Church in Boston. Recognizing the need to diagnose organic ailments, they associated a board of physicians with their work. Then in 1906, by special worship services, counseling, and pastoral visitation, they began a broad program in which ministers, doctors, and psychotherapists cooperated. With the publication of *Religion and Medicine* in 1908 and other books soon after, the leaders of the Emmanuel

14. Harry Emerson Fosdick's case is similar. Though an eminent churchman and intellectual, several of his most widely sold titles belong in this genre. He, like Jones, took care to keep his counsels within the bounds of Christian theology in its liberal form. Most relevant of Fosdick's many works is *On Being a Real Person* (1943), though his very widely read *Twelve Tests of Character* (1923) and *As I See Religion* (1932) show the continuity of his thought.

15. Born in Maryville, Missouri, Dale Carnegie (1888–1955) was educated first at the State Teachers College at Warrensburg, Missouri, then at the Columbia School of Journalism, the New York University School of Journalism, and the Baltimore School of Commerce and Finance. In 1912 he began to conduct courses in effective speaking and applied psychology, a labor which, during the next thirty-three years, took him into several foreign countries. He became known nationally through his daily syndicated newspaper column and his radio programs in the 1930s and '40s, but he gained his widest audience through three enormously popular books: *Public Speaking and Influencing Men in Business* (1926), *How to Win Friends and Influence People* (1936), and *How to Stop Worrying and Start Living* (1948). After his death, a large organization carried on his work, and the "Dale Carnegie Course" virtually became an American institution.

movement made their influence nationwide. During the next half-century these not always compatible interests in spiritual healing and psychotherapy became a powerful new element in the pastoral work of many denominations. The "revival" of the 1950s provided an especially favorable climate for such emphases. In the more troubled sixties, the development of "sensitivity training" promoted still another psychotherapeutic revival.

THE PHENOMENON OF PEALE

In terms of sheer capacity for exploiting the many-sided interests of the New Thought tradition, the unrivaled leader in the period after World War II was Norman Vincent Peale (b. 1898). Peale was born into a Methodist parsonage in Ohio, attended Ohio Wesleyan University and the Boston University School of Theology, and conducted increasingly successful pastorates in Methodist churches before being called in 1932 to the Marble Collegiate Church on Fifth Avenue. This move involved a transfer from Methodism to the Dutch Reformed church, but the austere predestinarianism of the Belgic Confession does not seem to have been the attraction. Indeed, only in these new surroundings did he begin to test his powers as a prophet of positive thinking. *You Can Win* (1938) was his first major effort, and though its sales were relatively small, its preface gave the clue to his entire message: "Life has a key, and to find that key is to be assured of success in the business of living. . . . To win over the world a man must get hold of some power in his inward or spiritual life which will never let him down." Naming this key, detailing procedures for using it so as to achieve various personal ends, and recounting anecdotes of people who had done so became the highly successful business with which Peale, according to his own rather low estimate, had "reached" thirty million Americans by the mid-1950s.

No medium of communication was overlooked as Peale presented his message in sermons and lectures to crowded assemblies, on the radio, phonograph records, and television. Most important, however, was his use of the printed word: sermons, books, articles in the mass circulation magazines, a newspaper column, testimonies and further articles in his own widely distributed *Guideposts,* booklets, tracts, and even little "How Cards" in which his procedures were tersely summarized for those who read while they run. Probably his most significant audience was reached with his two best sellers: *A Guide to Confident Living* (1948) and, above all, *The Power of Positive Thinking* (1952), which hit the two-million mark during the Eisenhower years. All considered, it was appropriate that the story of Mr. and Mrs. Maurice Flint's great success should appear in Peale's most successful book. This enterprising couple, after being reached by Peale, had built up a successful business marketing "Mustard Seed Remembrancers" to be worn as a kind of charm or amulet, calling to mind the parable of the mustard seed (Matthew 17:20)—from tiny beginnings, large results can flow. Of Peale it could certainly be said that he made very much out of very little. By comparison, Trine was an abstruse philosopher.

Yet the exposition of mind-cure was not Peale's only work. In an external way he took psychiatry seriously, and he collaborated with Dr. Smiley Blanton both in books and in a clinic affiliated with the Marble Church.[16] He was also active in support of conservative political causes. In the fall of 1960, Peale closed out the decade by presiding in New York City over an ad hoc conference of conservative Protestants who injected an acrid stream of anti-Catholicism into the presidential campaign of John F. Kennedy.

Pealeism, as it spread abroad in the land, was strenuously criticized in many quarters despite the fact that Peale himself was, like Billy Graham, remarkably adept at disarming his potential critics. Theological liberals attacked his accent on techniques and his reactionary social views. Theological conservatives objected to his Pelagian reliance on self-help. Neo-orthodox critics found his optimism fatuous. And all of these critics were embarrassed by the image of Christianity that he conveyed.

At least one immensely popular exponent of religion-in-general who escaped such criticism was Anne Morrow Lindbergh, whose *Gift from the Sea* appeared in 1955. The shells she had gathered by the ebbing and flowing sea became symbols of her themes as she invoked a tradition that was both ancient and modern, Catholic, Protestant, and pagan. As a woman who had borne her share of woe, she brought quiet counsel to Americans—especially women—through a discussion of selfhood, inner growth, and fully personal relationships. She too recognized the threat of the overcharged life, "the *Zerissenheit,* the torn-to-pieces-hood" of modern living. "The space is scribbled on, . . . the time has been filled." She then dwelt upon Rilke's insistence that solitude "is not something that one can take or leave. We *are* solitary . . . even between the closest human beings, infinite distances continue to exist." Yet to her it was that inner space which enables each person to become "a world to oneself" and thus become whole. "Two solitudes will surely have more to give each other than when each was a meager half." "To the possession of the self the way is inward, says Plotinus. The cell of self-knowledge is the stall in which the pilgrim must be reborn, says

16. See chap. 56, n. 6.

St. Catherine of Siena." So woman is called to be the pioneer in bringing "extrovert, activist, materialistic Western man . . . [to] realize that the kingdom of heaven is within." [17]

Unlike most of the popular soothsayers, Mrs. Lindbergh, far from deepening the "suburban captivity of the churches," was seeking to release the captives. The immense popularity of her book, moreover, reveals the degree to which Americans have fundamental religious needs that the churches do not answer. When old-time revivalism seemed anachronistic, Neo-orthodoxy too austere, neighborhood parishes too wrapped up in togetherness, and Pealeism too superficial, she provided a thoroughly modern guide to a deeper harmonial current. Evelyn Underhill once said that some men and women run away to God as boys used to run away to sea. And it is well to remember that a long and deep tradition does flow beneath even the most utilitarian perversions. Indeed, Underhill, through her many widely read writings on mysticism, is only one of many who have helped chart the way to the more enduring expressions of the *philosophia perennis.* In 1946 Aldous Huxley served the same end with an excellently conceived and widely read anthology of this great tradition.[18]

But the American who brought the mystical tradition to full expression in a way that won the attention of young and old alike and who reached into the 1960s with surprising force was Thomas Merton (1915–68). Born to artist parents in France, educated in France, at Cambridge and at Columbia University, he became a Catholic in 1938 and entered the Trappist silence of Gethsemani Monastery at Bardstown, Kentucky, in 1941. In many widely read books he then expounded the mystic way, showing not only great learning and philosophical insight, but also a sensitive understanding of contemporary spiritual dilemmas and, what is more unexpected, a deep concern for American social and political problems. Yet it must be added that his best-selling autobiography, *The Seven Storey Mountain* (1948), does much to make Merton's keen sense of relevance less surprising.[19]

17. *Gift from the Sea* (New York: New American Library, Signet Books, 1957), pp. 23, 56–58, 93–97. See also p. 956 above.

18. Evelyn Underhill, *Mysticism: A Study in the Nature and Development of Man's Spiritual Consciousness,* 12th ed. (Cleveland and New York: World Publishing Company, 1969); Aldous Huxley, *The Perennial Philosophy* (London: Chatto and Windus, 1946). Huxley's opening words define the term: "PHILOSOPHIA PERENNIS—the phrase was coined by Leibniz; but the thing—the metaphysic that recognizes a divine Reality substantial to the world of things and lives and minds; the psychology that finds in the soul something similar to, or even identical with, divine Reality; the ethic that places man's final end in the knowledge of the immanent and transcendent Ground of all being—the thing is immemorial and universal."

19. Merton's father was a New Zealander, his mother American. His education, in addition to much traveling and reading, included an interrupted novitiate as a Franciscan and a

In harmonial religion as in so many other traditions, one can thus discern a wide spectrum of ideas ranging from the prudential to the profound. Yet the full richness and variety of this religious current cannot be perceived unless we proceed to consider a parallel stream of esoteric thought which, though equally ancient, has been much rejuvenated in very recent times.

---

period of service with Friendship House (founded by Catherine de Hueck in Harlem during the 1930s), which burned lessons on white oppression and black suffering deep into his consciousness. Among his later works were *Conjectures of a Guilty Bystander* (1966), *Mystics and Zen Masters* (1967), and *Contemplative Prayer* (1969).

61

PIETY FOR THE AGE OF AQUARIUS: THEOSOPHY, OCCULTISM, AND NON-WESTERN RELIGION

On 6 October 1962 a disc by the Beatles—"Love Me Do" and "P.S. I Love You"—first hit the English popularity charts. The date, according to their biographer, is one which "some maintain should be an international celebration, a parade-picnic holiday." Before the decade was out the Beatles were clearly among the world's leading cultural subversives, irreverently, joyously, and pensively filling the air with freedom, exposing social cruelty, asking deeply personal questions. Yet by a strange paradox they were also both leading and reflecting a new religious impulse, not only in their music, but with their lives. One of their press agents said in 1964 that "they are so anti-Christ they shock me, which isn't an easy thing." But four years later, to the great surprise of many, they were gathered by the banks of the Ganges, seeking spiritual peace through the ancient but modernized disciplines of Hindu religion.[1]

This turning away from the religious traditions of the West was a major sign of the times. Simultaneously, the displays of countless novelty shops were providing evidence that a lively religious counterrenaissance was advancing under the sign of Aquarius. A popular revival of astrology was in progress, and with it renewed prestige for the Cabala and the Thrice-Greatest-Hermes. Because all of these interrelated movements are very old, and because America has long provided them a hospitable environment, an historical view is illuminating.

1. Anthony Scaduto, *The Beatles* (New York: New American Library, 1968), pp. 1–27.

Nineteenth-century scholars and philosophers were understandably obsessed with the problem of classifying religions. Because they invariably found religions to exist in distinct institutional, cultural, and linguistic contexts, they tended to stress the uniqueness of each. Yet scheme after scheme of classification proved unacceptable for reasons John Baillie has suggested:

> The more closely we study these seemingly exclusive and diverse systems and the more intimately we come to understand them from the inside, the more they appear to us as but partially divergent expressions of a common impulse and principle.[2]

So it is with the religious movements discussed in this chapter. They do have much in common with those grouped in the preceding chapter—indeed, the concept of harmonial religion embraces both. Yet a distinction can be made. The impulses now to be considered either explicitly place themselves outside of the Judaeo-Christian tradition, or they claim to absorb the truths of all historical religions. They tend to relate themselves positively to the great Eastern religions. (For this reason the religions of Asian Americans are also considered here.) Despite strong rational and empirical interests, they emphasize esoteric doctrines, astrology, flamboyant symbolism, occult powers, and/or secret organizational structures. Yet time and again one is impressed by similarities to Christian Science and New Thought as well as to many venerable traditions of Christianity and Judaism.

THEOSOPHY

The origins of Western theosophical religion are as obscure as its ramifications over the centuries are diverse. Some Rosicrucians trace their brotherhood to the reign of Thutmose III in ancient Egypt, while Madame Blavatsky considered Lao-Tzu and the Buddha to be relatively late "transmitters" of "the one Primeval, universal wisdom" that she, after "long aeons and ages," was unveiling; and undoubtedly some elements of esoteric religion are very ancient. But a more basic source is the great flowering of Neoplatonic and Gnostic speculation which occurred during the first three Christian centuries, in which the body of writings attributed to the legendary Thrice-Greatest-Hermes (Hermes Trismegistus) holds a central place. This "Hermetic" corpus of syncretistic religious thought has in fact been a great religious and cosmological alternative to Christinity ever since apostolic times. It dealt with all the classic topics: God, the Divine powers,

2. John Baillie, *The Interpretation of Religion* (New York: Charles Scribner's Sons, 1928), p. 414.

Creation, the ordering of the universe, the nature of the elements, man, soul, sin, salvation, and the symbolic interrelationships of all things. From earliest times even orthodox Christians and Jews have taken it into account, incorporating what they could, denouncing what was unacceptable, and disagreeing as to which was what.

Throughout the Middle Ages this enormously imaginative and unitive view of reality maintained itself. Though constantly held suspect, it provided a lively dialogue with Christian and Judaic orthodoxy. It is the chief Western fountainhead of theosophy, that viewpoint which holds divinity or God to be the decisive and pervading force in the universe, and which makes special mystical insight into the divine nature and its constitutive moments and processes the key to religious, philosophical, and scientific knowledge. This wisdom is given to adepts or initiates by divine illumination or perceived by them due to the operation of higher faculties.[3] As passed on and elaborated, it constitutes a vast "Secret Tradition" with ramifications into alchemy, astrology, necromancy, magic, and the "black arts" as well as into highly creative forms of theology, philosophy, mysticism, and science.

As a world view the hermetic tradition tended toward an idealistic form of pantheism which saw divine meanings and correspondences in every natural thing and found celestial wisdom in the most outwardly prosaic passages of Scripture. It blended with many forms of mysticism and sometimes inspired or informed whole philosophical systems. The Jewish Cabala, compiled from both Christian and Jewish sources in the later Middle Ages, was a major vehicle for transmitting this heritage to various Christian thinkers. During the age of the Renaissance men like Pico della Mirandola,

3. In her "Proem" to *The Secret Doctrine* Madame Blavatsky, in her own distinctive way, sets forth the three basic ideas of theosophy: "(1) An Omnipresent, Eternal, Boundless and Immutable PRINCIPLE, on which all speculation is impossible, since it transcends the power of human conception. . . . (2) The Eternity of the Universe *in toto* as a boundless plane; periodically 'the playground of numberless Universes incessantly manifesting and disappearing, called the 'Manifesting Stars,' and the 'Sparks of Eternity.' . . . The absolute universality of that law of periodicity, of flux and reflux, ebb and flow, which physical science has observed and recorded in all departments of nature. (3) The fundamental identity of all Souls with the Universal Over-Soul, the latter being itself an aspect of the Unknown Root; and the obligatory pilgrimage for every Soul. . . . The pivotal doctrine of the Esoteric Philosophy admits no privileges or special gifts in man, save those won by his own Ego through personal effort and merit throughout a long series of metempsychoses and reincarnations."

An Adept is one "who has reached the power and degree and also the purification which enables him to 'die' in his physical body, and *still live and lead a* conscious life in his Astral Body." In the Judaeo-Christian tradition "Enoch is the type of the dual nature of man—spiritual and physical." Theosophists thus prize the biblical book of Jude for recognizing Enoch, and the Fourth Gospel for at least seeming to. Interestingly, theosophists (like Anabaptists) regard the Emperor Constantine as an archvillain; but their complaint is that he throttled "the old religions in favor of the new one, built on their bodies" (H. P. Blavatsky, *The Secret Doctrine*, 3 vols., 3d ed. [New York, 1893–95], 1 : 42–45, 27, 559–61).

Paracelsus, and Reuchlin stimulated a veritable "hermetic" and "Cabalistic" revival which was advanced still farther in each succeeding century by both Protestants and Catholics. Jacob Boehme, the Protestant mystic, was a vital link in the tradition; Swedenborg was at least an offshoot from it; and some of the nineteenth century's greatest minds (Schelling, Novalis, Victor Hugo, Balzac, Franz Baader, and Joseph de Maistre) showed deep continuous interest in it. Masonic lodges and other secret fraternal orders often provided an institutional setting. Spiritualism, mesmerism, and faith healing aroused further interest in the spiritual unity of all things and hence in man's latent powers.

In modern times this syncretistic approach to religion inevitably appealed to those who were fascinated or troubled by the increase of knowledge about other world religions. Emerson and his Transcendental friends inspired a revival of serious scholarly study of the Eastern religions. Later in the century, both in Europe and in America, the alluring message of the Hindu and Buddhist scriptures began to be known—especially after Max Müller's multivolume edition of Eastern scriptures (1875–1901) became available. Not only did "reincarnation," "Karma," and "nirvana" enter the American religious vocabulary, but one or another of the Eastern religions often became a live alternative for those who were dissatisfied with or untouched by the more traditional forms of Judaeo-Christian religion.

Theosophy took shape in America as a specific organized religion in 1875, with the founding of the Theosophical Society in New York, but the wide dispersion of theosophic teaching resulted chiefly from the indefatigable efforts of two remarkable women: Madame Helena Petrovna Blavatsky (1831–91) and Annie Wood Besant (1847–1933). Madame Blavatsky had left her first husband and her native Russia by the time she was twenty, and for the next two decades she was a wanderer. By her own account she visited every continent, including South America. Questions as to what she did during these formative years, and how decorous her behavior was, are much debated; but it is certain that when she appeared in New York in 1872 she had become steeped in esoteric lore and was widely known as a wonder-worker and a medium of spiritual communications from the mahatmas. By this time her legendary beauty (which seems to have figured in many amatory adventures) had yielded to a very considerable obesity; yet her charismatic powers in matters esoteric had suffered no diminution. Her apartment soon became a theosophic center, and out of the resulting associations came the decision to unveil and to organize the "secret" theosophic tradition.

An illumination suggesting to Madame Blavatsky that she form an organization like the Rosicrucian or Masonic lodges may have been the occasion.

In any event, Colonel Henry S. Olcott (1832–1907), a sometime spiritualist leader of New York City, at her instigation took the formal steps in 1875 and became the first president of the Theosophical Society and Universal Brotherhood, with HPB as secretary. Its constitution, as well as HPB's *Key to Theosophy* (1889), states the purpose of modern theosophy; to establish a nucleus of the universal brotherhood of humanity, to promote the study of comparative religion and philosophy, and to make a systematic investigation of the mystic potencies of man and nature. Spiritualism had been a strong interest of Olcott, and up to then of HPB as well; but she soon repudiated its claims in her influential book *Isis Revealed* (1877). In the same work she also expounded the chief new emphasis of modern theosophy—its concern for the Hindu and Buddhist traditions of India and Ceylon—and her belief that direct illumination was received from a hierarchy of Hindu masters of the past and present. It was in response to this Oriental interest that HPB and Colonel Olcott departed for India in 1878, leaving the society's American chapter to flounder without leadership. The two founders maintained the society in India, however, until accusations of fraud led to their departure in 1885. Madame Blavatsky retired in Europe, studying and writing; then in 1888 she published her major work, *The Secret Doctrine,* a vast compendium of theosophic teaching. She remained in Europe and devoted herself to theosophy and the "Blavatsky lodge" or Esoteric Society, leaving the exoteric society and its organizational problems to Colonel Olcott.

After HPB's death in 1891 the movement's second great leader soon moved to the fore. Annie Wood Besant was the daughter of an Anglican priest and a sometime adherent of the Oxford Movement. She had turned to atheism, secularism, feminism, and socialism; and then after becoming interested in spiritualism, had been captivated by Madame Blavatsky and her *Secret Doctrine.* In 1893 Mrs. Besant and a representative of the society from India made a strong impression at the World Parliament of Religions in Chicago, but she returned to India to become head of the society after Olcott's death in 1907. During the next twenty years the society's membership grew to forty thousand, scattered in forty-three different countries, including over seven thousand in the United States, with headquarters in Wheaton, Illinois. During these years Mrs. Besant also strengthened the bond between Hinduism and theosophy and became a significant proponent of Indian nationalism.

In America, however, strong resistance to this oriental emphasis developed. Division followed, with the American group reorganizing itself on a more universal basis. This group, whose headquarters were in Point Loma, California, enjoyed considerable growth under their successive presidents

William Q. Judge and Katherine Tingley. In Germany similar resistance developed; and Rudolf Steiner (1861–1925) led most of its Theosophical Society membership into a separate Anthroposophical movement, which he understood as "the Esoteric Movement of the Reformation." As its name suggests, this movement stressed the *natural* accessibility of divine wisdom. Indeed, Goethe was Steiner's hero—and the "Goetheanum" was the name for its central temple, near Basel, Switzerland. Most of Steiner's works appeared in American editions, and his intellectual impact among theosophists was considerable.[4] In Germany this movement achieved a fairly solid institutional base which survived Hitler's efforts to suppress it. There is also a small Anthroposophical movement in America.

Aside from the divided Theosophical Society, still another movement stemmed from Madame Blavatsky's efforts. Oddly enough, its name is the Liberal Catholic Church. Its founders were Charles W. Leadbeater, a long-time associate of Mrs. Besant, and James I. Wedgewood, an English bishop of the Old Catholic Church who, after becoming a convinced theosophist, consecrated Leadbeater as a bishop of this church. His purpose was to give a positive ecclesiastical form to the theosophical impulse.[5] In "Liberal Catholicism" the historic ceremonial and vestments of the church were taken over in detail but given theosophical meanings. The chief substance of its eclectic and extremely tolerant doctrinal stance follows the same pattern. It thus became possible for an "orthodox" theosophist to worship in the precise forms of high Anglo-Catholicism. Bishop George S. Arundale of the Liberal Catholic Church succeeded to the international presidency of the Theosophical Society in 1933; and C. Jinarajadasa (Leadbeater's protégé) succeeded *him* in 1945; but the church and the society remained separate. By that time, however, the theosophical movement in all of its institutional manifestations was losing its force, becoming more a current of thought than an organized religion. The basic ideas of theosophical religion thus flowed far beyond organizational boundaries. Isis had, indeed, been unveiled, and occultism in various forms became the sparetime preoccupation of hundreds of thousands of Americans. Some, as we shall see, were organized in distinctive groups; but very many others pursued the subject alone, some as passionate believers, others as dabblers and hobbyists, yet all together they constituted a huge reservoir of interest which able organizers could rally.

Aside from the Theosophical Society and its offshoots, there are many other movements that are or claim to be based on the wisdom of the

4. See Ernst Boldt, *From Luther to Steiner;* and Steiner's *Theosophy* (New York: Rand-McNally and Co., 1910).

5. The Old Catholic Church was formed by Roman Catholics who dissented from the proclamation of papal infallibility by the Vatican Council of 1869–70. The Liberal Catholic Church, therefore, looks upon the ordination of its clergy as being more clearly in the apostolic succession than that of the Anglicans.

mahatmas. They conceptualize reality in similar terms and offer the same promises of greater personal power, health, and composure to their adherents. The "I Am" movement, founded in 1930 by Guy and Edna Ballard, was certainly not the most impressive or durable of American movements, but it demonstrated the prevalence of a certain kind of religious hunger in the United States, as well as the appeal of theosophic doctrines. Both of the Ballards had had longtime connections with innumerable forms of occultism before Guy Ballard published *Unveiled Mysteries* in 1934, in which he claimed to have received revelations from Saint Germain, the "ascended master" who continuously held the place of honor (along with Jesus, who is also an ascended master) in the writings and public ceremonies of the Ballards.[6] Through excellent organization, press-agentry, and theatrical meetings that filled the largest halls in one city after another, the Ballards may have reached as many as three million people with their message. They organized "classes" of thousands of interested followers. Like Christian Science, their program emphasized healing; like the later New Thought, it stressed the vast powers latent in man by virtue of his unity with Being (I AM) and the aid to be received from ascended cosmic beings. Guy Ballard's death in 1939 and a succession of lawsuits for fraudulent use of the mails brought to an end the sensational success of the movement.[7]

6. The real Comte de Saint-Germain (1710?–80?), a figure to stir anyone's imagination, was an adventurer in a half-dozen courts of Europe who reached his apogee of influence while in the confidence of Louis XV of France. He was a chemist, alchemist, and wonder worker, the alleged founder of freemasonry, the initiator of Cagliostro thereinto, and an authority on the Secret Tradition. Invocation of his name would ring bells for knowledgeable occultists everywhere.

7. The notorious Legion of Silver Shirts initially had much the same appeal during the 1930s. William Dudley Pelley (1885–1965) was a Hollywood screen writer and real estate promoter who in a sensational article in the *American Magazine* in March 1929 claimed that he had died and been reborn after "seven minutes in Eternity." From then on he became a medium of the wisdom of the mahatmas. Convinced that Hitler was the leader to whom his divine instructions pointed, he shaped his following to very outspoken fascistic and anti-Semitic ends. After legal problems disrupted Pelley's organization, the Ballards drew away many of his adherents. Upon release from prison Pelley resumed his earlier religious interests, and in 1954 he published a message he had allegedly received from Mary Baker Eddy. In an interesting way it affirms the unity of harmonial religion: "What I should like to see achieved is the extension of Christian Science as an earth-study of Matter and Materialisms into realms of the psychically abstruse, if I may use that term. I am not a Spiritist in the popular sense of the term. I am not a therapeutic religious teacher, even. I am a contrite and devout woman who wishes to transfer to my brothers and sisters on the earth-plane an agenda of what I believe to be true in respect to the eternal survival of the human spirit for great and greater performings in flesh and out of it as the age progresses into the Millennia of Beauty" (W. D. Pelley, *Why I Believe the Dead Are Alive* [Noblesville, Ind.: Soulcraft Chapels, 1954], p. 285).

The remarkable little movement which Professor Festinger and his associates infiltrated in the 1950s and then described in a brilliant book showed again how a similar set of interests, augmented by the issue of flying saucers, could hold a group together despite great adversities (see Leon Festinger et al., *When Prophecy Fails* [Minneapolis: University of Minnesota Press, 1956]).

ROSICRUCIANISM

If poetic justice had prevailed, this chapter on the Secret Tradition would have begun with Rosicrucianism, for that half-legendary fraternity and its possibly nonexistent "founder" constitute ideal material for beginning the history of modern occultism. In 1618 Johan Valentin Andrea (1586–1654), a Lutheran pastor-theologian of Württemberg, obviously fascinated by esoteric lore, published an account of one Christian Rosenkreuz, who had culminated an adventurous life (strongly resembling that of Paracelsus) by founding the Fraternity of the Rose Cross in 1408. Whatever may have been Andrea's purpose, he aroused widespread interest in occultism and provoked a revival of the hermetic tradition, especially among German Protestants of pietistic inclination. Secret lodges were also founded, and after 1750 Rosicrucianism found an important institutional "home" in many of the Masonic lodges.

Rosicrucianism came to America with considerable éclat in 1694 when Johann Kelpius (1673–1708), a student of Jacob Boehme and other sources of hermetic wisdom, arrived from Germany at the head of a party of pietistic millennialists. Their settlement on the Wissahickon Creek near Philadelphia attracted much attention and exerted a strong influence on the surrounding community. The claims of later Rosicrucian leaders of a secret succession of Rosicrucian councils running back to Kelpius can be neither proved nor disproved, but there is no doubt whatever that a fairly lively interest in theosophical and cabalistic doctrines was maintained by private enthusiasts, in the Masonic lodges, among Swedenborgians, and elsewhere, and that a renewal of interest occurred during the nineteenth century. To this end General Ethan Allen Hitchcock (1798–1870) became an especially effective expositor of the serious philosophical and religious views that underlay the occult tradition.[8] One pioneer organizer of this revived interest was R. Swinburne Clymer of Quakertown, Pennsylvania, who published a history of Rosicrucianism in 1902 and then founded the Fraternitatis Rosae Crucis, which has continued to sponsor a considerable literature on the subject. In 1915 another American expositor of the tradition, H. Spencer Lewis, founded the Ancient Mystical Order Rosae Crucis (AMORC) in San Jose, California. Still a third arose in Oceanside, California, through the efforts

8. Hitchcock was a Vermont-born grandson of Ethan Allen whose half-century of distinguished military service did not prevent wide-ranging research on alchemy and many related subjects (see especially his *Swedenborg, a Hermetic Philosopher . . . with a Chapter Comparing Swedenborg and Spinoza* [1858]). On the Wissahickon Hermits, see Julius F. Sachse, *The German Pietists of Provincial Pennsylvania, 1694–1708*.

of Max Heindel, a German follower of Steiner whose elaborate and very widely read tome, *The Rosicrucian Cosmo-Conception; or, Mystic Christianity* (1909; 3d ed., 1911), provides both a major textbook on the tradition and a doctrinal norm for the Rosicrucian Fellowship which he founded. All three of these groups, and several lesser ones, maintain the concept of membership in an "order," "fraternity," or "fellowship"; but they are usually anything but secretive in their efforts to create a constituency. National advertising and the distribution of literature have become major modes of "evangelism."

It is as propagandists for the venerable tradition of theosophical wisdom that Rosicrucians are most significant. In this role they join other theosophical organizations and the broad New Thought impulse in sustaining throughout America a vast amorphous constituency that overlaps other denominations and faiths. Leading Rosicrucian themes are evident in the following passages from *Mastery of Life,* a booklet that AMORC sends free to the inquirer:

> Since we are part of an orderly universe, with its majestic and immutable laws, *above and below,* then there also exists for man as part of this great cosmic scheme, a true purpose in life. By knowing this purpose, by relating it to his existence each day, man discovers himself. He becomes the rightful master of his dominion—this world—and relegates suffering, misery, and ignorance to their proper places—and apart from himself. . . . Those who continuously suffer misfortunes and whose lives are not as progressive or inspiring as they would want them can experience marked changes when [the] cosmic blueprint is followed.[9]

Then with an accent on its rational and scientific character, the booklet partially unveils the ancient Egyptian wisdom on the nature of cosmic law and the hidden powers of man.

COSMIC CONSCIOUSNESS AND THE SCIENCE OF SPIRITUAL MAN

In 1901 Richard Maurice Bucke, a Canadian-born wanderer and self-educated seer, expounded the results of his study of the literature of ecstatic illumination in a large volume entitled *Cosmic Consciousness.* With evidence drawn from Buddha, Jesus, Paul, Boehme, Saint John of the Cross, Balzac, and various unidentified Americans, he delineated the experience of

9. *Mastery of Life* (San Jose, Calif.: Department of Publication, Supreme Grand Lodge of the Ancient and Mystical Order Rosae Crucis, 1965), p. 7.

Cosmic Consciousness as a "new plane of existence" that results from an "illumination" of cosmic life and order and a sense of immortality.[10] Bucke thus sought, like so many before him, to counteract and absorb scientific materialism in a highly generalized form of mysticism. He does not seem to have founded any organization to perpetuate his teaching, but the ancient impulse he represented was later given institutional form by Dr. Walter Russell (1871–1963), who received his illumination in 1921, and his wife Lao Russell (b. 1904), who received hers in 1946.

With the motto "World Peace through World Balance" the Russells founded their University of Science and Philosophy in 1957 with its headquarters in Swannanoa, a neorenaissance palace in the Virginia Blue Ridge. An important aspect of the university's teaching is indicated in a tribute written by Lao Russell in 1957:

> My husband, Dr. Walter Russell, is a consummate Illuminate. God gave him an innersensory perception which reaches around the entire 360 degrees of the light spectrum. He can "see" within the atom without need of microscope or cyclotron—or within all the stars and nebulae of space without need of telescope or spectroscope. More than that he can see and know the geometry of space and the means by which the invisible universe absolutely controls the visible universe. That means that the riddle of the universe which no man has ever solved, regarding the mystery of the emergence of matter from space, and of its being swallowed by space, is as clear to him as the light of the sun is clear.[11]

In 1926 Walter Russell first presented to the world the two periodic charts of the elements which underlay his cosmological conceptions. This intuitional scientific interest in the natural order, however, is complemented by a more directly religious message that Dr. Russell described in an answering tribute:

> It was [my wife's] destiny to search from early childhood for the illusive secret which alone would free man from his belief in EVIL, which seemingly enslaved. . . . She looked only into the Light of [man's] illumined Soul. And it was there . . . she found the Holy Grail. . . . For behold! all that she found was GOOD—naught but GOOD.[12]

10. Richard M. Bucke, *Cosmic Consciousness* (Philadelphia: Innes & Sons, 1905), p. 2. On Bucke, see also William James, *Varieties of Religious Experience*, pp. 308–09.

11. Walter and Lao Russell, *Atomic Suicide?* (Waynesboro, Va.: University of Science and Philosophy, 1957), p. xxv.

12. Lao Russell, *God Will Work* With *You But Not* For *You* (Waynesboro, Va.: Walter Russell Foundation, 1955), p. xi.

The moral and religious implications of these discoveries were more fully expounded by Lao Russell in her magnum opus of 1955, *God Will Work* With *You But Not* For *You:*

> The new way of life, which is based upon God-awareness within, is now necessary, else we perish. . . . Your divine immortal Soul is ONE with the Creator of the Universe. . . . You are the spiritual Intelligence of the ONE mind of the Creator of all things, which centers your body as a seat of Consciousness. . . . That is why you eventually become what you think. When you have finally reached the stage of complete unity with your God-Self you will become One with God and lose your desire to manifest individuality. However, this state may be thousands of lives ahead, for it is the Ultimate.[13]

These familiar central doctrines of the harmonial tradition she associates with Emerson and Whitman, who, she says, "were both cosmic conscious Illuminates." More distinctive was the Russells' belief in the coequality of man and woman, caused by a balance of elemental forces based on Dr. Russell's philosophy of nature.

The Russells' outlook is also marked by a fairly strident apocalypticism, which, along with their stand on women's rights, even won them a hearing in the student protest movements of the 1960s. They designated 1960 as "the crucial year" for reversing man's way of life "to serving man instead of preying upon him," and they regarded 1963 as the "point of no return" in this race with time. The white race they considered "on the eve of its downfall" and in need of drastic transformation, despite its persistent belief in itself as the "world master." For instruction in this religious outlook the Russells maintain an extensive and rather expensive homestudy course. Adherents in any one locality may be brought in contact with each other by their common religious interests, but there are no organized "churches" to unite the hundreds of thousands who thank the Russells for having given them religious peace in a troubled world.

RELIGIONS OF THE EAST IN AMERICA

One of the perennial features of harmonial religion, as we have seen, is its intense interest in Eastern religion. Some scholars of India trace this Western fascination for the light of Asia back to ancient times. Through Plato and the Neoplatonists, they claim an influence on the entire mystical tradition, and thus see the West's modern interest in Hinduism and

13. Ibid., pp. 13–20.

Buddhism as a kind of religious nostalgia.[14] Be that as it may, American interest in Oriental wisdom has mounted steadily since the days of Transcendentalism. In the twentieth century both Vedanta and Buddhism had not only eloquent expositors but an increasing number of converts. The enormously complex religious history of India, Iran, China, and Japan cannot even be touched upon here, but some channels by which Asia's religions came to America can be at least briefly considered.

Vedanta

Though emigrants from India have moved in large numbers to Africa and British Guiana, very few have come to the United States. Their religions, however, have gained a significant foothold. A very impressive missionary of Hindu religion, the Swami Vivekananda (1862–1902), who came to the World Parliament of Religions in 1893, was a disciple of the great mystic theologian Ramakrishna (1836–86), and the Vedanta Society which he founded in 1897 has continued to maintain centers in many American cities. By its publications and lectures this society has not only created a dedicated constituency, but has given many Americans a larger appreciation of Indian religion generally. The poetry of Rabindranath Tagore (1861–1914) also helped to accommodate Vedanta to Western ways of thought. But it was Mohandas Gandhi (1869–1948), the spiritual leader of Indian nationalism, who with unprecedented success made Hindu religion a significant theological and ethical option the world over, but especially in Christian countries. In America Martin Luther King, Jr., underlined Gandhi's significance for the racial justice movement. Aldous Huxley has probably been the most widely read Western advocate of a philosophy which, though not expressly Vedantic, does stress the essential unity of the world's great mystical religions.

Considerably less elevated in its aims is the Self-Realization Fellowship organized in 1914 by another Indian swami, Paramhansa Yogananda. In contrast to the austere Ramakrishna monastery near Laguna Beach, Yogananda's interpretation of Yoga had its institutional center in a former luxury hotel near Los Angeles. Like the Vedanta Society, it posits the essential unity of all religions, but its message has a practical accent on peace, health, and greater personal power. By the 1960s the fellowship claimed two hundred thousand members. No small part of its success and prosperity was due to

14. The "fundamental truth" of the Upanishadic religion of India on the eve of Buddhism's rise, writes Kenneth K. S. Ch'en, is the doctrine that "Brahma, the inner essence of the universe, is the same *atman*, the inner essence of man" (*Buddhism: The Light of Asia*, pp. 8–9). Here are the key concepts of the harmonial tradition which led so many of its followers to embrace the Hindu logic of future existence and the transmigration of souls.

the efforts and largesse of a Kansas City millionaire who became not only a convert, but the successor of Yogananda.

Transcendental Meditation was the name by which still another wave of American interest in Vedantic wisdom came to be known. Its widespread following was due almost entirely to one remarkable guru, the Maharishi Mashesh Yogi, who belongs to the order of Shankara (or Shankaracharya) and is the leader of the International Meditation Society or Spiritual Regeneration Movement, with headquarters in Rishikesh, Uttar Pradesh, India. The Maharishi continued to hold longer, more advanced classes in Rishikesh, but he made his reputation as the "chief guru of the Western world" by dint of an extraordinarily busy itinerary in Europe and America and by founding hundreds of meditation centers in dozens of countries.

Shankara, the eighth-century philosopher and commentator on the Hindu scriptures, is known for his doctrine of absolute monism: Brahma alone is real; the phenomenal world is mere illusion. He stands, thus, at the opposite extreme from those dualistic and theistic forms of Hindu thought which have often interested ecumenical Christians. The Maharishi claims only to have modernized this ancient philosophy and to have developed modes of meditation that enable people to find the secret of life so that their living can be full and complete. No small part of his success stemmed from his having interested the Beatles in his message and method. That his name was also linked with many other popular figures helped to win him a large following among university students. Yet Transcendental Meditation was by no means limited to the counterculture of a protesting generation. It was simply a modern form of the recourse to Eastern harmonialism. Emerson and Thoreau were among its most distinguished American prophets, but for two thousand years it has been embraced in one form or another by those who found little solace in orthodox forms of the Judaeo-Christian tradition.

Bahá'i

The religion now known as Bahá'i or Bahaism arose within a messianic sect of the Shiite Islam of Iran. It began with the announcement by 'Ali Muhammad (1819–50) that he was a divine messenger, or the Báb (Gate). He then claimed that he was the last successor of Muhammad who would lead the way into the messianic kingdom; but later he declared that he, like Muhammad himself, was a manifestation of God, that the laws of Muhammad's dispensation were abrogated, and that he was the founder of a new religion. During the long period of turmoil that followed the Báb's death, one of his disciples, Husayn 'Ali (1817–92), took the title Bahá'u'lláh (Glory of God), and while exiled at Acre in Turkish-ruled Palestine, won increasing acceptance of his claim to be the one whom God would manifest. He left behind a large body of writings which defined the religious outlook of his following. He was succeeded by his son, Abdu'l-Bahá (1844–1921), who had been born on the date designated as the time of the new dispensation. It was he who through lecturing and writing gave most definitive expression to Bahá'i teaching and established it as an independent and worldwide religious movement. After 1921 his grandson, Shoghi Effendi, became the guardian of the faith.

Bahá'i teachings are syncretistic by intention, emphasizing the essential similarity of the great world religions, conceding the inspiration of the prophet or messiah of each, and ostensibly providing only a more perfect indication of the basis or nature of their essential unity. Bahá'i is thus committed to seek rational harmony in religion and the unity of mankind. Its aim is the establishment throughout the world of peace, equality, mutual love, and personal holiness. Its means for achieving a synthesis of world religions are monotheistic, and its basic theology expresses the major themes of Judaism, Christianity, and Islam in a modern, somewhat philosophic mode that deemphasizes the more sharply distinctive features of these religions.

Bahá'i was first brought to America through the World Parliament of Religions in 1893. It gained a significant number of adherents in the Chicago area, which was visited by 'Abdu'l-Bahá in 1908 and again in 1912, when he broke ground in suburban Wilmette for the ambitious nonagonal temple which was finally dedicated in 1953. This temple is projected as a center for educational and welfare institutions as well as a national headquarters. The World Center is in Haifa, Israel. In 1947 Baha'i membership in the United States was numbered at five thousand; but during the 1960s it has shown marked growth, especially among thoughtful, ethically concerned people who desire a religious affiliation free from dogmatism and the sectarian spirit. In 1969 there were 440 local assemblies in the United States and members in 2,570 cities.

Buddhism

Asia's religious heritage has often come to America through Buddhism—and in a form that reflects the passage of that impulse from India to China and then to Japan. No other "Eastern religion" is maintained in the United States by an ethnic minority so large as that constituted by Japanese-American Buddhists. Dominant among this group is the Jodo Shinshu school founded by Shinran Shonin in the twelfth century and now the most widespread form of Buddhism in Japan. The arrival of two priests in San Francisco in 1898 marks its American beginnings, and by 1970 it had a membership of about one hundred thousand served by eighty active ministers, a publishing house, and magazines in both English and Japanese. Though it is organized on a national basis, nearly three-fourths of its churches are located in the Pacific coast states.[15] Among America's half-million Japanese as among its quarter-million Chinese, the tendency to Christian affiliation has been very strong. Especially since 1945 ethnic religious commitments have not figured prominently in their self-consciousness as peoples. White antioriental hostility has also markedly waned.

After World War II, and especially during the 1960s, Zen Buddhism began to command the interest of many nonoriental Americans. The reasons for this unmistakable tendency were diverse. A half-articulated countercultural animus undoubtedly accelerated the trend, notably among college students. Yet the so-called Zen boom was not just a protest movement, nor was it just an exotic fad.[16] As many distinguished thinkers came to realize, Zen answered to very important religious needs of a secular age. It was direct, practical, and nonmetaphysical. In the words of one of its most effective Japanese expositors,

> Zen has no God to worship, no ceremonial rites to observe, no future abode to which the dead are destined, and, last of all, Zen has no soul whose welfare is to be looked after by somebody else and whose immortality is a matter of intense concern.[17]

At the same time, however, Zen is a way of bringing men to know the absolute oneness and allness of God by acquainting them with the real nature of their own minds. Christian theologians and psychoanalytical theorists could enter into meaningful dialogue and find a profound complement to Western mysticism.

15. Bishop Kenyru T. Tsuji, *The Buddhist Churches of America* (San Francisco: Buddhist National Headquarters, n.d.). Probably not more than 10 percent of the country's Japanese Americans maintain an active relationship to Buddhism.

16. William Johnston refers to the "Zen boom" in *The Mysticism of "The Cloud of Unknowing"* (New York: Desclee Co., 1967), p. 12. See also Aelred Graham, *Conversations: Christian and Buddhist;* Heinrich Dumoulin, *A History of Zen Buddhism.*

17. Daisetz T. Suzuki, *An Introduction to Zen Buddhism,* pp. 35–39. Zen (Chan) Buddhism is usually traced to Bodhidharma, who around A.D. 520 came from India to China, where his teachings were significantly influenced by Taoism. During the twelfth century it became a strong influence in Japan, especially among the military, who found in it a method of self-discipline. In Japan, whence its influence in the West has chiefly stemmed, it tended increasingly to free itself from the complex and otherworldly metaphysics of Indian Buddhism. During the last century this trend toward secularity has accelerated. The object of its discipline, as expressed through seemingly cryptic sayings or stories (*koans*) posed by its teachers, was the experience of enlightenment (*satori*), that is, a new viewpoint for looking into the essence of things (ibid., pp. 88–89).

Far less demanding and hence far more popular as manifestations of the countercultural spirit were several other ancient religious impulses. Most important, perhaps, both as symptom and as substance, was a sweeping resurgence of astrological interest. Separating dabblers from true believers is impossible, but the existence of over 10,000 full-time and 175,000 part-time astrologers indicates that this most ancient of sciences was exerting a powerful influence on the outlook and life styles of Americans.[18] Quite different in form but similarly popular was a revived interest in spiritualism.[19] Of at least equal significance to either of these was the greatly increased use of LSD and other hallucinogenic drugs and the rise of "psychedelic mysticism." LSD was practically unknown to the public until 1963, when Timothy Leary and Richard Alpert, both psychology professors at Harvard, were discharged for involving students in questionable experiments. In 1966 Leary founded the League for Spiritual Discovery and became the drug movement's most famous advocate. By 1970 drugs had become a national concern, and the religious states which some of them could induce had become the experience of thousands, though by that time Leary himself was warning against the use of drugs (aside from marijuana) and urging the disciplines of Eastern religion. Drugs nevertheless continued to be at once a powerful element in the search for religious peace and a path to the destruction of both peace and personhood.[20] For the American Indian, however, the peyote cult gained a special kind of cultural significance.[21]

18. As the one clearly predictable phenomenon in a mystery-filled universe, the movement of heavenly bodies has always figured prominently in the religious life of mankind. Theosophy and astrology, moreover, have almost always been closely linked. Christianity's swift growth in the Roman Empire is in part explained by the freedom it promised from astrological determinism. The prison-like character of modern technocratic society, on the other hand, conduces to the revival of this determinism, computerized horoscopes included. On the other hand, the Age of Aquarius, calculated from the westward procession of the equinoxes to begin sometime in the twentieth century, is variously interpreted by astrologists to be a time of peace, joy, love, and freedom—which, if true, might, by an interesting irony, bring mankind's release from the fateful power of the stars as well as from man-made tyrannies.

19. Perhaps the most sensational convert to spiritualism during the 1960s was the Episcopal Bishop James Pike. Spiritual Frontiers Fellowship, founded in 1956 with its offices in Evanston, Illinois, is one of many organizations fostering these interests, but nobody knows how many million Americans take spiritualist claims more or less seriously.

20. In addition to Leary's league at least two psychedelic churches have been founded: in 1963 the Church of the Awakening in New Mexico, which has a conservative but activistic membership, and the Neo-American Church, which professes a frank "drop out and turn on" otherworldliness (see William Braden, *The Private Sea: LSD and the Search for God*, pp. 90, 174).

21. The most significant church to stress psychedelic experience arose from the peyote cult of the American Indians. Its immediate background was the powerful and syncretistic Ghost Dance movement led by the prophet Wovoka, a Nevada Paiute who envisioned an apocalyptic return to a kind of Indian golden age. His movement, however, led to the Sioux Outbreak of 1890–91 and a terrible massacre by federal troops. By this time two other prophets of the Southwest, Quanah Parker and John Wilson (both part white), were setting

Lonely housewives and overworked businessmen were as much a part of the harmonial tide as hippies and protesting students. Statistics on these seekers can never be gathered, but the way in which many people are reached by prophets of inner peace is suggested in a simple yet poignant letter sent by an elderly lady to the editor of a small Ohio newspaper in 1970:

> I hope this letter will help someone.
>
> Our only son was killed in Vietnam in September, 1968. The time since has been very difficult but as Jim wrote from Vietnam when real lonely, "Life is too important to let loneliness get the best of you. That's why we take each day as it comes and make the best of it." We must do that for our little grandson.
>
> My mother found help in Rosicrucian teachings, including reincarnation. Since 1950 I have read psychic books. My mother left me her books and many new books are being written by doctors, ministers, psychologists, psychics and many others. Surely God is trying to get some new beliefs to the world since so many people are having psychic experiences. The Bible is full of psychic occurrences. Jeane Dixon is able to read people's thoughts and make future predictions. Many thoughts surely are not for the good of the world.
>
> Recently Jeanne Gardner from Elkins, W. Va., has appeared on TV. A voice has given her information and future predictions since 1961. The proceeds from songs, books and TV appearances are to be used to build a million dollar cathedral for all faiths near Elkins. The voice has given her specifications for this temple. Each part in it will have a meaning to the world.
>
> Lao Russell had a vision of Christ and with her husband Walter sculptured this vision at Swannanoa in Waynesboro, Va., at their University of Science and Philosophy. A home study course and their books are available from there. Both had Cosmic Consciousness (they talked with God), which is very, very rare. (That happened to Paul in the Bible.) Walter Russell could do everything. He died not long ago at 92. Lao Russell is younger and lectures and writes to help people know God.

---

another, more distinctly Christian, pan-Indian movement in motion—one in which peyote had a central sacramental place as a gift of God. As further shaped by former students of Carlisle and Haskell institutes, it became a strong post-tribal and hence "modernizing" impulse. After 1910 it spread widely in the trans-Mississippi region, and in 1918 it was incorporated in Oklahoma as the Native American Church. In 1934 an interstate federation under that name began to be achieved. In 1970 it was "the most influential, most important, and largest Indian religious body, directly involving more Indians than any other pan-Indian group" (Hazel W. Hertzberg, *The Search for an Indian Identity: Modern Pan-Indian Movements*, p. 295).

> Some ideas from their books follow. Love is Mind (God) and this cannot die—and we are all extensions of that one Great Mind. All knowledge exists. Man is what he thinks, what he desires to be. When man comprehends God's ways and processes and lives them, he has all the power of his Creator. God will work with you but not for you.
>
> I challenge youth to read and study psychic books and see if they can't find a help for our world. Many books are available in paperback. Don't use alcohol and drugs but keep your mind alert so we can be proud of our future leaders. Love one another! Help one another! [22]

Not to appreciate the distress exposed in a letter such as this is to miss a fundamental aspect of modern technocratic society. Not to see that the spiritual impulses that sustained this woman were an ascendant aspect of American religion is to overlook a major historical fact.

22. *Wilmington* (Ohio) *News-Journal*, 22 January 1970. Jeane Dixon (b. 1918) is the Wisconsin-born daughter of well-to-do German immigrants, and a Roman Catholic. She divides her time in Washington, D.C., between a very successful real estate business and well-publicized crystal-ball prophesying. Her predictions showed little more than average prescience, but due to their conservative political slant and persistent religious tone, her great popularity was an important sign of the times (see Ruth Montgomery's highly uncritical account, *The Gift of Prophecy: The Phenomenal Jeane Dixon;* and James Bjornstad, *Twentieth-Century Prophecy: Jeane Dixon and Edgar Cayce*).

Jeanne Gardner (b. 1930) teaches a broad religious message through all available media, including her book *A Grain of Mustard* (New York: Trident Press, 1969), which she summarizes in a sentence: "We have two wills: our will, which leads to nowhere, and God's will, a bumpy, rocky road which leads to peace of mind and happiness." Following the VOICE that first spoke to her mother and then to her, she seeks to build a large cathedral for all faiths near Elkins, West Virginia (quoted from a letter to the author, 15 July 1970).

62
BLACK RELIGION IN THE TWENTIETH CENTURY

The rise of the black churches in the half-century after the Civil War was accompanied by a steady erosion of the nation's will to make the Emancipation Proclamation a meaningful document. The collapse of the Freedman's Bureau, the Compromise of 1877, the Supreme Court's virtual invalidation of the Civil Rights Act in 1883, and President Wilson's extension of racial segregation to the federal civil service in 1913 are milestones on the road away from liberty and equality. The Fourteenth and Fifteenth amendments —and in a sense even the Thirteenth—became dead letters.

The twentieth century has witnessed a double transformation of this history. First of all, the scene was changed by an immense movement of people from southern farm lands to the cities of both the North and the South. Second, the civil rights movement became a more potent force. Around 1900 a more militant mood began to appear in the black community, and within fifty years it had become a decisive factor in the life of the entire country. Each of these trends has had profound consequences for Afro-American religious history.

THE GREAT MIGRATION: NORTHWARD AND CITYWARD

Migration and urbanization have been the major social facts of the twentieth century for Americans generally. But for no part of the population was the change so drastic as for the southern blacks who moved not only to the city but to the North. This migration was chiefly the result of the nationwide growth of industrialism and sweeping technological changes in southern agriculture, with the relative unattractiveness of southern race relations a strong contributing factor. The Negro population in the rural South was, of course, declining even before 1914 (77 percent in 1890; 72 percent in 1900; 66 percent in 1910), but World War I and generally changing employment patterns accelerated the trend. During the Depression the greater availability of public relief in the North introduced still another incentive. The second, third, and fourth decades of the century involved respectively 440,000, 680,000, and 403,000 blacks in the movement northward. World War II and the great economic expansion which followed brought a further increase. Between 1950 and 1960 a million Negroes left the South. By 1965 three-fourths of the black population was living in cities, and about half of it was in the urban North.

This gigantic transformation of location, occupation, and status was, if anything, a more traumatic experience for black Americans than the Civil War and emancipation. One way of life, its social system and economic setting, its moral and spiritual atmosphere, was exchanged for another. Family structures lost the reinforcement provided by familiar neighbors, the local church, and the necessities of domestic agriculture. Despite the constant crushing fact of discrimination, many new possibilities for employment presented themselves, and a new kind of class structure emerged. Black Americans also discovered the scope and variety of American life, though they could obtain few of the means for participation. Since 1900 nearly every new development in black religion has been a corollary of the great migration and the resulting shift of life styles. Even in the South, cities like Montgomery, Little Rock, New Orleans, and Birmingham became the chief arenas of conflict and change.

THE CHANGING SHAPE OF EVANGELICALISM

With a migrant people came a migrant church. The Baptist and Methodistic traditions which had held sway in the old rural situation of the South continued to predominate. Even the storefront and single-residence churches that sprang up on crowded city streets bore these denominational affiliations overwhelmingly. Almost two-thirds of the black church membership continued to be Baptist, and nearly one-third reflected Wesleyan origins. The prevailing piety of the members and the theology of the preachers witnessed to the same continuities. As with the other masses of migrants in America's growing cities, including whites from American rural areas and foreigners from abroad, the Negro strove to preserve and to duplicate the spirit and forms of his traditional religious institutions. Yet inevitably there were changes proportionate to the vast shift of social circumstance. What these former rural folk experienced is perhaps best understood if we consider two very basic trends: secularization and social differentiation.

The term "secularization" has recently undergone profound shifts of meaning, but it is here used to designate some unmistakable city-bred pressures on rural religion. Put simply, twentieth-century city life was not church-centered; the alternative opportunities for diversion, recreation, cultural satisfaction, and social grouping were far more diverse and seductive than in the country. Complex institutions, machines, the mass media including metropolitan newspapers and radio, more varied types of education, and wider ranges of entertainment all served to diminish an otherworldly view of life. In the environment itself the works of man closed out the mysteries of the natural world and the more elemental human confrontations with nature and nature's God. The supernatural lost its immediacy. In this strange new urban world with its hurried tempo and its anonymous crowds, the fixed norms of the older moral order also disintegrated. They appeared now as but one way of life among several others, and they lost their authority.

Nothing illustrates the changed situation better than the way in which jazz and public dancing took America by storm in the twenties. In this realm Negroes played a continuously creative role, greatly enriching American culture in the process. As New Orleans competed with Harlem for primacy, a new kind of popular music emerged, and with it exuberant new forms of dancing and the commercial "ballroom." Indeed, could anything in Harlem vie with the Savoy in its heyday? Ministers and prohibitionists, both black and white, wailed and railed; but with assists from radio and phonograph, jazz "gave the Negro his first victory in America."

Yet there are important bridges connecting "Steal Away to Jesus" with "The Saint Louis Blues." William C. Handy, the "father of the blues"—as well as the son and grandson of black preachers—alternated the publication of spirituals and blues all through his career. A rich background of experience in the small towns of the Mississippi Delta and the big southern and northern cities had taught him that the two genres were related:

> I think rhythm is our middle name. . . . When darktown puts on its new shoes and takes off the brakes, jazz steps in. If it's the New Jerusalem and the River Jordan we're studying, we make the spirituals. . . . In every case the songs come from way down deep. . . . The dove descended on my head just as it descended on the heads of those who

got happy at camp meeting. The only difference was that instead of singing about the New Jerusalem my dove began to moan about high-brown women and the men they tied to their apron strings.[1]

Charles Keil points both to a vital spiritual relationship and to the importance of religious institutions when he insists that "every contemporary blues singer, with perhaps a few exceptions, has received his musical socialization in the church and sees little or no conflict between the secular and sacred musical traditions." [2]

As a result of such forces, however, not only did the old folk religion lose its unchallenged claim on people's lives; but that powerful personage in the Negro's "free" past, the folk preacher, experienced a steady decline in his authority. To maintain a semblance of his power he would have to develop his showmanship or his sophistication; but even these strategies could only retard an inexorable process. Secularization, then, may be understood as a general atmospheric aspect of city life that did not conduce to the flourishing of traditional piety.

Social differentiation as the Negro experienced it in the city was, on the other hand, a rather hard objective circumstance. In contrast to the rural South, urban conditions produced a fairly definite class structure, though with rather marked differences among individual cities. The major sociological studies tend to agree in charting the emergence of a relatively small upper class (largely professional, well educated, and usually with considerable white ancestry), a somewhat larger middle class (skilled laborers, clerical personnel, and salaried government employees of various types), and a very large lower class (unskilled laborers, service employees, and those only partially employed or on welfare). As residential patterns and standards of behavior varied among these classes, so did each class have its characteristic religious affiliations. The upper class tended strongly toward membership in churches of predominantly white denominations, especially the Episcopal, Presbyterian, or Congregational. The Negro middle class also made these affiliations, but remained far more loyal to the independent black denominations, the African Methodist churches, and to a somewhat lesser degree, the Baptist. The individual congregations of these churches differed widely; but those with middle-class orientation tended to become more sedate in their worship, to have better educated ministers, to show a stronger interest in social reform, and to be less strict in enforcing pietistic

1. William C. Handy, *Father of the Blues*, ed. Arna Bontemps (New York: Macmillan Co., 1941), pp. 31, 83.

2. Charles Keil, *Urban Blues* (Chicago: University of Chicago Press, 1966), p. 40.

moral taboos. The highly developed organizational life of most congregations tended to sharpen the status consciousness of nearly everyone.[3]

The more dramatic changes in the black religious tradition occurred among the newer migrants to the city and among the very poor. To them was due the rapid increase of small storefront and residential churches. In the study of Mays and Nicholson (1933) 45 percent of the churches in Detroit and 72 percent of those in Chicago were of this type. Obvious economic factors go far to explain the rise of such churches; but their small size and intimate atmosphere was an important attraction.[4] Also important was the outlet they provided for imaginative leadership. From apostolic times on through the Middle Ages the Church had provided leadership opportunities for the lowly born. In America, among Protestants and Catholics alike, the clerical role was always an important route to social advancement. Because blacks in the growing urban ghettos had far fewer opportunities to exercise their diverse talents, the institutions of religion became especially important.

BLACK PENTECOSTALISM

Between 1906 and 1908 at a church on Azusa Street in Los Angeles occurred the great outpouring of the Spirit from which the twentieth-century revival of Pentecostalism flowed. The pastor of that Apostolic Faith Gospel Mission, whose influence spread across the nation and even abroad, was William J. Seymour, a Negro. Seymour thus personifies a process by which black piety exerted its greatest direct influence on American religious history, for the gift of tongues came during those years to black and white alike. Just as Pentecostal doctrines and church ways answered to the spiritual and social needs of blacks, so did they to other disinherited or suppressed people all over the world, most notably the underprivileged people of Latin America. During the later 1960s yet another Pentecostal revival would come to the United States. In the America of 1908, however, a new religious movement was not likely to remain more than momentarily integrated, and Pentecostalists soon began to organize segregated churches and associations. Given the extraordinary tendency of a "charismatic" movement to develop charismatic leaders, Pentecostalism from the first provided an especially fertile field for sensational and highly independent preachers to develop a distinctive following. As in white Pentecostalism, the gift of tongues con-

3. See the comparative pyramidal charts in E. Franklin Frazier, *The Negro in the United States*, pp. 293–97.

4. See Benjamin Elijah Mays and Joseph William Nicholson, *The Negro's Church*.

duced to extreme subjectivism. As a result, many Spirit-favored leaders proclaimed themselves to have received special revelations. This often led to the founding, not only of new congregations, but in cases where an effective organizer was at hand, of new sects or denominations. The very tendencies that accentuated radical congregationalism and a powerful laity also provided opportunities for self-proclaimed bishops to develop strong and financially lucrative bases of ecclesiastical power (see pp. 816–22 above).

The resultant situation among black Pentecostalists was chaotic. Yet certain representative bodies merit mention. Probably largest is the Church of God in Christ, founded by Charles H. Mason, a former Baptist who joined the Holiness movement in the 1890s. After participating in the movement in Los Angeles, Mason converted his Holiness congregation in Memphis to Pentecostal views and made it the nucleus of a rapidly expanding circle of churches. In its teaching on doctrine and morals this church stands near the center of normative Pentecostalism. By 1965 its general assembly reported 4,150 churches and nearly 420,000 American members, plus a sizable foreign constituency located largely in Africa and the Caribbean.

The Ethiopian [later, Apostolic] Overcoming Holy Church of God was founded in Alabama in 1916 by a former Methodist, W. T. Phillips. It followed standard Pentecostal lines except that Bishop Phillips retained an unusual degree of authority. He appointed the ministers of the denomination's three hundred churches and even received the tithes of his membership, which had reached seventy-five thousand by 1965.

In addition to these various large, medium, and small organizations there were literally countless independent congregations. Taken as a whole, the black Holiness-Pentecostal impulse probably included a million adherents. It constituted perhaps the most dynamic and socially functional element in black Protestantism; and its strict pietistic moral demands made it a considerable factor in the upward social mobility of its members. On the other hand, as these churches began to have a second generation membership, they tended toward greater sobriety and less otherworldliness in their faith and practice. Such accommodation to the standards of historic evangelicalism, however, led to the continuous founding of new gatherings as the flow of in-migrants continued, or as competition with the city's other attractions required more unrestrained forms of worship. During the later 1960s, however, black militancy was creating an atmosphere which was less favorable to ecstatic and otherworldly forms of religion.

THE FLOWERING OF CULTS

Pentecostalism was by no means the only religious impulse that took institutional form in the urban ghettos. The desperate circumstances of a people so incarcerated also led to far more drastic innovations, in particular, to the founding and development of unusual and sometimes brilliantly organized cults. Whether or not "Jack-leg preachers," sensational "healers," purveyors of spiritualistic frauds, and other types of religious showmen have found more avid constituencies among blacks or whites would be hard to say. Yet the "black gods of the metropolis" have undoubtedly had a character and appeal of their own. They have also tended to justify the disdain that Ira Reid displayed in a widely read and often quoted article, "Let Us Prey!"

> The whole group is characterized by the machinations of impostors who do their work in great style. Bishops without a diocese, those who heal with divine inspiration, praying circles that charge for their services, American Negroes turned Jews "over night," theological seminaries conducted in the rear of "railroad" apartments, Black Rev. Wm. Sundays, Ph.D., who have escaped the wrath of many communities, new denominations built upon the fundamental doctrine of race—all these and even more contribute to the prostitution of the church. And there seems to be no end to their growth. Already have five new institutions been opened for business. One thinks of the much advertised cinema production "Hell Bent for Heaven." [5]

Some of the references in this passage are to groups that do not even pretend to be Christian, yet their charismatic leadership and institutional form link them with many of the more radical evangelical organizations. The "cult" phenomenon, therefore, deserves separate discussion, even though a meaningful distinction between sects and cults is notoriously difficult to establish and maintain. To summarize definitions made in a previous chapter,[6] one may use the term sect to designate a restoration or intensification of certain emphases in an older or larger tradition. The term cult, on the contrary, refers to more radical departures, often virtually new religions with new doctrines and new grounds for authority, including new scriptures and even new messiahs. In the Afro-American tradition cults are important

5. Ira de A. Reid, "Let Us Prey!" *Opportunity* 4 (September 1926): 274–78. See also his *In a Minor Key* (Washington: American Council on Education, 1940).

6. See pp. 230–32, 472–76 above.

not only for their direct influence on many people, but also for the light they shed on the actualities of race in America.

Father Divine

By far the most widely publicized of the black cults was the Father Divine Peace Mission. This movement serves to illustrate the way in which various motifs taken from Holiness, New Thought, Perfectionist, and Adventist movements could be combined with utterly new elements so as to constitute, in effect, a small but distinct religion which could maintain itself even after the founder had "passed." George Baker, later known as Major J. Morgan Divine, and later still as Father Divine, was born on a Savannah River island around 1878–80. He showed religious interests very early, but the decisive turn came when he was about twenty and serving as a part-time Baptist minister in Baltimore. There he met Samuel Morris, an itinerant preacher who declared that he *was* the Father Eternal (1 Cor. 3:16). As Father Jehoviah, Morris founded a church of his own, and then associated George Baker with him as his "Messenger," or second person. In 1908 one Saint John the Vine Hickerson joined them, but the trio soon broke up because of quarrels over their places in the Godhead.

Around 1912 Baker alone gathered a following in Valdosta, Georgia, but three years later he was forced to move north to Brooklyn, then to Sayville, Long Island. Here for twelve years (1919–31), with an evangelism strategy that consisted of offering bountiful chicken dinners free, the movement's popularity increased, while the world wondered how the bounty was paid for. Then in 1931, with the Depression almost at its worst, Baker moved to Harlem, where the Peace Mission enjoyed a decade of expansion. "The part-time hedge-keeper of Baltimore had become a full-time heaven-keeper in New York." After 1941 legal problems required a transfer of Father Divine's residence and headquarters to Philadelphia, but the Peace Mission continued to thrive. When he died in 1965, the major heavens of his kingdom were still in New York and Philadelphia, but there were farms in New York State and other "extensions" in various northern and western cities.

The tenets of the Peace Mission issued chiefly from two sources. Most important was Father Divine's flamboyant personality, his free-flowing prodigality, and his alleged divinity. He was the incarnation of God, whose words, transcribed by secretaries and published in *New Day,* were sacred scripture. Heaven is now on earth; Holy Communion is celebrated at banquets with God himself; the age of the Church and of baptism by water is over. In theory, no hierarchy divided the blessed, except that God's two wives, *seriatim,* held a privileged position. His widow continued to lead the movement after his death as Mother Divine. (Edna Rose Ritchings was a golden blonde of twenty-one whom Father Divine married in 1946, to the consternation of many followers. Born in Vancouver, Canada, she had joined the Peace Mission, and as "Sweet Angel," had become a dedicated Rose Bud in Father Divine's entourage.) As a practical matter, membership of two sorts did evolve in the Peace Mission: an inner circle of those who gave over all their worldly possessions and became a sort of company of heaven entirely at the Father's bounty, and a wider membership of those who continued their worldly occupations.

A vital yet secondary source of Peace Mission teachings were theological principles with marked similarities to New Thought, though they were modified by perfectionist doctrines stemming from the Holiness impulse. Sin, sickness, and death are consequences (and signs) of unfaith; true faith is victorious and holiness is within reach:

> PEACE shall flow like a river [said Father Divine in 1939], and shall continue to extend this way, and sorrow and misery shall no longer be, when you all wholeheartedly accept ME and live exactly according to MY teaching universally. . . . You have to harmonize with ME in opposition to your sense of feeling.[7]

The moral implications of such "harmonizing" were clearly and, according to most observers, effectually laid down:

> One must refrain from stealing, refusing to pay just debts, indulging in liquor in any form, smoking, obscene language, gambling, playing numbers, racial prejudice or hate of any kind, greed, bigotry, selfishness, and lusting after the opposite sex.[8]

Most distinctive among these rules were the prohibitions of racial bigotry (the words "Negro" and "white" were not even to be used) and of lust (dancing, copulation, and marriage were forbidden since they would only increase the amount of misery in the world). Father Divine has been criticized as the sponsor of an essentially escapist movement; yet he did sponsor a Righteous Government Convention in 1936, worked for the election of Mayor LaGuardia and President Eisenhower (not least because Eisenhower had once quoted Father Divine's slogan, "Peace, It's Wonderful"),

7. Quoted from banquet messages given in Joseph R. Washington, Jr., *Black Religion: The Negro and Christianity in the United States*, pp. 122–25. "Christian Science is the half-truth, and Father Divine is the whole truth," declared one admiring convert (quoted in Sara Harris and Harriet Crittenden, *Father Divine, Holy Husband*, p. 287). These authors also found that most of the devoted members interviewed had a long history of experimenting with Christian Science, Unity, yoga, etc.

8. Arthur H. Fauset, *Black Gods of the Metropolis: Negro Cults of the Urban North*, p. 64.

actively sought to modify racial conflict, and successfully brought order and dignity into the lives of many adherents. Considerably less can be said of a rival cult often compared with the Peace Mission.

Sweet Daddy Grace

The United House of Prayer for All People (Isaiah 56:7) was the creation of Bishop Charles Emmanuel "Sweet Daddy" Grace, who, as his assumed name implied, invested himself with almost as much importance as Father Divine.

> Never mind about God [he said]. Salvation is by Grace only. . . . Grace has given God a vacation, and since God is on His vacation, don't worry Him. . . . If you sin against God, Grace can save you, but if you sin against Grace, God cannot save you.[9]

Grace's origins were humble; as his speech betrayed, he had come from Portugal or the Azores. He alleged himself to be white and often spoke patronizingly of the blacks who were baptized into his church. In 1925 he left a railroad job to begin preaching in the poorest urban districts of the Atlantic states, first in the South, later in the North. Over the years his wealth increased, as did the splendor of his living and the exaltedness of his place in the worship of his congregations as he toured from city to city, maintaining discipline, performing acts of healing, receiving gifts, collecting money, and selling a wide range of wonder-working Daddy Grace commodities.

The basic tenet of the House of Prayer is the sovereign power of its bishop, from whom all blessings flow. But the blessings (unlike Father Divine's) were intangible: healings on occasion, but more predictably ecstasies of the spirit, various ceremonial honors, and the vicarious pleasures of "sharing" Sweet Daddy's sumptuous life in a mansion-studded realm. What vestiges of Christianity remain suggest an extreme form of Pentecostalism. Worship services consist chiefly of frenzied dancing to very lively instrumental music—catalepsy, jerks, and the award of a white robe being the desired culmination. The House of Prayer demanded of its members only abject obedience and a willingness to part with money; consequently it had very little moral or social impact. Its success seemed to depend on the psychic needs of the more depressed elements of the black ghetto communities and the ability of a charismatic leader to satisfy those needs, in part by providing frequent lively meetings as well as splendid parades, public baptismal services with fire hoses, and monarchical pomp in worship.

9. Quoted, ibid., p. 26.

The great crisis in the House of Prayer came in 1960 when Daddy Grace died. For a time it appeared that tax litigation and conflicts between rival successors would end the cult's history and disperse its twenty thousand or so followers. After a year or two, however, Bishop Walter McCollough succeeded in extending its life, and in 1969 he dedicated a splendid new headquarters with an adjacent old people's home in Washington, D.C. At the national conclave there in 1969 a great parade and fire-hose baptisms in the street indicated that the church continued to win a lively following. Yet by this time the changing temper of the ghetto and the rise of black militancy were subjecting such forms of religious organization to increasingly severe criticism. Extensive future growth seemed improbable unless considerable changes in spirit and practice were effected.[10]

Cults such as the Peace Mission and the House of Prayer are unusual chiefly for their relative success and extreme individuality; but similar groups, often ephemeral and local, are constantly arising whenever some leader with the necessary gifts gathers a following. Some of them, but for their unusually charismatic leadership or extreme emphasis on faith healing, might be regarded simply as Holiness or Pentecostal churches. Like all such manifestations, white or black, they tap large reservoirs of human insecurity and anxiety. Yet students of black religion tend to stress three particular factors: their appeal to the special frustrations of the poorest and most culturally deprived elements in the ghetto; their response to the need of the more recent in-migrants for small, intimate contexts where the full range of feeling can find expression; and finally, their provision of a realm in which natural leaders can exercise organizational and entrepreneurial skills without white hindrance or competition.

Until or unless profound social changes occur, so that the energies and aspirations of urban blacks can find more meaningful expression, the cults (and kindred Christian movements) will no doubt continue to find many devoted adherents. The future of larger independent churches, however, as well as that of the rapidly growing Holiness-Pentecostal sects, depends on the larger question of the continued strength of Christian commitment in the black community as a whole. Since World War II problems of race rela-

10. At the time of Daddy Grace's death on 12 January 1960, the newspapers reported the membership of the House of Prayer as from three to six million; but Marvin A. Eisengart doubts that there were more than 25,000 regular members ("The House of Prayer" [Scholar of the House essay, Yale University, 1962]). Walter McCollough, who had joined the House of Prayer in 1930 at the age of fifteen, was in 1956 appointed by Daddy Grace as the pastor of the mother House of Prayer in Washington, D.C. At a meeting of the General Assembly on 6 February 1960, he was elected bishop, but Elder John McClure challenged the legitimacy of the election and declared himself bishop—a claim which he pressed for more than a year (see Eisengart, pp. 29–30).

tions and urban existence have become so intense that this question cannot even be addressed without prior consideration of the protest movement, which during the 1960s put the whole question of black religion in a new perspective. And mediating between the realm of cultic religion and the protest movement was the "protest cult" itself.

BLACK NATIONALISM AND THE BLACK MUSLIMS

The Nation of Islam, to give the Black Muslims their proper name, belongs in a class by itself among black religious movements. Not only has it been unusually successful in combining an appeal to blackness with an affirmation of Islam, but more than any other cultic religious movement it became a potent, even seminal, element in the rising protest movement. Its complex history, however, is so hidden from public view that it may never be entirely freed of confusion and controversy.

In its present form the Nation of Islam stems from two converging lines of influence. One of these can be traced to the "African dream" of Bishop Henry Turner, as well as to the later efforts of Marcus Garvey (1887–1940), a Jamaican who in 1914 founded a Universal Negro Improvement Association and African Communities League, with the motto "One God! One Aim! One Destiny!" Garvey's aim was to awaken the self-esteem of blacks everywhere and to redeem Africa for all Africans at home and abroad. Between 1916 and 1923 he recruited members in the United States with phenomenal success, using every means at his command, from flashy military parades to an extensive network of cooperative business ventures. His measures even included the organization of an African Orthodox church, with a militant Episcopal priest, George Alexander McGuire, being consecrated as its bishop by Archbishop Vilatte of the Syrian Orthodox church. McGuire bade the faithful to "forget the white Gods" and provided them with pictures of a black Madonna and Child.[11] Garvey meanwhile concentrated on more tangible objectives, and at a convention in 1920 he was elected the provisional president of Africa. Numerous frauds led to his deportation in 1927, yet far more effectively than earlier colonizationists, he had awakened the spirit of African nationalism among the urban masses. Like the organizations and churches of many ethnic minorities, Garvey's also contributed powerfully to the self-respect and group-consciousness of his followers and in the process exposed the degree to which many Afro-

11. See E. David Cronon, *Black Moses: The Story of Marcus Garvey and the Universal Negro Improvement Association.* In 1960 the African Orthodox church still had a membership of about seven thousand (C. Eric Lincoln, *The Black Muslims in America,* p. 65).

Americans were alienated from the white culture around them. After he had demonstrated the potentialities of this appeal, countless smaller movements, some more esoteric than others, most of them with strong religious overtones, stressed Ethiopian, Abyssinian, or more generally African themes. It is not surprising, therefore, that Black Muslims recognize Garvey as a forerunner in black nationalism.

More direct links seem to exist between the Black Muslims and the Moorish Science Temple of America, though they are by no means clear or undisputed. Its founder was a North Carolinian named Timothy Drew (1866–1929), who had somehow developed an interest in Islamic religion and become convinced that American "Negroes" should abandon that name and declare their "Asiatic" origins as Moors or Moorish Americans. To advance these interests he took the name Noble Prophet Ali Drew (Noble Drew Ali) and published *The Holy Koran,* a small pamphlet containing Islamic, Christian, and Garveyite passages along with his own interpretations. The basic message has had far-reaching implications, for it departed from Garvey's form of black nationalism in its insistence that the designations Negro, colored, Ethiopian, etc., be abandoned, that an Asiatic or Moorish identity be affirmed, and that the self-defeating life styles of the black subculture be abandoned. For those who took this new allegiance, salvation and self-respect were assured. The first Moorish Science Temple was founded in Newark in 1913, and others were planted elsewhere. In Chicago the movement flourished best, but with success came factionalism and violence. In 1929 one of Drew's major deputies was murdered, and shortly thereafter the prophet himself was killed. The Moorish Temple continued, however, and thirty years later his followers still maintained an expectant vigil at his grave in Lincoln Cemetery, Chicago.[12]

After Drew's death, a struggle for the succession to leadership and a splintering of the movement ensued. Among the claimants was Wallace D. Fard (or Wali Farad Muhammad), who began to gather a following in Detroit in 1930. Claiming (it is said) to be a reincarnation of Drew and a sometime visitor in Mecca, he preached a message very similar to that of Noble Drew Ali, founded a Temple of Islam in Detroit with possibly eight thousand members, and then a second in Chicago, where his most trusted lieutenant took charge. Farad's mysterious disappearance in 1934 opened another period of very slow growth. But amid the contention among rival

12. The Church of God (Black Jews), founded in Philadelphia by the Southern-born prophet F. S. Cherry, holds Adam, Jacob, and Jesus to have been black. Its cultic sobriety, moral teachings, and use of a Semitic language and scriptures resemble various Moorish and Islamic movements (see Fauset, *Black Gods,* chap. 4).

elements of the black Islamic impulse, the leader of Temple Number Two in Chicago gradually became dominant. He was Robert Poole (b. 1897), the son of a Baptist minister in Georgia, who had taken the name Elijah Muhammad. Having led the faction ascribing the most exalted status to the departed Farad, he now became the movement's leader, though the founding of Detroit's Temple Number One in 1931 was still accepted as the movement's beginning and Farad's birthday, 26 February, was in due course appointed as Saviour's Day.

Elijah Muhammad's authority rested on a unique claim that the will of Allah himself had been communicated to him and published in *The Supreme Wisdom* and successive issues of *Muhammad Speaks.* According to these teachings the Negroes of North America (the Black Nation) are to be led into their true inheritance as members of the ancient tribe of Shabazz, which looks to Abraham as its patriarch and to which all the world's non-white peoples belong. They will be led by the Nation of Islam, the followers of Elijah Muhammad. Caucasian people are an inferior, latter-day offshoot of the Black Asiatic Nation. The American Negro's self-hate (his negative estimate of blackness) is thus replaced by a strong sense of triumphant peoplehood. Black Muslim eschatology teaches that God has come; there is no life after this life; heaven and hell are only two contrasting earthly conditions; the hereafter (which will begin to appear about A.D. 2000) is but the end of the present "spook" civilization of the Caucasian usurpers, including the Christian religion. It will be followed by the redemption of the Black Nation and their glorious rule over all the earth.

Because of his refusal to kill on any orders but Allah's, Elijah Muhammad and a number of followers went to prison during World War II, while the movement languished—except behind bars, where it has always recruited effectively. The Nation of Islam, therefore, dates in a practical way to 1946, when Elijah Muhammad resumed leadership of a membership that had fallen to a thousand or less. In the changed atmosphere of the later 1950s the Black Muslims' outspoken message began to gain a new kind of relevance. Official membership statistics are not released, but responsible estimates made around 1960 spoke of a hundred thousand disciplined, relatively young, and predominantly male followers of whom was expected unquestioning obedience to the Messenger of Allah, regular attendance at meetings, and at least a tithe in money. Affiliated with the Chicago temple were many small business enterprises and the University of Islam, which provided a complete education through high school and beyond. Plans were projected for a major Islamic center and the acquisition of extensive farmlands.

The man who most effectively brought this message to the black multitudes of the urban ghettos and to the world at large was Malcolm X (1925–

65). Malcolm Little was born in Omaha, Nebraska, the son of a Baptist preacher who had supported Marcus Garvey. He spent most of his youth in Michigan, but he really discovered the black community only after completing the eighth grade and moving to the Boston area. He went to prison on a burglary charge in 1946. While he was in prison the Muslim's message came to him as a veritable gospel, and for over a decade after his release in 1952 he was an untiring apostle of the movement in New York and across the nation. Then in March 1964 he left the Black Muslims, founding first the Muslim Mosque, Incorporated, and later the nonreligious Organization of Afro-American Unity, both of which aimed to awaken and unify the movement for black liberation. He was assassinated in New York on 21 February 1965, but through his posthumously published autobiography and speeches he continued to be one of the decade's most prophetic voices.[13]

The appeal and importance of the Black Muslims, according to E. U. Essien-Udom, depends not so much on their "esoteric" doctrines and cultic practices as on their "exoteric" moral and social teachings, especially their rigorous standards of personal behavior, family responsibility, and occupational stability.[14] Robert Vernon made a related point five years later:

> So long as the movement had meaning to the ghetto poor in terms of their own experiences, and provided psychological and material therapy against the ravages of a white-dominated hell called America, the religion could have been Black Buddhism or Black Brahmanism or Black Anything with equal effect.[15]

The growth of the movement thus testifies to the alienation and despair bred by America's racial discrimination. In this sense the Black Muslims are a kind of bridge between the escapist cults and the main tradition of black

13. See *The Autobiography of Malcolm X* and *Malcolm X Speaks*, ed. George Breitman.

14. *Black Nationalism* (Chicago: University of Chicago Press, 1962). Its prohibitions of alcohol, narcotics, and sexual profligacy, like its demands of respect for womanhood in the context of a strong patriarchal family, of occupational responsibility, and of quiet, decorous behavior, are precisely those of the traditional Puritan-American mainstream. Black Muslims are thus summoned to the moral standards of the Caucasian devils; in this sense it is a "cultural sect" calling Negroes out of their subculture.

The relations of Black Muslims with traditional Islam are controversial. Many followers of the original Muhammad (A.D. 570–632), a large proportion of whom are Caucasian, insist that the racism of the Black Muslims as well as their leader's claim to authority contradict the basic nature of this most widely propagated and most interracial of world religions. Yet certain Arab leaders have shown some deference to Black Muslim leaders and their University of Islam in Chicago. On the other hand, Malcolm X's personal experience of the Islam of Mecca itself seems to have alienated him from the Chicago version (see *The Autobiography of Malcolm X*, pp. 323–88).

15. Robert Vernon, "Malcolm X: Voice of the Black Ghetto," *International Socialist Review* (Spring 1965); quoted in George Breitman, *The Last Year of Malcolm X: The Evolution of a Revolutionary* (New York: Merit Publishers, 1967), p. 7. This does not mean, of course, that Malcolm's conversion, like any number of others, did not have a deep religious dimension.

militancy. In theory, the movement offers a message of deliverance for blacks the world over; in reality, it is an island of disciplined security that is at once radical and bourgeois. Whether the esoteric features of the Black Muslims will survive the death of the movement's charismatic leader or whether the movement will move toward the social-political goals that Malcolm X advocated during his last days remains to be seen. Crucial to the denouement will be the protest movement on whose success not only black religion but the future of American democracy may be said to depend.

THE RISE OF THE PROTEST MOVEMENT

On 4 July 1881 Booker T. Washington called to order Tuskegee Institute's first class in a battered AME Zion church. Only three years later he addressed the National Education Association on "The Educational Outlook in the South," and from that time until his death he was the chief American spokesman for the Negro. His most celebrated statement was made in 1895 at the Atlanta Exposition, where he bade the whites of the New South "Cast down your bucket where you are":

> Cast it down among the eight millions of Negroes whose habits you know, whose fidelity and love you have tested in days when to have proved treacherous meant the ruin of your firesides. . . . While doing this you can be assured in the future as in the past that you and your families will be surrounded by the most patient, faithful, law-abiding, and unresentful people the world has seen. . . . In all things that are purely social we can be as separate as the fingers, yet one as the hand in all things essential to mutual progress.[16]

Accepting political inequality and social segregation (though not the denial of constitutional rights), he pleaded to all men everywhere to help make the Negro a trained, literate, and useful component of the new society. Though no churchman himself, he thus accepted and strengthened the arrangements which nearly all of the major Negro denominations and sects, including their educational leaders, then accepted—and which they by and large continued to accept down to World War II, and even after.

Ever since the days of the antislavery crusade, however, there have been men and women, black and white, who took a more radical view; and during the racial-justice nadir of the Progressive Era the first important challenge to the Washingtonian view of things came from W. E. Burghardt

16. Given in full in August Meier et al., eds., *Black Protest Thought in the Twentieth Century*, pp. 3–8.

DuBois (1868–1963), a Massachusetts-born Harvard Ph.D. who had become a professor of sociology at Atlanta University in 1897. In *The Souls of Black Folk* (1903) DuBois condemned the "Atlanta Compromise" and the whole notion that the pre–Civil War strategy of the free Negroes should now be changed "from a by-path into a veritable Way of Life." He saw, too, that religion was a fundamental part of this way of life, and in the same year published *The Negro Church,* the first scholarly work in the field. Except for his heavy emphasis on the need for liberal (as against technical) education and his emphasis on the leadership role of the "Talented Tenth," his words and ideas strike a trenchant contemporary note even a half-century later. Besides leading the anti-Bookerite "Niagara Movement," DuBois also helped to found the National Association for the Advancement of Colored People in 1909. As the only Negro on the national staff, he became editor of its magazine, the *Crisis.*

By 1915 DuBois had repudiated the notion that "God or his vice-gerent the White Man" should define the Negro's goals, and was seeking to awaken the self-consciousness of the Negro masses. In this sense he was frankly a "race man"; and in 1934 he broke with the NAACP by taking a position on the "segregation issue" which was then held by only a small black minority and almost no whites:

> There should never be an opposition to segregation pure and simple unless that segregation does involve discrimination. . . . Never in the world should our fight be against association with ourselves, because by that very token we give up the whole argument that we are worth associating with.[17]

During the next three decades the court battles of the NAACP brought considerable progress in the realms of integration, civil rights, and economic opportunity. World War II, to be sure, was fought by an utterly segregated army and navy, but the efforts of Adam Clayton Powell, Jr., in Harlem, a new wave of organized protest, and a series of urban riots had significant effects.[18] In 1949 two executive orders of President Truman integrating the armed services and the federal civil service achieved some of the most decisive reforms since the Reconstruction amendments were passed. Then in 1954 the Supreme Court culminated a long series of important decisions with its epoch-making unanimous ruling against "separate but equal" public

17. W. E. B. DuBois, "Segregation," *Crisis* 41 (January 1934); quoted by Meier et al., *Black Protest Thought,* pp. 159–60.

18. See Powell's *Marching Blacks: An Interpretive History of the Rise of the Black Common Man.* In 1941 he was elected to the New York City Council, and in 1944 to Congress. Succeeding his father, he was minister of the Abyssinian Baptist Church from 1937 to 1971.

schools. In one sense Ralph Bunche's pessimistic observation that Negroes were "wards of the Supreme Court" became more appropriate than in 1935 when he uttered it; but in the 1950s a new awakening of the national consciousness began to manifest itself, and a more general protest movement took shape.

THE WHITE REVOLUTION AND THE BLACK REVOLUTION

The revolutionary stage in the movement for racial justice in America has two relatively distinct aspects, both of them with great importance for religious history. The first may well be called the White Revolution because it involved a dramatic shift of viewpoint by leaders of the white community and a very considerable shift in public opinion. As complacency began to yield to guilt and concern, the basically racist character of American institutions came to be recognized to an unprecedented degree. The depth of this response should not be exaggerated, for reactionary movements also gained strength, yet doubts of the gravest sort began to corrode the old assumption that American ideals of equality had been achieved and that increased production would painlessly make all Americans happy. Especially effective in jogging the public conscience was President Eisenhower's decision in 1957 to move federal troops into Little Rock, Arkansas, in support of a court order integrating that city's Central High School. This widely publicized confrontation rallied the civil rights movement as had no other event for over a century. As a result, the churches slowly awoke from the complacency induced by the postwar revival. The National Council of Churches wrote a new chapter in the history of its concern for social issues. The "silent generation" of students began to be heard. But the chief impetus for change stemmed from an awakening in the black community.

The Black Revolution came into existence almost apart from organized efforts as sudden unanticipated events gradually transformed a hopeless passive minority into a self-conscious force. Blacks grew impatient with the almost imperceptible gains made through the strategies of Tuskegee, the Talented Tenth, or the NAACP. Direct action by the many rather than inductive research and legal maneuvers by the few became the order of the day. Due to this momentous shift of strategy, a long list of leaders, organizations, campaigns, and historic confrontations entered the annals of American history. And out of it all came a new sense of racial identity and purpose.

The real heroes of these many events—those who marched, picketed, protested, went to jail, and suffered pain and inhuman indignities—are innumerable and anonymous. They registered their courage, however, at places that deserve remembrance along with Valley Forge and Gettysburg. Hence Americans remember Montgomery, where Rosa Parks's exasperation with Jim Crow buses led to a successful transportation boycott and the emergence of Dr. Martin Luther King, Jr., as a racial leader. In February 1957 King became the first president of the Southern Christian Leadership Conference. Later that year came the events at Little Rock. The student sit-in movement dated back as far as 1943 when the newly organized Congress of Racial Equality (CORE) began its work in Chicago; but in 1960 this movement of passive resistance spread throughout the South despite more than a thousand arrests. In that year the Student Nonviolent Coordinating Committee (SNCC) began its "Jail, No Bail" activities and together with students in CORE began to make "freedom rides" so as to eliminate segregated interstate transportation facilities. The first bus was bombed and burned near Anniston, Alabama, on 14 May, and the National Guard was called into Montgomery. Through 1962 the voter registration drive was increasingly pressed, despite resistance and violence; and in October, after many legal maneuvers and a night of rioting in which two lives were lost, James H. Meredith registered as the first Negro student of the University of Mississippi. Incidents multiplied during 1963 with Birmingham, Alabama, most prominently in the news; but the culminating event was the peaceful convergence on Washington, D.C., of over 250,000 freedom marchers. Martin Luther King's moving depiction of his dream to this vast audience did not bring peace and equality to America, however; and in 1964 the chief centers of activity were in the North, as riots in New York, Jersey City, and Rochester set the stage, as it were, for the devastating outbreak in the Watts district of Los Angeles in the summer of 1965.

The year 1965 also witnessed the culminating demonstration of the civil rights movement, when twenty-five thousand people from all over the country converged on Selma, Alabama. This event brought President Johnson himself to declare that "We shall overcome." For the many who were there it took on almost pentecostal significance. Yet it also marked the beginning of the end of joint interracial protest. In the following summer, on 9 June, the shooting of James Meredith as he walked from Memphis to Jackson led to a convergence of black leaders on that highway march—and from that time forward a new sense of *black* responsibility became manifest. CORE dropped the term "multiracial" from its statement of purpose, and SNCC became even more black in its makeup and orientation. Both organizations lost their force, moreover, as opposition to the war in Vietnam began to absorb the attention of white student protests. New strategies came to the fore in the black liberation movement as the ideas of Malcolm X, who had been assassinated on 21 February 1965, began to replace those of Martin Luther King, who would be assassinated on 4 April 1968.

"Black Power" became the chief slogan during the next cycle of years. One notable example of the new spirit was the July 1966 meeting of forty Negro churchmen in the Bethel AME Church of Harlem. Responding to the changed temper of the times, they issued a powerful statement on the nature and promise of Black Power. They conceded that "too often the Negro church has stirred its members away from the reign of God in *this world* to a distorted and complacent view of *an otherworldly* conception of God's power." They insisted that black religion must no longer function as an institutional accommodation of white supremacy. Then without apology they compared their demands to Irish, Polish, Italian, and Jewish efforts at achieving group leverage in both public and private affairs. They pledged themselves to advance this cause and bade their white brethren regard it as a contribution to the future health of the American social order.[19]

Neither leaders nor spokesmen were much in evidence during the summer of 1967, when pent-up frustration and rage erupted in fire and violence in Newark and Detroit. After this "long hot summer," however, a three-day conference of black leaders was convened in the Episcopal Cathedral of Newark, again with the Reverend Nathan Wright as chairman. Among the several resolutions they issued was one which urged a boycott of all churches not working for the "black revolution." Yet this seemingly clear warning left many dilemmas even for those black churchmen who actively sought to rectify the entire American "system" of racial oppression. In part, the black churches faced the question of which road to follow.[20] For decades they had been accused of retarding the achievement of equality. "When one encounters the Negro church," the sociologist E. Franklin Frazier had declared, "one encounters the most important barrier to integration and the assimilation of members." [21] But by 1967 these same black churches were on the defensive for the opposite reason. They could proudly accept Frazier's statement and point to the fact that from time immemorial it was religion

19. The statement is explained and presented as an appendix in Nathan Wright, Jr., *Black Power and Urban Unrest.*

20. Needless to say, the white churches faced the same dilemma, especially as they responded to the "inside" demands made by their own black laity and clergy for special funds and separate organizational status. Still more provocative were the "outside" demands for "reparations" pressed upon them by James Forman and the Black Economic Development Conference. Born in Chicago (1929) and educated at Roosevelt University (degree in Public Administration, 1957), Forman worked at the Institute for Juvenile Research (Chicago) and taught school before being appointed executive director of the Student Nonviolent Coordinating Committee, 1961–66. After leaving SNCC he became active in the Black Economic Development Conference, and in April 1969 presented a Black Manifesto which demanded $500,000,000 in reparations from the churches and synagogues of America.

21. *The Negro Church*, pp. 70–71.

(organized and unorganized) that had held the Afro-American heritage together and preserved black solidarity.

At the same time, candid observers wondered if the churches could still perform that cultural function in the later twentieth century. Joseph R. Washington, for example, declared that the two large Baptist conventions merely "maintain church chaos via dictatorship perpetuated for personal gain" and that dictatorial regimentation in the Methodist bodies "inspires mediocrity."[22] Given the modern radical revolution, Vincent Harding wondered if the leaders of the black church hierarchy could "hold on to their already shaky grounds."[23] The otherworldly preoccupations of the sects and cults, meanwhile, despite their continued growth, seemed to increase both the chaos and the mediocrity. Church attendance and affiliation were declining just as they were in the white churches, except that they had started from a lower level and were proceeding at a swifter pace. The crisis was aggravated by the widening gap between the educational level of the clergy and that of the laity, with no improvement of the theological seminary situation in sight.[24]

In addition to the new social, economic, and intellectual factors which affected all churches, the black churches were profoundly involved in a reassessment of their particular theological and ideological situation. Among the options before them were, first of all, the two extremes: a single-mindedly pious concern for the development of a church that preached only a message of otherworldly salvation, or a secularist outlook in which the institutional church was regarded as no more than an assembly-point for community action. Between these extremes, however, diverse positive conceptions of the church's role were expounded by several very thoughtful men.

Most in accord with America's Reformed and Puritan heritage was that

22. Joseph R. Washington, *Black Religion*, pp. 67–69, 76–77.

23. Vincent Harding, "The Religion of Black Power," in *The Religious Situation: 1969*, ed. Donald R. Cutler, p. 13.

24. Reliable comparisons of black and white church membership in recent years are lacking; but the United States religious censuses of 1926 and 1936 indicated that the differences were very small, and that among men the black percentage was lower. In 1936 the overall figures were 44 percent (black) and 42.4 percent (white). In 1963 the Harris poll found that among Negroes regular church attendance (once a week) stood at 49 percent. Since the average congregation numbered two hundred, as against five hundred for whites, at least a thousand new ministers a year would be needed for the fifty-five thousand black churches; but only about a hundred a year were being graduated from seminaries (see William Brink and Louis Harris, *The Negro Revolution in America;* H. Richard Niebuhr et al., *The Advancement of Theological Education* [New York: Harper & Row, 1957]; and Fauset, *Black Gods*, chap. 10). *Theological Education* 4 (Spring 1970), with supplement, surveys black theological education. It reports 665 seminarians enrolled for a black membership of 10 million gathered in forty thousand congregations (p. S–10).

view which saw the Church's orthodox, pietistic, and moral message as the proper guide to constructive living in the social and political order. When coupled with pride of race and a strong concern for social justice, this might well be taken as the characteristic theology of most participants in the churches' civil rights effort. "We shall overcome" could be taken as its theme song. Yet it could draw on both the spirituals and traditional preaching tradition. From the lips of Ralph Abernathy, who succeeded Martin Luther King, Jr., as head of the SCLC, it would have great power and effectiveness.

Dr. King himself drew heavily on these same rich evangelical resources; yet the uniqueness of his theology owed much to the idealistic personalism and the Hegelian view of history which he studied while seeking his doctorate at Boston University. With further reading in Paul Tillich, the existentialists, and, at some point, Mohandas Ghandi, King developed a profound view of the office of black suffering and the meaning of historical travail, and a faith in God's ultimate victory. This standpoint suggested to him that Christian love must always be at the heart of the struggle. Yet he never failed to keep these "liberal" views in touch with the Baptist nurture of his youth. Almost the last words he uttered on the motel balcony in Memphis where he was assassinated were a request that Thomas Dorsey's gospel song, "Precious Jesus, Take My Hand," be on the program for that evening's scheduled rally. As his coffin was borne to its last resting place through the streets of Atlanta in a mule-drawn farm wagon, a sad and distracted America would remember the day five years before when a vast throng stretching out before the steps of the Lincoln Memorial had heard of his dream—that "We will be free one day":

> This will be the day when all of God's children will be able to sing with new meaning, "let freedom ring." . . .
>
> When we allow freedom to ring—when we let it ring from every city and every hamlet, from every state and every city, we will be able to speed up that day when all of God's children, black men and white men, Jews and Gentiles, Protestants and Catholics, will be able to join hands and sing in the words of the old Negro spiritual, "Free at last, Free at last, Great God a-mighty, We are free at last." [25]

In retrospect, it would seem that his theology went far to clarify his role as leader during a crucial decade of American history.

When Martin Luther King, Jr., died, one stage in the history of American

25. Martin Luther King, Jr., *I Have a Dream* (Los Angeles: John Henry and Mary Louise Dunn Bryant Foundation, 1963).

race relations also ended, though to many (possibly to most) Americans, both black and white, his way was still the best road to amity and justice. The more militant and separatistic spirit of the later sixties had no single theologian with anything like King's steady sustaining power. Black nationalism has from time to time had strong Christian support ever since the founding of the AME church in 1816. The Reverend Adam Clayton Powell, Jr., added his eloquent voice to the tradition for two decades, and very notably in March 1966; but in subsequent years his place in the black liberation movement became very uncertain. In 1968 the Reverend Albert B. Cleage, Jr., pastor of Detroit's Shrine of the Black Madonna (a church associated with the UCC), published *The Black Messiah,* a series of forceful sermons addressed to black Christians.[26] In these addresses Cleage contended that Jesus was a "revolutionary black leader" and that blacks should not look to "the Resurrection of the physical body of Jesus but the Resurrection of the Black Nation which He started." Here was a message in which a major accent of Garvey's African Orthodox church and even the Black Muslims was echoed.

James H. Cone, on the other hand, was far more effective in developing a theology that would give Christian substance to black consciousness and provide an ethical basis for Black Power:

> It is not my thesis that all Black Power advocates are Christians or even wish to be so. Nor is it my purpose to twist their language or to make an alien interpretation of it. My concern is, rather, to show that the goal and message of Black Power is consistent with the gospel of Jesus Christ. Indeed, I have even suggested that if Christ is present among the oppressed, as he promised, he must be working through the activity of Black Power. This alone is my thesis.[27]

Cone poses urgent questions: "Is there a message from Christ to the countless number of blacks whose lives are smothered under white society? Is it possible to be *really* black and still feel any identity with the biblical tradition expressed in the Old and New Testaments?" Against those who would abandon the faith as an opiate of the people, he provides a theology of revolution that "begins and ends with the man Jesus—his life, death, and resurrection." He professes his faith in the One who was sent "to proclaim release

26. Born in Indianapolis in 1911, Cleage attended Wayne State University (Detroit) and Oberlin Graduate School of Theology (Ohio). After serving as pastor of churches in Lexington, Kentucky, San Francisco, and Springfield, Massachusetts, he returned to Detroit in 1952 to serve as minister of the Central Congregational Church. Cleage became active in the NAACP, but in the 1960s his church was linked more explicitly with the cause of black liberation.

27. James H. Cone, *Black Theology and Black Power,* p. 48; see also pp. 32–35.

to the captives and recovering of sight to the blind, to set at liberty those who are oppressed, to proclaim the acceptable year of the Lord" (Luke 4:18–19). Without depriving the gospel of its comfort, Cone would animate the black churches—and the white churches, too, if they would listen—with grounds for faithful social action.

A final consideration is the religious dimension of Black Power itself, which Vincent Harding has so profoundly articulated. He describes the movement as an apocalyptic awakening to the fact that "now is the fullness of time . . . a day of destruction demanded by a just God," a time when armed and marching black saints conceive of their task no differently than those Puritans "who cut off unrepentant heads in old England or now burn 'suspected' children in Vietnam." He also sees—and calls for—a more positive religious response to the oft-reiterated affirmation that "We are a spiritual people," wondering if a broader identification with the world's oppressed will not lead Black Power to a rediscovery of Africa's religion "which seeks unity and harmony with the forces of God in the universe." [28]

The search for religious roots that are unrelated to the middle-class technocratic culture of Christendom goes on among white Americans as well—and for similar reasons that are discussed in the next chapter of this book. Yet these trends in black religion, like the revolutionary aims that accompany them, will depend on the nation's progress in abating racial oppression. No one can speak confidently of the future. What is certain is that the awakening of black America which became so prominent a fact of the sixties did more than anything else to make that decade a turning point in American religious history.

28. Harding, "The Religion of Black Power," pp. 3–38.

63

THE TURBULENT SIXTIES

The decade of the sixties seems in many ways to have marked a new stage in the long development of American religious history. Not only did this intense and fiercely lived span of years have a character of its own, but it may even have ended a distinct quadricentennium—a unified four-hundred-year period—in the Anglo-American experience. A Great Puritan Epoch can be seen as beginning in 1558 with the death of Mary Tudor, the last monarch to rule over an officially Roman Catholic England, and as ending in 1960 with the election of John Fitzgerald Kennedy, the first Roman Catholic president of the United States. To underline the same point, one might note that the age of the Counter-Reformation began in 1563 with the adjournment of the Council of Trent and ended in 1965 with the closing of the Second Vatican Council. Histories of the rise of organized Puritanism begin their accounts with the decisive first decade in the reign of Queen Elizabeth; and the terms "post-Puritan" and "post-Protestant" are first popularly applied to America in the 1960s.

This is not to say that only the vicissitudes of Puritanism are vital to an understanding of the intervening years; but it *is* to say that the exploration and settlement of those parts of the New World in which the United States took its rise were profoundly shaped by the Reformed and Puritan impulse, and that this impulse, through its successive transmutations, remained the dominant element in the ideology of most Protestant Americans. To that tradition, moreover, all other elements among the American people—Catholic, Orthodox, Lutheran, Jewish, infidel, red, yellow, and black—had in some way, negatively or positively, to relate themselves. Or at least they did so *until the 1960s,* when the age of the WASP, the age of the melting pot, drew to a close. Let us then look more closely at this momentous decade, this seeming watershed and alleged turning point in American history, this moment of truth for "the nation with the soul of a church."

THE RADICAL TURN IN RELIGION AND MORALS

Like many of its elegant, gay, or roaring predecessors, the decade of the 1960s will probably gain a name or two. Men will, of course, identify it with President Kennedy's New Frontier and President Johnson's Great Society (though not without irony), and with the war in Southeast Asia. Adjectives like "secular" or "permissive" will probably commemorate other aspects of these ten eventful years. The decade may also be remembered for the "death of God" or the "Great Moral Revolution"; and these terms will rest on actualities far more pervasive than, say, the gaiety of the troubled nineties or the elegance of the eighties. New cosmic signs *were* being read in the sixties. The decade *did* experience a fundamental shift in American moral and religious attitudes. The decade of the sixties was a time, in short, when the old foundations of national confidence, patriotic idealism, moral traditionalism, and even of historic Judaeo-Christian theism, were awash. Presuppositions that had held firm for centuries—even millennia—were being widely questioned. Some sensational manifestations came and went (as fads and fashions will), but the existence of a basic shift of mood rooted in deep social and institutional dislocations was anything but ephemeral.

There were also many specific events which registered a traumatic impact. A Roman Catholic was elected to the presidency of the United States—and then at the peak of his public favor was struck down and laid to rest while the nation and the world, half stupefied by the succession of events, joined in a concert of grief such as human technology could never before have made possible. In the meantime, an aged cardinal who had been elevated to the papacy in 1958 was carrying out a revolution in the Roman Catholic Church whose reverberations rumbled back and forth across the Christian world with implications for the future that defy human calculation. In 1967 Israel's Six-Day War brought about not only a dramatic renewal of Jewish self-consciousness, but a marked deterioration of Jewish-Christian relations—and at a time when Negro-Jewish relations were being put under severe strain by population shifts in the cities.

At the same time, the Protestant Establishment was absorbing the shock of two epoch-marking Supreme Court decisions. In 1962 a ruling on the one man–one vote principle cut deep into the rural strongholds of Protestant political power. In 1963 the Court dealt even more decisively with long-established and prevailingly Protestant practices by ruling religious ceremonies in the public schools unconstitutional. Then, as if to demonstrate the revolutionary import of the nation's pervasive pluralism, the civil rights movement itself was transformed. The culmination of its interracial phase was the great demonstration in Selma, Alabama, in March and April 1965; yet the virtual end of that movement and the emergence of Black Power as an organizing principle lay only a year away—on the other side of the Watts riot in Los Angeles and the Meredith march from Memphis to Jackson. Finally, as if fate were determined to make the decade a turning point in history, President Johnson authorized the bombing of North Vietnam in February 1965, and by the end of the year escalated the American troop strength there to two hundred thousand men. By 1969 this figure had passed the half-million mark, and the war had become America's longest. By 1970 the nation's sense of unity had fallen to its lowest point since 1861.

The full significance of these several compound events will not be knowable until the end of time, but it was perfectly clear to any reasonably observant American that the postwar revival of the Eisenhower years had completely sputtered out, and that the nation was experiencing a *crise de conscience* of unprecedented depth. The decade thus seemed to beg remembrance for having performed a great tutelary role in the education of America, for having committed a kind of maturing violence upon the innocence of a whole people, for having called an arrogant and complacent nation to time, as it were, and for reminding it that even Mother Nature is capable of dealing harshly with her children when they desecrate and pollute her bounty. There are good reasons for believing that the decade of the sixties, even at the profoundest ethical and religious levels, will take a distinctive place in American history.[1]

Given this situation, the historian is obliged to accept his traditional twofold task: first, to clarify the new elements which came to pervade America's moral, intellectual, and religious atmosphere; and then to suggest why the country found itself in such revolutionary circumstances at this particular time. Much that will be said would of course apply, *mutatis mutandis,* to Western civilization generally or even to the whole world. This sense of global unity, indeed, is a fundamental feature of the times. Our chief focus, nevertheless, shall be on the American scene, where the transition seems to have come first and been especially abrupt.

Lest the reader's expectations become too exorbitant, however, a warning is in order. The truth is that phenomena of this scope could be "ex-

1. The nature and impact of the sixties are discussed in three overlapping essays of my own: "The Radical Turn in Theology and Ethics: Why It Occurred in the 1960s," in *The Sixties: Radical Change in American Religion,* ed. James M. Gustafson; "The Moral and Theological Revolution of the Sixties and Its Implications for American Religious Historiography," in *The State of American History,* ed. Herbert Bass; and "The Problem of the History of Religion in America," *Church History* 39 (June 1970): 224–35.

plained" only if one had a "God's-eye view" of the whole past and the whole future. Teilhard de Chardin rightly observed that "not a thing in our changing world is really understandable except in so far as it has reached its terminus." [2] In the strict sense, our situation is historically inexplicable. We face the *mysterium tremendum*. We can only speculate as to the place of the sixties in some ultimate roll call of decades. Yet we know that these years were turbulent—that they brought excitement and liberation to some, bewilderment and pain to others. Nearly every American at some time or other wondered why this "almost chosen people" should have encountered so much unsettlement at just this juncture in history. No law can explain why a New World nation experiences such an upheaval in the thirty-sixth decade of its life; but perhaps a telling of the many-stranded *histoire* that led up to this crisscross crisis of the sixties can have more explanatory value than the characteristic findings of more scientific disciplines.

WHAT'S NEW?

The most widely publicized aspect of the decade's religious history was the emergence of a radical movement in theology which betokened (even if it did not cause) a major reappraisal of the most assured grounds of the historic Judaeo-Christian consensus. From beyond the grave Dietrich Bonhoeffer's demand for a "secular interpretation" of biblical language was answered by a deluge of serious efforts to meet the needs of a "world come of age." In America it was H. Richard Niebuhr who, at the age of sixty-six, delivered the crucial inaugural address to the sixties with his great essay *Radical Monotheism* (1960); but it was Gabriel Vahanian who first brought Nietzsche's famous phrase into public currency in his book *The Death of God: The Culture of Our Post-Christian Era* (1961). Far more conspicuous were three startlingly popular best sellers: Bishop J. A. T. Robinson's *Honest to God* (1963) in Great Britain, Pierre Berton's *The Comfortable Pew* (1965) in Canada, and Harvey Cox's *The Secular City* (1965) in the United States. Equally provocative were the works of three or four rather diverse thinkers who either proclaimed the "death of God," or insisted on an entirely "secular" interpretation of the gospel, or thoroughly "demythologized" the biblical message.[3] In the meantime, the same themes were

2. Pierre Teilhard de Chardin, *Panthéisme et Christianisme* (Paris, 1923), p. 8. Arthur C. Danto makes the same point in his *Analytical Philosophy of History* (Cambridge: At the University Press, 1965), chap. 1. See also Marcus Cunliffe, "American Watersheds," *American Quarterly* 13 (Winter 1961).

3. See Dietrich Bonhoeffer, *Letters and Papers from Prison* (New York: Macmillan Co., 1953), especially the later letters; Schubert M. Ogden, *Christ Without Myth* (New York: Harper & Row, 1961); Paul Van Buren, *The Secular Meaning of the Gospel* (New York: Macmillan Co., 1963); Thomas J. J. Altizer and William Hamilton, *Radical Theology and the Death of God;* Van A. Harvey, *The Historian and the*

being popularized in the mass media—and rendered more erudite in the treatises of a wide range of writers, both lay and clerical, of all faiths. A critical, sometimes exceedingly hostile literature of equal proportions soon arose, yet the movement won support both at the grassroots and in the halls of learning. A massive credibility gap in matters of faith and religion opened up.

Contemporaneous with this development, and closely related to it, was a tidal wave of questioning of all the traditional structures of Christendom, above all, of the so-called parish church. After Peter Berger's sounding of an early tocsin in *The Noise of Solemn Assemblies* (1961), "morphological fundamentalism" became the key concept of the new critics. Local churches, they said, were irrationally and stubbornly committed to structures and strategies inherited from the Middle Ages. Relevant and effective social action was almost impossible. Even more seriously, traditional methods of nurture were forcing laymen to divorce faith and theology from the modes of thought by which they dealt with other problems of life and work in the world. With cities in crisis, men accepted Gibson Winters's diagnosis of *The Suburban Captivity of the Churches* (1961). Recognizing the moribund state of the old institutions and traditions, Martin Marty wrote of *The Second Chance for American Protestants* (1963). This profound self-examination was not restricted to Protestants, moreover. Thomas O'Dea, among many others, wrote of *The Catholic Crisis* (1968). Jews, too, were soon involved in an equally drastic process of theological and institutional reformation. In *After Auschwitz* (1966), Rabbi Richard Rubenstein denied that religion as usual was any longer possible.

The ecumenical significance of these trends was considerable but in some ways untoward. Secularizing trends, even if moderate, tended to undermine old confessional commitments and make interchurch cleavages anachronistic. At the same time, the urgency of the social crisis made interchurch and interfaith cooperation imperative—even involuntary. Between 1960 and 1970, therefore, the officially supported Consultation on Christian Union (COCU) was able to propose highly acceptable terms of reunion for ten major denominations as widely separated as the Protestant Episcopal, the African Methodist Episcopal, and the Disciples of Christ. Catholic-Protestant dialogue proceeded so favorably that the president of Notre Dame predicted in 1970 that church reunion would come before the century's end. Even with such ecumenical "progress," however, the quality

---

Believer (New York: Macmillan Co., 1966); Edward Farley, *Requiem for a Lost Piety;* William A. Beardslee, ed., *America and the Future of Theology;* Brevard S. Childs, *Biblical Theology in Crisis;* and, as indicative of related matters, William Braden, *The Private Sea: LSD and the Search for God;* and Jacob Needleman, *The New Religions.*

of theological dialogue deteriorated and the laity's concern for reunion diminished. The National Council of Churches was cutting its budget for lack of support. Astonishingly little feeling either for or against the COCU proposals arose—except among Fundamentalists and Neo-evangelicals, who regarded all of these trends as demonstrations of flagging commitment. Since these conservatives also opposed the rising current of social concern evinced by the mainstream churches, the old liberal-conservative polarization was intensified and also given a strong socio-political dimension.

An equally significant shift could be noted in both ethical theory and actual behavior. Not only did the mass media devote much time and space to a "new morality," but even in doing so they often exploited a new permissiveness by dealing frankly with long-forbidden subjects. In schools, colleges, and universities, this "moral revolution" first took the form of opposition to the traditional doctrine that schools and colleges operate *in loco parentis*. Students demanded and received greater freedom, and then moved on, often with strong faculty support, to question the structures and value priorities of higher education generally. Questions of loyalty and obedience to constituted authority, even to the national state itself, were also opened with new intensity. Ethical thinkers, meanwhile, tended toward less legalistic, more situational modes of guiding the moral life.[4] As a corollary of these developments nearly every church body in America (as well as many in Europe, including the Vatican) decided that the time had come to appoint a commission for the reexamination of positions on sexual ethics that had been relatively unchallenged for two thousand years.

Far more fundamental than the revising of various sexual attitudes and prohibitions was the new vitality that came into the movement for women's liberation. As in so many cases, the churches felt the first effects as pressure to ordain women to the ministry became a steady feature of the decade—with widespread positive results. Then late in the sixties the movement took on broader and more truly revolutionary dimensions both by renewing the older (but widely ignored) demands for equality and by posing deeper questions about the moral structure of Western culture. Out of this new perspective for considering male and female values emerged a line of inquiry and action whose implications were at least as profound as that which stemmed from the black revolution.

No account of the decade's radicalism, especially at the ethical level, is

4. See Joseph Fletcher, *Situation Ethics: The New Morality* (Philadelphia: Westminster Press, 1966); Paul Lehmann, *Ethics in a Christian Context* (New York: Harper & Row, 1963); Harvey Cox, ed., *The Situation Ethics Debate;* James M. Gustafson, *Christ and the Moral Life* (New York: Harper & Row, 1968).

complete, however, unless it also takes cognizance of a vast and long overdue moral renewal. A revolt against the hypocrisies and superficiality of conventional moral codes by no means resulted in nihilism or libertinism, though both of the latter were defended and practiced by some especially alienated groups. Much of the violence and organized protest of the sixties arose from intense moral indignation, a deep suspicion of established institutions, and a demand for more exalted grounds of action than social success, business profits, and national self-interest. America's patriotic "civil religion," which Will Herberg in the mid-fifties had quite rightly designated as the basic faith of most Americans, was subjected to extremely severe criticism.[5] The old nationalistic rhetoric was widely repudiated as hollow and deceitful. Nor did this civic faith die only in youthful hearts, for superannuated legislators were at the same time transforming the calendar of national holy days into a convenient series of long or lost weekends. On the other hand, there arose a veritable "great awakening" to the threat of environmental pollution and of the widespread depredations of nature which were robbing "America the Beautiful" of its truth. Yet it was in connection with governmental priorities that sharpest conflict developed. Probably nothing did more to divest "The Star-Spangled Banner" of its unifying power than the subordination of social and economic needs to those of war and military might. Even flag-flying became a divisive symbol of the debates on law-and-order versus social justice.

In summary, one may safely say that America's moral and religious tradition was tested and found wanting in the sixties. For Protestants the theological solutions which Neo-orthodoxy had developed ceased to satisfy, with the result that problems of science and biblical criticism returned. For Roman Catholics the same fate overcame the stern condemnations of liberalism and "modernism" propounded by the Vatican Council of 1869–70 and a long series of encyclicals extending from Pius IX's *Quanta Cura* (1864) to Pius XII's *Humani Generis* (1950). After Pope John's call for *aggiornamento* had made its mark, and increasingly after the vernacular liturgies and other innovations of Vatican Council II had been absorbed, a new spirit manifested itself among the laity and clergy alike. When Pope Paul VI in July 1968 issued *Humanae Vitae,* his fateful encyclical condemning artificial methods of birth control, he was confronted by an unprecedented resistance. Many devout Catholics seemed more inclined to follow the counsel of theologians and moral philosophers than simply to obey the pope's instruction. Everywhere the need for greater intellectual honesty and deeper foundations of belief was exposed.

5. See pp. 954–55 above.

Of course, one must not exaggerate the depth and extent of change whenever the reference is made to a whole national population—or even to all churchgoers. If common observation were not enough, there are surveys to prove that most adult Americans, though deeply troubled, still held—in some outward formal sense—to the religious convictions of earlier years.[6] On the other hand, the declining growth rates and widespread budgetary problems of all the large denominations clearly revealed a loss of institutional vitality—though this loss was also experienced by every other institution as well. Parallel to these trends was a marked tendency among the clergy and religious of all faiths to leave their churchly callings for work in the world. Among seminary students the same tendency was noticeable. Between 1966 and 1969 the number of Roman Catholic sisters decreased by fourteen thousand and the number of seminarians by 30 percent. At the same time, youth of high school and college age were showing a strong sense of estrangement from traditional forms of Christian and Judaic nur-

6. See Andrew M. Greeley et al., *What Do We Believe? The Stance of Religion in America;* and Greeley, *Religion in the Year 2000.* Superficially my statement about the continuity of majority attitudes may seem to be contradicted by the incontestable growth of interest in astrology, spiritualism, and the occult. The contradiction, however, is more apparent than real (on the harmonial and theosophical traditions, see chaps. 57 and 58 above). The revival of these "esoteric" traditions is more "rational" than it seems, especially when they are understood as corollaries of cultural and institutional alienation.

Equally relevant was the many-faceted evangelical revival that manifested itself in the late 1960s. Appearing first was a charismatic revival that soon flowed beyond the Pentecostal churches into staid middle-class denominations and the student population. By 1971 there were even ten thousand or more Roman Catholic Pentecostals, with both clergy and nuns among them. Appearing somewhat later, chiefly among those of student age, was the so-called Jesus Movement, and it too was highly variegated. The more spontaneous groups showed little interest in clerical leadership or doctrinal fine points, took Jesus as an example, worked for peace and social justice, stressed love and charity in warmly personal terms, rescued derelicts of the drug culture, founded communes, adopted counter-cultural life styles, and flouted many legalistic forms of code morality. Expressive of their theology and outlook were the music and lyrics of two young Englishmen, Andrew Lloyd Webber and Tim Rice, whose rock opera, *Jesus Christ Superstar,* appeared as an enormously popular record album in 1969 and as a Broadway stage production in 1971.

Other groups were of more orthodox—or even Fundamentalist and Pentecostal—tendency. These often evidenced somewhat more continuity with older American revival movements, picketed *Jesus Christ Superstar* on both moral and doctrinal grounds, often attended conservative Bible institutes and seminaries, and frequently participated in local churches and in organized evangelistic efforts. They remained critical of the older leadership, however, and accepted many elements of the youth culture, including individualistic apparel, the bearded, long-haired look of conventional portraits of Jesus, new forms of poster art, and a penchant for guitars and rock music. They could thus be very effective missioners among those who were thoroughly disillusioned with ecclesiastical institutions.

The Jesus People soon gained widespread attention and provoked a deluge of published commentary, but their long-term significance cannot be known. Whether they should be considered in a footnote (as here) is a question which only the future will answer. To grim, tormented times they brought the blessings of joy and love; but there is no apparent reason for seeing them as an exception to the larger generalizations attempted in this chapter. Yet surprises are the stuff of history.

ture. In the same circles marrying outside one's faith became more prevalent, and Catholic regulations on mixed marriages were made less inflexible. The prospect of "the vanishing Jew" heightened rabbinic stringency, but the trend nevertheless continued.

The three basic but closely intertwined elements that pervade or characterize this steady rise of religious antitraditionalism are profound matters of outlook; they seem to involve a deep shift in the presuppositional substructures of the American mind. One can designate them as metaphysical, moral, and social:

1. A growing commitment to a naturalism or "secularism" and corresponding doubts about the supernatural and the sacral
2. A creeping (or galloping) awareness of vast contradictions in American life between profession and performance, the ideal and the actual
3. Increasing doubt as to the capacity of present-day ecclesiastical, political, social, and educational institutions to rectify the country's deep-seated woes.

Rich natural resources, technological marvels, vast productive power, great ideals, expanding universities, and flourishing churches seem to have resulted only in a country wracked by fear, violence, racism, war, and moral hypocrisy. Nor was this simply the diagnosis of a few black militants and campus radicals. The sense of national failure and dislocation became apparent to varying degrees in all occupational groups and residential areas.

The question returns: Why should a moral and intellectual revolution that was centuries in the making have been precipitated in the 1960s? Why should the complacency and religiosity of the Eisenhower years have faded so swiftly? Why did shortcomings of American society that had aroused reformers since the eighteenth century suddenly become explosive? Why, in summary, did so many diverse processes drop their bomb load on the sixties?

THE DEVELOPING PROBLEM

Radical theology, whether Catholic, Protestant, or Jewish, is fundamentally an adjustment of religious thought to an ordered understanding of the natural world that had been gaining strength at an accelerating rate for over four hundred years. The most basic element in this process is the attitude toward the physical universe typified by Galileo's telescopic observations of the moon's rocky surface in 1610. Three centuries later, when Henry Adams reflected on the intellectual revolution that separated the age of the Virgin of Chartres from the age of the dynamo, he became one of America's early death-of-God theologians: "The two-thousand-years failure of Christianity roared upward from Broadway, and no Constantine the Great was in sight." [7]

Even more troubling was the steady advance of knowledge in the biological realm, especially after Charles Darwin placed the "descent of man" within that area of intensified investigation. Until the nineteenth century the idea of providential design had easily turned man's knowledge of the animate as well as of the inanimate world to the uses of natural theology. With the rise of evolutionary theory, however, this grand structure of apologetical theory began to crumble before the incoming tide of naturalism. As the twentieth century wore on, the full force of still another long effort began to be felt: the attempt of historians, anthropologists, sociologists, and psychologists to explain the *behavior* of man in scientific terms.

In the churches there were more specific sources of intellectual consternation. Serious threats to the inerrancy of Scripture had been raised by the "Copernican revolution" which Isaac Newton had consolidated; other threats provoked the Genesis-and-Geology controversy. But these problems were mild compared to the impact of biblical criticism, the history of world religions, and developmental studies of religion and doctrine. In the churches of the United States the crisis of relativism which these investigations portended was staved off by liberalism's roseate world view, by widespread certainty of America's glorious destiny, and by the tendency of popular evangelical revivalism to ignore the problems. A new flourishing of idealistic philosophy also blunted the force of this new impulse for a time. Americans were even spared the devastating blows which World War I brought down upon the notion of Christendom's triumphant world role. Even in 1929, when the great economic collapse did finally bring this message home, the resurgent forces of Fundamentalism and Neo-orthodoxy—each in different ways to separate constituencies—staved off the accounting for yet another generation. During the Eisenhower years Norman Vincent Peale, Monsignor Fulton J. Sheen, Rabbi Joshua Loth Liebman, and Billy Graham could link hands, as it were, and preside over an Indian summer of confident living and renewed religious interest. Beneath the affluence and the abundant piety, however, a vast range of unresolved issues remained. Since these were the very years in which the mass media, notably television, were having an unprecedented effect upon the popular awareness of social and intellectual change, and in which a college education was becoming an expected, even necessary, stage in the life of every moderately ambitious American youth,

7. *The Education of Henry Adams* (Boston: Houghton Mifflin Co., 1918), p. 500.

the day was fast disappearing when traditional religious views would be accepted without serious questioning.

Almost as basic to the rise of radical theology as the cultivation of the modern mind was the inexorable development of what was often referred to as modern technocratic society. Max Weber performed a great office by turning men's attention to the ways in which the Judaeo-Christian world-view in general and the Protestant Reformation in particular accelerated the rationalization of social and economic life which underlies the rise of organized technology.[8] The United States, moreover, provided a living demonstration of the fact that, if unhindered by medieval notions of class and status, if animated by sufficiently powerful belief in the virtues of work and exploitation, and if blessed with natural resources in sufficient abundance, a "nation of immigrants" could outstrip the world in achieving technocratic maturity. Yet because of the strongly agrarian terms in which the American idea of the good life has been couched, as well as the relentlessness with which industrialism fostered the growth of cities, American history, especially during the last century, has necessarily experienced harsh confrontations of urban and rural values. In the sectional crisis of the 1860s, again in the 1890s, and still again in the 1920s, these value conflicts were exceedingly severe. In the 1960s the clash became especially intense.

In 1940 Waldo Frank predicted the intensification of these conflicts in *A Chart for Rough Waters:* "The collectivising trend of society under machine production, whether that society calls itself democratic, fascist, or socialist, is irrevocable." Roderick Seidenberg reiterated this warning a decade later in his work on *Posthistoric Man* (1950). He found "the full implications of science, technology, and the world of machinery . . . so vast as to defy . . . the possibility of sensing their ultimate meaning or their final impact upon our ways of life and thought." [9] Since then technological inroads on old ways of life have steadily advanced all over the world, from Arkansas to China. Regardless of governmental forms, this process has destroyed primordial social structures and modes of understanding human existence, and despite protest and violence it was proceeding apace to make "organization men" of the entire human race, with that portion of the race living in the United States and Canada feeling every major transition first.

In addition to these two worldwide trends—one intellectual, the other technological—there is another major transformatory process which the

8. See Benjamin Nelson, "Conscience, Revolutions, and Weber," *Journal for the Scientific Study of Religion* 7 (Fall 1968): 157–77, which cites much of the recent literature.

9. Roderick Seidenberg, *Posthistoric Man* (Chapel Hill: University of North Carolina Press, 1950), pp. 1, 95. Herbert W. Richardson's *Toward an American Theology* (New York: Harper & Row, 1967) addresses the intellectual problems of the "sociotechnic age."

United States shares with few, if any, other countries, namely, the eclipse of the Protestant Establishment which presided over its early colonial life, its war for independence, and its nineteenth-century expansion. In theory, the federal Union has been from its origins a nation of minorities, a land of freedom and equality. But it has never been so in fact. Radical inequality and massive forms of oppression have been features—fundamental features —of the American Way of Life. The election of the first American legislature and the first importation of African slaves took place in Virginia in 1619, and from that time forward the rhetoric of American democracy has been falsified by the actualities of racism and bondage. Catholics were subjected to disabilities, intolerance, and violence from the earliest times; and anti-Semitism began to grow virulent as soon as the Jewish immigration rate started to rise during the 1880s. The American Indian has been excluded from American life from the start, while Spanish-speaking citizens, whether gained by annexation of their territory or by immigration, have been consistently relegated to subordinate status. During the past century, however, the social structures, legal arrangements, patterns of prejudice, and power relationships that maintained the older establishment have been gradually undermined. The steady acculturation of the newer ethnic communities contributed much to this denouement, but the largest single factor in effecting the changed relationships was the urban explosion of the twentieth century.

A final long-term factor stems from the very dominance of Puritanism in the American religious heritage. One *can* imagine a different turn of affairs, for example, if English authorities, in the manner of the French, Spanish, and Dutch, had kept their dissenters at home and peopled the New World colonies only with orthodox conformists. But it was not so, and the future United States was settled and to a large degree shaped by those who brought with them a very special form of radical Protestantism which combined a strenuous moral precisionism, a deep commitment to evangelical experientialism, and a determination to make the state responsible for the support of these moral and religious ideas. The United States became, therefore, the land *par excellence* of revivalism, moral "legalism" and a "gospel" of work that was undergirded by the so-called Puritan Ethic. The popular revivalistic tradition of America tended, moreover, to be oblivious to the intellectual and social revolutions of the modern world. In its church life, as in its forms of popular democracy, intellectualism was deprecated and repressed. Since higher education was under the control of these same forces, many of the most powerful sources of modern thinking lagged far behind those of continental Europe, even though America's cash outlay for education led the world. And due to the strength of these ideas in overrepresented rural constituencies, they had a kind of illicit hold on the national life even after their actual strength had waned. By the mid-twentieth century, therefore, the circumstances were such that a pluralistic post-Puritan situation could rapidly develop.

None of these several long-term developments, however, explains why the 1960s should have experienced anything more than the same gradual adjustments that befell each preceding decade. Processes that are centuries old hardly constitute a sufficient account for the outbreak of a revolution. One is led, therefore, to the more immediate question: What precipitated so violent and sudden a moral and theological transformation in this particular decade? To satisfy such questioning one must point to special contingencies and partly accidental convergences which together might plausibly be designated as catalytic in their effects.

THE CATALYSIS OF THE SIXTIES

Each of the long-term processes already discussed was brought to a critical stage by the enormous economic expansion and rapid social change that the United States experienced and, for the most part, thoughtlessly enjoyed during the affluent years that followed World War II. Here again the phenomenon can be subdivided for clarity's sake by reference to five diverse but very familiar sequences.

1. The long-developing problems of rampant, unregulated urban and industrial growth began to create social conditions with which American political and fiscal practices could not cope. Problems of bureaucratic organization, political process, crime, medical care, education, sanitation, communication, housing, pollution, and transportation rendered American cities barely capable of sustaining minimum levels of existence and popular acquiescence. This situation had a timetable of its own, and crises were developing even in cities where race conflict was almost nonexistent.

2. Technological developments in agriculture and industry produced migrations of people that led the national electorate to repudiate many of the arrangements that had hindered equality of participation in American life. And what voters did not do, the Supreme Court accomplished. The John F. Kennedy family in the White House and Pope John XXIII in the Vatican symbolized or brought about a drastic alteration of old interfaith relationships. Between 1954 and 1963 the Supreme Court removed crucial legal supports from the power structure of the Protestant Establishment. The legal and political basis of equality, liberty, civil rights, censorship, and freedom

from arbitrary arrest were greatly strengthened. Most important by far, black America first in the context of the civil rights movement and then after 1966 under the banner of Black Power began to seek rectification of the historic inequalities that had featured its situation. For the first time in American history, in other words, the traumatic implications of true pluralism began to be realized. As a result of these traumas, radical discontent, militancy, and violence became as never before common features of American life. John Kennedy, Martin Luther King, Jr., and Robert Kennedy—all of them men on whom vast multitudes pinned their hopes for a better world—were assassinated.

3. Rapid technological development and widely publicized advancements in science also contributed to creating the national mood. Their impact was enormously increased by sensational accomplishments that aroused the popular imagination. Successful trips to the moon, for example, capped a decade of technical triumphs, while genetic discoveries dramatized progress in the study of human life. In this way the cumulative educative effects of television and of vastly expanded enrollments at the college level were suddenly magnified. Modern science and technology seemed to have no conceivable bounds. For many the idea of the supernatural lost its force, while these and still others came to doubt that human existence had any transcendent reference.

4. Less benign achievements, on the other hand, mitigated whatever remained of humanistic optimism in its older liberal forms. Nazi extermination camps and American atomic bombs on Japan, writes Robert Jay Lifton, inaugurated a new era in human history—a time in which man is devoid of assurance that he will live on as a species. His "self-destructive potential" seemed to be without limit. And in the 1960s not only was the memory of Auschwitz and Hiroshima renewed, but its implications were interiorized and expanded. A "New History" was being shaped.[10] The Cuban missile crisis, continued nuclear testing, indecisive attempts to achieve international control of nuclear armaments, and the construction of vast offensive and defensive missile systems underlined the tentativity of mankind's earthly existence. Meanwhile the alarming facts of overpopulation and environmental pollution called attention to still other ways in which mankind's future was threatened.

5. And finally, as the supreme catalyst, President Lyndon Johnson in 1965 began a drastic escalation of the war in Southeast Asia. This not only

10. See Robert Jay Lifton, "Notes on a New History," *New Journal* 3, no. 1 (September 1969): 5–9; and idem, *Death in Life: Survivors of Hiroshima* (New York: Random House, 1968).

prevented an assault on the problems of poverty, racism, and urban dislocation, but it also exposed the terrible inequities of selective service regulations. When added to other signs that military considerations were determining American priorities, these policies not only activated the student protest movement, but led to an unprecedented loss of confidence in American institutions, even among those charged with their custody and extension. As the viability of the entire "system" came into question in ever-widening circles, the population as a whole became increasingly polarized. Traditional patriotism and the American dream lost their credibility among several large minority groups, one of which was defined by its youthfulness.

THE SPIRITUAL RESULT

In the area of religion and morals the catalytic power of these converging developments proved to be enormous. The sharp crescendo of social strife seemed to demonstrate that the time-honored structures of American church life were "irrelevant" to the country's actual condition. By many critical observers, moreover, churchgoing America—both black and white—came to be regarded not as a moral leaven but as an obstacle to change. The seeming social irrelevance of the church brought profound and widespread disillusion to the ministers in nearly all denominations, but especially to those in whom the Social Gospel tradition was strong. Yet even to conservatives who believed that the mission of the church was to "save souls" and not to save society, very grave problems were evident. Not only did the universe seem unmindful of man's plight, but man's best achievements—including the educative measures on which so much effort and money had been lavished—rather suddenly began to produce an intellectual atmosphere in which the traditional faith did not flourish. Evil seemed triumphant. There seemed to be no place under the sun, or beyond the sun, for a "God who acts." Evidence of God's love for the world was hard to find.

As the decade of the sixties yielded to the 1970s, dissensus was more visible than consensus. The profound depths of racism lay open and exposed. Doubts, despair, and moral confusion were endemic. One great portion of the population wondered if a just society could ever be achieved; another portion felt that law and order had been needlessly and foolishly sacrificed. Among those "under thirty" and their many allies a counterculture struggled to be born, with the accent on spontaneity and freedom from dogma—whether theological or social. Yet militancy in the student movement and among the oppressed seemed to have become counterproductive. In the misnamed Bible Belt of the South and Midwest, in the lower middle classes, in organized labor, and among ethnic minorities whose economic and social status seemed (to them) very insecure, an inchoate conservative tendency could be noted, though no one could say what this frightened and perplexed multitude portended as a political force.

Americans, whether conservative, liberal, or radical, found it increasingly difficult to believe that the United States was still a beacon and blessing to the world.[11] Even less were they prepared to understand themselves as "chosen" to suffering and servanthood. Amid fears of genocide and the advent of a police state, a new kind of secular apocalypticism gained strength. In this context, the inducements to nihilism were strong. Because the national situation looked hopeless, and because so many hopeful leaders lay prematurely in their graves, the tendency to irrational destructiveness or withdrawn communalism was also very strong. Otherworldliness arose in many new forms. Radical theology, meanwhile, sent down its roots and drew its nourishment from the yearnings that underlay these responses and these temptations. It sought to bring a measure of transcendence, hope, and community to those who were alienated from technocratic society generally, from the American "warfare state," and from outworn forms of churchly life and practice. Religious interest and moral intensity were by no means waning in the Age of Aquarius; but neither the rejuvenated profession of astrology nor the burgeoning "science" of futurology were very definite about the prospects. One could only be assured that radically revised foundations of belief were being laid, that a drastic reformation of ecclesiastical institutions was in the offing, and that America could not escape its responsibilities as the world's pathbreaker in the new technocratic wilderness.

CONCLUDING REFLECTIONS ON THE PREDICAMENT OF THE WRITER AND THE READER OF HISTORY

"It is one of the great charms of books," observes Frank Kermode in his essay on eschatology and fiction, "that they have to end." [12] And so this book, too, has its charm. It ends, however, in a rather somber mood, for we have been considering a time of calamities. As the American people moved toward the bicentennial of the nation's independence, they could see few

11. An unusually thorough public survey conducted from January through April 1971, *The Hopes and Fears of the American People* (New York: Universe Books, 1971), revealed "new and urgent concern over national unity, stability and law and order." Of those questioned, 47 percent feared "a real breakdown." The average American for the first time believed that the United States had "slid backwards" during the previous five years and that the trend would continue (*New York Times*, 27 June 1971).

12. Frank Kermode, *The Sense of an Ending: Studies in the Theory of Fiction* (New York: Oxford University Press, 1967), p. 23.

living signs of the self-confidence and optimism that had marked the centennial observances of 1876, and even less of the revolutionary generation's bold assurance. Still more attenuated was the Puritan's firm conviction that America had a divine commission in the world. The nation's organic connections with the sources of its idealism and hope were withered.

The demarcation of historical periods, to be sure, is a heuristic, semifictional device. It is almost always a way of calling attention to the rise and fall of important ideas, beliefs, and institutions. But the historian who describes his own times as the *end* of an epoch makes a more daring venture. Because he finds the present to be in some sense a turning point in history, his words also acquire faintly apocalyptic connotations. He thus risks future disconfirmation. We know, furthermore, that the idea of a Puritan Epoch cannot be universally applied. To a large degree it refers only to the United States. In other parts of the globe—notably in the Third World—the present time of crisis is linked, not with Puritanism, but more broadly with the rise and fall of Western imperialism, colonialism, and capitalism. Yet for nearly everyone the impulse to see the present as the end of a period stems from an awareness of living in a time of radical transition. We survey the national experience from the kind of pseudo-future that a sense of crisis provides. As Kermode says, "We project ourselves—a small humble elect, perhaps—past the End, so as to see the structure whole, a thing we cannot do from our spot of time in the middle." [13]

The concept of a Puritan Epoch, however, does not release us from the constant obligation to reinterpret the American past. Because each morning's newspaper adds new events to the historian's agenda and hence alters his angle of vision, it joggles the past a little. For this reason historical work is an endless, Sisyphean task. And which events—if any—will turn out to be decisive for the spiritual history of the future, and hence also for interpreting the past, is intrinsically unknowable.[14] Yet the provocations of this

13. Ibid., p. 8.

14. In April–May 1970 the final two weeks of my course on American religious history were swallowed up in the turmoil of demonstrations and protest related to a widely publicized trial of several Black Panthers in New Haven, the American invasion of Cambodia, the National Guard's killing of four students at Kent State University, and the police slaying of two more at Jackson State College. The course, in other words, merged with the subject matter of this concluding chapter. In subsequent discussions as to what had actually happened in New Haven, the impossibility of producing an historical account of the events became manifest. Too few introspective diaries were kept, too many levels of action were proceeding at once, too many conflicting forces impinged on the university community. It meant too many different things to various groups of people; and from beginning to end the events had no physical or spiritual boundaries. Only with the passage of time, if ever, will it become clearer which elements of the situation had the most enduring effects and which ones, therefore, should have registered their impact on would-be historians. How much more impossible is it to account for a whole nation's turmoil during an entire decade!

predicament remind the writer and reader alike of the ways in which the historical enterprise is fundamentally relevant to nearly every major question of human existence. A history book that comes down to our own time is thus a tantalizing challenge—and an invitation.

As an active participant in contemporary history, the reader can hardly escape the responsibility for seeking to understand his present circumstance. Beyond that, as an observer of continuity and change in the conditions of his own existence, he may exercise the privilege that Carl Becker underlined when he spoke of "Everyman his own historian." [15] In this exciting role he will soon discover that the American experience does not explain itself. Whether as amateur or as professional, he will be a pioneer on the frontiers of postmodern civilization. Even his life style and moral stance will be elements in an interpretation of the religious situation—and hence of the past. Beyond all thoughts of epochs and endings and turning points, moreover, one may hope that such future interpreters, as well as later readers of these words, will see increasing evidence that the American people, in their moral and religious history, were drawing on the profounder elements of their traditions, finding new sources of strength and confidence, and thus vindicating the idealism which has been so fundamental an element in the country's past.

15. Carl L. Becker, *Everyman His Own Historian* (Chicago: Quadrangle Books, 1966), pp. 233–55. This was his presidential address to the American Historical Association in 1931. The book of essays bearing this title appeared in 1935.

BIBLIOGRAPHY

§ 1, Bibliographies. § 2, General Histories of Religions. § 3, Catholic Europe, New Spain, and New France. § 4, The European Protestant Background. § 5, The Reformation and Puritanism in England. § 6, General Works of American History. § 7, General Works of American Religious History. § 8, Church and State and Civil Religion in America. § 9, Indians, Indian Policy, and Indian Missions. § 10, Roman Catholicism: General American and Colonial Histories. § 11, Judaism in America. § 12, Eastern Orthodoxy in America. § 13, Protestant Denominational Histories and Studies. § 14, Long-Term Themes in Protestant History. § 15, Early Colonial Religion, § 16, American Puritanism. § 17, Later Colonial Religion. § 18, Jonathan Edwards and the New England Theology. § 19, Antebellum Protestantism. § 20, Transcendentalism and Other Romantic Currents. § 21, New Movements in Religion: Nineteenth Century. § 22, Sectional Issues and the Civil War. § 23, Slavery, the Negro, and the Black Churches. § 24, Roman Catholicism in the Nineteenth and Twentieth Centuries. § 25, Protestantism since the Civil War. § 26, Liberal Trends in Nineteenth-Century Religious Thought. § 27, Ecumenical and Inter-Faith Developments. § 28, Religious History from World War I to the Vietnam War. § 29, Twentieth-Century Theological Currents. § 30, Black Movements and Voices in the Twentieth Century. § 31, Spanish-Speaking Americans. § 32, Religion in the 1960s and 1970s. § 33, Biographies and Autobiographies.

One is staggered by the thought of a bibliography of American religious history that would include all of the relevant documents, published primary materials, periodicals, historical works, and scholarly articles. Fortunately, it is not necessary to undertake anything of this sort, since guides to the literature of nearly every major period, theme, and subject exist. Most important is Nelson R. Burr's two-volume *Critical Bibliography of Religion in America* (1961), which provides information on other bibliographical aids, has a table of contents, and includes a complete author index. Older but still valuable are Peter G. Mode's *Sourcebook and Bibliographical Guide for American Church History* (1921) and the *Bibliographical Guide to the History of Christianity* (1931) edited by Shirley Jackson Case, with an American section by William W. Sweet. Of the older bibliographies, none are more valuable than those which accompany each of the denominational histories contained in the thirteen-volume American Church History Series (ACHS, 1893–97) edited by Philip Schaff et al., volume 12 of which contains a general bibliography. (See below, sec. 1, for full titles of works mentioned here as well as other bibliographies.)

Due to the availability of these works as well as other compilations referred to in section 1, the suggestions for further reading provided in this volume, though comprehensive, are relatively modest. The bibliography which follows includes only a small fraction of the works consulted. Of the titles mentioned in footnotes, it usually repeats only recent secondary works which serve the purposes described below. Emphasis, with rare exceptions, has been placed upon important book-length secondary works in English, most of them recent, which themselves contain extensive and critical introductions to the primary and secondary literature of the subjects they treat. These titles are gathered in thirty-three sections, beginning with general topics and proceeding to more delimited areas in a broadly chronological manner. Because historians do not write with such classification schemes in mind, the reader with some special interest is advised to consult several related sections. Since nearly all of the works included are deemed to be of great value both for their substantive content and for their bibliographical contribution, comments on individual items are very rarely made.

Biographies, though they exist in immense profusion and constitute one of the most valuable approaches to periods and movements, have not been included in great number because of their accessibility through the catalogues of any good library, and because the *Dictionary of American Biography*, general and specialized encyclopedias, and other similar reference works provide critical guidance in this area. Yet because biographies and autobiographies provide a unique form of illumination, a few representative works in this important genre are given in section 33.

Relatively few histories of individual denominations and other smaller groups are included, but they are listed in most general works on American religion (sec. 7), in encyclopedias of several sorts, and, again, in library catalogues. Also of great value in this regard are the several general works or handbooks which deal systematically with churches, denominations, sects, and cults. Especially to be recommended is that of F. E. Mayer.

This bibliography does not contain a section on theory and method, despite the fact that the intersection of historical investigation and religious subject-matter has always raised formidable theoretical questions which have often provoked scholars, philosophers, and theologians to profound intellectual innovation. The reasons for my negative decision are quickly stated: the literature on this subject is not only vast and variegated but it is almost by definition controversial. Any brief list of books would be misleading or tendentious or both. Every item in this bibliography, moreover, does exemplify one or another methodological position to some degree, while some of them (such as those by Weber and Troeltsch) have exerted great influence on how historians have dealt with matters of religion and on what aspects they have chosen to study. In part to illustrate the multiplicity of ways in which a religious movement can be fruitfully studied, sections 5 and 16 on English and American Puritanism have been somewhat expanded. Not only has Puritanism in the broad sense of the term received more careful and mature concern than any other subject in the American field, but it is an area in which many historians have posed fundamental questions of theory and method and produced works of lasting significance.

It has taken much inner restraint to keep this bibliography within reasonable bounds; and countless deeply prized books—not even to mention articles—have been painfully omitted. Yet I believe that easily followed paths to the whole terrain have been marked out by those which are listed. My concluding hope is that some of the excitement and seriousness of purpose that motivated the many historians who are represented will be contagious, and that those who consult these books will find their interest in American religious history enlivened. To anyone so responding it can be guaranteed that he will find problems of intense human consequence at every turn, and that only very rarely, if ever, will he find a subject that has been definitively treated. For the analytical historian answers become questions.

1. BIBLIOGRAPHIES

Burr, Nelson R. *A Critical Bibliography of Religion in America.* 2 vols. Princeton, N.J.: Princeton University Press, 1961. [Part One, pp. 3–84 on bibliographical guides.]

Cadden, John Paul. *The Historiography of the American Catholic Church, 1785–1943.* Washington, D.C.: Catholic University of America Press, 1944.

Ellis, John Tracy. *A Guide to American Catholic History.* Milwaukee: Bruce Publishing Co., 1959.

Handlin, Oscar, et al. *Harvard Guide to American History.* Cambridge, Mass.: Harvard University Press, 1955.

Mode, Peter G. *Source Book and Bibliographical Guide for American Church History.* Menasha, Wis.: George Banta Publishing Co., 1921.

Rischin, Moses. *An Inventory of American Jewish History.* Cambridge, Mass.: Harvard University Press, 1954.

Schaff, Philip, et al., gen. eds. *The American Church History Series.* 13 vols. New York: Christian Literature Co., 1893–97. [Each denominational history contains a bibliography; general bibliography in vol. 12.]

Vollmar, Edward R. *The Catholic Church in America: An Historical Bibliography.* 2d ed. New York: Scarecrow Press, 1963.

2. GENERAL HISTORIES OF RELIGIONS

Baron, Salo W. *A Social and Religious History of the Jews.* 12 vols. New York: Columbia University Press, 1952–67.

Chadwick, Henry, ed. *The Pelican History of the Church.* 6 vols. Baltimore: Penguin Books, 1960–70.

Ch'en, Kenneth K. S. *Buddhism: The Light of Asia.* Woodbury, N.Y.: Barron's Educational Series, 1968.

Dolan, John P. *Catholicism: An Historical Survey.* Woodbury, N.Y.: Barron's Educational Series, 1968.

Dumoulin, Heinrich. *A History of Zen Buddhism.* Boston: Beacon Press, 1969.

Guttmann, Julius. *Philosophers of Judaism, from Biblical Times to Franz Rosenzweig.* New York: Holt, Rinehart and Winston, 1964.

Latourette, Kenneth Scott. *A History of Christianity.* New York: Harper & Brothers, 1953.

———. *A History of the Expansion of Christianity.* 7 vols. New York: Harper & Brothers, 1937–45.

Margolis, Max, and Marx, Alexander. *History of the Jewish People.* New York: Meridian Books, 1960.

Schaff, Philip, ed. *The Creeds of Christendom.* 3 vols. New York, 1877.

Smart, Ninian. *The Religious Experience of Mankind.* New York: Charles Scribner's Sons, 1969.

Sohm, Rudolf. *Outlines of Church History.* Boston: Beacon Press, 1958.

Trepp, Leo. *Eternal Faith, Eternal People: A Journey into Judaism.* Englewood Cliffs, N.J.: Prentice-Hall, 1962.

Troeltsch, Ernst. *The Social Teaching of the Christian Churches.* Translated by Olive Wyon. New York: Macmillan Co., 1931

Walker, Williston. *A History of the Christian Church.* Rev. ed. New York: Charles Scribner's Sons, 1959.

3. CATHOLIC EUROPE, NEW SPAIN, AND NEW FRANCE

Bolton, Herbert E. *The Mission as a Frontier Institution in the Spanish American Colonies.* Academic Reprints. El Paso, Tex.: Texas Western College Press, 1960.

———. *The Spanish Borderlands: A Chronicle of Old Florida and the Southwest.* New Haven: Yale University Press, 1921.

Bouyer, Louis. *The Roman Socrates: A Portrait of Saint Philip Neri.* Translated by Michael Day. Westminster, Md.: Newman Press, 1958.

Braden, Charles S. *Religious Aspects of the Conquest of Mexico.* Durham, N.C.: Duke University Press, 1930.

Bremond, André. *A Literary History of Religious Thought in France from the Wars of Religion to Our Own Time.* 3 vols. London: Macmillan & Co., 1928–36.

Brodrick, James. *The Origin of the Jesuits.* London: Longmans, Green and Co., 1940.

———. *The Progress of the Jesuits.* London: Longmans, Green and Co., 1947.

———. *Saint Ignatius Loyola: The Pilgrim Years, 1491–1538.* New York: Farrar, Straus and Cudahy, 1956.

Brou, Alexandre. *Saint Madeleine Sophie Barat: Her Life of Prayer and Her Teaching.* Translated by Jane Wynne Saul. New York: Desclee Co., 1963.

Burns, Edward M. *The Counter-Reformation.* Princeton, N.J.: Princeton University Press, 1964.

Elliott, J. H. *Imperial Spain, 1469–1716.* New York: Saint Martin's Press, 1963.

Hallett, Paul H. *Catholic Reformer: A Life of Saint Cajetan of Thiene.* Westminster, Md.: Newman Press, 1959.

Janelle, Pierre. *The Catholic Reformation.* Milwaukee: Bruce Publishing Co., 1949.

Kennedy, John Hopkins. *Jesuit and Savage in New France.* New Haven: Yale University Press, 1950.

Ozment, Stephen. *The Reformation in Medieval Perspective.* Chicago: Quadrangle Books, 1971.

Picón-Salas, Mariano. *A Cultural History of Spanish America, from Conquest to Independence.* Translated by Irving A. Leonard. Berkeley and Los Angeles: University of California Press, 1966.

Talbot, Francis X. *Saint Among the Hurons: The Life of Jean de Brébeuf.* New York: Harper & Brothers, 1949.

Walsh, Henry H. *The Christian Church in Canada.* Toronto: Ryerson Press, 1956.

Wright, J. Leitch. *Anglo-Spanish Rivalry in North America.* Athens, Ga.: University of Georgia Press, 1971.

Wrong, George M. *The Rise and Fall of New France.* 2 vols. New York: Macmillan Co., 1928.

4. THE EUROPEAN PROTESTANT BACKGROUND

Bainton, Roland H. *Here I Stand: A Life of Martin Luther*. Nashville, Tenn.: Abingdon Press, 1950.

———. *The Reformation of the Sixteenth Century*. Boston: Beacon Press, 1952.

Bergendoff, Conrad. *The Church of the Lutheran Reformation: A Historical Survey of Lutheranism*. Saint Louis: Concordia Publishing House, 1967.

Courvoisier, Jacques. *Zwingli: A Reformed Theologian*. Richmond: John Knox Press, 1971.

Dillenberger, John, and Welch, Claude. *Protestant Christianity Interpreted through Its Development*. New York: Charles Scribner's Sons, 1954.

Green, Robert W. *Protestantism and Capitalism: The Weber Thesis and Its Critics*. Boston: D. C. Heath, 1959.

Grimm, Harold J. *The Reformation Era, 1500–1650*. New York: Macmillan Co., 1965.

Heppe, Heinrich. *Reformed Dogmatics*. Introduction by Karl Barth. London: G. Allen and Unwin, 1952.

Hunt, George L., ed. *Calvinism and the Political Order*. Philadelphia: Westminster Press, 1965.

Jones, Rufus M. *Spiritual Reformers in the Sixteenth and Seventeenth Centuries*. New York: Macmillan Co., 1914.

Littell, Franklin H. *The Origins of Sectarian Protestantism: The Anabaptist View of the Church*. New York: Macmillan Co., 1960.

McNeill, John Thomas. *The History and Character of Calvinism*. New York: Oxford University Press, 1954.

Niesel, Wilhelm. *The Theology of Calvin*. Philadelphia: Westminster Press, 1956.

Ong, Walter J. *Ramus: Method and the Decay of Dialogue*. Cambridge, Mass.: Harvard University Press, 1958.

Schmid, Heinrich. *The Doctrinal Theology of the Evangelical Lutheran Church*. Translated from the 5th ed. by Charles A. Hay and Henry E. Jacobs. Philadelphia, 1876.

Schwiebert, E. G. *Luther and His Times*. St. Louis: Concordia Publishing House, 1950.

Spitz, Lewis W. *The Renaissance and Reformation Movements*. Chicago: Rand-McNally, 1971.

Tawney, R. H. *Religion and the Rise of Capitalism*. 1926. Reprint. New York: New American Library, 1947.

Torrance, Thomas F., ed. and trans. *The School of Faith: The Catechisms of the Reformed Church*. New York: Harper & Brothers, 1959.

Walton, Robert C. *Zwingli's Theocracy*. Toronto: University of Toronto Press, 1967.

Watson, Philip S. *Let God Be God! An Interpretation of the Theology of Martin Luther*. Philadelphia: Muhlenberg Press, 1947.

Weber, Max. *The Protestant Ethic and the Spirit of Capitalism*. London: G. Allen and Unwin, 1930.

Wendell, François. *Calvin: The Origins and Development of His Religious Thought*. New York: Harper & Row, 1963.

Whale, John Selden. *The Protestant Tradition*. Cambridge: At the University Press, 1955.

Williams, George H. *The Radical Reformation*. Philadelphia: Westminster Press, 1962.

Wilson, Charles. *The Dutch Republic and Its Civilization of the Seventeenth Century*. New York: McGraw-Hill Book Co., 1968.

5. THE REFORMATION AND PURITANISM IN ENGLAND

Ames, William. *The Marrow of Theology.* Translated from 3d Latin ed., 1629, and edited by John D. Eusden. Boston: Pilgrim Press, 1963.

Barbour, Hugh. *The Quakers in Puritan England.* New Haven: Yale University Press, 1964.

Cragg, Gerald R. *From Puritanism to the Age of Reason: A Study of Changes in Religious Thought within the Church of England, 1660–1700.* Cambridge: At the University Press, 1950.

Donaldson, Gordon. *The Scottish Reformation.* New York: Cambridge University Press, 1960.

George, Charles and Katherine. *The Protestant Mind of the English Reformation, 1570–1640.* Princeton, N.J.: Princeton University Press, 1961.

Haller, William. *The Elect Nation: The Meaning and Relevance of Foxe's Book of Martyrs.* New York: Harper & Row, 1963.

———. *The Rise of Puritanism.* New York: Columbia University Press, 1938.

Hill, Christopher. *The Century of Revolution, 1603–1714.* New York: W. W. Norton & Co., 1961.

Hughes, Philip. *The Reformation in England.* 3 vols. London: Hollis and Carter, 1954.

Knappen, Marshall Mason. *Tudor Puritanism: A Chapter in the History of Idealism.* Chicago: University of Chicago Press, 1939.

Little, David. *Religion, Order, and Law: A Study in Pre-Revolutionary England.* New York: Harper & Row, 1969.

MacCaffrey, Wallace. *The Shaping of the Elizabethan Regime.* Princeton, N.J.: Princeton University Press, 1968.

Moorman, John R. H. *A History of the Church in England.* London: A. and C. Black, 1953; New York: Morehouse-Barlow, 1959.

Morgan, Irvonwy. *The Godly Preachers of the Elizabethan Church.* London: Epworth Press, 1965.

Notestein, Wallace. *The English People on the Eve of Colonization.* New York: Harper & Brothers, 1954.

———. *The Scot in History: A Study of the Interplay of Character and History.* New Haven: Yale University Press, 1947.

Nuttall, Geoffrey F. *The Holy Spirit in Puritan Faith and Experience.* Oxford: Basil Blackwell, 1946.

———. *Visible Saints: The Congregational Way, 1640–1660.* Oxford: Basil Blackwell, 1957.

O'Connell, Marvin R. *Thomas Stapleton and the Counter-Reformation.* New Haven: Yale University Press, 1964.

Parker, Thomas M. *The English Reformation to 1558.* New York: Oxford University Press, 1950.

Powicke, Frederick M. *The Reformation in England.* New York: Oxford University Press, 1941.

Prall, Stuart E., ed. *The Puritan Revolution: A Documentary History.* Garden City, N.Y.: Doubleday & Co., Anchor Books, 1968.

Ridley, Jasper G. *Thomas Cranmer.* Oxford: Clarendon Press, 1962.

Rowse, A. L. *The Elizabethans and America.* New York: Harper & Row, 1959.

Trinterud, Leonard J., ed. *Elizabethan Puritanism*. New York: Oxford University Press, 1971.

Walzer, Michael. *The Revolution of the Saints: A Study of the Origins of Radical Politics*. Cambridge, Mass.: Harvard University Press, 1965.

Wright, Louis B. *Religion and Empire: The Alliance between Piety and Commerce in English Expansion, 1558–1625*. Chapel Hill: University of North Carolina Press, 1943.

6. GENERAL WORKS OF AMERICAN HISTORY

Bailyn, Bernard. *Education in the Forming of American Society*. Chapel Hill: University of North Carolina Press, 1960.

Bancroft, George. *History of the United States*. 6 vols. 2d ed., rev. Boston: Little, Brown and Co., 1876.

Bass, Herbert, ed. *The State of American History*. Chicago: Quadrangle Books, 1970. [Historiographical essays.]

Bernstein, Barton J., ed. *Towards a New Past: Dissenting Essays in American History*. New York: Random House, 1968.

Blau, Joseph L., ed. *American Philosophical Addresses, 1700–1900*. New York: Columbia University Press, 1946.

———. *Men and Movements in American Philosophy*. Englewood Cliffs, N.J.: Prentice-Hall, 1952.

Blum, John Morton, et al. *The National Experience: A History of the United States*. 2d ed. New York: Harcourt, Brace & World, 1968.

Clark, Thomas D. *Frontier America*. New York: Charles Scribner's Sons, 1959.

Cremin, Lawrence A. *American Education: The Colonial Experience*. New York: Harper & Row, 1970.

Curti, Merle. *The Growth of American Thought*. New York: Harper & Brothers, 1943.

Davis, David B. *The Fear of Conspiracy: Images of UnAmerican Subversion from the Revolution to the Present*. Ithaca: Cornell University Press, 1971.

Gabriel, Ralph Henry. *The Course of American Democratic Thought*. New York: Ronald Press, 1940.

Handlin, Oscar. *The Uprooted: The Epic Story of the Great Migrations that Made the American People*. New York: Grosset & Dunlap, 1951.

Hofstadter, Richard. *Anti-Intellectualism in American Life*. New York: Alfred A. Knopf, 1963.

Kraditor, Aileen, ed. *Up from the Pedestal: Writings in the History of Feminism*. Chicago: Quadrangle Books, 1968.

Parrington, Vernon L. *Main Currents in American Thought*. 3 vols. New York: Harcourt, Brace & Co., 1927, 1930.

Pochmann, Henry A. *German Culture in America: Philosophical and Literary Influences, 1600–1900*. Madison, Wis.: University of Wisconsin Press, 1957.

Potter, David M. *People of Plenty: Economic Abundance and the American Character*. Chicago: University of Chicago Press, 1954.

Schlesinger, Arthur M., and Fox, Dixon R., eds. *A History of American Life*. 13 vols. New York: Macmillan Co., 1927–48.

Schneider, Herbert W. *A History of American Philosophy*. New York: Columbia University Press, 1946.

Wittke, Carl. *We Who Built America: The Saga of the Immigrant*. New York: Prentice-Hall, 1939.

7. GENERAL WORKS OF AMERICAN RELIGIOUS HISTORY

Ahlstrom, Sydney E., ed. *Theology in America: The Major Protestant Voices from Puritanism to Neo-orthodoxy*. Indianapolis: Bobbs-Merrill Co., 1967.

Bach, Marcus. *They Have Found a Faith*. Indianapolis: Bobbs-Merrill Co., 1946.

Bacon, Leonard W. *A History of American Christianity*. New York: Christian Literature Co., 1897.

Baird, Robert. *Religion in America*. 1844. Critical abridgement with introduction by Henry W. Bowden. New York: Harper & Row, 1970.

Braden, Charles S., ed. *Varieties of American Religion*. Chicago: Willett, Clark and Co., 1936.

Brauer, Jerald C. *Protestantism in America: A Narrative History*. Rev. ed. Philadelphia: Westminster Press, 1965.

———, ed. *Reinterpretation in American Church History*. Chicago: University of Chicago Press, 1968.

Clark, Elmer T. *The Small Sects in America*. Rev. ed. New York: Abingdon-Cokesbury Press, 1949.

Clebsch, William A. *From Sacred to Profane America: The Role of Religion in American History*. New York: Harper & Row, 1968.

Gaustad, Edwin S. *Historical Atlas of Religion in America*. New York: Harper & Row, 1962.

———. *A Religious History of America*. New York: Harper & Row, 1966.

Hudson, Winthrop S. *American Protestantism*. Chicago: University of Chicago Press, 1961.

———. *Religion in America*. New York: Charles Scribner's Sons, 1965.

Marty, Martin E. *Righteous Empire: The Protestant Experience in America*. New York: Dial Press, 1970.

Mead, Frank S. *Handbook of Denominations in the United States*. 5th ed. Nashville, Tenn.: Abingdon Press, 1970.

Mead, Sidney E. *The Lively Experiment: The Shaping of Christianity in America*. New York: Harper & Row, 1963.

Moberg, David O. *The Church as a Social Institution: The Sociology of American Religion*. Englewood Cliffs, N.J.: Prentice-Hall, 1962.

Olmstead, Clifton E. *History of Religion in the United States*. Englewood Cliffs, N.J.: Prentice-Hall, 1960.

Smith, Hilrie Shelton, Handy, Robert T., and Loetscher, Lefferts A. *American Christianity: An Historical Interpretation with Representative Documents*. 2 vols. New York: Charles Scribner's Sons, 1960–63.

Smith, James W., and Jamison, A. Leland, eds. *Religion in American Life*. 4 vols. Princeton, N.J.: Princeton University Press, 1961. [Two of these volumes contain topical and thematic essays on American churches and religious thought. The other two are bibliographical.]

Sontag, Frederick, and Roth, John K. *The American Religious Experience: The Roots, Trends, and the Future of American Theology*. New York: Harper & Row, 1972.

Sweet, William W. *The Story of Religion in America*. New York: Harper & Brothers, 1950.

Weigle, Luther A. *American Idealism*. New Haven: Yale University Press, 1928.

8. CHURCH AND STATE AND CIVIL RELIGION IN AMERICA

Cherry, Conrad. *God's New Israel: Religious Interpretations of American Destiny.* New York: Prentice-Hall, 1971.

Drinan, Robert F. *Religion, the Courts, and Public Policy.* New York: McGraw-Hill Book Co., 1963.

Healey, Robert M. *Jefferson on Religion in Public Education.* New Haven: Yale University Press, 1962.

McLoughlin, William G. *New England Dissent, 1630–1833: The Baptists and the Separation of Church and State.* 2 vols. Cambridge, Mass.: Harvard University Press, 1971.

Nagel, Paul C. *One Nation Indivisible: The Union in American Thought, 1776–1861.* New York: Oxford University Press, 1964.

———. *This Sacred Trust: American Nationality, 1798–1898.* New York: Oxford University Press, 1971.

Pfeffer, Leo. *Church, State, and Freedom.* Boston: Beacon Press, 1953.

Smith, Elwyn A., ed. *The Religion of the Republic.* Philadelphia: Fortress Press, 1971.

Stokes, Anson Phelps. *Church and State in the United States.* New York: Harper & Brothers, 1950.

Tuveson, Ernest Lee. *Millennium and Utopia: A Study in the Background of the Idea of Progress.* Berkeley and Los Angeles: University of California Press, 1949.

———. *Redeemer Nation: The Idea of America's Millennial Role.* Chicago: University of Chicago Press, 1968.

9. INDIANS, INDIAN POLICY, AND INDIAN MISSIONS

Beaver, R. Pierce. *Church, State, and the American Indians.* Saint Louis: Concordia Publishing House, 1966.

Benedict, Ruth. *Patterns of Culture.* Boston: Houghton Mifflin Co., 1934.

Berkhofer, Robert F., Jr. *Salvation and the Savage: An Analysis of Protestant Missions and American Indian Response, 1787–1862.* Lexington, Ky.: University of Kentucky Press, 1965.

Brown, Joseph E. *The Sacred Pipe: Black Elk's Account of the Seven Rites of the Oglala Sioux.* Norman, Okla.: University of Oklahoma Press, 1953.

Carroll, Peter N. *Puritanism and the Wilderness: The Intellectual Significance of the New England Frontier.* New York: Columbia University Press, 1969.

Driver, Harold. *Indians of North America.* Chicago: University of Chicago Press, 1961.

Harrod, Howard L. *Mission among the Blackfeet.* Norman, Okla.: University of Oklahoma Press, 1971.

Hertzberg, Hazel W. *The Search for an American Indian Identity: Modern Pan-Indian Movements.* Syracuse, N.Y.: Syracuse University Press, 1971.

Hinman, George W. *The American Indian and Christian Missions.* New York: Fleming H. Revell Co., 1933.

Jackson, Helen Hunt. *A Century of Dishonor.* 1881. Reprint. Edited by Andrew F. Rolle. New York: Harper & Row, Torchbooks, 1965.

Osborn, Chase S. and Stellanova. *"Hiawatha" with Its Original Indian Legends.* Lancaster, Pa.: Jacques Cattell Press, 1944.

Pearce, Roy Harvey. *The Savages of America.* Baltimore: Johns Hopkins Press, 1953.

Priest, Loring B. *Uncle Sam's Stepchildren: The Reformation of United States Indian Policy, 1865–1887.* New Brunswick, N.J.: Rutgers University Press, 1942.

Vaughan, Alden T. *The New England Frontier: Puritans and Indians, 1620–1675.* Boston: Little, Brown and Company, 1969.

10. ROMAN CATHOLICISM: GENERAL AMERICAN AND COLONIAL HISTORIES

Burns, James A. *The Growth and Development of the Catholic School System in the United States.* New York: Benziger Brothers, 1912.

Ellis, John Tracy. *American Catholicism.* 2d ed., rev. Chicago: University of Chicago Press, 1969.

———. *Catholics in Colonial America.* Baltimore: Helicon Press, 1965.

———. *Documents of American Catholic History.* Milwaukee: Bruce Publishing Co., 1956.

Gleason, Philip, ed. *The Catholic Church in America.* New York: Harper & Row, 1970.

———. *Contemporary Catholicism in the United States.* Notre Dame, Ind.: University of Notre Dame Press, 1969.

Greeley, Andrew M. *The Catholic Experience: An Interpretation of American Catholicism.* Garden City, N.Y.: Doubleday & Co., 1967.

Maynard, Theodore. *The Catholic Church and the American Idea.* New York: Appleton-Century-Crofts, 1953.

Melville, Annabelle M. *John Carroll of Baltimore: Founder of the American Catholic Hierarchy.* New York: Charles Scribner's Sons, 1955.

Shea, John Gilmary. *The Catholic Church in Colonial Days.* 2 vols. New York, 1886.

11. JUDAISM IN AMERICA

Blau, Joseph L. *Modern Varieties of Judaism.* New York: Columbia University Press, 1966.

———, and Baron, Salo W. *The Jews of the United States, 1790–1840. A Documentary History.* 3 vols. New York: Columbia University Press, 1966.

Eisenstein, Ira, and Kohn, Eugene, eds. *Mordecai M. Kaplan, An Evaluation.* New York: Jewish Reconstructionist Foundation, 1952.

Finkelstein, Louis. *The Jews: Their History, Culture, and Religion.* New York: Harper & Brothers, 1949. [Includes section on the United States.]

Gay, Ruth. *Jews in America: A Short History.* New York: Basic Books, 1965.

Glazer, Nathan. *American Judaism.* Chicago: University of Chicago Press, 1957.

Handlin, Oscar. *Adventure in Freedom: Three Hundred Years of Jewish Life in America.* New York: McGraw-Hill Book Co., 1954.

Hapgood, Hutchins. *The Spirit of the Ghetto,* with drawings by Jacob Epstein, 1902. New edition with commentary by Harry Golden. New York: Schocken, 1965.

Heschel, Abraham Joshua. *Between God and Man: An Interpretation of Judaism.* Edited with introduction by Fritz A. Rothschild. New York: Free Press, 1959.

Hirshler, Eric E., ed. *Jews from Germany in the United States.* New York: Farrar, Straus and Cudahy, 1955.

Karp, Abraham J., ed. *The Jewish Experience in America: Selected Studies from the Publications of the American Jewish Historical Society.* 5 vols. New York: Ktav Publishing House, 1969.

Learsi, Rufus. *Israel: A History of the Jewish People*. Cleveland: Meridian Press, 1968.

Levy, Beryl Harold. *Reform Judaism in America*. New York: Bloch Publishing Co., 1933.

Malin, Irving. *Jews and Americans*. Carbondale, Ill.: Southern Illinois University Press, 1965.

Philipson, David. *The Reform Movement in Modern Judaism*. New York: Macmillan Co., 1931.

Rischin, Moses. *The Promised City: New York's Jews, 1870–1914*. Cambridge, Mass.: Harvard University Press, 1962.

Rose, Peter I., ed. *The Ghetto and Beyond: Essays on Jewish Life in America*. New York: Random House, 1969.

Sherman, Charles B. *The Jew within American Society*. Detroit: Wayne State University Press, 1961.

Sklare, Marshall. *Conservative Judaism: An American Religious Movement*. Glencoe, Ill.: Free Press, 1955.

Wirth, Louis. *The Ghetto*. Chicago: University of Chicago Press, 1956.

Wischnitzer, Mark. *To Dwell in Safety: The Story of Jewish Migration since 1800*. Philadelphia: Jewish Publication Society of America, 1948.

Zborowski, Mark, and Herzog, Elizabeth. *Life Is with People: The Culture of the Shtetl*. New York: International Universities Press, 1952.

12. EASTERN ORTHODOXY IN AMERICA

Benz, Ernst. *The Eastern Orthodox Church: Its Thought and Life*. Translated by Richard and Clara Winston. Chicago: Aldine Publishing Co., 1963.

Bespuda, Anastasia. *Guide to Orthodox America*. Tuckahoe, N.Y.: Saint Vladimir's Seminary Press, 1965.

Bogolepov, Alexander A. *Toward an American Orthodox Church: The Establishment of an Autocephalous Orthodox Church*. New York: Morehouse-Barlow Co., 1963.

Bolshakov, Serge. *The Foreign Missions of the Russian Orthodox Church*. New York: Macmillan Co., 1943.

Bulgakov, Sergius. *The Orthodox Church*. Milwaukee: Morehouse Publishing Co., n.d. [ca. 1935].

Emhardt, Chauncey, et al. *The Eastern Church in the Western World*. Milwaukee: Morehouse Publishing Co., 1928.

Saloutos, Theodore. *The Greeks in America*. Cambridge, Mass.: Harvard University Press, 1964.

Schmemann, Alexander. *The Historical Road of Eastern Orthodoxy*. New York: Holt, Rinehart & Winston, 1963.

Ware, Timothy. *The Orthodox Church*. Baltimore: Penguin Books, 1964.

13. PROTESTANT DENOMINATIONAL HISTORIES AND STUDIES

Albright, Raymond W. *A History of the Evangelical Church*. Harrisburg, Pa.: Evangelical Press, 1942.

———. *History of the Protestant Episcopal Church*. New York: Macmillan Co., 1964.

Bacon, Margaret Hope. *The Quiet Rebels: The Story of the Quakers in America*. New York: Basic Books, 1969.

Baxter, Norman A. *History of the Freewill Baptists: A Study in New England Separatism.* Rochester, N.Y.: American Baptist Historical Society, 1957.

Bloch-Hoell, Nils Egede. *The Pentecostal Movement: Its Origin, Development, and Distinctive Character.* New York: Humanities Press, 1964.

Bucke, Emory Stevens, ed. *The History of American Methodism.* 3 vols. Nashville, Tenn.: Abingdon Press, 1964.

Drury, Augustus W. *History of the Church of the United Brethren in Christ.* Dayton, Ohio: Otterbein Press, 1924.

Garrison, Winifred E., and DeGroot, Alfred T. *The Disciples of Christ: A History.* Saint Louis: Christian Board of Publication, 1948.

Jones, Rufus. *The Quakers in the American Colonies.* London: Macmillan & Co., 1911.

Kromminga, John Henry. *The Christian Reformed Church: A Study in Orthodoxy.* Grand Rapids: Baker Book House, 1949.

Lewis, Arthur J. *Zinzendorf, The Ecumenical Pioneer: A Study in the Moravian Contribution to Christian Mission and Unity.* London: SCM Press, 1962.

Loetscher, Lefferts A. *The Broadening Church: A Study of Theological Issues in the Presbyterian Church since 1869.* Philadelphia: University of Pennsylvania Press, 1954.

McConnell, S. D. *History of the American Episcopal Church, 1600–1915.* 11th ed. Milwaukee: Morehouse Publishing Co., 1916. [First edition appeared in 1890.]

Manross, William Wilson. *A History of the American Episcopal Church.* 2d ed., rev. and enl. New York: Morehouse-Gorham, 1950.

Meuser, Fred W. *The Formation of the American Lutheran Church.* Columbus, Ohio: Wartburg Press, 1958.

Murch, James D. *Christians Only: A History of the Restoration Movement.* Cincinnati: Standard Publishing Co., 1962.

Nelson, Eugene C. *The Lutheran Church among Norwegian Americans.* Minneapolis: Augsburg Publishing House, 1960.

Nichol, John Thomas. *Pentecostalism.* New York: Harper & Row, 1966.

Olsson, Karl A., ed. *The Evangelical Covenant Church.* Chicago: Covenant Press, 1954.

Peters, John L. *Christian Perfection and American Methodism.* Nashville, Tenn.: Abingdon Press, 1956.

Schaff, Philip, et al., eds. *The American Church History Series.* 13 vols. New York: Christian Literature Co., 1893–1898. [Eleven of these volumes contain histories of major denominations.]

Schneider, Carl E. *The German Church on the American Frontier.* Saint Louis: Eden Publishing House, 1939.

Smith, Timothy L. *Called unto Holiness: The Story of the Nazarenes, The Formative Years.* Kansas City, Mo.: Nazarene Publishing House, 1962.

Stephenson, George M. *The Religious Aspects of Swedish Immigration: A Study of Immigrant Churches.* Minneapolis: University of Minnesota Press, 1932.

Sweet, William W., ed. *Religion on the American Frontier:* Vol. 1, *The Baptists* (New York: Henry Holt & Co., 1931). Vol. 2, *The Presbyterians* (New York: Harper & Brothers, 1936). Vol. 3, *The Congregationalists* (Chicago: University of Chicago Press, 1939). Vol. 4, *The Methodists* (Chicago: University of Chicago Press, 1946). [These works consist of documents with introductions by the editor.]

Thompson, Ernest T. *Presbyterians in the South.* Richmond, Va.: John Knox Press, 1963.

Tietjen, John H. *Which Way to Lutheran Unity? A History of Efforts to Unite the Lutherans of America.* Saint Louis: Concordia Publishing House, 1966.

Torbet, Robert G. *A History of the Baptists.* Philadelphia: Judson Press, 1950.
Wentz, Abdel R. *A Basic History of Lutheranism in America.* Philadelphia: Muhlenberg Press, 1955.
Winehouse, Irwin. *The Assemblies of God.* New York: Vantage Press, 1959.

On groups claiming a distinct break with the Protestant tradition, see section 21: Christian Science, Jehovah's Witnesses, Mormons, New Thought, Shakers, Swedenborgians, Theosophy, etc.

14. LONG-TERM THEMES IN PROTESTANT HISTORY

Ahlstrom, Sydney E. *The American Protestant Encounter with World Religions.* Beloit, Wis.: Beloit College, 1962.
Bailey, Albert B. *The Gospel in Hymns: Background and Interpretation.* New York: Charles Scribner's Sons, 1950.
Baltzell, Edward Digby. *The Protestant Establishment: Aristocracy and Caste in America.* New York: Random House, 1964.
Brumm, Ursula. *American Thought and Religious Typology.* New Brunswick, N.J.: Rutgers University Press, 1970.
Handy, Robert T. *A Christian America: Protestant Hopes and Historical Realities.* New York: Oxford University Press, 1971.
Hudson, Winthrop S. *The Great Tradition of the American Churches.* New York: Harper & Brothers, 1953.
Latourette, Kenneth Scott. *Missions and the American Mind.* Indianapolis: National Foundation Press, 1949.
Lynd, Staughton, ed. *Nonviolence in America: A Documentary History.* Indianapolis: Bobbs-Merrill Co., 1966.
McLoughlin, William G. *Modern Revivalism: Charles Grandison Finney to Billy Graham.* New York: Ronald Press Co., 1959.
Marty, Martin E. *The Infidel: Freethought and American Religion.* Cleveland, Ohio: Meridian Books, 1961.
Meyer, Donald B. *The Positive Thinkers: A Study of the Quest for Health, Wealth, and Personal Power from Mary Baker Eddy to Norman Vincent Peale.* Garden City, N.Y.: Doubleday & Co., 1965.
Mode, Peter G. *The Frontier Spirit in American Christianity.* New York: Macmillan Co., 1923.
Niebuhr, H. Richard. *The Kingdom of God in America.* New York: Harper & Brothers, 1937.
———. *The Social Sources of Denominationalism.* New York: Henry Holt & Co., 1929.
Osborn, Ronald E. *The Spirit of American Christianity.* New York: Harper Brothers, 1958.
Perry, Ralph Barton. *Puritanism and Democracy.* New York: Vanguard Press, 1944.
Shea, Daniel B., Jr., *Spiritual Autobiography in Early America.* Princeton, N.J.: Princeton University Press, 1968.
Smith, Hilrie Shelton. *Changing Conceptions of Original Sin: A Study in American Theology since 1750.* New York: Charles Scribner's Sons, 1955.
———. *Faith and Nurture.* New York: Charles Scribner's Sons, 1941.

Stewart, Randall. *American Literature and Christian Doctrine.* Baton Rouge: Louisiana State University Press, 1958.

Sweet, William W. *Revivalism in America: Its Origin, Growth and Decline.* New York: Charles Scribner's Sons, 1944.

Weisberger, Bernard A. *They Gathered at the River: The Story of the Great Revivalists and Their Impact upon Religion in America.* Boston: Little, Brown and Co., 1958.

15. EARLY COLONIAL RELIGION

Andrews, Charles M. *The Colonial Period of American History.* 4 vols. New Haven: Yale University Press, 1934–38.

Bailyn, Bernard. *New England Merchants in the Seventeenth Century.* Cambridge, Mass.: Harvard University Press, 1955.

Baird, Charles W. *History of the Huguenot Emigration to America.* 2 vols. New York, 1885.

Bertelson, David. *The Lazy South.* New York: Oxford University Press, 1967.

Condon, Thomas J. *New York Beginnings: The Commercial Origins of New Netherland.* New York: New York University Press, 1968.

Craven, Wesley F. *The Southern Colonies in the Seventeenth Century, 1607–1689.* Baton Rouge: Louisiana State University Press, 1949.

Davidson, Elizabeth H. *The Establishment of the English Church in the Continental American Colonies.* Durham, N.C.: Duke University Press, 1936.

Johnson, Amandus. *The Swedish Settlements on the Delaware.* 2 vols. Philadelphia: University of Pennsylvania Press, 1911.

Sachse, Julius F. *The German Pietists of Provincial Pennsylvania, 1694–1708.* Philadelphia, 1895.

———. *The German Sectarians of Pennsylvania.* 2 vols. Philadelphia, 1899–1900.

Tolles, Frederick B., and Alderfer, E. Gordon. *The Witness of William Penn.* New York: Macmillan Co., 1957.

Wertenbaker, Thomas J. *The Founding of American Civilization.* 3 vols. New York: Charles Scribner's Sons, 1938–47.

16. AMERICAN PURITANISM

Erikson, Kai T. *Wayward Puritans: A Study in the Sociology of Deviance.* New York: John Wiley & Sons, 1966.

Foster, Stephen. *Their Solitary Way: The Puritan Social Ethic in the First Century of Settlement in New England.* New Haven: Yale University Press, 1971.

Hall, David, ed. *The Antinomian Controversy: A Documentary History.* Middletown, Conn.: Wesleyan University Press, 1968.

Langdon, George D., Jr. *Pilgrim Colony: A History of New Plymouth, 1620–1691.* New Haven: Yale University Press, 1966.

Miller, Perry. *Errand into the Wilderness.* Cambridge, Mass.: Harvard University Press, 1956.

———. *The New England Mind: From Colony to Province.* Cambridge, Mass.: Harvard University Press, 1953.

———. *The New England Mind: The Seventeenth Century.* New York: Macmillan Co., 1939.

———. *Orthodoxy in Massachusetts, 1630–1650.* Cambridge, Mass.: Harvard University Press, 1933.

———. *Roger Williams: His Contribution to the American Tradition.* Indianapolis: Bobbs-Merrill Co., 1953.

———, and Johnson, Thomas H., eds. *The Puritans: A Sourcebook of Their Writings.* Bibliographies revised by George McCandlish. 2 vols. Rev. ed. New York: Harper & Row, 1963.

Morgan, Edmund S. *The Puritan Dilemma: The Story of John Winthrop.* Boston: Little, Brown and Co., 1958.

———. *Roger Williams: The Church and the State.* New York: Harcourt, Brace & World, 1967.

———. *Visible Saints: The History of a Puritan Idea.* New York: New York University Press, 1963.

Morison, Samuel Eliot. *Builders of the Bay Colony.* Boston: Houghton Mifflin Co., 1930.

———. *The Founding of Harvard College.* Cambridge, Mass.: Harvard University Press, 1935.

Murdock, Kenneth. *Literature and Theology in Colonial New England.* Cambridge, Mass.: Harvard University Press, 1949.

Pettit, Norman. *The Heart Prepared: Grace and Conversion in Puritan Spiritual Life.* New Haven: Yale University Press, 1966.

Rutman, Darrett B. *American Puritanism: Faith and Practice.* Philadelphia: J. B. Lippincott Co., 1970.

———. *Winthrop's Boston: Portrait of a Puritan Town.* Chapel Hill: University of North Carolina Press, 1965.

Schneider, Herbert W. *The Puritan Mind.* Ann Arbor: University of Michigan Press, 1958.

Simpson, Alan. *Puritanism in Old and New England.* Chicago: University of Chicago Press, 1955.

Walker, Williston. *The Creeds and Platforms of Congregationalism.* Introduction by Douglas Horton. Boston: Pilgrim Press, 1960.

Winslow, Ola E. *Master Roger Williams: A Biography.* New York: Macmillan Co., 1957.

———. *Meetinghouse Hill, 1630–1783.* New York: Macmillan Co., 1952.

17. LATER COLONIAL RELIGION

Akers, Charles W. *Called unto Liberty: A Life of Jonathan Mayhew, 1720–1766.* Cambridge, Mass.: Harvard University Press, 1964.

Aldridge, Owen. *Benjamin Franklin and Nature's God.* Durham, N.C.: Duke University Press, 1967.

Bailyn, Bernard. *The Ideological Origins of the American Revolution.* Cambridge, Mass.: Harvard University Press, 1967.

Baldwin, Alice M. *The New England Clergy and the American Revolution.* Durham, N.C.: Duke University Press, 1928.

Boorstin, Daniel J. *The Lost World of Thomas Jefferson.* New York: Henry Holt & Co., 1948.

Bridenbaugh, Carl. *Mitre and Sceptre: Transatlantic Faiths, Ideas, Personalities, and Politics, 1689–1775*. New York: Oxford University Press, 1962.

Bushman, Richard L. *From Puritan to Yankee: Character and the Social Order in Connecticut, 1690–1765*. Cambridge, Mass.: Harvard University Press, 1967.

Carroll, Peter N., ed. *Religion and the Coming of the American Revolution*. Waltham, Mass.: Ginn & Co., 1970.

Cassirer, Ernst. *The Philosophy of the Enlightenment*. Princeton, N.J.: Princeton University Press, 1951.

Cousins, Norman, ed. *In God We Trust: The Religious Beliefs and Ideas of the American Founding Fathers*. New York: Harper & Brothers, 1958.

Cross, Arthur L. *The Anglican Episcopate and the American Colonies*. New York: Longmans, Green and Co., 1902.

Gaustad, Edwin Scott. *The Great Awakening in New England*. New York: Harper & Row, 1957.

Gay, Peter. *The Enlightenment: An Interpretation, The Rise of Modern Paganism*. New York: Random House, 1966.

Gewehr, Wesley M. *The Great Awakening in Virginia, 1740–1790*. Durham, N.C.: Duke University Press, 1930.

Goen, Clarence C. *Revivalism and Separatism in New England: Strict Congregationalists and Separate Baptists in the Great Awakening*. New Haven: Yale University Press, 1962.

Heimert, Alan E. *Religion and the American Mind from the Great Awakening to the Revolution*. Cambridge, Mass.: Harvard University Press, 1966.

Henry, Stuart C. *George Whitefield: Wayfaring Witness*. New York: Abingdon Press, 1957.

Koch, Gustav A. *Republican Religion: The American Revolution and the Cult of Reason*. New York: Henry Holt & Co., 1933.

Loveland, Clara Olds. *The Critical Years: The Reconstruction of the Anglican Church in the United States of America, 1780–1789*. Greenwich, Conn.: Seabury Press, 1956.

McLoughlin, William G. *Isaac Backus and the American Pietistic Tradition*. Boston: Little, Brown and Co., 1967.

Maxson, Charles H. *The Great Awakening in the Middle Colonies*. Chicago: University of Chicago Press, 1920.

Morais, Herbert M. *Deism in Eighteenth-Century America*. New York: Columbia University Press, 1934.

Ray, Sister Mary Augustina. *American Opinion of Roman Catholicism in the Eighteenth Century*. New York: Columbia University Press, 1936.

Tanis, James R. *Dutch Calvinistic Pietism in the Middle Colonies: A Study in the Life of Theodorus Jacobus Frelinghuysen*. The Hague: Martinus Nijhof, 1967.

Thompson, Henry P. *Into All Lands: The History of the Society for the Propagation of the Gospel in Foreign Parts, 1701–1950*. London: SPCK, 1951.

———. *Thomas Bray*. London: SPCK, 1954.

Tolles, Frederick B. *Meeting House and Counting House: The Quaker Merchants of Colonial Philadephia, 1682–1763*. Chapel Hill: University of North Carolina Press, 1948.

Trinterud, Leonard J. *The Forming of an American Tradition: A Re-Examination of Colonial Presbyterianism*. Philadelphia: Westminster Press, 1949.

18. JONATHAN EDWARDS AND THE NEW ENGLAND THEOLOGY

Boardman, George N. *A History of the New England Theology*. Chicago, 1899.

Carse, James. *Jonathan Edwards and the Visibility of God*. New York: Charles Scribner's Sons, 1967.

Cherry, Conrad. *The Theology of Jonathan Edwards: A Reappraisal*. Garden City, N.Y.: Doubleday & Co., Anchor Books, 1966.

Davidson, Edward H. *Jonathan Edwards: The Narrative of a Puritan Mind*. Boston: Houghton Mifflin Co., 1966.

Delattre, Roland A. *Beauty and Sensibility in the Thought of Jonathan Edwards*. New Haven: Yale University Press, 1968.

Elwood, Douglas J. *The Philosophical Theology of Jonathan Edwards*. New York: Columbia University Press, 1960.

Faust, Clarence H., and Johnson, Thomas H., eds. *Jonathan Edwards, Representative Selections*. Rev. ed. New York: Hill & Wang, 1962.

Foster, Frank H. *A Genetic History of the New England Theology*. Chicago: University of Chicago Press, 1907.

Haroutunian, Joseph. *Piety versus Moralism: The Passing of the New England Theology*. New York: Henry Holt & Co., 1932. Reprint. Introduction by Sydney E. Ahlstrom. New York: Harper & Row, Torchbooks, 1970.

Levin, David, ed. *Jonathan Edwards: A Profile*. New York: Hill & Wang, 1969.

Mead, Sidney E. *Nathaniel William Taylor, 1786–1858: A Connecticut Liberal*. Chicago: University of Chicago Press, 1942.

Miller, Perry. *Jonathan Edwards*. New York: William Sloan Associates, 1949.

Winslow, Ola E. *Jonathan Edwards*. New York: Macmillan Co., 1940.

19. ANTEBELLUM PROTESTANTISM

Ayres, Anne. *The Life and Work of William Augustus Muhlenberg*. New York, 1880.

Billington, Ray A. *The Protestant Crusade 1800–1860: A Study of the Origins of American Nativism*. New York: Macmillan Co., 1938.

Bodo, John R. *The Protestant Clergy and Public Issues, 1812–1848*. Princeton, N.J.: Princeton University Press, 1954.

Cleveland, Catharine C. *The Great Revival in the West, 1797–1805*. Chicago: University of Chicago Press, 1916.

Cole, Charles C., Jr. *The Social Ideas of the Northern Evangelists, 1826–1860*. New York: Columbia University Press, 1954.

Cross, Whitney R. *The Burned-Over District: The Social and Intellectual History of Enthusiastic Religion in Western New York, 1800–1850*. Ithaca: Cornell University Press, 1950.

Eaton, Clement. *The Mind of the Old South*. Rev. ed. Baton Rouge: Louisiana State University Press, 1967.

Ekirch, Arthur. *The Idea of Progress in America, 1815–1860*. New York: Columbia University Press, 1944.

Elsbree, Oliver W. *The Rise of the Missionary Spirit in America, 1790–1815*. Williamsport, Pa.: Williamsport Printing Co., 1928.

Ferm, Vergilius. *The Crisis in Lutheran Theology: A Study of the Issue between American Lutheranism and Old Lutheranism.* New York: Century Co., 1927.

Foster, Charles I. *An Errand of Mercy: The Evangelical United Front, 1790–1837.* Chapel Hill: University of North Carolina Press, 1960.

Goodykoontz, Colin B. *Home Missions on the American Frontier, with Particular Reference to the American Home Missionary Society.* Caldwell, Idaho: Caxton, 1939.

Griffin, Clifford S., *Their Brothers' Keepers: Moral Stewardship in the United States, 1800–1865.* New Brunswick, N.J.: Rutgers University Press, 1960.

Howe, Daniel W. *The Unitarian Conscience: The Harvard Moral Philosophers, 1805–1861.* Cambridge, Mass.: Harvard University Press, 1970.

Johnson, Charles A. *The Frontier Camp Meeting: Religion's Harvest Time.* Dallas, Tex.: Southern Methodist University Press, 1955.

Keller, Charles Roy. *The Second Great Awakening in Connecticut.* New Haven: Yale University Press, 1942.

Krout, John Allen. *The Origins of Prohibition.* New York: Alfred A. Knopf, 1925.

Ludlum, David M. *Social Ferment in Vermont, 1791–1850.* New York: Columbia University Press, 1939.

Marsden, George M. *The Evangelical Mind and the New School Presbyterian Experience.* New Haven: Yale University Press, 1970.

Mathews, Lois Kimball. *The Expansion of New England: The Spread of New England Institutions to the Mississippi River, 1620–1865.* Boston: Houghton Mifflin Co., 1909.

Miller, Perry. *The Life of the Mind in America: From the Revolution to the Civil War.* New York: Harcourt, Brace & World, 1965.

Miyakawa, T. Scott. *Protestants and Pioneers: Individualism and Conformity on the American Frontier.* Chicago: University of Chicago Press, 1964.

Ratner, Lorman. *Antimasonry: The Crusade and the Party.* Englewood Cliffs, N.J.: Prentice-Hall, 1969.

Rice, Edwin W. *The Sunday School Movement and the American Sunday School Union.* Philadelphia: Union Press, 1917.

Rosenberg, Carroll S. *Religion and the Rise of the City: The New York City Mission Movement.* Ithaca: Cornell University Press, 1971.

Silverman, Kenneth. *Timothy Dwight.* New York: Twayne Publishers, 1969.

Smith, Timothy L. *Revivalism and Social Reform in Mid-Nineteenth-Century America.* Nashville, Tenn.: Abingdon Press, 1957.

Smith, Wilson. *Professors and Public Ethics: Studies in Northern Moral Philosophers before the Civil War.* Ithaca: Cornell University Press, 1956.

Stephenson, George M. *The Puritan Heritage.* New York: Macmillan Co., 1952.

Sweet, William W. *Religion in the Development of American Culture, 1765–1840.* New York: Charles Scribner's Sons, 1952.

Taylor, William R. *Cavalier and Yankee: The Old South and American National Character.* New York: George Braziller, 1967.

Tewksbury, Donald G. *The Founding of American Colleges and Universities before the Civil War, with Particular Reference to the Religious Influences Bearing on the College Movement.* New York: Columbia University Press, 1932.

Tyler, Alice F. *Freedom's Ferment: Phases of American Social History to 1860.* Minneapolis: University of Minnesota Press, 1944.

Wright, Conrad. *The Beginnings of Unitarianism.* Boston: Beacon Press, 1955.

20. TRANSCENDENTALISM AND OTHER ROMANTIC CURRENTS

Bishop, Jonathan. *Emerson on the Soul.* Cambridge, Mass.: Harvard University Press, 1964.

Brown, Jerry W. *The Rise of Biblical Criticism in America, 1800–1870: The New England Scholars.* Middletown, Conn.: Wesleyan University Press, 1969.

Carpenter, Frederic I. *Emerson Handbook.* New York: Hendricks House, 1957.

Cross, Barbara M. *Horace Bushnell: Minister to a Changing America.* Chicago: University of Chicago Press, 1958.

Crowe, Charles. *George Ripley: Transcendentalist and Utopian Socialist.* Athens, Ga.: University of Georgia Press, 1967.

Easton, Loyd D. *Hegel's First American Followers: The Ohio Hegelians.* Athens, Ohio: Ohio University Press, 1966.

Fairweather, Eugene R., ed. *The Oxford Movement.* Library of Protestant Thought. New York: Oxford University Press, 1964.

Frothingham, Octavius Brooks. *Transcendentalism in New England: A History.* 1876. Reprint. Introduction by Sydney E. Ahlstrom. Philadelphia: University of Pennsylvania Press, 1972.

Furst, Lilian R. *Romanticism in Perspective: A Comparative Study of Aspects of the Romantic Movements in England, France, and Germany.* London: Macmillan & Co., 1969.

Hochfield, George, ed. *Selected Writings of the American Transcendentalists.* New York: New American Library, 1966.

Hutchison, William R. *The Transcendentalist Ministers: Church Reform in the New England Renaissance.* New Haven: Yale University Press, 1959.

Matthiessen, F. O. *The American Renaissance.* New York: Oxford University Press, 1941.

Miller, Perry, ed. *The Transcendentalists: An Anthology.* Cambridge, Mass.: Harvard University Press, 1959.

Nichols, James Hastings. *Romanticism in American Theology: Nevin and Schaff at Mercersburg.* Chicago: University of Chicago Press, 1961.

———, ed. *The Mercersburg Theology.* New York: Oxford University Press, 1966.

Rusk, Ralph L. *The Life of Ralph Waldo Emerson.* New York: Charles Scribner's Sons, 1949.

Stanton, Phoebe B. *The Gothic Revival and American Church Architecture 1840–1856.* Baltimore: Johns Hopkins Press, 1968.

Swift, Lindsay. *Brook Farm: Its Members, Scholars, and Visitors.* New York: Macmillan Co., 1900.

White, James F. *The Cambridge Movement.* New York: Cambridge University Press, 1962.

Williams, Norman P., and Harris, Charles, eds. *Northern Catholicism: Centenary Studies in the Oxford and Parallel Movements.* New York: Macmillan Co., 1933.

21. NEW MOVEMENTS IN RELIGION: NINETEENTH CENTURY

Andrews, Edward D. *The People Called Shakers.* New York: Oxford University Press, 1953.

Bates, Ernest Sutherland, and Dittemore, John V. *Mary Baker Eddy: The Truth and the Tradition.* New York: Alfred A. Knopf, 1932.

Bestor, Arthur Eugene, Jr. *Backwoods Utopias: The Sectarian and Owenite Phases of Communitarian Socialism in America, 1663–1829*. Philadelphia: University of Pennsylvania Press, 1950.

Block, Marguerite. *The New Church in the New World: A Study of Swedenborgianism in the New World*. New York: Henry Holt & Co., 1932.

Boldt, Ernst. *From Luther to Steiner*. London: Methuen & Co., 1923.

Braden, Charles S. *Spirits in Rebellion: The Rise and Development of New Thought*. Dallas, Tex.: Southern Methodist University Press, 1963.

———. *These Also Believe: A Study of Modern American Cults and Minority Religious Movements*. New York: Macmillan Co., 1949.

Brodie, Fawn. *No Man Knows My History: The Life of Joseph Smith, the Mormon Prophet*. New York: Alfred A. Knopf, 1945.

Cole, Marley. *Jehovah's Witnesses: The New World Society*. New York: Vantage Press, 1955.

Dresser, Horatio W. *History of the New Thought Movement*. New York: Crowell, 1919.

Ferraby, John. *All Things Made New: A Comprehensive Outline of the Bahá'i Faith*. New York: Macmillan Co., 1958.

Flanders, Robert Bruce. *Nauvoo: Kingdom on the Mississippi*. Urbana, Ill.: University of Illinois Press, 1965.

Fornell, Earl Wesley. *The Unhappy Medium: Spiritualism and the Life of Margaret Fox*. Austin, Tex.: University of Texas Press, 1964.

Holloway, Mark. *Heavens on Earth: Utopian Communities in America, 1680–1880*. 2d ed. New York: Dover Publications, 1966.

Kennedy, Hugh A. Studdert. *Mrs. Eddy: Her Life, Her Work, and Her Place in History*. San Francisco: Farallon Press, 1947.

Kuhn, Alvin Boyd. *Theosophy: A Modern Revival of Ancient Wisdom*. New York: Henry Holt & Co., 1930.

Leopold, Richard W. *Robert Dale Owen*. Cambridge, Mass.: Harvard University Press, 1940.

McMurrin, Sterling M. *Theological Foundations of the Mormon Religion*. Salt Lake City: University of Utah Press, 1955.

Mayer, Frederick E. *Jehovah's Witnesses*. Saint Louis: Concordia Publishing House, 1952.

Martin, Walter R. *The Truth about Seventh-Day Adventism*. Grand Rapids, Mich.: Zondervan Publishing House, 1960.

Miller, William M. *Bahá'ism: Its Origin and Teachings*. New York: Fleming H. Revell, 1931.

Mullen, Robert. *The Latter-Day Saints: The Mormons Yesterday and Today*. Garden City, N.Y.: Doubleday & Co., 1966.

Nichol, Francis David. *The Midnight Cry: A Defense of the Character and Conduct of William Miller and the Millerites*. Washington, D.C.: Review & Herald Publishing Association, 1944.

O'Dea, Thomas. *The Mormons*. Chicago: University of Chicago Press, 1957.

Peel, Robert. *Mary Baker Eddy: The Years of Discovery*. New York: Holt, Rinehart & Winston, 1966.

Porter, Katherine H. *Through the Glass Darkly: Spiritualism in the Browning Circle*. Lawrence, Kans.: University of Kansas Press, 1958.

Schneider, Herbert W. *A Prophet and a Pilgrim: Being the Incredible History of Thomas Lake Harris and Laurence Oliphant*. New York: Columbia University Press, 1942.

Spaulding, W. W. *A History of Seventh-Day Adventists.* 2 vols. Washington, D.C.: Review & Herald Publishing Association, 1949.

West, Ray B. *Kingdom of the Saints: The Story of Brigham Young and the Mormons.* New York: Viking, 1957.

22. SECTIONAL ISSUES AND THE CIVIL WAR

Barnes, Gilbert H. *The Antislavery Impulse, 1830–1844.* New York: D. Appleton-Century Co., 1933.

Blied, Benjamin J. *Catholics and the Civil War.* Milwaukee: Privately Printed, 1945.

Duberman, Martin, ed. *The Antislavery Vanguard: New Essays on the Abolitionists.* Princeton, N.J.: Princeton University Press, 1965.

Dumond, Dwight L. *The Antislavery Origins of the Civil War in the United States.* Ann Arbor: University of Michigan Press, 1959.

Dunham, Chester F. *The Attitude of the Northern Clergy toward the South, 1860–1865.* Toledo, Ohio: Gray Co., 1942.

Filler, Louis. *The Crusade Against Slavery, 1830–1860.* New York: Harper & Row, 1960.

Fredrickson, George M. *The Inner Civil War: Northern Intellectuals and the Crisis of the Union.* New York: Harper & Row, 1965.

Korn, Bertram W. *American Jewry and the Civil War.* Cleveland: Meridian Books, 1961.

Mathews, Donald G. *Slavery and Methodism: A Chapter in American Morality, 1780–1845.* Princeton, N.J.: Princeton University Press, 1965.

Pressly, Thomas J. *Americans Interpret Their Civil War.* New York: Collier Books, 1962.

Silver, James W. *Confederate Morale and Church Propaganda.* Tuscaloosa, Ala.: Confederate Publishing Co., 1957.

Stampp, Kenneth M. *And the War Came: The North and the Secession Crisis, 1860–61.* Chicago: University of Chicago Press, 1950.

———. *The Era of Reconstruction, 1865–1877.* New York: Alfred A. Knopf, 1967.

Staudenraus, P. J. *The African Colonization Movement, 1816–1865.* New York: Columbia University Press, 1961.

Wolf, William J. *The Almost Chosen People: A Study of the Religion of Abraham Lincoln.* Garden City, N.Y.: Doubleday & Co., 1959.

Zilversmit, Arthur. *The First Emancipation: The Abolition of Slavery in the North.* Chicago: University of Chicago Press, 1967.

23. SLAVERY, THE NEGRO, AND THE BLACK CHURCHES

Bardolph, Richard. *The Negro Vanguard.* New York: Random House, 1959.

Bracey, John H., Jr., Meier, August, and Rudwick, Elliott, eds. *Black Nationalism in America.* Indianapolis: Bobbs-Merrill Co., 1970.

Davie, Maurice R. *Negroes in American Society.* New York: McGraw-Hill Book Co., 1949.

Davis, David B. *The Problem of Slavery in Western Culture.* Ithaca: Cornell University Press, 1966.

DuBois, W. E. Burghardt. *The Souls of Black Folk.* 1903. Reprint. New York: Fawcett World Library, 1961.

———. *The Negro Church.* Atlanta, 1903.

Franklin, John Hope. *From Slavery to Freedom: A History of Negro Americans.* New York: Alfred A. Knopf, 1967.

Frazier, E. Franklin. *The Negro Church in America.* New York: Schocken Books, 1964.

———. *The Negro in the United States.* New York: Macmillan Co., 1949.

Gossett, Thomas F. *Race: The History of an Idea in America.* Dallas: Southern Methodist University Press, 1963.

Johnson, Clifton H., ed. *God Struck Me Dead: Religious Conversion Experiences and Autobiographies of Ex-Slaves.* Philadelphia: Pilgrim Press, 1969.

Jordan, Winthrop D. *White over Black: American Attitudes toward the Negro, 1550–1812.* Chapel Hill: University of North Carolina Press, 1968.

Lapides, Frederick R., and Burrows, David, eds. *Racism: A Casebook.* New York: Thomas Y. Crowell, 1971.

Mays, Benjamin E. *The Negro's God, as Reflected in His Literature.* New York: Atheneum Publishers, 1968.

———, and Nicolson, Joseph W. *The Negro's Church.* New York: Institute of Social and Religious Research, 1933.

Meier, August. *Negro Thought in America, 1880–1915.* Ann Arbor: University of Michigan Press, 1963.

Murray, Andrew E. *Presbyterians and the Negro: A History.* Philadelphia: Presbyterian Historical Society, 1966.

Nelsen, Hart M., Yokley, Raytha, and Nelsen, Anne. *The Black Church in America.* New York: Basic Books, 1971.

Pelt, Owen D., and Smith, Ralph Lee. *The Story of the National Baptists.* New York: Vantage Press, 1960.

Pipes, William H. *Say Amen, Brother! Old-Time Negro Preaching: A Study in Frustration.* New York: William-Frederick Press, 1951.

Redkey, Edwin S. *Black Exodus: Black Nationalist and Back-to-Africa Movements, 1890–1910.* New Haven: Yale University Press, 1969.

Reimers, David M. *White Protestantism and the Negro.* New York: Oxford University Press, 1965.

Rose, Arnold. *The Negro in America.* Boston: Beacon Press, 1956. [A Condensation of Gunnar Myrdal, *The American Dilemma,* 1944.]

Washington, Joseph R., Jr. *Black Religion: The Negro and Christianity in the United States.* Boston: Beacon Press, 1964.

Weinstein, Allen, and Gatell, Frank O. *American Negro Slavery: A Modern Reader.* New York: Oxford University Press, 1968.

Woodson, Carter G. *The History of the Negro Church.* 2d ed. Washington, D.C.: Associated Publishers, 1921.

Woodward, C. Vann. *The Strange History of Jim Crow.* 2d rev. ed. New York: Oxford University Press, 1966.

24. ROMAN CATHOLICISM IN THE NINETEENTH AND TWENTIETH CENTURIES

Abell, Aaron I., ed. *American Catholic Thought on Social Questions.* Indianapolis: Bobbs-Merrill Co., 1968.

———. *American Catholicism and Social Action: A Search for Social Justice, 1865–1950.* Garden City, N.Y.: Hanover House, 1960.

Bell, Stephen. *Rebel, Priest, and Prophet: A Biography of Dr. Edward McGlynn.* New York: Devin-Adair Co., 1937.

Browne, Henry J. *The Catholic Church and the Knights of Labor.* Washington, D.C.: Catholic University of America Press, 1949.

Callan, Louise. *Philippine Duchesne: Frontier Missionary of the Sacred Heart, 1769–1852.* Westminster, Md.: Newman Press, 1957.

Cross, Robert D. *The Emergence of Liberal Catholicism in America.* Cambridge, Mass.: Harvard University Press, 1958.

Flynn, George Q. *American Catholics and the Roosevelt Presidency, 1932–1936.* Lexington, Ky.: University of Kentucky Press, 1968.

Gleason, Philip. *The Conservative Reformers: German-American Catholics and the Social Order.* Notre Dame, Ind.: University of Notre Dame Press, 1968.

Koenker, Ernest B. *The Liturgical Renaissance in the Roman Catholic Church.* Chicago: University of Chicago Press, 1954.

McAvoy, Thomas T. *The Formation of the American Catholic Minority.* Philadelphia: Fortress Press, 1967.

———. *The Great Crisis in American Catholic History, 1895–1900.* Chicago: Henry Regnery Co., 1957.

———, ed. *Roman Catholicism and the American Way of Life.* Notre Dame, Ind.: University of Notre Dame Press, 1960.

Marx, Paul B. *Virgil Michel and the Liturgical Movement.* Collegeville, Minn.: Liturgical Press, 1957.

Moynihan, James H. *The Life of Archbishop John Ireland.* New York: Harper & Row, 1953.

O'Brien, David J. *American Catholics and Social Reform: The New Deal Years.* New York: Oxford University Press, 1968.

Ong, Walter J. *American Catholic Crossroads.* New York: Macmillan Co., 1959.

———. *Frontiers in American Catholicism: Essays on Ideology and Culture.* New York: Macmillan Co., 1957.

Phillips, Charles S. *The Church in France, 1848–1907.* New York: Macmillan Co., 1936.

Sheean, Arthur. *Peter Maurin, Gay Believer.* New York: Hanover House, 1959.

Shields, Currin. *Democracy and Catholicism in America.* New York: McGraw-Hill Book Co., 1958.

Shuster, George N. *The Catholic Spirit in America.* New York: Dial Press, 1927.

Vidler, Alec R. *The Modernist Movement in the Roman Church.* Cambridge: At the University Press, 1934.

Ward, Leo R., ed. *The American Apostolate.* Westminster, Md.: Newman Press, 1952.

Weber, Ralph E. *Notre Dame's John Zahm.* Notre Dame, Ind.: University of Notre Dame Press, 1961.

25. PROTESTANTISM SINCE THE CIVIL WAR

Abell, Aaron I. *The Urban Impact on American Protestantism, 1865–1900.* Cambridge, Mass.: Harvard University Press, 1943.

Barnes, William Wright. *The Southern Baptist Convention, 1845–1953.* Nashville, Tenn.: Broadman Press, 1954.

Bass, Clarence B. *Backgrounds to Dispensationalism: Its Historical Genesis and Ecclesiastical Implications.* Grand Rapids, Mich.: William B. Eerdmans Co., 1960.

Buck, Paul H. *The Road to Reunion.* Boston: Little, Brown and Co., 1947.

Cochran, Thomas C. *The Inner Revolution.* New York: Harper & Row, 1967.

Cross, Robert D. *The Church and the City, 1865–1910.* Indianapolis: Bobbs-Merrill Co., 1967.

DeGroot, Alfred Thomas. *New Possibilities for Disciples and Independents, with a History of the Independents, Church of Christ Number Two.* Saint Louis: Bethany Press, 1963.

Dombrowski, James. *The Early Days of Christian Socialism in America.* New York: Columbia University Press, 1936.

Farish, Hunter D. *The Circuit Rider Dismounts.* Richmond, Va.: Dietz Press, 1938.

Findlay, James F., Jr. *Dwight L. Moody: American Evangelist, 1837–1899.* Chicago: University of Chicago Press, 1969.

Handy, Robert T., ed. *The Social Gospel in America, 1870–1920: Gladden, Ely, Rauschenbusch.* Library of Protestant Thought. New York: Oxford University Press, 1966.

Higham, John. *Strangers in the Land: Patterns of American Nativism, 1860–1925.* New Brunswick, N.J.: Rutgers University Press, 1955.

Hopkins, Charles H. *A History of the YMCA in North America.* New York: Association Press, 1951.

———. *The Rise of the Social Gospel in American Protestantism, 1865–1915.* New Haven: Yale University Press, 1940.

Kraus, C. Norman. *Dispensationalism in America: Its Rise and Development.* Richmond, Va.: John Knox Press, 1958.

MacKenzie, Kenneth M. *The Robe and the Sword: The Methodist Church and the Rise of American Imperialism.* Washington, D.C.: Public Affairs Press, 1961.

Mann, Arthur. *Yankee Reformers in the Urban Age: Social Reform in Boston, 1880–1900.* Cambridge, Mass.: Harvard University Press, Belknap Press, 1954.

May, Henry F. *Protestant Churches and Industrial America.* New York: Harper & Brothers, 1949.

Sandeen, Ernest R. *The Roots of Fundamentalism, British and American.* Chicago: University of Chicago Press, 1970.

Sinclair, Andrew. *Prohibition: The Era of Excess.* Boston: Little, Brown and Co., 1962.

Spain, Rufus. *At Ease in Zion: Social History of Southern Baptists.* Nashville, Tenn.: Vanderbilt University Press, 1967.

Thompson, Ernest Trice. *The Spirituality of the Church: A Distinctive Doctrine of the Presbyterian Church in the United States.* Richmond, Va.: John Knox Press, 1961.

Weisenburger, Francis P. *Ordeal of Faith: The Crisis of Churchgoing America, 1865–1900.* New York: Philosophical Library, 1959.

Woodward, C. Vann. *The Burden of Southern History.* Baton Rouge: Louisiana State University Press, 1960.

26. LIBERAL TRENDS IN NINETEENTH-CENTURY RELIGIOUS THOUGHT

Bixler, J. Seelye. *Religion in the Philosophy of William James.* Boston: Marshall Jones Co., 1926.

Bowden, Henry W. *Church History in the Age of Science.* Chapel Hill: University of North Carolina Press, 1971.

Brown, Ira. *Lyman Abbott.* Cambridge, Mass.: Harvard University Press, 1953.

Buckham, John Wright, *Progressive Religious Thought in America: A Survey of the Enlarging Pilgrim Faith.* Boston: Houghton Mifflin Co., 1919.

Carter, Paul A. *The Spiritual Crisis of the Gilded Age.* DeKalb, Ill.: Northern Illinois University Press, 1972.

Cauthen, Kenneth. *The Impact of American Religious Liberalism.* New York: Harper & Row, 1962.

Foster, Frank H. *The Modern Movement in American Theology.* New York: Fleming H. Revell Co., 1939.

Greene, John C. *Darwin and the Modern World View.* Baton Rouge: Louisiana State University Press, 1961.

———. *The Death of Adam: Evolution and Its Impact on Western Thought.* Ames, Iowa: Iowa State University Press, 1959.

Hofstadter, Richard. *Social Darwinism in the United States, 1860–1915.* Philadelphia: University of Pennsylvania Press, 1945.

Hutchison, William R., ed. *American Protestant Thought: The Liberal Era.* New York: Harper & Row, 1968.

McGiffert, Arthur C., *The Rise of Modern Religious Ideas.* New York: Macmillan Co., 1915.

Moore, Edward C. *An Outline of the History of Christian Thought since Kant.* New York: Charles Scribner's Sons, 1912.

Persons, Stow, ed. *Evolutionary Thought in America.* New Haven: Yale University Press, 1950.

———. *Free Religion: An American Faith.* New Haven: Yale University Press, 1947.

Post, Albert. *Popular Free Thought in America, 1825–1850.* New York: Columbia University Press, 1943.

Radest, Howard B. *Toward Common Ground: The Story of the Ethical Societies in the United States.* New York: Frederick Ungar Co., 1969.

Roth, Robert J. *American Religious Philosophy.* New York: Harcourt, Brace & World, 1967.

Smith, John E. *The Spirit of American Philosophy.* New York: Oxford University Press, 1963.

White, Edward A. *Science and Religion in American Thought: The Impact of Naturalism.* Stanford, Calif.: Stanford University Press, 1952.

Wiener, Philip P. *Evolution and the Founders of Pragmatism.* Cambridge, Mass.: Harvard University Press, 1949.

Williams, Daniel Day. *The Andover Liberals: A Study in American Theology.* New York: King's Crown Press, 1941.

Young, Frederic H. *The Philosophy of Henry James, Sr.* New York: Bookman Associates, 1951.

27. ECUMENICAL AND INTER-FAITH DEVELOPMENTS

Bell, George K. A. *The Kingship of Christ: The Story of the World Council of Churches.* Baltimore: Penguin Books, 1954.

Brown, Robert McAfee, and Scott, David H., comps. and eds. *The Challenge to Reunion.* New York: McGraw-Hill Book Co., 1963.

———, and Weigle, Gustave. *An American Dialogue*. Garden City, N.Y.: Doubleday & Co., 1960.

Cavert, Samuel McCrea. *The American Churches in the Ecumenical Movement, 1900–1968*. New York: Association Press, 1968.

Douglass, H. Paul. *Church Unity Movements in the United States*. New York: Institute of Social and Religious Research, 1934.

Eckardt, A. Roy. *Elder and Younger Brothers: The Encounter of Jews and Christians*. New York: Charles Scribner's Sons, 1967.

Gilbert, Arthur. *A Jew in Christian America*. New York: Sheed & Ward, 1966.

Handy, Robert T. *We Witness Together: A History of Cooperative Home Missions*. New York: Friendship Press, 1956.

Hutchison, John A. *We Are Not Divided: A Critical and Historical Study of the Federal Council of the Churches of Christ in America*. New York: Round Table Press, 1941.

Lee, Robert. *The Social Sources of Church Unity*. Nashville, Tenn.: Abingdon Press, 1960.

Macfarland, Charles S. *Christian Unity in the Making: The First Twenty-Five Years of the Federal Council of the Churches of Christ in America, 1905–1930*. New York: Federal Council of Churches of Christ in America, 1948.

Murch, James D. *Cooperation without Compromise: A History of the National Association of Evangelicals*. Grand Rapids, Mich.: William B. Eerdmans Co., 1956.

Rosenzweig, Franz. *Judaism Despite Christianity: The "Letters on Christianity and Judaism" between Eugen Rosenstock-Huessy and Franz Rosenzweig*. Edited by Eugen Rosenstock-Huessy. University, Ala.: University of Alabama Press, 1969.

Rouse, Ruth, and Neill, Stephen C. *A History of the Ecumenical Movement, 1517–1948*. Philadelphia: Westminster Press, 1954.

Schoeps, Hans J. *The Jewish-Christian Argument*. New York: Holt, Rinehart & Winston, 1963.

Visser 't Hooft, Willem Adolph, ed. *The First Assembly of the World Council of Churches*. New York: Harper & Brothers, 1949.

28. RELIGIOUS HISTORY FROM WORLD WAR I TO THE VIETNAM WAR

Abrams, Ray H. *Preachers Present Arms*. New York: Round Table Press, 1933.

Allen, Frederick L. *Only Yesterday: An Informal History of the 1920s*. New York: Harper & Brothers, 1931.

———. *Since Yesterday*. New York: Harper & Brothers, 1940.

Atkins, Gaius Glenn. *Religion in Our Times*. New York: Round Table Press, 1932.

Bailey, Kenneth K. *Southern White Protestantism in the Twentieth Century*. New York: Harper & Row, 1964.

Bennett, David H. *Demagogues in the Depression: American Radicals and the Union Party, 1932–1936*. New Brunswick, N.J.: Rutgers University Press, 1969.

Braeman, John, et al., eds. *The 1920's*. Columbus: Ohio State University Press, 1968.

Brown, William A. *The Church in America: A Study of the Present Condition and Future Prospects of American Protestantism*. New York: Macmillan Co., 1922.

Carter, Paul A. *The Decline and Revival of Social Gospel, 1920–1940*. Ithaca: Cornell University Press, 1956.

Clark, Walter Huston. *The Oxford Group: Its History and Significance.* New York: Bookman Associates, 1951.

Dabney, Virginius. *Dry Messiah: The Life of Bishop Cannon.* New York: Alfred A. Knopf, 1949.

Eckardt, A. Roy. *The Surge of Piety in America: An Appraisal.* New York: Association Press, 1958.

Furniss, Norman K. *The Fundamentalist Controversy, 1918–1931.* New Haven: Yale University Press, 1954.

Gasper, Louis. *The Fundamentalist Movement.* The Hague: Mouton & Co., 1963.

Gatewood, William B., Jr., ed. *Controversy in the Twenties: Fundamentalism, Modernism, and Evolution.* Nashville, Tenn.: Vanderbilt University Press, 1969.

Ginger, Ray. *Six Days or Forever? Tennessee v. John Thomas Scopes.* Boston: Beacon Press, 1958.

Gusfield, Joseph R. *Symbolic Crusade: Status Politics and the American Temperance Movement.* Urbana, Ill.: University of Illinois Press, 1966.

Herberg, Will. *Protestant, Catholic, Jew: An Essay in American Religious Sociology.* Garden City, N.Y.: Doubleday & Co., 1955.

Hocking, William Ernest, ed. *Rethinking Missions: A Laymen's Inquiry after One Hundred Years, by the Commission of Appraisal.* New York: Harper & Brothers, 1932.

Howlett, Duncan. *The Fourth American Faith.* New York: Harper & Row, 1964.

Landis, Benson Y. *The Third American Revolution.* New York: Association Press, 1933.

Lenski, Gerhard. *The Religious Factor: A Sociological Study of Religion's Impact on Politics, Economics, and Family Life.* Garden City, N.Y.: Doubleday & Co., 1961.

Machen, J. Gresham. *Christianity and Liberalism.* New York: Macmillan Co., 1923.

McLoughlin, William G., ed. *Religion in America.* Boston: Houghton Mifflin Co., 1968.

Marty, Martin E. *The New Shape of American Religion.* New York: Harper & Brothers, 1959.

Mecklin, John Moffatt. *The Ku Klux Klan: A Study of the American Mind.* New York: Harcourt, Brace & Co., 1924.

Merz, Charles. *The Dry Decade.* Garden City, N.Y.: Doubleday, Doran & Co., 1931.

Meyer, Donald B. *The Protestant Search for Political Realism, 1919–1941.* Berkeley and Los Angeles: University of California Press, 1960.

Miller, Robert M. *American Protestantism and Social Issues, 1919–1939.* Chapel Hill: University of North Carolina Press, 1958.

Nash, Ronald H. *The New Evangelicalism.* Grand Rapids, Mich.: Zondervan Publishing House, 1963.

Riesman, David, with Glazer, Nathan, and Denney, Reuel. *The Lonely Crowd: A Study of the Changing American Character.* New Haven: Yale University Press, 1950.

29. TWENTIETH-CENTURY THEOLOGICAL CURRENTS

Bridges, Hal. *American Mysticism from William James to Zen.* New York: Harper & Row, 1970.

Ferm, Vergilius, ed. *Contemporary American Theology.* New York: Round Table Press, 1932.

Hammar, George. *Christian Realism in American Theology: A Study of Reinhold Niebuhr, W. M. Horton, and H. P. Van Dusen*. Uppsala: Appelberg, 1940.

Henry, Carl F. H. *Fifty Years of Protestant Theology*. Boston: W. A. Wilde Co., 1950.

Hoedemaker, Libertus A. *The Theology of H. Richard Niebuhr*. Boston: Pilgrim Press, 1970.

Kegley, Charles W., and Bretall, Robert W., eds. *Reinhold Niebuhr: His Religious, Social, and Political Thought*. New York: Macmillan Co., 1956.

———. *The Theology of Paul Tillich*. New York: Macmillan Co., 1952.

Nash, Arnold S., ed. *Protestant Thought in the Twentieth Century*. New York: Macmillan Co., 1951.

Soper, David W. *Major Voices in American Theology*. Philadelphia: Westminster Press, 1953.

Wieman, Henry N., et al. *Religious Liberals Reply*. Boston: Beacon Press, 1947.

30. BLACK MOVEMENTS AND VOICES IN THE TWENTIETH CENTURY

Breitman, George. *The Last Year of Malcolm X: The Evolution of a Revolutionary*. New York: Merit Publishers, 1967.

Brink, William, and Harris, Louis. *The Negro Revolution in America*. New York: Simon & Shuster, 1964.

Cleage, Albert B., Jr. *The Black Messiah*. New York: Sheed & Ward, 1968.

Cone, James H. *Black Theology and Black Power*. New York: Seabury Press, 1969.

Cronon, E. David. *Black Moses: The Story of Marcus Garvey and the Universal Negro Improvement Association*. Madison: University of Wisconsin Press, 1955.

Drake, St. Clair, and Cayton, Horace R. *Black Metropolis: A Study of Negro Life in a Northern City*. New York: Harcourt, Brace & Co., 1945.

Essien-Udom, E. U. *Black Nationalism: The Search for an Identity*. Chicago: University of Chicago Press, 1962.

Fauset, Arthur H. *Black Gods of the Metropolis: Negro Cults in the Urban North*. Philadelphia: University of Pennsylvania Press, 1944.

Fullinwider, S. P. *The Mind and Mood of Black America*. Homewood, Ill.: Dorsey Press, 1969.

Harris, Sara, and Crittenden, Harriet. *Father Divine, Holy Husband*. Garden City, N.Y.: Doubleday & Co., 1953.

Katz, Schlomo, ed. *Negro and Jew*. New York: Macmillan Co., 1966.

Lincoln, C. Eric. *The Black Muslims in America*. Boston: Beacon Press, 1961.

Little, Malcolm. *The Autobiography of Malcolm X*. New York: Grove Press, 1965.

———. *Malcolm X Speaks*. Edited by George Breitman. New York: Grove Press, 1966.

Lomax, Louis E. *The Negro Revolt*. New York: Harper & Row, 1962.

Meier, August, Rudwick, Elliott, and Broderick, Francis L., eds. *Black Protest Thought in the Twentieth Century*. 2d ed. Indianapolis: Bobbs-Merrill Co., 1971.

Powell, Adam Clayton, Jr. *Marching Blacks: An Interpretive History of the Rise of the Black Common Man*. New York: Dial Press, 1945.

Wright, Nathan, Jr. *Black Power and Urban Unrest*. New York: Hawthorne Books, 1967.

31. SPANISH-SPEAKING AMERICANS

Grebler, Leo, et al. *The Mexican American People: The Nation's Second Largest Minority*. New York: Free Press-Macmillan, 1970.

Lewis, Oscar. *A Study of Slum Culture: Backgrounds for La Vida.* New York: Random House, 1968.
Moore, Joan W. *Mexican Americans.* Englewood Cliffs, N.J.: Prentice-Hall, 1970.
Rand, Christopher. *The Puerto Ricans.* New York: Oxford University Press, 1958.
Scotford, John R. *Within These Borders: Spanish-Speaking Peoples in the U.S.A.* New York: Friendship Press, 1953.
Sexton, Patricia Cayo. *Spanish Harlem.* New York: Harper & Row, 1965.
Steiner, Stan. *La Raza: The Mexican-Americans.* New York: Harper & Row, 1968.

32. RELIGION IN THE 1960S AND 1970S

Altizer, Thomas J. J., and Hamilton, William. *Radical Theology and the Death of God.* Indianapolis: Bobbs-Merrill Co., 1966.
Beardslee, William A., ed. *America and the Future of Theology.* Philadelphia: Westminster Press, 1967.
Bjornstad, James. *Twentieth-Century Prophecy: Jeane Dixon and Edgar Cayce.* Minneapolis: Bethany Fellowship, 1969.
Braden, William. *The Private Sea: LSD and the Search for God.* Chicago: Quadrangle Books, 1967.
Callahan, Daniel. *The New Church: Essays in Catholic Reform.* New York: Charles Scribner's Sons, 1966.
———, ed. *The Secular City Debate.* New York, Macmillan Co., 1966.
Childs, Brevard S. *Biblical Theology in Crisis.* Philadelphia: Westminster Press, 1970.
Christ, Frank L., and Sherry, Gerard E., eds. *American Catholicism and the Intellectual Ideal.* New York: Appleton-Century-Crofts, 1961.
Cooper, John Charles. *Radical Christianity and Its Sources.* Philadelphia: Westminster Press, 1968.
———. *The Roots of the Radical Theology.* Philadelphia: Westminster Press, 1967.
Cox, Harvey, ed. *The Situation Ethics Debate.* Philadelphia: Westminster Press, 1968.
Cutler, Donald R., ed. *The Religious Situation: 1969.* Boston: Beacon Press, 1969.
Farley, Edward. *Requiem for a Lost Piety.* Philadelphia: Westminster Press, 1966.
Glazer, Nathan, and Moynihan, Daniel P. *Beyond the Melting Pot: The Negroes, Puerto Ricans, Jews, Italians, and Irish of New York City.* Cambridge, Mass.: MIT Press, 1963.
Gleason, Philip, ed. *Contemporary Catholicism in the United States.* Notre Dame, Ind.: University of Notre Dame Press, 1969.
Graham, Aelred. *Conversations: Christian and Buddhist.* New York: Harcourt, Brace & World, 1968.
———. *The End of Religion: Autobiographical Explorations.* New York: Harcourt Brace Jovanovich, 1971.
Greeley, Andrew M. *Religion in the Year 2000.* New York: Sheed & Ward, 1969.
———, et al. *What Do We Believe? The Stance of Religion in America.* New York: Meredith Press, 1968.
Gustafson, James M., ed. *The Sixties: Radical Change in American Religion. Annals of the American Academy of Political and Social Science* 387 (1970)
Hales, Edward E. Y. *Pope John and His Revolution.* Garden City, N.Y.: Doubleday & Co., 1965.
Hamilton, Kenneth. *God Is Dead: The Anatomy of a Slogan.* Grand Rapids, Mich.: William B. Eerdman's Co., 1966.

Hill, Samuel S., Jr. *Southern Churches in Crisis.* New York: Holt, Rinehart & Winston, 1967.

Lambert, Richard D., ed. *Religion in American Society. Annals of the American Academy of Political and Social Science* 332 (1960).

Marty, Martin E., and Peerman, Dean G. *New Theology.* 9 vols. New York: Macmillan Co., 1964–72.

Marty, Martin E. *Second Chance for American Protestants.* New York: Harper & Row, 1963.

Merton, Thomas. *Mystics and Zen Masters.* New York: Farrar, Straus, and Giroux, 1967.

Montgomery, Ruth. *The Gift of Prophecy: The Phenomenal Jeane Dixon.* New York: Bantam Books, 1966.

Needleman, Jacob. *The New Religions.* New York: Doubleday & Co., 1970.

Neusner, Jacob. *Judaism in America: Adventure in Modernity.* Englewood Cliffs, N.J.: Prentice-Hall, 1972.

Niebuhr, H. Richard. *Radical Monotheism and Western Culture, with Supplementary Essays.* New York: Harper & Brothers, 1960.

Noonan, John T., Jr. *Contraception: A History of Its Treatment by Catholic Theologians and Canonists.* Cambridge, Mass.: Harvard University Press, 1965.

O'Connor, John. *The People versus Rome: Radical Split in the American Church.* New York: Random House, 1969.

O'Dea, Thomas F. *American Catholic Dilemma: An Inquiry into the Intellectual Life.* New York: Sheed & Ward, 1958.

———. *The Catholic Crisis.* Boston: Beacon Press, 1968.

Ogletree, Thomas W. *The Death of God Controversy.* Nashville, Tenn.: Abingdon Press, 1966.

Reich, Charles. *The Greening of America.* New York: Random House, 1970.

Revel, Jean François. *Without Marx or Jesus: The New American Revolution.* Garden City, N.Y.: Doubleday & Co., 1970.

Roszak, Theodore. *The Making of a Counter-Culture: Reflections on the Technocratic Society and Its Youthful Opposition.* Garden City, N.Y.: Doubleday & Co., 1969.

Suzuki, Daisetz T. *An Introduction to Zen Buddhism.* Foreword by C. G. June. New York: Grove Press, 1964.

Vahanian, Gabriel. *The Death of God: The Culture of Our Post-Christian Era.* New York: George Braziller, 1961.

Wakin, Edward, and Scheuer, Joseph F. *The De-Romanization of the American Catholic Church.* New York: Macmillan Co., 1966.

33. BIOGRAPHIES AND AUTOBIOGRAPHIES

Allen, Alexander V. G. *The Life and Letters of Phillips Brooks.* 2 vols. New York: E. P. Dutton & Co., 1900.

Anderson, Courtney. *To the Golden Shore: The Life of Adoniram Judson.* Boston: Little, Brown and Co., 1956.

Beecher, Lyman. *Autobiography of Lyman Beecher.* Edited by Barbara Cross. 2 vols. Cambridge, Mass.: Harvard University Press, 1961.

Cahan, Abraham. *The Rise of David Levinsky.* 1917. Reprint. Introduction by John Higham. New York: Harper & Row, Torchbooks, 1960.

Cartwright, Peter. *Autobiography of Peter Cartwright.* Edited by Charles L. Wallis. Nashville, Tenn.: Abingdon Press, 1956.

Channing, William Henry. *The Life of William Ellery Channing.* Boston, 1880.

Cheney, Mary Bushnell. *Life and Letters of Horace Bushnell.* New York, 1880.

Day, Dorothy. *The Long Loneliness.* New York: Harper & Row, 1952. [An autobiography.]

DuBois, W. E. B. *Dusk of Dawn: An Essay toward an Autobiography of a Race Concept.* New York: Harcourt, Brace & World, 1940.

Dupree, Hunter. *Asa Gray.* Cambridge, Mass.: Harvard University Press, 1959.

Earhart, Mary. *Frances Willard: From Prayers to Politics.* Chicago: University of Chicago Press, 1944.

Ellis, John Tracy. *The Life of James Cardinal Gibbons, Archbishop of Baltimore, 1834–1921.* Milwaukee: Bruce Publishing Co., 1952.

Forbush, Bliss. *Elias Hicks: Quaker Liberal.* New York: Columbia University Press, 1956.

Fosdick, Harry Emerson. *The Living of These Days: An Autobiography.* New York: Harper & Brothers, 1956.

Fox, George. *The Journal of George Fox.* Edited by John L. Nickalls. Cambridge: At the University Press, 1952.

Frothingham, Octavius B. *Boston Unitarianism, 1820–1850: A Study of the Life and Work of Nathaniel Langdon Frothingham.* New York, 1890.

Gannett, William C. *Ezra Stiles Gannett: Unitarian Minister in Boston, 1824–1871.* Boston, 1875.

Guilday, Peter. *The Life and Times of John Carroll, Archbishop of Baltimore, 1735–1815.* New York: Encyclopedia Press, 1922.

Holden, Vincent F. *The Yankee Paul: Isaac Thomas Hecker.* Milwaukee: Bruce Publishing Co., 1958.

Lurie, Edward. *Louis Agassiz: A Life in Science.* Chicago: Chicago University Press, 1960.

Mathews, Basil J. *John R. Mott: World Citizen.* New York: Harper & Brothers, 1934.

Merton, Thomas. *The Seven Storey Mountain: An Autobiography.* New York: Harcourt, Brace & Co., 1948.

Middlekauf, Robert. *The Mathers: Three Generations of Puritan Intellectuals, 1596–1728.* New York: Oxford University Press, 1971.

Morgan, Edmund S. *The Gentle Puritan: A Life of Ezra Stiles, 1727–1795.* New Haven: Yale University Press, 1962.

Murdock, Kenneth B. *Increase Mather: The Foremost American Puritan.* Cambridge, Mass.: Harvard University Press, 1925.

Nethercot, Arthur H. *The First Five Lives of Annie Besant.* Chicago: University of Chicago Press, 1960.

———. *The Last Four Lives of Annie Besant.* Chicago: University of Chicago Press, 1963.

Noyes, George W., ed. *The Religious Experience of John Humphrey Noyes.* New York: Macmillan Co., 1923.

Omer, Englebert. *The Last of the Conquistadors: Junipero Serra, 1713–1784.* New York: Harcourt, Brace & Co., 1956.

Perry, Ralph Barton. *The Thought and Character of William James.* 2 vols. Boston: Little, Brown and Co., 1935.

Philipson, David. *Max Lilienthal.* New York: Bloch Publishing Co., 1915.

Repplier, Agnes. *Mère Marie of the Ursulines: A Study in Adventure.* Garden City, N.Y.: Literary Guild of America, 1931.

Rusk, Ralph L. *The Life of Ralph Waldo Emerson.* New York: Charles Scribner's Sons, 1949.

Stevenson, Dwight E. *Walter Scott: Voice of the Golden Oracle.* Saint Louis: Christian Board of Publication, 1946.

Stonehouse, Ned B. *J. Gresham Machen: A Biographical Memoir.* Grand Rapids, Mich.: William B. Eerdmans Co., 1954.

Thomas, Benjamin. *Abraham Lincoln.* New York: Alfred A. Knopf, 1952.

Weiss, John. *Life and Correspondence of Theodore Parker.* New York, 1864.

Wise, Isaac Mayer. *Reminiscences.* Translated and edited by David Philipson. 2d ed. New York: Central Synagogue of New York, 1945.

Woolman, John. *The Journal and Major Essays of John Woolman.* Edited by Phillips P. Moulton. New York: Oxford University Press, 1971.

Ziff, Larzer. *The Career of John Cotton: Puritanism and the American Experience.* Princeton, N.J.: Princeton University Press, 1962

Zwierlein, F. J. *Life and Letters of Bishop McQuaid, Prefaced with the History of Catholic Rochester before His Episcopate.* 3 vols. Rome and Louvain, 1925.

INDEX